Trade unions in the European Union

Picking up the pieces of the neoliberal challenge

PETER LANG

Lausanne · Berlin · Bruxelles · Chennai · New York · Oxford

Jeremy Waddington, Torsten Müller and
Kurt Vandaele (eds.)

Trade unions in the European Union

Picking up the pieces of the neoliberal challenge

Work & Society
Vol. 86

This book offers a comprehensive comparative overview of the development, structure, and policies of trade unions in all the 27 Member States of the EU from 2000 to 2020. It presents an in-depth analysis of the neoliberal challenges facing these organizations and their strategic and policy responses.

This publication has been peer-reviewed.

The European Trade Union Institute (ETUI) is financially supported by the European Union.

Published by Peter Lang Éditions scientifiques internationales - P.I.E. SA
1 avenue Maurice, B-1050 Brussels, Belgium
www.peterlang.com; info@peterlang.com

ISSN 1376-0955
ISBN 978-2-87574-634-4
ePDF 978-2-87574-635-1
ePub 978-2-87574-636-8
DOI 10.3726/b20254
D/2022/5678/60

PETER LANG Open

Peter Lang Group AG
International Academic Publishers
Bern

Foreword

More than twenty years ago I edited a book entitled *Trade Unions in Europe* with Jeremy Waddington. That book identified the challenges facing trade unions as a result of the implementation of neoliberal policies within nation states and the European Union. This volume is a timely update on developments since the millennium. Based around twenty-seven country chapters the book highlights both the challenges posed by neoliberalism to trade unions and the wide range of policy responses implemented by unions to adapt to new circumstances. It demonstrates the dangers to European social models arising from neoliberal policies and identifies what needs to be done if this model is to be protected. I recommend the book to all those interested in ensuring that the unique features of Europe's social models can be retained in a viable form.

Reiner Hoffmann

Former President of the German Trade Union Confederation (DGB)

Contents

List of figures

List of tables

List of contributors

Dragan Bagić is Associate Professor at the Department of Sociology, Faculty of Humanities and Social Sciences, University of Zagreb. He is one of the rare scholars in Croatia dealing with industrial relations issues. In addition to industrial relations, his research interests include political sociology, sociology of migration and social research methodology.

Tapio Bergholm was Visiting Fellow at the Industrial Relations Research Unit at the University of Warwick in 1990–1991. He completed his PhD in Finnish and Scandinavian History in 1997, and then a PhD in Sociology in 2015. He is docent at the University of Helsinki and the University of Eastern Finland. His research interests are the history of industrial relations, transport history and, at the moment, a biography of former President of Finland Mauno Koivisto.

Lisa Berntsen is researcher at the Scientific Bureau for the Dutch Trade Union Movement, De Burcht. She has a double PhD degree in Sociology and Economics and Business from the University of Groningen and the University of Jyväskylä. Her research interests are in the field of industrial relations and migration, with a special focus on trade union renewal and changing conditions and regulations regarding migrant work.

Inga Blažienė is Senior Researcher at the Labour Market Research Division of the Lithuanian Centre for Social Sciences in Vilnius. She holds a PhD in Economics from Gediminas Technical University, Vilnius. Inga was a visiting scholar at Corpus Christi College, Oxford University. Currently, she is a national correspondent for Lithuania in various EU networks, including the European Observatory of Working Life and European Centre of Expertise in the field of labour law, employment and labour market policies. Inga's research focuses on employment and labour market policies, industrial relations and working conditions.

Živa (née Filej) Broder has been employed at the University of Ljubljana, Faculty of Social Science, in the Centre for Public Opinion

Research as an expert administrative worker and researcher since 1999. She is a member of the Slovenian national team on ESS, EVS, WVS, ISSP and is a national representative for WAPOR. She has a Masters degree in Sociology.

Jan Czarzasty PhD (2010, SGH) is an economist and assistant professor at the Institute of Philosophy, Sociology and Economic Sociology, SGH Warsaw School of Economics, Poland. Chief expert in the field of labour relations and social dialogue at the Institute of Public Affairs (ISP) in Warsaw. His main areas of academic interest include economic sociology, industrial relations and social dialogue studies, comparative studies of modern capitalism. He has authored/co-authored over 50 articles and book chapters. He supervises the SGH unit in the research team working at the NCN-funded project COV-WORK (www.covwork.uni.wroc.pl) on Poles' life strategies and socio-economic consciousness in the context of the (post)pandemic crisis.

Paul de Beer is Henri Polak Professor of Industrial Relations at the University of Amsterdam (UvA). He is scientific director of the Scientific Bureau for the Dutch Trade Union Movement, De Burcht, and is affiliated with the interdisciplinary labour research institute AIAS-HSI at the UvA. He holds a PhD in economics at the University of Amsterdam. Formerly, he worked as a researcher at the Netherlands Institute for Social Research (SCP) and at the Scientific Council for Government Policy (WRR). His research interests include industrial relations, labour market evolution and policy, social policy, solidarity, and the value of work.

Manwel Debono is Associate Professor at the University of Malta and a former director of its Centre for Labour Studies. He has been involved in numerous national and European research projects dealing with industrial relations and working conditions. He is also a veteran contributor to the European Foundation for the Improvement of Living and Working Conditions and the European Employment Policy Observatory.

Roland Erne is Professor of European Integration and Employment Relations at UCD's College of Business and PI of the ERC Project 'Labour Politics and the EU's new Economic Governance Regime' at the UCD Geary Institute for Public Policy.

Carlos J. Fernández Rodríguez is Associate Professor in Sociology at the Universidad Autónoma de Madrid, Spain. His research interests are sociology of consumption and organizations, and industrial relations.

Luke Anthony Fiorini is Director of the Centre for Labour Studies (CLS), University of Malta. He is also a resident academic at the same Centre. He has written several peer-reviewed papers, presented at international conferences and also contributes towards the CLS's Eurofound commitments. Dr Fiorini represents Malta on the Worker Participation Network of the European Trade Union Institute.

Vera Glassner is a sociologist at the Vienna Chamber of Labour and a lecturer at the University of Vienna. Her research focus is on gender inequalities in working life and labour relations.

Julia Hofmann works as a researcher at the Vienna Chamber of Labour and is a lecturer in sociology at the University of Vienna. Her research focus is social inequality, the sociology of work and labour relations.

Rafael Ibáñez Rojo is Senior Lecturer in Sociology at the Universidad Autónoma de Madrid, Spain. His research interests are the sociology of work and consumption, and industrial relations.

Gregoris Ioannou is a sociologist and a Research Fellow at the University of Glasgow. He is also an external Expert for Eurofound on 'Working Conditions and Sustainable Work' and for the European Commission. His research focuses on labour relations and trade unionism, class conflicts and contentious politics. Aspects of his work have been published as books, articles in international peer-reviewed journals, chapters in collective academic volumes, reports and commentaries. His latest research monograph, entitled *Employment, Trade Unionism and Class: The Labour Market in Southern Europe since the Crisis*, was published by Routledge in 2021.

Marta Kahancová, PhD, is Founder and Managing Director of the Central European Labour Studies Institute (CELSI) in Bratislava, Slovakia. Her research interests include the sociology of organizations and work; in particular, she studies industrial relations, trade unions, working conditions, and atypical and undeclared forms of work. She also serves as a labour market expert for the European Commission (European Centre of Expertise in the field of labour law, employment and labour market policies) and the European Labour Authority (European Platform for Tackling Undeclared Work). Her publications have appeared in international peer-reviewed journals on industrial relations, sociology and human resource management. She completed her PhD under the supervision of Professor Jelle Visser at the University of Amsterdam in 2007.

Epp Kallaste, PhD, is Director and Senior Researcher at the Estonian Centre for Applied Research CentAR. Her main areas of expertise are labour relations, labour market, social protection and education.

Ioannis Katsaroumpas is a Lecturer in Employment Law at the University of Sussex. His research focuses on international, comparative and European labour law.

Anders Kjellberg is Professor of Sociology at Lund University, Sweden. His research deals with the Swedish model of industrial relations in a historical and internationally comparative perspective. Among the studied dimensions are self-regulation versus state regulation, union density and coverage of collective agreements.

Herman Knudsen is professor emeritus at Aalborg University. He has been active researching industrial relations and working life since the 1970s, notably with studies of industrial conflict, trade unions, workers' participation and European Works Councils.

Aristea Koukiadaki is Professor of Labour Law and Industrial Relations in the Department of Law and member of the Work and Equalities Institute at the University of Manchester. Her research expertise is in comparative labour law and industrial relations, EU labour law and social policy and socio-legal research. Her most recent work is on enforcement of EU labour law, labour dispute resolution and precarious work.

Salvo Leonardi is Senior Researcher at the Fondazione Di Vittorio, where he is in charge of industrial relations. A member of numerous international research networks and a project manager, he is author of many publications, including articles in academic journals, and chapters in collective volumes on labour law and industrial relations.

Jens Lind is Professor Emeritus at the Department of Sociology and Social Work, Aalborg University, Denmark. His main interests and research areas are in industrial relations, focusing on labour market policy, collective bargaining, trade unions and unemployment.

Vincenzo Maccarrone is a researcher in industrial relations, political economy and sociology of work. He is currently a Marie Skłodowska-Curie Postdoctoral Fellow at the Scuola Normale Superiore, with a project on global governance of labour.

Miguel Martínez Lucio is Professor at the University of Manchester and is involved in its Work and Equalities Institute. He researches and publishes on the changing nature of worker representation, union renewal, the state, and social issues within labour relations.

Monika Martišková is a researcher at the Central European Labour Studies Institute (CELSI) in Bratislava, Slovakia, and is a PhD candidate at the Department of Social Geography and Regional Development at Charles University in Prague, Czechia. She is interested in labour market institutions and collective bargaining in Central and Eastern European (CEE) countries.

Tibor T. Meszmann is a researcher at the Central European Labour Studies Institute, Bratislava, member of the Public Sociology Working Group 'Helyzet', Budapest, and member of the editorial board of *LeftEast*.

Adam Mrozowicki, PhD (2009, CESO KU Leuven, Belgium), is Associate Professor at the Institute of Sociology, University of Wrocław, Poland. His academic interests lie in the sociology of work, economic sociology, comparative employment relations, precarity, critical social realism and biographical methods.

Torsten Müller is Senior Researcher at the European Trade Union Institute in Brussels, where he is responsible for the area of wages, collective bargaining and trade unions in Europe.

Reinhard Naumann is an independent researcher and consultant in industrial relations and employment policies. He is Portuguese correspondent of the European Centre of Expertise in the field of labour law, employment and labour market policies (ECE) and of the European Observatory of Working Life (EURWORK). From 1996 until 2021 he has been Director of the Friedrich-Ebert-Stiftung office in Portugal.

Jelena Ostojić is a teaching assistant at the Department of Sociology, Faculty of Humanities and Social Sciences, University of Zagreb. Her research interests focus on the sociology of labour and industrial relations.

Maria da Paz Campos Lima, PhD (Sociology), is an integrated researcher at the Instituto Universitário de Lisboa (ISCTE-IUL), DINÂMIA'CET– IUL. She was an EIRO correspondent (2006–2014) and has been a correspondent of the European Observatory of Working Life (EurWORK) since 2014. She has participated in European comparative research projects on labour market reforms, social dialogue and collective bargaining. Her research interests include comparative industrial relations, collective bargaining, tripartite concertation, trade unionism and social movements.

Roberto Pedersini is Professor of Economic Sociology and Head of the Department of Social and Political Sciences at the Università degli Studi di Milano, Italy. He has long and extensive experience in the field of employment and industrial relations. His main current research interests concern labour market regulation and policies and industrial and employment relations.

Andreja Poje is a macroeconomist and researcher. She was an executive secretary for economics of the Association of Free Trade Unions of Slovenia (ZSSS) for nine years. She holds a Master's degree and is a PhD candidate at the University of Ljubljana, with research centred on labour economics, wages, income inequalities, gender pay gaps, collective bargaining and public finances.

Bjarke Refslund is Associate Professor in Sociology at Aalborg University, specializing in industrial relations and working life studies. He has a PhD degree in Political Science from Aalborg University. His main research areas include industrial relations, labour migration and labour market sociology.

Udo Rehfeldt is a political scientist and associated researcher at the IRES (France). He is the French correspondent of the ETUI network on Worker Participation in Europe and has taught comparative industrial relations at the University of Paris-X-Nanterre. His research fields are comparative and transnational industrial relations.

Thorsten Schulten is Head of the Collective Agreements Archive of the Institute of Economic and Social Research (WSI) within the Hans Böckler Stiftung, Düsseldorf. He also teaches political science as an Honorary Professor at the University of Tübingen.

Sertac Sonan is an Associate Professor at the Political Science and International Relations Department of Cyprus International University. He is the Director of Centre for Cyprus and Mediterranean Studies at the same university. His research interests include political clientelism, corruption, Cyprus conflict, and Turkish Cypriot politics and economy.

Slavina Spasova is Senior Researcher at the European Social Observatory and a Research associate at Université Libre de Bruxelles (CEVIPOL; ULB). She holds a PhD in political science (ULB) which explored the Europeanization of the Bulgarian trade unions. Her research agenda focuses on various social policy issues, and in particular on social protection.

Miroslav Stanojević is a retired Professor of Industrial Relations. He was a Head of the Organizations and Human Resources Research Centre at the Faculty of Social Sciences, University of Ljubljana. He is involved in projects and networks dealing with comparative employment relations, focused mainly on the central and eastern European countries.

Adam Šumichrast is a doctoral candidate at the Institute of History, Faculty of Arts, Masaryk University, Brno specializing in comparative labour and social history. He is also a junior researcher at the Central European Labour Studies Institute. He is also interested in research into industrial unrest and collective action in present-day Slovakia and Czechia.

Imre G. Szabó is a postdoctoral research fellow in the ERC Project 'Labour Politics and the EU's new Economic Governance Regime' at the UCD Geary Institute for Public Policy and School of Business.

Adrien Thomas, PhD, is a Research Scientist in the Labour Market Department at the Luxembourg Institute of Socio-Economic Research (LISER). His research focuses on trade unions in a comparative perspective, employment relations and the social dimensions of sustainable development.

Aurora Trif is an Associate Professor in International Employment Relations and Human Resource Management at Dublin City University Business School, Dublin City University, Ireland. Her research interests include comparative employment relations in Eastern Europe, precarious work, trade union innovation, work conflict, workplace partnership, and compassion at work. She has published widely in international scholarly journals.

Monika Uhlerová, PhD., is Vice-President of the Confederation of Trade Unions in the Slovak Republic (KOZ SR) (since 2016). She is also Vice-President of the Economic and Social Council of the Slovak Republic. Her research interests include institutionalized social dialogue and the role of trade unions in transforming labour markets.

Kurt Vandaele is Senior Researcher at the European Trade Union Institute in Brussels. His research interests include workers' resistance and their collective action repertoire, trade union revitalization, the platform economy and the political economy of Belgium and the Netherlands.

Catherine Vincent is a sociologist and senior researcher at IRES (Noisy-le-grand, France). Her current research interests focus on collective bargaining, employee workplace representation and HRM in the private and the public sector. She recently authored the French chapter of the ETUI book on collective bargaining in Europe.

Jeremy Waddington is Emeritus Professor of Industrial Relations, University of Manchester. During much of the period of preparation of this volume he was also Project Coordinator at the European Trade Union Institute.

Preface

In 2000 the European Trade Union Institute published its initial volume on trade unions in Europe (Waddington and Hoffmann 2000), which identified elements of the then nascent neoliberal challenge to trade unions. Since the publication of that volume unions have repeatedly been challenged by neoliberal programmes implemented within Member States of the European Union (EU) and at European level. At the heart of this challenge is the neoliberal assumption that trade unions, collective bargaining and other forms of regulation set by collective actors constitute 'labour market rigidities', the effects of which must be removed or minimized if economies are to thrive. This book charts the impact of the neoliberal challenge on trade unionism and the measures implemented by trade unionists in their attempts to adapt to changed circumstances. This book also takes into account the successive enlargements of the EU that have taken place since 2000. Central to the book are thus twenty-seven chapters, each of which examines trade unionism in a Member State of the EU.

The neoliberal agenda pursued by employers and policymakers at national and European levels is a macroeconomic policy comprising trade liberalization, fiscal discipline and prioritization of the control of inflation at the expense of full employment. In addition, the neoliberal programme includes wide-ranging political initiatives designed to free markets from bureaucratic or corporatist control. As trade unions were integral to these forms of control within the EU Member States, they were subject to challenge. Within Member States the liberalization and privatization of public services led to reduced public sector employment, which traditionally is densely unionized; labour market reforms reduced employment protections and accelerated low wage and atypical employment; collective bargaining was decentralized and, in some instances, de-unionized; and the state and political parties 'distanced' unions from involvement in policy formulation. There is no uniformity to these features of the neoliberal challenge between Member States, nor is there uniformity in the unions' capacity to respond and the form of their responses to these challenges. The twenty-seven country chapters at the core of this book chart the features of the national neoliberal challenge and the various trade union responses. The main analysis in each chapter covers the two decades from 2000. The cut-off point of the analysis is early 2021, which means that any post-Covid dynamics and trends could only be touched upon.

Four interrelated arguments resonate throughout the book. First, the neoliberal programmes pursued within the Member States are uneven and vary by degrees. The direction of travel within Member States may be similar, but the distance covered differs markedly. Second, the impact of the neoliberal challenge is influenced by this unevenness and by the state of trade unions at the time the different elements of the neoliberal challenge were implemented. Third, trade unions in Central and Eastern Europe (CEE) were not as embedded in social market–style industrial relations systems as their counterparts elsewhere in the EU when neoliberal programmes were enacted. Furthermore, trade unions in CEE had to adapt to enlargement and, in general, had access to fewer material and political resources. As a consequence, the impact of the neoliberal challenge has been harder felt by trade unions in CEE than elsewhere. Fourth, the impact of the EU has not always been benign. To the contrary the EU has distanced itself in practice, if not rhetorically, from the promotion of a European social dimension, especially between 1999 and 2014; the social policy measures that were adopted comprised many soft law elements, weak minimum standards and no attempt to upwardly harmonize social policy. Furthermore, a series of decisions made by the European Court of Justice have downgraded the rights of labour in relation to the operation of the single market.

In developing the different variants of these arguments each of the country chapters comprises material grouped under the same nine headings: the historical background and principal features of the system of industrial relations; the structure of trade unions and union democracy; unionization; union resources and expenditure; collective bargaining and unions at the workplace; industrial conflict; political relations; societal power; and trade union policies towards the EU. This framework accentuates the analytical similarities between chapters, while also facilitating the identification of different developments in the various Member States. The authors of each chapter determined the order in which the material is presented according to specific country characteristics. To further encourage consistency in analytical practice, the authors of each country chapter reviewed, via Zoom and physical meetings, drafts of other country chapters. Together with the reviewing conducted by the editors this approach ensured that each country chapter was peer reviewed by a minimum of six people.

The scale of this publication has necessitated the involvement of a wide range of people in addition to the editors and authors of the country chapters. The editors express their heartfelt thanks to these contributors. The ETUI acted as the hub of the research and funded the numerous meetings of authors and editors over the three years of production. Initially, Kristel Vergeylen and latterly Angélique Vanhoutte organized the workshops and convened the meetings with quiet efficiency. Specific responsibilities were distributed throughout the networks operated by the ETUI. In particular, James Patterson was responsible for the English editing of the country chapters and some of the pre-publication layout. Birgit Buggel-Asmus also assisted with the layout, while Giovanna Corda worked through the bibliography of each chapter. Needless to say, responsibility for the final manuscript rests with the editors.

Jeremy Waddington — Brussels, May 2022
Torsten Müller
Kurt Vandaele

Reference

Waddington, J. and Hoffmann, R. 2000. (eds). *Trade Unions in Europe.* Brussels: European Trade Union Institute.

Chapter 1

Trade unions in the European Union: Identifying challenges

Jeremy Waddington, Torsten Müller and Kurt Vandaele

Within most industrialized societies trade unions historically occupied a key position. In helping to construct modern liberal democracies unions struggled for collective representation, participation and universal suffrage. The widespread coverage of collective bargaining was associated with a diminution in inequality, an increasing wage share of national income and negotiated outcomes that informally linked inflation, productivity growth and wages. Within the workplace, unions negotiated protection against risks of illness and accidents as well as ensuring a degree of procedural fairness by means of grievance and disciplinary procedures. In alliance with Social Democratic, Labour and, in some countries Christian-democratic and Communist Parties, unions sought and secured rhetorical, if not political, commitments to seek full employment.

Within Western Europe analyses of the European social model emphasize a number of core features including forms of policy coordination that promote economic growth and consensual labour market development; the integration of social and welfare policy with economic policy; minimum terms and conditions of employment, more often than not underwritten by the state; and the independent representation of workers (Crouch 1993; Hyman 2005; Lane 1989). Central to each of these features is the role of trade union organizations[1] and collective bargaining (Crouch 1999: 32–47; Sassoon 1996), characteristics that separate

1 The term 'trade union organizations' is used throughout this publication to refer collectively to all trade unions: that is, at European level the ETUC and the ETUFs,

Europe from neoliberal forms of economic management, typified by the United States (Coates 2000: 77–106; Crafts and Toniolo 1996b), and contribute positively to long-term economic performance (Eichengreen 2007; Gamble 2014). This book explores whether trade union organizations are in a position to sustain their role within the national variants of the European social model.

The shift towards neoliberalism after about 1980 threatened the position of unions within the European Union (EU).[2] Views on the impact of this threat vary. At one extreme it is argued that neoliberalism has fundamentally altered industrial relations institutions and practices (Baccaro and Howell 2017), whereas others highlight the resistance and adaptation to the neoliberal project (Dølvik and Martin 2015) and the variation in its impact (Müller et al. 2019). What is clear is that trade unions in the EU are not in a good place. Unionization rates are at their lowest level since 1950 (Visser 2019a) and, at best, the resources deployed to organizing and recruitment campaigns have merely slowed national rates of decline (Holgate et al. 2018; Phelan 2007; Urban 2012). Mobilization in the form of strike activity to defend workers' interests is also at low ebb in most Member States of the EU (Vandaele 2016; van der Velden et al. 2007). Furthermore, the 'standard' union pursuit of improved pay and conditions for workers has been jeopardized by a decline in the coverage of collective bargaining and the decentralization of much of the collective bargaining that remains (Waddington et al. 2019). As a consequence, unions set the terms and conditions of employment for a smaller proportion of the workforce. The trust expressed by various groups of workers in unions, however, has not diminished in most countries (Frangi et al. 2017; Gorodzeisky and Richards 2019). The decentralization of collective bargaining requires trade unions to coordinate the settlement of decentralized collective agreements to ensure a degree of parity between workers who were previously covered by the same industrial agreement. In practice these developments mean that there are fewer resources available

---

and at national level trade union confederations, and national, regional or local trade unions.

2 Some would argue that the EU is a neoliberal project by definition (Gray 2004; Streeck 2019). While this argument is rejected here, it is acknowledged that neoliberal policies have informed the direction of travel of the EU over the period of interest of this publication: that is, since 2000.

to unions at a time when more wide-ranging tasks, the coordination of settlements, necessitating increased resources are required.

This publication assesses the position of trade unions in the EU since 2000. As such, it 'follows on' from an earlier European Trade Union Institute (ETUI) publication on European trade unionism (Waddington and Hoffmann 2000) and incorporates analysis of the impact of adopting the Euro and successive EU enlargements. The publication argues that the viability of the trade union pillar within some national variants of the European social model is threatened. To situate unions within a historical perspective this chapter comprises three sections. The first section reviews the historical bases of unionism during the 'golden age' between 1945 and 1975 and outlines the features of the subsequent neoliberal challenge to unionism to introduce the changing position of unions. The second section charts the changes in the labour market, economic outcomes and collective bargaining concurrent with the neoliberal project since the year 2000. These two sections thus identify the challenges faced by trade unions within the EU. The country chapters that form the body of the book and the concluding chapter examine in more detail how the neoliberal project has impinged on trade unionism within each Member State of the EU and identify how trade unionists have responded to these challenges. The third section reviews the themes addressed by the country experts in their chapters on the twenty-seven Member States of the EU and outlines the structure of the publication.[3] Throughout all the chapters in this publication reference is made to data available in Appendix A1.

From 'golden age' to neoliberal challenge

During the 'golden age' (Marglin and Schor 1990) or 'trente glorieuses', 1945 to 1975, trade unions in Western Europe advocated reform centred on workers' rights, improvements in terms and conditions of employment and industrial citizenship in economic management.

3 We acknowledge that the United Kingdom was a Member State of the European Union for much of the period under review here. Brexit, however, distanced the United Kingdom from the European Union and led to changes in the relationship between the European Trade Union Confederation and the Trades Union Congress. For these reasons there is no Chapter on the United Kingdom included in this volume. Examples from the United Kingdom are included in both Chapters 1 and 29 to illustrate arguments of wider scope.

Against the counterpoint of the command economies dominant within Central and Eastern Europe (CEE), the noteworthy feature of the period within market capitalism was the extent to which trade unions in Western Europe realized ambitions in these fields (Ross and Martin 1999: 6). In contrast, in much of CEE trade unions were incorporated into systems of governance dominated by Communist Parties, to which the unions were largely subservient. This section identifies the key features of the 'golden age' as a means of identifying the extent of the challenge to unions inherent in neoliberalism and, in particular, the threat to the legitimacy of trade unions.

From the 'golden age' to ...

Underpinning trade union progress in Western Europe during the 'golden age' was economic growth. Although this growth was cyclical, it was characterized by relatively long upswings and relatively short downswings (Crafts and Toniolo 1996a). Multinational companies (MNCs) were drivers of economic growth, basing their activities on 'fordist' mass production of goods, which were primarily intended for sale in national markets. Within MNCs 'affluent workers' were able to secure higher wages and enhanced job security in return for their cooperation at work, required by management to meet the demand arising from rising living standards (Goldthorpe et al. 1969). While rarely formally agreed or made explicit, wage growth became associated with a trade-off involving inflation and productivity growth (Marglin and Schor 1990). The increasing coverage of collective bargaining facilitated such trade-offs within all companies. This 'virtuous circle' powered high rates of economic growth until the late 1960s when rates of growth slowed and then subsequently dived as the impact of the oil crisis hit home and stagflation resulted (Eichengreen 2007: 198–251) coupled to a resurgence of industrial conflict (Crouch and Pizzorno 1978).

Accompanying the high rates of economic growth during the 'golden age' was the broadening of the role of the state informed by Keynesian policies (Howell 2005: 86–130). The welfare state was extended in scope and depth (Esping-Andersen 1990), and, at least, rhetorical commitments were made to securing full employment by parties of the political left and right. Trade unions participated in decisions made by the state at the centre and within the localities, particularly, but not exclusively, when left-of-centre parties were in power. Corporatist or tripartite arrangements afforded trade unions influence within national policy making, which promoted alliances between unions and political parties. Many unionists, for example, sought election to public office as representatives of the political party with which the unions were in alliance. Under pressure predominantly from unions, the state broadened industrial citizenship in the form of board-level employee representation, works councils, health and safety committees and other forms of workplace representation. This was particularly the case in the public sector where the state acted as a 'model employer' to promote similar developments in the private sector.

Trade unions benefitted from these developments. From a principally male, full-time, manual and manufacturing core membership unions extended organization to include some white-collar and women members. With the exception of the countries with variants of the Ghent system, where unions were involved in the administration of unemployment insurance, large segments of private sector services remained unorganized. Retail, hospitality, catering and tourism, for example, were low union density segments of most economies. Burgeoning membership allowed unions to finance and offer a wider range of services to members encompassing research, legal and training departments. Similarly, full-time officers and lay representatives[4] with extensive time-off provisions 'serviced' the growing membership by means of increasingly formalized grievance and disciplinary procedures.

Although pleas to internationalize became louder towards the close of the 'golden age' (Levinson 1972), trade unions remained national in orientation. Engagement with the nation state afforded the only opportunities to secure improvements in welfare provisions and legislation on union security. Similarly, collective bargaining arrangements were reliant on national industrial settlements, thus accentuating the national focus of unionists. The linkage between wages, inflation and productivity growth that informed collective bargaining was also based on national data and comparisons. Although some MNCs engaged in company bargaining, most were signatories to national industrial agreements and none introduced transnational settlements for the entire MNC. While the establishment of the European Trade Union Confederation (ETUC) in 1973 constituted a step towards greater European trade union

4 The term lay representative is used to refer to shop stewards, works councillors or their equivalents.

internationalization, the initial limited affiliation and the rudimentary structures were indicators of the limits to trade union internationalization, (Degryse and Tilly 2013; Dølvik 1999).

The potential for rapid economic growth in CEE after 1945 was present in the form of catch-up effects as largely agricultural economies industrialized and, as in the West, made good the damage wrought by the Second World War (Eichengreen 2007: 131–162). This potential of 'input capitalism' was not realized. The central planning system in which all major industries were owned by the state resulted in the rapid creation and expansion of the industrial base, but economic growth became dependent upon ever-greater inputs of labour and capital from about 1960 (Aldcroft and Morewood 1995). The subsequent failure to invest in modern machinery, labour shortages and poor management practices further impaired economic growth (Berend 1996).

In this context, the situation of trade unions in CEE differed markedly from their counterparts in the West. As close, yet subservient, allies of the various national Communist Parties, unions became integral to the system of exhortation directed towards productivity growth. In the absence of rising living standards, marked limits to consumption, underinvestment in housing and communications, and poor power provisions (Eichengreen 2007: 140; Mazower 2000: 253–289), unions were associated with the failures of central planning rather than institutions concerned to raise the living standards of members. Instead, trade unions in CEE emphasized a social role. The provision of convalescent homes, facilities at holiday resorts and extensive child-care arrangements exemplified the social aspect of union practice. These provisions coupled to advantages to members through trade union links to the Communist Party ensured high levels of union density. In 1970, for example, union density was estimated at 80.0 per cent or higher in each of the CEE countries where Communist Parties were in power.[5] Trade union density was thus markedly higher in CEE than in Western Europe.

Throughout most of CEE trade unions at the workplace were concerned to meet productivity, output and other targets required within the terms of central planning. Union involvement was thus an element of workplace management. It should be noted, however, that training

---

5 This figure is based on estimations provided by members of the network that produced this publication from CEE.

provisions were extensive with the consequence that significant proportions of the workforce were relatively highly skilled in some countries, notably Czechoslovakia and Hungary. The exception to the managerial function performed by unions in CEE was Yugoslavia where a system of self-management was implemented with each self-managed enterprise managed by an elected works council. Yugoslav self-management led to a degree of democratic rather than bureaucratic planning and the emergence of market relationships between self-managed enterprises (Moore 1970; Singleton and Topham 1963). Initially self-management was independent of Yugoslav unions, which occupied a similar position to their counterparts elsewhere in CEE, but after about 1970 Yugoslav trade unions supported unofficial strikes called against incomes policies implemented to curb inflation (Coates and Topham 1972: 244).[6]

In summary, the 'golden age' was a phenomenon of Western Europe that enabled trade unions to consolidate economic and political positions that hitherto they had not achieved. Within CEE the position of unions was also consolidated in a subservient relation to the Communist Party. The contrast between trade unionism in Western Europe and CEE was thus marked. Furthermore, these differences were accentuated when the Soviet bloc disintegrated and the system within which trade unions were consolidated was replaced.

... the neoliberal challenge

The neoliberal policy agenda impacted all Member States, albeit to different degrees dependent *inter alia* upon the resilience of trade union organization, the degree of union embeddedness in labour market and welfare institutions, and the intensity of the adopted neoliberal programme. At the core of the neoliberal agenda was the rejection of Keynesian assumptions, including the rejection of full employment as a desired political target and the prioritization of the control of inflation (Baccaro and Howell 2017). Post-1980 levels of unemployment have thus been consistently higher than those recorded during most of the 'golden age' with a subsequent weakening of the bargaining position of trade unions (see Table A1.J).[7] In pursuit of reduced inflation governments sought

6 Chapters 5 and 26 examine whether this different pattern of development impinges on trade union practices in Croatia and Slovenia after 2000.

7 All tables marked A1 are available in the appendix.

increases in labour market 'flexibility'. In this context trade unions and collective bargaining were viewed as labour market rigidities, which were to be reduced in effect. Accompanying attempts to reduce the coverage of collective bargaining were initiatives to promote the decentralization of collective bargaining, which were generally supported by employers. In CEE where unions and collective bargaining were at a different level of development compared to Western Europe, measures were taken to limit their development with adverse consequences for union density, which plummeted immediately after the transformation, and the coverage of collective bargaining, which remained sparse. Only in Romania and Slovenia were industrial bargaining arrangements established and these were short-lived in Romania (Trif and Paolucci 2019). Elsewhere in CEE where collective bargaining was established it tended to operate at company level.

Employers lobbied hard for these political changes and took advantage of the political opportunity to introduce a range of policies that further inhibit union organization, particularly in the form of human resource management (HRM) practices designed to enable managers to speak directly with workers rather than through their union workplace representative or works councillor, and so-called flexible working based on neoliberal legislation that limits job security. Although the extent to which Fordist production will disappear is debated (Coriat 1995; Hirst and Zeitlin 1991), it is clear that other production regimes, incorporating flexible specialization, are becoming embedded, again requiring a shift in union organization (Boyer and Drache 1996; Iversen and Soskice 2019: 136–215).

A further objective of the neoliberal programme is a reduction in the size and the role of the state. Privatization of industries and services owned by the state was commonplace in Western Europe after 1980, together with the introduction of mechanisms intended to promote internal markets within the remaining public sector. In CEE the extent of privatization was more wide-ranging, an impact compounded by the high rates of foreign direct investment from Western European- and United States (US)-owned MNCs (Bohle and Greskovits 2012: 262–267). In practice, throughout much of Europe public sector employment contracted as a proportion of the labour force, thereby shifting employment from economic segments of union strength to segments of relative union weakness.

Regarding the role of the state the neoliberal intention was to 'distance' the state from trade union engagement. In Western Europe many tripartite and corporatist institutions were dismantled or downgraded in influence, thus limiting union involvement in policy formulation (Baccaro and Howell 2017). In CEE tripartite institutions were established ostensibly to generate political support for the transformation to market economies, to settle minimum wages, to manage welfare provisions and to establish systems of industrial relations. Many of these tripartite institutions, however, were shown to be illusory, a means to generate neoliberal outcomes and a contraction of the welfare state, and a mechanism to ensure that labour recognized the weakness of its position (Bohle et al. 2007; Ost 2000).

During the 'golden age' the focus of trade union activity was within the nation state. Concurrent with the ascendency of the neoliberal policy agenda were further developments towards globalization and internationalization that rendered obsolete a sole union focus on the nation state. For unions, however, a focus on the nation state remained imperative as welfare provisions, legislation on social security and most collective bargaining institutions and practices remained national, albeit often taking international developments into account. While the nature and impact of globalization are contested (Munck 2002; Nichols and Cam 2005), it is apparent that the absence of agreed global regulation or a 'global compact' (Held 2004: 55–72) promotes regime competition as MNCs seek sites from which to base their activities more competitively (Greer and Hauptmeier 2016). In this context, national regulations sought by unions and labour unrest may act to encourage MNCs to locate activities where regulations are less demanding, which, in turn, may create conditions favourable for further unionization (Silver 2003). Regime competition results in operating standards below those sought by unions and, beyond Europe, the exclusion of trade unions from the workplace. The challenge for unions is to establish, or be integral to, a global regulatory framework, which ensures decent standards, however these may be defined.

Within the EU, integration, enlargement and the adoption of a wider range of European regulation has necessitated trade union interventions at European level. Trade unionists could no longer defend their interest by acting solely within the nation state. The ETUC and the European Trade Union Federations (ETUFs), which operate at industry level, are relatively 'immature' organizations that are in the process of establishing a *raison d'être* at a time when resources are limited. To ensure an articulated response to EU-level policy proposals the ETUC and the ETUFs must liaise with affiliated trade union organizations operating at national level. In short, to formulate coherent EU-level policies, additional resources are required at a time when membership decline effectively curtails the resources available to trade unionism. This pressure is felt most markedly in CEE where unions are relatively poorly resourced. Furthermore, the different 'starting points' of Western European and CEE trade unions as they emerged from the 'golden age' raises questions about how a unified union position might emerge and the form it might take (Adamczyk 2018; Müller and Platzer 2020). Similarly, differences in national industrial relations systems have led to intense debates within the ETUC as to the form European regulation preferred by trade unions might take (Lovén Seldén 2020; Seeliger 2019).

Concurrent with the neoliberal challenge was the weakening of the links between trade unions and social democratic or labour parties, as left-of-centre parties abandoned rhetorical demands for 'full employment' in favour of assigning preference to the control of inflation with adverse consequences for the bargaining position of unions (Haugsgjerd Allern and Bale 2017). The idea of trade unions working in conjunction with left-of-centre political parties in a labour movement has become increasingly open to question. In Germany and the United Kingdom (UK), for example, The 'Agenda 2010' adopted in 2003 by the Social Democratic-led coalition government of Chancellor Schröder and the 'third way' strategy of the Labour government of Prime Minister Blair were effectively programmes that copied many of the policies of their right-of-centre predecessors (Spier 2017; Webb and Bale 2017). Also in the political sphere, large numbers of unionists and potential members now vote for far-right nationalist and populist parties, albeit among unionists at a lower rate than among the population as a whole, further eroding the political position of trade unions (Mosimann et al. 2019; Oesch 2008).

Within the polity at EU-level the Alliance of Socialists and Democrats (S&D) was the largest parliamentary group until 1999,[8] but, with the exception of the fifth European Parliament 1999–2004, has operated as

[8] The title Alliance of Socialists and Democrats was adopted in 2009. While there were several name changes beforehand the most longstanding was the Party of European Socialists (PES), which is still used in some circles today.

part of a grand coalition with the Christian-democratic and conservative European People's Party (EPP), most recently as a means to limit the influence of the populist and nationalist right-of-centre. The price of this coalition is adherence to the neoliberal economic agenda advocated by the EPP and the absence of any recent significant progress on a European social policy agenda.[9] This pattern of development is characterized by an increasing reliance on 'soft' law regulation (Sapir 2014), an asymmetry between market enforcing and market correcting measures (Scharpf 2009), the 'social deficit' apparent in economic and social union (Hinarejos 2016), and the limited aspirations of the EU Pillar of Social Rights (Lörcher and Schömann 2016). It remains to be seen whether the European Commission led by Ursula von der Leyen will significantly change course, despite far-reaching initiatives such as the directives on adequate minimum wages in the EU and on platform workers.

The ascendency of the neoliberal political agenda is associated with a shift in the pattern of regulation in Western Europe involving the abandoning of Keynesian policies and in CEE the rejection of command economies. Throughout the EU trade unions are thus in the process of adjustment to radically changed circumstances. At its core, the neoliberal project intends to remove the state from intervening in the relation between capital and wage labour. From the neoliberal perspective the role of unions and collective bargaining thus needs to be curbed. Differences in the strength of trade unions, their institutional embeddedness and the intensity with which the neoliberal agenda is pursued ensure that neoliberalism has had varied national effects on unionism. Further exacerbating this situation are the uneven effects of digitalization, environmental change and migration. Examination of this variation between Member States is central to the country chapters. To introduce these analyses this chapter now elaborates the scale of changes in labour markets, economic outcomes and collective bargaining concurrent with the neoliberal project.

9 It should be noted in this context that when the PES was relatively stronger than currently, it followed the 'third way' or 'neue mitte' policies that embraced many of the assumptions of the neoliberal project, with the consequence that progress of social policy was limited.

Charting the scale of change

In outlining the ascendency of neoliberal policies, the previous section acknowledged historical differences between CEE and Western Europe, and between Member States within these two groups. This section enumerates the scale of these differences by reference to the labour market, economic outcomes and collective bargaining. In so doing the section maps in data terms the situation within each Member State, which is then elaborated within the country chapters. The data are presented in two forms: within the section graphically and separately for Western (EU16) and Eastern (EU11) Europe covering the period 2000 to 2020,[10] and in the Appendix, which includes data, where available, showing the averages for the 1960s, 1970s, 1980s, 1990s together with annual data from 2000 for each Member State. Data on individual Member States presented in this chapter are drawn from Appendix A1 unless otherwise stated.

The changing composition of the labour market

As well as diminishing the impact of trade unions and collective bargaining, the shift away from Keynesian economics inherent in the neoliberal project has required increasing flexibility and insecurity within the labour market. Within the EU the pursuit of increasing flexibility is associated with attempts to maintain some security for workers within the labour market, hence the promotion of 'flexicurity' by the European Commission (Wilthagen and Tros 2004). Accompanying and, in part, driven by the requirements of the neoliberal project are marked changes to the composition of the labour market and a weakening of the contractual position of workers. Changes in the composition of the labour market, whether they are a result of neoliberal policies or have other origins, have interacted with the diminished impact of trade unions and collective bargaining. The power resources approach, for example, demonstrates that high unemployment and shifts in the composition of the labour market away from the traditional model of male full-time

10 The EU16 comprises Austria, Belgium, Cyprus, Denmark, Finland, France, Germany, Greece, Ireland, Italy, Luxembourg, Malta, the Netherlands, Portugal, Spain and Sweden. The EU11 comprises Bulgaria, Czechia, Estonia, Hungary, Latvia, Lithuania, Poland, Romania, Slovakia and Slovenia.

employment in manufacturing weakens the structural and organizational power resources of workers and, hence, trade unions (Lehndorff et al. 2018; Schmalz et al. 2018). Structural power resources refer to the strategic location of workers within the labour process and their bargaining power within the labour market resulting from the scarcity of workers, which is diminished at times of high unemployment. Organizational power resources refer to the numerical strength of unions and their ability to successfully mobilize members. Organizational power resources are negatively affected by changes in the composition of the labour market because some sections of the labour market are more difficult for unions to organize (Levesque and Murray 2010).

Quantitative changes in the composition of the labour market are examined in five stages. The first stage assesses the impact of neoliberal policies on unemployment rates, while the second stage analyzes changes in employment rates. The third stage charts the feminization of employment. The fourth stage enumerates shifts in employment away from manufacturing towards private sector services, the so-called 'tertiarization of employment'. The fifth stage maps the growth of part-time and temporary employment and discusses the rise of contractual forms that differ from 'standard' employment. It is acknowledged from the outset that there are significant interrelationships between the changes charted here. As the country chapters show, the form of these interrelationships varies between countries. The argument that resonates throughout is that there have been marked changes in the labour market since the 1960s many of which have made it more difficult to sustain trade union organization (Ebbinghaus and Visser 1999).

Unemployment

Integral to the shift away from Keynesian policies was the political downgrading of the pursuit of full unemployment and the priority assigned to controlling inflation. The move away from controlling unemployment served an additional political purpose of weakening the bargaining position of trade unions when unemployment rates rose. Figure 1.1 shows the movements in the weighted averages of the unemployment rate from 2000.

Figure 1.1. Weighted average in the unemployment level in EU Member States (%), 2000–2020

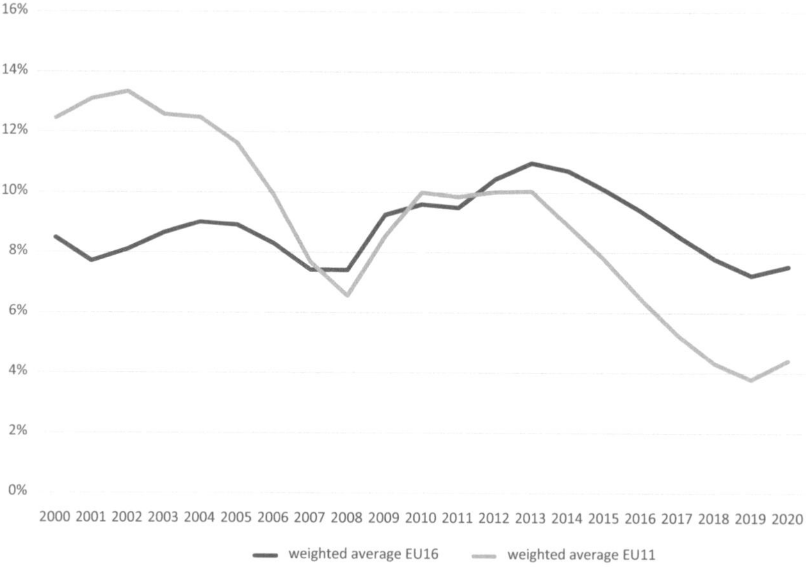

Among the EU16 the rate of unemployment varied within a relatively narrow range between 2000 and 2020. Unemployment increased following the sub-prime and financial crisis of 2008–2009, declined thereafter before rising again as the Covid pandemic hit. Although unemployment tended to rise throughout the EU16 after 2008, Table A1.J demonstrates that particularly sharp increases were recorded in the countries in which the Troika imposed neoliberal austerity measures.[11] Post-2008 unemployment peaks in these countries were markedly higher than elsewhere in the EU16: Cyprus, 16.1 per cent (2014); Greece, 27.5 per cent (2013); Ireland, 15.5 per cent (2012); Portugal, 16.4 per cent (2013); and Spain, 26.1 per cent (2013).

Compared with the 1960s and 1970s, unemployment rates in the EU16 during the twenty-first century were universally higher. In nine

[11] The Troika comprised the International Monetary Fund (IMF), the European Central Bank (ECB) and the European Commission. The Troika implemented a series of neoliberal austerity policies in countries within which a sovereign debt crisis arose as a result of the sub-prime and banking crisis of 2008.

Member States the average annual rate of unemployment after 2000 was higher than that recorded during the 1980s, whereas in five Member States recent rates are lower than during the 1980s.[12] This varied pattern suggests that considerable temporal variation remains within Member States regarding movements in the business cycle and the policies implemented to limit unemployment. It is noteworthy that Ireland and the Netherlands, two of the countries with high rates of unemployment during the 1980s, implemented the Programme for National Recovery in 1988 and the Wassenaar Agreement in 1982 (Bruff 2008; Visser and Hemerijck 1999), respectively, as coordinated responses involving the state and social partners. These measures led to marked reductions in unemployment, albeit accompanied by wage moderation (Eichengreen 2007: 388–393). Such initiatives have not been replicated during the twenty-first century among the EU16. Indeed, the Irish Programme for National Recovery persisted in the form of social partnership agreements until 2009 when it was disbanded as a result of the programme of reforms demanded by the Troika (Maccarrone et al. 2019). In the few countries in which tripartite 'crisis-corporatist' responses to the sub-prime and financial crisis were sought, it was not possible to conclude tripartite agreements at national level because of the marked divisions among the actors involved, although some bilateral company-level arrangements were concluded when the workers' side made concessions to safeguard employment (Urban 2012).

Figure 1.1 shows that the unemployment rate in the EU11 was relatively high during the early years of the twenty-first century, suggesting a long-term impact of the transition towards market economies and the struggle for competitiveness (Bohle and Greskovits 2012). The sub-prime and financial crisis acted to reverse the decline in the EU11 unemployment rate experienced between 2002 and 2008. The post-2008 unemployment rate, however, has yet to reach pre-2005 levels, unlike in the EU16, reflecting the relatively limited direct exposure of the EU11 to the sub-prime and financial crisis (Bohle and Greskovits 2012). In contrast,

[12] The nine Member States with higher rates of unemployment after 2000 than during the 1980s are: Austria, Finland, France, Germany, Greece, Italy, Luxembourg, Portugal and Sweden. The five Member States with lower recent rates are: Belgium, Denmark, Ireland, the Netherlands and Spain. No data are available for Cyprus and Malta for the 1980s, hence these two countries are excluded.

compared with the unemployment rate during the 1990s, twenty-first century average annual unemployment rates are higher in six of the EU11 Member States and lower in three,[13] confirming the impact of the wide range of political approaches intended to lower unemployment in these countries (Bohle and Greskovits 2012). It should also be acknowledged that large-scale emigration from several of the EU11 to the EU16 Member States has mitigated unemployment rates within the EU11 (Ther 2016: 246–248, 308–311).

Employment

Following the terms of the Amsterdam Treaty, at the Luxembourg jobs summit of November 1997 the EU launched the European employment strategy, which at the Lisbon summit of March 2000 was linked by the European Council to the European strategy for a knowledge-based economy. At the subsequent Nice summit in 2001 a range of key structural indicators were adopted as measures of progress towards the implementation of the Lisbon strategy. Among these indicators were targets for an overall employment rate of 70 per cent and a 60 per cent employment rate for women aged between 16 and 64 by 2010. In 2010 the European Council adopted the Europe 2020 strategy integral to which was the achievement of an employment rate of 75 per cent for adults aged between 20 and 64 years for each Member State by 2020.

Figure 1.2 maps the weighted average of the employment rate for the EU16 and EU11 since 2000. The employment rate for the EU16 rose steadily after 2000 from 66.1 to over 71.9 per cent. In quantitative terms, there is no apparent adverse effect on the aggregate employment rate from the sub-prime and financial crisis. Keeping up the level of employment, however, came at the price of deteriorating job quality marked in particular by an increase in nonstandard forms of employment and with average levels of job quality in the EU remaining below pre-crisis levels (Piasna 2017). Where the Troika intervened, however, the employment rate declined markedly between 2008 and 2012: Cyprus, 76.5 and 70.2 per cent; Greece, 66.3 and 55.0 per cent; Ireland, 73.5 and 64.5 per

---

13 The six Member States in which twenty-first century unemployment rates are higher than during the 1990s are: Bulgaria, Czechia, Estonia, Latvia, Lithuania and Slovakia. The three Members States in which the reverse is the case are: Hungary, Poland and Romania. In Slovenia the unemployment rates in the two periods were the same, while no data are available for the 1990s for Croatia.

cent; Portugal, 73.1 and 66.3 per cent; and Spain, 68.5 and 59.6 per cent. These declines suggest that actions taken across Europe to secure some jobs in particular through the widespread use of short-time work schemes, albeit on reduced terms and conditions to cut costs during the financial and sub-prime crisis were insufficient in countries where the Troika intervened (Hijzen and Venn 2011; Theodoropoulou 2018).

Figure 1.2. Weighted average in the employment rate in EU Member States (%), 2000–2020

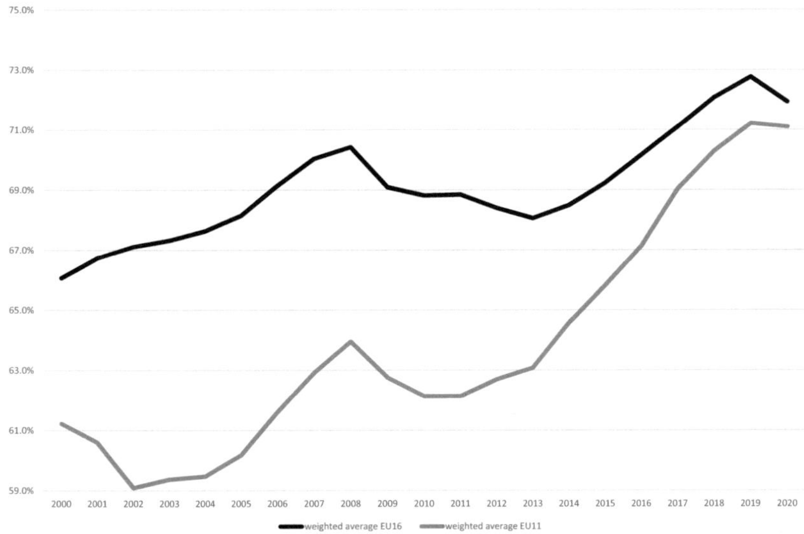

The employment rate in the EU11 declined sharply from 2000 to 2004 due to the impact of recession and post-1990 adjustment. Thereafter the employment rate consistently rose to more than 71.1 per cent in 2020, thus reaching a similar level to that in the EU16 in 2020. In all EU11 Member States the employment rate was higher in 2020 than in 2000, suggesting that irrespective of the chosen economic policy options the employment rate was generally protected. The current range of employment rates within the EU11, however, varies markedly from 67.1 per cent in Croatia to 79.3 per cent in Estonia in 2020. The quantitative development tells only part of the story, however. Despite the overall positive development of employment since 2000, which, in principle, should create favourable conditions for union organization, it should be noted once again that much of the increases in employment is due to the growth of 'atypical' jobs such as part-time and temporary employment, which are dealt with in more detail below (Piasna and Myant 2017; Rubery 2015).

Feminization of the employed labour force

From the 1960s the position of women within society and the labour market has changed markedly (Cunnison and Stageman 1995; Lewenhak 1980). In particular, regarding current purposes more women have participated in the labour market, albeit with considerable national variations in the rate of participation (see Table A1.L). Figure 1.3 illustrates two different plots on the feminization of the employed labour force in the EU11 and EU16 after 2000. In relative terms, the proportion of women in the employed labour force in the EU11 rose between 2000 and 2020 from 55.1 to 66.4 per cent of the labour force. Between 2000 and 2008, however, the proportion of women in the employed labour force tended to decline, a decrease that was reversed as men lost jobs in the period following the financial crisis. The range in the extent of feminization of the employed labour force in 2020 varies from 61.0 per cent in Romania to 75.8 per cent in Lithuania, indicating the impact of different social structures and welfare state regimes within the EU11.

Figure 1.3. Weighted average in the share of women in employment in EU Member States (%), 2000–2020

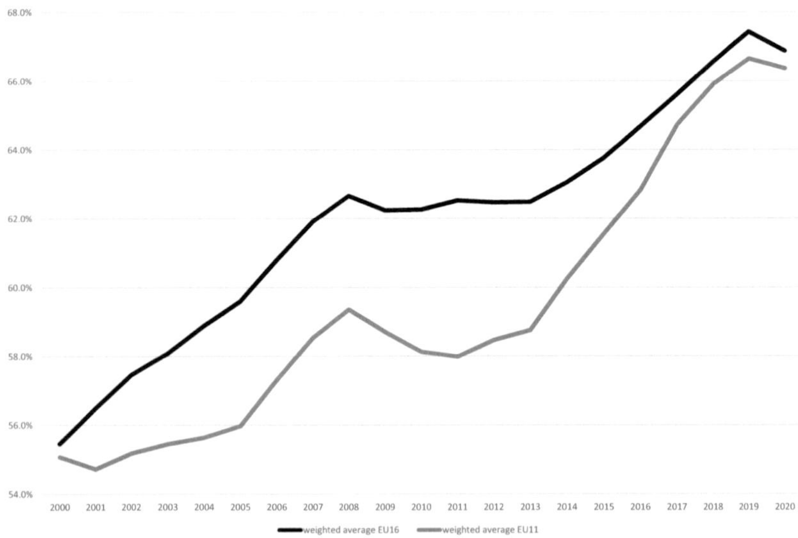

In contrast, Figure 1.3 shows an almost uninterrupted rise in the rate within the EU16 from 55.5 to 69.9 per cent by 2020. Although the rate of increase accelerated following the financial crisis, suggesting that men were most likely to lose their jobs in this period, it slackened thereafter as men subsequently found work. As with the EU11 there is considerable variation in the feminization rates among the EU16 Member States. Above-average feminization rates are found in the Nordic countries (Denmark, 74.3 per cent; Finland, 75.0 per cent; Sweden, 78.3 per cent), reflecting the long-term presence of policies designed to support gender equality at home, at work and in public life (OECD 2018b). Some Southern European countries exhibit relatively low feminization rates (Greece, 51.8 per cent; Italy, 52.7 per cent) again suggesting an impact of different social structures and welfare state regimes (Ferrera 2005).

Changing sectoral composition of the labour force

Figure 1.4 shows the shifts in the composition of the labour force by reference to industry and private sector services. It is acknowledged from the outset that these measures implicitly incorporate changes that are not quantified. The growth of employment in private sector services, for example, is associated with increases in employment at small workplaces, in labour turnover rates and the feminization of the labour force. In essence, there is a similar pattern in the EU11 and EU16: the share of employment in industry is contracting while that in private sector services is increasing. Within the EU11 and EU16 private sector services is now larger than industry. Whereas the financial crisis of 2008 marked the point when employment in private sector services overtook that in industry within the EU11, this point had occurred before 2000 in the EU16. Figure 1.4 illustrates the more marked impact of the financial crisis on employment in industry than private sector services. The rate of growth in employment in private sector services between 2000 and 2020 is similar in the EU16 and EU11 at around 10.0 percentage points.

Figure 1.4. Weighted average of employment in industry and private sector services in EU Member States (%), 2000–2020

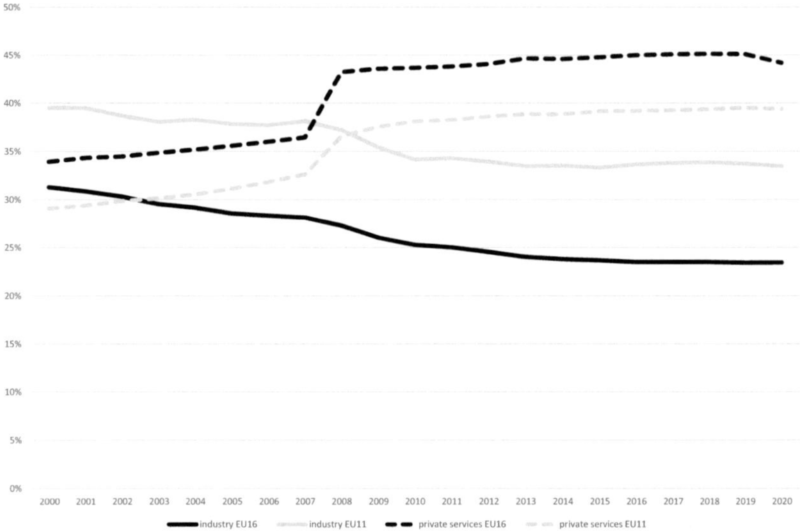

In every Member State of the EU11 the share of employment in industry declined between 2000 and 2020 (Table A1.M). It is noteworthy, however, that the declines in Czechia (3.2 percentage points) and Slovakia (2.0 percentage points) were small compared to elsewhere, reflecting the presence of skilled workforces working in relatively high value-added occupations (Bohle and Greskovits 2012: 138–181). Only in Slovakia, however, was employment in industry in 2020 more numerous than in private sector services within the EU11 (Tables A1.M and A1.N). In every Member State of the EU16 private sector services constitutes a larger proportion of employment than industry.

Part-time and temporary employment

About 76 per cent of part-time workers in Europe aged between 20 and 64 years are women (Eurostat 2020). Part-time work is thus a means whereby the employment rate is increased by encouraging the participation of women. In several countries part-time workers were initially discriminated against in the form of inferior terms and conditions of employment, particularly regarding pay, sickness, holiday leave and job security (Rogers and Rogers 1989; Standing 1999). Inferior job security encouraged the growth of part-time work in some countries, as employers viewed the ease of hiring and firing as a source of flexibility (Rubery and Fagan 1994). Legislation was enacted by some Member States to address these inequities and, in essence, set out to ensure that part-time work was pro-rata to full-time work at the same establishment. These national legislative initiatives were consolidated by the Part-time Work Directive (97/81/EC) in 1987, introduced as an anti-discrimination measure, which put part-time workers in Europe on a pro-rata footing with their full-time counterparts. The employer-driven flexibility of part-time work thus diminished over time, although it is apparent that discrimination against part-time workers has yet to disappear (Karamessini and Rubery 2014). Temporary work is also viewed as a source of flexibility insofar as short-term contracts may or may not be renewed dependent upon perceived economic circumstances, thereby enabling employers to vary the number of employees without reference to redundancy procedures (Standing 1999). Figures 1.5 and 1.6 illustrate the share of total employment that was part-time and temporary between 2000 and 2020.

Figure 1.5. Weighted average in the share of employment that is part-time in EU Member States (%), 2000–2020

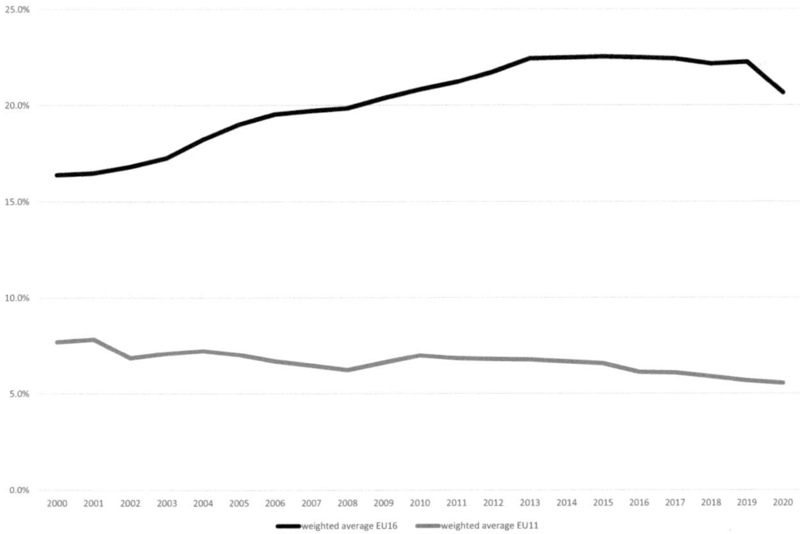

Figure 1.5 shows that part-time work comprised almost 21.0 per cent of all employment in the EU16 in 2020, having steadily risen from under 17.0 per cent in 2000. With the exceptions of France and Portugal, where the share of total employment comprising part-time employment remained fairly constant, the share of part-time employment increased in every Member State of the EU16 after 2000. The consistency implied by this pattern of development is absent when comparing countries. In the Netherlands, for example, 50.8 per cent of employment consists of part-time workers (Visser 2002), whereas, at the other extreme, part-time work comprises only 7.5 per cent of total employment in Portugal.

Figure 1.5 also demonstrates that part-time work occurs less frequently within the EU11 than the EU16.[14] Furthermore, within the EU11 the share of total employment that is part-time declined by almost 2 percentage points between 2000 and 2020. The pattern of development within the EU11 is disparate, however, with declines recorded in six countries between 2000 and 2020 (Bulgaria, Croatia, Latvia, Lithuania, Poland, Romania) and increases recorded in five countries (Czechia, Estonia, Hungary, Slovakia, Slovenia). Given the overall levels of part-time employment in the EU11 are much lower than in the EU16, it is not surprising that the range of occurrence is also narrower, varying from 1.8 per cent of employment in Bulgaria to 12.3 per cent in Estonia in 2020.

Figure 1.6 illustrates that temporary employment remained a fairly constant proportion of all employment within the EU16 between 2000 and 2020. By 2020 about 12.5 per cent of all employment was temporary, a significant proportion, but lower than that comprised by part-time employees. The wide-ranging effect of different national policy choices is also apparent (OECD 2019). In 2000, for example, Spain was an outlier with 25.8 per cent of employment composed of temporary work compared with 14.1 per cent in Finland and 13.8 per cent in France in the next two positions in the ranking and the minimum of 3.5 per cent in Malta. By 2020 Spain was less of an outlier with 20.4 per cent temporary employment compared to 15.3 per cent in Portugal, 14.9 per cent in the Netherlands and a minimum of 7.3 per cent in Austria (see Table A1.P).

---

[14] Several factors are cited by members of the network to explain the low rates of part-time work within the EU11 including the relatively low levels of pay, a reluctance among employers to engage part-time workers and the legacy effects of the extensive child care provisions established before 1990 which promoted full-time employment.

Figure 1.6. Weighted average in the share of temporary employment in EU Member States (%), 2000–2020

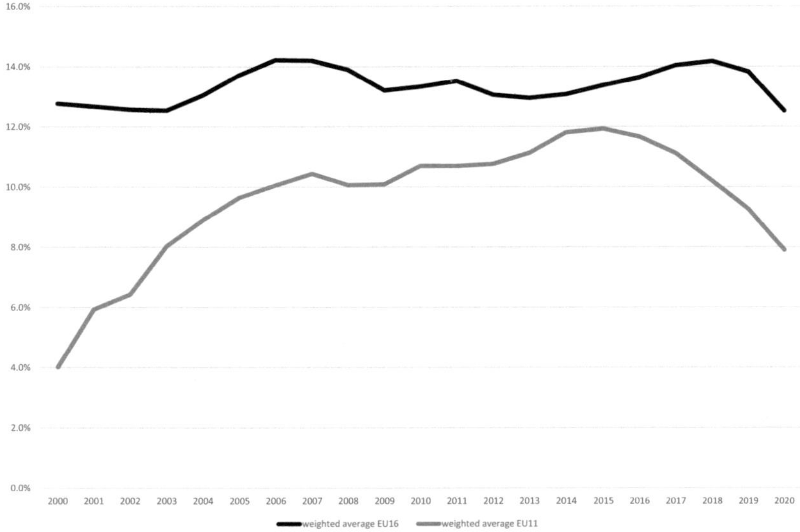

Although temporary work rose from 4.0 per cent to almost 8.0 per cent in the EU11 it did not reach the levels recorded within the EU16. Within the EU11 there are distinct patterns of development regarding temporary work in 2020. In Bulgaria, the Baltic States and Romania, for example, temporary work does not exceed 4 per cent of the employed labour force, whereas in Poland (14.7 per cent), Croatia (13.4 per cent) and Slovenia (9.5 per cent) the rates of temporary employment are comparable with the averages of the EU16. Poland, Croatia and Slovenia, however, are outliers within the EU11 as eight of the nine Member States with the lowest rates of temporary employment are EU11 Member States.[15]

[15] The eight EU11 Member States among the nine Member States with the lowest rates of temporary employment are Romania, Lithuania, Latvia, Estonia, Bulgaria, Hungary, Slovakia and Czechia. Malta is the only Member State from the EU16 included among these nine Member States.

Economic outcomes

The neoliberal pursuit of labour markets regulated to increase flexibility, including reductions in the coverage of trade unionism and collective bargaining, was directed towards improvements in economic performance (European Commission 2012; Minford 1990). This section examines three aspects of economic performance to assess the impact of neoliberal policies on unions: real wage and productivity development; wage share; and income inequality.

Within the EU three strands of development have facilitated the pursuit of neoliberal policies within Member States. First, the 'negative integration' (Scharpf 1996) that characterizes EU integration comprises deregulation and measures to guarantee the 'four freedoms' within Member States.[16] In combination, these factors generated pressures for wage moderation as competition intensified between Member States (Keune 2008). Second, pressures for wage moderation were also generated by the terms of economic and monetary union (EMU). Before EMU economic imbalances and diverging developments in national competitiveness could be addressed by devaluing national currencies. Within EMU this is no longer possible with the consequence that 'internal devaluation' by way of wage moderation to reduce labour costs became a 'functional substitute to currency devaluation' (Armingeon and Baccaro 2012: 256). Similarly, the strict requirements within EMU regarding public expenditure and public debt exert pressures to limit public sector wage increases through limits on government expenditure (Müller and Schulten 2015; Streeck 2015). These pressures for wage moderation are amplified by the European Central Bank policy of assigning primacy to the maintenance of low inflation, which, as was demonstrated above, has contributed to persistently high rates of unemployment. A third factor associated with the neoliberal agenda and influential within the EU was the sovereign debt crisis that followed the banking crisis of 2008 (Flassbeck and Lapavitsas 2015). The sovereign debt crisis resulted in a series of short-term demands that exacerbated pressures for the developments mentioned above. The objective here is to present the aggregate effects of these policies on labour.

---

16 The four freedoms cover the movement of goods, persons, services and capital within the EU.

Real wage and productivity growth

The relationship between the growth of real wages and productivity growth is an indicator of labour's capacity to ensure that workers receive a 'fair' share of the wealth they helped to generate. A higher rate of increase in productivity compared to that of real wages suggests that labour has a limited capacity to extract benefits from productivity growth. Raising the rate of productivity growth has also been a long-term objective of the neoliberal programme with labour market flexibility, reductions in the coverage of collective bargaining and unions, and bargaining decentralization among the policy means whereby such increases could be secured. Figure 1.7 charts the movements in real wages and productivity growth for the EU16 and EU11 since 2000.

Figure 1.7. Weighted average of annual change in real wages and labour productivity in EU Member States (%), 2000–2020

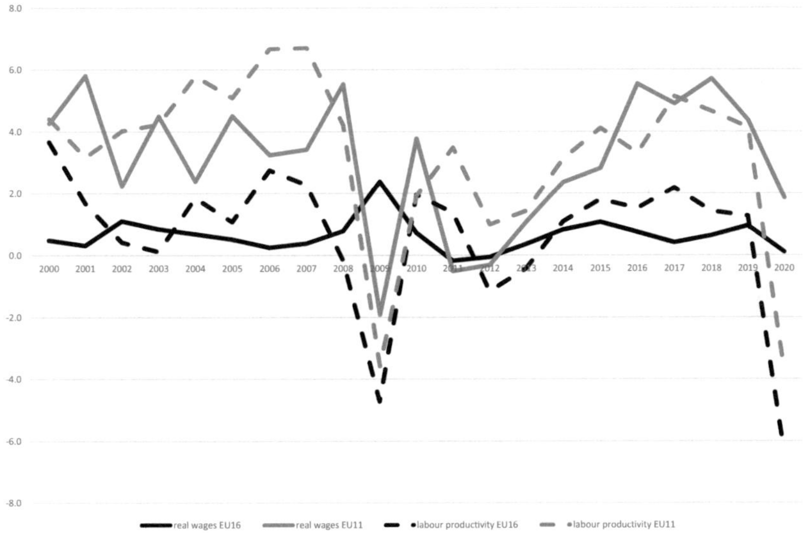

Until the sub-prime and financial crisis of 2008 movements in real wages lagged behind productivity growth in the EU16 but were broadly comparable. The rate of productivity growth dipped sharply in 2008–2009 as the impact of the crisis became apparent. After labour productivity recovered in 2010 real wages developed broadly in line with labour productivity until 2015 when productivity started to outpace real wage growth. This trend continued until 2020 when productivity took another hit from the Covid pandemic. In policy terms the decoupling of real wage growth from productivity development was the result of neoliberal austerity measures implemented as a response to the crisis. They restricted the growth of real wages and, in some countries, cut real wages, particularly among public sector workers (Flassbeck and Lapavitsas 2015; Keune et al. 2020).

Within the EU11 for much of the period between 2000 and 2009 productivity growth outstripped the growth in real wages. As in the EU16 the rate of productivity growth dipped sharply after 2007 within the EU11 before rising after 2009. Unlike the EU16, however, real wage growth also dipped markedly during the sub-prime and financial crisis in the EU11. Productivity growth rose more steeply than real wages until about 2013 after which real wage growth accelerated more quickly than productivity growth. For much of the period after 2000 within the EU11 the rate of real wage growth thus was greater than productivity growth. This suggests that adjustments to the market economy after the transformation are benefitting the living standards of those in employment within the EU11 irrespective of the relatively low coverage of collective bargaining and low union density rates. This effect is likely to be accentuated by emigration.

Wage share

The decoupling of real wage increases from labour productivity growth is reflected in the long-term development of the wage share as a measure of the share of the national income accounted for by labour compensation in the form of wages, salaries and other benefits (OECD 2018). Figure 1.8 charts the wage share accruing to labour in the EU16 and EU11 between 2000 and 2020. The plot for the EU16 indicates a slight decrease between 2000 and 2007 reflecting that real wage development lagged behind the movements in labour productivity. The short-term rise in the plot immediately after 2007 is primarily due to the countercyclical nature of the wage share which means that it tends to fall when output increases and rise when output decreases. After this short-term recovery, however, the wage share resumed its decreasing tendency in the EU16 until the Covid pandemic. It thus appears that the economic and political pressures arising from neoliberal crisis management after the financial crisis of 2008, based on a combination of austerity policies and political interventions into national collective bargaining systems meant that workers did not benefit appropriately in the wealth they created (Schulten and Müller 2015). Reference to Table A1.S shows that in Greece, Ireland, Portugal and Spain there were marked declines in the wage share, particularly after 2010, indicating that labour bore the brunt of the economic reforms demanded by the Troika.

Figure 1.8. Weighted average in wage share in EU Member States (%), 2000–2020

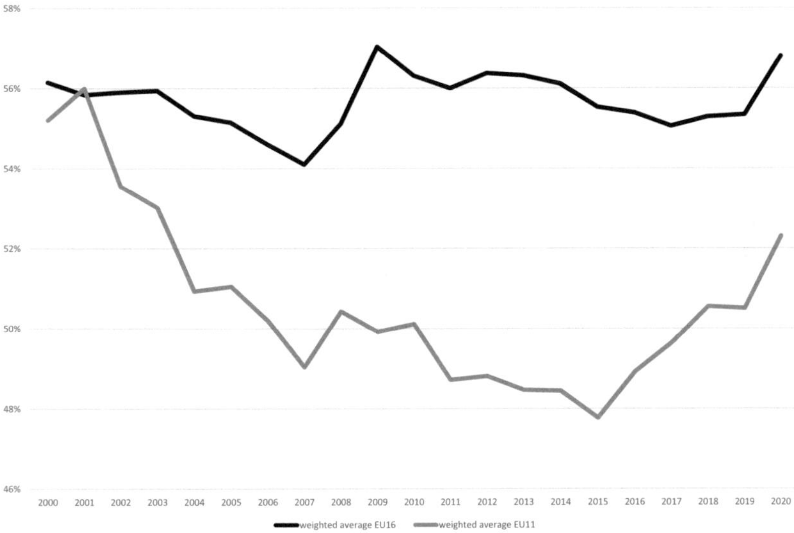

Table A1.S includes data from the 1960s and thus allows an assessment of the long-term impact of the neoliberal programme. With the single exception of Greece during the 1970s in every Member State within the EU16 for which data are available the average annual wage share for the 1970s and 1980s was greater than that for 2020. Furthermore, the extent of the decline between the 1960s and 2020 was marked in several countries: Ireland, –33.0 percentage points; Greece, –10.7 percentage points; Portugal, –10.7 percentage points; Finland, –13.0 percentage points; and Austria, –6.0 percentage points. The long-term effect of the neoliberal programme is thus the decline in the wage share accruing to labour within the EU16. The reasons for the long-term decline of the wage share and the corresponding shift in income distribution from labour to capital are manifold. They include the financialization of the economy (Grady and Simms 2019; Kollmeyer and Peters 2019), the liberalization of capital markets (Stockhammer et al. 2018), the deregulation of labour markets (Deakin et al. 2014) and the decentralization of collective bargaining (Checci and García Peñalosa 2010). All these factors share one common characteristic: they have helped to shift the balance of power from labour to capital and thus decreased union bargaining power (Lübker and Schulten 2018).

Turning to the EU11 reveals a different pattern of development. The plot in Figure 1.8 shows that the wage share in the EU11 fell between 2000 and 2015 by about 7.0 percentage points before rising 4.0 percentage points to 2020. Labour was thus unable to retain its wage share for much of the period after 2000 and between 2000 and 2015 sustained marked losses compared with labour in the EU16. Table A1.S shows that only in Croatia, Hungary, Poland and Romania the wage share accruing to labour was lower in 2020 compared to both the average for the 1990s and for the year 2000. The decline was particularly steep in Romania, 19.1 percentage points between 2000 and 2020, where the state eliminated industrial bargaining and union density plummeted. In Bulgaria, Czechia, Estonia, Latvia and Lithuania the wage share accruing to labour was higher in 2020 than the average for the 1990s and for the year 2000. EU membership, mediated by a range of institutional factors, has thus had a mixed effect on the wage share within Member States of the EU11 (Bohle and Greskovits 2012; European Commission 2018).[17]

Income inequality

Figure 1.9 shows the development of inequality of disposable income in the EU16 and EU11 between 2000 and 2020 using the Gini coefficient.[18] Two points are immediately apparent from the plots. First, inequality within the EU11 between 2005 and 2016 was greater than that within the EU16 but has fluctuated throughout. Second, in contrast there has been a steady rise in inequality within the EU16 since about 2002. Neoliberal policies are thus associated with rising inequality within the EU16. The extent of inequality within the EU is generating macroeconomic inefficiencies, as well as accelerating rates of poverty (Ostry et al. 2016; Piketty 2014).

---

[17] In Slovakia the wage share in 2020 was higher than that recorded for the 1990s but lower than that for 2000, whereas the reverse was the case for Slovenia.

[18] The Gini coefficient takes a value between zero and one. The data are reported here as percentage points for ease of explanation.

Figure 1.9. Income inequality in EU Member States (%), 2000–2020

As anticipated from Figure 1.9 the highest rates of inequality are found in the EU11 in Bulgaria, Estonia, Latvia, Lithuania and Romania, with Bulgaria at the peak of European inequality at 40.0 per cent in 2020 (Table A1.T). It is also noteworthy that the three Baltic States where neo-liberal policies have been in the forefront since 1990 are included among the Member States with the highest rates of inequality. The Visegrad nations, Croatia and Slovenia have income inequality rates comparable with those of the EU16. Although unionization rates and the coverage of collective bargaining tended to decline in EU11 Member States following the financial crisis, there is no single pattern of either increasing or decreasing income inequality after 2008. The Member States that were subject to intervention from the Troika were all positioned towards the top of the ranking of inequality within the EU16.

The neoliberal assault on collective bargaining

Collective bargaining is central to an analysis of trade unions in the EU on two key counts. First, the pursuit of improved terms and conditions of employment for members, and employees more generally, by means of collective bargaining is a core union activity (Webb and Webb

1920). Second in pursuit of flexibility within the labour market, advocates of the neoliberal agenda seek to reduce the influence or eliminate collective bargaining, thus removing the rigidities they view as arising from its presence. The tension between these two positions is examined in two stages, which assess the coverage of bargaining and the level of bargaining. The argument here is that huge disparities in the coverage of bargaining between the EU16 and EU11 effectively underpin a different set of objectives for unions within the two groups of Member States. Furthermore, the decentralized bargaining arrangements in the EU11 and the process of decentralization underway in several Member States within the EU16 create additional pressures on the articulation and coordination capacities of unions. A third stage examines the implications of these developments for unions.

The coverage of bargaining

Figure 1.10 shows movements in the weighted coverage of collective bargaining, defined as the number of employees whose terms and conditions of employment are set by collective bargaining expressed as a proportion of the labour force. The plot for the EU16 remains relatively constant between 2000 and about 2009. After 2009 there was a shallow decline in coverage until 2014, after which the decline was more marked. The activities of the Troika explain the decline in the coverage of collective bargaining after 2009. The coverage in Cyprus declined from 57.3 to 45.4 per cent between 2008 and 2012, for example, while in Greece and Ireland coverage fell from 83.1 to 21.9 per cent and from 40.5 to 32.5 per cent between 2008 and 2014. This 'frontal assault' on collective bargaining (Marginson 2015) resulted from the rigorous application of neoliberal economic priorities in these countries by the Troika. It is also noteworthy that collective bargaining coverage data tends to overstate the actual rate of coverage in countries where the Troika intervened. Contrary to the requirements of collective agreements, the terms and conditions of some employees were set by collective agreements that had not be updated for several years by employers concerned to reduce costs (Campos Lima 2019; Ioannou and Sonan 2019; Katsaroumpas and Koukiadaki 2019). Elsewhere coverage rates remained stable after 2000 in the EU16.

Figure 1.10. Weighted average in collective bargaining coverage in EU Member States (%), 2000–2020

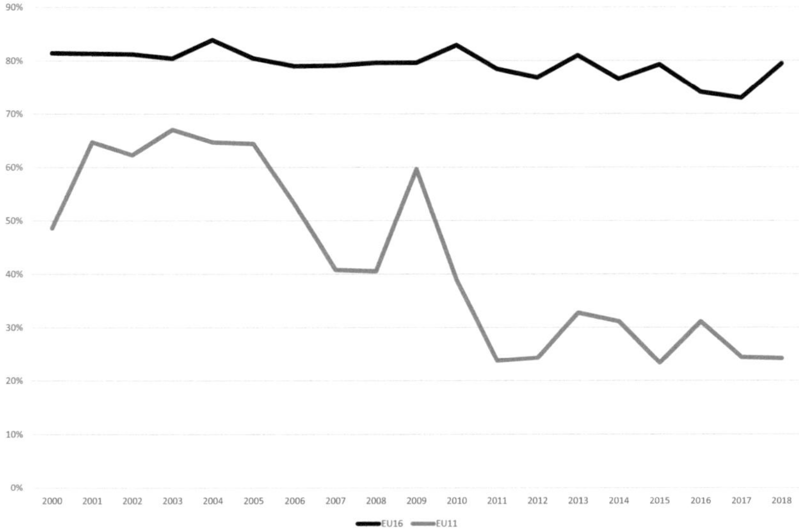

Two further points are apposite vis-à-vis coverage data in the EU16. First, with the exception of the countries mentioned above, the coverage of collective bargaining has remained relatively constant since 1960 (Table A1.H). As becomes apparent below, consistency in the coverage of collective bargaining masks significant changes in collective bargaining practices and the regulatory capacity of the institution. Second, there are significant differences within the EU16 in coverage rates, ranging from a constant 98.0 per cent in Austria in 2020 to around 50.0 per cent in Malta. Furthermore, the relative position in the rank order of Member States among the EU16 remained fairly constant after 1960. Austria, Belgium, Denmark and Sweden, for example, were towards the top of the ranking regarding the coverage of collective bargaining in 2000 and 2020, whereas Ireland, Luxembourg and Malta were towards the bottom of the ranking within the EU16 for both years. There is no Member State among the EU16 for which was recorded a marked move up the ranking between 2000 and 2020.

Compared to the plot for the EU16, the plot for the EU11 varies considerably between 2000 and 2018. The absence of consistency in the plot is indicative of the relative immaturity of collective bargaining systems in these Member States, the wide-ranging impact of changes in government, and the actions of employers.[19] During the period after 2000 until about 2005 the coverage of collective bargaining in the EU11 tended to converge with that of the EU16. Following the sub-prime and banking crisis of 2008 the coverage of collective bargaining in the EU11 declined, with particularly steep falls between 2008 and 2015 in Romania, from 100.0 to 22.6 per cent, in Slovenia, from 100.0 to 67.5 per cent, and in Slovakia from 40.0 to 24.0 per cent. The decline in the coverage of collective bargaining in Romania and Slovenia are particularly noteworthy because until 2008 coverage in these two countries was comparable with the highest coverage rates among the EU16. It is also apparent that collective bargaining coverage rates in the Baltic States, where neoliberal policies have been implemented to wide-ranging effect (Bohle and Greskovits 2012: 96–137; Kallaste and Woolfson 2013), failed to reach 35 per cent after 2008, and in Lithuania was at 12.5 per cent in 2020. By 2016 only in Slovenia among the EU11 did collective bargaining cover more than half of the labour force. In short, collective bargaining is absent for many workers in the EU11, which has marked implications for trade union objectives and activities.

Level of bargaining

Table 1.1 shows developments in the level of bargaining since 1960 for the EU16 and EU11. The data indicate the principal level or levels at which bargaining is conducted, not the only level. In the period until 1980 the principal level of collective bargaining was industry level or above for all EU16 countries except Cyprus and Luxembourg, where bargaining alternated between company and industry levels, and Malta, where company bargaining prevailed. The 'golden age' was thus associated with the establishment or maintenance of industry bargaining, which effectively took wages out of competition.

Table 1.1 illustrates that between 2000 and 2019 the level of bargaining has remained constant in fourteen of the EU16 countries. In ten countries industry bargaining remains dominant: in Cyprus and Luxembourg industry and company bargaining take place, while in Malta bargaining is principally conducted at local and company levels. In Belgium and Finland, two countries where the level of bargaining has varied since 2000, collective bargaining remains centralized but varies between industry and cross-industry levels. In contrast, in Greece and

[19] Missing data are also problematic for the EU11 plot, particularly in the period between 2006 and 2008.

Ireland, countries adversely affected by sovereign debt crises and subsequent intervention by the Troika, bargaining was decentralized, particularly after 2010.

Table 1.1. The principal level of bargaining since 1960

	1960	1970	1980	1990	2000	2005	2010	2015	2019
Austria	4	4	4	3	3	3	3	3	3
Belgium	4	4	3	4	4	5	4	5	4
Bulgaria	n.a.	n.a.	n.a.	n.a.	3	3	3	2	2
Croatia	n.a.	n.a.	n.a.	n.a.	2	2	2	2	2
Cyprus	n.a.	n.a.	2	2	2	2	2	2	2
Czechia	n.a.	n.a.	n.a.	n.a.	2	2	2	2	2
Denmark	5	5	5	3	3	3	3	3	3
Estonia	n.a.	n.a.	n.a.	n.a.	1	1	1	1	1
Finland	3	5	3	4	3	4	3	4	3
France	3	3	3	3	3	3	3	3	3
Germany	3	3	3	3	3	3	3	3	3
Greece	3	3	3	4	4	4	4	2	2
Hungary	n.a.	n.a.	n.a.	4	2	2	1	1	1
Ireland	1	5	5	5	5	5	1	1	1
Italy	5	3	3	3	3	3	3	3	3
Latvia	n.a.	n.a.	n.a.	n.a.	1	1	1	1	1
Lithuania	n.a.	n.a.	n.a.	n.a.	1	1	1	1	1
Luxembourg	2	2	2	2	2	2	2	2	2
Malta	1	1	1	1	1	1	1	1	1
Netherlands	5	3	3	3	3	3	3	3	3
Poland	n.a.	n.a.	n.a.	2	1	1	1	1	1
Portugal	n.a.	n.a.	3	4	3	3	3	3	3
Romania	n.a.	n.a.	n.a.	n.a.	3	5	5	2	2
Slovakia	n.a.	n.a.	n.a.	n.a.	3	2	2	2	2
Slovenia	n.a.	n.a.	n.a.	n.a.	5	5	3	4	3
Spain	n.a.	n.a.	5	3	3	4	3	3	3
Sweden	5	5	5	3	3	3	3	3	3

Notes:
1. bargaining takes place predominantly at local or company level;
2. intermediate or alternating between industry and company bargaining;
3. bargaining predominantly takes place at sector or industry level;
4. intermediate or alternating between central and industry bargaining;
5. bargaining predominantly takes place at central or cross-industry level with binding norms for lower level agreements.

Source: OECD/AIAS (2021).

These data thus portray a relatively stable situation since 2000 within the EU16. More detailed analyses suggest that the extent of stability is exaggerated by these data. In particular, the favourability principle, whereby the standards set in higher level agreements cannot be overridden by the terms of lower level agreements, has been relaxed for an increasingly wide range of issues effectively ensuring that agreements concluded at lower levels set actual terms and conditions of employment (Müller et al. 2019: 632). In France, for example, where this pattern of development is pronounced, pressure is placed on unions to maintain links between the industry and company levels of agreement setting. This is increasingly difficult in smaller companies with a limited union presence (Vincent 2019).

In addition to relaxing the favourability principle, decentralization has been promoted by altering the terms of industry agreements to make them less demanding than agreements concluded at company level. In this regard a variety of mechanisms have been implemented including: agreements that set only minimum standards, leaving the detailed negotiation of terms and conditions to the company level; figureless agreements, which leave the determination of wages to the company level; corridor agreements that specify the minimum and maximum standards between which company agreements must be settled; derogation clauses to industrial agreements, which delegate the settlement of particular issues to the company level; opening or hardship clauses enabling company-level actors to conclude agreements that are inferior to the industry level standard; and opt-out clauses allowing companies to postpone or not apply certain terms of the industrial agreement (Ibsen and Keune 2018: 10; Müller et al. 2019: 632; Visser 2016). In each of these instances industrial agreements remain in place but are no longer the means whereby all terms and conditions are settled.

Reference to the EU11 data in Table 1.1 demonstrates that local or company bargaining has been dominant since 2000 in Estonia, Hungary, Latvia, Lithuania and Poland. In Bulgaria and Slovakia bargaining tends to vary between industry and company levels, with the latter becoming increasingly more influential (Bernaciak 2013; Kahancová 2013). The much-publicized initiatives supported by the European Commission and the International Labour Organisation (ILO) (Bernaciak 2015; Vaughan-Whitehead 2003) to establish industry level bargaining as the basic means to settle terms and conditions of employment have thus failed, ensuring a disparity of structure between the EU16 and the EU11. Only in Romania and Slovenia were central and industry level bargaining arrangements established on a wide-ranging basis, hence the relatively high collective bargaining coverage rates in these countries noted in Table A1.H. The Romanian cross-industry bargaining arrangements were underpinned by legislation and were dismantled in 2011 by a centre-right government. Furthermore, measures were introduced that precluded the social partners from negotiating any further cross-industry agreements. These actions were taken without parliamentary debate (Trif 2013; Trif and Paolucci 2019) and resulted in a steep decline in coverage between 2010 and 2011. Among the EU11 it is thus only in Slovenia that relatively longstanding industrial bargaining arrangements have been sustained (Stanojevic and Poje 2019). In summary, in both Western Europe and CEE wages are now increasingly part of competition and unilaterally set by management.

The impact of changes in collective bargaining on trade unions

The diminution in the coverage of collective bargaining coupled to the decentralization within the EU16 and the failure to establish industry bargaining within the EU11 have profound implications for trade union organization and policy. The diminution in the coverage of collective bargaining in some Member States of the EU16 reduces the opportunities for unionists to set terms and conditions of employment, which, in turn, suggests a reduced likelihood of potential members joining, and existing members maintaining membership of, a union. Similarly, the failure to achieve high collective bargaining coverage rates in most EU11 Member States acts to reduce the attraction of union membership.

The relatively high, but declining, coverage of collective bargaining in some EU16 countries and the low coverage in most EU11 countries highlights the absence of uniformity in trade union positions. With exceptions, unions within the EU16 can reasonably claim to set terms and conditions for a substantial proportion of the labour force and use this position to promote membership. In contrast, the opportunities to use collective bargaining and the capacity of unions to negotiate terms and conditions of employment are more restricted in the EU11. This disparity also raises policy issues concerning union purpose. In broad terms, the central policy challenge for trade unions within the EU16 is retaining extant collective bargaining coverage and extending coverage to specific economic segments, primarily in private sector services, where collective bargaining has yet to be established or consolidated. The policy challenge for unions in the EU11 is to establish collective bargaining arrangements throughout the economy, rather than extend coverage to specific segments.[20]

The decentralization of bargaining is also problematic for union organization. Irrespective of the form taken by decentralization in the EU16, more issues are settled at company level and more agreements need to be agreed compared to 'classic' industrial bargaining. The coordination of collective agreements becomes more complex with decentralization, as trade unions attempt to maintain a degree of comparability across a range of company agreements, whereas beforehand the basis of comparability was written into the industrial agreement.[21] Furthermore, decentralization increases the pressure on local union organization. Industrial level bargaining requires local union representatives to negotiate the terms of implementation of the industrial agreement at company level. If bargaining is decentralized it is the basic terms of the agreement that must be negotiated at company level. Assuming the presence of union representatives within the company, the negotiation of these basic terms may require additional skills and training for these representatives. In the absence of union representatives within the company the decentralization of bargaining may result in the deployment of full-time officers to conduct the bargaining, which raises the questions are there enough full-time officers and/or is the union in a position to employ additional full-time officers? Alternatively, employees may be mandated to act on behalf of the union and to conduct company-level bargaining. This option also raises questions concerning the availability of skills, training and resources, as well as issues concerned with the ratification by the workforce and the relevant unions of any agreement concluded. If trade union organization is weak or non-existent the prospect of terms and conditions unilaterally determined by management becomes more likely.

While decentralized bargaining is predominant throughout the EU11 the position of trade unions differs from that in the EU16. Three points are of particular salience in this regard. First, apart from relatively short periods in Romania and Slovenia, industry level bargaining has not been

---

[20] Chapter 29 examines the issues associated with divergent collective bargaining arrangements and policy formulation at European level.

[21] It is acknowledged that local bargaining may have led to supplements to industrial agreements with the consequence that terms and conditions may have varied among those covered by an industrial agreement.

present on a wide-ranging basis within the EU11. Trade unions thus are not having to adjust to decentralization but have to take decentralized bargaining as the point of departure. Second, many unions based in the EU11 have neither the resources nor accumulated skills to conduct company bargaining at all the sites where members are present. Third, given the low rates of unionization in most EU11 Member States (Vandaele 2019), it is apparent that unionists will not be present in many companies with the consequence that the likelihood of unilateral setting of terms and conditions by management is increased. In short, to broaden the coverage of collective bargaining in most EU11 Member States, unions are required to secure a presence on a company-by-company basis: a resource-intense approach that many trade unions are unable to implement.

Two further features linked to collective bargaining coverage and structure impinge on union activity in both the EU16 and EU11. First, the coordination of decentralized agreements may be complicated in dual systems by the presence of works councils, particularly if non-unionists populate the works councils. Furthermore, some works councils have the regulatory underpinning to enable them to conclude collective agreements independently of unions. Regulations enabling such arrangements were designed to restrict union engagement at company level in some countries (Borbély and Neumann 2019). Second, low collective bargaining coverage, decentralization or a combination of the two has resulted in increased support for legally regulated minimum or living wages among unionists (Schulten 2006; Schulten and Müller 2019; Sellers 2019). Even where industry agreements are in place, the difficulties of policing the terms of these agreements have led to support for the introduction of a legal minimum wage, particularly within unions based in private sector services, as they often organize a sparse membership employed at a huge number of small workplaces. The preference for a legal minimum wage or living wage compensates for the absence of unionists at many sites insofar as the responsibility for policing minimum wages systems is formally transferred to the state. The absence of sufficient inspectors, however, brings into question the realism of the assumption of the transfer of responsibility to the state.

Unionization and mobilization

Within the EU16 the shift from the 'golden age' to the neoliberal challenge represents a change of position for trade unions within Member

States. From involvement in national policy making and securing gains for members and organization within Western Europe, unions became 'part of the problem' for advocates of neoliberalism who viewed them as a source of rigidity within the labour market. Within CEE a different but similarly dramatic transformation took place, as unions moved away from a subservient position to the Communist Party within command economies to an independent position within market economies. Throughout the EU these wide-ranging shifts were concurrent with the marked changes to labour markets, the diminution of the wage share accruing to labour, rising inequality and decentralized bargaining documented above. This section charts shifts in the pattern of unionization and industrial conflict: that is the effects of the changes mentioned above on trade union mobilization.[22]

Unionization

Figure 1.11 charts the weighted average of union density since 2000 for the EU16 and EU11. There is a downward trend apparent in both plots with that for the EU16 showing a relatively consistent decline, while that for the EU11 exhibits more variation. Throughout, density for the EU11 is lower than that among the EU16. In combination, the weighted average density level of almost 23.0 per cent in the EU16 and 14.5 per cent in the EU11 in 2018 constitute the lowest levels of union density recorded since 1945 and have led some to suggest that unions are no longer representative of working men and women (Meardi et al. 2021; Minford 1990).

---

[22] Of course, these measures are only partial indicators of union mobilization. A range of alternative measures could also be used. At this juncture, the point is to emphasize the challenges faced by trade unionists in the current economic and political climate. These measures facilitate the identification of these challenges and their scale.

Figure 1.11. Weighted average in net trade union density in EU Member States (%), 2000–2018

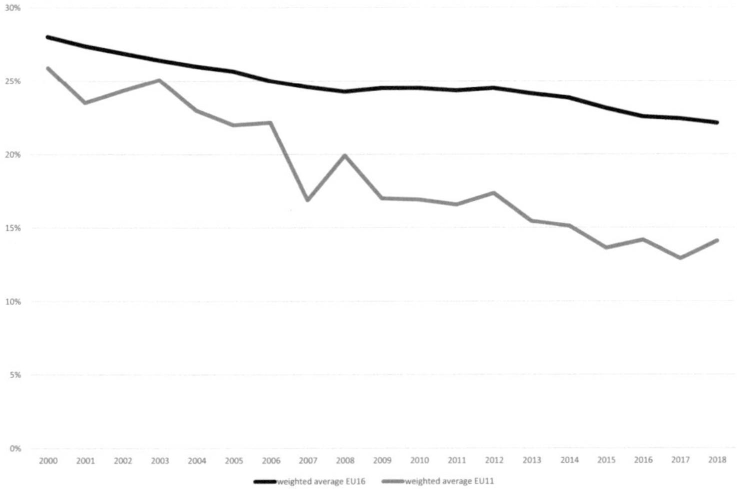

Reference to Table A1.D puts these plots into a longer-term context. The decline in density recorded in Figure 1.11 is clearly a continuation of a long-term trend of decline that commenced in most EU16 countries for which data are available during the 1980s. Only in Belgium and Denmark is the level of union density during the 2010s comparable with that of the 1970s. The Ghent system enabled trade unions in Belgium and in Denmark (Shin and Böckerman 2019; Vandaele 2006; Van Rie et al. 2011) to maintain density levels. In Finland the relatively late introduction of a Ghent system during the late-1960s effectively promoted the unionization rate, which peaked during the mid-1990s. A similar Ghent-style system in Sweden has not prevented a decline of more than 10 percentage points from the peak, in no small part because governments have introduced measures that have weakened these systems (Høgedahl and Kongshøj 2017). The transition to democracy during the 1970s explains the Portuguese and Spanish cases (Bermeo 1986; Fishman 1990). Density levels in these countries peaked during the late-1970s following the transition to democracy and thereafter tended to decline.

Declines in union density among the EU11 have been steeper than those recorded in the EU16 (Vandaele 2019), suggesting that trade unions, which were an integral institution of the pre-1990 command economies, have been hard-hit by the transition to market economies and have yet to adapt to changed circumstances. Where data are available, for example, for the period immediately before or immediately after the transformation, density levels in excess of 80 per cent were commonplace: Estonia, 1992, 93.9 per cent; and Hungary, 1990, 88.6 per cent (Appendix A1.D). It is also noteworthy that steep falls in union density were recorded in Poland before 1990. Throughout the EU11 during the period immediately after 1990 many workers viewed trade unions as a part of the pre-1990 system that had been rejected (Bernaciak and Kahancová 2017; Crowley and Ost 2001). In consequence, workers left unions in large numbers. As the country chapters illustrate, it remains problematic for some unions to rid themselves of the association with the command economies and recruit, particularly young, workers employed in the new market economies of the EU11.

It is also apparent from Tables A1.D and A1.H that national differences between union density and the coverage of collective bargaining are marked, which illustrates variations in the extent of 'free riding'. France is an extreme case in this instance with 8.0 per cent union density and 98.5 per cent coverage in collective bargaining in 2014, resulting in a free rider rate of 90.5 per cent (for details, see Sullivan 2009). At the other extreme is Cyprus where union density and the coverage of collective bargaining are almost identical, resulting in a free rider rate of zero. Higher free rider rates tend to occur where industrial bargaining remains in place, often coupled to the frequent use of extension mechanisms or functional equivalents, and unions have failed to recruit workers whose terms and conditions of employment they set. Some of the country chapters demonstrate that this group of workers are now being targeted in recruitment and organizing campaigns (Ibsen and Tapia 2017).

Figure 1.3 and Table A1.L demonstrate the rising employment rates among women throughout the period since 1960. Women have tended to form a larger proportion of trade union membership in the EU11 than in the EU16 due to the concentration of membership in the EU11 Member States within the public sector where large numbers of women are employed (Bernaciak and Kahancová 2017). In contrast, membership in the EU16 is relatively more evenly distributed across the three sectors and is thus also present in segments of the economy where men constitute the majority of employees and unionists.

Industrial conflict

Figure 1.12 plots the weighted average of strike volume between 2000 and 2020 for the EU16 and EU11. Strike volume is defined as the number of days not worked due to industrial action per 1,000 employees. Both the EU16 and EU11 plots fluctuate markedly, indicating the effects of specific and large-scale strikes. Strike volume in the EU16 tends to decline after 2000, albeit irregularly, while that for the EU11 remains low throughout and by 2017 strikes were relatively rare events, although a peak in strike activity was recorded thereafter. Three factors have been cited to explain these trends: the structural changes in the composition of the labour force detailed earlier in this chapter; a downsizing of the remaining direct workforce in manufacturing through subcontracting and outsourcing; and the impact of more intense competition resulting from the development of national and transnational production networks (Dribbusch and Vandaele 2007). These factors are closely connected to globalization and the neoliberal policy agenda. In terms of the argument developed in this publication, the diminished extent to which trade unions are able to mobilize strike action suggests a period of 'labour quiescence' (Shalev 1992) in which the defence of trade union interests must incorporate means additional to strike activity. Some argue that integral to these additional means is a shift from a labour repertoire to one based on citizens' rights (Gentile and Tarrow 2009; Vandaele 2016).

Figure 1.12. Weighted average in days not worked due to industrial action in EU Member States, 2000–2020

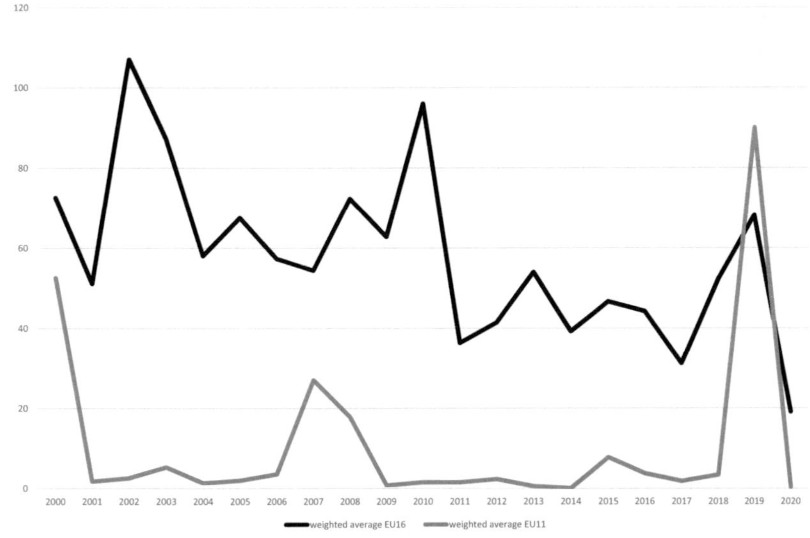

Reference to Table A1.I illustrates the effects of specific national bargaining rounds on strike volume. In Sweden in 2003 and Denmark in 2013, for example, public sector settlements to industrial agreements were achieved only after large-scale industrial action, hence the sharp increases in strike volume for these years (Hamark 2021). Annual peaks in strike volume for some countries are also indicative of general strikes called as a means to resist neoliberal policy initiatives (Hamman et al. 2016) and resistance to austerity measures in the public sector (Vandaele 2016). It is also apparent that some countries are not as strike prone as others: Germany and the Netherlands among the EU16, for example, consistently have relatively low annual strike volumes compared with France and Finland.

The structure of the publication

At the core of this publication are twenty-seven country chapters, which map and explain developments in trade unionism in each Member State of the EU since the year 2000. Each of these chapters has been written by national experts and peer reviewed by both the editors and the authors of other country chapters. In practice, each country chapter places the developments introduced in this chapter into a national context and explains specific national peculiarities by reference to economic, social and political developments. Each country chapter and the concluding chapter emphasize the range of responses implemented by trade unionists to the challenges outlines in this chapter.

In order to ensure a degree of consistency between chapters each country chapter comprises nine sections presented in an order of the author's choosing. Each of these sections arises from points raised in this chapter. The sections cover:

- the historical background and principal features of the system of industrial relations,
- the structure of trade unions and union democracy,
- unionization,
- union resources and expenditure,
- collective bargaining and trade unions at the workplace,
- industrial conflict,
- political relations,

- societal power, and
- trade union policies towards the EU.

In addition, the authors of the country chapters were asked to categorize each country by reference to Visser's (2019b) four categories on the future of European trade unionism: marginalization, dualization, substitution and revitalization. It is acknowledged that there are difficulties with these categories, as more than one may be present concurrently within a Member State. Analysis of the responses comprises the final section of a concluding chapter to the entire publication, which presents an overview of the state of unions in the EU in 2022, reviews the impact of the responses to the neoliberal challenge implemented by trade unionists and speculates on future developments.

The argument present in every chapter is that these are difficult times for unions in Europe. The neoliberal project has weakened and is continuing to weaken fundamental features of the national variants of the European social model within the EU16 and has prevented the establishment of elements of the European social model within the EU11. A range of quantitative measures indicate the extent of the challenge faced by unionists in terms of declining unionization; a restricted capacity to mobilize industrial action; a declining wage share for labour, particularly in the EU11; and a decline in the coverage of collective bargaining coupled to its decentralization. The increasing 'distance' between unions and Social Democratic and Labour Parties exacerbates the difficulties of union renewal, as legislative support is not readily forthcoming. Concurrently, climate change is a challenge that particularly affects industries where unions are still relatively strong, while the shift towards a low-carbon society promotes industries that are currently sparsely unionized. Similarly, digitalization poses challenges for unions on a wide front, but particularly concerning the protection of employment rates and the quality of work (Degryse 2016; Drahokoupil and Vandaele 2021; Jepsen and Drahokoupil 2017; Vandaele 2018).

This bleak situation, however, is mitigated. The banking crisis of 2008, for example, demonstrated the failure of the unregulated markets favoured by the neoliberals (Gamble 2014; Piketty 2014). Similarly, the increases in rates of productivity growth anticipated by the neoliberals to result from labour market flexibility have failed to materialize. In short, the internal contradictions of the neoliberal project are becoming increasing evident (Pedersini 2019), although the political elites in several Member

States and at European level remain wedded to the basic assumptions of the project (Crouch 2011; Lehndorff 2015). More recently, the Covid-19 crisis has prompted a wide range of responses many of which have involved unions in national decision-making.

Within this context it is apparent that unionists are searching for new approaches to adjust to changed circumstances. Internally, a wide range of recruitment and organizing campaigns are underway directed towards bringing workers often outside of unions in the past into membership, horizontal forms of union democracy have been introduced to supplement traditional vertical forms, and mergers have consolidated and sometimes transformed union structure. Externally, political alliances have been sought beyond social democratic and labour parties, particularly with organizations campaigning on environmental, sustainability and equality issues. As becomes apparent from the country chapters these initiatives take a wide range of forms and have generated mixed results as the country chapters illustrate.

References

Adamczyk, S. (2018) 'Inside The Trade Union Family: The 'Two Worlds' within the European Trade Union Confederation', *European Journal of Industrial Relations*, 24 (2), 179–192.

Aldcroft, D. and Morewood, S. (1995) *Economic Change in Eastern Europe since 1918*. London: Routledge.

Armingeon, K. and Baccaro, L. (2012) 'Political Economy of the Sovereign Debt Crisis: The Limits of Internal Devaluation', *Industrial Law Journal*, 41 (3), 254–275.

Baccaro, L. and Howell, C. (2017) *Trajectories of Neoliberal Transformation: European Industrial Relations since the 1970s*. Cambridge: Cambridge University Press.

Berend, I. (1996) *Central and Eastern Europe, 1944–1993: Detour from the Periphery to the Periphery*. Cambridge: Cambridge University Press.

Bermeo, N. (1986) *The Revolution within the Revolution: Workers' Control in Rural Portugal*. Princeton: Princeton University Press.

Bernaciak, M. (2013) 'Social Dialogue Revival or "PR" Corporatism? Negotiating Anti-Crisis Measures in Poland and Bulgaria', *Transfer*, 19 (2), 239–251.

Bernaciak, M. (2015) *Beyond the CEE 'Black Box': Crisis and Industrial Relations in the New EU Member States*. ETUI Working Paper 2015.05. Brussels: European Trade Union Institute.

Bernaciak, M. and Kahancová, M. (2017) 'Introduction: Innovation Against All Odds?', pp. 1–20 in Bernaciak, M. and Kahancová, M. (eds). *Innovative Union Practices in Central-eastern Europe*. Brussels: European Trade Union Institute.

Bohle, D. and Greskovits, B. (2012) *Capitalist Diversity on Europe's Periphery*. Ithaca: Cornell University Press.

Bohle, D., Radice, H. and Shields, S. (2007) 'Introduction', *Competition and Change*, 11 (2), 81–87.

Borbély, S. and Neumann, L. (2019) 'Neglected by the State: The Hungarian Experience of Collective Bargaining', pp. 295–314 in Müller, T., Vandaele, K. and Waddington, J. (eds). *Collective Bargaining in Europe: Towards an Endgame*. Brussels: European Trade Union Institute.

Boyer, R. and Drache, D. (1996) 'Introduction', pp. 1–30 in Boyer, R. and Drache, D. (eds). *States against Markets: The Limits of Globalization*. London: Routledge.

Bruff, I. (2008) *Culture and Consensus in European Varieties of Capitalism. A 'Common Sense' Analysis*. London: Palgrave Macmillan.

Campos Lima, M. (2019) 'Portugal: Reforms and the Turn to Neoliberal Austerity', pp. 483–504 in Müller, T., Vandaele, K. and Waddington, J. (eds). *Collective Bargaining in Europe: Towards an Endgame*. Brussels: European Trade Union Institute.

Checchi, D. and García Peñalosa, C. (2010) 'Labour Market Institutions and the Personal Distribution of Income in the OECD', *Economica*, 77 (307), 413–450.

Coates, D. (2000) *Models of Capitalism: Growth and Stagnation in the Modern Era*. Cambridge: Polity Press.

Coates, K. and Topham, T. (1972) *The New Unionism: The Case for Workers' Control*. Harmondsworth: Penguin.

Coriat, B. (1995) 'Incentives, Bargaining and Trust: Alternative Scenarios for the Future of Work', *International Contributions to Labour Studies*, 5: 131–151.

Crafts, N. and Toniolo, G. (1996a) 'Postwar Growth: An Overview', pp. 1–37 in Crafts, N. and Toniolo, G. (eds). *Economic Growth in Europe since 1945*. Cambridge: Cambridge University Press.

Crafts, N. and Toniolo, G. (1996b) 'Reflections on the Country Studies', pp. 576–581 in Crafts, N. and Toniolo, G. (eds). *Economic Growth in Europe since 1945*. Cambridge: Cambridge University Press.

Crouch, C. (1993) *Industrial Relations and European State Traditions*. Oxford: Clarendon.

Crouch, C. (1999) *Social Change in Western Europe*. Oxford: Oxford University Press.

Crouch, C. (2011) *The Strange Non-death of Neoliberalism*. Cambridge: Polity.

Crouch, C. and Pizzorno, A. (eds) (1978) *Resurgence of Class Conflict in Western Europe since 1969*. London: Macmillan.

Crowley, S. and Ost, D. (2001) 'Introduction: The Surprise of Labor Weakness in Postsocialist Society', pp. 1–12 in Crowley, S. and Ost, D. (eds). *Workers after Workers' States: Labor and Politics in Postcommunist Eastern Europe*. Lanham: Rowman and Littlefield.

Cunnison, S. and Stageman, J. (1995) *Feminizing the Unions*. Aldershot: Avebury.

Deakin, S., Malmberg, J. and Sarkar, P. (2014) 'How Do Labour Laws Affect Unemployment and the Labour Share of National Income? The Experience of Six OECD countries, 1970–2010', *International Labour Review*, 153 (1), 1–27.

Degryse, C. (2016) *Digitalisation of the Economy and its Impact on Labour Markets*. Working Paper 2016.02. Brussels: European Trade Union Institute.

Degryse, C. and Tilly, P. (2013) *1973–2013: 40 years of History of the European Trade Union Confederation*. Brussels: European Trade Union Institute.

Dølvik, J. E. (1999) *An Emerging Island? ETUC, Social Dialogue and the Europeanisation of the Trade Unions in the 1990s*. Brussels: European Trade Union Institute.

Dølvik, J. E. and Martin, A. (eds). (2015) *European Social Models from Crisis to Crisis*. Oxford: Oxford University Press.

Drahokoupil, J. and Vandaele, K. (2021) *A Modern Guide to Labour and the Platform Economy*. Cheltenham: Edward Elgar.

Dribbusch, H. and Vandaele, K. (2007) 'Comprehending Divergence in Strike Activity: Employers' Offensives, Government Interventions and Union Responses', pp. 366–381 in van der Velden, S., Dribbusch, H.,

Lyddon, D. and Vandaele, K. (eds). *Strikes Around the World, 1968–2005.* Amsterdam: Aksant.

Ebbinghaus, B. and Visser, J. (1999) 'When Institutions Matter: Union Growth and Decline in Western Europe, 1950–95', *European Sociological Review*, 15 (2), 135–158.

Eichengreen, B. (2007) *The European Economy Since 1945: Coordinated Capitalism and Beyond.* Princeton: Princeton University Press.

Esping-Andersen, G. (1990) *The Three Worlds of Welfare Capitalism.* Cambridge: Polity Press.

European Commission. (2012) *Labour Market Developments in Europe 2012, European Economy No. 5.*, Brussels, Directorate-General for Economic and Financial Affairs.

European Commission. (2018) *Labour Market and Wage Developments in Europe: Annual Review 2018.* Brussels: European Commission.

Ferrera, M. (2005) *Welfare State Reform in Southern Europe: Fighting Poverty and Social Exclusion in Italy, Spain, Portugal and Greece.* London: Routledge.

Flassbeck, H. and Lapavitsas, C. (2015) *Against the Troika: Crisis and Austerity in the Eurozone.* London: Verso.

Fishman, R. (1990) *Working-class Organization and the Return to Democracy in Spain.* Ithaca: Cornell University Press.

Frangi, L., Koos, S. and Hadziabdic, S. (2017) 'In Unions We Trust! Analysing Confidence in Unions across Europe', *British Journal of Industrial Relations*, 55 (4), 831–858.

Gamble, A. (2014) *Crisis Without End? The Unravelling of Western Prosperity.* New York: Palgrave MacMillan.

Gentile, A. and Tarrow, S. (2009) 'Charles Tilly, Globalization, and Labor's Citizen Rights', *European Political Science Review*, 1 (3), 465–493.

Goldthorpe, J., Lockwood, D., Bechhofer, F. and Platt, J. (1969) *The Affluent Worker in the Class Structure.* Cambridge: Cambridge University Press.

Gorodzeisky, A. and Richards, A. (2019) 'Do Immigrants Trust Trade Unions? A Study of 18 European Countries', *British Journal of Industrial Relations.* https://doi.org/10.1111/bjir.12466

Grady, J. and Simms, M. (2019) 'Trade Unions and the Challenge of Fostering Solidarities in an Era of Financialisation', *Economic and Industrial Democracy*, 40 (3), 490–510.

Gray, A. 2004. Unsocial Europe: Social Protection or Flexploitation. London: Pluto Press.

Greer, I. and Hauptmeier, M. (2016) 'Management Whipsawing: The Staging of Labor Competition Under Globalization', *Industrial and Labor Relations Review*, 69 (1), 29–52.

Hamark, J. (2021) 'Strikes and lockouts: The need to separate labour conflicts', *Economic and Industrial Democracy*, https://doi.org/10.1177/0143831X211049274

Hamman, K., Johnston, A. and Kelly, J. (2016) 'The Electoral Effects of General Strikes in Western Europe', *Comparative Politics*, 49 (1), 63–82.

Haugsgjerd Allern, E. and Bale, T. (eds). (2017) *Left-of-centre Parties and Trade Unions in the Twenty-first Century*. New York: Oxford University Press.

Held, D. (2004) *Global Covenant*. Cambridge: Polity.

Hijzen, A. and Venn, D. (2011) *The Role of Short-Time-Work Schemes during the* 2008–*09 Recession*. OECD Social, Employment and Migration Working Papers, No. 115. Geneva: OECD Publishing.

Hinarejos, A. (2016) 'Changes to Economic and Monetary Union and their Effects on Social Policy', *The International Journal of Comparative Labour Law and Industrial Relations*, 32 (2), 231–249.

Hirst, P. and Zeitlin, J. (1991) 'Flexible Specialisation versus Post-Fordism: Theory, Evidence and Policy Implications', *Economy and Society*, 20 (1), 1–56.

Høgedahl, L. and Kongshøj, K. (2017) 'New Trajectories of Unionization in the Nordic Ghent Countries: Changing Labour Market and Welfare Institutions', *European Journal of Industrial Relations*, 23 (4), 365–380.

Holgate, J., Simms, M. and Tapia, M. (2018) 'The Limitations of the Theory and Practice of Mobilization in Trade Union Organizing', *Economic and Industrial Democracy*, 39 (4), 599–616.

Howell, C. (2005) *Trade Unions and the State: The Construction of Industrial Relations Institutions in Britain, 1890–2000*. Princeton: Princeton University Press.

Hyman, R. (2005) 'Trade Unions and the Politics of the European Social Model', *Economic and Industrial Democracy*, 26 (1), 9–40.

Ibsen, C. and Tapia, M. (2017) 'Trade union revialisation: where are we now? Where to next?', *Industrial Relations Journal*, 59 (2), 170–191.

Ibsen, C. and Keune, M. (2018) *Organised Decentralisation of Collective Bargaining: Case Studies of Germany, the Netherlands and Denmark*. OECD Social, Employment and Migration Working Papers, No. 217. Paris: OECD Publishing.

Ioannou, G. and Sonan, S. (2019) 'Cyprus: A Divided Nation, Diverging Collective Bargaining Patterns, Weakened yet still Standing', pp. 109–130 in Müller, T., Vandaele, K. and Waddington, J. (eds). *Collective Bargaining in Europe: Towards an Endgame*. Brussels: European Trade Union Institute.

Iversen, T. and Soskice, D. (2019) *Democracy and Prosperity: Reinventing Capitalism through a Turbulent Century*. Princeton: Princeton University Press.

Jepsen, M. and Drahokoupil, J. (2017) 'The Digital Economy and Its Implications for Labour: 2, The Consequences of Digitalisation for the Labour Market', *Transfer*, 23 (3), 249–262.

Kahanková, M. (2013) 'The Demise of Social Partnership or a Balanced Recovery? The Crisis of Collective Bargaining in Slovakia', *Transfer*, 19 (2), 171–183.

Kallaste, E. and Woolfson, C. (2013) Negotiated Responses to the Crisis in the Baltic Countries', *Transfer*, 19 (2), 253–266.

Karamessini, M and Rubery, J. (eds). (2014) *Women and Austerity: The Economic Crisis and the Future for Gender Equality. London*: Routledge.

Katsaroumpas, I. and Koukiadaki, A. (2019) 'Greece: 'Contesting' Collective Bargaining', pp. 267–294 in Müller, T., Vandaele, K. and Waddington, J. (eds). *Collective Bargaining in Europe: Towards an Endgame*. Brussels: European Trade Union Institute.

Keune, M. (2008) 'Introduction: Wage Moderation, Decentralization of Collective Bargaining and Low Pay', pp. 1–35 in Keune, M. and Galgóczi, B. (eds). *Collective Bargaining on Working Time: Recent European Experiences*. Brussels: European Trade Union Institute.

Keune, M., Romas Martin, N. and Mailand, M. (2020) *Working under Pressure – Employment, Job Quality and Labour Relations in Europe's Public Sector since the Crisis*. Brussels, European Trade Union Institute.

Kollmeyer, C. and Peters, J. (2019) 'Financialization and the Decline of Organized Labor: A Study of 18 Advanced Capitalist Countries, 1970 to 2012', *Social Forces*. 98 (1), 1–30.

Lane, C. 1989. Management and Labour in Europe. Aldershot: Edward Elgar.

Lehndorff, S. (2015) 'Europe's Divisive Integration: An Overview', pp. 7–38 in Lehndorff, S. (ed.). *Divisive Integration: The Triumph of Failed Ideas Revisited.* Brussels: European Trade Union Institute.

Lehndorff, S., Dribbusch, H. and Schulten, T. (2018) European Trade Unions in a Time of Crises – An Overview, pp. 7–38 in Lehndorff, S., Dribbusch, H. and Schulten T (eds). *Rough Waters – European Trade Unions in a Time of Crises.* Brussels: European Trade Union Institute.

Lévesque, C. and Murray, G. (2010) 'Understanding Union Power: Resources and Capabilities for Renewing Union Capacity', *Transfer*, 16 (3), 333–350.

Levinson, C. (1972) *International Trade Unionism.* London: George Allen and Unwin.

Lewenhak, S. (1980) *Women and Work.* Basingstoke: MacMillan.

Lörcher, K. and Schömann, I. (2016) *The European Pillar of Social Rights: Critical Legal Analysis and Proposals, Report 139.* Brussels: European Trade Union Institute.

Lovén Seldén, K. (2020) 'Challenges Posed by the EU Minimum Wage Initiative to the ETUC and European Trade Union Cooperation', *Transfer*, 26 (3), 325–343.

Lübker, M. and Schulten, T. (2018) *Europäischer Tarifbericht des WSI – 2017–2018, WSI-Report Nr. 42, September 2018.* Düsseldorf: Wirtschafts- und Sozialwissenschaftliches Institut.

Maccarrone, V., Erne, R. and Regan, A. (2019) 'Ireland: Life after Social Partnership', pp. 315–335 in Müller, T., Vandaele, K. and Waddington, J. (eds). *Collective Bargaining in Europe: Towards an Endgame.* Brussels: European Trade Union Institute.

Marginson, P. (2015) 'Coordinated Bargaining in Europe: From Incremental Corrosion to Frontal Assault?', *European Journal of Industrial Relations*, 21 (2), 97–114.

Marglin, S. and Schor, J. (eds). (1990) *The Golden Age of Capitalism.* Oxford: Clarendon.

Mazower, M. (2000) *Dark Continent: Europe's Twentieth Century.* London: Allen Lane.

Meardi, G., Simms, M. and Adam, D. (2021) 'Trade Unions and the Precariat: Representative Claims', *European Journal of Industrial Relations*, 27 (1), 41–58.

Minford, P. (1990) 'Ideology and Pragmatism in Economic Thatcherism', pp. 191–203 in Clark, J. (ed.). *Ideas and Politics in Modern Britain.* Basingstoke: MacMillan.

Moore, R. (1970) *Self-management in Yugoslavia.* Fabian Research Series Pamphlet, No. 281. London: Fabian Society.

Mosimann, N., Rennwald, L, and Zimmermann, A. (2019) 'The Radical Right, the Labour Movement and the Competition for the Workers' Vote', *Economic and Industrial Democracy*, 40 (1), 65–90.

Müller, T. and Platzer, H.-W. (2020) 'The European Trade Union Federations within the European Polity: ETUFs and International Trade Union Activity', *Transfer*, 26 (3), 289–306.

Müller, T. and Schulten, T. (2015) *The Public-private Sector Pay Debate in Europe.* Working Paper 2015.08. Brussels: European Trade Union Institute.

Müller, T., Vandaele, K. and Waddington, J. (2019) 'Conclusion: Towards an Endgame', pp. 625–668 in Müller, T., Vandaele, K. and Waddington, J. (eds). *Collective Bargaining in Europe: Towards an Endgame.* Brussels: European Trade Union Institute.

Munck. R. (2002) *Globalisation and Labour: The New Great Transformation.* London: Zed Books.

Nichols, T. and Cam, S. (2005) 'Labour in a Global World', pp. 206–238 in Nichols, T. and Cam, S. (eds). *Labour in a Global World.* Houndsmills: Palgrave MacMillan.

OECD. (2018a) *OECD Employment Outlook 2018.* Paris: OECD Publishing.

OECD. (2018b) *Is the Last Mile the Longest? Economic Gains from Gender Equality in Nordic Countries.* Paris: OECD Publishing

OECD. (2019) *OECD Employment Outlook 2018: The Future of Work.* Paris: OECD Publishing.

OECD/AIAS. (2021) OECD/AIAS ICTWSS database. https://www.oecd.org/employment/ictwss-database.htm.

Oesch, D. (2008) 'Explaining Workers' Support for Right-wing Populist Parties in Western Europe: Evidence from Austria, Belgium, France, Norway, and Switzerland', *International Political Science Review*, 29 (3), 349–373.

Ost, D. (2000) 'Illusory Corporatism in Eastern Europe: Neoliberal Tripartism and Postcommunist Class Identities', *Politics and Society*, 28 (4), 503–530.

Ostry, J., Loungani, P. and Furceri, D. (2016) 'Neoliberalism Oversold?', *Finance and Development*, 53 (2), 38–41.

Pedersini, R. (2019) 'International Organisations and the Role of Collective Bargaining', *Transfer*, 25 (2), 181–203.

Phelan, C. (2007) *Trade Union Revitalisation: Trends and Prospects in 34 Countries*. Oxford: Peter Lang.

Piasna, A. (2017) *'Bad Jobs' Recovery? European Job Quality Index 2005–2015*. Working Paper 2017.06. Brussels: European Trade Union Institute.

Piasna, A. and Myant, M. (eds). (2017) *Myths of Employment Dderegulation: How it neither Creates Jobs nor Reduces Labour Market Segmentation*. Brussels: European Trade Union Institute.

Piketty, T. (2014) *Capital in the Twenty-first Century*. Cambridge: The Belknap Press of Harvard University Press.

Rogers, G. and Rogers, J. (eds). (1989) *Precarious Jobs in Labour Market Regulation: The Growth of Atypical Employment in Western Europe*. Geneva: International Institute for Labour Studies.

Ross, G. and Martin, A. (1999) 'European Unions Face the Millenium', pp. 1–25 in Martin, A. and Ross, G. (eds). *The Brave New World of European Labor: European Trade Unions at the Millennium*. New York: Berghahn Books.

Rubery, J. (2015) 'Change at Work: Feminisation, Flexibilisation, Fragmentation and Financialisation', *Employee Relations*, 37 (6), 633–644.

Rubery, J. and Fagan, C. (1994) 'Does Feminization Mean a Flexible Labour Force?', pp. 140–166 in Hyman, R. and Ferner, A. (eds). *New Frontiers in European Industrial Relations*. Oxford: Blackwell.

Sapir, A. (2014) 'Still the Right Agenda for Europe? The Sapir Report Ten Years On', *Journal of Common Market Studies*, 52 (1), 57–73.

Sassoon, D. (1996) *One Hundred Years of Socialism*. London: I.B. Tauris Publishers.

Scharpf, F. (1996) 'Negative and positive integration in the political economy of European welfare states', pp. 15–39 in Marks, G., Scarpf, F., Schmitter, P. and Streeck, W. (eds.). London: Sage.

Scharpf, F. (2009) *The Double Asymmetry of European Integration. Or, Why the EU Cannot be a Social Market Economy*. MPIfG Working Paper 09/12. Cologne: Max Planck Institute for the Study of Societies.

Schmalz, S., Ludwig, C. and Webster, E. (2018) 'The Power Resources Approach: Developments and Challenges', *Global Labour Journal*, 9 (2), 113–134.

Schulten, T. (2006) 'Statutory and Collectively Agreed Minimum Wages in Europe: An International view', pp. 1–26 in Schulten, T., Bispinck, R. and Schäfer, C. (eds). *Minimum Wages in Europe*. Brussels: European Trade Union Institute.

Schulten, T. and Müller, T. (2019) 'What's in a Name? From Minimum Wages to Living Wages in Europe', *Transfer*, 25 (3), 267–284.

Seeliger, M. (2019) *Trade Unions in the Course of European Integration*. London: Routledge

Seller, P. (2019) 'Trade unions and the Living Wage in the UK', *Transfer*, 25 (3), 367–372.

Shalev, M. (1992) 'The Resurgence of Labour Quiescence', pp. 102–132 in Regini, M. (ed.). *The Future of Labour Movements*. London: Sage.

Shin, Y.-K. and Böckerman, P. (2019) 'Precarious Workers' Choices about Unemployment Insurance Membership after the Ghent System Reform: The Finnish Experience', *Social Policy & Administration*, 53 (7), 921–939.

Silver, B. (2003) *Forces of Labor: Workers' Movements and Globalization since 1870*. Cambridge: Cambridge University Press.

Singleton, F. and Topham, T. (1963) 'Yugoslav Workers' control: The Latest Phase', *New Left Review*, 18: 73–84.

Spier, T. (2017) 'Growing Apart? Trade Unions and Centre-left Parties in Germany', pp. 130–148 in Haugsgjerd Allern, E. and Bale, T. (eds). *Left-of-Centre Parties and Trade Unions in the Twenty-First Century*. Oxford: Oxford University Press.

Standing, G. (1999) *Global Labour Flexibility: Seeking Distributive Justice*. Houndsmills: MacMillan.

Stanojević, M. and Poje, A. (2019) 'Slovenia: Organised Decentralisation in the Private Sector and Centralisation in the Public Sector', pp. 545–562 in Müller, T., Vandaele, K. and Waddington, J. (eds). *Collective Bargaining in Europe: Towards an Endgame*. Brussels: European Trade Union Institute.

Stockhammer, E., Kohler, K. and Guschanski, A. (2018) *The Impact of Financialisation on the Wage Share: A Theoretical Clarification and Empirical*

Test. PKES Working Paper 1802. Bristol: Post-Keynesian Economics Society.

Streeck, W. (2015) 'Why the Euro Divides Europe', *New Left Review*, 95: 5–26.

Streeck. W. (2019) 'Progressive Regression: Metamorphoses of European Social Policy', *New Left Review*, 118: 117–139.

Sullivan, R. (2009) 'Density Matters: The Union Density Bias and Its Implications for Labor Movement Revitalization', *Mobilization*, 14 (2), 239–260.

Theodoropoulou, S. (ed.). (2018) *Labour Market Policies in the Era of Pervasive Austerity. A European Perspective*. Bristol: Policy Press.

Ther, P. (2016) *Europe since 1989*. Princeton: Princeton University Press.

Trif, A. (2013) 'Romania: Collective Bargaining Institutions under Attack', *Transfer*, 19 (2), 227–237.

Trif, A. and Paolucci, V. (2019) 'Romania: From Legal Support to Frontal Assault', pp. 505–524 in Müller, T., Vandaele, K. and Waddington, J. (eds). *Collective Bargaining in Europe: Towards an Endgame*. Brussels: European Trade Union Institute.

Urban, H.-J. (2012) 'Crisis Corporatism and Trade Union Revitalisation in Europe' pp. 219–241 in Lehndorff, S. (ed.). *A Triumph of Failed Ideas*. Brussels: European Trade Union Institute.

Vandaele, K. (2006) 'A Report from the Homeland of the Ghent System: The Relationship between Unemployment and Trade Union Membership in Belgium', *Transfer*, 12 (4), 647–657.

Vandaele, K. (2016) 'Interpreting Strike Activity in Western Europe in the Past 20 Years: The Labour Repertoire under Pressure', *Transfer*, 22 (3), 277–294.

Vandaele, K. (2018) *Will Trade Unions Survive in the Platform Economy? Emerging Patterns of Platform Workers' Collective Voice and Representation in Europe*. Working Paper 2018.5. Brussels: European Trade Union Institute.

Vandaele, K. (2019) *Bleak Prospects: Mapping Trade Union Membership in Europe since 2000*. Brussels: European Trade Union Institute.

van der Velden, S., Dribbusch, H., Lyddon, D. and Vandaele, K. (eds). (2007) *Strikes Around the World*. Amsterdam: Aksant.

Van Rie, T., Marx, I. and Horemans, J. (2011) 'Ghent Revisited: Unemployment Insurance and Union Membership in Belgium and the Nordic countries', *European Journal of Industrial Relations*, 17 (2), 125–139.

Vaughan-Whitehead, D. (2003) *EU Enlargement versus Social Europe? The Uncertain Future of the European Social Model.* Cheltenham: Edward Elgar.

Vincent, C. (2019) 'France: The Rush Towards Prioritising the Enterprise Level', pp. 217–238 in Müller, T., Vandaele, K. and Waddington, J. (eds). *Collective Bargaining in Europe: Towards an Endgame*. Brussels: European Trade Union Institute.

Visser, J. (2002) 'The First Part-time Economy in the World: A Model to Be Followed?', *Journal of European Policy*, 12 (1), 23–42.

Visser, J. (2016) 'What Happened to Collective Bargaining during the Great Recession?', *IZA Journal of Labour Policy*, 5 (9), 1–35.

Visser, J. (2019a) *Trade Unions in the Balance*. ILO ACTRAV Working Paper. Geneva: International Labour Organization.

Visser, J. (2019b) *ICTWSS Database*. version 6.1. Amsterdam: Amsterdam Institute for Advanced Labour Studies (AIAS), University of Amsterdam.

Visser, J. and Hemerijck, A. (1999) '*"A Dutch Miracle". Job Growth, Welfare Reform and Corporatism in the Netherlands*'. Amsterdam: Amsterdam University Press.

Waddington, J. and Hoffmann, R. (eds). (2000) *Trade Unions In Europe*. Brussels: European Trade Union Institute.

Waddington, J., Müller, T. and Vandaele, K. (2019) 'Setting the Scene: Collective Bargaining under Neoliberalism', pp. 1–32 in Müller, T., Vandaele, K. and Waddington, J. (eds). *Collective Bargaining in Europe: Towards an Endgame*. Brussels: European Trade Union Institute.

Webb, S. and Webb, B. (1920) *History of Trade Unions*. London: Longmans.

Webb, P. and Bale, T. (2017) 'No Place Else to Go: The Labour Party and the Trade Unions in the UK', pp. 246–264 in Haugsgjerd Allern, E. and Bale, T. (eds). *Left-of-Centre Parties and Trade Unions in the Twenty-First Century*. Oxford: Oxford University Press.

Wilthagen, T. and Tros, F. (2004) 'The Concept of 'Flexicurity': A New Approach to Regulating Employment and Labour Markets', *Transfer*, 10 (2), 166–186.

Abbreviations

CEE Central and Eastern Europe

EMU Economic and Monetary Union

EPP	European Peoples Party
ETUC	European Trade Union Confederation
ETUF	European Trade Union Federation
ETUI	European Trade Union Institute
EU	European Union
HRM	Human Resource Management
MNC	Multinational Company
S&D	Alliance of Socialists and Democrats
UK	United Kingdom
US	United States

Chapter 2

Austria: Trade unions in a world of 'contested stability'?

Vera Glassner and Julia Hofmann[1]

By European comparison, the Austrian trade union system is the most unitarian, with only one organization, the Austrian Trade Union Federation (ÖGB, *Österreichischer Gewerkschaftsbund*). The ÖGB incorporates seven sectoral[2]/industry[3] trade unions. Austrian trade unions are embedded in a complex system of industrial relations and workers' participation. The representation of labour interests rests on three formally independent pillars: first, the national trade union federation ÖGB and its (multi-)sectoral/industry organizations; second, the Austrian Chamber of Labour (AK, *Arbeiterkammer*), membership of which is mandatory, and which acts as the statutory employee interest organization of all employees; and third, employee interest representation at the company level, which comprises board-level representation through employee representation on supervisory boards and works councils (*Betriebsräte*). Unions usually negotiate at national (or regional) industry level on pay and other working conditions, while works councils negotiate at enterprise level on issues such as additional benefits related to pay or work pensions.

Like most of European unions, Austrian unions have been confronted with a process of constant membership decline over the past thirty years. Since 2016, however, unions have been able to halt this trend and now

---

1 The authors would like to thank Susanne Pernicka (JKU Linz) and colleagues of the department for economic science and statistics at the Chamber of Labour Vienna for their valuable comments on this chapter.

2 Broad sectors of economic activities such as private/public.

3 Industry (within a sector), for instance, metalworking, finance/insurance, health care.

have around 1.2 million members. The Covid-19 crisis has once more led to membership losses, totalling around 20,000 people between 2019 and 2021. Because of the uncertain future of the pandemic and its effects on the labour market at the time of writing (2022), it was not yet clear whether this was just a one-off event or whether it heralds a longer trend of membership decline.

While net union density in Austria is moderate in European comparison (around 26 per cent in 2020), collective bargaining coverage is extraordinarily high. Around 98 per cent of workers are covered by collective agreements. The encompassing scope of collective bargaining results mainly from companies' obligatory membership of the Chamber of the Economy (WKO, *Wirtschaftskammer*) and the legal extension of collective bargaining coverage to employees who are not union members. Collective bargaining generally takes place at the industry level and is highly coordinated and synchronized within and between industries. The wage agreement in metalworking serves as an orientation mark for bargaining actors in other manufacturing industries, as well as in commerce and the public sector. Together with Germany, the Netherlands, Norway, Sweden and Switzerland, Austria belongs to the group of 'persistently low-strike countries' (Vandaele 2016), which means that strikes and industrial conflicts are generally rare.

Even though on the surface it seems that unions have been fairly successful in enforcing their interests, a closer look at the dynamics in the country shows that the 'Austrian model' is contested on both the political and the collective bargaining level. The general power shift from labour to capital has induced changes in economic and social policies, as well as attempts to decentralize collective bargaining. Political power shifts to the right have further challenged the role of social partnership and the culture of compromise and balancing interests. Over the coming years, unions will thus be well advised to adapt to these multiple challenges.

Table 2.1 Principal characteristics of trade unionism in Austria

	1980	2000	2020
Total trade union membership	1,661,000	1,442,000	1,199,000
Women as a proportion of total membership	30 %	32 %	36 %*
Gross union density	59 %	45 %	32 %*
Net union density	52 %	37 %	26 %*
Number of confederations	1	1	1
Number of affiliated unions (federations)	15	13	7
Number of independent unions	0	0	0
Collective bargaining coverage	95 %	98 %	98 %
Principal level of collective bargaining	Cross-industry/ industry	Industry	Industry
Days not worked due to industrial action per 1,000 workers	0**	1	0

Notes: *2019; **Average value 1980–1984.

Sources: Appendix A1, ETUI (2020), OECD (2007), ÖGB (2020, 2021a).

Historical background and principal features of the industrial relations system

In international comparison, the Austrian industrial relations system is often characterized as well-developed and highly stable over time. One reason for this lies in the 'post-war consensus' which tried to avoid a repetition of the bitter pre-Second World War divisions by guaranteeing different forms of power sharing between the relevant societal actors and the strong inclusion of various interest groups in political decision-making. This intention and the economic situation after the Second World War– including weak private capital– fostered cooperative relations between labour and capital in the post-war period (Talós and Hinterseer 2019). It found expression in so-called 'Austro-corporatism' (Pernicka and Hefler 2015).

One of the main features of Austro-corporatism is the chamber system and related to this the important role of social partnership. The ÖGB is one of four acknowledged social partners. The other three are the Chamber of Labour (AK), the WKO and the Chamber of Agriculture (LK, *Landwirtschaftskammer*). The Austrian chamber system has a long history and was re-established after the Second World War with the aim of representing the interests of (mainly occupational) interest groups vis-à-vis other interest groups and the state. These chambers ensure that the interests of specific groups are included in policymaking processes and offer services such as legal advice and representation for their members. Unions benefit especially from the Chamber of Labour and employers' mandatory membership in the Chamber of the Economy because one of the WKO's main tasks is to negotiate collective agreements (see below).

The AK, which acts as the statutory employee interest organization of all employees in Austria, provides free legal advice on issues such as labour law and social benefits, and offers workers legal protection in labour court cases. Although such services are also provided by trade unions, the relationship between trade unions and the AK is supportive rather than competitive. They regard each other as partners acting on sometimes similar, sometimes different fronts. Unions tend to be more combative, while the AK relies more on its role as an expert organization. In general, the AK supports unions (which have fewer material and personal resources) in their interest representation policies and through its expertise on a wide range of issues, such as collective bargaining, for example by providing data on macroeconomic and industry developments. As many employees have access to legal advice via their obligatory chamber membership, becoming a union member in Austria is rather a question of individual norms and values or a sign of support for the work of unions or works councils. Moreover, in recent years unions have tried to organize vulnerable labour market groups (for example, one-person businesses in package deliveries), which by employment status are non-AK members (as they are classified as 'employers', not 'employees' in a strictly legal sense), but work under highly dependent and vulnerable working conditions.

The industrial relations system was especially successful in the so-called 'golden age of Fordism', when political and social reforms were based on a demand-driven economic policy, including a strong state, nationalized industries and a large public sector, characterized by high levels of economic growth (Pernicka and Hefler 2015). From the beginning of the late 1980s, but especially since Austria's accession to the European Union (EU) in 1995, there was a shift from 'demand-side corporatism' to 'supply-side corporatism' (Traxler 1995), through which the industrial relations system– and especially the employee side – came under increasing pressure. Privatization policies and internationalization, as well as growing unemployment and rising inequality weakened labour organizations. Moreover, political shifts since the 2000s – such as two periods with right-wing government coalitions involving the conservative

People's Party (ÖVP, *Österreichische Volkspartei*) and the extreme-right Freedom Party (FPÖ, *Freiheitliche Partei Österreich*) (2000–2007 and 2017–2019) – have also challenged the role of social partnership and put pressure on labour organizations in particular. The dependence of the social partners and the chamber system on legal and political support became particularly evident during these periods.

Structure of trade unions and union democracy

The Austrian union system is the most unitarian in European comparison, with one single organization, the ÖGB. There are virtually no other trade unions outside the ÖGB.[4] The ÖGB covers – de facto – all trade unions and union members in Austria. Legally, the ÖGB is an autonomous association that is an umbrella organization of independent trade unions (Karlhofer 2001). The ÖGB has budgetary and personnel autonomy and may authorize strikes. In European comparison, the ÖGB exhibits a high degree of formal centralization. The ÖGB's affiliated unions, however, are densely integrated into decision-making structures. They enjoy, depending on their membership strength, autonomy with regard to their membership and financial policies vis-à-vis the ÖGB. For instance, the affiliates autonomously collect fees from their members. In collective bargaining, the relationship between the ÖGB and its affiliates is more balanced in favour of the latter; while the ÖGB formally signs all collective agreements actual negotiations are carried out by the trade unions.

Three criteria are relevant for the demarcation of trade unions' organizational domains: political/ideological alignment, employee status and sectors/industries (Traxler et al. 2001: 40). The ÖGB encompasses the entire party-political spectrum, including social democratic, Christian, leftist-communist, independent-green, and right-wing Freedom Party–affiliated unionists, as well as (party-politically) independent unionists. Thus, the ÖGB incorporates a wide variety of political and ideological

4 The Austrian Freedom Party set up its own trade union in 1998. The majority of its members were from the police. The trade union was not entitled to conclude collective agreements and had 10,000 members (Traxler et al. 2001: 45), but it was dissolved a couple of years later. Today, there are two employee organizations outside the ÖGB, neither of which is entitled to engage in collective bargaining: (i) an employee organization linked to the Freedom Party (the *Freie Exekutivgewerkschaft*), which has members almost exclusively among the armed forces, and (ii) an employee organization for medical doctors (*Asklepios*) founded in 2015 and having around 2,000 members.

views, within which social democrats are dominant in all industries, with the exception of the public sector, in which Christian trade unionists are in the majority (see subsection 'Political relations').

The ÖGB incorporates seven sectoral/industry trade unions. The GPA Union (formerly: Union of Salaried Private Sector Employees) (GPA, *Gewerkschaft GPA*), which is the largest union, organizes (mostly) private sector employees from all industries, as well as journalists and all *workers and employees in* the graphical industry. The Union of Public Services (GÖD, *Gewerkschaft Öffentlicher Dienst*) organizes civil servants and employees in public administration, health care, education and other professions at federal and state (or provincial) level. The Union of Production Workers (PRO-GE, *Die Produktionsgewerkschaft*) organizes mainly blue-collar workers from manufacturing industries. Younion (*Die Daseinsgewerkschaft*) covers public sector workers from districts and municipalities, as well as workers in arts, media, sports and the free professions. Vida (*Gewerkschaft vida*) organizes mostly blue-collar workers in private services and transport. The GBH (*Gewerkschaft Bau–Holz*) union organizes construction and woodworkers. And the GPF (*Gewerkschaft der Post- und Fernmeldebediensteten*) organizes postal and telecommunication workers. Because of the unified union system and the de facto non-existence of unions not affiliated to the ÖGB, inter-union competition is low.

Table 2.2 Membership of sectoral/industry trade unions, 2003– 2020

	2003		**2012**		**2020**
GPA	285,601	GPA-djp	273,970	GPA	279,965
GÖD	229,262	GÖD	234,346	GÖD	255,910
GMT	205,418	PRO-GE	230,878	PRO-GE	230,268
GdG	172,549	GdG-KMSfB	152,592	Younion	144,480
GBH	149,784	GBH	116,376	GBH	114,269
GdE	92,627	Vida	144,492	Vida	130,528
GPF	66,756	GPF	50,787	GPF	43,499
HGDP	48,697				
ANG	37,593				
GdC	32,747				
HTV	34,236				
GDJP	18,327				
KMSfB	11,603				
Total ÖGB	**1,385,200**		**1,203,441**		**1,198,919**

Source: ÖGB (2021b).

While demarcation based on sector (private/public), industry and (within an industry) branch[5] is most relevant for structuring trade union organization, employee status has lost its formally important role. Since the late 1990s, a process of harmonization of the pay and conditions of blue- and white-collar workers has taken place, mostly through collective bargaining but also by legislation. Formally, separate agreements remain to be concluded for both groups of workers, but wages and conditions, such as terms of notice, have been aligned in many cases. This process is still ongoing, however. In organizational terms, there is no strict separation of unions organizing exclusively blue- or white-collar workers.

According to its statutes, the federal congress is the highest-level body of the ÖGB. Around 500 delegates entitled to vote decide on the ÖGB's policy goals and elect the president, vice presidents, ÖGB executive and controlling commission. The federal executive board is the highest-level decision-making body and decides on important issues, such as strikes. Representatives of the (multi-)industry unions, as well as of the women's, pensioners' and youth departments are represented in the federal executive board. The board nominates, together with the trade unions, delegates entitled to vote in the congress. The executive board manages the current policies and assets of the ÖGB. The controlling commission monitors compliance with the ÖGB's statutes and its financial and economic activities. Rank-and-file members are usually not involved in the ÖGB's political decision-making (although they are not formally excluded from decision-making by the statutes).

The trade unions have adapted their organizational structures to workforce changes. The interests of working women were traditionally addressed in women's departments within the ÖGB and its affiliates, analogous to special departments for young people and pensioners. Against the background of the growing share of women in the total labour force, however, the ÖGB decided in 2005 that women should be represented on ÖGB bodies in accordance with their share in membership. Likewise, GPA implemented a positive action plan, including a women's quota in all bodies in 1997. Gender mainstreaming plans were adopted in several unions in the 2000s (Blaschke 2015; Traxler and Pernicka 2007).

---

5 Economic activity within an industry; for instance, within the metalworking industry automotive production constitutes a branch.

Transnationalization of the labour market and increasing east–west labour migration have raised awareness among trade unions of the need to address migrant workers (Griesser and Sauer 2017). The ÖGB has no specific formal structures to represent migrant workers and rather pursues a policy of regarding them as 'normal members'. Workers without Austrian citizenship (or EU/European Economic Area citizenship since Austria's accession to the EU in 1995) have been allowed to stand as candidates in Chamber of Labour and works council elections since 2006. Nevertheless, migrant workers are underrepresented in employee representation bodies (Michenthaler et al. 2013).

Mergers began to gain momentum in the 2000s (see Table 2.3). The Union of Metal, Mining and Energy Workers (GMBE, *Gewerkschaft Metall-Bergbau-Energie*) merged with the Textiles and Garments Trade Union (TLB, *Gewerkschaft Textil-Leder-Bekleidung*) in 2000 to form the Metalworking and Textiles Union (GMT, *Gewerkschaft Metall-Textil*). The main reasons underlying trade union mergers were changes in economic structure and in the composition of the labour force, as well as expected efficiency gains by scale and synergy effects arising from unified trade union structures and bundling of resources (Traxler and Pernicka 2007: 208). Another driver of union mergers was the big financial losses of the union-owned BAWAG bank in 2006, which resulted in a severe financial crisis for the ÖGB. Thus, three mergers took place in the same year, resulting in the Metalworking, Textiles and Food-processing Union (GMTN), the Union of Salaried Employees, Printing, Journalism and Paper (GPA), and the Transport and Service Union Vida (see Table 2.3). In 2009, two other mergers took place. The Municipal Employees' Union (GdG) merged with the Trade Union for the Small Arts, Media, Sports and Liberal Professions (KMSfB) to become 'Younion' (*Die Daseinsgewerkschaft*) in 2015, while the Metalworking, Textiles, Agriculture and Food-processing Union (GMTN) merged with the Union of Chemical Workers (GdC) to form the manufacturing industries union PRO-GE.

In strategic terms, the organization of a larger share of workers in a larger number of industries was supposed to increase inter-branch coordination in collective bargaining and membership strategies. In most cases, mergers involved at least one large and powerful union and one or more smaller unions. Mergers were also aimed at ensuring the viability of smaller unions (the merger between the Metalworking, Textiles, Agriculture and Food-processing Union and the Chemical Workers' Unions, however, rather resembled an amalgamation, that is, a merger between equals). Merger processes were not free of conflicts. Initially, in the mid-1990s the ÖGB planned to reduce the number of unions from fourteen to three, covering manufacturing, services and the public sector. These plans were not supported by their affiliates, however. For instance, the breaking up of the Private Services Union GPA to establish the principle of industry-wide unionism (for instance, one union per company) was not carried out because of union resistance (Traxler and Pernicka 2007). In particular, mergers involving powerful unions, such as the GPA and the Metalworking and Textiles Union, were the outcome of bottom-up processes driven by sector/industry unions (Traxler 2001). This underscores that the ÖGB's influence is not all-encompassing; rather trade unions were able to maintain a certain level of autonomy.

Table 2.3 Trade union mergers in Austria since 2000

Year	Merging trade unions	New trade union
2000	**Gewerkschaft Metall-Bergbau-Energie (GMBE)** Union of Metal, Mining and Energy Workers **Gewerkschaft Textil-Leder-Bekleidung (TLB)** Textiles and Garments Trade Union	**Gewerkschaft Metall-Textil (GMT)** Metalworking and Textiles Union
2006	**Gewerkschaft Metall-Textil (GMT)** Metalworking and Textiles Union **Gewerkschaft Agrar-Nahrung-Genuß (ANG)** Food and Agrarian Workers' Union	**Gewerkschaft Metall-Textil-Nahrung (GMTN)** Metalworking, Textiles and Food-processing Union
2006	**Gewerkschaft der Privatangestellten (GPA)** Union of Salaried Employees **Gewerkschaft Druck, Journalismus, Papier (GDJP)** Printing, Journalism and Paper Union	**Gewerkschaft der Privatangestellten, Druck, Journalismus, Papier (GPA-djp)** Union of Salaried Employees, Printing, Journalism and Paper 2020 renamed: GPA Union

(*Continued*)

Table 2.3 Continued

Year	Merging trade unions	New trade union
2006	**Gewerkschaft der Eisenbahner (GdE)** Union of Railway Employees **Gewerkschaft Handel, Transport, Verkehr (HTV)** Commerce and Transport Union **Gewerkschaft Hotel, Gastgewerbe, Persönlicher Dienst (HGPD)** Hotels, Catering and Personal Services Union	**Gewerkschaft vida** Transport and Service Union
2009	**Gewerkschaft der Gemeindebediensteten (GdG)** Municipal Employees' Union **Gewerkschaft für Kunst, Medien, Sport und freie Berufe (KMSfB)** Trade Union for the Small Arts, Media, Sports and Liberal Professions	**Gewerkschaft der Gemeindebediensteten - Kunst, Medien, Sport, freie Berufe (GdG-KMSfB)** Union for Municipal Employees and the Small Arts, Media, Sports and Liberal Professions 2015 renamed: **Die Daseinsgewerkschaft (Younion)**
2009	**Gewerkschaft Metall-Nahrung-Genuss (GMTN)** Metalworking, Textiles, Agriculture and Food-processing Union **Gewerkschaft der Chemiearbeiter (GdC)** Union of Chemical Workers	**Produktionsgewerkschaft (PRO-GE)** Union of Production Workers

Source: Authors' compilation based on Stückler (2000) and Adam (2006, 2007).

Unionization

One important indicator of trade union strength is net union density, that is, the share of union members in the total of active, employed people. Net union density is also used as a proxy indicator for a union's organizational power resources. As in most European countries, union membership in Austria has declined over time. According to ÖGB data, there were 1,442,400 union members in 2000, falling to 1,198,919 in 2020 (ÖGB 2021a). Net trade union density was around 37 per cent in 2000 and declined to 27 per cent in 2019 (OECD 2021).

The factors involved in the union membership decline are manifold. Structural changes in the labour market, such as the sectoral and occupational composition of the workforce, an increasing share of (often part-time employed) female employees and a partial precarization of employment relations have resulted in a shrinking of organizational power. Privatization of formerly state-owned companies and industries and EU economic liberalization policies have eroded former union strongholds. Finally, social factors such as individualization, a pluralization of values and orientations and the disintegration of traditional political affiliations have reduced the number of workers who become trade union members (Bacher et al. 2019; Peetz 2010;).

De-industrialization and 'tertiarization' of the economy – that is, the growth of services – have changed the composition of the labour force (Mesch 2004). While in 2004, 26.9 per cent of the total workforce was employed in manufacturing, this share had fallen to 22.7 per cent by 2018 (AK 2005; WKÖ 2019). In contrast, the share of employees in public and private services rose from 68.5 per cent in 2004 to 73.8 per cent in 2018. The share of blue-collar workers in manufacturing declined from 64 per cent in 2004 to 53.5 per cent in 2018. Developments in employment are largely mirrored in the membership figures of ÖGB unions. The GPA, organizing largely white-collar workers in manufacturing, has gained members, while PRO-GE and Vida, organizing mainly blue-collar workers in manufacturing, private services and transport, report declining memberships. Likewise, membership has grown in the public sector union GÖD and the private sector union GPA, while the postal and telecommunications union GPF, the woodworkers' union (GBH), the transport and services workers' union vida and younion (municipal workers) are recording membership losses. Since 2016, the trend towards a constant decline in ÖGB membership has been reversed. The Covid-19 pandemic, however, has led to a recurring membership loss of around 18,000 people. Because of the uncertain future of the pandemic and its effects on the labour market, it is not yet clear whether this was just a one-off event or a precursor of a longer trend of membership decline.

Table 2.4 Female union members and their share in total membership, 2003–2019

	2003			2012			2019	
GPA	124,749	43.7 %	GPA-djp	122,486	44.7 %	GPA-djp	131,767	46.7 %
GÖD	111,858	48.8 %	GÖD	125,191	53.4 %	GÖD	142,310	55.8 %
GMT	35,963	17.5 %	PRO-GE	34,281	14.8 %	PRO-GE	35,177	14.9 %
GdG	88,701	51.4 %	GdG-KMSfB	75,905	49.7 %	younion	75,875	51.8 %
GBH	6,497	4.3 %	GBH	3,574	3.1 %	GBH	3,936	3.3 %
GdE	5,818	6.3 %	Vida	46,961	32.5 %	Vida	43,171	32.2 %
GPF	16,106	24.1 %	GPF	11,880	23.4 %	GPF	10,372	23.4 %
HGDP	35,921	73.8 %						
ANG	8,614	22.9 %						
GdC	4,663	14.2 %						
HTV	12,634	36.9 %						
GDJP	3,429	18.7 %						
KMSfB	3,669	31.6 %						
Total ÖGB		**33.1 %**			**34.9 %**			**36.4 %**

Source: ÖGB (2019a, 2021b).

The 'feminization' of the labour force – the share of women in total employment grew from 43.7 per cent in 2000 to 47 per cent in 2019 (Statistik Austria 2020a) – has also affected trade union membership. The share of women among union members constantly increased from 32 per cent in 2000 to 36.4 per cent in 2019 (ÖGB 2021a). In the public sector, female members constitute the majority, and among salaried employees in the private sector almost half of all members are women. Although union organization is higher among men (34 per cent), density rates of female workers are declining to a lesser extent than those of men (in 2018: 774,700 union members were men, and 436,800 were women). The share of women among new members was 42.2 per cent in 2019, and the annual increase in membership was highest among young people (ÖGB 2020).

In 2017, around a quarter (24 per cent) of dependently employed persons were migrants, in other words, without Austrian nationality[6]

6 The largest share of workers (2017) are German (11 per cent), around one-quarter (24 per cent) are from the former Yugoslavia (excluding Slovenia) and Central-Eastern Europe (23 per cent: with 9 per cent from the EU8, excluding Romania and Bulgaria), as well as 9 per cent from Turkey and 10 per cent from Romania and Bulgaria. The rest are citizens of other western European and non-European countries.

(Titelbach et al. 2018). The share of migrant workers is significant in agriculture, hotels/restaurants and company-based services, such as cleaning, construction and among agency workers in manufacturing. Large numbers of migrants are working in private households (for example, old-age care). According to estimates based on the European Social Survey (2018), the union density of foreign workers is significantly lower than among non-foreign workers: approximately 17 per cent of non-Austrian citizens versus 28 per cent of Austrian citizens. Moreover, in line with the general trend towards a membership decline in recent years, migrant membership has also declined.

The growth of atypical employment, such as part-time work, fixed-term and freelance agency work and contingent work, is a particular challenge for trade unions. Part-time work, which is particularly widespread among women, has increased the most, from 16 per cent in 2000 to 28 per cent in 2019 (Statistik Austria 2020b). Between 2008 and 2017, contingent employment (fewer than 12 hours per week) grew by 33.6 per cent, fixed-term work by 31.8 per cent and agency work by 22 per cent (Knittler 2018). Since the harmonization of social security contribution regulations for fixed-term and regular work the former type of work has declined. Atypically employed workers are often employed for a limited time period, labour turnover is high and workers are physically dispersed or separated from core labour forces. This makes it difficult for trade unions to approach them. According to European Social Survey (ESS) data (2018), 15 per cent of workers with fixed-term contracts were union members, compared with 26.5 per cent of workers with open-ended contracts, and only 6 per cent of self-employed workers were members, compared with 25.5 per cent of employed workers.

Confronted with continuing declines in membership and financial losses, trade unions increased their efforts and repertoires of action in addressing (potential) members. They began to exchange experiences about practices in organizing and campaigning with unions from other countries such as the United States and Germany in the early 2000s. Centrally orchestrated, industry-wide organizing campaigns have been rare in Austria, however. Rather, trade unions have expanded educational training for works councils, including also a shift in focus from legal knowledge to practical action, including membership recruitment.

Trade union membership strategies vary between industries (Pernicka and Stern 2011). Usually, unions' approaches are a combination of campaigns to raise awareness of union representation, questioning workers about their problems and wishes at work, collective bargaining and mobilization for collective action, often making use of social media. Unions in health care and social services are most active and visible, for instance, engaging in public action in shopping streets or city centres to raise awareness of workers' issues, such as the 'care crisis' resulting from understaffing and bad working conditions. More recently, the PRO-GE union initiated the *Sezonieri* campaign, focusing on agricultural workers, in addition to the ÖGB-linked 'UNDOK' platform fighting undocumented work. Unions provide advice on legal matters, mostly in labour and social law, but also in other areas, such as tax and residence regulations, in several languages (mainly Turkish, Serbo-Croatian/Bosnian, Hungarian). Most unions employ bi- or multi-lingual officers.

The GPA has responded to the growing diversity of its membership by establishing special interest bodies, so-called interest groupings, such as self-employed and temporary agency workers, IT specialists, professional and executive staff, and migrants (Pernicka 2005). In the meantime, however, resources for interest groupings have been cut and their intra-organizational influence has further decreased. The focus now lies more on recruiting new members.

To summarize, collective bargaining and representation by works councils still dominate trade union policies. Campaigning, organizing and membership participation approaches are advancing and becoming increasingly professionalized (especially by the efforts of committed individuals). These activities largely remain small-scale, however.

Union resources and expenditure

Austrian unions are financed mainly from voluntary membership fees. A much smaller part of union revenues (around 8 per cent) comes from sales and operational income. Members pay a monthly fee of 1 per cent of their gross income, including overtime bonuses and other surcharges, excluding special payments such as Christmas or holiday bonuses, as well as compensation of expenses. Under special circumstances, such as parental leave or civilian services, members are exempted from paying membership fees. There are also possibilities to reduce fees, for instance, for unemployed/marginally employed people, retirees, pupils or students or persons on sickness benefits. Trade union fees are fully tax deductible.

The sectoral/industry trade unions collect fees from their members, while the ÖGB receives a share of total membership fees. Legally, the affiliates are not separate associations but part of the ÖGB. But both the ÖGB as the peak-level organization, as well as the trade unions have their own budgets. The ÖGB's financial resources were severely threatened when BAWAG, a large bank owned by the ÖGB, lost a huge amount of money in financial speculation, which was made public in 2006. The bank's bailout plan, however, legally required the ÖGB to sell BAWAG, as well as its shares in the Central Bank, and to be liable to the extent of its assets. Moreover, the ÖGB was obliged to inform the Central Bank about its strike fund, previously a well-kept secret (Traxler and Pernicka 2007: 212). Burdened with huge liabilities, the ÖGB had to sell much of its properties and followed an austerity programme during the ensuing years. Nevertheless, austerity policies have focused mainly on sales and consolidation of assets rather than cutting staff or services for members.

As outcomes from collective bargaining, such as annual wage increases, apply not only to trade union members, but to all workers belonging to a particular collective agreement's domain, getting higher wages are not a big incentive for workers to join a trade union (Traxler and Behrens 2002). Nevertheless, unions always refer to the fact that high union membership as an integral part of their organizational power is essential for their position in collective bargaining. In addition, they offer their members services, such as free legal protection in labour law cases, legal advice and consultation, as well as several benefits for purchases, leisure and culture. Because Austrian workers are also mandatory members of the Austrian Chamber of Labour, becoming a union member is often more likely to be a question of norms and values (being part of a bigger community) than a question of direct material benefits.

Making up around 92 per cent of annual revenues, membership fees are essential for trade unions' survival. Thus, structural changes in the labour market and the general economic situation have a direct impact on their financial resources. In economic downturns and periods of high unemployment, on the one hand, union resources generally decrease because of the reduced fees for unemployed members or because members leaving the union when they lose their job. In economic upswings, on the other hand, union resources generally increase.

Unions were fairly successful in stabilizing their financial resources over the past ten years. Revenues from membership fees increased between 2009 and 2019 from €195 million to €247 million; liabilities continuously decreased.

The ÖGB is an association and is thus non-profit-orientated. The annual revenues cover, more or less exactly, annual (mostly personnel and operational) expenses, which were €120 million (personnel expenses) and €132 million (operational expenses) in 2019. The ÖGB had around 1,800 employees in 2018. The number of employees has slightly declined in the past ten years, as has the number of local offices (ÖGB 2019b).

The effects of the current Covid-19 pandemic on their financial resources are not yet clear. The strong increase in unemployment – despite the widespread use of short-time work and a decline in union membership rates in 2020 and 2021, may lead to a slight financial loss over the coming years.[7]

Collective bargaining and unions at the workplace

The negotiation of wages and working conditions is one of the central tasks of trade unions. Collective bargaining takes place within a dual system for the representation of labour interests, with the ÖGB and the sector/industry unions carrying out negotiations, for example on collective agreements, while works councils (or specific employee representation bodies in the public sector) represent employees' interests at the workplace. While trade unions settle wages and a wide range of working conditions in collective agreements, works councils are entitled to conclude company/works agreements (*Betriebsvereinbarung*) with the management on certain legally prescribed issues devolved upon them by labour law and collective agreements. Although works councils are formally independent from unions, the vast majority of works councillors are also union members. Usually, there is close cooperation between trade unions and works councils. Works councils benefit from unions' expertise and organizational power, while works councils provide access to the rank-and-file and are essential for recruiting members.

---

7 Even though the use of short-time working has played an important role in saving jobs – at the peak of the pandemic in spring 2020 approximately 1 million people were on short-time working (Tamesberger and Moser 2021) – the average unemployment figure in 2020 increased considerably from around 300,000 in 2019 to around 400,000 in 2020 (AMS 2021).

An indicator of the workplace organization of employees is the density of works councils, measured by the share of workers represented by a works council in the total workforce. The representational density of works councils has decreased slightly since 2000. Roughly, 55 per cent of workers were represented by a works council in 2000 (Hermann and Flecker 2009), falling to 52.5 per cent in 2019.[8] Employee representation at the workplace (2016) varies between industries, and is highest in the public sector (90 per cent), industry and crafts (61 per cent) and lowest in retail (30 per cent) and tourism (15 per cent). In addition, works council density varies with size of firm in terms of the number of employees, increasing with company size. According to a study on working conditions in Austria, a declining share of workers say that they have contact with works council representatives at the workplace (Eichmann and Saupe 2014).

Collective bargaining takes place in a multi-level hierarchical legal framework, whereby minimum standards in basic working conditions, such as maximum working time, health and safety or dismissals, are regulated by law. Collective agreements set legally binding minimum standards of pay for the entire wage scale and a wide range of working conditions, such as working time, and special bonuses such as holiday and Christmas remuneration. Social partners agreed on a minimum wage of €1,500 in collective agreements in 2017. Currently, all collective agreements (with very few exceptions) provide for a minimum wage above this mark. The goal of a new minimum wage of €1,700 was included in the ÖGB's working programme in 2018 (Hofmann and Zuckerstätter 2019). Works councils are entitled to negotiate works agreements on issues such as working time, telework/home office or surveillance procedures, at company level. They monitor adherence to collective agreements at the workplace and ensure workers' voice and codetermination in certain areas of company policy. Usually, conditions set at decentralized levels can only be favourable to employees ('favourability principle'). Only under exceptional circumstances, and in agreement with the social partners, can collective agreements permit downward derogation at the company level.

---

8 These figures derive from the Working Climate Index 4/2016 and 4/2019, a survey initiated by the Chamber of Labour for Upper Austria in 1997, which is updated on a regular basis (AK 2016, 2019).

Around 98 per cent of workers are covered by collective agreements. The broad scope of collective bargaining results from companies' obligatory membership of the WKO and the legal extension of collective bargaining coverage to employees who are not union members (Glassner and Hofmann 2019; Traxler and Behrens 2002). Besides the WKO a number of voluntary employers' organizations, for instance in finance and banking and in social services, conclude collective agreements, provided they are of significant economic relevance in terms of their memberships. On the employees' side, the ÖGB and its seven affiliated industry unions negotiate collective agreements. Usually, collective agreements are settled at industry level between (multi-)industry unions and the industry/branch associations of the WKO. Collective bargaining law allows for company-level collective agreements only in exceptional cases (mostly for big, formerly stated-owned companies, such as airlines and railway companies). Collective agreements are legally binding for all workers employed in a company that is a member of an association that is a signatory party to a collective agreement. In the first half of the 2000s, trade unions actively contributed to the stabilization of the collective bargaining system by concluding agreements in formerly uncovered industries such as Information and Communications Technology (ICT), universities, non-university research, social services and agency work (Hermann and Flecker 2006). For a small fraction of workers not covered by collective agreements minimum wage norms stipulated by the federal arbitration agency apply (for instance, for janitors and caretakers).

Collective bargaining is highly coordinated and synchronized within and between industries (Traxler et al. 2008). The annual negotiation round starts in autumn in the metal industry. The wage agreement in metalworking serves as an orientation mark for bargaining actors in other manufacturing industries, as well as in commerce and the public sector. Since the turn of the century, the pattern-setting effect of the metal industry has lost ground and multiple smaller 'pattern-setting rounds', such as the public sector and social services, or the 'spring round', starting with the electronics and chemical industries, have emerged (Glassner and Hofmann 2019).

Despite the formal stability and inclusiveness of the collective bargaining system signs of erosion and increasing conflicts may be observed. The long-term fall in trade union density has weakened labour's bargaining position. In addition, the share of workers represented by a works council has declined over time. Trade unions point to the problem that some employers in metalworking and other industries attempt to apply agreements– such as the crafts agreement– that are more favourable for them, rather than agreements, such as the industrial agreement, that should apply on the basis of the company's size and mode of production (Pernicka et al. 2020). The diversity of employers' positions in international production chains, their profitability and market positions has widened with the internationalization of the metal industry. The growing divergence of employers' and employees' interests is increasingly hampering the conclusion of an industry-wide agreement. An open conflict erupted in metal that resulted in the dissolution of the industry's bargaining platform, comprising the WKO industry associations of the metal industry and the unions PRO-GE and GPA in autumn 2011. The metalworking and machinery industries, dominated by small- and medium-sized companies, rejected the union wage demands and terminated the practice of joint negotiations. The trade unions in response mobilized for industrial action, the first strike in metal for many years. Separate agreements had been concluded in metal since autumn 2012. To date, wage increases had been equal for the entire industry, while an increasing number of qualitative issues, such as working time arrangements, became more diversified.

Negotiations in the metal industry have been more contested and conflict-ridden since then (Pernicka et al. 2020). For trade unions, the annual settlement of a uniform wage increase for metal has become a feat of strength. Representatives of some industry associations have publicly complained that collective agreements are too rigid and costly. The unions have responded by announcing company assemblies and warning strikes, most recently in 2018. One year before, the government unilaterally changed working time regulations and unions sought to compensate the emerging disadvantages for workers with a favourable collective agreement. Collective bargaining has also become more conflictual in other industries, such as social services and banking.

To conclude, collective bargaining is less stable than the extraordinarily high level of bargaining coverage might suggest. Despite its– in European comparison– outstandingly encompassing bargaining system, support has waned over the years among some employers, and beneath the surface of the almost full bargaining coverage, some are withdrawing from collective bargaining and circumventing collective agreements (for instance, in metalworking and foundries, bakeries). Finally, political attacks on statutory membership of the chambers underscore the 'borrowed stability' of industrial relations (Glassner and Hofmann 2019).

Industrial conflict

Together with Germany, the Netherlands, Norway, Sweden and Switzerland, Austria belongs to the group of 'persistently low-strike countries' (Vandaele 2016), which means that strikes and industrial conflicts are generally rare. Their negligible role in industrial relations is because of so-called 'Austro-corporatism' and social partnership, which was based on cooperation and compromise. In 'normal' collective bargaining rounds the sheer threat of a strike by unions is usually sufficient to persuade the employers' side back to the negotiation table and to reach a compromise. Also in socio-political disputes (such as disputes over the pension or health care system) trade unions usually rely on their connections to political parties or the government or on social partnership negotiations. Thus, unions strongly rely on their institutional power resources (Glassner and Hofmann 2019).

Since 1945, strikes and industrial action have rarely been used to pursue workers' interests in Austria. Also in the period from 2000 to 2020 analysed here, the number of days not worked was generally very low: from 2000 to 2009 the average was 41 days, and from 2010 to 2017 it was only two days (Appendix A1). While internationally 'days not worked' are used as an important indicator of strike frequency, this indicator is not very helpful to grasp the few signs of industrial action in Austria as it is often zero (see Figure 2.1). The ÖGB thus uses an alternative indicator: total strike hours. For the Austrian case this is especially useful as most strikes are so-called warning strikes, which last only a few hours and are thus not included in the 'days not worked' indicator. Besides, unions often call for works assemblies instead of (warning) strikes. This is a very 'Austrian way' of interrupting work. In these work assemblies, important company issues are discussed while actual work is stopped, but they do not appear in official strike statistics.

Figure 2.1 Days not worked and workers involved in industrial action, 2000–2019

Note: Data regarding the days not worked per 1,000 employees is calculated with the Eurostat indicator for the number of employees.
Source: ÖGB (2019a), WKO (2019), see also appendix.

Figure 2.1 shows strike activity per year between 2000 and 2019. We only see three peaks in the data: 2003, 2011 and 2018. The 2003 peak was because of bigger, nationwide political confrontations. Since 2000, Austria had had its first neoliberal-conservative government with the participation of the extreme-right FPÖ, which tried to weaken the unions' institutional power and to abolish compulsory membership of the chambers, one of the fundamental principles of social partnership (Astleithner and Flecker 2017). The government also tried to reshape and downsize social security systems by emphasizing a stronger role for individual private provision. During this time, there was a lot of political tension in the air. One reform attempt in 2003 caused the situation to escalate. The ÖVP-FPÖ government had planned a pension reform disadvantaging employees, which was followed by huge protests and strikes organized by the interest organizations of labour and civil society. This major resistance was partly successful, as it forced the government to take back some planned reform steps. Thus, these rare, but in part successful political protest experiences still play an important role in trade unions' collective memory and were re-activated several times later on (Hofmann 2017).

While these forms of protests and strikes aimed at political initiatives, there was also some industrial action in relation to collective bargaining. Especially in the metal industry tensions increased during collective bargaining rounds. These growing tensions explain the peak in strike indicators in 2011. In this context, the re-introduction of the public announcement of wage claims by the unions to build up public support, as well as strike threats became a more important part of unions' 'action repertoires'.

The 2018 peak points to the autumn collective bargaining round, which was highly influenced by the new legislation on the so-called '12-hour-day'. Unions tried to correct the 'social imbalance' of this law. They demanded compensation via higher wages, as well as more influence for workers over working time arrangements in companies and more vacations. They were rather quick to use the threat of measures such as works assemblies or (warning) strikes as employers did not want to make such concessions.

In recent years, there have been some signs of a 'tertiarization of industrial conflicts' as employees in the social and health care systems, whose professional ethos usually prevents them from striking, have become more and more protest prone. In early 2019 the bargaining round in social services was accompanied by strikes before a compromise was reached. In the following year, collective bargaining in social and health care was again highly conflictual: the unions demanded a reduction of weekly working time to 35 hours, with full wage compensation. Followed by a campaign called '35 hours are enough', they drew attention to the fact that in the social and health care sector (in which employees are predominantly female) most employees work part-time as their job is physically and psychologically too demanding to work a full 40-hour week. As the employers, mostly non-profit organizations, argued they could not finance a 35-hour week, care workers went on strike in February 2020. The protests stopped dead due to the Covid-19 pandemic, however, and the bargaining partners agreed on a compromise, including wage increases and a working time reduction to 37 hours.

Political relations

Because of the closely interwoven system of Austro-corporatism, trade union relations with politics are generally close in Austria. Their political influence unfolds along two paths: (i) via their role as social partners and (ii) via their personal and organizational links to political parties. Within the (and because of the country's small size) closely connected political system, trade unions are very well equipped with institutional power resources.

The ÖGB is one of four acknowledged social partners. The other three are the Chamber of Labour, the Chamber of the Economy and the Chamber of Agriculture. Trade union membership is voluntary, but membership of the other social partner organizations is mandatory. While all organizations are generally open to all political ideologies, traditionally, the ÖGB and the AK lean towards social democracy, with the exception of the two most Western states Tyrol und Vorarlberg, which are more conservative in their orientation. In the other chambers Christian-conservative ideologies dominate.

Political critique of the influence of social partners on Austria's political system has gained momentum since the 1980s: the 'Austrian model' has become increasingly contested at the political level. Especially the extreme-right party FPÖ, which was in government once in the 1980s and twice since 2000 (2000–2007; 2017–2019), has tried to minimize the social partners' influence. At the beginning of the 2000s, the government of the conservative Austrian People's Party (ÖVP) and the extreme-right FPÖ actively challenged social partnership. Social and labour policies were for the first time negotiated without properly involving the social partners (especially the labour side). The FPÖ has repeatedly tried to abolish compulsory membership of chambers, an institutional feature that helps to maintain the extraordinarily high collective bargaining coverage (Glassner and Hofmann 2019), but it has not been successful so far.

Although it has become more and more evident in recent years that the normative commitment to social partnership could reach its limits when power relations change, unions still stick to the system of social partnership at the political level. It has guaranteed them an institutionalized channel to influence social policymaking and labour legislation. Moreover, public attitudes are generally in favour of social partnership (Profil 2018). The power shift because of the sudden end of the right-wing coalition between the FPÖ and the ÖVP in 2019 and the entry of the Green Party as coalition partner of the ÖVP might have fostered hopes of a revival of social partnership. Lo and behold, the management of the Covid-19 pandemic has been strongly shaped by the social partners, including the legislation on short-time working (Schnetzer et al.

2020; Tálos and Hinterseer 2019). It still remains to be seen, however, how long this 'revival' will last.

The connections between trade unions and political parties are traditionally strong. Especially the historical alliance with the Social Democratic and Christian Democratic parties has helped unions to bring their influence to bear. Around 30 per cent of all ministers from 1945 to 2015 had a social partner background, including two ÖGB presidents. Through their individual party membership, several unionists were and still are also members of the Austrian Parliament. Two presidents of the ÖGB even became (vice-)presidents of the parliament. While the Social Democratic Party of Austria (SPÖ, *Sozialdemokratische Partei Österreich*) predominantly recruited ministers and members of parliament from the ÖGB and the AK, the ÖVP recruited from the WKO and the LK (Ennser-Jedenastik 2017). Moreover, within the Social Democratic and the Christian-conservative party there are 'union and employee related subgroups'. For instance, there are union representatives in the party executive of the SPÖ, and one sub-organization of the ÖVP is the Austrian Federation of Employees (ÖAAB, *Österreichischer Arbeitnehmerinnen- und Arbeitnehmerbund*), which is not a trade union but rather an 'interest group' for employee concerns organized within the ÖVP.

When Sebastian Kurz became leader of the ÖVP in 2017, he tried to limit the influence of different interest groups within the party. This included a reduction of the influence of the ÖAAB (Puller 2018). But, recent developments, such as the coalition government with the Green Party which is in power since 2019 and the management of the Covid-19 pandemic, have entailed a reinvigoration of ties between the ÖVP leadership and the ÖAAB. Traditionally, social and labour policy is not strong in Green parties, but the Austrian Greens also have union connections via the independent-green faction in the ÖGB (including one Green MEP) and the Chamber of Labour. FPÖ also has a 'union-wing' (the *Freiheitliche Arbeitnehmer*), but their influence is low giving its Janus-faced social and economic orientation. While FPÖ voters are more likely to support (ethnocentrist) social policies, the party's leadership tends more towards neoliberal economic positions and is thus not much in favour of trade unions (Flecker et al. 2019). There is another party in the Parliament, which is not particularly union-friendly: the small liberal party New Austria and Liberal Forum (NEOS, *Das Neue Österreich und Liberales Forum*). Similar to the FPÖ, NEOS is against compulsory chamber membership and habitually describes unions as 'modernization blockers'.

Societal power

As institutional power and relations to politics were well-developed trade union resources in Austria, for a long time the extension of societal power was not a strategic union focus. Nevertheless, awareness of the need to enter into coalitions with other civil society actors has grown over the past twenty years. The general power shift from labour to capital, as well as special political situations such as governments with FPÖ participation in the early 2000s encouraged a rethink on this issue. Emerging transnational social movements (such as the Alter Europe movement) have also contributed to unions' rising awareness of the importance of coalition-building (Hofmann 2017).

Since the beginning of the 2000s, the ÖGB or its affiliates have been co-organizers or supporters of numerous demonstrations, such as the protests against the two ÖVP/FPÖ governments or against right-wing extremism and fascism. Unionists have been active in social movements such as the Alter Europe movement and in longer-term alliances, such as the alliance 'Paths out of the crisis', which was formed during the financial and economic crisis from 2008 onwards, or the campaign for the rights of seasonal migrant workers in agriculture (*Sezonieri*). In recent years, there has rarely been a big, civil society demonstration without the participation of the ÖGB or at least one of its affiliates. Campaigning know-how is also continuously being built up, for example via union education courses. Sometimes, the coalitions with civil society actors have even had a clearly visible outcome, such as a drop-in centre for undocumented workers (UNDOK), which was initially set up by a group of civil society actors, unionists and political activists and is now located at ÖGB headquarters in Vienna.

Contacts between central civil society actors (such as Attac or the national poverty conference – an umbrella organization of social NGOs) and unions are thus fairly well developed (Strickner 2014). Here, the fact that Austria is spatially and demographically modest in size might also play an important role. The number of activists is manageable and thus networks are easier to build up. Having said all that, we would still argue that the associational power of unions is low, for two reasons: first, the influence of civil society engagement on politics is in general modest, whereas the unions' influence on politics as a social partner was strong until the recent past. This provoked and still provokes unions to focus their efforts on the latter. Second, it is often only a handful of unionists who are active in coalition-building with civil society. Thus, to date, coalition-building as a strategy has not really penetrated the depths of union organizational structures.

According to the literature, 'real' social movement unionism (Kelly 1998) would involve not only unions building alliances with other progressive forces, but also that they 'recreate themselves as social movements' (Frege and Kelly 2004: 137). This would mean changing their strategies to influence politics not only from the negotiation table but also and perhaps even more so through protests in the streets and at enterprises. Such a strategic shift has not yet manifested itself in Austria. Indeed, from time to time, unions organize massive campaigns. One recent example are the demonstrations against the extension of the working day to 12 hours, in which more than 100,000 people participated (Stern and Hofmann 2018). Collective bargaining rounds have also become more and more conflictual in recent years. Nevertheless, these campaigns are selective and do not indicate a substantial shift of strategies, rather an extension of the unions' repertoire of contention.

Another way of gaining societal power is to expand discursive power (Urban 2010). If unions are able to intervene in public debates, their societal power gains strength. The use of traditional media channels (via TV, adverts or their own print media) is very well developed in Austria. Nowadays, however, social media is rapidly gaining discursive power. Unions jumped on the social media train quite late, but they have shown a high degree of professionalization in this area in recent years. Public relations via social media are now part of established union marketing. Several campaigns are already designed as online-only; existing print media is now also available as an online version. Still there is room for improvements: while the Facebook accounts of the ÖGB or its affiliates do not receive more than 60,000 likes, the ÖGB has over 1 million members who need to be reached.

Trade union policies towards the European Union

Trade unions have been rather supportive of European integration since the 1990s. The ÖGB contributed to the largely positive public vote in favour of the country's accession to the EU in 1995. The unions have been much more reserved vis-à-vis the Europeanization of social and labour market policy and the EU's 'eastern enlargements', however. The ÖGB, against the background of large gaps in wage levels and working conditions between Austria and its CEE neighbouring countries, pressed for long transition periods before the Austrian labour market was fully opened. Nevertheless, Austrian unions were, and still are among the most active in their (financial and organizational) support for CEE trade unions.

The ÖGB's transnational work focuses on shaping interest policies at European level through formal institutional channels, such as the ÖGB's office in Brussels, the European Economic and Social Committee, and the European Trade Union Confederation (ETUC) on a broad range of issues, such as European labour market and social policy. Furthermore, ÖGB regional offices participate in nine interregional trade union councils (IRTUCs) together with unions from Italy, Slovenia, Hungary, the Czech Republic, Germany and Switzerland. The aim of this interregional cooperation is to counter wage and social dumping, exchange information on collective bargaining and wage developments, and provide advice on workers' rights. The union council between western Hungary and Burgenland, the most eastern region of Austria, functions particularly well and has established cross-border networks in various industries and at company level (Hammer 2010).

The transnational coordination of collective bargaining to counter wage competition between countries within the euro zone was the main aim of interregional trade union networks set up to coordinate wage polices in a number of industries (Glassner and Pochet 2011; Pernicka and Glassner 2014). The Austrian metalworking union was among the most active, together with unions from Germany and the Benelux countries, in shaping policies for the European coordination of wage setting (the collective bargaining committee of the European Metalworkers' Federation/IndustriAll has been headed by an Austrian unionist since 2007). The transnational coordination of wage bargaining has lost much of its relevance since the financial crisis of 2008/09. In political terms, the focus has meanwhile shifted from bargaining policy coordination towards a European minimum wage policy at the level of the ETUC (Schulten et al. 2015). One network, however, the 'Vienna Memorandum Group', founded in 1999 by metalworking unions from Austria, Germany, Slovenia, Slovakia, the Czech Republic and Hungary, is still active. Unionists continue to meet biannually to fight wage and social dumping and to exchange information on collective bargaining developments.

Furthermore, the European Federation of Building and Woodworkers (EFBW) has established a European database on wages and basic working conditions, providing information in many languages.

Industry unions' transnational activities are usually less formalized and rather issue-specific. One example is the 'Fair work' platform of the construction and woodworkers union's (GBH) regional office in Styria, which provides (online and face-to-face) bilingual information for migrant and posted workers to promote equal wages for equal work in industries prone to wage and social dumping (Krings 2019). Ensuring fair working conditions for agricultural workers is the aim of the *Sezonieri* campaign, initiated by the PRO-GE, Vida and NGOs in 2014.

The traditionally strike-averse ÖGB unions usually do not take industrial action during European Action Days. Usually, they send delegates to the assemblies or solidarity notes. This contrasts with the approach of southern European unions that often call for Europe-wide strikes and industrial action (Pernicka and Hofmann 2014; Hofmann 2017). It is noteworthy that during the general strike in 2003 the Austrian railway union successfully mobilized the Hungarian railway union for transnational strike action (Hammer 2010).

All (multi-)industry unions engage with their respective industry-level European trade union federations. Engagement is far-reaching in the metal industry, with PRO-GE regularly participating in meetings called by IndustriAll, as well as in construction and forestry (GBH), in private services (GPA, Vida) and in the public sector, for example, in health care, social services, gas and electricity (Younion). Likewise, unions participate in European sectoral social dialogue. Involvement, however, depends on the degree of activity of the – currently – 43 sectoral social dialogue committees. It may vary considerably between industries and over time.

European works councils (EWCs) are important institutional resources for transnational labour action. EWCs have been particularly active in the automotive sector to avoid competition between multinational companies in different countries (Greer and Hauptmeier 2012; Pernicka et al. 2017). Trade unions perceive EWCs as an important institutional resource and tend to express pro-active attitudes towards transnational labour cooperation.

Conclusions

From an international comparative perspective, Austrian trade unions still enjoy largely favourable conditions. Particularly in collective bargaining, trade unions are influential actors equipped with far-reaching bargaining autonomy and supportive institutional conditions, such as companies' mandatory membership of the Chamber of the Economy and the legal bindingness of collective agreements for non-unionized workers, which ensures bargaining coverage of the vast majority of workers. Labour law provides for high standards of worker protection and working conditions. Precarious employment is increasing but is still only of minor importance in comparison with other countries. The monitoring of working conditions is supported by state agencies, such as the Labour Inspectorate, and is fairly effective in European comparison. At the company level, works councils enjoy comparatively broad codetermination rights and the support of a unified union movement. The large (but declining) majority of works councillors are union members.

Referring to the four possible futures of trade unions presented by Visser (2019), which path will Austrian trade unions take? The dangers of 'marginalization', 'substitution' or 'dualization' do not seem to be too great considering the strong institutional backing trade unions still enjoy. 'Revitalization' as a probable future scenario of the union movement, however, seems to be too optimistic, as membership-focused approaches and organizational renewal have not been fully embraced by unions. Thus, a future of 'stability', added to Visser's (2019) four futures of trade unions, seems to be most probable for unions at this point in time. This future does not follow automatically, however. Rather, it requires continued efforts on the part of trade unions in order to strengthen membership, in particular among young, migrant and female workers, and to pursue inclusive strategies of collective bargaining and representation of labour's interests vis-à-vis employers and the government.

Trade unions in Austria are affected – as all European unions are – by global structural change and growing economic and social inequalities, driven by increasing international competition, market liberalization, the emergence of monopolistic platform companies, and an increasingly heterogeneous labour force. The rise in unemployment, the closure of production sites, national and European digitalization and decarbonization policies are exacerbating structural change. To date, unions have been negatively affected by many of these processes. Overall, these developments have accelerated the shift of power relations to the detriment of organized labour.

Looking more closely at labour relations, multiple challenges come to the fore. The constant decline in union density, the dependence on institutional resources that ensure a high collective bargaining coverage, and the subordinate importance of membership policies are some of the most important. The weakening of social partnership and the side-lining of organized labour, as well as changing values among younger generations of managers, politicians and journalists that are hostile towards or ignorant of the idea of social partnership and negotiated compromise have contributed to the trade unions' loss of relevance as powerful societal actors.

To summarize, we would like to highlight three densely interrelated challenges.

First, and starting from a rather abstract level, unions are confronted with a dilemma between a membership logic and a logic of influence unfolding in a very specific way. Comparatively extensive institutional resources for instance in collective bargaining have led to a fairly passive reliance on them and a neglect of organizational renewal. At the same time, the withdrawal of institutional power in national social dialogue has forced unions out of political decision-making and into an oppositional role, a role into which the unions have not yet grown. Unions, largely lacking experience in industrial action, have to gain further experience in mobilization, protest and building alliances with civil society actors in order to strengthen their institutional power.

Second, reliance on institutional power is risky. Changes in governmental coalitions with far-right and neoliberal parties might induce a withdrawal of institutional resources, as previous – and persistent – attacks on statutory membership of chambers have shown. Trade unions in Austria, a small and export-dependent economy, traditionally support a moderate wage policy, aiming at macroeconomic stability and international competitiveness. Unions, having deeply internalized their role in social partnership, are traditionally strike-adverse.

Third, statutory membership of chambers does not automatically translate into smooth and conflict-free collective bargaining and outcomes favourable for organized labour. Neither does it imply the quasi-automatic conclusion of collective agreements, as recent conflicts in metalworking – in which every year the employers publicly question the negotiation procedures – have shown. Nor does it guarantee all-encompassing compliance by companies or parts of industries, as illustrated by, for instance, the initial refusal of foundry companies to recognize the metalworking agreement in 2019.

The current Covid-19 pandemic has deepened long-standing problems. In the short term, unions are suffering from membership losses arising from mass unemployment. The current resurgence of social partnership has indeed allowed the trade unions to assert themselves in crisis management, as indicated, for example, by the rapid conclusion and implementation of short-time working agreements. As experience from the 2008–2010 crisis shows, however, 'crisis corporatism' might be transitory and built on borrowed stability.

The Austrian labour movement rests upon three pillars; works councils at the company level, collective bargaining at industry level, and trade unions at sectoral/industry and national levels. All three areas of action are densely intertwined and have to be strengthened synchronously. Trade unions have to address processes of erosion in all three areas. The question of how to do so successfully remains of the utmost importance for trade unions, and not only in Austria.

References

All links were checked on 20 April 2021.

Adam G. (2006) Union merger announced. https://www.eurofound.europa.eu/publications/article/2006/union-merger-announced

Adam G. (2007) Latest union merger part of ongoing process. https://www.eurofound.europa.eu/publications/article/2007/latest-union-merger-part-of-ongoing-process

AK (Arbeiterkammer) (2005) Wirtschafts- und Sozialstatistisches Taschenbuch 2005, Wien, AK Wien.

AK (Arbeiterkammer) Oberösterreich (2016) Arbeitsklima Index 2016, 4/2016, Linz, AK OÖ.

AK (Arbeiterkammer) Oberösterreich (2019) Arbeitsklima Index 2019, 4/2019, Linz, AK OÖ.

AMS (Arbeitsmarktservice) (2021) Arbeitsmarkt. http://www.statistik.at/web_de/statistiken/menschen_und_gesellschaft/arbeitsmarkt/index.html

Astleithner F. and Flecker J. (2017) From the golden age to the gilded cage? Austrian trade unions, social partnership and the crisis, in Lehndorff S., Dribbusch H. and Schulten T. (eds) Rough waters: European trade unions in a time of crises, Brussels, ETUI, 173–195.

Bacher J., Grausgruber J., Haller A., Höllinger F., Prandner D. and Verwiebe R. (eds) (2019) Sozialstruktur und Wertewandel in Österreich. Trends 1986–2016, Wiesbaden, VS Verlag für Sozialwissenschaften.

Blaschke S. (2015) Female representation in the decision-making structures of trade unions: the influences of sector, status and qualification, Journal of Industrial Relations, 57 (5), 726–747.

Eichmann H. and Saupe B. (2014) Überblick über Arbeitsbedingungen in Österreich: follow-up-studie, Wien, ÖGB Verlag.

Ennser-Jedenastik L. (2017) Die personelle Verflechtung zwischen Sozialpartnern und Bundesregierung in Österreich 1945–2015, Österreichische Zeitschrift für Politikwissenschaft, 45 (3), 29–44.

ETUI (2020), European works councils data base. www.ewcdb.eu.

Flecker J., Hentges G., Grajczjar I., Altreiter C. and Schindler S. (2019) Extreme und populistische Rechtsparteien und die soziale Frage – Entwicklungen in Frankreich, Österreich, Ungarn und den Niederlanden, WSI-Mitteilungen, 72 (3), 212–219.

Frege C. and Kelly J. (2004) Varieties of unionism: strategies for union: revitalization in a globalizing economy, New York, Oxford University Press.

Glassner V. and Hofmann J. (2019) Austria: from gradual change to an unknown future, in Müller T., Vandaele K. and Waddington J. (eds) Collective bargaining in Europe: towards an endgame, Brussels, ETUI, 33–51.

Glassner V. and Pochet P. (2011) Why trade unions seek to coordinate wages and collective bargaining in the Eurozone: past developments and future prospects, Working Paper 2011.03, Brussels, ETUI.

Greer I. and Hauptmeier M. (2012) Identity work: sustaining transnational collective action at General Motors Europe, Industrial Relations, 51 (2), 275–299.

Griesser M. and Sauer B. (2017) Von der sozialen Neuzusammensetzung zur gewerkschaftlichen Erneuerung? MigrantInnen als Zielgruppe der österreichischen Gewerkschaftsbewegung, Österreichische Zeitschrift für Soziologie, 42 (2), 147–166.

Hammer N. (2010) Cross-border cooperation under asymmetry – the case of an Interregional Trade Union Council, European Journal of Industrial Relations, 16 (4), 351–367.

Hermann, C. and Flecker, J. (2006) Neue Flächentarifverträge in neuen Branchen: Erfahrungen aus Österreich, WSI-Mitteilungen, 59 (7), 396–402.

Hermann C. and Flecker J. (2009) Betriebliche Interessenvertretung in Österreich, in Hermann C. and Atzmüller R. (eds) Die Dynamik des 'österreichischen Modells': Brüche und Kontinuitäten im Beschäftigungs- und Sozialsystem, Berlin, Edition Sigma, 93–110.

Hofmann J. (2017) Gewerkschaften ohne Grenzen? Die Instrumente der European Action Days im Länder- und Zeitvergleich, Wien, ÖGB Verlag.

Hofmann J. and Zuckerstätter S. (2019) Living wages: a reasonable goal or a surrender of minimum wages? An Austrian perspective, Transfer, 25 (3), 373–379.

Karlhofer F. (2001) Österreich: Zwischen Korporatismus und Zivilgesellschaft, in Reutter W. and Rütters P. (eds) Verbände und Verbandssysteme in Westeuropa, Wiesbaden, Verlag für Sozialwissenschaften, 335–354.

Kelly J. (1998) Rethinking industrial relations: mobilisation, collectivism and long waves, London, Routledge.

Knittler K. (2018) Atypische Beschäftigung 2017 – allgemein und im Familienkontext, Statistische Nachrichten, 9, 744–753.

Krings T. (2019) Posted workers in Österreich: Grenzüberschreitende Entsendearbeit im Spannungsfeld von offenen Märkten und (supra-) nationaler Regulierung, Österreichische Zeitschrift für Soziologie, 44 (1), 21–41.

Mesch M. (2004) Vertikale und intraindustrielle Lohn- und Gehaltsstreuung in Österreich 1995–2000, Wirtschaft und Gesellschaft, 30 (1), 99–132.

Michenthaler G. Dawid E., Schuster C. and Kaiser D. (2013) Betriebliche Mitbestimmung in Österreich 2012, Vienna, AK Wien.

OECD (2007) Strikes, in Society at a glance 2006: OECD social indicators, Paris, OECD Publishing.

OECD (2021) OECD/AIAS ICTWSS Database. www.oecd.org/employment/ictwss-database.htm.

ÖGB (2019a) Österreichische Streikstatistik seit 1945, Vienna, ÖGB.

ÖGB (2019b) Jahresabschluss 2019. ÖGB-Gesamt, Vienna: ÖGB.

ÖGB (2020) Mitgliederstatistik gesamt nach Gewerkschaften (2019), Vienna, ÖGB.

ÖGB (2021a) Mitgliederstatistik und Mitgliederbewegung seit 1945, Vienna, ÖGB.

ÖGB (2021b) Mitgliederstatistik gesamt nach Gewerkschaften (2020), Vienna, ÖGB.

Peetz D. (2010) Are individualistic attitudes killing collectivism?, Transfer, 16 (3), 383–398.

Pernicka S. (2005) The evolution of union politics for atypical employees, Economic and Industrial Democracy, 26 (2), 205–228.

Pernicka S. and Glassner V. (2014) Transnational trade union strategies towards European wage policy: a neo-institutional framework, European Journal of Industrial Relations, 20 (4), 317–334.

Pernicka S. and Hefler G. (2015) Austrian corporatism: erosion or resilience, Austrian Journal of Political Science, 44 (3), 39–56.

Pernicka S. and Hofmann J. (2014) Ein soziales Europa? Möglichkeiten und Grenzen transnationaler Solidarität von Gewerkschaften, in Kneuer M. and Masala C. (eds) Solidarität, Sonderheft Zeitschrift für Politikwissenschaften, Baden-Baden, Nomos, 134–163.

Pernicka S. and Stern S. (2011) Von der Sozialpartnergewerkschaft zur Bewegungsorganisation? Mitgliedergewinnungsstrategien österreichischer Gewerkschaften, Österreichische Zeitschrift für Politikwissenschaft, 40 (4), 335–355.

Pernicka S., Glassner V. and Dittmar N. (2017) When does solidarity end? Transnational labour cooperation during and after the crisis – the GM/Opel case revisited, Economic and Industrial Democracy, 38 (3), 375–399.

Pernicka S., Glassner V., Dittmar N. and Neundlinger K. (2020) Interessen und Anerkennung in der Lohnpolitik aus feldtheoretischer Perspektive, Industrielle Beziehungen, 27 (4), 461–480.

Puller A. (2018) Die Österreichische Volkspartei unter Sebastian Kurz, Kurswechsel, 3/2018, 9–18.

Profil (2018) Umfrage: Zwei Drittel der Österreicher sehen die Sozialpartnerschaft positiv. https://www.profil.at/oesterreich/umfrage-sozialpartnerschaft-positiv-10046175.

Schnetzer M., Tamesberger D. and Theurl S. (2020) Mitigating mass layoffs in the COVID-19 crisis: Austrian short-time work as international role model. https://voxeu.org/article/mitigating-mass-layoffs-covid-19-crisis-austrian-short-time-model.

Schulten T., Müller T. and Eldring L. (2015) Prospects and obstacles of a European minimum wage policy, in van Gyes G. and Schulten T. (eds) Wage bargaining under the new European economic governance: alternative strategies for inclusive growth, Brussels, ETUI, 327–359.

Statistik Austria (2020a) Bevölkerung nach Erwerbstatus und Geschlecht seit 1994. http://www.statistik.at/web_de/static/bevoelkerung_nach_erwerbsstatus_und_geschlecht_seit_1994_063253.pdf.

Statistik Austria (2020b) Erwerbstätige und unselbständig Erwerbstätige nach Vollzeit/Teilzeit und Geschlecht seit 1994. https://www.statistik.at/web_de/statistiken/menschen_und_gesellschaft/arbeitsmarkt/arbeitszeit/teilzeitarbeit_teilzeitquote/062882.html.

Stern S. and Hofmann J (2018) Speed kills slowly: Sozialpartnerschaft unter Schwarz-Blau II, Kurswechsel, 3/2018, 38–46.

Strickner A. (2014) Building resistance: Ansätze EU-weiter Protestkoordination, Kurswechsel 1/2014, 11–20.

Stückler A. (2000) Metalworking and textiles unions to merge. https://www.eurofound.europa.eu/sr/publications/article/2000/metalworking-and-textiles-unions-to-merge.

Tálos E. and Hinterseer T. (2019) Sozialpartnerschaft Ein zentraler politischer Gestaltungsfaktor der Zweiten Republik am Ende?, Vienna, Studienverlag.

Tamesberger D. and Moser R. (2021) Job-retention schemes in Europe: Austria, Brussels, European Trade Union Institute. http://dx.doi.org/10.13140/RG.2.2.17906.84164

Titelbach G., Fink M., Hyee R. and Valkova K. (2018) Beschäftigungsentwicklung von Inländer/inne/n und Ausländer/inne/n am österreichischen Arbeitsmarkt, Vienna, Projektbericht des Instituts für Höhere Studien.

Traxler F. (1995) Two logics of collective action in industrial relations?, in Crouch C. and Traxler F. (eds) Organized industrial relations in Europe: what future?, Aldershot, Avebury, 23–45.

Traxler F. (2001) Far-reaching union restructuring under discussion. https://www.eurofound.europa.eu/sr/publications/article/2001/far-reaching-union-restructuring-under-discussion.

Traxler F. and Behrens M. (2002) Collective bargaining and extension procedures. https://www.eurofound.europa.eu/publications/report/2002/collective-bargaining-coverage-and-extension-procedures.

Traxler F. and Pernicka S. (2007) The state of unions: Austria, Journal of Labor Research, 28 (2), 207–232.

Traxler F., Blaschke S. and Kittel B. (2001) National labour relations in internationalized markets, Oxford, Oxford University Press.

Traxler F., Brandl B. and Glassner V. (2008) Can cross-border bargaining coordination work? Analytical reflections and evidence from the metal industry in Germany and Austria, European Journal of Industrial Relations, 14 (2), 217–237.

Urban H.J. (2010) Wohlfahrtsstaat und Gewerkschaftsmacht im Finanzmarkt-Kapitalismus: Der Fall Deutschland, WSI Mitteilungen, 63 (9), 443–450.

Vandaele K. (2016) Interpreting strike activity in western Europe in the past 20 years: the labour repertoire under pressure, Transfer, 22 (3), 277–294.

Visser J. (2019) Trade unions in the balance, ILO ACTRAV Working Paper, Geneva, ILO.

WKO (Wirtschaftskammer Österreich) (2019) Österreichs Industrie Kennzahlen 2019, Vienna, WKO.

Abbreviations

AK	Arbeiterkammer (Chamber of Labour)
FPÖ	Freiheitliche Partei Österreich (Freedom Party Austria)
GBH	Gewerkschaft Bau–Holz (Union of Construction and Woodworkers)
GdG	Gewerkschaft der Gemeindebediensteten, Kunst, Medien, Sport und freie Berufe (Municipal Employees' Union)
GÖD	Gewerkschaft Öffentlicher Dienst (Union of Public Services)
GPA	Gewerkschaft GPA (GPA Union)
GPF	Gewerkschaft der Post- und Fernmeldebediensteten (Union of Postal and Telecommunications Workers)
LK	Landwirtschaftskammer (Chamber of Agriculture)
NEOS	Das Neue Österreich und Liberales Forum (New Austria and Liberal Forum)
ÖAAB	Österreichischer Arbeitnehmerinnen- und Arbeitnehmerbund (Austrian Federation of Employees)

ÖGB	Österreichischer Gewerkschaftsbund (Austrian Trade Union Federation)
ÖVP	Österreichische Volkspartei (Austrian People's Party)
PRO-GE	Die Produktionsgewerkschaft (Union of Production Workers)
SPÖ	Sozialdemokratische Partei Österreich (Social Democratic Party of Austria)
Vida	Gewerkschaft vida (Transport and Service Union)
WKO	Wirtschaftskammer Österreich (Chamber of the Economy Austria)
Younion	Die Daseinsgewerkschaft (Union for municipal employees and the small arts, media, sports and liberal professions)

Chapter 3

Belgium: Trade unions coping with workplace fissuring and opposing wage moderation in a tottering political system

Kurt Vandaele*

Belgian trade unions are still faring well compared with most other countries in the European Union (EU). A benevolent institutional setting at the workplace and industrial level proves relative robustness. First, *union-only* representative structures – union representatives, health and safety bodies and works councils – allow unions to establish and maintain a social norm of union membership, especially in large companies. Second, management has relatively lower incentives to openly resist unions at the workplace as the industry is the predominant level for collective bargaining (Western 1999). Third, unions are involved in paying out unemployment benefits, a variant of the 'Ghent system', stimulating unionization of the unemployed and workers with relatively higher unemployment risks and allowing unions to offer various services outside the workplace. Notably, the 'institutional stickiness' of this union security is buttressed by union activism and unions' considerable mobilization capacity, as large-scale demonstrations and political mass strikes exemplify. Also, ideas of 'social partnership' underpinning a tradition of social dialogue and political advocacy enable unions to influence the political process, although success largely depends on the political parties currently in power. Finally, unions' organizational learning probably needs to be brought into the equation to understand why union density has shown notable long-term stability, hovering around 55 per cent from the mid-1990s to the mid-2010s.

---

* I am grateful to Jean-Marie De Baene, Raf De Weerdt, Chris Serroyen and Guy Van Gyes for their comments and suggestions.

Table 3.1 Principal characteristics of trade unionism in Belgium

	1980	**2000**	**2019**
Total trade union membership	2,645,000	3,096,000	3,295,000
Women as a proportion of total membership	n.a.	38 %	46 %*
Gross union density**	87 %	90 %	80 %
Net union density	53 %	57 %	49 %
Number of confederations		3	
Number of affiliated unions (federations)	30	20	17
Number of independent unions		>1	
Collective bargaining coverage		96 %	
Principal level of collective bargaining		Industry	
Days not worked due to industrial action per 1,000 workers	71**	77	107

Note: *2018.

Source: Appendix A1; **ETUI.

Most indicators in Table 3.1 suggest that the industrial relations system remain fairly unchanged. But the challenges are mounting today. Union membership and density deteriorated during 2014–2019, although this has perhaps set in later than expected by observers who anticipated such a weakening at the dawn of the twenty-first century (Van Gyes et al. 2000). Net union density fell below a symbolic 50 per cent level in 2019. In addition, apart from reforms in unemployment insurance, labour market deregulation and flexibility have been incrementally promoted over time, giving rise to a tendency towards workplace fissuring (Weil 2014). This indirectly undermines union security and complicates union efforts to organize workers. Moreover, political parties, such as the Flemish nationalists, who are adversely disposed towards Belgium's neocorporatist socio-economic decision-making, have been on the rise. Finally, unions' room for wage negotiations is curtailed by a central wage norm, established in 1996 and tightened up in 2017, which has provoked fierce union opposition since then.

Historical background and principal features of the industrial relations system

Union pluralism and regional variation, a strong mobilization capacity, formal links with political parties and embeddedness in labour market and welfare institutions mark Belgian unionism historically (Faniel 2010). Union organizations have developed along three ideological lines. The segmentation of society into 'pillars' implied that they belonged to a broad organizational network, based on the same subculture, supporting workers 'from the cradle to the grave' (Strikwerda 1997). The ideological origins of the socialist General Federation of Belgian Labour (ABVV/FGTB, *Algemeen Belgisch Vakverbond*) are rooted in anti-capitalism and representing the interests of the working class *as a whole*.[1] Christian unions *for workers only* developed when the Catholic Church recognized the importance of the *question sociale* with the publication of the papal encyclical *Rerum Novarum* in 1891 and a fierce competition with the socialist unions started. The roots of the Confederation of Christian Trade Unions (ACV/CSC, *Algemeen Christelijk Vakverbond*) lay in rejecting socialist 'class conflict' and in emphasizing integration within and with society. The ideological orientation of the General Confederation of Liberal Trade Unions of Belgium (ACLVB/CGSLB, *Algemene Centrale der Liberale Vakbonden van België*) rests on countervailing power within the labour market, highlighting direct benefits and gains for its members. The three union confederations could *ideally* be attributed to one edge of Hyman's (2001) triangle on union identities, but in reality each confederation has been oscillating between two edges in Figure 3.1 over time, while variations in identities are also geographically relative, not absolute.

---

1 Full French names of institutions or organisations that can be abbreviated are not provided in the main text for reasons of space; they can be found in the abbreviations list.

Figure 3.1 Regional differences in union identities

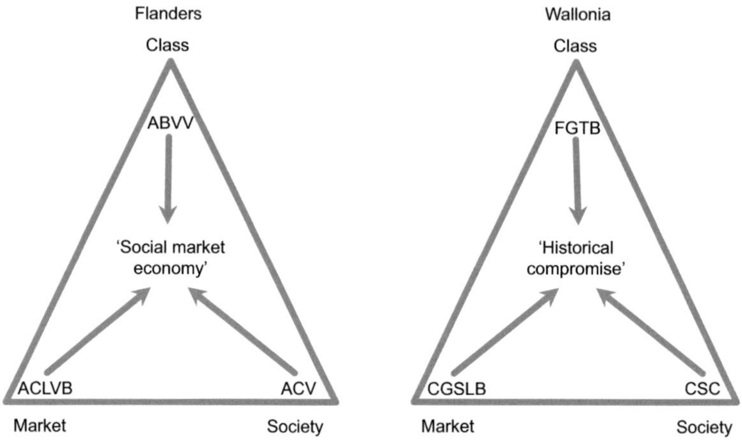

Source: Vandaele and Hooghe (2013).

Besides the different socio-demographic and political context, also uneven geographical industrialization typified Belgian unionism and membership dynamics from the outset (Mort Subite 1990). The shifting centre of economic gravity from French-speaking Wallonia to Dutch-speaking Flanders since the 1930s reinforced the ACV/CSC in the latter region and Belgium generally; ACV/CSC affiliates also commenced early on to organize workers beyond those employed in large factories. Deindustrialization eroded the ABVV/FGTB's historical stronghold within manufacturing in Wallonia so that union pluralism would be stronger here. Relationships between the confederations nevertheless became less stressful over time (Pasture 1996): the practice of a 'common union front' at the national level vis-à-vis the employers' associations and the state developed from 1936 onwards. Being facilitated by the 'Social Pact', an informal agreement concluded after clandestine negotiations between union and business leaders in 1944, union security gradually strengthened after the Second World War (Cassiers and Denayer 2010). Governance of the social security system by the 'social partners' was established, with the 'Ghent system' metamorphosing into a 'quasi-Ghent system' as unions retained a role in the now compulsory unemployment system by paying out unemployment benefits alongside a state agency (Vandaele 2006). Also, establishing health and safety committees and works councils was legally made possible, while joint committees for collective bargaining were institutionalized at the industrial level and extended to more industries. Union pluralism was secured in 1952: representativeness criteria stipulated that confederations and their affiliates are entitled to bargain if they cover the whole country, and have a mandate in the two social dialogue institutions at the national level, the Central Economic Council (CRB/CEC, *Centrale Raad voor het Bedrijfsleven*) for economic matters and the National Labour Council (NAR/CNT, *Nationale Arbeidsraad*) for social affairs (Blaise 2010). The state thus promoted a consensual approach via a dense neocorporatist architecture, subordinating strike action to bargaining (Vercauteren 2007). A similar approach would later be followed in the three economic-based Regions and three language-based Communities in a federalized Belgium (Installé et al. 2010). An 'institutionalization of conflict' rather than an 'institutionalization of cooperation' has marked Belgian 'social partnership', however (Therborn 1992). Union mobilization continued in a still 'pillarized' society after the Second World War, and industrial action did not wither away.

In hindsight, the ABVV/FGTB, leading in Wallonia, has interpreted the 'Social Pact' as only a *temporal* 'historical compromise' between the two sides of industry in anticipation of structural reforms within capitalism (Hemmerijckx 1995). Its understanding of being instrumental for the development of a 'social market economy' has traditionally been dominant in Flanders due to the ACV/CSC's predominance. In practice, biennial bipartite negotiations between the 'social partners' at the cross-industrial level, outside the formal social dialogue institutions, resulted in seven interprofessional agreements (IPA/AIP, *interprofessioneel akkoord*) between 1960 and 1976, boosting a Keynesian growth regime based partly on increasing domestic demand. IPA/AIPs are not binding; they offer a framework for Belgium's multi-level bargaining system. IPA/AIPs can also lay down minimum standards for all employees in the private sector, to be translated into collective agreements at the cross-industrial level. For example, a cross-industry agreement, given legal force via a Royal Decree, introduced a guaranteed average monthly minimum wage in 1975. The industrial level is considered dominant, however, because its collective agreements are broad in scope, including non-wage issues, and provide legal content following cross-industry agreements (Vandekerckhove and Van Gyes 2012).

State 'intervention' in wage-setting became increasingly important when an IPA/AIP could not be agreed in 1976. The practice of concluding IPA/AIPs revived in 1986, however, and a more established biennial collective bargaining cycle started. 'Economic vulnerability' is a common assumption among the economic and political elites, given Belgium's small open economy (Jones 2008). Hence, introducing a wage norm in the private sector, the 'competitiveness law' of 1989, was strengthened in 1996 to ensure entry to the European Monetary Union (Vilrokx and Van Leemput 1998); Belgium entered the eurozone in 1999. The new law consolidated the return to an export-oriented growth regime based on supply-side wage moderation since the early 1980s (Van den Broeck 2010). It anchored state 'intervention' in wage-setting and institutionally modelled collective bargaining on 'competitive corporatism' by curtailing multi-employer bargaining through calibrating wage developments in France, Germany and the Netherlands. Simultaneously, Belgium is one of the few EU countries in which the principle of wage indexation has largely remained intact in settled collective agreements. Wages and social benefits still 'automatically' adjust to changing prices of goods and services via a 'health index', introduced in 1994, which excludes heavily tax-influenced commodities such as alcohol, motor fuel and tobacco. Wage indexation linked to the 'health index', operationalized via diverse arrangements at the industrial level, thus sets a floor for wage-setting, whereas the wage norm provides a centralized ceiling.

Structure of trade unions and union democracy

Two idiosyncrasies of Belgian unionism are noteworthy from a comparative EU perspective. First, based on *publicly available self-reported membership figures*, the ACV/CSC is the *only* confessional confederation that surpassed a socialist one in member size from 1958 to 2018. The ACV/CSC and the ABVV/FGTB – with 1,534,199 and 1,547,325 members in 2020, respectively – dominate the union landscape. Second, the much smaller ACLVB/CGSLB, with 307,805 members in 2020, is the *only* liberal confederation in the EU (Faniel and Vandaele 2011), whereby solely public sector workers and teachers in non-state organized schools have specific unions; workers in other industries are direct members of the confederation. The quasi-monopoly position of these three confederations implies that not many independent unions are active. Although their exact number and membership are unknown, most are small occupational unions presenting themselves as 'neutral'. They are active mainly in the public sector except for the National Confederation of Staff (NCK/CNC, *Nationale Confederatie van het Kaderpersoneel*) organizing managerial staff in the private sector.

Union members are simultaneously part of their union within the ABVV/FGTB and the ACV/CSC, with internal divisions organizing members into subindustries, and regional structures, which are local branches geographically defined by the place where members live. Manual workers are organized by unions per industry, whereas non-manual workers have their own unions that group them occupationally across industrial boundaries. The legal distinction that formerly existed between employment statutes explains this organizing principle. Unions anticipated the labour law change of 2013 for a unified employment status and partial harmonization of existing statutes via swapping members in certain industries over the years. Member transfers continue today: this process materializes gradually, given its influence upon relationships between unions and vis-à-vis employers' associations at the industrial level.

Most unions are still national: they organize workers throughout the country. There are some noteworthy exceptions. The white-collar unions in the ACV/CSC have been divided virtually from the outset, but separated formally in 1984, while educational unions split in the early 1990s at the subnational level so they would be able to lobby political authorities more effectively. Notably, internal discord over policies instigated a formal regional divide in the ABVV/FGTB metal union into a Brussels, Flemish and Walloon 'entity' in 2006. A federal umbrella structure, with competence only for federal matters, is kept for liaising with the confederation, while the Brussels 'entity' is *de facto* a subunit of the Walloon 'entity'. The Flemish and Walloon/Brussels 'entities' are considered to be separate unions here. ABVV/FGTB and ACV/CSC affiliates organizing solely within one Region increased their overall member share from 18.5 to 23.9 per cent from 2000 to 2019.

Figure 3.2 ABVV/FGTB and ACV/CSC affiliates and mergers, 2000–2020

	Trade unions	2000	2001	2002	2003	2004	2005	2006	2007	2008	2009	2010	2011	2012	2013	2014	2015	2016	2017	2018	2019	2020
ABVV/FGTB	AC/CG	321.188	→	→	→	→	→	→	→	→	→	→	→	→	→	→	→	→	→	→	→	419,382
	TKD/TVD	48.886	→	→	→	→	→	→	→	→	→	→	→	29.706 ↗								
	BBTK/Setca	290,670	→	→	→	→	→	→	→	→	→	→	→	→	→	→	→	→	→	→	→	437,616
	ACOD/CGSP	251,994	→	→	→	→	→	→	→	→	→	→	→	→	→	→	→	→	→	→	→	307,210
	Metaal/Métal	176,143	→	→	→	→	→	ABVV-Metaal		→	→	→	→	→	→	→	→	→	→	→	→	148,410
								FGTB Métal		→	→	→	→	→	→	→	→	→	→	→	→	
	Horval	82,380	→	→	→	→	→	→	→	→	→	→	→	→	→	→	→	→	→	→	→	136,178
	BTB/UBT	29,423	→	→	→	→	→	→	→	→	→	→	→	→	→	→	→	→	→	→	→	59,075
	Jongeren/Jeunes	7,558	→	→	→	→	→	→	→	→	→	→	→	→	→	→	→	→	→	→	→	39,454
ACV/CSC	ACV Puls	254,608	→	→	→	→	→	→	→	→	→	→	→	→	→	→	→	→	→	→	280,077	
	ACV-Bouw - Industrie & Energie/CSC-Bâtiment - Industrie & Energie	225,698	→	→	→	→	→	→	→	→	232,699	ACVBIE/CSCBIE			→	→	→	→	→	→	257,976	
	ACV Energie Chemie/CSC Energie Chemie	56,591	→	→	→	→	→	→	→	→	52,055											
	ACV Metaal/CSC Métal	197,335	→	→	→	→	→	→	→	→	174,026	ACV-CSC METEA			→	→	→	→	→	→	159,750	
	ACV Textura/CSC Textura	73,138	→	→	→	→	→	→	→	→	47,350											
	ACV Voeding en Diensten/CSC Alimentation et Services	208,384	→	→	→	→	→	→	→	→	→	→	→	→	→	→	→	→	→	→	247,266	
	ACV Openbare Diensten/CSC Services publics	130,043	→	→	→	→	→	→	→	→	→	→	→	→	→	→	→	→	→	→	162,989	
	CSC CNE	120,930	→	→	→	→	→	→	→	→	→	→	→	→	→	→	→	→	→	→	153,061	
	ACV Transcom	78,004	→	→	→	→	→	→	→	→	→	→	→	→	→	→	→	→	→	→	78,854	
	ACV COV	41,463	→	→	→	→	→	→	→	→	→	→	→	→	→	→	→	→	→	→	35,942	
	ACV COC	38,293	→	→	→	→	→	→	→	→	→	→	→	→	→	→	→	→	→	→	41,227	
	CSC FIC	17,872	→	→	→	→	20,349	CSC-Enseignement			→	→	→	→	→	→	→	→	→	→	42,933	
	CSC CEMNL	9,648	→	→	→	→	9,686															
	CSC CCPET	8,064	→	→	→	→	8,702															
	CSC UCEO	2,601	→	→	→	→	2,651															
	ACV Enter/CSC Enter	25,278	→	→	→	→	→	→	→	→	→	→	→	→	→	→	→	→	→	→	36.019	

Note: The listed union names are those stated in 2021; full names can be found in the abbreviations list.
Source: ABVV/FGTB, ACV/CSC.

Seven unions are affiliated to the ABVV/FGTB today. This confederation has historically weak authority over its affiliates, with each union maintaining a strike fund; a relatively higher turnover also marks the confederal leadership in the period considered here. The membership share of the three largest unions increased from 72 to 77 per cent from 2000 to 2020. Only the multi-sector General Workers Union (AC/CG, *Algemene Centrale*) has been involved in a merger by 'acquiring' a small occupational union facing perpetual membership decline (see Figure 3.2). Their membership share, together with that of private service sector unions, has increased, whereas the metal unions, as the only industrial unions left within the ABVV/FGTB, are losing ground. They have established close cooperation with the transport union, which was formalized in 2018 and reinforced two years later as regards 'organizational matters and politico-syndical standpoints'.

Turning to the ACV/CSC, with 10 affiliated unions today, the locus of its power is equally not at the confederal level but rests with the affiliates, although arguably less so than in the socialist confederation; the ACV/CSC operates a centralized strike fund.[2] Membership concentration grew, with the share of the three largest unions rising from 47 to 54 per cent from 2000 to 2019. Mergers have made the ACV/CSC less fragmented. Unions organizing within education in the French Community 'amalgamated' in 2006. Union mergers in various industries, resulting in two new multi-industry union, can be considered 'acquisitions'. Figure 3.3 shows that there are no genuine industrial unions left in the Christian confederation. A new merger is under way between the metal and textiles union and the union organizing in construction, energy and chemicals, which will boost membership concentration by more than 10 percentage points. The Flemish white-collar union will then become the second-largest ACV/CSC affiliate instead of the largest, giving way to the new multi-industry union will have the lead.

2 ACV Puls formally joined the fund in 2002.

Figure 3.3 Membership distribution by union type and Region (averages), 2000–2009 and 2010–2019

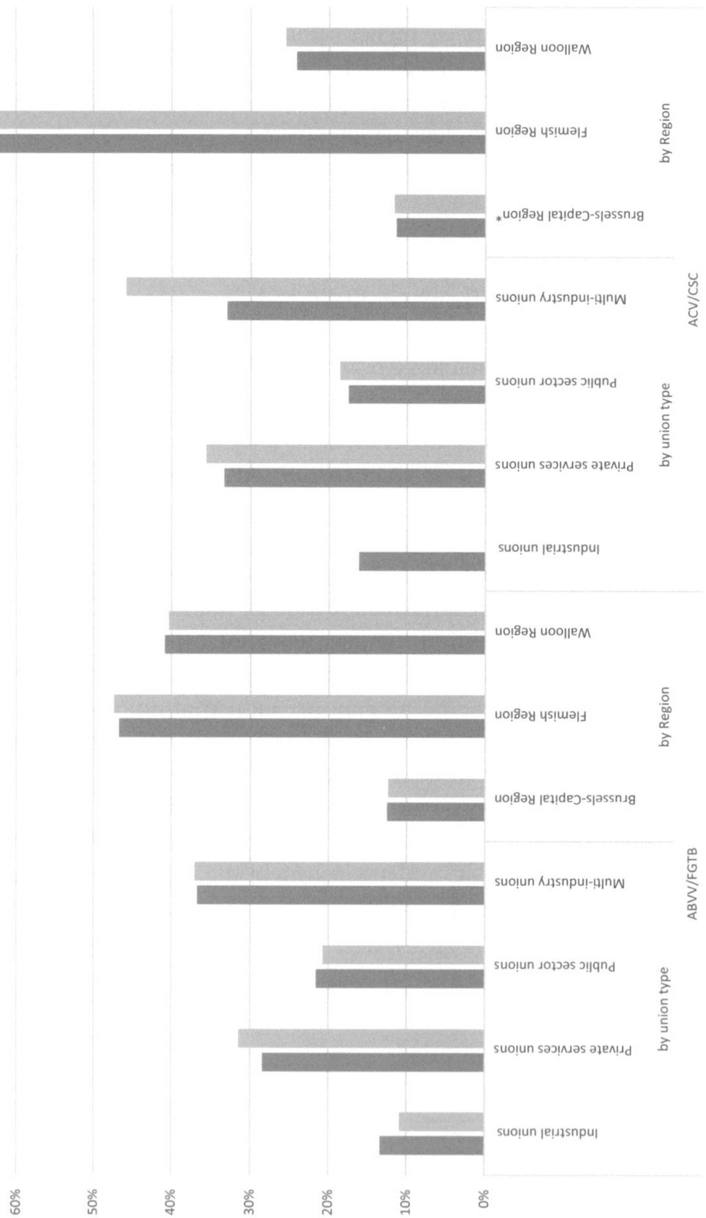

Note: * The Brussels- Capital Region includes part of the Flanders Region (Halle- Vilvoorde).
Source: ABVV/FGTB, ACV/CSC.

Local branches constitute the 'interprofessional structure': they are geographically grouped across affiliated unions. A process of upscaling has marked this structure, especially in the ACV/CSC.[3] Branches have an important administrative and coordinating role within their geographical areas of operation. They provide advice and services to union members via an extended network of service centres, and offer educational work and support for union activists and unions. Branches also identify and campaign around collective issues within and *beyond* the workplace, and seek alliance-building with civil society actors. Local branches are part of the confederations' regional and linguistic sub-structures, which have gained considerably in importance following the devolution of the Belgian state (Vandaele and Hooghe 2013). The regional membership distribution is fairly stable in both the ABVV/FGTB and the ACV/CSC (see Figure 3.3). The francophone member share is substantial in the ABVV/FGTB, although still in a minority in all affiliates except for the public sector union, whereas 'Flanders' is predominant in the ACV/CSC and the ACLVB/CGSLB. At the confederal level, one-third of the mandates are assigned to the Brussels, Flemish and Walloon sub-structures, whereas unions account for two-thirds.

Unions, regional sub-structures and confederations in principle hold congresses every four years. Union decision-making is characterized by bottom-up processes of interest aggregation and agenda-setting, providing room for union activists – labelled 'militants' – and procedures of indirect democracy, whereby every decision-making level chooses its representatives at higher levels, based on membership size. Within the ACV/CSC, for instance, its affiliates and local branches and the regional and confederal decision-making levels should be composed at least 50 per cent of activists, with proportional representation of women and representation of young people, the unemployed and workers with a migrant background (ACV 2019b). Feedback-loops and ratification procedures are also built into union decision-making processes for concluding collective agreements and IPA/AIPs. Unions sometimes also use surveys to better gauge the interests and needs of the rank-and-file regarding the bargaining agenda, or to evaluate their services.

---

3 The number of branches shrank from twenty-one to thirteen from 2000 to 2020, while declining from eighteen to sixteen in the ABVV/FGTB.

Specific structures are in place for women, young people, the unemployed, migrants, workers on early retirement and pensioners (the latter only within the Brussels and Walloon ACV/CSC sub-structures). All three confederations signed a charter on gender mainstreaming in 2004 to promote gender equality of men and women at the workplace and in their decision-making structures. Still, although the share of women in unions has increased (Appendix A1), and the first female leader at the confederal level was elected in the ABVV/FGTB in 2002, women are still underrepresented and their participation in decision-making structures is low (Ravesloot 2012). Students and young people have their own separate structures, set up after the Second World War, within the ABVV/FGTB and the ACV/CSC, whereas the ACLVB/CGSLB caught up in 2010 (Pulignano and Doerflinger 2014). Confederation actions and lobbying on issues regarding young people indicate that their interests and needs are looked after, although the situation of dedicated youth structures within individual unions is more patchy, with some being more energetic than others (Berntsen 2019). The unemployed have had their own 'jobless workers' commissions' since the early 1980s, but their working is 'somewhat erratic', influenced by regional unemployment dynamics (Faniel 2012a). Finally, regarding migrant workers, confederations and their affiliates over time have promoted polices on equal treatment and opportunities, citizenship, antiracism and social clauses against discrimination (Martens and Pulignano 2008).

Union resources and expenditure

Little is publicly known about the financial performance of union organizations. Besides returns on financial investments, a distinction can be made between three other income sources, although their relative size and changes over time are unspecified. First, members' subscriptions themselves are the unions' main source of income. Local branches in the ABVV/FGTB decide upon lump-sum rates, whereas this is done by union affiliates in the ACV/CSC. Subscription rates are set rather low, and the competitive union landscape disincentivizes wide variations between unions. The ACV/CSC endeavours to achieve further harmonization among its affiliates today. Also, this confederation has been setting subscriptions for young workers (between 18 and 25 years of age) since 2019 and has lowered them (ACV/CSC 2019b). It is unsure, however, whether this approach recruits workers beyond those already convinced of the benefits of membership (Delespaul and Doerflinger 2019). Rates are also reduced for other member categories, such as the part-time employed, the unemployed, workers on long-term sick leave or early retirement and pensioners. Membership is free for students in all confederations except for most ABVV/FGTB Walloon local branches.

Member dues are typically paid by direct debit to the union or its local branch – the latter is common in the ACV/CSC.[4] Financial flows between union structures depend on the membership categories and union organization in question. In the ACV/CSC (2019b), for example, based on a full-time working member 20 years of age, the financial flow is as follows: the union and local branch receive each 36 per cent, while 11 per cent goes to the confederal level and 7 per cent is allocated to the central strike fund; the remaining 10 per cent is budgeted for member magazines and affiliation fees to other (union) organizations and international solidarity. In order to run the union apparatus and offer services, the ACV/CSC (2020) and the ACLVB/CGSLB[5] employed 3,283 and 594 staff in 2019 and 2020, respectively. Unions offer a wide range of professionalized services, often oriented towards employability, such as career guiding and training. Unions have held webinars during the Covid-19 pandemic, as their service centres were (partly) closed. Services also include providing information about employment contracts, legal assistance in case of labour disputes, and help in completing tax forms. Furthermore, unions pay out strike benefits, and other benefits could include small bonuses such as on the occasion of marriage or moving in together, childbirth or adoption, and retirement, as well as reductions for members in union-run holiday residences or for other leisure activities, and shopping discounts.

Second, bipartite welfare funds are instrumental for providing indirect support to union membership and activities. Employers finance the funds, which are jointly administered by employers' associations and unions at the industry level. They are established and regulated by collective agreements so that the degree of union support varies between industries. The funds annually pay out a 'union premium' in several, but not all industries, which is an additional benefit for *union*

---

4 Dues can also be deducted directly from wages.

5 See https://www.aclvb.be/nl/structuur-en-kerncijfers-van-de-aclvb#kerncijfers

members only.[6] Although payment is subject to compliance with 'social peace' clauses in collective agreements, this is barely applied in practice. The premium can substantially decrease union dues in particular industries, so that union membership comes at a low cost. Obtaining membership is hence instrumentally strengthened and free-riding is lessened in a system in which industrial collective agreements are almost always extended. Welfare funds usually supplement unemployment and early retirement benefits, too (Van Rie et al. 2011). These top-up benefits are in theory available to non-union members, but unions sometimes charge for administrative costs on that account. Thus, in practice, union membership is incentivized, also because it is more convenient to receive unemployment or early retirement benefit and top-ups via the same agency. Finally, funds also typically finance skill-based education for workers and training for members of the health and safety bodies and works councils; collective agreements regulate the conditions and modalities for granting facility time.

Third, the state (indirectly) supports the unions financially, either as an employer or otherwise. Thus, similar arrangements are in place regarding the 'union premium' for civil servants and facility time for union representatives in state administration and state-related organizations. Furthermore, union dues are tax deductible in case of unemployment, as they can be deducted from unemployment benefit, or if the taxpayer opts to include the cost in their tax declaration. Unions can also be granted certain subsidies for educational activities, international development cooperation, specific projects or youth work. Most importantly, the 'quasi-Ghent system' implies that the state reimburses agents for their involvement in the administration of unemployment-related benefits, based on a complex formula (Vandaele 2006). These agents are run either by the union confederations or the state via the branch office for unemployment benefits (HVW/CAPAC, *Hulpkas Voor Werkloosheidsuitkeringen*), which is governed by the 'social partners' as part of the social security system. The HVW/CAPAC guarantees that receiving unemployment-related benefits is not contingent on union membership. Although this state agency supports the non-unionized for free, its share in benefit administration is rather low and even declined slowly until 2019 (see Figure 3.4).

6 The premium is not subject to taxation up to a certain maximum, which has been set at 145 euros since 2018.

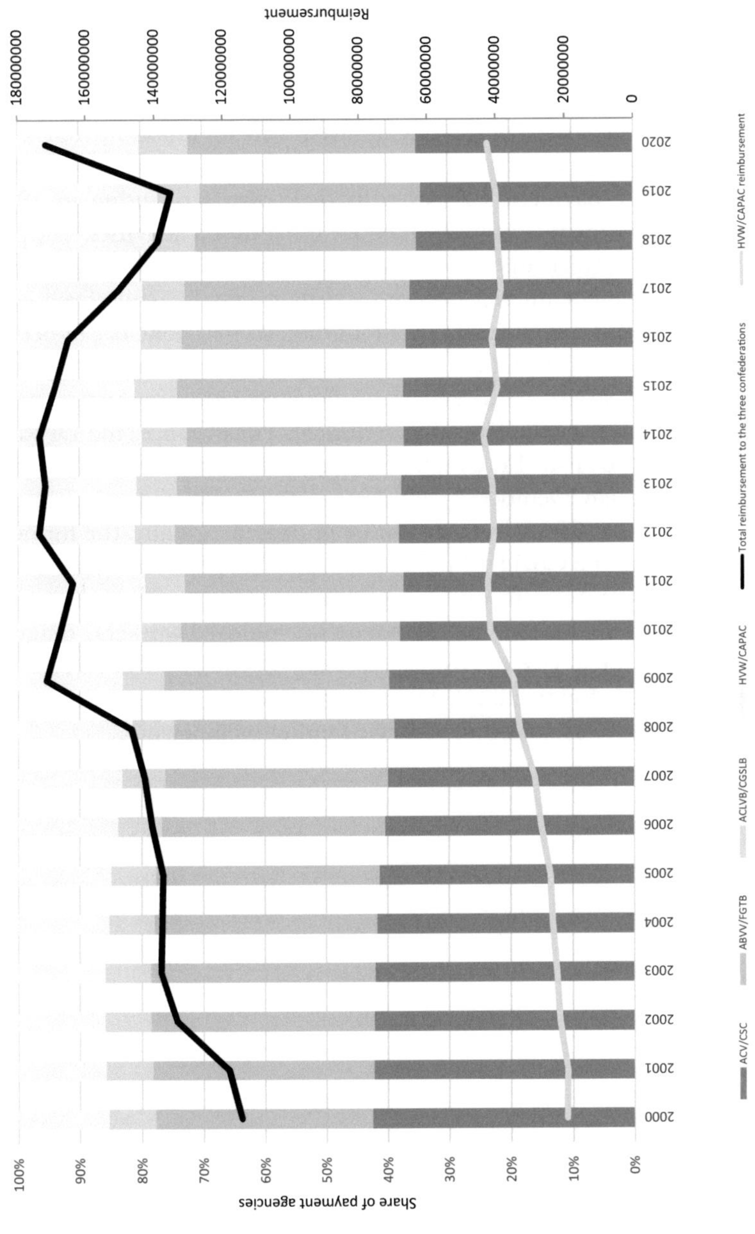

Figure 3.4 Share of agents in the provision of unemployment insurance and reimbursement, 2000–2020

Source: RVA/ONEM.

Unions are considered to be more efficient than the HVW/CAPAC, irrespective of scale effects (*De Tijd* 3 May 2016). Union dominance is explained by the historical identification of unions with benefit payment, their dense network of payment services and ability to pay benefits slightly earlier than the HVW/CAPAC, and (perceptions of) better service. The percentage of the unemployed who are union members has scarcely changed, standing at 87 per cent in 2020. Confederations established separate payment services with their own accounting in 1996; legally, disbursements cannot be used for other union activities. The procyclical link between unemployment and membership entails that falling unemployment implies decreasing disbursements, while fixed costs for staff and ICT investments are mounting, so that deficits can occur.[7] Every so often, the formula for calculating disbursements is subject to change, which is largely dependent on the economic circumstances and balance of power in the federal government. For instance, the Di Rupo government (2011–2014, comprising social democrats, economic liberals and Christian Democrats) introduced an annual reduction in disbursements from 2013, but this can be mitigated.[8] Finally, the furlough scheme during the Covid-19 pandemic highlights how the 'quasi-Ghent system' is also subject to unemployment law reforms. The scheme has entailed a massive increase in 'temporary unemployed workers', resulting in difficulties in service provision, especially in the HVW/CAPAC (De Federale Ombudsman 2021). Even so, 31 per cent turned to the state agency (RVA 2021), and thus eschewed union membership.

---

7 The overall correlation between disbursements and gross union membership stands at 0.91 in the period 2000–2019 but is 0.69 for net membership.

8 Also, decreasing disbursements because of falling unemployment have been made to slow down in 2022 (*De Tijd* 22 October 2021).

Unionization

Membership data can be retrieved only from union administrative records or occasional surveys. Unions have historically inflated member figures for reasons of mutual competition or the sometimes delayed and irregular payment of union dues (Ebbinghaus et al. 2000). This practice should not be overestimated, however: the coefficient for inflating membership has gradually decreased, while concealing membership trends is impractical. The ABVV/ FGTB claims no longer to apply a coefficient, and the ACLVB/CGSLB declares that it has gradually reduced this practice since the 1990s (Faniel and Vandaele 2012). The ACV/CSC has publicly stated that it no longer uses it, and revised its figures from 2000 onwards, resulting in a lower figure for membership.[9] Overall membership achieved its highest number ever recorded in 2014, at 3,400,359 (see Figure 3.5).[10] The continuous membership growth registered since the Second World War (except for some years in the 1980s) has halted, however.[11] The ACV/CSC[12] has experienced a membership decline since 2011, the ABVV/FGTB from 2014 onwards. Both lost 176,543 members overall (excluding students) during 2013–2019. The ACLVB/CGSLB, by contrast, has enjoyed ongoing membership gains, although its growth rate nearly halved in the 2010s compared with the previous decade.

---

9 A comparison between old inflated and new data reveals a coefficient of between 11 and 12 per cent.

10 This figure excludes students, except in the case of the ACLVB/CGSLB as its share of students is unknown. If students are included, there were 3,488,624 members in 2014.

11 ABVV/FGTB membership also declined in 1961–1962.

12 As one of the first policy responses to decline, the 'administrative cleaning' of membership records has produced some additional reductions.

Figure 3.5 Union membership and density since 2000 and changes in membership (%), 2001–2010 and 2011–2020

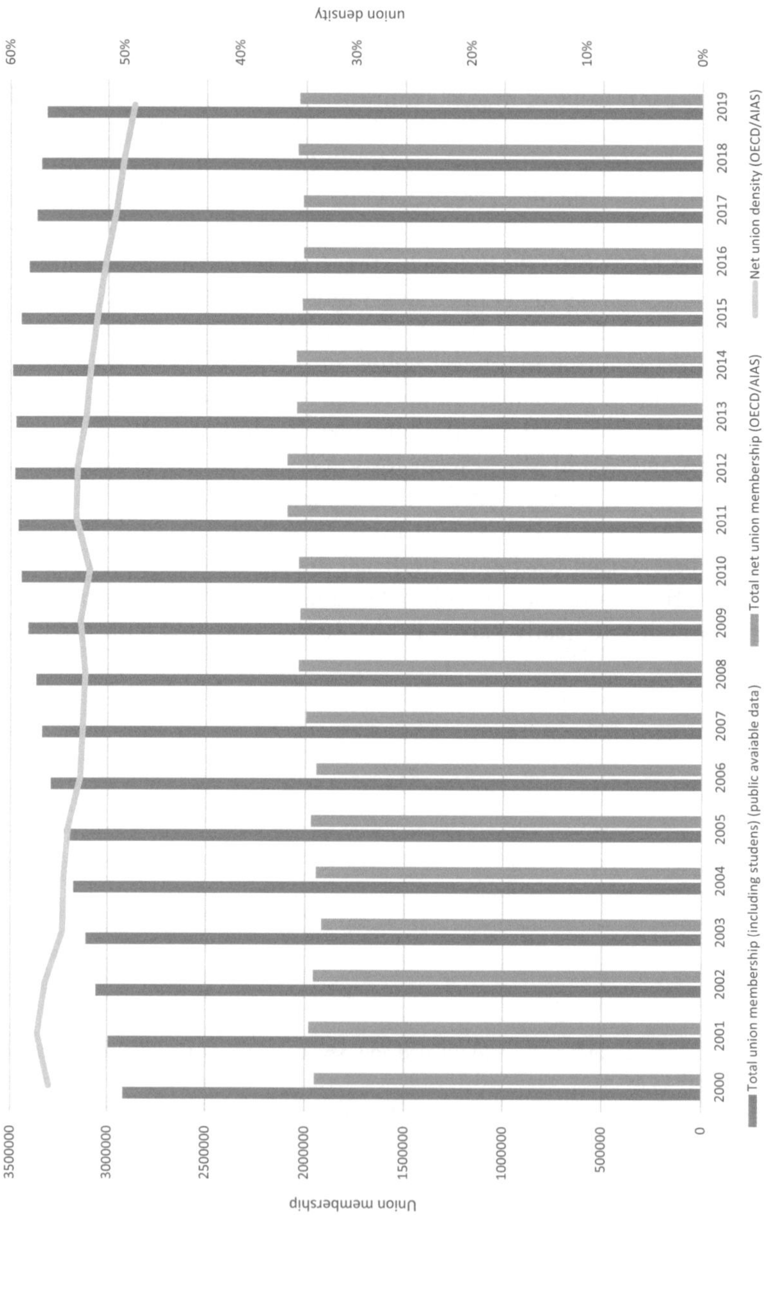

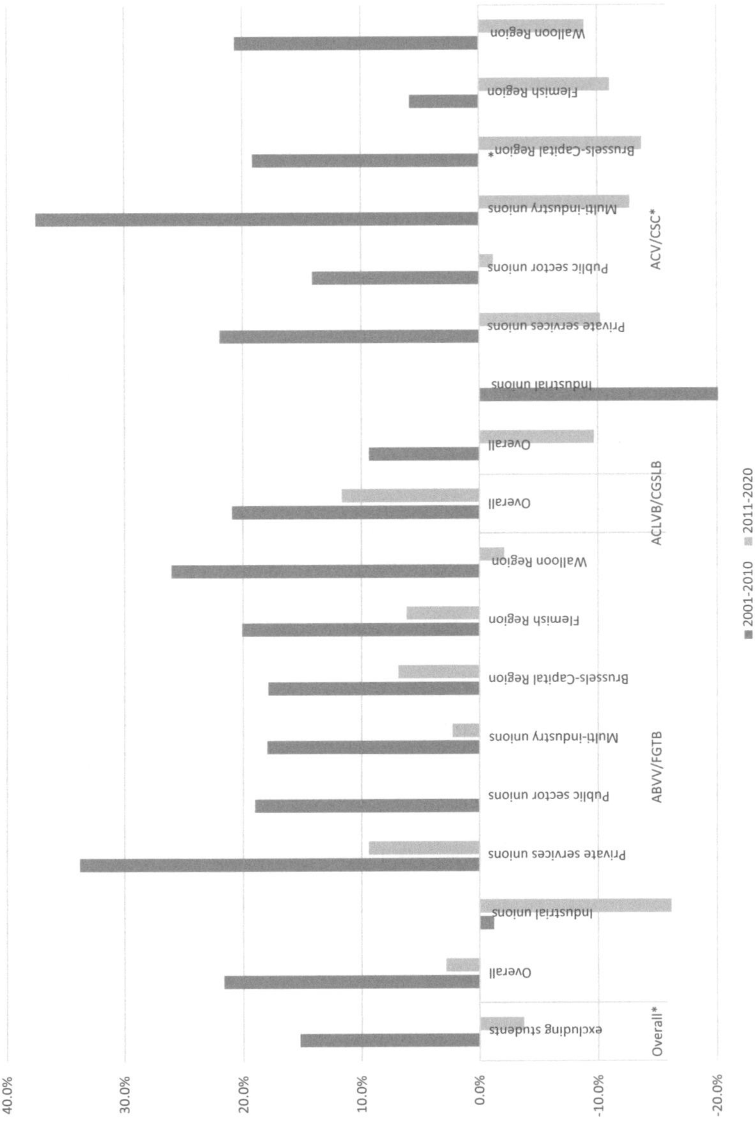

Note: * 2011–2019.
Source: Appendix A1; ABVV/FGTB, ACLVB/CGSLB, ACV/CSC.

Membership increases have slowed down considerably at the ABVV/ FGTB, and this confederation is no longer making progress in Wallonia. Falling membership or meagre rises marked ACV/CSC affiliates in the 2010s, while membership decreased in all regions. Industrial and multi-industry unions in particular have seen a plunge in membership in both confederations. Overall membership growth resumed again in 2020, making up over one-third of losses, especially among white- collar unions and unions organizing in hospitality and transport. This is because of the furlough scheme's impact on the 'quasi- Ghent system'. As decline is more marked in the Christian confederation, the membership ratio with the ABVV/FGTB has diminished, in particular in Flanders. Some ambiguity remains concerning the latter's use of a coefficient, however (OECD and Visser 2021). Thus the ACV/CSC can still be considered the largest confederation.

While net unionization has been fluctuating at around 55 per cent since the early 1990s, union density stood at 49.1 per cent in 2019. Taking into account non-active members, such as the unemployed and pensioners, gross density is considerably higher. Belgian unions are encompassing organizations, and about one-third of their members are (temporally) not in employment (Faniel and Vandaele 2012). Differences in unionization rates based on gender, age or company size are compressed compared with other EU countries (Van Gyes et al. 2000), but rates are more diverse between education levels (Vendramin 2007) or occupational status as a result of different levels of job insecurity (De Witte 2005). The 'quasi-Ghent system' thus incentivizes certain worker categories to unionize and to remain in membership, especially those with higher unemployment risks or with lower educational attainment (Van Rie et al. 2011), whereas 'middle- and upper-class employees' are underrepresented (Strøby Jensen 2020).

Parental socialization has become a less important motive for unionization among younger age categories over time (Swyngedouw et al. 2016), although it still plays a certain role (Delespaul and Doerflinger 2019). Also, membership decline might be generated virtually 'automatically' by large and highly unionized cohorts reaching early retirement or pension age and leaving the labour market. Based on annual administrative reports, the ACV/CSC data indeed show an ageing membership, although the share of members younger than 25 years of age has been improving since 2017. Moreover, ongoing deindustrialization, also affecting Flanders, where the ACV/CSC is relatively stronger, presumably contributes to membership weakening, especially among multi-industry unions.[13] Membership gains in private services no longer seemed able to compensate for this in 2010–2019; the same holds true for the public sector, in which austerity measures stalled employment growth. Also, the ACV/CSC's share in the benefit administration of the 'quasi-Ghent system' has been steadily deteriorating over time, which has resulted in closures of service centres (ACV 2019a). Certain categories of (unemployed) workers might thus be less likely to join this confederation. Although the duration of unemployment benefit payment remains, in principle, unlimited, tighter restrictions on entitlement to unemployment and early retirement benefits (Lefebvre 2019), especially in the aftermath of the 2007–2008 financial and economic crisis, might further explain overall union decline. Being numerous in Brussels-Capital and the Walloon Region, the long-term unemployed can be excluded from receiving benefits more rapidly today, making it necessary for them to turn to social services.[14] Arrangements regarding the activation allowance for graduates, paid out by either the unions or the HVW/CAPAC, have also changed since 2012. The 'waiting period' has been lengthened for new graduates entitled to the allowance, while the entitlement period is no longer unlimited: early unionization of young people via the 'quasi-Ghent system' is thus discouraged.

Tactics associated with an organizing approach are not unfamiliar to Belgian unions. They have an institutionally driven interest in identifying future (young) union activists for inviting them to be candidates on the social election lists. The period prior to the quadrennial social elections for health and safety committees and works councils provides unions with an opportunity to reach out to workers and prioritize their issues. Union education focuses mainly on union representatives and elected candidates, however. There are generally no dedicated programmes for non-elected ones or ordinary members, or for finding potential activists in the years between elections. Also, a considerable percentage of workers have no direct union exposure in their workplace as elections are held only in companies in the private sector above a certain employment threshold. Union representatives in some industries might nevertheless

---

[13] The same reasoning applies to ABVV/FGTB, especially regarding membership dynamics in Wallonia.

[14] Anecdotical evidence suggests that social services advise people to cancel union membership to cut costs.

be active in smaller companies, and union density is relatively high here compared with non-Ghent countries. This cannot be attributed solely to the Belgian 'quasi-Ghent system' ; specific union strategies also play a role. These include holding local meetings in an effort to reach members in smaller companies; 'network unionism', which involves joint meetings between unionists in subcontractors and principal companies; and coaching and mentoring of activists in smaller companies by activists in larger ones (Van Gyes 2010).

Union activities and campaigns sometimes target specific worker categories, with a particular focus recently on platform workers (Vandaele 2020b). The ACV/CSC established a new unit 'United Freelancers' in 2019 to organize freelancers, including platform workers. Various projects focussing on the membership dimension had already been initiated in all confederations before membership decline set in (Faniel 2012b). In particular, a renewed focus on students started in the early 2000s, offering free membership, advice and legal assistance, and targeted policies to raise awareness about unionism, for example, at schools and music festivals (Berntsen 2019; Vendramin 2007). Free membership for students has resulted in rapid membership growth in the ACV/CSC and, later on, the ABVV/FGTB, but their shares have declined since 2009 and 2017, respectively. Finally, individual union activists or full-time officials might be inspired by US-style organizing, but a systematic approach, going beyond social elections, with drives in targeted weakly unionized industries, has been nearly absent so far. Using organizing tactics avant-la-lettre since the end of 1980s, the branch within the ACV/CSC affiliate organizing in the not-for-profit sector in Flanders might be an exception (Vanhooren and Deceunynck 2005). Other ACV/CSC affiliates, in particular the white-collar union in Flanders, are showing a growing interest in experimenting with US-style (digital) organizing (ACV 2019a). Research is also under way.

Collective bargaining and unions at the workplace

Centralization, which provides strong coordination between interlinked hierarchical bargaining levels, is one of the main feature of Belgium's collective bargaining system in the private sector.[15] Union

[15] Employment terms and conditions in the public sector are set by law; its bargaining cycle is different from that of the private sector, and bargaining can include consultation or negotiation.

density is high, as is the organization rate of the employers' associations, the latter standing at 82 per cent in 2018 (Vandaele 2019a). Collective agreements at the industrial and cross-industrial levels are nearly always extended, which results in a stable bargaining coverage of 96 per cent. The law on the 'promotion of employment and the preventive safeguarding of competitiveness' of 1996 (henceforth: the 'competitiveness law') curtails lower bargaining levels via a 'wage norm'. Calculating the norm at the cross-industrial level has been an entirely 'technocratic' exercise since the revision of the competitiveness law in 2017. It is no longer CRB/CCE as a whole – in which the 'social partners' are represented on a parity basis – that provides negotiating flexibility, but solely its secretariat, which is entrusted with estimating the wage norm and predicting national inflation for two-year periods. Also, the norm is no longer considered indicative. Wage increases are now bound to it, whereas before increases could be agreed above the norm in well-performing companies or industries. Setting the norm itself is part of the biennial IPA/AIP negotiations among the 'Group of Ten', an informal group comprising the general-secretary and president of both the ABVV/FGTB and the ACV/CSC, the ACLVB/CGSLB president and five representatives from four employers' associations.[16]

Concluding an IPA/AIP is considered symbolic for Belgium's bipartite 'social partnership' model. Domestic inflationary wage developments exceeding the wage norm; wage moderation in the three reference countries, especially in Germany; and sombre economic prospects can all cast negotiations into disarray from the start. If a draft IPA/AIP is concluded, then ABVV/FGTB and ACV/CSC affiliates, the ACLVB/CGSLB and regional union sub-structures vote on the draft. This occasionally exposes divides and tensions between union organizations or sub-structures. Deadlocked negotiations are cited time and again in the media to call its legitimacy into question. This denies, however, the longstanding practice of collective bargaining within the NAR/CNT and at lower levels. Failed negotiations trigger state 'intervention': the federal government is authorized to suspend negotiations and to propose a compromise or, ultimately, to set an imperative wage norm, mainly following the draft IPA/AIP, especially if it is supported by most 'social partners'. Six IPA/AIPs have been

16 'Ceci n'est pas un group des 10': in a typically Belgian (surrealistic) manner, there are eleven people at the negotiating table. The president of the main employers' association traditionally acts as the president of the 'Group of Ten' and does not represent its organisation.

concluded successfully since 1996, but this has to be set against eight (partial) failures. All negotiations have been unsuccessful since the 2007–2008 financial and economic crisis except for the 2016 IPA/AIP.

State-sponsored coordination seems a necessary yet insufficient condition for facilitating IPA/AIP agreements. Because other types of state sponsorship are challenging as a result of Belgian devolution (Arcq and Pochet 2000) – education and labour market policies are subnational competences – state sponsorship focused mainly on cutting employers' social security contributions before the 2007–2008 crisis. Being strongly dependent on budgetary and fiscal policies, this type of state sponsorship has now reached its limits, especially as employers' social security contributions were *structurally* reduced by a tax shift in 2016. Above all, the Michel I government (2014–2018, composed of economic liberals, the Flemish nationalists and Flemish Christian Democrats) strengthened the competitiveness law in 2017 by building into the wage norm calculation an ex-ante safety margin and ex-post correction mechanisms, thereby further reducing negotiating flexibility. Persistent wage restraint via state-imposed coordination has been the outcome since then, as IPA/AIP negotiations failed in 2018, 2020 and 2022.

Wage restraint is linked to a restricted scope for wage negotiations at lower bargaining levels and a bargaining system that is becoming more fragmented. Negotiating flexibility is therefore often sought in non-wage demands and remuneration types that are omitted from wage norm calculations and commonly partly exempted from social security contributions and taxes, such as luncheon and other vouchers and bonuses, especially at the company level (Van Gyes et al. 2021). Company-level bonus plans were introduced in 2008; Figure 3.6 demonstrates their extraordinary growth. So-called 'cafeteria plans' are increasingly being used in an attempt to replace current benefits and wage increases via a set of individualized alternative benefits. A tax-favourable 'profit premium' set unilaterally by management has also been possible since 2018. All these variable pay schemes are helping to exacerbate wage inequality. Finally, fragmentation also comes in as a result of the devolution of the Belgian state, which implies that bargaining units in certain industries, in particular related to the public sector, only cover the Region or Community. This tests trade union bargaining coordination as different Regions are gradually developing different employment terms and conditions. Yet, a genuinely disorganized decentralization has not been a policy option so far, also because of the unions' institutional embeddedness in the workplace, especially in large companies.

Figure 3.6 Number of collective agreements at the company and industrial levels, 2000–2020

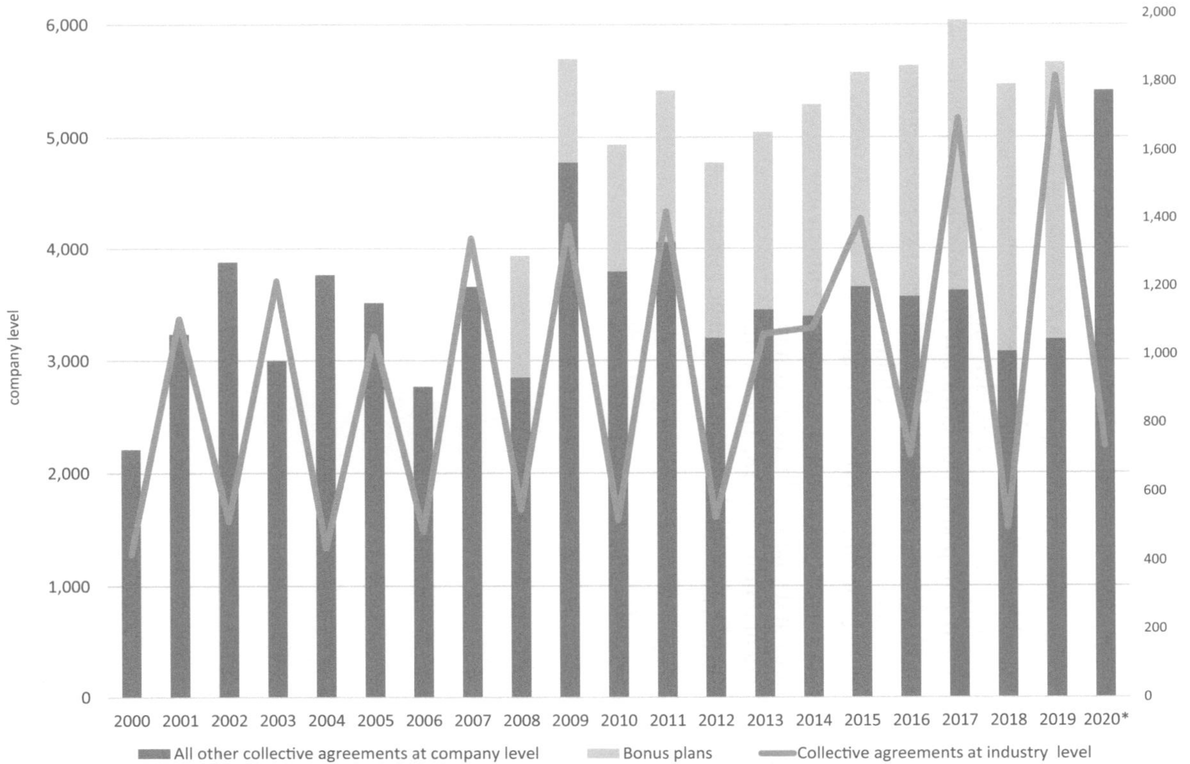

Note: * Bonus plans are included, but their number was unknown at the time of writing.
Source: FOD WASO/SPF ETCS.

Turning to workplace democracy, whereas board-level employee representation is absent (except at the public railway company until 2002), there is a union-dominated dual system of worker representation. First, union representatives are normally active in companies with at least fifty employees; this threshold is lowered in various industries by collective agreement. Second, health and safety committees (since 1952) are legally required in private sector companies with fifty employees or more and works councils (since 1948) in companies with 100 employees or more.[17] Quadrennial elections, taking place since 1950, determine the composition of these bodies (Op den Kamp and Van Gyes 2010). Only the three union confederations can propose candidates. There are two exceptions. Since 1987 a separate electoral college can be established at companies with managerial staff comprising a minimum of fifteen members: the NCK/CNC or staff themselves can nominate candidates, though without much electoral success. Elections in the national railway company were equally not successful for independent unions in 2018. This was the first time elections were held. No elections take place in the rest of the public sector.

[17] Transposing the 2002 EU directive on informing workers has meant that health and safety committees in smaller companies are taking over some of the competences of work councils, if one is not in place.

Figure 3.7 Participating rate and social election results for works councils, 2000–2020

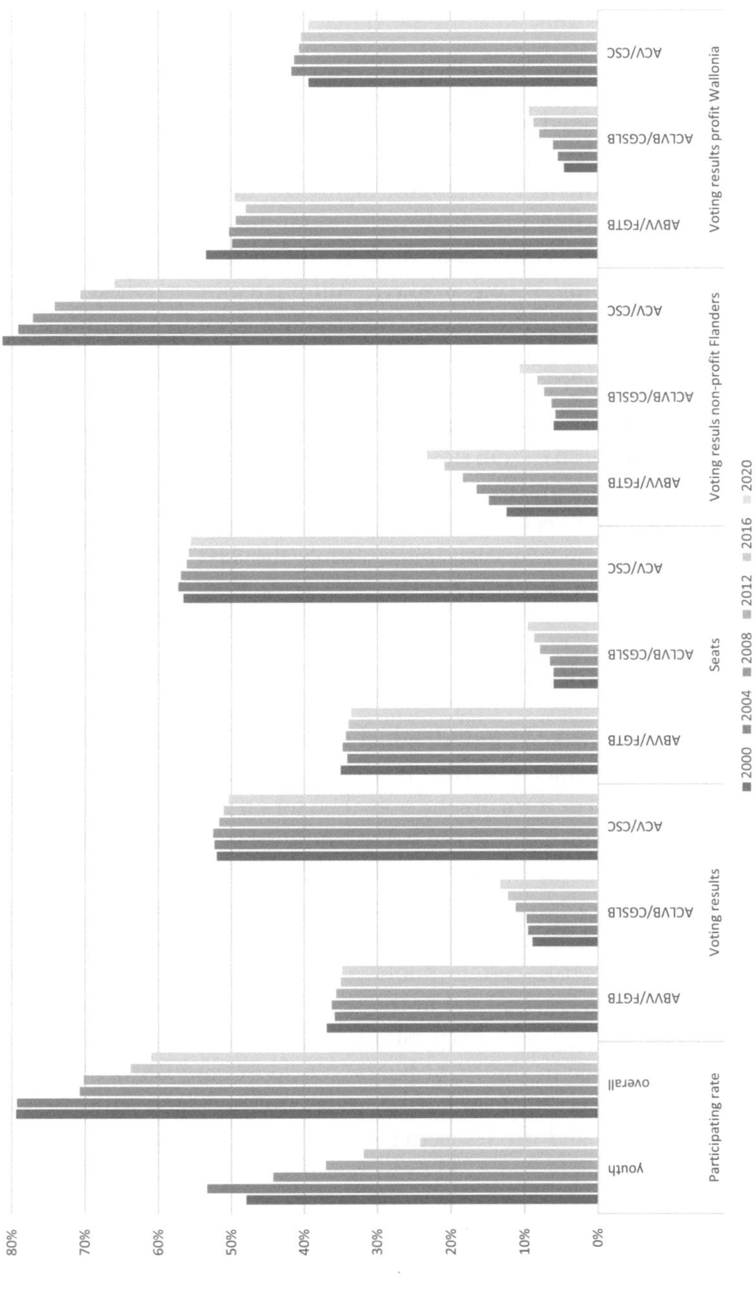

Source: FOD WASO/SPF ETCS.

Social election candidates, whether elected or not, are protected against dismissal. They are considered the 'heart of trade unions', together with union representatives. Both ideally aggregate workers' interests and needs in the workplace, and discuss union standpoints with them. Their presence is associated with, for instance, more occupational training and stronger knowledge of individual and collective workers' rights and their application (Hermans et al. 2020). Figure 3.7 demonstrates a declining election participation rate, however. Unions are also increasingly experiencing difficulties convincing workers to run as candidates, especially among women and young workers. Although non-standard contracts might partly explain this, it also reveals how member recruitment of young workers has become a challenge.[18] The election results illustrate that the ACLVB/CGSLB has steadily risen in popularity, resulting probably in a stronger union pluralism in workplaces. ABVV/FGTB and ACV/CSC results show an overall slow-moving weakening, but with differences between industries and Regions. The ACV/CSC's share is decreasing in the non-for-profit sector in Flanders, which is marked by institutions associated with the Christian 'pillar', while the ABVV/FGTB's share in the profit sector in Wallonia has also been weakening, at least until 2016.

Industrial conflict

The right to strike is an individual right, and considered fairly liberal in Belgium (Humblet and Rigaux 2016). If their union has recognized the action, which is normally the case, then union members are entitled to strike benefits, which rise as the strike continues. Case law has laid down rules on industrial action as unions fear the liability that goes along with legal personality. Legislative proposals for stricter regulation of industrial action have a long history, however (Humblet 2007). Recently regulation has become stricter in certain public services, including laws on a guaranteed minimum service level in the case of industrial action in railways and prisons in 2017 and 2019. Similar minimum service arrangements have been in place in the main public transport companies in Flanders and Wallonia since 2021 and 2017, respectively, via covenants between these companies and the respective subnational governments stipulating certain requirements that need to be met in case of industrial action.

---

18 Temporary agency workers have been entitled to vote at their place of work since 2020.

Apart from a notice period for preventing labour disputes, collective agreements contain 'social peace' clauses, although industrial action is usually still possible in practice; there is no legal distinction between legal and illegal action. Secondary action is possible as well. Also, joint committees at the industry level usually have conciliation bodies, through which national officials of the 'social partners' advise local parties on how to end disputes. In addition, labour conciliators of the Federal Public Service Employment, Labour and Social Dialogue (FOD WASO/SPF ETCS, *Federale Overheidsdienst Werkgelegenheid, Arbeid en Sociaal Overleg*) can be called in for mediation in the case of stalled labour disputes. These conciliators also act as chairs of joint committees and their conciliation body.

Lockouts seldom occur but are possible. Employers are not allowed to replace workers while they are on strike. Instead, they have been using the civil courts to break strikes since the mid-1980s through the unilateral imposition of substantial fines on picketing workers. Under pressure from the federal government, the 'social partners' agreed to halt this juridification of industrial action by concluding a non-binding 'gentlemen's agreement' in 2002 (Palsterman 2002). As juridification continued, again under government pressure, the 'partners' promised to 'modernize' the agreement in 2016 but negotiations failed. Recent court rulings have also put pressure on the right to take industrial action: for example, ABVV/FGTB activists were convicted for the 'malicious obstruction of traffic' during industrial action against austerity measures by the Michel I government in 2015–2016.

Belgian unions are real 'mobilization machines' (Andretta et al. 2016). This has been exemplified by various large-scale demonstrations against, for instance, labour market reforms and austerity measures, especially since 2011. Participation in union-staged demonstrations is commonly covered by strike benefits, which mainly incentivizes strongly union-committed members. Those are predominantly union activists who act as mobilization facilitators, but unions have difficulties mobilizing beyond this network of often middle-aged activists. This has been described as a 'crisis behind the figures' (Faniel 2012b).

The years 2001, 2005 and 2014 are three particular peaks in industrial action since 2000 (Appendix A1). Strikes against reforms in education, especially in Wallonia, explain the 2001 upsurge. The 2005 peak was the result of a general strike arising from failed negotiations between the 'social partners' and federal government about the 'Generational Pact' to reform early retirement pension schemes.[19] Another 24-hour general strike took place against the austerity measures imposed by the Di Rupo government in early 2012. Its rather low participation can be explained by a large public sector strike at the end of 2011. A third general strike clarifies the 2014 peak. The Michel I government unilaterally decided to gradually increase the retirement age from 65 to 67 years, and to impose several austerity measures. The strike was preceded by supposedly the largest union-staged demonstration since 1986, with about 120,000 participants, and rotating industrial action at the county level. This remarkable union mobilization yielded hardly any results, however, as the government's ideological and organizational alignment with the unions was minimal. Nevertheless, measured by days not worked due to industrial action, the Michel I government has been the second most contested since 1991 (Vandaele 2019b), the year from which the new data series are available.

National demonstrations and strike actions, mainly about pension-related reforms, reappeared from 2016 onwards but they did not reach the 2014 participation level. They were less coordinated, and there was union discord about the exact timing of the strike weapon and its effectiveness. Tensions arose not only between affiliates and the regional substructures within the confederations, but also between the latter, although their relations are generally pragmatic. While the ABVV/FGTB called a national 24-hour strike against government pension policies in 2016, this did not excluded ACV/CSC members from taking industrial action as well, especially in Wallonia. The latter Region, though dominated by two counties, Hainaut and Liège, has been more strike-prone than Flanders (Vandaele 2021), although reliable data on industrial action by Region has only been available since 2017. A 'united union front' restored afterwards, however, and union mobilization at the national level has recently taken a more 'offensive' character. Grievances have centred around restoring purchasing power and against the strictness of the competitiveness law since its reform. Notable industrial action for higher wages took place in manufacturing in late 2018 and in the private sector via 24-hour national strikes after the failure of IPA/AIP negotiations in both early 2019 and 2021. Union organizations started a petition in early 2022 to initiate a parliamentary debate on the current competitiveness law. In general, union organizations have increasingly turned to actions beyond industrial action, especially litigation, though with mixed results.

---

[19] A general strike is defined here as a strike called by all three union confederations for all industries in both the private and public sector.

Figure 3.8 Share of days not worked because of industrial action by industry or sector and their strike-proneness*, 2007–2020

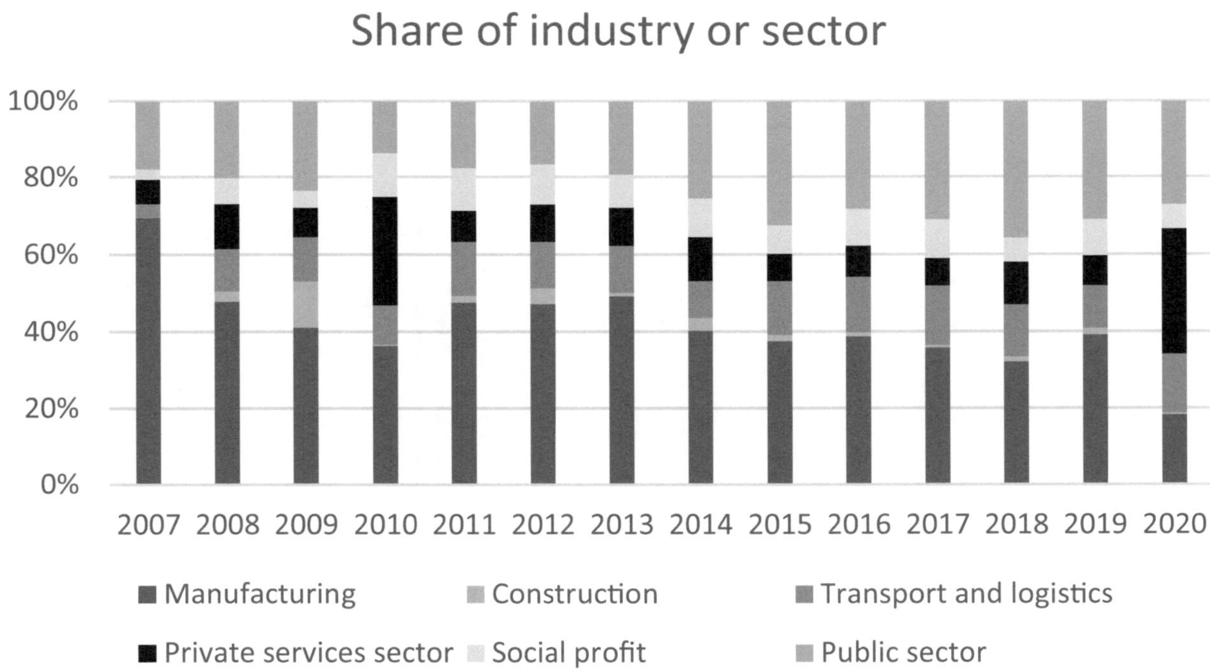

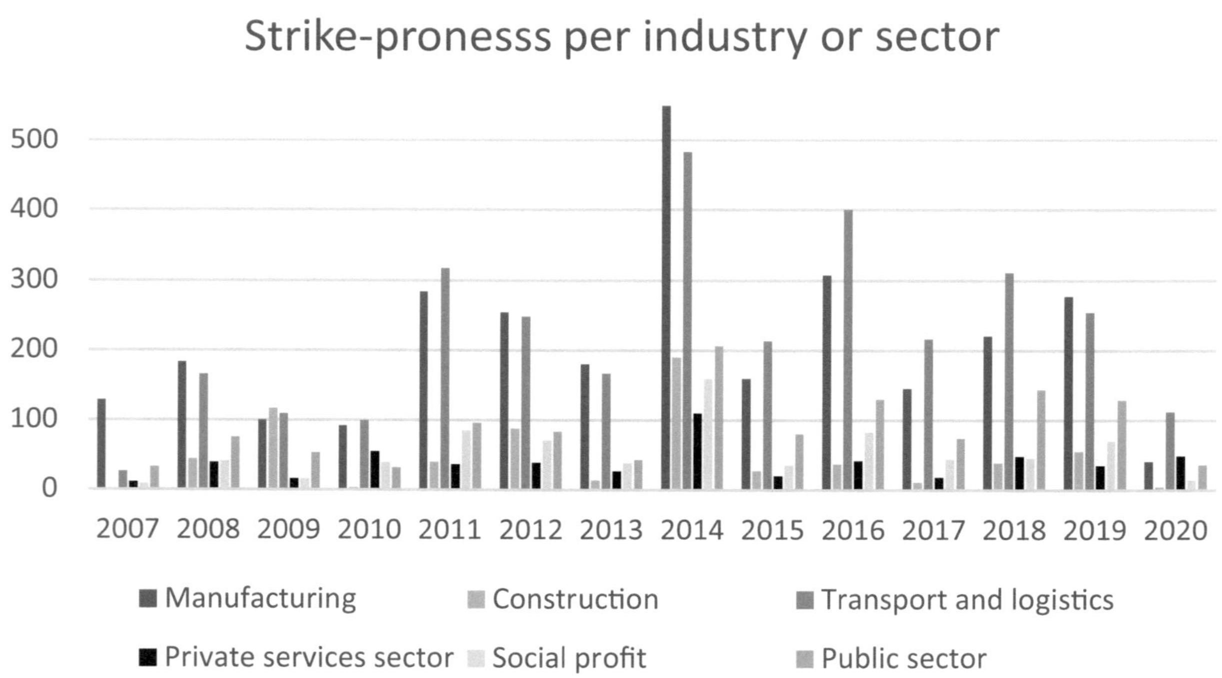

Note: * Measured per 1,000 employees in the respective industry or sector. Data available since 2007. Grouping based on joint committees. Series break in 2013.
Source: RSZ/ONSS.

Belgium traditionally belonged somewhere in the middle of the EU 'strike league table' up to the 1990s (Scheuer 2006). This has changed: the country has now moved above the EU average. Its ranking is the result of unions' continued use of a 'labour repertoire' that includes general 24-hour strikes to impose *political pressure*, while strike activity has declined in most EU countries (Vandaele 2016). Public sector strikes have gained as well in importance since 2014, when austerity measures mainly hit this sector (see Figure 3.8). Whereas political mass-strikes, either public sector or general, dominate statistics, industrial action to put *economic pressure* is linked to the biennial bargaining cycle in Belgium. The strike level is thus noticeably higher in the first semester of uneven years when negotiations usually take place for collective agreements at the industry level (Vandaele 2019a). Transport and logistics, and manufacturing, which often faces restructuring and closures, are the most strike-prone industries. The shares of both the private service and the not-for-profit sector – the latter implying a feminization of the strike weapon – are fairly stable. The only exception is 2010 because of a large strike within the supermarket Carrefour against restructuring plans. This strike together with, for example, the first industry-wide strike in domestic cleaning in 2019 demonstrate that Belgian unions are able to organize industrial action in fragmented industries. Finally, construction is a strike-calm industry except for 2009 when an industry-wide strike – the first since 1968 – was called over a new collective agreement that unions considered too 'unbalanced'.

Political relations

Belgium's consociational democracy for accommodating religious and language cleavages has been mirrored in the socio-economic realm via neocorporatist arrangements, oriented equally towards piecemeal policy adjustment. Composed on a parity basis of delegates from the union confederations and main employers' associations, the NAR/CNT is the most influential social dialogue institution at the national level (De Vos et al. 2003). As Belgium's 'social parliament', the NAR/CNT advises the federal parliament or government on labour and social security law. Cross-industry collective agreements can also be concluded in the NAR/CNT, and they are almost always extended by Royal Decree. The NAR/CNT together with other collective bargaining arrangements are part of Belgium's neocorporatist system, traditionally buttressed by the social- and Christian-democratic political parties. Both 'political families' historically have ideological and organizational links with the respective confederations, although those alignments have been structurally weakened over time (Faniel and Gobin 2020).[20] Proportional representation and coalition governments have nevertheless so far provided at least one political party in the federal government with historical ties to the ABVV/FGTB or the ACV/CSC. This partisan leaning largely guarantees the endurance of the neocorporatist system, although electoral shifts alongside labour market reforms are putting pressure on its regulatory capacity. Four interrelated matters linked to those shifts are forcing union organizations to reconsider their strong integration with the political domain.

---

20 Party–union links in the 'liberal family' were abandoned in 1962, although informal links still exist.

Figure 3.9 Party standing in the Chamber of Representatives since 1999

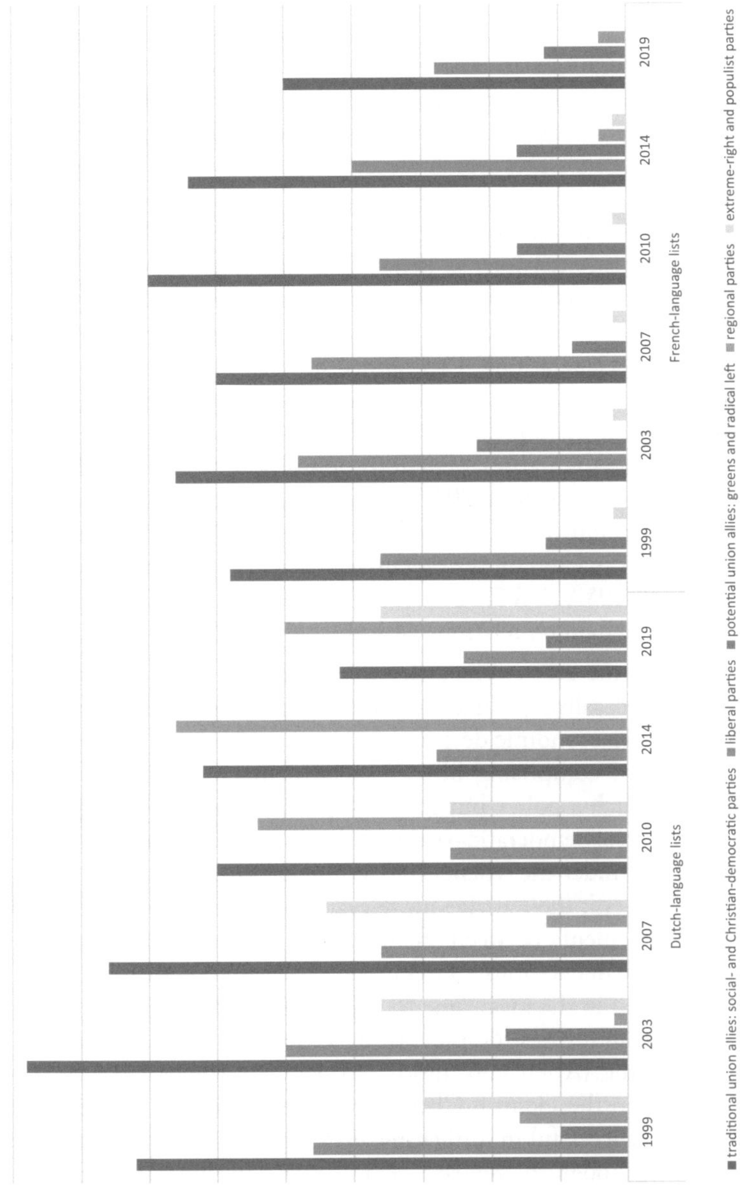

Source: Federal election results.

First, electoral support is declining for the traditional allies of the ABVV/FGTB and the ACV/CSC, especially among the Dutch-language lists in Belgium's split party system (see Figure 3.9). Consequently, union organizations are also working together with other political parties to represent their members, especially since social- and Christian-democratic parties when in power have promoted labour market reforms and austerity measures which are detrimental to the union agenda. The Flemish social democratic party was closer to 'Third Way' policies in the early 2000s. This caused friction with the ABVV/FGTB and internal ethnic-linguistic tensions as the French-speaking sub-structure accused the Flemish one of being too receptive to such polices (Faniel and Gobin 2020). Party–union links were particularly tense during the general strike against the 'Generational Pact' aimed at strengthening early retirement schemes in 2005 and later when austerity measures affected the 'quasi-Ghent system' in 2011 (Brepoels 2015). Tensions lessened when the social democratic parties went into opposition in 2014, and once they came into power again in 2020. Party–union links can still be considered structural, as illustrated by the fact that the ABVV/FGTB has a seat (in an advisory capacity) on the executive board of the social democratic parties. Some ABVV/FGTB branches, especially in Wallonia, nevertheless favour strengthening relations with the radical left.

Second, the ascent of parties that embrace neoliberalism and thus favour the so-called 'primacy of politics' has been colliding with neocorporatist socio-economic decision-making. The Verhofstadt I government (1999–2003, comprising liberal, social democratic and green parties) promoted such a policy but this was quickly abandoned under pressure from the social democratic parties. A drift away from neocorporatism was undeniable under the Michel I government. Little room was left for the 'social partners': their advice on relevant policy issues was overruled and several agreements between them became 'implementation agreements for government decisions' (Van Gyes et al. 2018: 85). Their autonomy has been restored in the meantime to cope with (un)lockdowns within companies and industries, despite strong government 'intervention' during the pandemic (Ajzen and Taskin 2021). Nevertheless, the ACV/CSC has perceived the Flemish Christian Democrats in the Michel I government as unsuccessful in mitigating austerity measures and labour market reforms. Although the reforms seem comparatively modest (Simoni and Vlandas 2020), they have contributed to workplace fissuring. Informal networks still exist between individual Christian Democrats who have sympathies with the Christian labour movement and the ACV/CSC, especially in Flanders, but the 'exclusive partnership' between the confederation and the Christian-democratic party was abandoned in the 1990s. Green parties are generally perceived as an alternative ally, even though their standpoints are not always unequivocally pro-union.

Third, the electoral rise of the New Flemish Alliance (N-VA, *Nieuw-Vlaamse Alliantie*) has made it more difficult to form federal governments, as illustrated by various periods of caretaker government since 2007 and mounting pressures on Belgian solidarity structures. Initially, this Flemish pro-independence and conservative party pursued social policies to promote nation-building in Flanders in the early 2010s (Vandaele and Hooghe 2013). This swiftly failed because of a shift towards austerity policies, including skimping on subsidies for civil society organizations (including unions), in the aftermath of the 2007–2008 financial and economic crisis. Advancing a neoliberal agenda and further devolution puts the N-VA in direct opposition to union organizations, especially as devolution is synonymous with attempts to sideline social dialogue institutions in Flanders, despite their stronger neocorporatist underpinning there than in the other Regions. Further devolution would supposedly endanger the position of the 'social partners' in governance bodies of the social security system, including the 'quasi-Ghent system', which is still organized primarily at the federal level, as unions nurture solidarity between all workers in Belgium.

Finally, the electoral gains of the extreme right in Flanders since the late 1980s have exposed the limits of member–union relations based predominantly on instrumental motives. The extreme right has made several futile attempts to break the quasi-monopoly of confederations by establishing their own 'unions', appointing their own candidates in social elections or hijacking union symbols such as International Workers' Day. Social policies aimed at native workers and against migrants have become more prominent in propaganda. Such welfare chauvinism was seen as part of the electoral success in 2019. Union organizations try to counteract the extreme right through union education aimed at union activists, and anti-racist campaigns. Confederations also jointly adopted a code of conduct in 1994 permitting them to exclude union representatives who are known to have run as candidates for the extreme right via union by-laws. This was extended to ordinary members after the 2006 municipal elections. These efforts and union solidarity rhetoric do not make members immune to the siren calls of the extreme right, however. There is generally no negative union membership effect when it comes to voting for them in Belgium compared with other European countries, although middle-class voters are an exception (Mosimann et al. 2019; Oesch 2008).

Societal power

Critical or positive support for unions is relatively high, although less so in Flanders, and seems quite stable (Swyngedouw et al. 2016). Their legitimacy is nevertheless regularly contested in the mainstream press and media and by the liberal parties, N-VA and the extreme right. These parties all favour decentralized collective bargaining – a policy preference they share with the Flemish employers' association VOKA – and replacing the 'quasi-Ghent system' with a single state agency. The latter is ironic given their neoliberal or libertarian preferences for 'free market' policies. Union organizations sometimes find themselves caught up in a short media storm defending the 'quasi-Ghent system': they especially emphasize the cost-efficiency of union-run paying agents compared with the HVW/CAPAC. The abovementioned parties also openly question neocorporatist arrangements, such as the exemption of the 'union premium' from taxes, or take any opportunity to delegitimize the unions in relation to financial issues.

Above all, the heightened union mobilization during the Michel I government has given rise to so-called 'union bashing' (Zienkowski and De Cleen 2021). The N-VA and extreme right portray union mobilization also in ethnic-linguistic terms, thereby homogenizing Wallonia and disregarding differences in mobilization in Flanders (Abts et al. 2019). No longitudinal empirical data exist to make an assessment on whether such bashing has become more frequent or fierce, or both, although the electoral successes of the N-VA and the extreme right and the 'primacy of politics' discourse have certainly fed into this view. Unions' discursive power has recently become more prominent as mobilization as such has brought only meagre results. Unions keep using leaflets, brochures and paper or (digital) member magazines to inform their members, and traditional media-oriented tactics to influence public opinion. They are also increasingly using social media, although progress can still be made here given the gap between the social media engagement and number of members. Furthermore, unions regularly launch public campaigns targeting specific groups of workers, such as employees in small and medium-sized enterprises, agency workers, women, migrant and student workers, aiming to strengthen their employment terms and conditions. Inspired by the US 'Fight for 15' campaign, one of the most recent campaigns was the ABVV/FGTB-campaign for a 'decent minimum wage' to tackle in-work poverty (Flohimont 2019).

Broadening the union agenda beyond the labour market is part of the identity of Belgian union organizations. This is rooted in their 'pillarized' past: they fell into a cauldron containing dense networks and union–community collaboration from the outset, and they have remained there via their local branches and union activists. They also forge coalitions with grassroots and progressive movements beyond the own 'pillar', proving that institutional embeddedness can go hand in hand with social movement unionism (Pasture 2009). Largely following societal developments, union organizations cooperate with, for instance, non-governmental organizations in international development, the antiracism movement and migrant associations, the environmental and climate movement and the other-globalization movement, anti-austerity and poverty movement. Grassroots and progressive movements can rely on unions' mobilization capacity, if needed, while coalitional unionism is also often structural and institutionalized. The latter implies that unions as 'policy insiders' are often sharing seats with civil society organizations in advisory bodies, especially at subnational levels (Willems et al. 2021).

Trade union policies towards the European Union

Belgium is a country that traditionally supports the European integration project, and union organizations are no exception: they subscribe to the supranational logic of the European Trade Union Federations (ETUFs) and the European Trade Union Confederation (ETUC), of which the ABVV/FGTB was a founding member.[21] The simple geographical fact that Brussels hosts the ETUFs and the ETUC almost naturally provides union organizations with close links.[22] Also, the language skills of Belgian union representatives and their occasional migrant

---

21 The ACV/CSC joined the ETUC in 1974, after its first enlargement, and the ACLVB/CGSLB in 2002. The ACV/CSC is also member of the European Union of Christian Democratic Workers.

22 Geographical proximity also provides relatively easy access to policymakers at the European level, although influencing decision-making regarding the European Semester is strongly contingent on the federal government coalition (Peña-Casas and Ghailani 2019).

background, and union leadership socialized into finding compromises in a country on the cultural boundary of Germanic and Latin Europe, might facilitate the search for a common understanding in EU organizations (Jouan and Tilly 2017). Bi- and multilateral coordination with unions from neighbouring or other countries is also a strategy advanced by Belgian unions. Thus, the 1996 competitiveness law has indirectly resulted in strengthening wage coordination with unions in two neighbouring countries, Germany and the Netherlands, as well as Luxembourg since 1998 and France since 2002. Although this so-called 'Doorn initiative' has faded over time, it inspired the launch of a Committee for the Coordination of Collective Bargaining within the ETUC in 1999.

The only publicly known wrong note in the relationship since 2000 has been the non-participation of the ABVV/FGTB in the 2003 ETUC Congress. While their nominated but not endorsed candidate for the ETUC Secretariat was the immediate cause of this, its roots lay in lingering discord from the early 1990s, when the socialist confederation but also the ACV/CSC stressed the shortage of organizational adaptation of the ever more heterogeneous ETUC and demanded more strategical coherence (Jouan and Tilly 2017). Belgian confederations thenceforward developed a more pragmatic and less prescriptive stance towards the ETUC, but they continue to be at the forefront of defending a 'social Europe'. Nevertheless, although Belgium was the first country to transform the European Works Council directive into national legislation, there are fewer European Works Councils (EWCs) than one would have expected based on the multinational companies headquartered in Belgium. This is the outcome of the lack of knowledge about EWCs, a low perceived added value of European-level information and consultation, or prioritizing worker representation at the local level (Olijslagers and De Spiegelaere 2019).

Together with their relatively robust membership figures, mobilization capacity and vast resources, Belgian union organizations have been instrumental in organizing European demonstrations or other actions by the ETUFs or ETUC, and are present in relatively large numbers. The effective protests and political advocacy against the Port Directive and the Services Directive in the 2000s have been quintessential in this regard (Leiren and Parks 2014). Judgements by the Court of Justice of the European Union on the Belgian system of recognizing dockworkers remain an enduring concern for transport unions, however. Also, in coordination with unions from Central and Eastern Europep, the

Inter-Regional Trade Union Councils, ETUFs or ETUC – in particular, unions organizing in construction, food processing and transport – have increased their efforts to better regulate the free movement of workers and tackle 'social dumping' in the EU (Jouan and Tilly 2017). Like increased national labour market deregulation and flexibility, liberalization and 'social dumping' have contributed to workplace fissuring, tending to undermine Belgium's neocorporatist arrangements and their regulatory capacity.[23] Recent initiatives such as the European Pillar of Social Rights, the European Labour Authority or the European minimum wage are therefore all welcomed by the Belgian union organizations.

Conclusions

It is probably no coincidence that Belgium is referred to in a recent book on how to rejuvenate the American labour movement (Madland 2021): Belgian union organizations have somehow 'unawares' incorporated many US-inspired ideas on unionism considered vital for a vibrant labour movement. They combine robust embeddedness in labour market and welfare institutions, political advocacy strategies and litigation with some organizing tactics, although almost solely related to social elections, and strong union mobilization, featuring a wide action repertoire. Their 'pillarized' past is resilient within the framework of today's coalitional and community unionism within and beyond their 'pillar' and a 'whole-worker approach' that goes beyond the workplace and a solely economic focus, especially via local branches and the inclusion of, for instance, students, the unemployed and pensioners as members. All of this has arguably contributed to a high and exceptionally longstanding stable union density rate until 2014 demonstrating how Belgian unions kept membership levels in line with the growth of wage- and salary-earners, and compositional shifts within it.

A 'belated' de-unionization has nevertheless set in, which has adversely affected union revenue. No academic studies have yet examined the reasons for recent membership losses, and the extent to which membership in- or outflows, or both, are causing this. But young workers in particular

---

23 One exception to negative integration might be EU policies promoting formal gender equality and integration of women in the labour market, with gender equality provisions being adopted in cross-industry collective agreements and IPA/AIPs over time (Lemeire and Zanoni 2021).

are clearly a growing concern, as also shown by their decreasing participation rate in social elections. Membership dynamics in the ABVV/FGTB and the ACV/CSC have gone together with more member concentration, less union fragmentation and a reconfiguration of internal relationships between affiliates. For example, the ABVV/FGTB undergoing internal alliance-building: weakening metal unions are cooperating with the transport union that has growing membership. Industry unions joining forces with multi-industry ones has been another way of reinforcing their influence, in terms of which white-collar unions in particular are – relatively – losing ground. Thus, mergers are typically an organizational response of ACV/CSC affiliates in industries mainly with declining employment and confronted with sustained membership decline.

In terms of Visser's (2019) four future union scenarios, although based solely on the union membership dimension, *substitution* is unlikely in the near future. This scenario would also imply a weakening of the quasi-monopoly of the three confederations. Belgian unions are simply too large, and there are no rival organizations or institutions. The considerable influx into the HVW/CAPAC of 'temporary unemployed workers' as a result of the Covid-19 furlough scheme demonstrates how certain worker categories are 'union evasive', however. Unions' comprehensive nature, with identities and strategies emphasizing inclusiveness, not only calls into question insider/outsider models of behaviour, but also excludes outspoken dualization and marginalization scenarios for now. Unions are simply still strong among their traditional membership bases, although *dualization* tendencies could develop if they do too little to recruit among growing new worker categories, either at the lower or the higher end of the labour market. In this respect, labour market reforms and the influence of EU policies on Belgium's neocorporatist arrangements and employment relations are not very helpful as they contribute to workplace fissuring.

A rapid and pronounced decline in union membership would result in *marginalization*, which would probably be generated by imperilling unions' institutionally based security, especially the 'quasi-Ghent system'. This security remains largely intact as the traditional political allies of union organizations are still electorally strong enough to veto destabilizing policy proposals that would impact *directly* on union security. Governments largely respected neocorporatist traditions of social dialogue before the 2007–2008 financial and economic crisis. Political advocacy and union mobilization have at best only weakened the tightening of (early) pension arrangements and labour market reforms, however. Equally, political mass strikes demonstrated their limitations during the Michel I government. For union organizations it was a matter of 'sweating it out'. The Michel I government's legacy is clear, however: a restricted right to take industrial action in certain industries, more labour market deregulation and flexibility, undermining the neocorporatist system's regulatory capacity, and a collective bargaining system increasingly typified by state 'intervention' in wage-setting, wage restraint and fragmentation.

There might be reasons for some positivity in the wake of the pandemic. The De Croo government, which came to power in 2020 and includes economic liberals, socialists, the greens and Flemish Christian Democrats, mainly subscribes to neocorporatist traditions. Equally, resuming union growth also seems to imply a return to 'normal', with net union density, in all likelihood, having again risen above the symbolic level of 50 per cent since 2020. It would perhaps be too much to claim that this return to a more open political opportunity structure and renewed membership increase has set the unions on the road to revitalization, however. Easier trade union access to socio-economic decision-making might only amount to a temporary reprieve until the next elections. Also, one-off pandemic-related growth should not blind the unions to the underlying weakening of membership. The 'quasi-Ghent system' is therefore a double-edged sword for unions. It provides them with an almost 'automatic' inflow of members. Conversely, the unions might also be 'giants with feet of clay', with large memberships but weak organizational power, reducing their effectiveness, especially if their relationships with (unemployed) newcomers and existing members are predominantly instrumental (Vandaele 2020a). Unless the unions engage seriously with organizing, especially in new industries, with the aim of increasing union effectiveness in the workplace and beyond, all of this points to a continuation of the Belgian *Sonderweg* rather than clear-cut *union revitalization*.

References

All links were checked on 6 April 2022.

Abts K., Dalle Mulle E. and Laermans R. (2019) Beyond issue diversification: N-VA and the communitarisation of political, economic and cultural conflicts in Belgium, West European Politics, 42 (4), 848–872.

ACV (2019a) Nieuwe aanpak voor ledenwerving en ledenzorg, Vakbeweging, Speciale uitgave 906, Brussel, ACV.

ACV (2019b) Wie is en wat doet het ACV, Vakbeweging, Speciale editie 913, Brussel, ACV.

ACV (2020) Administratief verslag 2019. Organisatie, rekeningen en ACV-leden, Brussel, ACV.

Ajzen M. and Taskin L. (2021) La concertation sociale au temps du coronavirus: enjeux et perspectives du premier confinement en Belgique, Revue française de gestion, 298, 79–95.

Andretta M., Bosi L. and della Porta D. (2016) Participants in trade union-staged demonstrations: a cross-country comparison, Transfer, 22 (3), 295–313.

Arcq E. and Pochet P. (2000) Toward a new social pact in Belgium?, in Fajertag G. and Pochet P. (eds) Social pacts in Europe. New dynamics. Second edition, Brussels, ETUI, 113–134.

Berntsen L. (2019) Vakbonden en jongeren. Belgische inspiratie voor de Nederlandse vakbeweging, Publicatie 19, Amsterdam, De Burcht.

Blaise P. (2010) Le cadre institutionnel de la concertation sociale, in Arcq E., Capron M., Léonard E. and Reman P. (eds) Dynamiques de la concertation sociale, Bruxelles, Centre de recherche et d'information socio-politiques, 43–74.

Brepoels J. (2015) Wat zoudt gij zonder 't werkvolk zijn? De geschiedenis van de Belgische arbeidersbeweging 1830–2015, Leuven, Van Halewyck.

Cassiers I. and Denayer L. (2010) Concertation sociale et transformations socio-économiques depuis 1944, in Arcq E., Capron M., Léonard E. and Reman P. (eds) Dynamiques de la concertation sociale, Bruxelles, Centre de recherche et d'information socio-politiques, 75–92.

De Federale Ombudsman (2021) De Federale Ombudsman Jaarverslag 2020. Houvast bieden in onzekere tijden. https://www.federaalombudsman.be/nl/jaarverslag-2020

Delespaul S. and Doerflinger N. (2019) Een verlaagde prijs als motief voor vakbondslidmaatschap voor jongeren? Inzichten uit België, Tijdschrift voor Arbeidsvraagstukken, 35 (1), 40–54.

De Vos M., De Hert P., Humblet P. and Lenaerts L. (eds) (2003) Vijftig jaar nationale arbeidsraad, Brugge, Die Keure.

De Witte H. (ed.) (2005) Job insecurity, union involvement and union activism, Aldershot, Ashgate.

Ebbinghaus B., Visser J., Pasture P. and Slomp H. (2000) Belgium, in Ebbinghaus B. and Visser J. (eds) Trade Unions in Western Europe since 1945, London, Macmillan, 111–155.

Faniel J. (2010) Caractéristiques et spécificités des syndicats belges, in Arcq E., Capron M., Léonard E. and Reman P. (eds) Dynamiques de la concertation sociale, Bruxelles, Centre de recherche et d'information socio-politiques, 93–119.

Faniel J. (2012a) Inside or outside trade unions? The mobilization of the unemployed in Belgium, in Chabanet D. and Faniel J. (eds) The mobilization of the unemployed in Europe: from acquiescence to protest?, Basingstoke, Palgrave Macmillan, 89–107.

Faniel J. (2012b) Crisis behind the figures? Belgian trade unions between strength, paralysis and revitalisation, Management Revue, 23 (1), 14–31.

Faniel J. and Gobin C. (2020) Les relations entre syndicats et partis politiques: un frein à la mobilisation sociale ?, in Faniel J., Gobin C. and Paternotte D. (eds) Se mobiliser en Belgique. Raisons, cadres et formes de la contestation sociale contemporaine, Louvain-la-Neuve, Academia-L'Harmattan, 117–139.

Faniel J. and Vandaele K. (2011) Histoire de la Centrale générale des syndicats libéraux de Belgique (CGSLB), Courrier hebdomadaire du CRISP 2123–2124, Bruxelles, Centre de recherche et d'information socio-politiques.

Faniel J. and Vandaele K. (2012) Implantation syndicale et taux de syndicalisation (2000–2010), Courrier hebdomadaire du CRISP 2146–2147, Bruxelles, Centre de recherche et d'information socio-politiques.

Flohimont O. (2019) 'Fight for 14'. The campaign for a decent minimum wage of €14 per hour in Belgium, Transfer, 25 (3), 381–386.

Hemmerijckx R. (1995) De socialistische vakbeweging en het Sociaal Pact, in Luyten D. and Vanthemsche G. (eds) Het Sociaal Pact van 1944. oorsprong, betekenis en gevolgen, Brussel, VUB Press, 227–245.

Hermans M., Desiere S. and Lenaerts K. (2020) Maakt de vakbond het verschil? Effecten van werknemersvertegenwoordiging op organisatieniveau, Leuven, HIVA-KU Leuven.

Humblet P. (2007) Regulering van de staking: noodzaak, provocatie of windowdressing, in Devos C. and Humblet P. (eds) Arbeid vs kapitaal: een kwarteeuw staking(srecht), Gent, Academia Press, 121–143.

Humblet P. and Rigaux M. (2016) Introduction to Belgian labour law, Antwerpen, Intersentia.

Hyman R. (2001) Understanding European trade unionism: between market, class and society, London, Sage.

Installé M., Ongena O. and Verlinden M. (2010) La concertation socio-économique au sein des Régions et Communautés, in Arcq E., Capron M., Léonard E. and Reman P. (eds) Dynamiques de la concertation sociale, Bruxelles, Centre de recherche et d'information socio-politiques, 291–319.

Jones E. (2008) Economic adjustment and political transformation in small states, Oxford, Oxford University Press.

Jouan Q. and Tilly P. (2017) The Belgian trade union organisations: national divisions and common European action, in Ciampani A. and Tilly P. (eds) National trade unions and the ETUC: a history of unity and diversity, Brussels, ETUI, 119–137.

Lefebve V. (2019) Les réformes de l'assurance chômage (2011–2019), Courrier hebdomadaire du CRISP 2438–2439, Bruxelles, Centre de recherche et d'information socio-politiques.

Leiren M.D. and Parks L. (2014) When trade unions succeed: cases of blocked liberalisation in the common market, European Journal of Political Research, 53 (3), 465–479.

Lemeire V. and Zanoni P. (2021) Beyond methodological nationalism in explanations of gender equality: the impact of EU policies on gender provisions in national collective agreements in Belgium (1957–2020), European Journal of Industrial Relations, 28 (1), 47–64.

Madland D. (2021) Re-union: how bold labor reforms can repair, revitalize and reunite the United States, Ithaca, Cornell University Press.

Martens A. and Pulignano V (2008) Immigration and trade unions in Belgium: historical trends and new challenges, Transfer, 14 (4), 665–675.

Mosimann N., Rennwald L. and Zimmermann A. (2019) The radical right, the labour movement and the competition for the workers' vote, Economic and Industrial Democracy, 40 (1), 65–90.

Mort Subite (1990) Barsten in België: een geografie van de Belgische maatschappij, Berchem, EPO.

OECD and J. Visser (2021) OECD/AIAS ICTWSS Database. Note on definitions, measurement and sources, Paris, OECD.

Op den Kamp H. and Van Gyes G. (2010) Een halve eeuw sociale verkiezingen. Een trendanalyse van 1950 tot 2008, Leuven, HIVA.

Oesch D (2008) Explaining workers' support for right-wing populist parties in Western Europe: Evidence from Austria, Belgium, France, Norway and Switzerland, International Political Science Review, 29 (3), 349–373.

Olijslagers C. and De Spiegelaere S. (2019) Why aren't there more European Works Councils? A Belgian perspective, ETUI Policy Brief 7, Brussels, ETUI.

Palstermans P. (2002) L'accord sur le droit de grève, Courrier Hebdomadaire du CRISP 1755, Bruxelles, Centre de recherche et d'information socio-politiques.

Pasture P. (1996) Belgium: pragmatism in pluralism, in Pasture P., Verberckmoes J. and De Witte H. (eds) The lost perspective? Trade unions between ideology and social action in the new Europe. Vol. 1. Ideological persistence in national traditions, Aldershot, Avebury, 91–135.

Pasture P. (2009) Belgian trade unions: between social movement and service centre, in Phelan C. (ed.) Trade unionism since 1945. Towards a global history, Vol. 1, Western Europe, Eastern Europe, Africa and the Middle East, Frankfurt am Main, Peter Lang, 3–35.

Peña-Casas R. and Ghailani D. (2019) National trade unions and the European Semester: reciprocal influence and 'something for everyone': case study Belgium, Working Paper Series – Research Paper 40, Brussels, European Social Observatory.

Pulignano V. and Doerflinger N. (2014) Belgian trade unions and the youth: initiatives and challenges, Leuven, Centre for Sociological Research. https://soc.kuleuven.be/ceso/ceso-reports-1/141001belgium-trade-unions-and-the-youth-final.pdf

Ravesloot S. (2012) Still facing discrimination: Impediments to women's representation in Belgian trade unions, in: Ledwith S. and Hansen L.L. (eds) Gendering and diversifying trade union leadership, Oxford, Routledge, 285–302.

RVA (2021) De RVA in 2020. Volume 1: Activiteitenverslag, Brussel, Rijksdienst voor Arbeidsvoorziening.

Scheuer S. (2006) A novel calculus? Institutional change, globalization and industrial conflict in Europe, European Journal of Industrial Relations, 12 (2), 143–164.

Simoni M. and Vlandas T. (2020) Labour market liberalization and the rise of dualism in Europe as the interplay between governments, trade unions and the economy, Social Policy & Administration, 55 (4), 637–658.

Strikwerda C. (1997) A house divided. Catholics, socialists, and Flemish nationalists in nineteenth-century Belgium, Lanham, Rowman and Littlefield.

Strøby Jensen C. S. (2020) Trade unionism in Europe: are the working class still members?, European Journal of Industrial Relations, 26 (1), 107–120.

Swyngedouw M., Abts K. and Meulemen B. (2016) Syndicats et syndicalisme: perceptions et opinions, Courrier hebdomadaire du CRISP 2298, Bruxelles, Centre de recherche et d'information socio-politiques.

Therborn G. (1992) Lessons from 'corporatism' theorizations, in Pekkarinen J., Pohjola M. and Rowthorn B. (eds) Social corporatism. a superior economic system? Oxford, Clarendon Press, 24–43.

Van den Broeck M. (2010) Le Conseil central de l'économie, in Arcq E., Capron M., Léonard E. and Reman P. (eds) Dynamiques de la concertation sociale, Bruxelles, Centre de recherche et d'information socio-politiques, 193–209.

Van Gyes G. (2010) Trade union strategies to recruit new groups of workers – Belgium, Dublin, Eurofound.

Van Gyes G., De Witte H. and van der Hallen P. (2000) Belgian trade unions in the 1990s: does strong today mean strong tomorrow?, in Waddington J. and Hoffmann R. (eds) Trade unions in Europe. Facing challenges and searching for solutions, Brussels, ETUI, 105–142.

Vandaele K. (2006) A report from the homeland of the Ghent system: the relationship between unemployment and trade union membership in Belgium, Transfer, 12 (4), 647–657.

Vandaele K. (2016) Interpreting strike activity in western Europe in the past 20 years: the labour repertoire under pressure, Transfer, 22 (3), 277–294.

Vandaele K. (2019a) Belgium: stability on the surface, mounting tensions beneath, in Müller T., Vandaele K. and Waddington J. (eds) Collective bargaining in Europe: towards an endgame, Brussels, ETUI, 53–76.

Vandaele K. (2019b) Annexe: Les jours de grèves en 2018, in Gracos I., Grèves et conflictualité sociale en 2018 II. Conflits d'entreprise, Courrier hebdomadaire du CRISP 2424–2425, Bruxelles, Centre de recherche et d'information socio-politiques, 101–106.

Vandaele K. (2020a) Newcomers as potential drivers of union revitalization: survey evidence from Belgium, Relations Industrielles/Industrial Relations, 75 (2), 351–375.

Vandaele K. (2020b) From street protest to improvisational unionism: platform-based food-delivery couriers in Belgium and the Netherlands, Berlin, Friedrich-Ebert-Stiftung.

Vandaele K. (2021) Annexe: Les jours de grèves en 2020, in Gracos I., Grèves et conflictualité sociale en 2020 II. Conflits d'entreprise, Courrier hebdomadaire du CRISP 2513–2514, Bruxelles, Centre de recherche et d'information socio-politiques, 67–74.

Vandaele K. and Hooghe M. (2013) L'appel de la voie communautaire: syndicats, organisations patronales et nouveaux mouvements sociaux dans une Belgique redimensionnée, in Dandoy R., Matagne G. and Van Wynsberghe C. (eds) Le fédéralisme belge. Enjeux institutionnels, acteurs socio-politiques et opinions publiques, Louvain-la-Neuve, Academia-Bruylant, 139–176.

Vandekerckhove S. and Van Gyes G. (2012) Collective agreed wages in Belgium: indicators and trends, Background Paper European Policy Conference 'Collectively agreed wages in Europe: Challenges in the statistical and political field', 29 November 2012, Leuven, Onderzoeksinstituut voor Arbeid en Samenleving.

Van Gyes G., Van Herreweghe D., Smits I. and Vandekerckhove S. (2018) Opposites attract? Decentralisation tendencies in the most organised collective bargaining system in Europe: Belgium in the period 2012–2016, in Leonardi S. and Pedersini R. (eds) Multi-employer bargaining under pressure: decentralisation trends in five European countries, Brussels, ETUI, 67–103.

Van Gyes G. et al. (2021) Rapport over de resultaten van het sectoraal overleg in 2019–2020, Brussel, Federale overheidsdienst Werkgelegenheid, Arbeid en Sociaal Overleg, Algemene directie Collectieve Arbeidsbetrekkingen.

Vanhooren P. and Deceunynck J. (2005) Bedienden in beweging: een geschiedenis van de Landelijke bedienden centrale, Antwerpen, Gevaert.

Van Rie T., Marx I. and Horemans J. (2011) Ghent revisited: unemployment insurance and union membership in Belgium and the Nordic countries, European Journal of Industrial Relations, 17 (2), 125–139.

Vendramin P. (2007) Les jeunes, le travail et l'emploi – Enquête auprès des jeunes salariés de moins de 30 ans en Belgique francophone, Namur, Fondation Travail-Université/CSC.

Vercauteren G. (2007) In naam van de sociale vooruitgang: de rol van de overheid in het sociale overleg in België (1944–1981), Leuven, Acco.

Vilrokx J. and Van Leemput J. (1998) Belgium: the great transformation, in Ferner A. and Hyman R. (eds) Changing industrial relations in Europe, 2nd edn, Oxford, Blackwell, 315–347.

Visser J. (2019) Trade unions in the balance. ILO ACTRAV Working Paper, Geneva, ILO.

Weil D. (2014) The fissured workplace. Why work became so bad for so many and what can be done to improve it, Cambridge, Harvard University Press.

Western B. (1999) Between class and market: postwar unionization in the capitalist democracies, Princeton, Princeton University Press.

Willems E., Beyers J. and Heylen F. (2021) Interest representation in Belgium: mapping the size and diversity of interest group population in a multi-layered neocorporatist polity, Politics of the Low Countries, 3 (1), 32–72.

Zienkowski J. and De Cleen B. (2021) The polyphonic critique of trade unions: unpacking the logics of union critical discourse, Critical Discourse Studies, 8 (5), 519–537.

Abbreviations

Some organizations or institutions also have an official name in Belgium's third official language, German. These are omitted here for reasons of space.

ABVV/FGTB	Algemeen Belgisch Vakverbond/Fédération générale du travail de Belgique (General Federation of Belgian Labour)
AC/CG	Algemene Centrale/Centrale Générale (General Workers Union)
ACOD/CGSP	Algemene Centrale der Openbare Diensten/Centrale Générale des Services Publics (General Union of Public Services)

ACLVB/CGSLB	Algemene Centrale der Liberale Vakbonden van België/Centrale Générale des Syndicats Libéraux de Belgique (General Confederation of Liberal Trade Unions of Belgium)
ACV COC	Algemeen Christelijk Vakverbond Christelijke Onderwijscentrale (Christian Education Federation–Flemish)
ACV COV	Algemeen Christelijk Vakverbond Christelijk Onderwijzersverbond (Christian Union Federation of Teachers–Flemish)
ACV/CSC	Algemeen Christelijk Vakverbond/Confédération des syndicats chrétiens (Confederation of Christian Trade Unions)
BBTK/Setca	Bond van Bedienden, Technici en Kaderleden/ Syndicat des Employés, Techniciens et Cadres (Union of Clerical, Technical and Supervisory Staff of Belgium)
BTB/UBT	Belgische Transportbond/Union Belge du Transport (Belgian Union of Transport Workers)
CRB/CCE	Centrale Raad voor het Bedrijfsleven/Conseil central de l'économie (Central Economic Council)
CSC CCPET	Confédération des syndicats chrétiens Centrale chrétienne du personnel de l'enseignement (Christian Union of Staff in Technical Colleges–francophone)
CSC CEMNL	Confédération des syndicats chrétiens Centrale de l'enseignement moyen et normal libre (Christian Union Federation in Free Secondary and Primary Education–francophone)
CSC FIC	Confédération des syndicats chrétiens Fédération des instituteurs chrétiens (Christian Union Federation of Teachers–francophone)
CSC CNE	Confédération des syndicats chrétiens Centrale nationale des employés (National Union of Employees–francophone)

CSC UCEO	Confédération des syndicats chrétiens Union chrétienne des membres du personnel de l'enseignement officiel (Christian Union Federation of Staff in Public Education–francophone)
EU	European Union
EWCs	European Works Councils
FOD WASO/SPF ETCS	Federale Overheidsdienst Werkgelegenheid, Arbeid en Sociaal Overleg/Service public fédéral Emploi, Travail et Concertation sociale (Federal Public Service Employment, Labour and Social Dialogue)
HORVAL	Centrale van de Voeding, Horeca & Diensten/Centrale Alimentation, Horeca & Services (Union of Workers in Food Production, Hotels and Services)
HVW/CAPAC	Hulpkas voor werkloosheidsuitkeringen/Caisse auxiliaire de Paiement des Allocations de Chômage (Branch Office for Unemployment Benefits)
IPA / AIP	interprofessioneel akkoord/accord interprofessional (interprofessional agreement)
NAR/CNT	Nationale Arbeidsraad/Conseil national du travail (National Labour Council)
NCK/CNC	Nationale Confederatie van het Kaderpersoneel/Confédération nationale des cadres (National Confederation of Staff)
N-VA	Nieuw-Vlaamse Alliantie (New Flemish Alliance)
TKD/TVD	Centrale voor Textiel, Kleding en Diamant/ Centrale du Textile, Vêtement et Diament (Textiles-Clothing-Diamant)

Chapter 4

Bulgaria: Trade unions establishing legitimacy through institution-building and the usages of 'Europe'

Slavina Spasova

Since 1989, there have been two trade union confederations in Bulgaria: the Confederation of Independent Trade Unions of Bulgaria (CITUB, Конфедерация на независимите синдикати в България) and the Confederation of Labour Podkrepa (CL Podkrepa, КТ 'Подкрепа').[1] CITUB was established in February 1990: it is the successor to the trade union organization that existed under the communist regime. CL Podkrepa was a political movement, established in 1989 by dissidents opposed to the former regime. It was registered as a union confederation because the Bulgarian constitution of the time was less rigid about the possibility of establishing such an organization. Today there are no ideological or significant differences between the two confederations in terms of strategy or presence in industries.

Modern, democratic trade unionism in Bulgaria has developed from two starting points. First, opposition to the communist past on the part of CL Podkrepa, and a strong commitment to reform on the part of CITUB; and second, robust conflict with the government over representation and the function of social dialogue. The Bulgarian transition process during the 1990s differed from most other countries in Central

---

1 This chapter contains more information on CITUB than on KT Podkrepa, as CITUB is the largest confederation in Bulgaria, undertakes more initiatives and has been the subject of more research. Moreover, CITUB runs the Institute for Social and Trade Union Research (ISTUR), which provides information and publications on the activities of the confederation.

and Eastern Europe (CEE). Privatization and restructuring were implemented relatively late because of several stop-and-go reforms in a context of political and economic instability. In 1997 this situation led to the introduction of a currency board by the International Monetary Fund (IMF), which is still in place and has had a significant impact on the trade unions' room for manoeuvre (Gradev 2001). The currency board has also affected social dialogue, often assessed as 'a tool for a more equitable distribution of the negative effects of the reforms rather than a process in which everyone wins' (Tomev 2017: 23). The government accepted 'market radicalism' (Bohle and Greskovits 2012: 221), not because of an outright pursuit of a neoliberal agenda but mainly because of the general weakness of institutions and the state. In this context, the two confederations have sought mainly to legitimize and maintain their role in the political and industrial relations system, primarily through institution-building, often using foreign resources, most of which originate from within the European Union (EU) (Spasova 2015). This strategy has been only partly successful: union density and collective bargaining coverage have remained relatively stable in the past decade (2010–2020), although there has been a fall in membership in the previous decades (1989–2010), largely because of the restructuring and privatization of the economy in the 1990s and 2000s (see Table 4.1).

Table 4.1 Principal characteristics of trade unionism in Bulgaria

	1991	2000	2019
Total trade union membership	2,681,000	652,000	407,000
Women as a proportion of total membership	n.a.	50 %[a]	n.a.
Gross union density	n.a.	27 %	15 %
Net union density	n.a.	27 %	15 %
Number of confederations	2	2	2
Number of affiliated unions (federations)	78 (only CITUB)	n.a.	62
Number of independent unions	n.a.	n.a.	n.a.
Collective bargaining coverage	n.a.	45 %	23 %[b]
Principal level of collective bargaining		Company	
Days not worked because of industrial action per 1,000 workers	n.a.	n.a.	n.a.

Notes: [a] 2003; [b] 2018.

Source: Appendix A1; Kirov (2005, 2019); NIPA (2021).

Historical background and principal features of the industrial relations system

During the communist period (1945–1989) Bulgarian unions were built on the model of the Soviet trade unions, to serve as a 'transmission belt' for Communist Party ideology. The communist period, however, is only a part – although an essential one – of path-dependent union development after 1989, which stems from two main historical characteristics of the Bulgarian union movement before communist times.

The first characteristic, linked to an inherent feature of the context of early Bulgarian unionism, is the reliance on foreign support and the pervasiveness of foreign ideas, models and ideologies throughout union history.[2] The second characteristic of Bulgarian unions throughout their history is the particular link with the state. There were only very brief periods before 1989 when democratic unionism existed in Bulgaria and the many unions founded during the interwar period were mainly 'yellow' unions that were 'incorporated' into the state and served government interests and territorial expansion (Launey 1990). 'Incorporation' into the communist-led state was also the main characteristic of unionism during the period 1945–1989. The unions' main function was to provide services and benefits for workers, such as food vouchers, work equipment and the organization of holidays. Core union activities, such as collective bargaining, industrial conflict and workers' representation, did not exist (Pavlov 1991).

The significant foreign influence and unions' use of foreign resources and networks, as well as (conflictual) relations with the government in the context of building tripartism, have remained among the most important features of modern Bulgarian union history since the fall of the communist regime in 1989. This was visible first in the creation of the two confederations, CITUB and KT Podkrepa. The transformation of CITUB occurred mainly because of the organizational structure and expertise it inherited from the communist unions, but also the reformist vision and international academic and unions network of its first president Krastyo

---

[2] The very first Bulgarian unions were created in a particular economic context. Bulgaria, which became an independent state in 1879, emerged from the Ottoman Empire, characterized by a rural and feudal economy. Only 5 per cent of its population worked in crafts or trade – this was not a strong enough foundation for the development of industrial action (Kaloara 1973).

Petkov (Spasova 2015). Expertise has indeed been crucial for CITUB's survival and transformation. In this respect, it is important to note that, since 1989, CITUB's Institute for Social and Trade Union Research (ISTUR) has played a crucial role in providing expertise on industrial relations and social policies, not only for the union but in Bulgaria more generally. ISTUR is also one of the most active trade union research institutes in CEE (Kirov 2015; Spasova et al. 2020). CL Podkrepa was originally more of a political and civic movement. It was one of the founding members of the Union of Democratic Forces (UDF, Съюз на демократичните сили), the largest liberal political party in opposition – in a bipartisan political system up until 2001 – to the Bulgarian Socialist Party (BSP, Българска Социалистическа Партия), which is the reformed Bulgarian Communist Party. CL Podkrepa's main purpose in the beginning was to influence the political replacement of managers of state-owned companies in an economic system that remained largely state-owned until 1997. Its transformation as a trade union was significantly supported by ideological and financial support from the American Federation of Labor–Congress of Industrial Organizations (AFL-CIO) and its Solidarity Centre (Spasova 2015).

During the 1990s, the restructuring of the industrial relations system took place in a general context of political instability, delays in economic restructuring and privatization, and 'shadow economic conglomerates', which operated in the grey area between the state and the private sector, leading to the mafia infiltration of the economy (Dimitrov 2001). In this context, the Bulgarian situation differed considerably from that of other CEE countries and emerged as a 'weak state' (Bohle and Greskovits 2012). Thus, until the privatization process started in 1997, industrial relations were strongly politicized, and conflicts were related to changes of management in public companies, which superseded everything else in industrial relations (CITUB 1993).

In this context, the trade unions were the main protagonists promoting tripartite social dialogue. They were the main instigators of social dialogue–based institution-building, a process that they perceived as guaranteeing their legitimacy. The salience of foreign assistance was also essential in this process and more generally in the setting up of a new structure of industrial relations, mainly by the ILO, which coupled its tripartite 'philosophy' with the deployment of considerable technical assistance. The two trade union organizations were the main actors advocating the creation of such institutions to ensure their role in state-level decision-making (Spasova 2015). In their endeavours, they made successful use of a constellation of personal foreign union contacts of the presidents of the two confederations.[3]

The introduction of a currency board in 1997 gave the IMF a prominent role in the tripartite system, which de facto became 'quadripartite' (Gradev 2001). The content of social dialogue was constrained by the limitations of the board, especially regarding wages. Unions accepted a role as guardians of 'social peace'[4] in a context of macroeconomic restrictions, on condition that they would be consulted in the areas that directly concerned their members. The 'Stabilization Agreement' of 1997, signed by the government and the IMF, took into account EU accession criteria and requirements. It also reflected discussions with the 'social partners' on the agreement's degree of conformity with the European Social Model, which the two confederations used as a template for their role in decision-making (Spasova 2015).

After the simmering politicization of industrial relations during the first years of the transition, until 1997, the relationship between trade union confederations and party politics faded away. Since then there has been no link between the declared political orientation of governments and the development and efficacy of social dialogue (Detchev et al. 2005). This is because of two factors. First, until 1997 there was no real privatization, and large enterprises were still state-owned. Second, almost all the governments during the 1990s implemented anti-union policies, presenting the unions as the main obstacles to the establishment of a market economy and hindering the functioning of tripartite structures. Governments used tripartite institutions to legitimize their own position, and not to resolve social conflicts or allow the social partners to be involved in privatization (Iankova 2002). The deteriorating relationships with political parties and governments also led to the breaking away of some affiliated unions from both confederations. The context of the 1990s determined the fate of the unions for the next 20 years, during which unions continued to struggle for recognition and to build institutions in a context of government hostility by mobilizing foreign support.

---

3 A significant role was played by the International Confederation of Free Trade Unions (ICFTU), the ETUC, AFL-CIO, Force Ouvrière (FO) from France, and the Fédération Générale du Travail de Belgique (FGTB).

4 This also includes 'ethnic peace', given the significant Turkish minority in Bulgaria and the war in the former Yugoslavia.

Political relations

Trade union political relations since 1997 have been characterized by two main, interlinked features: conflict with the government over the legal criteria for union representativeness for participating in social dialogue at national level, and the struggle for a well-functioning social dialogue.

The issue of representativeness in national level social dialogue became salient in 1996–1997, during the economic crisis, when the government authorized the participation of several breakaway unions in the National Council for Tripartite Cooperation (NCTC, Национален съвет за тристранно сътрудничество). Both confederations made salient use of their international contacts, which became involved in the conflict to defend the functioning of the tripartite institutions. Following this conflict, the legal criteria for union representativeness were enshrined in the revised Labour Code (Кодекс на труда) in 2001, not least because of international pressure, as well as the favourable attitude of Labour Minister Neykov, former vice-president of CITUB (Spasova 2015). Soon afterwards, despite the existence of representativeness criteria, the Simeon II government (2005–2009) authorized another organization, supportive of government policies, to participate in the tripartite institutions. This exacerbated the conflicts between the unions and government. Again, as in 1996–1997, the two confederations called on the European and international union movement to support them in this struggle (Spasova 2015). This situation resulted in further legal changes and was the last episode of political non-compliance with the representativeness criteria. Since 1998, the census of union membership has shown that CITUB and CL Podkrepa are the only organizations fulfilling the relevant criteria and thus recognized as nationally representative.

While the criteria for a trade union confederation to be nationally representative have changed over the years, they are as follows in 2021: (i) to have at least 50,000 individual members; (ii) to have workplace unions in at least one-quarter of the activities in the Classification of Economic Activities, with members numbering no less than 5 per cent of employees in each economic activity or at least fifty union organizations with no fewer than five members in each economic activity; (iii) to have regional organizations in more than a quarter of the municipalities in the country and a national governing body; and (iv) to be recognized as a legal entity at least three years before the submission of the request for recognition of representativeness.

The second line of conflict between unions and government has been the struggle over the meaningful functioning of social dialogue. The two trade union confederations have been the main actors pushing for social dialogue institution-building at all levels. They have made significant use of the ILO 'tripartite paradigm' and their international contacts in the European and international union movement. After the privatization process was launched, coupled to the progress of Bulgaria towards EU accession, the main paradigm became the EU's insistence on developing social dialogue at all levels, and especially bipartite social dialogue, which was still very new at the beginning of 2000, during the early days of privatization. Both confederations and employers' associations embraced the social dialogue paradigm and their role as 'social partners', and strove to make them work (Spasova 2015). Even employers' associations stressed that until 2000 the social partners were 'in the grip of the state' and that only during the accession process and with considerable pressure from the EU could the unions and employers negotiate autonomously outside the government's 'clutches' (Spasova and Tomini 2013).

As during the previous decade, in the 2010s, there were several turbulent periods for social dialogue at national level, with either the union confederations or the employers leaving the NCTC for several months, especially regarding stop/go reforms, ongoing for more than a decade, such as those in the healthcare and pension systems. Conflict between unions and government was salient especially in 2008 at the beginning of the Great Recession, when the unions opposed the government's measures (Spasova and Tomini 2013; Tomev 2017). There was some improvement in 2010–2011 through the creation of a standing working group on improving social dialogue and the involvement of the union confederations and employers in anti-crisis decision-making. The government conducted tripartite negotiations in 'hard times' to maximize its popularity and guarantee its re-election by demonstrating loyalty to a consensual mode of policymaking. This period is described as 'PR corporatism', although it failed to enhance the quality of social dialogue (Bernaciak 2013). Indeed, the period that followed, between 2013 and 2017, was characterized by political instability, as the unions instigated several protests, mainly because of the government's austerity measures, enshrined in the so-called Financial Stability Pact of 2011 (Tomev 2017: 26).

The recurrent conflictual situation in tripartism was at least slightly counterbalanced by the development of bipartite national dialogue. It was only after EU accession in 2007 that favourable conditions were created for the development of autonomous bipartite dialogue (Tomev et al. 2008). The first bilateral agreement on the indexation of wage growth in the private sector was signed in 2007, which led to an increase in the average wage (Detchev 2007; Tomev 2017). Back then, these first bipartite agreements were considered to be an important step towards autonomous bipartite dialogue and a success for the unions, which had been striving for it for years, brandishing the EU recommendations during the accession process (Spasova 2015; Tomev et al. 2008). The first bipartite agreements were seen as having restored hope that social dialogue in Bulgaria could achieve more than just safeguarding 'social peace' (Detchev 2007). Moreover, in the context of the political instability during the period 2013–2017 unions and employers continued to conclude bipartite agreements, several of which were linked to European instruments and international agreements (EU and ILO). Nevertheless, relations between the unions and the employers, which were cooperative at the beginning of the crisis, deteriorated in 2016 when the employers refused to negotiate a National Agreement on Violence and Stress in the Workplace (a draft of which was prepared by the unions in 2012 as a result of the European Social Dialogue on the issue), the so-called 'minimum insurance income' in 2016 (MII, see below) (Tomev 2017), as well as the increase in the statutory minimum wage (Kahancová and Kirov 2021; Tomev et al. 2019).

Despite the frequent struggles in the NCTC, mainly between the government and the social partners, there have also been periods of smooth collaboration. Social dialogue persists and has never been called into question. This is exactly what the unions have been struggling for: in a context of political instability that has shaken the Bulgarian state, to continue to reinforce the social dialogue institutions which are among the guarantees of their existence. For instance, in recent years, some important decisions have resulted in structural improvements to social dialogue being enshrined in the Labour Code in 2015 and 2020 (Labour Code 2021, CITUB 2020). During the Covid-19 pandemic, both confederations have been very active with jointly proposal measures and a whole package of measures was developed in collaboration with them within the NCTC (Eurofound 2021).

Structure of trade unions and union democracy

Both CITUB and CL Podkrepa are made up of national union federations. These union federations are the main affiliates of the confederations and, in general, cover an industry in the public or private sector. The confederal level is responsible for the organization's overall strategic orientation, and the affiliated federations are fairly autonomous in defining their priorities and strategies. CITUB and CL Podkrepa are the only representative confederations at the industrial and cross-industry level. The two confederations also have a local base, with 'regional representations' in almost all administrative regions. These regional unions bring together all the union sections in the territory of the respective region. They have administrative and legal staff who help the affiliated organizations in their work. There are some very small workplace unions which are not affiliated to one of the two main union confederations, but there is no data on their prevalence or functioning. There have been no mergers in the modern history of Bulgarian trade unions.

There is some fragmentation in CITUB, with parallel federations in certain industries (Kirov 2015). The duplication in CITUB of affiliates within the same economic activity, such as food and beverages, transport and education, is the result of historical factors and interpersonal conflicts. As soon as independence from the Communist Party was proclaimed, the confederation began a profound reorganization of its industrial structures. In just a few months, between December 1989 (fall of the communist regime) and the first months of 1990, the number of federations grew from fourteen to seventy-eight, and finally ended up at thirty-five in the 2010s (Petkov 2011). There were three reasons for this fragmentation. First, with union democratization the new leaders allowed the splitting up of former large federations that grouped together several industries, often in competition with each other, in order to facilitate decentralization and to give more power to grassroots organizations. Second, to prevent workers with different political visions leaving for CL Podkrepa at the beginning of the transition process, the union leadership allowed duplication or even triplication of federations in the same industry. Third, there were leadership conflicts: the former state company managers wanted to safeguard their power in a changing context and tried to use unions to this end (Petkov 2011; Spasova 2015).

Both confederations have similar collective governing bodies. From the outset, the leaders of the confederations wanted to develop a balance of power between the affiliated federations and the confederal level (Spasova 2015). The affiliates are represented in various confederation governing bodies. Confederation leaderships are elected by delegates appointed by the federations' decision-making bodies once every five years (CITUB) or four years (CL Podkrepa). The grassroots members do not directly elect the federation and confederation leaderships. Between congresses (Конгрес), both confederations are governed by a Coordinating Council (Координационен съвет), which includes the leaders of most federations and representatives of the associated members, which have an advisory vote. The Executive Council (Изпълнителен комитет), with representatives of the federations and regional unions, is a permanent governing body that organizes the confederation's general activities between the Confederal Councils. Clearly, these bodies are perceived by the federation leaders to be well-functioning and facilitate the democratic functioning of the various structures (Interview CITUB 23 March 2021; Spasova 2015).

CITUB has also been very active on gender issues. The latter became more visible over the period 2012–2017 through the work of the Commission for Equality, Family, Women and Children and the 'Public Women's Parliament 21st Century' at CITUB, which organizes frequent debates on the role of women. In general, there is a gender balance within the affiliates of the confederations (see Table 4.1), which is partly explained by the widespread union organizing in education and state administration, whose employees are predominantly women. As for the union decision-making bodies, 37 per cent of the members of CITUB's Executive Committee are women, as are 42 per cent of the presidents of union federations affiliated to CITUB (interview 23 March 2021). Nevertheless, no woman has yet been elected confederal secretary of CITUB. At CL Podkrepa, there has been an important change over the past ten years: the completely male confederal secretariat is now far more balanced, with two women and three men. Among the presidents of the affiliated federations 33 per cent are women.

The federations have a similar organizational structure to the confederations (Congress, Coordination Commission, Executive Committee). Their main activity is to negotiate collective agreements, sharing and defending their positions on socio-economic, labour and professional issues; to ensure socio-economic, labour and professional protection of union members; and to organize protests, demonstrations, and strikes. In general, the federation presidents are satisfied by relations with the confederation level; they feel effectively involved in the decision-making process and rely on support from staff at confederal level. Moreover, in most cases, the federation offices are located in the same building as those of the confederations, which makes contact much easier (Spasova 2015). CITUB also has as associate members small organizations seeking representation vis-à-vis the state in defence of some of their interests, as well as expertise. As these organizations do not pay a membership fee, they have only an advisory vote. In practice, associate members pay the confederation a fee based on a contract for the services they receive from the confederation (CITUB 2017). Over the years, in addition to its main affiliates, CITUB has accepted associate member unions, which represent a large range of interests, from craft, small 'entrepreneur unions' such as hairdressers and artists to civil society organizations, such as those representing disabled people and since 2019 a union representing the financial sector (CITUB 2022).

The main activity of workplace unions is to negotiate collective agreements and protect their members' labour rights. The workplace union is represented by a president and takes its decisions through a delegates' meeting. In general, they are not paid and do not have their own paid staff. Workplace leaders are generally satisfied with their relationship with the federation and regional levels and their access to them. They rely on the federation mainly for legal and expert support, as well as taking part in seminars and training organized by the federation and sometimes by the confederation (Spasova 2015).

Unionization

Union density in Bulgaria stood at 15.4 per cent in 2016, based on the most recent union census: CITUB affiliates have 271,312 members and CL Podkrepa affiliates 79,567 members (CITUB 2022). Density has declined markedly since 1989, but this baseline is not representative, as during the communist period almost all the workers were union members. The most important period to be considered is after 2000 when the privatization process started: over the period 2003–2016 union density decreased by 11 percentage points (Table 4.2). In both confederations, the highest membership figures are in the public sector, and, in particular, in education. The largest federation in CITUB is the Union of

Bulgarian Teachers (Синдикат на Българските учители) and similarly in CL Podkrepa it is the Teachers' Trade Union (Синдикат 'Образование'). Both represent 25 per cent of union membership in each confederation (Spasova 2015). The federations of both confederations accept pensioners, the unemployed, self-employed and students as members. CITUB recently changed its statutes (2017) to underline that it accepts 'forms of work in the digital economy'.

Table 4.2 Trade union membership and density, 1989–2016[a]

	1989	1995	1998	2003	2012	2016
CITUB	4 million	1 million	607,883	380,000	275,762	271,312
CL Podkrepa	*Year of foundation*	250,000	154,900	120,000	91,738	79,567
Union density	98 %	41 %	36 %	26 %	19–20 %	15 %

a The scheduled 2020 census was postponed because of the Covid-19 pandemic.

Source: Kirov (2005), CITUB (2022).

The rapid decline in membership during the 1990s was the result of three main factors. First, the process of restructuring and privatization led to a significant decline in employment, which fell by 31.5 percentage points between 1989 and 1993. Second, the industrial sector was particularly hard hit by a dramatic decline in workforce between 1989 and 1999: worker numbers halved in textiles, electronics and machinery. Finally, the spectacular growth of small and medium-sized enterprises caused a drop in union membership during the 1990s. In 2019 the proportion of micro-enterprises was 92.6 per cent (up to nine persons), with 'small' companies of between ten and forty-nine employees making up 6 per cent, and enterprises with more than fifty employees less than 3 per cent. No fewer than 56.5 per cent of the Bulgarian workforce is employed in micro- and small-enterprises (NSI 2021). The fragmentation of the Bulgarian economy into micro and small enterprises has been highlighted by the trade unions as one of the main hindrances to unionization, coupled with the significance of the informal economy, which represented 21 per cent of GDP in 2019, although it was considerably higher before 2016 (BICA 2020). In addition to the informal economy, anti-union actions and the negative attitudes towards unionization among some employers are highlighted as reasons for declining membership in recent years (Spasova 2015).

Over the past five years, the tobacco industry has been among those hardest hit by restructuring and redundancies. At the same time, CITUB points out that its own record for the past five years (2012–2017) is fairly positive, and the number of new members, including several in the public and cultural sectors, has made up for those that have left. For the first time, CITUB managed to halt its membership decline and even extended organization to previously non-unionized industries. Almost half of its affiliated federations recorded membership rises. Three new national trade unions were established and affiliated to CITUB during the period 2012–2017. Among the greatest successes is the unionization of part of the Information and Communications Technology (ICT) sector, which joined in 2016. The unions had been fighting for this for years and it represented a crucial step for the confederation, giving it a foothold in this area of services that comprises mainly young workers (Spasova 2015). Other federations were created in other sectors, including culture, national administration and fire services (CITUB 2017). Other recent affiliates of CL Podkrepa include priests and church employees, represented by the Trade Union of Sacred and Church Employees (Синдикат на свещено и църковни служители).

This success in halting membership decline can be attributed to the implementation of a unified confederal policy on unionization for 2012–2017. The confederation has developed an innovative approach based on a combination of organizing and servicing instruments. Organizing through targeting became vital: planning of the approach to be taken for each company had to become more individual and pragmatic (CITUB 2017; Tomev 2017). CITUB has provided the possibility of maintaining union membership during labour market transitions, for example, during periods of unemployment or training, or after retirement. Moreover, it has become possible for certain labour market groups, such as the self-employed, homeworkers, unemployed people, those with disabilities and workers in non-unionized companies, to join the union through the regional union organizations affiliated to CITUB. This was not previously. Finally, an extensive training programme was established on organizing and campaigning for union leaders, activists and experts at regional, industrial and company levels, conducted in cooperation with the Swiss union Unia. CITUB also created a database of companies, covering many details of ownership, connections, economic prospects, investment intentions and financial indicators (CITUB 2017). In addition to the usual methods of workplace unionization, both confederations also used broad public campaigning (2010–2020) in an effort to appeal as much as possible to young people. Some of these campaigns were conducted jointly by the two confederations, and some even with employers' associations, as these were often based on EU funding aimed at raising awareness of information and consultation rights. For instance, the national information and consultation campaign 'Be Info' was managed together with the Bulgarian Industrial Association (Българска индустриална асоциация). More than 200 companies were visited at which there were no trade unions, and information and consultation systems[5] were developed in 30 per cent of them. This campaign has been evaluated by the confederations as a positive example of cooperation with the employers (CITUB 2017; Interview CITUB 22 March 2021).

The provision of services has always been a priority and was inherited from the communist past. Both confederations and most federations provide a number of services, such as legal assistance, different kinds of funds for certain social risks, and training. Thus, CITUB has prioritized the improvement and development of new services in its unionization strategy since 2012, and the confederation launched an individual legal protection fund, a mutual assistance fund and a mutual life insurance scheme in 2014 (Tomev 2017). The mutual assistance fund grants financial assistance to their members up to an amount of BGN 3,000 (€1,533). CITUB also operates a legal protection fund, which provides support and legal representation from trusted CITUB lawyers, including an e-portal, on which several legal services can be accessed online (CITUB 2022). In April 2020, during the Covid-19 pandemic, CITUB launched an ad hoc assistance fund for members infected with the disease, who received a lump sum of at least BGN 150 (€75).

Union income and expenditure

The main source of income for the confederations, at both the confederal and federation level, are membership fees, followed by financing from national and European projects in which they become involved. In CITUB, the individual membership fee is set at 1 per cent of net monthly wages, 15 per cent of which is supposed to be transferred from the affiliated federation to the confederation. The workplace union transfers to

5 These are union-dominated. For more information, see section 'Collective bargaining and unions at the workplace'.

the federation a share that varies considerably by federation, but ranging between 15 and 70 per cent. In CL Podkrepa, the membership fee is set at minimum 0.7 per cent of net monthly wages, meaning that workplace organizations can set a fee above this threshold. Unlike CITUB, the statutes of CL Podkrepa precisely define the share which is transferred from the workplace union to the federation to which it is affiliated: 55 per cent. Of the amount received by the federation, not less than 10 per cent is allocated to a strike fund (Statutes CL Podkrepa).

Revenues from fees have been decreasing over recent years because of declining membership, officially reported low wages in some industries, non-payment or delays of wages, or organizational problems (Kirov 2005). Thus, there has been a progressive diversification of the sources of union finance. European and national projects have become a second main source of income at confederal and federation level. For example, funding from projects had increased from 2 per cent of overall revenues in 1998 to 26 per cent by 2000, at the beginning of the EU accession process (Kirov 2005). Union leaders stress the importance of these projects in a context in which no public subsidies are allocated to the confederations. The leaders often compare this situation to that of certain other EU Member States in which unions do receive public subsidies, at least indirectly (Spasova 2015).

Other sources of income at confederation and federation level include real estate,[6] but this is not particularly significant; income from economic activity, such as consultancy; printing activities; occasionally, social recreation and tourism;[7] and donations (Statutes CITUB; Statutes CL Podkrepa; Interview 22 March 2021). At the end of the 1990s, both confederations also participated actively in privatization schemes, through management–employee buy-outs (MEBO), which also served as a source of income (Iankova 2002). In addition, with the establishment of the three-pillar pension system in the early 2000s, the confederations became involved in private pension funds. CITUB participated in the establishment of the private pension insurance company 'Doverie' (Spasova 2013).

---

6 The exact share of this funding is not publicly available.

7 The law allows non-profit organizations to engage in commercial activity only with a view to supporting their own activity, with no redistribution of profit. The proceeds are used by trade unions to organize seminars and business trips, as well as recreation activities, such as tourism.

Collective bargaining and unions at the workplace

The modalities of collective bargaining are enshrined in the Labour Code (2001). Negotiations take place and collective agreements are concluded at enterprise, industry and municipal levels. The main level of bargaining is the company level. Collective bargaining can take place only between trade unions and employers and their representatives. At the industry level, unions and employers' associations[8] have to be affiliates of the respective national umbrella organizations. At enterprise level, however, other unions that are not members of the national representative organizations can also take part in collective bargaining. In fact, this possibility is only rarely used, as only a few unions are not members of CITUB or CL Podkrepa. These few unions seem in general to be opposed to the two confederations and consider that workers should be covered by collective agreements without paying a fee to the unions that concluded the agreement (Interview 22 March 2020).

Freeriding is not really possible, because, under the Labour Code (2001), there is a procedure that allows employees who are not union members to join the collective agreement. In general, non-unionized employees must pay a fee, which may be a share of their gross wages or a set amount, usually[9] to a union organization that is a signatory to an agreement, in order to benefit from this agreement (Kirov 2019). Data for 2018 show that 90.6 per cent of all collective agreements included a procedure for coverage of non-unionized workers (NIPA 2019).

In general, in enterprises in which collective agreements exist, 92 per cent of workers were covered (NIPA 2021). Since the promulgation of the new Labour Code in 2001, collective agreements at industry level can be extended to all enterprises in the industry, under certain conditions, but this possibility was rarely used. Employers were opposed to this procedure as it extends rights to an entire sector (Kirov 2019). Because of privatization, restructuring and the fall in union density in the ten years between 2002 and 2012 collective bargaining coverage decreased by 11 percentage points (Kirov 2019). In total, 12,728 collective agreements

---

8 There have been several changes in the structure and number of employers' organizations in Bulgaria. In 2021, there were five nationally representative employers' organizations.

9 The fee can be also paid to an enterprise fund called 'Social, welfare and cultural services for employees'.

were concluded over the period 2010–2018 (NIPA 2021), with an average national coverage rate of 28 per cent. During the same period, the main level of bargaining remained the company, accounting for 96.5 per cent of the agreements signed; followed by agreements at municipal level, with 2.5 per cent, and finally, at the industrial level, with 1 per cent. The number of collective agreements at company level has been falling slightly since 2010, from a peak of 1,707 agreements in 2012 (because of the anti-crisis agreements) to 1,130 agreements in 2018. It remains stable overall, however (see Figure 4.1). For the period 2011–2018 the average coverage at company level was 14.5 per cent, with 13.8 per cent in 2018 (NIPA 2021). At industry level the average coverage of concluded agreements was 13 per cent for the period 2010–2018.

Figure 4.1 Number of collective agreements at company level, 2000–2018

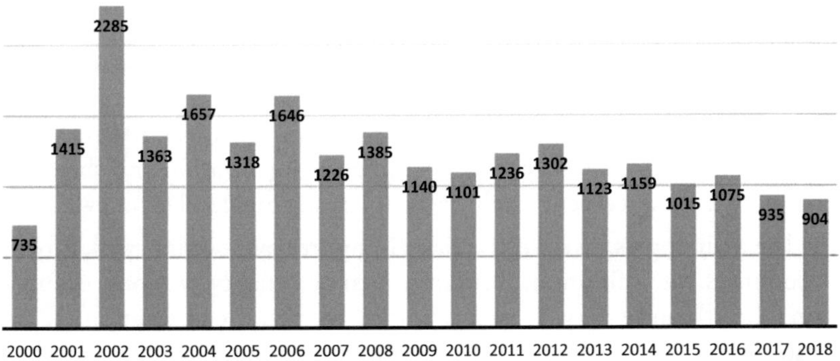

Note: Excluding annexes.
Source: Author's calculations based upon NIPA (2019, 2021) and personal communication with the Bulgarian Labour Inspectorate (March 2021).

There is a clear association between the number of agreements and unionization in the public sector. In 2018, 84.9 per cent of all agreements were concluded in the public sector and 15.1 per cent in the private sector. Collective bargaining coverage in the public and private sectors is 39.7 and 6.5 per cent, respectively (NIPA 2019). The association is even clearer if one looks into the different industries: for the period 2010–2018, 45 per cent of all collective agreements were signed in education, followed by health care (15 per cent) and manufacturing (8.4 per cent). During the period 2011–2018, collective bargaining coverage was highest in education at 33 per cent, where union density is highest (NIPA 2021). Coverage in education is followed by civil servants at 31 per cent and health care at 27.2 per cent, while 'industry'[10] is at 16.8 per cent. A recent survey conducted by the Union of Bulgarian Teachers (Синдикат на българските учители), affiliated to CITUB, shows that 93 per cent of the clauses in the collective agreements at industry and workplace level in education are respected (interview CITUB 23 March 2021). Within private industry the highest coverage is in mining and quarrying (67.7 per cent), the 'production and distribution of electricity and heat' (62.2 percent) and in 'water supply' (46.5 per cent).

Although the figure has remained stable since 2010, the number of collective agreements concluded since the 2000s has decreased for a number of reasons: the mass privatization process which started in 1997 and continued into the 2000s; the subsequent fall in union density; the fragmentation of employers into six organizations and the lack of organization of employers in some industries; the predominance of micro-enterprises in the economy, as well as the size of the informal economy. Moreover, in some cases, employers oppose the creation of unions at the workplace or refuse to conduct negotiations (Spasova 2015). Many employers are not members of any employer organization and therefore do not observe agreements at the industry or sectoral level (Tomev 2017).

The main topics for collective bargaining are wage-setting, with a focus on bonuses, the minimum insurance income, quality of work, occupational health and safety, as well as information and consultation (Kirov 2019; NIPA 2019). Wage-setting has never been successfully established as a bargaining topic. In 2018, only 31.1 per cent of agreements set a negotiated minimum wage for the enterprise higher than the statutory minimum wage. Regarding individual industries, the most successful collective agreements regarding wage-setting are again in education: 47.6 per cent of all agreements were negotiated in the sector (NIPA 2019). In general, when it comes to remuneration, collective agreements have provisions on higher additional payments in respect of working conditions, night work, overtime, different types of bonuses, length of service, rather

---

[10] In Bulgaria, economic activity is classified in seven categories: (1) agriculture, forestry and fishing; (2) industry; (3) trade, transport, tourism and services; (4) government; (5) education; (6) health care; (7) culture and others. We use this classification as provided in NIPA statistics. Thus, the category 'Industry' comprises all activities (such as manufacturing, mining and quarrying) not included in the previous categories.

than wage increases. These features reflect a visible trend towards achieving greater flexibility and individualization in determining employees' individual wages (CITUB 2017; Tomev 2017).

Another important topic of collective bargaining, especially important for the trade unions, is bargaining on the MII, which is used as a basis for calculating the minimum social security contributions for the nine professional categories for each economic activity. If the social partners at industry level do not reach agreement on the MII, the standards are established by the Ministry of Labour and Social Policy (Tomev 2017). Industry-level collective agreements have not been able to provide sufficient mechanisms for wage increases, although they are a very important means of improving some legal standards. They do not ensure actual income growth in line with inflation and labour productivity, however. The currency board system has also restricted autonomous bargaining and social dialogue (Kirov 2019; Tomev et al. 2008).

Work councils are not strongly present in companies, partly because of implicit opposition from the trade union confederations (Kirov 2019) to the transposition of the four EU directives on information, consultation and workers' participation in companies during the Bulgarian accession process (Spasova 2015). This implicit reluctance should be seen against the backdrop of years of struggle with different governments to develop legal criteria on trade union representativeness. Between 2003 and 2006, the European Commission (EC) insisted on the urgent need to adopt the law transposing the directives (Spasova 2015). The main union arguments were that there were no clear rules in the Labour Code that would allow this EU requirement to be accepted. The two confederations had also observed the situation in other CEE countries, where several governments proposed laws that sought to replace union prerogatives in companies. In the end, only Bulgaria and Estonia introduced 'double representation' by unions and works councils (Meardi 2012). A separate law on works councils was adopted in 2006, which allows for a 'transfer of competences', meaning that the general assembly of employees, or the assembly of elected delegates with the same functions, can decide to give these new rights to the existing union organizations at the workplace, or to existing employee representatives elected to represent employees' social and economic interests. In most cases, these delegates are union representatives. Thus, in practice, through the 'transfer of competences' mechanism introduced in the legislation, unions remain the only channel of representation in most companies (Spasova 2015).

Industrial conflict

The right to strike has existed in Bulgaria since 1993.[11] Nevertheless, civil servants were not entitled to go on strike. It is only since 2016, after years of negotiations, that civil servants, with some exceptions, have obtained the right to strike under specific conditions. In 2006, budgetary restructuring in the public sphere and new laws on the status of civil servants led to social tensions. The government refused to extend the right to strike to the public sector, and to repeal its ban on strikes in health care, energy and telecommunications, and for public sector employees. In this context, CITUB and CL Podkrepa again looked for foreign support, and with the help of the European Trade Union Confederation (ETUC) jointly lodged a complaint with the Social Rights Committee of the Council of Europe. Following this action, the Law on the Regulation of Collective Conflicts at Work was amended and the right to strike was established in health care, energy and telecommunications. Civil servants were given the right to strike only ten years later, in 2016. The different forms that industrial action can take in Bulgaria are enshrined in the Labour Code (2001): direct negotiations between the parties, mediation or arbitration, or both, a symbolic strike, a warning strike lasting an hour, and strikes proper, for which the union should provide a written warning at least seven days in advance (NIPA 2015b).

Table 4.3 Strikes and labour disputes, 2011– 2019

	2011	2012	2013	2014*	2015	2016	2017	2018	2019
Strike frequency	4	5	14	2	4	1	3	0	0
Days not worked because of industrial action per 1,000 employees	5	6	18	<1	1	<1	<1	0	0
Collective labour disputes	16	24	51	47	24	25	13	9	7

Note: * Information available only for the first four months regarding days not worked.

Source: Author's elaboration based on NIPA (2015b, 2021).

[11] The Communist regime banned strikes.

Industrial action and particularly strikes were frequent in the economically and socially turbulent period 1989–1997. Afterwards, strike activity became far less frequent. In the period 1997–2001, during the first years of the currency board, strikes declined significantly because of political and economic stabilization and the improvement of tripartite social dialogue (Kirov 2005). Very clearly in the first years of CITUB, the leadership stance, enshrined in policy programmes, was that workers should first be protected through legislation, meaning that CITUB was committed to building up laws and institutions to maintain social peace, seeing strikes as only a very last resort (Spasova 2015).

Among the memorable strikes of the 2000s were the teachers' strike for better pay and working conditions in 2007, which lasted forty-two days and whose demands were met, as well as the railway workers' strike for unpaid salaries over several months in 2009. After 2011, most labour disputes, including strikes, took place during the crisis years 2012–2014. The number has fallen steeply since then (Table 4.3). Since 2015, the main reasons for strikes have been failure to conclude a collective agreement (50 per cent), followed by non-compliance with an agreement (23 per cent) and refusal to bargain (13 per cent) (NIPA 2015b, 2021). The main reasons for collective labour disputes since 2015 include restructuring and redundancies, health and safety conditions at work, changes in pay rates, non-payment of 'extra payments or bonuses' rather than unpaid wages (NIPA 2021). Both confederations provide strike benefits.

In general, however, strikes are rare and used by unions as a last resort, although they do often organize national protests. During the economic crisis years of 2010–2014, the unions led several national protests, mainly related to the successive pension reforms and the anti-crisis austerity measures. For instance, the tripartite National Agreement on Pension Reform in 2010 was signed following strong pressure through protests from the two confederations. (Tomev 2017). In 2015, in an event unprecedented in Bulgaria, the employers' organizations organized a national protest against a planned increase in electricity prices for businesses. It was supported by the unions, which argued that the new financial burdens could lead to company bankruptcies, dismissals and cuts in workers' wages and social benefits (Tomev 2017).

Societal power

Bulgarian union confederations always emphasize their importance not only as workers' organizations, but also as broader organizations playing an important role in 'civil society'. For instance, the president of CITUB often underlines that it is the largest 'non-governmental/public organization' in Bulgaria. This discourse should be understood in connection with the recurrent struggles with the government over the past thirty years. The main channel for interaction with civil society is the Economic and Social Council of Bulgaria (ESC, Икономическия и социален съвет). The ESC is an independent consultative body, funded by the state budget, which includes representatives of the union confederations, employers' associations and NGOs, and is a forum for consultation on economic and social policies (ESC 2022). The idea of creating such a body in Bulgaria, in addition to the NCTC, emerged at the end of the first Social Dialogue programme funded by the European PHARE programme (1993–1998). Both sides of industry, and particularly the union confederations, pushed for the creation of such an institution at the end of 1998, in the context of the debate on representativeness. They wished to create a space for participation free from state influence. Another important factor was the legitimacy of the two confederations among the 'various interests' in civil society: both confederations also have associate members, which are not trade unions (Spasova 2015).

Both confederations actively work with NGOs in networking and alliances, as well as with local authorities and academic organizations in long-term joint projects representing common interests. In 2014, CITUB, together with CL Podkrepa and seventeen NGOs, formed a 'National Semester Alliance' as part of the 'EU Alliance: For a Democratic, Social and Sustainable European Semester' to improve their involvement and impact on the European Semester process. The confederations are satisfied with this cooperation, particularly because it was already taking place with many of these NGOs in the Economic and Social Council (Tomev et al. 2019). CITUB has been especially active in establishing CITUB-related civic and charity associations. Another major channel for participation in civil society are the youth organizations of the two confederations, which are also very active in this context. The CITUB youth organization established in 1999, the NGO 'Youth Forum 21st Century' ('MF 21 century'), is among the most active in Bulgaria.

One of the most important areas of activity has always been communication with the media. Since the early days, trade union leaders have tried to maintain a presence in the media. This approach has significantly boosted CITUB's public presence. According to the confederation, these expanded media activities and the use of modern communication channels have been quite successful (CITUB 2017). Both confederations also try to be active on social media and in 2015 CITUB launched an internet platform, 'Electronic Trade Union CITUB', which, according to the organization, makes it possible to reach workers not only through the 'factory gates' but also through 'the computer monitor in their homes' (Tomev 2017).

Trade union policies towards the European Union

While CITUB and CL Podkrepa have expressed strong criticisms of certain EU policies, especially those linked to austerity during the 2008 crisis and, more recently, to the Green Deal, they have always had a positive and proactive attitude towards 'Europe', both EU institutions and ETUC (Kirov 2005; Spasova 2015). The EU has been seen as the guarantor of the rule of law in a 'weak state', and especially as a means of fostering the creation of social dialogue institutions. During the years of EU accession both confederations saw themselves as 'watchdogs', monitoring state compliance with EU rules during the accession process (Kirov 2005; Spasova 2015). EU accession was particularly important in curbing ultra economic-liberal measures, shifting the accent to the importance of social partnership and social dialogue, promoting the regulatory fight against certain criminal economic practices, and providing technical assistance to improve the administrative and political efficiency of the state (Bohle and Greskovits 2012). Thus, 'Europe' can be seen as a generic term in the confederations' attitudes and practices, a broad paradigm that includes, depending on the specific discourse and policies or situations, three elements: the ETUC, the EU, and a broader vision of Europe as a civilizing influence (Spasova 2015).

The confederations have made considerable use of Europe's political, legal and financial resources to help transform their organizations and to fight for their legitimacy vis-à-vis often hostile governments. First, the transformation of CITUB and the creation of CL Podkrepa were broadly related to the international socialization of pro-European intellectual union elites. Second, references to Europe have been crucial in power struggles with the government, especially during the accession process, incorporating European standards and practices, and constructing new institutions to maintain union legitimacy and participation in the decision-making process, such as the establishment of autonomous bipartite dialogue, the creation of ESC and the right to strike. References to 'Europe' have been firmly present in union programmes since 1991. Particularly during the accession period, several unions' documents (including dedicated chapters in their programmes) and resolutions discussed the issues at stake, linked mainly to the transposition of the EU *acquis* in the social area and the importance of cooperation with ETUC. There was only one area of the social *acquis*, information and consultation, with regard to which the confederations were implicitly reluctant to push for quick transposition, and where the *acquis* was perceived as a constraint rather than an opportunity. Participation in European projects is also significant for the funding of confederations and federations. Some federation experts specialize only in the drafting of European projects (Spasova 2015). ISTUR's expertise has also further developed as a result of their close involvement in projects at European level (Tomev et al. 2019). Recently the Bulgarian unions have been quite active regarding the idea of pushing for an EU directive linked to collective bargaining (Interview CITUB 22 March 2021).

As for the participation of Bulgarian unions in European Works Councils (EWCs), only a few companies have representatives in EWCs, which are relatively new. Before Bulgaria's EU accession in 2007 Bulgarian worker representatives had the status of observers. CITUB is the most active in the domain of EWCs. It initiated a network of union leaders in multi-national corporations, together with various projects to prepare and integrate Bulgarian representatives into EWCs (Kirov 2015). Regarding participation in, and relations with, European trade union federations, almost all the Bulgarian federations are affiliated to them. Leaders generally express satisfaction with this, mainly with the training, common actions and projects in which they are involved thanks to these organizations (Spasova 2015).

Unions have also been involved in transactional campaigning and cross-border cooperation, especially regarding Bulgarian workers in EU countries. An interregional council representing workers in Bulgaria and Romania has been set up by CITUB and the National Confederation of Free Trade Unions of Romania – Brotherhood (Confederația Națională a Sindicatelor Libere din România-Frăția or CNSLR-Frăția*)*. The aim is to boost employment and to ensure free access to the labour markets of the two neighbouring countries through joint initiatives and measures such as mutual legal assistance, as well as providing advice and targeted support for Bulgarians working in Romania and vice versa. Another recent collaboration is between CITUB and the Cyprus Workers Confederation

(SEK, Συνομοσπονδία Εργαζομένων Κύπρου) concerning seasonal Bulgarian workers in Cyprus. Joint centres have been established centres for informing and advising workers. Similar centres have been set up in Germany and Austria, in cooperation with, respectively, the German Trade Union Confederation (*Deutscher Gewerkschaftsbund*) and the Austrian Trade Union Federation (*Österreichischer Gewerkschaftsbund*). An agreement for trade union cooperation has also been signed with the Romanian confederation Cartel Alpha (CITUB 2017).

The Bulgarian confederations have become among the most proactive among other unions in the EU regarding their involvement in the EU Semester (Spasova et al. 2020). Again, the main conflicts are with the government and the confederations try to use EU channels directly, through the European Semester officials or ETUC, to further their interests (Tomev et al. 2019). In 2020, however, the confederations were very active in meetings with government representatives and media presentations in order to lobby the state not to vote in favour of the Green Deal's new binding EU target for a net domestic reduction of greenhouse gas emissions of at least 55 per cent by 2030 compared with 1990 levels. In Bulgaria there are still coal and other mines at which trade unions have an important pool of members and high collective bargaining coverage. Both confederations strongly emphasize the need to prepare, as soon as possible, a National Action Plan for a just transition to a low-carbon economy, access to the latest technologies at European level, as well as the creation of a flexible set of state aid rules linked to investments to achieve the objectives of the Green Deal (CITUB 2022; News.bg 2020).

Conclusions

Bulgarian trade unionism has gone through several historical transformations. Nevertheless, two main characteristics have persisted over time: conflicts with the state on meaningful involvement in social dialogue, and considerable use of international, mainly European, resources to build up social dialogue institutions and maintain their role in Bulgarian political decision-making processes.

All in all, the unions' proactive involvement in developing laws and institutions that have enshrined their economic and social role has been successful. This, however, offered no guarantee about the actual functioning of these institutions and the unions' effective involvement and impact. Union density has decreased over the years, although it has more or less stabilized over the past ten years. Unions are most powerful in the public sector, but fairly weak in the private sector. This is also reflected in the low and decreasing collective bargaining coverage. There are, however, some positive prospects, such as developments in CITUB, with new members from traditionally non-unionized sectors, such as ICT, finance and culture. Until recent years, the main conflicts were with the state, but since the privatization process was largely completed, the unions are now at odds with the employers. The low number of collective agreements in the private sector and the rare extensions of agreements speak volumes about the difficult relations.

While the transition process can be considered complete, and there has always been dualization between trade unions organizing in the private and in the public sectors, two future – and fairly contradictory – scenarios are most likely for Bulgarian unions, based on Visser's typology (2019): 'marginalization' or 'revitalization', depending on the unions' capacity to seize the opportunity for transformation in the critical juncture opening up with the Green Deal, digitalization and the Covid-19 pandemic. The 'marginalization' scenario is plausible, as membership is diminishing. *Formal* marginalization is fairly unlikely as the unions' role is well enshrined in a network of social dialogue institutions and legally established representativeness criteria at national level. Despite recurrent conflicts with the government, these institutions have never been called into question and there have even been some legal improvements since 2015. In fact, they are protected by representativeness criteria. De facto marginalization could happen fairly quickly, however, if the unions do not find a means of revitalization: the question is not only 'how many people' are represented by them but also who joins trade unions. Indeed, a revitalization scenario is also possible, as there have been some promising signs: CITUB has made the unionization policy a top priority during the past decade and there have been some positive developments, mainly in the public sector. Moreover, both confederations have allowed affiliates for, for example, the self-employed, pensioners, the unemployed and disabled people. Nevertheless, revitalization will happen only if unions are revived across Europe, in a wide-ranging and solidaristic response to both old and new challenges. This would also require a strong political commitment, at both national and European level, to the importance of unionism, and more generally to social partnership, in the functioning of the European democracies.

One of the most plausible scenarios for the more distant future is yet another transformation of Bulgarian unions. There may be mergers and evolution towards more 'hybrid' organizations of workers and broader social groups, as they have been opening up membership more and more to other groups than wage-earners, making it possible to address the transitions between activity statuses. Now when the transition and EU accession processes are over, the challenge is how to redefine and reaffirm union objectives, and especially how to present new 'persuasive visions' in a 'new language' (Gumbrell-McCormick and Hyman 2013: 205), especially in the context of the Green Deal, which will have a significant impact on the most unionized industries. Moreover, there is a need to focus firmly on empowering collective bargaining at the workplace, rather than on law and institution-building which, at least on paper, have been successful.

References

Bernaciak M. (2013) Social dialogue revival or 'PR corporatism'? Negotiating anti-crisis measures in Poland and Bulgaria, Transfer, 19 (2), 239–251.

BICA (2020) BICA: gray economy in Bulgaria continues to decrease, Bulgarian Industrial Capital Association News, 15 December 2020. https://bica-bg.org/bica-gray-economy-in-bulgaria-continues-to-decrease/?lang=en

Bohle D. and Greskovits B. (2012) Capitalist diversity on Europe's periphery, Ithaca, Cornell University Press.

CITUB (1993) Report of the Coordination Council at the 3rd Congress of KNSB, 8–10 October 1993.

CITUB (2017) Report of the Coordination Council at the 8th Congress of KNSB, 2–3 May 2017.

CITUB (2020) CITUB and CL Podkrepa: A quick assessment of the impact of the Green Deal and the establishment of a fair transition board is needed, CITUB, 14 February 2020. https://knsb-bg.org/index.php/2020/02/14/knsb-i-kt-podkrepa-neobhodima-e-barza-oczenka-na-vazdejstvieto-ot-zelenata-sdelka-i-sazdavane-na-bord-za-spravedliv-prehod/

CITUB (2022) Official site, https://knsb-re-dial.net/

Detchev T. (2007) Voluntary agreements between employers and trade unions give new sense to the social dialogue, Detchev Blog [in Bulgarian]. https://news.bg/columnists/za-noviyasmisal-na-sotsialniya-dialog.html

Detchev T., Gladicheva R. and Ilkov V. (2005) The evolving structure of collective bargaining in Europe 1990–2004. Research project co-financed by the European Commission and the University of Florence. National report Bulgaria.

Dimitrov V. (2001) Bulgaria: The Uneven Transition, London, Routledge.

Economic and Social Council of Bulgaria (2022) Official site, https://esc.bg/en/home/

Eurofound (2021) Covid-19: implications for employment and working life, Covid-19 series, Luxembourg, Publications Office of the European Union.

Gradev G. (2001) Bulgarian Trade Unions in transition: the Taming of the Hedgehog, in Crowley S. and Ost D. (eds) Workers after workers' states: Labor and politics in postcommunist Eastern Europe, Oxford, Rowman & Littlefield Publishers, 121–141.

Gumbrell-McCormick R. and Hyman R. (2013) Trade unions in Western Europe. hard times, hard choices, Oxford, Oxford University Press.

Iankova E. (2002) Eastern European capitalism in the making, Cambridge, Cambridge University Press.

Kahancová M. and Kirov V. (2021) Shaping minimum wages in Central and Eastern Europe, in Dingeldey I., Grimshaw D. and Schulten T. (eds) Minimum wage regimes: statutory regulation, collective bargaining and adequate levels, Abingdon, Routledge, 87–112.

Kaloara B. (1973) Materiali po istoria na profsyuznoto dvijenie v Balagaria [History of the Trade unions in Bulgaria], Sofia, Profizdat.

Kirov V. (2005) Facing EU Accession: Bulgarian Trade Unions at the Crossroads, in Dimitrova D. and Vilrokx J. (eds) Trade union strategies in Central and Eastern Europe: towards decent work, Budapest, ILO, 111–153.

Kirov V. (2015) The integration of the Bulgarian Trade Union Confederation of Independent Trade Unions of Bulgaria (CITUB) into European Union (EU) Governance structures, in Landgraf C. and Pleines H. (eds) Interest representation and Europeanization of trade unions from EU Member States of the Eastern enlargement, Stuttgart, Ibidem Verlag, 217–237.

Kirov V. (2019) Bulgaria: collective bargaining eroding, but still existing, in Müller T., Vandaele K. and Waddington J. (eds) Collective bargaining in Europe: towards an endgame, Brussels, ETUI, 77–92.

Launey M. (1990) Le syndicalisme en Europe, Paris, Imprimerie nationale.

Meardi G. (2012) Social failures of EU enlargement. A case of workers voting with their feet, London, Routledge.

NSI (2021) Data on business statistics, Sofia, National Statistical Institute. https://www.nsi.bg/en/content/11237/business-statistics.

News.bg (2020) https://news.bg/about/zelena-sdelka.

NIPA (2015b) Analiz na registriranite ot Nacionalnia institute za pomirenie i arbitraj slucai nq kolektivni trudovi sporove, vklucitelno stachki (Analysis of the cases of collective labor disputes registered by the National Institute for Conciliation and Arbitration, including strikes).

NIPA (2019) Annual report of the National Institute for Conciliation and Arbitration (NIPA) on collective agreements and collective labor disputes (2017–2018).

NIPA (2021) Database on collective agreements and collective labor disputes (2010–2020).

Pavlov D. (1991) Ot sindikalizym kym politicheski infantilizym, [From syndicalism to political infantilism], Istoricheskii pregled, Bulgarian Academy of Sciences, 3, 25–44.

Petkov K. (2011) How we created CITUB? A historical and sociological study, Personal blog of Petkov K. https://web.archive.org/web/20120710040414/http://www.kpetkov.eu/.

Spasova S. (2013) Les réformes des retraites dans les pays d'Europe centrale et orientale: entre influences internationales et déterminants nationaux, La Revue de l'IRES, (77), 129–163.

Spasova S. (2015) Professionnalisation à travers la socialisation internationale et les 'usages de l'Europe', Le cas des organisations syndicales en Bulgarie, CITUB et CL Podkrepa, après 1989, Doctoral thesis, Université Libre de Bruxelles, publicly defended, 24 September 2015.

Spasova S. and Tomini L. (2013) Building social dialogue institutions in Bulgaria: between EU conditionality and domestic social actors, Debatte: Journal of Contemporary Central and Eastern Europe, 21 (1), 3–24.

Spasova S., Sabato S. and Porchez M. (2020) Going European: domestic politics and expertise matter. National trade union strategies for involvement in the European Semester, Analytical Report Work Package 3 – INVOTUNES project, OSE Working Paper Series, Research Paper 46, Brussels, European Social Observatory.

Tomev L. (2017) Innovative trade union practices in Bulgaria: a remedy for falling membership and declining institutional power?, in Bernaciak M. and Kahancová M. (eds) Innovative union practices in Central-Eastern Europe, Brussels, ETUI, 21–38.

Tomev L., Daskalova N., Mihailova T. and Ivanova V. (2008) Wages and collective bargaining in Bulgaria, SEER: Journal for Labour and Social Affairs in Eastern Europe, 11 (2), 219–237.

Tomev L., Daskalova N., Kostov L. and Ivanov M. (2019) 'What Europe says matters': the European Semester as a catalyst to overcome national social dialogue blockages?, Case Study Bulgaria, OSE Research Paper 36, Brussels, European Social Observatory.

Visser J. (2019) Trade unions in the balance, ACTRAV Working Paper, Geneva, ILO.

List of interviews

Interview with the vice-president responsible for labour rights and collective bargaining (CITUB), 22 March 2021.

Interview with the president of the Union of Bulgarian Teachers (CITUB), 23 March 2021.

Abbreviations

AFL-CIO	Congress of Industrial Organizations
CITUB	Confederation of Independent Trade Unions of Bulgaria
CL Podkrepa	Confederation of Labour Podkrepa
ESC	Economic and Social Council of Bulgaria
ETUC	European Trade Unions Confederation
FGTB	Fédération Générale du Travail de Belgique
FO	Force Ouvrière
ICFTU	International Confederation of Free Trade Unions
ILO	International Labour Organization
IMF	International Monetary Fond
MII	Minimum Insurance Income
NCTC	National Council for Tripartite Cooperation

Chapter 5

Croatia: Trade unions able to retain influence despite loss of resources

Dragan Bagić and Jelena Ostojić

It is well known from the extensive literature that during the transition process trade unions in most former socialist states failed to impose themselves as strong actors in industrial relations and ensure themselves a voice in shaping the political economies of these states (Crowley and Ost 2001). Within the framework of this predominantly negative image of trade unions in Central and Eastern Europe (CEE), only a few cases stand out, such as Slovenia and Poland. There has been relatively little evaluation of Croatian trade unions' success in this area in the international literature and the Croatian union movement is rarely mentioned as an exception to the dominant pattern of weak trade unions in the region. In this chapter, we sketch some arguments for a more optimistic view of the trade union movement in Croatia.

In the transition from socialism to capitalism, Croatian unions managed to maintain a relatively high level of union density, keeping it above the European weighted average and well above the average for other former socialist states (Vandaele 2019). This was despite strong deindustrialization and changes in employment towards tertiarization and smaller enterprises. The trend in union density in Croatia was still negative, but the unions managed to maintain a stable level of membership and union density for prolonged periods (Table 5.1; see also Figure 5.1).

Table 5.1 Principal characteristics of trade unionism in Croatia

	1999	2008	2017
Total trade union membership	502,000	485,800	330,000
Women as a proportion of total membership	n.a.	47 %	49 %
Gross union density	n.a.	n.a.	n.a.
Net union density	41.8 %	34.7 %	22.6 %
Number of confederations	5	5	3
Number of affiliated unions (federations)	180	180	109
Number of independent unions	320	320	390
Collective bargaining coverage[3]	70 %	68 %	53 %
Principal level of collective bargaining	Mixed; industry and company		
Days not worked due to industrial action per 1,000 workers	n.a.	n.a.	n.a.

Source: 1999: Authors' estimation; 2008: Bagić (2010); 2017: Bagić (2019).

When it comes to the most important trade union activity, collective bargaining, Croatia again stands out from most other CEE countries in terms of collective bargaining coverage, matching the European average and well above the average of former socialist states (Vandaele 2019). As we described in our earlier work (Bagić 2019), at the onset of the transition process Croatian trade unions managed to establish a highly centralized and coordinated collective bargaining system, which guaranteed a very high level of coverage. In the mid-1990s, however, they lost the battle and allowed the single centralized system to fall apart and fragment into several different sub-systems.

Although the Croatian trade union movement is highly fragmented at all levels, and there is a high level of competition between the relevant actors, the most important divisions among trade unions have been overcome and there are no major or long-lasting conflicts. Furthermore, cooperation and coordinated action are on the increase. This latter development has also resulted in the renewal of the unions' societal power, which they utilize successfully to prevent the imposition of policies detrimental to workers. For the time being, this power is mostly defensive, used to block further deterioration of workers' rights. Unions have failed, for now, to shift the balance in the political economy in favour of workers and such optimistic scenarios are not foreseeable at the moment. The state of affairs presented in this chapter, however, does not make such expectations entirely illusory.

Historical background and principal features of the industrial relations system

At the beginning of transition process in the 1990s the formation of an entirely new industrial relations system began, with very little from the previous period to rely on, other than the trade unions themselves. In Croatia, as in most other socialist countries, trade unions did not play their original role in representing workers' interests during the socialist period. Instead, their task was primarily to provide social services to workers through enterprises. Socialist unions entered the new system with a large membership and a significant number of union professionals, as well as certain assets. The socialist trade unions had begun to prepare for change, and when it came, they seemed ready for it, at least when it came to retaining membership but also to retaining a dominant position, despite the fact that new independent unions were established before the formal change of system and the galloping fragmentation of the union movement in its wake.

Industrial relations formation in the early years was marked primarily by the peculiarities of the transition. Economic transformation had a secondary role compared with other aspects. The transition in Croatia is marked primarily by the struggle for independence and secession from Yugoslavia. Therefore, in the first years of the transition, the new elites focused primarily on achieving political independence and waging war, and after that on rebuilding war-affected parts of the country. Economic reforms and transformation made it onto the agenda only in the mid-1990s, when other processes were almost completed or running in the background of major processes. For that reason, Croatia's transition in earlier years is not marked by economic 'shock doctrine', as was the case in some other CEE countries, nor by a negative attitude on the part of the new political elite towards trade unions, except perhaps some scepticism about the reformed socialist trade unions. This allowed unions to impose themselves as a relevant social actor from the beginning. In the early years of transition, this made it possible to establish a system of industrial relations resembling 'informal corporatism' (for further details see Bagić 2019). Nevertheless, in the second half of the 1990s this industrial relations system rapidly disintegrated, losing all essential features of a corporatist system. This disintegration occurred primarily because political elites no longer had an interest in maintaining social peace in wartime and institutions were neither stable nor formalized. When the industrial relations institutions became formalized, in the mid-1990s, the system lost its clear structure and was gradually transformed by the end of that decade.

The subsequently established system is characterized by heterogeneous patterns and processes. In the public sector, the established industrial relations system had strong trade unions with great influence, both on workers' direct rights and on the way the system itself was structured and governed. In the private sector, patterns were established depending on whether a particular activity was dominated by large enterprises left over from the socialist period or by a 'new economy', established after the transition. In the former, unions retained a certain influence over workers' rights through collective bargaining, while the latter is dominated by the individualization of labour relations, without collective workers' action towards employers. Working conditions and the level of rights protection maintain the aforementioned hierarchy. This means that public sector employees enjoy relatively the best working conditions and the highest level of rights protection, followed by employees in industries with a traditional union presence and in larger companies. The worst and most diverse working conditions, conversely, are found in the rest of the private sector. In this labour market segment, violations of basic workers' rights, as provided for in the Labour Act and other regulations, are frequent.

Structure of trade unions and union democracy

The Croatian trade union movement is extremely fragmented at all levels. According to the latest available data, there are about 640 registered trade unions. This number of officially registered unions is increasing (compare Bagić 2010).[1] Despite the high number of registered trade unions, the estimated number of active unions is around 250, of which 109 are members of the three representative trade union confederations

1 Keep in mind that Croatia has about four million inhabitants and about 1.3 million employed.

(Official Gazette 2018). The majority of registered individual trade unions are company unions, which organize all workers within a company regardless of occupation. Most of the membership, however, belongs to a small number of industrial unions. The trade union structure as regards type and level of organization differs significantly depending on the type of activity and ownership sector. While the public sector in the narrow sense (public services and public administration) is dominated by industrial unions, public enterprises (owned by the central state or local self-governments) are dominated by company unions or quasi-industrial unions. Their membership comes from a number of different employers within the same sector, but they originated from an in-house trade union during the restructuring of large systems, when an enterprise was divided into several legal entities and/or, partially privatized. The private sector, in turn, is marked by a combination of industrial and company unions. In some industries company trade unions have greater influence and in others – such as construction, tourism, trade, food processing and the metal industry – the industrial ones have more influence.

Unionism at the peak level, however, has been marked by a trend towards centralization over the past two decades, as a result of the falling number of representative confederations. The new act on representativeness raised the bar for union confederation representativeness, resulting in a loss of status by the Union of Croatian Trade Unions (URSH, *Udruga radničkih Sindikata Hrvatske*) in 2013, and in the Croatian Trade Union Association (HURS, *Hrvatska udruga radničkih sindikata*) in 2017.

The three trade union confederations that have maintained representativeness at the national level to the present day have been operating since the beginning of the transition. They represented a total of about 252,000 members of 109 affiliated unions at the end of 2017.[2]

---

2 The term 'representativeness of trade union confederations' refers to representation in the national tripartite body, the Economic and Social Council, in operation since 1993. There were no clear criteria for determining representativeness to begin with, so all union confederations participated in a tripartite dialogue. As relations between them were bad and differences between their respective memberships were large, in the second half of the 1990s a conflict arose among the confederations over the representativeness criteria. This blocked the work of the tripartite body and so legal regulation was essential. The problem was resolved by adopting a special act on determining union representativeness. The new act, adopted in 2012 (with minor amendments in 2014), imposed somewhat stricter criteria, which led to a reduction in the number of representative confederations to the current three.

The oldest trade union confederation is the Union of Autonomous Trade Unions of Croatia (SSSH, *Savez samostalnih sindikata Hrvatske*), founded jointly in May 1990 by the reformed unions operating in the former socialist system and the new, independent unions, founded already in 1989, before the socialist system was formally abandoned (Kokanović 2001: 148). Because the first union confederation was founded jointly by the former socialist trade unions and the newly established ones, there was hope that a monolithic union movement would be established, avoiding fragmentation. This would certainly have strengthened workers' collective voice during the transition. The 'old' and the 'new' trade unions could not agree on the degree of centralization of the new union confederation at the founding congress, however, and the new unions soon left SSSH and founded new union confederations (Bagić 2010). At first, SSSH consisted mainly of reformed old socialist unions, organized by industries and represented in their branches in large enterprises in various industrial activities. Most of these unions still form the basic structure of SSSH. In the meantime, several newly established trade unions have joined the confederation, as well as unions whose foundation was instigated by the confederation itself to increase its representation in some industries or to encourage certain groups of workers to organize themselves. In 2021, 25 trade unions were SSSH affiliates. The main notable feature of this confederation is that the share of public sector employees in its total membership is smaller than in the other two confederations. Although SSSH was the dominant trade union confederation in terms of number of members during the 1990s, having more than half of the membership of all representative confederations, now it has almost the same number of members as the Independent Trade Unions of Croatia (NHS, *Nezavisni hrvatski sindikati*) (see Table 5.2).

The NHS is the largest trade union confederation, bringing together 58 unions in public enterprises, public administration and public services. Although the bulk of union membership is made up of public sector employees, a smaller proportion of affiliated unions also bring together private sector employees. Most affiliates are company unions, which means that this confederation has the lowest average number of members per affiliated union. NHS was formally established at the end of 1999, but it was building on the work of two previous confederations established in the early 1990s, which merged to establish the new confederation.[3]

The third representative trade union confederation is the Association of Croatian Trade Unions (Matica, *Matica hrvatskih sindikata*). Matica was created primarily as a confederation that brings together trade unions from education and other public services, such as health care, culture and social security. In the meantime, it has expanded its profile and today also brings together 26 trade unions from the private sector and public enterprises. About three-quarters of its membership comes from three trade unions from the education sector, representing workers in primary education, secondary education and science and higher education. This still gives this confederation a recognizable identity.

In all three confederations the affiliated unions have significant autonomy and confederations cannot interfere in how they represent their members (see Bagić 2010). The union leaders define the confederations' policies and they elect the leadership, with no direct influence of the rank-and-file members. The membership also has limited influence on the management of individual unions, because the leadership is elected by shop stewards and not individual members. In general, therefore, Croatian unions can be described as top-down organizations.

Table 5.2 Basic information about the three representative confederations

	Year	**SSSH**	**NHS**	**Matica**
Number of affiliated unions	2012	20	59	10
	2017	25	58	26
Number of workers represented	2012	99,682	116,837	61,411
	2017	94,622	96,870	60,648
Membership domain		Predominantly representing unions from the private sector	Representing unions from different sectors, with a significant share of unions of public companies	Predominantly representing unions from public services

Source: Official documents on representativeness of confederations.

[3] These were the Confederation of Independent Trade Unions of Croatia (*Konfederacija nezavisnih sindikata Hrvatske*) and the Coordination of the Croatian Trade Unions of Public Servants and Employees (*Koordinacija hrvatskih sindikata javnih službenika i namještenika*).

Relations among the union confederations have evolved significantly over the past 30 years, as have their lines of division. At the very beginning, the main line of division was between the old, reformed unions and the new unions with no heritage from the socialist system. Furthermore, the new unions developed their own divisions between those representing public services and public administration, and those representing public enterprises. At the beginning of the transition certain political divisions emerged as well, which were partly 'sponsored' by the ruling centre-right party at the time, the Croatian Democratic Union (*Hrvatska demokratska zajednica*). SSSH and its affiliated unions, as the confederation of the majority of unionized workers, organized a series of strikes and protests related to wage harmonization (as a result of high inflation) already in the early 1990s. The authorities' reactions were very negative and hostile, and SSSH and its affiliates were labelled remnants of the 'former system' who were working against the interests of the newly established independent state. Consequently, authorities encouraged the establishment of new confederations and unions, which contributed to fragmentation and mistrust among the union confederations and their leaders (see Bagić 2010).

In the second half of the 1990s, a new line of division emerged on the issue of trade union cooperation with political parties. While some confederations, such as Matica and SSSH, showed a readiness to establish partnerships with individual political parties as a necessary mechanism for implementing union goals, other confederations, led by NHS, opposed this and insisted that unions should remain politically neutral. In the late 1990s, Matica and SSSH established close relations with opposition parties, mainly parties of the centre and centre-left, while NHS maintained neutrality. This line of division slowly disappeared about ten years ago, when all confederations gradually distanced themselves from all political parties.

With the arrival of the global financial crisis of 2008–2009, there was a brief division between unions and confederations on the issue of austerity policies. Union confederations that predominantly represented private sector workers supported austerity policies and public sector reforms, while trade unions which predominantly represented public sector employees opposed such policies. This division also disappeared relatively quickly, as all confederations gradually adopted a predominantly negative attitude towards austerity policies, but also towards liberalization of labour relations in the private sector. Since then, rapprochement has been on the rise among trade union confederations and the establishment of better cooperation. For the past five years cooperation among confederations has been at its highest level since 1990.

The positive trend of cooperation among confederations and the weakening of the divisions that resulted in fragmentation have created the preconditions for fostering mutual association at the level of union confederations. Thus, two union confederations that lost their representative status initiated merger proceedings with other confederations. If these processes are accomplished successfully, we can expect that representative confederations will again represent a huge majority of union members and that the number of independent unions will decrease.

Unionization

At the end of 2018, net union density in Croatia was 22.6 per cent,[4] which means that Croatian trade unions had about 330,000 members in total.[5] As shown in Figure 5.1, there has been a significant decline in union density in the past ten years, especially from 2009 to 2014. In 2009, union density was estimated at about 35 per cent, while five years later it had declined by about one-quarter or 9 percentage points. After this sharp decline, the like of which had not been recorded since the early 1990s, the negative trend halted or slowed down significantly between 2014 and 2018.[6]

In the socialist period, union membership was not mandatory in Croatia (and the rest of the former Yugoslavia), but membership was usually automatic upon employment and the worker could withdraw from membership on request. About 90 per cent of employees are estimated to have been union members before the beginning of the transition

---

4 The source of membership data is an unpublished survey conducted by Dragan Bagić, co-author of this chapter. The survey was conducted in November and December 2018 on a nationally representative sample of 2,000 respondents over 15 years of age. Data was collected by the Ipsos agency as part of its omnibus survey. When sampling error is taken into account, estimated actual union density ranges from 19.6 to 25.6 per cent.

5 The number refers only to members who are dependently employed. The number of members was calculated based on an estimate of 1.45 million dependently employed persons in 2018 (CBS 2019). Taking into account sampling error, the actual number of trade union members at the end of 2018 was between 285,000 and 372,000.

6 Taking into account sampling errors, the change in union density from 2014 to 2018 is not statistically significant: $\lambda^2 = 1.747$; df = 1; p = 0.186.

(Kokanović 1999; 2001). After the start of the transition, all previous union members had to re-join, and re-enrolment was also implemented by reformed socialist trade unions. This led to a drop in union density but not a drastic one, of the kind seen in other post-socialist countries. This can be considered the first important success. During the 1990s, however, union density declined rapidly, falling to about 42 per cent by the end of the period. This is largely attributable to the effects of the restructuring and privatization of enterprises and industries that formed the basis of the socialist economy and to the transition of the labour force to the 'new economy', particularly newly established private companies, mainly small and medium enterprises (SMEs). Union density remained stable in the next decade, which may be considered the second significant success of Croatian trade unions, given that negative trends in union density continued in Europe. Unions clearly failed to attract as members new workers who replaced those who retired. From 2009 to 2014, for example, the average age of union members increased from 43.8 to 46.8.[7] An optimistic sign in this regard, however, is the fact that the average age of union members has not fallen between 2014 (46.8 years) and 2018 (45.1 years).[8]

Figure 5.1 Union density in Croatia, 1990–2018

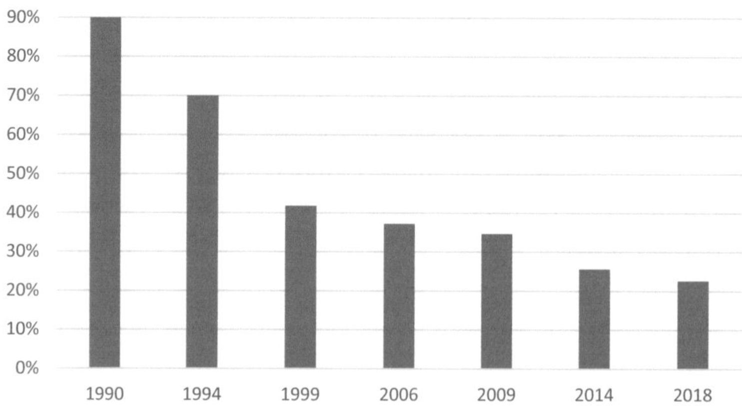

Source: 1990–1994: unions' administrative data (Kokanović 1999); 2006–2018: national surveys (Bagić 2010, 2016).

---

7 $t = -3.752$; $df = 386$; $p < 0.01$.

8 $t = 1.443$; $df = 334$; $p = 0.150$.

As Table 5.3 illustrates, there are significant differences in union density with regard to type and size of employer, and industry. When it comes to type of employer, the highest union density is found in public institutions in education, health and social care, followed by public enterprises, owned by the central government or cities and municipalities. In state administrative bodies or units of local/regional self-government, union density is around 39 per cent. In private enterprises, which make up the majority of employees, union density is only about 10 per cent. Among private enterprises, key differences exist with regard to the number of employees. In micro enterprises (up to ten employees), there is virtually no union membership; in small enterprises (ten to ninety-nine employees) one in ten workers is a union member and union density grows significantly as size of establishment increases. Private enterprises in financial services and insurance (29 per cent), manufacturing (15 per cent), and construction and utilities (15 per cent) have above-average union density. Industries comprising a significant number of employees, such as retail and hospitality and tourism, have union density below average for the private sector (8 and 5 per cent, respectively).

Table 5.3 Union density by type of employer and enterprise size in private sector, 2018

	Union density (%)
All employees	*22.6*
Public institutions (schools, hospitals, social care and so on)	55.7
Public enterprises	45.3
State/local/regional administrative bodies	38.7
Private enterprises total	10.3
<10 employees	*0.0*
10–99 employees	*10.4*
100–249 employees	*17.1*
>250 employees	*23.9*
Other*	3.8

Note: * NGOs, international organizations, individual employees and so on.

Source: Authors' survey.

With regard to workers' personal characteristics, there is no significant difference in union density between men (22 per cent) and women (23 per cent). There are substantial differences in terms of workers' age, however: among those under 30, union density is only about 11 per cent, while among the oldest age group it is three times that. These data clearly show that Croatian unions have not been successful in recruiting new workers and still rely predominantly on cohorts that joined unions at the very beginning of the transition.

Table 5.4 Union density by employee characteristics, 2018

		Union density (%)
All employees		*22.6*
Gender	Male	22.3
	Female	23.0
Age group	<30	10.6
	30–49	21.3
	50>	36.7
Education level	Primary	32.8
	Secondary	18.9
	Tertiary	27.9

Source: Authors' survey.

With regard to labour market status, data show that workers who are not at the core of the labour market but at its margins are significantly less involved in trade unions. Thus, survey data from 2018 show that only 5.5 per cent of employees with a fixed-term employment contract were union members, while the same percentage is almost five times higher among those with a permanent employment contract.

Union resources and expenditure

Union finances are based largely on membership fees, which generally range around 1 per cent (gross or net) of union members' wages. As a rule, membership fees are the main and, for some trade unions, the only source of funding. Less important sources of revenue are financial assets and real estate, but also project activities that have been taking place through the European Social Fund for the past six years, since Croatia's accession to the European Union (EU) in 2013. Such project activities allow unions to implement or expand their activities, as well as, in some cases, to temporarily increase the number of employees through project employment.

Although the operational logic of confederations differs somewhat from that of individual unions, income structures largely coincide: confederations are funded predominantly from the membership fees of affiliated trade unions. Depending on the confederation, they are the sole or the predominant source of its income. Confederations are particularly interested in having large trade unions as affiliates and are inclined to adjust membership fees for that purpose. At a rough estimate, affiliates pay confederations fees of up to 20 per cent of their own membership fees. Such income provides the income base for confederations, and their entire organizational structure, in terms of number of employees, overhead and main activities, is governed by it. A confederation's financial sustainability depends on this. Project activities and their potential employment boost are supplementary to this.

As already mentioned, trade unions were one of the target beneficiaries of the European Social Fund. During the implementation of related schemes, unions often participated in cooperation with non-governmental organizations (NGOs), educational institutions and research institutes. Project financing involves temporary, strictly earmarked funds, limited to project implementation. Although from the accounting perspective they represent a source of union income, they cannot be used to cope with infrastructure issues or cover overheads. This ultimately means that such funds cannot be used to cover the reduction in union and confederations' income caused by a decline in membership. While some trade unions rely on project income to a larger extent, they represent a much smaller share in total income than membership fees. Unions' loss of income because of falling membership has been particularly pronounced in the past three years, although overall, falling income is a longer-term process.

Turning to reasons why unions are harder hit in some industries than in others, one might mention layoffs due to the restructuring of some of the largest companies (prominently in the road-building sector), closure of factories and production (metal and textile industries), and pronounced emigration of labour from Croatia to other European countries. Some trade unions, however, such as those in the telecommunications industry, have seen a rise in income as a result of rising membership in 2020 compared with three years earlier.

Declining membership in affiliated unions has affected confederations in various ways. Where a confederation's sole source of income comprises fees from affiliates, income decline has been linear. Confederations may also provide affiliates with other services, however, in which case the latter's contributions may be subject to negotiations.

The structure of union expenditures primarily comprises their employees' wages and overhead costs, and for some trade unions also office rental. In addition to these basic expenses – which may also include shop stewards' fees (for extra work not covered by their wages), solidarity assistance to trade union members (Christmas or Easter bonus, Christmas presents for members' children, support for new-born babies, support for long tern sick leave) – we must also mention membership fees for higher-level associations. This includes fees for membership of national confederations, as well as international union organizations. Trade unions also partially cover training costs for union representatives and works councils, although in some collective agreements, the bulk of training costs are borne by the employer.

The number of permanent staff in trade unions is falling, mainly because of declining income. Often, new people are not hired as jobs fall vacant following a retirement or employment termination by mutual agreement. There are no significant fluctuations in the number of full-time employees, but temporary employment has increased through project work. In the absence of their own infrastructure, trade unions often outsource part of their services, such as accounting or legal services, as well as some activities contracted on a project basis.

Collective bargaining and unions at the workplace

In general, trade union activities and interests are largely at the company level, except for unions in public services and public administration, where they are primarily at the national level, which corresponds to the level of collective bargaining. Even for industry trade unions that conduct collective bargaining at that level, most activities are organized by company-level branches and most resources, such as membership fees, are at the company level. Outside public services and public administration, both trade unions that bargain collectively at the company level and those that bargain only at the industrial level carry out activities at the company level. This includes monitoring the implementation of collective agreements and laws, and mediating in individual complaints and problems, which may include representing workers in labour disputes.

Croatia has a dual system of employee interest representation. Unions have a monopoly on collective bargaining and strike action, while works councils have a monopoly on the right to information, consultation and codetermination. Given that most unions outside the public sector have a strong presence at the company level, in practice unions often control works councils. In many cases, unions exercise an option made available by the Labour Code to substitute for the works council without elections. There have also been rare cases in which unions were pushed out by employers using works councils for workers' interest representation.

According to the latest available data from 2014, collective bargaining coverage in Croatia is around 53 per cent, a decrease of around 10 percentage points in comparison with 2009 (Bagić 2016). In general, the level of collective bargaining coverage has been stable for a relatively long period, without a clear negative trend or a trend towards decentralization, which is already high. The decrease of bargaining coverage in the past decade is mainly the consequence of two factors: the decrease in the share of unionized industries in the total labour force and the abolition of the industry-level agreement for retail (Bagić 2019).

Although collective agreements regulate working conditions for most workers, wage setting itself is not prominent in collective bargaining. In many cases, wages are not negotiated in detail for the main job positions; sometimes (around 15 per cent of cases), even the minimum wage is not negotiated. The majority of collective agreements are signed for a period longer than two years, and a significant proportion of agreements with relatively long validity do not have mechanisms for wage adjustments for inflation and the cost of living. It is not uncommon for employers to increase wages unilaterally, even when there is a collective agreement. Exceptions are collective bargaining in public services and public administration and some private companies, where wages are agreed annually or biennially. As there is no uniform system of collective bargaining (see details in Bagić 2019), there is no formal or informal mechanism of wage coordination.

Trade unions have been unsuccessful in controlling wage levels, especially during the 1990s, when wage increases were very rare and employees' purchasing power decreased constantly, especially for those on low wages. Unions, therefore, lobbied for the introduction of minimum wage regulations. The minimum wage was introduced in 1998 with the Collective Agreement on the Level of the Minimum Wage, which applied to all employers in the Republic of Croatia. Until 2003, the Ministry of Finance de facto set the minimum wage independently, whereas subsequently the minimum wage was set at 35 per cent of the average gross wage in eight months of the previous year. The minimum wage system was changed in 2008 with the adoption of the Minimum Wage Act, which has been amended several times since then (Nesić and Blaževi Burić 2018). The current minimum wage system entitles the government to set the minimum wage on an annual basis after consulting the social partners. For 2021, the net minimum wage is set at around 450 euros a month, which is about 49 per cent of the average net wage.

In addition to interest representation, a significant trade union activity in the workplace is the provision of financial assistance to members. In addition, unions organize various leisure activities for their members at the workplace, such as joint trips, annual sports meetings and cultural events, especially for members' children at Christmas.

Industrial conflict

Data on strikes and other forms of industrial conflict in Croatia are not easily accessible, and the literature on them is sporadic and rare. Figure 5.2 shows the number of strikes and strike participants over the past three decades by bringing together two data sources: the Workers' Struggle Archives[9] and the work of Dolenec et al. (2020).

Figure 5.2 Overview of number of strikes and strike participants, 1990–2017

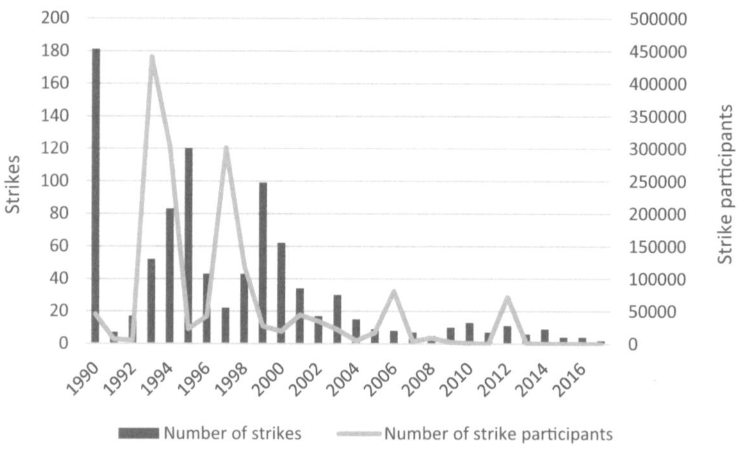

Note: There is an interruption in the data series in 2000.
Source: 1990–1999: Workers' Struggle Archives; 2000–2017: Dolenec et al. (2020).

9 http://arhiv-radnickih-borbi.org/

Croatia entered the 1990s after a wave of strikes caused by the reforms implemented there, in common with other Yugoslav republics under pressure from international financial institutions and creditors. These reforms resulted in wage cuts or stagnation, while prices continued to increased (Grdešić 2007). After Croatia declared independence in 1991, workers' strikes and revolts went on until the beginning of the armed conflict. In response to the latter the trade unions concluded an agreement on cooperation and action during a state of war or imminent threat to the independence and unity of the Republic of Croatia. Under this, in cooperation with the government, they suspended their activities and committed themselves to social peace during the war. The agreement was terminated by a general strike organized by union confederations and several individual trade unions on 12 March 1993. In addition to large membership mobilizations through general strikes organized by union confederations, a large number of strikes took place in the 1990s at lower levels as well. The Archive of Workers' Struggles has evidence of over 700 strikes and over 500 other industrial conflicts in this period, but the real numbers are likely to be much higher. At that time, strikes were most often initiated because of unpaid wages and to keep companies and their production going. Data on the frequency of strikes and the number of strike participants (Figure 5.2) clearly show that workers were actively responding to unfolding processes: they opposed privatization and deindustrialization because of their negative experiences, and protested over job losses and rising unemployment.

Work stoppages were often a response to privatization and the installation of new management boards and heads of companies whose interests often did not include maintaining production and preserving jobs. Strike action sometimes proved counterproductive as a means of workers' resistance, however. Therefore, workers resorted to new methods that allowed production to continue, and jobs to be preserved. Perhaps the most prominent new approach were the so-called 'headquarters for the defence of companies'.[10] The first headquarters appeared in 1998 in Kutina at the Petrokemija factory as a form of in-company struggle that overcame trade union divisions and included all workers' organizations in a joint fight against privatization. The aim was to retain majority state

10 'Headquarters for the defence of companies' are a special form of industrial conflict in Croatia which, among other things, meant workers' taking control of the company.

ownership in the company. This became the dominant pattern of industrial conflict in the subsequent period (Grdešić 2007; Ivandić and Livada 2014; Lončar 2013).

Croatia entered its second decade of independence with large workers' strikes similar to those that had marked the end of the previous decade (Figure 5.2). The year 2000 is one of the turning points in post-independence Croatian history because the centre-right government was replaced by a social democratic one, with which union confederations had signed a social agreement just before the elections.

Numerous strikes marked the first year of the second decade of independence; as many as sixty-two were recorded in 2000. Since then, the annual number of strikes has been significantly lower. Although there were thirty-four strikes in 2001 and thirty in 2003, the largest number of strike participants was recorded in 2006, when over 80,000 workers took part in a three-day strike of civil servants (Dolenec et al. 2020). The most frequent strike activity, recorded in the early 2000s, does not coincide with the largest mobilization of people for strike action.

The global financial crisis, which hit Croatia in 2008 and lasted until 2014, had extremely negative consequences for the economy, employment and the quality of work. The unemployment rate reached 17.4 per cent in 2013, and the number of job losses compared with the last pre-crisis year amounted to 231,000 (Matković and Ostojić 2019). These trends were accompanied by intensified strike activities in particular in the public sector such as primary and secondary schools, faculties, scientific institutions and health care.

Industrial conflict over the past 30 years has been characterized by the following key trends. The first years after Croatian independence, the 1990s, were marked by numerous strikes and other industrial conflicts. Mass participation in strikes came as the result of trade union confederations organizing general strikes, which have not occurred subsequently. Throughout the period 2000–2017, with the exception of the first few years, the number of strikes was significantly lower, but their intensity increased during the global financial crisis. We may thus conclude that they continue to be a response to attacks on labour and material rights. The larger scale strike mobilization since 2000 has been linked to strikes in the public sector in which union density remains relatively high and trade unions play a significant role in defending workers' interests.

Political relations

The unions' main mechanism for influencing public policy is the national tripartite Economic and Social Council (GSV, *Gospodarsko-socijalno vijeće*). The GSV has been operating, with shorter or longer interruptions, since 1993. The intensity and quality of the dialogue has varied at different stages. The current phase of tripartite social dialogue began with political changes in 2000.[11] It is characterized by stabilization and more routine functioning. Social partners, union confederations and employers' associations have the opportunity to give their opinions on a wide range of laws (in addition to labour issues, the GSV discusses laws in other policy areas, such as public finance, economic policy, education, health care, social policy, pension policy, and environmental protection) prepared by ministries before proposals are submitted for formal adoption by the government through parliamentary procedures. In this way, the social partners have a formal opportunity to shape a wide range of public policies. Especially at critical moments, such as the response to the Covid pandemic, the government uses the GSV for consultation with social partners. In addition, the social partners nominate representatives to working groups in many areas. They work on drafting laws, especially regulations governing public services such as education, health care and social welfare or public administration. The GSV holds meetings relatively regularly, usually once a month, giving leaders of trade unions and employers an opportunity to meet regularly with ministers in charge of the most important portfolios, such as labour, social policy, education, health care, finance and the economy.

The trade unions thus have a relatively stable institutional framework for influencing public policy and for regular interaction with government representatives at the highest level (deputy prime minister and ministers). To date this institutional framework has failed to result in compromise solutions to disputed issues in the domain of labour relations or social policy. This applies primarily to a number of amendments to the Labour Act (ZOR, *Zakon o radu*) that have led to increased labour market flexibility and reduced workers' legal protection, as well as efforts by various

---

11 In early 2000, parliamentary elections were held, resulting in the first change of government since 1990. The united opposition removed the then-ruling Croatian Democratic Union, a centre-right party. These elections are seen as a significant milestone in terms of democratization.

governments to reform the pension system or privatize segments of the public sector within the framework of austerity policies (often under pressure from the European Commission). Because direct union opposition through institutional consultation channels has proved unfruitful, they have been forced to use non-institutional and political mechanisms of pressure in a number of such cases, with greater or lesser success (see the next section).

The social partners also have representatives in the most important committees of the Croatian Parliament, through which they can present their views on certain public policies before MPs.[12] The social partners also have representatives in the governing bodies of certain institutions important for regulating the labour market, such as the Croatian Employment Service.

Attempts were made to establish political partnership between trade unions (confederations) and political parties in the late 1990s and early 2000s, but these efforts did not result in any significant boost for trade union influence on public policies. The rapprochement of the two confederations, Matica and SSSH, with the opposition centre and centre-left parties began in 1997, resulting in the signing of pre-election agreements between those parties and the confederations before the 2000 elections. Opposition parties committed to implement certain reforms and consult with trade unions in implementing public policies, while confederations committed to support opposition parties in the upcoming elections. After the opposition parties won the elections, pre-election cooperation was transformed into a tripartite reform accord. But soon, the social partners became dissatisfied with the manner and speed of certain reforms, and the union confederations withdrew only a few months after signing the accord (first SSSH, and then the others). Thus this most significant attempt to establish political exchange ended in failure.

Some trade unions and union leaders have not completely given up on some kind of political engagement. They believe that, although current political parties do not (sincerely) advocate workers' interests, a political party may at some point emerge with which trade unions could establish closer cooperation.

---

12 An interesting feature of the Croatian parliament are so-called 'expert/external members' of parliamentary committees, who can participate in discussions about proposed laws and policies, albeit without voting rights.

The possible realization of such hope emerged in 2010 with the establishment of a new left-wing political party, the Croatian Labour Party (Laburisti, *Hrvatski laburisti*), whose programme included as one of its priorities the protection of workers and, in particular, promoting the trade unions' role in protecting workers' rights (Hrvatski Laburisti 2010). The founder of Laburisti, Dragutin Lesar, was a prominent union leader from the 1990s and the current leadership is also dominated by union activists (Hrvatski Laburisti 2020). But after promising results in the 2011 parliamentary elections (5.8 per cent of the vote at the national level and six seats out of 151), they lost support rapidly and today the party is very marginal.

The failure of Laburisti called for some reflection on the modalities of political representation of workers' and trade unions' interests. For example, in 2016, Matica organized a round table entitled 'Is it time for the political organization of trade unions?'. Vilim Ribič, confederation head, said at the round table 'Let's do something! Our society is disintegrating, our future is disintegrating. Political activism of some sort is imperative' (Matica hrvatskih sindikata 2016). The fact that no such moves have yet been made indicates indirectly that opinions are divided on this issue within the unions themselves.

Societal power

Some prominent (neo)liberal activists take the view that trade unions in Croatia, and in particular public sector unions, have excessive societal power, which they use to block fiscal policy reforms or supposed improvements in public sector efficiency.[13] To support such assertions they cite examples of trade union actions over the past ten years in opposition to various reforms or proposed legal amendments. For example, from 2010 to 2019, the unions organized four (one in 2010, two in 2014 and one in 2019) successful initiatives to call referendums on certain

13 Davor Hujić, founder and leader of the Taxpayers' Association, and one of the most active liberal activists, has repeatedly said publicly that public sector unions have a 'veto power', with which they can block any type of reform (of the public sector). See his argument in the text published on 31 October 2019 at www.index.hr 'Hujić: Trade unions are interest groups run by well-paid lobbyists': https://www.index.hr/vijesti/clanak/huic-sindikati-su-interesne-skupine-koje-vode-dobro-placeni-lobisti/2128316.aspx

government reform initiatives that, from a union perspective, were detrimental to workers' interests.[14] The unions collected enough signatures to instigate the referendum process on each occasion and as a result the proposed legal amendments were halted. In one case, an already adopted law was amended, formally on the government's initiative. The level of union power is illustrated by the fact that in all four initiatives they collected a significantly larger number of signatures than the minimum (around 400,000). For example, the first initiative in 2010, when the trade unions opposed amendments to the Labour Act (ZOR) that would have ended the continuing validity of collective agreements beyond their expiry dates – the so-called 'after-effect' – collected over 800,000 signatures, over 20 per cent of all voters. The most recent trade union initiative, launched in 2019, which demanded the repeal of already adopted amendments to the pension insurance law, which shortened the transition period for extending the retirement age, collected about 750,000 signatures.

In addition to union confederations, which jointly organized the collection of signatures, NGOs also participated in the initiative, to a lesser extent. Cooperation between trade unions and NGOs – for example, the latter offered support to Kamensko textile factory workers, who went on hunger strike in September 2010 because their wages had not been paid for several months – intensified in 2013. A significant step in this direction was the public support of nineteen associations for the great May Day protest organized by all union confederations. Shortly afterwards, at its session in June 2013, the SSSH Presidency adopted organizational and action guidelines, including cooperation and joint action with NGOs in activities of common interest (Ivandić and Livada 2014). This cooperation was particularly evident in one of the two initiatives

---

14 According to Croatian regulations, non-governmental organizations or citizens' groups have the right to initiate a referendum with the aim of amending existing laws or provisions of the Constitution, or adopting new provisions of the law or the Constitution. The initiator of such a referendum must formulate one or more potential referendum questions and must collect the signatures of at least 10 per cent of the total number of eligible voters (about 400,000) within two weeks. Once the collected signatures are submitted, the validity and exact number of signatures is determined, and the parliament may ask the Constitutional Court for an opinion on the constitutionality of the proposed question before deciding to call a referendum. If the government decides to withdraw the bill or changes it on its own initiative initiators of the referendum may withdraw their initiative (see more in Čepo and Nikić Čakar 2019).

implemented in 2014, both directed against privatization in the public sector, which collected 600,000 and 530,000 signatures, respectively (see Čepo and Nikić Čakar 2019). The 'We won't give up our motorways' initiative, established to oppose the leasing of motorways as concessions, saw the participation of NGOs known for fighting to maintain resources in public hands, in addition to the trade unions directly interested.

In general, besides exhibiting their societal power, through these initiatives unions demonstrated the possibility of good mutual cooperation; several trade unions and union confederations participated in all of them. Trade unions' relative societal power is also shown by their success in collecting enough signatures for referendum initiatives (see above). Of the nine initiatives launched in the past ten years, only two others were successful, apart from the four launched by trade unions.

Union representatives, primarily leaders and experts from trade union confederations, are often featured in the media and are the standard interlocutor regarding the labour market, the pension system, living standards and related issues. Their frequent media appearances have a twofold effect on trade unions' reputation and influence. On one hand, they have significant public visibility, giving the impression that they are an important and influential stakeholder. On the other hand, the fact that it is more or less the same union leaders who appear again and again (some since the beginning of the transition) often has a negative effect on public opinion. Nevertheless, the fact is that Croatian unions have not lost their presence in the public arena and are still able to express and try to impose their opinions on certain topics. Since the global financial crisis and the introduction of austerity measures by various governments, union leaders have become participants in heated public debates regarding austerity policies, often publicly attacking the authorities, but also entering into fierce debates with civil society actors and other stakeholders who support austerity measures or favour of deep public sector reforms, including the reduction of the welfare state.

Public trust in trade unions is not strong. According to a survey from the beginning of 2020, about half of all citizens over the age of 18 do not trust trade unions, while only about one-sixth of respondents expressed confidence in them.[15] According to their average value on the trust scale,

---

15 Data from a hitherto unpublished survey conducted by the Faculty of Political Science, University of Zagreb, on a nationally representative sample of 979 respondents.

trade unions are in the bottom half (ninth out of fourteen institutions surveyed) with an average score of 2.27. In this survey, citizens expressed a lower level of trust in political institutions such as political parties, the government, national parliament, courts and public administration. General trust in NGOs is slightly higher than in trade unions. This indicates that unions' status in the eyes of the public is lower than their media presence and political influence might suggest. At the same time, paradoxically, the unions are able to mobilize a large number of citizens for such actions as referendum initiatives, despite this relatively negative public standing.

Trade union policies towards the European Union

When it comes to the trade unions' attitude towards Croatia's integration in the EU and European institutions, the prevailing view seems to be that EU accession was inevitable. That was the consensus among parliamentary parties, and the unions did not raise a dissenting voice. Trade union criticism is often directed at domestic political elites regarding their lack of preparation for integration, as a result of which Croatia continues to have poorer living and working standards than other EU member states.

Croatia's accession to the EU happened during a period of prolonged recession, with high unemployment rates and other negative trends. The gradual opening up of the labour markets of core EU countries caused massive labour emigration, especially from the regions where industry has been shutting down for decades. Labour migration is one of the main issues that the unions have been trying to highlight at the EU and regional levels. Lower living standards than in other EU member states, poorer labour market indicators – such as a high share of temporary employment – are so-called push factors for emigration to the more affluent parts of the EU. On the other hand, labour emigration led to a growing need for foreign workers who can compensate for the country's shortages. That dynamic might lead to social dumping but also falling working conditions (see Eurofound 2017a, 2017b). For the same reason, the SSSH was against the Croatian parliament's 2016 decision to join the countries that showed the yellow card to the Posted Workers Directive. The parliament made its decision in order to preserve Croatian companies' and workers' competitiveness in EU by keeping the labour costs of Croatian workers low. Together with the European Trade Union Confederation (ETUC) and the European Economic and Social Committee, SSSH highlighted concerns about unfair competition and boosting competitiveness at the expense of wages and workers' rights.

The issue of the labour migration of foreign workers to Croatia, predominantly from neighbouring countries, is also a topic of debate between the members of the Regional Trade Union Council *Solidarnost*. *Solidarnost* was founded in 2011 in Ljubljana and brought together the former Yugoslavia trade unions. The Council was initially formed by Slovenian colleagues to provide support to trade unions in countries in the process of EU accession. Today, Croatia and Slovenia play the same role in guiding other countries in the region. The Regional Trade Union Council 'Solidarity' is an informal body that provides a platform for equal cooperation among its members. All agreements are adopted by unanimity.

During the global financial crises, union leaders, especially those from the public sector, were very critical of austerity policies in Croatia. They blamed the European Commission for using the European semester as a tool to put pressure on governments to implement austerity measures.

Today, all three national trade union confederations – SSSH, NHS and Matica – are full members of the ETUC. Croatian unions are present in eight out of ten industry-level European trade union federations (ETUFs). The only ETUFs of which Croatian unions are not members are the European Arts and Entertainment Alliance and the European Confederation of Police.

Conclusions

Croatian trade unions are at a crossroads. On one hand, they have the potential to start using their societal power. This has been proven over the past decade – despite their significant resource losses in terms of membership and funding – by a number of successful initiatives to reverse certain trends in political economy and to improve workers' living and working conditions. Declining labour supply because of the mass emigration of workers since Croatia's accession to the EU (estimated at more than 300,000 new emigrants since 2013) has helped in this (labour shortages are obvious from the rapid decrease in the number of unemployed and increasing demand for immigrant workers). There has also been a general shift in economic policy away from the neoliberal matrix. This could result in trade union revitalization, according to Visser's (2019) classification. On the other hand, the risk remains that the trade unions may become irrelevant and lose influence if membership continues to fall, along with financial and human resources. There does not appear to be a constant negative trend as regards union density, but there have been occasional crisis episodes characterized by a sudden loss of membership over a shorter period, alternating with periods of stagnating union density. Some future crisis episode could result in a new steep decline in membership, which could lead trade unions to the edge of marginalization (Visser 2019).

Which of these two paths Croatian unions will take, and with them the entire system of industrial relations, depends largely on four key issues.

The first issue concerns systemic efforts to recruit newly employed workers in the workplaces where unions already operate. Data suggest that the decline in union density is occurring in the core of the union movement, where trade unions have affiliates, already have a large membership and ensure benefits for workers through collective agreements.[16] Recruiting new generations of workers at the traditional union core is a matter of survival. Unless this is successful, the chance of recruiting members in firms with no experience and tradition of union organizing is significantly reduced.

The second key issue is the challenge of developing serious and effective union organizing campaigns in workplaces and occupations that lack a union tradition. Although there are unions in Croatia that can brag about their success in organizing previously unorganized workers, even among small employers, they are mainly in the public sector or enterprises experiencing business problems. There are few examples of successful union organizing in relatively stable and successful companies with no union tradition.

The third challenge that unions will face at the national level in the coming years is generational change among union leaders. Two out of three union confederations have leaders who have been around since the

16 Results from previously cited unpublished research by one of the authors. Research conducted in 2009 demonstrated that union density in work organizations in which there was at least one trade union confederation was around 70 per cent. By 2014 that was down to 60 per cent, and in 2018 to 54 per cent.

very beginning of the transition. Their imminent departure from these positions creates new opportunities, in the sense that the public are perhaps weary of them, but on the other hand their experience and relationships will depart with them. Generational change can also be expected in several large affiliated unions.

The fourth challenge concerns trade union reputation. As the data show, the average Croatian citizen does not have a positive opinion of unions. Despite that, the unions have managed to mobilize a significant part of the public in several major actions over the past decade. This suggests that trust has not been lost irretrievably. But in order for the trade unions to reverse negative trends in public policies and industrial relations, a systematic approach to reputation management is also needed, by both individual organizations and the union movement in general.

It is worth mentioning that there have been several experiences and achievements over the past decade that can serve as a positive basis for the first of the two paths leading to revitalization. First of all, the establishment of mostly good relations and successful cooperation between trade unions, especially among the three representative union confederations at the national level. There is also greater union confidence in their ability to mobilize the public for workers' interests, as exhibited by the four successful referendum initiatives. Also valuable is the establishment of cooperation with NGOs, but also the emergence of new NGOs focused directly on strengthening unionism or promoting ideas that will help strengthen the unions' position. We should also add the increased openness of some individual political actors towards union positions or the emergence of new political actors advocating policies that also imply strong and influential trade unions. Although this process is external to the unions, they can take some credit for it, based on the harsh criticisms they have directed towards certain political actors in previous years.

References

All links were checked on 6 July 2021.

Bagić D. (2010) Industrijski odnosi u Hrvatskoj – društvena integracija ili društveni sukob, Zagreb, Tim Press.

Bagić D. (2016) Obilježja kolektivnog pregovaranja u Republici Hrvatskoj: usporedba javnog sektora i gospodarstva, in Barjašić Špiler L. and Radek I. (eds) Utjecaj kolektivnih ugovora na prava radnika u RH, Zagreb, Matica hrvatskih sindikata, 107–162.

Bagić D. (2019) Croatia: stability amidst heterogeneous collective bargaining patterns, in Müller T., Vandaele K. and Waddington J. (eds) Collective bargaining in Europe: towards an endgame, Brussels, ETUI, 93–108.

Čepo D. and Nikić Čakar D. (2019) Direct democracy and the rise of political entrepreneurs: an analysis of citizens' initiatives in post-2010 Croatia, Anali Hrvatskog politološkog društva: Časopis za politologiju, 16 (1), 27–48. https://doi.org/10.20901/an.16.02

Crowley S. and Ost D. (eds) (2001) Workers after workers' states: labor and politics in postcommunist Eastern Europe, Oxford, Rowman & Littlefield.

Dolenec D., Balković A., Kralj K., Širinić D., Romanos E. and Fernandes T. (2020) Protest event dataset for Croatia, Portugal, Serbia and Spain: focus on strike data, Politička misao: casopis za politologiju, 57 (4), 155–168. https://doi.org/10.20901/pm.57.4.07

Eurofound (2017a) Fraudulent contracting of work: abusing the posting of workers (Belgium, Finland and Italy), Eurofound, Dublin.

Eurofound (2017b), Pay inequalities experienced by posted workers: challenges to the 'equal treatment' principle, Eurofound, Dublin.

Grdešić M. (2007) Uspon i pad stožera za obranu kompanija u Hrvatskoj, Revija za sociologiju, 38 (1/2), 55–69.

Hrvatski laburisti (2010) Programske smjernice. https://laburisti.com/programi/programske-smjernice/

Hrvatski laburisti (2020) Predsjedništvo. https://laburisti.com/sredisnja-tijela/predsjednistvo/

Ivandić M. and Livada I. (2014) Linije (dis)kontinuiteta – Kratak prikaz formi radničkog organiziranja I metoda borbe (1990–2014), Zarez 381, 10 April 2014.

Kokanović M. (1999) Croatian Labour Realities, 1990–1999, SEER – South-East Europe Review for Labour and Social Affairs, 2 (3), 185–208.

Kokanović M. (2001) The cost of nationalism: Croatian labour, 1990–1999, in Crowley S. and Ost D. (eds) Workers after workers' states: labor and politics in postcommunist Eastern Europe, Oxford, Rowman & Littlefield.

Lončar J. (2013) Petnaest godina borbe – Povijest stožera za obranu kompanije Petrokemija u Kutini, Le Monde Diplomatique [Croatian edition], 5 March 2013.

Matica hrvatskih Sindikata (2016) Okrugli stol: Je li vrijeme za političko organiziranje sindikata?, 18 January 2016. https://www.matica-sindikata.hr/okrugli-stol-je-li-vrijeme-za-politicko-organiziranje-sindikata/

Matković T. and Ostojić J. (2019) Tko što radi sada? Dob i rod kao odrednice položaja na tržištu rada u Hrvatskoj 2007–2018, in Puljiz V. (ed.) Socijalno-demografska reprodukcija Hrvatske, Zagreb, Projekt Centar za demokraciju i pravo Miko Tripalo.

Nestić D. and Blažević Burić S. (2018) Radnici na minimalnoj plaći i siromaštvo u Hrvatskoj, Revija za socijalnu politiku, 25 (3), 235–262. https://doi.org/10.3935/rsp.v25i3.1547

Official Gazette (2013/2018) Povjerenstvo za utvrđivanje reprezentativnosti, Narodne novine, 41/2013, 59/2018).

Vandaele K. (2019) Bleak prospects: mapping trade union membership in Europe since 2000, Brussels, ETUI.

Visser J. (2019) Trade unions in the balance, ILO ACTRAV Working Paper, Geneva, ILO.

Abbreviations

ETUC European Trade Union Confederation

ETUF European trade union federations

GSV Gospodarsko-socijalno vijeće (Economic and Social Council)

HURS Hrvatska udruga radničkih Sindikata (Croatian Trade Union Association)

Matica Matica hrvatskih sindikata (Association of Croatian Trade Unions)

NGOs non-governmental organizations

NHS Nezavisni hrvatski sindikati (Independent Trade Unions of Croatia)

SSSH Savez samostalnih sindikata Hrvatske (Union of Autonomous Trade Unions of Croatia)

URSH Udruga radničkih Sindikata Hrvatske (Union of Croatian Trade Unions)

ZOR Zakon o radu (Labour Act)

Chapter 6

Cyprus: A divided society with trade unions on a slow retreat

Gregoris Ioannou and Sertac Sonan

Cyprus is a small island in the eastern Mediterranean with a population of about 1 million. The main languages are Greek and Turkish. The island, which had come under British rule in 1878, became an independent republic in 1960. The political antagonism between the two main communities of the island, the Greek Cypriots and the Turkish Cypriots – who in 1960 accounted for 77 and 18 per cent of the population, respectively – resulted in inter-communal violence and the forced withdrawal of the Turkish Cypriot community from state institutions in 1964. The interventions of Greece and Turkey in 1974 led to the island's de facto territorial division and the total separation of the two communities, thus completing a process that had begun in the late 1950s. Consequently, roughly 37 per cent of the northern part of the island came under Turkish control. The island remains divided as all attempts to conclude a reunification agreement have thus far failed.

Whereas the Greek Cypriot community in the South, maintaining control of the Republic of Cyprus, achieved significant economic growth in the 1980s and 1990s and joined the European Union (EU) in 2004 and the euro zone in 2008, the Turkish Cypriot community has been unable to follow a similar route, largely because of the refusal of the international community to legitimize its secessionist initiative in the form of the establishment of the Turkish Republic of Northern Cyprus (KKTC, *Kuzey Kıbrıs Türk Cumhuriyeti*) in 1983, which is recognized and bankrolled only by Turkey.

Both sides' economies are oriented towards services, which account for almost 80 per cent of total employment (Eurostat and State Planning

Organisation 2020), and both have sizeable migrant labour populations; in the North around one-fourth of the registered workforce is made up of migrant workers (two-thirds from Turkey), while in the South the proportion is around 20 per cent. The labour force in the southern part of the island is currently just over 400,000 people, while the northern part has a smaller labour market with a labour force of around 150,000. As of 2019, Turkish Cypriot GDP per capita was $12,649 (Statistical Institute 2020), slightly less than half that of the Greek Cypriots, which was $27,858 (World Bank 2021).

In the South a fully fledged tripartite system of industrial relations was constructed and strengthened after 1974 with strong collective bargaining, while in the North the peculiar political situation and the public sector's economic dominance has resulted in weaker institutionalization and weaker collective bargaining. There are also significant differences in the structure and operation of the trade unions across the divide (Ioannou and Sonan 2017).

Since the 1980s substantial development has occurred, resulting in the expansion of the economy and the labour force in the South. Total trade union membership also increased and the proportion of women within it, but at a much slower rate than the labour force until the onset of the financial crisis, when it decreased slightly. Union density and collective bargaining coverage, however, dropped from around 80 per cent to around 40 per cent over a period of four decades (Table 6.1). The three main confederations[1] retained their dominant role in the trade union landscape, but the number of small independent trade unions expanded in this period.

In the Turkish Cypriot case, thanks to immigration, the labour force almost tripled between 1980 and 2019. Union membership, however, went up by only 25 per cent (Table 6.2). Therefore, although there are no comparable data with which to calculate the exact density figures, it is safe to say that there has been a remarkable decline in both union density and collective bargaining coverage. Female labour force participation seems to have been stuck at around 40 per cent since 2004, when reliable data

---

1 There is an issue of terminology here as both PEO and DEOK call themselves federations of trade unions, while SEK, a confederation of trade union industrial federations, is further subdivided into local trade unions. For the purposes of this chapter and for clarity, international consistency and comparative value we will treat PEO and DEOK as confederations as well.

collection started. The trade union landscape has traditionally been fragmented: there are three confederations,[2] which currently have nineteen affiliated trade unions, while there are twenty-nine independent unions, almost all exclusively organized in the public and semi-public sectors.

Table 6.1 Principal characteristics of trade unionism in Cyprus (South)

	1980	**2000**	**2019**
Total trade union membership	123,000	170,000	180,000
Women as a proportion of total membership	30 %*	36 %	38 %
Gross union density[1]	80 %	65 %	43 %*
Net union density[2]	80 %	65 %	43 %*
Number of confederations	3	3	3
Number of affiliated unions (federations)	22	21	21
Number of independent unions	30	70	100
Collective bargaining coverage[3]	80 %	65 %	43 %*
Principal level of collective bargaining	Industry level and company level		
Days not worked due to industrial action per 1,000 workers	534	4	62**

Note: * Estimate; ** 2018. Various figures in Table 6.1 are approximations based on various fragmented available sources (Trade Union Registrar 2021; Eurofound 2020; Republic of Cyprus 2004). As unemployment was very low in 1980 and 2000 and relatively low in 2019, gross union density and net union density tend to converge – also many unionized workers retain their union membership while being unemployed without paying dues. Because there are no extension mechanisms the same figure can be used for collective bargaining coverage. The number of functioning independent unions is an estimate based on the Trade Union Registrar 2021 catalogue, which lists the legal entities, including district labour centres, according to year of initial registration. There is high fluctuation in the strike statistics from year to year and the three yearly snapshots captured in Table 6.1 cannot be used to identify a trend.

2 All three call themselves federations.

Table 6.2 Principal characteristics of trade unionism in Cyprus (North)

	1980	2004	2019
Total trade union membership	19,120	21,756	24,937
Women as a proportion of total membership	n.a.	n.a.	44 %
Gross union density[1]	n.a.	29 %	20 %
Net union density[2]	n.a.	34 %	22 %
Number of confederations	0	0	0
Number of affiliated unions (federations)	3	3	3
Number of independent unions	n.a.	n.a.	29
Collective bargaining coverage[3]	n.a.	34 %	22 %
Principal level of collective bargaining	Company level (for semi-public institutions and municipalities); sectoral level (for public sector)		
Days not worked due to industrial action per 1,000 workers	n.a.	n.a.	n.a.

Note: All figures are calculated by the authors based on official statistics (trade union membership figures are from Statistical Yearbooks (various years); the share of women among trade union members in 2019 is provided by the Trade Unions' Registrar; the number of salaried employees, total labour force and unemployment figures (used to calculate the trade union density) come from annual Household Labour Force Surveys conducted by the Statistical Institute (İstatistik Kurumu) (various years)).

Historical background and principal features of the industrial relations system

The industrial relations system in the South is of the voluntarist type, influenced by the British model as its roots go back to the colonial period. Collective bargaining enjoys procedural and political support at the institutional level but does not have legal force per se. Established at a time when trade unions were strong, the Greek Cypriot industrial relations system assigns the state a mediating role, leaving substantial scope to organized employers and trade unions to regulate employment relations themselves. The Code of Industrial Relations, agreed on a tripartite basis and in operation since 1977, itself an instrument with no legal force, describes the procedures, the time frames for dispute resolution, restraining but not stifling industrial conflict. In the North, industrial relations are regulated by law rather than voluntarism, inspired more by the Turkish model. The fact that trade unions are almost exclusively organized in the public sector, in effect means that, in the absence of union protection, employees in the private sector enjoy much more limited rights than employees in the public sector. The only social dialogue mechanism that covers private sector employees is the minimum wage determination commission, which is composed of representatives of government, employers and employees, and meets at least once a year to determine the statutory minimum wage.

The origins of the trade union movement in Cyprus can be traced back to the 1920s in committees springing out of spontaneous strikes in the mines and construction sites, in which communist militants had a key role. In 1932 the first legislation was introduced but it took another decade before the institutionalization of trade unionism could begin, when the union movement expanded significantly, and the colonial authorities proceeded to liberalize and expand labour-related legislation. The initial trade unions were ethnically mixed, but the rising nationalism and the developing conflict between the elites of the two communities resulted in the separation of Greek Cypriots and Turkish Cypriots within the trade unions, a process which was completed by the late 1950s (Fantis 2006; Slocum 1972).

As the two communities' trade union landscapes are almost entirely different from one another, in the rest of this chapter they will be analysed separately, apart from in the concluding section where both sides will be evaluated together.

The South

In the Greek Cypriot community, another split took place on parallel ideological lines at the time when the trade unions were attempting to confederate. By the mid-1940s the 'new trade unions' had been formed on an anti-communist platform denouncing the communist control of the old unions led by the Pancyprian Trade Union Committee (Παγκύπρια Συντεχνιακή Επιτροπή, ΠΣΕ), which subsequently became the Pancyprian Federation of Labour (Παγκύπρια Εργατική Ομοσπονδία, ΠΕΟ). This was the time of the civil war in Greece, which affected the Greek Cypriot community in Cyprus, and the Cold War, which resulted in the split up of the trade union movement at a global level. The new trade unions subsequently became the Cyprus' Employees Confederation

(Συνομοσπονδία Εργαζομένων Κύπρου, ΣΕΚ). PEO and SEK have since then been the two main confederations in the Greek Cypriot community.

Whereas PEO is affiliated with the left-wing Progressive Party of the Working People (Ανορθωτικό Κόμμα Εργαζομένου Λαού, ΑΚΕΛ), SEK is positioned on the centre-right of the political spectrum, which in the post-1974 era has been dominated by Democratic Rally (Δημοκρατικός Συναγερμός, ΔΗΣΥ) and the Democratic Party (Δημοκρατικό Κόμμα, ΔΗΚΟ). In the early 1960s a split from SEK established a third small trade union confederation, the Democratic Labour Federation of Cyprus (Δημοκρατική Εργατική Ομοσπονδία Κύπρου, ΔΕΟΚ). This is now aligned to the small social democratic party Movement for Social Democracy Party (EDEK), which was formed a few years later. The close connection of the unions with political parties is a principal feature of the trade union movement and has evolved largely without changing (Ioannou 2016). This connection is more customary than formal and determines the recruitment of union personnel, the direct lines of communication between union and party leaders and, in the case of the Left, the combination of trade union and political careers. In the case of SEK, a relatively recent constitutional clause prohibits the holding of union and party posts simultaneously, but transitions from the one to the other, ordinary membership and activism continue.

Structure of trade unions and union democracy

Both PEO and SEK are centralized organizations and although they have some differences of structure and name, power ultimately rests at the central level. PEO is a confederation composed of eight trade unions, organized on an industry basis. SEK is a confederation composed of seven trade union 'federations', some of which are subdivided into other, smaller trade unions covering specific groups of workers. The largest and most significant independent trade unions are also listed in Table 6.3. It is important to note that while in PASYDY and ETYK internal factions aligned to political parties are unofficial, in the public-sector education trade unions such factions – both party and non-party aligned – are institutionalized (Ioannou 2016). The number of independent trade unions has increased in recent decades, but most remain small and cover particular groups of workers, comprising altogether less than one-third of total union membership, with PEO and SEK exceeding two-thirds of total union membership.

Whereas trade unions all operate under democratic rules governed by

Table 6.3 Main trade union organizations in Cyprus (South)

Full name	Acronym	Type	Membership
Pancyprian Federation of Labour (Παγκύπρια Εργατική Ομοσπονδία, ΠΕΟ)	PEO	Confederation	61,656 (2019)
Cyprus' Employees Confederation (Συνομοσπονδία Εργαζομένων Κύπρου, ΣΕΚ)	SEK	Confederation	60,635 (2019)
Pancyprian Union of Civil Servants (Παγκύπρια Συντεχνία Δημοσίων Υπαλλήλων, ΠΑΣΥΔΥ)	PASYDY	Independent (public sector)	14,024 (2019)
Organisation of Greek Secondary Education Teachers (Οργάνωση Ελλήνων Λειτουργών Μέσης Εκπαίδευσης Κύπρου, ΟΕΛΜΕΚ)	OELMEK	Independent (public-sector secondary education)	5,757 (2019)
Pancyprian Organisation of Greek Teachers (Παγκύπρια Οργάνωση Ελλήνων Δασκάλων, ΠΟΕΔ)	POED	Independent (public-sector primary education)	6,287 (2019)
Union of Bank Employees Cyprus (Ένωση Τραπεζικών Υπαλλήλων Κύπρου, ΕΤΥΚ)	ETYK	Independent (banking)	9,195 (2018)

Source: Eurofound (2020).

their constitutions, with congresses and elections, a series of factors often erect obstacles that may at least partially hollow out substantive internal democracy. Oligarchic elements are, to be sure, present in all mass organizations, but competing with democratic elements. The indifference and passivity of a large section of the rank-and-file members means in practice that, at most times, only a minority engages in trade union politics. Salaried trade union officials compose an overtly large and crucial segment of the trade union leadership at all levels, while the bureaucratization and drift of trade unionism into the role of service provision, in combination with centralization in place, enhances the distance between trade unions as organizations and their members (Ioannou 2015). Although workplace committees and workplace assemblies, especially in times of industrial conflict, are forums for dialogue, deliberation and voting, the views of professional trade unionists tend to weigh more than those of ordinary members.

There have been no significant mergers in recent decades. The last trade union restructuring within PEO took place in 2002 when some smaller trade unions were merged and a new one was formed covering workers in the service sector and transferring members from other existing trade unions. Nor has there been a significant breakaway from the two main confederations, although some groups of workers in various industries and sectors are mobile across trade union boundaries. The most significant such mobility has been in the public sector in recent decades, from PASYDY to small independent unions. This has also affected SEK, which traditionally has dominated in the semi-public sector, both winning and losing members, especially peripheral or special groups of workers who are employed irregularly.

Unionization

The main trend in trade union membership in the past few decades has been stagnation. The fall in union density, however, has been dramatic, from 65 per cent in 2000 to around 40 per cent today because of the growing workforce. There are multiple reasons for the decline of union density: first, economic restructuring, bringing the decline of traditionally unionized industries, such as light manufacturing, and the rise of numerous service industries where unionization is more difficult; second, the weakening of collectivism and political identities and the rise of individualistic mentalities and worldviews; third, the weakening institutional power of trade unions and the increasing difficulty of protecting workers, which makes trade union membership less attractive; fourth, the increasing proportion of migrant, young and precarious workers in the labour force, who are more difficult to organize (Ioannou 2015; Ioannou and Charalambous 2019). Although some attempts have been made to reverse or at least slow down the decline, with trade unions attempting to enter new workplaces and new industries, as well as implementing information campaigns in universities, there has been no systematic, resourceful and comprehensive campaign in that direction.

The official definition of a trade union member, according to the Trade Union Registrar, is a person who has paid at least a monthly membership contribution in the past two years. Thus it includes many unemployed people. When people become unemployed, they tend to distance themselves from trade unions, however, and do not participate in union life. Pensioners are not formally counted as union members, although PEO has a separate pensioners' organization which is sometime active as a pressure group. As the proportion of women in the labour force expanded significantly in the last quarter of the twentieth century, this was also reflected in trade union membership: the proportion of women rose from around a quarter in the 1970s to more than 35 per cent by 2000. Although women are overrepresented in several industries that are highly unionized, such as public administration, banking and education, they are also overrepresented in industries that are typically non-unionized, such as sales and services and are more likely to be in non-standard and precarious employment, which again tends to be non-unionized.

Trade union membership in absolute numbers had been expanding following the expansion of the total working population until the onset of the economic crisis in 2011. This expansion in the 1990s and 2000s however, was far below the expansion of the workforce, resulting in a decline of union density (Ioannou and Sonan 2014). The revision of the trade union law in 2012 strengthened the right to unionization in two ways: it eases unionists' access to workplaces and it allocated more time for elected workers to carry out their trade union duties, instituting a procedure for obligatory union recognition if more than 40 per cent of workers are willing to opt for union membership (Yannakourou 2016). Yet the improvement achieved in trade union legislation, which was beneficial to organizing efforts, was insufficient to arrest the trend in membership decline in relation to the expansion of the labour force. In the crisis decade of the 2010s trade unions lost members and faced even greater difficulty recruiting new ones to replace them.

Some progress was achieved in terms of recruitment of migrant workers in unionized industries such as hotels and construction in the 2010s, but not so with regard to precarious workers, Cypriots or migrants (Ioannou 2017; Trimikliniotis and Demetriou 2011). There is limited, if any platform work in the southern part of Cyprus; in any case, freelancers and the self-employed generally tend to be non-unionized. In a best-case scenario, some groups of bogus self-employed may join trade unions to demand employee status or set up independent associations, which then ask for trade union and more broadly social support in their efforts to gain employee status. Really self-employed professionals are not represented by trade unions; at best they may set up an association for lobbying rather than bargaining purposes.

As far as sectors and industries are concerned there is significant variation. Unionization is relatively very high in industries such as banking, medium to high in construction, and hotels, and relatively low in retail trade and services. It is much higher in the public and semi-public sector than in the private sector and there is significant variation within industries. It is, for example, very high in public education and much lower in private education at all levels. Unionization tends to be higher in bigger than in smaller workplaces and is almost non-existent in small and micro companies. Some employers are firmly and actively anti-union; in such settings, workers are typically too afraid to join trade unions and unions too reluctant to put resources into recruitment campaigns.

Union resources and expenditure

Union funding comes primarily from membership fees, which typically constitute 0.5–1 per cent of a worker's monthly salary and are deducted directly from the employing firm's accounts office. In PEO, fees are collected by its affiliates organized in district labour centres; out of this revenue, 30 per cent is allocated to the central confederation. In SEK which has its affiliates organized into federations in addition to the district labour centres, the central confederation is allocated 15 per cent, while an additional 10 per cent is kept at the trade union middle 'federal level'. There have been no significant changes in this model in recent decades. As PEO, SEK and DEOK are all centralized and politically unified structures internally, little can be deduced about internal power relations from formal organizational structures and internal resource allocation.

Sometimes, to avoid competition in certain unionized workplaces, PEO and SEK may agree dual membership, with the fee divided 50/50 between the two confederations. This practice was instituted not long ago to deal with some workers' reluctance to be identified with one union because it might serve as a proxy for political affiliation. This practice is neither widespread nor formalized. It is a practical tool aimed to help unions to embark on collaborative recruitment campaigns and it tends to be temporary. PEO and SEK do not have reduced rates for special categories of workers, but they do not charge membership fees to unwaged (unemployed) members. Both confederations operate various benefit schemes for their members, such as subsidized holidays, and provide some services, such as subsidized health care and pharmaceutical provision. Both were significant factors in slowing down union decline in the 1990s and 2000s by persuading otherwise discontented workers to retain their union affiliation. Whereas the subsidized holidays continue to be important, perhaps more so in austerity and post-austerity times – and unions also receive a subsidy from the state's social security holiday fund to keep the scheme going – trade unions' health care and pharmaceutical role is expected to become redundant as the General Health Service introduced in 2019 develops fully in the current decade. Trade union organizations own some buildings, but these assets do not bring in significant income as they are primarily used for offices (Tombazos 2020).

The state also directly and indirectly supports the trade unions financially, to a small extent. Union subscriptions are tax deductible and so are employer and employee contributions to provident and pension funds, where they exist, creating incentives to workers to join both trade unions and provident and pension funds. Trade unions are usually involved directly or indirectly via unionized workers, along with employer representatives, in the administration of these funds, which vary in size from industry to firm level. In non-unionized workplaces and non-unionized industries provident and pension funds are rare. Additionally, the state subsidizes some of the training functions of trade unions, both directly in terms of trade union education and indirectly in terms of subsidizing workers' training by union trainers and the holiday schemes mentioned above. Employers, both state and private ones, can also be considered an alternative source of minimal indirect support in the sense that they are obliged to provide trade union representatives with time off.

Collective bargaining and unions at the workplace

Collective bargaining is conducted at the industry and company levels and as there is no extension mechanism, coverage rates tend to coincide with trade union density. In the past three decades following its decline from around 75 per cent in the early 1990s to around 40 per cent today

(Ioannou and Sonan 2019). The absence of extension mechanisms means that some employers can avoid being bound by industrial collective agreements and this tends to occur more frequently in smaller companies. Trade unions have been trying to get the government to institute an extension mechanism for almost two decades but have been unsuccessful as employers objected and the right-wing government in office since 2013 has been unwilling to push it through. Recently however, trade unions did manage to make some terms of the collective agreements universally applicable and legally binding: starting wages in the hotel industry and working time and other monetary benefits in construction.

The two bargaining levels rarely co-exist – in some industries, such as manufacturing and transport bargaining, takes place at company level, in others such as hotels and constructions at industry level. So, unlike other southern European countries the predominance of the two levels has not arisen during the crisis. While this means that there is no free riding, it must also be said that often collective bargaining does tend to exert some positive indirect influence on the wages of non-unionized workers who are not formally covered by it. Although there is disorganization among employers in some industries, and some employers opt out of their associations to avoid being bound by industry-level collective bargaining, overall, employers' associations at industry level are sufficiently solid. Trade unions usually have more difficulty finding interlocutors at the company level.

In industries where there is no collective bargaining, again trade union pressure may result in some improvements in terms and conditions of employment, or at least force the employer to abide with the legal minimum. This in a sense has mixed implications for trade union organization, providing workers with both incentives and disincentives for joining. Health and safety issues are typically not a domain in which trade unions play an institutionalized role, but industries with frequent accidents, such as construction, do constitute focal points for union campaigns.

Over time trade union power at the workplace level has declined as in many workplaces the proportion of non-unionized, precariously employed workers has expanded; subcontracting has also contributed to further fragmentation (Ioannou 2015). The fact that there are more non-unionized workplaces has encouraged some employers in unionized workplaces to partially evade collective agreements by making other arrangements for newly hired staff or not enforcing some clauses for all staff. The incidence of employers refusing to negotiate collective agreements or to re-negotiate renewal of collective agreements has increased over the years.

This has made PEO and SEK more ready to resort to the state, both to make collective agreements and to have them enforced to protect their members. PEO shifted its position in the late 2000s and joined with SEK to lobby to strengthen collective bargaining via legislative means. During the crisis in the 2010s both unions campaigned for the introduction of a legislative floor on wages and basic benefits. The trade unions were unsuccessful with the first issue, although they did secure improvements on the organizational front with the 2012 trade union law. With respect to minimum wages, progress was achieved in the industrial collective bargaining in 2019 resulting in the institution of a legislative minimum wage floor for a series of occupations in hotels in 2020. In construction, the main violations of the collective agreement concerned working time and overtime pay, public holidays, bonuses and the refusal or delay of some employers to contribute to the Provident Fund. The trade unions' decade-long campaign led to an agreement in 2019, which made these 'key terms' of the sectoral collective agreement legally enforceable in 2020 (Ergatiko Vima, 2020).

Industrial conflict

Strike action has not traditionally been frequent in Cyprus. When it does take place in highly unionized industries, however, they are typically successful in terms of participation. When this concerns big industries, such as construction or public services, the number of lost workdays shoots up. A very long construction strike in 2013 resulted in the record number of 605,464 workdays lost. In the past decade there have been some smaller spikes, such as in 2012 with 48,294 workdays lost and in 2016 with 35,801 workdays lost. There are no significant restrictions on strike action, with some exceptions regarding 'essential services' and generally no other major legal or institutional obstacles (Ioannou and Sonan 2019). At the same time, there is no tradition of general strikes or solidarity strikes, although it is common in cases of long strikes in one industry for strikers to be supported by trade unions in other industries via public statements, contributions to the strike fund and also, in rare cases, with participation in protests. The trend at both the industrial and the company levels has been for strike action to be used as a threat and as a bargaining weapon, usually conducted during the period of the renewal of collective agreements, starting with a warning three-hour or four-hour stoppage, then moving to twenty-four hours or forty-eight hours, but rarely going beyond that.

During the crisis years, however, another observed trend was numerous local strikes, usually about the non-payment or delayed payment of wages and against employer unilateralism, typically by cutting wages, benefits or reducing contributions to provident or pension funds (Ioannou and Charalambous 2017). Although the bigger picture, after the beginning of public-sector cuts in 2010–2011, was that trade unions acquiesced or negotiated and signed interim austerity agreements in numerous industries and workplaces, in some cases when they were strong enough, they challenged employer aggression with indefinite strikes. These were mostly defensive actions, however, usually merely inducing the state to enforce the law. Overall, at least as far as unionized workplaces are concerned, most employers have showed an interest in maintaining stable labour relations. As long as trade unions signalled their willingness to retreat, in principle accepting voluntary redundancies and cuts, employers did not engage in union busting and frontal assaults on collective bargaining, opting instead for negotiations and temporary compromises.

An exception to this was the construction industry in 2013, where employers questioned industrial collective bargaining as an institution, provoking a defensive – even existentially defensive, for that matter – strike, which turned out to be very long in duration, wide in scope and unrelated to any law violations. Construction was the industry worst hit by the crisis and by late 2012 was on its knees, with thousands of workers laid off and employers refusing to renew collective agreements. The strike launched in 2013, which lasted more than a month, was a strategic rearguard action that was really about the defence of collective bargaining as such rather than any specific demands (Ioannou 2021).

Big trade unions do distribute strike benefits to their members but usually only in cases of prolonged strikes of more than four to five days. There are no separate member contributions to strike funds, nor are these kept separately in union budgets; funds for this purpose are raised by open appeals when needed.

Political relations

All three general trade union confederations are closely linked to political parties, in one way or another. In the big independent trade unions, where a general party direction is absent, the political parties again exert some influence through their formal or informal factions. Even small independent trade unions that have no political party affiliations also need to resort to political parties and lobbying, especially when industrial relations drift into conflict. The connection of the union confederations to political parties gives them access to information about government plans and parliamentary discussions, while their participation in the social dialogue system and the numerous tripartite committees allows them to have a say on a wide range of labour and social policy issues (Sparsis 1998). The organizational implications of this are mixed. On one hand, trade unions can present themselves as powerful institutional forces that are able to influence things at the state level. While this may help to attract some workers, it may alienate others, who see them as part of a system that is not working in favour of workers' interests.

Tripartite corporatism and social partnership have not been working as extensively and as thoroughly as in the past. Whereas in the 1960s, and more so in the 1970s and 1980s, tripartite social dialogue was fairly elaborate and significant, albeit not sufficiently institutionalized as it was also conducted in the spirit of voluntarist industrial relations, in the 1990s and 2000s, as Cyprus became more subjected to international economic pressures and political and ideological influences, the trust and commitment of both the employers and the state was gradually eroded. In the crisis years of the 2010s social dialogue suffered major blows and its weakening has not been fully reversed in the post-crisis years (Ioannou 2021). In the heyday of corporatism, trade unions, employers and the state reached formal tripartite agreements at the national level on several issues – such as the dispute resolution procedures, social insurance reforms, and labour and welfare legislation – and were frequently consulted on matters of social and employment policy. The initiative always rested with the government, and bringing the social partners on board before legislating was considered beneficial. Although still in place, social dialogue has become rarer and thinner. The crisis and subsequently since 2013 the right-wing government's lack of commitment to the usefulness of social dialogue, has meant not only fewer tripartite agreements but also less consultation, at least with the trade unions, which has been minimal and less substantive.

Trade union objections against the austerity measures adopted before and during the Troika years were completely ignored. Instead, state actors were happy to get on board with the employers' viewpoint that social dialogue was a luxury that could not be afforded in times of emergency.

The fact that a left-wing government was in office at the time prevented PEO from mobilizing, while SEK and DEOK also restricted themselves to rhetorical rather than actual protests. After the change of government in 2013, and once the impact of the austerity measures began to take its toll, PEO and DEOK did engage in some street protests along with other unions and civil society groups, but unlike in other southern European countries this was neither comprehensive nor frequent or sufficiently large-scale; nor did it replace workplace conflict. In any case, as in other southern European countries, demonstrations were not effective in impacting policymaking at the state level.

Even after the end of the emergency period, the government took a lot of social and labour policy decisions unilaterally and less so via meaningful social dialogue. Meetings of the tripartite committees became rarer and often were held after the decisions had been taken by the government, just before their submission for formal approval by the Council of Ministers. Social dialogue and consultation in the context of the European Semester process, contrary to the formally stated desire of the European Commission to have the social partners involved, was even thinner. Typically, the policy text is so diametrically opposed to the unions' viewpoint that it is difficult to engage with it substantially. In any case, even when state officials do receive feedback from the trade unions, it rarely finds its way into the final text (Ioannou 2021).

Something else that needs mentioning and that illustrates the continued weakness of trade unions to effectively lobby political institutions and exert political influence is the long-drawn-out attempt to strengthen labour inspections by establishing an Independent Labour Inspection Service. After many years of social dialogue, in 2019 the trade unions managed to persuade the government to stop delaying and prepare the relevant bill instituting the Service with an increased range, scope and depth of authority, only to be defeated by a parliamentary majority of the right and centre-right parties, including the governing party. After one more year of delay the bill was finally voted on in 2020 and its implementation – the re-organization of the Labour Inspection Service – is currently in process.

Societal power

Trade unions have been a little more successful at retaining their societal power rather than their institutional power over the past two decades. Although neoliberal discourse has gained ground in the public sphere since its emergence in the 1990s and had escalated by the 2010s, trade unionism was not delegitimized. Most attacks by employers, politicians and the press concerned or were focused on public-sector unionism and aimed to present public-sector unions as representing vested interests of the privileged and their leaderships. The fact that the power in PASYDY was seen to be concentrated in the hands of its leader, serving as general secretary for almost three decades before losing the leadership election in 2020, was used to tarnish the image of all trade unions. The fact that top-level civil servants and often ministers were ex-PASYDY members, and the fact that lobbying was PASYDY's main form of action, led to accusations of backdoor deals and collusion with the political elite. This delegitimized them in the eyes of broader society (Papanastasiou 2017). Although attempted, it was more difficult to do this effectively with respect to the education trade unions, as was evident with their popular mass protests in 2018.

PASYDY has been challenged in multiple ways as it has been unable to maintain good working conditions in the public sector and its leadership is considered to promote the interests of a more privileged core against those of an expanding periphery of younger, newly recruited and irregularly employed workers. PASYDY has lost members over the past decade and the new trade unions that have emerged, ASDYK and ISOTITA, have not been able to make a breakthrough. Overall, density has declined in the public sector. PASYDY has maintained its privileged role in negotiating with the government, not only on labour issues but also on broader organizational matters.

ETYK in the banking industry has been under increasing pressure. During the crisis the employers went as far as disbanding their association for a few years (Rougala 2015), forcing the decentralization of collective bargaining from industry to company level. After the cooperative societies were converted into branches of a state bank, PEO and SEK entered the banking industry and competed with ETYK. The antagonism among the trade unions is ultimately not helpful in the long-drawn-out battle to defend and maintain the universalist logic of wage rises against the performance-related approach promoted by some banks.

Trade unions are heedful of the importance of communications and frequently issue statements on various labour and social policy issues, which usually find their way into the media. Although late-comers and still struggling with the internet and social media, they have advanced in the past decade on this front as well. There has been no systematic campaign in recent years, however, in the sense of allocating substantial energy and resources to a set of specific targets. Nor have they engaged in any systematic coalition-building with NGOs and other civil society organizations beyond some occasional or annual events. It must be said that NGOs and civil society organizations acting truly independently from political parties are limited in number and significance, while environmental activism, although on the rise in recent years, has focused mainly on specific issues rather than on developing a comprehensive agenda with which to seek institutional support and coalition-building.

Trade union policies towards the European Union

While all trade unions, as one might expect, oppose the dominant neoliberal policy framework of the EU, they also differ in their viewpoints, relations and policies towards the EU as an institution. Whereas SEK and DEOK are members of the European Trade Union Confederation (ETUC), PEO, which is affiliated to the World Federation of Trade Unions (WFTU), is not. As small trade unions from a small country, however, neither of them has a particularly active role within European-level trade union confederations and federations. They do follow developments, receive information, send delegates and all maintain international relations departments. Their engagement is, however, minimal and their involvement in European social dialogue remains limited. That also applies to their expectations of the ETUC and the European trade union federations at industry level. SEK, which is more EU-oriented and active in the ETUC, lobbies for more attention and institutional support to be given to the second pillar of pensions, especially the provident funds (Argyrides 2020). As a result of the structure of the Cyprus economy, overwhelmingly dominated by small and medium-sized enterprises – with micro-enterprises having a substantially enhanced role – European works councils are largely absent.

Although the economic crisis and its painful political management in Cyprus provoked a general rise in Euroscepticism, it did not last more than a few years. Like elsewhere, trade unions in the south of Cyprus did not adopt populist positions and refrained from developing populist narratives, preferring instead to refer to more classic 'workers and welfare' themes both in their mobilizations and in their rhetoric in general (Ioannou and Charalambous 2019). Although neither of the two main confederations is, formally speaking, social democratic in orientation, as PEO leans towards the left-wing AKEL and SEK towards the centre-right parties DISY and DIKO, their politics are pragmatic and usually support a progressive agenda in terms of employment relations and social policy. PEO, although embracing a soft Euroscepticism at times, which is to some extent why it keeps a distance from the ETUC, does follow developments at EU level and its research centre, the Cyprus Labour Institute (INEK), is Cyprus' national partner of Eurofound. SEK is more conservative ideologically and politically it is currently more constrained because of its association with a government that is not friendly towards workers' interests.

The North

The trade union movement in the northern part of the island was shaped by the dynamics of the inter-communal conflict between the two communities, which turned violent in the 1950s. This hindered the development of modern institutions, including trade unions, until 1974 (see Ioannou and Sonan 2014, 2017) when the island was divided geographically. Although the union movement had started as a common struggle of Cypriots during British colonial rule, starting in the aftermath of Second World War, and in parallel with the intensification of calls for union with Greece among Greek Cypriots, calls for separate Turkish Cypriot trade unions became vocal within the Turkish Cypriot community. The first ethnically homogenous Turkish Cypriot unions emerged in the 1940s, under the roof of the Cyprus Turkish Workers Unions Federation, which was later renamed the Cyprus Turkish Trade Unions Federation (*Türk-Sen, Kıbrıs Türk İşçi Sendikaları Federasyonu*) in December 1954 (Türk-Sen 2020). Collaboration with bigger (Greek Cypriot) confederations, particularly PEO, continued nevertheless. This eventually came to an end towards the end of the 1950s, once the Turkish Cypriot paramilitary organization the Turkish Resistance Organization (TMT, *Türk Mukavemet Teşkilatı*) took control of the union movement, along with all other political and social institutions. This marked the end of cooperation between the two communities and deprived Turkish Cypriot workers of the protection provided by bigger and more organized (now solely Greek Cypriot) trade unions. Although a common state – the Republic of Cyprus – was formed in 1960, the ethnic division continued in almost every aspect of life, and subsequently an even deeper crack emerged after

1964 when the Turkish Cypriot leadership ordered all Turkish Cypriots to gather in enclaves/ghettoes following violent clashes between the two communities at Christmas 1963.

In parallel with the decrease in tension between the two communities, a few other unions started to emerge in the Turkish Cypriot enclaves after 1968, and the first Trade Union Law was passed in 1971 by the Turkish Cypriot authorities. Until 1974, however, the TMT maintained its dominance over Turkish Cypriots' social, economic and political affairs, and only after the relative normalization and demilitarization of the post-1974 period did trade unions start to gain more autonomy and a more class-based orientation. Even then, a split between the right-wing and left-wing unions continued, and right-wing unions maintained their nationalistic character.

Structure of trade unions and union democracy

For a small island economy with a total workforce slightly below 150,000 in 2020 (İstatistik Kurumu 2020) and trade union membership at 25,000 (Statistical Institute 2020: 232), it might be said that the northern part of Cyprus has too many trade unions, resulting in a fragmented union landscape. As of 2017, there were eighty-three registered trade unions, fifty-three of which were active (Güler 2017). In the Trade Union Registrar's latest list for 2019, forty-nine trade unions are listed, although one is for employers, so forty-eight is perhaps a more accurate figure. The high number of trade unions can be attributed to the ease of setting up a trade union; only twenty members are required to establish a new union. Another possible reason is the lack of a culture of democracy and problem-solving within unions, which leads to the splitting off of disgruntled members (KTAMS leader Ahmet Kaptan, cited in Güler 2017); one very recent example of such splintering took place following the general assembly of a trade union at which, having lost the leadership, the defeated chair set up a new one to lead. Furthermore, politicians have traditionally encouraged fragmentation as it undermines the strength of the larger unions and of the union movement in general (Güler 2017).

Table 6.4 Main trade union organizations in Cyprus (North)

Full name	Acronym	Type	Membership
Federation of Free Trade Unions (Hür İşçi Sendikaları Federasyonu)	Hür-İş	Confederation	4,752
Federation of Cyprus Turkish Trade Unions (Kıbrıs Türk İşçi Sendikaları Federasyonu)	Türk-Sen	Confederation	1,611
Federation of Revolutionary Trade Unions (Devrimci İşçi Sendikaları Federasyonu)	Dev-İş	Confederation	1,138
Cyprus Turkish Primary School Teachers Union (Kıbrıs Türk Öğretmenler Sendikası)	KTÖS	Independent (public-sector primary education)	2,261
Cyprus Turkish Secondary School Teachers Union (Kıbrıs Türk Orta Eğitim Öğretmenler Sendikası)	KTOEÖS	Independent (public-sector secondary education)	2,516
Cyprus Turkish Civil Servants Trade Union (Kıbrıs Türk Amme Memurları Sendikası)	KTAMS	Independent (public sector)	3,593
Cyprus Turkish Public Officials Trade Union (Kıbrıs Türk Kamu Görevlileri Sendikası)	Kamu-Sen	Independent (public sector)	2,107
Public Workers Trade Union (Kamu İşçileri Sendikası)	Kamu-İş	Member of Hür-İş	2,750
Municipal Workers Trade Union (Belediye Emekçileri Sendikası)	BES	Independent	1,541

Source: Trade Union Registrar (2020) and Statistical Institute (2020).

There are three trade union confederations, which account for 30 per cent of overall trade union membership: the Federation of Cyprus Turkish Trade Unions (Türk-Sen, *Kıbrıs Türk İşçi Sendikaları Federasyonu*), the Federation of Revolutionary Trade Unions (Dev-İş, *Devrimci İşçi Sendikaları Federasyonu*), and the Federation of Free Trade Unions (Hür-İş, *Hür İşçi Sendikaları Federasyonu*). The biggest, right-leaning Hür-İş, has seven affiliated unions and a total of 4,752 members, while the smallest, the leftist Dev-İş, has three affiliated unions and a total of 1,138 members (Statistical Institute 2020). The left-leaning Türk-Sen, which is the oldest federation, has nine affiliated unions with a total membership of 1,611.

Around 70 per cent of trade union members are organized in twenty-nine independent unions (Statistical Institute 2020: 236). The organizations with the biggest membership and influence among the independent unions are those of the teachers, who are organized in two separate unions, the Cyprus Turkish Primary School Teachers Union (KTÖS, *Kıbrıs Türk Öğretmenler Sendikası*) and the Cyprus Turkish Secondary School Teachers Union (KTOEÖS, *Kıbrıs Türk Orta Eğitim Öğretmenler Sendikası*), and of civil servants, who also have two unions based along ideological lines, the left-leaning Cyprus Turkish Civil Servants Trade Union (KTAMS, *Kıbrıs Türk Amme Memurları Sendikası*) and the right-leaning Cyprus Turkish Public Officials Trade Union (Kamu-Sen, *Kıbrıs Türk Kamu Görevlileri Sendikası*). With over 1,500 members, the Municipal Workers Union (BES, *Belediye Emekçileri Sendikası*) is another notable trade union. Other independent unions have fewer than 1,000 members.

Two of the confederations, Türk-Sen and Dev-İş, cooperate with each other on a regular basis as both are members of the Trade Union Platform (Sendikal Platform), which brings together left-leaning unions and confederations. KTAMS, KTÖS and KTOEÖS, as well as BES are also part of this loose umbrella organization. The platform can be seen as the continuation of the 'This Country Is Ours Platform' (*Bu Memleket Bizim Platformu*), which brought together left-wing political parties and civil society organizations in the late 1990s to resist growing Turkish influence in the political and economic life of Turkish Cypriots. The platform played a major role in mobilizing the wider public towards a pro-reunification stance regarding the solution of the Cyprus problem in the early 2000s. During this process, for the first time, a left-wing political party, the Republican Turkish Party (CTP, *Cumhuriyetçi Türk Partisi*) became the senior partner in a coalition government. The fact that one of the leading forces in the platform came to power led to its transformation, and trade unions within it coalesced as a loose organization to resist austerity measures towards the end of the 2000s, forming the Trade Union Platform (Felek 2020). Although they never joined the Trade Union Platform, from time to time, the right-leaning Hür-İş and Kamu-Sen cooperated or acted together with the Platform in its anti-austerity struggle. The Platform makes its decisions on a consensus basis and its spokesperson is changed on a rotational basis.

In the recent past, there has been no merger among trade unions; on the contrary, existing unions have continued to splinter and new unions have continued to emerge. When it comes to union democracy, at the confederation level, in Hür-İş, for instance, consensus is sought and secured on most decisions at the executive board level, but some decisions are made by majority vote. In the broader assembly, which is the main decision-making body, all member unions are represented in proportion to their membership (with a minimum of one and a maximum of five representatives). The assembly elects the president, two vice-presidents, the secretary general, the treasurer and the organizational secretary of the confederation (who are usually, but not always the heads of the individual unions). At the executive board level, these are joined by the representatives of the individual unions.

Unionization

The structural and politico-economic characteristics of this services-based small island economy have seriously hindered unionization in the private sector, and therefore trade unions are organized almost exclusively in the public and semi-public sectors, as well as in local administrations. The membership figures seem to have got stuck at around 25,000 since the 1990s, while the labour force has kept growing.

An overwhelming majority of primary school teachers working at state schools (roughly 90 per cent), for instance, are members of KTÖS (Gelener 2020); KTOEÖS has a similar proportion. Retail and construction, on the other hand, are dominated by migrant workers and almost completely non-unionized. Virtually no construction workers are members of a trade union; in retail, only employees of a small supermarket chain, which is itself a joint venture of various trade unions, are unionized. In a similar vein, in tourism, there is only one relatively big hotel, at which the employees are unionized, and it has been run by the union itself – the Tourism Workers Union (TES, *Turizm Emekçileri Sendikası*) – following privatization of the hotel in 2008.

After the introduction of a scheme by the Ministry of Labour in 2018 aimed at promoting unionization, union membership in the private media sector also expanded. The scheme basically grants financial incentives in the form of the government paying employees' social security premiums on behalf of the employers, if the media company agrees to sign a collective agreement with its employees. One of the downsides of the scheme was that it did not cover employees who are not citizens of the KKTC. The scheme was initially planned to last for three years and its long-term success can be better analysed once it expires, but it is safe to say that it led to the expansion of unionization in the private media sector (Faustmann et al. 2020: 9–10). Although the extension of this scheme to other industries was proposed by the Ministry of Labour in February 2019, the draft legislation was eventually shelved when the governing coalition collapsed (Faustmann et al. 2020: 10).

An overwhelming majority (70 per cent) of trade union members who are affiliated with one of the three confederations are men; in the remaining trade unions membership is almost equal between men and women. An overwhelming majority of union leaderships are still composed of men, however. On a more positive note, the current chair of KTÖS and the secretary general of KTOEÖS are women. In this respect, the two public education unions are exceptions. Having said that, although around 65 per cent of teachers' union members are women, it is still not possible to talk about gender equality at the union administration level.

There are no clear statistics about the proportion of pensioners among the members but former unionists interviewed for this study estimated it at around 5–10 per cent at KTÖS and around 20 per cent at KTAMS. As almost all trade union members are employed in the public or semi-public sector, where redundancies are quite rare, unemployed people are not likely to constitute more than a negligible presence in the trade unions.

Union resources and expenditure

Turkish Cypriot trade unions rely on their members' fees to finance their activities. As almost all members are in the public sector, fees are deducted by the Ministry of Finance and transferred to the unions in line with the checkoff system (with the exception of KTÖS, which prefers to collect its members' fees itself). In the few unionized workplaces in the private sector, fees are also deducted directly by the employer and transferred to the account of the union in charge (Felek 2020).

The Trade Unions Law does not regulate fees, and therefore the rates vary from union to union. KTÖS's rate for instance is 1.25 per cent of the gross salary, whereas KTOEÖS's rate is 0.4 per cent of the net salary (KTAMS' membership fee is 0.8 per cent of the gross salary whereas its rival Kamu-Sen's fee is 0.7 per cent). In a similar vein, confederations receive their funding from their affiliates. At Hür-İş, individual unions are required to pay 1/500 of the minimum wage for each of their members to the confederation (Latifoğlu 2020). Dev-İş has a more centralized structure; all membership fees (1 per cent of gross salary) are transferred directly to the Confederation (Felek 2020).

A few larger trade unions, such as KTAMS, also generate revenue by renting out their facilities and buildings. Major trade unions also have credit cooperatives, which provide their members with lower than market interest rates. Although everyone can join these cooperatives, in the words of a former union board member, 'the cooperation between the union and the cooperative creates a synergy' and helps in retaining members (Gelener 2020).

According to the constitution of KTAMS (Article 35), 15 per cent of membership fees are allocated to the strike fund. There is also a health fund, which can be used to donate or lend money to members experiencing health problems. Other unions have similar schemes. Trade unions also provide discounts and promotions for their members via agreements made with various businesses, particularly private hospitals and hotels, in both Cyprus and Turkey.

One of the major expenses for unions is the running costs of their headquarters, which also includes the employees' wages. None of the unions or confederations have more than a handful of full-time professional employees. Currently, KTÖS has three full-time employees and two to three part-timers at its radio station. In a similar vein, KTAMS has three professionals, namely a secretary and two other personnel dealing with press relations and statistics. According to the trade unionists interviewed for this chapter, legal services also constitute an important expense.

As in the South, trade unions organized in the public sector are indirectly subsidized by the state in the form of paid leave granted to elected union representatives. By law, three to four board members (it can be either three full-time or two part-time and two full-time) of the two biggest unions in the public administration are granted paid leave during their stint at the union administration. In the case of teachers, the number of part-timers can be up to three; the number of full-timers is the same. Those public-sector unions with more than 100 members are also entitled to have four members with an extra twenty days of paid leave to be used for union activities. The three trade unions affiliated with Dev-İş all have full-time presidents as the confederation is organized mainly in the private sector.

Expenses are under the control of the executive board; particularly the chair/secretary general and treasurer are authorized to incur expenses. Union accounts are subject to external auditing. At the end of the year, all trade unions are required to submit their accounting reports to the Trade Unions' Registrar under the Ministry of Labour.

Collective bargaining and unions at the workplace

The right to collective bargaining is protected by the constitution. Having said that, signing a collective agreement has largely been the privilege of a small group consisting mainly of manual workers in the public and semi-public sectors (Faustmann et al. 2020; Ioannou and Sonan 2019). As far as the number of employees and social benefits covered are concerned, 'the most comprehensive of all collective agreements in the northern part of Cyprus is the one agreed between the Ministry of Finance and Kamu-İş [which is affiliated with Hür-İş, and has 2,750 members], which represents public sector workers' (Ioannou and Sonan 2019: 122). At local government level, too, collective agreements are signed regularly between individual municipalities and various trade unions, of which BES, which has over 1,500 members, is the biggest. Therefore, the process is more decentralized and takes place at the workplace level. The same applies to a few collective agreements signed in the private sector.

White collar employees in the public sector are subject to a fairly centralized collective bargaining mechanism called 'protocol talks', which cover a large segment of the working population. In accordance with Article 135 of the Public Employees Law (1979), a meeting is held annually between the Ministry of Finance and the two civil servant unions with the largest membership (KTAMS and Kamu-Sen). Recently, the teachers' and health sector unions have also been invited to these talks. If the unions and the Ministry of Finance come to an agreement, they sign a protocol whose provisions come into force following the legislature's approval, if the issues agreed require legislation (Sonan 2018). No protocol has been signed since 2007, however, and in some years no meeting is convened by the Ministry of Finance. This can be attributed to the austerity policies implemented since 2010 (for more on this, see Sözen and Sonan 2019).

Collective bargaining and agreements are very rare in the private sector. There is a statutory minimum wage, and

> this sets a benchmark for the non-unionized workforce in the private sector. Migrant workers, who make up a quarter of the labour force, are the most vulnerable group and the statutory minimum wage is probably the only safety net they can rely on. The minimum wage is determined 'at least once a year', by a commission made up of 15 members: five representatives from the largest union [confederation, which is Hür-İş], five representatives from the employers' association and five members representing the government [chaired by the undersecretary of the Ministry of Labour]. (Ioannou and Sonan 2019: 123)

One reason behind employees' recent reluctance to remain union members is the absence of collective agreements in the public administration proper. In terms of rights, working conditions and remuneration, it is possible to divide this group into two sub-groups: those who entered the public service before 2011 and those who did so afterwards. Those who have joined since 2011 are subject to the unpopular Law Regulating the Monthly Salary, Wage and Other Allowances of Public Employees, which substantially reduced entry-level salaries in the public sector and introduced new conditions for new entrants and in doing so 'further restricted the scope of collective bargaining for public sector' employees' (Ioannou and Sonan 2019: 121; see also Sonan and Gökçekuş 2020). According to a former trade unionist interviewed for this chapter, those in the former group have gained almost everything that could have been gained from membership. Therefore, they tend to cancel their membership to avoid the membership fee. Those in the second group, on the other hand, tend to join unions and remain there as unions can still help them to advance their rights and interests (Barçın 2020).

Industrial conflict

The unions frequently come together to issue joint statements and hold protests to show solidarity with each other. General strikes, which are usually organized by the Trade Union Platform, are resorted to particularly when the government renews economic protocols with Turkey (which is done every three years), which include austerity and privatization (see Ioannou and Sonan 2014; Sonan and Gökçekuş 2020). Usually, these do not last more than one day as this would deplete the strike funds. One recent tactic used by the unions is to go for longer strikes where it hurts the government most, namely at workplaces where the Ministry of Finance collects money, such as tax offices or the motor vehicle registry.

One of the most important public assets whose privatization is envisaged in the economic protocols is the electricity authority (Kıb-Tek, *Kıbrıs Türk Elektrik Kurumu*). Lately, El-Sen, which is the trade union organized in Kıb-Tek, has increasingly been using the strategy of cutting the electricity of institutions – both public and private – running substantial debts with the electricity authority (see, for instance, Kıbrıs Manşet 2013 and Havadis 2019). This is meant to increase the profitability of Kıb-Tek and to draw the attention of the public to the fact that the real problem is the reluctance of the government, which controls the board of the authority, to collect bills, not inefficiency of production and distribution. In this endeavour, the union is supported by the confederation which it is affiliated with (Türk-Sen), as well as other members of the Trade Union Platform.

The decision to go to strike is made together with the rank-and-file members, for whom a strike entails considerable sacrifices (Felek 2020). Larger unions with bigger strike funds also tend to consult with their members before they take the decision to go on strike (Barçın 2020). At Dev-İş, the strike fund is controlled by the confederation but it does not pool this fund. Rather, member unions rely on the contributions they have made when they go on strike (Felek 2020).

Though there is lack of continuous historical data regarding the frequency of strike action, a quick analysis of the number and duration of strikes between 2008 and 2017, provided by the Ministry of Labour's activity reports, show that there has not been much of a change in pattern over this limited period. Unless there is a major political development, which leads to a general strike and possibly a wider mobilization called for by the Trade Union Platform, or a major financial crisis in a particular workplace, which leads to relatively long strikes (such as the one in the Nicosia Municipality in 2012, which led to a total of 35 days of strikes), most strikes last between a few hours and a few days. The number of strikes per year registered in the activity reports of the Ministry of Labour for the period 2008–2017 ranged between ten and thirty-nine, with an average of twenty-one.

Political relations

The nature of the relationship between the trade unions and political parties is different from that in the South; there is no organic link. Generally speaking, left-leaning trade unions have good relations with left-leaning political parties, and the same applies to a considerable extent to their right-leaning counterparts. Trade unions are good at organizing mass protests, which may create some impact on broader social and political issues. For instance, they played a major role in mobilizing people to demonstrate in favour of the reunification of the island and joining the EU in the period 2002–2004. This was a major achievement with permanent effects on the political scene. Although in the end reunification and EU membership did not materialize because of the 'no' vote of the Greek Cypriot community in the referendum held in 2004 (in which Turkish Cypriots voted in favour), the island as a whole has become a part of the EU, and pro-reunification parties came to power as senior coalition partners for the first time. Furthermore, pro-reunification candidates won the presidential elections twice between 2005 and 2015 (Faustmann et al. 2020).

Trade union capacities to have a lasting impact on economic policymaking has been historically low, however. Unlike the situation in the South, trade unions have never been involved in political decision-making in the context of tripartism and social dialogue. This leaves direct action in the form of organizing mass protests as the only option in trying to influence government policies. This has been in further decline over the past decade in the face of the growing influence of neoliberalism, in the form of austerity policies, which have been imposed by Ankara with growing determination. Initially (in 2010–2011), the Trade Union Platform, which brought together unions across the political spectrum, managed to mobilize public support against these policies and organized rallies attended by tens of thousands of people, but they failed to stop the implementation of austerity measures (Faustmann et al. 2020). As a result, 'in the face of Ankara's resolve, public anger gradually changed to cynicism and anti-austerity protests subsided' (Sonan and Gökçekuş 2020).

Societal power

To reach out to their members and the wider public, trade unions rely on text messages, internet and social media. One of the major unions,

KTÖS, has its own radio station (Radyo Mayıs), web TV and an online newspaper. Hür-İş also recently started a web TV service. KTAMS had its own weekly TV show, which lasted for two years (entitled 'KTAMS Evaluating the Week').

As admitted by unionists themselves, the trade unions' credibility in the eyes of the wider public has been in decline. According to the quarterly surveys conducted by the Centre for Migration, Identity and Rights Studies, they are among the least trusted institutions, along with the parliament, political parties, religious institutions and financial institutions (cited in Faustmann et al. 2020). The unions are blamed for not doing anything beyond protecting the narrow interests of their own members, who are overwhelmingly working in the public and semi-public sectors, while ignoring precarious employment in the private sector. There have been no attempts at lasting coalition-building with NGOs either. Having said that, despite their declining credibility, and failure to expand to the private sector and to influence economic policymaking, trade unions still remain the most potent and dynamic elements of civil society and the backbone of social opposition, particularly in relation to major political issues, such as relations with Turkey and the solution of the Cyprus problem. The recent revival of the 'This Country Is Ours' Platform following a highly contested presidential election can be seen as an embodiment of the trade unions' underlying strength.

Trade union policies towards the European Union

The northern part of the island has a unique position with regard to the EU. Although in legal terms, the island as a whole became part of the EU in 2004, in practice, the northern part is still outside the EU because of the failure to reach a comprehensive settlement of the Cyprus problem. In other words, the implementation of the *acquis communautaire* has been suspended in the North, pending the solution of the Cyprus problem; for the same reason, it has not gone through a harmonization process to adopt the EU's *acquis*.

Having said that, following the failed Annan plan (2004), the Council of the EU stated its determination to 'put an end to the isolation of the Turkish Cypriot community and to facilitate the reunification of Cyprus by encouraging the economic development of the Turkish Cypriot community'. Accordingly, the European Commission has been implementing an aid programme for the Turkish Cypriots, which aims to facilitate the reunification of Cyprus by encouraging the economic development of the Turkish Cypriot community, with particular emphasis on, among other things, preparations for transposing the EU body of laws following a comprehensive settlement of the Cyprus issue. Given this state of limbo, it is not possible for Turkish Cypriot unions to be actively involved in EU-level politics.

Left-leaning and pro-reunification unions also have a vision of being part of the EU, and from time to time visit Brussels to lobby for this. One of the three confederations, Türk-Sen, is a member of the ETUC. According to its website, the confederation regularly attends general assemblies and takes part in various ETUC committees (Türk-Sen 2020). KTAMS is a member of European Public Service Union (EPSU), while KTÖS, KTOEÖS and DAÜ-SEN (Eastern Mediterranean University Union of Academic Staff) are members of European Trade Union Committee for Education (ETUCE). Furthermore, the pro-reunification unions have regular contacts with the unions in the South and they co-organize activities to mark Labour Day, for instance. The right-leaning unions, such as Hür-İş Confederation, on the other hand, have closer ties with Turkish trade unions.

Conclusions

Analyses of the trade unions in the South and the North were kept separate in this chapter because objectively they operate in separate political and economic contexts, in different institutional orders and essentially have built diverging traditions. This makes cross-border collaboration difficult even for trade unions interested in reunification. In the past two decades, however, common statements and gatherings in support of reunification by left-wing unions have been constant, while in 2015, the All Trade Unions Forum, initially founded in 1995, issued a joint Memorandum supporting a standardized and unified system of employment and work relations, wages and benefit specifications, health and social security at the level of the united federal state, reiterating this position at the peak of the peace negotiations in 2016 (Ioannou 2020). In this concluding section, as in the Introduction, we merge the two sides in Cyprus and bring the analysis of the two parts together.

Table 6.5 provides an overview of the chapter before we move to future projections.

Table 6.5 Comparing the two parts of the country

	South	North
Relations with politics	Tripartite corporatism surviving but hollowed out	Social dialogue, which has never been strong, has been further weakened
Collective bargaining	Declining collective bargaining coverage and increasing dependence on legal regulation	Declining trade union density goes hand in hand with shrinking collective bargaining coverage, both limited to public and semi-public sectors
Labour force and trade union structure	Fragmentation of labour force but less so of the trade union landscape	Fragmentation of both labour force and trade unions
Trade union power resources	Trade union power reduced especially at associational and institutional levels	Declining influence of trade unions in the face of growing Turkish influence through economic austerity programmes
Strikes and collective action	No significant restrictions to striking but no tradition of general and political strikes – strikes typically used defensively, locally, and tactically	No significant restrictions to striking in the public and semi-public sectors; declining capacity in organizing mass political mobilization in the past decade

Source: authors' elaboration.

Predictions about the future are always difficult. Elements of the current of state of trade unions in the South point to all four trends identified by Visser (2019). Marginalization and dualization processes have been under way for at least two decades, while in the past decade there have also been modest signs of revitalization as the trade unions have begun to realize that an active effort was needed, even if only to hold their ground. Furthermore, in recent years some trade unions have come to the fore, primarily those representing more excluded workers in the broader public sector: smaller, younger, and somewhat more oriented towards social movements rather than to traditional trade union work. Although these are still engaged in trade unionism in the broad sense, and not merely campaigning and advocacy, they have much looser membership structures and, in addition to voice mechanisms provided by some employers, can be seen to be fulfilling not only a revitalization but also a substitution function.

Taking a bird's eye view and somewhat schematically dualization seems the strongest of the four trends. Not because protecting insiders is the unions' primary aim, but because of the political and economic environment of increased instability and declining institutional support they find themselves in (Doellgast et al. 2018). Trade unions face multiple challenges. In addition to the erosion of their structural power, in the past two decades their associational and institutional power has declined as well, creating a harsh context. Employers have become more aggressive and the state less interested in social cohesion, as well as more ready to sacrifice rights for the promotion of national competitiveness. This, coming at a time of increasing difficulty in maintaining their organizational reach and societal appeal, has rendered trade unions overtly vulnerable to further weakening in the years ahead.

As far as the northern part of the island is concerned, dualization and then marginalization seem to be the most likely trends in the future. Since the beginning, one of the biggest problems of the Turkish Cypriot labour market has been its dualization/segmentation along public–private lines. The fact that unionization is almost non-existent in the private sector has led to a serious decline in union density in the past two decades as the private sector has grown faster than the public sector. In this period, trade unions, which are extremely fragmented, could not take any meaningful action to expand towards the private sector in the face of employers' hostility and the government's indifference in upholding constitutional rights; unless unions find a way to break through and reach employees in the private sector they are likely to become less relevant in the growing labour market.

In the public and semi-public sectors, in which trade unions have been operating safely, they are likely to face challenges in defending their existing – and diminishing – power, too. The growing influence of the neoliberal policies imposed by Ankara, and particularly possible privatization of certain semi-public institutions, such as Kib-Tek, is likely to lead to a further decline in union membership.

References

All links were checked on 20 April 2021.

Argyrides P. (2020) SEK General Organisation Secretary, interview, June 2020.

Barçın D. (2020) Former KTAMS Secretary General, interview, September 2020.

Doellgast V., Lillie N. and Pulignano V. (eds) (2018) Reconstructing solidarity. Labour unions, precarious work, and the politics of institutional change in Europe, Oxford, Oxford University Press.

Ergatiko Vima (2020) Η δικαίωση των οργανωμένων αγώνων των εργαζομένων στην Οικοδομική Βιομηχανία [The victory of the organised struggles of workers in the construction], Ergatiko Vima, 11 June 2020.

Eurofound (2020) Working life in Cyprus. https://www.eurofound.europa.eu/country/cyprus#working-life

Fantis A. (2006) Το Συνδικαλιστικό Κίνημα στα Χρόνια της Αγγλοκρατίας 1878–1960, Λευκωσία [The Trade union movement in the British times 1878–1960].

Faustmann H., Ioannou G. and Sonan S. (2020) Cyprus: Trade Union Monitor, FES Briefing October 2019, Berlin, Friedrich Ebert Stiftung.

Felek H. (2020) Former Dev-İş President, interview, September 2020.

Gelener S. (2020) Former KTÖS Executive Board Member, interview, September 2020.

Güler A. (2017) Sendika Bolluğu [Profusion of Trade Unions], Yenidüzen, 6 September 2017.

Havadis (2019) El-Sen Maliye Bakanlığı'nın elektriğini kesti [El-Sen cut the electricity of the Ministry of Finance], 29 August 2019. https://www.havadiskibris.com/el-sen-maliye-bakanliginin-elektrigini-kesti/ [accessed on 2 May 2021]

Ioannou G. (2015) Labor force fragmentation in contemporary Cyprus, Working USA: Journal of Labor and Society, 18 (4), December, 595–612.

Ioannou G. (2016) The connection between trade unions and political parties in Cyprus, in Charalambous G. and Christophorou C. (eds) Party-society relations in the Republic of Cyprus: political and societal strategies, London, Routledge, 110–128.

Ioannou G. (2017) Employment in crisis: Cyprus and the extension of precarity, in Schierup C. and Bak Jørgensen M. (eds) Politics of precarity: migrant conditions, struggles and experiences, Brill, 138–159.

Ioannou G. (2020) The normalization of Cyprus' partition among Greek Cypriots: political economy and political culture in a divided society, Basingstoke, Palgrave Macmillan.

Ioannou G. (2021) Employment, trade unionism and class: the labour market in Southern Europe since the crisis, New York, Routledge.

Ioannou G. and Charalambous G. (2017) The social and political impact of the Cyprus economic crisis (2010–2017), Bonn, Friedrich-Ebert-Stiftung.

Ioannou G. and Charalambous G. (2019) West European trade unions, labour and 'the people': from the golden era to the times of austerity, in Charalambous G. and Ioannou G. (eds) Left radicalism and populism in Europe, London, Routledge, 204–222.

Ioannou G. and Sonan S. (2014) Trade unions in Cyprus: history and environment of division, common challenges ahead, Bonn, Friedrich-Ebert-Stiftung.

Ioannou G. and Sonan S. (2017) Trade unions and politics in Cyprus: an historical comparative analysis across the dividing line, Mediterranean Politics, 22 (4), 484–503.

Ioannou G. and Sonan S. (2019) Cyprus: a divided island – diverging collective bargaining patterns, weakened yet still standing, in Waddington J., Müller T. and Vandaele K. (eds) Collective bargaining in Europe: towards an endgame, Brussels, ETUI, 109–129.

İstatistik Kurumu (KKTC) (2020) Hanehalkı İşgücü Anketi – Bülten 2020 [Household Labour Force Survey – Bulletin 2020]. http://www.stat.gov.ct.tr/HIA-BULTEN-YIL-7.aspx

Kıbrıs Manşet (2013) 'El-Sen 22 Devlet Dairesi ve 3 Bakanlığın Elektrik Akımını Borcundan Dolayı Kesti' [El-Sen cut the electricity of 22 government offices and 3 ministry due to their unpaid debts], 4 February 2013. https://www.kibrismanset.com/guncel/el-sen-22-devlet-dairesi-ve-3-bakanligin-elektrik-akimini-borcundan-dolayi-kesti-h26309.html [accessed on 26 September 2020].

Latifoğlu, Y. (2020) Former Hür-İş President, interview, September 2020.

Papanastasiou S. (2017) Συνδικαλισμός, πολιτική, πλακάκια [Trade unionism, politics, hooking up] Phileleftheros 26/3/2017. https://www.philenews.com/f-me-apopsi/arthra-apo-f/article/367220/syndikalismos-politiki-plakakia

Republic of Cyprus (2004) Labour Statistics 2002, Nicosia, Printing Office of the Republic of Cyprus.

Rougala T. (2015) The end of the Banks' employers association, Sigmalive, 10 December 2015. http://capital.sigmalive.com/story/12633785

Slocum J. (1972) Labour relations in Cyprus, Nicosia, Government Printing Office.

Sonan S. (2018) Assessment of social dialogue environment in the Turkish Cypriot community, Cyprus Dialogue Forum (unpublished).

Sonan S. and Gokcekus O. (2020) Socio-economic and political impact of austerity policies in North Cyprus: a brief assessment, Nicosia, Friedrich Ebert Stiftung.

Sözen A. and Sonan S. (2019) Yet another case of electoral and government epidemic? The Turkish Cypriot legislative election of January 2018, South European Society and Politics, 24 (1), 129–154.

Sparsis M. (1998) Tripartism and industrial relations: the Cyprus experience, Nicosia, Sparsis M.

State Planning Organization [Devlet Planlama Örgütü] (2020) Ekonomik ve Sosyal Göstergeler 2018 [Economic and Social Indicators 2018], Lefkoşa.

Statistical Institute (2020) Statistical Yearbook 2019, North Cyprus. http://www.stat.gov.ct.tr/IST-YIL-2019.aspx

Tombazos C. (2020) PEO General Organisation Secretary, interview, June 2020.

Trimikliniotis N. and Demetriou C. (2011) Labour integration of migrant workers in Cyprus: a critical appraisal, in Pajnic M. and Campani G. (eds) Precarious migrant labour across Europe, Ljubljana, The Peace Institute, 73–96.

Trade Union Registrar (2020) Unpublished document, North Cyprus.

Trade Union Registrar (2021) Κατάλογος εγγεγραμμένων συντεχνιών [List of registered Trade Unions]. http://www.mlsi.gov.cy/mlsi/dlr/dlr.nsf/page26_gr/page26_gr?OpenDocument

Türk-Sen (2020) Tarihçe [History]. http://turk-sen.org/turk-sen-tarihce/ [accessed on 26 September 2020].

Visser J. (2019) Trade unions in the balance, ILO ACTRAV working paper, Geneva, ILO.

World Bank (2021) GDP Per Capita – Cyprus, 2019. https://data.worldbank.org/indicator/NY.GDP.PCAP.CD?locations=CY [accessed on 2 May 2021]

Yannakourou S. (2016) Κυπριακό Εργατικό Δίκαιο [Cyprus Labour Law], Athens, Nomiki Vivliothiki.

Abbreviations

ΔΕΟΚ	Δημοκρατική Εργατική Ομοσπονδία Κύπρου (Democratic Labour Federation of Cyprus)
BES	Belediye Emekçileri Sendikası (Municipal Workers Trade Union)
Dev-İş	Devrimci İşçi Sendikaları Federasyonu (Federation of Revolutionary Trade Unions)
Hür-İş	Hür İşçi Sendikaları Federasyonu (Federation of Free Trade Unions),
Kamu-İş	Kamu İşçileri Sendikası (Public Workers Trade Union)
Kamu-Sen	Kıbrıs Türk Kamu Görevlileri Sendikası (Cyprus Turkish Public Officials Trade Union)
KKTC	Kuzey Kıbrıs Türk Cumhuriyeti (Turkish Republic of Northern Cyprus)
KTAMS	Kıbrıs Türk Amme Memurları Sendikası (Union of Turkish Cypriot Public Servants)
KTÖS	Kıbrıs Türk Öğretmenler Sendikası (Cyprus Turkish Primary School Teachers Union)
KTOEÖS	Kıbrıs Türk Orta Eğitim Öğretmenler Sendikası (Cyprus Turkish Secondary School Teachers Union)
OEB	Ομοσπονδία Εργοδοτών και Βιομηχάνων (Federation of Employers and Industrialists)
ΠΕΟ	Παγκύπρια Εργατική Ομοσπονδία (Pancyprian Federation of Labour)
ΣΕΚ	Συνομοσπονδία Εργαζομένων Κύπρου (Cyprus' Employees Confederation)
Türk-Sen	Kıbrıs Türk İşçi Sendikaları Federasyonu (Federation of Cyprus Turkish Trade Unions)

Chapter 7

Czechia: Trade unions escaping marginalization

Monika Martišková and Adam Šumichrast

In common with other Central and Eastern European (CEE) countries, Czechia has experienced turbulent change over the past thirty years. The transformation from a centrally planned to a market-oriented economy have put trade unions in a difficult position. On one hand, the trade unions understood the need to transform institutions and liberalize the economy, but on the other, many of the economic reforms being imposed were in conflict with their core task of protecting workers. Trade unions were expected to cope with the new economic structures alongside their old mainly communist era management and experience. It is no surprise that today a significant part of society in the region regard trade unionism as a relic from the past (Martišková and Sedláková 2017). Nevertheless, some features of the trade union movement have been revitalized, especially in recent years.

After 1990 the trade unions were reborn within a fairly favourable institutional framework, which provided their activities with institutional support and gave them tools to protect employees in the transformation period. In 1990, a Collective Bargaining Act (ZKV, *Zákon o kolektivním vyjednávání*) and a Tripartite Consultations Act (ZTK, *Zákon o třístranných konzultacích*) were adopted, creating a framework for social dialogue in the former Czechoslovakia. This framework was adopted by the two countries that emerged from the division of this country in 1993, the Czech Republic (now Czechia) and the Slovak Republic (or Slovakia) (see Chapter 25). The system of collective bargaining then established was such that labour legislation was considered a minimum and better working conditions could be negotiated at lower levels. This structure was supposed to support collective bargaining at the industry and company levels. Trade unionists were granted protection at their workplaces, and at the national level tripartite consultations were held regularly. This institutional setting has changed only a little since its establishment (Myant 2019).

Despite this favourable institutional setting for collective bargaining, trade unions often opted for legislative solutions for improving working conditions, especially for vulnerable groups, such as agency workers. Moreover, the dominant level of collective bargaining became the company level, which fosters labour market dualization, in which only organized workplaces guarantee better working conditions beyond the Labour Code (*Zákoník práce*) regulations. At the same time, industry-level collective bargaining has almost lost relevance for regulating working conditions (Myant 2019), although in finance a new industry-level agreement helped to improve working conditions in the industry as a whole. At the national level, only social partners are consulted and there is no collective bargaining.

The trade unions did not tend to openly support any political party, although their representatives have had direct links to – mainly – the Czech Social Democratic Party (ČSSD, *Česká strana sociálně demokratická*) for the past three decades. In recent years, with the diminishing power of traditional right-wing and left-wing parties, trade unions have sought to remain as independent as possible in the political sphere.

A constant decline in membership means that trade unions have to fight for their place in society. Total trade union membership declined from 2.35 million in 1995 to 500,000 in 2018, with the result that trade union density fell from 45 to 11 per cent. Concurrently, collective bargaining coverage decreased from 47 to 33 per cent. There has also been a decrease in the number of trade unions federations, although the number of trade union confederations has remained stable (see Table 7.1).

Table 7.1 Principal characteristics of trade unionism in Czechia

	1995	2000	2020
Total trade union membership	2,350,000	1,200,000	500,000*
Women as a proportion of total membership	n.a.	47 %**	49 %***
Gross union density	56 %	30 %	11 %
Net union density	45 %	27 %	11 %
Number of confederations	3	3	3
Number of affiliated unions (federations)			
ČMKOS	50	30	32
ASO	3	n.a.	13
KUK	12	n.a.	14
Number of independent unions****	5	n.a.	10
Collective bargaining coverage	47 %	28 %	35 %
Principal level of collective bargaining	company		
Days not worked due to industrial action per 1,000 workers	1.3	n.a.	n.a.

Note: *2018; **2002; ***2014; ****Estimate.

Source: Appendix A1.

In response to these unfavourable developments trade unions have sought ways to remain relevant. In recent years, there has been a shift from a reliance on political lobbying and addressing legislation to efforts to become an independent stakeholder in society. To this end the main trade union confederation mobilized its analytical and organizational capacities and launched a long-term campaign for pay rises. This was later translated into international cooperation with trade unions from other CEE countries in articulating a European solution to wage differentials within the European Union (EU). This mobilization brought several thousand new members, improved the image of trade unions in society and, from some perspectives, can be interpreted as a form of trade union revitalization. As this chapter shows, however, such positive assessments of trade unions in Czechia are problematic. In particular, because the trade unions have not been able to recruit vulnerable labour market groups as members, and because the process of property delimitation from the 1990s has yet to be completed, internal revitalization has stalled.

Historical background and principal features of the industrial relations system

Labour movements in the Czech lands developed within the Austro-Hungarian Empire during the second half of the nineteenth century and were fully established within an independent, democratic Czechoslovak state between 1918 and 1939. This period could be called a 'golden age of unionism', in which the labour movement reached 2.3 million members and comprised more than 500 different unions, 318 trade union magazines were published, and strikes were very common (ČSÚ 2018). The fall of the Czechoslovak Republic in March 1939 was a fatal blow for trade unionism. The long-standing demand for the unification of the trade union movement and overcoming fragmentation was satisfied, but in a grotesque form compared with what the trade unions had envisaged. Under Nazi occupation, the imposition of compulsory unified trade unions ended the 'class struggle' and ensured the subordination of the working class to the economic interests of the state (Šumichrast 2018: 101).

After the end of the war, new united unions, under the aegis of the Revolutionary Trade Union Movement (ROH, *Revoluční odborové hnutí*), emerged and became the link between the Communist Party of Czechoslovakia (KSČ, *Komunistická strana Československa*) and the working population. The Communists seized power with the active help of the ROH (Čapek 2008: 212). Throughout the period until 1989 the ROH performed all its tasks in accord with the instructions of the KSČ. ROH's main role was to provide individual members with leisure activities. For that purpose, ROH owned a wide variety of holiday properties intended for trade union members, providing leisure activities and holiday facilities. ROH was expected to encourage effort and commitment among employees. Collective bargaining was not undertaken in these times and so employee protection could be performed only at individual level, for example, in case of maltreatment at the workplace (Myant and Drahokoupil 2011: 5).

After the first events of the Velvet Revolution on 17 November 1989, around 6,000 strike committees organized a general strike and created a base for an All-Trade Unions Congress held on 2–3 March 1990. This movement took over the apparatus and assets of the former ROH, such as buildings, clubs and vacation resorts (Pokorný 2015, 2019) but there was also continuity at the level of representatives. At the Congress, the delegates of the forty-one unions present formally established two organizations: a successor of ROH responsible for property delimitation, the Property Delimitation Association of Trade Unions (MSDUOS,

Majetková, správní a delimitační unie odborových svazů) and a new trade union confederation. From 1993 after the division of Czechoslovakia the name of the confederation was the Czech and Moravian Chamber of Trade Unions (*Českomoravská komora odborových svazů*), and at the second Congress in 1998 the current name was adopted, the Czech and Moravian Confederation of Trade Unions (ČMKOS, *Českomoravská konfederace odborových svazů*) (Stark and Bruszt 1998). Since its re-establishment the trade union movement has been concerned with the fundamental economic and social problems related to the overall transformation of society, switching to the principles of pluralist democracy and a market economy, and vocally opposing radical neoliberal reforms (Pokorný 2019).

After 1989 entrepreneurs established a several employers' associations, which allowed them to participate in newly formed collective bargaining and tripartite consultative institutions. The new system was modelled on the conventions of the International Labour Organization regarding collective bargaining. In this regard, developments in Czechia were similar to those in the majority of post-socialist countries (Myant 2010). Post-socialist Czechoslovakia was the first country in the region to establish tripartite institutions, and these institutions have maintained their vitality in the post-independence period (Stark and Bruszt 1998: 183). The establishment of the tripartite Council of Economic and Social Agreement (RHSD, *Rada hospodářské a sociální dohody České republiky*) was one of the unions' demands. The tripartite system was settled for the first time in October 1990. It does not function smoothly but, in essence, it is a tool to streamline communication between social partners and the government, with a potential to limit various disputes (Pokorný 2015: 200–201).

Tripartite members do not engage in collective bargaining, but within their consultative role they can influence government policy. In addition to representatives from ČMKOS, the RHSD also includes the chair of the trade union headquarters of the Association of Independent Trade Unions (ASO, *Asociace samostatných odborů*) and representatives of two employer's federations, the Confederation of Employers' and Entrepreneurs' Associations (KZPS, *Konfederace zaměstnavatelských a podnikatelských svazů*) and the Confederation of Industry (SP, *Svaz průmyslu*).

The industrial relations system in Czechia is currently classified as 'embedded neoliberal', indicating a mixture of 'pro-market' reforms with a strong neoliberal narrative. There is also vocal resistance to these reforms from various social movements, within which trade unions dominate (Bohle and Greskovits 2012). Similarly, Eurofound (Voss et al. 2018) has allocated Czech industrial relations to a country cluster called 'transition economy', characterized by politicized social partners that are involved irregularly with collective bargaining, conducted primarily at the company level. The Czech industrial relations system can be also described as 'statist', highlighting the strong role of government in social and economic issues, which does not always consult with the social partners (Kahancová and Kirov 2021). In what follows we show that, despite diminishing influence, trade unionism keeps searching for ways to revitalize and remain an important player in society.

Structure of trade unions and union democracy

The avoidance of over-centralization was a fundamental objective in the development of the trade union movement during the 1990s. The result was considerable autonomy afforded to basic organizations and federations, while confederations remained important political stakeholders with limited impact on affiliated federations. Besides ČMKOS, established from federations previously associated in ROH, in 1990 a Confederation of Arts and Culture (KUK, *Konfederace umění a kultury*) was established to which initially twelve industrial trade unions affiliated. KUK representatives stated publicly that they were concerned that trade union centralization in ČMKOS might resemble the former state socialist trade unions affiliated to ROH (Pokorný 2015). In 1990 another two trade unions confederations were established, the pro-communist Trade Union of Bohemia, Moravia and Silesia (OSČMS, *Odborové sdružení Čech, Moravy, Slezska*) and the Independent Christian Trade Union, now the Christian Trade Union Coalition (KOK, *Křesťanská odborová koalice*).

Further fragmentation of the trade union movement resulted from differing views on ČMKOS's internal functioning. In 1995, three affiliates left ČMKOS and established ASO, to which another four industrial trade unions subsequently affiliated, creating the second largest confederation in Czechia, with around 80,000 members (ASO 2020).[1] The reason cited for the establishment of ASO was that the functioning of ČMKOS

---

1 Trade Union of Workers in Agriculture and Food (OSPZV, *Odborový svaz pracovníků zemědělství a výživy Čech a Moravy*), United Union of Private Employees (JSSZ, *Jednotný svaz soukromých zaměstnanců*) and Trade Union of Northwestern Power Station Workers (OSSE, *Odborový svaz severozápadních energetiků*). In the following years, other trade unions joined this new trade union confederation, including the Flat Glass Trade Union (OSPS, *Odborový svaz ploché sklo*), the Nuclear Energy Workers' Trade Union (OSZJE, *Odborový svaz zaměstnanců jaderné energetiky*) and

was 'too expensive', as the fees requested from affiliated trade unions were high (Hospodářské Noviny 1995). The fragmentation of ČMKOS was caused partially by different views on ČMKOS' involvement in politics, because trade union members had different views on the liberal reforms introduced by the centre right-wing parties in the government (Myant 2010). ASO tried to secure a place on the RHSD shortly after its formation, but it did not succeed until 2000, when it replaced KUK.

Several grassroots protest movements were also established. Currently active and visible in the public debate are smaller independent trade unions, such as the New Trade Union (*Nové odbory*), operating mostly in the eastern part of Czechia, and the Trade Union of the Self-employed (*Podnikatelské odbory*), which recruits among the self-employed. The membership of these unions totals several thousand workers from different industries and does not represent competition to the three established confederations. Currently, three confederations operate in Czechia: the largest ČMKOS and smallest ASO participate in tripartite structures, whereas the third, KUK, is an international confederation as two federations from Slovakia are affiliated to it but it is not a member of tripartite body in either country (see Table 7.2).

Table 7.2 Trade union organizations in Czechia, 2020

Confederation/ union	Private sector, productive industries	Private sector, services	Public sector	Number of members
ČMKOS	All of mining, manufacturing, and construction, except agriculture, print and glass	Retail, finance, catering, hotels, media, culture, and recreation	State administration, education, health, road and air transport, power generation, railways	287,000
ASO	Agriculture, food, glass	Retail, finance, culture	Health, power, road transport, railways	80,000
KUK		Culture and recreation	Culture and recreation	31,000
Independent unions	Glass, print, food	Self-employed	Road and transport, police, railways	

Source: Myant (2010), updated; membership numbers: Kyzlinková et al. (2017).

the Czech Air Traffic Controllers' Association (ČSRLP, *České sdružení řídících letového provozu*). In 1998, a very large and strong Trade Union of Railway Workers (OSŽ, *Odborové sdružení železničářů*) also transferred from ČMKOS.

There is no specific membership domain in any of the three confederations. All represent workers from the public and private sectors. The division between blue- and white-collar workers has never applied to the Czech trade union movement. Federation domains are usually based on industries; no other demarcation is applied within the confederations. Direct member participation is possible primarily at the company level, while federation and confederation levels apply hierarchical structures within systems of delegates and elected representatives.

ČMKOS is the principal trade union confederation in Czechia and represents almost 300,000 members, which is around 70 per cent of all trade union members (Table 7.2). Members are distributed among thirty-two affiliated trade union federations covering various industries (Table 7.3). Several of these federations are small; for instance, five different federations cover different segments of the culture industry, but they associate between twenty to seventy basic trade union organizations each. Affiliated unions are independent from the confederation in decision-making, finance and personnel. The main motivation for industrial unions to affiliate to the confederation is access to tripartite consultations and the possibility of lobbying for workers' interests in different industries. The high level of independence of affiliated trade unions is further pronounced in ASO, where they apply 'the rule of minority', which guarantees that collective decisions taken by ASO do not have to apply to those trade unions which do not agree with the decision (ASO 2016).

The supreme body of ČMKOS is the Congress (*Sjezd*), which meets every four years. In the period between Congresses, the supreme body of ČMKOS is the Assembly (*Sněm*). The Assembly consists of members of the leadership, the Council (*Rada*) and delegated representatives of affiliated unions. The Assembly may convene a Congress, declare a general strike, accept new affiliates of ČMKOS and cancel membership. The Council is the executive body of ČMKOS, which runs the activities of the confederation between sessions of the Assembly. The structure also includes fourteen Regional Councils, which represent members in the regions. The structure of ASO is simpler. The supreme body is the *Valná hromada,* while the executive body is the Presidency (*Předsednictví*) which consists of an elected president and vice-presidents. In KUK, the supreme body is the Congress of Confederated Unions (*Kongres konfederovaných*) and the executive body is the Presidium (*Prezídium*).

Representatives are elected for four years in both ČMKOS and ASO; in KUK it is five years.

Trade union federations are assigned to a specific industry but vary in size depending on the industry covered and, consequently, the membership base. In the case of smaller trade unions, the industrial specification is more detailed – covering, for example, only library workers or professional singers, than in the case of the larger trade union federations, such as those covering the entire metal, education, retail and healthcare industries. Despite specified domains company-level trade unions have the liberty to affiliate to any trade union federation. Trade union federations comprise basic level organizations which operate at workplace level. Basic organizations can either cover one workplace, or several workplaces of one employer. Thus, several trade unions could be established within one employer in different workplaces, but also one trade union could be present at several workplaces of one employer. There are 5,920 basic trade unions registered as independent subjects (ARES 2021).

The minimum requirement to establish a basic trade union is three members. In 20 per cent of workplaces where trade unions operate more than one organization is present (Myant 2019). The plurality of trade union organizations might create problems in collective bargaining as the ZKV requires the agreement of all trade union organizations. Theoretically this might serve as an incentive to establish 'yellow' trade unions, but this does not often occur in Czechia (Myant 2019).

Basic organizations in all three trade union confederations are relatively independent from the federation level. They conclude collective agreements covering all employees at the workplace level. There is very informal coordination between the federation level and basic organizations when it comes to collective bargaining. The federation level may offer services in the form of consultations, legal advice, training and informal exchanges about practices and working conditions at different workplaces within specific industries to basic organizations.

Several mergers and dissolutions have occurred in the modern history of trade unions, which are presented in Table 7.3. In general we can say that some mergers are still to be expected given the high number of small trade unions. Many of them are members of the property delimitation organization MSDUOS established in 1990 (for details see section on union resources) and do not want to lose their shares, which would happen if they disappeared through merger.

Table 7.3 ČMKOS affiliates and their industrial coverage

Sector	Industry	Current name	Mergers or split
Private sector	Hotels, restaurants (HORECA)	*Českomoravský odborový svaz pohostinství, hotelů a cestovniho ruchu* (Czech-Moravian Trade Union of Restaurants, Hotels and Tourism)	Re-founded in 1990
Private sector	Food processing	*Nezávislý odborový svaz pracovníků potravinářského průmyslu a příbuzných oborů Čech a Moravy* (Independent Trade Union of Workers in the Food Industry and Related Sectors of Bohemia and Moravia)	Formed by splitting the *Odborový svaz pracovníků zemědělství a potravinářského průmyslu* (Trade Union of Workers in Agriculture and the Food Industry) in 1990
Private sector	Chemical industry	*Odborový svaz ECHO* (Trade Union ECHO)	Formed by merging *Odborový svaz chemie ČR* (Trade Union of Workers in the Chemical Industry) and *Odborový svaz energetiků* (Trade Union of Workers in Power Generation) in 2004
Private sector	Services (translation)	*Odborová Jednota tlumočníků a překladatelů* (Interpreters and Translators Union)	Formed in 1990, joined to ČMKOS in 2019.
Private sector	Steel, engineering, electrical industry	*Odborový svaz KOVO* (Czech Metalworkers' Federation KOVO)	Transformed from *Odborový svaz kovoprůmyslu* (Trade Union of Workers in the Metal Industry) in 1990
Private sector	Mining	*Odborový svaz pracovníků hornictví, geologie a naftového průmyslu* (Union of Workers in Mining, Geology and Oil Industries)	Re-founded in 1990

Table 7.3 Continued

Sector	Industry	Current name	Mergers or split
Private sector	Banking, insurance	*Odborový svaz pracovníků peněžnictví a pojišťovnictví* (Trade Union of Banking and Insurance Employees)	Re-founded in 1990 by split from OSSOPZO, *Odborový svaz státních orgánů, peněžnictví a zahraničního obchodu* (Trade Union of State Organs, Finance and Foreign Trade)
Private sector	Textiles, garments, footwear	*Odborový svaz pracovníků textilního, oděvního a kožedělného průmyslu Čech a Moravy* (Trade Union of Textile, Clothing and Leather Industry Workers)	Re-founded in 1990 (previously named *Odborový svaz textilního, oděvního a kožedělního průmyslu*) (Trade Union of Workers in the Textile, Garment and Leather Industries)
Private sector	Construction	*Odborový svaz Stavba České republiky* (Building Workers Union of the Czech Republic)	Transformed from *Odborový svaz Stavebnictví a ve výrobě stavebních hmot* (Trade Union of Workers in Construction and the Production of Construction Materials) in 1990
Private sector	Coal mining	*Severočeské sdružení odborových organizací důlního průmyslu* (North Bohemian Association of Trade Union Organizations of the Mining Industry)	Formed by split from *Odborový svaz pracovníků hornictví, geologie a naftového průmyslu* (Union of Workers in Mining, Geology and Oil Industries) in 2007
Private sector	Trade, retail, logistics, social care	*Unie zaměstnanců obchodu, logistiky a služeb* (Employees of Trade, Logistics and Service Union)	Renamed in 2018 from *Odborový svaz pracovníků obchodu* (Trade Union of Trade Workers)
Public sector	Military	*Českomoravský odborový svaz civilních zaměstnanců armády* (Czech-Moravian Trade Union of Civilian Employees of the Army)	Re-founded in 1990

(*Continued*)

Table 7.3 Continued

Sector	Industry	Current name	Mergers or split
Public sector	Education	*Českomoravský odborový svaz pracovníků školství* (Czech and Moravian Union of School Workers)	Founded in 1990
Public sector	Fire service workers	*Odborový svaz hasičů* (Firefighters Union)	Founded in 1990
Public sector	Public broadcasting company employees	*Odborový svaz Media* (Media Union)	Renamed in 2002, previously named *Odborový svaz pracovníků hromadných sdělovacích prostředků ČR* (Trade Union of Mass Media Workers in the Czech Republic)
Public sector	Culture	*Odborový svaz pracovníků knihoven* (Union of Library Workers)	Founded in 1990, from 1990 to 1996 affiliated to KUK, since 2002 affiliated to ČMKOS
Public sector	Science and research	*Odborový svaz pracovníků vědy a výzkumu* (Trade Union of Science and Research Workers, TUSRW)	Founded in 1990
Public sector	Local and central government administration	*Odborový svaz státních orgánů a organizací* (Trade Union of State Organs and Organizations)	Founded in 1990 by split from *Odborový svaz státních orgánů, peněžnictví a zahraničního obchodu* (Trade Union of State Organs, Finance and Foreign Trade)
Public sector	Culture	*Unie orchestrálních hudebníků České republiky* (Orchestra Musicians Union of the Czech Republic)	Founded in 1990, since 1990 affiliated to KUK, later left and since 2003 affiliated to ČMKOS
Public sector	Education	*Vysokoškolský odborový svaz* (University Trade Union)	Founded in 1990
Public/ private sectors	Railways	*Aliance drážního provozu* (Railway Traffic Alliance)	Created by split from *Odborové sdružení železničářů* (Trade Union of Railway Workers) in 2013
Public/ private sectors	Culture	*Herecká asociace* (Actors' Association)	Founded in 1990, since 1990 affiliated to KUK, later left and since 2002 affiliated to ČMKOS

Table 7.3 Continued

Sector	Industry	Current name	Mergers or split
Public/ private sectors	Transportation	*Odborový svaz dopravy* (Transport Workers' Union)	By merging *NOS pracovníků veřejné silniční dopravy ČM* (Independent Trade Union of Public Road Transport of Bohemia and Moravia), *Odborový svaz pracovníků civilního letectví* (Trade Union of Workers in Civil Aviation) and *Odborový svaz pracovníků vodní dopravy* (Trade Union of Workers in Water Transport) in 1994. In 2007 *Odborová organizace Dopravního podniku Metro* (Trade Union Organization of the Public Transport Enterprise Metro) joined
Public/ private sectors	Forestry	*Odborový svaz pracovníků dřevopracujících odvětví, lesního a vodního hospodářství v ČR* (Wood, Forestry and Water Industries Workers' Trade Union in Czech Republic)	Founded in 1990
Public/ private sectors	Culture	*Odborový svaz pracovníků kulturních zařízení* (Trade Union of Workers in Cultural Institutions)	Founded in 1990, during 1990 to 1999 affiliated to KUK, since 2001 affiliated to ČMKOS
Public/ private sectors	Culture	*Odborový svaz pracovníků kultury a ochrany přírody* (Trade Union of Workers in Culture and Protection of Nature)	Founded in 1990, during 1990 to 1999 affiliated to KUK, since 2001 affiliated to ČMKOS

(*Continued*)

Table 7.3 Continued

Sector	Industry	Current name	Mergers or split
Public/ private sectors	Services	*Odborový svaz UNIOS* (Trade Union UNIOS, TU UNIOS)	Formed by merging the *Českomoravský odborový svaz pracovníků služeb* (Czech-Moravian Trade Union of Service Workers), the *Odborový svaz pracovníků zahraničního obchodu* (Trade Union of Foreign Trade Workers) and *Sdružení plynárenských odborů v ČR* (Association of Gas Trade Unions in the Czech Republic) in 1994
Public/ private sectors	Aviation	*Odborový svaz zaměstnanců letectví* (Union of Aviation Employees)	Founded in 1991 by split from *Odborový svaz dopravy a silničního hospodářství* (Trade Union of Workers in Transport and Roads)
Public/ private sectors	Post, telecom, newspapers distribution	*Odborový svaz zaměstnanců poštovních, telekomunikačních a novinových služeb* (Trade Union of Workers in Postal, Telecom and Newspaper Services Czech Republic)	Founded in 1990
Public/ private sectors	Health care, social care	*Odborový svaz zdravotnictví a sociální péče v České republice* (Trade Union of the Health Service and Social Care of the Czech Republic)	Founded in 1990
Public/ private sectors	Culture	*UNIE Odborový svaz profesionálních zpěváků České republiky* (Trade Union of Professional Singers of the Czech Republic)	Founded in 1990, during 1990 to 1995 affiliated to KUK, since 2002 affiliated to ČMKOS

Table 7.3 Continued

Sector	Industry	Current name	Mergers or split
			ASO
Private	Finance	*Odborové sdružení zaměstnanců finančních orgánů* (Trade Union of Employees of Financial Authorities)	n.a.
Private	Retail	*Odborové sdružení zaměstnanců Jednoty* (Trade Onion of employees of Jednota)	n.a.
Private		*Regionální odborový svaz* (Regional Trade Union)	Founded in 2002
Private	Energy	*Český odborový svaz energetiků* (Czech Trade Union of Power Engineers)	Formed by split from *Odborový svaz energetiků* in 1992 (Trade Union of Workers in Power Generation), co-founder of ASO in 1995
Private	Finance	*Odborový svaz zaměstnanců pojišťoven* (Trade Union of Insurance Employees)	n.a.
Public/ private sectors	Public transportation	*Odborové sdružení pracovníků elektrických drah a autobusové dopravy* (Trade Union of Workers of Electric Railways and Bus Transport)	Founded in 2003, later affiliated to ASO
Public/ private sectors	Transportation	*Nezávislý odborový svaz automobilové dopravy* (Independent Trade Union of Automobile Transport)	Founded in 2003, later affiliated to ASO
Private sector	Agro	*Odborový svaz pracovníků zemědělství a výživy - ASO* (Trade Union of Agricultural and Nutrition Workers, ASO)	Formed by split the *Odborový svaz pracovníků zemědělství a potravinářského průmyslu* (Trade Union of the Workers in Agriculture and the Food Industry) in 1990, in 1995 co-founder of ASO

(*Continued*)

Table 7.3 Continued

Sector	Industry	Current name	Mergers or split
Public/ private sectors	Health care, social care	*Lékařský odborový klub - Svaz českých lékařů* (Medical Trade Union Club – Association of Czech Physicians)	Merged with *Svaz českých lékařů* in 2001
	Glass	*Odborový svaz Ploché sklo* (Trade Union Flat Glass)	Split from *Odborový svaz zaměstnanců sklářského, keramického, bižuterního průmyslu a porcelánu* (Trade Union of Employees of Glass, Ceramic, Costume Jewellery and Porcelain Industries) in 1997
Private		*Jednotný svaz soukromých zaměstnanců* (United Trade Union of Private Employees)	Founded in 1990, co-founder of ASO in 1995
Public/ private sectors	Railways	*Odborové sdružení železničářů* (Trade Union of Railway Workers)	Founded in 1990, transferred from ČMKOS to ASO in 1998

Source: Authors' compilation based on Myant (2010) confederation websites.

Unionization

Unsurprisingly, immediately after the fall of the communist regime trade union membership was wide-ranging, amounting to about 80 per cent of the working population or 2.8 million members (Pokorný 2015). The transformation during the 1990s was accompanied by a sharp membership decrease because of the privatization of state companies and, in many cases, their subsequent bankruptcy, and the emergence of private companies with no interest in collective bargaining or social dialogue at workplace level. The arrival of multinational companies after 2000 also did not increase trade union membership significantly, although new trade unions were established in the automotive, retail and banking sectors. Only in 2015 did trade union membership stabilize at about 500,000 members or about 11 per cent of working population (see Figure 7.1). It is suspected that many of these members are retired, thus further undermining an active membership base for the Czech trade unions (Myant 2019).

Figure 7.1 Trade union membership and density, 1993–2018

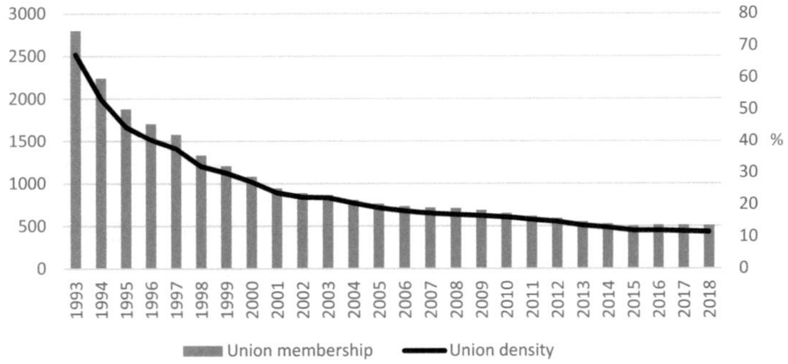

Source: Appendix A1.

In terms of gender and industrial composition, women are represented in trade unions at a slightly higher rate than their participation in the labour market: 49 per cent of women are trade union members, while 66 per cent of women participate in the economy in 2014 (see Appendix A1). This situation results from the strong trade union presence in the public sector, especially in education and health care, which are highly feminized. In the private sector, trade unions dominate in the metal industry and are vocal also in the retail, chemical industry and construction. This distribution partially corresponds to the industrial composition of the Czech economy, in which manufacturing industry employs 28 per cent of the total working population, wholesale and retail 11 per cent, health and social care 7.2 per cent, and similar proportions in education and transport (Eurostat 2021, [lfsa_ergan]).

Trade unions are experiencing difficulties in recruiting new type of workers. The unions have tried to improve the working conditions of temporary agency workers, the number of which has increased rapidly since the economic recession of 2008/2009, but they have not sought to recruit them. The main obstacle to the recruitment of temporary agency workers are the industrial-based structures of unions, which create difficulties when temporary workers switch jobs and industries (Martišková and Sedláková 2017). Many temporary agency workers are also seeking permanent employment and thus have no interest in engaging with trade unions as temporary workers; they prefer to obtain core employee status first. For these reasons trade unions in Czechia – and in Slovakia (see Chapter 25) – favour legislation to increase the protection of agency workers rather than try to recruit them (Martišková and Sedláková 2017). Similar obstacles are observed regarding other new workers within the labour market, such as platform economy workers, who are even more unreachable for trade unions, as their engagement is outside big workplaces, the traditional strongholds of trade unions (Kahancová et al. 2020). Foreigners are also poorly represented in trade unions, despite their rising numbers within the labour market after 2010. This is explained by the protectionist stance of trade unions, which argue that the influx of foreigners disrupts trade union efforts to increase the low wages of domestic workers (Čaněk 2017). Nevertheless, trade unions consistently show solidarity with migrants and condemn anti-immigrant rhetoric.

Czech trade unions have not developed comprehensive recruitment strategies in relation to new groups of employees or to employees in more stable jobs. One explanation lies in the structure of their power resources. During the transformation period trade unions acquired strong institutional powers, which allowed them to follow their agenda without a significant membership base (Mrozowicki 2011). Another explanation lies in the resource allocation approach. CEE trade unions have a strong tradition of member service provision, which prevents them from allocating significant resources and activities to outsiders (Ost 2005). Moreover, existing members prefer the service model, and consider recruitment campaigns too expensive, and not to be paid for from their membership fees (Mrozowicki 2011).

The absence of recruitment strategies does not mean that trade unions are not interested in recruiting new members, however. As a matter of course, each year trade unions organize contact campaigns on the streets where they inform the public about trade union activities and offer legal advice to passers-by. Trade unions were also able to recruit 26,000 workers in 2015 and 2016 through increased visibility by means of the ČMKOS campaign 'An End to Cheap Labour' (*Konec levné práce*) (ČMKOS 2018). The strongest industrial trade union KOVO (OS KOVO, *Odborový svaz KOVO*) also reported increased interest in establishing new basic trade unions in the metal industry, pointing out that this was happening without any recruitment campaign (OS KOVO 2020b). The problem with these unorganized approaches is that they lack a strategic element and do not allow trade unions to increase membership in specific industries or at specific employers. This includes the premises of foreign-owned companies known for their maltreatment of employees, or in strategic industries, such as automotive.

To summarize, despite decreasing a membership base trade unions are seeking ways to recruit members. Their approach, however, could be assessed as unsystematic. In their efforts to increase membership trade unions do not avoid any group on the labour market, but at the same time do not focus specifically on vulnerable employees, such as migrants, agency workers and other precarious employees, which means that they tend to be underrepresented in the trade union movement.

Union resources and expenditure

From a historical point of view, it is significant whether and to what extent trade unions participated in the redistribution of ROH property after 1990. For this reason, notable differences between the different unions' headquarters persist today. Before 1989, ROH had assets of 16 billion Czechoslovak crowns (about €614,000,000) and employed 2,308 employees at the central office and another 1,083 employees in the federations (Pokorný 2015). The Czech and Slovak Confederations of Trade Unions, the legal predecessor of ČMKOS, took over the membership and trade union assets, which now represent 80 per cent of all the organization's assets (Pokorný 2015). Other confederations that were established after the so-called 'delimitation' of trade union property and so did not have access to ROH property are materially disadvantaged.

Property management has been the subject of several conflicts within Czech trade unions (Myant 2010). In 1990, the Property Delimitation Association of Trade Unions (MSDUOS) was established by thirty federations to manage the property inherited from ROH, including prominent hotels, relaxation centres, offices and flats. Each of the thirty unions involved in MSDUOS was previously an affiliate of ROH (Myant 2010). MSDUOS operates today with twenty trade union federations as members and a principal function of facility management and rental of remaining hotels, relaxation centres and office buildings. MSDUOS does not accept new members and ČMKOS is not a member organization. In 2019, MSDUOS sold the House of Trade Unions in Prague, the head office of ČMKOS and other trade union federations for around 1 billion Czech crowns, or around €40 million (MSDUOS 2019). According to MSDUOS representatives, the capacity of the building was several times higher than current trade union needs (assessed at only 20 per cent of the office space available). The cost of running this building was therefore regarded as unsustainable and MSDUOS board members decided to sell. Interestingly, ČMKOS did not have any say in this decision, and their representatives had to explain to the public that it was not ČMKOS who had sold their main office.

Redistribution of MSDUOS revenues from property management is calculated on a historical basis and benefits MSDUOS members unequally. The biggest trade union federation KOVO has a 30 per cent share, while the construction trade union STAVBA and the mining trade union both have 10 per cent shares; 4 per cent goes to the chemicals trade union ECHO (website for political journalism in Czechia) and another 4 per cent to the trade union of state employees. A further 42 per cent is distributed among another 15 federations (Balajová 2012). Other federations, created after 1990, do not receive anything from this property redistribution. Historical property delimitation from ROH thus creates disparities within the trade union movement today. Nevertheless, individual federations and some company-level trade unions also own various smaller properties from ROH not managed by MSDUOS.

ČMKOS's main annual revenue comes from membership fees paid by affiliated federations and from project base financing (Table 7.4). Each of the affiliated unions pays 0.422 per cent of the average wage in the economy in a given year for each of its members, excluding unemployed members, retirees or members on parental leave (ČMKOS statute, 2018).[2] To compare, ASO demands from its affiliated members an annual €0.08 per member, which is significantly less than affiliated organizations pay to ČMKOS (approximately €5 per employed member). Each year, ČMKOS receives around €1.15 million in membership fees (Table 7.4). In 2019, ČMKOS employed 102 (full-time equivalent) employees (of whom thirty-seven were core employees) (ČMKOS 2019a). ASO had approximately ten employees and KUK reports five but only two full-time equivalents (ASO 2019; KUK 2020). The annual budget of ČMKOS is around €2 million (Table 7.4), while ASO reports €743,000 and KUK has an annual budget of around €15,000 (ASO 2019; KUK 2020). The budget revenues include all sources of financing, especially membership fees and project financing.

---

2 ČMKOS Statut: https://or.justice.cz/ias/ui/vypis-sl-detail?dokument=52863322&subjektId=737679&spis=322906

At the level of basic organizations in federations affiliated to ČMKOS 1 per cent of members' monthly wages is collected, while ASO affiliated company-level trade unions collect a fixed fee typically lower than 1 per cent of employees' monthly wages. Between 20 to 30 per cent of collected fees go to the federation level.

Table 7.4 Financial situation of ČMKOS (in euros), 2015–2019

	2015	2016	2017	2018	2019
Membership fees paid by federations	1,053,953	1,058,817	1,076,984	1,167,219	1,196,596
Projects (state budget and European funds)	790,749	742,907	990,809	1,128,222	926,301
Number of employees (full-time equivalent)	85	108	115	137	102

Note: for EUR/CZK currency conversion an average exchange rate published by the Czech National Bank for the given year was used. Data before 2015 are not available. Data do not include ČMKOS affiliated federations.

Source: ČMKOS annual reports (2015–2019).

Trade union organizations and employers' organizations that are members of the RHSD are also entitled to state budget funds 'to support social partners' mutual negotiations at the state and regional level regarding workers, especially their economic, production, employment, wage and social interests' (Labour Code §320a). Part of the revenues of ČMKOS and ASO come from this source and form a significant part of their project financing.

At company level, trade unions are entitled to material support from employers 'to an extent appropriate for the performance of trade union activities, such as providing them with premises (furnished and equipped as necessary) and bearing costs related to their maintenance and technical operations' (LC §277). Trade union representatives are released from their regular work to perform work for the trade union only if agreed with the employer. Wage compensation is set by agreements between trade unions and employers. Even in large companies, trade unionists are often released only partially from their regular work. In other cases a trade union leader may be formally employed in the HR department of the company so that their salary is paid by the employer. In general, trade union representatives at the company level try to avoid spending membership fees on their own salaries and seek ways of obtaining payment from the employer. If unsuccessful they do the job only as volunteers, which reduces their accessibility to members and their ability to cover all important issues at the company level.

To conclude, the financing of trade union federations and confederations has three main sources: membership fees, project financing and revenues from communist period ROH property. The last of these resources is managed by only twenty trade union federations. At the company level, trade unions are financed mainly from membership fees and could be partially supported by the employer, but this depends on agreement with trade unions operating at the workplace.

Collective bargaining and unions at the workplace

Company-level collective bargaining is the most important level in setting working conditions in the Czech industrial relations system. Working conditions set at company level may only improve on provisions set in national legislation and/or at the industry level. From one point of view this does not create enough space for bargaining because the Labour Code already provides a detailed set of working condition provisions. On the other hand, the Labour Code offers reasonable protection to those not covered by a collective agreement (Colling 2009). Company-level agreements covered 788,000 employees in 2019 (MPSV 2020) or 18 per cent of the working population. Between 10 and 20 per cent of employees are covered by one of the twenty multi-employer agreements (Myant 2019). Collective agreements typically regulate pay, working time and other benefits paid by employers at the company level beyond the minimum set by the Labour Code and the statutory minimum wage. In the public sector, however, pay is defined by government decree and is not the subject of collective agreements. In this case public sector trade unions can only lobby political representatives and engage in protest actions if needed to gain higher wages for public sector workers (Martišková 2020).

In 2019, 85.5 per cent of company-level agreements contained provisions that increased pay and 78 per cent defined fixed minimum wages for different categories of workers within the company (Table 7.5). A significant number of agreements also defined severance payments above the minimum legal level. The majority of agreements also contained working time regulations, although working time accounts, conferring more employment flexibility, were regulated by only 7 per cent of agreements. In the context of labour market transformation and the requalification of employees this requires, only 1.8 per cent of collective agreements define specific conditions for employee education. In effect, employees' further training is highly dependent on employer programmes and is rarely bargained at company level (SANEP 2019).

Table 7.5 Content summary of collective agreements, 2019

Provisions in company-level collective agreements	**Absolute number of collective agreements**	**Collective agreements (%)**
Employer contribution to food	1,204	95.6
Working time arrangements	1,155	91.7
Holidays beyond Labour Code	1,113	88.4
Payment provisions	1,077	85.5
Wage fixes	982	78.0
Employer contribution to supplementary pension insurance	827	65.7
Severance payment (employed more than one year)	637	50.6
Conditions for employees' professional development	425	33.8
- of which specific conditions for employees' development	*23*	*1.8*
Severance payment (employed less than two years)	422	33.5
Severance payment (employed less than one year)	411	32.6
Employer contribution to life insurance	319	25.3
Working time account provisions	93	7.4
Employer contribution to commuting	88	7.0
Reduction of agency work	37	2.9

Source: Authors' compilation based on data from information on working conditions survey (IPP (kolektivnismlouvy.cz)

Company-level bargaining, as the dominant level of wage setting, tends to foster labour market dualization in Czechia. The trade union bargaining priority is to protect members, the vast majority of whom are full-time employees, while those with temporary contracts are rarely unionized. As a result, collective agreements contain provisions on lay-off policies that disadvantage fixed-term and temporary workers, who are laid off before full-time workers as a matter of course (Bernaciak 2015). This was especially visible in the aftermath of the financial crisis and a similar bargaining strategy was also used in the economic slowdown caused by the Covid-19 pandemic.

Besides company-level bargaining, the provisions of the Labour Code play an important role in defining working conditions. In recent years trade unions have increasingly sought to improve working conditions through legislative reform rather than collective bargaining. This strategy has been driven by falling trade union membership and collective bargaining coverage (Martišková et al. 2021). In this case, in particular weak workplace-level trade unions simply control the correct implementation of Labour Code provisions, rather than aim to improve working conditions at the workplace.

Free-riding at the company level is an issue because unionization at company level oscillates between 10 and 20 per cent, while collective agreements cover all employees. Trade unions thus seek ways of compensating their members. Larger trade union federations still retain their regional structures, employ lawyers and negotiators, and provide members with legal services free of charge in individual disputes with employers. Trade unions also offer members various vouchers and discounts for leisure time activities such as massage, spa or shopping facilities, but also organize free-time activities for their members (Arendas 2016).

In the workplace employees can also be represented by works councils, regardless of a trade union presence. Works councils have operated in Czechia since the 1920s and were re-established in 2001 as a part of the synchronization of the Czech law with European law in the pre-accession period. Works councils must be set up in enterprises with at least fifty employees, provided that 10 per cent of the workforce requests this in writing. Works councils have a right to information about working conditions, pay or employment, but cannot participate in collective bargaining (Drahokoupil and Kahancová 2017). Because only trade unions are granted collective bargaining rights, work councils do not represent competition to trade unions at the workplace level. Often trade unions and works councils operate at the same employer, but in this case only the trade union can initiate bargaining and conclude collective agreements.

Multinational corporations are dominant in several industries, most notably automotive, retail and banking. Trade union interaction with multinational corporations' management depends on how the company was established (privatized or direct investment), the origin of the company and the strength of trade unions at workplace. As Myant (2020) concludes, the interaction of trade unions with multinational corporations has brought mixed results, varying from recognition and continuing collective bargaining after privatization (Škoda in automotive), initial difficulties with recognition (Bosch in automotive), to gaining better outcomes under foreign ownership compared with domestic ownership (Mitas in the rubber industry). During the privatization process in the 1990s, trade unions often perceived the takeover of a company by a foreign investor as an advantage; local managers were inexperienced and that often resulted in companies going bankrupt (Falbrem 2011). What also helped trade unions to gain recognition was media pressure and international pressures in specific cases of maltreatment, but also legislation, which guarantees a relatively easy process for establishing trade unions and collective bargaining rights.

Industrial conflict

In Czechia, employees have a right to strike but the current legal regulations minimize their occurrence. There have been only minor changes to the legal regulation of strikes since 1991, when the provisions were introduced in the ZKV (Myant 2019). Based on the Act, strike action is possible only after collective bargaining or mediation fail and a two-thirds majority of at least 50 per cent of the relevant workforce voted for it (ZKV §17). Fulfilling these conditions is a time- and resource-consuming process, which significantly constrains strike activity. When employees go on strike, they also forfeit wages and compulsory social contributions are not paid by the employer (ZKV §22). Therefore, strike participation necessitates a significant financial commitment by strike participants or by trade unions, which usually discourages employees from participating. Alternatively, employees can call a strike outside the legal framework of the Collective Bargaining Act. In these circumstances the strike is based only on the provisions of the Charter of Human Rights, which can be disputed in court by employers (Myant 2019). Strike funds are created by trade unions from their own resources, but there is no regulation or coordinated approach from federations or confederations.

Trade unions at company level often use a strike warning instead of actual strike action to advance negotiations. A strike warning is not a legally recognized term but serves as a powerful tool to more negotiations forward because it attracts media attention and through public relations pressure may force management to conclude a collective agreement and prevent a strike. When a collective agreement is concluded the law prohibits strike action. Strikes outside the legal framework of the Collective Bargaining Act thus occur rarely and only in symbolic form, lasting perhaps one hour or a maximum of one day.

Looking at developments over time, trade unions at the national level used a form of general strike during the 1990s and early 2000s, lasting from one hour to one day. Several large demonstrations have also been called during the past 30 years: for instance, against pension reform in 1994, social reform in 1995, and against the policies of the right-wing government in 1997. In each case there were about 100,000 participants. Most of the demonstrations occurred when right-wing governments were in office (Myant 2010; Pokorný 2015). The last huge demonstration organized by Czech trade unions was in 2012, called to protest against austerity measures following the financial crisis of 2008/2009 and, in particular, wage cuts in the public sector, proposed by the then right-wing 'austerity' government. The demonstration in Prague was considered an exceptional success given the low participation in protests in previous years (Martišková and Sedláková 2017; Myant 2013).

Given the limitations on strike activity, trade unions mobilize employees in other ways, such as organizing petitions, demonstrations or issuing strike warnings if collective bargaining seems likely to fail. The following analysis, based on newspaper records of trade union protest activities between 1988 and 2017, shows the frequency with which these tools were used (strike warning are not included here). As Figure 7.2 shows, the demonstration was the dominant way of showing discontent for Czech trade unions, particularly during the 1990s, while later on petitions gained in importance. Strike activity is low; the only exceptional year is 2008, with twenty-three strikes organized by trade unions. Between 2001 and 2017 trade unions organized 107 strikes, most lasting a day, while longer strikes were exceptional.[3]

3 Exceptional was the 42-day strike in 2001, and the 22-day strike at Czech Television, the national broadcaster company, in 2000/2001, as well as another 22-day strike at mining company Koh-i-noor in 2000. Then there were two strikes that lasted seven days, two that lasted nine days and one that lasted five days.

Figure 7.2 Trade union protest actions, 1988–2017

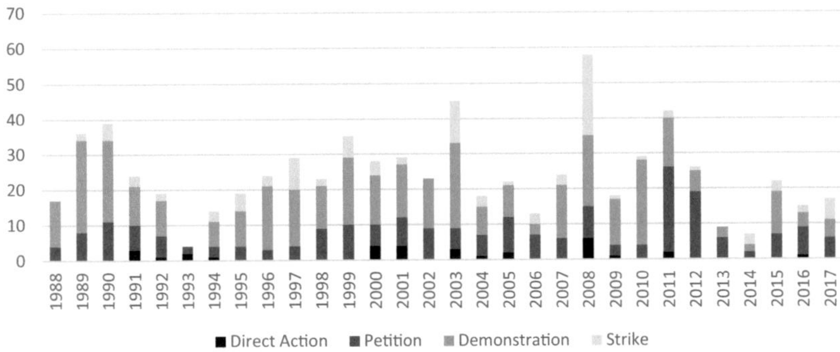

Source: Authors' compilation based on data from Císař et al. (2012) and own updates.

In recent years trade unions have explored alternative ways of showing discontent (Martišková and Sedláková 2017). A significant alternative means of protest was undertaken by doctors who conducted a campaign under the banner 'Thank You We Are Leaving' during which 3,837 doctors had submitted their resignation letters by the end of 2010. The reason why standard protest activity was not applied was the legal strike ban on employees in health care and social care facilities (ZKV §20g), but also an absence of industrial bargaining in the sector (Martišková and Sedláková 2017). The campaign was coordinated by the Doctors Trade Union Club and the Union of Czech Doctors (LOK-SČL, *Lékařský odborový klub, svaz českých lékařu*), a professional trade union affiliated to ASO. It ended with agreement with the Ministry of Health Care (*Ministerstvo zdravotnictví ČR*), which promised 15 per cent wage increases in return for the withdrawal of the doctors' resignations. Another example of alternative ways of showing discontent was a big national gathering of trade unionists from ČMKOS to support collective bargaining at company level and demand increases in the statutory minimum wage set at national level. As this action also increased ČMKOS's societal power, it is discussed below.

Political relations

Most of political relations in Czechia are conducted through consultations within the Czech tripartite body RHSD, which is composed of seven representatives each of the trade unions, the employers and the government. The RHSD has only a consultative role, but it is the main communication channel between the social partners and the government and thus has special importance in Czech industrial relations. At the RHSD the social partners discuss and suggest amendments to proposed legislation related to economic and social issues. It is also the place where the statutory minimum wage is negotiated, although the final decision and approval rests with the government alone.

Unsurprisingly the functioning and outcomes of the tripartite meetings are dependent on the government's attitude to social dialogue. Several times since its establishment in 1990, the RHSD has been dysfunctional or neglected by politicians, especially by those from the political right. Political animosities between the centre and right-wing governments and the trade unions are evident and have materialized in several strikes and demonstrations (Myant 2010).

Although trade unions state that they are apolitical, most of the trade union agenda is consistent with that of the social democratic ČSSD, with which trade unions have ideological commonalities. These commonalities were especially important during the 1990s and 2000s when neoliberal reforms aimed at privatization, the pension system, health care, the tax system and working conditions were proposed by right-wing governments. The trade unions put up substantial opposition, calling demonstrations and strikes. In recent years, especially since 2012, tripartite consultations have taken a more predictable form with no pitfalls and mutual animosities. This is also thanks to the ČSSD presence in the government, albeit only as a junior coalition partner. ČSSD also proved to be a partner for basic trade unions when campaigning for better working conditions in multinationals operating in Czechia. One illustrative example was the involvement of ČSSD Prime Minister Bohuslav Sobotka in a dispute about wages and working conditions in the Ahold retail chain in 2017. The Prime Minister personally approached the Dutch ambassador in Czechia with an urgent request to improve working conditions and wages in this retail chain owned by the Dutch multinational (Myant 2020).

In addition to ideological similarities, there was also a strong personal connection between ČMKOS and the ČSSD, although ČMKOS has not declared for any party at any election. Richard Falbr, ČMKOS chair from 1994 to 2002, was a member of the Czech Senate from its formation in 1996 to 2004 and of the European Parliament from 2004, both times supported by the ČSSD. Milan Štěch was ČMKOS chair from 2002 to 2010 and a senator for the Social Democrats from 1996 to 2020. Jaroslav Zavadil, chair of ČMKOS between 2010 and 2013, became a ČSSD Deputy in 2013 and adviser to President Zeman on social issues. Since 2020 neither ČMKOS nor any other trade union confederation has had elected representatives in parliament.

Constructive cooperation since 2017 with the government of Andrej Babiš of the political movement Action of Dissatisfied Citizens(Akec nespokojenych obcanu) (ANO), in which the ČSSD is a junior coalition partner, has resulted in some successes in improving working conditions, including regular increases in the minimum wage and the adoption of the Retail Opening Hours Act (*Zákon o prodejní době v maloobchodě*) on closing large retail stores during several state holidays (Pokorný 2019). ČMKOS is trying, however, to become a more independent political stakeholder without, if possible, open ties with politicians. An important context is the long-term decline of ČSSD, which electorally is currently oscillating around the 5 per cent threshold for entering parliament. Trade unions' declared independence is appreciated by members and may help them to stabilize or even improve their position in society in the future (ibid.).

Societal power

Despite falling membership and difficulties in increasing collective bargaining coverage, trade unions have not been forgotten in Czech society. According to the annual survey on trust in trade unions almost half of the respondents trust or mostly trust in this institution. This number increased constantly from 30 per cent in 2001 to almost 45 per cent in 2020 (Figure 7.3). Similarly, 60 per cent of the population think that trade unions are needed and useful in society (STEM 2014).

Figure 7.3 Trust in trade unions, 2001–2020

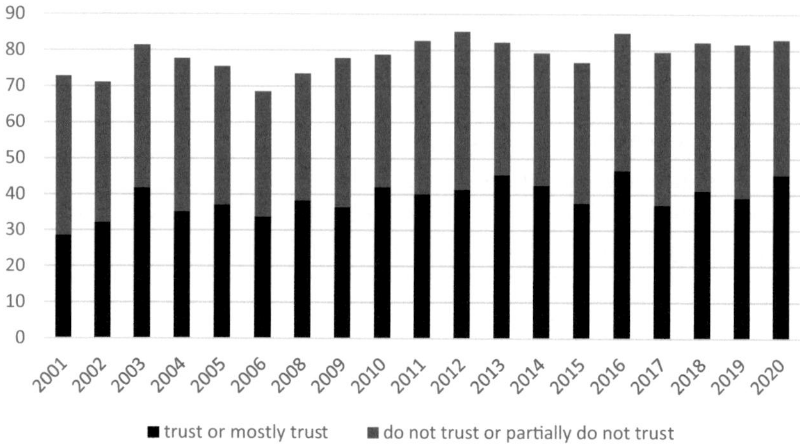

Source: Authors' compilation based on data from annual surveys of the Centre for Public Opinion Research (CVVM).

Improved perceptions of trade unions in recent years might also be attributed to their improved communication and self-presentation strategy, especially since 2015, when ČMKOS ran a long-term campaign for pay rises under the banner 'An End to Cheap Labour'. This campaign is perceived as innovative in the Czech context (Martišková and Sedláková 2017) as for the first time it established a theme in the public space usually occupied by politicians (Myant and Drahokoupil 2017). Trade unions launched this campaign based on their own analyses, which showed that Czech wages on average were only one-third of German wages. ČMKOS identified a set of measures that could improve living conditions in Czechia, including the strategic goal of nominal wage increases to achieve wage convergence with the EU average (Fassmann and Ungerman 2015). A flagship event of the campaign was the annual organization of a members' meeting in Prague, which brought together about 1,500 trade unionists. The aim of the meeting was to activate trade union negotiators before the new collective bargaining round to demand significant wage increases, inspired by the Austrian ÖGB and German DGB confederations (ČMKOS 2015). The annual event attracts significant media interest, which contributes to ČMKOS's public visibility. Although this campaign cannot be categorized as traditional protest activity, it demonstrates the trade unions' mobilization potential and highlights their goals to the public. This campaign also helps to recruit members, resulting in increased membership levels. It may also have contributed to the stabilization of membership (Myant and Drahokoupil 2017).

There is no tradition of trade union cooperation and coalition-building with non-governmental organizations (NGOs). During the 1990s when trade union structures were being rebuilt, NGOs were not a developed force in Czech society. This made it harder to establish connections with these organizations at a later date. Trade unionists mention a lack of professionalism in NGOs as a reason for the very weak links. The only exception was short-term cooperation with the leftist movement ProAlt during the protests against the right-wing government of 2010–2013 and its proposal for budget cuts in 2012. Together, ProAlt and the trade unions managed to involve the public in various protest actions, culminating in a massive 'Stop the Government' demonstration on 20 April 2012, which led to the fall of the government. Nevertheless, this cooperation did not last because the activists and trade unionists did not find common interests beyond the protests. The ProAlt movement was dissolved a few years later.

Cooperation with the climate change movement is even more problematic. Within ČMKOS the Trade Union of Workers in Mining Industry, Geology and Diesel Industry (OS PHGN, *Odborový svaz pracovníků hornictví, geologie a naftového průmyslu*) and ASO affiliate the Czech energy sector trade union ČOSE (*Český odborový svaz energetiků*) are very vocal on this topic. This openly undermines the climate movement by pushing the position in arguing that the end of coal mining in Czechia would lead to enormous increases of energy prices and demanding the building of nuclear plants to replace coal-fired power stations (Souček 2020). In 2019, when a Coal Commission (*Uhelná komise*) was established for Czechia with a brief to set a date for ending coal mining, the one place allocated to trade unions was occupied by the representative of OS PHGN. At EU level, however, ČMKOS supports climate goals and recognizes the need to take action to preserve the environment. This illustrates the differences of opinion on the issue within the trade union movement. Despite this, climate NGOs, such as Greenpeace, are trying to include trade unions in the coal mining and energy industry in discussions about a Just Transition in the sector (Greenpeace 2021). The second largest trade union confederation, ASO, engages mainly in the debate on agriculture and the problem of water sufficiency caused by climate change, demanding restrictions on large farming enterprises, which exert intense pressure on resources through intensive farming. The smallest confederation KUK is not vocal on this issue.

Trade union policies towards the European Union

During the 1990s it was vital that Czech trade unions generate international recognition. Formal acceptance within international structures was perceived as a confirmation of their credibility (Myant 2010). On 14 December 1995, ČMKOS was formally accepted as a member of the European Trade Union Confederation (ETUC), an important milestone for the organization. Later, international cooperation gained importance in industries in which foreign capital is dominant, such as automotive, retail, banking and other services. This cooperation is important beyond European works councils, especially in cases in which employers banned trade union activities at the workplace, for instance at the automotive supplier Bosch in Jihlava or the recent case of trade unions established in Ryanair (Liebreich 2020; Myant 2020). The active involvement of the industrial level trade union federations and cooperation with respective partner unions based in the country of the company's headquarters proved to be an efficient means of improving trade union recognition in Czech subsidiaries, especially in retail (Myant 2020). ASO is neither affiliated to the ETUC nor the European Confederation of Independent Trade Unions (CESI) at confederal level, although affiliated unions that represent doctors and railway workers participate in European level organizations.

ČMKOS and ASO affiliates, especially the larger ones, are members of international and EU-level organizations and are involved in EU-level social dialogue structures. Nevertheless, most trade unions report that a lack of personnel capacity and financial resources prevent them from participating more actively in EU social dialogue structures (Akgüç et al. 2019). Moreover, because of insufficient capacity, there is usually only one international secretary with no other support staff within trade unions (ibid.). Language barriers also often prevent elected representatives from more active involvement. Despite these drawbacks, Czech trade unionists regard international cooperation as an important tool for improving working conditions, especially in industries in which multinational corporations dominate.

At the regional level, cooperation has developed with trade unions from the other Visegrad countries (Hungary, Poland and Slovakia), especially in industries with a high incidence of cross-border working, such as construction and health care (Akgüç et al. 2019; Kahancová et al. 2019). For trade unions in the metal industry regional cooperation within the Vienna Memorandum, which encompasses Austrian, Czech, German, Slovak and Slovenian metalworkers' trade unions, is exceptionally important as a mechanism for preventing social dumping and deterioration of working conditions in the automotive industry.

In 2019, ČMKOS president Josef Středula was elected a vice-president of the ETUC. This could be perceived as an outcome of the recent efforts of trade unions from CEE to improve their integration in European social dialogue structures and to articulate topics specific to the region, particularly low wages. CEE trade unions have been active in articulating this issue since 2017 when, following demands from Czech and Slovak trade unions and partially inspired by the ČMKOS campaign 'An End to Cheap Labour', the ETUC adopted a resolution on promoting increases in the lowest wages and launched the campaign 'Europe Needs a Pay Rise'. The idea of a European minimum wage has become official ETUC policy, although not yet translated into any specific measures, primarily because of opposition from Nordic trade unions (Czarzasty et al. 2020). On this issue, ASO supports ČMKOS at the EU level and both demand minimum wages be set at 50 per cent of the average wage (ASO 2021).

Conclusions

Similarly to their counterparts in other CEE countries, Czech trade unions have experienced a turbulent thirty years, marked by economic transformation from a planned to a market economy, which has affected their functioning and position in society. Internally they have undergone a transformation from centralized organizations subordinated to the Communist Party of Czechoslovakia (*Komunistická strana Československa*) to an independent societal entity defending its place in the new political and economic order. Externally, trade unions have adapted to the changing labour market, which is reflected in altered working conditions and a quickly diminishing membership base. Looking at the Czech trade unions' future prospects, we discuss four possible scenarios suggested by Visser (2019): marginalization, dualization, replacement or revitalization.

Given the decline in membership over the past thirty years and decreasing bargaining coverage, we might conclude that trade union marginalization is inevitable in Czechia. Nevertheless, we argue that the trade unions are seeking ways of avoiding this fate and remain relevant. Based on the analysis in this chapter, there are at least four arguments to support this claim. First, trade unions have been able to attract new members in important industries within the economy even without focused recruitments campaigns. This inflow has not yet translated into significant membership growth, however, because of the high number of members that are leaving the labour market, and thus union membership. Second, despite a significant decrease in protest activities, trade unions have been able to demonstrate their relevance, boost collective bargaining outcomes and attract media attention through innovative campaigns and public gatherings. Third, they aim to remain independent actors with no open ties to political parties, despite historically strong links with social democrats, who in the past ten years have lost a significant share of their electorate. Fourth, trade unions remain one of the most trusted institutions in Czechia.

The question is, what is the future of trade unions if they escape marginalization. Their ability to innovate and modernize their public presence in the 2015 campaign 'An End to Cheap Labour' would suggest that revitalization is the new path. Nevertheless, there is little evidence of a capacity to address recruitment problems, exacerbated by unequal property inheritance and redistribution of revenues. In addition, trade unions might find it difficult to address upcoming challenges, such as climate change and technological unemployment. Furthermore, the unions have shown no interest in establishing partnerships with civil society organizations that are much more vocal on these issues. These considerations may preclude revitalization.

Alternatively, trade unions may escape marginalization by remaining relevant in predominantly public industries of the economy, and by protecting core employees rather than the more vulnerable. This would suggest a dualization path. This is currently supported by the decentralization of collective bargaining, resulting in heterogeneous outcomes as regards improving working conditions and guaranteed protection of core workers in organized workplaces, while precarious and platform workers remain at the mercy of market forces. The Czech trade unions have not, however, abandoned the protection of vulnerable employees, despite their difficulties recruiting them. They have tried to protect them through legislative solutions instead of collective bargaining. Changes in legislation are achieved mainly through tripartite negotiations, political lobbying, public action and protest activities. Trade unions have thus created a symbiotic structure of collective bargaining backed by a legislative framework and legislative solutions that help to improve working conditions and partially to escape the dualization path. The risk of this path is that trade unions achievements in legislation are highly dependent on political representation and government's political orientation.

The replacement scenario also seems unlikely, although, in the case of migrant workers, we observe that trade unions are being replaced by civil society organizations that specialize in protecting migrant workers' rights. Migrant workers, however, remain a small part of the labour market and there are no signs of trade unions being replaced by other organizations or institutions.

Czech trade unions have undergone some turbulent times during the past thirty years. Nevertheless, they are expected to face even more dramatic changes in the future, the most significant of which will be climate change and ensuring a Just Transition of the economy for domestic employees. Given the contradictions with which this issue is fraught, trade unions may experience difficult times when attempting to protect both the environment and workplaces.

References

All links were checked on 27 May 2021.

Akgüç M., Martišková M., Szüdi G. and Nordlund C. (2019) Enhancing the effectiveness of social dialogue articulation in Europe (EESDA). Stakeholders' views on and experiences with the articulation of social dialogue and its effectiveness, Brussels, European Centre for Political Studies. https://www.celsi.sk/media/datasource/D2.2_EESDA_Stakeholders-views_n1bPRAR.pdf

ARES (2021) Database of economic subjects in the Czech Republic. https://wwwinfo.mfcr.cz/ares/ares_es_form.html.cz (Trade unions code 707)

Arendas Z. (2016) Industrial relations in car-manufacturing industry: a comparative case study of Audi Hungaria, Gyor and Mercedes Benz, Kecskemet, Budapest, Centre for Policy Studies/Central European University. https://cps.ceu.edu/sites/cps.ceu.edu/files/cps-working-papers-industrial-relations-audimercedes-hungary-2016.pdf

ASO (2016) Stanovy ASO schválené Valnou hromadou dne 12. prosince 2016 [Association of independent unions by-law], Prague, Asociace samostatných odborů. https://www.asocr.cz/obsah/63/stanovy-aso-schvalene-valnou-hromadou-dne-12-prosince-2016/17854

ASO (2019) Výroční zpráva [Annual report], Prague, Asociace samostatných odborů. https://or.justice.cz/ias/ui/vypis-sl-firma?subjektId=743599

ASO (2020) Cíle a poslání [Aims and mission], Prague, Asociace samostatných odborů. https://www.asocr.cz/obsah/64/cile-poslani/881

ASO (2021) The role of collective bargaining in securing working conditions, including fair remuneration at work, Praha, Asociace Samostatnyeh Odboru.

Balajová K. (2012) Chyť mě když to dokážeš [Catch me if you can], Euro.cz, 24 May 2012. https://www.euro.cz/archiv/chyt-me-kdyz-to-dokazes-2-780825

Bernaciak M. (2015) Beyond the CEE 'black box': crisis and industrial relations in the new EU member states, Working Paper 2015.05, Brussels, ETUI.

Bohle D. and Greskovits B. (2012) Capitalist diversity on Europe's periphery, Ithaca, Cornell University Press.

Čaněk M. (2017) Trade unions and migration in the Czech Republic, 2004–15, in Marino S., Roosblad J., Penninx R. (eds) Trade unions and migrant workers, Cheltenham, Edward Elgar Publishing, 307–329.

Čapka F. (2008) Odbory v českých zemích v letech 1918–1948, Brno, Masarykova univerzita.

Císař O., Navrátil J. and Vráblíková K. (2012) Collective action and protest in East-Central Europe. Czech Science Foundation Project GAP404/11/0462, Brno, Masaryk University.

ČMKOS (2015) Vize změny hospodářské strategie ČR, Prague, ČMKOS. https://www.cmkos.cz/obsah/223/vize-zmeny-hospodarske-strategie-cr/14318

ČMKOS (2018) Výroční zpráva 2017, Prague, ČMKOS. https://or.justice.cz/ias/ui/vypis-sl-detail?dokument=52601935&subjektId=737679&spis=322906

ČMKOS (2019a) Konec levné práce v ČR, Prague, ČMKOS. https://www.cmkos.cz/cs/obsah/219/konec-levne-prace-v-cr/12791

ČMKOS (2019b) Výroční zpráva, Prague, ČMKOS.

Colling T. (2009) Court in a trap? Legal mobilisation by trade unions in the United Kingdom, Warwick Papers in Industrial Relations 91, Coventry, University of Warwick. https://www.econstor.eu/bitstream/10419/48542/1/60401631X.pdf

ČSÚ (2018) První republika. Zlatý věk odborů, Prague, Český statistický úřad. https://www.czso.cz/csu/stoletistatistiky/prvni-republika-zlaty-vek-odboru

Czarzasty J., Adamczyk S. and Surdykowska B. (2020) Looking for European solutions. Trade unions in Central and Eastern Europe striving for cross-border solidarity, Transfer, 26 (3), 307–323.

Drahokoupil J. and Kahancová M. (2017) Worker participation in Czechia and Slovakia, in Berger S., Pries L. and Wannöffel M. (eds) The Palgrave handbook of workers' participation at plant level, Basingstoke, Palgrave Macmillan, 301–322.

Eurostat. 2021. Employment and Unemployment Data. https://ec.europa.eu/eurostat/web/ifs/data/database

Falbrem R. (2011) Dialog o transformaci [Dialogue about transformation], Prague, Institut pro péči o kulturní a intelektuální dědičství. https://www.ippkid.cz/2011/04/15/dialog-o-transformaci-s-richardem-falbrem/

Fassmann M. and Ungerman J. (2015) Vision of the economic strategy change in the Czech Republic. Economic and political priorities, Prague, ČMKOS. https://ipodpora.odbory.info/soubory/dms/ukony/14982/6/VISION-Vision%20of%20the%20Economic%20Strategy%20Change%20in%20the%20Czech%20Republic.pdf

Greenpeace (2021) Dvě třetiny lidí podporují výsluhové dávky pro uhelné horníky a energetiky. Odbory a ekologické organizace žádají spravedlivou transformaci [Two-thirds of people support dismissal rent to coal miners and coal power plant workers. Trade unions and NGOs demand just transition], Prague, Greenpeace Česká republika. https://www.greenpeace.org/czech/tiskova-zprava/13641/dve-tretiny-lidi-podporuji-vysluhove-davky-pro-uhelne-horniky-a-energetiky-odbory-a-ekologicke-organizace-zadaji-spravedlivou-transformaci/

Hospodářské noviny (1995) Zemědělci vystoupili z odborové komory [Agrarians have withdrawn from trade union chamber], Hospodářské noviny, 16 February 1995. https://archiv.ihned.cz/c1-834732-zemedelci-vystoupili-z-odborove-komory

Kahancová M. and Kirov V. (2021) Shaping minimum wages in Central and Eastern Europe: giving up collective bargaining in favour of legal regulation?, in Dingeldey I., Grimshaw D. and Schulten T. (eds) Minimum wage regimes: statutory regulation, collective bargaining and adequate levels, Abingdon Oxon, Routledge, 87–112.

Kahancová M., Martišková M. and Szüdi G. (2019) Enhancing the effectiveness of social dialogue articulation in Europe (EESDA). EESDA National Report: Slovakia, Bratislava, Central European Labour Studies Institute. https://www.celsi.sk/media/datasource/D3.2_EESDA_National_Report_SK.pdf

Kahancová M., Meszmann T.T. and Sedláková M. (2020) Precarization via digitalization? Work arrangements in the on-demand platform economy in Hungary and Slovakia, Frontiers in Sociology, 5, article 3.

KUK (2020) Výroční zpráva 2019, Prague, KUK. https://or.justice.cz/ias/ui/vypis-sl-firma?subjektId=739062

Kyzlinková R., Pojer P. and Veverková S. (2017) Industrial relations in the Czech Republic. Recent developments and future challenges [Industriální vztahy v České republice: Nedávný vývoj a budoucí výzvy]. Prague, RILSA. https://katalog.vupsv.cz/Fulltext/ul_2078.pdf

Liebreich J. (2020) V Ryanairu se nemůžete cítit bezpečně, natož mu důvěřovat, říká šéf českých odborů Pizzolato, E15.cz, 7 June 2020. https://www.e15.cz/byznys/doprava-a-logistika/v-ryanairu-se-nemuzete-citit-bezpecne-natoz-mu-duverovat-rika-sef-ceskych-odboru-pizzolato-1370379

Martišková M. (2020) Czech public sector industrial relations in the aftermath of the crisis: keeping the status quo as a successful strategy to protect working conditions, in Keune M., Ramos Martin N.E. and Mailand M. (eds) Working under pressure employment, job quality and labour relations in Europe's public sector since the crisis, Brussels, ETUI, 35–72.

Martišková M. and Sedláková M. (2017) Reinventing the role of the Czech trade unions: halfway through the journey, in Bernaciak M. and Kahancová M. (eds) Innovative union practices in Central-Eastern Europe, Brussels, ETUI, 57–72.

Martišková M., Kahancová M. and Kostolný J. (2021) Negotiating wage (in) equality: changing union strategies in high-wage and low-wage sectors in Czechia and Slovakia, Transfer, 27 (1), 75–96.

MPSV (2020) Informace o pracovních podmínkách, Ministerstva práce a sociálních věcí, Louky, MPSV ČR. http://kolektivnismlouvy.cz/download/2020/IPP_2020.pdf

Mrozowicki A. (2011) Trade union organizing in Eastern Europe: a viable pathway to trade union revitalization? A case study of the automotive sector, Emecon Employment and Economy in Central and Eastern Europe, 2 (1), 1–20.

MSDUOS (2019) Výroční zpráva 2019, MSDUOS, Prague. https://or.justice.cz/ias/ui/vypis-sl-detail?dokument=62258421&subjektId=739080&spis=324309

Myant M. (2010) Trade unions in the Czech Republic. Report 115, Brussels, ETUI.

Myant M. (2013) Vzestup a pád českého kapitalismu: ekonomický vývoj České republiky od roku 1989, Prague, Academia.

Myant M. (2019) Czechia: bargaining supplements legal protection, in Müller T., Vandaele K. and Waddington J. (eds) Collective bargaining in Europe: towards an endgame. Volume I, Brussels, ETUI, 131–149.

Myant M. (2020) European multinational companies and trade unions in eastern and east-central Europe. Working Paper 2020.03, Brussels, ETUI. https://www.etui.org/sites/default/files/2020-07/WP-2020.03-Myant-WEB.pdf

Myant M. and Drahokoupil J. (2011) Transition economies: political economy in Russia, Eastern Europe, and Central Asia, Oxford, Wiley-Blackwell.

Myant M. and Drahokoupil J. (2017) 'An end to cheap labour' – How a public campaign may become a turning point for Czech unions' strength, Berlin, FES. https://library.fes.de/pdf-files/iez/13816.pdf

OS KOVO (2020b) Zaměstnanci se stále častěji zajímají o to, jak založit odbory, Prague, OS KOVO. https://www.oskovo.cz/aktuality/zamestnanci-se-stale-casteji-zajimaji-o-jak-zalozit-odbory

Ost D. (2005) The defeat of solidarity. anger and politics in postcommunist Europe, Ithaca, Cornell University Press.

Pokorný J. (2015) Pracovat a nebát se! Kapitoly z dějín odborů v českých zemích [To work and not to be afraid! Chapters from the history of trade unions in the Czech lands], Prague, ČMKOS.

Pokorný J. (2019) 30. výročí generální stávky a vznik nových odborů, Prague, ČMKOS.

SANEP (2019) Průzkum 'Průmysl-Společnost 4.0' [A survey Industry-Society 4.0]. https://www.cmkos.cz/cs/obsah/785/pruzkum-prumysl-spolecnost-40/111802 -https://ipodpora.odbory.info/dms/soubory/index?file=PRUZKUM%20-Prumysl-Spolecnost%204.0_20190715082106.pdf

Souček P. (2020) Franta: Uhelnou komisi ovlivňuje nikým nezvolená skupina [Fanta: Coal commission is influenced by non-elected group], IUHLI.cz, 2 November 2020. https://iuhli.cz/franta-uhelnou-komisi-ovlivnuje-nikym-nezvolena-skupina/

Stark D. and Bruszt L. (1998) Postsocialist pathways. Transforming politics and property in East Central Europe, Cambridge, Cambridge University Press.

STEM (2014) Názory občanů na odbory [Citizens opinions on trade unions], Prague, STEM. https://www.stem.cz/nazory-obcanu-na-odbory/

Šumichrast, A. (2018) Transformácia či zánik? Vývoj odborov v Slovenskom štáte (1939-1945) v kontexte vybraných európskych diktatúr [Transformation or extinction? Development of Trade Unions in the Slovak State (1939–1945) in the context of selected European dictatorships], in Studia historica Brunensia. Brno, Masaryk university, 85–102.

Visser J. (2019) Trade unions in the balance. ILO ACTRAV working paper, Geneva, ILO.

Voss E., Broughton A., Pulignano V., Franca V. and Rodriguez Contreras R. (2018) Exploring the connections between EU- and national-level social dialogue, Luxembourg, Publications Office of European Union. https://www.eurofound.europa.eu/publications/report/2018/exploring-the-connections-between-eu-and-national-level-social-dialogue

Abbreviations

ASO	Asociace samostatných odborů (Association of Independent Trade Unions)
ČMKOS	Českomoravská konfederace odborových svazů (Czech and Moravian Confederation of Trade Unions)
ČSSD	Česká strana sociálně demokratická (Czech Social Democratic Party)
ETUC	European Trade Union Confederation
KUK	Konfederace umění a kultury (Confederation of Arts and Culture)
MSDUOS	Majetkové, správní a delimitační unie odborových svazů (Property Delimitation Association of Trade Unions)

OS PHGN	Odborový svaz pracovníků hornictví, geologie a naftového průmyslu (Trade Union of Workers in Mining Industry, Geology and Diesel Industry)
RHSD	Rada hospodářské a sociální dohody České republiky (Council of Economic and Social Agreement)
ROH	Revoluční odborové hnutí (Revolutionary Trade Union Movement)
ZKV	Zákon o kolektivním vyjednávání (Act on Collective Bargaining)

Chapter 8

Denmark: Trade unions still afloat at ebb tide

Herman Knudsen, Jens Lind and Bjarke Refslund

Looked at in a European context in which trade union power is rapidly deteriorating, Danish trade unions remain strong, with relatively high union density and an enduring and strong institutional position (see Table 8.1). Collective bargaining is the centrepiece of the primary wage-setting model, and overall the industrial relations model remains based on a consensual approach between employers and unions. Trade unions remain an influential societal actor in Denmark and are perceived by the large majority of citizens as an important and legitimate actor. Union density has declined in recent decades, however, particularly in certain industries, while there is also a growing share of union members in 'yellow' unions, as well as migrant workers who are largely not unionized. On the other hand, unionization has been growing among white-collar workers with a university degree, and there has been an increasing union consciousness among white-collar segments of the economy.

Using the typology developed by Crouch (1993), the Danish (and Nordic) unions form part of an industrial relations system characterized by 'bargained corporatism' rather than 'contestation' or 'pluralist bargaining'. Among the five types of industrial relations used by Welz and colleagues to describe differences among European Union (EU) member states, Denmark (and the other Nordic countries) is of the type 'organized corporatism' (Welz et al. 2016). A further label often assigned to the Danish industrial relations system is that of 'flexicurity' because of a purported 'golden' balance between flexibility for employers and security for workers (Knudsen and Lind 2018; Madsen 2002).

Table 8.1 Principal characteristics of trade unionism in Denmark

	1980	2000	2019
Total trade union membership	1,794,000	1,870,000	1,868,000
Women as a proportion of total membership	n.a.	n.a.	52 %
Gross union density	n.a.	n.a.	n.a.
Net union density*	68 %	66 %	64 %
Number of confederations	3	3	2
Number of affiliated unions (federations)	n.a.	n.a.	95
Number of independent unions	n.a.	n.a.	19
Collective bargaining coverage	n.a.	85 %	83 %
Principal level of collective bargaining	Cross-industry	Industry	Industry
Days not worked due to industrial action per 1,000 workers	78	46	3

Source: Authors' calculations on the basis of Statistisk Tiårsoversigt, various years, and Statistics Denmark (Statistikbanken). 2000 membership figures from Ibsen et al. (2013).
* Number of trade union members in the labour force as a proportion of all participants in the labour force (employed, unemployed and self- employed persons).

Historical background and principal features of the industrial relations system

Unionization in Denmark took off around 1870. The first trade unions were craft based, but they were soon followed by a unionization wave among unskilled workers. In 1898 the great majority of the existing unions came together in the Confederations of Danish Trade Unions (DsF, *De samvirkende Fagforbund*), which later, similar to Sweden and Norway, changed its name to LO (*Landsorganisationen i Danmark*). The employers' side also united in 1898, with the creation of the Danish Employers' Confederation (today DA, *Dansk Arbejdsgiverforening*).

The DsF/LO first and foremost organized skilled and unskilled manual workers. Skilled office workers also joined unions affiliated to the LO, whereas unions for professions such as nurses, teachers and many other 'white-collar' groups remained outside. In 1952 unions for these groups of salaried/white-collar employees formed the Confederation of Professionals in Denmark (FTF, *Funktionærernes og Tjenestemændenes Fællesråd*). A third confederation, exclusively for professions with a university degree, was established in 1972, the Danish Confederation of Professional Associations (AC, *Akademikerne*). A major distinction between the three confederations was that the members of the blue-collar unions in the DsF/LO were workers paid by the hour (*timelønnede*), whereas the members of the FTF and the AC were salaried employees paid by the month (*funktionærer*). In 2018 an amalgamation was agreed between LO and the FTF leading, in 2019, to the establishment of one large confederation, the Danish Trade Union Confederation (FH, *Fagbevægelsens Hovedorganisation*). This leaves Denmark with only two major confederations, the large FH and the much smaller AC.

Already by 1952, an American scholar had identified a number of central peculiarities of the Danish system (Galenson 1969). He found that trade unions and employer associations played a remarkably prominent role in the regulation of labour relations in Denmark, in particular by means of collective agreements. He also noted that relations between the two sides were relatively harmonious, characterized by a cooperative spirit and with a minimum of state regulation, which was aimed mainly at facilitating institutions set up by the parties themselves.

The same features nowadays are often described as 'the Danish model', as those pinpointed by Galenson were also emphasized later by several Danish scholars (Andersen et al. 2014; Due et al. 1993; Jensen 2007; Kristiansen 2014; Lind and Knudsen 2018). The centrality of collective bargaining is no doubt the most important feature. The rules governing collective bargaining have been established by the parties and are supported by the state. A central document in this respect is the Main Agreement (*Hovedaftalen*), which sets the frame for the Danish industrial relations regulation. It has been renewed several times and dates back to its first version, the September Agreement (*Septemberforliget*), which was the result of the first generalized conflict between capital and labour in Denmark, the great lock-out of 1899. This was a long and bitter confrontation between unions and employer associations in which the latter aimed to eliminate the unions' tactics of exploiting the combined strength of one or more unions to target one employer at a time through strike action (*omgangsskruen*). The conflict resulted in a compromise between the combatants: the union side had to recognize the right to manage as an employer's prerogative, while the employers had to acknowledge national unions as legitimate bargaining partners.

While substantive collective agreements dealing with wages, working time and working conditions are treated in a separate section below, another collective agreement dealing with procedures and rights, such as the Main Agreement, is the Cooperation Agreement (*Samarbejdsaftalen*).

The first cooperation agreement was concluded between the DsF (LO) and the DA in 1947 and covered workers in the private sector. Later it was supplemented by a similar agreement for the public sector. Cooperation agreements regulate the setting up and functioning of cooperation committees in individual workplaces. These committees consist of management and employee representatives and have the aim of furthering both enterprise and employee interests through an ongoing dialogue. The birth of this institution was strongly influenced by the German works councils, which were reintroduced in Germany shortly after the Second World War (Knudsen 1995).

The establishment over the years of viable industrial relations institutions by the labour market parties themselves has resulted in a high degree of consensus among unions, employer associations and the main political parties that parliament and government should intervene as little as possible in industrial relations. In fields with legislation, such as occupational health and safety, unions and employer associations are normally given the opportunity to influence the contents of the legislation in decisive ways. A strong norm, although not always adhered to, says that only labour legislation that can muster the support of both sides should be introduced (Knudsen and Lind 2018).

Structure of trade unions and union democracy

Structurally, trade unionism in Denmark ranges from the workplace level (shop stewards, and in some instances workplace clubs), via the local branch level and the national federation level, to the confederal level. In unions with a complex structure there are also substructures along sectoral, professional and/or occupational lines.

Historically, the organizational principles and structure of trade unions followed trades, and later in particular professional or educational patterns. This has been supplemented to a limited degree by other factors, such as gender, religion and political ideology. Originally there were unions for skilled workers and later for unskilled male workers (1896) and female workers (1901). There are also a few examples of industrial unions, notably in the food industry and finance, but they have never become decisive for union structures, as in Germany.

The FTF, founded in 1952 (and merged with the LO in 2019 to form the FH) was a confederation of unions organizing mainly, but not exclusively, public sector workers with a medium-high education, such as social workers, nurses and teachers, while its largest membership private sector union was the Finance Workers Union. When the FTF merged with the LO there were eighty affiliated unions. A main historical difference from LO was, apart from the professions, that the FTF-affiliated unions did not approve the close relationship between the LO and the Social Democratic Party (*Socialdemokratiet*). The FTF claimed to be politically neutral, so when LO gradually abandoned the intimate relationship with the Social Democrats the road was clear for a merger between the two confederations.

The creation of FH signalled a turning point in several respects. First, it happened at a time when the LO, historically virtually synonymous with Danish unionism, had lost its position as the umbrella organization within which a majority of union members were organized. Second, for the first time a woman was elected leader of the peak confederation of Danish unions. Third, for the first time the leader did not come from 'blue-collar' ranks but from the commercial and clerical workers' union and had a 'white-collar' background. Overall, the creation of FH indicates deeper changes in the structure of the Danish union movement, with lower to medium paid white-collar workers, such as nurses, clerks and teachers, gaining a more prominent role, although manufacturing remains the level-setting sector in collective bargaining rounds. White-collar workers have become more attentive to unionism as a means of improving their working conditions, which have been steadily declining because of increased work pressure and the reduced prestige of public sector employment. A major motive for the merger was to be able to show strength through unity: to have one confederation representing a majority of union members, rather than the more fragmented picture of three 'minority' peak organizations.

AC is a confederation founded in 1972 primarily of unions organizing employees with an academic education, such as engineers, medical doctors, economists, architects and university staff. When LO and FTF merged in 2019 some FTF-affiliated unions did not approve. In consequence, unions of physiotherapists, occupational therapists and midwifes joined AC instead of FH, while the union for workers in banking and finance, with some 40,000 members, became independent (until it joined FH in 2022).

Table 8.2 presents the confederations' respective shares of total union membership, as well as the shares of independent unions. Among the unions outside the confederations, some adhere to different principles from the unions in the confederations, such as the Christian Union (Krifa, *Kristelig Fagforening*), which for example, opposes resort to strike action. The shares of 'yellow' unions and of unions ideologically at odds with the traditional unions grew from 7 per cent in 2007 to 18 per cent in 2019. The remaining 10 percentage points of union members outside the confederations in 2019 are accounted for by the Danish Association of Managers (LH, *Ledernes Hovedorganisation*) and other traditional unions, including the Financial Sector Union (*Finansforbundet*) and the Danish Union of Journalists (DJ, *Dansk Journalistforbund*). These unions are thus not 'yellow' unions, but rather alike the other FH unions.

Table 8.2 Trade union membership: shares by confederations and independent unions

	1980		2000		2019	
	Members	**Share (%)**	**Members**	**Share (%)**	**Members**	**Share (%)**
LO	1,250,000	70	1,167,000	62	–	–
FTF	277,000	15	350,000	19	–	–
FH	–	–	–	–	1,092,000	58
AC	70,000	4	150,000	8	259,000	14
Independent unions	197,000	11	203,000	11	669,000	28
All trade unions	1,794,000	100	1,870,000	100	1,868,000	100

Note: As trade unions have joined and left the confederations, and the membership statistics are not directly comparable with earlier years, figures cannot be directly compared across years. LO and FTF merged in 2019 to form FH.

Source: Danmarks Statistik, FH: https://fho.dk/om-fagbevaegelsens-hovedorganisation/medlemstal/

In 2019, 64 trade unions were affiliated to FH. The four biggest (representing more than 50 per cent of FH membership) were former LO unions, namely the United Federation of Workers (3F, *Fagligt Fælles Forbund*), the Union of Commercial and Clerical Employees in Denmark (HK, *Handels- og Kontorfunktionærernes Fagforbund*), the union for mainly health and care workers (FOA, *Fag og Arbejde*) and the Danish Metalworkers' Federation (Metal, *Dansk Metalarbejderforbund*). 3F organizes manual workers of many kinds, both skilled and unskilled, HK clerical and sales staff, FOA mainly public sector manual workers and Dansk

Metal skilled metal workers. 3F originally organized unskilled manual workers but over the past thirty years or so, a number of unions – such as those of bricklayers, carpenters, plumbers and other traditional skilled workers – have joined 3F. Apart from nurses, schoolteachers and social workers most unions initially affiliated to FTF were very small and specialized, such as surgical appliance makers (forty-seven members), the Royal Court staff (forty-eight members) and radio telegraphists (313 members). The Danish Society of Engineers (IDA, *Ingeniørsammenslutningen i Danmark*) (78,000 members) and the lawyers' and economists' union (DJØF, *Dansk Jurist- og Økonomforbund*) (64,000 members) are the biggest unions in AC.

Mergers have been a permanent feature, leading to changes in trade union structure. Besides the abovementioned merger between the two largest confederations, important amalgamations and acquisitions have also taken place among the national federations, especially in the LO domain. By the time of the confederation merger in 2019 there were seventeen LO-affiliated unions compared with twenty-two in 2000. Most of the mergers in the period after 2000 involved 3F, with unions representing female unskilled workers, brewery and restaurant workers, building workers and others joining this union, thus contributing heavily to 3F's transformation into a general union.

Both FH and AC are confederations with a wide variety of members. Accordingly, the complexity inside the confederations makes it difficult to maintain a centralized decision-making structure. One obvious example of this is the fact that collective bargaining is not conducted directly by the confederations, unless the member unions ask them to do so. The confederations' functions include coordination of collective bargaining and formal relations with the government in tripartite negotiations.

The leaders of FH are elected by the affiliated unions at a Congress held every four years, while those of AC are selected by the main committee every two years. The biggest unions have the most votes and influence. In FH, the main committee has some seventy-eight members from the most important unions and the Executive Committee twenty-five members. The AC Executive Committee has eleven members, so power is more centralized than in FH.

The typical structure of democracy in manual trade unions is that local unions elect their leaders at a general assembly. Local trade union leaders and section leaders can be represented at a Congress, at which the union national leadership is elected. In the larger unions various sections elect an Executive Board which is responsible for leadership between congresses. This structure, for instance, can be seen in 3F.

In most AC affiliates, members elect the union leadership in general elections. This is, for instance, the case in the Union of Professionals from Arts and Science (DM, *Dansk Magisterforening*). This union is divided into five sectors, whose leadership (Chair and Executive Committee) is also elected. DM's policy is decided at a Congress held every three years, delegates to which are selected by the sectors.

In general, trade unions in Denmark are democratic organizations, although indirect elections for leaderships being the dominant principle. The main problem is that membership participation in elections is often sparse and provides a good opportunity for the development of a kind of 'oligarchy', or at least that is the impression among some members. The relatively low level of participation can also be seen in the ballots on new collective agreements. It varies among unions, but it is not unusual that under 50 per cent actually participate, although it has been above 50 per cent in recent ballots (Andersen and Hansen 2020).

Unionization

Trade union density peaked during the mid-1990s at around 73–75 per cent and has gradually declined since to 64 per cent in 2019.[1] Membership decline may be observed first and foremost among the LO-affiliated unions, whereas FTF and AC have gained members, together with independent unions. The general decline is not as dramatic as elsewhere, as a union density of 64 per cent is still high. Nevertheless, the loss of members at LO – now FH – is a major concern in the union movement, particularly in light of the growth of the 'yellow' unions now potentially challenging the overall functioning of the Danish industrial relations model. If only the traditional, or mainstream, trade unions are counted, the unionization rate was down at 52.6 percent in 2019.

1 If we exclude the self-employed, which would make a lot of sense because they are rarely unionized, the current net union density is 67–68 per cent (depending on how many self-employed we count in). Arnholtz and Navrbjerg (2021) set the net unionization density at 68.4 per cent without the self-employed. Pensioners and students may have been included in the historical figures, so it is difficult to compare union density over time.

One main reason for the loss of members among the former LO-affiliated unions is the shift of occupational structure from manufacturing to the service sector and occupations that require higher levels of education. This development has resulted in fewer union members in the LO-organized area and more in the FTF and AC areas. There are also industries that typically come from within the LO-organized area, such as cleaning, hotels and restaurants, and agriculture, in which unionization has traditionally been lower and where membership has declined, partly because of a strong increase in the inflow of migrant workers, who are much less unionized and remain difficult for the unions to organize (Refslund 2016).

LO membership decline can also be ascribed to the changes in the so-called Ghent system of unemployment insurance (Lind 2004b, 2009). The Ghent system was introduced in Denmark in 1907. As voluntary insurance it was based upon membership of unemployment funds set up by the trade unions and funded by members' contributions. In the post-war period membership of such funds was increasingly made more attractive as the state financed higher proportions of the cost and the level of unemployment benefits increased in relation to wages. By that time, in other words, Denmark had a highly state-subsidized unemployment insurance system of the Ghent type which 'is indeed associated with higher rates of unionization' (Rasmussen and Pontusson 2018: 813). Furthermore, during the late 1970s an attractive early retirement scheme was introduced that covered only members of unemployment funds. Since the early 1980s, however, membership fees have increased, the early retirement scheme has been virtually abandoned, unemployment insurance has been made less attractive, and the ties between unemployment funds and trade unions have been loosened. This has weakened the unemployment funds as a recruitment vehicle for many of the former LO-affiliated trade unions. The bonds between FTF- and AC-affiliated unions and the unemployment funds have never been as tight as in the case of LO, with the result that these two confederations have not lost as many members due to this reason (Ibsen et al. 2013).

Apart from not unionizing at all, an alternative to union membership of a confederation affiliate is to join a union outside the confederations. Some of these are traditional unions, but around seven are completely outside the 'Danish model', and hence not part of the regulatory framework erected by the traditional unions and their employer counterparts. These unions, in general, do not call industrial action, and only offer their members legal help and advice. They often also have more limited member democracy, and rarely sign collective agreements. Such 'yellow' unions are obviously not popular among the traditional unions and are described as free-riding on the latter's gains, in particular those arising from collective bargaining (Caraker 2013; Ibsen et al. 2013). It can be disputed whether 'yellow' unions qualify as genuine trade unions: a more accurate label might be 'insurance companies'. Nevertheless, they also differ among one another: the Christian Union (Krifa, *Kristelig Fagforening*) dating back to 1899, does sign collective agreements, whereas others do not, such as the ASE. These unions attract members by their much lower membership fees and 'non-political' orientation, which also includes their attitudes to collective bargaining (Caraker 2013). Five 'yellow' unions, in particular the Christian Union, three unions under the Trade Union House,[2] and ASE have recorded significant membership growth since 2002, when the conservative-liberal government made it possible to establish interprofessional unemployment insurance funds (Lind 2003), and since the outlawing of closed-shop agreements in 2006 (see Ibsen et al. 2013).

Overall, the total membership share of 'yellow' unions increased from 7 per cent of total union membership in 2007 to 18 per cent in 2019. In particular, the Trade Union House and ASE, originally an unemployment fund for the self-employed, have flourished as a result of liberalization of the rules on unemployment insurance. The growth of these unions is a by-product of the expansion of the interprofessional unemployment funds. It is possible to be a member of an unemployment fund without joining a union, but many decide to take 'the whole package'. In Table 8.3 below some key characteristics of the largest trade unions in Denmark are presented.

[2] Trade Union House is an organization that consists of three organizations for various kinds of employees, one for the self-employed and two unemployment funds.

Table 8.3 Largest twenty trade unions in Denmark, 2019

	Members	Women share (%)	Confederation	Category	Sector
3F (general union)	222,060	25	FH	Blue-collar	Mainly private
HK (office & commerce)	176,276	76	FH	White-collar	Both
FOA (various occupations)	151,348	85	FH	Blue-collar	Mainly public
Krifa (Christian; general union)	115,396	51	'Yellow'	Both	Both
LH (managers)	104,567	29	Outside	White-collar	Both
IDA (engineers)	78,069	26	AC	White-collar	Both
Metal	72,071	4	FH	Blue-collar	Mainly private
Nurses	71,973	96	FH	White-collar	Public
DJØF (lawyers and economists)	63,626	55	AC	White-collar	Both
2B Trade Union House (general union)	58,795	48	'Yellow'	Both	Both
ASE Employees (general union)	58,757	40	'Yellow'	White-collar	Both
Teachers' Union	58,146	71	FH	White-collar	Public
Child care workers	54,228	83	FH		Public
Danmark Trade Union House (general)	51,504	35	'Yellow'	Both	Both
Finance Union	39,360	50	Outside	White-collar	Private
DM (Arts and Science)	35,832	64	AC	White-collar	Public
Social care workers	35,602	75	FH		Public
Electricians	23,867	0.1	FH	Blue-collar	Private
Business Danmark (salespersons)	23,496	28	'Yellow'	White-collar	Private
Technicians	22,146	44	FH	White-collar	Mainly private

Source: Statistics Denmark (Statistikbanken, LONMED3).

Around 48 per cent of the labour force are women, but more than half of union members are women (52 per cent). The female workers' union (KAD, *Kvindeligt Arbejderforbund i Danmark*), established in 1901, existed for more than 100 years until it merged into 3F in 2005. Now all unions organize both men and women, but with a strongly varying gender composition in line with the gender segmentation in the labour market. Manual blue-collar, private sector unions have the smallest proportion of female members – for instance, the electricians and the metal workers union – while the highest proportions of female members are found in white-collar public sector unions. In this way the gender segmentation of the labour market is reflected in the unions' gender profile.

The main criterion for being permitted to become a member of a specific trade union is to have had a special education or to be employed in a specific area of work, often synonymous with the coverage area of a collective agreement signed by the union. Most unions only recruit members with that sort of profile. The unions and confederations have specific rules to regulate the system and resolve conflicts about membership recruitment to avoid too much competition in their efforts to recruit new members. In contrast, most 'yellow' unions accept all sorts of employees as members.

The impact on unionization of 'new' groups in the labour market, such as migrants, precarious workers, platform workers, self-employed and freelancers varies considerably, but the number of migrant workers, in particular from Central and Eastern Europe (CEE), has increased substantially in the past decade in certain industries, including construction, cleaning and agriculture. While these groups have much lower unionization levels, the unions have become much more attentive to them. For most unions, attention is directed towards migrants, precarious workers and the self-employed, while platform workers and freelancers typically are more relevant for HK and other unions organizing professional workers. The unions are still seeking appropriate strategies to reach these workers.

To organize migrant workers, unions have resorted to their traditional measures, seeking to convince migrants at the workplace to join the union, but they have also supplemented their efforts with targeted information campaigns. While the Danish unions have always been attentive to organizing workers, as reflected in their high union density, increasing attention has been paid to the methods and approaches applied to organizing different workers. Here some inspiration has been drawn from the 'organizing approach', even though it was developed for low union density settings and Danish unions have adapted and cherry-picked elements from it (Arnholtz et al. 2016). An example of such a process, where unions have improved their approach to organizing, is the struggle for decent working conditions for all foreign workers involved in the construction of the new metro line in Copenhagen from 2011. The main contractor was a consortium of Italian companies, CMT, which subcontracted the work to numerous subcontractors from twenty-four countries. CMT was hostile to union involvement, so the Danish unions tried to convince the workers, publicize the poor working conditions, and take a case to the labour court. They won the case and could then distribute the fine imposed on the employer among the workers, which helped convince them that it was worth joining a union. Around 30 per cent of the transnational workers in the metro construction project became union members, in comparison with the normal rate among other transnational workers in Copenhagen of around 6–7 per cent (Arnholtz and Refslund 2019).

Union resources and expenditure

Union accounts are usually not publicly available. In the Danish union movement, there is a long tradition of concealing information about economic resources, so that the employer counterpart cannot estimate accurately, for example, how long unions can pay out strike benefits in case of a major conflict.

Economically, unions rely almost entirely on membership fees. Fees vary from union to union, with a cash sum between €60 and €70 per month being typical, although the fee is considerably less in 'yellow' unions (in the unions set up by the Trade Union House less than 10 euros per month). Most unions have reduced rates for part-time workers and students/apprentices. It can be estimated that Danish unions in total receive between €1 billion and €1.5 billion per year in fees, which makes them financially powerful organizations. Since the early 2000s, decreasing membership in the traditional unions, combined with increased price competition from 'yellow' unions, have made resources less abundant than in previous decades, particularly among unions that used to affiliate to LO. The merger between LO and FTF was not driven primarily by financial considerations, but it was certainly one of the motives behind it.

Among the unions in the former LO-organized area, union fees are normally paid to the local union or branch. From there some of the income is channelled to activities at company level, union clubs and shop stewards, and to the national and confederation level. In unions with a complex structure, such as 3F, resources are also devolved to occupational subgroups. In unions affiliated to FTF and AC fees are typically paid to the federation at national level; from there some of the resources are allocated to local activities. The confederations FH and AC are financed by contributions from the member unions. Union membership is subsidized in the sense that members can deduct the fee, and payments to the unemployment fund, from their income before they pay income tax.

A further, but minor income source stems from institutions established and administered jointly with employer organizations. Pension funds and training funds, as determined in collective agreements, are run by various boards consisting of union officials and employer representatives. Other union leaders may sit on boards in public companies or cooperatives. Fees from board membership often constitute a considerable extra income for union officials, and several unions, including FH, have rules that limit how much of this income may be kept by the board members themselves. Amounts above the limit must be passed on to the union organization in question.

At company level, collective agreements and legislation provide for shop stewards, cooperation committee members, work environment representatives and employee members on company boards to be compensated by time-off from work for the time they spend on union matters and on representing workers. There are no fixed norms for this time compensation, except that the employer shall make sure that the representatives are given the 'necessary time' to fulfil their tasks (Kristiansen 2014), so, in reality, it is a bargaining issue at workplace level.

Part of union resources can be used as strike funds to pay members while they are conflicting and not receiving any wages. Normally, unions do not publish anything about the size of their strike funds, or resources that may easily be made available for strike benefits, but sometimes they may see an advantage in doing so. This seemed to be the case in 2007 in the early stages of the process of renewing collective agreements in the private sector. Unions were quoted in the press as having money enough to ensure member strike benefits for several weeks should a conflict break out. Likewise, employer organizations highlighted *their* ability to support their members during a conflict (Berlingske Tidende 2007). In a twenty-five-day-long lock-out of teachers in 2013, the Teachers' Union paid out about €70 million in benefits (DR 2018). If normal funds should prove too small to cover strike benefits, other resources can be drawn upon. Many unions own their office buildings; the large unions own training facilities as well and would be able to obtain bank loans on that basis, at least from Arbejdernes Landsbank, Denmark's sixth largest bank, owned by unions and union members. Furthermore, a group of unions own an investment company with investments in real estate and a range of funds and production companies. In 2019 the company had assets worth about €600 million (AKF-Holding 2020).

Union resources are spent mainly on maintaining a union apparatus staffed by a combination of elected union officials and union officers employed to handle various union tasks. The union apparatus is geared primarily to providing services to the members, such as negotiating and monitoring collective agreements, preparing and taking part in meetings and labour court cases related to dispute resolution, and dealing with individual grievances to ensure that members receive the compensation they are entitled to in case of unfair dismissals, work accidents, company closures and bankruptcies.

In recent years, a new job title has appeared among union officers, that of 'organizer'. Organizing used to be a task undertaken mainly by local union activists and shop stewards, but the growing influx of foreign workers, as well as new, less union-friendly attitudes among young workers, have spurred unions to establish jobs specifically designed to recruit new members. More resources are also spent on recruitment campaigns through advertisements in the media and on increasing unions' visibility through sponsorships of sports activities and teams. A further activity worth mentioning is internal training. Among the FH-affiliated unions most training is aimed at the elected leaders at local level and workplace representatives: shop stewards, members of cooperation and work environment committees, and members who are elected to company boards.

Collective bargaining and unions at the workplace

The most important collective bargaining takes place at industry and national level: in the private sector between employers' organizations in four or five industries and bargaining cartels of various trade unions, and in the public sector in three areas: state, region and municipality. In the private sector, the DA and its affiliates have successfully refused to negotiate collective agreements with AC organizations at national level, and for HK (clerical and commercial workers) a special clause determines that the national agreement shall apply only in workplaces where union membership is at least 50 per cent. According to most agreements, wages are also bargained at company level (see below).

Collective bargaining coverage in the private sector is around 65 per cent and in the public sector close to 100 per cent. There is no legislation on minimum wages in Denmark, and collective wage-setting is left entirely to unions and employers' associations. It is a widespread opinion, also held by employers, that governments should not intervene in these matters. This makes arrangements such as legislation on a minimum wage very unpopular among the social partners.

In the private sector, the traditional bargaining parties were the confederations LO and DA. In the course of the 1980s, however, this changed, as the trade union federations took over to avoid the many conflicts and state interventions of the 1970s. This 'decentralization', as it was called, led to a relatively stable structure during the early 1990s when DA implemented a major reorganization and the unions had to adjust to the new DA bargaining bodies (Lind 1995). The unions created five bargaining bodies that represented various unions. The most important of these bargaining bodies is CO-Industry (established already in 1912), which bargains with the Danish Industry (DI, *Dansk Industri*), the most powerful organization on the employers' side. At a later stage in the 1990s the collective bargaining system was further transformed to provide more room for local negotiations at company level, although this decentralization is regulated via agreements at the industry level. The present system has been termed 'centralized decentralization', 'multilevel bargaining' (Due and Madsen 2006) or 'coherent fragmentation' (Lind 2004a) to emphasize that, although decentralized and local elements are in place, it is a misunderstanding to call collective bargaining in Denmark decentralized.

Collective agreements are normally bargained for two to three years and the bargaining normally starts with aiming at reaching a compromise between Danish Industry and CO-Industry. This agreement then sets the level for the remaining bargaining areas. The argument for this is that manufacturing is exposed to international competition and accordingly should set a level that can secure competitiveness. This joint understanding draws on the principles agreed upon in the Joint Declaration (*Fælleserklæringen*) of 1987, in which wage development is adjusted over time and one of the main aims is to avoid inflation through high-wage growth. The metal industry agreement accordingly still sets the bargaining standard for the rest of economy through pattern bargaining (Müller et al. 2018).

Bargaining used to take place in the public sector in the same years as in the private sector, but over the past 20 years public sector bargaining has taken place in the following year. The idea is that the public sector then can adjust its level of agreements to the current level in the private sector. Public sector bargaining includes central state, regions and municipalities and on the union side FH and AC have formed joint bargaining bodies, the Central Bargaining Unit (*Centralorganisationernes Fællesudvalg*) for central government and the United Bargaining Body (*Forhandlingsfællesskabet*) for regions and municipalities.

In both the private and the public sector wages set by national collective agreements can be adjusted locally. In the private sector this depends on the pay system for manual workers, which can be either 'minimum wage' or 'normal wage'. Some white-collar workers have so-called 'figureless agreements', in principle leaving wage-setting entirely to the local level.

Before the 1990s unskilled manual workers generally had a 'normal wage' system, meaning that their wages were set at the national level for the entire bargaining period and not adjusted locally. Skilled manual workers normally had a 'minimum wage' system, in which a minimum wage was set in the national bargaining round, typically followed by local negotiations. DA wanted a more flexible and decentralized system and during the 1990s they managed to reduce the areas with a 'normal wage' system. For white-collar workers organized in HK, who traditionally had a more individualized system, almost like a 'minimum wage', the employers were able to bargain 'figureless agreements'. This means that wages are adjusted to the capacity to pay at the individual workplace, resulting in a far more differentiated pay structure. 'Normal wage' is mainly used in low-skill/low-wage industries, and the collective agreement in the transport industry sets the standard for wage development in bargaining areas with 'normal wage'.

In the public sector the implementation of the neoliberal model, in particular New Public Management, which imposes mechanisms on the public sector that are supposed to emulate the dynamics of the market and competition, has since the early 1990s led to the introduction of pay systems to be bargained locally – so-called 'local pay' and 'new pay'. This is supposed to grant individual pay supplements for especially productive and valuable staff. This local bargaining plays only a minor role in the public sector, especially in periods of austerity.

Such flexible wage-setting arrangements currently apply to around 80 per cent of the Danish workforce: figureless agreements apply to 20 per cent and the minimum wage system to 60 per cent (Ibsen and Keune 2018: 27). This in turn means that in a majority of cases the wage levels bargained at national industry level are only a floor for the wages bargained at local level, often several times during the term of an agreement.

Unions were reluctant to adopt these pay systems in both the private and the public sector because they were a clear breach of the traditional solidaristic wage policy and undermined the importance of national agreements. But they have now accepted them because they make trade unions, particularly shop stewards, more visible and important in local negotiations. This, in turn, illustrates the role of the unions for the members, and hence contributes to membership retention.

If an employer has signed a collective agreement all workers within the occupational area defined by the agreement are covered, regardless of whether they are union members or not. This system of course faces a high risk of 'free-riding': a worker does not have to pay the union membership fee to be paid according to the agreement.

Unions and employers' organizations are very keen on avoiding any weakening of collective bargaining. Therefore, it is important for them to have as many issues as possible settled through collective bargaining, not just pay and working time, but also pensions, training, holidays and parental leave. The importance of issues beyond wages and working conditions have been growing over recent decades and they now constitute an important element of collective bargaining, where the unions have achieved substantial gains. The demarcation lines between legislative regulation of the labour market and collective bargaining are in fact flexible when it comes to pensions, holidays, redundancy, training, maternity leave, employment and unemployment policies. Wages and working time, however, are almost entirely a matter for collective bargaining.

Industrial conflict

The right to strike is a collective right, as are many labour rights. For instance only unions and employers' associations can bring a case to the labour court. Collective rights, as opposed to individual legal rights, make the Danish industrial relations system different from most other legal systems (Dølvik et al. 2018; Høgedahl 2020). Only trade unions can call an industrial conflict, bargain collective agreements and 'own' a collective agreement. And if the labour court decides that the employer has not acted according to a collective agreement, the union, not the workers affected, will receive the compensation (and then pay the members affected).

The right to strike is confined to 'conflicts of interest' as opposed to 'conflicts of rights', which must be solved through mediation and arbitration (Kristiansen 2014). Conflicts of interest are defined as conflicts connected to the conclusion or renewal of collective agreements, while conflicts of rights are related to disagreements that may occur over the interpretation of collective agreements and management decisions.

The distinction between the two types of conflict, and the different procedures set up to regulate them, was laid down by the 1899 September Agreement and regulations based on the work of a public commission, with representatives from unions and employers' associations, established in 1908. Besides an agreement on 'norms guiding industrial conflicts and their resolution', this work in 1910 resulted in two important industrial relations acts establishing the labour court and the Conciliation Board (*Forligsinstitutionen*), which essentially are institutions aimed at helping the parties themselves to resolve conflicts (Kristiansen 2014).

The right to strike and the right to lock out workers to a large extent mirror each other. In processes of renewal of industry-level or sector-level collective agreements, unions will typically at a certain stage give notice of a strike. To avoid straining strike funds too much, typically only a minor fraction of the members will be called out on strike, hitting strategic areas in which employers and/or society will soon experience negative effects. Subsequently, the strike notice will often be followed by the employers' association giving notice of a much broader lock-out hitting the entire labour force, or a large share of it, within the area concerned. In most cases neither the strike nor the lock-out is implemented as the parties reach agreement at the negotiation table. If a conflict breaks out, however, a high number of working days is likely to be lost.

As long as a collective agreement is in force, strikes and lock-outs are not allowed: a so-called peace obligation applies. Strikes and lock-outs are allowed only when agreements are being renewed, or if used as a weapon to achieve a collective agreement in an industry or, more typically, in a company not hitherto covered by collective bargaining (Kristiansen 2014). In the latter case, the employer will typically not belong to an employer organization and not want to be bound by a collective agreement. If it is a workplace in which workers are not unionized, or only weakly, a direct strike against the employer may not be feasible. In such cases, secondary industrial action is a recognized weapon: 'the sympathetic work stoppage, so important in Denmark because of the strength of organization among workers and employers…' (Galenson 1969: 244). In secondary industrial action or sympathy action (*sympatistrejke*) union members not directly involved in a conflict may be called upon by their union to block the delivery of materials, goods and services to a firm that refuses to conclude a collective agreement (Kristiansen 2014). In contrast to countries in which a ballot among workers is needed, or the majority of workers need to be union members before a demand for a collective agreement can be raised, secondary industrial action provides Danish unions with a strong weapon that helps to increase union membership, as well as collective bargaining coverage. Not least within the large 3F union this weapon is frequently used for instance by the section for building workers at local branch level.

While strikes connected to collective bargaining are the most important ones in Danish industrial relations, accounting for the majority of working days lost, they are not the most frequent. The vast majority of strikes are unofficial or wildcat strikes, which breach collectively agreed norms regarding industrial conflict. An unofficial strike is usually confined to workers – perhaps only members of a single union – at an individual workplace. The decision to strike is taken by the workers themselves, sometimes spontaneously as a reaction to conditions that are experienced as unfair, and sometimes as part of local pay negotiations where, although constituting the local element of collective bargaining, no strike right exists. If an unofficial strike runs longer than a short period in which the relevant union and employers' association first attempt to find a solution, it will be brought before the labour court. The court will typically order a return to work and, in addition, impose a fine on the striking workers (Kristiansen 2014). In principle, all strikes at workplaces where there is a collective agreement are unofficial, but there are no official statistics distinguishing official and unofficial strikes.

Galenson (1969) found Danish industrial relations to be a case of 'industrial peace' when studying the conditions prevailing in the first half of the twentieth century, and peace rather than conflict is still often stressed as a core feature of 'the Danish model'. More recent international comparisons, however, place Denmark among the rather conflict prone countries. For the period since 2000, Denmark is situated closer to the top than the bottom of a European league of working days lost due to industrial conflict (Appendix A1). In a historical perspective, however, the conflict level in Denmark, as in Europe as a whole, has decreased radically. Working days lost to industrial conflict were down to 49 per 1,000 employees in the period 2010–2018, compared with 103 during the 2000s, and 212 in the peak period of the 1970s (Appendix A1; Knudsen and Lind 2012a).

Table 8.4 presents data on conflicts for the two decades from 2000 to 2019. As official Danish statistics do not distinguish between strikes and lock-outs the concept of 'work stoppage' is used to cover both categories. While almost all work stoppages are strikes, lock-outs may contribute substantially to the number of working days lost. This was the case not least for the period 2010–2019, in which the lock-out of teachers in 2013 resulted in approximately 900,000 lost working days, or more than 80 per cent of all cases in the decade. In the private sector, lock-outs were part of the major conflicts in 1973 and 1998 but have not been practised to any significant extent since 1998. This is not because lock-outs have not been called, but because unions and employers have managed to renew the collective agreements at the negotiation table.

Table 8.4 shows a clear trend towards fewer conflicts and fewer working days lost because of conflicts. The incidence of industrial conflict has changed substantially, as has the overall pattern. Historically, the great majority of conflicts have occurred in the private sector, notably in manufacturing, and the major ones, with many working days lost, have also taken place in that sector, since 1945 notably in the years 1956, 1973, 1985, and 1998. They were all in connection with the renewal of national collective agreements. But in the past twenty years or so the public sector has taken the lead regarding large conflicts connected to collective bargaining and working days lost.

Table 8.4 Work stoppages in Denmark, 2000–2009 and 2010–2019

	Work stoppages	**Workers involved**	**Working days lost**
2000–2009, annual average	716	63,320	261,870
2010–2019, annual average	238	14,865	107,250

Source: Statistics Denmark (www.statistikbanken.dk/10324).

While most strikes used to take place in manufacturing this is no longer the case. During the period 2000–2004, 57 per cent of all conflicts took place in manufacturing but by 2015–2019 the share had fallen to just 23 per cent (Statistics Denmark n.a.). Contributing to the radical decrease in strike frequency in manufacturing was no doubt the fact that the bargaining agents in the industry, Dansk Industri and CO Industry (CO-Industri), agreed stricter procedures in relation to unofficial strikes in the 2004 bargaining round (Due and Madsen 2006). Furthermore, the sharp fall in inflation no doubt played a role in bringing down the number of strikes: the rationale behind many unofficial strikes – the fact that wages were lagging behind prices – simply no longer applied. Throughout the period 2000–2019 unions managed to secure increases in real wages, except for the years 2010–2012. But even in these austerity years workers and unions largely refrained from using the strike weapon. Faced with steeply rising unemployment following the 2008 financial crisis the unions instead showed restraint, awaiting better times, which came from 2013, with real wages growing about 10 per cent from 2012 to 2019 (Thomsen 2019).

Since 1998 there have been no large conflicts connected to collective bargaining in the private sector, whereas there have been two major conflicts in the public sector. For the period 2000–2019 the public sector contributed more than 80 per cent of the total number of working days lost because of industrial conflict (Altinget 2018; Statistics Denmark).

The rising conflict level in the public sector has partly been due to workers' dissatisfaction with pay and conditions, often influenced by cuts in public expenditure, and partly by more aggressive tactics on the part of public employers. In 2008, nurses and staff working in care institutions for children and the elderly went on strike, demanding a pay rise of 15 per cent over the next three years. The strike went on for fifty-nine days before it ended with pay rises of around 13 per cent (Altinget 2018). Another spectacular conflict occurred in 2013 when the association of municipalities, with the backing of the government, locked out some 43,000 teachers for twenty-five days, until, as the teachers' union refused to cave in, the conflict was ended by legislation (Altinget 2018). In this way public employers got rid of the so-called Working Time Agreement, which defined how much time teachers should spend on teaching compared with preparation and other job-relevant activities. This conflict, so clearly aimed at increasing individual teachers' workload, led to much resentment among teachers. Only in 2020 did the parties manage to reach a new national agreement on working time.

Again in 2018 a major conflict in the public sector was imminent. Unions had given strike notice to 155,000 workers, and public employers had responded with a massive lock-out notice covering no fewer than 440,000 public employees (Altinget 2018). In the end, the action was called off after protracted negotiations and a major effort by the Conciliation Board. The rising level of conflict in the public sector has triggered discussion over whether it should have the same industrial relations system as the private sector, particularly given that relations between public negotiators and public legislators, who may choose to end a strike by legislation, are very close (Høgedahl 2019).

General strikes, being prominent in Belgium, France and Spain, are not part of the repertoire of Danish unions. There is a generally respected mutual understanding between the political system and the industrial relations system about non-interference.

Political relations

Historically, the LO-affiliated section of the Danish union movement developed long-standing and very close relations with the Social Democratic Party (*Socialdemokratiet*). Similar to the other Nordic countries, this close alliance was characterized as a key feature of Nordic social democratic capitalism (Korpi 1978, 1983). Often union representatives would have a political role in the Social Democratic Party. LO was officially represented in the executive bodies of the Party and vice versa. The other confederations, AC and FTF, were less political, smaller and, in general, played a less important role in the overall governance of society, because LO – and in particular unions in manufacturing – formed the core of the 'social democratic capitalism model'. The ties with the Social Democratic Party have weakened since the 1970s, and in 2002 LO removed the reference to the Social Democratic Party in its constitution (Allern et al. 2007). The Social Democrats have additionally become more prone to introduce policies that run against unions' demands, such as non-Keynesian economic policies and retrenchment policies in unemployment benefits, as well as cutbacks in welfare provisions (Klitgaard and Nørgaard 2014; Refslund and Lind 2021).

Given the declining official and political ties between LO/FH and the Social Democratic Party, the union movement nowadays seeks broader coalitions and engages more actively with other political parties. Nevertheless, many political overlaps remain with the Social Democratic

Party, and the party is still more aligned and attentive to union claims than right-wing parties (Klitgaard and Nørgaard 2014). Segments of the union movement leadership feel stronger connections with the smaller left-wing parties, the Socialist People Party (*Socialistisk Folkeparti*) and Left Unity (*Enhedslisten*); notably some of the more 'belligerent' parts of 3F are more closely aligned with the political left, in particular Left Unity.

Overall, the union movement today appears to take a more pluralist approach, seeking broader cooperation in parliament and to influence the most relevant political actors. The unions thus have some relations with most major political parties and actively seek to influence most parties. There is also some variation across unions: low-wage unions such as 3F and FOA have closer ties with the left-wing, while the high-wage unions, such as those in the bargaining cartel CO-Industri, notably Dansk Metal, have stronger relations with the Social Democratic and the centre-right parties, because they share more political views, such as wage restraint to increase competitiveness. The anti-immigrant right-wing party Dansk Folkeparti (DF) has become increasingly important for the union movement, and vice versa, because of its recent preparedness to make political deals not just with the other right-wing parties, as was their traditional position, but also with the Social Democrats. DF's anti-immigrant political agenda has also largely been accepted by the Social Democratic government in power since 2019.

Corporatist policymaking has, in general, declined, while other actors have gained more access to the policymaking process (Binderkrantz and Christiansen 2015; Jørgensen and Larsen 2014; Klitgaard and Nørgaard 2014; Refslund and Lind 2021). But the labour market parties, not least the unions, have played a huge role in policies addressing the labour market disruptions caused by the Covid-19 pandemic since spring 2020, through several tripartite agreements to mitigate the effects of the crisis on the labour market. Overall, the social partners maintain an active role in policymaking, in particular on labour market policies, although less so than in the heyday of Danish corporatism in the 1970s (Mailand 2020; Refslund and Lind 2021). In line with the more pluralist interest representation, unions are actively seeking political influence, irrespective of the party affiliation of the government. Social dialogue may be stronger when a weak government, in a fragile coalition, is in power, particularly if it is from the centre-right (Mailand 2020). Unlike the trend since the 1990s, marked by negative reforms from a trade union perspective, the Social Democratic government that came to power in 2019 initiated several policies that can be termed union-friendly, for instance on differentiated early retirement, which has been a union demand for years. Other demands, however, such as improvements in the strongly eroded unemployment benefits, have not been met.

Societal power

Overall, unions still play an important role as a societal actor, and the idea of unionism and the inclusion of unions in societal problem-solving is still influential. Most Danes continue to see unions as a vital and legitimate actor (Caraker et al. 2014). Since unions still have significant traditional institutional, associational and structural power resources, however, they rely less on societal and coalitional power than union movements that are deprived of such power resources (Bieler 2018). A study of the power elite in Denmark found four union leaders to be among the ten most powerful people in the country (Larsen et al. 2015). The study reached this conclusion by studying networks and interactions in central economic and political decision-making fora. It thus probably underestimates economic and political power, notably capital, parliament and government. Nevertheless, the study signals that the union movement is strongly integrated in the power structures of Danish society.

The unions are aware of the importance of public debates and discourse, and occasionally run large-scale public campaigns to influence public opinion on working conditions and wages, but also other issues they consider relevant for their constituency, such as the retirement age. Here the unions have been able to influence the political debate. Public debates are used more directly to influence industrial relations. The unions often create negative publicity on social dumping, such as underpayment of migrant workers, for instance in construction (for an example, Arnholtz and Refslund 2019). In addition, in the highly publicized public sector industrial dispute in 2013 on teachers' working hours the unions actively tried to use the media – also social media – to influence the outcome (Hansen and Mailand 2019).

Additionally, unions remain an important societal voice in public and media discussions, and leaders of the main unions and confederations participate in public and media debates on societal issues, reflecting the fact that most wage-earners are union members. At the industrial level, unions are also frequently included in public debates, when the issues affect union members. Nevertheless, the range and scope of topics that are deemed relevant for unions may have diminished somewhat over recent decades. While there has been some historical engagement on the part of the unions in issues beyond the labour market, such as nuclear power, apartheid in South Africa and other transnational issues, this is currently limited. For example, the unions do not act as a pivotal actor in the climate change discussion. Regarding climate change FH has developed a plan for the 'green transition of the economy', but this is confined to union perspectives and does not include much 'coalition-building'. Just to illustrate the relevant internal union disputes, the metal workers union and the employers' association Dansk Industri jointly stated they are against a special Danish CO_2 fee, because they fear it will reduce competitiveness (Kaergaard 2020).

Much research on coalitions and unions has emphasized coalitions on issues including austerity and privatization (Ibsen and Tapia 2017). While the union movement has been partly engaged in protests on these issues, it has not developed any large-scale coalitions with other societal actors. In the Danish context, however, unions remain the key actor, and most of the protests outside the union realm on austerity and privatization probably originate from union activists.

Unions are increasingly paying attention to communication with members and others via social media. In recent collective bargaining rounds, some of the more critical union activists, who demanded stronger positions from unions in bargaining – for example, on social dumping – were very active online on Facebook and managed to engage in and influence discussions. Likewise, union leaders have sought to improve communications with members online. Recently the union movement made the members' ballot on the collective bargaining results available online for the first time. They are thus trying to adapt their communication with members to the new online reality, although they have not yet found the perfect formula for online communication (Andersen and Hansen 2020).

Trade union policies towards the European Union

European Union (EU) policies and legislation, and in particular Court of Justice of the European Union case law, have influenced the Danish labour market. Since the 1990s, there have been strong concerns that Europeanization would cause upheaval in Danish industrial relations. Initially, the fear was that that the implementation of EU directives would undermine some of the essential features of 'the Danish model', while later the notorious '*Laval* quartet' were viewed as very damaging because they challenge collective bargaining. Major disturbances, however, did not materialize following *Laval* (Refslund 2015). The increasing 'Europeanization' of labour law and labour market systems is also influential in Denmark, illustrated by the recent EU Directive on paternal and maternal leave (EU/2019/1158) and the discussions on an EU-wide minimum wage. There is a great commotion over the proposed EU minimum wage, which is widely seen by employers, unions and politicians as a direct assault on the Danish wage-setting system and the broader industrial relations system (Müller and Schulten 2020).

While there have been challenges on implementing European legislation, a consensus between employers' associations, unions and policymakers on how to implement European legislation persists. Their point of view is that European legislation must be introduced within the framework of collective agreements, which remain imperative in Danish labour market regulation. The intention is to ensure that the implementation of EU legislation is handled bilaterally via collective agreements, and that the parliament adopts legislation to cover the residual workers not covered by collective agreements, if that is needed (Knudsen and Lind 2012b). The unions have accepted the basic idea of the free movement of labour, but avoiding social dumping is a recurrent issue. Transnational labour, like posting of workers, is used to circumvent national regulation, in particular collective agreements (Arnholtz and Lillie 2020; Arnholtz and Refslund 2019; Refslund 2016).

The Danish labour market parties have in general rather dragged their feet in their engagement with EU debates and peers, as they have prioritized the national partnership in preserving the Danish model of industrial relations (Knudsen and Lind 2012b). This has come at the cost of engaging in some European-wide discussions, which indicates that the unions have had a somewhat passive and more sceptical approach to the European Union cooperation, along with the other Nordic unions (Larsson 2015; Vulkan and Larsson 2018). Danish unions are nevertheless active in European cooperation. FH and AC are members of the ETUC, and the national union federations are in general members of the ETUFs, which they utilize for information sharing. But they find direct European cooperation with other unions on collective bargaining less germane. Their overall perception is that they cannot gain much from European cooperation because of the lack of power resources available to unions in many other EU countries. This also means that unions typically prioritize national solutions and actions over supranational and European solutions (Gumbrell-McCormick and Hyman 2013), for instance engaging in national discussion with companies rather than in European works councils.

There has historically been a strong bond between the Nordic unions, among the LO confederations in particular, institutionalized in the Council of Nordic Trade Unions (*Nordens Facklige Samorganisation*), which also occasionally serves as a coordination forum for the Nordic unions on their EU policy (Larsson 2015: 105). Moreover, Nordic and hence Danish unions often prioritize their own Brussels offices over the ETUC and ETUFs (Larsson 2015). While Nordic cooperation is important, unions also engage in particular with German unions in manufacturing because developments in Germany are highly influential on working conditions in neighbouring countries, including Denmark (Andersen et al. 2015; Müller et al. 2018).

Conclusions

The Danish unions' enduringly strong societal and associational position shows that unionism is not under severe threat. Danish unions remain firmly embedded in society and the labour market institutions, and there is a strong consensus between the unions and employers on the overall governance of the labour market and working conditions. Union density also remains high, at 64 per cent, and has been fairly stable over the past decade, although it has declined steadily since the peak in the 1990s. Hence, there is no frontal attack on unions and unionism in the Danish context, and the unions have also played a significant role in the labour market policy adjustments during the Covid-19 crisis.

Nevertheless, there are challenges, such as increasing membership of 'yellow' unions that do not form part of the collective bargaining system or the basic agreements that govern the relations between the parties, including the labour court. Growing numbers of unorganized migrant workers are also seen by many unions as a strong challenge to unionism. In certain industries, the impact of the unions and the reach of collective bargaining appear to be close to critical so that a substantial number of workers find themselves outside the protection offered by unions and collective agreements. The unemployment benefit system has also been eroded and institutionally changed to the detriment of the traditional unions.

In sum this does not suggest that unionism in Denmark is unequivocally on a declining trajectory, although the role and power of the unions have diminished since the heyday of Danish social democratic capitalism (before the neoliberal turn), when unions played a key role in political and economic life (Esping-Andersen 1985, 1990). Whether these incremental challenges over time will undermine the unions' important role in Danish political economy is an open question. To date, the challenges have been accommodated within the system, with accompanying alterations and some limitations on union influence, rather than resulting in trade union marginalization.

Regarding the future, none of Visser's (2019) four scenarios fit the Danish case well. As mentioned above, *marginalization* is hardly on the horizon. Some tendencies towards *dualization* between organized and unorganized parts of the labour market may be a growing feature. We may also see more *substitution* in its specific Danish form, where voice through traditional unions is being replaced by a much meeker representation through 'yellow' unions. *Revitalization* will continue to be a feature, regarding both structures and practices. At least for the next decade or two, however, continuing strength and relevance will probably be more apt descriptions than any of Visser's four scenarios.

References

All links were checked on 5 May 2021.

AKF-Holding (2020) Årsrapport 2019, Copenhagen, AKF Holding A/S. https://akf-holding.dk/wp-content/uploads/2020/04/4468_akf_ar19_web.pdf.

Allern E., Aylott N. and Christiansen F. (2007) Social Democrats and trade unions in Scandinavia: the decline and persistence of institutional relationships, European Journal of Political Research, 46 (5), 607–635.

Altinget (2018) Her er tre af de mest spektakulære konflikter – og den, der ikke blev til noget, Altinget, 17 April 2018. https://www.altinget.dk/artikel/her-er-tre-af-de-mest-spektakulaere-konflikter-og-den-der-ikke-blev-til-noget

Andersen S.K. and Hansen N. (2020) OK20: Livsfaseoverenskomsten udfoldet, dumping uforløst og corona som joker, FAOS-report 177, Copenhagen, Københavns Universitet.

Andersen, S.K., Dølvik, J.E. and Ibsen, C. (2014) Nordic labour market models in open markets. Report 132, Brussels: ETUI.

Andersen S.K., Ibsen C., Alsos K., Nergaard K. and Sauramo P. (2015) Changes in wage policy and collective bargaining in the Nordic Countries – Comparison of Denmark, Finland, Norway and Sweden, in van Gyes G. and Schulten T. (eds) Wage bargaining under the new European economic governance, Brussels, ETUI, 139–168.

Arnholtz J. and Lillie N. (2020) Posted work in the European Union: the political economy of free movement, Abingdon, Routledge.

Arnholtz J. and Navrbjerg S. (2021) Lønmodtageres faglige organisering 2000–2018, FAOS-report 184, Copenhagen, Københavns Universitet.

Arnholtz J. and Refslund B. (2019) Active enactment and virtuous circles of employment relations: how Danish unions organised the transnationalised Copenhagen Metro Construction Project, Work, Employment and Society, 33 (4), 682–699.

Arnholtz J., Ibsen C. and Ibsen F. (2016) Importing low-density ideas to high-density revitalisation: the 'organising model' in Denmark, Economic and Industrial Democracy, 37 (2), 297–317.

Berlingske Tidende (2007) Lønmodtagernes strejkekasser bugner af penge, Berlingske Tidende, 26 January 2007. https://www.berlingske.dk/virksomheder/loenmodtagernes-strejkekasser-bugner-af-penge.

Bieler A. (2018) Agency and the power resources approach: asserting the importance of the structuring conditions of the capitalist social relations of production, Global Labour Journal, 9 (2), 243–248.

Binderkrantz A. and Christiansen P. (2015) From classic to modern corporatism. Interest group representation in Danish public committees in 1975 and 2010, Journal of European Public Policy, 22 (7), 1022–1039.

Caraker E. (2013) Kristelig Fagforening og aftalesystemet, Økonomi og Politik, 86 (1), 31–44.

Caraker E., Høgedahl L., Jørgensen H. and Møberg R. (2014) Fællesskab før forskelle, research report, Aalborg, CARMA.

Crouch C. (1993) Industrial relations and European state traditions, Oxford, Clarendon Press.

Dølvik J., Marginson P., Alsos K., Arnholtz J., Meardi G., Müller T. and Trygstad S. (2018) Collective wage regulation in northern Europe under strain: multiple drivers of change and differing responses, European Journal of Industrial Relations, 24 (4), 321–339.

DR (2018) Fagforeningerne har lagt milliarder i strejkekasserne, DR, 9 March 2018. https://www.dr.dk/nyheder/penge/fagforeninger-har-lagt-milliarder-i-strejkekasserne Danish national broadcaster

Due J. and Madsen J. (2006) Fra storkonflikt til barselsfond: den danske model under afvikling, Copenhagen, Jurist- og Økonomforbundets Forlag.

Due J., Madsen J. and Jensen C. (1993) Den danske model: en historisk sociologisk analyse af det kollektive aftalesystem, Copenhagen, Jurist- og Økonomforbundets Forlag.

Esping-Andersen G. (1985) Politics against markets: the Social Democratic road to power, Princeton, Princeton University Press.

Esping-Andersen G. (1990) The three political economies of the welfare state, International Journal of Sociology, 20 (3), 92–123.

Galenson W. (1969) The Danish system of labor relations – a study in industrial peace, New York, Russell & Russell.

Gumbrell-McCormick R. and Hyman R. (2013) Trade unions in Western Europe: hard times, hard choices, Oxford, Oxford University Press.

Hansen N. and Mailand M. (2019) Overenskomstfornyelsen 2018. Musketered, magtbalancer og modelforandringer, FAOS-report 166, Copenhagen, Københavns Universitet.

Høgedahl L. (2019) Den danske model i den offentlige sektor: Danmark i et nordisk perspektiv, Copenhagen, Jurist- og Økonomforbundets Forlag.

Høgedahl L. (2020) The Danish labour market model: is the Bumblebee still flying?, in Christiansen P., Elklit J. and Nedergaard P. (eds) Oxford Handbook of Danish Politics, Oxford, Oxford University Press, 559–576.

Ibsen C. and Keune M. (2018) Organised decentralisation of collective bargaining: case studies of Germany, Netherlands and Denmark, OECD Social, Employment and Migration Working Papers 217, Paris, OECD Publishing.

Ibsen C. and Tapia M. (2017) Trade union revitalisation: where are we now? Where to next?, Journal of Industrial Relations, 59 (2), 170–191

Ibsen F., Høgedahl L. and Scheuer S. (2013) Free riders: the rise of alternative unionism in Denmark, Industrial Relations Journal, 44 (5–6), 444–461.

Jensen C. (2007) Arbejdsmarkedsrelationer i Danmark – fra konfliktbaseret konsensus til konsensusbaseret konflikt: industrial relations traditionen og de industrielle relationer i en dansk kontekst, Copenhagen, Jurist- og Økonomforbundets Forlag.

Jørgensen H. and Larsen F. (2014) Ny politisk-institutionel regulering: reformer, partsindflydelse og dansk model, in Jørgensen H. (ed.) Arbejdsmarkedsregulering, København, DJØF Forlag, 287–319.

Kaergaard V. (2020) DI og Dansk Metal fraråder dansk særafgift på CO2, Energywatch.dk, 29 September 2020. https://energiwatch.dk/Energinyt/Politik___Markeder/article12446199.ece.

Klitgaard M. and Nørgaard A. (2014) Structural stress or deliberate decision? Government partisanship and the disempowerment of unions in Denmark, European Journal of Political Research, 53 (2), 404–421.

Knudsen H. (1995) Employee participation in Europe, London, Sage.

Knudsen H. and Lind J. (2012a) De danske modeller. Plus ca change, plus c'est la même chose?, Tidsskrift for Arbejdsliv, 14 (2), 9–30.

Knudsen H. and Lind J. (2012b) Is the Danish model still a sacred cow? Danish trade unions and European integration, Transfer, 18 (4), 381–395.

Knudsen H. and Lind J. (2018) Danish flexicurity: not the same today as yesterday, in Sander G., Tomljenovics V. and Bodiroga-Vukobrat, N. (eds) Transnational, European, and National Labour Relations, Cham, Springer, 197–213.

Korpi W. (1978) The working class in welfare capitalism: work, unions and politics in Sweden, London, Routledge & Kegan Paul.

Korpi W. (1983) The democratic class struggle, London, Routledge & Kegan Paul.

Kristiansen J. (2014) Den kollektive arbejdsret, Copenhagen, Jurist- og Økonomforbundets Forlag.

Larsen A., Ellersgaard C. and Bernsen M. (2015) Magteliten – hvordan 423 danskere styrer landet, Copenhagen, Politikens Forlag.

Larsson B. (2015) Trade union channels for influencing European Union policies, Nordic Journal of Working Life Studies, 5 (3), 101–121.

Lind J. (1995) The modernisation of trade unions in Denmark, Transfer, 1 (1), 44–63.

Lind J. (2003) Arbejdsmarkedsreformen og vejen til det frie valg på arbejdsmarkedet, Tidsskrift for Arbejdsliv, 5 (2), 73–77.

Lind J. (2004a) Das dänische Tarifvertragssystem zwischen Kohärenz und Fragmentierung, WSI Mitteilungen, 57 (7), 367–373.

Lind J. (2004b) The restructuring of the Ghent model in Denmark and consequences for the trade unions, Transfer, 10 (4), 621–625.

Lind J. (2009) The end of the Ghent system as trade union recruitment machinery?, Industrial Relations Journal, 40 (6), 510–523.

Lind J. and Knudsen H. (2018) Denmark: the long-lasting class compromise, Employee Relations, 40 (4), 580–600.

Madsen P. (2002) The Danish model of flexicurity: a paradise with some snakes, in Sarfati H. and Bonoli G. (eds) Labour market and social protections reforms in international perspective: parallel or converging tracks?, Farnham, Ashgate, 243–265.

Mailand M. (2020) Corporatism since the great recession: challenges to tripartite relations in Denmark, the Netherlands and Austria, Cheltenham, Edward Elgar.

Müller T. and Schulten T. (2020) The European minimum wage on the doorstep, ETUI Policy Brief 1/2020, Brussels, ETUI.

Müller T., Dølvik J., Ibsen C. and Schulten T. (2018) The manufacturing sector: still an anchor for pattern bargaining within and across Countries?, European Journal of Industrial Relations, 24 (4), 357–372.

Rasmussen M. and Pontusson J. (2018) Working-class strength by institutional design? Unionization, partisan politics, and unemployment insurance systems, 1870 to 2010, Comparative Political Studies, 51 (6), 793–828.

Refslund B. (2015) Adjusting the Danish industrial relations system after Laval: recalibration rather than erosion, Transfer, 21 (2), 247–251.

Refslund B. (2016) Intra-European labour migration and deteriorating employment relations in Danish cleaning and agriculture: industrial relations under pressure from EU8/2 labour inflows?, Economic and Industrial Democracy, 37 (4), 597–621.

Refslund B. and Lind J. (2021) Denmark: enduring institutionalised wage coordination in a changing corporatist context, in Ebbinghaus B. and Weishaupt T. (eds) The role of social partners in managing Europe's great recession: crisis corporatism or corporatism in crisis?, Abingdon, Routledge.

Thomsen J. (2019) Stærk fremgang i dansk realløn [Confederation of Danish Industry, employers association], DI Analyse, September 2019. www.danskindustri.dk/arkiv/analyser/2019/9/stark-fremgang-i-dansk-reallon/

Visser J. (2019) Trade unions in the balance, ILO ACTRAV Working Paper, Geneva, ILO.

Vulkan P. and Larsson B. (2018) Patterns of transnational trade union cooperation in Europe: the effect of regimes, sectors and resources, European Journal of Industrial Relations, 25 (2), 147–162.

Welz C., Fromm A., Rodriguez Contreras R. and Boehmer S. (2016) Mapping key dimensions of industrial relations, Luxemburg, Publications Office of the European Union.

Abbreviations

3F	Faglig Fælles Forbund (United Federation of Workers)
AC	Akademikerne (Danish Confederation of Professional Associations)
ASE	Arbejdsløshedskassen for selvstændige (Union connected to unemployment fund for self-employed)
CO-Industri:	Centralorganisationen af Industriansatte (Central Organization of Industrial Employees in Denmark)
DA	Dansk Arbejdsgiverforening (Confederation of Danish Employers)
Dansk Metal	Dansk Metalarbejderforbund (Danish Metalworkers' Federation)
DI	Dansk Industri (Federation of Danish Employers in Manufacturing Industry)
DJØF	Dansk Jurist- og Økonomforbund (Danish Association of Lawyers and Economists)
DM	(earlier Dansk Magisterforening) (Federation of Professionals in Arts and Science)
DsF	De samvirkende Fagforbund (Confederations of Danish Trade Unions)
EU	European Union
ETUC	European Trade Union Confederation
ETUF	European Trade Union Federation
FH	Fagbevægelsens Hovedorganisation (Danish Trade Union Confederation)
FOA	Fag og Arbejde (The union for mainly health and care workers)

FTF Funktionærernes og Tjenestemændenes Fællesråd (Confederation of Professionals in Denmark)

HK Handels- og Kontorfunktionærernes Fagforbund (Union of Commercial and Clerical Employees in Denmark)

IDA Ingeniørsammenslutningen i Danmark (Danish Society of Engineers)

Krifa Kristelig Fagbevægelse (Christian Union)

LH Ledernes Hovedorganisation (Danish Association of Managers)

LO Landsorganisationen i Danmark (Danish Confederation of Trade Unions)

Chapter 9

Trade unions in Estonia: Less than meets the eye

Epp Kallaste

After the dissolution of the Soviet Union trade unions in Estonia had to find their role in the new economic system. In response to people's fears of losing social protection in turbulent times most minimum working conditions were regulated by law, depriving the unions of a substantial part of their role. Subsequently, union membership and collective bargaining gradually declined and recently union membership has stabilized at the very low level of around 5–7 per cent of employment (see Table 9.1). Estonia's unions are concentrated in the public sector, among the older workforce and in a few industries. Estonian trade unionism is too fragmented for such a small country with low union membership. As a result, resources are thinly spread, which hinders the effective representation of employees. Most trade unions are too small to afford even one employee of their own. The trade unions that operate at industry level are more successful in concluding collective agreements and representing their members. Striving towards structural changes and movement from company-based trade union organizations to industry unions has had some limited success. In order to bring about change to current trends of trade unionism and collective bargaining, some kind of major structural change must take place, either in the organization of employees or the regulation and role of collective bargaining.

Table 9.1 Principal characteristics of trade unionism in Estonia

	2000	2019
Total trade union membership	75,000	30,000
Proportion of women in total membership	60 %	57 %*
Gross union density	17 %	5 %
Net union density	14 %	4 %
Number of confederations	2	2
Number of affiliated unions (federations)	35	24
Number of independent unions**	n.a.	4
Collective bargaining coverage	32 %***	6 %****
Principal level of collective bargaining	company	company
Days not worked due to industrial action per 1,000 workers	2	2

Notes: *Data from 2015; **The number of company unions not affiliated to industry trade unions is higher. The four are essential independent unions that have visibility, activity and impact. These are the Estonian Doctors Union (EAL, Eesti Arstide Liit), the Estonian Nurses Union (EÕL, Eesti Õdede Liit), the Estonian Educational Personnel Union (EEPU, Eesti Haridustöötajate Liit) and the Federation of the Estonian Universities Universitas (Universitas Eesti Kõrgkoolide, Teadus-Ja Arendusasutuste Ametiliitude Ühendus). No data available for 2000, but EEPU and Universitas were at this time members of TALO and the other two were independent; ***Data from 2001; ****Data from 2018.

Source: Appendix A1, Kallaste (2004, 2019), web pages of the confederations, and Estonian Statistical Office (Labour Force Survey).

Historical background and principal features of the industrial relations system

In Estonia, as in the other former Soviet Bloc countries, the history of the current industrial relations system started with the regaining of independence at the beginning of the 1990s. In the market economy, trade unions have a different role from the one they had in the planned economy, where nominally all the means of production were owned by the workers. During the course of the 1990s, the entire legislative basis for industrial relations, as for the other fields of the economy and civic participation, was developed from scratch. Even though the role and functions of trade unions were reinvented for the market economy, industrial relations in practice and the trade union movement and its members have been influenced by their Soviet past in many ways. Although several trade unions and professional unions claim to be the legal successors of trade union organizations that existed before the Soviet occupation, the structure of trade unionism was inherited from the Soviet era rather than from what preceded it.

The influence of the Soviet era on trade unions in the new economic system was multifaceted. On one hand the trade unions inherited the name (*ametiühing* in Estonian), the organization and the image of the Soviet era trade unions, which impacted negatively on people's attitudes to the trade union movement in the new economic reality. On the other hand, the trade union confederation, the Estonian Trade Union Confederation (EAKL, *Eesti Ametiühingute Keskliit*), inherited large properties accumulated during the Soviet era and administered by the Central Council of Trade Unions of the Estonian Soviet Socialist Republic (*Eesti Nõukogude Sotsialistliku Vabariigi Ametiühingute Kesknõukogu*). This legacy still constitutes the unions' main source of income.

During the transformation of the state, a smaller trade union confederation separated from EAKL in 1993, the Estonian Employees' Unions' Confederation (TALO, *Teenistujate Ametiliitude Keskorganisatsioon*). The Estonian word *teenistuja* signifies a public servant and reflects TALO's recruitment focus on representing white-collar public sector employees, more specifically employees in the fields of culture, education and science. At present, however, there is no clear division of labour or membership between the two confederations. Another split from EAKL occurred in 1997 with the separation of the Food and Rural Workers' Trade Union Confederation (ETMAKL, *Eesti Toiduainete ja Maatöötajate Ametiühingute Keskliit*). This Confederation, however, has never been very active and was officially dissolved in 2021.

In the Soviet era, trade unions were formed in companies and company-level representation was the predominant form that continued into the new economic system at the beginning of the 1990s. Company unions united into industry-level organizations, forming associations of trade unions. Thus, at the beginning of the 2000s, the dominant form for an affiliate of a union confederation was a federation of company trade unions. Another form of trade union comprised professional organizations, such as those for doctors, journalists and actors, which incorporated trade union activities and collective bargaining into their agenda. Professional organizations that acquired trade union and collective bargaining roles were, however, in the minority and in some cases existed side by side with company unions in the same industry. In some industries – for example, electricity and oil-shale mining – the privatized monopoly companies which continued their activities in the same role covered almost the whole industry and, therefore, a trade union formed in the monopoly company almost coincides with an industry-level trade union.

Structure of trade unions and union democracy

The two Estonian trade union confederations are EAKL and TALO. In addition, there are some important independent trade unions, such as: the Estonian Doctors Union (EAL, *Eesti Arstide Liit*), the Estonian Educational Personnel Union (EEPU, *Eesti Haridustöötajate Liit*), the Estonian Nurses Union (EÕL, *Eesti Õdede Liit*), and the Federation of the Estonian Universities (*Eesti Kõrgkoolide, Teadus- ja Arendusasutuste Ametiliitude Ühendus,* UNIVERSITAS). TALO is much smaller than EAKL, both in number of members and in organizational resources. Both EAKL and TALO have lost some industry unions, but the loss has been greater in TALO. EAKL included seventeen industry unions or federations of unions in 2020 and TALO 7, whereas in 2003, the reported numbers of members were, respectively, eighteen and twelve (Kallaste 2004). Trade unions affiliated to EAKL had around 20,000 members in 2019 and TALO around 3,000, as reported by confederations, whereas in 2003 the respective estimates had been 43,000 and 35,000 members (Kallaste 2004). Thus, trade union members represented by EAKL declined around half and those represented by TALO by 90 per cent in the period 2003–2019. ETMAKL was reported to represent 4,000 members in 2006 (Carley 2009), but this confederation has never been an active social partner at state level. EAKL and TALO have discussed some years ago a possible merger in the form of TALO becoming an affiliate of the EAKL, but the discussions have not borne fruit.

There have been different movements among confederation affiliates (Figure 9.1): mergers, dissolutions, a change of confederation, and splits from confederations. Some of the trade unions that affiliated to TALO and EAKL at the beginning of the 2000s were independent by 2019. Most notable of these are EEPU, with over 10,000 members, and Universitas, with around 1,200 members, which split from TALO in 2009. With this move, there were no trade unions in education left in TALO. The nurses' union EÕL split from EAKL in 2016. The Estonian Association of Journalists (EAJ, *Eesti Ajakirjanike Liit*) that initially affiliated to TALO joined EAKL in 2012. Affiliates that had previously been members of the confederations have either just dissolved or merged into some existing union. Those affiliates that were not listed in 2003 are, in the case of EAKL, the Chemical Workers' Union (*Keemikute Ametiühing*) that split from the Industry and Metal Workers' Union (IMTAL, *Industriaal- ja Metallitöötajate Ametiühingute Liit*) and in the case of TALO one union that has a double affiliation: one in TALO and the other in the Federation of the Trade Unions of State and Municipal Agencies Employees (ROTAL, *Riigi- ja Omavalitsusasutuste Töötajate Ametiühingute Liit*), which, in turn, affiliated to EAKL. Two new unions in TALO were previously members of an association of trade unions, but the association was terminated.

Figure 9.1 Number of affiliates of EAKL and TALO and main independent trade unions in 2019 and their affiliation in 2003

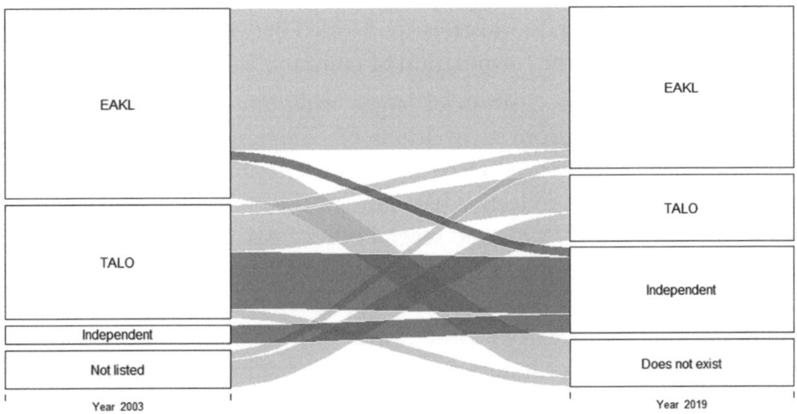

Note: Size of the boxes indicates the number of unions and not their membership.
Source: EAKL and TALO web page, Kallaste (2004).

Trade union membership has declined proportionately more than the number of affiliates of confederations, indicating shrinking trade union size. The only trade unions for which data are available and which have grown compared with the beginning of the 2000s are the Estonian Seamen's Independent Union (EMSA, *Eesti Meremeeste Sõltumatu Ametiühing*) and EÕL. All other trade unions have lost members.

EAKL is trying to persuade affiliates to merge and unite forces in order to increase the capacity and viability of trade unions and reduce bureaucracy. Trade unions in Estonia operate in a decentralized manner and there are no substantial levers available to the confederation to promote mergers. Thus, while there have been some mergers, there have also been splits.

In some cases, several affiliates of one confederation operate in the same industry at company level, but do not cooperate to develop a united industry policy. For example, there are two trade unions in retail and services: the Estonian Association of Communications and Service Workers' Trade Unions (ESTAL, *Eesti Side- ja Teenindustöötajate Ametiühingute Liit*) and the Estonian Trade Union of Commercial and Servicing Employees (ETKA, *Teenindus- ja Kaubandustöötajate Ametiühing*). ETKA conducts collective bargaining with hotels in Tallinn. In addition, EMSA, entered into an agreement in the hotel industry with Tallin, whose main activity is the operation of passenger ships on the Baltic Sea. Even though industry-level union structures have clearly taken shape in some industries, several industries are divided between trade unions that do not cooperate in the formulation of common industry policy.

In addition to the creation of larger trade unions through mergers, the aim is to move from associations of company unions to industry unions, which have proved to be more efficient and persistent in representing employees in collective bargaining. This move was made in road transport during the 1990s and several other EAKL affiliates are moving towards this. For example, ESTAL and the Association of Industrial and Metal Workers' Trade Unions (IMTAL, *Industriaal- ja Metallitöötajate Ametiühingute Liit*) are in the process of transformation from a federation of trade unions into an industry trade union, resulting in one legal entity that individuals may join as trade union members, while company unions are still associated. In medicine, the only trade union, the Association of Healthcare Professionals Trade Unions (*Tervishoiualatöötajate Ametiühingute Liit*), was dissolved and now only three industry-wide professional unions operate in the field (EÕL, EAL and the Union of Estonian Healthcare Professionals [*Eesti Tervishoiutöötajate Kutseliit*]).

With the decline of trade union membership, there has been a decline in the overall number of trade unions (legal entities), although this decline has been slower than in the case of membership. There have been some trade union mergers, but dissolutions have been more common. Because of the larger proportional decrease in membership compared to the decrease in the number of organizations, the remaining organizations are smaller and weaker. It should be noted that, despite the general trend of decline, there have also been some new trade unions formed (see Figure 9.2).

Figure 9.2 Number of registered, dissolved and created trade unions in the non-profit associations and foundations register, 2009–2018

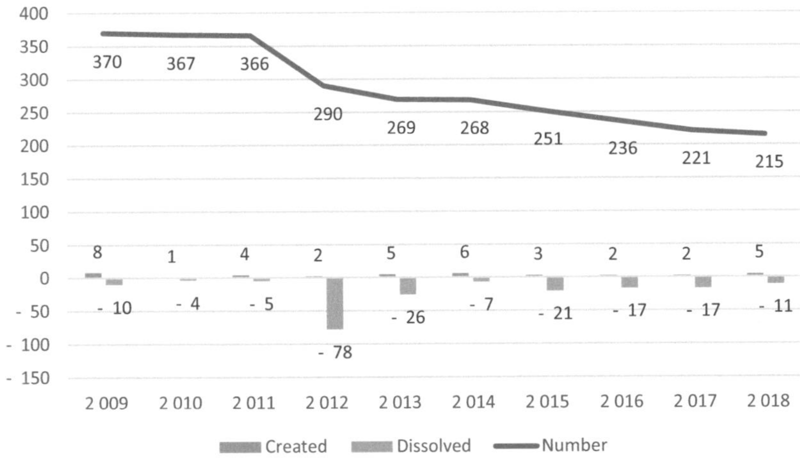

Source: Järve (2019).

The total number of trade unions registered in the non-profit associations and foundations register was 215 in 2018 (Figure 9.2). This has declined by 155 during the past ten years. The total number of organizations functioning as trade unions – that is, that represent employees and bargain collectively – is higher than the number of registered trade unions. Some professional unions operate as trade unions but are registered as general non-profit organizations and not specifically as trade unions. There is no information on how many other non-profit associations operate as trade unions.[1] Registered trade unions are divided roughly equally between company-level unions and trade unions that may be formed on the basis of profession, industry or region or a combination of these. The

1 The number of non-profit associations in the activities of business, employers and professional organizations was 1,667 in 2008 (Hallemaa and Servinski 2009: 78), which is 4.5 times higher than the number of trade unions. This includes, however, all kinds of professional organizations – which also do not engage at all in employees' representation and bargaining with employers – and also employers' organizations. It is hard to tell how many of these organizations act as trade unions.

trade unions that are not company unions may have individuals or company unions or associations of trade unions as their members.

Unionization

Trade union membership has declined overall. Total membership is between 33,000 and 39,000 members, making up 5–6 per cent (previously between 5 and 7 per cent) of employees, as reported in the Labour Force Survey (LFS) (Figure 9.3).

Figure 9.3 Union members as a percentage of employees, 2000–2019

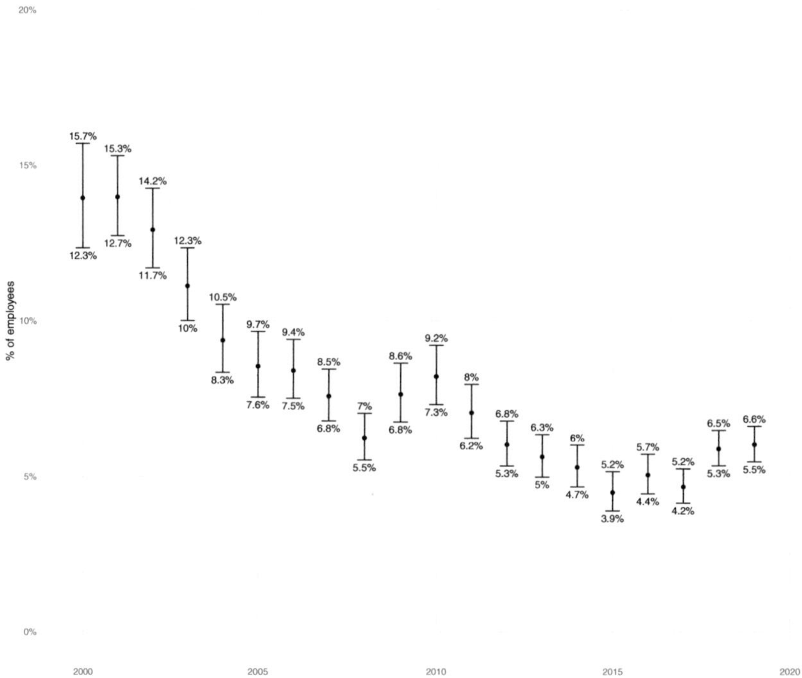

Note: 95 per cent confidence intervals.
Source: Estonian Labour Force Survey, Statistics Estonia, author's calculations.

In Estonia, official membership statistics are not collected from trade unions. The only data sources are the unions themselves and the Estonian

Labour Force Survey, but trade unions do not publish their membership figures. Therefore, there is no overview of specific groups of trade union members, such as the retired or unemployed. It must be admitted that some trade unions do not even have adequate up-to-date information on their members. Even though the situation has improved markedly since the beginning of the 2000s, there are still cases in which union dues are withheld from wages by the employer and only the employer is aware of union members' identity.

Based on the LFS, it is apparent that unionization is more common in the public sector and in state- or municipality-owned establishments (Figure 9.4). As is usual elsewhere, union membership is more common in larger enterprises. Union membership is concentrated in the public sector or public services that are privately operated but publicly financed, for example public transport.

Figure 9.4 Trade union membership by type of establishment, 2019

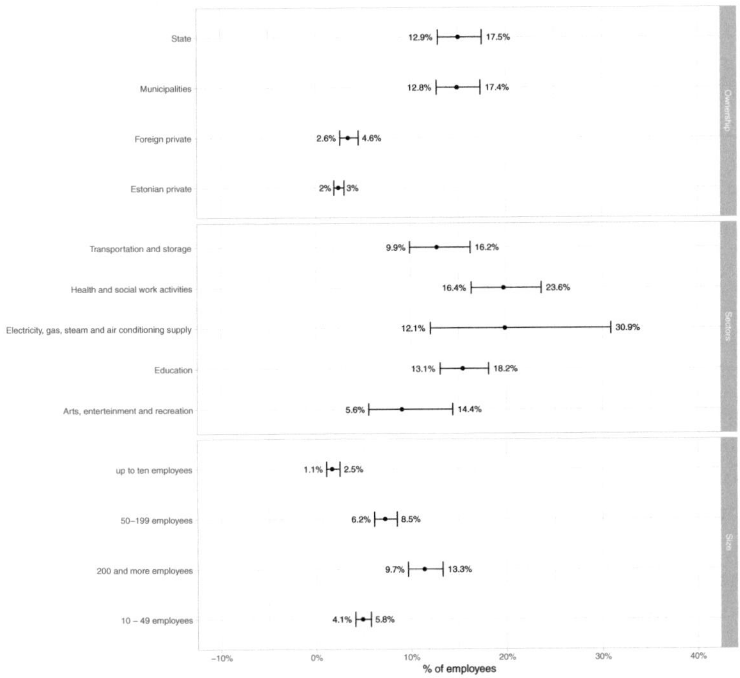

Note: Percentage of employees.
Source: Estonian Labour Force Survey, Statistics Estonia, author's calculations.

Unionization is higher among older and more educated workers (Figure 9.5). The small gender difference indicates that women are slightly more unionized. This is partly connected to the more unionized industries of health care and education in which female workers dominate. There is a clear difference between employees who have worked for a long time in one company and those with a short tenure. Trade unions are more successful in retaining members in establishments where their presence has been long-term. When people change jobs, they are easily lost to the union. In order to maintain unionization levels, organizing staff changing jobs must improve and the move away from company unions towards industry unions is an essential step in this direction.

The foreign-born population has a slightly higher unionization rate in Estonia than native people. This is probably related to the workers settled in Estonia in the Soviet era. The new immigrants' profile is somewhat different. EAKL has an immigration policy, but the focus is not on the unionization of new immigrants but rather on labour market regulation, which is not being complied with for many immigrant workers. Estonia has turned from a net emigration country to a net immigration country during the past five years. It is doubtful that emigration and immigration have had an essential impact on unionization in Estonia. Work-related emigration from Estonia is mainly to the Nordic countries, some of it in the form of commuting. This might bring about higher unionization in Estonia if the experience of a highly unionized labour market abroad is transferred to the local labour market, but there are no signs of this yet.

Estonian trade unions represent some industries in which freelancing is the traditional form of working, for example actors and journalists. Thus, depending on the industry, there might be some unionization among freelancers. The LFS has too few observations for an estimation.

At the confederation level and depending again on industry, the unionization of self-employed platform workers, such as taxi drivers and food couriers, is high on the agenda. In 2018 a strike of Bolt taxi drivers, who operate as service providers to the Bolt ridesharing platform and are not salaried employees, took place with no trade union involvement. The strike was against a change in company pricing policy that lowered drivers' incomes. The drivers stopped driving and picketed company headquarters, demanding dialogue with the management. Trade unions, however, have not been able to organize these platform workers. Trade unions have considered the introduction of a service for platform workers by means of which employers' data on orders and pricing is systematized and presented to the worker. This could be attractive to platform workers. There is insufficient leadership within unions and staff to provide this service, thus restricting the number of such workers who become union members.

Figure 9.5 Trade union membership by type of member, 2019

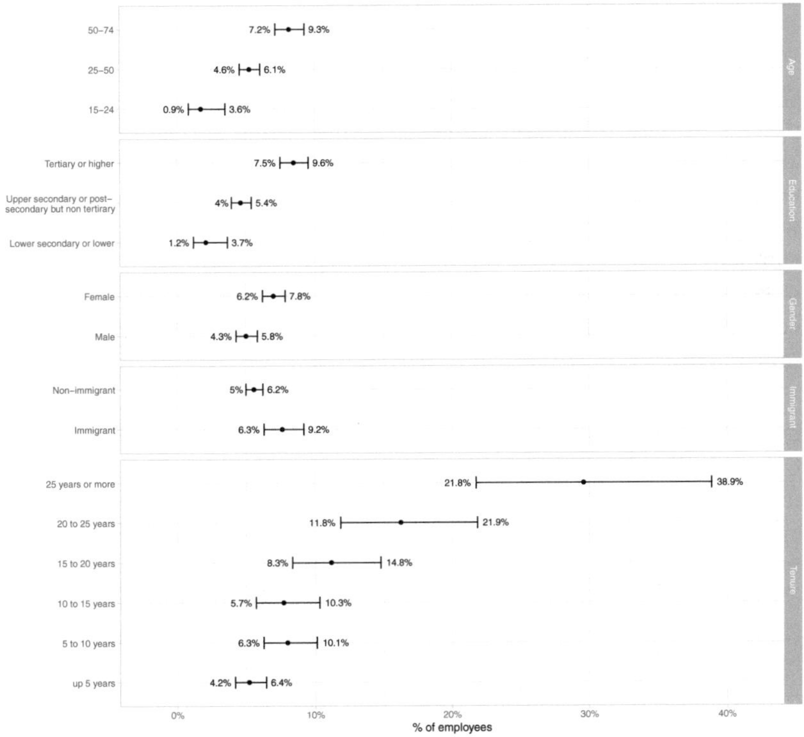

Note: Percentage of employees.
Source: Estonian Labour Force Survey, Statistics Estonia, author's calculations.

Organizing new members is high on EAKL's agenda. Each year EAKL runs a recruitment campaign. The campaigns include organizing meetings in public locations and workplaces, together with media promotion on different channels. The campaigns have not generated a significant increase in membership. At the same time, the decline has not continued either and the unionization rate among employees has not declined markedly since 2008. There are not yet signs of organizing people employed in new forms of work, even though this is on EAKL's agenda. Thus, union membership is in decline and concentrated in traditional segments. Even though there are yearly organizing campaigns there has been no increase in union membership and new forms of work are not organized.

Union resources and expenditure

Most trade unions depend entirely on membership fees, which are usually 1 per cent of the member's gross wage and paid monthly to unions. In some professional unions an annual fixed amount is collected and different rates apply to retired or unemployed members. Usually, fees are paid by the members directly to the trade union account. There are some exceptions left from the Soviet era, where the employer withholds company union fees from the monthly wage and transfers them to the trade union account. The fees of federations and confederations are calculated from union membership, usually, but each organization decides individually.

Unlike most of the other unions EAKL also has substantial income from the management of real estate. While TALO income in 2019 was €10,463 (TALO 2020), entirely from membership fees, EAKL's income in 2018 was €605,947, of which 93 per cent was from real estate management (EAKL 2019). Some additional income besides membership fees is also secured by some other unions: for example, in 2016 around 35 per cent of the Estonian Theatre Union's (*Eesti Teatriliit*) income (Eesti Teatriliit 2018) and in 2019, 65 per cent of Network of Estonian Nonprofit Organisations' (EMSL) income (EMSL 2020) was from fees. The rest of their income came from real estate management, public project funding, and the sale of publications. European Union (EU) and international projects have sometimes contributed to trade union budgets, with specific spending restrictions, but at confederal level these are currently a minor source of income. The additional income of most unions, if they have any, comes mainly from real estate management or government grants in the case of the Theatre Union, or employers' contributions in the case of EMSA. But most unions have no other sources of income than member contributions. The Estonian Transport and Road Workers Trade Union (ETTA, *Eesti Transordi ja Teetöötajate Ametiühing*), for example, obtains 99 per cent of its income from membership fees (ETTA 2020).

As unions depend almost entirely on union fees, membership decline has had a detrimental impact on union organization. According to the non-profit organizations register, only 38 per cent of trade unions employed at least one employee. In most cases there was only one (Järve 2019). Even the confederation TALO has only one full-time employee (TALO 2020). Only twenty-three trade union organizations had more than one employee. As already explained, there may be some professional organizations that operate as general non-profit organizations that also have employees, and stronger organizations for which there are no data. In general, the capacity of trade unions in Estonia is very limited and so they must concentrate their resources.

According to the chair of EAKL, membership contributions from about 500 union members are needed to hire one full-time staff member. At a lower ratio of members per employee, a union cannot pay a competitive wage and members would not be interested in working as trade union officials. Estonian trade unions are very small and changes in trade union structure are difficult to implement. Even though there are many trade unions with fewer than 500 members they still operate as separate trade unions.

The main expenditure items for unions are office costs and payroll. Some larger trade unions offer additional security or support mechanisms to their members. These may include support, additional unemployment insurance, legal aid or additional insurance for sick days, which are the responsibility of employees in Estonia. EAKL also provides legal aid to some extent. The demand for legal aid at central level has declined somewhat. The reason for this is the change of union membership structure to larger companies and the focus on dialogue with employers. Peep Peterson, the current EAKL Chair, argues that where relations with the employer are strong and discussions take place there is no need for the trade union to provide legal assistance to members. The State Labour Inspectorate (TI, *Tööinspektsioon*) also provides free legal consultation in Estonia, which has also probably lowered demand for similar union services. Legal aid, however, is still an important part of trade union activities, and EMSA, for example, established a separate limited company for providing legal aid and training in 2016.

According to the chair of EAKL most trade unions, including EAKL, now have a strike fund. Strike funds are financed from unions' internal resources and are not publicly disclosed. The unions that have called strikes or issued strike threats have all created a strike fund. There are no regulations or mutually agreed conditions concerning the size or use of strike funds and there is no overview of the amount of such funds.

To summarize, Estonian trade unions are small and their resources are scattered. Most trade unions do not have even one employee. As most trade unions depend entirely on members' fees, they have been adversely affected by membership decline. Some industry unions and confederations, however, have additional income from real estate management, employers or other activities.

Collective bargaining and unions at the workplace

The decline in trade union membership has been accompanied by a decline in the number of collective agreements (Figure 9.6) as well as coverage. Each year fewer agreements are registered in the collective agreements register. Compliance with the obligation of registering signed agreements is likely to be less than complete, however, which might also partly explain the decline in registered agreements.[2]

Looking back over the preceding ten years shows that while union density was the same in 2019 as it was in 2008 (Figure 9.3), the number of concluded and registered collective agreements had declined by 40 or 59 per cent of the 2008 level (Figure 9.6).

---

2 For example, from a query to the Collective Agreements Register it appeared that the last collective agreement of which one signatory party was ETL (Theatre Union) was signed more than 10 years ago. From the ETL web page it appears that at least in 2017 some agreements were concluded in which ETL participated as a representative of the employees' side.

Figure 9.6 Number of new collective agreements registered in the register of collective agreements, 2001–2019

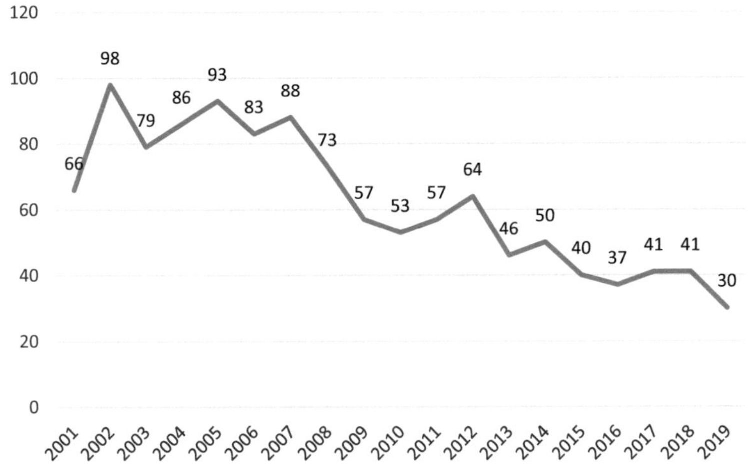

Source: 2002–2015: Kaldmäe (2017: 76), based on register of collective agreements; 2016–2019: data forwarded to the author from the collective agreements register.

According to the Law on Collective Agreements (*Kollektiivlepingu seadus*) workplace collective agreements shall be entered into by the relevant trade union. If employees are not represented by a trade union an authorized employee representative shall sign the agreement. Usually, the agreement is concluded by the trade union, but there have also been cases in which an authorized representative elected by the general assembly of employees signed it (Kallaste 2019). With changes to trade union structure union representatives are increasingly likely to participate in collective bargaining at the workplace. At the same time, collective bargaining coverage has declined and there are fewer companies with collective agreements (Kallaste 2019).

Collective bargaining takes place in Estonia at different levels. The principal level is still the company, where the highest proportion of collective agreements are concluded. Some bargaining takes place at industry level, but in several of these instances the industry comprises only one company. Although Estonia has very loose conditions for extending collective agreements (Kallaste 2019), there are extended agreements in only two industries: bus transport and medicine. Industry-level agreements are accompanied in transport by a second layer of company-level agreements.

During the 1990s, state-level collective agreements were wider than the minimum wage and often the signed agreements were tripartite. Some agreements also stipulated tax-exempt minimum incomes and details on labour policy financing (Taliga et al. 2002). Since the beginning of the 2000s, regular state-level collective bargaining has been bipartite and concentrates on the state minimum wage, which is agreed in a collective agreement and extended throughout the country. Regular bargaining on the minimum wage is conducted by the Estonian Employers' Confederation (ETK, *Eesti Tööandjate Keskliit*) and EAKL. Other issues have moved to the sphere of bipartite or tripartite social dialogue and result occasionally in agreements.

The minimum wage agreement is also enacted by Government decree, which always includes the same terms as agreed in the collective agreement. Thus, even though the collective agreement should be applied in its own right, it is enacted and thus reinforced through a decree. The minimum wage agreement has a wide-ranging impact on the labour market and also influences other fields through the benefits or taxes tied to the size of the minimum wage. For example, in many municipalities in Estonia the kindergarten fee for parents is linked to the minimum wage. The latest minimum wage agreement signed in 2019 stipulated the increase of the minimum wage to 40 per cent of the average wage in 2021. This would mean a monthly minimum wage of €571, given the forecast for the average wage of €1,428 in 2021. Taking into account the current economic crisis employers' and employees' confederations have proposed to freeze the minimum wage at the 2020 level (ETK 2020). With the rapid increase in the unemployment rate because of the Covid-19 pandemic the trade unions' focus has shifted from wage increases to job maintenance. Minimum wage increases have thus been halted.

The general principle is that in collective agreements only conditions that improve on those stipulated in the law are agreed (favourability principle). During the transformation from a planned to a market economy a large set of conditions were legally stipulated as mandatory to protect minimum working standards. This included working and rest time pauses, length of vacation, redundancy notice periods and pay. Therefore, the scope for collective bargaining became fairly narrow. In 2008 the new Employment Agreement Act (TLS, *Töölepingu seadus*) was passed, which introduced the possibility of agreeing different conditions from those stipulated in law if this is done in a collective agreement. As a result, some working and rest time conditions, and terms for advance notice of cancellation of individual employment contracts that differ from the

Figure 9.7 Monthly national minimum gross wage and average gross wage (in euros), 2000–2021

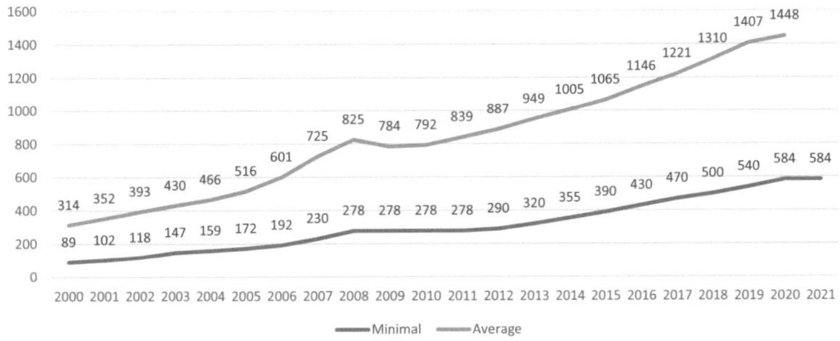

Source: Average wage 2000–2008: Statistics Estonia web database, table PA5311; average wage 2009–2017: Statistics Estonia web database, table PA5211; average wage 2019–2020: Statistics Estonia web database, table PA001; minimum wage 2000–2020: Estonian Tax and Customs Board web page; minimum wage in 2021: ETK (2020).

legislation may be agreed in collective agreements. This has not created any significant additional interest in collective bargaining. The additional scope for conditions that could be agreed on more flexibly in collective agreements is under discussion with the government and employers in the retail trade. The other social partners, however, do not envisage that collective agreements should be the instrument that confer flexibility.

Collective agreements on wages, working and rest time conditions in Estonia usually apply to all employees in the workplace, regardless of their unionization. Free-riding is therefore a worrying problem for trade unions. A few means are available for using collective agreements with employers to promote unionization. The reasons for joining a trade union must usually lie elsewhere, including a sense of solidarity or common interests.

There have been attempts to restrict non-unionized employees benefits from collective agreements and to limit free-riding. In 2008 the Supreme Court ruled in the litigation between Estonian Railway Trade Union (*Eesti Raudteelaste Ametiühing*) and Estonian Railway AS that the employer has an obligation to apply the collective agreement to all employees, whether or not they belong to a trade union.[3] Applying a collective agreement

3 Riigikohtu tsiviilkolleegiumi otsus 09. jaanuarist 2008 nr 3-2-1-133-07 MTÜ Eesti Raudteelaste Ametiühing kassatsioonkaebus Tallinna Ringkonnakohtu 31.08.2007. a otsusele.

only to employees belonging to a trade union is contrary to the prohibition of unequal treatment of employees. The Estonian Railway Trade Union had concluded a collective agreement with Estonian Railway AS that required the employer to collect a fee of 0.5 per cent of the monthly wage from non-unionized employees who want to be subject to the collective agreement. The employer had to transfer the collected fees into a solidarity fund managed by the trade union. The employer extended the agreement to all employees without collecting such a fee and the court ruled this to be lawful.

EMSA has implemented a number of successful practices to restrict the extension of collective agreement coverage to non-unionized employees. There are three types of practice in use and stipulated in collective agreements. The first is the provision whereby the employer and EMSA extend the collective agreement to non-EMSA employees if the employee has expressed such a wish in writing and to pay a collective agreement fee of 1 per cent of their wages. The second approach involves the employer paying annually into a welfare fund operated by the trade union. This approach does not directly motivate employees to unionize, but gives the union wider possibilities for supporting and organizing members. According to EMSA's annual accounts the support paid through this welfare fund operated by trade unions in 2019 was €79,600. This formed 16 per cent of collected membership dues. The third solution involves the collective agreement covering only union employees with the exception of some specific pay, working and rest time conditions that apply to all employees (Lember 2020). Thus, even though free-riding is hard to beat, trade unions have found ways of restricting collective agreements to union members only or to extend coverage by making non-union members pay for this directly or indirectly through the employer's welfare fund.

To summarize, the number of collective agreements has declined and most are still concluded at company level. There are collective agreements covering different levels: state-level minimum wage agreements, industry-level agreements and company-level agreements. In Estonia the prevalent attitude is that it is better to regulate by law than to leave important terms and conditions of employment to collective bargaining. Even the minimum wage is enacted through government decree. Some trade unions have been able to fight free-riding by restricting the extension of collective agreements to non-unionized employees.

Industrial conflict

Estonian law regulates three types of strike activity: warning strikes, of up to one hour; support strikes, of up to three days' duration; and strikes proper. A support strike is allowed when a strike is already under way. Warning strikes must be announced three working days before they take place and support strikes by five working days. Strikes may be organized only if there is no industrial peace obligation and must be preceded by conciliation conducted by the Public Conciliator (*Riiklik lepitaja*). Strikes must be announced at least two weeks before they take place.

Strikes are fairly rare in Estonia and most industrial conflicts are resolved by Public Conciliation. All in all, during the whole period 2000–2020 there were only five strikes in Estonia: one strike by train drivers in 2004, two by teachers in 2003 and 2012, one by health care professionals in 2012 and one by Rakvere Lihakombinaat (HKScan) slaughterhouse workers in 2018. In addition, there was one strike organized by EAKL in 2012, which had wider scope and was not preceded by conciliation. This strike aimed to guarantee a balanced budget in unemployment insurance funds to stop the revision of the Employment Agreements Act (*Töölepingu seadus*) and to add amendments to the Collective Agreements Act demanded by the trade union confederation. This raised the question of the legality of strikes and the boundaries of political strikes, to which clear answers have yet to be found.

In addition to strikes, pickets are usually organized in combination with warning strikes or strikes, but sometimes without a strike. For example, in 2018 rescue workers organized a series of small pickets in order to ask for a pay rise from the state budget. On 19 September 2019 around twenty rescue workers gathered in front of the Government building in order to support their demand for higher wages within state budget negotiations and on 9 December 2019 they picketed in front of the Estonian Rescue Board. In 2016 medical workers launched a campaign that involved taking a pillow to their workplace to direct attention to their working and rest time conditions. Even though this was not organized by trade unions, it was an effective campaign.

While state-owned and state-financed industries such as education, health care, cultural and rescue workers mainly try to influence the government, in the private sector Nordic corporations are sometimes involved and, in these cases, support is sought from the headquarters of the Nordic trade unions. In the case of Rakvere Lihakombinaat (HKScan), with the aid of the Finnish Food Workers' Union (SEL, *Suomen Elintarviketyöläisten Liitto*) a picket was organized in front of the headquarters of HKScan in Finland and working meetings held in three factories in Finland that brought about a 1–1.5 hour production stoppage (Herm 2018). This was organized to support the demands of the striking employees in Estonian meat processing plants. Similarly, the Finnish PAM (*Palvelualojen ammattiliitto*) supported workers who were having trouble in collective bargaining with the employer in Sokos Hotel Viru (Pealinn 2015). In the case of Nordea Bank a picket was organized in front of the bank's Swedish headquarters by the Estonian trade union without the help of the Nordic trade unions (Pealinn 2017). The efficiency of local and international pickets is not clear, but they certainly attract attention if done effectively.

Political relations

Several leaders of trade union confederations joined political parties in the 1990s: Siim Kallas, who was the leader of EAKL in 1989–1991, became leader of the Reform Party (*Reformierakond*) from 1994 to 2004 and Estonian Prime Minister at the beginning of the 2000s. The leaders of EAKL during 1991–2000, Raivo Paavo, and 2000–2003, Kadi Pärnits, and the leader of ETTA in 1989–1992, Eiki Nestor, were members of the Social Democratic Party (*Sotsiaaldemokraadid*) and the two later individuals are still politically active. The current chair of EAKL, Peep Peterson, has been a member of the Social Democratic Party and the leader of their youth organization. Thus, more individual connections exist between the trade union movement and the Social Democratic Party than other political parties.

EAKL, however, has remained politically neutral since 2003. It entered into discussions with all political parties in order to put its own agenda onto their electoral platforms during recent parliamentary elections. In 2019 EAKL managed to negotiate with four parties out of six and concluded an agreement with three parties (Social Democratic Party, Eesti 200 and Central Party). The agreement was designed so that parties included themes from EAKL's proposals in their electoral platforms. For example, both the Social Democratic Party and the Central Party incorporated – with the same wording – the clauses from the agreement with the EAKL in their platform for the extension of unemployment insurance conditions and the enhancement of the Estonian Unemployment Insurance Fund's capacity to offer career and training services.

Social dialogue involving trade unions is multifaceted in Estonia and includes several historical stages. The first stage ran up to the beginning of the 2000s and included several tripartite agreements on different national issues. At the beginning of the 2000s, the so-called Socio-Economic Council (*Sotsiaalmajandusnõukogu*) was founded to formalize social dialogue between different stakeholders. This, however, was not very effective, the council's role and power were not clear, and it quietly disappeared, being terminated in 2011 (statement by the Secretary of State 2011). At the same time, several tripartite boards were introduced for public bodies such as the Council of the Unemployment Insurance Fund (*Töötukassa*) and the Health Insurance Fund (*Haigekassa*). Also, trade union input was sought on different public policies. Thus, the official role provided by these boards and the government search for input into regulatory and policy design were the main forms of social dialogue. In recent years social dialogue in the form of regular tripartite meetings of EAKL, the Employers' Confederation and the Ministry of Social Affairs, as well as tripartite meetings with the Prime Minister, have been introduced. Meetings with the Minister of Social Affairs prepare the meetings with the Prime Minister and set the agenda for the following months. Meetings with the Minister of Social Affairs take place around one to two months apart and those with the Prime Minister quarterly. The themes are raised by both parties and cover different topical issues. Peep Peterson, the Chair of EAKL, argues that this kind of scheduled set-up ensures that social dialogue is more effective and makes it possible to raise issues spontaneously.

EAKL and the Employers' Confederation have had some bilateral negotiations and agreements in an effort to set policy, but they have not been very successful. An example of this bilateral approach concerns the extension mechanism for collective agreements. This has long been under discussion in Estonia. Some argue that it violates the Constitution as there is no possibility for non-unionized parties to contribute to the debate or acquire information about the conditions included in the agreement prior to its enactment and publication in official announcements (Kallaste 2019). At the beginning of 2018, the employers and union confederations concluded an agreement on how the parties should inform and consult all stakeholders in cases in which the agreement should be extended. In 2020 the Supreme Court ruled that the extension of collective agreements to employers that are not members of the employers' association that concluded the agreement is not valid, stating in essence that the relevant clause of the act is not valid.[4] The reason is that an employer that is not a member of the employers' association that concluded the agreement had no possibility of finding out about the terms of the agreement or influencing them beforehand. The Supreme Court reviewed the situation and, with one dissenting opinion, did not consider the social partners' agreement on information and consultation conditions of extension. On 29 April 2021 the government introduced a draft amendment to the Collective Agreements Act to restrict the extension terms of collective agreements.

To conclude with trade unions' ties with political parties, these were stronger in the first years of Estonian independence. Currently, trade unions have no direct links to any political party and try to establish good dialogue and find common ground with a range of parties. Regular social dialogue in the form of social partners' tripartite meetings takes place with the current government. In addition, formal participation in tripartite boards, such as the Unemployment Insurance Fund and the Health Insurance Fund, gives the social partners an established role in policy making. Bipartite dialogue between the social partners, however, has a role through minimum wage negotiations. Outside that, however, it is rather formal. Their bipartite resolution on the extension of collective agreements was not even taken up by the Supreme Court when deciding on the conditions of extensions. This confirms the fears of those who demand legal regulation rather than bipartite agreements.

Societal power

Project-based initiatives are the main form of trade union cooperation with other NGOs. Trade unions participate in a number of social movements with links to the labour market and employee working conditions. EAKL is currently negotiating with a coalition on the gender wage gap. This involves EAKL working with a number of NGOs campaigning for women's rights and work.

---

4 Riigikohtu tsiviilkolleegiumi otsus 15. juunist 2020 nr 2-18-7821 Aktsiaseltsi Temptrans kassatsioonkaebus Tallinna Ringkonnakohtu 30. oktoobri 2019. a otsusele.

Trade unions participate and influence employment, social and education policy also through their involvement in numerous commissions, committees and working groups. In addition to the abovementioned councils of the Unemployment Insurance Fund and the Health Insurance Fund, EAKL and TALO have appointed members sitting, for example, on the Estonian Qualifications Authority Council, the Adult Education Council, the Study on Estonian Labour Market, Today and Tomorrow (OSKA) (applied research surveys on sectoral needs for labour and skills) Coordination Council, and also the Monitoring Committee for the Operational Programme for Cohesion Policy.

At the industry level trade unions give their opinions and provide input to national industry regulation and policy projects and participate in the work of international organizations. In Estonia and internationally, demand for trade union information, consultation and participation is higher than trade union resources effectively allow. Thus, their societal power could be greater if trade unions' capacities were able to grow, but by the same token will decline even further if there is not structural change.

Trade union policies towards the European Union

Even though Estonian trade unions are small and have restricted resources, international cooperation has been active in the direction of the EU, Nordic countries and the other Baltic countries. EAKL is a member of seven EU Commission advisory committees (including Safety and Health at Work, Freedom of Movement for Workers, Social Fund, Social Dialogue), the European Economic and Social Committee and the national boards of EU institutions such as Eurofound, the European Agency for Safety and Health at Work and the European Centre for the Development of Vocational Training.

EAKL cooperates closely with Latvian unions (Free Trade Union Confederation of Latvia) and enjoys slightly looser cooperation with Lithuanian unions (Lithuanian Trade Union Confederation). With Latvia, there are efforts to develop joint learning from best practices. It is harder to find common ground with Nordic countries, whose industrial relations systems are very different from those of the Baltic countries. Nordic trade unions also tend to keep international cooperation within narrow confines, for example in the case of discussions on European minimum wage initiatives.

At industry level industrial unions have their own international activities, which, in turn, are dependent on capacity. With small unions and few employees success depends on the specific persons involved and their abilities. Sometimes there are considerable shortcomings in language skills. Despite their small size, however, Estonian trade unions try to take part in international trade union meetings.

EAKL values cooperation and representation within the European Trade Union Cooperation (ETUC) highly. The ETUC's agenda corresponds to large extent to EAKL's interests, and cooperation and discussions with the European Commission are constructive. The ETUC has also sought support and cooperation together with EAKL from the Estonian government, which has also been important to all parties.

Conclusions

Estonia is a very small country with low trade union membership, and this sets essential limits to the capacity of trade unions. As most trade unions depend almost entirely on union membership contributions, the decline of membership has had a detrimental impact. The movement from small company unions and associations of unions to industry-level organization and industry-level trade unions is an essential development if the potential of trade unionism is to be realized. Even though there are some signs of simplification of trade union structure and some revitalized interest in trade unions among academics, there has not yet been a revival in unionization rates. Although the presence of new unorganized groups of workers has been recorded by trade unionists, efforts to organize these groups have been minimal. At the same time, it must be noted that in Estonia most of 'traditional' employment is not organized.

In addition to the structural shift from company unionism to industry unionism, the mergers of the unions have to happen in order to create capacity for unions to act as capable partners to employers. There is no meaningful reason to keep two trade unions confederations, especially with such an unequal membership, financial and human resources. With small unions resources are scattered and union capability is severely limited.

The future of trade unions depends essentially on the changes that they are able and willing to bring about. Without essential changes to the structure of unions the current situation will continue as it has continued for around ten years now. Some industry unions or professional unions with industry-wide activities have more power and capacity and will continue with their activities as they have done up to now while in the rest of the economy trade unions fade away. Confederal trade unionism in the form of EAKL will continue in its present form because the confederation has an alternative income to union dues and its input is demanded at national and international level. In 2020 there are not yet very clear signs to predict different outcome for trade unions in Estonia than has been the trend for the past ten years. Thus, the gradual phasing out continues or, in terms of Visser's (2019) four possible futures, the marginalization continues.

Acknowledgements

Many thanks are due to Peep Peterson, current EAKL chair, for the interview he granted on 10 July 2020.

References

All links were checked on 14 June 2021.

Carley M. (2009) Trade union membership 2003–2008, Dublin, European Foundation for the Improvement of Living and Working Conditions. http://adapt.it/adapt-indice-a-z/wp-content/uploads/2013/09/eurofound_20091.pdf

EAKL (2019) Majandusaasta aruanne 01.01.2018–31.12.2018 [Annual accounts for the fiscal year]. https://www.eakl.ee/media/2018 EAKL majandusaasta aruanne.pdf

Eesti Teatriliit (2018) Majandusaasta aruanne 01.01.2017-31.12.2017 [Annual accounts for the fiscal year]. http://media.voog.com/0000/0040/2501/files/Majandusaasta%20aruanne%202017.pdf

EMSL (2020) Annual accounts for the fiscal year 01.01.2019–31.12.2019, requested by the author from the Business Register.

ETK (2020) Tööandjad ja ametiühingud teevad ettepaneku alampalk külmutada [Employers' and trade unions' propose to freeze the minimum wage], News, 2 September 2020. https://www.employers.ee/seisukohad/tooandjad-ja-ametiuhingud-teevad-ettepaneku-alampalk-kulmutada/

ETTA (2020) Annual accounts for the fiscal year 01.01.2019–31.12.2019, requested by the author from the Business Register.

Hallemaa H. and Servinski M. (2009) Mittetulundusühendused ja kodanikuühiskonna areng [Non-profit organizations and civil society], Quarterly Bulletin of Statistics Estonia, (1/09), 58–89.

Herm T. (2018) Rakvere lihakombinaadi töötajad lähevad Soome möllama [Employees of Rakvere meat processing plant go to Finland to roam], Virumaa Teataja, 20 February 2018. https://virumaateataja.postimees.ee/4415911/rakvere-lihakombinaadi-tootajad-lahevad-soome-mollama

Järve J. (2019) Eesti ühingute statistiline ülevaade [Statistical overview of Estonian associations]. https://centar.ee/wp-content/uploads/2019/08/2019.06.13-Eesti-%C3%BChingute-statistiline-%C3%BClevaade-l%C3%B5plik-1.pdfDetailed data tables made available by the author

Kaldmäe L. (2017) Kollektiivsed töösuhted [Collective labour relations], in Sotsiaalministeerium (ed.) Eesti tööelu-uuring 2015 [Estonian work-life survey 2015], Tallinn, Sotsiaalministeerium, 64–85. https://www.sm.ee/sites/default/files/content-editors/Ministeerium_kontaktid/Uuringu_ja_analuusid/eesti_tooelu_uuring_2015.pdf

Kallaste E. (2004) Ametiühingute mõju töötingimustele Eestis [Trade union impact on working conditions in Estonia], MA Dissertation 94, Tartu, Faculty of Economics, Institute of Public Economics, Tartu University.

Kallaste E. (2019) Estonia: simultaneous institutionalization and waning of collective bargaining, in Müller T., Vandaele K. and Waddington J. (eds) Collective bargaining in Europe: towards an endgame, ETUI, 173–195.

Lember J. (2020) E-mail from Jüri Lember, Chairman of the Estonian Seamen's Independent Union to the author, 14 December 2020.

Pealinn (2015) Viru hotelli töötajad korraldavad piketi [Viru Hotel employees organise a picket], Pealinn, 18 May 2015. https://pealinn.ee/2015/05/18/viru-hotelli-tootajad-korraldavad-piketi/

Pealinn (2017) Nordea Eesti ametiühing korraldab Rootsi peakorteri juures piketi [The Nordea Estonian trade union is organizing a picket at the Swedish headquarters], Pealinn, 4 January 2017. https://pealinn.ee/?s=Nordea+Eesti+ameti%C3%BChing+korraldab+Rootsi+peakorteri+juures+piketi

Statement by the Secretary of State (2011) Adopted on 01.07.2011, RT III, 09.07.2011, 1. https://www.riigiteataja.ee/akt/309072011001

Taliga H., Kallas S. and Vare T. (2002) 10 aastat sotsiaaldialoogi Eestis [10 Years of Social Dialogue in Estonia], Tallin, Eesti Ametiühingute Keskliit.

TALO (2020) Majandusaasta aruanne 01.01.2019–31.12.2019 [Annual accounts for the fiscal year], requested by the author from the Business Register.

Visser J. (2019) Trade unions in the balance, ILO ACTRAV Working Paper, Geneva, ILO.

Abbreviations

EAKL	Estonian Trade Union Confederation (E*esti Ametiühingute Keskliit)*
EAL	Estonian Doctors Union (*Eesti Arstide Liit*)
EAJ	Estonian Association of Journalists (*Eesti Ajakirjanike Liit*)
EEPU	Estonian Educational Personnel Union (*Eesti Haridustöötajate Liit*)
EMSA	Estonian Seamen's Independent Union (*Eesti Meremeeste Sõltumatu Ametiühing*)
EÕL	Estonian Nurses Union (*Eesti Õdede Liit*)
ESTAL	Estonian Association of Communications and Service Workers' Trade Unions (*Eesti Side- ja Teenindustöötajate Ametiühingute Liit*)
ETK	Estonian Employers' Confederation (*Eesti Tööandjate Keskliit*)
ETKA	Estonian Trade Union of Commercial and Servicing Employees (*Teenindus- ja Kaubandustöötajate Ametiühing*)
ETMAKL	Food and Rural Workers' Trade Union Confederation (*Eesti Toiduainete ja Maatöötajate Ametiühingute Keskliit*)
ETTA	Estonian Transport and Road Workers Trade Union (*Eesti Transordi ja Teetöötajate Ametiühing*)
ETUC	European Trade Union Cooperation
IMTAL	Association of Industrial and Metal Workers' Trade Unions (*Industriaal- ja Metallitöötajate Ametiühingute Liit*)
KLS	Collective Agreements Act (*Kollektiivlepingu seadus*)
LFS	Labour Force Survey
ROTAL	Federation of the Trade Unions of State and Municipal Agencies Employees (*Riigi- ja Omavalitsusasutuste Töötajate Ametiühingute Liit*)

TALO	Estonian Employees' Unions' Confederation (*Teenistujate Ametiliitude Keskorganisatsioon*)
TI	State Labour Inspectorate (*Tööinspektsioon*)
TLS	Employment Contracts Act (*Töölepinguseadus*)
UNIVERSITAS	Federation of the Estonian Universities UNIVERSITAS (*UNIVERSITAS Eesti Kõrgkoolide, Teadus- ja Arendusasutuste Ametiliitude Ühendus*)

Chapter 10

Finland: Trade unions struggling within a Ghent system

Markku Sippola and Tapio Bergholm

Since the year 2000, the Finnish trade union movement has witnessed four key trends: a significant fall in membership, the feminization of membership, a decline in strike activity and the growing assertiveness of employers' organizations in pushing for the decentralization of collective bargaining. The most notable issue here is the fall in union membership. Finnish union membership peaked during the mid-1990s, when unemployment was high and the country was in a deep recession. The main reason for this – comparatively recent – success was the unemployment insurance system associated with unions, the so-called 'Ghent system'. Simultaneously, the profiles of union members have changed since the 1990s, as many potential union members in core positions have opted to join an independent unemployment insurance fund rather than a union. As a consequence, union density declined from its absolute peak of 78.5 per cent in 1994 to around 60 per cent in 2017 (Ahtiainen 2019a). Meanwhile, the General Unemployment Fund (YTK, *Yleinen työttömyys-kassa*), which is not affiliated with trade unions, has gained around half a million members since its establishment in 1991. Paradoxically, because of the universally binding nature of collective agreements, collective bargaining coverage has increased, at the same time as union membership has declined (Ahtiainen 2019b; Table 10.1).

Table 10.1 Principal characteristics of trade unionism in Finland

	1980	2000	2019
Net union membership	1,332,000	1,498,000	1,330,000
Net union density	69 %	74 %	60 %
Women as a proportion of total membership	43 %	46 %*	55 %**
Number of confederations	4	3	3
Collective bargaining coverage	70 %	85 %	89 %***
Principal level of collective bargaining	Centralized	Centralized / industry	Industry
Days not worked due to industrial action per 1,000 workers	442****	124	99***

Notes: * 1998; ** 2013; *** 2017/2018; **** 1990 (there are great annual variations because of the bargaining situation, although the trend is declining).

Sources: Appendix A1; Ahtiainen (2019a: 38; 2019b: 76).

The second key trend is the feminization of the union movement and the decrease in male membership. Although Finland is a dual-earner society, men are in the majority as a proportion of the labour force and employment. Because of developments since the 1990s recession, however, the share of women has increased on both counts. The decrease in male union membership has been larger proportionally than the fall in female membership. Today, the majority of active union members in Finland are female (Table 10.1). The third feature of Finnish unionism is the declining trend of working days lost as a result of industrial action, which indicates less conflictual industrial relations. While during the 1970s and 1980s, Finland had one of the highest high strike rates in Europe, this picture started to change dramatically in the early 1990s when the number of strikes and working days lost decreased substantially and began to resemble average European strike figures (see Table 10.1).

Since 1991, the union movement has been on the defensive and the employers' organizations have become more assertive. Concession bargaining about pensions, unemployment insurance and social security payments have dominated during this period. Whereas labour costs have decreased, social security payments for employees were introduced and have gradually increased. The strategy of employers' organizations to decentralize collective bargaining gained momentum during the concession bargaining period of the 1990s and 2000s. Employers abandoned centralized agreements between confederations, first in principle in 2005 and then in practice in 2017. The Covid-19 pandemic offered employers an opportunity to push for more decentralization and to shift the locus of bargaining to the local level. In autumn 2020, forestry employers decided to abandon collective agreements at the industry level and to opt for company-level bargaining. This was followed by a decision by an influential employers' association, Technology Industries in Finland, (*Teknologiateollisuus ry*) to split into two organizations in March 2021. Since autumn 2021, Technology Industries of Finland has represented only those employers who want to carry out collective bargaining at the local level, while the Employers of Technology Industries (*Teknologiateollisuuden työnantajat ry*) represents those employers who wish to continue industry-level collective agreements. The decision might serve as a precedent for other industries and exacerbate the erosion of the system of centrally binding collective agreements in Finland.

Historical background and principal features of the industrial relations system

Finland's trade union structure derives from a century-long labour market trajectory, from the domination of industry to the proliferation of white-collar professions. After the Second World War, there were three trade union confederations in Finland: the Confederation of Finnish Trade Unions (SAK, *Suomen Ammattiliittojen Keskusjärjestö*), the Confederation of Intellectual Employment (HTK, *Henkisen Työn Keskusliitto*) and the Finnish Confederation of Technical Salaried Employees (STTK, *Suomen Teknisten Toimihenkilöiden Keskusliitto*). A fourth confederation was created in 1950 to represent professional employees with relatively high levels of education and training: the Confederation of Unions for Academic Professionals (AKAVA, *Korkeakoulutettujen Työmarkkinakeskusjärjestö*). In 1956, HTK changed its name to the Federation of Clerical Employees' and Civil Servants' Organizations (TVK, *Toimihenkilö- ja virkamiesjärjestöjen Keskusliitto*). TVK, which at the time was the second largest confederation, went bankrupt in 1992 as a result of failed investments in property and shares. Its largely female-dominated affiliates subsequently joined the largely male-dominated and much smaller STTK. This move not only changed the internal membership structure of STTK but also increased the confederation's influence under its new name the Finnish Confederation of Professionals (preserving the previous acronym, STTK).

SAK, the largest and most powerful confederation, suffered a decade-long split in the 1960s when many unions left the confederation. Some unions remained independent, and some formed a breakaway confederation, the Finnish Trade Union Federation (SAJ, *Suomen Ammattijärjestö*). The division was short, however. In 1969 unification was made possible when SAK changed its statutes and name to become the Central Organization of Finnish Trade Unions (the acronym SAK remained the same). In the new organization the affiliated unions are more independent in taking decisions on collective bargaining and industrial action. Developments within AKAVA have been more stable because it has remained unified throughout its half-century long history. AKAVA is the youngest confederation and the one with the most dynamic membership development. While at the beginning of the 2000s AKAVA was till the smallest of the three confederations, today it represents more members than STTK (see Table 10.2).

The organization of Finnish employers mirrors the structure of Finnish trade unions, with a limited number of confederations to which industry-level associations are affiliated. The currently largest and most influential organization, the Confederation of Finnish Industries (EK, *Elinkeinoelämän keskusliitto*), consists of nineteen industry-level associations representing 15,300 companies, which employ around 900,000 people (EK 2021). EK was established in 2005 as a merger of the Employers' Confederation of the Service Industries (PT, *Palvelutyönantajat*) and the Confederation of Industry and Employers (TT, *Teollisuuden ja Työnantajain Keskusliitto*). TT was itself the result of a merger between the Finnish Confederation of Employers (STK, *Suomen työnantajain keskusliitto*) and the Confederation of Industry (TKL, *Teollisuuden Keskusliitto*) in 1993, which illustrates the process of organizational consolidation on the employer side in the private sector. Today, there are three main employers' (con)federations: EK, the Employers' Organization of Local Authorities (KT, *Kunta- ja hyvinvointialuetyönantajat*) and the Office for the Government as Employer (VTML, *Valtion työmarkkinalaitos*). There is, furthermore, a lobbying organization, the Federation of Finnish Enterprises (SY, *Suomen Yrittäjät*), but this is not a party to collective bargaining (Jonker-Hoffrén 2019).

Finland can be characterized as a representative of the 'Nordic class compromise' prevailing among the labour market parties, manifested in the alliances between social democrats and agrarian parties, as well as the consolidation of collective agreements between employers' and workers' representatives (Kettunen 2001: 145). In Finland, however, the compromise saw its complete fulfilment much later than in the other Nordic countries, where such compromises were reached during the 1930s (see Chapters 4 and 28). The two Employees' Pension Acts in 1961 (*Työntekijäin eläkelaki*), agreed as a result of a tripartite process, laid the foundation of a class compromise between the labour market parties (Bergholm 2009). This can be seen as an overarching feature of unionism in Finland and Nordic societies more generally. The idea of party symmetry was naturally considered to be applied between the labour market parties, however, backed by political parties, the trade unions and employers' associations. Therefore, unions achieved a strong and legitimate role alongside employers' associations (Kettunen 2004: 295). In the heyday of this development, union representatives were even regarded as carriers of 'universal' interests against particular capitalist interests (Kettunen 2004: 295).

The notion of class compromise is reflected in the two central pillars of the Finnish model of industrial relations: national collective agreements and the strong involvement of unions and employers in policy-making on social security for employees. National collective agreements became common after the government wage resolution of 1945. This first pillar of the Finnish model is characterized by strong government involvement in wage formation and policy. During the early 1960s, negotiation relationships improved between labour market organizations and they gained influence. Social security reforms of unemployment insurance (1960), pension schemes for private-sector employees (1961) and guidelines for collective agreements for the years 1961 and 1962 were the result of compromises between STK and SAK. This created the basis for the second pillar of the Finnish model in which the social partners established a strong position in the design of the social security system.

The two pillars of the Finnish model were simultaneously in play after a significant internal devaluation policy was introduced. The first incomes policy agreements in the late 1960s strengthened Finland's competitiveness and improved the operating conditions of the union movement. The incomes policy system can be seen as an institutionalized tripartite arrangement between government, unions and employers, leading to tripartite, centralized agreements (TUPO, *Tulopoliittinen ratkaisu*). In the 1990s, the Finnish state usually saw centralized agreements as a way to limit inflation (Kauppinen 2005), and after joining the euro in 1999 to keep a check on 'competitiveness'. The centralized incomes policy system was, furthermore, seen as a tool for ensuring more peaceful industrial relations and supporting a solidaristic wage policy (Jonker-Hoffrén 2019).

The strong trade union role in the social security system is reflected in the so-called 'Ghent system', under which unions are responsible for the administration of the public unemployment insurance system. This has important implications for unionization (Crouch 1993: 85; D'Agostino 1992: 40).[1] The only countries among the twenty OECD members that managed to increase their union density between the 1970s and early 2000s were countries with a Ghent system: Belgium, Denmark, Finland and Sweden (see Chapters 2, 8 and 28) (OECD 2004: 144; Visser 2006).[2] Since the late 1980s, however, it has been possible for people in Finland to affiliate to an unemployment insurance fund without joining a union. The emergence of independent employment funds was the major factor behind the 10 percentage point decline in union density in Finland between 1993 and 2002 (Böckerman and Uusitalo 2006). The establishment of the General Unemployment Fund in 1992, which was supported by some employers, has contributed to the erosion of union membership in Finland (Bergholm 2012).

Structure of trade unions and union democracy

Currently, there are three trade union confederations in Finland: the industrial union-based SAK, the profession/occupation-based STTK and the academic/occupation-based AKAVA. The union landscape thus has a more or less status-based structure. When it comes to organizational profile, both industrial and professional unions are represented.

---

1 The union administered insurance fund system was adopted as Belgium's national policy, and similar systems were introduced in several European countries prior to the First World War. With the Ghent system, unions were able to carry on the medieval tradition in which guilds assisted and supported their unemployed members by means of so-called gifts or travel benefits (D'Agostino 1992: 40).

2 The Ghent system was adopted in Nordic countries in the following sequence: Norway in 1906, Denmark in 1907, Finland in 1916 and Sweden in 1934, although Norway replaced its prior system with a state insurance system in 1938 (D'Agostino 1992: 40–41).

Table 10.2 Organizational structure and membership of the main confederations, 2020

	Members	Affiliates (membership)
SAK*	880,574	PAM (207,326), Teollisuusliitto (211,801), JHL (181,881), Rakennusliitto (69,060), AKT (43,509), Sähköalojen ammattiliitto (34,663), Paperiliitto (33,826), SEL (30,047), PAU (25,004), Merimies-Unioni (9,056), KEY (7,901), Teme (4,976), IAU (3,939), RAU (3,853), Suomen Muusikkojen Liitto (3,605), SHU (1,625), SSSL (271), Yleinen Lehtimiesliitto (173)
STTK	ca. 500,000	Tehy (160,000), Pro (120,000), SuPer (90,000), Jyty (50,000), ERTO (15,000), Unio (9,000), MVL (3,000), SLPL (1,800), Kirkon alat ry (n.a.), METO (n.a.), RIA (n.a.), SKL (n.a.), SPAL (n.a.), VvL (n.a.), Yhteistyöjäsen Agrologien Liitto (n.a.)
AKAVA	ca. 600,000	Opetusalan Ammattijärjestö OAJ (117,351), Tekniikan akateemiset TEK (72,178), Insinööriliitto IL (69,327), Suomen Ekonomit (53,311), Tradenomiliitto TRAL (31,441), Suomen Lääkäriliitto (27,399), Akavan Erityisalat (26,484), Sosiaalialan korkeakoulutettujen ammattijärjestö Talentia (25,994), Myynnin ja markkinoinnin ammattilaiset MMA (18,950), Suomen Lakimiesliitto (16,045), Luonnon-, ympäristö- ja metsätieteilijöiden liitto Loimu (14,282), Yhteiskunta-alan korkeakoulutetut (12,543), Esimiehet ja Asiantuntijat YTY (11,217), Suomen Poliisijärjestöjen Liitto SPJL (10,942), Kuntoutusalan asiantuntijat (9,336), Suomen Farmasialiitto (7,961), KTK Tekniikan Asiantuntijat (7,835), Suomen Psykologiliitto (7,548), Suomen Hammaslääkäriliitto (7,426), Suomen Terveydenhoitajaliitto (7,143), Tieteentekijöiden liitto (7,130), Upseeriliitto (6,289), Agronomiliitto (6,016), Kirkon Akateemiset AKI (5,272), Ammattiliitto Ava (5,054), DIFF Ingenjörerna i Finland (3,269), Päällystöliitto (3,447), Suomen Eläinlääkäriliitto (2,876), Akavan sairaanhoitajat ja Taja (2,842), Suomen Arkkitehtiliitto SAFA (2,771), Professoriliitto (2,559), Suomen Puheterapeuttiliitto (1,740), Diakoniatyöntekijöiden Liitto DTL (1,685), Suomen Työterveyshoitajaliitto (1,327), Kasvatuksen ja nuorisotyön asiantuntijat KNT (1,072), Akavan Yleinen Ryhmä AYR (749)

Note: * As of 1 January 2020.

Source: SAK https://www.sak.fi/ammattiliitot/jasenliitot/jasenmaarat

As a result of mergers SAK and STTK are dominated by their three largest affiliates (see Table 10.2). In SAK, the Service Union United (PAM, *Palvelualojen ammattiliitto*), the Industrial Union (*Teollisuusliitto*), and the Trade Union for the Public and Welfare Sectors (JHL, *Julkisten ja hyvinvointialojen liitto*), each have about 200,000 members, which combined amounts to more than two-thirds of SAK's membership. PAM was founded in 2000 as a merger of four unions (shop workers' union, hotel and restaurant workers' union, property maintenance workers' union, and technical and special workers' union).[3] The Industrial Union Teollisuusliitto was founded in 2017 from three unions. The biggest of them was the Metalworkers Union, with around 140,000 members, second was Industrial Trade Union, with around 53,000 members (chemical, leather, shoe, rubber, textiles workers and printers), and third was the Wood and Allied Workers Union (*Puuliitto*), with around 33,000. In STTK, the Union of Health and Social Care Professionals in Finland (*Tehy*) is by far the largest affiliate, with 160,000 members. Tehy, with Trade Union Pro (*Ammattiliitto Pro*), representing professionals, experts and managerial staff, and the Finnish Union of Practical Nurses (SUPER, *Suomen lähi- ja perushoitajaliitto*) combined account for about 73 per cent of the employees represented by STTK affiliates.

AKAVA's structure is more heterogeneous. The four largest unions account for some 52 per cent of members represented by the confederation. The biggest union is the Trade Union of Education in Finland (OAJ, *Opettajien ammattijärjestö*), which has united all kinds of teachers under its roof, from kindergartens to vocational training and universities of applied sciences (polytechnics). No fewer than twenty-one unions are affiliated to Akava, with fewer than 10,000 members. With thirty-six affiliates, AKAVA is the confederation with the highest number of affiliated unions.

Many trade unions have abandoned big conferences at which all affiliated locals have at least one representative. Instead of these conferences there are elections to union councils (*edustajisto*) by secret ballot. Councils elect presidents and boards of unions. The biggest and most powerful unions in SAK, STTK and AKAVA have this council election system as their union democracy structure.

---

3 Liikealan ammattiliitto, Hotelli- ja ravintolahenkilökunnan liitto (HRHL), Kiinteistötyöntekijäin liitto (KTTL) and Teknisten- ja erikoisammattien liitto (Tekeri).

The three trade union confederations dominate the union landscape in Finland. Independent unions outside the confederations have a small proportion of total membership and miniscule influence over collective bargaining outcomes and other matters. The most notable independent union is the Union of Journalists (*Journalistiliitto*), which has nearly 14,000 members. It was formerly a member of the professional employees' confederation (at that time TVK) but was expelled in 1974 because of its refusal to support a general strike.

Unionization

Trade union membership peaked during the mid-1990s, when unemployment was high and the country was in a deep recession. The main reason for this comparatively recent success was the Ghent-style unemployment insurance system associated with unions. After this peak, union density declined from 78.5 per cent (1994) to around 60 per cent (2017). Another trend is the feminization of union membership. Finland is a dual-earner society. As a proportion of the labour force and employment men are in the majority, but since the recession in the 1990s the proportion of women has increased on both counts. The decrease of the male union membership rate has been proportionally larger than the decline of the female membership rate. Today, based on Finanssivalvonta's (2020) figures, the majority of union members (57 per cent) active in the labour force are women.

Table 10.3 Gender composition of union confederations, 2019

	SAK	STTK	AKAVA	Independent
Women	254,538	282,394	275,066	11,728
Men	298,207	93,656	214,094	7,160
Women	46.0 %	75.1 %	56.2 %	62.1 %
Men	54.0 %	24.9 %	43.8 %	37.9 %

Note: Aggregate numbers are different from Table 10.2. These numbers concern trade union members in the labour force, while Table 10.2 presents total membership figures.

Source: Finassivalvonta (2020).

In 2020, trade union membership was more female and more formally educated than 20 or 30 years previously. The decline in aggregate membership has been greatest among blue-collar workers. This has particularly affected SAK, which mainly organizes blue-collar workers and therefore recorded a decrease in membership. STTK, by contrast, mainly has members with college or university of applied sciences degrees and a high proportion of female members (see Table 10.3). The share of total union membership organized by STTK has remained fairly stable even though actual numbers have declined. AKAVA, which was traditionally the confederation of people with university degrees has gained new strength as a consequence of the structural shift in employment (see Table 10.4). Today, AKAVA is competing with STTK for professionals with lower qualifications (Ahtiainen 2019a; Finanssivalvonta 2020)

Table 10.4 Members represented by confederations, 2006, 2009 and 2019

	SAK	STTK	AKAVA	Independent	Total
2006	798,817	471,325	392,328	13,917	1,676,387
2009	757,250	468,431	415,479	13,694	1,654,854
2019	552,745	376,050	489,160	18,888	1,436,843
2006	47.7 %	28.1 %	23.4 %	0.8 %	
2009	45.8 %	28.3 %	25.1 %	0.8 %	
2019	38.5 %	26.2 %	34.0 %	1.3 %	

Note: Trade union members in labour force.

Source: Finanssivalvonta (2020).

There are several reasons for the decreasing attachment to unions. While in the 1970s, union attachment coincided with a clear increase in union power in society and active participation of unions in strike movements and party politics, the attachment of subsequent generations of workers has been much more instrumental (Kevätsalo 2005: 34).[4] Trade unions are not as attractive to young people. The problem is clearly seen in union membership statistics. Research on youth activity in Trade Union Pro shows that activities organized by the union compete with other uses of free time (Lönnqvist-Ahvonen 2019). Long working hours

4 Also Bruun (1990: 31) argues that membership of a union does not necessary imply any political inclination, for the trade unions have been transformed from a fighting organization (army) to a social security institution (church) and a defender of workers' rights (solicitor's office), and consequently, a worker can bear in mind any of these functions when affiliated to unions.

and family life need to be reconciled, which does not leave much room for other activities, except for particularly interesting ones; moreover, there appears to be little knowledge among workers of the events organized by the union.

In fact, the fall in trade union membership since the 1990s is partly the result of potential members opting for the independent unemployment insurance fund YTK rather than joining unions. For many wage-earners, unemployment insurance associated with union membership long provided an incentive for joining a union. There seems to be an overall trend of trade union membership falling, while membership of union-administered or other unemployment funds has remained at the same level (Ahtiainen 2019a: 12). Much of the diminishing commitment to unions is related to the establishment of the YTK in 1991, which made it possible to join an unemployment fund without joining a union. The declining trend in union membership since the mid-1990s, associated with the rising popularity of 'independent unemployment funds' has been noted in other studies (e.g. Böckerman and Uusitalo 2006). In 2019, the YTK had around 470,000 members, which corresponded to about 20 per cent of wage-earners (Finanssivalvonta 2020) and closely corresponds to the drop in union membership between 1994 and 2017 mentioned above.

Furthermore, unions have not been able to attract young workers (Ahtiainen 2019a: 49–50); nor have they been able to fully grasp the needs of marginal groups of workers, such as freelancers, zero-hours workers, agency workers, (bogus) self-employed and migrant workers, the kinds of groups utilized in outsourced labour processes and peripheral segments of the labour market. The unionization of migrant workers in Finland has remained low. For example, in the construction industry, which has been strongly unionized, with generally a 70 per cent unionization rate, union density among migrant workers was still at 12–14 per cent in 2012 (Alho 2013). As parts of work processes are outsourced and supply chains lengthened, the grip of grassroots shop stewards and work safety officials on workplaces has weakened in construction and manufacturing, while they have always been relatively weak in the service sector.

In previous decades, Finnish unions have benefitted from a high-density passive recruitment environment rather than unions actively organizing workers. To encourage more active union engagement, not just passive union membership, some Finnish unions have adopted the 'organizing model' typical of some other European countries. The organizing model entails stimulating activism and mobilizing existing union members, as well as targeted organizing campaigns in workplaces. For example, the Finnish Metalworking Union Metalliliitto has adopted organizing model tactics, while the Service Union PAM has arranged organizer training and activities in accordance with the principles of the organizing model (Kall et al. 2019).

Union income and expenditure

The decline in membership made affiliated unions more critical of spending by their confederations. A case in point is the decision at the SAK Congress in 2016 to cut the membership fee of affiliates to the confederation from 7 per cent of net membership fee income to 6 per cent. Trade union financial resources are concentrated within the nationally affiliated unions, not the confederations. The confederations are dependent on fees from affiliates, although in some years their capital gains or profits from investments can be substantial.

Unions have favourable tax treatment in two ways. First, membership fees of unions are tax-deductible because the state considers that unions by their very nature develop their members' skills and professional ability. Second, the capital income of all non-governmental organizations (NGOs), non-profit foundations and common-good organizations is tax-free. This increases the income of unions, which are non-profit NGOs according to Finnish law.

Unions obtain their income mainly from membership fees. Some unions have large investment portfolios because they have accumulated strike funds over several decades. The profits from these investments vary quite a lot. For example, the Industrial Union, OAJ and Pro had good returns on their investments in 2018 when a social housing company originally owned by the unions went public on the stock exchange.

Membership fees normally have two components: first the fee for the union and second the fee to the unemployment fund. In many national unions this combined membership fee increased during the crisis of the 1990s but decreased gradually in later decades. This development was halted during the Finnish recession decade of 2008–2017. The basis of membership fees varies substantially. Unions affiliated to SAK collect about 1.2–1.6 per cent of members' gross salary. Within AKAVA, OAJ has the same system, but membership fees in many other unions affiliated to AKAVA consist of a fixed sum instead. There are also mixed arrangements for membership fees. For example, Pro collects 1.25 per cent of income but a maximum of €49 per month, including the contribution to the unemployment insurance scheme.

The overview of the income and expenditure of TEHY, one of the largest unions, provided in Table 10.5 gives an example of union finances more generally. The union has increased its membership in recent decades and is one of the flagships of the feminization of the Finnish trade union movement. It is to some extent exceptional as it can cover all expenditures from its own general income. Some unions with declining membership use investment earnings to cover their running costs. Personnel, operations and office expenses are the biggest items of expenditure in TEHY's accounts, as well as they are at other Finnish unions. As Table 10.5 illustrates, income from investments fluctuates strongly.

Table 10.5 Income and expenditure ('000 euros), TEHY, 2018 and 2019

	2018	**2019**
General income (mainly membership fees)	26,064	27,390
Income from activities	792	878
Personnel	–10,910	–11,464
Operation expenses	–10,115	–9,450
Office expenses	–2,846	–2,598
Office space expenses	–1,010	–1,007
Income from strike fund investment	6,479	25,654
Result for the financial year	7,850	28,790

Source: TEHY Financial statement 2020, https://www.tehy.fi/system/files/mfiles/muu_dokumentti/tehyn_tilinpaatos_vuodelta_2019_id_14877.pdf

Collective bargaining and unions at the workplace

Finland has a tradition of centralized bargaining, with negotiations at the cross-industry, confederational level. Employers' and trade union confederations have been active in a number of social policy areas, but one of the main activities was the negotiation of tripartite centralized income agreements (TUPOs, *Tulopoliittiset kokonaisratkaisut*). These were concluded regularly between 1968 and 2007 and were the backbone of the Finnish bargaining model. The government introduced the first version of TUPOs in 1967 (Bergholm 2007: 391). TUPOs were essentially framework agreements for bargaining at the industry level (Böckerman and Uusitalo 2006; Malmberg 2002: 194).[5] Besides serving as agreements between union confederations and employers' associations, TUPOs involved the government and the Bank of Finland, and were aimed at coordinating wage policy, tax and other matters. TUPOs were a form of political exchange because, in addition to bargaining guidelines, they included state guarantees for farmers' income development, government promises to introduce new social policy reforms and sometimes development projects in housing and day care for children below school age. As the era of centralized income policy agreements began, many features of the 'Nordic model' became a reality in Finland (Kettunen 2004: 299).

More recently, collective bargaining has become more decentralized. In 2015, EK made a unilateral decision that it would no longer take part in TUPOs. Although tripartite TUPOs have been buried, bipartite centralized income agreements have been concluded subsequently. In 2016, after being pressurized by a newly elected centre-right government, the peak-level unions and employers' organizations agreed on a 'competitiveness pact', which de facto set up inferior labour conditions compared with earlier bargaining rounds. This was the first such occurrence in Finland's industrial relations history. Centralized wage coordination is regarded as an important tool for maintaining price competitiveness among companies in Finland, which, as a member of the euro zone, cannot resort to currency devaluation. This means that wage drift in certain industries can harm the country's price competitiveness. That is why the export industry–led 'Finnish model' of industrial bargaining has gained ground. The bargaining pattern is characterized nowadays as 'centralized decentralization', indicating that the dominant level of negotiations has shifted from the general confederal level to industry-level 'pattern bargaining', driven by export sector organizations (Jonker-Hoffrén 2019: 197).

The Finnish model of collective bargaining nowadays corresponds to the two-tier bargaining model typical of the other Nordic countries

---

5 The Communist 'minor wing' of the Finnish trade union movement did not at first agree to generally binding centralized collective agreements. Their catchphrase was 'Down with incomes policy, down with concessions of class!' [*Alas tulopolitiikka, alas luokkasopu!*] (Koskela 2019: 7).

(Dølvik and Marginson 2018). An industry-level collective agreement sets the national standard and wage increases, as well as laying down procedural and economic guidelines for local or firm-level pay arrangements. These higher-level 'distributive' negotiations run parallel with workplace-level 'partnership' codetermination processes (Sippola 2012). In other words, a single channel system – via trade unions and shop stewards – prevails in Finland, while workplace cooperation on technical and organizational issues is carried out with union shop stewards or other employee representatives.

There are some voices in employers' associations that support shifting the locus of bargaining even further to the local level. A practical move towards this goal occurred in October 2020, when Finnish Forest Industries (*Metsäteollisuus*), the employers' federation for forestry, which is not affiliated to any employers' confederation, announced that it would shift negotiations from the industry to the local level. The federation's decision came as a surprise to other labour market parties in Finland, including other employers' associations. To some extent Technology Industries of Finland (*Teknologiateollisuus*) has made a similar move. These breaks have been warmly welcomed by the Federation of Finnish Enterprises (SY, *Suomen Yrittäjät*), which regarded such a development as natural and self-evident. It is yet to be seen whether and within what timeframe this decision will be followed by similar announcements by other employers' associations. Forestry is, after all, an industry in which collective bargaining already largely takes place at the local level, whereas in other industries such a tendency has been less prominent.

Collective agreements in Finland are universally binding. In 1970, the extension mechanism – which makes an agreement generally applicable – was introduced into Finnish labour law. After the conclusion of a private-sector collective agreement, the parties are obliged to send it to an Extension Committee (*yleissitovuuden vahvistamislautakunta*), operating independently under the Ministry of Social and Health Affairs, whose task it is to judge whether the agreement can be extended to the whole industry (Jonker-Hoffrén 2019: 204). Public sector collective agreements are, by definition, already extended to all civil servants without such a procedure (Jonker-Hoffrén 2019: 250). Employers that are unorganized in terms of collective bargaining also have to comply with the national agreements of their industry. At around 89 per cent, the coverage of Finnish collective agreements is not only very high but also remarkably stable in European comparison (Ahtiainen 2019b).

In recent years, EK and the business-promoting lobbying organization SY have often criticized the extension mechanism. They have, for example, proposed the inclusion of continental European-style opening clauses in industry agreements. Such clauses have not been implemented directly, although it is now possible to introduce more limited 'survival clauses' with the consent of unions and employers at industry level (Jonker-Hoffrén 2019: 205). A survival clause can materialize in local-level negotiations, conditions for which are set up in the industry-level agreement, for a limited time period.

Topics open to local-level bargaining are stipulated in the industry-level agreement except for wages, which are regarded as minimum wages for the industry. Wage bargaining above the minimum level is possible and widely used in manufacturing (Jonker-Hoffrén 2019: 212). EK and, especially, SY have promoted extension of the scope of local bargaining to companies that are not members of employers' associations and to non-unionized worker representatives. The goal of such proposals is to invest individual firms with the power to set local wage levels, and to eliminate the national minimum wage–setting mechanism based on industry-level agreements. Despite strong lobbying by SY, the proposals have not materialized in amendments to labour legislation.

Even though collective bargaining coverage is nearly 90 per cent, however, it is realistic to ask how the conditions of workers not covered by agreements are defended. These include workers who are insufficiently covered by agreements: for example zero-hours or posted workers. A step towards wider coverage of collective agreements for posted workers was the 2015 *Sähköalojen ammattiliitto vs Elektrobudowa* ruling by the European Court of Justice, which underscored the legitimacy of legally binding agreements to cover posted workers in Finland. On the other hand, clauses concerning zero-hours contracts have appeared belatedly in service sector collective agreements, which raises concerns that collective agreements are not keeping pace with the conditions prevailing in new forms of work (Sippola et al. forthcoming). The new types of work are so far of minor significance in the labour market, and the main types of worker not covered by collective agreements are in private-sector professional groups, such as accountants, fitness centre workers, beauticians/cosmeticians, commercial work and veterinary clinics.

International trade union initiatives concerning green jobs and just transition have gained some visibility by means of proclamations by

Finnish confederations and larger trade unions, but they have not really been integrated into the bargaining agenda. Similarly, the issue of the gender wage gap has not achieved a high profile, except for the health care unions in recent bargaining rounds. This may be explained partly by Finnish unions' defensive posture, as employers have become more assertive in pushing their agendas. During this power struggle such 'new' issues have not achieved priority. When it comes to the labour market effects of digitalization, Finnish unions are likely to be pragmatic in the sense that industries affected by digital transformation have already been subject to restructuring; old jobs have been destroyed and new ones created, and the Finnish labour force has been sufficiently flexible and versatile.

Industrial conflict

During the term of an agreement, employers and unions are obliged to enforce industrial peace. Industrial action concerning matters settled in collective agreements represents a breach of the agreement and the Labour Court (*Työtuomioistuin*) can impose fines on employers or trade unions in such cases. In extreme cases the Labour Court can annul the whole collective agreement if a party to the agreement continuously violates the peace obligation by taking industrial action. The national mediation system, which is peculiar to the Nordic industrial relations model more generally, deals with disputes over collectively bargained labour conditions. The Finnish National Mediator (*Valtakunnansovittelija*) is based on an analogous system of dispute settlement, although it holds somewhat wider powers than its Swedish counterpart (Elvander 2002). In Finland, if a dispute settlement procedure begins, the parties to the issue are obliged to participate, but there is no obligation to reach an agreement.

The 1970s saw a proliferation in the number of strikes in Finland. At the time, Finland was among those European countries with the most working days lost due to industrial action. Most of the strikes were 'wild cat' and locally based. Particularly sensitive to industrial action was the metal industry, which was under considerable pressure to raise wages as they lagged behind those in Sweden (Koskela 2019: 66). A prominent example of the wide effect of strikes was the seven-week 1971 metal industry strike, leading to implementation of holiday compensation (*lomaltapaluurahat*), which was later also introduced in other industry agreements.

The dynamics of industrial relations have changed substantially since the 1970s and 1980s, when there were still some 'low trust' elements in Finnish industrial relations, leading to a high strike incidence compared with other Nordic countries (Kettunen 2004: 292). In the early 1990s, the number of strikes and working days lost decreased dramatically (Figure 10.1), largely corresponding to average European figures (Koskela 2019: 71). The economic crisis in the early 1990s and permanent high levels of unemployment even after the crisis prompted a 'new realism' in unions. Since the beginning of the 2000s, employers' organizations have been more assertive and the unions mainly in a defensive position during bargaining rounds and in public debates about changes concerning the social wage, especially pensions. This low level of industrial conflict persists today. There is still some fluctuation in the number of strikes and lockouts and the number of working days lost, but the peaks are much lower than in the 1970s and 1980s (see Figure 10.1).

The patterns and tactics of industrial conflict have changed over the past twenty years. Most recent strikes have been short. Many strikes are demonstrations without any concrete demands. They are sympathy strikes, when employers start so-called 'change negotiations' about dismissals. At the end of these negotiations the number of redundancies is announced. Sympathy strikes also occur when employers close down factories or other workplaces for good. These sympathy strikes are a ritualistic way of showing solidarity with your workmates without any intention of influencing the outcome (Bergholm 2017).

As part of collective bargaining, trade unions have introduced German-style short warning strikes. Some of these have been successful, but when the Paper Workers Union (*Paperiliitto*) carried out a warning strike in 2005, employers in the paper industry responded with a long lockout. The employers have learned to respond to short warning strikes with equally short and painful targeted lockouts. Political demonstration strikes are legal in Finland and during the period of a right-wing government 2015–2019 there were several of them. Some involved masses of workers meeting in the capital Helsinki, although proper general strikes did not take place.

Figure 10.1 Working days lost and number of conflicts, 1970–2019

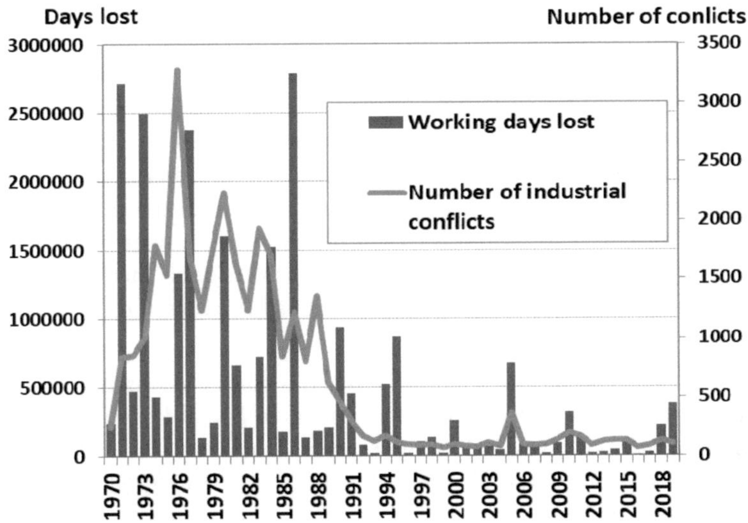

Source: Statistics Finland.

Since the 1990s, politically oriented strikes have generally been publicly condemned in Finland. A comparison of expressions of public opinion regarding two strikes – the 1991 Transport Workers' Union's (AKT, *Auto- ja Kuljetusalan työntekijäliitto*) dockworkers' strike and TEHY's 2007 industrial action in health and social care – shows that the majority, especially young people, supported the latter as long as it did not become associated with partisan politics (Koskela 2019: 31–32). The former, however, was perceived negatively by a majority of respondents mainly because of Finland's poor economic situation and the overt rationale of the strike as a protest against the government. More recently, however, politically oriented strikes have received a more positive reception. A mass demonstration organized by SAK, STTK and many affiliates of AKAVA against the Finnish government's allegedly worker-hostile policies in September 2015 gained wide public acceptance. The media coverage, which supported low-paid female-dominated occupations, was mainly positive towards the demonstrators. A similar phenomenon was witnessed in the mass demonstration called by SAK against the government-imposed 'active employment model' in February 2018.

Political relations

All trade union confederations and their affiliates in Finland are officially politically independent. In practice this means that organizational structures are not based on party affiliation. Many unions and confederations, however, have historically had close direct links to various parties, which have gradually loosened over time. The de-politicization of union organizations has occurred at the level of the confederations more than at the affiliated union level; for example, SAK no longer recruits officials on a political basis but rather recruits professionals meritocratically. Simultaneously, political youth organizations have ceased to serve as talent pools for the unions.

Political division lines still matter when it comes to unions' representative structures. Within SAK, the members of Social Democratic Party (*Sosialidemokraatit*) clearly dominate and the majority of SAK affiliates are led by Social Democrats. The Left Alliance (*Vasemmistoliitto*) is the other major player in SAK and its affiliates. According to recent surveys, the populist immigration-opposing party the Finns Party (*Perussuomalaiset*) has gained more union support than the Left Alliance measured as a proportion of the membership. In AKAVA the strongest party is the conservative National Coalition Party (*Kokoomus*). Until the 1990s, the social democrats and conservatives were nearly equally strong in STTK, but gradually the social democrats have gained the upper hand in the largest unions affiliated to STTK. As the membership of AKAVA has increased proportionally, the National Coalition Party has gained a stronger position within affiliated trade unions than the Left Alliance.

The strength of the National Coalition Party in the Finnish union movement is interesting. It has weakened ties between left-wing parties and union members. On the other hand, conservative union leaders and members have some influence on the policies of the National Coalition Party. For instance, employers were frustrated when 'their own party' supported special wage increases for nurses in 2007 and this very same party was then unwilling to support EK's proposals to change labour law.

Since 1990 there have been a few moments when industrial relations in Finland were put to a test. At the beginning of the 1990s, the economic depression, the centre-right government and the fall of the Soviet Union inspired the employers' federation to demand a complete revision of the whole industrial relations system. That time, the Finnish Employers' Confederation (STK, *Suomen Työnantajain Keskusliitto*) proposed a new agreement policy. Prime Minister Esko Aho (Centre Party, *Keskusta*) proposed replacing the tripartite model of cooperation between the government, the employers' associations and trade unions with a new division of labour in which the Bank of Finland would be responsible for monetary policy and interest rates, the government for fiscal policy and the labour market organizations only for wages. The depth of the recession, the heterogeneity of the employers' federations and the difference between export industry and domestic market prevented the STK from pushing through its proposed policy. In the pre-euro era, devaluations restored export competitiveness. A profound change in the labour market system seemed to disappear from the employers' arsenal of strategic goals, as the Social Democratic Party returned to government in 1995 after success in the general elections.

The early 2000s saw relatively stable economic development in Finland, and trade union political relations remained relatively unchanged. Most trade union members identified with particular political parties, as was the case in previous decades: Social Democratic Party and Left Alliance members maintained relationships with SAK-affiliated unions, and National Coalition Party members with AKAVA (Tiihonen 2015). The Finns Party, a new party in the Finnish political arena, generated a strong attachment among members of unions affiliated to SAK and STTK. The government party coalition had a direct effect on whether employers' organizations or trade unions were able to influence the government programme. An employers' confederation EK managed to include many of their goals in the programme of the 2007 right-wing government, whereas SAK and STTK influenced the programme of the 2011 multi-party (so-called 'sixpack') coalition.

There were particular antagonisms between Finnish trade unions and the government under Juha Sipilä's prime ministership in 2015–2019, as the right-wing government proposed emergency legislation if certain concessions were not made during the centralized bargaining round in 2015–2016. The government advocated 'competitiveness' and 'austerity' policies, which had repercussions for the industrial relations atmosphere (Jonker-Hoffrén 2019: 200). In autumn 2015, the three trade union confederations SAK, STTK and AKAVA organized a mass demonstration against the proposed legislation, in which 300,000 workers gathered around Finland. Ultimately, Finnish trade union confederations and employers' associations regarded it as a lesser evil to conclude a 'competitiveness pact' than to accept the government's proposal to cut social and employment subsidies. The pact signified a 4 per cent decrease in labour costs; it also included clauses alleviating company-level collective bargaining (ibid.). The tensions between the Sipilä government and unions remained until the end of the government. In spring 2018, when the government proposed a new unemployment subsidy scheme, SAK once again organized a demonstration of 10,000 workers against the proposal.

Union confederations still have much negotiating power concerning social policy: for example, on pensions, unemployment insurance and parental leave. This power is connected to the tradition of tripartite negotiations on legislation in these fields (Bergholm 2009). Although tripartite centralized incomes policy agreements, TUPOs, have been officially rejected by the employers' associations, labour market parties engage in activities closely resembling TUPOs in times of crisis. The competitiveness pact of 2016 was a manifestation of that, and even more so the 'crisis package' in spring 2020. When the Covid-19 pandemic began in March 2020, the government asked union confederations and employers' confederations to sketch a labour market policy package to avoid unemployment and bankruptcies. The resulting proposal that involved a temporary decrease in employers' pension fees, postponing the payment of pension insurance fees, temporary flexibilization of dismissals, furlough procedures and temporary strengthening of the subsistence of laid-off persons, was in large part approved by the government.

Societal power

Especially in Anglo-Saxon countries, unions have sought revitalization by establishing new coalitions with other social movements, to compensate for the loss of power resources connected with national collective bargaining and policymaking (Ibsen and Tapia 2017). For Finnish unions policymaking in different arenas and collective bargaining still play a dominant role compared with the development of new forms of activity in the face of a declining membership base. Attention has been directed, however, towards retaining and gaining new members, particularly young people and male blue-collar workers.

Besides shaping the public image of institutions, media visibility and social media campaigns are capable of influencing public debates. Hence, public campaigning may influence the power positions of labour market parties, and eventually state-level regulation. Finnish trade unions have lately become active in publicizing their negotiation goals. One such campaign with broad publicity was the nurses' industrial action in 2007, in which nurses made a strong argument against the low levels of wage compensation they saw as embedded in societal structures. The action made visible the vested interests of different stakeholders within the corporatist regime (Koskinen-Sandberg and Saari 2019).

While Finnish labour market parties have traditionally been regarded as backward in relation to gender equality issues, they have assumed a new role in enhancing gender equality by participating in debates on equality issues within and outside tripartite negotiations (Elomäki et al. 2019). Of the trade union confederations, SAK has pointed out structural biases and discrimination and AKAVA has paid attention to individuals and prevailing attitudes. On the employers' side, proposals concerning gender equality have been rarer. A remarkable contribution to the debate on gender equality from the latter, however, was a 2017 EK model for reforming family leave schemes (ibid.).

In terms of themes or agendas in public campaigning, individual trade unions have been active in putting forward the interests of vulnerable groups, such as part-time workers, zero-hours workers and immigrants. One example is the cooperation between the service union PAM and an activist food couriers' rights network 'Justice for Couriers' (*Oikeutta läheteille*). The network regards its interests as being close to the unions, with the consequence that it has expressed the aim of attracting couriers to labour unions such as PAM (Saksela-Bergholm 2021). Also, Finnish trade unions affiliated to AKAVA, SAK and STTK have established a network entitled 'Itset' with the aim of ensuring improved rights for self-employed workers, such as freelancers. The network aims to revise Finnish competition law to allow self-employed workers to negotiate their labour conditions and compensation collectively (Ilsøe et al. 2020).

Finnish unions have been active in collaboration with NGOs on the issue of corporate social responsibility (CSR). In 2018 the Trade Union Solidarity Centre of Finland SASK (on this organization, see next section) announced a campaign 'To the Starting Lineup' (*Ykkösketjuun*) with seventy other civil society organizations to highlight Finnish corporations' CSR. Furthermore, SASK and a number of Finnish human rights and environmental NGOs support the work of a corporate global conduct reporting organization, Finnwatch. Although Finnish trade unions regard the concept of CSR itself as vague, they take the phenomena revolving around it seriously in their public campaigning, and they have managed to involve business partners in jointly organized media events on decent work (Lämsä and Viljanen 2014).

A new arena for societal discussion is participation in social media debates. A survey study of thirty-four trade unions on their use of social media found that it had not become a consolidated communication channel, nor had social media been taken as an element of strategic planning for union communication (Jouppi 2016). Nevertheless, social media and other media have played a role in various campaigns that unions have taken part in, such as 'The Kingdom of Free People' (*Vapaiden valtakunta*) the goal of which was to advocate more a worker-friendly political direction in Finland, and 'Let's Behave' (*Ollaan ihmisiksi*) to change clients' attitudes to become friendlier towards salespeople. Some progress has been evidenced since the beginning of the 2000s, when few initiatives were taken by unions to use Information and Communications Technology (ICT) to strengthen interaction and community spirit (Aalto-Matturi 2005). Clearly, the internet has not developed into a new 'Workers' Hall' or 'Community Hall' of the union movement.

Trade unions are still in the phase of experimenting with the new channels of influence and making innovations in recruiting new members on these grounds. The involvement of the service sector union PAM in the Finnish Big Brother programme created a sensation in 2010, as a union official was prepared to drop young people from the Big Brother house for seeking employment. The idea for this came from the observation that the PAM's potential membership base includes those who watch reality TV shows. Worth noting is also the Finnish industrial union's 'The Man from the Union' campaign in 2019, a TV advertisement in which a trade union member defended a young shop customer 'Niko' in various situations. This campaign evoked massive criticism from EK affiliates. Similarly in 2020, when a few unions supported the '430 million' campaign directed at preventing tax avoidance among Finnish firms, it provoked critical comments mainly among business circles. These examples illustrate that the unions have lately become involved in societal debates and have managed to provoke reactions from employers, in a manner that has made people recognize that there are divergent interests among the labour market parties.

Trade union policies towards the European Union

International cooperation among Finnish trade unions is at a modest level, focussing on Nordic, European Union and international arenas.

Nordic unions are passive in cross-national union action compared with their continental and Southern European counterparts (Larsson et al. 2012). This may be because of their sceptical stance towards the confederalist ambitions of giving power to the European Trade Union Confederation (ETUC) to negotiate on behalf of their members. Finnish, and overall Nordic, cooperation with the ETUC is at an average level, below that of Austria, Belgium, Germany and Spain. Confederations are the most frequent partners for influencing EU policies; also manufacturing sector unions are more engaged than the others in transnational cooperation (Larsson et al. 2012).

Union confederations have adopted different profiles in their attitudes towards workers' transnational mobility. They have acted as gatekeepers in the country's immigration politics, and SAK has sought to prevent labour immigration from non-EU or EEA countries (Alho 2015). Yet, STTK and AKAVA have pursued less protectionist policy attitudes towards labour immigration. The stance of Finnish union confederations towards EU-level labour mobility has thus been somewhat more conservative than in other Nordic countries. In another EU policy-related matter, the 2019/2020 European minimum wage initiative, Finnish confederations have assumed a deviant stance compared with their Nordic neighbours. Collective bargaining is seen in the Nordic countries as a more effective means of gaining better results for workers than statutory minimum wages (Furåker 2020). For example, SAK supported the minimum wage initiative as long as it acknowledges the features of the Finnish bargaining system, while other Nordic unions were more categorically against the idea. Therefore, the Finnish confederations do not consider the EU's minimum wage initiative as being at odds with the Finnish system of collective bargaining.

A natural framework for cooperation has traditionally been the Nordic region, in which the Council of Nordic Trade Unions has played a major role. Nordic cooperation became even more coordinated in the aftermath of Denmark, Finland and Sweden joining the EU (Helander 2008). Finnish unions' transnational cooperation in many international and European issues has occurred mainly within a Nordic framework. These issues were related to institutional cooperation within the International Labour Organization, World Trade Organization and matters concerning European Works Councils (ibid.).

In 1986, the SAK founded the Trade Union Solidarity Centre of Finland (SASK), which became the solidarity and development cooperation organization for Finnish trade unions. Nowadays, two confederations (SAK and STTK), as well as thirty-five unions are affiliated members, paying either 1 per cent for confederations or 0.1 per cent of membership fees to SASK. Contrary to the union confederations of the other Nordic countries, the Finnish SAK urged its members to use their right to vote to join the EU in 1994 (Boldt 2008: 39–40). In general, SAK has been for multilateral trade systems and a gradual liberalization of global trade, while opposing protectionism (Boldt 2008: 43).

Finnish unions have also been active in Estonia. Their contacts with Estonian counterparts are probably as intense as with those from Denmark, Norway and Sweden (Helander 2008). In the 1990s, Finnish unions tended to regard their system as a superior model to be emulated by the weaker labour movements in the Baltic states. Finnish-Estonian cooperation evolved under various EU initiatives, the Baltic Sea Trade Union Network (BASTUN) and bilateral initiatives (Kall et al. 2019). Lately, cooperation has developed from ad hoc bilateral joint action into a more coherent organizing campaign in the context of the Baltic Organizing Academy (BOA). Activities in the Baltic area must be seen against the backdrop of the potential threat of the Baltic neoliberal regime and its labour market consequences for the future of Finnish industrial relations. The proximity of an almost trade union free zone in close proximity, combined with the expectation of a massive influx of Estonian immigrant workers in Finland after Estonia joined the EU in 2004 have, in all likelihood, contributed to Finnish-Estonian joint projects and organizing efforts.

Transnational solidarity, as essential as it would prove in the common European market, is difficult to embed among Finnish trade unions, as there is a historical trajectory of national compromise and a nation-level basis for union membership. Difficulties in engaging in transnational cooperation were seen at the Olkiluoto 3 construction site, operated by a French-German consortium Areva-Siemens, when Polish posted workers sought help from various organizations, including the Finnish Construction Trade Union (*Rakennusliitto*) and the European Migrant Workers' Union. The inaction on the part of the Finnish union, as the Poles experienced it, raised questions concerning the ethnocentric character of Finnish unions (Lillie and Sippola 2011).

One possible answer to the inability of the Finnish unions to look after posted workers at the time was the European Court of Justice (ECJ) ruling on the *Laval un Partneri* case, which led to a hesitance to demand wage increases for posted workers (Lillie and Sippola 2011). The 2015 ECJ ruling on the *Sähköalojen ammattiliitto vs. Elektrobudowa* case, however, prompted the Finnish unions to use their power to demand the extension of national collective agreements also to posted workers.

Conclusions

A Nordic-type 'class compromise' characterizes the Finnish trade union movement in the post-War era, although recent decades have witnessed signs of disintegration. In line with the other Nordic countries, Finland's unions have been deeply involved in tripartite negotiations on various policy issues, most notably social policy. A distinctive feature of the Finnish industrial relations system was the era of TUPOs, high-level tripartite packages that not only included incomes policy, but also penetrated other areas of industrial, social and employment policies. Such agreements were concluded almost uninterruptedly from 1968 to 2007, when EK's withdrawal marked the end of the system.

The societal power of the Finnish labour market parties has remained strong, although the forms of influence have changed: processes that were once carried out in a rather non-transparent way behind closed doors have become more visible. The power resources that the parties used to employ no longer remain unquestioned, but need to be legitimated in public discussions, lobbying and campaigning. One might wonder whether the unilateral arena of influence has taken precedence over the traditional bilateral and tripartite arenas (see Ilsøe 2017), as a result of which labour market parties increasingly seek to influence legislation from their own perspective, thereby undermining the processes of collective bargaining and social dialogue. This development is rather alarming from a trade union point of view. Business organizations' lobbying networks at Finnish ministries and government bodies are denser than those of trade unions (Hirvola et al. 2021: 143).

The peak year of Finnish trade union power was 1990, when both blue-collar and white-collar unionism was at its peak. Since then, male blue-collar workers have become rarer as working age paying members of trade unions. Somewhat compensating this trend, although not fully, has been the increase in female, white-collar unionism. This tendency might be expressed as 'more female, less male, white-collar, beyond-the-peak trade union movement'.

None of Visser's (2019) possible futures for trade unions correspond to the Finnish trade union movement, but the future is likely to have elements of each of them. Visser's scenarios include: (i) marginalization (fading away and losing relevance); (ii) dualization (unions end up promoting job security for their insider members at the expense of outsiders); (iii) substitution (unions will be replaced by other forms of social action and representation); and (iv) revitalization (unions regain their vitality and youthfulness).

Marginalization looks the most unlikely development. Finnish unions are by no means losing their relevance or fading away, and they will probably maintain their established role as defenders of labour interests in society. Unions have been blamed for preferring insiders at the expense of precarious workers. In fact, the fall in union membership since the 1990s is the result of potential members in core positions opting for the independent unemployment insurance fund YTK rather than joining a union. Therefore, unions have not been able to attract young full-time workers in permanent employment into membership. Neither they have been able to fully grasp the needs of marginal groups. Nevertheless, there are signs that unions are taking up a role as defenders of more vulnerable groups, such as zero-hours workers, platform workers and the (bogus) self-employed. The substitution argument is not really viable, although the independent unemployment fund YTK has taken a prominent role as unemployment insurance administrator, a role undertaken by unions during the 1970s and 1980s, since YTK cannot take over from the unions as defender of workers' interests. A more likely scenario is that a void will open up if joining an unemployment insurance fund is not associated with union membership.

What about the revitalization scenario in relation to the Finnish union movement? Finland, as a Nordic country, can be characterized as 'institutionally secure' (Ibsen and Tapia 2017: 179). Unions can develop organizing strategies while defending their traditional strongholds of collective bargaining and corporatist policymaking. But how long will their strong power resources endure in the face of falling unionization rates or accusations of having an inclination to defend mainly the interests of male insiders? Revitalization is needed, but is a movement towards Anglo-Saxon type coalitions with other social movements the right direction? New efforts are needed to maintain the membership base, and for example, the potential of ICT and the internet have not been exhausted as forums for networking, support and exerting influence (Aalto-Matturi 2005).

One possible direction would be the 'organizing model', which has proved attractive to unions in the United States, the Netherlands, Germany and Denmark, as well as the Baltic states. It would represent a departure from Finnish unions' previous strategies to maintain their membership base (Kall et al. 2019). The model encompasses strategic targeting of companies, one-on-one conversations with workers, recruiting 'natural leaders', following progress and – perhaps most importantly – engaging in an extended process of identity work, in which old national jurisdictions and partnerships are complemented or substituted by new forms of aggressive campaigning and cooperation. In a way, such a model is nothing new, but rather a return to the labour movement's formative years before the Second World War, when organizers were used and new union structures were established.

References

Aalto-Matturi S. (2005) The Internet and new opportunities for the Finnish trade union movement, Working USA, 8 (4), 469–481.

Ahtiainen L. (2019a) Palkansaajien järjestäytyminen vuonna 2017, Työ- ja elinkeinoministeriön julkaisuja 2019: 10. https://julkaisut.valtioneuvosto.fi/bitstream/handle/10024/161433/TEM_10_2019_Palkansaajien%20jarjestaytyminen.pdf?sequence=1&isAllowed=y

Ahtiainen L. (2019b) Työehtosopimusten kattavuus vuosina 2017/2018, Työ- ja elinkeinoministeriön julkaisuja, 2019: 62. http://julkaisut.valtioneuvosto.fi/bitstream/handle/10024/161945/TEM_2019_62.pdf

Alho R. (2013) Trade union responses to transnational labour mobility in the Finnish-Estonian context, Nordic Journal of Working Life Studies, 3 (3), 133–153.

Alho R. (2015) Inclusion or exclusion? Trade union strategies and labor migration, PhD thesis, University of Turku.

Bergholm T. (2007) Sopimusyhteiskunnan synty II: Hajaannuksesta tulopolitiikkaan (The birth of contract society II: from split to income policy), Helsinki, Otava.

Bergholm T. (2009) The making of the Finnish model: The qualitative change in Finnish corporatism in the early 1960s, Scandinavian Journal of History, 34 (1), 29–48.

Bergholm T. (2012) The country report of Finnish trade unions 2012: strong trade union movement in gradual decline, Friedrich Ebert Stiftung study. http://library.fes.de/pdf-files/id-moe/09545.pdf

Bergholm T. (2017) Ovatko työtaistelut vakava yhteiskunnallinen ongelma? in Pyöriä P. (ed.) Työelämän myytit ja todellisuus, Gaudeamus, 184–196.

Boldt P.J. (2008) SAK:n globalisaatiostrategiasta, in Helander M. (ed.) Going Global – Ay-liikkeen menestysresepti globaalissa ajassa, Minerva Kustannus Oy, 33–48.

Böckerman P. and Uusitalo R. (2006) Erosion of the Ghent system and union membership decline: lessons from Finland, British Journal of Industrial Relations, 44 (2), 283–303.

Bruun S. (1990). Den nordiska modellen för facklig verksamhet, in Bruun N., Fodgren B., Halvorsen M., Hydén H. and Nielsen R. (eds) Den Nordiska modellen: Fackföreningarna och arbetsrätten i Norden – nu och i framtid- en, Malmö, Liber.

Crouch C. (1993) Industrial relations and European state traditions, Oxford, Clarendon Press.

D'Agostino H. (1992) Why do workers join unions? A comparison of Sweden and OECD countries, Swedish Institute for Social Research 22, Edsbruk, Akademitryck.

Dølvik J.E. and Marginson P. (2018) Cross-sectoral coordination and regulation of wage determination in northern Europe: Divergent responses to multiple external pressures, European Journal of Industrial Relations, 24 (4), 409–425.

EK (2021) Mitä ek tekee? https://ek.fi/tietoa-meista/mika-on-ek/mika-on-ek/

Elomäki A., Koskinen Sandberg P., Kantola J. and Saari M. (2019) Työmarkkinajärjestöt valtiollisen tasa-arvopolitiikan tyhjiötä täyttämässä? Työmarkkinakeskusjärjestöjen tasa-arvoulostulot vuosina 2010–2017, Sosiologia, 56 (2), 122–140.

Elvander N. (2002) The labour market regimes in the Nordic countries: a comparative analysis, Scandinavian Political Studies, 25 (2), 117–137.

Finanssivalvonta (2020) Työttömyyskassat. Tilastot kassoittain 2019 (excel). https://www.finanssivalvonta.fi/tilastot/vakuutus/tyottomyysvakuutus/

Furåker B. (2020) The issue of staturory minimum wages: views among Nordic trade unions, European Journal of Industrial Relations, 41 (2), 419–435.

Helander M. (2008) Suomalaisen ay-liikkeen kansainväliset yhteydet, in Helander M. (ed.) Going global – Ay-liikkeen menestysresepti globaalissa ajassa, Helsinki, Minerva Kustannus Oy, 99–140.

Hirvola A., Mikkonen S., Skippari M. and Tiensuu P. (2021) Kohti avoimempaa lobbausta: Lobbauksen nykytila Suomessa valtiollisella tasolla, Selvityksiä ja ohjeita 2021:6, Helsinki, Oikeusministeriö.

Ibsen C.L. and Tapia M. (2017) Trade union revitalisation: where are we now? Where to next? Journal of Industrial Relations, 59 (2), 170–191.

Ilsøe A. (2017) The digitalisation of service work – social partner responses in Denmark, Sweden and Germany, Transfer, European Review of Labour and Research, 23 (3), 333–348.

Ilsøe A., Jesnes K. and Hotvedt M. (2020) Social partner responses in the Nordic platform economy, in Jesnes K. and Nordli Oppegaard S.M. (eds) Platform work in the Nordic models: issues, cases and responses, TemaNord 2020:513, Copenhagen, Nordic Council of Ministers, 56–63.

Jonker-Hoffrén P. (2019) Finland: Goodbye centralised bargaining? The emergence of a new industrial bargaining regime, in Müller T., Vandaele K. and Waddington J. (eds) Collective bargaining in Europe: towards an endgame, Brussels, ETUI, 197–216.

Jouppi J. (2016) Hyvin suunniteltu on puoliksi tehty. Työntekijöiden ammattiliittojen sosiaalisen median käyttö ja suunnittelu, Master's thesis in Organizational Communications, University of Vaasa.

Kall K., Lillie N., Sippola M. and Mankki L. (2019) Overcoming barriers to transnational organizing through identity work: Finnish-Estonian trade union cooperation, Work, Employment and Society, 33 (2), 208–225.

Kauppinen T. (2005) Suomen työmarkkinamalli, Helsinki, WSOY.

Kettunen P. (2001) Kansallinen työ. Suomalaisen suorituskyvyn vaalimisesta, Helsinki, Yliopistopaino.

Kettunen P. (2004) The Nordic model and consensual competitiveness in Finland, in Castren A.-M., Lonkila M., Peltonen M. and Alapuro R. (eds) Between sociology and history: essays on microhistory, collective action, and nation-building, Helsinki, Finnish Literature Society, 289–309.

Kevätsalo K. (2005) Yhdestoista hetki. Uuden vuosituhannen ay-liike paikallistasolla, Helsinki, Käyttötieto.

Koskela A. (2019) Hanskat tippui. Lakkojen historia ja vaikutus yhteiskunnassa, Helsinki, Kalevi Sorsa –säätiö.

Koskinen-Sandberg P. and Saari M. (2019) Sisters (can't) unite! Wages as macro-political and the gendered power orders of corporatism, Gender, Work & Organization, 26 (5), 633–649.

Lämsä A.-M. and Viljanen S. (2014) Finland: positive union engagement with CSR, in Preuss L., Gold M. and Rees C. (eds) Corporate social responsibility and trade unions: perspectives across Europe, Abingdon, Routledge, 31–48.

Larsson B., Bengtsson M. and Lovén Seidén K. (2012) Transnational trade union cooperation in the Nordic countries, Management Revue, 23 (1), 32–48.

Lillie N. and Sippola M. (2011) National unions and transnational workers: the case of Olkiluoto 3, Finland, Work, Employment and Society, 25 (2), 292–308.

Lönnqvist-Ahvonen S. (2019) Nuorten, alle 35-vuotiaiden jäsenten aktiivisen toiminnan kehittäminen Ammattiliitto Pron paikallisyhdistyksessä, Final thesis, Saimaa University of Applied Sciences.

Malmberg J. (2002) The collective agreement as an instrument for regulation of wages and employment conditions, in Wahlgren P. (ed.) Stability and change in Nordic labour law: legal abbreviations, Scandinavian Studies in Law 43, Stockholm, Stockholm Institute for Scandinavian Law, 189–213.

OECD (2004) Employment outlook 2004, Paris, OECD Publications.

Saksela-Bergholm S. (2021) Finland, in Sanz de Miguel P., Bazzani T. and Arasanz J. (eds) The definition of worker in the platform economy: exploring workers' risks and regulatory solutions: study, Brussels, EESC, 106–114.

Sippola M. (2012) Local bargaining and codetermination: Finnish experience in comparative perspective, European Journal of Industrial Relations, 18 (1), 53–69.

Sippola M., Jonker-Hoffrén, P. & Ojala, S. (2023) "The varying national agenda in variable hours contract regulation: implications for the labour market regimes in the Netherlands and Finland", special issue in *European Journal Industrial Relations* (final version submitted 30 January 2023).

Tiihonen A. (2015) Etujärjestöjen, puolueiden ja yhteiskuntaluokkien suhde Suomessa 2000–luvulla, Master's thesis, School of Management, University of Tampere.

Visser J. (2006) Union membership statistics in 24 countries, Monthly Labor Review, 129 (1), 38–49.

Abbreviations

AKAVA Confederation of Unions for Academic Professionals (Korkeasti koulutettujen työmarkkinakeskusjärjestö)

AKT Transport Workers' Union (Auto- ja kuljetusalan työntekijäliitto)

EK Confederation of Finnish Industries (Elinkeinoelämän keskusliitto)

HTK Confederation of Intellectual Employment (Henkisen työn keskusliitto)

JHL Trade Union for the Public and Welfare Sectors (Julkisten ja hyvinvointialojen liitto)

LTK Business Employers' Confederation (Liiketyönantajain keskusliitto)

OAJ Trade Union of Education in Finland (Opettajien ammattijärjestö)

PAM Service Union United (Palvelualojen ammattiliitto)

SAK Confederation of Finnish Trade Unions (Suomen ammattiliittojen keskusjärjestö)

STK Finnish Employers' Confederation (Suomen työnantajain keskusliitto)

STTK Finnish Confederation of Professionals (Toimihenkilökeskusjärjestö)

SUPER Finnish Union of Practical Nurses (Suomen lähi- ja perushoitajaliitto)

SY Federation of Finnish Enterprises (Suomen Yrittäjät)

TEHY Union of Health and Social Care Professionals in Finland

TUPO Income policy agreement; bipartite or tripartite national agreement on salaries and other general terms and conditions of employment (Tulopoliittinen kokonaisratkaisu)

TVK Federation of Clerical Employees' and Civil Servants' Organisations (Toimihenkilö- ja virkamiesjärjestöjen keskusliitto)

YTK General unemployment fund (Yleinen työttömyyskassa)

Chapter 11

France: Fragmented trade unions, few members, but many voters and much social unrest

Udo Rehfeldt and Catherine Vincent

Historically, industrial relations in France have been characterized as adversarial between trade unions and employers, complemented by strong state intervention. The latter has now diminished, however, and collective bargaining has developed with a strong tendency towards decentralization. With a very low, but stable unionization rate (see Table 11.1), elections have become the main source of union legitimacy. Union action is supported by public funding and by strong legal rights, in particular for multi-channel employee representation at workplace level, which is in practice coordinated by the unions. Union power is weakened, however, by the persistent fragmentation of the union confederations and by polarization between union strongholds in large companies and in the public sector, on one hand, and the large number of small and medium-sized enterprises (SMEs) without union presence on the other. Union power has also been weakened by recent legal reforms of the industrial relations system, which have undermined the role of centralized bargaining by abolishing the favourability principle. Tripartite concertation at peak level, which had nearly achieved a neo-corporatist character, has lost its impetus, and industrial conflict, although still high by European comparison, has lost its efficacy.

Table 11.1 Principal characteristics of trade unionism in France

	1980	2000	2019
Total trade union membership	3,481,000	2,212,000	2,151,000*
Proportion of women in total membership	n.a.	44 %	46 %
Gross union density	20 %	11 %	9 %
Net union density	19 %	10 %	9 %
Number of confederations	5	7**	7**
Number of affiliated unions (federations)***	100	73	72
Number of independent unions	Many	Few	Few
Collective bargaining coverage	85 %	98 %	98 %
Principal level of collective bargaining	Industry	Erosion of industry level	Industry and company
Days not worked due to industrial action per 1,000 workers	84	120	113*

Note: * 2018; ** including 'quasi-confederations'; *** Based upon CFDT, CGT and FO.

Source: Appendix A1.

Historical background and principal features of the industrial relations system

The central features of the French industrial relations model are multi-channel employee representation, fragmented trade unions and employers' organizations, and adversarial relations between trade unions and employers, compensated by strong state interventionism. Historically, employee representation and collective bargaining developed rather late in France compared with other European countries. Industrial relations were characterized by mistrust and conflict. For a long time, employers refused to grant access to the workplace and to recognize unions as bargaining partners. In consequence, unions initially developed outside companies and workplaces. The union movement reacted to state and employer hostility with hostility towards both bourgeois democracy and the capitalist order. The initial syndicalist orientation, based on a revolutionary unionism programme, was abandoned during the First World War, and led to a reformist transformation of the movement. In 1936, the Popular Front government introduced laws on employee delegates and the extension of collective industrial agreements, signed by the most representative unions.

After the Liberation in 1944, the programme of economic and social democracy of the Resistance, in which the unions played an active role, was implemented by a series of nationalizations with tripartite management and by the introduction of works councils with information and consultation rights. Union representatives at the workplace level have existed in a number of large companies since the 1950s, but as a right they were introduced by law only as late as 1968, as a result of the general strike of May 1968 and the tripartite 'Grenelle' agreements, which put an end to it. The 1982 'Auroux' laws, adopted after the left-wing parties had come to power, attempted to create a synergy between works councils and unions by strengthening both works councils' consultation rights and trade union delegates' bargaining rights. But in contrast to the legislators' intentions and the unions' hopes, the legislative provision for trade union presence at the workplace did not lead to a renewal of unionism. On the contrary, trade union density, already weak by European standards, continued to decline, falling to only 8 per cent. On the other hand, the Auroux laws led to an increase in workplace-level bargaining, which revealed a strategic change on the part of the employers, who understood the merits of decentralized workplace bargaining, not only because such bargaining met their demands for flexibility, but also because they could now exploit the unions' weakened bargaining power.

Since the 1980s, there has been a slow departure from French 'exceptionalism' in the form of state dominance after a series of reforms, adopted under pressure from the unions in the 1980s and under pressure from employers' organizations in the period 2004–2017. After 2008, there was even a short-lived move towards neo-corporatism, through the development of tripartite concertation at peak level, which came to a provisional halt in 2016–2017, when a reversal of the hierarchy of norms between the industry and enterprise levels was imposed by law without prior concertation.

Structure of trade unions and union democracy

To analyse trade union structure and internal democracy this section assesses in turn political, religious and occupational fragmentation; mergers and breakaways; and union structures and democracy.

Regarding fragmentation, in the private sector there are five 'representative' trade union confederations at the national level:[1]

- The General Confederation of Labour (CGT, *Confédération Générale du Travail*) was founded in 1895 and is the oldest and, for a long time, the largest confederation. After the Second World War, communists occupied the leading positions in the confederation and its affiliates. After 1996, the CGT officially marked its autonomy from the Communist Party (*Parti communiste français*) and adopted a dual strategic orientation, both as a social movement union and as a negotiating union (de Comarmond 2013). Despite its continuous decline in membership since the 1970s, the CGT remains one of the two largest confederations.
- The French Democratic Confederation of Labour (CFDT, *Confédération Française Démocratique du Travail*) is now the largest confederation. It is the result of the transformation, in 1964, of the French Confederation of Christian Workers (CFTC, *Confédération Française des Travailleurs Chrétiens*), initially created in 1919. This renaming symbolized its official departure from the social doctrine of the Catholic Church. In the 1970s, the CFDT saw itself as a leftist trade union by establishing the goal of self-management socialism (*autogestion*), but in 1978 it initiated a reformist reorientation labelled 're-unionization' (*resyndicalisation*). Its aim was to return to purely trade union aims and methods, which were to be realized above all through collective bargaining (Barthélemy et al. 2012; Defaud 2009; Guillaume 2014).
- Worker Force (FO, *Force Ouvrière*, officially CGT-FO) was created in 1948 as an anti-communist union after a split in the CGT. For a long time, a preferential bargaining partner of employer associations and governments (Dreyfus and Pigenet 2011), FO has pursued a more autonomous trade union policy since the 1990s, sometimes in unity of action with the CGT.
- The CFTC is the organization of the minority who refused to accept its transformation into the CFDT in 1964 and continues the Christian tradition under the old name.
- The General Confederation of Clerical and Managerial Staff (CGC, *Confédération Générale des Cadres*) was founded in 1944 and renamed the French Confederation of Supervisors-General

1 In France, the status of 'representativeness' gives a union the legal right to participate in collective bargaining and to present lists for workplace relations (see below).

Confederation of Clerical and Managerial Staff (CFE-CGC, *Confédération Française de l'Encadrement-Confédération Générale des Cadres*) in 1981. It regards itself as a non-political representation of clerical and professional staff (Béthoud et al. 2013). In France, such groups of employees are called *cadres* and include mainly managers, supervisors, engineers and technicians.

In France this large number of confederations has coexisted with an even greater number of autonomous unions, particularly in the public sector. Many of them were initially affiliated to the CGT but refused to take a position in the 1948 split. They simply disaffiliated from the CGT in order to preserve their unity. The most important was the Federation of National Education (FEN, *Fédération de l'Education Nationale*), which itself split in 1993, when two communist-led sub-federations were excluded by the socialist majority. Most of the autonomous unions are now affiliated to two groupings, which do not consider themselves confederations because they have not – or not yet – developed a complete dual structure of professional federations and local representations:

- The first was the *Groupe des 10*, created in 1981. In 1998, it transformed itself into the 'Solidaires' Union of Trade Unions (USS, *Union Syndicale Solidaires*) after the affiliation of a number of radical autonomous unions (Béroud and Denis 2012). Some of them were left-wing breakaways from the CFDT, named 'Supportive, Unitary, Democratic' (SUD, *Solidaires, unitaires, démocratiques*). The first was *SUD-PTT*, founded in 1989 after the exclusion of the militant part of the CFDT postal and telecommunication federation (Denis 2003). Another important breakaway led to the creation of railway union *SUD-Rail* in 1995 (see the controversial assessment by Connolly and Darlington 2012 and Denis 2012).
- Some of the more moderate federations left the *Groupe des 10* and in 1993 created the National Union of Autonomous Trade Unions (UNSA, *Union Nationale des Syndicats Autonomes*), together with other unaffiliated federations, the most important of which was FEN, now renamed *UNSA-Education.*

After the creation of these two quasi-confederations, only a few autonomous unions remain unaffiliated. The largest is the Unitary Trade Union Federation (FSU, *Fédération Syndicale Unitaire*), created in 1993 at the initiative of the unions excluded from FEN. The FSU is now the most important union in education.

Figure 11.1 Evolution of French union organizations, 1947–2015

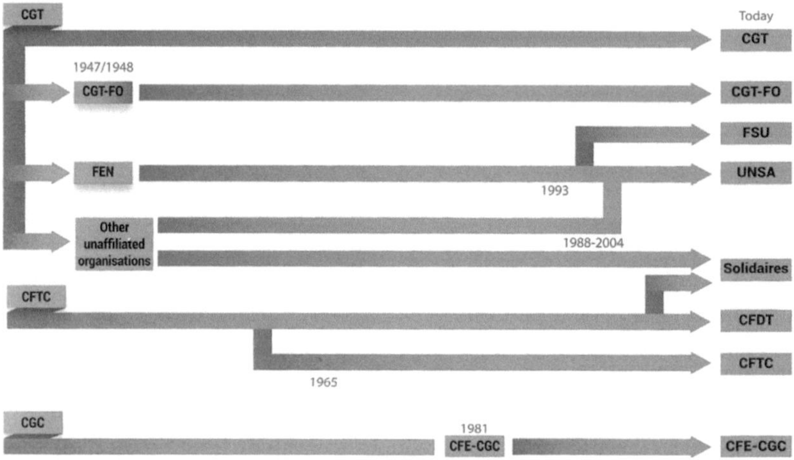

Source: IRES et al. (2015).

The academic literature and the media distinguish between 'reformist' and 'revolutionary' unions. Initially, the term 'reformist' was used for unions that explicitly championed a gradual improvement of workers' situations through reforms, in contrast to the CGT, which historically defined itself as 'revolutionary', long a synonym for syndicalist unionism. Later, the term 'revolutionary' was used to characterize the communist-dominated CGT. From the 1930s, however, the French Communist Party no longer pursued revolutionary goals, and today even the CGT admits that all trade unions are 'reformist in essence', as stated by CGT secretary general Philippe Martinez (interview in *Le Monde*, 12 September 2015). Interestingly, in the media, the initial meaning of the word 'reformist' has undergone a reversal in recent decades. Trade unions are now classified as 'reformist' if they accept employers' and the government's demands for reforms aimed at partially rolling back historical workers' rights obtained by previous reforms. In this chapter, we will concentrate mainly on the three largest confederations, CFDT, CGT and FO.

Turning to mergers, the CFDT has reduced the number of federations, from twenty-nine in 1980 to sixteen in 2019. During that period, the CGT also reduced the number of its federations, but its present number (thirty) remains significantly higher, at a similar level to that of FO (twenty-six). Most of these mergers were for financial reasons, merging unions in declining with those in expanding industries. Initially, mergers in the CFDT also had a political aim, which was to create larger entities in an effort to transcend a narrow craft consciousness and promote a broader class solidarity.

Mergers between confederations have been initiated repeatedly but have always failed. After the legal introduction of electoral criteria for union representativeness in 2008, CFE-CGC and UNSA initiated a merger process in order to be able to pass the new 8 per cent hurdle in the private sector. Ultimately, the majority of CFE-CGC members rejected this project, which would have meant its transformation from a professional into a general union. Indeed, the CFE-CGC had no need for a merger because, under the 2008 Law, a specific rate of representativeness is calculated for the category of managerial staff alone, and in this category the CFE-CGC has never had any difficulty in exceeding 8 per cent. Breakaways are more frequent than mergers.

The renewed split of the trade union movement regarding the labour law reforms in 2016–2017 led to the emergence of two union poles. On one side, cooperation between 'reformist' unions CFDT, CFE-CGC, CFTC and UNSA has become quasi-permanent. On the other, coordination is now frequent between the oppositional organizations CGT, FSU and USS, joined more and more often by FO. Coordination across all union organizations has become rare.

The basic unit of all organizations for union democracy is the 'union' (*syndicat*). It is generally constituted outside companies by all the workplace union sections of the same industry at the level of a certain territory. In the CGT, a basic union can also be constituted at the level of a single workplace or a single company or public service. Consequently, the CGT has more basic unions than the CFDT. In the past decade, the CGT has included more than 17,000 basic unions with an average of around thirty members, whereas the CFDT has had around 1,300 basic unions, mainly at *département* level, but with an average of 340 members (Andolfato and Labbé 2011).

In a confederation, all basic unions are affiliated at the same time to an industry federation and to a cross-industry body at *département* level, called a UD (*union départementale*), as well as at regional level, called a UR (*union régionale*). At local level, several basic unions can also constitute a local cross-industry body called a *union locale*, although this level is losing its importance. The CGT's territorial structures are less centralized than those of the CFDT and the CFTC, in which regional unions play a more important role than departmental ones.

Historically, French unions first emerged as craft unions, which were gradually transformed into general industrial union confederations. The three largest confederations have retained separate structures for managerial staff, which is at the same time integrated into the different industry federations. This specific structure allows these confederations to compete successfully with the CFE-CGC and to contest its pretention to be the exclusive representative of these workers. Compared with countries such as the United Kingdom or Germany, confederations play a stronger role in the French trade union movement. They negotiate nationwide cross-industry or tripartite agreements and participate in the bipartite or tripartite management of social security funds. The confederation's policy and its congress decisions are generally taken as guidelines by the federations.

According to union statutes, internal democracy is exercised by the congress. Each UD and UR, each federation and finally each confederation hold their own congresses, generally every three years. The congress adopts or modifies the statutes, defines union strategy and elects its executive. Congress delegates are mandated by the different basic unions and have voting rights proportionate to their fee-paying membership. In the case of a confederal congress, representatives of the federations, the UDs and the URs also participate in the congress, but without voting rights. In the CGT, mandates for basic unions are the result of a majority vote that does not reflect divergent opinions. This voting principle amplifies the final votes in the congress. In practice, congress elections are controlled by local activists with an elective and/or union mandate in companies and the civil service.

Because of their common history, CGT and FO on one hand, and CFDT and CFTC on the other, have the same internal structures. The different bodies are similar, but sometimes have different names. Every federation and territorial union elects a delegate for the union parliament, with voting rights corresponding to the number of members that have regularly paid their membership fees. In CGT and FO, this parliament is called the National Confederal Committee, and in the CFDT the National Council. The union structures for specific groups, such as managers, civil servants, pensioners, women and young people, also send delegates to the parliament. In practice, the parliament is dominated by the intermediate union bureaucracy. It meets regularly two or three times a year and controls the activities of the executive body. This control is not merely formal. In recent times, union parliaments have not only contested decisions by the Secretary General, but in some cases (CGT in 2015, FO in 2018) they have even forced him to resign after only a few months in office.

The intermediate union bureaucracy also plays an important role in the election of the executive by the confederal congress. For this purpose, the federations and the UDs have the right to draw up lists of candidates. The past executive also has the right to present candidates. Other lists sometimes emerge, but never have a chance to be elected. Members of the executive thus are, in practice, co-opted rather than elected. In the CGT before 1999, this co-optation system was paradoxically intended to prevent all seats being occupied by communists and to reserve a few seats for Catholics or members of the Socialist Party.

At workplace level, there is more possibility of voice for individual members. Here, a 1968 Law gives union members present at the workplace the right to create a union section and to have regular meetings. In practice, however, the union section meetings are attended mainly by activists (Pignoni 2017). For each workplace, the law allows the nomination of a union delegate by the union, in practice by the federation, which can also withdraw this mandate. Since the 2008 Law, the federation's choice has been limited, however, as they can only nominate a worker who has previously individually obtained at least 10 per cent of the votes at the workplace elections (see below).

Unionization

Apart from periods of social unrest (as in 1936 or 1944), the French trade union movement has never experienced mass unionization and the long-term unionization rate has always been relatively low compared with other European countries. After a peak of 20 per cent during the 1970s, it declined continuously to 8 per cent during the 1990s.

In France, three non-homogeneous statistical series are available for the evolution of unionization. Figure 11.2 shows estimations for 1996–2005, 2008 and 2010, and survey results for 2013 and 2016. They confirm the stabilization of the unionization rate since 1996, now estimated at around 11 per cent (DARES 2018; Pignoni 2016;).

Figure 11.2 Net unionization rates in France, 1949–2016

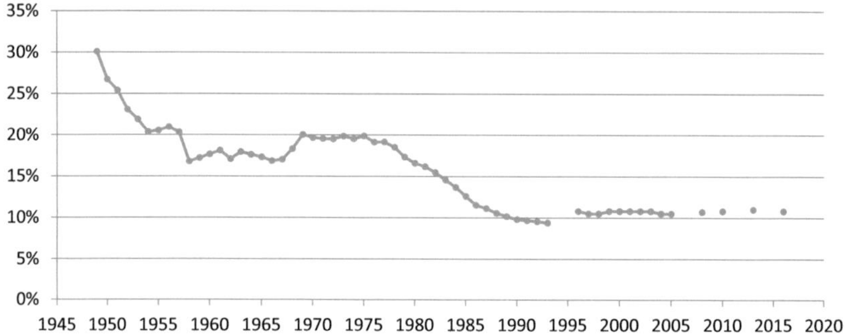

Source: DARES (Ministry of Labour) (2018).

The number of members is tending to come closer to the number of activists, which explains why unionization did not continue to decline after 1995. In the year 2000, the CFDT had 3,000 confederal and federal officials, 7,000 quasi officials or activists with full time-off for activities related to their elective or union mandate in companies and the civil service, and 200,000 activists with an elective or union mandate (Andolfatto and Labbé 2011). Thus more than half of the declared members had the profile of activists or officials.

The internal membership structure of the confederations has been affected by structural changes in the French economy and workforce. Initially, unions represented mainly male manual industrial workers, with the exception of the CFTC-CFDT, which represented mainly service sector workers, including female workers in the commercial sector. Because of industrial decline, workers in manufacturing now represent only 13 per cent of the total workforce. But they still represented 28 per cent of active union members in 2013. Unionization was initially forbidden for civil servants. Later in the twentieth century, the public sector became another stronghold for all the trade unions, in particular for the autonomous unions, but also for the CGT and the FO. Even in the CFDT, the weight of the public sector grew during the 1980s. Nearly half of all active trade union members, 43 per cent in 2013, work in the public sector.

Given the importance of the public sector for trade unions, members there have the biggest influence on socio-occupational differences.

The comprehensive membership rate in the public sector is 20 per cent, against only 9 per cent in the private sector. A quarter of trade union members in the civil service are categorized as professional and managerial staff, mainly teachers. The membership rates of all occupations are systematically higher in the public than in the private sector. In the public sector, the highest rates are found in the police (49 per cent) and in financial administration (38 per cent).

If one considers the private sector alone, manual workers and office workers have a higher unionization rate than professional and managerial staff, 9.2 and 7.4 per cent, respectively, compared with 7.2 per cent. Qualified manual workers have a higher rate, at 11 per cent, than unqualified workers, at 6 per cent. Membership rates are correlated with employment status. The rates are 12 per cent for full-time workers, 8 per cent for part-time workers, but only 3 per cent for workers with fixed-term employment contracts and a mere 1 per cent for temporary agency workers. The average unionization rate in manufacturing is 13 per cent. Relatively high rates are found in transport at 18 per cent and finance at 12 per cent; the lowest rates occur in construction at 2.5 per cent and wholesale and retail trade at 2.6 per cent.[2]

In contrast to the public sector, unionization in the private sector correlates strongly with workplace size, ranging from 5 per cent in workplaces with fewer than fifty employees to 14.4 per cent in workplaces with more than 200 employees. This is closely correlated with the presence of a union delegate. Previous editions of the REPONSE survey[3] show that the stronger the trade union presence, the greater is the propensity to join a union. In 2001–2005, union presence at the workplace was as high as 73 per cent in state-owned companies, but only 33 per cent in private companies (Wolff 2008). Until 2005, the rate of union presence was increasing regardless of workplace size, but after 2005 declined again from 37.6 to 30.6 per cent in 2017 (DARES 2020).[4]

Like everywhere in Europe, membership rates are also strongly correlated with age. Only 2.5 per cent of young people between 18 and

---

2 For statistical reasons, there is no breakdown for all industries.

3 REPONSE is a survey on industrial relations at workplace level carried out by DARES every six years since 1992.

4 Because of the importance of multi-workplace companies, union presence is systematically 10 percentage points higher at company level, but this does not necessarily guarantee proximity to all employees.

24 years are trade union members. This percentage has not changed much since the 1980s (Pignoni 2017). According to opinion polls, young people are not more hostile to unions than older ones, on the contrary. But they prefer involvement in other fields, such as alternative social movements or NGOs (Contrepois 2015). When young people find a job, at the beginning they are often precarious, which does not favour unionization. If they find a stable job, for example in the public sector, their unionization rate tends to be closer to that of older workers (Béroud et al. 2008). Union members have an average age of 45, compared with 40 for the whole workforce. The unionized workforce is also ageing faster. In 2013, 39 per cent of union members were between 50 and 65 years of age, compared with 25 per cent for the whole workforce. Twenty years earlier, the difference was only 21 to 19 per cent.

There are no detailed figures on the proportion of migrant workers in union membership. Collecting statistics based on ethnicity is forbidden in France. Some sources report the proportion of non-French workers in trade union membership as 2 per cent (Contrepois 2017).

The only field in which the situation has improved over the years is the unionization of women (see Table 11.2). The high percentage for female participation in the governance of the CGT in 2005 is an effect of the 1999 congress decisions on parity. The CFDT had taken such a decision for a 30 per cent quota as early as 1982, then parity in 2014. These decisions, however, had no significant effects on female participation at the lower levels (Guillaume and Pochic 2013). According to the ETUC Annual Gender Equality Survey 2019, based on affiliate declarations, the share of women in membership has recently risen in all confederations, particularly in the CGT (Fulton and Sechi 2019).

Recruitment difficulties were closely related to membership decline until 1996. Analytically, one can distinguish between exogenous and endogenous factors. The former factors are essentially related to structural changes in the economy and society. They are the same for all industrial countries, primarily the decline in manufacturing, the employment crisis and the increase of individualism.

The REPONSE survey 2017 quotes the fear of discrimination in their professional career amongst the four main reasons that prevent workers from joining a union (Pignoni 2019). Discrimination and repression by the management have always accompanied the development of unionism in France. In 2011, unionists from CGT, FO, CFTC, FSU and USS,

Table 11.2 Participation of women in trade union membership in 2005 and 2016–2018 and in different union confederation bodies in 2005

	CGT (%)	CFDT (%)	FO (%)	CFTC (%)	CFE-CGC (%)
Total membership 2005	28	44.2	45	40	18.5
Total membership 2016–18	38	50	45	44	n.a.
Congress	29	37	45	31	8.7
National council or committee	25	28.3	8.8	31	17.5
Executive committee	50	26.5	12	13	30
Select executive committee	50	30	23	12.5	11.1
Secretaries general of federations	19	11.8	7.4	10	14.8
Secretaries general of UDs	8.3	8.5	7.6	–	–

Source: 2005: Silvera (2006); 2016–2018: Fulton and Sechi (2019).

together with a series of academics and researchers created an 'Observatory on anti-union discrimination and repression'. Their report (Observatoire 2014) shows that repression takes the form of psychological and even physical violence. Since 2004, the Ministry of Labour no longer publishes statistics on dismissals of protected worker representatives. In this last year, more than 10,000 unionists were sacked even though as union delegates or elected representatives they were protected by law against unfair dismissal. There are very few condemnations by the courts of such practices. Thus, especially in times of mass unemployment, the fear of dismissals acts as a powerful obstacle to unionization. In recent times, anti-union discrimination has taken more subtle forms, such as the slowdown of professional careers and wage cuts for union activists. The 2008 Law has made it an obligation for big companies to negotiate agreements that secure union rights and the careers of activists or former activists. Some companies have done so, but at the workplace level, difficulties persist in their implementation and in reversing adversarial management practices (Amossé and Denis 2016; Chappe et al. 2019).

Endogenous factors are those in respect of which unions take their own responsibility. Some are specific to France. Opinion polls and the REPONSE survey mention the lack of attractiveness of unions as a main obstacle that prevent workers from joining them. They are criticized for their 'politicization', their internal divisions and their sectarianism. Researchers also criticize their growing 'institutionalization' (Adam

1983; Béroud and Yon 2013; Giraud et al. 2018), with more and more activists in positions of quasi full-time officials completely absorbed by their bargaining activities and neglecting their day-to-day relations with the ordinary members and workers in general (Andolfatto and Labbé 2011; Dufour and Hege 2010). Some academics have analysed this as the inevitable transformation of unions from a social movement into a 'social agency' (Rosanvallon 1988), based on elections and state recognition.

The historical decline of unionism, together with its institutional achievements, gives new explanatory power to the free-rider paradigm. But the reality is more ambiguous. The main reason for not joining a union, quoted by 40 per cent of workers in the 2017 REPONSE survey, is that they 'do not need to be member of a union to defend themselves'. On the other hand, when there are worker representatives at the workplace, about 48 per cent of the workers consider that unions are useful and provide services. If there are no representatives, this opinion declines to 26 per cent. These arguments can be paraphrased as 'the unions work for me at the workplace, so I do not need to join them', but a second argument states the contrary: 26 per cent of workers say that they did not join a union because 'there are no unions present in the company' (Pignoni 2019). This is confirmed by the correlation of union presence and membership stated above.

This situation shows the fragility of union power at the workplace. Unions are finding it more and more difficult to find candidates for employee representation. The most experienced activists often retire without being able to ensure successors. If the unions are unable to recruit younger members, they run the risk of no longer being present in many workplaces, where, in turn, it will be impossible to submit lists for workplace elections or to recruit new members.

After some hesitation, unions now give high priority to union organizing. All union confederations prioritize organizing workers in SMEs, young people and precarious workers. Up to now, the Anglo-Saxon organizing model has had limited influence in France (Thomas 2016). CFDT and CGT have tried to improve their image among workers by changing their ideological references and orientations. The political moderation of the CFDT leadership seems to be paying in the long run. But this membership drive has its limits, because the union has recruited essentially where it was already present, turning part of its voters into members.

The CGT also adopted a new reformist course in 1998, and in 2004 launched a national organizing plan. Unionization was not considered a priority by its basic structures, however, and the new congress orientations were largely ignored (Piotet 2009). So far, it remains unclear to what extent the membership increase in both the CFDT and the CGT can be attributed to the use of new organizing tools.

Some researchers regard the creation of new radical 'grassroots' unions as a form of union renewal (Connolly 2010; Yon 2016). One must consider, however, that this has consisted mainly of the transfer of activists from one union to another, essentially from CFDT to SUD. Once established, these unions did not show a significant increase in membership. They remained essentially unions of activists.

Elections are a major source of union legitimacy. In the year 2000, the CGT and the CFDT repeatedly demanded that the criteria of union representativeness should be based on the results of workplace elections and that a majority principle should be introduced for collective bargaining. Thus, they indirectly endorsed the earlier writings of academics who had concluded that union legitimacy and power were already based more on elections and legal institutions than on membership (Adam 1983; Rosanvallon 1988). In 2008, the two confederations came to an agreement with the employers' organizations to ask the government to prepare a new law on representativeness, which was voted on the same year as the 'Law on Social Democracy' (see below).

In 2013 and 2017, the government published the aggregated results of the first two four-year cycles of workplace elections in the private sector. The representativeness rules still differ in the civil services, but representativeness was already grounded on a three-year cycle of elections when it was changed in 2010 into a similar four-year cycle. Since 2014, the elections take place on the same day for the three branches of the civil service: the state civil service, local authorities and public hospitals. Table 11.3 shows the result for the last two cycles in all sectors. At national cross-industry level in the private sector, all five trade union confederations, including the CFE-CGC,[5] were able to pass the new 8 per cent hurdle in the private sector and could secure their previous

[5] In 2016–2020, the CFE-CGC secured its representativeness by obtaining 21.2 per cent for the category of professional and managerial staff, although this was far behind the CFDT (27.7 per cent). The CFE-CGC also obtained growing votes in the other categories of white-collar workers.

representativeness status. The autonomous unions UNSA, USS and FSU did not, but they did manage to secure their representativeness in the civil service. In 2017, the CFDT ousted the CGT from first place in the private sector and claimed to be the leading confederation nationwide, not only in terms of membership – as it had been since 1995 – but also in terms of accumulated votes. This 'victory' had its limits, however, because it was due only to the fact that the CFDT lost fewer votes than the CGT.

Table 11.3 Results of workplace elections in the private sector and civil service, 2013–2020

	Private sector		**Civil services**	
	2013–2016 (%)	**2017–2020** (%)	**2014** (%)	**2018** (%)
CGT	24.9	23.0	23.1	21.8
CFDT	26.4	26.8	19.3	19.0
FO	15.6	15.2	18.6	18.1
CFTC	9.5	9.5	3.3	2.9
CFE-CGC	10.7	11.9	2.9	3.4
UNSA	5.4	6.0	10.4	11.2
USS	3.5	3.7	6.8	6.3
FSU	–	–	7.9	8.7
Other	4.0	3.8	7.7	8.6
Participation	42.8	38.2	52.9	49.8

Source: Ministry of Labour, DGAFP (General Direction of Public Administration and Civil Service).

Union resources and expenditure

French trade unions have traditionally been noted for the paucity of their financial and organizational resources (Pernot 2018). With the development of consultative bodies and of bargaining at all levels, and therefore of time-off for trade union officials to perform their duties, the number of officials has increased, and it has become possible to make a career as a trade unionist. This development has led several researchers to make accusations of trade union bureaucratization (Andolfatto and Labbé 2011; Béroud and Yon 2013) and to conclude that unionists are doomed to become professionals (Rosanvallon 1988). Further evidence of this integration comes from trade union financing, the latter coming mainly from the unions' position in different institutions.

Membership fees have never been the main source of funding of French trade unions. As a result, paradoxically, declining membership is not putting their financial position under strain. Based on trade union accounts published since 2011, it is estimated that membership fees constitute, on average, one-third of confederal budgets (Andolfatto and Labbé 2017). The level of fees and the rules for distribution between the different organizational levels (confederations, federations and territorial unions) vary among unions. The CFDT was the first to centralize the collection of membership fees and to standardize their allocation by creating a dedicated central service during the 1970s. The fee is 0.75 per cent of annual net wages and the rules of allocation between the various bodies are decided at confederal congress. Since its forty-seventh confederal congress in 2003, the CGT has also opted for a common rule for the distribution of fees, the amount of which is 1.0 per cent of annual net wages. Both organizations ensure that minimum resources are guaranteed to basic unions whose members have low incomes. FO is the confederation that leaves the most autonomy to its unions: it is at this level that both the amount and the distribution of membership fees are set, subject to guaranteeing a minimum amount for the confederal level. The three confederations apply free membership in exceptional cases: for example, to part-time and unemployed workers.

The main source of union funding is public financing. For a long time, the various subsidies provided by public authorities remained more or less opaque. They corresponded to funding received for the operation of the joint institutions of social protection and vocational training, for union training but also for participation in the design and implementation of public policies. This opacity about the origin of union funds fuelled many media smear campaigns. To make state funding more transparent, a 2008 Law made it mandatory for unions with a certain level of resources to publish an annual financial report. The Law of 5 March 2014 went further. A national fund for financing social dialogue was created. Managed jointly by representative trade unions and employers' organizations, it brings together all public subsidies from the state, as well as a contribution based on private sector payroll.[6] The joint body is responsible for distributing

---

[6] The contribution rate is 0.016 per cent of the payroll with a minimum national fundraising of 73 million euros. The difference is made up by a state subsidy, if necessary. This has not been necessary to date because in the first year, 2015, fundraising brought in 84.3 million euros.

the proceeds of such levies. The sums are distributed between the representative trade unions and employers' organizations, 20 per cent being reserved for non-representative unions that have obtained between 3 and 8 per cent of the votes in professional elections. Each organization receives a fixed share, as well as an amount calculated on the results of workplace elections. The total subsidy is paid to the confederations. This can change the internal balance of resource distribution to the benefit of the central level. Financial flows that escaped the attention of the confederal bodies are now centralized. The rules on financial transparency have strengthened the rationalization of union resources and the use of centralized management tools, including databases and accounting software, that previously had been rejected (Bourguignon and Yon 2018). Moreover, local authorities often allocate subsidies or material resources to local unions.

Last but not least, an important, albeit non-monetary, resource comprises employers' contributions resulting from the strengthening of trade union rights in recent decades. These include paid hours off for elected representatives or union mandates in companies or the civil service that activists partly use outside their workplace, such as federations or local unions. In addition, material means of support or training facilities are granted by employers. In large companies, collective agreements often provide union sections with means of support well above legal requirements. French trade unions offer some services, such as legal advice on work and employment, help in case of lay-offs and training. Often, they are not confined to members.

Collective bargaining and unions at the workplace

In France, collective bargaining has had a statutory basis since 1936, although it did not become the normal mode of industrial relations until later on. During the so-called 'Trente Glorieuses' (the thirty years from 1945 to 1975), industry-level bargaining emerged as the pillar of French industrial relations. Despite one of the lowest rates of union density, the French bargaining coverage rate stands at 96 per cent in the private sector, and 98 per cent including public enterprises.[7] The high coverage

---

7 It is worth noting that there was no real collective bargaining in the civil service in France up to the 2010 Law on social dialogue renewal (*rénovation du dialogue social*), despite the fact that it accounts for almost 20 per cent of the total employed workforce. Renewal remains incomplete, however, as the law did not confer legally binding status on agreements, as only their legislative or regulatory implementation grants them normative scope (Vincent 2016).

level results from two factors. First, collective agreements apply to all employees of a company covered by them regardless whether or not they are trade union members. Second, and above all, bargaining coverage has been broadened by the general use of administrative extension of industrial agreements. The state has compensated for employers' hostility to bargain using two other tools. First, in order to level social inequalities and to compensate for a deficient bargaining process, a statutory national minimum wage was implemented, by a 1950 Law revised in 1970. The government annually sets its rate according to strictly established rules. The minimum wage increase more or less set the pace for wage industry agreements (Delahaie and Vincent 2021). Second, until the late 1990s, representative unions had a monopoly in collective bargaining at all levels. More recently, new rules for union representativeness and the validity of agreements have also sought to support the security of bargaining. Paradoxically, these supporting measures have often proved detrimental by removing the incentive for individuals to join unions, promoting a unionism based on the strength of a community of activists rather than on a mass membership, and finally encouraging further dependence on state support (Pernot 2018).

Nevertheless, until the 1970s, collective bargaining hardly existed without conflicts, and collective agreements were often signed after strikes. The promotion of contractual policy, traditionally advanced by the CFTC, CGC and CGT-FO, also became the spearhead of the CFDT in the 1980s. The conversion of the CGT to bargaining was more gradual but was achieved in the early 1990s. All the confederations favoured reaching agreement at industry level.

During the following decades, collective bargaining experienced a twofold evolution. On one hand, it was extended to the national inter-industry level and its content shifted from wage issues to new topics, such as employment or working hours. This new kind of concertation, often with more or less explicit government incentives and the results of which are consolidated in legislative texts, can be considered a kind of 'pre-legislation'. Moreover, after the Second World War, in order to increase their social and political influence, unions were granted a role in the administration of the welfare state, giving them legitimacy beyond the sphere of collective bargaining. During the 1970s, jointly managed institutions were the main state approach to governance in the fields of social protection, unemployment benefit and training.[8] All the social partners are devoted to it, including employers' organizations (Daniel et al. 2000).

On the other hand, there was an early development, compared with most continental European countries, towards the decentralization of collective bargaining to company level through a catalogue of issues for which derogations are possible. At the same time, the legal possibilities for negotiations with non-union representatives at the workplace were extended.[9] During the past two decades, employers have chosen to prioritize company-level bargaining to weaken the constraints imposed by legislation or even by sectoral bargaining, but the industry level has remained important in determining employment and working conditions. The number of workplace-level agreements increased substantially from 3,900 in 1984 to 36,600 in 2015. Since then, the number of agreements concluded has continued to increase each year. In 2015, negotiations took place in only 15 per cent of workplaces with more than ten employees; however, these workplaces employed 61.9 per cent of the workforce, proving that, in SMEs, there is often no collective bargaining because there are no unions (Daniel 2017).

Even if the changing pattern of collective bargaining has gradually loosened the coupling between industry and company levels, until recently, coordination among the different levels was still ensured by the 'favourability' principle (Tallard and Vincent 2014). The 2016 El Khomri Law and the 2017 Macron Ordinances introduced a reversal of the hierarchy of norms and gave more autonomy to company bargaining. This overhaul of collective bargaining will certainly hasten the decline of the regulatory capacity of industry agreements. Currently, the situation in practice is that the use of derogations remains limited. Three reasons may explain derogations' lack of success at company level (Vincent 2019). First, union delegates, supported by their union federations have refused to sign them. Second, the standards imposed at industry level are already the result of minimal compromises and leave little room for less favourable agreements. Last but not least, derogation agreements are not relevant tools for management. In large companies, as long as economic

8 Joint institutions have managed employees' supplementary pension funds and the unemployment compensation scheme since the conclusion of national agreements in 1947 and 1958, respectively. This management method was extended to vocational training in 1971.

9 Since the early 2000s, successive legislation has extended the possibilities for non-union representatives to negotiate in non-unionized workplaces. The Macron ordinances drastically extended the scope of the device.

survival is not at stake, opening negotiations on derogation clauses sends a very negative message both for unions and employees. SMEs are less likely to sign their own agreements, whether or not they include derogations, because maintaining the reference to industry-level agreements seems less time-consuming and risky.

Regarding inter-industry collective bargaining, the actors involved in negotiating and signing agreements have not changed much, despite the 2008 Law on representativeness and the introduction of a majority criterion regarding the validity of agreements, whatever their level. The picture is somewhat different at industry and workplace levels, where most collective bargaining takes place. The CGT and the CFDT maintain representativeness in almost all the bargaining industries, unlike other trade unions. The diversity of the combinations of trade unions representativeness at workplace level is greater and may change from election to election.

Representatives of trade union federations lead industry-level bargaining and are usually under tight control from their confederation officers. The picture is much less simple at workplace level. As noted above, three types of actors can negotiate at the workplace: union delegates, works council members or employees mandated by a union. Most workplace agreements are still signed by union delegates. The presence of union delegates, however, does not provide any information on their day-to-day practices. In many enterprises, unionists have little contact with union structures outside the company. Sometimes, union presence is confined to a single delegate, isolated from the organization that is supposed to have chosen them (Dufour and Hege 2010). In fact, negotiations in small companies are often only pseudo-negotiations, in which union delegates simply accept the employer's choices. Genuine negotiations take place only in companies in which unions are strong enough, meaning the large ones. Even in the latter, union federations do not have detailed knowledge of the contents of the growing number of company agreements. Information is more complete on annual wage negotiations, on which the federations send out regular reminders to their activists to complete their databases. HR managers have put a wide range of measures on the bargaining agenda to increase flexibility, moves facilitated by the continuous relaxation of labour market regulations. Add to this the increase in topics for mandatory bargaining and many unionists complain that these negotiations often exhaust local representatives, who thus lose time needed for putting the employees' daily demands on the agenda. These new bargaining topics are often controversial between unions, and even inside individual unions. For representatives of federations, it is quite impossible to establish common rules for concession bargaining, because local activists must judge whether such a concession is compensated in a complex agreement by advances for employees in other areas. Some union federations take a more rigorous stance, refusing to accept concessions of any kind. Checking these instructions is not always easy, however, and may sometimes end with the withdrawal of the delegate's mandate (Rehfeldt and Vincent 2018).

Combined with the trend towards decentralization, the economic crisis has constrained collective bargaining, because employers seek to erode past union achievements by introducing more flexibility (especially on working time), more mobility and more productivity, and also by dampening wage dynamics. The unions for their part have set new priorities in order to obtain guarantees on employment and skills. This explains the growing number of collective agreements focused on employment and training. As a matter of fact, recent reforms have utterly changed the legal framework of the French collective bargaining system. For now, these changes have not altered social actors' practices much (Delahaie et al. 2021).

Industrial conflict

In France the right to strike is an individual right guaranteed by the Constitution. In the majority of cases, however, strikes are called by unions. In the public sector and transport, there are a few legal restrictions, such as mandatory strike notices, guaranteed minimum services and a minimum one-day pay reduction for strikers in order to discourage short-duration stoppages. Despite these restrictions, wildcat strikes still persist in transport and are justified by the legal 'right of withdrawal in case of immediate danger'.

The low unionization rate has always been compensated by a high mobilization capacity on the part of the unions. The strike rate declined from the 1970s to the 1990s, however, despite a peak attributable to the social movement of December 1995. After 2000 it went up again. On average, the strike rate remains one of the highest in Europe, together with other Mediterranean countries (Vandaele 2016). This is mainly because of a high strike propensity in the public and transport sectors (see Figures 11.3 and 11.4). This remarkable strike performance is achieved despite the weakness of union strike funds. Such funds are generally organized locally only after the beginning of a strike, appealing to wider solidarity. The CFDT, which is not very strike-prone, is the only confederation that has set up a permanent strike fund. In the public sector, if a strike is successful, unions are sometimes able to negotiate partial compensation for wage losses. This is less frequent now.

Figure 11.3 Number of days not worked due to industrial action per 1,000 employees in the private sector, 2005–2016

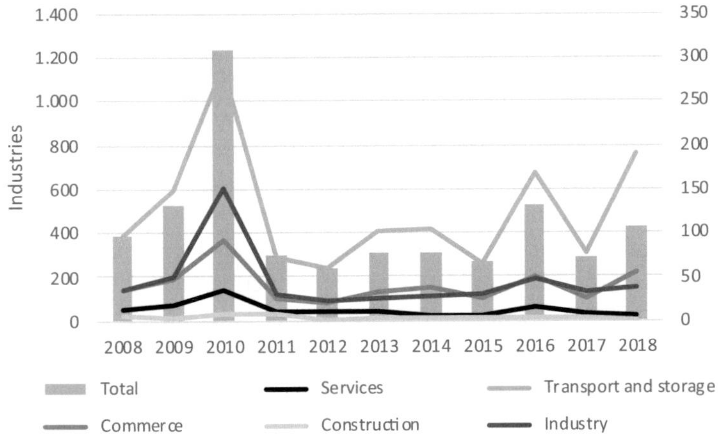

Source: DARES (2018).

Figure 11.4 Number of days not worked due to industrial action in the state civil service, 1999–2018

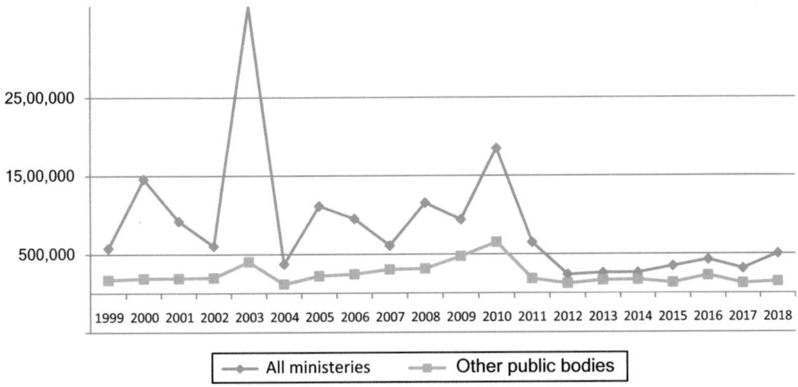

Note: * Other public bodies are mainly the state-owned companies Poste and France Telecom/ Orange. There are no series for public hospitals and local authorities.
Source: Le Goff (2019).

After 2000 there were four strike peaks in 2003, 2010, 2016 and 2018, all related to social movements against reforms of pension law (2003 and 2010) or labour law (2016 and 2018). The 2003 and 2010 movements were the most important. They were backed by all the unions and were only partially successful. The 2016 and 2018 movements were backed by only half of the trade unions and were unsuccessful (see below).

The six-year REPONSE survey provides greater detail about strikes. In the 2010 survey, 29 per cent of workplaces with more than ten employees had notified an industrial conflict, a much higher proportion than the 21 per cent in the first survey in 1998. Conflicts could take various forms: brief work release, demonstration or refusal of overtime. All these forms increased during the period 1998–2010, except for strikes lasting more than two days (Giraud et al. 2018). As workers become more precarious, unions now favour shorter conflicts, which are less costly and less risky for workers, but in many cases are still costly for the management, in particular if they disrupt just-in-time production (Béroud et al. 2008).

Although regular collective bargaining is more and more frequent in larger companies, strikes are often the only way for unions to force management to negotiate (Pernot 2010). Violent action is generally in decline. Only 1 per cent of the conflicts notified in the REPONSE survey took that form. They can include occupation or blocking of factories, sequestration of management and even, in very rare cases, threats of destruction. These are generally associated with protecting jobs and production sites (Contrepois 2011; Hayes 2012).

In 2004, the last year for which such information is available, 62 per cent of all strikes in the private sector were initiated by the CGT, more than half of them together with other unions. The CFDT initiated 35 per cent, FO 25 per cent, both mainly together with other unions. Only 13 per cent of strikes were spontaneous and not initiated by one of the unions (Carlier and De Oliveira 2005).

Political relations

In the application of the so-called *Charte d'Amiens*, adopted by the syndicalist majority of the 1906 CGT congress, union members are asked not to introduce into the union political opinions they are free to 'profess outside'. Unions should stay apart from political parties. Today, all unions officially subscribe to these principles of political autonomy and non-interference of parties in union affairs. In reality, however, things have developed somewhat differently. After the great split of the workers' movement in 1919–1920, the reformist majority of the CGT was close to the reformist minority of the socialist party SFIO, and the syndicalist union minority was close to the majority that subsequently created the French Communist Party (PCF, *Parti Communiste Français*) and adopted the Leninist principle that unions are simply a transmission belt of party decisions. The rise of communists in the reunified CGT led to the breakaway of FO in 1949. Officially, FO put forward the Amiens principle of political autonomy, but in reality, most of its leaders, including its secretary general, were members of the Socialist Party, even if there were also syndicalist, Trotskyist or Gaullist activists. In the Christian union family, similar union–party links were established with the Catholic Centre party, which loosened after its transformation into the CFDT. In the CFDT, the choice between an autonomous strategy and an alliance with the Socialist Party (PS, *Parti Socialiste*) was a matter of dispute in the 1970s (Mouriaux 1985).

At the end of the 1990s, the links between unions and parties began to loosen. After the collapse of the Soviet Union and the decline of the PCF, the CGT leadership officially ended its organic links with the leadership of the Communist Party, symbolized by the presence of union leaders in party governance. Many union leaders and activists remained party members, however. In 2015, for the first time the CGT elected a Secretary General who was not a member of the Communist Party. Tensions also appeared between CFDT and PS. All the unions have now officially abandoned their practice of recommending that members vote for certain parties in elections. Until 2017, despite the absence of official electoral recommendations, members and supporters of CGT, CFDT, FO, UNSA, USS and FSU continued to vote en masse for left-wing parties, mainly the PS. The 2017 presidential elections, which led to a collapse of the PS, have interrupted this continuity. In the first election round, a majority of the supporters of CGT, USS, FSU and even FO voted for the candidate of the extreme left, Jean-Luc Mélenchon, whereas a majority of the supporters of CFDT and UNSA voted for Emmanuel Macron, following the recommendations of some Socialist and union leaders.

From 2000 until 2015, both left- and right-wing governments pronounced themselves in favour of concertation with the unions on labour policy, and legislation in support of union representation and collective bargaining. After 2000, reforms were accelerated under pressure from the employers' organizations, which reiterated demands to negotiate with the unions on an overhaul (*refondation*) of the industrial relations system. Their main objective was to eliminate state interventionism in social regulation and to replace it with the primacy of collective bargaining at workplace level. The unions agreed to negotiate a series of cross-industry agreements, afterwards transposed into law, in which employers were able to impose most of their demands. These agreements were signed by the three 'reformist' trade unions CFDT, CFTC and CFE-CGC, and some of them also by FO.

In 2007, the practice of pre-negotiation of labour law reform was secured by the Larcher Law. It commits the government, in case of a legislative initiative in the field of employment relations, to give the social partners the opportunity to negotiate a cross-industry collective agreement on this issue, which the government then has to implement by law.[10] The Larcher Law, inspired by the Maastricht Social Protocol of 1992, gave a kind of neo-corporatist flavour to the practice of tripartite concertation. It led to another series of cross-industry agreements, some of which were also co-signed by the CGT (Freyssinet 2017). Tripartite concertation at peak level, however, came to a halt under President Hollande in 2015. The 2016 El Khomri Law and the 2017 Macron Ordinances were adopted without prior concertation. The El Khomri Law was supported only by the CFDT, as was the first draft of the Macron reform. The final bill was opposed by all the unions, although they were unable to prevent its adoption by the Parliament (Rehfeldt 2018a).

Societal power

Some of the authors mentioned in this chapter have helped to spread a vision of a definitive institutionalization of French trade unionism increasingly cut off from the reality of employees at work and social movements. Analysis of the current influence of unions and their ability to share their conception of social change tempers this judgement.

On one hand, unions still have a relatively good image among workers, in any case much better than that of political parties. In addition,

---

[10] The government can, however, circumvent this obligation by declaring a reform bill 'urgent'.

unions know how to mobilize beyond strikers when it comes to opposing reforms that have an impact on the world of work. French unions have long found support among the general public. On the other hand, forms of mobilization have been renewed within the workforce, as illustrated by the recurrent practice of coordination which has developed during numerous struggles since the end of the 1980s, including among railway workers and nurses. Going beyond unions and their traditional scope of action is not entirely new but has not subsequently prevented unions from successfully managing these movements. These include recently the creation of the Inter-health-emergencies group (CIU, *Collectif Inter-Urgences*), a social movement within public hospitals since 2019. This group brings together non-unionized allied health professionals motivated by improving working conditions and reception within emergency structures. With the support of hospital unions CGT, FO and USS, it managed to coordinate several national strikes of unprecedented scale in 2019 and 2020. The so-called 'yellow vests' (*gilets jaunes*) movement is, from this point of view, something apart because from the start it has denied any rapprochement with the trade unions, even if many union activists participated in the mobilization, at least in the first weeks. This movement, named after the high-visibility road safety vests worn by protesters, emerged in October 2018 after calls on social media to protest against a tax reform bill generating rising prices of automotive fuels. Soon, the movement's demands widened, including measures to improve the living standards of the working and middle classes. The main action of the movement has been to hold demonstrations every Saturday, which quickly led to violent episodes, especially in Paris. From November 2018, the protest was also organized around illegal blockades of roads and roundabouts and mainly mobilized the inhabitants of rural and peri-urban areas. These two movements, although very different, have both succeeded in launching powerful mobilizations independently of any trade union. They are also characterized by transgressive forms of action that have made it possible to obtain results. These movements are largely based on new digital media that can trigger actions spontaneously and quickly.

To conclude, we can add that the French trade unions have always built coalitions with NGOs but most recently, the Covid-19 pandemic and its social and economic aftershocks have accelerated the construction of coalitions of unions, associations and environmental organizations, all left out by the government in managing the health crisis. In early March 2020, the

Pacte du pouvoir de vivre (whose aims were defined as 'a new environmental, social and democratic model of society') was launched at the initiative of nineteen organizations, including a number of NGOs working in the social field or for the climate (the most famous is the *Fondation Nicolas Hulot*) and three trade unions: CFDT, CFTC and UNSA. The aim of the pact is to reconcile social justice and ecological transition, including the fight against inequalities. It also proposes a new sharing of power in the making of public policy and within companies. For its part, at the end of March 2020, CGT, USS, FSU and the Peasant Confederation (*Confédération paysanne*) also published an appeal, together with several environmental organizations, such as Greenpeace. In total, eighteen trade unions, associations and environmental organizations are calling for the relocation of production, the strengthening of public services and the conditioning of aid paid to companies on their ecological and social conversion.

Trade union policies towards the European Union

When the ETUC was created in 1973, FO was the only French affiliate, as it had been among the forerunners of the ETUC. FO was reluctant to assent to ETUC enlargement, fearing that the arrival of Catholic and Communist unions would dissolve its ideological homogeneity, but it could not avoid the arrival of other French affiliates: CFDT (1974), CFTC (1990), CGT (1999), and UNSA (1999). The CFE-CGC created its own European organization in 1989, now called CEC European Managers, but some of its federations – such as the metal, textile, mining and energy federations – are now affiliated to IndustriAll Europe. The FSU is also affiliated to an ETUF, the European Trade Union Committee for Education (ETUCE), as well as to Eurocadres. Only one French union organization remains unaffiliated: USS.[11] Because of the large number of their organizations, and benefitting from the generous ETUC statutes, the French affiliates carry a certain weight in the Executive Committee and the Congress, despite the small number of workers they represent. At the 2019 Vienna Congress, the French delegation was the third largest (twenty-five delegates), after those from Italy (thirty-nine) and Germany

11 Its public finance and customs federations are affiliated to the Union of Finance Personnel in Europe (UFE), which cooperates with the European Confederation of Independent Trade Unions (CESI). The CESI also affiliates some other French autonomous unions.

(twenty-seven). Until 2019 and with the exception of 2011–2015, one member of the ETUC secretariat always came from a French affiliate (1973–1975 FO, 1975–2003 CFDT, 2003–2011 CGT, 2015–2019 CFDT).[12]

All the French union confederations, except the CGT, were from the beginning in favour of European integration, both for economic and political reasons. European integration was seen as a vehicle for prosperity, peace and protection from the 'communist threat', both inside and outside. Since its affiliation to the ETUC, the CFDT has been the French union with the most active involvement in European integration and consequently in the ETUC. The CFDT was, and still is, the most active supporter of European social dialogue, both at cross-industry, industry and company level. It supported the initiative for the creation of European WorksCouncils, long before the adoption of the European directive in 1994 (Rehfeldt 2009). It also strongly supports transnational company agreements. This partly explains why half of all European framework agreements have been signed by French multinationals (Rehfeldt 2018b).

A more critical attitude on the part of FO vis-à-vis European policies coincided with the arrival of Jacques Delors in Brussels in 1985. It was heightened by the CGT's affiliation to the ETUC in 1999, which has led to a certain marginalization of FO (Pernot 2001). In 2004, FO was the only affiliate to vote in the ETUC executive committee against the Constitutional Treaty, but it did not recommend voting against it in the French referendum. At the same meeting, the CGT abstained on the Constitutional Treaty, but this position, defended by its Secretary General, was defeated by its union assembly, which adopted a motion in favour of organizing a campaign against it. When in 2012 the ETUC rejected the Fiscal Compact, FO and CGT were relieved, because they were able to ask the French Parliament (albeit unsuccessfully) to reject its ratification. CFDT and UNSA were the only affiliates to defend the Compact. They continued to denounce austerity, however, and the absence of a European social vision. This allowed both to participate in the European action day of 29 February 2012, together with the CGT, FSU and USS (Pernot 2013). At the Athens Congress of May 2019, the

12 In 2011–2015, the ETUC secretary general was the Frenchwoman Bernadette Ségol. She had passed her whole professional career as an official of different ETUFs. It remains unclear whether she had previously been a member of any French union.

ETUC found unity again. The same month, however, the congress of the CGT exhibited deep divergences about its international affiliations. Delegates criticized the ETUC policy and asked for a re-affiliation to the World Federation of Trade Unions (WFTU), which it had left in 1995 with observer status. An amendment putting the WFTU at the same level as the ETUC was finally adopted by a 54 per cent majority, against the wishes of the executive committee, which was able to gather the support of only 34 per cent of the delegates.

Conclusions

Examining the situation critically, French trade unions could hardly exist without support from the state. Although this support has now diminished, the institutionalization of the trade union confederations has enabled them to maintain their capacity for action and their influence. To conclude, we may cast some doubt on the durability of the French model. In discussing the four scenarios presented by Visser (2019), three of them – *marginalization*, *substitution* and *revitalization* – do not seem particularly likely. Undoubtedly the state has reduced legal rights for employees and weakened unions, so that on the whole the protection of employees has diminished. But to date this trend has not led to a *marginalization* of unions. The current crises show that the state still needs partners in the world of work. Furthermore, French unions have lately chosen a realistic strategy of coalition-building with NGOs to meet new challenges, such as climate change.

Faced with the reversal of their social gains, workers in certain areas are organizing themselves in more direct forms of representation. Nonetheless, the presence/support of trade unions is still evident in these movements, which means that there has not yet been *substitution*. On the contrary, these social movements are sometimes rather an opportunity for unions to establish new links with workers on the periphery of the *salariat*, as in the case of the struggles over delivery riders. Nonetheless, there are no real signs of *revitalization*.

The most likely scenario for French trade unions, then, is polarization, rather than *dualization*, as Visser calls his last scenario. The French model has polarized in two ways. On one hand, a world of small companies without a union presence stands over against a world of large companies in which the unions continue to exert influence. The current weakening of industry bargaining, the level that plays a decisive role in SMEs, reinforces this polarization. The main challenge for unions in the coming decades should be to find ways to fight against the fragmentation of the workforce. Moreover, the world of work has itself polarized between compromise-oriented and more oppositional unions. This polarization is more accentuated at the cross-industry and industry level than at the company level, where more unitary practices remain, usually in a defensive posture.

References

All links were checked on 14 June 2121.

Adam G. (1983) Le pouvoir syndical, Paris, Dunod.

Amossé T. and Denis J.-M. (eds) (2016) La discrimination syndicale en question: la situation en France, Travail et Emploi, (145), 1–214.

Andolfatto D. and Labbé D. (2011) Sociologie des syndicats, 3rd edn, Paris, La Découverte.

Andolfatto D. and Labbé D. (2017) Le financement des partenaires sociaux après la loi Sapin du 5 mars 2014, Droit Social, (3), 255–264.

Barthélemy M., Dargent C., Groux G. and Rey H. (2012) Le réformisme assumé de la CFDT: enquête auprès des adhérents, Paris, Presses de Sciences Po.

Béroud S. and Denis J.-M. (2012) Le développement interprofessionnel de Solidaires: entre volonté d'expérimentation et reproduction du 'modèle' confédéral, La Revue de l'IRES, 75, 67–92.

Béroud S. and Yon K. (2013) Institutionnalisation et bureaucratisation du syndicalisme: pour une lecture dialectique, in Mezzi D. (ed.) Nouveau siècle, nouveau syndicalisme, Paris, Syllepse, 35–51.

Béroud S., Denis J.-M., Desage G., Giraud B. and Pelisse J. (2008) La lutte continue? Les conflits de travail dans la France contemporaine, Broissieux, Editions du Croquant.

Béthoux E., Desage G., Mias A. and Pélisse J. (2013) Sociologie d'un syndicalisme catégoriel: la CFE-CGC ou la fin d'une exception? Paris, Armand Colin.

Bourguigon R. and Yon K. (2018) The political effects of accounting normalisation on trade unions: an analysis of financial transparency reform in France, British Journal of Industrial Relations, 56 (2), 418–441.

Carlier A. and De Oliveira V. (2005) Les conflits du travail en 2004, les salaires, premier thème de revendication, Premières Synthèses 45.1, Paris, Dares.

Chappe V.-A., Denis J.-M., Guillaume C. and Pochic S. (2019) La fin des discriminations syndicales? Luttes judiciaires et pratiques négociées, Paris, Editions du Croquant.

Connolly H. (2010) Renewal in the French trade union movement: a grass-roots perspective, Frankfurt am Main, Peter Lang.

Connolly H. and Darlington R. (2012) Radical political unionism in France and Britain: a comparative study of SUD-Rail and the RMT, European Journal of Industrial Relations, 18 (3), 235–250.

Contrepois S. (2011) Direct action in France: a new phase in labour-capital conflict, in Gall G. (ed.) New forms and expressions of conflict at work, Basingstoke, Palgrave Macmillan, 152–170.

Contrepois S. (2015) Mobilised but not unionised? An analysis of the relationships between youth and trade unionism in France, in Hodder A. and Kretsos L. (eds) Young workers and trade unions: a global view, Basingstoke, Palgrave Macmillan, 90–106.

Contrepois S. (2017) France: the assimilationist model called into question, in Marino S., Roosblad J. and Penninx R. (eds) Trade unions and migrant workers: new contexts and challenges in Europe, Cheltenham, Edgar Elgar, 128–157.

Daniel C. (2017) La négociation collective d'entreprise en 2015. Stabilité de la part des entreprises qui négocient, Résultats 66, Paris, Dares.

Daniel C., Rehfeldt U. and Vincent C. (2000) La régulation paritaire à la française, Revue française des affaires sociales, 3–4, 119–133.

Dares (2018) La syndicalisation. https://dares.travail-emploi.gouv.fr/donnees/la-syndicalisation

Dares (2020) Les institutions représentatives du personnel. https://dares.travail-emploi.gouv.fr/donnees/les-institutions-representatives-du-personnel

de Comarmond L. (2013) Les vingt ans qui ont changé la CGT, Paris, Denoël.

Defaud N. (2009) La CFDT (1968–1995). De l'autogestion au syndicalisme de proposition, Paris, Presses de Sciences Po.

Delahaie N. and Vincent C. (2021) The SMIC as a driver for collective bargaining: the interplay of collective bargaining and minimum wage in

France, in Dingeldey I., Schulten T. and Grimshaw D. (eds) Minimum wage regimes: statutory regulation, collective bargaining and adequate levels, London, Routledge, 162–188.

Delahaie N., Farvaque N., Fretel A., Guillas-Cavan K., Messaoudi D., Petit H., Tallard M. and Vincent C. (2021) Vers un basculement de la branche vers l'entreprise? Diversité des pratiques de négociations collectives et pluralité des formes d'articulation entre entreprise et branche, Rapport pour la Dares, Noisy, IRES.

Denis J.-M. (2003) Les syndicalistes de SUD-PTT: des entrepreneurs de morale?, Sociologie du Travail, 45 (3), 307–325.

Denis J.-M. (2012) The case of SUD-Rail: the limits of 'radical political unionism', European Journal of Industrial Relations, 18 (3), 267–272.

Dreyfus M. and Pigenet M. (eds) (2011) Les meuniers du social: Force ouvrière, acteur de la vie contractuelle et du paritarisme, fin des années cinquante-début des années quatre-vingt, Paris, Publications de la Sorbonne.

Dufour C. and Hege A. (2010) The legitimacy of collective actors and trade union renewal, Transfer, 16 (3), 351–357.

Freyssinet J. (2017) Social dialogue in the shadow of the State in France, in Guardiancich I. and Molina O. (eds) Talking through the crisis: social dialogue and industrial relations trends in selected EU countries, Geneva, ILO, 107–130.

Fulton L. and Sechi C. (2019) ETUC annual gender equality survey, Brussels, ETUC.

Giraud B., Yon K. and Béroud S. (2018) Sociologie politique du syndicalisme, Paris, Armand Colin.

Guillaume C. (ed.) (2014) La CFDT: sociologie d'une conversion réformiste, Rennes, Presses Universitaires de Rennes.

Guillaume C. and Pochic S. (2013) Breaking through the union glass ceiling in France: between organisational opportunities and individual resources, in Ledwith S. and Hansen L.L. (eds) Gendering and diversifying trade union leadership, London, Routledge, 245–263.

Hayes G. (2012) Bossnapping: situating repertoires of industrial action in national and global contexts, Modern & Contemporary France, 20 (2), 185–201.

IRES, CGT CFDT, FO, CFDT and UNSA (2015) Trade unions in France, Paris, IRES. http://gesd.free.fr/syndires15.pdf

Le Goff T. (ed.) (2019) Rapport annuel sur l'état de la fonction publique: politiques et pratiques de ressources humaines: faits et chiffres. Edition 2019, Paris, Direction générale de l'administration et de la fonction publique.

Mouriaux R. (1985) Syndicalisme et politique, Paris, Editions Ouvrières.

Observatoire de la discrimination et de la répression syndicales (2014) De la discrimination individuelle à l'action collective. Propositions pour garantir le respect des droits syndicaux et salariés: rapport 2014, Paris, Observatoire de la discrimination et de la répression syndicales. https://observatoire-repression-syndicale.org/?p=1585

Pernot J.-M. (2001) Dedans, dehors, la dimension internationale dans le syndicalisme français, Thèse de doctorat, Université de Nanterre – Paris X.

Pernot J.-M. (2010) Syndicats: lendemains de crise? Nouvelle édition revue et augmentée, Paris, Editions Gallimard.

Pernot J.-M. (2013) France. L'Europe, une influence diffuse sur les relations professionnelles mais un sujet de discorde syndicale, Chronique internationale de l'IRES, 143–144, 75–92.

Pernot J.-M. (2018) France's trade unions in the aftermath of the crisis, in Lehndorff S., Dribbusch H. and Schulten T. (eds) Rough waters. European trade unions in a time of crisis, 2nd and updated edition, Brussels, ETUI, 39–64.

Pignoni M.-T. (2016) La syndicalisation en France: des salariés deux fois plus syndiqués dans la fonction publique, Analyses 25, Paris, Dares.

Pignoni M.-T. (2017) De l'adhérent au responsable syndical: quelles évolutions dans l'engagement des salariés syndiqués?, Analyses 15, Paris, Dares.

Pignoni M.-T. (2019) Les représentants du personnel dans l'entreprise: des salariés comme les autres?, Analyses 2, Paris, Dares.

Piotet F. (ed.) (2009) La CGT et la recomposition syndicale, Paris, PUF.

Rehfeldt U. (2009) European works councils in France, in Hertwig M., Pries L. and Rampeltshammer L. (eds) European works councils in complementary perspective: new approaches to the study of European interest regulation, Brussels, ETUI, 153–185.

Rehfeldt U. (2018a) Industrial relations in France: from the underdevelopment of collective bargaining to the failure of neo-corporatist concertation, Employee Relations, 40 (4), 617–633.

Rehfeldt U. (2018b) A mapping of the transnational company agreements: inventory and dynamic, in Guarriello F. and Stanzani C. (eds)

Trade unions and collective bargaining in multinationals. From international legal framework to empirical research, Milan, Franco Angeli, 46–59.

Rehfeldt U. and Vincent C. (2018) The decentralisation of collective bargaining in France: an escalating process, in Leonardo S. and Pedersini R. (eds) Multi-employer bargaining under pressure: decentralisation trends in five European countries, Brussels, ETUI, 151–184.

Rosanvallon P.(1988) La question syndicale, Paris, Calmann-Lévy.

Silvera R. (2006) Le défi de l'égalité hommes/femmes dans le syndicalisme, Mouvements (43), 23–29.

Tallard M. and Vincent C. (2014) Les branches professionnelles sont-elles toujours un lieu pertinent de négociation des normes d'emploi?, Droit Social, 3, 212–216.

Thomas A. (2016) The transnational circulation of the 'organizing model' and its reception in Germany and France, European Journal of Industrial Relations, 22 (4), 317–333.

Vandaele K. (2016) Interpreting strike activity in western Europe in the past 20 years: the labour repertoire under pressure, Transfer, 22 (3), 277–294.

Vincent C. (2016) France: the crisis speeds up public service reform and adjustment, in Bach S. and Bordogna L. (eds) Public service management and employment relations in Europe, emerging from the crisis? Abingdon, Routledge, 112–135.

Vincent C. (2019) France: the rush towards prioritising the enterprise level, in Müller T., Vandaele K. and Waddington J. (eds) Collective bargaining in Europe: towards an endgame, Bruxelles, ETUI, 217–238.

Visser J. (2019) Trade Unions in the Balance, ILO ACTRAV Working Paper, Geneva, ILO.

Wolff L. (2008) Le paradoxe du syndicalisme français: un faible nombre d'adhérents, mais des syndicats bien implantés, Premières Synthèses 16.1, Paris, Dares.

Yon K. (2016) A long awaited homecoming: the labour movement in social movement studies, in Fillieule O. and Accornero G. (eds) Social movement studies in Europe. The state of the art, New York, Berghahn Books, 54–68.

Abbreviations

CEC Confédération Européenne des Cadres (European Confederation of Professional and Managerial Staff)

CESI Confédération Européenne des Syndicats Indépendants (European Confederation of Independent Trade Unions)

CFDT Confédération Française Démocratique du Travail (French Democratic Confederation of Labour)

CFE-CGC Confédération Française de l'Encadrement – Confédération Générale des Cadres (French Confederation of Supervisors – General Confederation of Professional and Managerial Staff)

CFTC Confédération Française des Travailleurs Chrétiens (French Confederation of Christian Workers)

CGT Confédération Générale du Travail (General Confederation of Labour)

CIU Collectif Inter-Urgences (Inter-health-emergencies group)

DARES Direction de l'animation de la recherche, des études et des statistiques (Research and statistical department of the French Ministry of Labour)

DGAFP Direction générale de l'administration et de la fonction publique (General Direction of Public Administration and Civil Service)

DGB Deutscher Gewerkschaftsbund (German Trade Union Confederation)

ETUC European Trade Union Confederation

ETUCE European Trade Union Committee for Education

ETUF European Trade Union Federation

FEN Fédération d'Education Nationale (Federation of National Education)

FO Force Ouvrière (Worker Force, officially CGT-FO)

FSU Fédération Syndicale Unitaire (Unitary Trade Union Federation)

NGO Non-governmental organization

PCF Parti Communiste Français (French Communist Party)

PS Parti Socialiste (Socialist Party)

PSU Parti Socialiste Unifié (Unified Socialist Party)

REPONSE Relations professionnelles et négociations d'entreprise (Industrial relations and company-level bargaining, survey carried out by DARES)

SFIO Section Française de l'Internationale Ouvrière (French Section of the Worker International) former name of PS

SMEs small and medium-sized enterprises

SUD Solidaires, Unitaires, Démocratiques (Supportive, Unitary, Democratic)

UD Union départementale (cross-industry union body at départment level)

UR Union régionale (cross-industry union body at regional level)

UNSA Union Nationale des Syndicats Autonomes (National Union of Autonomous Trade Unions)

USS Union Syndicale Solidaires ('Solidaires' Union of Trade Unions)

WFTU World Federation of Trade Unions

Chapter 12

Germany: Different worlds of trade unionism

Torsten Müller and Thorsten Schulten

Writing twenty years ago in the predecessor of the present volume, Hoffmann (2000) described the state of German trade unions as relatively stable. This was based on the strong institutional framework of the dual system of interest representation, with works councils at the company level and multi-employer bargaining at industry level, ensuring high collective bargaining coverage. At first sight, the union landscape today still gives an impression of strength, particularly from an international comparative perspective. Germany is home to two unions – IG Metall and Ver.di – which in terms of membership are among the largest in the world. Furthermore, unions played an essential role in securing jobs and safeguarding industries during the Great Recession in 2008/2009 and more recently in the Covid-19 pandemic. Partly as a consequence of this, Germany is still among the countries with the most positive public perception of unions in the European Union (EU) (European Commission 2019).

A closer look at developments during the past twenty years yields a more nuanced picture. The first qualification concerns membership development. The affiliates of the German Trade Union Confederation (DGB, Deutscher Gewerkschaftsbund), the largest union confederation, lost around one-fifth of their membership in the first decade of the 2000s. Unions managed to halt – and in some cases reverse – the loss of membership after 2010, however. The Covid-19 pandemic has recently led again to a somewhat greater loss of membership (Specht 2022). Overall, net union density has decreased by almost 10 percentage points during the past twenty years to around 16 per cent (see Table 12.1), which has considerably weakened the unions' organizational strength.

Moreover, the employers' weakening support for or even resistance to core institutions of German industrial relations represents a major challenge to the unions' institutional power resources. The employers' increasing reluctance to engage in industry-level collective bargaining has contributed to the decentralization, fragmentation and ultimately erosion of collective bargaining. As a consequence, collective bargaining coverage has decreased substantially, from 68 per cent in 2000 to 51 per cent in 2020.

Furthermore, the principal features of the German industrial relations model and its impact on unions differ considerably by industry and even region. It is therefore an oversimplification to speak of the German unions as an entity, treating them as a homogenous actor. On the contrary, there is a growing divergence which has led to a growing polarization of different worlds of industrial relations and unionism within Germany (Hassel and Schroeder 2018). At one end of the spectrum are the export-oriented industries and the public sector, where the traditional features of the German industrial relations system are still largely in place: strong collective actors on both sides of industry, industry-level collective agreements and a strong presence of works councils. At the other end, large parts of the services and crafts sector and, from a regional perspective, eastern Germany are characterized by a far-reaching erosion of the traditional model of German industrial relations more generally and union presence more specifically. The remainder of this chapter analyses the multi-faceted challenges to unions and their responses in trying to adapt to a changing world of work.

Table 12.1 The principal characteristics of trade unionism in Germany

	1991	2000	2020
Total trade union membership	13,748,600	9,330,000***	7,448,567
Women as a proportion of total membership*	33 %	32 %	34 %
Gross union density	38 %	25 %	n.a.
Net union density	36 %	25 %***	16 %
Number of confederations	4	4	3
Number of affiliated unions (federations)	n.a.	n.a.	DGB: 8 DBB: 40 CGB: 13****
Number of independent unions	n.a.	n.a.	6 (2018)
Collective bargaining coverage	85 %**	68 %	51 %
Principal level of collective bargaining	Industry level	Industry level but increasing importance of company level	
Days not worked due to industrial action per 1,000 workers	11	0	9

Note: * data available only for DGB-affiliated unions; **1990; ***2001; ****2018.

Source: Appendix A1.

Historical background and principal features of the industrial relations system

The development of industrial relations is closely linked to the specific German variant of 'Rhenish capitalism' (Albert 1993), which is traditionally based on strong political and societal support for the concept of the 'social market economy' (Müller-Armack 1947). According to this originally 'ordoliberal' concept, the state defines the rules of the game to ensure competitive markets, while at the same time supporting a dense network of institutions and civil society actors in generating 'most of the regulations and collective goods that circumscribe, correct and underpin the instituted markets of … the social market economy' (Streeck 1997: 39). German industrial relations have been characterized as a system of 'conflictual partnership' (*Konfliktpartnerschaft*) (Müller-Jentsch 1999), whereby class conflict is embedded in a wide range of legally backed institutions that enable and constrain the unions' and employers' capacity to act. Its most important feature is the so-called 'dual system of interest representation', comprising collective bargaining, which takes place mainly at industry level, and worker representation at the company and workplace level. The principal idea behind this arrangement is to keep distributional conflicts between capital and labour out of day-to-day labour relations at company level. In light of their far-reaching participation rights and opportunities, unions usually follow a more cooperative attitude of 'partnership' but from a position of strength, which always allows them to change to a more confrontational strategy and to take industrial action.

The most important legal basis of industrial relations is Article 9(3) of the German Constitution (Basic Law), which guarantees freedom of association and thus the autonomy of trade unions and employers in regulating employment conditions (*Tarifautonomie* or 'free collective bargaining'). The German constitution therefore largely excludes direct state intervention in determining terms and conditions of employment and guarantees far-reaching regulatory competences of the two sides of industry. By defining distinct arenas for the autonomous regulation of the employment relationship, legislation also underpins the dual structure of employee interest representation as the most fundamental feature of industrial relations. The legal basis of collective bargaining is the Collective Agreements Act of 1949 (TVG, *Tarifvertragsgesetz*) and employee representation at workplace level is based on the Works Constitution Act (BetrVG, *Betriebsverfassungsgesetz*), which was first introduced in 1952 and substantially amended in 1972 and 2001. These two laws establish a formal division of labour between unions, which, as a rule, negotiate collective agreements with employers' associations at industry level, and works councils, which are statutory, non-union bodies elected to represent employees in the workplace.

The broad-based nature of trade unions and employers' associations is reflected in their organizational principle, which as a rule follows an industrial logic. Interest representation on the employers' side rests on three pillars: chambers of industry and commerce (*Industrie- und Handelskammern*), business associations, and employers' associations (Jacobi et al. 1998; Schröder and Weßels 2017). The key industrial relations actors on the employers' side are the employers' associations because they negotiate collective agreements with trade unions. The Confederation of German Employers' Associations (BDA, *Bundesvereinigung der Deutschen Arbeitgeberverbände*) is the national peak-level organization, comprising forty-eight national industry associations and fourteen regional cross-industry associations. Like the DGB on the union side, the BDA is not directly involved in negotiating collective agreements. Negotiations are undertaken by its industry-level affiliates. The employers' association density rate is remarkably stable over time and with 68 per cent in 2018 (OECD and AIAS 2021) substantially higher than union density. In order to stabilize membership levels about half of German employers' associations introduced a special so-called 'OT membership' (Behrens and Helfen 2019). 'OT' stands for *ohne Tarif*, which means membership without being bound by a collective agreement. This essentially gives employers the opportunity to remain a member of the association without having to apply an industry-level agreement signed by the respective employers' association. There is little information about the actual uptake of this kind of special membership. Evidence from the metalworking industry, however, shows that the proportion of companies making use of OT membership increased from 24 per cent in 2005 to 52 per cent in 2017 (Schulten 2019).

For most of the post-war period, industrial relations enjoyed a high degree of stability. In the past twenty years, however, they have come under increasing pressure. While formally the legal framework governing the dual system of interest representation remained largely unchanged, below the surface, the employers' waning support for 'conflictual partnership' and its two main institutional pillars – works councils and industry-level collective bargaining – has considerably undermined the unions' institutional power resources. At the heart of the unions' capacity to act, however, is their own organizational strength. The principal political and economic features have also changed considerably. Liberalization and deregulation in social and labour market policy have led to a weakening of social and employment protection and to a strong increase in precarious employment, representing a major challenge for union organizing. Unions have also been faced with a fundamental shift in the economic and employment structure, resulting from the tertiarization of the economy, the twin challenge of the green and digital transitions and the increasing liberalization and privatization of the public sector.

Structure of trade unions and union democracy

After the Second World War, trade unions were reconstituted as unitary, non-partisan and industrial organizations (*Einheits- und Industriegewerkschaft*) which are, as a rule, affiliated to the DGB. This means that unions are not affiliated to or financed by any political party and that they, in principle, organize all workers in one industry irrespective of their status, profession and political or ideological orientation. The principle of industrial unionism finds its clearest expression in the slogan: 'one company, one union'. The primary purpose of these organizational principles is to avoid political divisions and inter-union demarcation conflicts about organizing members and collective bargaining responsibilities. The principle of industrial unionism, however, has never been implemented in its pure form. Already in the early stages of the reconstitution of the German union movement, there were three organizations besides the DGB that organized workers on the basis of status or ideological orientation. These were: the German Salaried Employees' Union (DAG, *Deutsche Angestelltengewerkschaft*), established in 1945, the German Civil Service Federation (DBB, *Deutscher Beamtenbund und Tarifunion*), founded in 1950, and the Christian Trade Union Confederation (CGB, *Christlicher Gewerkschaftsbund*), established in 1955.

Today, the union landscape consists of three confederations, their sixty-four affiliates and fourteen independent professional unions which, at the end of 2020, together represented more than 7.5 million employees (Table 12.2). By far the largest of the three confederations is the DGB

Table 12.2 Trade union structure and membership, 2001, 2010 and 2020

	2001	**2010**	**2020**
Deutscher Gewerkschaftsbund (DGB) German Trade Union Confederation	**7,899,000**	**6,193,252**	**5,850,167**
Eight DGB affiliates:			
Industriegewerkschaft Metall (IG Metall) German Metalworkers' Union	2,710,000	2,239,588	2,214,662
Vereinte Dienstleistungsgewerkschaft (Ver.di) United Services Union	2,807,000	2,094,455	1,941,071
Industriegewerkschaft Bergbau, Chemie, Energie (IG BCE) Mining, Chemicals and Energy Industrial Union	862,000	675,606	606,348
Industriegewerkschaft Bauen-Agrar-Umwelt (IG BAU)Building, Agriculture & Environmental Workers' Union	510,000	314,568	231,663
Gewerkschaft Erziehung und Wissenschaft (GEW) Union of Education and Science	268,000	260,297	280,452
Gewerkschaft Nahrung-Genuss-Gaststätten (NGG) Food, Tobacco, Hotel & Allied Workers Union	251,000	205,646	194,145
Eisenbahn- und Verkehrsgewerkschaft (EVG) Railway and Transport Union	306,000	232,485	184,090
Gewerkschaft der Polizei (GdP) Trade Union of the Police	185,000	170,607	197,736

Table 12.2 Continued

	2001	2010	2020
Deutscher Beamtenbund und Tarifunion (dbb)* German Civil Service Association 40 affiliates – Main DBB affiliates:	**1,211,000**	**1,280,000**	**1,312,000**
Verband Bildung und Erziehung (VBE) Education and Training Association			164,000
Deutsche Polizeigewerkschaft (DPolG) German Police Union			94,000
Komba Gewerkschaft (komba) Local authority union			90,000
Deutscher Philologenverband (DPhV)German Philologists' Association			90,000
Deutsche Steuergewerkschaft (DStG) German Tax Trade Union			70,000
Gewerkschaft der Sozialversicherung (GdS) Trade Union for Social Security			42,000
Gewerkschaft Deutscher Lokomotivführer (GDL) German Train Drivers' Union	33,000	33,000	34,000
Kommunikationsgewerkschaft DPV (DPVKOM) Communications Trade Union DPV			27,000
Christlicher Gewerkschaftsbund Deutschlands (CGB)* Christian Trade Union Confederation of Germany (fourteen affiliates)	**n.a.**	**275,000**	**280,000**
Independent professional trade unions*	**220,000**	**255,000**	**286,000**
	70,000	106,000	128,000
Marburger Bund (MB) Union of Salaried Medical Doctors			33,000
Deutscher Journalisten-Verband (DJV)German Journalists' Association			
Deutscher Bankangestellten-Verband (DBV) German Association of Banking Staff			21,000
Unabhängige Flugbegleiter Organisation (UFO) Independent Flight Attendants' Organization			13,000
Vereinigung Cockpit (VC) Cockpit Association			9,600
Gewerkschaft der Flugsicherung (GdF) Union of Air Traffic Controllers			3,800
In total	**9,330,000**	**8,003,252**	**7,728,167**
Net union density	23.7 %	18.9 %*	16.3 %**

Note: *Data for 2018; **data for 2019.

Source: DGB (2021), Dribbusch and Birke (2019); OECD and AIAS (2021).

with 5.8 million members, followed by the DBB with 1.3 million members and the CGB with 270,000 members.

Until 1989 the German trade union structure remained remarkably stable. The DGB originally had sixteen affiliates and this composition remained almost unchanged during the first forty years after its establishment in 1949. The union landscape changed, however, through mergers

Table 12.3 Union mergers since 1989

Year	Merging trade unions	New trade union
1989	IG Druck und Papier (IG DruPa) Printing and Paper Union Gewerkschaft Kunst (GK) Arts Union	IG Medien Media Union
1996	IG Bau-Steine-Erden (IG BSE) Construction Workers' Union Gewerkschaft Gartenbau, Land- und Forstwirtschaft (GGLF) Agriculture and Forestry Union	IG Bauen-Agrar-Umwelt (IG BAU) Building, Agriculture & Environmental Workers' Union
1997	IG Chemie-Papier-Keramik (IG CPK) Chemical, Paper and Ceramics Industry Union IG Bergbau und Energie (IG BE) Miners' Union Gewerkschaft Leder (GL) Leather Workers' Union	IG Bergbau, Chemie, Energie (IG BCE) Mining, Chemicals and Energy Industrial Union
1998/2000	IG Metall (1998) Metalworkers' Union Gewerkschaft Textil-Bekleidung (GTB) (1998) Textil and Clothing Workers' Union Gewerkschaft Holz und Kunststoff (GHK) (2000) Wood and Plastics Union	IG Metall German Metalworkers' Union
2001	Gewerkschaft Öffentliche Dienste, Transport und Verkehr (ÖTV) Public Services, Transport and Traffic Union IG Medien Media Union Deutsche Postgewerkschaft (DPG) German Postal Workers' Union Gewerkschaft Handel, Banken und Versicherungen (HBV) Retail, Banking and Insurance Workers' Union Deutsche Angestellten Gewerkschaft (DAG) German Salaried Employees' Union	Vereinte Dienstleistungsgewerkschaft (Ver.di) United Services Union

Table 12.3 Continued

Year	Merging trade unions	New trade union
2010	Gewerkschaft Transport, Service and Netze (Transnet) Transport, Service and Networks Union Verkehrsgewerkschaft Deutscher Bundesbahnbeamten und Anwärter (GDBA) Union of civil servants within German Rail	Eisenbahn- und Verkehrsgewerkschaft (EVG) Railway and Transport Union

Source: Authors' own compilation based on Waddington et al. (2005) and Keller (2012).

that took place mainly in the second half of the 1990s, which halved the number of DGB affiliates from seventeen in 1989 to eight in 2010 (see Table 12.3).

Two mergers are particularly noteworthy: first, the amalgamation between the DGB-affiliated Transnet and the DBB-affiliated Union of Civil Servants within German Rail (GDBA, *Verkehrsgewerkschaft Deutscher Bundesbahnbeamten und Anwärter*) in railways in 2010. This was the first merger of unions from two competing confederations (Keller 2012). Second, because of the sheer size of the newly created organization, in 2001 the merger of five service sector unions to form Ver.di as one united service sector union covering both private and public services (Keller 2001; Waddington et al. 2005). With 2.8 million members in 2001, Ver.di not only was the largest individual DGB affiliate, surpassing even IG Metall with 2.7 million members at the time, but in the whole Western world.

The union mergers prompted the 'rise of conglomerate unions' (Streeck and Visser 1997), which extend their organizational domains to various industries. IG Metall, for instance, has its main constituency in metal manufacturing, including the automobile industry as its organizational stronghold. IG Metall also covers steel, textiles and wood processing, however. Ver.di is even more diverse and represents, apart from the public sector, about 200 industries in private services (Dribbusch and Birke 2019; Dribbusch et al. 2018). The emergence of conglomerate, or multi-industry, unions which, particularly in the case of Ver.di, represent 'mini-DGBs' within the DGB, changed power relationships between the confederation and its affiliates. The two largest affiliates, IG Metall and Ver.di, which today have about 2 million members each, together represent around 70 per cent of all DGB union members. The DGB's already relatively weak position in relation to its affiliates was further weakened and largely restricted to representational matters and political lobbying (Müller and Wilke 2014). The DGB, for instance, does not negotiate collective agreements. DGB affiliates organize workers, are active at the workplace and are engaged in collective bargaining and industrial action. The DGB, furthermore, is financially dependent on its affiliates, which, according to the DGB statutes, finance the DGB by transferring 12 per cent of their annual income from membership fees to the DGB (DGB 2018). Internally, the DGB coordinates cross-industrial policies and mediates between affiliates in the case of inter-union conflicts about the representation of members and collective bargaining responsibilities (Schroeder and Greef 2014).

Germany has also seen a certain revival of occupational unions that, with the exception of the DBB-affiliated German Train Drivers' Union (GDL, *Gewerkschaft Deutscher Lokomotivführer*) do not belong to any of the three confederations (Keller 2018; Schröder et al. 2011). Most of them have transformed themselves from occupational associations with mainly lobbying and servicing functions to real unions with collective bargaining competences (Dribbusch et al. 2018; Schroeder and Greef 2014). The renaissance of professional unions took place in industries such as health care, rail and air traffic which all share certain facilitating characteristics: they were confronted with far-reaching changes by liberalization and privatization of services, which negatively affected wages and working conditions and threatened the status of the professional group represented by these organizations. Furthermore, all organizations felt that the particular interests of their membership were no longer adequately represented by the larger and more encompassing DGB unions. All five occupational unions had the necessary organizational power resources and capacity to mobilize their members to force reluctant employers to negotiate an agreement with them. Their organizational strength is based on high union density facilitated by organizing fairly homogenous professional groups with high labour market power because of their scarce qualifications, which are indispensable for the provision of essential goods and services and cannot easily be substituted (Dribbusch and Birke 2019; Keller 2018; Schroeder and Greef 2014). While employers are often worried about the German system being affected by the 'British disease' of the 1960s and 1970s, with many strong and strike-prone occupational unions (Keller 2018), the emergence of professional unions has been limited to certain industries with specific conditions.

Unionization

Total DGB membership reached its all-time high of almost 12 million members after German re-unification in 1991 following the integration of East German union members, only to slump shortly afterwards (Dribbusch et al. 2018). The reasons for the sharp decline in the East in the 1990s include job losses as a result of privatization, deindustrialization and the end of the construction boom, decreasing labour market participation of women, early retirement of older employees, the disappearing of large enterprises and the parallel emergence of SMEs (Ebbinghaus and Göbel 2014). DGB membership dropped for the first time below the 6 million mark in 2007. The rate of membership decline decreased, however: whereas between 2001 and 2010 the DGB lost more than 20 per cent of its members, this rate was 5.5 per cent between 2010 and 2020. Of the three confederations, DBB was the only one whose membership has increased over the past twenty years (see Table 12.2), reflecting the stable employment situation among civil servants (Dribbusch and Birke 2019).

The aggregate figures for the DGB mask very different membership developments among its affiliates. First, there are the police union GdP and the education union GEW (*Gewerkschaft Erziehung und Wissenschaft*), which managed to increase their membership. Second, there are IG Metall and the food workers' union NGG (*Gewerkschaft Nahrung-Genuss-Gaststätten*), which have consolidated their membership and considerably decreased the rate of membership decline. The third category comprises the remaining four unions, Ver.di, IG BCE, the railway and transport union EVG (*Eisenbahn- und Verkehrsgewerkschaft*) and in particular the construction workers' union IG BAU (*Industriegewerkschaft Bauen-Agrar-Umwelt*), all still struggle with considerable membership losses. In contrast to the DGB-affiliated industrial unions, the smaller professional unions have continuously increased their membership. Nevertheless, overall net union density dropped from 23.7 per cent in 2001 to 16.3 per cent in 2020.

Reasons for the negative long-term trend in union membership are manifold. First, changes in the economic structure involving the deindustrialization and tertiarization of the economy with a substantial shift in employment from union strongholds in manufacturing to the private services sector. A large part of IG BCE's continued membership decline, for instance, can be explained with the phasing-out of the coal industry.

Second, there is the growing importance of employment patterns hampering unionization. This involves the increase in atypical employment forms, widespread in the private service sector, and the growing importance of smaller establishments without union presence or works councils. The key reason for employees to join a union is direct contact with unions in the workplace (Behrens 2009; Dribbusch 2003). Whereas in large-scale industries, such as metalworking and chemicals, unions are generally well represented on works councils and among employees, establishing a presence in the private service sector is much more difficult because workers are more likely to be spread across a large number of often very small workplaces. Rationalization, restructuring and outsourcing of service operations, however, also led to the shrinking or disappearance of large establishments in manufacturing, negatively affecting membership of the manufacturing unions IG Metall and IG BCE. Finally, privatization of formerly state-owned companies, such as Deutsche Bahn, Deutsche Post and Deutsche Telekom, led to substantial job cuts, negatively affecting membership developments in EVG and Ver.di organizing in railways and in postal and telecommunication services, respectively. Ver.di's more fundamental problem, however, is that

Figure 12.1 Proportion of female members in German unions (%), 2001 and 2020

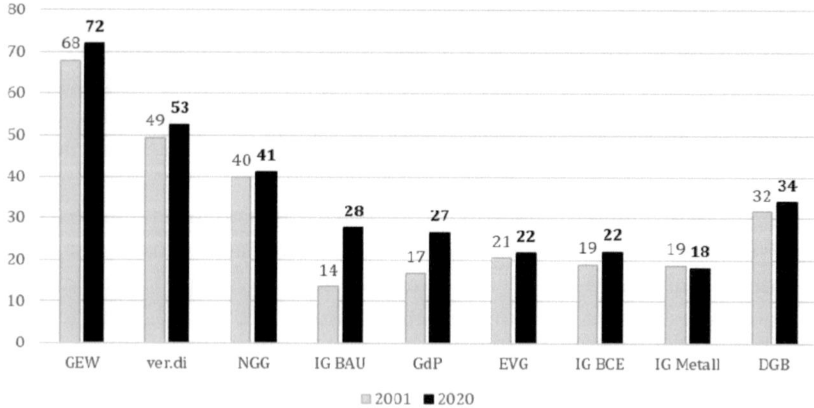

Source: DGB (2021).

membership gains in some industries, such as health care and social and educational services, could not compensate the continuing membership decline in areas such as public administration and retail (Dribbusch and Birke 2019: 11).

Disaggregating union membership figures illustrates another fundamental problem: the membership structure no longer matches the current employment structure. For instance, the increasing labour market participation of women over the past twenty years is not reflected in the structure of union membership (Hassel and Schroeder 2019). While the female employment rate increased by more than 13 percentage points – from 58.8 per cent in 2001 to 71.9 per cent in 2020 (Destatis 2021), the overall proportion of women in unions increased only marginally from 31.7 per cent in 2001 to 34.1 per cent in 2020 (see Figure 12.1). The only DGB-affiliate which substantially increased its share of female members from 13.5 per cent in 2001 to 27.8 per cent in 2020 is IG BAU due to the growth in the female-dominated cleaning industry and the simultaneous decline of membership in the male-dominated construction industry (Hassel and Schroeder 2019). Overall, the share of women in the unions' membership reflects the industry-specific differences in female labour market participation. Given the higher proportion of female employees in their industries, the proportion of female members in GEW, Ver.di and NGG is much higher than in the traditionally male-dominated manufacturing unions, such as IG Metall and IG BCE.

Unions also face the problem that membership tends to be 'overaged' and younger workers are significantly underrepresented (Biebeler and Lesch 2015; Lesch and Winter 2021). As a result of demographic developments, unions have to recruit more and more members every year just to keep their level of organization constant. Furthermore, unions are also underrepresented among white-collar workers, especially among those with an academic background; they also have significant problems organizing the more precarious workers in the services industries.

Unions responded to these representation gaps with new strategic membership policies to become more attractive and relevant for traditionally underrepresented worker categories. A stronger focus on campaign-based organizing methods involves participation-oriented forms of action designed to involve (potential) members in the building of union structures (Dribbusch and Birke 2019). Ver.di, for instance, links organizing initiatives with a more confrontational style of collective bargaining. The idea behind the concept of 'organizing through conflict'

(Kocsis et al. 2013) is to use a collective conflict situation in which there is a greater necessity for workers to act in unity to achieve their objectives to mobilize and organize employees. This strategy has been successfully applied in social and child care services. A variant of this strategy is Ver.di's concept of 'conditional' collective bargaining (*bedingungsgebundene Tarifpolitik*), which is mainly aimed at individual companies and establishments without collective bargaining and poor unionization. This strategy implies that Ver.di will start negotiating an agreement only if enough workers join the union beforehand so that there is a realistic chance of success in a dispute over a collective agreement. This strategy has proven to be successful in a number of privatized hospitals, which contributed to the positive membership development in the health sector (Dribbusch and Birke 2019).

IG Metall has pursued similar campaign-based and participation-oriented strategies by starting campaigns for whole industries or groups of employees. In 2008, IG Metall started a temporary agency work campaign with the slogan 'Equal work – equal pay', with the aim of directly approaching the temporary agency workers to unionize them and to improve their conditions by ensuring that they get the same pay as the workers of the hiring company.

In 2015, IG Metall started a comprehensive organizing campaign with several regional and local projects based on a budget of €170 million used to employ 140 organizers who in cooperation with local union activists targeted specific companies (Schroeder and Fuchs 2019). The aim of these union development projects was not just to recruit new members but also to initiate a cultural and organizational change to help the union to tailor its activities and services to workers' needs and interests. Another element of the strategy to foster more participation-oriented forms of action are membership and employee surveys to capture the preferences and interests of (potential) members. In 2017, a broad-based employee survey was conducted in preparation for the 2018 bargaining round to gauge the actual interests of the rank-and-file; to foster more ownership of the demands; to improve the capacity to mobilize the membership; and finally to strengthen the legitimacy of the demands vis-à-vis employers and government (Hassel and Schroeder 2018).

Ver.di and IG Metall also intensified their activities for solo self-employed and, in particular, for platform workers by opening up membership for this category of workers and by providing specific services, setting up online platforms for the solo self-employed (Vandaele 2021).

More recently, in 2019 IG Metall cooperated with the YouTubers Union, a self-organized group of professional content creators, in a joint campaign labelled 'FairTube' to make YouTube's algorithmic management and cash nexus fairer and more transparent (Vandaele 2021).

Union resources and expenditure

Writing about union finances is a difficult task. Although unions such as IG Metall and Ver.di are very transparent in their activity reports, most unions stopped reporting financial information in their activity reports at the beginning of the 2010s or never did so in the first place. The financial organization of unions is also very complex, covering different areas that are organized in different legal entities with separate budgets. At the most general level one can distinguish the political area that covers the unions' day-to-day activities from the trustee activities that cover real estate and property management. At IG Metall, for instance, there are two further areas with separate budgets: first, a non-profit area dealing with the promotion of youth welfare and international cooperation, as well as links with science and research; and second, investments in companies that provide different kinds of services for IG Metall members and third parties that go beyond the services defined in the statutes (IG Metall 2019a: 268). Publicly available data refers almost exclusively to the first area of political activities and varies widely across unions.

This section therefore deals with the political activities of unions as defined in their statutes and deals mainly with developments at IG Metall and Ver.di. Where data is available developments in the DGB will also be referred to in order to illustrate the financial link with its affiliates.

In principle, unions mainly finance their day-to-day activities through membership fees. For example, the share of DGB income received from its affiliates is around 90 per cent of total income. The rest of its income comes from interest payments and 'other' income, which is not further specified. The DGB does not charge membership fees. It receives 12 per cent of the membership income of each of its eight affiliates. The individual unions' membership fee as a rule is 1 per cent of the members' monthly gross wage, although IG BAU charges 1.15 per cent and GEW and GdP – both organizing in the public sector – charge less than 1 per cent. All unions have to varying degrees reduced fees for members who receive social security benefits, such as the unemployed and pensioners.

Most unions also specify a minimum fee, applying mainly to students, members who are temporarily on parental leave and junior staff. In absolute terms the income of IG Metall and Ver.di is much larger than that of the DGB. In 2012, for instance, the last year for which data for all three organizations is publicly available, the income of the DGB was €164 million compared with IG Metall with €496 million and Ver.di with €423 million. Put differently, the contributions of the two largest affiliates account for two-thirds of the DGB's total income.

Between 2002 and 2010, membership decline in IG Metall and Ver.di negatively affected their income. After 2010, however, membership and income development diverged as both unions managed to increase their income considerably despite more or less stagnating membership. Between 2011 and 2018, Ver.di's total income increased by 13 per cent from €415.3 to €471 million and IG Metall's total income by 28 per cent from €480 to €614.4 million (IG Metall 2012, 2019a; Ver.di 2012, 2019). This is because both unions managed to halt the rapid decline in membership, while the particularly sharp income increase in IG Metall is because of the disproportionately strong increase in members who pay the full fee of 1 per cent of the monthly gross wage (IG Metall 2012, 2019a). The second main reason for the rise in income is the wage increases ensured by collective agreements. Because membership fees are directly linked to members' gross wage, any collective agreed wage increase also increases the union's income (IG Metall 2019a; Ver.di 2019).

The allocation of income from membership fees across the different levels and functional units of the organization is usually specified in the statutes or budgetary guidelines, which vary considerably from union to union. At IG Metall, for instance, the statutes clearly outline that local branches should receive: (i) a base amount not linked to membership fees; (ii) 20 per cent of the membership fees paid by the members who pay the 1 per cent fee in their organizational domain; (iii) 30 per cent of the membership fees paid by the members who pay a reduced membership fee (IG Metall 2019b). To strengthen branches' capacity to act and to create a level playing field between 'strong' and 'weak' branches, IG Metall has also set up regional structural funds. Further support for 'weak'

Figure 12.2 IG Metall's structure of expenditure (as % of total expenditure), 2018

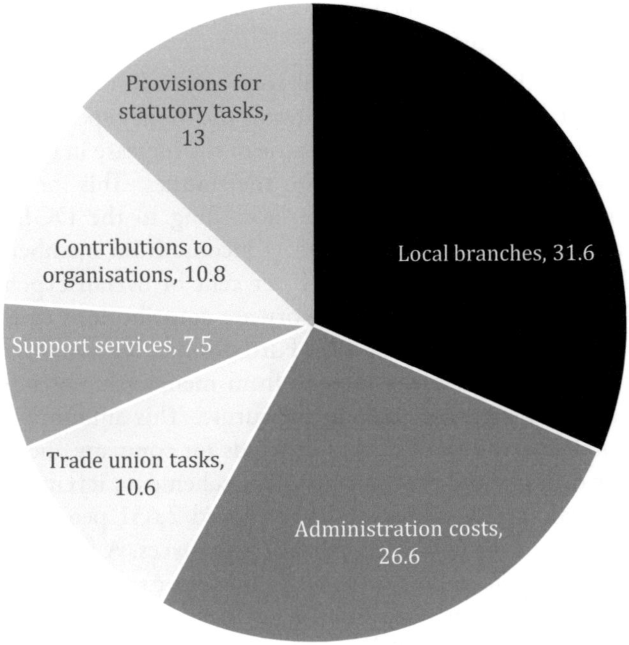

Source: IG Metall (2019a).

branches is provided via IG Metall's project 'Presence on the ground' (*Präsenz in der Fläche*), initiated in 2017 to strengthen its local structures. The income allocated to local branches was increased from €156.9 million in 2002 to €214.2 million in 2018 (IG Metall 2019a). Because IG Metall's total income has also increased considerably, the local branches' share in total income remained stable at 35 per cent.

Figure 12.2 illustrates that, in 2018, the largest share of IG Metall's total expenditure is allocated to local branches, followed by almost 27 per cent spent on administrative costs, of which personnel costs, (legal) fees as well as rents are the largest items. Personnel costs account for two-thirds of administrative costs and approximately 18 per cent of total expenditure. A bit more than 10 per cent was spent on 'trade union tasks', comprising expenditure for day-to-day union activities, such as union training centres, shipping costs for union documents, costs of training courses, travel expenses and printing costs. 'Support services' covers the union's financial support for members, such as in the case of industrial action. This category of expenditure can vary considerably and depends heavily on strike frequency.

Over time, the various shares of total expenditure have remained remarkably stable, while in absolute terms the money spent on each category has increased considerably because of the increase in total income. Some expenses are fixed according to the statutes. This includes 'contributions to organizations' because, according to the DGB statutes, IG Metall has to pay 12 per cent of its income from membership fees to the DGB. This amounts to 10.4 per cent of overall expenses. The remaining 0.4 per cent in this category are contributions to European and international union federations. Furthermore, IG Metall statutorily puts aside 15 per cent of its income from membership fees to ensure that it can fulfil statutory tasks in the future. This amounts to 13 per cent of total expenditure: it sets aside funds for company and collective bargaining disputes and provides a pension scheme for its employees (IG Metall 2019a). In 2018, IG Metall employed 2,631 people. The local branches account for half of IG Metall's employees. A fifth work at the union's headquarters in Frankfurt, while the union's training centres and regional offices account for 10 and 8 per cent of overall employment, respectively (IG Metall 2019a).

The DGB spends the largest share – around 40 per cent – of its expenditure on the provision of legal advice and representation in court for the almost 6 million union members. For this purpose the DGB established a subsidiary company, DGB Rechtsschutz GmbH, which employs more than 700 people in more than 100 offices across Germany. This does not mean that the affiliates do not provide legal support to their members, but the provision of legal advice to all union members is a statutory task of the DGB. The second largest share of the DGB budget – around 30 per cent – goes on personnel costs for the roughly 800 employees, almost a quarter of whom work at DGB headquarters in Berlin.

Collective bargaining and unions at the workplace

Collective bargaining at industry level and worker participation at company and establishment level are the central pillars of the traditional dual channel of interest representation. They represent two distinct arenas with a clear formal division of labour between trade unions, which conclude collective agreements with employers' associations or individual employers, and works councils, which represent the employees' interest within companies and establishments through a multi-level system of information, consultation and codetermination rights. Works councils, which can be set up in establishments with more than five employees, are allowed to conclude only so-called 'works agreements' (*Betriebsvereinbarung*), which 'may not deal with remuneration and other conditions of employment that have been fixed, or are normally fixed, by collective agreement'. Furthermore, works councils are obliged to work with management 'in a spirit of mutual trust for the good of the employees and of the establishment'.

Despite this formal legal separation between trade unions and works councils, there are close ties of mutual dependency between the two, both personally and functionally. Although works councils are not genuine union bodies, the majority of works councillors are union members (Emmler and Brehmer 2019). In practice, works councillors fulfil important union functions at the company and workplace level, such as monitoring compliance with collective agreements and recruiting new union members. They are also often ex officio union lay officials actively involved in internal union policymaking and members of union collective bargaining committees (*Tarifausschuss*), which formally decide the union's demands in negotiations and have to approve new collective agreements. Unions, in turn, provide training and legal advice for works council members (Jacobi et al. 1998).

In addition to representation at workplace level, there is a system of board-level employee representation based on the 1976 Codetermination act (MitbestG, *Mitbestimmungsgesetz*), which in companies with at least 2,000 employees entitles employee representatives to 50 per cent of the seats on a company's supervisory board. In smaller companies, with 500–2,000 employees, the BetrVG provides for one-third employee representation on supervisory boards. Even though employee representatives do not have the majority of votes, board-level representation gives the employees' side privileged access to strategic information and therefore some influence over management decisions.

In the past, this dual system has ensured a high degree of stability and provided unions with institutional power resources to regulate the employment relationship. Over the past 20 years, however, both pillars of the dual system have experienced processes of erosion and geographical and industrial fragmentation, not only weakening unions' capacity to act but also increasingly blurring the division of labour between unions and works councils (Müller and Schulten 2019a). Today, broad-based collective actors on both sides of industry, which ensure both high bargaining and works council coverage, are restricted to core areas of the public sector and western German manufacturing industry, with the automotive and chemical industries as its core.

According to data provided by the Establishment Survey of the Institute of Employment Research of the German Federal Employment

Figure 12.3 Collective bargaining coverage (%), 1998–2020

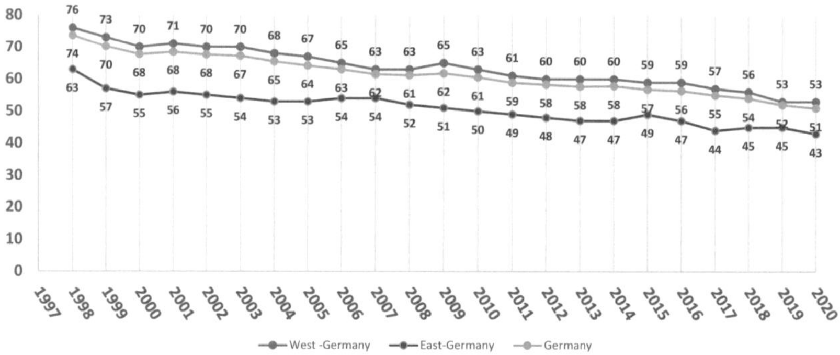

Note: Workers covered by collective agreements as a percentage of all workers.
Source: Ellguth and Kohaut (2020, 2021).

Agency (IAB), Germany has experienced a dramatic decline in collective bargaining coverage, from 74 per cent in 1998 to 51 per cent in 2020 (see Figure 12.3). There are considerable regional differences, however, with coverage being traditionally more than 10 percentage points higher in western than in eastern Germany. The decline over the past 20 years, however, has been more or less the same: falling in western Germany from 76 per cent in 1998 to 53 per cent in 2020, and in eastern Germany from 63 to 43 per cent.

Bargaining coverage also differs considerably across industries. In some industries, such as public administration, energy or finance, more than three-quarters of workers are still covered by a collective agreement. In some traditional union strongholds, such as chemicals and the automotive industry, coverage also remains very high. In a large section of private services, such as hospitality, commerce and IT services, however, at best 40 per cent of the workforce have their terms and conditions set by collective agreements (Müller and Schulten 2019a).

In addition to geographical and industrial fragmentation, the bargaining system has undergone a process of decentralization. The declining bargaining coverage is caused by the drop in the number of workers covered by industry-level agreements, which decreased between 2000 and 2020 (Ellguth and Kohaut 2021). Thus, while the industry-level still dominates, the relative importance of company-level agreements has increased. This quantitative development has been advanced by the frequent use of so-called 'opening clauses', allowing company-level agreements to deviate from industry agreements (Schulten and Bispinck 2018). While opening clauses were an attempt by unions to regain control over an increasing number of company-level derogations, which were agreed between management and works councils without the involvement of the industry-level bargaining parties, it also changed the traditional division of labour between unions and works councils (Dribbusch et al. 2018; Müller and Schulten 2019a). The latter are increasingly involved in negotiations about wages and working time, which previously, at least formally, was the sole prerogative of unions at industry level. Furthermore, a central precondition of ensuring a process of controlled decentralization in which industry-level agreements define the conditions under which company-level derogations are possible, is close articulation between industry-level unions and the works councils at company level (Müller and Schulten 2019a). This is where the erosion of worker participation comes into play.

While works council representation was never the norm, the share of establishments with a works council dropped further from 12 per cent in 2000 to 9 per cent in 2019 (Ellguth and Kohaut 2020), while the workers covered by works councils declined even more drastically. Whereas 50 per cent of West German and 41 per cent of East German workers were covered by a works council in 2000, the figures dropped to 41 per cent in western Germany and 37 per cent in eastern Germany in 2020. Unions have particular difficulties establishing works councils where they are hardly present, such as in the fragmented private service sector (Ellguth and Kohaut 2020), while the increasing resistance against works councils, in particular by employers in owner-led SMEs, further explains the declining coverage (Behrens and Dribbusch 2019).

Table 12.4 Workers covered by a works council and a collective agreement in the private sector (%), 2000, 2010 and 2020

	Western Germany			Eastern Germany		
	2000 (%)	2010 (%)	2020 (%)	2000 (%)	2010 (%)	2020 (%)
WC and CA	43	37	30	33	28	25
WC but no CA	7	8	11	8	9	12
No WC but CA	26	22	19	19	16	14
Neither WC nor CA	24	32	41	39	47	50

Note: As a percentage of all workers; WC = works council; CA = collective agreement.

Source: Ellguth and Kohaut (2011, 2021)

A further sign of a more critical approach by employers towards worker participation is the decline in the number of companies covered by parity board-level representation, which stood at 652 in 2019, down from 767 in 2002 (Emmler and Misterek 2020). Using legal loopholes such as the European Company Statute, or simply purposefully avoiding existing obligations, more and more companies openly circumvent German codetermination laws (Sick 2020)

The decline in the share of the workforce in private industry covered by both a works council and a collective agreement illustrates the extent of the erosion of the German dual system as an institutional power resource of unions. The blank spots in collective bargaining and worker participation without any coverage of collective agreements and works councils has increased considerably: in western Germany from 24 to 41 per cent, and in eastern Germany from 39 per cent to half the workforce (Table 12.4). Some 53 per cent of the workforce in western German manufacturing were still covered by both a works council and a collective agreement in 2019 compared with 26 per cent in the western German private service sector (Ellguth and Kohaut 2020). In eastern Germany, the corresponding figures are 27 per cent in manufacturing and 26 per cent for the private services sector.

The erosion of interest representation and deteriorating union density go hand in hand. The erosion is particularly pronounced in eastern Germany and the private services sector where unions find it difficult to gain a strong foothold. What used to be a mutually supportive virtuous circle of developing strong institutions and broad-based unions has turned into a mutually undermining vicious circle. In many regions and industries unions are simply too weak to counter the employers' more hostile approach to industry-level collective bargaining and to worker participation by forcing the employers to the negotiation table and by blocking employers' attempts to prevent the establishment of employee participation structures. Another part of this more critical approach is the introduction of 'OT membership' by some employers' associations, which on one hand helps to stabilize their membership but on the other advances the decline of collective bargaining coverage.

The key challenge for unions in strengthening collective bargaining and worker participation is therefore to break the vicious circle by closing the geographical and industrial representation gaps that have opened up outside the core area of the western German manufacturing sector. In order to strengthen collective bargaining, the unions demand political reforms, such as a less restrictive procedure for the extension of collective agreements (Schulten 2019) and stronger labour clauses in public procurement laws, so that public contracts are awarded only to companies that apply collective agreements (Schulten 2021).

Industrial conflict

Compared with other European countries, Germany is not a very strike-prone country (Vandaele 2016). The reasons for Germany's traditionally low strike rate include the unitary union movement, with a limited number of industrial unions; the dominance of industry-level collective agreements based on mutual support for the concept of conflictual cooperation; and the fairly restrictive regulation of strikes (Dribbusch 2019). Unions can call strikes only on issues directly related to the content and form of a collective agreement. From this follows the prohibition of political strikes and this also means that civil servants, who are not permitted to engage in collective bargaining, cannot go on strike. In addition, there is a relatively high quorum for strike activity: a call for a strike needs the approval of 75 per cent of the union members in a secret ballot. During a strike, unions support their members with strike pay. Every union has its own rules for strike pay. The amount of strike pay, however, usually depends on the length of union membership and the membership fee paid.

The pattern of strike action has changed markedly since the mid-2000s in response to a changing industrial relations landscape. The pattern is characterized by three interlinked trends: first, German industrial relations have become more conflictual, even though in a European context this is

Figure 12.4 Workers involved and days not worked because of industrial action per 1,000 employees, 2006–2021

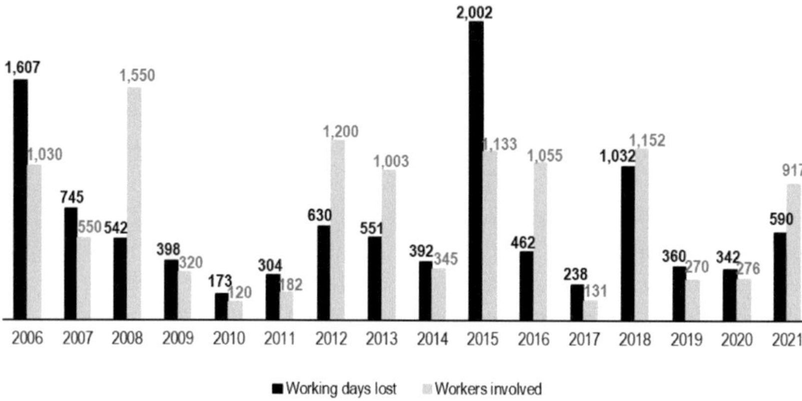

Source: Frindert et al. (2022).

still fairly modest. Compared with the period before the mid-2000s, the number of strikes has increased, while at the same time the number of days not worked has declined (Frindert et al. 2022; Figure 12.4). This indicates that the number of large-scale industry-wide strikes has decreased, while the number of smaller disputes in the context of single-employer bargaining has increased. Second, strike activity has shifted increasingly to the service sector; and third, strikes are spreading to new groups of employees, which used to be less involved in strike activities.

The fragmentation and decentralization of collective bargaining led to an increase in bargaining arenas, which in turn increased the potential for industrial conflict. As a consequence of the privatization and liberalization of important areas of the public sector, such as postal services, railways and health care, a small number of often national-level collective agreements were replaced by a large number of industry-level agreements and hundreds of company agreements (Brand and Schulten 2008). Furthermore, in manufacturing, the outsourcing of activities previously performed in-house led to the emergence of whole new service industries, such as contract logistics and contract manufacturing (Dribbusch 2019). By either withdrawing from collective agreements or demanding cuts in negotiated terms and conditions to cope with intensified competition, the employers' increased readiness to engage in conflict has contributed to more conflictual industrial relations. Over time the maintaining or establishing of collective bargaining in particular in individual companies has become an increasingly important issue for strike action alongside the still dominant issues of pay and working time (Dribbusch 2019).

This applies in particular to the service sector which since the mid-2000s accounts for more than two-thirds of days not worked because of industrial action. This 'tertiarization' of strike action can be traced to various factors. First, the absence of large-scale strike action in manufacturing, which dominated strike statistics up to the mid-2000s (Dribbusch 2019). Second, unions in the service sector embarked on a more assertive approach in combating low pay, bad working conditions and employers' flat refusal to engage in collective bargaining at all. Amazon is just the most prominent example of a general problem of how to get individual employers in the service sector to the negotiation table. This more assertive strategy also includes the pursuit of more conflictual, traditionally 'Anglo-Saxon' recruitment and campaigning initiatives (Kocsis et al. 2013). Third, a new, more critical awareness among previously less strike-prone groups of employees. Examples are the strikes in social and child care in 2009 and 2015 conducted by Ver.di to fight the structural undervaluing of the work performed by the predominantly female employees in those industries (Schulten and Seikel 2020), and the various strikes by doctors and nurses for better working conditions and the establishment of collective bargaining more generally in the health sector, which is characterized by a highly fragmented bargaining structure. Finally, there is the renaissance of professional unions, such as in hospitals, railways and aviation in response to the privatization and liberalization of services. Even though, often in contrast to public perceptions, the professional unions in these industries were not disproportionally strike-prone (Bispinck 2015), their more active role still contributed to the changing pattern of strike activity.

Political relations

The trade unions' role in the political realm relies on different courses of action to influence political decision-making. First, as an interest group unions try to establish links with political parties and governments to influence policymaking; second, as corporate actors, unions are directly involved in the decision-making processes of many institutions that are an integral part of the social market economy; and third, as social movements, unions try to mobilize their members and build alliances with other civil society organizations in order to build political pressure on governments. Unions cultivate all three channels for influencing political decisions fairly pragmatically.

German unions consider themselves to be non-partisan organizations: they are not officially linked to nor financed by any political party. In practice, however, the DGB and its affiliates traditionally have close links with the Social Democratic Party (SPD, *Sozialdemokratische Partei Deutschlands*), which forms a kind of a 'privileged partnership' (Schroeder 2008). The close link between DGB unions and the SPD rests on large overlaps of their respective political values and programmes and close personal ties based on mutual memberships. All presidents of the DGB unions are also members of the SPD. The only exception was from 2001 to 2019, Frank Bsirske, the president of Ver.di, who was a member of the Green Party. Among the four current members of the DGB board, however, two (including the DGB president) are members of the SPD, one of the Green Party and one of the Christian Democrats (CDU).

Both pillars of the 'privileged partnership' started to crumble in the 1990s when the proportion of unionized SPD members of parliament decreased from 90 per cent at the end of the 1980s to less than 60 per cent in the mid-2000s (Schroeder 2008). The biggest blow to the 'privileged partnership' came from the substantial revision of the German welfare state as a consequence of the so-called 'Agenda 2010' introduced by the SPD–Greens coalition government under Chancellor Schröder in 2003 (Bäcker 2018; Bosch 2015). Agenda 2010 entailed cuts in unemployment benefits, the active expansion of the low-wage sector by introducing, for instance, so-called 'mini jobs', and the raising of the pensionable age to 67 in 2007 under the centre-right CDU/CSU–SPD coalition government (Dribbusch and Birke 2019). Agenda 2010 altered the SPD–union relationship in two respects: first, it changed the political landscape because it led to the establishment of *Die Linke* ('The Left') as a new party left of the SPD on the political spectrum with the active support of many disappointed unionists who had left the SPD. Second, Agenda 2010 showed the unions that they could no longer rely on the SPD to advance their objectives in the political arena. They have therefore kept their options open: from 2005 onwards the DGB abstained from its traditional electoral recommendation of the SPD, acknowledging that it has to seek the support of all governments (Dribbusch et al. 2018).

An important part of the unions' political relations is their institutional embeddedness in advisory and decision-making bodies of various (quasi-)public institutions, such as the boards of the labour administration and social insurance institutions, the labour courts, broadcasting councils, advisory boards of ministries and even the board of the state bank Kreditanstalt für Wiederaufbau (Wiesenthal 2014). The involvement of unions (and employers) in this dense network of semi-autonomous self-governing bodies is a defining characteristic of Germany's social market economy. It enables unions to perform a broader societal role that goes far beyond their core business of collective bargaining. For instance, the unions' involvement in the (shared) administration and partly the regulation of the social security system – involving unemployment, health care, pension and care insurance – provides unions with an institutionalized voice in social policymaking. This should not be confused with real decision-making power: it rather provides unions with an institutionalized channel to ensure that workers' interests are heard. Unions' 'institutional voice', for instance, was not strong enough to prevent the neoliberal welfare state reforms pursued by Agenda 2010, which also restricted unions' influence in the self-governing bodies of the social security systems through stronger state intervention, in particular in decisions on the budget and benefit design (Trampusch 2009). Despite these recent further restrictions of unions' institutional power, their institutional embeddedness in the network of self-governing bodies is still an important factor in representing the interests of the wider workforce, which in turn strengthens unions' organizational legitimacy (Jeanrond 2014).

Finally, tripartite arrangements of political exchange between unions, governments and employers are very rare in Germany. In the past fifty years there have been only three instances: in the context of so-called 'concerted action' (*Konzertierte Aktion*) in 1967–1977; the so-called 'Alliance for Jobs, Training and Competitiveness' (*Bündniss für Arbeit, Beschäftigung und Wettbewerbsfähigkeit*) in 1998–2003; and the short-lived tripartite management of the 'Great Recession' in 2008/2009. A common feature of all three tripartite arrangements is that they were based on the joint interests of unions and employers in defending the competitiveness of German industry (Dribbusch et al. 2018). To achieve this objective, unions accepted wage moderation in exchange for employment security. From a union perspective, the results of these tripartite arrangements have been mixed, as the example of 'crisis corporatism' (Urban 2015) in 2008/2009 illustrates. The tripartite arrangement helped to safeguard employment, which in the international press was heralded as the 'German job miracle' (The Economist 2010; for a critical assessment see Dörre 2014). Its success came at considerable cost, however. First, the 'job miracle' was restricted mainly to the core workforce, especially in manufacturing, while many temporary jobs were cut (Urban 2015). Second, even the core workers who kept their jobs had to make considerable concessions as regards moderate wage increases (Bispinck 2011) and worse working conditions because 'employment security was linked to accelerated enterprise restructuring, leading to far-reaching performance intensification and an adverse impact on workers' health' (Urban 2015: 273). Third, unions could not realize any of their more long-term political objectives such as the proposal of a public fund for investment, a re-regulation of agency work and a significant extension of company-level codetermination rights (Dribbusch et al. 2018). In the public perception, however, the unions proved themselves to be 'crisis managers', which considerably improved their image in the wider population. Even though unions have not engaged in another tripartite arrangement since then, the 2008/2009 'crisis corporatism' helped them, especially IG Metall, to gain new prestige and self-confidence. It is therefore viewed as a strategic tool to return to in the future, if needed.

Societal power

Societal power refers to unions' capacity to successfully influence the public discourse and agenda-setting through public campaigns and building alliances with other civil society organizations. Societal power is not new for German unions. There have been broad-based political campaigns in the past, such as the high-profile campaigns on working time, including the DGB-led campaign for a five-day working week in the 1950s/1960s and the IG Metall-led campaign for a thirty-five-hour working week in the 1980s (Futh 2018). Overall, however, to pursue their political objectives, unions have traditionally relied more heavily on their institutional power resources through their involvement in the dense network of corporatist arrangements (Rehder 2014).

Public campaigns have been more important in unions' action repertoire since the beginning of the 2000s. This strengthened focus on campaigning is linked to the partial erosion of Germany's model of industrial relations. First, one might mention the continuous decline in membership and collective bargaining and works council coverage, especially outside the traditional core areas of union representation. Second, the unions' more difficult situation in the corporatist framework that made them realize the need to develop alternative ways to pursue (potential) members' interests outside the well-established institutional channels.

The pursuit of public campaigns was seen as a new strategy to bolster unions' organizational power resources as an essential prerequisite of increasing their institutional power resources. Unions pursue two different kinds of public campaigns. First, there are campaigns directly addressed to individual anti-union companies, which are embedded in a broader organizing strategy to recruit new members among industries and categories of workers that are traditionally difficult to organize. Their objective is to put public pressure on companies that obstruct organizing initiatives or the establishment of works councils, or that refuse to become (or stay) part of industry-level collective agreements. A prominent example is Ver.di's high-profile campaign against the retail discounter Lidl, which started in 2004 (for details, see Rehder 2014; Schreieder 2007). Since then there have been a range of similar campaigns pursued by other unions, such as in security services, industrial cleaning, retail, hospitals and the wind energy industry (Bremme et al. 2007; Wetzel 2013).

The second type of public campaign is concerned with broader political issues that appeal to the broader public, going beyond the interests of the core workforce. They are dealing with broader political issues, aimed at generating public support to put pressure on companies and policymakers. Examples include the campaign on the introduction of a statutory minimum wage, the 'equal work, equal pay' campaign in the agency work industry, driven by IG Metall (Benassi and Dorigatti 2015), and NGG's campaign for better working conditions in the meat industry (Erol and Schulten 2021). A common characteristic of these campaigns is that their success was based on unions' success in scandalizing bad pay and working conditions, and the fact that the issue was perceived publicly as a 'just cause', reaching beyond the unions' core constituency. In recent times, the most successful political campaign by German unions was the minimum wage campaign which, after a battle lasting more than fifteen years, ultimately led to the introduction of a statutory minimum wage on 1 January 2015 (Bosch 2018).

More recently, the unions have tried to find new allies in their campaigns for social and ecological transformation. IG Metall has published several position papers on social and green transition, together with two leading environmental organizations, the *Bund für Umwelt und Naturschutz Deutschland* (Friends of the Earth Germany) and the *Naturschutzbund Deutschland* (IG Metall 2021). Ver.di and Fridays for

Future also launched a joint campaign to extend public transport and to improve the working conditions of public transport workers (Liebig and Lucht 2022).

Trade union policies towards the European Union

German unions' general view of the EU is fairly ambiguous. On one hand, they strongly support European integration, which for them is a peace project that ensures social progress and is therefore more than just a common market (Hoffmann and Botsch 2021). Furthermore, they have strong economic reasons to support integration because in particular the German export-oriented industries benefit from the European single market. On the other hand, the unions are highly critical of the European policies pursued in the past twenty years. They criticize the asymmetry of market-enforcing and market-correcting policies (Scharpf 2009), which have turned European integration largely into a neoliberal project by promoting policies of deregulation, liberalization and privatization, which have subordinated social objectives to the imperatives of price competitiveness and fiscal discipline (DGB 2017). This is why German unions have been extremely critical of the incomplete Economic and Monetary Union (EMU) without an integrated fiscal and social policy and of the supply side–oriented management of the financial crisis in 2008/2009, which was based on austerity, internal devaluation and the dismantling of collective bargaining systems.

The key objective of German unions was and still is to implement an alternative model of European integration based on the idea of a social and solidaristic Europe (Hoffmann and Botsch 2021). For this reason, they have always been strong supporters of including a social progress protocol in the European treaties giving social rights the same status as economic rights and ensuring minimum social standards across the EU. Recognizing the interdependence of the European economies, the alternative model aimed for by the unions cannot be based on national solutions but on the European regulation of the internal market. This view is succinctly summed up in Ver.di's 2010 European policy manifesto: 'not less, but more Europe, just not more of the same' (Ver.di 2010: 44). 'More Europe' in this sense entails not only strengthening the European social dimension institutionally, but also boosting cross-border European cooperation and coordination among unions to prevent social dumping and to safeguard their members' interests.

To achieve the objective of a more social Europe, unions use different channels to influence developments at European level (Mittag 2017). One channel is the ETUC and the industry-level European Trade Union Federations (ETUFs). The DGB and its affiliates are founding members of the respective EU organizations and they are actively engaged in all their working structures and committees. By their sheer size in terms of membership and their affiliation fees, German unions naturally play an important role in the European federations' policymaking. The DGB, for instance, was one of the key driving forces behind the ETUC's push for an alternative model of economic governance and supply-side policies in the aftermath of the 2008/2009 economic crisis. To boost investment, and as an alternative to the dominant austerity policies at the time, the DGB developed its Marshall Plan for Europe (DGB 2012), which inspired the ETUC campaign 'A new path to Europe' (ETUC 2013). In addition to providing conceptual input into the ETUC's policy debates, the DGB also financially and organizationally supported successive ETUC campaigns such as the 'Europe needs a pay rise' campaign in 2017/2018. These multilateral activities were complemented by close bilateral contacts with unions from other countries. They served a dual purpose: to provide direct organizational support, for instance, in the aftermath of the crisis to unions in the crisis countries; and to agree on a common position in order to support the DGB's position in the ETUC's internal policy discussions. The bilateral contacts are mainly ad hoc and issue-specific. More institutionalized exchanges exist between the DGB and the British, French and Polish unions via annual union forums.

To varying degrees, DGB affiliates pursue a similar mix of multilateral activities under the umbrella of their respective ETUFs and bilateral activities with unions from other countries. A good example is provided by IG Metall's activities regarding collective bargaining and company policy. IG Metall was a key driving force of the European Metalworkers' Federation's (EMF) collective bargaining coordination approach and the adoption of bargaining guidelines as early as 1996 (Platzer and Müller 2011). To prevent downward pressure on wages and social standards, IG Metall strongly supported the EMF policy to agree on a common European policy approach, according to which national bargaining should at least compensate for price increases and secure an adequate share of productivity gains. These multilateral activities were accompanied by bilateral activities such as the establishment of 'inter-regional' collective bargaining networks of IG Metall districts with unions from neighbouring countries. The most active networks today are those with Belgian and Dutch unions and the Vienna Memorandum Group with IGM Bavaria, Austria, Czechia, Hungary, Slovakia and Slovenia (Müller and Schulten 2019b). A similar approach involving common European guidelines was pursued in the field of company policy, and in particular European Works Councils (EWCs), to minimize cross-border competition and the resulting downward pressure on working conditions. To improve cross-border coordination IG Metall strongly supported the adoption of common EMF guidelines for the negotiation of EWCs in the 1990s and in 2005 the ten EMF principles on socially responsible company restructuring (Platzer and Müller 2011). The active role of IG Metall, and the other German unions more generally, in pushing for improved European coordination of EWC-related union activities is not surprising, given that of the currently approximately 1,250 active EWCs roughly three-quarters include a representative from Germany and roughly one-quarter of the currently active EWCs are headquartered in Germany (ETUI 2022).

The DGB and its largest affiliates IG Metall and Ver.di also have their own European liaison officers in Brussels to represent the union's interests vis-à-vis the European institutions. The main objectives of these liaison officers are to gather information about European legislative initiatives and to feed the union's position into the European policymaking process. The liaison officers are another channel for influence European policymaking processes to achieve the dual objective of protecting the interests of German workers and to achieve a more general policy change at European level.

For unions such as IG Metall, which represent workers in highly internationalized industries, characterized by a dense network of European regulation, the EU is just another level in a multi-level structure of decision-making. They extend their national policies and practices to the European level under the organizing, facilitating and unifying umbrella of the European trade union organizations (Rüb 2009). This integral view of Europe is also reflected in the union-internal organization. European issues are treated as a cross-cutting theme dealt with by issue-specific departments as an additional dimension of their national activities. At IG Metall, European aspects of collective bargaining and company policy, for instance, are dealt with by the respective departments. By the same token, at Ver.di, European issues are dealt with by the various sectoral departments (*Fachbereiche*) (Dittmar 2017, 2021). Ver.di, however, also illustrates the varying significance of European issues for day-to-day activities. In the highly internationalized transport sector European issues are much more integrated into the day-to-day activities of the respective *Fachbereich* than, for instance, in the *Fachbereich* dealing with the less internationalized public sector (Dittmar 2017, 2021).

Conclusion

The past twenty years can be divided into two distinct periods. The first period covers the years from 2000 until the beginning of the Great Recession in 2008. During this period, unions' organizational strength and capacity to act was under attack. The first and most important indicator of their defensive position was the sustained substantial decrease in union membership during this period. This was partly a consequence of the unions' own problems in retaining existing members and in gaining new members in the newly emerging market segments. It was also a consequence of the unfavourable economic and political environment at the time. Economically, this period was characterized by limited economic growth and a continuous increase in unemployment, which peaked at more than 11 per cent in 2005, creating difficult conditions for unions to retain their membership level. Politically, under Chancellor Schröder the unions lost the SPD as their traditional political ally and were consequently side-lined by the government in order to pursue its 'Agenda 2010'. Furthermore, the employers' declining acceptance of traditional German industrial relations institutions contributed to the decentralization of collective bargaining and a continuous decrease of collective bargaining coverage, thereby further undermining one of the central pillars of the unions' capacity to act. In a nutshell, the situation between 2000 and 2008 was characterized by a decline in the unions' organizational, institutional and structural power resources. The severity of this general trend varied by industry, leading to a consolidation or even deepening of the different worlds of unionism. Strong unions prevailed in the export-oriented industries and the public sector, but in parts of the service and crafts sectors unions struggled to get a foothold. Thus, in terms of Visser's (2019) categories this period up to the Great Recession was characterized by a further union dualization. In some industries and regions there were even signs of marginalization.

The 2008/2009 Great Recession marked a turning point as it proved an opportunity for unions to strengthen their position. To a certain extent the dire situation the unions were in at the beginning of the crisis, with continuing loss of organizational and institutional power resources, prompted a strategic shift inside the unions by making recruiting and retaining members the overarching goal of all union activities. Unions pursued new paths by embracing the organizing model. This involved not only a new focus on membership recruitment and retention, but also a cultural shift in the pursuit of new forms of action, such as more participation-oriented forms of internal decision-making, more conflictual strategies for bringing companies to the negotiation table, and a broader political agenda that goes beyond the interests of the traditional core constituency in collective bargaining and in campaigns. This new approach contributed to a more positive membership development than during the period before the crisis – thereby strengthening unions' organizational power.

The fact that the German economy was not exceptionally hard hit by the crisis and recovered quickly, furthermore, strengthened the unions' structural power, enabling them to negotiate higher wages. Even though unions did not manage to stop the decline in collective bargaining and works council coverage as the central elements of their institutional power, the Great Recession offered an alternative institutional channel to exert influence by engaging in a corporatist arrangement to mitigate the negative impact of the crisis for workers. This specific form of 'crisis corporatism' improved their public image and increased their acceptance in the political sphere. This increase in their societal power created favourable conditions for the unions' new, more campaign-oriented approach. Thus, the unions' development since 2008 has been characterized by signs of stability and revitalization.

These signs of revitalization are fragile, however. Whether this can be sustained in the future depends very much on how unions cope with current and future challenges. The Covid-19 pandemic wiped out much of the unions' organizing successes in only one year. Demographic change and the twin digital and ecological transformation are two other major challenges with potentially far-reaching implications for employment, especially in the union strongholds of the manufacturing sector. Whether they can maintain their role depends largely on the capability of German manufacturing industry to manage the twin transformation in a sustainable and inclusive way, retaining a certain level of employment. Moreover, unions are facing challenges from ongoing changes in the employment structure, which has to be mirrored in the composition of their membership. Finally, to maintain their role, unions need to find ways to overcome the cleavage between the different worlds of unionism. In view of the increased blurring of industrial demarcations and the challenges raised by the twin transition this is a task not only for unions organizing in underrepresented industries, but for all German unions.

References

All links were checked on 27 July 2022.

Albert M. (1993) Capitalism against capitalism, London, Whurr Publishers.

Bäcker G. (2018) Dauerbaustelle Sozialstaat: Chronologie gesetzlicher Neuregelungen in der Sozialpolitik 1998–2017, Duisburg, Institut Arbeit und Qualifikation.

Behrens M. (2009) Still married after all these years? Union organizing and the role of works councils in German industrial relations, ILR Review, 62 (3), 275–293.

Behrens M. and Dribbusch H. (2019) Avoiding the union at the workplace – evidence from surveys amongst German trade unions, in Behrens M. and Dribbusch H.(eds) Industrial relations in Germany – dynamics and perspectives, WSI-Mitteilungen, Special Issue, Baden-Baden, Nomos, 31–50.

Behrens M. and Helfen M. (2019) Small change, big impact? Organisational membership rules and the exit of employers' associations from multiemployer bargaining in Germany, Human Resource Management Journal, 29 (1), 51–66.

Benassi C. and Dorigatti L. (2015) Straight to the core: explaining union responses to the casualization of work: the IG Metall campaign for agency workers, British Journal of Industrial Relations, 53 (3), 533–555.

Biebeler H. and Lesch H. (2015) Organisationsdefizite der deutschen Gewerkschaften, Wirtschaftsdienst, 95, 710–715.

Bispinck R. (ed.) (2011) Zwischen ‚Beschäftigungswunder' und ‚Lohndumping'? Tarifpolitik in und nach der Krise, Hamburg, VSA-Verlag.

Bispinck R. (2015) Wirklich alles Gold, was glänzt? Zur Rolle der Berufs- und Spartengewerkschaften in der Tarifpolitik, Gegenblende, 11.05.2015. https://gegenblende.dgb.de/++co++ebcfc60c-f7b6-11e4-bce0-52540066f352

Bosch G. (2015) The German welfare state from an inclusive to an exclusive Bismarckian model, in Vaughan-Whitehead D. (ed.) The European Social Model in crisis, Cheltenham, Edward Elgar, 175–229.

Bosch G. (2018) The making of the German minimum wage: a case study of institutional change, Industrial Relations Journal, 49 (1), 19–33.

Brand T. and Schulten T. (2008) Liberalisierung und Privatisierung öffentlicher Dienstleistungen und die Erosion des Flächentarifvertrags, WSI-Mitteilungen, 61 (10), 570–576.

Bremme P., Fürniß U. and Meinecke U. (eds) (2007) Never work alone. Organizing – ein Zukunftsmodell für Gewerkschaften, Hamburg, VSA-Verlag.

Destatis (2021) Erwerbstätigenquoten 1991 bis 2021. https://www.destatis.de/DE/Themen/Arbeit/Arbeitsmarkt/Erwerbstaetigkeit/Tabellen/erwerbstaetigenquoten-gebietsstand-geschlecht-altergruppe-mikrozensus.html

DGB (2012) Ein Marshallplan für Europa, 08.12.2012. https://www.dgb.de/themen/++co++985b632e-407e-11e2-b652-00188b4dc422

DGB (2017) Geschäftsbericht 2014–2017, Berlin, Deutscher Gewerkschaftsbund.

DGB (2018) Satzung des Deutschen Gewerkschaftsbundes, Stand Mai 2018, Berlin, Deutscher Gewerkschaftsbund. https://www.dgb.de/uber-uns/dgb-heute/satzung

DGB (2021) Die Mitglieder der DGB-Gewerkschaften. https://www.dgb.de/uber-uns/dgb-heute/mitgliederzahlen

Dittmar N. (2017) Europaarbeit der Gewerkschaft ver.di – Vorschlag einer feldtheoretischen Perspektive, Österreichische Zeitschrift für Soziologie, 42, 183–193.

Dittmar N. (2021) Europaarbeit der Gewerkschaft ver.di – Eine feldtheoretischen Perspektive, Wiesbaden, Springer VS.

Dörre K. (2014) The German job miracle a model for Europe?, Brussels, Rosa Luxemburg Stiftung. https://rosalux.gr/sites/default/files/publications/german-job-miracle.pdf

Dribbusch H. (2003) Gewerkschaftliche Mitgliedergewinnung im Dienstleistungssektor. Ein Drei-Länder Vergleich im Einzelhandel, Berlin, edition sigma.

Dribbusch H. (2019) New militancy in a changing industrial landscape, in Behrens M. and Dribbusch H. (eds) Industrial relations in

Germany – Dynamics and perspectives, WSI-Mitteilungen Special Issue, Baden-Baden, Nomos, 95–122.

Dribbusch H. and Birke P. (2019) Trade unions in Germany – challenges in a time of transition, Berlin, Friedrich-Ebert-Stiftung. http://library.fes.de/pdf-files/id/ipa/15399.pdf

Dribbusch H., Lehndorff S. and Schulten T. (2018) Two worlds of unionism? German manufacturing and service unions since the Great Recession, in Lehndorff S., Dribbusch H. and Schulten T. (eds) Rough waters – European trade unions in a time of crisis, Brussels, ETUI, 209–233.

Ebbinghaus B. and Göbel C. (2014) Mitgliederrückgang und Organisationsstrategien deutscher Gewerkschaften, in Schroeder W. (ed.) Handbuch Gewerkschaften in Deutschland, Wiesbaden, Springer VS, 207–239.

The Economist (2010) Inside the miracle – How Germany weathered the recession, 13.10.2010. https://www.economist.com/special-report/2010/03/13/inside-the-miracle

Ellguth P. and Kohaut S. (2011) Tarifbindung und betriebliche Interessenvertretung: Aktuelle Ergebnisse aus dem IABBetriebspanel 2010, WSI-Mitteilungen, 64 (5), 242–247.

Ellguth P. and Kohaut S. (2020) Tarifbindung und betriebliche Interessenvertretung: Aktuelle Ergebnisse aus dem IAB-Betriebspanel 2019, WSI-Mitteilungen, 73 (4), 278–285.

Ellguth P. and Kohaut S. (2021) Tarifbindung und betriebliche Interessenvertretung: Ergebnisse aus dem IAB-Betriebspanel 2020, WSI-Mitteilungen, 74 (4), 306–314.

Emmler H. and Brehmer W. (2019) The composition of works councils – Results from the WSI Works Council Survey, in Behrens M. and Dribbusch H.(eds) Industrial relations in Germany – dynamics and perspectives, WSI-Mitteilungen, Special Issue, Baden-Baden, Nomos, 51–71.

Emmler H. and Misterek F. (2020) Mitbestimmung in Zahlen, in I.M.U. (ed.) Mitbestimmung der Zukunft, Mitbestimmungsreport No 58, Düsseldorf, Institut für Mitbestimmung und Unternehmensführung, 6–10.

Erol S. and Schulten T. (2021) Renewing labour relations in the German meat industry. An end of 'organized irresponsibility'?, WSI Report, No. 61e. https://www.wsi.de/de/faust-detail.htm?sync_id=HBS-007928

ETUC (2013) A new path for Europe: ETUC plan for investment, sustainable growth and quality jobs, Brussels, ETUC. https://www.etuc.org/en/document/new-path-europe-etuc-plan-investment-sustainable-growth-and-quality-jobs

ETUI (2022) EWCDB – European Works Councils Database, Brussels, ETUI. https://ewcdb.eu/

Europäische Kommission (2015) Standard Eurobarometer 84 Anlage: Die öffentliche Meinung in der europäischen Union, Befragung November 2015, Brüssel, Europäische Kommission.

European Commission (2019) Standard Eurobarometer 91 Annex: Public opinion in the European Union, June 2019, Brussels, European Commission.

Frindert J., Dribbusch H. and Schulten T. (2022) WSI-Arbeitskampfbilanz 2021, WSI-Report No 74, Düsseldorf, Wirtschafts- und Sozialwissenschaftliches Institut. https://www.wsi.de/de/faust-detail.htm?sync_id=HBS-008309

Futh S.K. (2018) Strategische Kommunikation von Gewerkschaften – Die Kampagnen Samstags gehört Vati mir, 35-Stunden-Woche und Mindestlohn, Wiesbaden, Springer VS.

Hassel A. and Schroeder W. (2018) Gewerkschaften 2030 – Rekrutierungsdefizite, Repräsentationslücken und neue Strategien der Mitgliederpolitik, WSI Report, No. 44, Düsseldorf, Wirtschafts- und Sozialwissenschaftliches Institut. https://www.boeckler.de/pdf/p_wsi_report_44_2018.pdf

Hassel A. and Schroeder W. (2019) Trade union membership policy: the key to stronger social partnership, in Behrens M. and Dribbusch H. (eds) Industrial relations in Germany – dynamics and perspectives, WSI-Mitteilungen, Special Issue, Baden-Baden, Nomos, 73–93.

Hoffmann J. (2000) Industrial relations and trade unions in Germany: the pressure of modernisation and globalisation, in Waddington J. and Hoffmann R. (eds) Trade unions in Europe – facing challenges and searching for solutions, Brussels, ETUI, 249–275.

Hoffmann R. and Botsch A. (2021) Solidarisch ist man nicht alleine – Anforderungen an eine progressive Wirtschaftspolitik für Europa, in Gärber A. (ed.) Europa.Besser.Machen.: Vorschläge für eine progressive Wirtschaftspolitik, Frankfurt am Main, Campus Verlag, 43–54.

IG Metall (2012) Geschäftsbericht 2007–2010, Frankfurt am Main, IG Metall.

IG Metall (2019a) Geschäftsbericht 2015–2018, Frankfurt am Main, IG Metall

IG Metall (2019b) Satzung, Frankfurt am Main, IG Metall.

IG Metall (2021) IG Metall und BUND fordern zügige Mobilitätswende mit klaren Perspektiven für die Beschäftigten, Press Release, 22.10.2021. https://www.igmetall.de/presse/pressemitteilungen/ig-metall-und-bund-fordern-zuegige-mobilitaetswende

Jacobi O., Keller B. and Müller-Jentsch W. (1998) Germany: facing new challenges, in Ferner A. and Hyman R. (eds) Changing industrial relations in Europe, 2nd edn, Oxford, Blackwell Publishers, 190–238.

Jeanrond H. (2014) Gewerkschaften und soziale Sicherung, in Schroeder W. (ed.) Handbuch Gewerkschaften in Deutschland, Wiesbaden, Springer VS, 465–484.

Keller B. (2001) ver.di: Triumphmarsch oder Gefangenenchor? Neustrukturierung der Interessenvertretung im Dienstleistungssektor, Hamburg, VSA-Verlag.

Keller B. (2012) Der Zusammenschluß von Gewerkschaften im Eisenbahnsektor – Von Vernunftehen und unwilligen Dritten, Arbeit, 21 (4), 247–262.

Keller B. (2018) Professional unions in Germany: theoretical explanations and practical consequences for industrial relations, Transfer, 24 (4), 437–450.

Kocsis A., Sterkel G. and Wiedemuth J. (eds) (2013) Organisieren am Konflikt. Tarifauseinandersetzungen und Mitgliederentwicklung im Dienstleistungssektor, Hamburg, VSA-Verlag.

Lesch H. and Winter L. (2021) Gewerkschaften: Strukturdefizite verstärken sich, IW-Kurzbericht No. 50. https://www.iwkoeln.de/studien/hagen-lesch-strukturdefizite-verstaerken-sich-516253.html

Liebig S. and Lucht K. (eds) (2022) Fahren wir zusammen? Die öko-soziale Allianz von ver.di und Fridays for Future im ÖPNV, Hamburg, VSA-Verlag.

Mittag J. (2017) Flexible adaptation between political, social and economic interests: the multi-faceted europeanisation of German trade unions, in Ciampani A. and Tilly P. (eds) National trade unions and the ETUC: A history of unity and diversity, Brussels, ETUI, 19–44.

Müller H.-P. and Wilke M. (2014) Gewerkschaftsfusionen: der Weg zu modernen Multibranchengewerkschaften, in Schroeder W. (ed.) Handbuch Gewerkschaften in Deutschland, Wiesbaden, Springer VS, 147–171.

Müller T. and Schulten T. (2019a) Germany: parallel universes of collective bargaining, in Müller T., Vandaele K. and Waddington J. (eds) Collective bargaining in Europe: towards an endgame, Volume II, Brussels, ETUI, 239–265.

Müller T. and Schulten T. (2019b) Die Wiener Memorandum Gruppe – ein zentraler Baustein der tarifpolitischen Koordinierung in Europa, in IG Metall, OS KOVO, OZ KOVO, PRO-GE, SKEI und VASAS (eds) 20 Jahre Wiener Memorandum, Wien, PRO-GE, 7–8.

Müller-Armack A. (1947) Wirtschaftslenkung und Marktwirtschaft, Hamburg, Verlag für Wirtschaft und Sozialpolitik.

Müller-Jentsch W. (ed.) (1999) Konfliktpartnerschaft – Akteure und Institutionen der industriellen Beziehungen, 3rd edn, München, Rainer Hampp Verlag.

OECD and AIAS (2021) OECD-AIAS-ICTWSS database, Version 09/2021. https://www.oecd.org/employment/ictwss-database.htm

Platzer H.-W. and Müller T. (2011) Global and European trade union federations – a handbook and analysis of transnational union organizations and policies, Bern, Peter Lang.

Rehder B. (2014) Vom Korporatismus zur Kampagne? Organizing als Strategie der gewerkschaftlichen Erneuerung, in Schroeder W. (ed.) Handbuch Gewerkschaften in Deutschland, Wiesbaden, Springer VS, 241–264.

Rüb S. (2009) Die Transnationalisierung der Gewerkschaften – eine empirische Untersuchung am Beispiel der IG Metall, Berlin, edition sigma.

Scharpf F. (2009) The double asymmetry of European integration: or, why the EU cannot be a social market economy, MPIfG Working Paper 09/12, Cologne, Max Planck Institute for the Study of Societies.

Schreieder A. (2007) Die Lidl-Kampagne – ein Zukunftsmodell für Gewerkschaften, in Bremme P., Fürniß U. and Meinecke U. (eds) Never work alone: Organizing – ein Zukunftsmodell für Gewerkschaften, Hamburg, VSA-Verlag, 153–174.

Schroeder W. (2008) SPD und Gewerkschaften: Vom Wandel einer privilegierten Partnerschaft, WSI-Mitteilungen, 61(5), 231–237.

Schroeder W. and Fuchs S. (2019) Neue Mitglieder für die Gewerkschaften – Mitgliederpolitik als neues Politikfeld der IG Metall, OBS-Arbeitsheft 97, Frankfurt am Main, Otto-Brenner-Stiftung.

Schroeder W. and Greef S. (2014) Struktur und Entwicklung des deutschen Gewerkschaftsmodells: Herausforderung durch Sparten- und Berufsgewerkschaften, in Schroeder W. (ed.) Handbuch Gewerkschaften in Deutschland, Wiesbaden, Springer VS, 123–145.

Schroeder W. and Weßels B. (2017) Die deutsche Unternehmerverbändelandschaft: vom Zeitalter der Verbände zum Zeitalter der Mitglieder, in Schröder W. and Weßels B. (eds) Handbuch Arbeitgeber- und Wirtschaftsverbände in Deutschland, 2nd edn, Wiesbaden, Springer VS, 3–28.

Schroder W., Kalass V. and Greef S. (2011) Berufsgewerkschaften in der Offensive – Vom Wandel des deutschen Gewerkschaftsmodells, Wiesbaden, VS Verlag.

Schulten T. (2019) German collective bargaining – from erosion to revitalisation?, in Behrens M. and Dribbusch H.(eds) Industrial relations in Germany – dynamics and perspectives, WSI-Mitteilungen, Special Issue, Baden-Baden, Nomos, 11–30.

Schulten T. (2021) Social clauses in German public procurement – towards a Post-Rüffert regime?, in ETUC (ed.) Social clauses in the implementation of the 2014 public procurement directives, Brussels, ETUC, 26–41.

Schulten T. and Bispinck R. (2018) Varieties of decentralisation in German collective bargaining, in Leonardi S. and Pedersini R. (ed.) Multi-employer bargaining under pressure: decentralisation trends in five European countries, Brussels, ETUI, 105–149.

Schulten T. and Seikel D. (2020) Beyond austerity: upgrading German public services and the role of trade union campaigns and collective bargaining, in Keune M., Ramos Martín N. and Mailand M. (eds) Working under pressure: Employment, job quality and labour relations in Europe's public sector since the crisis, Brussels, ETUI, 145–182.

Sick S. (2020) Erosion als Herausforderung für die Unternehmensmitbestimmung, in I.M.U. (ed.) Mitbestimmung der Zukunft, Mitbestimmungsreport No 58, Düsseldorf, Institut für Mitbestimmung und Unternehmensführung, 13–17.

Specht F. (2022) DGB verliert rund 130.000 Mitglieder, Handelsblatt, 01.02.2022. https://www.handelsblatt.com/politik/deutschland/gewerkschaften-dgb-verliert-rund-130-000-mitglieder/28028788.html

Streeck W. (1997) German capitalism: does it exist? Can it survive?, in Crouch C. and Streeck W. (eds) Political economy of modern capitalism: mapping convergence and diversity, London, Sage, 33–54.

Streeck W. and Visser J. (1997) The rise of conglomerate union, European Journal of Industrial Relations, 3(3), 305–332.

Trampusch C. (2009) Der erschöpfte Sozialstaat. Transformation eines Politikfeldes, Frankfurt am Main, Campus Verlag.

Urban H.J. (2015) Between crisis corporatism and revitalisation: trade union policy in the era of European financial market capitalism, in Lehndorff S. (ed.) Divisive integration: the triumph of failed ideas in Europe – revisited, Brussels, ETUI, 269–294.

Vandaele K. (2016) Interpreting strike activity in western Europe in the past 20 years: the labour repertoire under pressure, Transfer, 22 (3), 277–294.

Vandaele K. (2021) Collective resistance and organizational creativity amongst Europe's platform workers: a new power in the labour movement?, in Haidar J. and Keune M. (eds) Work and labour relations in global platform capitalism, Cheltenham, Edward Elgar, 206–234.

Ver.di (2010) European policy manifesto, Berlin, Ver.di. https://www.verdi.de/themen/internationales/++co++d5ee55c6-c360-11e0-64ad-00093d114afd

Ver.di (2012) Geschäftsbericht 2007–2011, Berlin, Ver.di.

Ver.di (2019) Geschäftsbericht 2015–2018, Berlin, Ver.di.

Visser J. (2019) Trade unions in the balance. ILO ACTRAV Working Paper, Geneva, ILO.

Waddington J., Kahmann M. and Hoffmann J. (2005) A comparison of the trade union merger process in Britain and Germany: Joining forces?, Abingdon, Routledge.

Wetzel D. (ed.) (2013) Organizing – Die Veränderung der gewerkschaftlichen Praxis durch das Prinzip Beteiligung, Hamburg, VSA-Verlag.

Wiesenthal H. (2014) Gewerkschaften in Politik und Gesellschaft: Niedergang und Wiederkehr des „Modells Deutschland", in Schroeder W. (ed.) Handbuch Gewerkschaften in Deutschland, Wiesbaden, Springer VS, 395–421.

Abbreviations

BDA	Bundesvereinigung der Deutschen Arbeitgeberverbände (Confederation of German Employers' Associations)
BetrVG	Betriebsverfassungsgesetz (Works Constitution Act)
CDU	Christlich Demokratische Union (Christian Democratic Union)
CGB	Christlicher Gewerkschaftsbund Deutschlands (Christian Trade Union Confederation of Germany)
DAG	Deutsche Angestelltengewerkschaft (German Salaried Employees' Union)
dbb	Deutscher Beamtenbund und Tarifunion (German Civil Service Association)
DGB	Deutscher Gewerkschaftsbund (German Trade Union Confederation)
EMF	European Metalworkers' Federation
ETUC	European Trade Union Confederation
ETUF	European Trade Union Federation
EVG	Eisenbahn- und Verkehrsgewerkschaft (Railway and Transport Union)
EWC	European Works Councils
FDP	Freie Demokratisch Partei (Free Democratic Party)
GDBA	Verkehrsgewerkschaft Deutscher Bundesbahnbeamten und Anwärter (Union of civil servants within German Rail)
GDL	Gewerkschaft Deutscher Lokomotivführer (German Train Drivers' Union)
GdP	Gewerkschaft der Polizei (Trade Union of the Police)
GEW	Gewerkschaft Erziehung und Wissenschaft (Union of Education and Science)
GHK	Gewerkschaft Holz und Kunststoff (Wood and Plastics Union)
GL	Gewerkschaft Leder (Leather workers' union)
GTB	Gewerkschaft Textil-Bekleidung (Textil and Clothing Workers' Union)
IG BAU	Industriegewerkschaft Bauen-Agrar-Umwelt (Building, Agriculture & Environmental Workers' Union)

IG BCE	Industriegewerkschaft Bergbau, Chemie, Energie (Mining, Chemicals and Energy Industrial Union)
IG BE	Industriegewerkschaft Bergbau (Mining workers' union)
IG CPK	Industriegewerkschaft Chemie-Papier-Keramik (Chemical, Paper and Ceramics Industrial Union)
IG Metall	Industriegewerkschaft Metall (German Metalworkers' Union)
MB	Marburger Bund (Union of Salaried Medical Doctors)
NGG	Gewerkschaft Nahrung-Genuss-Gaststätten (Food, Tobacco, Hotel & Allied Workers Union)
SPD	Sozialdemokratische Partei Deutschlands (Social-Democratic Party)
TVG	Tarifvertragsgesetz (Collective Agreements Act)
Ver.di	Vereinte Dienstleistungsgewerkschaft (United Services Union)

Chapter 13

Greek trade unions during the period 2000–2020: Plus ça change?

Ioannis Katsaroumpas and Aristea Koukiadaki

This chapter traces the institutional trajectory of Greek trade unions during the period 2000–2020. The broader socio-political horizon of this period has been increasingly shaped by the dominance of what might be termed 'Europeanized neoliberalization'. This term captures the close entanglement of a process of neoliberal restructuring (Karamessini 2009; Kennedy 2016) with the discursive hegemony of European Union (EU)/ Economic and Monetary Union (EMU) membership obligations. While EMU entry was initially presented in the late 1990 and early 2000s as conditioned upon wage moderation and structural reforms, after 2010 its retention was more dramatically conditioned upon extreme austerity and the deconstruction of the protective character of Greek labour law (Katsaroumpas 2018; Koukiadaki and Kokkinou 2016a). This highly volatile conjuncture, juxtaposing periods of 'thickened history' (Beissinger 2002: chapter 4) – in the form of episodic bursts of legislative, political and social-movement activity (May 2010–2014) – and periods of relative stability (2000–May 2010 and 2015–2020) presented a challenging environment for unions. But despite the epoch-shifting 2010 crisis, which led to a new social and labour model characterized by political insecurity, instability and extensive social insecurity (Manitakis 2014), the following puzzle appeared: a pattern of structural continuity with regard to the trade union movement combined with an uneven effect in some functional areas, such as collective bargaining and union density, over others that experienced virtually no major changes (union structure and democracy, funding, action repertoire). Table 13.1 presents the principal characteristics of trade unions in Greece, as they have evolved in recent decades, covering the pre-crisis period and during the crisis. It is important to clarify here that there is no publicly available data on trade union membership since 2016.

Table 13.1 Principal characteristics of trade unionism in Greece

	1998	**2007**	**2016**
Total trade union membership (GSEE)	662,000	666,000	490,000
Total trade union membership (ADEDY)	241,000	311,200	253,600
Women as a proportion of total membership	n.a.	33.8 % (2008)	32.4 % (2012)
Union density	27.5 %	22.6 %	20.2 %
Number of confederations	2	2	2
Number of affiliated unions (GSEE federations)	62	62 (2005)	68
Number of affiliated unions (ADEDY federations)	n.a.	45 (2005)	45
Collective bargaining coverage	100 %	100 %	26 %
Principal level of collective bargaining	Company level		
Days not worked due to industrial action per 1.000 workers	126	314 (2002)	n.a.

Source: Visser (2019a).

This chapter seeks to complement the extensive literature on trade unions in Greece from the perspective of 'Hyman's triangle' (Bithymitris and Kotsonopoulos 2018; Hyman 2001), the power resource approach (Vogiatzoglou 2018), social-movement theory (see Malamidis 2021) and grassroots unionism (Kretsos and Vogiatzoglou 2015). There is also an extensive labour-law literature documenting the far-reaching post-2010 deconstruction of the protective character of Greek collective labour law and the associated use of law to restrict unions' functional space (Katsaroumpas 2018; Koukiadaki and Kokkinou 2016a; Papadimitriou 2013; Yannakourou and Tsimpoukis 2014).

Approaching unions as unitary actors in the Greek context is difficult. Unions are better regarded as 'open institutional fields of contestation' (Gallas 2018; Taylor et al. 2011); not only 'organizations of struggle, but also fields of struggle between competing forces of labour with different strategies' (Gallas 2018: 351). This conception is better suited for capturing the contradictory trends towards institutionalization, politicization and radicalization (Papadopoulos 2004) in Greece, as well as avoiding the risk of an automatic equation of union actions with the promotion of workers' interests (Gallas 2018). Furthermore, the following periodization is useful in the Greek context. The signing of the first Memorandum of Understanding with the International Monetary Fund (IMF)/EU in May 2010 can be used as a boundary between the pre-crisis period of relative stability (2000–May 2010) and the subsequent crisis period (May 2010–2020). The second period is in turn divided into three sub-periods: (1) the *first, 'deconstruction' period* (May 2010–2014), associated with successive waves of IMF/EU-imposed legal changes adopted by governments formed by the traditional political parties in various formations, the Panhellenic Socialist Movement (PASOK, Πανελλήνιο Σοσιαλιστικό Κίνημα) and New Democracy (ND, Νέα Δημοκρατία); (2) the *second, 'stasis' period* (2015–June 2019) in which the pace of labour-law reforms slowed down, partly because of the tensions between the Syriza-led (Coalition of the Radical Left, Συνασπισμός Ριζοσπαστικής Αριστεράς) government's commitment to unions/labour rights and lenders' demands; (3) a third period also characterized by deconstruction, beginning with the election of the right-wing New Democracy government in July 2019 that exhibits some early signs of a new round of neoliberalization.

Historical background and principal features of the industrial relations system

The history of the Greek labour movement has been broken down into five periods (Ioannou 2000). The first (1879–1918) begins with the outbreak of the first strikes on the island of Syros in 1879 and ends with the founding of the General Confederation of Greek Workers (GSEE, Γενική Συνομοσπονδία Εργατών Ελλάδας) in 1918, as the culmination of the struggles for organizational unity. As the beginnings of the labour union movement in Greece coincided with the economic crisis of the 1920s, during which the bourgeoisie hardened its attitude towards the labour movement, this deprived the union movement of democratic, political and trade union freedoms found in other European countries at that time (Katsoridas 2020: 127). The second period (1919–1940) ends with the establishment of state-controlled trade unionism during the Metaxas dictatorship (1936–1940). While social policy measures, involving the establishment of social security funds, the regulation of wages by collective agreements and a minimum wage, were adopted, unionism came under direct state control and state intervention in the regulation of industrial relations widened (Ioannou 2000). In this context, the third period (1940–1949) – which includes the years of the Second World War, the Occupation, Liberation, and the ensuing Civil War – was characterized by the increasing politicization of the labour movement, without leading to a formal division of the trade union movement. During the fourth period (1950–1974), however, which covers the course of the labour movement until the collapse of the military dictatorship in 1974, the state unionism system was accompanied by the expulsion from the unions of left-wing unions or unions influenced by the Communist Left and continuing divisions concerning union hierarchies. It was only during its fifth period – the era of parliamentary democracy from the fall of the dictatorship in 1974 until today – that the main parameters for union democratization were established (see section below on political relations).

Broadly speaking, union power has not traditionally derived from their membership levels and presence at the workplace, but from the existence, hitherto, of a wider political context that was favourable to unions and reflected the links between unions and political parties. Starting in the 1980s and consolidated in the 1990s, this was accompanied in turn by a to some extent favourable regulatory framework. The latter was structured on the basis of an inter-sectoral agreement responsible for determining the national minimum wage and the operation of a multi-level system of bargaining centred around the extension of higher-level agreements to a large number of employees. This ensured very high bargaining coverage despite low union density rates and a low incidence of company-level bargaining. In this sense, one of the most important elements of the Greek system was the way the notion of collective autonomy had evolved over the years and the way this related to the promotional role that the state had to develop early on to facilitate the settlement of industrial conflicts and to regularize patterns of industrial relations (Katsaroumpas and Koukiadaki 2019). At the same time, Greek industrial relations seemed to confirm some of the assumptions behind the 'Mediterranean varieties of capitalism' approach (Amable 2003), namely that 'a history of heavy state regulation may weaken the capacity of local actors to autonomously coordinate their activities' (Molina and Rhodes 2007). This was facilitated by the regulatory framework itself, in respect of the restrictive rules regarding the establishment of unions at the workplace, further encouraging recourse to political mobilization and general strikes (Kretsos and Vogiatzoglou 2015).

Political relations

Greek trade unions have traditionally been linked to the political process more through the operation of internal party-based factions that transform 'all unions to small replicas of the Parliament' (Mavrogordatos 1998: 56) rather than through social dialogue institutions. Consequently, the unitary structure of the union movement conceals an intense fragmentation due to the existence of well-organized factions around political party lines. The landmark Law 1264/1982 on the democratization of trade unions facilitates this fragmentation by requiring a proportional system of election of the members of executive bodies among lists and candidates. Since the 1990s, elements have been emerging of more 'consensual' structures in relations between the unions and the state (Kouzis 2007; Voulgaris 2012). The conclusion of the 2000 Confidence Pact between the government and social partners in an environment of wage moderation, which was needed for entry to Eurozone, was a notable innovation but it ultimately failed and was abandoned (Tsarouhas 2008; Yannakourou and Soumeli 2004: 9; Zambarloukou 2006).

The pre-crisis period witnessed a stable internal balance of power within both GSEE and the Civil Servants' Confederation (ADEDY, Ανώτατη Διοίκηση Ενώσεων Δημοσίων Υπαλλήλων), both dominated by the pro-PASOK faction Greek National Trade Union Movement for Workers' Defence (PASKE, Πανελλήνια Αγωνιστική Συνδικαλιστική Κίνηση Εργαζομένων). In the early 2000s, it was common practice for ex-GSEE leaders to become Ministers and MPs upon their retirement (Kretsos and Vogiatzoglou 2015: 225), thereby offering a personal 'governmental' link between unions and the government. In 1999, the Communist Party of Greece (KKE, Κομμουνιστικό Κόμμα Ελλάδας) established its own militant confederation, the All-Workers Militant Front (PAME, Πανεργατικό Αγωνιστικό Μέτωπο), while remaining within GSEE structures. In another example of internal division, however, PAME generally chooses to organize separate protests from GSEE (Kapsalis 2012: 23). During this period, continuing a trend whose origins can be traced back to the 1990s, the factions started operating less as 'transmission belts' of their political parties and more autonomously as pressure points for the government, including by capturing key policymaking areas, such as labour and pensions (Iordanoglou 2013; Sotiropoulos 2019: 643).

From 2010, the traditional PASOK and right-wing New Democracy two-party system collapsed after the two parties signed the increasingly unpopular austerity-driven Memoranda. This caused rifts in both main union factions, PASKE and the Democratic Independent Movement of Workers (DAKE, Δημοκρατική Ανεξάρτητη Κίνηση Εργαζομένων) with their parties (PASOK and ND, respectively) (Kousis and Karakioulafi 2013: 6–7). The rifts were more acute for PASOK. Despite PASOK's electoral annihilation and Syriza's victory in 2015 PASKE dominance and Syriza's marginal presence in GSEE continues, with Syriza failing to 'build a strong hold in interest groups' (Sotiropoulos 2019: 616). Potential explanations for this phenomenon can be found in Syriza's historical social-movement orientation, perceiving unions as bureaucratic and dominated by traditional political parties (Tsakatika and Eleftheriou 2013); Syriza's 'weak social base' among workers; and the collapse of clientelistic state–party–citizen relations during the crisis (Vogiatzoglou 2018: 125 ft 2). From 2016, the pro-ND DAKE emerged as the largest faction in ADEDY.

But the bitter divisions inside the union movement reached a dramatic climax in the violent interventions of PAME activists, twice leading to the abandonment of the 2019 GSEE conference. These interventions were made amid disputed allegations of the improper involvement of management in the elections of conference members by affiliated organizations. Eventually, a judicial decision was needed to allow GSEE administration to resume on a provisional basis until the 2020 conference. Another critical function that some militant unions played during the crisis was that of preventing the fascist Golden Dawn (Χρυσή Αυγή) – a pro-Nazi organization and political party recently declared a criminal organization by the Greek courts – from penetrating Greek unions. Bithymitris and Spyridakis (2020) provide an excellent account of how the militant PAME-leading Trade Union of Metal Workers of Attica and the Shipbuilding Industry of Greece succeeded in preventing the rise of a union created by Golden Dawn.

Turning to the issue of social dialogue, in the crisis period the unions' role in the design, adoption and implementation of the radical measures was marginal (Kapsalis 2012; Patra 2012). While for the first Memorandum in May 2010 (European Commission 2010) there was no social dialogue, for the second (March 2012) there were discussions among social partners, although their outcomes were considered by the lenders, in a somewhat paternalistic manner, as '[falling] short of expectations', with the result that the Troika suggested a unilateral imposition of reforms (European Commission 2012: 147). The general picture during the crisis period is that unions were not properly consulted (Koukiadaki and Kokkinou 2016a) as 'crisis negotiations were monopolized by the state, which further entrenched its dominant role in industrial relations' (Rigby and Calavia 2018: 137).

The persistence of party-based factions within unions illustrates the unclear boundaries between factionalism and politicization. Viewed positively, the presence of union factions in all major political parties reflects a cross-party legitimacy of the role of unions. But the PAME/GSEE tensions based on accusations of class betrayal and business unionism undermine unions' public image. Despite these rivalries, GSEE still maintains its hegemonic status at the top of the unions and hosts, in an inclusive manner, all relevant factions, including those supported by PAME and KKE. The unions' political relations have been characterized during the 2000s by continuity, displaying less volatility than the political party system.

Structure of trade unions and union democracy

Union structure and union democracy constitute elements of all trade union functions (Ewing 2005). One of the primary characteristics of the Greek union movement is its dual structure at confederal level: different confederations exist for the private (GSEE) and public sectors (ADEDY). In the private and the wider public sector, including state-owned enterprises, the representation of employees in unions within GSEE is structured at three levels. The first is the primary unions. Many are company-based groups, but they can also be branches of larger national or regional bodies or occupational unions. In addition, a 'new' form of workers' organization emerged with the implementation of the Memoranda, namely the 'Associations of Persons' (Law 4024/2011).[1] Then come secondary unions, namely federations (on the basis of industry or occupation) and the so-called 'labour centres' (on the basis of geographical area), both of which are formed by two or more primary unions. The third category, the confederal level, comprises GSEE. Workers' representation at the GSEE Congress takes place through the federations and the labour centres. At

---

1 Note that 'associations of persons' are not new institutions, strictly speaking. They were established through Law 1264/1982 but had no collective agreement powers as such (see Katsaroumpas and Koukiadaki 2019).

present there are eighty-one labour centres and seventy-three sectoral federations within GSEE. The biggest federations are the Greek Federation of Bank Employee Unions (OTOE, Ομοσπονδία Τραπεζοϋπαλλήλικών Οργανώσεων Ελλάδας), the Federation of Private Employees (OIYE, Ομοσπονδία Ιδιωτικών Υπαλλήλων Ελλάδας), the Federation of Personnel of the Public Power Corporation SA (GENOP/DEI, Γενική Ομοσπονδία ΔΕΗ Κλάδου Ηλεκτρικής Ενέργειας) and the Federation of Greek Builders and Associated Professions (OMOIKEL, Ομοσπονδία Οικοδόμων και Συναφών Επαγγελμάτων Ελλάδας).[2] Traditionally, industrial or occupational unions dominate, although there is a significant presence of company unions, both at primary level and the level of the federations and labour centres. Although there is no publicly available data on changes in the union membership structure and distribution across different levels of organization within the private sector, Table 13.2 shows that the number of labour centres and federations has steadily increased, while there has been a significant decline in the number of primary-level unions. In addition, the number of members actively participating in their unions has progressively declined.

Table 13.2 Changes in the membership of GSEE, 1989–2016

GSEE Congress	Number of primary-level union members (natural persons)		Number of primary-level unions	Number of labour centres	Number of federations
	Members who voted	Registered members			
1989	564,477	n.a.	3,020	69	47
1992	482,337	798,689	2,676	63	60
1995	430,581	775,115	2,318	66	53
1998	413,843	754,142	2,295	68	57
2001	420,610	768,484	2,264	68	58
2004	448,754	839,383	2,373	70	60
2007	472,304	870,415	2,245	74	83
2016	n.a.	n.a.	1,875	79	69

Source: Bithymitris and Kotsonopoulos (2018), Katsoridas (2020).

2 OTOE: total number of 'voting' members: 36,562 (data 2016); OIYE: total number of 'voting' members: 22,709 (data 2016); GENOP-DEI: total number of 'voting' members: 12,121 (data 2016); OMOIKEL: total number of 'voting' members: 12,139 (data 2016).

Similar to the private sector, the organization of workers in the public sector is structured at three levels: primary staff associations, which may be of a local, co-occupational or sectoral nature; secondary organizations, which are formed by the primary associations of employees and have an exclusively 'sectoral' dimension based on the formation and operation of federations; and the tertiary union organization, ADEDY, which is formed by the secondary organizations of civil servants. In 2020 there were a total of forty-six federations belonging to ADEDY. Out of all the federations under ADEDY, four – namely the Greek Primary Teachers' Federations (DOE, Διδασκαλική Ομοσπονδία Ελλάδας), the Secondary Education Teachers (OLME, Ομοσπονδία Λειτουργών Μέσης Εκπαίδευσης), the Public Hospital Employees (POEDIN, Πανελλήνια Ομοσπονδία Εργαζομένων Δημόσιων Νοσοκομείων) and the Employees in Local Government (POE-OTA, Πανελλήνια Ομοσπονδία Προσωπικού Οργανισμών Τοπικής Αυτοδιοίκησης) – represent over 65 per cent of the total strength of ADEDY, while the remaining 35 per cent is distributed over the other forty-two federations (Katsoridas 2020: 255).[3]

In the context of fragmentation at cross-sectoral level, there were attempts by ADEDY and GSEE in the early 2000s, with the creation of a consolidated bipartite National Coordinating Trade Union Council (or 'trade union congress'), to investigate and take decisions jointly on strategic options, priorities and far-reaching tactical options for the union movement. Despite cooperation in, among others, research activities, there has been no progress towards a merger between the two confederations. Union fragmentation at the confederal level is complemented by similar levels of fragmentation at secondary and primary levels as well. Despite plans for organizational simplification of the unions in the early 2000s (e.g. at the 31st Congress in 2002) no progress has been made on these objectives. Reasons for the continuing fragmentation include the existence of a great number of occupational unions and the loose interpretation of the notion of the 'branch', which allows space for more than one federation (Kouzis 2007). Furthermore, unlike other countries, where financial pressures have led to union mergers, such pressures have

3 DOE: total number of 'voting' members: about 59,625; OLME: total number of 'voting' members: about 37,500; POEDIN: total number of 'voting' members: about 37,500; POE-OTA: total number of 'voting' members: about 37,500. All data are from 2016.

been less noticeable in Greece, as unions have traditionally not depended so much on direct income from the membership base.

More importantly, the function of the unions is not confined to a simple struggle of ideological approaches, while political parties essentially function as organized forces within the unions (Kouzis 2007), the outcome being the intensification of factionalization and partisanship of the union movement (Katsoridas 2020). At the level of the confederations, during the 2000s and early 2010s, both GSEE and ADEDY boards had small majorities in favour of PASOK, which to some extent allowed closer cooperation between the two confederations (Ioannou 2005: 158). Recent evidence suggests, however, that changes in the composition of the confederations' boards have led to greater union antagonism at confederal level. The decision by ADEDY's executive board to declare a work stoppage and call on public sector employees to take part in a rally, organized by PAME,[4] so that the 37th GSEE Conference could not take place, illustrates these divisions well. Unions' political linkages had been extensively used in the past at other levels of union organization as well. This has been the case especially in respect of public sector unions and state-owned enterprises, where paradoxically unions have a significant membership base, indicating the long shadow of the close relationship between the political system and union leaderships.

From a regulatory perspective, Law 1264/1982 on the 'democratization of the trade-union movement and enshrinement of the trade-union freedoms of workers' remained largely unchanged during both the stability and crisis periods (2009–2018). Other changes (see section below on bargaining) seem to have intensified the antagonism between different segments of the union movement, however. Proposed changes, put forward recently by the New Democracy government (2019–present), may soon affect the internal organization of unions directly. This is because they include measures that can be seen as targeting the operations of unions per se, such as the requirement for registration of unions in a single register in order to be able to conclude collective agreements, the reduction of paid leave and the liberalization of dismissal protection for union officials.[5]

---

[4] At PAME's 2016 national conference, 536 trade unions participated: 12 federations, 15 labour centres, 457 trade unions and 52 'struggle committees'. A conference is also held in 2017 but there is no publicly available data on the participant organisations.

[5] Law 4635/2019. This possibility applies to all other types of decisions of the General Assemblies and of other unions' administrative bodies. The law stipulates that the

Unionization

The issue of unionization is directly related to trade unions' service and representation functions (Ewing 2005). There are no official figures on the number of union members in Greece. Instead, the data for calculating union density has traditionally been based on the unions' own figures on voting members in union elections for the administration boards (and not those registered as members or those that have paid their dues).[6] This is on the basis that the number of members voting indicates more active participation in union activities (Katsoridas 2020: 265). At the same time, concerns have been expressed that the union estimates may be inaccurate or distorted, inflating the actual number of their members in order to increase their legitimacy, enhance their chances in elections or receive funding, as these are often distributed according to the number of voting members (Koukoules 1994).

Historical data on union density in Greece suggests of increasing erosion during the period 2000–2020. Before the 2000s, unions were already experiencing challenges, as density had already been reduced from 48 per cent in 1977 to 24.9 per cent in 2001. During 2000–2016, the decline continued and intensified further during the economic crisis. According to the latest data, GSEE and ADEDY had 612,000 voting members in total in 2016: GSEE had 358,761 voting members eligible at its congress in March 2016 and ADEDY reported 253,564 voting members at its congress in November 2016. Based on the total number of employees – namely 237,192 in the first quarter of 2016 – this produces a union density figure of 25.8 per cent (Georgiadou 2021). The ICTWSS database, however, calculates union density in 2016 at 20.2 per cent (see Figure 13.1).[7] The figures also mask a marked difference between the public and private sectors. In the private sector, density does not exceed 15 per cent, while in the public sector it exceeds 90 per cent in some cases (for an analysis, see Katsoridas, 2020).

---

secrecy and transparency of members' voting shall be guaranteed, as shall be defined by the statutes of the trade union. By decision of the Minister of Labour the terms and conditions for the application of this regulation will be stipulated. This decision has not yet been adopted.

6 No data are publicly available on the actual number of people registered as union members or on those of them who have paid their dues.

7 The calculation excluded union members that are unemployed or retired and are not employees (Visser 2019a). See also Katsoridas (2020: 274) who calculated that union density stood in 2016 at 20.3 per cent.

Figure 13.1 Trade union density, 2000–2016

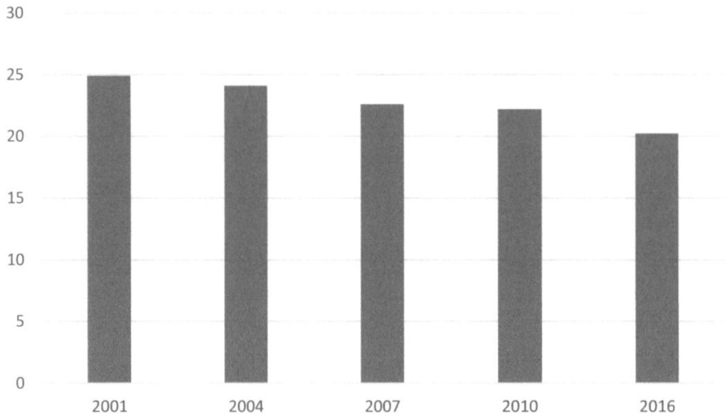

Source: Visser (2019a).

Low union density rates can be interpreted as the outcome of a number of interrelated elements of the labour market and industrial relations framework. First of all, the make-up of the workforce: the presence of a large number of irregular and undocumented workers in combination with a large percentage of bogus self-employed and atypical workers, has meant that in practice a large section of workers has not been unionized (Zambarloukou 2006). It is noteworthy that within the private sector, the largest sectors in terms of workforce size – commerce, services and food – have the lowest union density rates. The high percentage of small and micro companies in these industries, in combination with the characteristics described above, dissuade workers from organizing in primary industrial unions and company unions (Katsoridas 2020: 267). What is more, these groups of workers, who are often precarious, exhibit some of the elements identified by Standing (2011) regarding the 'modern precariat', including their lack of affiliation to unions or political parties. Recent analysis by Zisimopoulos et al. (2019) also suggests that the social classes that suffer most from exploitation – defined as belonging to different groups identified as working class – show a lower density rate than the union density of total workers in waged employment. In contrast, the highest level of union density was reported in lower level managers and supervisors in the private sector and to a larger extent civil servants (Zisimopoulos et al. 2019: 5).

As for the trade unions, there is evidence to suggest a reluctance on their part to accept various categories of precarious workers as members.

In the private sector, this involves, for example, excluding from union membership people employed through so-called voucher schemes and outsourcing in banking. The rationale is that they should avoid legitimizing such practices. Based on similar arguments about marginalizing such business practices, union federations in the public sector have in the past not accepted as members people on fixed-term contracts in local government (Koukiadaki and Kokkinou 2016b). Kapsalis (2012: 24) suggests that during the crisis there was growth of a new form of grassroots unionism that was more class-conscious and tried to operate on the basis of direct democratic principles without bureaucrats and professional leadership. These attempts were more prevalent in specific contexts, such as the service sector, where unionization has historically not been high (Koukiadaki and Kokkinou 2016b), or where there is a large number of atypical employees, or higher rates of labour-law violations. Part of this grassroots unionism contested the 'institutionalized official' unions (Karakioulafis and Kanellopoulos 2018) on the basis of the latter's closeness to political parties and inability to represent a growing number of precarious workers. Even in this case, however, grassroots unions have tended to focus in some respects on developing forms of political mobilization rather than mobilization at the workplace level (Kretsos 2011).

Unions' appeal to other categories of employees, for example young workers and women, is also not without its challenges. A 2015 nationwide survey reported that 82 per cent of union members are 40 years old or above. Even though workers aged between 25 and 29 years' old constitute 20 per cent of total employees, only 1 per cent are union members (Zisimopoulos 2018: 379–381). This compares badly with data from 1999, when 25 per cent of young workers were union members. Reasons cited include unions' relations with political parties and their inability to engage with the problems facing this category of workers (Katsoridas 2020). In a similar vein, unions have largely been unable to capitalize on the relative growth – from 39 per cent in 2000 to 45 per cent in 2018 – of female employment in recent decades. In 2015, men were represented in the union movement at a level almost 13 percentage points higher than women (Zisimopoulos 2018). A survey conducted by GSEE reported that the most important deterrent for becoming a union member among women was the lack of time to engage in union activities because of family obligations (85.8 per cent of respondents). The predominance of men in unions and in union leadership, pressure and discouragement on the part of their partners or their families, and devaluation by their colleagues, were also reported as factors preventing women from participating in unions (51 per cent, 49 and 38.3 per cent, respectively) (Varhalama et al. 2015).

Union resources and expenditures

Trade union funding is a major 'infrastructural' power resource (Schmalz et al. 2018: 119), essential for internal union capacities and financial autonomy. During 2000–2020, the comparatively 'exceptional' Greek tradition of extensive state-mediated union funding (Kouzis 2007)[8] proved resilient despite experiencing certain changes in its institutional form.

Union funding originated in the Greek authoritarian past, more specifically during the fascist Metaxas dictatorship in the late 1930s, when it was used as a class instrument for pro-government unions at the expense of dissident militant communist ones (Kouzis 2007; Lavdas 2005). This institution survived the post-1974 democratic transition and in its 2000 form it operated according to a complex system administered by the Ministry of Labour, which drew on employers' and workers' social security contributions (0.25 per cent for each party) on behalf of an organization called the Workers' Welfare Organization (OEE, Οργανισμός Εργατικής Εστίας). Besides union funding, OEE performed a 'service function' (Ewing 2005) by offering a range of services to workers, such as vouchers for recreational, tourist and cultural activities. The scope of eligible expenses for union funding was restricted to basic operational costs, payroll costs for a limited number of staff, conference or election expenses and other overheads, such as rent, cleaning and heating costs.

The availability of this funding contributed to – or at least reinforced – a *resource dualism* among unions, depending on their willingness to participate in the funding systems, eligibility and funding received. On one hand, GSEE and, to a lesser extent, secondary-level private sector associations (federations) drew heavily on OEE funding as their major sources of income, with voluntary membership subscriptions performing a secondary or symbolic role (Kritsantonis 1998). On the other hand, primary-level unions in the public sector derived most of their income

---

8 The term 'state-mediated funding' is used instead of 'state funding' because it better captures the fact that these funds are drawn from employer and/or employee contributions.

from voluntary membership subscriptions. Most of these unions were formally excluded as they failed to satisfy the required threshold of 500 voting members. And even if they did, they received minimal funding. Public unions at all levels and the banking unions in the private sector, however, did not receive OEE funding and rely significantly on membership subscriptions.[9]

This system experienced virtually no changes in the pre-crisis period (2000–2010). The only exception was a 0.05 rise in OEE contributions agreed by the 2002–2003 National General Collective Agreement. It is illustrative that during 2007–2009 GSEE sourced more than 95 per cent of its income from OEE compared with the miniscule 1 per cent that came from the subscriptions of affiliated members (Table 13.3).

Table 13.3 Total GSEE income from 1 April 2007 to 31 December 2009

Income source	Absolute number in euros	Total income (%)
Funding from Ergatiki Estia	20,250,000	95.2
Funding from other sources	180,000	0.9
Bank interest	612,000	2.9
Subscriptions of affiliated organizations	231,000	1.1
Total income	21,273,000	100

Note: Rounded data.

Source: GSEE (2010: 7).

This regime was subjected to an external challenge by the 'capture' of the Greek state IMF/EU-imposed conditionality established during the Greek debt crisis (Katsaroumpas 2018; Koukiadaki and Kretsos 2012). Memorandum II identified OEE as a 'non-priority social expenditure' and demanded its termination (European Commission 2012: 110). All duties, liabilities and resources were transferred to the Manpower Organization (OAED, Οργανισμός Απασχόλησης Εργατικού Δυναμικού). Employer contributions were abolished as part of the overall aim of reducing non-wage costs for employers (European Commission 2012). The ex-OEE contributions are now held under a special earmarked OAED account from which union funding is drawn. Despite this institutional

9 ADEDY collects a 0.3 euro subscription per person from affiliated secondary organisations.

reform, however, successive ministers have renewed this funding on a triannual basis (2013, 2016 and 2019). Law 4491/2017 also clarified that these funds do not constitute *state aid or funding* but a 'withholding of a resource', implying that the state here acts in a mediating capacity (Article 16).

In 2016, Syriza-led government minister George Katrougalos described this system as an 'unhealthy solution' and stated 'that trade unions should be self-funded, as to gain autonomy from the state' (Petropoulos 2016). This comment provoked a fierce response by GSEE, accusing him of 'blackmailing with economic asphyxiation the trade union movement, reminiscent of other eras and other "democracies" without "independent" or "autonomous trade unions"' (GSEE 2016).

The legal provision for union leave is another important institutional source for union activities. This is significant as unions tend to rely on their members' services for their operation rather than on full-time employees. In 2018 GSEE employed around fifty persons (Kostakos 2018), a figure not unrelated to the fact that state-mediated funding covers only a limited number of staff. Union leaders at secondary or tertiary levels are entitled to a full union leave with pay for their tenure subject to more generous provisions in collective agreements. In addition, with regard to the collection of membership subscriptions, Law 1264/1982 provided for an employer's duty to maintain check-off arrangements subject to more specific provisions by National General Collective Agreements. On the question of expenditures, Kouzis draws a link between the dominant status of state-mediated union funding covering only basic expenses and the relative absence of strike funds in unions along with the almost inexistent service provision to their members (Kouzis 2007: 187).

There is a striking absence of academic literature on union expenditure and other union resources, although some observations can be made. First, the state-mediated union funding exhibits a peculiar 'stickiness' despite its abolition in various historical periods and the recognition of its provisional nature by Law 1264/1982 (Kouzis 2007). This model can be seen as an instance of *statization* of union resources threatening their financial autonomy (Kouzis 2007; Stergiou 2002). Its origins are linked to an active class state supporting friendly unions against the communist threat. In its modern form, this institution typifies the close connection between state, law and administrative discretion. Secondly, it established various channels of state influence on unions. To begin with, this model helps the preservation of upper-level unions in that it shields them from membership changes. In this sense, it represents a peculiar institutional arrangement contributing to 'institutional embeddedness' that partially uncouples the organizational fortunes of unions from labour market strength (Baccaro et al. 2003: 120–121). The state also enjoys the ability to use the threat of economic asphyxiation as a leverage tool for pressuring unions as well as influencing their 'organizational flexibility' by controlling the expenses eligible for funding (Kouzis 2007).

Thirdly, union funding operates in the complex and opaque intersection between welfare law, this is social security contributions, and administrative law via Ministerial decisions. Even if one accepts in principle the thesis that a system of funding of unions by compulsory contributions is justified vis-à-vis their public role as vital democratic institutions, the current model seems to be far from this principle. It is dominated by the state's expanded discretionary role. The government controls the flow of contributions from employees to the social security provider and then to OAED from which only a part is channelled to unions based on administrative decisions. Hence, it is not managed by unions based on a direct and transparent reciprocal link between contributions and funding. And these contributions appear to employees in a bureaucratic guise as another state-imposed salary reduction with an obscure name. It should also not be ignored that the state enjoys an additional financial source to be used as needed for other budgetary purposes. In addition, unions are vulnerable to the charge that they are parasitic to the state which could be rhetorically mobilized by a future government embracing a Thatcherite-type assault on unions. Finally, a critique from freedom and authority would see this system as incompatible with the autonomous will of workers to choose their funding for their union representatives and their active and conscious participation in the union processes (Stergiou 2002).

Collective bargaining and unions at the workplace

The case of collective bargaining constitutes one of the prime areas where the role of the state, through primarily statutory intervention, has traditionally played a critical role in the framing of collective bargaining, including at workplace level. In the first period (2000–2010) the regulatory framework for collective bargaining was shaped by Law 1876/1990 that intended to promote collective autonomy and contain the dominant, until then, role of the state in the industrial relations system. In practice, the bargaining system was relatively stable in terms of its structure, coverage and operation. Bargaining coverage stood at around 80 per cent in contrast to union density that was estimated at around 24 per cent (Visser 2019a). But there was growing dissonance between legal stability and neoliberal economic change (Katsaroumpas and Koukiadaki 2019). From the perspective of union organization, there were considerable challenges in respect of their formation and operation, given that 96 per cent of firms employed fewer than twenty employees, which has been the minimum union membership demanded for a union to be established in a company (Kouzis 2000). Further, the provision of three levels of union organization, with a very large number of primary-level unions traditionally organized around occupations, contributed to organizational fragmentation (Yannakourou 2004). These in conjunction with the politically driven divisions within GSEE and ADEDY meant that the involvement of local union officers and shop stewards in the administration of collective agreements at workplace level was not extensive. In addition, the long-term secondment of union officials from the workplaces, their participation in various committees and councils and their political ambitions, among others, created an image among the workforce of senior trade unionists with significant benefits and privileges (Katsoridas 2020: 292–293). On the other hand, while legislation introduced in 1988 (Law 1767/1988) made for the first time provision for the establishment and operation of works councils, the take-up of these was minimal. This was attributed to the satisfaction of some unions with the informal joint consultation arrangements and the concern by the leadership of unions that the elected members of the works' council would not be under their control and could thus become their competitors (Jecchinis 1994).

The crisis period saw several changes in the regulatory framework for collective bargaining, indirectly challenging the role of unions at the workplace level. In the first 'deconstruction' period, crisis-related changes included a temporary suspension of the extension of industrial and occupational agreements and the principle of favourability,[10] and the provision of scope for all firms, including those employing fewer than fifty persons,[11] to conclude firm-level collective agreements through

---

[10] Law 4024/2011.

[11] In the previous system, there was no right to company-level bargaining in companies below 50 employees and only sectoral and occupational collective agreements could apply.

the so-called 'association of persons'. The Committee on Freedom of Association of the International Labour Organization expressed particular concerns about the granting of collective bargaining rights to such associations, as it was deemed that it could 'seriously undermine the position of trade unions as the representative voice of the workers in the collective bargaining process' (ILO 2012). While firm-level bargaining predominantly through associations of persons was initially taken up, the number of company-level agreements plummeted again as a result of further reforms that again reduced the incentive for employers to proceed to the conclusion of company-level agreements, even with associations of persons (Koukiadaki and Grimshaw 2016). What is more, the contraction of higher-level bargaining, and thus of bargaining coverage (see Table 13.1 above), had significant influence on the unions' associational capacity. It essentially reduced the incentive for certain unions at primary level to be part of the overall structure of GSEE, constraining even further the institutional power of the third-level federation and precipitating a crisis of credibility from the workers' point of view (Kapsalis 2012: 9). At the same time, this was combined with the intensification of grassroots movements at company level, with mixed results (Kretsos and Vogiatzoglou 2015).

In the 'stasis' phase, initial attempts by the Syriza-led government to implement a range of measures to promote collective bargaining were thwarted by continuing pressure from Greece's creditors in 2015. According to the 2017 agreement entered into by the then Greek government with its creditors, however, Law 4472/2017 reserved the right to reintroduce the favourability principle and extension of collective agreements at the end of the period of validity of the Memorandum of Understanding (MoU). These changes were duly introduced into law from August 2018. But given the wide-ranging effects of the previous reforms on unions' associational capacity and the fact that any extension decision has to follow strict legal conditions, very few agreements were extended, thus negatively impacting upon workers' protection at workplace level. These changes were short-lived, however. The new government led by New Democracy introduced legislation in 2019 that was again designed to remove the incentives for collective bargaining and to weaken further unions' regulatory function (Law 4635/2019). The legislative changes included the introduction of an exception to the favourability principle by local (occupational or industrial) collective agreements, a special extension regime in respect of companies in financial difficulty and non-profit organizations, and further restrictions on the unilateral right to arbitration. Evidence from 2020 confirms the irrelevance of collective bargaining as a method for determining terms and conditions of employment, including at company level.

Industrial conflict

Greek trade unions have traditionally deployed industrial action as a political rather than an industrial-economic tool (Kritsantonis 1998: 525). Such a preference may also reflect the perceived feasibility of state intervention for worker interests compared with their generally weaker industrial power (Katsaroumpas and Koukiadaki 2019: 274–278). The frequent use of 24-hour general strikes, often with symbolic effect, is a prominent manifestation of this (Vogiatzoglou 2018: 130). According to Hamann et al. (2013: 1032), thirty-three out of seventy-two general strikes in Western Europe between 1980 and 2006 took place in Greece. The comparatively high rate of general strikes is also enabled by the permissive legal framework, which requires only a decision of the GSEE or ADEDY administrative council. There are generally no reliable data on the level of strike participation overall and within specific industries and sectors to allow an in-depth and systematic analysis.

No alterations were made to the legal framework during the pre-crisis period. Reliable assessments of strike activity are impossible because the Ministry of Labour ceased to record strikes in 2000. But the successful mass strikes in 2000 against the proposed deregulatory pension reform proposed by PASOK minister Tasos Giannitsis are notable. The combined effects of union mobilization, plummeting government popularity and internal cabinet divisions led to the withdrawal of the reforms and caused the departure of Giannitsis (Tsarouhas 2012: 166–168). While for some scholars this event evidences privileged workers' aversion to reforms in Greece (Featherstone and Papadimitriou 2008; Giannitsis 2007; Matsaganis 2008), for unions it proved their ability to veto deregulatory reforms through a complementary use of industrial action and political pressure. These strikes appeared to be rather the exception than the rule in the pre-crisis period, however.

The post-2010 crisis period witnessed a radical transformation of the legal context. Successive waves of EU/IMF-imposed reforms that interfered directly in collective bargaining and its preconditions (Koukiadaki and Kokkinou 2016a; Katsaroumpas 2018) meant that unions' institutional security was eroded significantly. This was particularly the case with GSEE, following the attacks on the National General Collective Agreements as a universal minimum wage-setting system. Unions thus faced a dual exclusion. On one hand, their collective bargaining capacities were reduced by the destabilization of the collective bargaining system. On the other hand, the government became unresponsive to internal pressures owing to the IMF/EU bailout conditionality regime and the threat of Eurozone expulsion. In this context, industrial action appeared to the unions to be the last resort.

During 2010–2012, there was intense strike activity through general strikes (Kretsos and Vogiatzoglou 2015) and more conflictual actions (Papanikolopoulos et al. 2018), coinciding with the various rounds of proposed legislative reforms. This surge in strike activity was integrated into a wider mobilization strategy of resistance to austerity, along with 'demonstrations, clashes with the police and protests in the majority of Greek cities', to be followed by the *Indignados* movement, labour mobilization and civil disobedience (Psimitis 2011; Sergi and Vogiatzoglou 2013: 224). According to the GSEE press releases, the strikes on 19 October 2011 and 18 October 2012 had 100 per cent participation in the oil refinery, shipbuilding, maritime transport and port sectors, and 90 per cent in the steel, construction and retail sectors (GSEE 2011, 2012).

Within this period, the 272-day strike at Hellenic Steel in Aspropirgos by a 'militant' union against proposed wage cuts (by cutting working hours) and dismissals was characterized as an example of 'militant unionism' (Bithymitris 2016). Despite its failure, the strike became emblematic in the struggle against the injustice of austerity, gathering celebrity support and solidarity contributions from a variety of national and international actors, such as student unions and solidarity associations (Bithymitris 2016: 381). The period 2012–2015 witnessed a reduction in strikes and mobilization (Papanikolopoulos et al. 2018), however, which continued under the Syriza-led governments (2015–2019).

In their analysis, Papanikolopoulos et al. (2018: 66–70) attribute the retreat of mobilization to a combination of challenges of the Greek union movement. The identify among others the drastic impact of measures on employees' resources (which, along with the fear of unemployment, made them less likely to continue strike participation), the routinization of strikes, state suppression and the transfer of hopes from protests to the electoral arena with the election of the Syriza-led government.

While strike activity went on the decline after 2012, the legal framework for industrial action, which was curiously left untouched in 2010–2015 (see Katsaroumpas and Koukiadaki 2019: 274–278), became increasingly a Memorandum target after 2015. Potentially reflecting compromises between lenders and the Syriza government, committed to the existing framework, Memorandum II focused on procedural delaying tactics by requiring consultations, which should 'tak[e] into account best practices internationally and in Europe' (European Commission 2015: 21). Even though an Expert Consultation fell short of recommending any changes (Expert Group 2016), the 2018 Supplemental Memorandum called for adoption of 'legislation to increase the quorum for first-degree unions to vote on a strike to 50 per cent' (European Commission 2018: 23). The previous threshold was one-third and in some cases one-fifth (Zisimopoulos 2019: 99). Here it should be clarified that these thresholds apply to first-level unions, because a decision by the administrative council is sufficient for the peak confederations (GSEE and ADEDY). Union leaders warned that these steps may be the first in an overall deconstruction of the strike framework (Iefimerida 2018).

The right-wing New Democracy government, elected in 2019, is clearly intent on making a more substantial intervention in the industrial action framework. In 2020, the government presented a proposal for a substantial overhaul of the system. It called for a union obligation to provide remote balloting for strike decisions and imposed a requirement to justify industrial action. There were also proposals for a minimum of 40 per cent safety personnel in businesses whose function is critical for society and in the public sector, which will arguably reduce the effect of strikes. The law also proposes the general illegality of occupation of premises, which was used in the crisis, or any exertion of psychological or physical force (Enikos 2020). Union resistance to this law, along with health and safety complaints about inadequate protection from Covid-19, led to some notable strikes in 2020. Besides ADEDY strikes calling for the recruitment of additional personnel (doctors, teachers, cleaners and transport personnel), along with the requisition of private facilities (News247 2020a), there were teachers' strikes about the lack of sufficient Covid-19 measures at school and student safety (News247 2020b) and a doctors' strike complaining about poor medical facilities (CnnGreece 2020).

An overall assessment of the period 2000–2020 cannot but be struck by the resilience of the political use of industrial action as a political tool, but also note its failure to register its impact after the 2010 crisis. The Greek case offers an example of the utilization of industrial action as part of the 'governmental' function (Ewing 2005). The recent proposals for industrial action reform depart from the pre-existing consensus in this area, however, and may prefigure a more radical step-by-step attack on the right to industrial action.

Societal power

The prevailing academic narrative in Greece posits a 'colonization' of civic, non-governmental associations by political parties, shaped by the power of a strong state against a weak society (Diamandouros 1991; Makridimitris 2002; Mouzelis and Pagoulatos 2002: 8), including trade unions. Unions generally suffer from low public trust. While Malamidis' observation that unions 'have been identified as representatives of state interests and have often been associated with corruption and patronage' (Malamidis 2021: 70) should be treated as a generalization, a 2010 public survey found that only 25 per cent of respondents trusted unions. This figure is even lower for GSEE and ADEDY, at 23 per cent (VPRC 2010). NGOs were even less trusted because of scandals and accusations that they have benefited from non-transparent state funding (Loukidou 2014: 2; Sotiropoulos and Bourikos 2014).

With the exception of the anti-pension reform movement in 2010, the most important movements between 2000–2010 – namely those against globalization (between 1999–2003; see Malamidis 2021), against privatization of universities, by university students (2005–2006), and against police brutality, led by young people in 2008 (Vogiatzoglou 2018: 125) – were not led by unions. On the left, however, there was a sort of 'civil society turn' by both KKE and Syriza – both marginal parties at that time gathering around 3–6 per cent of the vote – which include 'a visible effort to reconfirm existing links and forge new links to trade unions and social movements' (Tsakatika and Eleftheriou 2013: 82). For KKE, this turn has taken the form of the PAME confederation's efforts to reach unorganized workers, while for Syriza, it takes the form of an alliance of environmental, anti-capitalist, feminist and other social movements.

The 2010 crisis is considered to be a turning point, prompting a revitalization of Greek society in the form of denser civil society network, with more state autonomy (Loukidou 2014; Simiti 2017). The union movement has taken a dual position in this revitalization: (i) a 'social movement turn' by GSEE and ADEDY 'from the top'; and (ii) the emergence of 'grassroot' unions and labour organizations 'from below'.

ADEDY/GSEE strikes between 2010 and 2012 became integrated into the 'anti-austerity social movement'. Kanellopoulos and Kostopoulos (2013: 10) identify three main clusters in their analysis of protest participation: unions, organized political forces (Syriza, Antarsya, KKE) and 'indignados' (*Aganaktismenoi*). They observe the complementary use GSEE/ADEDY made of calling the strike and the superior mobilization capacity of other organizations to bring participants to the demonstrations (Kanellopoulos and Kostopoulos 2013: 11). Here the permissive legal regime for general strikes was exploited to provide resources for social protest. But the GSEE decision to back 'yes' in the 2015 referendum called by Syriza brought it into conflict with most sections of Greek social movements.

Regarding activities 'from below', various unions of teachers, workers and pharmacists have engaged in coalition-building by providing volunteer services to the rising solidarity network, offering services to those in need (Kantzara 2014: 270). These networks cover both formal organizations – voluntary associations and NGOs – and informal networks seeking to remedy the 'social protection gap' created by the dramatic decline of the already weak welfare state (Sotiropoulos and Bourikos 2014: 34). There are militant, grassroots union organizations, informal workers' collectives and experimental cooperatives and self-management projects, including local-based Workers' Clubs (Εργατικές Λέσχες), which are able to get the message out to the hard-to-reach small-enterprise employees and the unemployed (Kretsos and Vogiatzoglou 2015: 226–230). The various unions of precarious workers maintain no links with traditional parties, operate in areas with low unionization and enjoy a contentious relationship with the GSEE, in which they participate reluctantly (Kretsos and Vogiatozlou 2015: 228). They have forged alliances with other organizations, however, such as smaller left-wing parties, student unions and NGOs through a union assembly and calls to its members for demonstrations during the general strike (ibid.: 229).

Moving to environmental issues, the 2004–2005 National General Collective Agreement (NGCA, Εθνική Γενική Συλλογική Σύμβαση

Εργασίας) established a clear duty of the parties to 'accept the need for compatibility of productive activities with environmental protection and sustainable development', while providing for permanent institutional structures with the government and local authorities. More recently, the 2018 NGCA explicitly referred to climate change, stating that 'the parties … agree to jointly request their participation in the National Council for Adaptation to Climate Change' through one employer representative and one GSEE representative. The NGCA stated that both parties accept the 'just transition of workers to an economy of low carbon emissions, which will ensure the necessary support for them when there is a need for redeployment, reskilling and redistribution'. These references appear to have a more declaratory/symbolic value than anything more substantial, however.

While there has been an overall trajectory of structural continuity during this period, it is notable that for a time there was closer alignment between GSEE/ADEDY and the emerging social movement. While this may be attributed to the loss of institutional security, the Greek case illustrates an interesting complementarity between GSEE/ADEDY – which possess 'legal-institutional resources' in the form of general strikes – and social movements, enabling a high level of mobilization. This alignment appears to have a short-term episodic nature, however, devoid of permanent links. As we move through the 2020s, it is an open and critical question, how the tensions will evolve between an emergent grassroots social-movement unionism and the more institutionalized union leadership.

Europeanization and trade unions

In the past 20 years, the EU question has largely come to define the industrial relations framework in Greece, including trade unions. The pre-crisis period (2000–2010) was characterized by an 'intended' Europeanization, understood as 'modernization', in which domestic actors simply responded to challenges emanating from the top (Gemenis and Lefkofridi 2013; Ioakimidis 2000). This was in the context of the formation at that time of attitudes towards European integration that understood it as a struggle between pro-EU modernizers and adherents of the 'underdog culture' (Diamandouros 1993), who lamented the 'loss of sovereignty' to the EU. The impetus towards modernization was transmitted to the industrial relations system in a top-down manner, through a variety of mechanisms. Their main characteristics were their soft- rather than hard-law nature;[12] that they were informed by ideas of adaptability and social partnership; and that their focus was primarily on promoting unions' governmental and public administration function. The main example here would be the European Employment Strategy (EES), which aimed at strengthening social partners' participation in the process of policy reform. The incorporation of the EES in Greece had limited success, as unions and employers played only a marginal role in the formulation and implementation of National Action Plans. This was because of the presence of historical and institutional factors blocking the re-articulation of policy preferences along conciliatory lines (Tsarouhas 2008).

From the trade union perspective, these developments could be interpreted as supporting the transition of the union movement from 'disjointed corporatism' (Lavdas 1997), as the main form of interest representation, to emancipation from state and political structures. At the same time, the support for a greater government and public administration function for unions had the potential to nurture contradictions, which, if not addressed adequately, could undermine their role and position in the industrial relations systems and in society more broadly (Papavlasopoulos and Spourdalakis 2008). Given how the relationship between unions and the political realm had evolved in previous years, it is easy to understand why the Europeanization of policy initiatives limited the unions' ability to engage and represent new categories of workers. The focus on entering a process of political exchange (albeit not always successful, see Zambarloukou 2006) in turn affected union density, which has decreased in recent years, while strengthening union bureaucracy and generating complications in terms of leadership renewal. All of the above seem to have led the unions into a crisis of representativeness that was dangerous for their future in light of the low levels of participation, limited mobilization and – especially – their inability to integrate dynamic categories, such as young people, women and immigrants (Papavlasopoulos and Spourdalakis 2008).

It is against this context that the economic crisis in the late 2000s had wide-ranging and radical implications for the union movement. This

---

[12] This does not take into account the role of EU Directives, as these did not primarily address the role of trade unions as such.

period can be distinguished from the period of stability in two ways. First of all, the role of the legal framework becomes pivotal in altering the institutional configurations in the industrial relations system and the role of the unions. Secondly, rather than witnessing a substitution in terms of trade union functions in the industrial relations system, what was promoted indirectly at first and later directly was the marginalization of unions as actors in the industrial relations system altogether. In relation to the former, this was brought about through the legal framework: it was almost exclusively state regulation, articulated in line with Greece's commitments in the MoU, that challenged the institutional arrangements for unions.

In relation to union marginalization, this came about firstly as a result of the absence of any union involvement in the discussions leading up to the drafting of the 'structural market reforms' that accompanied the loan agreements, thus limiting their governmental and public administration functions. Later on, legislative measures were implemented to constrain those functions even further, primarily through the removal of the regulatory function of cross-sectoral agreements and extended beyond them to target unions' regulatory function through a combination of measures affecting their role in bargaining. While mobilization attempts were developed by the unions in response to these developments, the 'consensual hegemony' of the trade union movement (Bithymitris and Kotsonopoulos 2018) was emphatically highlighted in the run-up to the 2015 referendum organized by the then Syriza-led government. Whereas GSEE condemned the EU's austerity policies in Greece, its official position was that the referendum was misguided and divisive, in direct contrast to the Greek public, who rejected the bailout agreement. While the post-crisis period is no longer ostensibly subject to the conditionality requirements applicable during the crisis, the current domestic agenda of labour reforms – which includes limiting even further unions' workplace representation – seems to be consistent with the priorities expressed in the context of the enhanced surveillance procedure, assessing Greece's progress with the policy commitments made at the Eurogroup meeting in June 2018 (see, for instance, European Commission 2020).

Overall, the trajectory of Greek trade unions during the years of Europeanization was marked by a set of contradictions that have had significant implications for the movement, once the country emerged from the crisis. The emphasis on the unions' governmental and public administration function, as part of Europeanization, without making an effort to organize more effectively a growing number of underrepresented workers, as well as the pre-existing co-dependence with political parties, amplified the unions' exposure to the drastic EU-mandated 'labour market reforms' during the crisis and subsequently.

Conclusions

Considering the density of events in the period under examination here, it is surprising that the architecture of Greek trade unions in 2020 would be strikingly familiar to an observer from the year 2000. While Greece struggled with the 'European question' in different guises in this period, historical contradictions persist. The contradictions between a unitary structure and intense political party factionalism; between a suspicion towards and dependence on the state; between the absence of social dialogue structures and politics as the privileged form of action; between the legitimacy of collective bargaining in public discourse and low union density rates; and between the 'upper' and 'lower' parts of the union movement are only some examples. The Greek case could be perceived as providing a warning of the perils of the routinization of class politics within the labour movement, which has the potential to act as a source of division and fragmentation. It also exposes the precarious boundaries between politicization, radicalization and factionalism. But equally it provides an ideal example of unions as institutional fields of contestation (Gallas 2018; Taylor et al. 2011).

Visser (2019b) has identified four possible scenarios or possible futures for trade unions: *marginalization, dualization, substitution*, or *revitalization*. The pattern of union development in Greece seems to suggest that the most likely scenarios there are marginalization or dualization, or both. Whereas the persistently high level in Greece of forms of unstable and non-standard employment (e.g. bogus self-employment) could open up opportunities to experiment with new forms of worker voice and representation, this does not seem to be the case in Greece (with limited exceptions, such as outsourced workers in the banking sector). This, in combination with the paternalistic ethos in the small and medium-sized enterprises, which account for 86 per cent of jobs in Greece (OECD 2017, cited in Visser 2019b) suggests that substitution is unlikely. Equally importantly, revitalization seems at best to be elusive at present, although the emergence of some promising elements of grassroots trade unionism should not be ignored.

The trade union movement has been performing comparatively badly across all areas, for example membership diversity, women and youth participation in union decision-making and innovative and effective organizing campaigns. This could act as springboard for a union renewal. Instead, there has been a gradual dualization and, more recently, marginalization of trade unions in recent decades. Dualization – unions promoting the job security of their 'insider' members potentially at the expense of 'outsiders' – has come about as a result of various interlocking internal and external factors and has become institutionalized through the now excessively decentralized bargaining system. In this context, the recently proposed changes to the trade union regulatory framework by the present government, in conjunction with developments during the crisis, have the potential to force unions into playing a marginal role or into managing ever smaller fringes of the public and administrative sector, and even losing their relevance for regulation altogether.

As Greece enters the 2020s, one may speculate that in future people may view this period as one in which the accumulated contradictions of the union movement merged with the disruptive legacy of the EU's neoliberal intervention in Greek collective labour law. It is an open question whether these contradictions will be resolved in a destructive or a transformative manner, or both, for the unions. Either way, it will be critical for Greek society and democracy.

References

All links were checked on 9 August 2021.

Amable B. (2003) The diversity of modern capitalism, Oxford, Oxford University Press.

Baccaro L., Hamann K. and Turner L. (2003) The politics of labour movement revitalization: the need for a revitalized perspective, European Journal of Industrial Relations, 9 (1), 119–133.

Beissinger M. (2002) Nationalist mobilization and the collapse of the Soviet State, Cambridge, Cambridge University Press.

Bithymitris G. (2016) Union militancy during economic hardship: the strike at the Greek steel company 'Hellenic Halyvourgia', Employee Relations, 38 (3), 373–389.

Bithymitris G. and Kotsonopoulos L. (2018) Μετασχηματισμοί του ελληνικού συνδικαλιστικού κινήματος από τη μεταπολίτευση μέχρι την κρίση: συνέχειες και ρήξεις, Greek Political Science Review, 44 (1), 99–122.

Bithymitris G. and Spyridakis M. (2020) Union radicalism versus the nationalist upsurge: the case of Greek shipbuilding workers, Dialectical Anthropology, 44, 121–135.

CNN Greece (2020) ΕΣΥ: Απεργία γιατρών και νοσηλευτών στις 15 Οκτωβρίου, CNN Greece, 13 October 2020. https://www.cnn.gr/ellada/story/238249/apergia-giatron-kai-nosileyton-stis-15-oktovrioy.

Diamandouros N. (1991) PASOK and state-society relations in post-authoritarian Greece, 1974–1988, in Vryonis S. Jr (ed.) Greece on the road to democracy: from the junta to PASOK, 1974–1986, New Rochelle, N.Y., published under the auspices of the Speros Basil Vryonis Center for the Study of Hellenism by Aristide D. Caratzas, 15–35.

Diamandouros N. (1993) Politics and culture in Greece, 1974–91: an interpretation, in Clogg R. (ed.) Greece 1981–1989: the populist decade, New York, St. Martin's Press, 1–25.

Enikos (2020) Νέος συνδικαλιστικός νόμος: Τι προβλέπει το νομοσχέδιο του υπουργείου Εργασίας, Enikos, 30 October 2020. https://www.enikos.gr/international/747025/neos-syndikalistikos-nomos-ti-provlepei-to-nomo schedio-tou-ypourg.

European Commission (2010) The economic adjustment programme for Greece, Occasional Papers 61, Brussels, European Commission.

European Commission (2012) The second economic adjustment programme for Greece, Occasional Papers 94, Brussels, European Commission.

European Commission (2015) Memorandum of understanding between the European Commission. Acting on behalf of the European stability mechanism and the Hellenic Republic and the Bank of Greece. https://ec.europa.eu/info/sites/info/files/01_mou_20150811_en1.pdf

European Commission (2018) Supplemental memorandum of understanding: Greece. third review of the ESM programme. https://ec.europa.eu/info/sites/default/files/economy-finance/third_smou_-_final.pdf

European Commission (2020) Enhanced surveillance report: Greece, Institutional Paper 137, Luxembourg, Publications Office of the European Union.

Ewing K. (2005) The function of trade unions, Industrial Law Journal, 34 (1), 1–22.

Expert Group (2016) Recommendations of the expert group for the review of Greek labour market institutions, 27 September 2016. https://www.ieri.es/wp-content/uploads/2016/10/Final-Report-Greece-September-2016.pdf

Featherstone K. and Papadimitriou D. (2008) Whose benefits? The elusive reform of the Greek pension system, in Featherstone K. and Papadimitriou D. (eds) The limits of Europeanization: reform capacity and policy conflict in Greece, Basingstoke, Palgrave Macmillan, 77–117

Gallas A. (2018) Class power and union capacities: a research note on the power resources approach, Global Labour Journal, 9 (3), 348–352.

Gemenis K. and Lefkofridi Z. (2013) Greece: a critical assessment of Europeanization, in Mannin M. and Bretherton C. (eds) The Europeanization of European politics, New York, Palgrave Macmillan, 95–106.

Georgiadou P (2021) Working life in Greece, Dublin, European Foundation for the Improvement of Living and Working Conditions.

Giannitsis T. (2007) Η χαμένη ευκαιρία του 2001, To Vima, 7 October 2007.

GSEE (2010) 34ο Πανελλαδικό Συνέδριο ΓΣΕΕ: Οικονομικός Απολογισμός, Προϋπολογισμός (ΓΣΕΕ, 18–21 Μαρτίου 2010)

GSEE (2011) Καθολική Συμμετοχή στη Γενική Απεργία της ΓΣΕΕ – ΑΔΕΔΥ, 19 October 2011, https://gsee.gr/?p=3479.

GSEE (2012) Καθολική Συμμετοχή στη Γενική Απεργία της ΓΣΕΕ – ΑΔΕΔΥ, 18 October 2012, https://gsee.gr/?p=2533.

GSEE (2016) Δελτίο τύπου – στα ψεύδη της κυβέρνησης που δεν έχουν τελειωμό εμείς απαντάμε με αλήθειες και στοιχεία, 22 August 2016. https://gsee.gr/?p=33733.

Hamann K., Johnston A. and Kelly J. (2013) Unions against Governments: explaining general strikes in Western Europe, 1980–2006, Comparative Political Studies, 46 (9), 1030–1057.

Hyman R. (2001) Understanding European trade unionism: between market, class and society, London, SAGE.

Iefimerida (2018) Τι προβλέπει η διάταξη για την προκήρυξη απεργίας -Γιατί αντιδρούν τα συνδικάτα, *Iefimerida,* 14 January 2018. https://www.iefimerida.gr/news/389061/ti-provlepei-i-diataxi-gia-tin-prokiryxi-apergias-giati-antidroyn-ta-syndikata

ILO (2012) Case No. 2820 (Greece): Reports in which the Committee requests to be kept informed of developments, in ILO, Reports of the Committee on Freedom of Association, 365th report of the Committee on freedom of association, 223–274. http://www.ilo.org/wcmsp5/groups/public/---ed_norm/---relconf/documents/meetingdocument/wcms_193260.pdf

Ioakimidis P.C. (2000) The Europeanization of Greece: an overall assessment, South European Politics and Society, 5 (2), 73–94.

Ioannou C. (2000) Trade unions in Greece: development, structures and prospects, Bonn, FES Library. http://library.fes.de/fulltext/bueros/athen/00740toc.htm

Ioannou C. (2005) Greece: from divided 'quangos' to fragmented 'social partners'. Explaining the absence of mergers, in Waddington J. (ed.) Restructuring representation: the merger process and trade union structural development in ten countries, Brussels, P.I.E. – Peter Lang, 139–164.

Iordanoglou C. (2013) State and interest groups, Athens, Polis.

Jecchinis C. (1994) Η συμμετοχή των εργαζομένων στη διοίκηση των επιχειρήσεων, Athens, OMED.

Kanellopoulos K. and Kostopoulos K. (2013) Alliance building in the Greek anti-austerity campaign 2010–2012, paper presented at the Political Networks Session, 7th ECPR General Conference 4–7 September 2013, Bordeaux.

Kantzara V. (2014) Solidarity in times of crisis: emergent practices and potential for paradigmatic change. Notes from Greece, Studi di Sociologia, 52 (3), 261–280.

Kapsalis A. (2012) Τα ελληνικά συνδικάτα στο περιβάλλον της οικονομικής ύφεσης και κρίσης. https://rosalux.gr/sites/default/files/kapsalis_greekfinal_0.pdf

Karakioulafis C. and Kanellopoulos K. (2018) Triggering solidarity actions towards contingent workers and the unemployed. The point of view of grassroots trade unionists and labour activist, Partecipazione e Conflitto, 11 (1), 121–144.

Karamessini M. (2009) From a state-led familistic to a liberal, partly defamilialized capitalism: the difficult transition of the Greek model, in Bosch G., Lehndorff S. and Rubery J. (eds) European employment models in flux: a comparison of institutional change in nine European countries, Basingstoke, Palgrave Macmillan, 223–246.

Katsaroumpas I. (2018) De-constitutionalising collective labour rights: the case of Greece, Industrial Law Journal, 47 (4), 465–503.

Katsaroumpas I. and Koukiadaki A. (2019) Greece: 'contesting' collective bargaining, in Muller T., Vandaele K. and Waddington J. (eds) Collective bargaining in Europe, Brussels, ETUI, 267–293.

Katsoridas D. (2020) Η σύνθεση της εργατικής τάξης στην Ελλάδα και το ζήτημα της συνδικαλιστικής εκπροσώπησης, PhD Thesis, Chios, University of Aegean.

Kennedy G. (2016) Embedding neoliberalism in Greece: the transformation of collective bargaining and labour market policy in Greece during the Eurozone crisis, Studies in Political Economy, 97 (3), 253–269.

Koukiadaki A. and Grimshaw D. (2016) Evaluating the effects of the structural labour market reforms on collective bargaining in Greece, Conditions of Work and Employment Series 85, Geneva, ILO.

Koukiadaki A. and Kokkinou C. (2016a) Deconstructing the Greek system of industrial relations, European Journal of Industrial Relations, 22 (3), 205–219.

Koukiadaki A. and Kokkinou C. (2016b) The rise of the dual labour market: fighting precarious employment in the new member states through industrial relations (PRECARIR) Country report: Greece, Research Reports 17, Central European Labour Studies Institute (CELSI).

Koukiadaki A. and Kretsos L. (2012) Opening Pandora's Box: the sovereign debt crisis and labour market regulation in Greece, Industrial Law Journal, 41 (3), 276–304.

Koukoules G. (1994) Ελληνικά συνδικάτα: οικονομική αυτοδυναμία και εξάρτηση (1938–1984), Athens, Odysseus.

Kostakos D. (2018) Ακριβέ μου συνδικαλισμέ…, Athina984, 05 June 2018. https://www.athina984.gr/2018/06/05/akrive-moy-syndikalisme/

Kousis M. and Karakioulafi C. (2013) Labour unions confronting unprecedented austerity in Greece, 2010–2013, conference paper presented at ECPR General Conference, Bordeaux, 4–8 September 2013.

Kouzis G. (2000) Εργασιακές σχέσεις και κοινωνικός διάλογος, in Kouzis G. and Robolis S. (eds) Ζητήματα κοινωνικού διαλόγου, Athens, Gutenberg, 89–167.

Kouzis G. (2007) Τα Χαρακτηριστικά του Ελληνικού Συνδικαλιστικού Κινήματος: Αποκλίσεις και συγκλίσεις με τον ευρωπαϊκό χώρο, Athens, Gutenberg.

Kretsos L. (2011) Union responses to the rise of precarious youth employment in Greece, Industrial Relations Journal, 42 (5), 453–472.

Kretsos L. and Vogiatzoglou M. (2015) Lost in the ocean of deregulation? The Greek labour movement in a time of crisis, Industrial Relations, 70 (2), 218–239.

Kritsantonis N. (1998) Greece: The maturing of the system, in Ferner A. and Hyman R. (eds) Changing industrial relations in Europe, 2nd edn, Oxford, Wiley-Blackwell, 504–528.

Lavdas K. (1997) The Europeanization of Greece: interest politics and the crises of integration, London, Palgrave Macmillan.

Lavdas K. (2005) Interest groups in disjointed corporatism: social dialogue in Greece and European 'competitive corporatism', West European Politics, 28 (2), 297–316.

Loukidou K. (2014) New examples of collective action in Greece: challenging the traditional patterns of civil society–state relationship, Paper presented at the 11th ISTR International Conference: 'Civil Society and the Citizen', Muenster, 22–25 July 2014.

Makridimitris A. (2002) Κράτος και Κοινωνία Πολιτών, Athens, Metamesonykties Ekdoseis.

Malamidis H. (2021) Social movements and solidarity structures in crisis-ridden Greece, Amsterdam, Amsterdam University Press. https://doi.org/10.1515/9789048551460

Manitakis A. (2014) Η κατάρρευση του μεταπολιτευτικού πολιυικού συστήματος, με επίκεντρο την κρίση αξιοπιστίας της πολιτικής, την εποχή της αλληλο-εξαρτώμενης, παγκόσμια, και επιμερισμένης, ευρωπαϊκά κυριαρχίας. https://www.constitutionalism.gr/manitakis-katareusi-politikou-sustimatos/

Matsaganis M. (2008) Progressive modernization defeated: failing to reform pensions (1996–2002), in Carlos M. (ed.) The challenge of social policy reform in the 21st Century, Athens, Sideris, 205–228.

Mavrogordatos G. (1998) Μεταξύ Πιτυοκάμπτη και Προκρούστη, Athens, Odysseas.

Molina O. and Rhodes M. (2007) The political economy of adjustment in mixed market economies: a study of Spain and Italy, in Hancké B., Rhodes M. and Thatcher M. (eds) Beyond varieties of capitalism: conflict, contradictions and complementarities in the European economy, Oxford, Oxford University Press, 223–252.

Mouzelis N. and Pagoulatos G. (2002) Civil society and citizenship in postwar Greece. http://www2.aueb.gr/users/pagoulatos/mouzelis%20civil%20society.pdf

News247 (2020a) ΑΔΕΔΥ: Απεργία στις 26 Νοεμβρίου- Στα αιτήματα και η προστασία της Υγείας, News247, 13 November 2020. https://www.news247.gr/koinonia/adedy-apergia-stis-26-noemvrioy-sta-aitimata-kai-i-prostasia-tis-ygeias.9049002.html

News247 (2020b) Απεργία των δασκάλων στις 15 Οκτωβρίου, News247, 10 October 2020. https://www.news247.gr/koinonia/apergia-ton-daskalon-stis-15-oktovrioy.9014770.html

OECD (2017) OECD Employment Outlook 2017, Paris, OECD Publishing.

Papadimitriou C. (2013) The Greek labour law face to the crisis [sic]: a dangerous passage towards a new juridical nature, European Labour Law Network Working Paper 3.

Papadopoulos A. (2004) Institutionalisation of social forces, in Charalambis D., Maratou-Alipranti L. and Hadjiyanni A., Recent social trends in Greece 1960–2000, Montreal, McGill-Queens's University Press, 391–424.

Papanikolopoulos D. et al. (2018) Το απεργιακό φαινόμενο στην Ελλάδα: Καταγραφή των απεργιών κατά την περίοδο 2011–2017, Athens, INE-GSEE Labour Institute.

Papavlasopoulos E. and Spourdalakis M. (2008) Κόμματα, ομάδες συμφερόντων και οι μετασχηματισμοί στο σύστημα εκπροσώπησης. Πέρα από τις θεωρίες της κρίσης, in Kontiadis X.I. and Anthopoulos C.T. (eds), Κρίση του ελληνικού πολιτικού συστήματος, Athens, Papazisis, 291–315.

Patra E. (2012) Social dialogue and collective bargaining in times of crisis: the case of Greece, Working Paper 38, Geneva, ILO.

Petropoulos A. (2016) Τι ισχύει για την χρηματοδότηση των συνδικάτων- «Πόλεμος» Κατρούγκαλου- ΓΣΕΕ', Newpost, 23 August 2016. https://newpost.gr/ellada/5c125cfa56dccb7e13e39c2e/ti-isxyei-gia-thn-xrhmatodothsh-twn-syndikatwn-polemos-katroygkaloy-gsee

Psimitis M. (2011) The protest cycle of spring 2010 in Greece, Social Movement Studies, 10 (2), 191–197.

Rigby M. and Calavia M. (2018) Institutional resources as a source of trade union power in Southern Europe, European Journal of Industrial Relations, 24 (2), 129–143.

Schmalz S., Ludwig C. and Webster E. (2018) The power resources approach: developments and challenges, Global Labour Journal, 9 (2), 113–134.

Sergi V. and Vogiatzoglou M. (2013) Thing globally, act locally? Symbolic memory and global repertoires in the Tunisian uprising and the Greek anti-austerity mobilizations, in Flesher-Fominaya C. and Cox L. (eds), Understanding European movements: new social movements, global justice struggles, anti-austerity protest, London, Routledge, 220–235.

Simiti M. (2017) Civil society and the economy: Greek civil society during the economic crisis, Journal of Civil Society, 13 (4), 357–373.

Sotiropoulos D. (2019) Political party-interest group linkages in Greece before and after the onset of the economic crisis, Mediterranean Politics, 24 (5), 605–625.

Sotiropoulos D. and Bourikos D. (2014) Economic crisis, social solidarity and the voluntary sector in Greece, Journal of Power, Politics & Governance, 2 (2), 33–53.

Standing G. (2011) The precariat: the new dangerous class, London, Bloomsbury Academic.

Stergiou A. (2002) Το ελληνικό Εργατικό Κίνημα Παθογένειες και Προοπτικές Το Βήμα των Κοινωνικών Επιστημών, (33), 5–34.

Taylor G., Mathers A. and Upchurch M. (2011) Beyond 'political economism': new identities for unions in Western Europe?, Capital and Class, 36 (1), 17–34.

Tsakatika M. and Eleftheriou C. (2013) The radical left's turn towards civil society in Greece: one strategy, two paths, South European Society and Politics, 18 (1), 81–99.

Tsarouhas D. (2008) Social partnership in Greece: Is there a europeanization effect?, European Journal of Industrial Relations, 14 (3), 347–365.

Tsarouhas D. (2012) Political discourse and path shaping in public policy: comparing pension reforms in Greece and Italy, Public Administration, 90 (1), 160–174.

Varhalama E., Mpoukouvalas K. and Papageorgiou I. (2015) Η Συμμετοχή των Γυναικών στα Όργανα Διοίκησης των Συνδικαλιστικών Οργανώσεων Δομής της Γενικής Συνομοσπονδίας Εργατών Ελλάδας, Μελέτες 46, Athens, INE-GSEE Labour Institute.

Visser J. (2019a) ICTWSS Database. version 6.1., Amsterdam, Amsterdam Institute for Advanced Labour Studies (AIAS), November 2019.

Visser J. (2019b) Trade unions in the balance, ACTRAV Working Paper, Geneva, ILO.

Vogiatzoglou M. (2018) Re-paving the path to hell: Greek trade unions amid crisis and austerity, in Lehndorff S., Dribbusch H. and Schulten T. (eds) Rough waters: European trade unions in a time of crises, 2nd and updated edition, Brussels, ETUI, 117–134.

Voulgaris G. (2012) *Η Ελλάδα από τη Μεταπολίτευση στην Παγκοσμιοποίηση*, Athens, Polis.

VPRC (2010) 'Συνδικαλισμός, συνδικάτα και συνδικαλιστική συμμετοχή στη συγκυρία της οικονομικής κρίσης' https://workersnet.files.wordpress.com/2010/09/syndicats_under_economic_crisis.pdf.

Yannakourou S. (2004) The evolution of labour law in the European Union: 1992–2003, Country study on Greece, Brussels, European Commission.

Yannakourou M. and Tsimpoukis C. (2014) Flexibility without security and deconstruction of collective bargaining: the new paradigm of labour law in Greece, Comparative Labor Law and Policy Journal, 35 (3), 331–370.

Yannakourou S. and Soumeli E. (2004) The evolving structure of collective bargaining in Europe 1990–2004, National report Greece and Cyprus. http://adapt.it/adapt-indice-a-z/wp-content/uploads/2014/08/matina_yannakourou.pdf .

Zambarloukou S. (2006) Collective bargaining and social pacts: Greece in comparative perspective, European Journal of Industrial Relations, 12 (2), 211–229.

Zisimopoulos I. (2018) *Ταξική Σύνθεση των Συνδικάτων και Προσδιοριστικοί Παράγοντες της Συνδικαλιστικής Πυκνότητας στην Ελλάδα*, PhD thesis, University of Patras.

Zisimopoulos I. (2019) Industrial relations in Greece: before, during and beyond the economic crisis, Journal of Economics and Business, 22 (2), 81–107.

Zisimopoulos I., Economakis G. and Androulakis G. (2019) The class composition of trade union movement in Greece: an empirical investigation, Discussion Paper Series 2019–2, Athens, Greek Association of Political Economy.

Abbreviations

ADEDY Ανώτατη Διοίκηση Ενώσεων Δημοσίων Υπαλήλων (Civil Servants' Confederation)

DAKE Δημοκρατική Ανεξάρτητη Κίνηση Εργαζομένων (Democratic Independent Movement of Workers)

DOE Διδασκαλική Ομοσπονδία Ελλάδας (Greek Primary Teachers' Federation)

EMU Economic and Monetary Union

GENOP-DEI Γενική Ομοσπονδία ΔΕΗ Κλάδου Ηλεκτρικής Ενέργειας (Federation of Personnel of the Public Power Corporation SA)

GSEE Γενική Συνομοσπονδία Εργατών Ελλάδος (General Confederation of Greek Workers)

KKE Κομμουνιστικό Κόμμα Ελλάδας (Communist Party of Greece)

ND Νέα Δημοκρατία (New Democracy)

OAED Οργανισμός Απασχόλησης Εργατικού Δυναμικού (Manpower Organisation)

OEE Οργανισμός Εργατικής Εστίας (Workers' Welfare Organization)

OIYE Ομοσπονδία Ιδιωτικών Υπαλλήλων Ελλάδας (Federation of Private Employees)

OLME Ομοσπονδία Λειτουργών Μέσης Εκπαίδευσης (Secondary Education Teachers federation)

OMOIKEL Ομοσπονδία Οικοδόμων και Συναφών Επαγγελμάτων Ελλάδας (Federation of Greek Builders and associated professions)

OTOE Ομοσπονδία Τραπεζοϋπαλληλικών Οργανώσεων Ελλάδας (Greek Federation of Bank Employee Unions)

PAME Πανεργατικό Αγωνιστικό Μέτωπο (All-Workers Militant Front)

PASOK Πανελλήνιο Σοσιαλιστικό Κίνημα (Panhellenic Socialist Movement)

POEDIN Πανελλήνια Ομοσπονδία Εργαζομένων Δημόσιων Νοσοκομείων (Public Hospital Employees Federation)

POE-OTA Πανελλήνια Ομοσπονδία Προσωπικού Οργανισμών Τοπικής Αυτοδιοίκησης (Employees in Local Government Federation)

Chapter 14

Hungary: After the end of illusions, trade unions on the brink of marginality

Tibor T. Meszmann and Imre G. Szabó

Few experts of industrial relations attain the standards of precision, balanced judgement and broad horizons that were characteristic of László Neumann's work on Hungarian trade unions. In 2005, fifteen years after the collapse of authoritarian state socialism and at the moment of the country's accession to the European Union (EU), he assessed the prospects of Hungarian trade unions with cautious optimism:

> The potential ensured by their remaining membership and assets, as well as the system of industrial relations institutions formed since the change of regime and help from their political allies may serve as the basis for renewal. With Hungary's joining the EU, domestic forces and institutions have been given powerful external support. (Neumann 2006: 56)

Indeed, having survived the freefall of membership numbers and widespread delegitimation in the course of capitalist economic transition, the position of Hungarian trade unions seemed to have stabilized around the turn of the millennium (see Table 14.1). They benefited from the relative strength of existing labour institutions. Tripartite consultation and social dialogue forums experienced a revival in the wake of EU accession, collective bargaining coverage stabilized, the pace of labour market liberalization slowed down, and a relatively generous welfare state compensated those who were pushed out of the labour market during the transition (Bohle and Greskovits 2012).

Table 14.1 Principal characteristics of trade unions in Hungary

	1990	2000	2020
Total trade union membership	3,989,000	966,000*	367,000**
Women as a proportion of total membership	n.a.	54 %	46 %
Gross union density	89 %	29 %*	9 %**
Net union density	89 %	20 %*	7 %**
Number of confederations	7	6	5
Number of affiliated unions (federations)	>117	189***	162
Number of independent unions	n.a.	n.a.	>5
Collective bargaining coverage	45 %****	38 %	22 %
Principal level of collective bargaining	n.a.	Company or establishment	Company or establishment
Days not worked due to industrial action per 1,000 workers	10	55	84**

Note: *2001; **2018; ***2010; ****1993.

Source: Appendix A1, Gimdt (1996), The Hungarian Labour Market – Yearly Review and Analysis by the Hungarian Academy of Sciences – Institute of Economics, KSH, Neumann (2018), self-reporting by trade unions and confederations or as published on their website.

Nevertheless, Neumann added a note of caution: 'it has to be clearly seen that these very same forces may help preserve the current organizational frameworks unchanged or even weaken them over time' (Neumann 2006: 65). Studies in the comparative employment relations literature also warned of the deceptiveness of the institutional power enjoyed by trade unions (Bohle 2011; Hassel 2007; Ost 2000). Following up on this point, this chapter examines the question of how Hungarian trade unions have coped with the challenges of renewal and dangers of marginalization, what organizational answers they have provided and how they may have changed in the process (Visser 2019). This inquiry is able to reflect on these questions from a historical perspective that is now fifteen years longer than at the vantage point of EU accession. The analysis commences with a brief historical overview outlining the development of Hungarian trade unions before the system change of 1989.

Historical background and principal features of the industrial relations system

The history of trade unions in Hungary over the past 150 years has been turbulent and dramatic. Unions emerged in the second half of the nineteenth century from craft-based associations with educational-cultural functions, which also provided mutual aid for their members. By the 1890s, operating with minimal organizational infrastructure concentrated in urban areas, the unions had become an integral part of the social democratic movement and were closely associated with the Hungarian Social Democratic Party (Lux 2008). Following a brief period of popular democracy in the wake of the Second World War, the communist dictatorship destroyed autonomous worker organizations and the social democratic tradition of trade unionism. The Communist Party installed trade unions in every company as a kind of 'transmission belt', tasked with promoting productivity increases in the process of rapid industrialization, distributing welfare benefits, as well as overseeing health and safety rules.

After 1989 three periods can be distinguished in which trade unions faced different external pressures in their political and economic environment. During the 1990s, trade unions had to meet the challenge of a fundamental transformation of the economic and political system. On the economic side, they had to deal with the transition from a state-managed economy with full employment to a market economy dominated by foreign capital and characterized by an unstable labour market. On the political side, the democratic transition put an end to trade unions' subordination to the party-state, but also to compulsory trade union membership of workers and a centralized trade union structure. Trade unions also had to face legitimacy issues in a discursive environment that regarded them as 'relics of the past'.

Hungary joined the EU in 2004, concluding the transition period and formally accomplishing the grand project of 'returning to the West', which the trade unions also wholeheartedly supported. By 2004 their position was consolidated in the new economy and polity. Despite their fragmentation, they were included in the polity through tripartite institutions, and besides defending their strongholds in the public sector, they also established new positions in some of the largest foreign-owned companies. The years around 2004 also turned out to be the final years of successful economic transformation (Bohle and Greskovits 2012). As early as 2006, fiscal austerity returned to Hungary, which again put confederations and trade unions under strain.

The global financial crisis propelled a conservative government into power in 2010. The Orbán government, with the Fidesz-led parliamentary supermajority (Hungarian Civic Alliance, *Fidesz–Magyar Polgári Szövetség*) had a quite different vision of the relationship between the polity and social partners. The relative institutional stability that Hungarian trade unions had previously enjoyed thus quickly evaporated after 2010, as new legislation radically weakened tripartite institutions to the status of symbolic bodies of social dialogue, and the government preferred to negotiate with trade unions according to its own pre-set agenda. Since 2010 there has been accelerated labour market liberalization, with legislative measures undermining trade union power at the firm level and restrictions on the right to strike and collective bargaining (Horváth and Kártyás 2021; Laki et al. 2013).

Structure of trade unions and union democracy

Hungarian trade unions are decentralized. Industrial unions have been losing their relevance and leading role to company-level unions, especially to unions in large companies. In addition, confederations have little authority over their affiliates. Originally, Hungarian trade unions regarded the German system of employment relations, dominated by industry-level unions, as the model to follow. In practice, industrial trade unions lost ground mostly because enterprises gained a high degree of autonomy to regulate work and employment at the expense of industry-level regulation during the privatization process. Coordination, let alone regulation with uninterested, competing employers or their loose associations proved difficult from the start. Different trades did not feel as if their interests were represented by large organizations. The autonomy and 'independence' of smaller union organizational units were also boosted by their leaders' politically motivated decision-making and by the competitive relations between confederations (Ladó 1994; Ladó and Tóth 1993; Szalai 1994; Tóth 1994; Tóth F. 1998; Tóth 2000a, 2000b). A dominant interpretation of democratization in the early 1990s thus translated into an extreme decentralization and fragmentation of the originally nineteen industry-level trade unions (MSZOSZ 2010; Szabó 2014).

Six stable trade union confederations had emerged by the first half of the 1990s.[1] The National Confederation of Hungarian Trade Unions (MSZOSZ, *Magyar Szakszervezetek Országos Szövetsége*), the Confederation of Autonomous Trade Unions (ASZSZ, *Autonóm Szakszervezetek Szövetsége*), the Confederation of Unions of Professionals (ÉSZT, *Értelmiségi Szakszervezeti Tömörülés*), the Democratic League of Independent Trade Unions (Liga, *Független Szakszervezetek Demokratikus Ligája*), the National Confederation of Workers' Councils (MOSZ, *Munkástanácsok Országos Szövetsége*), and the Trade Unions' Cooperation Forum (SZEF, *Szakszervezetek Együttműködési Fóruma*). Four confederations comprised mainly private sector unions – MSZOSZ, Liga, MOSZ, ASZSZ – while the public sector was represented by SZEF and ÉSZT. Confederations typically emerged as loose umbrella organizations, 'action-alliances' or forums, as indicated by the name of SZEF. Liga operated with the least defined structure, insisting on a grassroots model of unionism, allowing plant-level and territorially organized unions to become direct affiliates of the confederation from the beginning (LIGA 2013; Tóth 2000b).

Confederations have traditionally had only low authority over their union affiliates. In turn, industry-level federations face the challenge of maintaining authority over larger plant-level union members, as the latter increased their autonomy, being also aware of their own attractiveness to other, competing industrial unions or confederations. From the beginning of the transition, confederations tried to compensate for their lack of authority over affiliates by building direct links to the polity through tripartite institutions that secured visibility and financial resources. After 2010 the authority of confederations was further weakened as a result of the legislative and political changes implemented by the Orbán government. The lack of authority of confederations, but also of industrial unions over affiliates remains a stumbling block for uniting trade union power. Industry-level unions sometimes left or changed confederal affiliation. In addition, brand new hybrid unions were formed, mainly right-wing and nationalist in ideology, such as the National Trade Union of Employees Designed for Life (ÉTMOSZ, *Életre Tervezett Munkavállalók Országos Szakszervezete*). Thus, both industrial and some large company unions, such as the Audi Hungary Independent Trade Union (AHFSZ,

1 Seven confederations were active at the start of transition in 1990.

Audi Hungária Független Szakszervezet), emerged as increasingly autonomous organizations in the national arena, whose power approximates to that of confederations.

The Hungarian trade union movement is not only decentralized but also divided along political and sectoral lines. The separation between the public and private sectors has become less prominent over time, but the political cleavage has been a stable feature of the Hungarian trade union movement since 1990, splitting confederations into two camps. Figure 14.1 maps the main confederations, their distance from each other and how that distance developed between 1990 and 2020 along two main dimensions of ideological-political divisions (left-right) and sectoral composition (public-private). The size of the shapes approximates the membership numbers of each confederation. The horizontal axis separates the main confederations along political lines. After 1989, one group of confederations originated as reformed successors to the entrenched and massive pre-1989 official National Trade Union Council (SZOT, *Szakszervezetek Országos Tanácsa*). The other group emerged as grassroots movements of new organizations, established mainly by anti-communist dissenters. The former group maintained formal or informal links to the reformed successor of the Communist Party, the Hungarian Socialist Party (MSZP, *Magyar Szocialista Párt*). They were particularly pronounced in the case of MSZOSZ, but also partly true for SZEF. The 'grassroots' group of confederations had links to newly formed liberal and conservative political parties. Confederations also sought political party allies for practical reasons, mostly to influence strategically important legislation, such as the distribution of union assets inherited from SZOT to their own advantage (Ladó and Tóth 1996; Neumann 2006: 73; Tóth 2000b).

Figure 14.1 Development of confederation size and structure of cleavages, 1990–2018

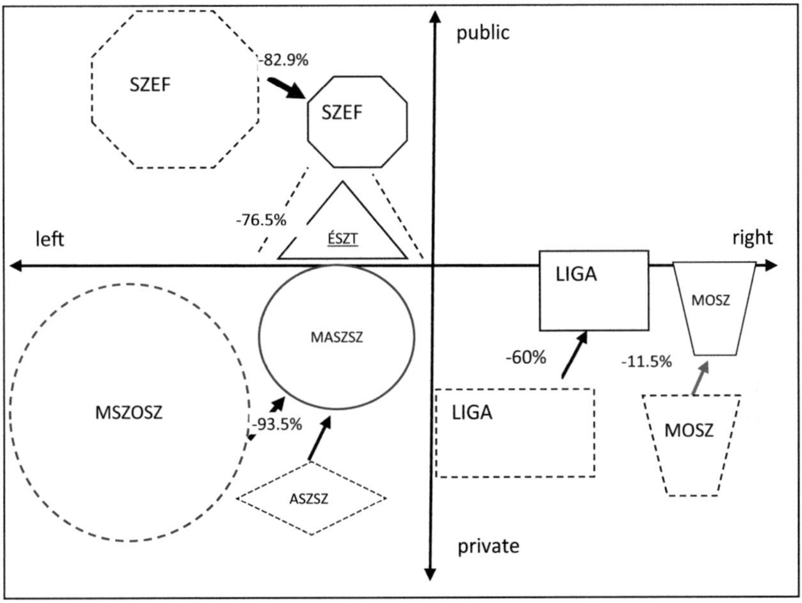

Note: Arrows indicate the change between 1990 and 2018 in position and size (membership in thousands) of confederations. Their position in 1990 is indicated in dashed lines, their position in 2018 in solid lines.
Source: Girndt (1996), Neumann (2018). Figure designed and calculations made by the authors data for 2020 from self-reporting by trade unions and confederations or as published on their website.

All major confederations had easily discernible political party allies from the early 1990s: confederations and political parties launched joint campaigning initiatives, from one-off street protests to national referenda, trade union leaders featured on the electoral list of parties and many of them were elected MPs (Tóth 2000b). Up until 2006 MSZOSZ also officially endorsed the Hungarian Socialist Party (MSZP, *Magyar Szocialista Párt*) manifesto before general elections. The political party landscape of Hungary has changed many times since 1989. What matters from our perspective is that asymmetrical union–party links have constantly hindered cooperation between confederations. In Figure 14.1, some movement is apparent in confederations' political positions between 1989 and 2020, but the distance between them remained large. As of 2020,

MASZSZ, SZEF and ÉSZT are in the 'centre-left' block, critical of the right-wing government in power since 2010, while LIGA and especially MOSZ have a more cordial relationship with the governing party.

None of the six historical confederations was ever dominant, whether in terms of membership, capacities or influence. The main competitors for a dominant role were the 'legacy-incumbent' confederation MSZOSZ and its main challengers Liga and MOSZ. The intense conflicts between the two camps in the early 1990s were followed by a relatively calm period when boundaries between them were stabilizing. Inter-confederation hostility peaked again after 2006, when Liga 'poached' affiliates from other confederations in both the public and the private sector by offering lower contribution rates, and also undermined consultation and agreements with the government through political action (LIGA 2009). A limited consolidation of confederation structures took place after 2010, as MSZOSZ and ASZSZ merged to form the Hungarian Trade Union Confederation (MASZSZ, *Magyar Szakszervezeti Szövetség*), reducing the number of confederations from six to five. The merger was shallow: affiliated unions did not merge, some of them even moved to other confederations. This partial consolidation happened within the left-wing section of the confederation spectrum, so it did not contribute to a relaxation of political tensions between confederations.

Along the vertical axis of Figure 14.1, a second, less pronounced cleavage runs between public sector and private sector unions. Public sector unions had to cope with at best a secondary role in interest representation and reconciliation. There is also fragmentation within the public sector as ÉSZT organizes the smaller branches of the public sector dominated by professionals, particularly scientists, and the main public sector confederation, SZEF, originally brought together the largest (successor) public sector unions, such as those in health care and education. At the same time, there are public sector unions that belong to majority private sector confederations or do not have a confederal affiliation at all.

Hungarian trade unions are registered as civil society organizations and therefore must follow formal statutory requirements of transparency and regular elections of officials. At the same time, union democracy is weak in substantive terms, with little strategic initiative to reinvigorate the relationship between officials and the rank-and-file. Elections of top officials are also rarely contested. Unions are aware of the need to increase the diversity of those who reach official positions within the hierarchy but their tools to achieve this are limited and quite traditional. While there are no quota systems, for example for women in leadership positions, some confederations and industrial unions have special youth and women sections, and support union members in launching corresponding plant-level committees.

Political relations

As in other states of the former Eastern bloc, for Hungarian trade unions the tectonic changes of 1989 implied a redefinition of their role in the new context of market economy and democracy. As they were associated with the authoritarian past, they faced a crisis of legitimacy and representation: among other things, legislation weakened their rights of representation.[2] They had no say in matters of privatization, and their influence at establishment level and on the labour market was fluid rather than stable.

But there were dissatisfied masses of workers who needed representation and this coincided with Hungary's EU integration process, entailing the construction of social dialogue and worker representation institutions. These institutions provided entry points for trade unions. The unions survived the difficult period of transition and stayed afloat by 'reorganizing their relationship with the new actors of democracy and the market' (Thoma 2001), getting involved in institutions of social dialogue and wage setting, and receiving rights and entitlements to represent employees' interests. Participation in tripartite bodies turned out to be crucial for confederations, as subsidies and employment opportunities from tripartite structures compensated for dwindling resources from affiliates, making it possible to maintain confederation staff numbers and physical infrastructure.

As in other Central and East European (CEE) states, a central institution for politically motivated trade union inclusion in the polity was the tripartite interest reconciliation body. This institution changed its name and exact role alongside successive governments, and its functions oscillated between social dialogue and national-level quasi-bargaining on wages (Héthy and Ónodi 2008). In its most powerful form, between 2002 and 2011, it existed under the name National Council for the

2 The Constitutional Court interpreted trade union representational rights as colliding with employees' individual freedoms. See: Kollonay and Ladó (1996); cf. Tóth (2000b).

Reconciliation of Interests (OÉT, *Országos Érdekegyeztető Tanács*). During the period around EU accession and the financial crisis, supplementary bodies of social dialogue were created to secure trade union involvement in broader matters of policymaking.[3] The most important of these was the Economic and Social Council (GSZT, *Gazdasági és Szociális Tanács*), established in 2004.

Between 2002 and 2011, the OÉT relied on an extensive mandate for information, consultation and negotiation in the area of labour market regulation. Every year, the government was obliged to negotiate and reach agreement with the social partners before setting the level of the statutory minimum wage. The OÉT also issued national wage increase guidelines. In this respect, the OÉT's mandate extended beyond strictly defined social dialogue into a weak version of centralized wage bargaining in the shadow of legislation.[4] This, in turn, raised questions of constitutionality, as the polity was sharing its sovereign power with interest groups outside the system of electoral representation. The OÉT's legitimacy was consequently weakened between 2006 and 2009 by a drawn-out constitutional court procedure scrutinizing the forum's legal basis (Berki and Neumann 2009).

During the period 2002–2006, trade unions were able to exert influence on the polity through these tripartite bodies, resulting in repeated statutory minimum wage increases, general wage increase recommendations and pro-worker amendments of the Labour Code (*Munka Törvénykönyve*).

Apart from these temporary successes, confederations tended to take a reactive position in these fora, at best slowing down labour market liberalization initiated by employers and successive governments. Public sector confederations faced similar challenges in terms of general economic developments, with a few important differences. Compared with the private sector, negotiations in the public sector have been even more exposed to political cycles, with more generous wage increases in election years and austerity between elections. Public

---

[3] For an extensive list of social dialogue bodies see Márkus and Tóth (2010).

[4] We define collective bargaining as negotiations on wages and working conditions between representatives of employers and employees. The agreed outcomes of collective bargaining are binding even without supporting legislation and breaching them can lead to industrial conflict. Social dialogue by contrast is non-binding; it necessarily involves governments as policymakers and its scope also tends to be broader.

sector employees were the targets of budget cuts in the wake of recurring fiscal crises of the Hungarian state in 1995, in 2006 and then again from 2008. In these periods, public sector confederations had to adopt a very defensive stance to protect jobs and often accepted wage freezes and nominal wage cuts in return. At the same time, they could not always expect solidarity from private sector unions interested in lower levels of taxation.[5]

An additional problem with tripartite institutions was that their ability to channel conflicting interests and manage conflict situations decreased over time (Berki and Dura 2012). In effect, this system especially harmed those trade unions that were the most committed to finding institutional solutions to social conflict and policymaking dilemmas.

Most accounts claim that the tripartite body's existence depended on successive governments' willingness to maintain it (Koltay and Neumann 2006: 32). The exposure of tripartism to different partisan conceptions of governance was a final and fatal weakness (Héthy and Ónodi 2008). This was proved in 2011 when the OÉT was abolished by the Orbán government and replaced with a tripartite body, the Standing Consultative Forum for the Competitive Sphere and the Government (VKF, *Versenyszféra és a Kormány Állandó Konzultációs Fóruma*), which is restricted to the private sector and has only a consultative role on minimum wages and average wage increases (Herczog 2017). Since 2010, there has been no tripartite institution covering the entire workforce. The National Economic and Social Council (NGTT, *Nemzeti Gazdasági és Társadalmi Tanács*), established in 2011, is a purely advisory body with broad participation from civil society, the church and academia (Szabó 2013). To compensate for their exclusion from decision-making, especially concerning the Labour Code, some confederations and industrial unions attempted to exert influence through protests. Without sufficient resources, however, these protests could not be sustained, and apart from immediate reactions to legislative changes, they could not compensate for the lost institutional voice.

Trade unions have been involved in the polity not only directly through tripartism, but also indirectly through their links with political parties. The latter relationship has been asymmetric (Avdagic 2004).

---

5 As its former chairman, Endre Szabó put it, SZEF constantly had to fight the dogma that value creation is based only on production of goods, and that the human sphere is only of secondary importance, of unequal value. See Szabó (2014, p. 28).

Even nominally left-wing parties repeatedly reneged on their pro-labour electoral promises once entering into government and trade unions lacked the capacity to credibly punish them for this. On the other hand, through their links to political parties, up until the mid-2000s, trade union leaders were often appointed to positions in the state bureaucracy, especially under left-wing governments, in line with earlier traditions (Bohle 2011). The relationship between MSZP and MSZOSZ was characterized by a 'revolving door' mechanism where key personalities held successive or often parallel positions in the trade union and state bureaucracy. The result was a schizophrenic situation in which people who opposed certain government measures as trade union leaders often had to go along with them as party members. The embeddedness in the state bureaucracy also undermined trade union leaders' credibility and exposed them to attacks from rival confederations (Bohle and Greskovits 2010: 352).

After Viktor Orbán came to power in 2010, Liga, and especially the MOSZ–FIDESZ relationship faced similar challenges to MSZOSZ–MSZP in earlier years: the new government introduced several measures hostile to the labour movement, with some highly controversial and compromising gestures (Rácz 2013). Confederation–party relationships often remain informal. In sum, confederation leaders on their part were forced to choose between two evils: temporary influence and access to decision-making and resources with long-term risks, or marginalization from decision-making. Understandably, no confederations opted for the second.

What were the main substantive positions that confederations represented in their relationship to the polity? The four, mainly private sector confederations did not differ significantly in their economic policies and social dialogue positions during the years of transformation. MOSZ insisted most strongly on worker participation in privatization and asset sharing. Liga was committed to developing a social market economy, including employee participation in decision-making at all levels (LIGA 2013). The position of MSZOSZ was the most defined: it had relied on union involvement on distributional issues in the state socialist period. Post-1989 MSZOSZ insisted on progressive taxation and the minimum wage to achieve a living wage. From the late 1990s, trade unions refocused their activities on collective bargaining and incomes policy, achieving some success on these issues with the help of their political allies in the period 2002–2006.

Unionization

Trade union membership in post-state socialist Hungary, similarly to other countries in the region, underwent a dramatic, continuing decline. From compulsory trade union membership common in the previous system, only 7.4 per cent of the employed population were members of trade unions by early 2020, almost exclusively full-time employees with permanent contracts. In manufacturing, trade unions suffered a great decline during the 1990s as a result of their inability to protect jobs in privatized companies. By 2001 unionization rates were already modest. In general, rising unemployment had an extremely negative effect on trade unions.[6] As Figures 14.2 and 14.3 indicate, trade unions in all economic segments lost members continuously from 2001. Being relatively sheltered from the job destruction of the 1990s, union membership declined more slowly in the public sector than in the private sector, but it followed the same trend. Public sector union density started from a higher level but declined rapidly after 2006.

Figure 14.2 Trade union density across industries and industry weight in total union membership, 2001

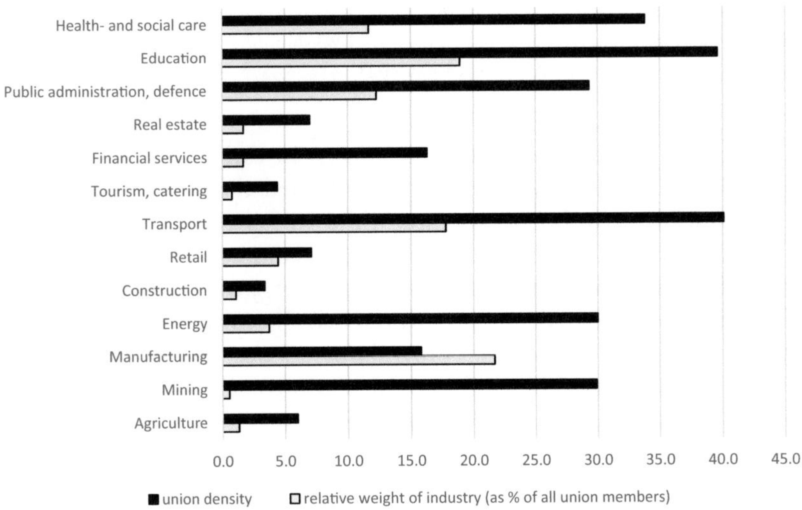

Source: KSH (2002).

6 There were somewhat late initiatives to tackle the issue of the unemployed, especially on the part of the two general unions MSZOSZ and LIGA.

Figure 14.3 Trade union density across industries and industry weight in total union membership, 2015

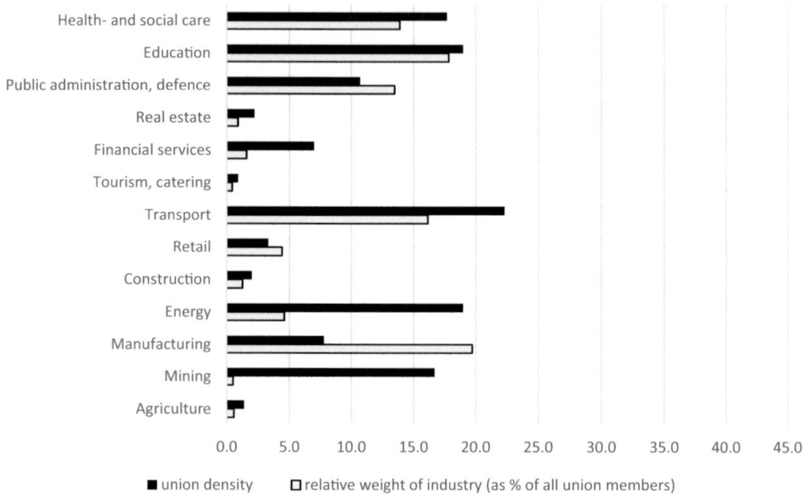

Source: KSH (2016). Stadat online spreadsheet set, Table 9.1.22. 15–64 éves alkalmazottak nemzetgazdasági ágak, nemek és aszerint, hogy tagjai-e valamelyik szakszervezetnek, 2015. II. negyedév [Employees aged 15–64 by industries of the national economy, gender and union membership, 2nd quarter of 2015.] https://www.ksh.hu/docs/hun/xstadat/xstadat_evkozi/e_szerv9_01_22.html Accessed 18 July 2021.

According to the latest statistical data,[7] in early 2020, only about 23.6 per cent of surveyed employees indicated that there was a trade union operating in their workplace, while 10.9 per cent did not know. Trade union presence continued to be more common in the public sector and in semi-state enterprises, such as in energy or transport. Business unit size also mattered for union presence. In workplaces with fewer than fifty employees in 2015 only about 15 per cent of them knew about a union presence (authors' calculations). Only in large workplaces, employing at least 500, was a union presence likely, with 55.3 per cent of employees acknowledging a union presence. Unionization

[7] KSH (2021) Stadat online spreadsheet set, Table 9.18.3.2. Employees aged 15–64 by membership of a trade union at the workplace, Q1 2020. https://www.ksh.hu/docs/eng/xstadat/xstadat_infra/e_munkmin_9_18_03_02.html (accessed: 19 July 2021).

is also more likely in private enterprises in manufacturing. Territorially, such a difference played out in uneven unionization rates in industrial centres, such as Győr, where Audi and some automotive suppliers are located, or administrative-university towns with comparatively higher unionization rates, compared with more depressed regions and rural areas. Interestingly, such sectoral-territorial unevenness is also reflected in male and female unionization rates. Thus, quite tellingly from the 2015 data it is in the south of Hungary, in the university town of Szeged, where female unionization rates are the highest – at 16.4 per cent – as a result of the concentration of public sector employment, whereas the male unionization rate is highest – at 18.8 per cent – in the most industrialized region, around the town of Győr, where Audi is centred.

As demonstrated in Figure 14.3, public administration, health care, education, transport and manufacturing were among economic activities with the largest union presence in 2015. These are the five economic segments in which the majority, 81 per cent, of union members are concentrated. Although energy has comparatively high union density, this economic segment has a small share of employment. The contrast here is sharpest with retail and manufacturing: both are large segments of the economy, in which density is lower than average. Interestingly, it is Pest, the county surrounding Budapest, where both male and female unionization rates are lowest (5.3 and 6.3 per cent, respectively). Business unit size, concentration, as well as product or service market security seem to explain this outcome. Trade unions, for their part, maintained their presence in larger companies, attracting members based on a mix of individual and collective interest representation, and special services. Unions adopted alternative ways of unionizing, such as US-style organizing only sporadically and rather late, in the 2010s, mostly in manufacturing and retail.

In general, there are fewer than ten Hungarian trade unions with more than 10,000 members (see Table 14.2). Very few reach 20,000 members, including pensioners. Of the ten largest trade unions three are not affiliated to a confederation, and only five have remained loyal to their confederations over the past three decades. It is also important to note that there is a company-level union in the top ten, with almost 10,000 members.

Table 14.2 Ten largest trade unions in Hungary, 2018

Trade union	Economic activity	Affiliation (changes)	Membership in 2018
PSZ	education	SZEF	24,317
Vasas	manufacturing	MASZSZ (MSZOSZ before merger)	22,000
EDDSZ	health care	SZEF-> Liga -> independent (own confederation)	15,075*
VDSZ	chemical industry	MASZSZ (ASZSZ before merger)	30,000
MTSZSZ	engineering	ÉSZT -> Liga	12,500
EVDSZ	electric power	ASZSZ-> Liga	9,500
VDSZSZ	railways	Liga -> Independent	8,500–9,000
KASZ	retail	MASZSZ (MSZOSZ before merger)	11,500
VSZ	railways	MASZSZ (MSZOSZ before merger)	10,457
AHFSZ automobile (company level)	automobiles	Independent	9,750

Note: * administrative data.

Source: Németh and Girndt (2018), AHFSZ (2020). For full names of trade unions see 'Abbreviations'.

Union resources and expenditure

After 1989 trade unions had five main sources of income: (i) a fairly large stock of real estate, including offices, hotels and holiday resorts at prestigious locations that they inherited and distributed among themselves from the monopoly state socialist confederation SZOT; (ii) external financial support from international organizations and foundations; (iii) state support; (iv) financial contributions at establishment-company level; and (v) membership fee inflows from the rank-and-file and from affiliates in the case of industrial unions and confederations. Table 14.3 summarizes the rather modest infrastructure and expert apparatus of the main trade union confederations and industry-level unions. Table 14.3 indicates the annual percentage of income from external finances in running the organizations compared with membership fees, and sheds light on absolute membership and change. Included in the data are the finances of one large industrial (Vasas) and one large company union (AHFSZ) in order to indicate the modest confederal finances and contrast them with the lower levels. Note, however, that among several hundred registered trade unions there are only about a dozen that have noticeable infrastructure (an office for example), paid officials and financial resources to cover them.

Table 14.3 Full-time staff and union income (confederations and some trade unions)

Confederation	Full-time staff (estimate)	Finances – income 2019, HUF (€ in brackets[8])	Membership, and change, thousands and per cent (1990*–2018)	Percentage of membership fee in annual income %
ÉSZT	2–5	158,432,000 (479,000)	27,000 (–93,000, -76.5%)	2.9
Liga	16	326,458,000 (988,000)	100,200 (–149,800, -60%)	14.2
MASZSZ	10–15	194,295,000 (588,000)	104,461 (-1,505,000, -93.5%)	16.1
MOSZ	10–15	636,543,000 (1.926,000)	53,112 (-6,888, -11.5%)	0.4
SZEF	6	220,796,000 (668,000)	65,000 (-315,000, -82.9%)	3.9
Industrial union (federation)				
Vasas*	23	587,449,000 (1,777,000)	22,000 (-482,000, -95.6%)	88.8
Company union				
AHFSZ	14 (officers)	280,333,000 (848,000)	9,145 (+8,725, +2,177%)	64.2

Source: Neumann (2018), AHFSZ website, Court data on Civil Society Organizations: https://birosag.hu/kozzetetel-kereso. Authors' own calculation.

Although the formula and distribution of the membership fee between levels of trade unions changed over the years, the basic principle behind membership fees was that union members were to pay 1 per cent of their gross monthly income to a plant-level union. Half of this sum,

8 Value in euros is estimated by taking the official central rate of the Central Bank of Hungary (Magyar Nemzeti Bank) on the last day of the reference period. For example, for 2019, the rate on 31 December 2019 was 1 EUR = 330.52 HUF.

in some cases less but increasingly more, remained with the plant-level union, and the remainder went to industrial unions, which were crucial for employing experts and running an organization and apparatus (Neumann 2017; Sauer 1993). Industrial unions and unions in different public sector activities then paid dues to confederations, and also to international organizations with which they were affiliated. In addition, some trade union leaders had additional incomes from their positions in various supervisory bodies.

With very few exceptions, industrial unions constantly had to cope with plummeting incomes from membership fees, but also adapted to increased autonomy and special deals concluded with large company-based affiliates. The negative tendencies culminated in fights for already unionized members and their fees at the confederal level, impacting further on the negative spiral in general finances. To poach affiliates from other confederations, probably most notoriously Liga decreased membership fees and allowed greater autonomy for affiliated unions, a practice that was most pronounced in 2006–2010 (Neumann and Tóth 2018: 138; Szabó-Morvai 2010: 17). The cumulative effect was that total membership and discipline declined further, as more autonomy was granted to affiliated unions by other confederations and industry unions, too.

To maintain their more and more modest but still costly infrastructure and apparatus, industrial unions and confederations increasingly had to sell their assets. During the past thirty years the formerly massive real estate assets, which were split among confederations, have largely disappeared. Finally, the relevance of and dependence on external support increased over time. Both international and state support became ever more important. The anti-union government that came to power in 2010 played on these massive dependencies. During 2010–2012 state support decreased radically. Originally this support had been designed to ensure trade union participation in various social dialogue bodies. The anti-union government, however, blocked funding to confederations and trade unions, in effect 'blackmailing' them to secure their consent to legislative and institutional changes (Lajtai 2017).

Finally, until 2012 an important share of trade union income at the company level came from the legally guaranteed working time allowance for union representatives, calculated according to the number of union members. If this time allowance was not fully used by the end of the year, it could also be cashed in: that is, it could be turned into company-level union income. From 2013, the new Labour Code prohibited the 'cashing-in' option. As indicated in Figure 14.4, external private funding fell after 2012.

Figure 14.4 Distribution and development of trade union income (HUF million), 2005–2018

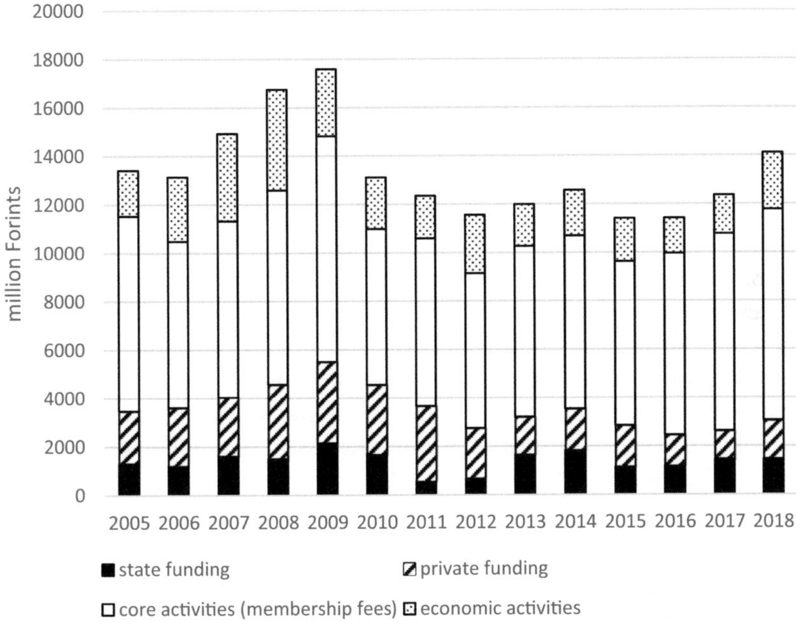

Source: KSH (2021). Stadat online spreadsheet set, Table 9.1.1.12. A nonprofit szervezetek száma és bevétele szervezeti forma szerint (2005–) [Number and income of not-for-profit organizations, according to legal form (2005–)] https://www.ksh.hu/stadat_files/gsz/hu/gsz0014.html Accessed 28 July 2021.

Figure 14.4 shows the changing share of external funds and state funds in the period 2005–2018 and also trade unions' total income. On average in 2018 trade unions operated with an annual budget of about HUF 21 million (€65,300).

Collective bargaining and unions at the workplace

There is a dual system of interest representation in Hungary: besides trade unions, there is an opportunity to establish and elect works councils in sufficiently large enterprises. Compared with the German model, however, works councils are much weaker: Still, they maintain information and consultation rights, some of which unions lost after 2012, but also decide on the use of company social funds. Whereas the relationship between works councils and trade unions was uneasy at the beginning, trade unions now typically occupy key positions in works councils, fielding their own candidates during works council elections. Trade unions are also in charge of collective bargaining. Conflicts still emerge in some cases, especially when pro-management works councils are established, and management does not recognize or include trade unions in collective bargaining.

Collective bargaining has a very modest regulatory impact on the labour market in Hungary, as the law considers individual bargaining to be dominant. Collective bargaining coverage is low, negotiations are decentralized to the company level and the agreements are often limited in scope. At the same time, collective bargaining is embedded in detailed regulation of the labour market bylaws and other statutory instruments that trade unions have been trying to influence with limited success through tripartite forums, as already discussed. The following sections review the role of trade unions in collective bargaining.

The main procedural rules for collective bargaining are laid down by national legislation, specified in the Labour Code (*Munka Törvénykönyve*). The Labour Code recognizes the autonomy of enterprises in regulating many aspects of employment, including bargaining without state intervention at the establishment or company level (Makó and Simonyi 1997: 222). Trade unions are entitled to bargain collectively with enterprise management if they reach a 10 per cent representativeness threshold. Certain groups in the public sector are excluded from the right to bargain collectively by their special employment statutes, including civil servants, members of the armed forces and – since 2021 – health care employees (Horváth and Kártyás 2021; Mélypataki 2019: 16–17). The Labour Code does not specify the level of bargaining but grants bargaining rights to individual trade unions, as well as to trade union confederations. Moreover, works councils are also entitled to sign collective agreements with the employer at workplaces where there is no valid union-negotiated collective agreement.

The company has been the predominant level of collective bargaining in the Hungarian private sector since the 1990s, with a small and declining number of industry-level agreements. The weakness of the industry level is partly because of employers' reluctance to engage in multi-employer bargaining and the rarity of compulsory extension mechanisms for collective agreements. Nevertheless, trade unions have also contributed to this situation by focusing their resources on defending key workers in large companies, while employees at the suppliers of the same company in the same industry often remained without collective representation. Procedurally, at least in manufacturing, the bargaining process, if sufficiently inclusive at all, tilted towards insider groups, that is male middle-aged employees, with the consequence that it strengthened a business unionist strategy to the exclusion of other social groups, especially the classic labour market outsiders, such as agency workers, young people, women, non-locals and Roma (Gerőcs et al. 2021; Neumann 2000; Neumann and Tóth 2018).

Confederations have tried to compensate for the weakness of industry-level bargaining by actively promoting national-level tripartite negotiations. The main vehicle through which tripartism influenced lower levels of bargaining was minimum wage setting. Tripartite negotiations were however not equivalent to collective bargaining; at best they could be called 'quasi' collective bargaining (Berki 2014: 127). They were forums of 'interest reconciliation' and the resulting agreements lacked the legal enforcement power of collective agreements, which are officially called 'collective contracts' (*kollektív szerződések*) in Hungary. Therefore, legislation and, in the case of minimum wage setting, government decrees followed up on these agreements to secure adherence. The government abandoned national-level tripartism in 2010, moved the negotiations on the minimum wage to a restricted private sector consultation forum, and opened up several formerly statutorily regulated aspects of the employment relationship to bargaining in 2012, thereby further decentralizing bargaining processes.

There has been no single dominant level of collective bargaining in the public sector, where the relevance of collective bargaining for wage setting has been overshadowed by government unilateralism. National legislation sets detailed pay scales for each group of public sector workers, leaving very narrow scope for local bargaining. The public sector has its own tripartite consultation forums, including the government and public service employers, but with their low enforceability and sensitivity to the relationship with the government, these forums faced the same issues as OÉT (Berki 2014: 127). The main change in public sector bargaining after 2010 was the centralization of public service provision: central government took over the management of most industries of the public service from the municipalities, with the result that the importance of negotiations in specific public sector industries increased, particularly in education and health care, in the context of even stronger government unilateralism.

Only around a quarter of employees are covered by collective agreements in Hungary, concentrated mainly in the shrinking public sector, as well as in larger companies, especially in state or mixed ownership. Coverage correlates with industries and workplaces with increased unionization rates. As collective agreements are binding for all employees at a given workplace, the coverage rate is also higher than unionization rates and has not fallen so radically in the past two decades, from 38 to 22 per cent. The trade union strategy in collective bargaining focused mainly on recurring issues of employment and job security, particularly fighting job losses, and wage/income–related issues. Apart from the brief period around EU accession – 2002–2006 – trade unions had to adopt a defensive stance, withstanding offensives on working time flexibilization, decentralization and the liberalization of labour law regulation that impacted on jobs and incomes. Overall, concession bargaining over wages, jobs and working time became the norm, especially in economically difficult periods, including the present period impacted by Covid-19 (1990s, 2008–2010, 2020–). The pandemic has had a disastrous impact, especially in parts of the private service sector, such as tourism and accommodation, where the unions have lost even the little leverage they had earlier. Many employers unilaterally terminated collective agreements in the second half of 2020, and in only one case could a trade union launch a collective dispute and strike for its reinstatement. Health sector employees lost their public employee status on 1 March 2021, and unions here also lost the chance to regulate employment collectively, and strikes became practically impossible.

In both the private and the public sector the scope of collective agreements is limited. Often the majority of provisions only repeat those of the Labour Code, so-called 'parrot clauses'. Rather than targeting the main wage, collective agreements in Hungary often focus on the supplementary elements of remuneration, such as fringe benefits, anniversary bonuses and holiday allowances (Fodor et al. 2008; Nacsa and Neumann 2008; Neumann 2006). These allowances were exempt from taxation until 2018.

Industrial conflict

Strikes were regulated for the first time in Hungarian history in 1989. The right to strike is recognized in Hungary's constitution and the main questions of strike legality are settled by Act 1989/VII, adopted in the year of the country's democratic transition. As Berki aptly summarizes, 'after its first 15 years in force, the concrete forms and methods had been defined and disagreements were overcome by practice or by Constitutional Court (*Alkotmánybíróság*) rulings, and norms were created that guided both actors involved, the media, the general public, and relevant authorities' (Berki 2019: 5).

Changes in the constitution (Fundamental Law, *Alkotmány, Alaptörvény*) and legislation since 2010 have had an impact on the frequency and character of strikes in different industries. The governing parliamentary majority amended the strike law in 2010, making provisions on essential services more difficult to meet. In practice, this meant that in the public services trade unions had to define with employers the level of essential services, or, in the absence of such agreement, demand a preliminary court ruling on essential services (Rindt 2012). The potential to use the strike weapon was thus significantly curtailed in the traditionally hot pockets of public transportation and public services, in which the required essential level of services is also set by law (Berki 2019: 16). This restrictive legislation translated into very low strike activity in the public sector, except for a national strike in education and childcare in 2016. There is no formal obligation for trade unions to ballot members before a strike. Practice depends on specific union by-laws and informal understandings, and whether and how the union leadership surveys the willingness of the rank-and-file before announcing industrial action. Because of unions' financial weakness and the generally short duration of strikes, the question of strike funds rarely features in public debates.

Particularly during the 1990s and until the early 2000s, as in other post-state socialist countries, job insecurity undermined the real potential of union strike action. Figure 14.5 shows data from the Hungarian Statistical Office on strike activity between 2000 and 2019, based on indicators for the number of participants and hours not worked due to strikes.[9] In terms of variation over time, between 2000 and 2019

9 Hungary has a low level of industrial conflict in European comparison. According to data standardized by Kurt Vandaele for the period 2000–2018, the Hungarian

Hungarian industrial relations alternated between periods of total acquiescence, when barely any work stoppages occurred, and peaks of relative unrest, with significant and well-reported strikes in strategic industries. After a prolonged railway strike in 2000, both strike indicators declined until 2006, when the austerity measures and social policy reforms of the socialist-liberal Gyurcsány government triggered a wave of strikes in public services (Neumann and Tóth 2018: 149). The financial crisis of 2008 ushered in a period of near-complete absence of strikes from Hungarian industrial relations. A single strike was reported to the Statistical Office in 2011 and 2013, two in 2015, while there were no work stoppages in 2014. Since 2015, the strike weapon has experienced a revival. Teachers' unions called a one-day national strike over school reform in 2016. In 2019, a week-long strike took place at the car manufacturer Audi, the fifth largest private sector employer in Hungary. Because of the Hungarian plant's key position in supply chains and the endurance of the organizers, the strike also brought production in the main Audi plant in Germany to a halt (Handelsblatt.com 2019).

Figure 14.5 Strike activity in Hungary, 2000–2019

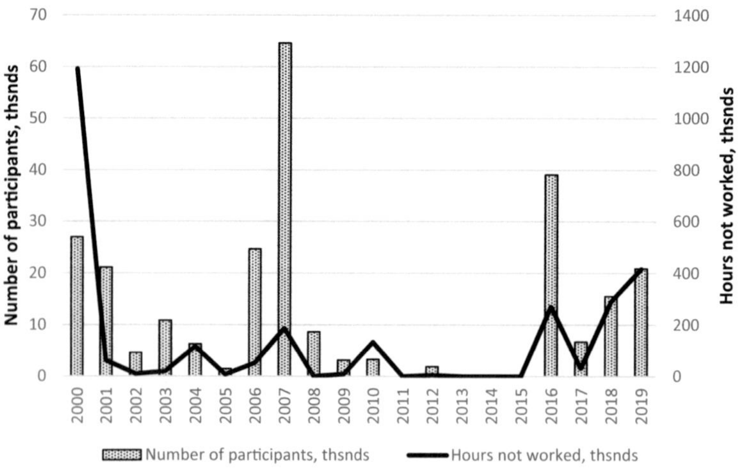

Source: KSH (2021). Stadat online spreadsheet set. Table 20.1.1.73, Strikes. https://www.ksh.hu/stadat_files/mun/en/mun0073.html Last accessed 27 July 2021.

---

economy lost 14 working days a year to industrial conflict per 1,000 employees, well below the weighted 22-country European average of 45 days. At the same time, this figure masks variations over time and across sectors, as well as the qualitative aspects of industrial conflict in Hungary.

Before the legislative changes in 2010, public services – particularly public transport, health care and education – were at the epicentre of industrial conflict, while in the private sector employee voice was constrained to company-level disputes. In the public sector, competing national trade unions and confederations also called strikes at different times, depending also on the political orientation of the government (Berki 2019: 16–22). Strikes increased after 2016 because of industrial action in the private sector, especially manufacturing. Warning strikes are especially numerous in the private sector and have proven to be a sufficient and relatively effective tool for giving weight to employee demands (Berki 2019: 17–21).

A partial explanation of the low level of strike activity is that industrial conflict was replaced with softer conflict, directed against state authorities. Available data suggest that, over time, demonstrations have become more prominent tools within Hungarian trade unions' protest repertoire. Street protests saw their peak in the period 2010–2014, in parallel with the almost complete absence of strike action (Berki 2019: 10). Public petitions and especially demonstrations were the main union weapon, which mobilized not only members but also sympathizers and the public in economically and politically hard times (Berki 2019; Greskovits 1998). Large mobilizations took place against changes in the Labour Code in 2001, against what were popularly known as the 'Servant law' (*cselédtörvény*) and the 'Slave law' (*rabszolgatörvény*) in 2018–2019, against health care reforms in 2006–2009 and against constitutional changes in 2011, even though some of these also caused friction within the movement.

Hungarian trade unions have also been involved in representing their members in individual cases at labour tribunals. Confederations and some industry-level unions maintain an extensive network of legal aid services and prioritize their maintenance when allocating limited financial and human resources (Németh and Girndt 2018: 9). In the period 2005–2010, Labour Tribunals (*Munkaügyi Bíróságok*) dealt with more than 30,000 cases every year, indicating the popularity of the court route of dispute resolution (Berki 2016: 279). The Orbán regime has restructured the system of labour tribunals, merging them into upper courts and also making it bureaucratically more burdensome and costly to file a case. Subsequently, the number of cases declined markedly, from 31,074 in 2010 to 4,615 in 2019 (Berki 2016: 279; Courts of Hungary 2019: 51). It seems that more burdensome and complicated legal procedures ensure that trade unions are less likely to take up individual cases. On the whole, workplace conflict is highly individualized and also tilts towards 'exit': alongside emigration to other EU countries, turnover, especially in manufacturing, increased markedly during 2016–2019.

Societal power

The importance of societal power resources in trade union politics is growing, as these resources could potentially compensate for the decline of organizational and institutional power resources (Visser 2019: 69; Wagner and Refslund 2016: 347). Hungarian trade unions seem to have recognized this link recently. Three aspects of societal power form the basis of the analysis here: public perceptions of trade unions, trade union use of communications and media, and trade union links to social movements.

The Hungarian public is divided and vacillating in its opinion of trade unions. Figure 14.6 shows the development of public opinion on Hungarian trade unions in a European comparison between 2005 and 2019, based on Eurobarometer survey data. After a moderate increase

Figure 14.6 Public opinion concerning trade unions in Hungary, 2005–2019

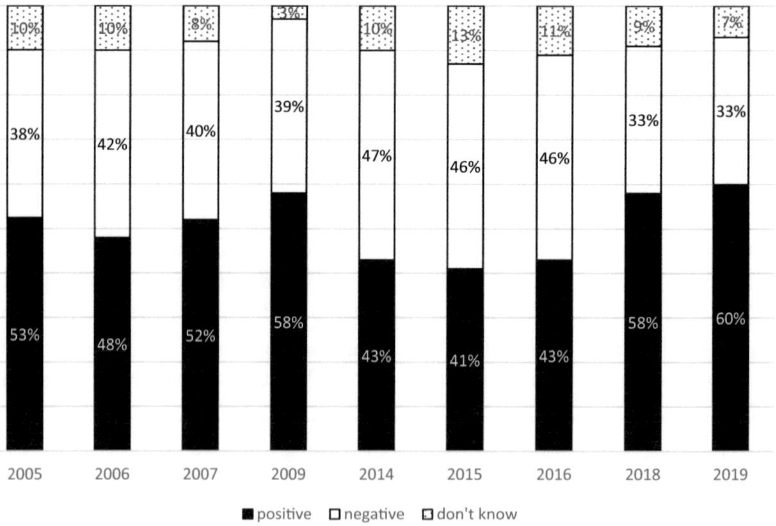

Source: Standard Eurobarometer surveys: 63, 65, 67, 72, 82, 84, 85, 90, 91.

in their popularity around EU accession, the popularity of trade unions fell to a low point in the wake of the financial crisis. The share of respondents with positive views on unions had fallen to 41 per cent by 2015. In recent years a considerable turnaround has taken place in the Hungarian public's attitude towards trade unions, as the share of favourable views increased to 60 per cent, which is also higher than the EU average.

Trade unions are typically better known by older generations. The perception and judgement of trade unions, however, has also changed over time within generations. In the 1990s, trade unions were poorly regarded by younger generations, which translated into low membership figures among this social cohort. Especially prone to individualism and self-reliance, young people were mistrustful of any established institutions or organizations, including trade unions, and indicated that they could rely on themselves or perhaps on the family (Gazsó 1995). The latest public opinion poll of 2019, however, indicated that perceptions of trade unions among young people have improved. In the sample, 66% of young people under 35 years of age did not agree with the statement that trade unions are a relic of the past. Probably even more importantly, 38% indicated that they had either joined a trade union, or would turn to a trade union at their workplace to address a problem at work (Kunert and Kiss 2019).

During the 1990s and 2000s Hungarian trade unions suffered from a public discourse that treated them as relics of the past and from a media landscape that was divided across political lines. After 2010, a more monolithic media landscape emerged, increasingly controlled by the government, which leaves even less space for critical voices. Trade unions usually achieve a more prominent public profile when they protest, for example during recent demonstrations against changes in the Labour Code (2018–2019), which improved public perceptions of trade unions, but only among opposition sympathizers and swing voters (Idea 2019).

Over the entire post-1989 period, trade unions have lacked the resources and know-how to shape public opinion, launch effective national media campaigns and 'rebrand themselves'. Confederations and industrial unions do not have public relations professionals among their permanent employees; at best, they periodically hire media specialists for the short term. Trade unions were slow to catch up with online communication and public relations tools, instead relying on printed newsletters. As of 2020, most trade unions operate a website, but with few exceptions, they have limited resources to update content and improve design. In 2010 research found most trade union websites to be very modestly informative (Szabó-Morvai 2010: 19–23). Indicatively the AHFSZ website – a company-level union – looks more transparent than the websites of most confederations and industrial unions. Hungarian trade unions have become more active recently in exploiting the opportunities provided by social media. Facebook has been increasingly used over the past five years, especially by some industrial unions, such as KASZ or Vasas. The unions representing social service workers have launched several campaigns in which workers posted selfies on Facebook, holding up a sheet of paper that showed their job title, years of experience and take-home pay (Neumann and Tóth 2018: 148).

Since the 1990s most confederations and many industrial unions have been rhetorically open to civil society organizations and social initiatives, but in reality, these links are fragile. Thus, trade unions in the 1990s established links with organizations of the unemployed (MSZOSZ 1997), but these alliances did not last. More recently, some trade unions have established weak ties with student and educational-activist groups. These ties are also very fragile because, on the trade union side, there are typically no policies and strategies for managing these ties.

Since 2010, there have been repeated attempts to broaden trade union activities in a more political, 'social movement' direction. The leadership of the trade unions representing police and firefighters started to restructure their organizations' activities into a social movement direction after the Orbán government attacked their members' early retirement rights without consultation in 2011. Nevertheless, after initial intense protests which gathered considerable media attention, the movement lost momentum and its leaders ended up leaving trade union organizing activities altogether (Neumann and Tóth 2018: 150). A similar situation occurred in nursing when a new trade union and a social movement organization developed simultaneously, a development that caused internal organizational friction within the health care union. The 2016 teachers' strike was also triggered by a grassroots protest movement of schoolteachers whose main grievance was not wages but the loss of professional autonomy in the wake of the centralization of the school system after 2010.

Trade union policies towards the European Union

Confederations were generally in favour of, and optimistic about, EU membership, as they believed in the promise of catching up with labour standards in the old EU Member States. Confederal Congress materials and conferences from the period 2002–2006 testify to this. They also held a joint celebration on the occasion of joining the EU in May 2004. Confederations welcomed new social dialogue institutions, the Industry-level Social Dialogue Committees (ÁPB, *Ágazati Párbeszéd Bizottság*) and the Economic and Social Council (GSZT, *Gazdasági és Szociális Tanács*). These were direct copies of the corresponding EU-level bodies. These institutions nudged the government and employers into acknowledging unions as negotiating partners in areas and at levels where they would otherwise not have done (Herczog 2017; Neumann 2008). Moreover, confederations also supported the setting up of transnational information and consultation bodies – European Works Councils (EWCs)– as part of the integration process. The overall impact of these forums on trade unions is nevertheless dubious. By creating parallel structures on top of already existing institutions, they complicated the landscape of employment relations and splintered the organizational resources of trade unions even further. Correspondingly, trade unions were unable to control these institutions, which did not contribute to the strengthening of industry-level bargaining or to more responsive government policy-making (Borbély 2015: 3; Herczog 2017; Neumann 2008).

Unions have also been the recipients of EU funding, in particular through the European Social Fund's capacity-building measures for social partners. Over the 2007–2013 multiannual financial framework period, HUF 3.7 billion (€12.46 million) were awarded to various trade union-led projects, including training and the establishment of employee legal aid networks. This funding was subsequently somewhat reduced as EU funds operated with different priorities for the 2014–2020 period. EU funding in 2007–2013 amounted to 3.8 per cent[10] of total trade union income during the period, notwithstanding that many of these projects also included employer organizations as consortium partners. While EU funds provide lifeline support for trade unions that are in a dire financial situation, they also deepen some of the problems of the trade union movement. First, these funds are controlled, administered and managed by the Hungarian government, further increasing the unions' dependence

---

[10] Authors' calculation based on the Hungarian government's EU-project awards database and on the Hungarian Statistical Office's data on trade union finances (STADAT table 9.1.1.12. on non-profit organisations, https://www.palyazat.gov.hu/tamogatott_projektkereso)

on state power. Second, there is no indication that EU projects have mitigated the internal conflicts within the Hungarian trade union movement. On the contrary, from the HUF 3.7 billion (€12.46 million) received from the EU, a single project led by the Liga confederation received HUF 1.6 billion (€5.39 million), raising concerns about the cordial relations between Liga's then leadership and the Orbán government.[11]

Already from late 1990s, cross-border international cooperation in terms of information flow, study exchanges and visits were thriving in particular in the two counties of Bács-Kiskun (with Romania and most states of former Yugoslavia, especially Serbia), and Vas (with Austria). Here territorial county-level organizations of confederations, especially of MSZOSZ and affiliated industrial unions, took a leading role. One of the most significant consequences of EU accession, combined with the 2008 financial and economic crisis, was the accelerating emigration of Hungarian workers to Western Europe (Bohle and Greskovits 2019: 1,083). This process spurred some action in terms of cross-border cooperation between trade unions in Hungary and in the 'old Member States'. Several cross-border initiatives were launched with the aim of tackling the exploitation of the Hungarian migrant workforce, with the involvement of home and host country trade unions, such as between MASZSZ and Austria's ÖGB. One particular issue is posted work, on which the Metalworkers' Federation (Vasas) cooperates with the German Trade Union Confederation and trade unions from some other new Member States in a project called 'Fair working conditions', also supported by the European Commission.[12] More recently, in 2018, all Hungarian confederations joined confederations of other Visegrad countries in a declaration calling for the reduction of the intra-EU wage gap, in line with the European Pillar of Social Rights. In more general terms, EU membership tightened the Hungarian economy's integration into European value chains and opened further opportunities for management whipsawing in the EU's core economies (Greer and Hauptmeier 2016). In a bid to counteract these pressures, a significant part of EU accession–related institution building took the form of participation in EWCs involving representatives from the Hungarian subsidiaries of multinational companies. As the cumulative data suggest, along with other works councils in the Visegrad countries, trade union

---

[11] See, for example, NOL (2013).

[12] See: https://www.fair-labour-mobility.eu/

representatives in multinational companies that relocated some of their production to Hungary viewed the involvement of their works councillors in EWCs very differently: opinions differed from very useful to not useful (Krzywdzinski and Schröder 2017).

Trade unions in the EU core can also prevent such pressures by helping labour organization in peripheral countries such as Hungary. The German and the Hungarian metalworkers' unions IG Metall and Vasas have launched initiatives in that direction. The two unions established joint offices in Hungary at major plants of German carmakers in 2016 and 2017, and promoted training and organizing activities at these sites (Silvia 2020: 413–414).

In terms of participation in the European Trade Union Confederation (ETUC) and engagement with EU institutions, Hungarian trade unions take a reactive position. Their leadership is represented at the European level; for example, Viktória Nagy of SZEF was elected president of the ETUC Youth Committee in 2017 (ETUC 2017). Nevertheless, whereas confederations regularly report to, and seek support from, EU-level trade union organizations, trade union leaders report little enthusiasm for EU issues from the rank-and-file. The participation of Hungarian trade unions in EU-level campaigns is also hindered by the fragmentation of the movement and by the uneasy relationship with political parties.

Conclusions

This chapter suggests that Visser's marginalization thesis applies to Hungary: 'marginalization is most likely where decline and ageing have reached extremes and where unions lack the backing of legal and social institutions and are confronted with a political and social climate of hostility or indifference' (Visser 2019: 71). Irrespective of opportunities arising in the wake of EU accession, the history of Hungarian trade unions during the past thirty years can be described as a continuous battle against marginalization. The economic shock of the capitalist transition confronted them with a real threat of marginalization from the 1990s. Marginalization in the context of economic and political regime transition meant a decline in trade union membership, the fragmentation of trade union structures, and a legitimacy crisis, in which unions had to redefine their role while facing a hostile or indifferent public opinion.

In this chapter two prominent strategies with which Hungarian trade unions attempted to counteract these initial challenges were highlighted, together with the reasons why these strategies failed to halt marginalization processes. The first strategy was market-based, the second state-based. First, trade unions from the beginning of the transition redefined themselves as market actors. In Hyman's framework of a triangular relationship between market, society and class, Hungarian unions firmly placed themselves in the corner of the market, with only a few shades of society and class (Hyman 2001). They redefined their role as market actors with the goal of improving terms and conditions of employment for members, either through collective bargaining or through direct lobbying of company management. Trade unions relied on a professional servicing model, based on the representation of core employees. This market-oriented strategy has been defensive, as it focused on already organized workers in core, competitive segments of the economy and was not able to deal with increasing labour market dualization. Because of capacity problems, interest representation of the most precarious employees and outsider social groups featured low on the union agenda (Neumann and Tóth 2018: 136). Furthermore, the core is shrinking as trade unions are unable to protect even core members in difficult times. 'Society' featured on their agenda only to the extent of embracing the idea of 'social partnership', but their capacity to influence social and economic policymaking has faded over time and was shattered by the government change in 2010. The increasing concentration of trade union membership in the public sector nevertheless pushes unions beyond a narrow market-based strategy, as issues of redistribution and social reproduction feature prominently in public sector industrial relations. Class antagonism, going beyond strictly defined issues of wage bargaining, has never featured in the vocabulary of Hungarian trade unions since 1989.

What the Hyman triangle is missing but which has been crucial for Hungarian trade unions in the past thirty years is their relationship to the polity. The second dominant reaction to membership decline, and to a weakening structural position within trade unions, was to build close political links, partly through tripartite channels, partly through political parties. Trade union confederations accepted incorporation or were co-opted into a whole spectrum of tripartite institutions that secured resources for them and could function in 'good' times, but not in crisis situations. The limits of this politically focused strategy were revealed already in the early years of transition, when the most important austerity, liberalization and privatization measures were implemented without trade union consent and through unilateral legislation. Furthermore, the reliance of the confederations on the polity constituted an unbalanced model of union capacities, with the majority of paid experts and bureaucrats concentrated at peak confederal level, although the peak-level lacked authority over affiliates. Industrial unions in privatized manufacturing had no institutionalized role, and typically no partners on the employer side to push for more comprehensive coordinated regulation. The weakness of industry- and sector-level organizations has remained the Achilles heel of Hungarian trade unionism.

More precisely, this chapter demonstrates that László Neumann's note of caution about Hungarian trade unions' reliance on institutions has been warranted by the experience of the fifteen years since 2005. The institutions that gave unions the illusion of power at the turn of the millennium proved ineffective in the face of political and economic crises in 2006 and 2008, and they were swept away by the conservative political forces that have governed Hungary since 2010. The key finding of this chapter is that from the 1990s Hungarian unions, especially confederations, depended too much on channels of inclusion in the polity, mediated through their relationship with political parties. As union strength was concentrated in the public sector, even greater political vulnerabilities came to the fore in situations of fiscal austerity and political crises. Losing direct institutional access to the polity, trade unions have been in a process of experimentation since 2010, including protest, co-option and attempts to regain power on the ground by relying on structural and societal power resources. As part of this experimentation, in recent years there has been a detectable increase in social support for unions, which could also be associated with their increased use of media and social spaces.

As they used to rely on involvement in tripartite institutions confederations have found it most difficult to adapt, while some industry- and company-level unions have been partly able to compensate for institutional weakness thanks to the economic recovery that started in the middle of the decade. For the first time since 1989 instead of unemployment, labour shortages were the main issue confronting the Hungarian labour market, causing tensions regarding work intensification and, in theory, giving increased structural power to workers and temporary collective action opportunities to unions (Silver 2003). In practice, rather than engaging in collective action and unionization, restrictive strike legislation and managerial unilateralism pushed workers into individualized forms of exit, as turnover mounted and emigration to other EU countries also increased. Such developments came to an abrupt end with the slowdown of the global economy in 2019 and with the Covid pandemic in 2020. As marginalization went hand in hand with the problem of declining organizational capacity, trade unions did not have the resources to tackle challenges of digitalization and green transition thoroughly. At best, conferences or workshops were organized on these issues, but these did not result in a sustainable strategy or outcome. Overall, trade unions have been unable to translate labour's market power at the end of the 2010s along solidaristic lines to increase bargaining power, and this has become even more difficult in the unfavourable economic circumstances post-2020.

References

All links were checked on 13 June 2021.

AHFSZ (2020) AHFSZ Hírek Az Audi Hungária Független Szakszervezet tájékoztatója January 28 2020 https://www.ahfsz.hu/uploads/dokumentumok/001_ahfsz_hirek_2020.01.28..pdf

Avdagic S. (2004) Loyalty and power in union-party alliances: labour politics in postcommunism, MPIfG Discussion Paper 04, Köln, Max-Planck-Institut für Gesellschaftsforschung. https://www.econstor.eu/handle/10419/19909

Berki E. (2014) The specifics of setting salaries and interest reconciliation in the public sector, in Neumann L. and Fazekas K. (eds) The Hungarian Labour Market. Review and Analysis, 124–135.

Berki E. (2016) Hogyan rendezzük munkaügyi vitáinkat?, Opus et Educatio, 3 (3), 277–286. http://opuseteducatio.hu/index.php/opusHU/article/view/111

Berki E. (2019) Munkaügyi akciók 2010 és 2019 között Magyarországon, Budapest, Friedrich Ebert Stiftung.

Berki E. and Dura M. (2012) Munkaügyi kapcsolatok közszolgálatban. Szeged, Pólay Elemér Alapítvány.

Berki E. and Neumann L. (2009) Constitutional Court ruling paves way for new social dialogue law, Dublin, Eurofound. https://www.eurofound.europa.eu/publications/article/2009/constitutional-court-ruling-paves-way-for-new-social-dialogue-law

Bohle D. (2011) Trade unions and the fiscal crisis of the State, Warsaw Forum of Economic Sociology, 2 (3), 89–105.

Bohle D. and Greskovits B. (2010) Slovakia and Hungary: successful and failed euro entry without social pacts, in Pochet P., Keune M. and Natali D. (eds) After the euro and enlargement: social pacts in the EU, Brussels, ETUI, 345–369.

Bohle D. and Greskovits B. (2012) Capitalist diversity on Europe's periphery, Ithaca, Cornell University Press.

Bohle D. and Greskovits B. (2019) Politicising embedded neoliberalism: continuity and change in Hungary's development model, West European Politics, 42 (5), 1069–1093.

Borbély S. (2015) Az ágazati párbeszéd nemzetközi és hazai helyzete és lehetőségei, Project report, Budapest, MKKSZ.

Courts of Hungary (2019) Ügyforgalmi Elemzés. [Analysis of Court Proceedings Data], Budapest.

ETUC (2017) Viktória Nagy elected ETUC Youth President. ETUC, Press release, 12 December 2017, Brussels, ETUC. https://www.etuc.org/en/pressrelease/viktoria-nagy-elected-etuc-youth-president

Fodor T.G., Nacsa B. and Neumann L. (2008) Egy és több munkáltatóra kiterjedő hatályú kollektív szerződések összehasonlító elemzése – országos összegző tanulmány, Budapest, SZMM, 17–19.

Gazsó F. (1995) Nemzedéki orientációk instabil társadalmi környezetben, Szociológiai Szemle, 1, 3–23. https://szociologia.hu/dynamic/9501gazso.htm

Gerőcs T., Meszmann T.T. and Pinkasz A. (2021) Uneven development in the European automotive industry labour fragmentation and value-added production in the Hungarian semi-Periphery, in Komlossy A. and Music G. (eds) Global commodity chains and labour relations, Studies in Global Social History 42, Leiden, Bril.

Girndt R. (1996) Hungary's trade unions division and decline, Labour Focus on Eastern Europe, 55, 47– 59.

Greer I. and Hauptmeier M. (2016) Management whipsawing. The staging of labor competition under globalization, ILR Review, 69 (1), 29–52.

Greskovits B. (1998) The political economy of protest and patience, Budapest, Central European University Press.

Handelsblatt (2019) Autobauer: Streik in Ungarn bringt Audi-Bänder in Ingolstadt zum Stillstand. Handelsblatt, 28 January 2019. https://www.handelsblatt.com/unternehmen/industrie/autobauer-streik-in-ungarn-bringt-audi-baender-in-ingolstadt-zum-stillstand/23917968.html

Hassel A. (2007) The curse of institutional security: the erosion of German trade unionism, Industrielle Beziehungen, 14 (2), 176–191.

Herczog L. (2017) Szociális párbeszéd a rendszerváltást követően, Szakszervezetek, 7 March 2017. https://szakszervezetek.hu/8-kiemelt-hirek/10763-herczog-laszlo-szocialis-parbeszed-a-rendszervaltast-kovetoen-2

Héthy L. and Ónodi I. (2008) Országos társadalmi párbeszéd – az Országos Érdekegyeztető Tanács és a Gazdasági és Szociális Tanács, Budapest, Foglalkoztatási és Szociális Hivatal. http://mek.oszk.hu/16100/16112/16112.pdf

Horváth I. and Kártyás G. (2021) Látlelet: Az egészségügyi szolgálati jogviszonyról és a szabályozás kérdőjeleiről, Munkajog, 1, 1–17. https://munkajogilap.huhttps://outlook.office.com/files/etui@etui.org//latlelet-az-egeszsegugyi-szolgalati-jogviszonyrol-es-a-szabalyozas-kerdojeleirol/

Hyman R. (2001) Understanding European trade unionism: between market, class and society, London, SAGE.

Idea (2019) Rabszolgatörvény' miatti tiltakozások: a bizonytalanok is ellenzéki állásponton. Idea Intézet. http://www.ideaintezet.hu/hirek-aktualis/13/---rabszolgatorveny----miatti-tiltakozasok--a-bizonytalanok-is-ellenzeki-allasponton

Kollonay C. and Ladó M. (1996) Hungary, in Carabelli U. and Sciarra S. (eds) New patterns of collective labour law in Central Europe: Czech and Slovak Republics, Hungary, Poland, Milano, Giuffre Editore, 101–161.

Koltay J. and Neumann L. (2006) Introduction. Industrial relations in Hungary – A close look in a wider perspective, in Fazekas K. and Koltay J. (eds) The Hungarian Labour Market: Review and Analysis, Budapest, Institute of Economics, HAS Hungarian Employment Foundation, 27–35.

Krzywdzinski M. and Schröder A. (2017) Globale Rahmenvereinbarungen in der europäischen Automobilzulieferindustrie, WZB Discussion Paper SP III 2017-2302, Berlin, Wissenschaftszentrum Berlin für Sozialforschung.

KSH (2002) Műszakrend, munkarend, szervezettség, Budapest, Központi Statisztikai Hivatal.

Kunert A. and Kiss N. (2019) Szakszervezeti trendforduló a láthatáron. Új Egyenlőség, 7 July 2019. https://ujegyenloseg.hu/szakszervezeti-trendfordulo-a-lathataron/

Ladó M. (1994) Workers' and employers' interests – as they are represented in the changing industrial relations in Hungary, Krakow, Krakow Academy of Economics.

Ladó M. and Tóth F. (1993) Szociális partnerek Magyarországon, Európai Szemle, 3, 26–36.

Ladó M. and Tóth F. (eds) (1996) Helyzetkép az érdekegyeztetésről. 1990–1994, Budapest, Érdekegyeztető Tanács Titkársága.

Lajtai Gy. (2017) Szakszervezeti jövő Európában és Magyarországon. A közelmúlt és a jelen, Paper presented at Lehet a szakszervezet újra társadalmi mozgalom? 11 March 2017, Budapest, SZEF-ÉSZT Akadémia. https://szefakademia.hu/esemenyek/lehet-a-szakszervezet-ujra-tarsadalmi-mozgalom

Laki M., Nacsa B. and Neumann L. (2013) Az új Munka Törvénykönyvének hatása a munkavállalók és munkáltatók közötti kapcsolatokra, Discussion Paper 2012/2, Budapest, Hungarian Academy of Sciences.

LIGA (2009) A LIGA Szakszervezetek beszámolója a LIGA XII. kongresszusára a 2006–2009 közötti tevékenységéről. https://www.liganet.hu/images/a5508/beszamolo.pdf

LIGA (2013) LIGA 25: Gaskó István ünnepi beszéde, VDSZSZ, 13 December 2013. https://www.youtube.com/watch?v=q1buvTSYaZY&feature=youtu.be&ab_channel=vdszsz

Lux J. (2008) A magyarországi szakszervezetek történetéből. Budapest, Friedrich Ebert Alapítvány. http://polhist.hu/wp-content/uploads/2017/11/lux2008.pdf

Makó Cs. and Simonyi Á. (1997) Inheritance, imitation and genuine solutions (institution building in Hungarian labour relations), Europe-Asia Studies, 49 (2), 221–243.

Márkus E. and M. Tóth L. (eds) (2010) A társadalmi párbeszéd intézményei és fórumai 2010, Budapest, Társadalmi Párbeszéd Koordinációs Iroda. http://mek.oszk.hu/08200/08203/08203.pdf

Mélypataki G. (2019) A munkaügyi kapcsolatok helyzete és szerepe a közszolgálatban. Budapest, Nemzeti Közszolgálati Egyetem.

MSZOSZ (1997) Munkanélküliség és a szakszervezetek, Budapest, MSZOSZ. http://library.fes.de/pdf-files/bueros/vifaost/a98-08311.pdf

MSZOSZ (2010) Az első húsz év. DVD, Budapest, MSZOSZ.

Nacsa B. and Neumann L. (2008) A kollektív szerződések ereje, a szabályozás hatékonysága, in Herczog L., Kaló J., Lux J., Mátraházi I. and Várkonyi J. (eds) Szociális párbeszéd új keretek között, Budapest Foglalkoztatási és Szociális Hivatal Társadalmi Párbeszéd Központ, 79–89.

Neumann L. (2000) Decentralizált kollektív alku Magyarországon. in Koltay J. (ed.) A munkaügyi kapcsolatok rendszere és a munkavállalók helyzete. Budapest, MTA Közgazdaságtudományi Kutatóközpont, 37–70.

Neumann L. (2006) The Hungarian trade unions and their future options, in The Hungarian Labour Market: review and analysis 2006, Budapest, Institute of Economics, HAS Hungarian Employment Foundation, 57–74. http://econ.core.hu/doc/mt/2006/en/infocus2006.pdf

Neumann L. (2008) Spotlight on four years of sectoral social dialogue, Dublin, Eurofound. https://www.eurofound.europa.eu/publications/article/2008/spotlight-on-four-years-of-sectoral-social-dialogue

Neumann L. (2017) Tagdíjak, támogatások, jövedelmek; a magyar szakszervezeti mozgalom finanszírozásának negyedszázados története, Paper presented at Lehet a szakszervezet újra társadalmi mozgalom? 11 March 2017, Budapest, SZEF-ÉSZT Akadémia. https://szefakademia.hu/esemenyek/lehet-a-szakszervezet-ujra-tarsadalmi-mozgalom

Neumann L. (2018) Annual review 2017 of labour relations and social dialogue in Hungary, Bratislava, Friedrich-Ebert-Stiftung.

Neumann L. and Tóth A. (2018) Hungarian unions under political and economic pressure, in Lehndorff S., Dribbusch H. and Schulten T. (eds) Rough waters: European trade unions in a time of crises, Brussels, ETUI, 135–159.

Németh E. and Girndt R. (2018) Félúton a rezignáció és a felemelkedés között, Budapest, Friedrich Ebert Stiftung. http://library.fes.de/pdf- files/bueros/budapest/14551-20180919.pdf

NOL (2013) A rendszerhibában bíznak, NOL.hu, 21 January 2013. http://nol.hu/belfold/20130121-a_rendszerhibaban_biznak-1360775

Ost D. (2000) Illusory corporatism in Eastern Europe: neoliberal tripartism and postcommunist class identities, Politics & Society, 28 (4), 503–530.

Rácz G. (2013) Hogyan vegyünk, és hogyan tegyünk tönkre szakszervezetet?, Idea Intézet, 4 November 2013.

Rindt Z. (2012) Amended strike law one year on, Dublin, Eurofound.

Sauer W. (1993) Um Legitimität und Vermögen. Zur Geschichte der ungarischen Gewerkschaftsbewegung 1988 bis 1993, Jahrbuch des Vereins für Geschichte der Arbeiterbewegung, 9, 114–160. https://homepage.univie.ac.at/walter.sauer/Publikationen-Dateien/Um_Legitimitaet_und_Vermoegen.pdf

Silver B. J. (2003) Forces of labor: workers' movements and globalization since 1870, Cambridge, Cambridge University Press.

Silvia S. J. (2020) The transnational activities of German trade unions and works councils: from foreign policy to active engagement, German Politics, 29 (3), 404–421.

Szabó E. (2014) A SZEF története 1989–2013, Budapest, SZEF.

Szabó I.G. (2013) Between polarization and statism – effects of the crisis on collective bargaining processes and outcomes in Hungary, Transfer, 19 (2), 205–215.

Szabó-Morvai Á. (2010) Szakszervezeti stratégia és megújulás. A munkavállalói érdekképviselet jelene és jövője Magyarországon. http://www.employmentpolicy.hu/resource.aspx?resourceID=252_merop_szakszervezetek_4

Szalai E. (1994) A civil társadalomtól a politikai társadalom felé. Munkástanácsok 1989–1993, Budapest, T-Twins Kiadó.

Thoma L. (2001) Régi söprűk, új szemét, Magyar Narancs, XIII (14), 5 May 2001. https://magyarnarancs.hu/publicisztika/thoma_laszlo_regi_sopruk_uj_szemet_a_szakszervezetekrol-54970

Tóth A. (1994) A munkaügyi kapcsolatok rendszere a poszt-szocialista Magyarországon, in Balogh I. (ed.) Törésvonalak és értékválasztások, Budapest, MTA Politikai Tudományok Intézete, 298–331.

Tóth A. (2000a) Üzemi tanácsok, szakszervezetek és munkáltatók, in Koltay J. (ed.) A munkaügyi kapcsolatok rendszere és a munkavállalók helyzete, Budapest, MTA Közgazdaságtudományi Kutatóközpont, 223–256. https://mek.oszk.hu/01500/01540/01540.pdf

Tóth A. (2000b) A magyar szakszervezetek a politika és a gazdaság viharában, Politikatudományi Szemle, 9 (1–2), 151–183. http://epa.niif.hu/02500/02565/00031/pdf/EPA02565_poltud_szemle_2000_1-2_151-184.pdf

Tóth F. (1998) Konszenzuskereső évek. Az Autonóm Szakszervezetek Szövetsége. Autonóm Szakszervezetek Szövetsége, Budapest, Autonóm Szakszervezetek Szövetsége.

Visser J. (2019) Trade Unions in the Balance. ILO ACTRAV Working paper, Geneva, ILO.

Wagner I. and Refslund B. (2016) Understanding the diverging trajectories of slaughterhouse work in Denmark and Germany: a power resource approach, European Journal of Industrial Relations, 22 (4), 335–351.

Abbreviations

AHFSZ *Audi Hungária Független Szakszervezet* (Audi Hungary Independent Trade Union)

ÁPB *Ágazati Párbeszéd Bizottság* (Sectoral Social Dialogue Committee)

ASZSZ *Autonóm Szakszervezetek Szövetsége* (Confederation of Autonomous Trade Unions)

EDDSZ *Egészségügyi Dolgozók Demokratikus Szakszervezete* (Democratic Trade Union of Healthcare Workers)

ÉSZT *Értelmiségi Szakszervezeti Tömörülés* (Confederation of Unions of Professionals)

ÉTMOSZ *Életre Tervezett Munkavállalók Országos Szakszervezete* (National Trade Union of Employees Designed for Life)

EVDSZ *Egyesült Villamosenergia-ipari Dolgozók Szakszervezeti Szövetsége* (Federation of Workers in Electricity Generation)

EWCs European Works Councils

FIDESZ *Magyar Polgári Szövetség* (Hungarian Civic Alliance)

GSZT *Gazdasági és Szociális Tanács* (Economic and Social Council)

KASZ *Kereskedelmi Alkalmazottak Szakszervezete* (Trade Union of Retail Employees)

KSH *Központi Statisztikai Hivatal* (Central Statistical Office)

Liga *Független Szakszervezetek Demokratikus Ligája* (Democratic League of Independent Trade Unions)

MASZSZ *Magyar Szakszervezeti Szövetség* (Hungarian Trade Union Confederation)

MOSZ *Munkástanácsok Országos Szövetsége* (National Confederation of Workers' Councils)

MSZOSZ *Magyar Szakszervezetek Országos Szövetsége* (National Confederation of Hungarian Trade Unions)

MSZP	*Magyar Szocialista Párt* (Hungarian Socialist Party)
MTSZSZ	*Mérnökök és Technikusok Szabad Szakszervezete* (Free Trade Union of Engineers and Technicians)
NGTT	*Nemzeti Gazdasági és Társadalmi Tanács* (National Economic and Social Council)
OÉT	*Országos Érdekegyeztető Tanács* (National Council for the Reconciliation of Interests)
PSZ	*Pedagógusok Szakszervezete* (Teachers' Trade Union)
SZEF	*Szakszervezetek Együttműködési Fóruma* (Trade Unions' Cooperation Forum)
SZOT	*Szakszervezetek Országos Tanácsa* (National Trade Union Council)
Vasas	*Vasas Szakszervezeti Szövetség* (Vasas Metalworkers' Trade Union Federation)
VDSZ	*Magyar Vegyipari, Energiaipari és Rokon Szakmákban Dolgozók Szakszervezeti Szövetsége* (Federation of Chemical Workers of Hungary)
VDSZSZ	*Vasúti Dolgozók Szabad Szakszervezete* (Free Trade Union of Railway Workers)
VKF	*Versenyszféra és a Kormány Állandó Konzultációs Fóruma* (Standing Consultative Forum for the Private Sector and the Government)
VSZ	*Vasutasok Szakszervezete* (Trade Union of Railway Workers)

Chapter 15

Ireland: Trade unions recovering after being tipped off balance by the Great Recession?

Vincenzo Maccarrone and Roland Erne[1]

This chapter describes the features and fortunes of the Irish trade union movement over the past thirty years. It highlights the issues it has faced and the strategic responses it has adopted. Whereas the collapse of social partnership agreements and the unilateral imposition of wage cuts after the financial crisis put unions very much on the defensive, it would be wrong to write off the Irish union movement.

From 1987 to 2008, Irish industrial relations were dominated by a series of centralized, tripartite social partnership agreements. In exchange for wage moderation, these agreements gave unions influence over policy-making. Most importantly, however, the wage moderation and industrial peace brought by these agreements also favoured a substantial increase in foreign direct investment. This national 'competitive corporatist' approach led to both substantial increases in Irish workers' real wages and a substantial decline in the share of GDP going to wage earners (Erne 2008; Teague and Donaghey 2009). As long as social partnership guaranteed a growing economy, Irish union leaders and workers accepted wage moderation, notably because the social partnership model compared favourably with developments in the United Kingdom, where the unions had been weakened by the onslaught of Thatcherism. The decades of

1 This project has received funding from the European Research Council under the European Union's Horizon 2020 research and innovation programme (grant agreement no. 725240, https://www.erc-europeanunions.eu). We would also like to acknowledge the helpful comments we received from the editors and colleagues at peer review meetings.

partnership agreements also saw a significant decline of unions' mobilization and organizational power, however, as evidenced by the significant fall in unionization rates and strike activity (Table 15.1). Furthermore, despite social partnership, the legislative framework for collective labour rights remained weak.

The 2008 financial crisis therefore caught the Irish union movement on the wrong foot. After all, accepting a 'smaller slice of a shrinking cake' hardly represents an attractive union strategy (Erne 2013). Social partnership and centralized collective bargaining collapsed in 2009, following the implementation of unilateral wage cuts in the public sector. Further austerity measures followed in subsequent years, when Ireland

Table 15.1 Principal characteristics of unionism in Ireland

	1990	2000	2019
Total trade union membership	491,000	549,000	552,000
Women as a proportion of total membership	34 %	43 %*	57 %*
Gross union density	57 %	40 %	28 %
Net union density	51 %	36 %	25 %
Number of confederations	1	1	1
Number of affiliated unions (federations)	50	n.a.	29
Number of independent unions	17	n.a.	7***
Collective bargaining coverage	63 %	44 %	34 % [2017]
Principal level of collective bargaining	National intersectoral level	National intersectoral level	Company level in private sector****; national level in public sector
Days not worked due to industrial action per 1,000 workers	264	72	18

Note: *2001; **2016; *** This is an estimate. Whereas Irish law prevents the unions of the Gardaí (police) and Defence Forces from joining ICTU, other representative bodies willingly choose to remain outside ICTU, namely the Psychiatric Nurses Association, the Irish Hospital Consultants Association, and the Irish Dentists Association. There is also the Independent Workers Union, which claims to have about 1,000 members and to uphold the syndicalist ideals of early trade unionists, such as James Connolly and Jim Larkin (Darlington 2008); **** In a few industries, namely in the construction, cleaning, and the security industry, industry-level bargaining persists.

Source: Appendix A1.

entered the Troika bailout programme of the European Commission, the European Central Bank (ECB) and the International Monetary Fund in 2010 and became subject to the European Union's (EU) commodifying new economic governance prescriptions (Jordan et al. 2021). To further complicate this picture, some employers launched successful legal challenges to the only existing industrial wage-setting mechanisms in Irish legislation. Ireland left the bailout programme at the end of 2013. With the Troika out of the country and an improved economic situation, unions faced a more favourable environment. In some cases, they even succeeded where they had hitherto failed, namely when they successfully collaborated with unions across borders to compel the low-cost Irish airline Ryanair to grant union recognition. Even so, the unions are still facing tough challenges, as they have not yet fully recovered from being tipped off balance by the 2008 crisis and from decades of social partnership, which has significantly hampered their mobilization and organizational power resources.

Historical background and principal features of the industrial relations system

The history of the Irish trade union movement is intertwined with the formation of the Irish state and the struggle for independence from the British Empire (Gumbrell-McCormick and Hyman 2013; O'Connor 2011).

Craft unionism dominated the scene throughout the 1800s. It was only towards the end of that century that British unions attempted to organize unskilled workers (O'Connor 2011). Meanwhile, intersectoral local trade councils were established throughout the island of Ireland. Irish delegates attended the British Trade Union Congress (TUC), founded in Manchester in 1868, but the reduced space devoted to Irish matters was reflected in their limited involvement. This led to attempts to create an Irish confederation, which culminated in the birth of the Irish Trade Union Congress (ITUC) in 1894. While the ITUC was initially dominated by the Irish branches of British craft unions, 1909 saw the birth of the Irish Transport and General Workers' Union (ITGWU), which organized workers irrespective of their trade and would soon become the largest Irish union. The ITGWU joined the Congress in 1910. Over time, industrial and general unions acquired increasing importance, although a tradition of craft unionism has persisted until today.

Following the creation of the Irish Free State and the partition of the island, the ITUC continued to represent both Irish- and British-based unions on both sides of the border (Roche et al. 2000). Yet, tensions remained between Irish and British unions (Ní Lochlaínn 2005), eventually leading to a split in 1945, with nationalist Irish unions creating the Congress of Irish Unions. The schism lasted until 1959 when the two confederations dissolved to form the Irish Congress of Trade Unions (ICTU) which continues to operate across the border. In what has been described as a 'distinctive complexity' (Gumbrell-McCormick and Hyman 2013), ICTU thus is a confederation of

> Ireland based unions who operate in the Republic of Ireland only, Republic of Ireland based unions who operate in both the Republic of Ireland and Northern Ireland, Northern Ireland based unions who operate in Northern Ireland only, unions headquartered in the UK who operate in both the Republic and Northern Ireland, or who operate only in Northern Ireland. (ICTU 2011: 7)

In this chapter, we focus on developments in the Republic of Ireland.

As in Britain, voluntarism dominated Irish industrial relations also after the creation of the Irish state, with employment conditions regulated by collective bargaining between employers and unions rather than by law (Von Prondzynski 1998). In such a context, the role of the state is to provide an adequate framework in which this can happen (Doherty 2014), for instance, by sponsoring various institutions for conflict resolution, such as the Labour Court.

In contrast to Britain, however, the main cleavage in Irish politics remained – until very recently – the national question rather than class. Thus, although the ITUC created the Irish Labour Party in 1912, this remained always a minoritarian force, occasionally going into government as junior partner of one of the two largest Irish parties, Fianna Fáil (FF) and Fine Gael (FG). Whereas both parties positioned themselves on the centre-right on socio-economic issues, they emerged from a bloody civil war over the Anglo-Irish Treaty in 1922–1923. With the support of Ireland's ruling class, the Catholic Church and large sections of the country's working people, Fianna Fáil – Ireland's republican party – dominated Irish politics from 1932 to 2011 (Allen 1997; Hardiman 1992; Roche 2009). Over the past decade, however, the Irish political spectrum has been re-aligning along more traditional left–right divides.

Since the late 1930s, trials of 'quasi-corporatism' (Gumbrell-McCormick and Hyman 2013) characterized Irish labour relations (Roche et al. 2000), despite the legacy of pluralist, British industrial relations traditions in the country. In 1987, a Fianna Fáil-led government brokered the first 'competitive corporatist' Social Partnership agreement (ibid.), involving ICTU and the two peak-level employer organizations, the Confederation of Irish Industry and the Federated Union of Employers.[2] Over time, however, Fianna Fáil's capacity to integrate all social classes declined, culminating in the collapse of national social partnership agreements under its watch in 2009.

Structure of trade unions and union democracy

Irish organized labour displays a variety of associational forms, ranging from large general unions to industrial unions, but also including craft and professional unions. Despite these differences, the structure of unions is broadly similar. Where unions are present at the workplace, members are represented by shop stewards who are either elected by their colleagues or appointed by the union. The basic unit of organization is the branch, organized on an industrial or a geographical basis. The governing authority of a union is usually the national executive council, which is elected by a conference of delegates of union members. The national executive council appoints a general secretary who manages the affairs of the union, along with a team of industrial officers and staff members.

In terms of union internal organization, centralizing and decentralizing tendencies co-exist. While the era of social partnership saw little direct involvement of workplace union members in collective bargaining (Doherty and Erne 2010), one side effect of the end of national wage agreements has been a greater engagement on the part of local shop stewards in the private sector in formulating claims and implementing collective agreements (Roche and Gormley 2020). Whereas public sector bargaining remains centralized at the national level, the agreements are subject to an aggregate ballot. Thus, rank-and-file members can overturn the result of an agreement, even against the recommendation of the

2 The two organizations merged in 1993 to form the Irish Business and Employers Confederation (Ibec), which is the largest employer organization in Ireland.

union leadership. This happened in 2013 with the concessionary 'Croke Park II' public sector agreement (Erne 2013).

With very few exceptions, unions in Ireland are affiliated to ICTU, which is the sole Irish affiliate of the European Trade Union Confederation (ETUC). In 2019, forty-three unions were affiliated to it, of which twenty-nine organize in the Republic of Ireland. ICTU's governing authority is the Executive Council, which is elected at a Biennial Delegate Conference by delegates of affiliated unions. The Executive Council appoints ICTU's general secretary, who runs the organization along with an assistant general secretary and a small number of officers based in Dublin and Belfast.

Like the British TUC, ICTU does not direct its affiliates. The conduct of collective bargaining is left to its affiliates, whereas the confederation is tasked with influencing the state, employers and society on matters of concern for labour. This includes not only individual and collective workers' rights but also other social issues, such as health and education policy, as well as European and international affairs (Maccarrone 2021). From 1987 to 2008, ICTU was more influential when its officers were central in the negotiation of national tripartite social partnership agreements. After their collapse, ICTU's Public Service Committee continued to coordinate collective bargaining in the public sector. By contrast, ICTU's Private Sector Committee was reconstituted only in 2015 to issue guidance on recommended pay targets for its affiliates (Higgins 2015).

Given the high number of ICTU affiliates, more than one union may represent workers in an industry or company. At times this can give rise to disputes, which are dealt with by a committee within the confederation. Even so, most members are concentrated in a few unions (see Table 15.2). The general Service Industrial Professional and Technical Union (SIPTU) – which originated from the ITGWU – accounts for over a third of ICTU's members in the Republic. Overall, in the private sector, SIPTU, the retail union Mandate, the engineering union Connect and the general (British-based) union Unite organize approximately 85 per cent of union members (Roche and Gormley 2020). In the public sector, the largest union is Fórsa (Gaelic for 'force', as well as 'leverage'), established in 2017 from the merger of three unions.[3] Fórsa represents approximately a third of ICTU-affiliated union members in the public sector. Sectoral trade unions organizing public sector workers, such

[3] These are the Irish Municipal, Public and Civic Trade Union (IMPACT), the Public Service Executive Union (PSEU) and the Civic and Public Services Union (CPSU).

as nurses and midwifes (INMO), doctors (IMO) and teachers (ASTI, INTU, TUI), also play an important role.

Table 15.2 Membership of ICTU and its largest affiliates, 2008 and 2018

Name	Type	Membership 2008	Membership 2018
Irish Congress of Trade Unions (ICTU)	Confederation	612,676	517,830
Services Industrial Professional and Technical Union (SIPTU)	General	209,881	173,000
FÓRSA	Service sector (predominantly public sector)	87,225[a]	89,401
Connect Trade Union	Craft (predominantly construction trades)	55,245[b]	39,000
Mandate	Service sector (mostly retail)	45,206	33,462
UNITE	General [UK-based]	40,363[c]	21,440
Irish Nurses and Midwifes Association (INMO)	Occupational	40,100	39,150
Irish National Teachers' Organization (INTO)	Occupational	31,345	38,546
Communication Workers' Union (CWU)	Occupational	19,550	15,003
Association of Secondary Teachers in Ireland (ASTI)	Occupational	18,064	16,849
Teachers' Union of Ireland (TUI)	Occupational	15,417	18,352
Financial Service Unions (FSU)	Service sector (financial industry)	15,052[d]	8,521
Irish Medical Organization (IMO)	Occupational	6,144	4,685

Note: Excluding membership in Northern Ireland; [a]Obtained as the sum of members of IMPACT (61,450), CPSU (13,775) and PSEU (12,000); [b] Sum of members TEEU (45,035) and the members of UCATT in the Republic of Ireland (10,210); [c] Sum of members of Amicus (28,500) and ATGWU (11,863) in the Republic of Ireland; [d] Members of the Irish Bank Officials' Association (IBOA).

Source: ICTU (2009, 2019a).

Hence, 'the double face of high concentration in few general unions and fragmentation in many small unions' (Roche et al. 2000: 345) still marks Irish unionism. Reducing fragmentation has been a concern for ICTU's leadership since its early days (O'Connor 2011). Over time, the number of its affiliates has declined through amalgamations. In 1959, the confederation included seventy affiliates that were operating in the Republic (Roche et al. 2000) by comparison with twenty-nine in 2019. The most notable merger took place in 1990, when the ITGWU merged with the Federated Workers Union of Ireland to create SIPTU. ICTU's representativeness has also increased over time, with the two largest independent unions – the nurses' union INO (now INMO) and the banking union IBOA (now FSU) joining it in the 1990s (Roche et al. 2000). Roche et al. (2000) calculate that throughout the 1990s ICTU included approximately 95 per cent of unions operating in Ireland, a figure that still stands today.

After the 2008 financial crisis, ICTU established a commission that proposed to reduce the number of affiliates to six larger federated sectoral organizations (Geary 2016; Hickland and Dundon 2016). Although its 2013 biennial conference adopted a plan to move in this direction, little has been done, with two exceptions: the merger between the (public) sector unions IMPACT, CPSU and PSEU, which led to the creation of Fórsa in 2017; and the merger of the Technical Engineering and Electrical Union (TEEU) and the Irish section of the British construction sector union UCATT, which led to the birth of Connect in 2018.

Unionization

There are two main data sources on unionization in Ireland. One is the administrative data reported by the unions themselves. Since the early 1990s, union density data is also available from the Labour Force Survey of the Central Statistics Office (CSO). The two sources differ, as unions may count among their members also the self-employed, pensioners and the unemployed, while CSO includes only employees.[4] Overall, CSO data consistently show a lower level of unionization in comparison with the data provided by the unions (Roche 2008; Walsh 2015). This also

4 This also explains the discrepancy between some of the data reported here and the data provided in Appendix A1.

explains the discrepancy in the data on unionization in Tables 15.1 and 15.2.

Even taking these differences into account, all statistical sources point to a decline in union density during recent decades. Having reached a peak of 62 per cent in 1980, union density in Ireland was still over 50 per cent at the beginning of the 1990s (Roche 2008). It subsequently diminished almost uninterruptedly until the Great Recession (Figure 15.1). By 2008, density was around 31 per cent, according to survey data. Union membership had increased significantly throughout the 1990s (Figure 15.1). Density decreased, however, because membership did not keep pace with the huge growth in employment recorded throughout the period of economic growth, when Ireland became known as the 'Celtic Tiger' (ibid.).

Figure 15.1 Net union density and membership, 1990–2020

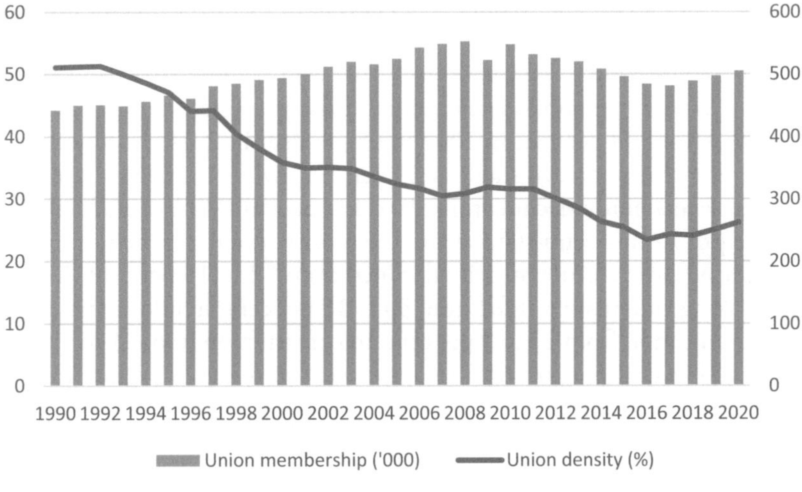

Note: employees only.
Source: OECD/AIAS (2021).

This downward trend reversed shortly following the 2008 financial crisis. Membership fell, but density increased slightly until 2011. This was probably because unionized occupations – such as those in the public sector – suffered a relatively minor contraction in terms of employment vis-à-vis non-unionized ones (Wallace et al. 2020). From 2012, however, density started to fall, as union membership dropped more than employment. In fact, the number of people in employment started to grow in 2013, while union membership continued to fall until 2016. It then recovered but remained well below 2008 levels. As a result, density had dropped to 23 per cent by 2016, before recovering slightly to 26 per cent by 2020 (CSO 2020). Such a low level of union density was seen last in the 1920s and 1930s (Roche 2008). The stark decline is important, as union density is a key determinant of the extent of collective bargaining in Ireland, given the limited role played by extension mechanisms (Maccarrone et al. 2019).

These overall trends mask further differences by sector. In general, union density is much higher in the public than in the private sector. In 2004, union density in the Irish public service was slightly below 70 per cent, whereas it hovered between 27 and 28 per cent in the private sector (Roche 2008; Walsh 2015). By 2014, density had fallen to 62.9 per cent in the public sector and to only 16.4 per cent in the private sector (Walsh 2015). As a result, the share of public sector workers in terms of total union membership rose from 40 to 55 per cent between 2004 and 2014 (ibid.). Within the public sector, union density in public administration declined from 78 per cent in 2007 to 65 per cent in 2018. In education, however, it has remained stable at 61 per cent, while the health-care sector has seen a minor decline from 49 to 43 per cent (Wallace et al. 2020). In the private and semi-state sector, the most relevant decline is in manufacturing, where union density declined from 32 to 19 per cent (ibid.). In banking and finance, it fell from 30 to 18 per cent; in information and communication from 22 to 9 per cent; in construction from 21 to 17 per cent; and in transport from 45 to 39 per cent in the same period (ibid.).

It is also interesting to break down the data by demographic characteristics. The growing importance of the public sector – where female employment is significantly higher than male – in defining trends in total union membership can account for the rising share of women as union members (Wallace et al. 2020). In 2005, women made up 48 per cent of total union membership (CSO 2020). By 2020, this percentage had climbed to 57 per cent (ibid., Figure 15.2.), although the male employment rate remains overall higher. Just as more generally across Europe (Vandaele 2019), unions in Ireland are struggling to unionize younger workers: according to CSO data, union density for the age group 15–34 was 15 per cent in 2018 by comparison with an overall density rate of 24 per cent (Wallace et al. 2020). Usually, density rises with age, reaching its highest level for workers older than 55 years (ibid.). This 'greying' of union membership poses obvious challenges for unions' prospects. Unions are also underrepresented among migrant workers, among whom density stood at 9 per cent in 2018.

Figure 15.2 Union membership by gender, 2005–2020

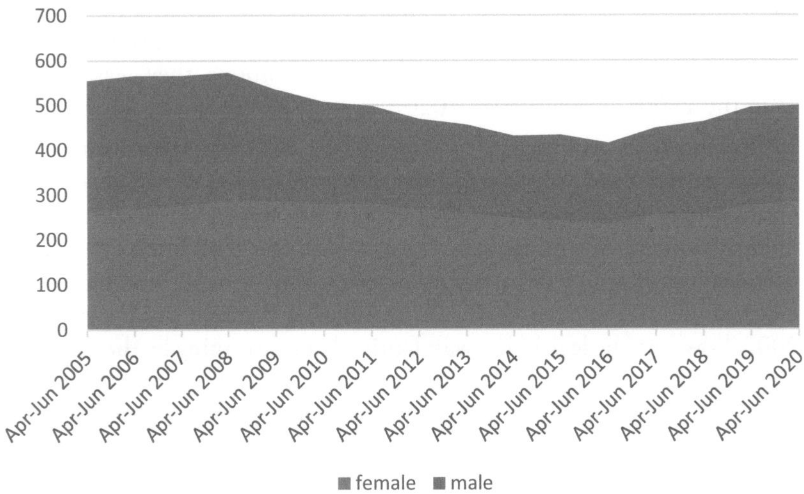

Note: employees only.
Source: Authors' elaboration on CSO (2020a) data.

Whereas the economic cycle is an important determinant in explaining trends in unionization, also structural factors – higher growth of employment in industries and occupations that are generally associated with lower unionization rates – may be at play (Ebbinghaus 2002). In the case of Ireland, these seem relevant to explain the decline that took place from the 1990s until the 2008 economic and financial crisis (Roche 2008), although evidence of the effect of structural factors for more recent years seems inconclusive (Walsh 2015, 2018).

In addition to cyclical and structural factors, institutional elements, such as the legal framework for union recognition and employers' attitudes towards collective bargaining, are relevant (Roche 2008). The Irish framework lacks an enforceable legal framework for union recognition, which hinders union presence in the workplace, arguably a key factor for unionization (Toubøl and Jensen 2014). While workers have a constitutional right to join a union, Irish law does not require employers to recognize or negotiate with them (Cullinane and Dobbins 2014). In this respect, the reliance of the Irish economy on foreign direct investment (FDI) has played a key role (D'Art and Turner 2005), as multinationals (especially of US origin) increasingly preferred to operate non-unionized workplaces (Gunnigle et al. 2009). The attitude of the government on the matter also shifted: whereas state agencies tasked with attracting FDI flows in the 1960s and the 1970s would routinely recommend that incoming multinationals recognize unions, they ceased to do so in the 1990s (Wallace et al. 2020).

To motivate employers to engage in collective bargaining, the Industrial Relations Acts 2001–2004 nevertheless provided that in workplaces where collective bargaining would not take place unions could obtain binding determinations on pay, working conditions and conflict resolution practices from the Labour Court instead (Cullinane and Dobbins 2014; Doherty 2016). Following a legal challenge by Ryanair in 2007, however, the legislation was deprived of its meaning by the Supreme Court. Its ruling accepted Ryanair's argument that it would not be bound by the determinations of the Labour Court, as Ryanair's engagement with its internal staff committees would be 'collective bargaining' in the sense of the law, despite union remarks on their lack of independence from the company management (O'Sullivan and Gunnigle 2009). Although the Industrial Relations Act was amended again in 2015, following a longstanding campaign by Irish unions, not much has changed in practice (Dobbins et al. 2020; Murphy and Turner 2020). By 2020, only four cases had been heard by the Labour Court, as a result of the new law's restrictions on unions' bringing up a case (Duffy 2019).

Attempts to provide a stronger legal basis for collective bargaining rights backed by opposition parties had been resisted by successive coalition governments. To complicate this situation further, even if a better law was to be approved by the Parliament, employers can still challenge its constitutionality in court, as happened in the case of a new law on Sectoral Employment Orders in 2020 (see section 'Collective bargaining and unions at the workplace' below). Given the difficulties in securing effective Irish labour laws, ICTU decided to campaign for an EU directive on collective bargaining (ICTU 2019). Accordingly, the confederation welcomed the Directive on 'adequate minimum wages in the European Union' (Directive (EU) 2022/2041), which also included provisions to improve collective bargaining in member states – such as Ireland – where bargaining coverage is less than 80 per cent. Although the directive has still to be implemented, it has already had some effect, with the establishment of a tripartite commission to improve the legislation on collective bargaining rights and the announcement of the phased introduction of a living wage that would be set at 60 per cent of the median wage in any given year.

In addition to an unfavourable legal framework and growing employer hostility towards union recognition, one must mention unions' own strategies towards the recruitment of new members. During the era of social partnership, as wage bargaining took place at the national level, Irish unions mostly displayed a passive attitude towards organizing and recruiting new members (Erne 2013; Roche 2008). While there was a growing awareness of this issue within the union movement already in the mid-2000s, the end of social partnership accelerated the urgency of tackling it (Murphy and Turner 2016).

Some unions have therefore adopted organizing models (Geary 2016; Hickland and Dundon 2016). SIPTU, for instance, created a new organizing department and appointed organizers from underrepresented groups, such as migrant workers (Murphy and Turner 2016). Beyond workplace organization, SIPTU and Mandate also launched public campaigns to raise awareness of poor working conditions in low-paid industries, such as hospitality, cleaning and retail, though with uneven success (Geary and Gamwell 2019; Murphy and Turner 2016; Murphy et al. 2019).

Unions have also paid more attention to the challenges brought by the rise of the platform economy. The former Irish Bank Official Association, which rebranded itself the Financial Service Union in 2016 to organize workers also in other industries (Hancock 2016), established a new branch for workers in the video game industry. SIPTU also supported the efforts of food delivery platform workers to ameliorate their working conditions.

ICTU and its affiliates have also worked towards legislative measures to tackle precarious work. Examples include the Irish Competition (Amendment) Act 2017, which extends collective bargaining rights to freelance workers, and the Employment (Miscellaneous Provisions) Act 2018 that limits the use of zero-hours contracts. By contrast to other European unions (see Bender 2020: 218), Irish unions also vetoed the inclusion of opt-out clauses by collective bargaining from the EU's equal treatment principle for atypical workers (temporary agency, fixed term, and part-time workers) during the transposition of the corresponding EU directives into Irish law.

The main challenge in terms of unionization, however, remains the organization of workers in multinational companies, which play an ever-increasing role in the Irish economy (Brazys and Regan 2017). Whereas there is a union presence in some foreign chemical and pharmaceutical companies, as well as Apple, which came to Ireland when the Irish Development Agency (IDA) was still recommending that multinationals recognize unions, the FDI-dominated sectors display very low unionization rates. Multinationals, especially of US origin, are increasingly using 'double breasting' practices, that is, adding new non-unionized plants to an older unionized establishment (Gunnigle et al. 2009). While recent developments in the US tech industry, such as the unionization drive at Google, might also have a positive impact in Ireland, it remains to be seen whether Irish unions will be able to capitalize on them.

Union resources and expenditure

The bulk of union resources in Ireland come from membership fees. As Hillery (1974: 345) observed in a rare piece on union finance in the Republic 'members cannot figure on a balance sheet, but they are nevertheless the union's real asset'. Table 15.3 shows the income of some of the main unions, highlighting the dominant role played by members' contributions.

Table 15.3 Union finances of ICTU and its five largest affiliates, 2019*

Name	Staff number	Members' contributions	Annual income
ICTU	25 (plus 7 at NERI)	2,339,825	3,582,431
SIPTU	303	33,828,115	34,632,554
Fórsa	119	16,692,574	16,752,635
INMO	74 (12 part-time)	10,751,303	11,011,301
Connect	31	3,566,802	3,610,641
Mandate	50	5,392,411	5,283,040

Note: *Or latest year available before that date; The annual income of a union might be lower than its members' contributions if other sources of income (e.g. net gains/loss on investment) contributes negatively to the total.

Source: Registrar of Friendly Societies.

Whereas Irish unions are financed by their individual members, their confederation is financed by its affiliates. As agreed at ICTU's Biennial Delegate Conference (BDC) in 2015, all ICTU-affiliated unions pay a flat fee (1,622 euros [€]), a variable amount based on the number of their members and BDC delegates, and a contribution for each member to fund the activities of the Nevin Economic Research Institute (NERI), the unions' research body. In addition, ICTU also receives government funding to sustain training activities.[5] Some of the largest unions benefit also from the funding for training, though this would constitute a minor share of their budget. The government's Department of Enterprise, Trade and Employment may also provide grants to favour union mergers, though the amount nowadays is insignificant (Frawley 2012).

Given the tight relationship between unionization and funding, staff numbers vary according to union size, as shown in Table 15.3. The headquarters for all Irish unions and the Irish offices of the British-based unions are in Dublin, but the largest unions have additional offices throughout the country. As ICTU and some unions operate also in the North, they have offices there – primarily in Belfast – too. The fact that the bulk of unions' resources come from membership also means that unions' finances have been negatively impacted by the fall in membership since the 2008 crisis, although this has happened unevenly, with unions in the private sector being more affected.

Every union has its own way of determining the level of fees, as well as the allocation of funds between the central level and the branches. Broadly speaking, fees are calculated proportionally to a member's income. The largest union, SIPTU, charges from one to five euros a week, with the lowest band being applied to those who earn under €127 per week, and the highest to those who earn more than €500 weekly. Thus, the highest rate corresponds approximately to a membership fee of €260 per year. Specific rates are applied to the unemployed, those on unpaid leave or retired. Union dues can be paid by the member to the union or, if the member chooses so and the employer allows it, can be deducted directly from the worker's salary. This is common in the public sector, though in 2010 – amid the tensions brought by the financial crisis – the government considered changing the rule that allowed deduction of union dues

---

5 Of an annual income of €3,582,431 in 2018, €900,000 came from the Department of Business, Enterprise & Innovation (ICTU Report of the Executive Council 2019).

at source (Sheehan 2010). While this was not acted upon, in 2011, the government abolished the tax relief on union subscriptions. Recently, ICTU has requested that the government reverse this decision to favour higher unionization (ICTU 2019).

As unions tend to own their own buildings, most of their spending goes on staff. Following the turn to organizing, some unions amended their rule books to specify that a share of expenditure must be devoted to organizing rather than service activities. SIPTU, for example, allocates 25 per cent of its income to strategic organizing. Unions usually have separate reserve funds to finance disputes, for instance through the provision of strike benefits, which is controlled centrally. Training is a benefit of union membership, with courses offered mostly on industrial relations issues but also on IT skills or English skills for migrant workers (Föhrer et al. 2021). The main service offered by unions is nevertheless the representation of its members through collective bargaining and assistance with individual or collective disputes.

Collective bargaining and unions at the workplace

From 1987 to 2009, the framework of collective bargaining in Ireland was dominated by social partnership, a series of seven centralized tripartite agreements that regulated pay in the public sector and in the unionized private sector. At the core of the agreements was an exchange between wage moderation and tax cuts. Over time, however, the scope was extended to cover broader areas of economic and social policy. While the agreements were voluntary, pay drift was limited, with a high degree of control exercised by national bargaining (Roche 2007). At workplace level, Ireland has a single-channel representation system, with some caveats. In unionized companies, workers are represented through their union, though the law also allows for the existence of staff internal committees, as shown in Ryanair's case. Throughout the social partnership era, the involvement of workplace union members was minimal (Doherty and Erne 2010). Whereas national agreements attempted to incentivize workplace partnership, the number of firms in the private sector that adopted local partnership agreements remained low (Roche and Teague 2014). Neither did the adoption of the EU Information and Consultation Directive help raise employees' voice, as regulatory loopholes enabled employers to devise their own 'counterbalancing forms of (pseudo) consultation' (Dundon et al. 2006: 492).

In addition to national bargaining, some industries have historically been covered by wage-setting mechanisms, which included legal extension mechanisms. The Industrial Relations Act of 1946 provided that low-paid industries where collective bargaining was not widespread could be covered by employment regulation orders (EROs), which provided legally enforceable minimum wage criteria and regulations for employment. Representing a form of de facto industry-level bargaining, EROs were drafted and submitted for approval to the Labour Court by a Joint Labour Committee (JLC) – a tripartite body composed of an equal number of representatives of employers and trade unions in the relevant industry, plus an independent chair from the Labour Court. In more recent decades, EROs applied especially to low-paid service industries, such as cleaning, security, retail and hospitality (O'Sullivan and Royle 2014). While collective agreements are not binding, unions and employers could make them legally binding by registering them with the Labour Court as a Registered Employment Agreement (REA). The most important REAs covered the construction industry. The firms represented by the Construction Industry Federation saw REAs as insurance for a level playing field. By 2008, 15 per cent of private sector employees were covered by EROs and 8 per cent by REAs (Duffy and Walsh 2011).

A national minimum wage was also introduced in 2000 within the framework of social partnership, partially out of concern that the existing legislation did not offer enough protection to low-paid workers. Initially set at £4.40 (€5.59) per hour, corresponding to 55 per cent of the median industrial wage, the national minimum wage was raised over time, usually following negotiations as part of social partnership agreements or unilateral government intervention based on a recommendation of the Labour Court (Erne 2006).

This structure of bargaining was put under considerable pressure by the outbreak of the 2008 crisis, followed by the arrival of the 'Troika' at the end of 2010. The first effect of the recession was the collapse of social partnership. In 2008, in the wake of the recession, social partners renegotiated the last agreement, introducing pay pauses (Regan 2012). In early 2009, however, the government unilaterally implemented pay cuts for public sector employees through the first of a series of 'Financial Emergency Measures in the Public Interest' (FEMPI) Acts. Following the announcement that the government would have sought further cuts to the public sector pay bill, the unions called a national public sector strike with high participation (Geary 2016; Szabó 2018). Negotiations thus reopened, but when talks reached a deadlock, the government moved to unilaterally cut public sector wages again in November 2009. As private sector employers had already announced that they would withdraw from the last national agreement, social partnership was now over. Since then, industrial relations have followed different dynamics.

In the public sector, centralized bargaining resumed in 2010 in the form of concession bargaining. Imposing a third unilateral pay cut within 20 months would have been difficult for the government. The unions had been weakened by the failure to stop wage cuts in 2009, however, and the threat of another pay cut from the government was still looming (Szabó 2018). As a result, the 2010 Croke Park Agreement was signed in which – in exchange for a pay freeze and a union commitment to public sector reform – the government excluded further pay cuts and compulsory redundancies for *existing* employees. Pay for new entrants in the public service was reduced by 10 per cent a few months later when Ireland was on the verge of entering a structural adjustment programme under the Troika.

A second concessionary agreement was signed in 2013 when Ireland was still in a bailout. Austerity policies depressed domestic demand and made the agreed deficit targets difficult to reach. Thus, at the end of 2012, the government proposed to renegotiate the Croke Park Agreement, seeking additional cuts to the public sector wage bill. The Croke Park II Agreement included pay cuts and increased working hours but was rejected by the aggregate ballot of union members (Erne 2013). Instead, a large majority of union members approved the Haddington Road Agreement (HRA), involving slightly less onerous concessions. This decision was hardly voluntary, as the government had in the meantime adopted a new FEMPI Act, which foresaw much harsher cuts in pay and worse working conditions for the members of unions refusing to sign the new agreement.

After Ireland left the bailout at the end of 2013, and the economic situation started improving markedly, public sector unions initiated a campaign for pay restoration. The Lansdowne Road Agreement (2015) and the Public Service Stability Agreement (2018) provided for a phased restoration of pay. Yet, some of the measures agreed in previous concession agreements, such as the increase in working hours, remained in place. Moreover, the negotiations failed to amend fully the two-tier pay system that had emerged throughout the recession. Some specific issues concerning recruitment of staff in the health-care sector also emerged. Hence, some underlying tensions remained, leading to strikes by teachers' and nurses' unions in recent years. At the end of 2020, in the context of the Covid-19 pandemic, a new 'transitional' agreement was reached, including pay increases between 2 and 3.4 per cent over the following two years (skewed towards the lower paid), a restoration of overtime rates, which had been cut in the recession, as well as the establishment of a committee to remove the additional working hours introduced by HRA in 2013 for those already employed at that time. The agreement has been backed by the members of most of ICTU's public service affiliates. The members of two teachers' unions (ASTI and TUI) rejected it in a ballot, however, because it does not remove fully the two-tier pay system for new entrants introduced during the recession. In the private sector and semi-state companies, the collapse of social partnership and the decentralization of collective bargaining allowed employers to impose easier adjustments at the firm level. Yet, since the end of 2010, unions in manufacturing have started to cautiously seek wage increases again, targeting firms in export-oriented sectors that had been sheltered from the worst effect of the recession, such as chemicals and pharmaceuticals (Geary 2016; Roche and Gormley 2020). Unions such as SIPTU and the TEEU sought increases in the order of 2 per cent a year, which was eminently affordable, consistent with the trends in similar industries in other EU countries and in line with the ECB's inflation target (Hickland and Dundon 2016; Roche and Gormley 2020). This strategy has since been followed by other unions, such as Mandate, the FSU and Unite, leading to the emergence of a form of coordinated pattern bargaining (Roche and Gormley 2020). The 2 per cent pay norm became further institutionalized through Labour Court recommendations in pay disputes (ibid.). While the mean of collectively agreed pay increases rose as the economic situation improved significantly in the past five years, average yearly increases remained below 3 per cent up until 2019.

Legal wage-setting mechanisms were also affected by the outbreak of the 2008 crisis and the subsequent imposition of the EU's 'new economic governance' regime (Jordan et al. 2021). As a result of a legal challenge launched by employers in the fast food sector, the High Court found JLCs 'unconstitutional' in 2011. Similarly, in 2013, the Supreme Court struck down REAs, following a legal challenge by a group of electrical contractors.

The government reintroduced JLCs with the Industrial Relations Act 2012, but with narrower scope and providing an opt-out clause from the terms set by EROs on the ground of financial hardship. To address the constitutionality issue, the Act introduced veto power for the competent minister, but thereby reduced the social partners' autonomy (Achtsioglou and Doherty 2014). Moreover, when setting EROs, JLCs had now to consider competitiveness factors as well. Crucially, there is no way to enforce new EROs if employers refuse to agree with the JLC's minimum wage rulings. New EROs have been signed only in two industries: cleaning and security. Large industries previously covered by JLCs, such as retail, hospitality and catering, are not covered by wage agreements because of employers' opposition. The reform was monitored by the Troika, as the request to review both EROs and REAs had been inserted already in the first Memorandum of Understanding.

The reform of REAs happened outside the context of the bailout, with the Industrial Relations Act 2015, which also reintroduced the 'right to bargain' legislation. While the Act re-established company-level REAs, sector-level REAs were replaced by new Sectoral Employment Orders (SEOs). SEOs have reduced scope, as they can only deal with remuneration, sick pay and pension schemes. Furthermore, while REAs were based on a collective agreement, a union or an employer organization can unilaterally ask the Labour Court to issue an SEO in a sector. Provided that the party is deemed to be representative, the Labour Court can then recommend the adoption of an SEO to the competent minister, who may or may not enact it. An opt-out clause for employers exists on the ground of financial hardship. Since the adoption of the 2015 Act, only two new SEOs have been enacted, in the construction and the electrical contracting industry, even though SIPTU, Connect and Unite intended to seek SEOs also in new industries (Higgins 2018a, 2018b). However, further legal challenges by different employers' groups against both the EROs and the SEOs have slowed-down the enforcement of new sectoral agreements.

The developments concerning extension mechanisms, coupled with the decline in union density, help to explain why collective bargaining coverage has diminished over recent decades (see Table 15.1). Estimated at 62.8 per cent in 1990, in 2009 coverage had fallen to 40.5 (OECD/AIAS 2021). It has further diminished after the Great Recession, standing at 34 per cent in 2017.

The national minimum wage has also been affected by the recession. The first Memorandum of Understanding of November 2010 committed the Fianna Fáil-led government to reduce the minimum wage by €1 per hour (a reduction of approximately 12 per cent). This cut, however, was reversed in 2011 by a new coalition government of Fine Gael and Labour, also following a campaign by unions and NGOs. Reinstatement was offset by reducing employers' social contributions to keep the effect on unit labour costs unchanged (Jordan et al. 2021). Furthermore, minimum wage development had effectively been frozen until 2015 when the government established a Low Pay Commission (LPC) composed of unions and employers' representatives, as well as academics, charged with making non-binding recommendations on the level of the national minimum wage. Between 2015 and 2019, in the context of a buoyant recovery, the LPC recommended moderate annual national minimum wage increases, which the government adopted. In 2020, however, ICTU left the LPC when other members of the committee refused to grant an increase greater than €0.1 per hour. As it stands, the Irish minimum wage remains well below the OECD threshold of adequacy for a decent standard of living (Müller and Schulten 2020).

Recently, the government asked the LPC to prepare a study on the establishment of a living wage, which should be higher than the national minimum wage. Meanwhile, union representatives have returned to the LPC. Whereas the establishment of a living wage was part of the current Fianna Fáil-Fine Gael-Green coalition's Programme for Government, this move can also be linked to the directive on adequate minimum wages in the EU (Prendergast 2021).

Industrial conflict

Irish law contains no explicit right to strike. Instead, the law provides for an immunity from sanctions for workers engaged in industrial action, if that happens within the parameters set by the law. Industrial action is currently regulated by the Industrial Relations Act 1990, which imposes rather stringent constraints. The Act prohibits political strikes, limits secondary picketing and does not provide immunity for sympathy action (Wallace et al. 2020). A secret ballot must be held for any form of industrial action, and a notice of one week should be provided to the employer (ibid.). Given these restrictions on industrial action, some unions, such as Mandate, have called for repeal of the Act. The police and defence forces are excluded from strike immunity. That said, the mere *threat* of a strike by police unions in 2016 led to pay concessions from the government.

Comparative analysis of strike action trends in Western Europe has placed Ireland in a middle position between 'strike-prone' Southern European countries and 'low-strike' Northern European countries (Vandaele 2016). Until the 1980s, strike activity in Ireland was broadly correlated with the economic cycle, with an increase in industrial action in periods of economic expansion (Wallace et al. 2020). This trend changed in the period of sustained economic growth from the 1990s, under the banner of the 'Celtic Tiger'.

Indeed, since the late 1980s, strike activity in Ireland has diminished significantly (see Figure 15.3). Looking at the frequency of strikes between 1922 and 2019, Wallace et al. (2020: 227) note that 'the number of strikes has been under 50 in only 30 years, 28 of which have occurred since the commencement of social partnership agreements in 1987'. Similar conclusions can also be drawn from the statistics on working days lost because of industrial action (ibid.; Figure 15.4). This decline in strike activity can be interpreted partly as a 'peace dividend' of centralized bargaining. Other factors were also at work, however, as strike activity diminished more generally across Western Europe in the same timeframe, despite institutional diversity (Vandaele 2016). For instance, 'structural' factors such as deindustrialization and increased competitive pressures resulting from globalization can help account for decreasing strike activity (ibid.). In the Irish case, unionization trends were affected by an unfavourable legislative framework and unions' own attitudes towards organizing during the era of social partnership.

Figure 15.3 Number of industrial disputes per year, 1985–2020

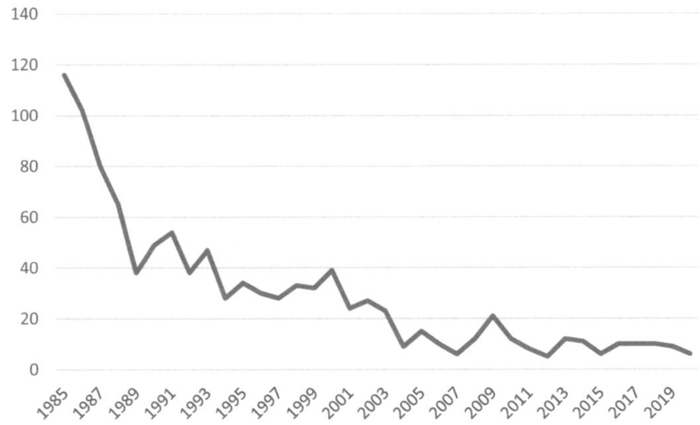

Source: CSO (2020b).

Industrial conflict remained low overall, even with the outbreak of the Great Recession and the end of social partnership, although with some isolated spikes. In early 2009, following the implementation of harsh austerity measures, unions attempted to coordinate a general strike. The attempt failed as some did not reach the required majority in strike ballots, most notably IMPACT, while others did not hold ballots at all (Geary 2016). More successful was a public sector general strike that took place a few months later, with approximately 265,000 workers participating (O'Kelly 2010) and involving 80 per cent of all public sector workers (Szabó 2018). This was the largest one-day strike in Irish history (Geary 2016). A second day of strikes was postponed following the reopening of negotiations with the government. The collapse of negotiations led to a new round of unilateral pay cuts for public service employees. Unions responded with prolonged work-to-rule, which triggered significant disruptions, for example in the passport office.

With the re-emergence of national collective bargaining in the public sector in 2010, however, industrial conflict dropped significantly. In the private sector, after the end of social partnership, ICTU and IBEC signed a protocol that 'prioritized job retention, competitiveness and orderly dispute resolution' (Roche and Gormley 2018: 447). Whereas by the end of 2009 the number of days not worked because of industrial action had reached 200 per 1,000 employees, it had fallen to only two per 1,000 employees by 2011 (Geary 2016). Strike figures continued to be low also in 2012 and 2013, while Ireland was still under Troika conditionalities (see Figure 15.4). In response to the Troika's commodifying labour policy prescriptions, ICTU focused on lobbying the government, and in particular the Labour Party, which was part of the ruling coalition (Geary 2016). But some ICTU affiliates,[6] together with NGOs and community groups, created the Coalition to Protect the Lowest Paid. The Coalition campaigned to reinstate the minimum wage at its original level and to defend industry-level wage-setting institutions. Some industry-specific campaigns evolved too, such as the one organized by SIPTU to protect industry wage agreements in the cleaning sector (Geary and Gamwell 2019).

Strike activity recovered slightly after the beginning of the economic recovery (Figure 15.4). The years 2016 and 2017 saw several strikes in transport (tram, bus and rail services) that had both proactive (demand for pay increases) and defensive features (resistance to restructuring and downsizing). It should be noted that this industry is still characterized by a relatively high trade union density and by a comparatively higher degree of workers' structural power (Vandaele 2016). Another notable example of industrial action in transport was the 2017 strike of Ryanair pilots and aircrew, as part of a coordinated transnational campaign (Golden and Erne 2022), which led to the historic Ryanair decision to grant union recognition at long last.

The two-tier pay structure for new entrants which had been included in national public sector agreements during the crisis was challenged by teachers' strikes in 2016 and 2020. In 2019, nurses and midwifes struck for better pay and working conditions to stop the emigration of Irish health-care staff, attracting considerable public support (Szabó 2019). Retail has been characterized by a certain degree of industrial action, with strikes in different supermarket chains organized by Mandate in 2015 and 2018. In 2020, workers of the retail multinational Debenhams staged a long strike to obtain enhanced redundancy payments, following the liquidation of the company's branch in Ireland. This has been the most visible industrial action taken during the Covid-19 pandemic.

---

6 SIPTU, Mandate, Communications Workers' Union, UNITE.

Figure 15.4 Days not worked due to industrial action (per 1,000 employees) and number of workers involved (thousands), 2000–2019

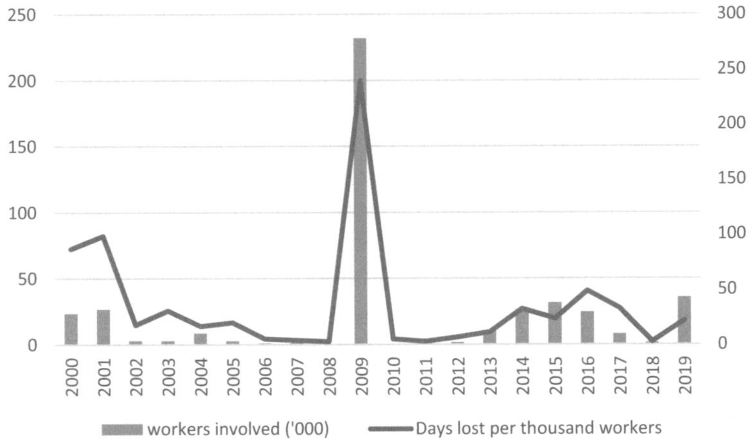

Source: CSO (2020b), data for 2019 are provisional.

Political relations

The Irish Labour Party has never been as strong as its British counterpart. Consequently, the union movement has not developed a symbiotic relationship with the party, although a handful of unions, most notably SIPTU, remained formally affiliated to it until recently. Relations between the party and the union movement were strained by Labour's stint in government in coalition with Fine Gael between 2011 and 2015, when a growing number of union members saw it as a co-manager of austerity. This led to a motion at the 2015 SIPTU Biennial Conference asking the union to disaffiliate from Labour. In any case, the Labour Party amended its constitution in 2017 and ceased all organizational affiliations. In turn, SIPTU decided to retain its political fund, but that it now could be used to support any union-related candidates, not only those running for Labour (Wall 2017). This also reflects the electoral growth in recent years of parties of the radical left (People before Profit – Solidarity) and the left-wing republican party Sinn Feín (SF), which is affiliated to the left-wing GUE group in the European Parliament and became the biggest party in the Irish parliament in 2020. SIPTU is currently one of the few Irish unions retaining a political fund, along with the two teachers' unions ASTI and INTO (Registrar of Friendly Societies 2019).

In terms of broader relations of the union movement with the polity, despite the collapse of the tripartite social partnership arrangements in 2009, many union leaders still see the partnership era in a positive light, also given the privileged access to government and influence on policymaking it granted. Over time, social partnership agreements became increasingly more comprehensive, and several tripartite bodies were set up to address different policy issues. But the social partnership era also saw a significant decline in union organizational power because of the decline of union density, while the framework for union recognition was weak and employment protection legislation remained among the lowest among the OECD countries. Additionally, there was also a significant reduction of the wage share (Allen 2007; Erne 2008). Therefore, some scholars wonder whether, retrospectively, social partnership was a 'Faustian Bargain' to make Ireland more competitive (D'Art and Turner 2011).

The picture of Irish unions' relations with the polity after the outbreak of the 2008 crisis and the end of social partnership is one of continuity and change. On one hand, the trends in industrial conflict over the past decade show that, even after the end of national tripartite agreements union leaders have, with some exceptions, continued to favour a logic of influence over one of mobilization in response to the austerity measures implemented by successive governments since the outbreak of the Great Recession (Geary 2016). On the other hand, faced with a decline in their institutional power, unions have been pushed to look for other sources of power, such as societal power. The end of tripartite agreements has also highlighted the urgency of addressing the issue of recruitment and organization in response to falling unionization. Moreover, while centralized bargaining re-emerged in the public sector, private sector unions have instead pursued strategies of local 'pattern bargaining' which have led to greater involvement of local members and shop stewards in the negotiation of agreements (Roche and Gormley 2018, 2020).

Given the above, a return of social partnership in the form of pre-2009 cross-sectoral wage agreements is unlikely. After some years of limited involvement of social partners in policymaking, however, both the government and employer organizations now seem readier to re-engineer forms of national social dialogue to address issues affecting the competitiveness of the Irish economy, such as housing and infrastructure. It might not be a coincidence that Fianna Fáil's return to power in 2020, as part of an historic 'post-civil-war' coalition with Fine Gael and the Greens, has also led to the re-establishment of a social dialogue unit within the Department of the Taoiseach (Prime Minister). The concrete exchange that would underlie a possible new social pact remains to be seen, however, as much as whether and how the union movement will decide to be involved.

Another aspect that might influence the future relationship between the union movement and politics in Ireland is the progressive re-alignment of the Irish political system towards a more traditional left–right divide, which has become evident over the past decade. What is more, the average Irish voter now leans towards the centre-left (Müller and Regan 2021). Although a viable left-wing coalition has not yet emerged, this might lead to changes in Irish unions' political involvement.

Societal power

The end of social partnership forced the Irish union movement to seek other sources of power. Beyond working on organizational power, unions attempted to boost their societal power. This has happened both through an improved use of public campaigning and communication, and through coalition-building with social movements and NGOs (Geary 2016).

With the outbreak of the 2008 crisis, the union movement faced a very hostile media environment (Mercille 2014). The social partnership process was identified as one of the culprits of the recession in Ireland, and part of the media began to denounce 'over-paid' public sector employees (Roche 2009). An analysis conducted by ICTU of editorial commentaries in the print press in the final quarter of 2009 found almost 90 per cent of union press coverage to be hostile (Culpepper and Regan 2014). Moreover, ICTU's alternative plan to austerity received very little traction in the public debate (Geary 2016). This seemed to have a feedback effect on public opinion: the 2009 'Eurobarometer' survey registered an increase in the number of people who associated a negative meaning with the term 'trade union' (Figure 15.5).

Figure 15.5 Public perception of trade unions in Ireland and the EU, 2006–2018

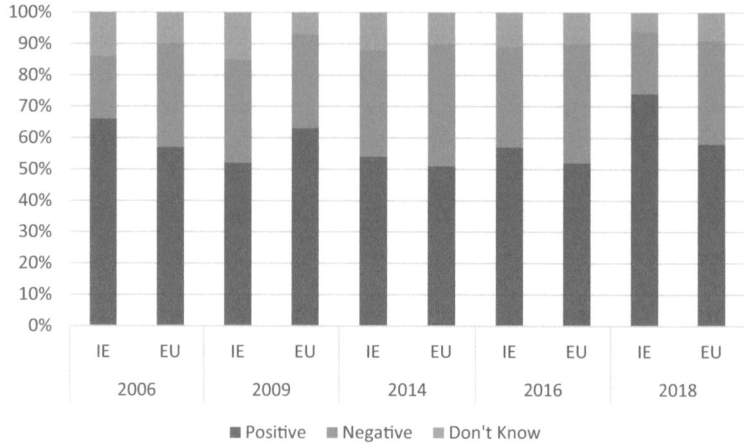

Source: Eurobarometer reports. (Some Eurobarometer surveys contain the question, 'Could you please tell me for each of the following, whether the term brings to mind something very positive, fairly positive, fairly negative or very negative?', including the term 'trade union'.)

In turn, Irish unions tried to strengthen their position in the battle of ideas, for instance, by establishing the NERI socio-economic research institute in 2012 (Geary 2016). Public sector unions also tried to improve their internal dialogue with their own members and their external communication activities to counteract media stereotypes about public sector workers (Harbor 2011). Meanwhile, the negative effect of the recession on public perception of unions seems to have disappeared. In 2018, 74 per cent of Irish respondents to the Eurobarometer survey associated a positive meaning with the term 'trade union', well above the values of 2006 and the EU average (see Figure 15.5). Interestingly, the positive perception is highest among young people aged 15–24.

Attempts to reach a broader public opinion have also been part of unions' organizing campaigns over the past decade, inspired by examples such as the US 'Justice for Janitors'. A public campaign in cleaning launched by SIPTU was part of a successful effort to restore an industry-level wage agreement in the industry. In hospitality, characterized by low union density and employers' hostility towards unions (Geary and Gamwell 2019), SIPTU launched a 'Fair Hotels' campaign based on an ethical consumerism approach, inviting consumers to support hotels employing fair work practices (ibid.; Murphy and Turner 2016). A similar approach was followed in Mandate's 'Fair Shop' campaign, launched in 2012. The effectiveness of this type of campaigning in relation to organizing remains unclear, however (Geary and Gamwell 2019; Murphy and Turner 2016). These campaigns also involved coalition-building with civil society organizations, such as the Migrant Rights Centre Ireland and the National Women's Council, which was also part of the 'Coalition to Protect the Lowest Paid', in which unions and NGOs joined forces to defend minimum wage institutions during the Troika conditionality (Maccarrone 2021). More recently, Irish union leaders joined an international campaign coalition for a four-day working week (https://fourdayweek.ie).

Unions also took part in social movements with a focus that went beyond traditional industrial relations issues. In 2014, the CPSU, the CWU, Mandate, Opatsi and Unite engaged – along with Sinn Fein and radical left parties – in the popular 'Right2Water' movement, which successfully fought against the introduction of water charges (Hearne 2015). More recently, ICTU and several affiliates have supported the 'Raise the Roof' campaign, which aims to tackle the dramatic housing crisis that the country is currently experiencing. Likewise, unions successfully supported a Yes-vote in both the 2015 gay marriage referendum and in the 2018 referendum on the right to abortion. In 2012, ICTU also supported the introduction of a Financial Transaction Tax (ICTU 2012), by contrast to the Labour Party, which as part of the governing coalition was afraid to question Ireland's status as a low-tax destination. Even so, in future, Irish unions arguably could play a greater role in European trade union campaigns for a fairer corporation tax system at the EU and OECD levels (Carr 2020).

Trade union policies towards the European Union

Gumbrell-McCormick and Hyman (2013: 177) note that 'as in several other member states, unions in Ireland have shifted from a primarily anti-EU stance to support for further integration'. When a referendum was held about joining the European Economic Community (EEC) in 1973, ICTU campaigned for a No-vote. Irish unions justified their position with concerns about the EEC's potentially negative effects on the weak Irish industrial system rather than on class-based arguments

(Golden forthcoming). Subsequently, ICTU did not take sides in the referendum on the Single European Act[7] but supported the Maastricht, Amsterdam and Nice treaties. In the 2000s, however, trade union Euroscepticism grew again (Béthoux et al. 2018). While a majority of ICTU's executive council voted to support the Lisbon Treaty, SIPTU did not forward this recommendation to its members, which was 'widely seen as a tacit call to reject the Treaty' (Gumbrell-McCormick and Hyman 2013: 178). Other unions expressing criticisms were Unite and the TEEU (Golden forthcoming). The debate was shaped by two major industrial relations disputes, involving the companies GAMA and Irish Ferries, which highlighted issues of compliance with the minimum wage legislation and fuelled unions' fears of a 'race to the bottom' because of increased labour mobility in a context of weak employment protection legislation (Béthoux et al. 2018). Fears of social dumping were also triggered by the '*Laval* quartet' of rulings of the European Court of Justice. In 2008, Irish voters rejected the Lisbon Treaty.

When a second referendum was held in 2009, the economic context had changed completely as the recession hit Ireland hard. In addition, the Labour Party promised to draft a new Industrial Relations Act as a prospective member of the next government that would implement the right to collective bargaining, if ICTU and SIPTU would actively campaign for a Yes-vote on Lisbon II, which they did (ibid.). Three years later, a referendum was held on the 'Fiscal Treaty' while Ireland was still under the 'Troika' conditionality. While the ETUC, for the first time in its history, opposed an EU Treaty, ICTU – while critical of the Treaty's austeritarian orientation – did not issue such a recommendation to its members (ibid.). The leadership of the Congress justified this choice on the grounds that access to the European Stability Mechanisms was conditional on ratification of the Fiscal Treaty (ibid.).

The participation of Irish unions in European affairs has traditionally been quite low (Golden forthcoming; Gumbrell-McCormick and Hyman 2013). Although unions are involved in European trade union federations and European works councils (Föhrer and Erne 2017), 'neither the Congress nor any of its affiliates has a dedicated international resource for Ireland, which is most unusual in the European Trade Union

7 As all changes to the Irish Constitution must be approved by referendum, the Supreme Court ruled in 1987 that the same would also apply to most European Treaty changes (Golden forthcoming).

Movement' (ICTU 2011: 13). This reduced participation in European affairs was reflected also in a limited involvement of Irish unions in European and transnational action at the height of the Eurozone crisis, even though Ireland was among the 'programme countries' which received conditional financial assistance (Maccarrone 2021).

In more recent years, however, both the Congress and some of its affiliates became more involved in European affairs. Esther Lynch, a former ICTU officer, was elected ETUC Confederal Secretary in 2015, to then become General Secretary in 2022, the first Irish trade unionist to do so. Moreover, the Tenth Congress of the European Federation of Public Service Unions (EPSU) was held in Dublin in 2019. There have also been instances of transnational collective action that involved Irish unions, such as the successful transnational campaign of Ryanair pilots that eventually forced Ryanair to recognize unions in 2017. Given the difficulties encountered in securing collective bargaining rights at the national level, ICTU is now looking to work harder at the European level to address this issue and it has strongly supported the directive on the European minimum wage.

Another aspect on which Irish unions are becoming more active at the EU level is that of European works councils (EWCs). Following Brexit, several multinational companies have relocated their headquarters from the United Kingdom to Dublin (EWC News 2021). This also reveals a poor transposition of the EU EWC Directive, however, as currently unions in Ireland have no right to take a company to court to compel it to allow the establishment of an EWC. For this reason, SIPTU asked the EU Commission to review the implementation of the EWC directive in Ireland (ibid.).

In terms of involvement in the consultation process within the new EU economic governance framework, ICTU's position has evolved over time. Irish unions were very critical of the process of consultation during the Troika conditionality, to the extent that, in 2012, the then president of SIPTU proposed boycotting further meetings with the international institutions (Sheehan 2012). When Ireland left the bailout programme at the end of 2013, the country was inserted within the ordinary procedures of the European Semester. In a context perceived as more favourable, ICTU tried to utilize the consultation process of the Semester to highlight some issues, such as precariousness and low pay, and generally as an additional opportunity to influence policymaking after the end of social partnership.

Conclusions

The picture that emerged after the collapse of social partnership in 2009, following the outbreak of the Great Recession, is one of both continuity and change. In response to the austerity measures that successive governments implemented in turn, ICTU and its major affiliates have, after a brief period of industrial strife in 2009, favoured a strategy of concession bargaining to at least remain at the bargaining table. As a result, the level of industrial conflict has remained low over the past decade. Conversely, however, the collapse of national wage agreements also accelerated processes of institutional change within the union movement. Many unions have re-organized themselves and turned towards new organizing and campaigning models. At the same time, Irish union density and membership is lower than a decade ago, although the data shows a small recovery in the most recent years on both accounts. Recent survey data also shows that public perceptions towards unions are today positive and above the EU average, especially among young people. So, where are Irish unions heading? Which of the union futures outlined by Visser (2019) – marginalization, substitution, dualization and revitalization – matches Irish unions?

Our answer is, none of them. We were simply not able to put the Irish union future into one box without suppressing important empirical evidence. The cycles of union protest and acquiescence in Ireland during the past decade do allow less Manichean conclusions (Erne 2019: 259), but only if we use Visser's typology 'as a heuristic tool to understand the tension between contention and interest intermediation that are present in all unions: and not as a classification device to put different unions into distinct boxes' (ibid.)

Irish unions have been put under pressure but have not been marginalized. As most of their membership is concentrated in the public sector and in traditional industries, however, they must find ways to counter the widespread union substitution drives that multinational corporations employ to prevent unionization. The successful transnational collective action in the Ryanair case illustrates that gaining union recognition is possible even in an anti-union company. Even so, the future of the Irish labour movement depends on comparable successes in other Ireland-based multinationals. In this respect, some hope might come from the news that a large group of Google's workers in Ireland recently unionized (Rogan, 2023).

Irish unions have also effectively resisted the introduction of opt-out clauses in Irish law from the EU equal pay requirements for temporary agency and other atypical workers. Hence, dualization is hardly the most likely union future.

Finally, some unions have also strengthened their collaboration with social movements or framed their campaigns for better working conditions in a way that would appeal to the wider public, as happened in the 2019 Irish nurses' strike. But even if union density has registered a slight increase since 2016, it remains to be seen whether these initiatives will be able to reverse the long-lasting decline in unionization and lead to revitalization.

References

All links were checked on 3 May 2021.

Achtsioglou E. and Doherty M. (2014) There must be some way out of here: the crisis, labour rights and Member States in the eye of the storm, European Law Journal, 20 (2), 219–240.

Allen K. (1997) Fianna Fáil and Irish Labour: 1926 to the present, London, Pluto Press.

Allen K. (2007) The corporate takeover of Ireland, Dublin, Irish Academic Press.

Bender B. (2020) Politisch-ökonomische Konfliktlinien im sich wandelnden Wohlfahrtsstaat. Positionierung deutscher Interessenverbände von 2000 bis 2014, Wiesbaden, Springer VS.

Béthoux E., Erne R. and Golden D. (2018) A primordial attachment to the nation? French and Irish workers and trade unions in past EU referendum debates, British Journal of Industrial Relations, 56 (3), 656–678.

Brazys S. and Regan A. (2017) The politics of capitalist diversity in Europe: explaining Ireland's divergent recovery from the euro crisis, Perspectives on Politics, 15 (2), 411–427.

Carr L. (2020) Breaking the impasse on corporate taxation, Social Europe, 27 November 2020. https://www.socialeurope.eu/breaking-the-impasse-on-corporate-taxation a large group of Google's workers in Ireland recently unionized (Rogan, 2023).

CSO (2020a) Labour force survey – Union membership Q2 2005 – Q2 2020, Cork, Central Statistics Office.

CSO (2020b) Industrial Disputes, Cork, Central Statistics Office.

Cullinane N. and Dobbins A. (2014) Considering the impact of the 'right to bargain' legislation in Ireland: a review, Industrial Law Journal, 43 (1), 52–83.

Culpepper P.D. and Regan A. (2014) Why don't governments need trade unions anymore? The death of social pacts in Ireland and Italy, Socio-Economic Review, 12 (4), 723–745.

D'Art D. and Turner T. (2005) Union recognition and partnership at work: a new legitimacy for Irish trade unions?, Industrial Relations Journal, 36 (2), 121–139.

D'Art D. and Turner T. (2011) Irish trade unions under social partnership: a Faustian bargain?, Industrial Relations Journal, 42 (2), 157–173.

Darlington R. (2008) Syndicalism and the transition to communism: an international comparative analysis, Aldershot, Ashgate.

Dobbins T., Cullinane N. and Sheehan B. (2020) Ireland's conundrum on union bargaining rights: assessing the Industrial Relations Amendment Act 2015, Industrial Relations Journal, 51(1–2), 75–91.

Doherty M. (2014) Can the patient survive the cure? Irish labour law in the austerity era, European Labour Law Journal, 5 (1), 81–94.

Doherty M. (2016) New morning? Irish labour law post-austerity, Dublin University Law Journal, 39 (1), 104–125.

Doherty M. and Erne R. (2010) Mind the gap: national and local partnership in the Irish public sector, Industrial Relations Journal, 41 (5), 461–478.

Duffy K. (2019) Trade unions and their collective bargaining conundrum: where to next?, Industrial Relations News, (12), 28 April 2019. https://www.irn.ie/article/24539.

Duffy K. and Walsh F. (2011) Report of independent review of employment regulation orders and registered employment agreement wage setting mechanisms, Dublin, Department of Business, Enterprise and Innovation.

Dundon T., Curran D., Ryan P. and Maloney M. (2006) Conceptualising the dynamics of employee information and consultation: evidence from the Republic of Ireland, Industrial Relations Journal, 37 (5), 492–512.

Ebbinghaus B. (2002) Trade unions' changing role: membership erosion, organisational reform, and social partnership in Europe, Industrial Relations Journal, 33 (5), 465–483.

Erne R. (2006) A contentious consensus: the establishment of the national minimum wage in Ireland, in Schulten T., Bispinck R. and Schäfer C. (eds) Minimum wages in Europe, Brussels, ETUI, 65–83.

Erne R. (2008) European unions: labor's quest for a transnational democracy, Ithaca, Cornell University Press.

Erne R. (2013) Let's accept a smaller slice of a shrinking cake. The Irish Congress of Trade Unions and Irish public sector unions in crisis, Transfer, 19 (3), 425–430.

Erne R. (2019) Social movements or state apparatus, in Kiess J.M. and Seeliger M. (eds) Trade unions and European integration: a question of optimism and pessimism?, Abingdon, Routledge, 259–266.

EWC News (2021) Mass exodus to Irish EWC jurisdiction, EWC News, (1), 14 April 2021. https://www.ewc-news.com/en012021.pdf.

Föhrer B. and Erne R. (2017) Training programmes for European works councillors in Germany, in Ireland and at EU level: transnational trade union action through education?, European Journal of Industrial Relations, 23 (3), 243–259.

Föhrer B., Erne R. and Finlay G. (2021) Transnational competence: a transformative tool? A comparison of German and Irish political trade union education programs, Labour Studies Journal, 46(2), 182–212.

Frawley M. (2012) Secretary-general defends union training grants, Industrial Relations News, (16), 4 April 2012. https://www.irn.ie/article/15812.

Geary J. (2016) Economic crisis, austerity and trade union responses: the Irish case in comparative perspective, European Journal of Industrial Relations, 22 (2), 131–147.

Geary J. and Gamwell S. (2019) An American solution to an Irish problem: a consideration of the material conditions that shape the architecture of union organizing, Work, Employment and Society, 33 (2), 191–207.

Golden D. and Erne R. (2022) Ryanair pilots: Unlikely pioneers of transnational collective action. European Journal of Industrial Relations, 28(4), 451–469.

Golden D. (2023, forthcoming) Labour Euroscepticism: Italian and Irish Unions' changing preferences towards the EU, London: ECPR Press.

Gumbrell-McCormick R. and Hyman R. (2013) Trade unions in Western Europe: hard times, hard choices, Oxford, Oxford University Press.

Gunnigle P., Lavelle J. and McDonnell A. (2009) Subtle but deadly? Union avoidance through 'double breasting' among multinational companies, in Lewin D., Kaufman B.E. and Gollan P. (eds) Advances in industrial and labor relations, Vol. 18, Bingley, Emerald Group Publishing, 51–73.

Hancock C. (2016) Irish Bank Officials' Association to rebrand itself, Irish Times, 6 May 2016.

Harbor B. (2011) And now for the bad news: trade union internal communications in a crisis, Industrial Relations News, (17), 4 May 2011. https://www.irn.ie/article/14759.

Hardiman N. (1992) The state and economic interests: Ireland in comparative perspective, Proceedings of the British Academy, (79), 329–358.

Hearne R. (2015) The Irish water war, Interface, 7 (1), 309–321.

Hickland E. and Dundon T. (2016) The shifting contours of collective bargaining in the manufacturing sector in the Republic of Ireland: government, employer and union responses since the economic crisis, European Journal of Industrial Relations, 22 (3), 235–249.

Higgins C. (2015) Congress private sector body revived, but no radical change in pay strategy, Industrial Relations News, (40), 4 November 2015. https://www.irn.ie/article/20011.

Higgins C. (2018a) Connect union seeks to expand SEO model into other sectors, Industrial Relations News (37), 11 October 2018. https://www.irn.ie/article/23766.

Higgins C. (2018b) SIPTU looking to expand use of sectoral wage orders across private sector, Industrial Relations News, (42), 15 November 2018. https://www.irn.ie/article/23929.

Hillery B. (1974) Trade union finance in the Republic of Ireland, Economic and Social Review, 5 (3), 345–352.

ICTU (2009) Report of the Executive Council Biennial Delegate Conference, Tralee, 7–10 July.

ICTU (2011) Report of the Commission on the Irish Trade Union Movement, Dublin, ICTU.

ICTU (2012) The case for a financial transaction tax, Dublin, ICTU.

ICTU (2019a) Report of Executive Council Biennial Delegate Conference, Dublin, 2-4 July.

ICTU (2019b) Realising the transformative effect of social dialogue and collective bargaining in Ireland. Route to Reform, Dublin, ICTU.

Jordan J., Maccarrone V. and Erne R. (2021) Towards a socialization of the EU's new economic governance regime? EU labour policy interventions in Germany, Ireland, Italy and Romania (2009–2019), British Journal of Industrial Relations, 59 (1), 191–213.

Maccarrone V. (2021) Common pressure and uneven trajectories. The commodifying impact of the European Union's new economic governance regime on Irish and Italian industrial relations, PhD thesis, Dublin, University College Dublin.

Maccarrone V., Erne R. and Regan A. (2019) Ireland: life after social partnership, in Müller T., Vandaele K. and Waddington J. (eds) Collective bargaining in Europe: towards an endgame, Brussels, ETUI, 315–335.

Mercille J. (2014) The role of the media in fiscal consolidation programmes: the case of Ireland, Cambridge Journal of Economics, 38 (2), 281–300.

Müller S. and Regan A. (2021) Are Irish voters moving to the left?, Irish Political Studies, 36:4, 535–555.

Müller T. and Schulten T. (2020) The European minimum wage will come – but how?, Social Europe, 15 September 2020. https://www.socialeurope.eu/the-european-minimum-wage-will-come-but-how.

Murphy C. and Turner T. (2016) Organising precarious workers: can a public campaign overcome weak grassroots mobilisation at workplace level?, Journal of Industrial Relations, 58 (5), 589–607.

Murphy C. and Turner T. (2020) Tipping the scales for labour in Ireland? Collective bargaining and the industrial relations (Amendment) Act 2015, Industrial Law Journal, 49 (1), 113–134.

Murphy C. et al. (2019) Trade union responses to zero hours work in Ireland, Industrial Relations Journal, 50 (5–6), 468–485.

Ní Lochlaínn A. (2005) A question of allegiance? Ideology, agency and structure: British-based union in Ireland 1922–1960, PhD thesis, Florence, European University Institute.

O'Connor E. (2011) A labour history of Ireland 1824–2000, Dublin, University College Dublin Press.

OECD/AIAS (2021) OECD/AIAS ICTWSS database. https://www.oecd.org/employment/ictwss-database.htm.

O'Sullivan M. and Gunnigle P. (2009) Bearing all the hallmarks of oppression: union avoidance in Europe's largest low-cost airline, Labor Studies Journal, 34 (2), 252–270.

O'Sullivan M. and Royle T. (2014) Everything and nothing changes: fast-food employers and the threat to minimum wage regulation in Ireland, Economic and Industrial Democracy, 35 (1), 27–47.

O'Kelly K.P. (2010) The end of social partnership in Ireland?, Transfer, 16 (3), 425–429.

Prendergast A. (2021) Green light for move from minimum wage to living wage, Industrial Relations News, (14), 15 April 2021. https://www.irn.ie/article/26916.

Regan A. (2012) The political economy of social pacts in the EMU: Irish liberal market corporatism in crisis, New Political Economy, 17 (4), 465–491.

Roche W.K., Larragy J. and Ashmore J. (2000) Ireland, in Ebbinghaus B. and Visser J. (eds) Trade Unions in Western Europe since 1945, London, Palgrave Macmillan, 339–369.

Roche W.K. (2007) Social partnership in Ireland and new social pacts, Industrial Relations, 46 (3), 395–425.

Roche W.K. (2008) The trend of unionisation in Ireland since the mid-1990s, in Hastings T. (ed.) The state of the unions: challenges facing organised labour in Ireland, Dublin, The Liffey Press, 17–46.

Roche W.K. and Gormley T. (2018) The advent of pattern bargaining in Irish industrial relations, Industrial Relations Journal, 48 (5/6), 442–462.

Roche W.K. and Gormley T. (2020) The durability of coordinated bargaining: crisis, recovery and pay fixing in Ireland, Economic and Industrial Democracy, 41 (2), 481–505.

Roche W.K. and Teague P. (2014) Successful but unappealing: fifteen years of workplace partnership in Ireland, International Journal of Human Resource Management, 25 (6), 781–794.

Roche W.K. (2009) Social partnership: from Lemass to Cowen, Economic and Social Review, 40 (2), 183–205.

Rogan A. (2023) `Large group' of Irish Google workers turn to union as tech crunch bites. Business Post, 5 February 2023.

Sheehan B. (2010) Union leaders & government officials meet, but long road ahead, Industrial Relations News, (4), 27 January 2010. https://www.irn.ie/article/13302.

Sheehan B. (2012) SIPTU leader wants Congress boycott of Troika 'bag-men', Industrial Relations News, (39), 24 October 2012. https://www.irn.ie/article/16476.

Szabó I. (2018) Trade unions and the sovereign power of the state. A comparative analysis of employer offensives in the Danish and Irish public sectors, Transfer, 24 (2), 163–178.

Szabó I. (2019) The Duty to Strike, Jacobin, 18 February 2019. https://www.jacobinmag.com/2019/02/ireland-nurses-strike-public-sector-austerity

Teague P. and Donaghey J. (2009) Why has Irish social partnership survived?, British Journal of Industrial Relations, 47 (1), 55–78.

Toubøl J. and Jensen C.S. (2014) Why do people join trade unions? The impact of workplace union density on union recruitment, Transfer, 20 (1), 135–154.

Vandaele K. (2016) Interpreting strike activity in western Europe in the past 20 years: the labour repertoire under pressure, Transfer, 22 (3), 277–294.

Vandaele K. (2019) Bleak prospects: mapping trade union membership in Europe since 2000, Brussels, ETUI.

Visser J. (2019) Trade unions in the balance, ACTRAV Working Paper, Geneva, ILO.

Von Prondzynski F. (1998) Ireland: corporatism revived, in Ferner A. and Hyman R. (eds) Changing industrial relations in Europe, 2nd edn, Oxford, Blackwell Publishing, 55–73.

Wallace J., Gunnigle P. and O'Sullivan M. (2020) Industrial relations in Ireland, 5th edition, Dublin, Institute of Public Administration.

Walsh F. (2015) Union membership in Ireland since 2003, Journal of the Statistical and Social Inquiry Statistical Society of Ireland, 44, 86–100.

Walsh F. (2018) Trade union density in Ireland since 2003: what do the statistics tell us?, Industrial Relations News, (27), 12 July 2018. https://www.irn.ie/article/23509

Wall M. (2017) SIPTU to keep political fund despite break from Labour Party, Irish Times, 25 May 2017. https://www.irishtimes.com/news/ireland/irish-news/siptu-to-keep-political-fund-despite-break-from-labour-party-1.3096827.

Abbreviations

ASTI Association of Secondary Teachers in Ireland
CPSU Civil and Public Services Union
CSO Central Statistics Office

CWU	Communication Workers' Union
ECB	European Central Bank
ERO	Employment Regulation Order
ETUC	European Trade Union Confederation
FDI	Foreign direct investment
FF	Fianna Fáil
FG	Fine Gael
FSU	Financial Service Union
IBEC	Irish Business and Employers' Confederation
IBOA	Irish Bank Officials' Association
ICTU	Irish Congress of Trade Unions
IMPACT	Irish Municipal, Public and Civil Trade Union
IMO	Irish Medical Association
INMO	Irish Nurses and Midwifes Association
INTO	Irish National Teachers' Organisation
ITGWU	Irish Transport and General Workers' Union
ITUC	Irish Trade Union Congress
JLC	Joint labour committee
MoU	Memorandum of understanding
NERI	Nevin Economic Research Institute
NMW	National Minimum Wage
PSEU	Public Service Executive Union
REA	Registered Employment Agreement
SEO	Sectoral Employment Order
SF	Sinn Feín
SIPTU	Services, Industrial, Professional and Technical Union
TEEU	Technical Engineering and Electrical Union
TUC	Trades Union Congress
TUI	Teachers' Union of Ireland

Chapter 16

Trade unions in Italy: Pluralism and resilience

Salvo Leonardi and Roberto Pedersini

The Italian system of industrial relations is characterized by a number of original traits, viewed in a comparative perspective. One such trait is the high degree of voluntarism and abstention of law – in the private sector, at least – on all the main pillars of the system: social partners' representativeness, the effects of collective agreements, minimum wages, the right to strike and employee participation. Over the post-war decades, trade unions moved from complete marginalization in the 1950s to the longest and most intense cycle of class struggles in the West, after the 1969 watershed (Crouch and Pizzorno 1977) and until the mid-1980s, when their institutional recognition finally attained the level of the most mature national systems (Bertuccelli et al. 2008). Since then, union power and density have declined, but more slowly than in many other countries, stabilizing around a relatively high 35–36 per cent (see Table 16.1). The three historical union confederations established in the first post-war decade – the General Italian Confederation of Labour (CGIL, *Confederazione Generale Italiana del Lavoro*), the Italian Confederation of the Workers' Trade Unions (CISL, *Confederazione Italiana Sindacati dei Lavoratori*) and the Italian Union of Labour (UIL, *Unione Italiana del Lavoro*) – remain the most representative labour organizations, dealing with a dozen peak employer associations. Their associative power resources are quite solid, with almost 12 million members, including pensioners, and so are their organizational structures and finances. CGIL, CISL and UIL remain committed to European Union (EU) integration, and their members offer some limited support to right-wing nationalists and populists, but less than in the past (Leonardi and Carrieri 2020). They often cooperate with other social movement organizations, especially in support of the social and economic integration of immigrants and refugees and for a fair transition to a green and decarbonized economy (Rugiero 2019).

The two-tier collective bargaining structure – with the national industry level prevailing over company bargaining – can still be considered centrally organized (Leonardi and Pedersini 2018) (see Table 16.1). Bargaining coverage is high and very stable at over 80 per cent, as is the ratio between minimum and median wages, which is one of the highest among the most industrialized countries (Garnero 2017). Although their political and societal power appears to be weakening, the unions are very active. They constantly press the government for social concertation, and promote campaigns, actions and mass rallies as they lobby for tax, welfare and labour law reforms. Important and sometimes successful battles focus on advocacy for over-exploited migrant workers, for instance in agriculture, aimed at obtaining more severe norms and penalties for unscrupulous employers, or on the recognition of employee status, with all the attendant rights, for platform workers in food delivery and logistics. They also support the introduction of conditional constraints on delocalization.

Table 16.1 Principal characteristics of trade unionism in Italy

	1980s	2000	2019
Total trade union membership (active members)	6,349,000	5,262,000	5,865,000
Women as a share of total membership	35.0 %	38.3 %	45.0 %
Gross union density	62.8 %	72.7 %	61.1 %
Net union density	43.8 %	34.8 %	32.5 %
Number of confederations	5*	7*	8**
Number of affiliated unions (federations)	82	52	47
Number of independent unions (confederations)	2	4	5
Collective bargaining coverage	80 %	80 %	80 %
Principal level of collective bargaining	Industry		
Days not worked because of industrial action per 1,000 workers	1,135	59	n.a.

Note: * Visser (2019); ** number of confederations regarded as representative in the public administration (ARAN 2019).

Source: Appendix A1.

The challenges of representing and organizing the new world of work, which often involves young people and precarious workers, is shown by the slow downward trend in membership, coupled with the increase in members' average age, and the differences in unionization by type of contract and level of education (Carrieri and Feltrin 2016; Leonardi 2018). Nowadays, a growing number of small workplaces, especially in private services, are short of representation, while the bogus self-employed are excluded from full legal and social protections. At the same time, the collective bargaining system, though still strong, is threatened by an unprecedented proliferation of industry-wide agreements signed by new actors of uncertain or nil representativeness (CNEL 2019). Industrial conflict is limited mainly to specific industries, in which minor unions compete intensively to gain visibility and public recognition. Unions' reputation in society appears, at least according to media surveys and polls, to have become tarnished. The old and once strong linkages with political parties have vanished almost completely, with broad sectors of the working class left without political representation. The intensive period of tripartite social pacts in the 1990s faded into weaker social dialogue, comprising mainly bilateral consultations, if not fully replaced by government unilateralism. Timid but important signs of a reversing trend emerged in 2020, however, when unions played a key role in managing the social and economic impact of the Covid-19 pandemic, both in tripartite concertation and in collective bargaining at all levels (CNEL 2021). Their involvement in the definition of the National Recovery Plan was disappointing, however, with trade unions now demanding to be taken much more seriously in consideration during the implementation phases.

Historical background and principal features of the industrial relations system

Although the birth of the first confederation dates back to 1906, it is in the years immediately following the end of the fascist dictatorship and of the Second World War that the national union landscape was defined (Turone 1988). In June 1944, with half of Italy still occupied by the Nazis, three union leaders, acting on behalf of socialists, communists and Christian Democrats, signed the 'Pact of Rome'. This was the refoundation act of the new CGIL, internally united and pluralist, with the communist Giuseppe Di Vittorio as General Secretary. In the climate of the mounting Cold War, that unity did not last too long. A harsh dispute about the introduction of political strikes in the new confederation statute led the Catholic component to leave when, in 1948, a wave of strikes racked the country in response to a failed attack on the life of Communist leader Palmiro Togliatti. This saw the birth of the second confederation, the CISL. Two years later, the Social Democrats – who in 1947 had split from the Socialist Party (PSI) to protest against the electoral alliance with the Communists – left the CGIL, which remained attached to the socialist-communist tradition only. In this way, the Social Democrats, with the supporters of the small Republican party, founded the third confederation, the UIL. This threefold articulation is still the core of the Italian union landscape, although it does not include it all, as several minor craft and independent unions have emerged over recent decades.

In terms of values and identity, CGIL, CISL and UIL have long reflected the main political divides of the post-war decades, but they have also expressed specific union ideologies and cultures (Accornero 1992; Cella 2008). CGIL has long represented a model of unionism rooted in the principles of Marxist classism, aimed at a general representation of labour, rejecting the former notion of acting as a 'transmission belt' with a view to conferring on the union the full dignity of a 'political subject', and refusing corporatist particularism, including when it assumes radical features (Pepe et al. 2003). These features translated into an inclusive idea of union democracy, which is not confined to 'members first', and includes centralization of collective bargaining and strike organization, and the search for structural reforms through political exchange under pro-labour governments. The CISL embodies a pluralist idea of union action, borrowed from Anglo-Saxon models, based on defence of collective autonomy from state interference, an historical vocation for decentralized bargaining, employees' participation and, today, for occupational welfare, a concept of union democracy as based on the primacy of members' voices (Baglioni 2011). Compared with the former two, the UIL originally had a less pronounced ideological stance (Turone 1990). In the post-1969 years, when CGIL and CISL rejected the German codetermination model, which was stigmatized as a form of subaltern participation, the UIL alone promoted its emulation. In the 1990s, it forged an original idea of a 'citizen's unionism' to represent people in the plurality of their social needs, beyond mere occupational status.

Despite divisions and even conflicts, which were fairly violent until the mid-1960s, cooperation and unity of action between the three confederations have usually prevailed, culminating in a Federative Pact between CGIL, CISL and UIL, which remained in place between 1972 and 1984. Since then, relations have been fluctuating and today are fairly cooperative again. A proposed merger to form a single confederation once the old political divides have been overcome, now and then returns to the agenda. The main hurdle seems to be the predictable impact of the possible merger on the three organizational structures.

As regards industrial relations, collective bargaining has undergone a series of different phases over recent decades. The initial strong centralization at the cross-industry level of the first two post-war decades was followed by a shift towards the primacy of the industry-wide agreement, with the first openings to the firm level in the early 1960s. With the 'hot autumn' of 1969, the hierarchy was reversed, with the achievements of decentralized bargaining being transposed to the industrial level, without any respect for top-down coordination or peace clauses. In the 1980s, the bargaining system moved in the opposite direction, with the attempted centralization of incomes policy negotiations to contain inflation, on one hand, and the decentralized micro-concertation of reorganization processes, on the other (Regini 1991). In the early 1990s, the current two-tier coordinated bargaining system was institutionalized. The watershed was the tripartite agreement of July 1993, still considered as a sort of 'Basic Agreement' of Italian industrial relations. Slightly amended over the years, it set out some fundamental pillars: the income policy framework for horizontal coordination (which remained in place until 2009), the two-tier vertically coordinated collective bargaining structure, and renewed workplace representation structures, as a key component of that vertical coordination.

Italy belongs to the small group of Member States of the EU in which there is no legal minimum wage. Pay floors are set by collective agreements at the national and industry level, according to job classification scales. Moreover, there is no administrative extension mechanism, although established jurisprudence fills this twofold gap, which only Denmark and Sweden share with Italy in the EU. Article 36 of Italy's Constitution lays down that remuneration must always be 'proportionate' to the work performed and, in any case, 'sufficient' to guarantee workers and their families a dignified existence. Judges and social security institutions have established the practice that industry-wide agreements signed by comparatively the most representative social partners satisfy such constitutional requirements. If a worker complains that they are unfairly paid, the yardstick is the remuneration set in the corresponding industrial agreement. Despite this indirect enforcement mechanism, the number of workplaces failing to apply collectively agreed wages and norms is growing, and so is the number of working poor, probably because of the lack of workers' representatives, job casualization and adequate public inspections. In some industries and territories, levels of avoidance of minimum wage rates can reach 20 and even 30 per cent, with an average of just over 20 per cent (Garnero 2017).

Finally, two other pillars of a mature industrial relations system are of importance: workers' participation and the right to strike. Both are recognized and framed by the Constitution (Articles 46 and 40, respectively), while evoking legal regulation of both. Because of the long reciprocal veto of the social partners, the envisaged possibility to introduce legislation in these domains has remained largely ignored and has been left, once again, to self-regulation through collective agreements. Under the influence of EU provisions, information and consultation rights eventually received legal backing, while no board-level employee representation exists, including in state-owned companies. Turning to the right to strike, it is considered a fundamental individual worker's right to be exercised collectively and lawful for all reasons, including political ones. Peace clauses are set in cross-industry protocols on collective bargaining and usually further defined by industry-wide agreements, while strict mandatory rules on the exercise of the right to strike are established by law for 'essential public services'.

Structure of trade unions and union democracy

Italian unions are fairly complex organizations, combining both the confederal horizontal/territorial criterion and the vertical/industrial one. In the three major confederations, union aggregation follows similar lines. The three main territorial levels are the local/provincial, the regional and the national, while since the 1990s traditional industrial demarcations have been affected by various processes, which led to reorganization and a number of mergers. The underlying driving forces include the liberalization and privatization of public utilities, the reconfiguration of the media and publishing industries following the digital revolution, labour-market deregulation and spreading non-standard employment. Other, subsequent mergers were intended to streamline representation and negotiations in broad industries, such as chemicals, energy, textiles and fashion, or simply to make better use of organizational resources. Table 16.2 shows the timeline of the establishment of the current union federations affiliated to the three major confederations and the date of subsequent mergers.

Table 16.2 Union federations in 2021: date of establishment and mergers

Union	Confederation	Sectors	Established	Number of previous organizations
Fiom	CGIL	Metalworking	1901	–
SPI	CGIL	Pensioners	1946	–
Fillea	CGIL	Construction, wood, cement, extraction	1948	–
Flaei	CISL	Electricity	1949	–
Fim	CISL	Metalworking	1950	2
Uilm	UIL	Metalworking	1950	–
Uilposte	UIL	Postal services	1950	–
Uiltucs	UIL	Commerce, hotels, services	1950	–
Fnp	CISL	Pensioners	1952	–
Filca	CISL	Construction, wood, cement, extraction	1955	3
Feneal	UIL	Construction, wood, cement, extraction	1958	2
Filcams	CGIL	Commerce, hotels, services	1960	2
Fir (FSUR)	CISL	Research	1972	–
Cisl Università (FSUR)	CISL	University	1972	–
Fisascat (Fist)	CISL	Commerce, hotels, catering, services	1973	4
Filt	CGIL	Transport	1980	6
FP	CGIL	Public administration	1980	–
Cisl Medici	CISL	Medical doctors	1982	–
Fisac	CGIL	Banking and insurance	1983	2
Fit	CISL	Transport	1985	6
Flai	CGIL	Agriculture and food industry	1988	2
Slp	CISL	Postal services	1993	–
Uila	UIL	Agriculture and food industry	1994	2
SLC	CGIL	Communication	1996	2
Fai	CISL	Agriculture and food industry	1997	2
FP	CISL	Public administration	1997	4

(*Continued*)

Table 16.2 Continued

Union	Confederation	Sectors	Established	Number of previous organizations
Cisl Scuola (FSUR)	CISL	Primary and secondary education and vocational training	1997	2
Nidil	CGIL	Atypical workers	1998	–
Uilca	UIL	Banking and insurance	1998	3
Femca	CISL	Chemicals, textiles, clothes and fashion, energy, public utilities,	2001	2
Flc	CGIL	Education and research	2004	2
Fistel (Cisl Reti)	CISL	Media, entertainment, communication	2005	2
Filctem	CGIL	Chemicals, textiles, clothes and fashion, energy, public utilities,	2006	3
Felsea (Fist)	CISL	Atypical workers	2009	2
Fns	CISL	Firefighters, prison guards, forestry guards	2009	3
Uiltec	UIL	Chemicals, textiles, clothes and fashion, energy, public utilities	2013	2
Uilcom	UIL	Media, entertainment, communication	2013	–
First	CISL	Banking and insurance	2015	2

Source: Authors' elaboration.

Since 1946, one of the peculiar features of Italian unionism has been the presence of a separate union federation for retired workers, with significant weight within the confederations. Each confederation today has a separate pensioners' union, which invariably constitutes the largest of the affiliated organizations. The Italian Pensioners' Union (SPI, *Sindacato Pensionati Italiani*) alone, affiliated to CGIL, has some 2.5 million members. Together, the three confederal pensioners' unions amount to 42 per cent of total union membership (see Table 16.3). Such a wide membership among pensioners is linked to the various services that unions provide, starting with administrative assistance at the time of retirement and then complemented with help in submitting annual tax declarations and relations with the public administration, for instance to obtain access to welfare benefits and care services. Moreover, pensioners' unions are active at local level in negotiating welfare benefits and social assistance schemes with municipalities and organizing different social and cultural initiatives. In order to maintain the predominance of active members within confederation governance, the weight of pensioners' federations in decision-making bodies, starting from the congress, is not proportionate to the total number of their affiliates.

A second peculiarity is the presence of specific non-standard workers' unions. These unions were established in the second half of the 1990s, when non-standard employment received a boost from labour-market reforms. They currently represent temporary agency workers and, notably, 'semi-autonomous' freelance workers, who are formally regarded as self-employed, although they are often economically and organizationally dependent. Fixed-term workers are not covered by these organizations, but by industrial unions. Temporary agency workers have their own national collective agreement, whereas freelancers benefit from service activities, legal advocacy and campaigns, as in the case of demands for the recognition of legal subordination and employee status. Last in order of time, they have contributed to the mobilization of food delivery workers, alongside the sectoral transport and logistics federations and, notably, independent grassroots unions.

The national confederation level is the most important, as it performs the essential roles of political guidance and operational coordination across federations and territorial structures. Clearly, confederations do not operate in a top-down manner but gather and process inputs from industries and territories. Industry federations, in particular, enjoy significant independence, namely in the fields of organizing and recruiting, collective bargaining and internal organization. Major federations can play a fairly significant role in confederations, through their voice in congresses and their presence in confederal bodies.

In the major confederations, the territorial structures, at both local and national levels, serve the dual purpose of promoting internal horizontal coordination across industrial federations and negotiating with the corresponding peak employer organizations, as well as engaging in dialogue with the government authorities. Conversely, the industrial federations at national level are responsible for negotiating industry-wide collective agreements, while at local level they are concerned mainly with vertical coordination of the implementation and administration of agreements by assisting workplace union structures, including in decentralized negotiations.

The territorial and industrial organizational levels do not complete the articulation of Italian unions. The company level complements the reach of industrial organizations, with an essential link with workers and workplaces. Furthermore, besides affiliated union federations, the major confederations include other types of affiliates and associations or subsidiary organizations, which cater to specific interests or perform special activities. Among the affiliates, as mentioned above, the two non-industrial federations characteristic of Italy's trade union scene are the federations of pensioners and the federation of 'a-typical' workers.

The principles of gender balance and the inclusion of young people and immigrants in governance bodies have been adopted in the articles of association of the major union confederations and federations. Women committees are very common at all levels (national, sectoral, territorial), whereas the formal establishment of youth and immigrant committees varies between confederations and federations and sometimes reflects the importance of young and immigrant workers among the workforce. At national level, all confederations organize either a specific association or a committee to represent the interests of migrant workers, especially with a view to influencing public policies and providing services and assistance. Internally, representation quotas and targets are meant to ensure and enhance inclusiveness in decision-making and better reflect members' diversity.

Besides workers' representation, the confederations provide a broad range of services, which are increasingly taking advantage of new digital technologies and address issues related to work and employment, but also cater to other needs that people may have through their life course. Individual services include employment services and counselling, assistance in retirement and welfare benefits procedures, legal advice and assistance in individual labour disputes, and fiscal services. Pension, welfare and tax services are provided by the so-called *patronati* and Tax Assistance Centres (CAF, *Centri Assistenza Fiscale*), which can be established by unions, as well as by other types of organization and association. These are particularly important and represent a fundamental link with all workers. These services are administered according to legislation and are provided to both members and non-members, with lower fees for the former, as an incentive to join a union. They entail a close relationship between the unions and the relevant public administration, so that they could be regarded as an Italian version of the Ghent system, which helps to preserve membership levels. Their contribution to recruiting and retaining members is probably one explanatory factor of the resilience of Italian unions' density and levels of affiliation (Frangi and Barisione 2015). Every year, the 'services system' helps to maintain membership levels and recruit hundreds of thousands of new members, who compensate for those who terminate their affiliation. Although this can be regarded as 'instrumental membership', short of ideal and value-based motivation, it seems to be a key approach to accommodating the growing individualization at work and in society, by giving the unions a semi-public role, in line with the logic of functional differentiation and social democracy.

The confederations perform other important activities through their research and training centres, their archival resources on the history of the labour movement, and their participation in a number of public bodies and institutes in an advisory capacity.

Although union confederations are peak organizations, they are not second-level organizations. Workers, pensioners and citizens, in particular matters, may directly join the confederations and exercise their membership rights in various ways. Basically, a worker may join a confederation through the union federation responsible for the industry in which they are employed. The confederations' basic organizational structures are set up in workplaces or at territorial level for pensioners, and other categories (depending on the confederation, for instance for non-standard workers and workers employed in agriculture or artisanal firms).

Italian unionism is characterized by pluralism, which extends beyond the three major union confederations. Besides – and in competition with – the three largest and historical confederations mentioned above, there are a multitude of independent or minor unions. Some are structured into umbrella confederations and represent the main independent unions in Italy, with a more or less pronounced political profile, from the traditional right-wing General Labour Union (UGL, *Unione Generale del Lavoro*) to the left-wing and grassroots unions (USB, *Unione Sindacale di Base*; COBAS, *Comitati di base*), which are now quite strong among migrant workers in the logistics sector. Independent unions also include two 'non-political' and 'autonomous' Workers' Confederations (CONFSAL and CISAL),[1] organizing and quite active in trade, tourism

1 See full names in the list of abbreviations.

and some manufacturing branches, respectively, and considered to be representative for participation in some tripartite institutions. Others are strong industrial or professional organizations, particularly in industries such as air traffic control, banks, public administration, schools and hospitals, and they often have an occupational character.

Article 39 of the Italian Constitution envisages the registration of unions and includes the requirement that their internal organization be democratic. Public registration was never actually introduced for unions, however, because they wanted to preserve their autonomy from any state interference. But certainly unions are large and participatory democratic organizations.

The bodies of the confederations can be distinguished according to different roles: deliberative, executive, control and jurisdiction. The most important deliberative body, for all three confederations, is the confederal *Congresso*, which takes place every four years. They set out action programmes and elect and appoint all organizational positions. The run-up to each congress starts with members' assemblies in the workplaces and local structures, which discuss the congress documents as laid down in a consultation process organized by the national governing bodies in connection with industrial and territorial structures. Members' assemblies elect representatives to the higher congress levels (territorial and industrial). The congress assemblies taking place at lower organizational levels, such as territorial structures or industrial federations, also elect the relevant governing bodies, including the secretary general and the secretariat. The process always takes several months before the final general congress at national level. Each confederation has its own rules and features, but this general framework applies in all cases. By means of this complex exercise, the confederations define their programmatic lines for the next four years and the leadership that will develop and implement them.

Unionization

Data on union membership is provided by union confederations, except in the case of the public administration, for which a system for assessing representativeness was introduced in 1997. The system involves the collection and certification of data on both membership and votes cast in the elections for workplace representation structures in the public administration. These rules provided the basic reference for the representativeness criteria and assessment procedures introduced by the inter-confederal joint text on representation of January 2014, signed by Confindustria, CGIL, CISL and UIL, and, at different times, by other employer associations and unions. These rules have yet to be implemented in full, however.

The latest membership data for the three major confederations show a total membership of 11.7 million in 2019, with some 6.5 million active workers and around 5 million retired members, or 42 per cent of total membership (Table 16.4). This section focuses on membership among active workers, although some reference to retired members is included, when relevant.

Considering the self-reported data on active workers from the three largest confederations, net union density was 32.5 per cent in 2019. In fact, total membership has been increasing over the past five years and this seems to confirm the relative resilience of Italian unions. Compared to the peaks achieved during the late 1970s and early 1980s, however, there has been an erosion of membership and density. Union density reached 50.5 per cent in 1976, in a period of widespread mobilization, and membership continued to increase in the following years, topping at almost 7.2 million workers in 1980. After that, union density and membership progressively declined until the end of the 1990s. The lowest membership was recorded in 1998, at some 5.1 million workers. After that, it rebounded, although density continued to decrease until reaching 33.1 per cent in 2006. Despite the temporary erosion that followed the economic and sovereign debt crisis in the early 2010s, both indicators started to rise again, especially thanks to an increase in membership in the private services sector, where employment creation concentrated, with growing demands for representation.

Today, total membership among active workers is almost 6.5 million, an increase of over 1 million members compared with the late 1990s, while density has remained steadily over one-third of employees in the past two decades, showing the unions' capacity to cope with the substantial increase in employment that took place in this period (3.1 million more employees since 1998). Although the drivers of this resilience are still to be thoroughly investigated, scattered evidence indicates a combination of organizing and servicing as a likely explanation. On one hand, despite the difficulties, unions seem to have gained a significant hold in some of the most difficult areas to organize: non-standard work and small enterprises. The federations organizing non-standard workers had almost 240,000 members in 2019, or 3.6 per cent of the overall membership, which represents a considerable success (Bordogna 2021). As for small and medium-sized enterprises, the extension since the 2009 crisis to this key segment of the Italian economy of the wage guarantee fund – which requires the conclusion of a collective agreement – has enabled unions to establish closer contacts with very small firms. More generally, membership has expanded considerably in the private services sector, thereby adapting to the changing composition of overall employment. Besides active workers, membership among pensioners is another remarkable feature of Italian unionism, as mentioned above. On the other hand, the wide range of services provided by local union structures, from legal advice to tax services, has consolidated workers' and citizens' confidence in and reliance on trade unions and represents a significant source of membership expansion.

The overall weight of independent unions, in terms of active members, is very uncertain and controversial, too. It is likely to be around 1 million, as certified members in the public administration alone number some 430,000, although their incidence in the private sector is thought to be much lower. This implies that the official data on Italian membership, usually calculated for the three historical confederations only, are underestimated. If we take these 1 million further union members into account, then union density in Italy could be close to 40 per cent of all employees.

Membership composition among active workers has changed markedly in recent decades. According to ICTWSS data (2019), in 1980 agriculture still represented 16 per cent of union membership (1.1 million), while industry accounted for 47 per cent (3.4 million) and services 36 per cent (2.7 million). After two decades, in 2000, agriculture was down to 8 per cent (0.45 million), services represented more than half of all members (51 per cent, 2.65 million) and industry covered 41 per cent (2.1 million). According to the latest data available for 2019 (Table 16.3), manufacturing and construction currently account for slightly over 37 per cent of membership (2.3 million). Private services, including non-standard workers, cover 35 per cent of members and the public administration includes almost one-quarter of all members of the three major confederations (altogether 3.5 million). It should be noted, however, that the federations covering school and health services, for instance, represent workers in the private sector, too, so that the share of public services is to some extent overestimated, and the actual weight of private services is certainly higher. This is in fact a general problem, as representation and collective bargaining do not usually follow the demarcation lines between industries set by official or formal definitions. This means that the correspondence between unions, membership and economic activities presented in Table 16.3 should be regarded as a general indication.

Certification of membership in the public sector allows further analysis. According to the latest assessment of union representativeness in the public administration for 2019–2021 (ARAN 2019), some 1,200,000 workers were union members among non-management staff, putting union density in the public sector at 50.3 per cent, well above the level in the private sector (Bordogna and Pedersini 2019). It is worth noting that representation in the public sector is very fragmented. This is because of the widespread presence in the public sector of special interest organizations, which base their representation on professional and even single administration-based identities. In this, they can often rely on their capacity to control administrative processes and on their key position and ability to disrupt service provision. Moreover, public employers are often more sensitive to workers' demands and there is no economic compatibility to preserve, although public budget constraints can become hard, for example, during periods of austerity (Bach and Bordogna 2016). The total number of registered unions in the whole public administration for non-management staff is 523 organizations. Only twenty-nine trade unions – around 6 per cent – were regarded as representative in the latest assessment, and can therefore sit at the bargaining table. Indeed, the introduction of a representativeness check does not seem to have substantially reduced the proliferation of independent unions, probably because of the role they can nevertheless play in local informal relations and negotiations. Overall, most members of the public administration are affiliated to CGIL (23.3 per cent), CISL (24.9 per cent) and UIL (16.3 per cent), reaching almost two-thirds of total membership. Independent unions, that is organizations which are not affiliated to the three major confederations, had some 430,000 members, which corresponded to around 36 per cent of the total.

Based on still unofficial data on 2020, membership does not seem to have suffered much from the pandemic. The ban on lay-offs introduced by the government from March 2020 to June 2021, and the massive use of short-time working schemes have limited the occupational impact of the crisis, at least for the time being.

Table 16.3 Union membership of major confederations by industry and affiliated federations, 2019

Industries, sectors or groups	**CGIL**	**2019**	**CISL**	**2019**	**UIL**	**2019**	**Total**	**%**
Metalworking	FIOM	309,127	FIM	205,320	UILM	99,605	*614,052*	*9.5*
Chemicals, textiles, energy	FILCTEM	187,917	FEMCA	106,411	UILTEC	117,607	*426,381*	*6.6*
			FLAEI	14,446				
Construction and wood	FILLEA	266,592	FILCA	228,865	FENEAL	158,511	*653,968*	*10.1*
Manufacturing and construction		763,636		555,042		375,723	1,694,401	26.1
Agro-industry	FLAI	259,643	FAI	204,532	UILA	229,508	*719,238*	*11.1*
			UGC	25,555				
Agro-industry		259,643		230,087		229,508	719,238	11.1
Commerce and services	FILCAMS	615,197	FISASCAT*	400,319	UILTUCS	139,911	*1,171,616*	*18.1*
			Sicurezza	16,189				
Transport	FILT	159,904	FIT	127,801	UILTRASPORTI	131,657	*419,362*	*6.5*
Communication	SLC	87,892	FISTel	44,795	UILCOM	38,503	*265,608*	*4.1*
			SLP	66,294	UILPOSTE	28,124		
Banking and insurance	FISAC	79,209	FIRST	90,466	UILCA	45,351	*215,026*	
Private services		942,202		745,864		383,546	2,071,612	31.9

Industries, sectors or groups	**CGIL**	**2019**	**CISL**	**2019**	**UIL**	**2019**	**Total**	**%**
Public administration, health and education	Funzione pubblica	379,397	Funzione pubblica	254,628	UILPA	55,608		
			Medici	6,924				
					UIL FPL	205,301		
					OOCC.	532		
	FLC	207,722	FSUR	256,891	UILSCUOLA	84,673	*558,935*	*8.6*
					UILRUA	9,649		
Public sector		587,119		518,443		355,763	1,461,325	22.5
Temporary and non-standard	NIDIL	122,993	FELSA*	43,945	UILTEMP	69,711	*236,649*	*3.6*
	Unemployed	4,678						
	Mixed	14,028	Various	286,490	Second affiliation	306,743**		
Non-standard and others		141,699		330,435		376,454	848,588	13.1
Active workers		*2,694,299*		*2,379,871*		*1,414,251*	6,488,421	100.0
Pensioners	SPI	2,652,272	FNP	1,699,619	UILPENSIONATI	560,361	4,912,252	42.0
	TOTAL	5,346,571		4,079,490		2,281,355	11,707,416	

Note: * FELSA and FISASCAT merged and jointly established the federation of tertiary unions (FIST) in 2014 but maintained their autonomy and independence.
** Second affiliation members: they are excluded from calculations of the number of active workers (which includes members of UILTEMP only), but added to the total membership of UIL.

Source: Authors' elaboration based on trade union confederation data.

Table 16.4 Membership by gender, nationality and age, Italy, 2019

Member characteristics		CGIL (%)	CISL (%)	UIL (%)
Gender	Men	51.4	51.4	55.0
	Women	48.6	48.6	45.0
Place of birth	Italy	89.6	85.1	91.7
	Abroad	10.4	14.9	8.3
Age	Up to 35 years	8.9	15.6	n.a.
	35–50 years	20.9	–	n.a.
	35–55 years	–	58.1	n.a.
	51–65	27.7	–	n.a.
	Over 55 years	–	26.3	n.a.
	Over 65 years	42.4	–	n.a.

Source: Authors' elaboration based on data from trade union confederations.

Union resources and expenditure

Confederations are large organizations with millions of members and thousands of officials. Their main financial resources are membership fees, which generally amount to 1 per cent of members' gross annual minimum collective wage rates. Revenues from membership fees are distributed between the various union levels, according to decisions taken by the top confederal statutory bodies and partly by federations, for their respective shares. For instance, within CGIL, the larger part of union fees remains at the territorial level of the union federation to which the members belong, while the rest is distributed across the various industrial and confederal levels. The various organizational levels of the union federation receive 76 per cent of membership dues, while the confederation obtains 24 per cent. The other major confederations probably follow a similar pattern, as their organizational structure is very similar.

A rough estimate of the union fees paid by active workers only would put the total amount at around 1.2 billion euros (Carrieri and Feltrin 2016), excluding retired members' fees, which are calculated at a reduced rate, and the revenues obtained through public contributions and user fees for services provided. Overall, estimates indicate total revenues for the three major confederations of around 2 billion euros. A comprehensive analysis of the resources and expenditures of the confederations is not possible, however, because union structures have separate financial reports and no consolidation is available.

If only the financial reports of the national level of confederations are considered, a partial examination comprising less than 5 per cent of the total estimate is possible. The volume of available resources at the national confederal level depends on the ways in which each confederation organizes the distribution of revenues across the various horizontal and vertical structures. Between 60 and 70 per cent of all revenues of the national confederations derive from membership fees.

Table 16.5 Distribution of membership fees: the case of CGIL

Union level	Union structure	Percentage
Federation	Territorial level	61
	Regional level	8
	National level	7
Confederation	Territorial level	20
	Regional level	4

Source: Dipartimento Politiche Organizzative. CGIL Lombardia, Struttura, sistema di finanziamento e sfide per il Sindacato in Italia.

Analysis of confederation expenditures at the national level is also heavily influenced by their internal organization, and data are not easily comparable.

Following the severe restrictions on movement and attendance of events in response to the Covid-19 pandemic, union confederations have made significant financial savings, although the massive use of short-time working schemes and social shock-absorbers have reduced workers' fees because of their lower wages.

The pension and welfare benefit services of *patronati* are provided essentially free of charge, with possible exceptions stipulated by law, and they involve a public contribution. Tax services by *CAFs* are generally provided for a fee, which is lower for union members, but they also receive a fixed sum for each tax declaration they process. These services represent a non-trivial source of revenues. According to the available estimations, the composition of overall revenues shows that membership fees represent 64 per cent of the total, tax services 17 per cent, including public compensation, the reimbursements *patronati* obtain for their public interest services total 12 per cent, while legal advice covers the remaining 7 per cent.

Collective bargaining and unions at the workplace

In Italy, collective bargaining is an essential expression of the constitutional principle of trade union freedom. The provisions concerning unions' ability to stipulate binding industry-wide agreements, under the condition of registration, in accordance with Article 39 of the Constitution, have never been implemented. The bargaining system has developed along very different lines than those envisaged by the Constitution, essentially, the free and mutual recognition of the parties, according to the principles of civil law. The *de facto* extension mechanism, guaranteed by established judicial practice of applying the constitutional principles of proportionality and adequate pay (Article 36) with reference to collectively agreed wages as the benchmark, ensures that all wage-earners tend to be covered, albeit indirectly, by a national industry-wide agreement. Figures and statistics all agree on coverage of 80 per cent (OECD 2019; Pedersini 2019) and even over 90 per cent (Birindelli 2016; CNEL-ISTAT 2016).

Regarding collective bargaining levels and coordination, the 1993 Protocol established a two-tier system, hierarchically coordinated: one national industry-wide agreement, *de facto* almost mandatory, and a decentralized and optional level, at the company or, alternatively, territorial levels. The signatory parties independently define the scope of the industrial bargaining unit, meticulously listing all the types of industries and jobs covered by the agreement. The industry-wide agreement establishes the basic rules that regulate the individual employment relationship: working time and pay in all their essential components, as well as the collective rights and duties of the signatory parties in the field of industrial relations. The industrial agreement defines the respective specialization of the two levels of bargaining; grants and specifies information and consultation rights; provides further trade union rights at workplace level above those guaranteed by law; and establishes and regulates national bilateral bodies and self-financed funds to manage occupational welfare, such as supplementary pension schemes and health care insurance.

An industry-wide agreement is normally a 'book' of around 250 articles and a dozen annexes. Its renewal takes place on a three-year basis, according to predefined procedures, which include peace clauses. The national agreement has the key function of safeguarding purchasing power, now based on the expected inflation rate, as forecasted by the National Institute of Statistics. Minimum wages are differentiated between industries and by professional qualifications at an average ratio of 100/200 within the same agreement. The average wage rate across the many industrial minima is estimated at around 9 euros gross (Birindelli 2018), but with strong differences between high- and low-paid industries.

As of June 2021, the national register of industry-wide agreements kept by the CNEL records 985 texts, compared with only 350 in 2008. Of these, barely one-third are signed by the federations affiliated to the three major confederations. Despite this multiplication of collective agreements signed by non-affiliated unions, only a minority are applied extensively, and all are signed by the most representative federations. Some 350 industry-wide agreements covered approximately 98 per cent of all employees at the end of 2019, while 60 per cent of all registered agreements are not even mentioned in the monthly social security declarations (INPS 2020).

Faced with the boom in agreements signed by minor organizations, the social partners' representativeness is now a hotly debated issue. So-called 'pirate agreements' are a concern and there are widespread demands to prevent them from putting downward pressure on genuine collective bargaining and wage setting. Experts and political parties, such as the Five Star Movement, are pushing for the adoption of a statutory minimum wage, and bills on *salario minimo* are under discussion in Parliament. After criticism from the social partners, wage setting prerogatives should be preserved and collectively agreed wages would continue to be the benchmark. The statutory minimum wage should be viewed as a safety net to prevent pay from falling below the legal wage floor. With a view to strengthening the enforcement of collective agreements, unions are currently more open to accepting a law on representativeness that would adopt the criteria established in the cross-industry framework agreements of 2011–2014, based on the national average between overall union membership and the percentage of votes received in the union workplace elections (see Chapter 27 on Spain). The threshold for admission to the bargaining table would be 5 per cent, while, according to the majority principle, 50 per cent plus one would be required for industrial agreements to be valid and binding.

Decentralized bargaining is carried out at group or company level, or alternatively at territorial level. The coverage of decentralized bargaining is estimated at around 20 per cent of enterprises and 35 per cent of workers, concentrated in the medium-large unionized enterprises of the centre-north (Birindelli 2016). It is worth underlining the weight and importance of territorial bargaining, which ensures second-level negotiations for industries structurally characterized by a discontinuous workforce or very small enterprises, or both (such as construction, agriculture, artisanal firms and tourism). The most important topic of decentralized bargaining is probably 'variable pay', but the range of subjects covered is very wide and embraces working time, restructuring, well-being at work and social benefits (CNEL 2020). The two levels – national and decentralized – are coordinated hierarchically, according to specialization and not duplication. Exit or derogation clauses are usually delimited by the national industry agreements.

To stimulate and expand decentralized bargaining, various reforms during the past decade have attempted to reduce the weight of national agreements and increase the room for manoeuvre at the firm and territorial levels. Some of these reforms were adopted autonomously by the social partners through cross-industry agreements (in 2009, 2011–2014 and 2018–2019). Others were introduced by government initiatives and laws (2011 and 2015), following the recommendations of supranational institutions, as in the case of the letter from the European Central Bank in summer 2011, or the country-specific recommendations, during the European Semester. Moreover, budget laws supported the expansion of firm-level bargaining through fiscal incentives for performance-related bonuses. These reforms have significantly promoted bargaining decentralization by introducing possibilities for exit clauses and derogations. Nevertheless, these possibilities do not seem to have had a major impact because of the main unions' reluctance. Moreover, flexibility in workforce management is already quite broad, and SMEs and artisanal enterprises resist opening up to firm-level bargaining. For all these reasons, although weakened, the system can still be labelled a case of coordinated decentralization (Leonardi and Pedersini 2018).

At the company or workplace level, the actor entitled to negotiate and sign agreements on the workers' and the union side is the Unitary Union Representation (RSU, *Rappresentanza Sindacale Unitaria*). It is a single-channel union structure elected by all employees, with no distinction between union members and non-members, and it is endowed with both bargaining and consultative rights. The 1970 Workers' Statute established fifteen employees as the threshold for setting up a union enterprise structure, with the possibility of freely carrying out union activities in the workplace. The election of RSUs takes place every three years on competing lists, presented by the unions that signed the industry agreement in force in the workplace, or otherwise with the collection of a minimum number of signatures. It has been estimated that about 80 per cent of the elected delegates belong to the industrial federations CGIL, CISL and UIL, but surveys are not very up to date. Minor unions have accumulated significant support in some industries, such as banks, schools, hospital, and transport and logistics.

The link between workplace representation and firm-level bargaining is very strong, as evidenced by the almost perfect overlap between their respective coverage rates of around 12 per cent of companies with more than ten employees (Pedersini 2019). The role and prerogatives of the workers' health and safety representative are established in detail by law. Joint committees are very common for addressing ad hoc issues, such as work organization, equal opportunities or training.

Industrial conflict

The collection of data on industrial conflicts in Italy was discontinued in 2010 and it has never resumed. This came after at least two decades of progressive reduction in strike activity, marked by a transition to 'tertiary' conflict, that is, a progressive shift of conflicts from manufacturing to services, thereby involving a 'third party' (the user), who bears most of the consequences of stoppages. This happens notably in public services, such as transport (Bordogna and Pedersini 2019). Such a transition involves a clear transformation of the nature of conflict, in terms of both indicators and of impacts. For instance, small groups of workers can provoke significant service disruptions, so that participation rates are not always relevant. Sometimes, even calling a strike and revoking it at the last minute can be as disruptive as an actual strike (this is known as the 'announcement effect'). Moreover, work stoppages do not necessarily produce losses for the employer. In some cases, they can even, paradoxically, improve the bottom line: think of subsidized public transport structurally operating at a loss. Saving on labour costs may effectively reduce the loss. Indeed, the burden of strikes is often shifted to users, who are prevented from using the service and therefore incur costs and inconvenience.

With a view to avoiding these consequences, Law No. 146/1990, later amended by Law No. 83/2000, was introduced to regulate the exercise of the right to strike in 'essential public services', which are defined in terms of activity and not ownership. They involve all services where the exercise of the right to strike may affect other citizens' fundamental rights, as recognized and protected by the Constitution, because the latter have to be equally preserved and protected. Examples include transport, public utilities, health and tribunals. Regulation is left to the social partners in the relevant industries, which establish the rules to balance conflicting rights. These essentially consist of mandatory self-regulation protocols, which include procedures to inform people about strikes and limitations to ensure minimum levels of service provision. The Guarantee Commission on the implementation of the law on strikes in essential public services (*Commissione di garanzia dell'attuazione della legge sullo sciopero nei servizi pubblici essenziali*) oversees the whole process and sanctions possible violations.

Despite this twofold change, a general decrease in strike levels and a shift to services, conflict remains an important tool for unions, which is regularly used when disputes arise. At the industrial level, conflicts usually mark agreement renewals, often for a few hours involving large numbers of workers. Harsher conflicts can arise in local disputes on company restructuring: they involve more stoppages, with lower participation rates, but longer duration. Mass mobilization seldom takes place. When it happens it usually concerns specific policies and is directed against government initiatives. This might represent a second shift: from the employment relation to the political arena, with a view to influencing policymaking. The lack of data, however, does not allow a proper analysis.

Focusing on the data on strikes in essential public services reveals an increase in the number of both called strikes and actual stoppages. The rate of cancelled strikes remained around 30–40 per cent of called strikes in the 2000s. The number of called strikes grew almost by one-third between 2004 and 2019, while actual strikes rose by 22 per cent (2,345 and 1,462, respectively, in 2019). Such trends show that conflict is far from a thing of the past in employment relations. Indeed, quite recently, new areas of mobilization emerged, especially in industries in which unionism is relatively weak, because they concern new activities (such as platform delivery workers; see Tassinari and Maccarrone 2017, 2020) or industries in which the fragmentation of the economic activity between many operators is high and non-standard jobs and work cooperatives prevail (such as warehousing in logistics).

Besides strikes, trade unions have a broad repertoire of activities to influence the quality and content of employment relations. The pandemic has affected the viability of some of them. There was increased attention to health and safety issues, however, with a wave of strikes in March 2020 to demand safe working conditions (De Sario et al. 2021). Similarly, in 2021, there was mobilization to support measures to protect employment and to demand extension of the ban on dismissals, which eventually ended on 30 June 2021. Union mobilization led to a union–employer joint opinion, which was endorsed by the government and included the commitment by enterprises to use all available shock-absorbers, and notably Covid-19 short-time working, before resorting to dismissals.

Hearings before the relevant parliamentary committees represent a traditional channel that social partners use to influence law-making, which has recently gained centrality because of the parallel weakening of tripartite social concertation. This is a formal and institutionalized way of voicing criticisms and bringing data and arguments to support the social partners' positions. It can be coupled with campaigns and mobilization, although it usually takes place following more technical and evidence-based approaches, which prevail in such contexts. Indeed, the social partners are not alone in these hearings, which usually involve public institutes and authorities, such as the National Institute of Statistics or the National Institute of Social Security, as well as civil society organizations and individual experts, depending on the issues at stake. This development highlights a new tendency, introducing a significant change in the relationships between interest organizations and the political arena: that is, the relative retreat of the government is bringing the parliament centre-stage and seemingly includes elements of a shift from neo-corporatism to a sort of competitive pluralism.

Political relations

The place and role of the confederations and their affiliates in the political arena can differ, and vary through time. As the confederations progressively acquired an independent and autonomous mobilization capacity in the 1960s and the central union thrust shifted from the national confederal level to the industrial and increasingly company levels, open links with political parties started to be regarded as problematic. Separation of confederations and parties became a priority and the incompatibility between union and party positions was introduced in the articles of association of the confederations at the end of the 1960s. This formal step was introduced to mark trade union autonomy and possibly turn them into independent political actors. Clearly, the ties between unions and parties were not terminated abruptly and remained significant in the following two decades.

Another relevant, rather symbolic step in the direction of weakening relations between unions and the party system was the termination of the internal political components of CGIL (the communist and socialist factions) in the early 1990s. A crucial contribution had come from the transformation of the Communist Party (PCI) into the Democratic Party of the Left (PDS), between 1989 and 1991. At the same time, the sudden overhaul of the traditional party system after the 1992 scandals, with the dissolution of the Christian Democrats (DC) and the Socialist Party (PSI) in 1994, and the further multiple reconfigurations of the political scene in Italy in the following decades have certainly pushed further the separation between unions and political parties, although a certain proximity remains with the centre-left of the political spectrum.

The progressive autonomy gained by unions vis-à-vis political parties has built into an independent political stance and role. During the 1990s, the relative political weakness of several governments confronted with dire economic situations, such as the currency and financial crisis of summer 1992, or challenging reforms, starting from the pension system and the labour market, was the catalyst of a series of social pacts in which unions gained a prominent position. Later, the second Berlusconi government, which took office in 2001, inaugurated a new unilateral stance, which significantly reduced the room for social concertation. In this new political climate, CGIL and sometimes its metalworking federation FIOM often took the lead in advancing critical positions and tried to oppose the government's initiatives. CISL and UIL, although critical, believed that it was necessary to maintain a dialogue with the government. Neither position proved particularly fruitful, although it could be maintained that the proposal for the most radical reform of the regulation of individual dismissals was stopped, as CGIL organized a mass mobilization reportedly gathering 3 million people on a Saturday in March 2002 and the three confederations called an eight-hour general strike on 16 April 2002, with extensive participation. Indeed, social concertation has progressively waned since the late 1990s, as most governments have maintained a mostly unilateral approach to economic and employment reforms. The most important reforms of the current decade have been introduced unilaterally, with little more than an announcement: collective bargaining and pensions (2011), labour market (2012 and 2015), the temporary anticipation of retirement and the introduction of the citizenship income (2019).

If this is the general trajectory of tripartite social concertation, relations between union members and political parties, as evident from political voting, are now fairly complex and the traditional support for parties belonging to the labour movement, broadly speaking, cannot be taken for granted. In the 2013 general elections, 40.9 per cent of employees opted for the centre-left, 20 per cent for M5S and 15 per cent for the right. In 2018, the situation changed significantly: the centre-left lost more than 10 percentage points, which were gained almost entirely by M5S, a cross-cutting and anti-establishment movement, which was the party receiving the most votes, both overall and among union members (29.5 per cent). Right-wing parties saw their support among employees increase, too, from 15.1 to 22.7 per cent. The right-wing populist *Lega* alone tripled its votes, from 4.8 to 12.9 per cent (Mattina 2019). In the European elections of 2019, M5S halved its votes, both in total and among union members (17 per cent). The Democratic Party (PD), which in total received 22.7 per cent of the votes cast, rose to 31 per cent among union members. Nearly 55 per cent of CGIL members voted for parties of the centre-left. *Lega* took a great leap forward (34.3 per cent), also among union members but, significantly, recorded eight points fewer than among non-members. The two political blocks totalled around 37 per cent each.

The intransigent policy and rhetoric on immigration from the ex-Minister of the Interior, Lega's leader Matteo Salvini, certainly played a key role in pushing his impressive growth in votes and popularity in 2019, but his support for reducing the retirement age and for the tax autonomy of regional administrations attracted wide support among the working class in Northern Italy. M5S has somehow limited the rightward shift of workers and union members, but it also reduced the political space for an expansion of the left and centre-left parties, for example, in its fight for a citizens' income and now for a statutory minimum wage of 9 euros. Despite these challenges, union membership still matters, and influences voting choices, as a result of the political and cultural socialization that organizations establish with their members (Leonardi and Carrieri 2020). At the time of writing, both Lega and M5S are declining in the polls of voters' preferences, while a new 'star' is rising in Italy's political sky, the far-right 'Fratelli d'Italia' (*Brothers of Italy*, whose name comes from the first line of the national anthem).

Societal power

Union political action is often tightly connected with civil society organizations, especially when it intersects with mobilization in favour of civil rights. This is the case of discrimination in the workplace, based, for instance, on gender, sexual orientation or national origin. Trade unions and civil rights movements join together in events such as marches, pride parades, sit-ins and flash mobs. In recent years, public discourse has been pervaded by references to immigrants and public order. In European surveys, Italians were often at the top of the list for migrant-related fears (IPSOS 2017). Surveys in metropolitan suburbs and industrial districts record widespread resentment and anger against migrants and Roma, also among former leftist voters and union activists. In 2013, 64 per cent of union members said they were in favour of accepting migrants from poorer countries. Today, 55 per cent say that Italy already accepts too many immigrants (Mattina 2019).

For trade unions, these developments represent a major concern and require new capacities to respond to the anxieties and expectations of their native constituency, safeguarding traditional values and attitudes in favour of hospitality, integration and social justice. It may be true that, historically, Italian unions have been less sensitive than other European unions in giving voice and representation to outsiders (Meardi 2012), but this position has changed over time. In their moral and political concept of solidarity (Morgan and Pulignano 2020), Italian unions are probably among those in Europe expressing stronger conviction when it comes to establishing the inclusion of migrants as one of the main objectives in their organizational and political agenda. 'Avoid war among the poor' is the union mantra. Their diagnosis is that 'the national anti-European, xenophobic and racist populisms that have grown up across the EU have sprung directly from the interplay between anarchic globalization and a short-sighted, cowardly European policy that, in the past decade, has clashed with the needs, expectations and hopes of wider areas of the population' (CISL 2019: 2–3). They are attempting, therefore, to produce narratives and policies that are distant both from the neutrality of the technocratic elites and the stigmatizing demagogy of right-wing populism.

Significant initiatives have been launched to support the regularization of migrant workers and there is a continuing mobilization against racism, which finds an organizational pillar in the special services and assistance provided by unions to migrant workers (De Sario and Galossi 2021). Taking a 'social movement unionism' approach, Italian unions are fighting for unconditional rescue at sea; abrogation of the strict *Security Decrees*; respect for asylum seekers' constitutional rights; abolition of the crime of 'illegal immigration'; closure of overcrowded detention centres; and recognition of *jus soli* for granting Italian citizenship to the children of migrants born in Italy.

Trade union policies towards the EU

European integration has become a central and very divisive theme in Italian politics around which nationalist and populist parties have built a decisive part of their broad consensus. Until the U-turn of 2020, the collective memory of the painful reforms suggested by the European Central Bank in August 2011, the strong constraints on national budgetary policies and Italy's isolation as it was left to cope with migrant landings on its own coasts represented effective references with which to stir up public anger against the EU. One of the most longstanding pro-EU Member States, Italy has seen a rapid and striking growth in 'Eurosceptic' dissatisfaction.

The unions, throughout the past ten years, have harshly criticized the neoliberal ideology of the new economic governance. The rigid constraints of the Stability Pact imposed fiscal austerity and compromised the possibility of using public expenditure to support economic recovery, thereby depressing wages and public investments, and hence domestic demand (Prosser 2019). With other Southern European unions, Italians were at the vanguard of attempts to organize actions and protests against austerity and in favour of a major change in EU policies.

Despite the great disillusionment of the past decade, the unions have never abandoned their trust in the European project. 'It's not the idea of Europe that has failed', according to former CISL General Secretary Annamaria Furlan, 'but the deviation from the ethical and political vision of its founding fathers. The answer to the problems cannot be that of national populism. It would be a regressive and reactionary choice to want to reverse an outdated historical phase. [CISL wishes to] relaunch the European dream of the United States of Europe'. A similar message has also come from the other two major confederations. Susanna Camusso, former CGIL General Secretary, says that: 'if we do not defend Europe, we will not reform it' and 'the need for Europe has not disappeared…'. 'Europe is needed.' UIL has the same stance, illustrated by the position of the current General Secretary of the ETUC, Luca Visentini, who reiterated this commitment at the last Congress of the European Trade Union Confederation (ETUC) in 2019.

On the eve of the European elections, in 2019, the three confederations intensified their pro-European commitment, signing an 'Appeal for Europe' with the largest employers' confederation Confindustria. It stated, among other things, that the European project 'must be relaunched clearly and strongly in its full significance for civilization'. For the Italian social partners: 'those who aim to call the European Project into question want to return to the isolation of nation states, trade barriers, fiscal dumping and currency wars, reviving the disturbing spectres of the twentieth century'. Criticism of the populist nationalists could not be clearer or more direct.

The steadfast support of the Italian unions for the European project was and remains far from uncritical of the policies adopted in recent years, expressly regarded as one of the main causes of the nationalist regression of large parts of European societies. According to the unions, the EU must be capable of redeeming its social and democratic profile in the eyes of the citizens. Unions recommend a new sustainable model of integration, to be achieved by strengthening the democratic legitimacy of the European institutions and placing the European Parliament at the centre of the decision-making process. European economic governance must be radically reconsidered, with the full and effective implementation of the European Pillar of Social Rights, fostering upward convergence through strengthening collective bargaining and coverage, reducing social and fiscal dumping and legal regime shopping.

Particularly strong is the concern about the insufficient development of wages and industry-wide bargaining in CEE. Although reluctant in relation to an unprecedented statutory minimum wage at domestic level – in defence of wages set by collective agreements – CGIL, CISL and UIL look favourably on the EC initiative for a Directive on adequate minimum wages, for example, because of the way it is conceived, respectful of national systems and focusing very much on achieving a high level of collective bargaining (no less than 80 per cent) in all Member States. The proposal is in fact considered a stepping-stone for reducing current EU wage gaps, not to mention social dumping. Moreover, Italian unions believe that wider and better use of international mobilization is needed: transnational company agreements are considered among the few positive innovations of recent years, while international mobilizations and campaigns, such as those at Ryanair or Amazon, have to be extended. Italy was the first country in which, after a wave of strikes and initiatives, Amazon was forced to negotiate with the unions and recognize them at the workplace level. This was a fairly successful example of organizing and union renewal. Compared with some other national organizations, Italians unions appear more open to greater transfer of decision-making sovereignty to supranational levels, such as the ETUC and the Global Union Federations, as an inescapable step towards a real internationalization of union action and effectiveness (Leonardi and Carrieri 2020).

Conclusions

Trade unions remain fairly important social actors in the Italian economic and political landscape. Despite some weakening of their public image as generally representative, which is mirrored in the difficulties they have encountered in playing a prominent role in policymaking in recent years, their presence is pervasive and they continue to enjoy significant institutional support. As Jelle Visser recently pointed out (Visser 2019: 59–71), the fate of trade unions today appears to include distinct parallel trajectories, which represent different viewpoints – and interpretations – of the challenges they face and their responses. As key social actors affected by economic, societal and political changes, they are constantly in danger of seeing their role downplayed and gradually sliding into marginalization. The erosion of membership and collective bargaining coverage are considered the main indicators of such a trajectory. As illustrated above, the signs in this direction are still limited, although an ageing membership and the double challenge of growing precarization and increased professionalism in certain industries and occupations represent critical factors. Dualization and revitalization can be considered the two faces of the underlying tensions which are putting trade unions under pressure in Italy, as elsewhere. On one hand, traditional strongholds and forms of representation are shrinking and losing effectiveness; on the other, unions are constantly striving to extend areas of representation and experimenting with new ways of voicing workers' demands.

The relative stability of membership and successes in extending membership to the private service sector in general, and to new occupations and workplaces – including temporary agency work, SMEs and some platform jobs – testify to the initiatives Italian trade unions have launched to address the risk of dualization through revitalization efforts.

Finally, the role of the unions does not seem to have been radically challenged by the emergence of new social actors. The multiplication of new actors in the field of industrial relations seems to indicate that the potential of labour representation is far from being exhausted. Rather, the trade unions' capacity to respond to the changing environment and to new challenges relies partly on developing forms of cooperation with civil society actors and on integrating emerging collective responses into their repertoires and even their own organizational structures. Trade unions are proactive and responsive collective actors. They represent a lively component of the Italian economic and political fabric, which is set to play a significant role in the coming decades and to support labour through the epochal changes that we are facing, above all digitization and sustainability. Even in the terrible pandemic crisis of the past two years, unions have been able to play a key role and avoid substantial erosion of membership. In fact, they have been able to strengthen their role by addressing health and safety issues in workplaces and defending the twofold measures of extended Covid short-time working and the ban on dismissals for over a year – a fairly unique case. All these elements ultimately encourage us to invest some timid hope in the future of trade unions in Italy.

References

Accornero A. (1992) La parabola del sindacato, Bologna, Il Mulino.

ARAN (2019) Accertamento provvisorio della rappresentatività. Triennio 2019–2021. https://www.aranagenzia.it/.

Bach S. and Bordogna L. (eds) (2016) Public Service Management and Employment Relations in Europe. Emerging from the Crisis, New York, Routledge.

Baglioni G. (2011) La lunga marcia della CISL: 1950–2010, Bologna, Il Mulino.

Bertuccelli L., Righi S. and Pepe A. (2008) Il sindacato nella società industriale, Roma, Donzelli.

Birindelli, L. (2016) Contrattazione integrativa e retribuzioni nel settore privato, Roma, Fondazione Giuseppe Di Vittorio.

Birindelli L. (2018) I "minimi" nei Contratti Collettivi Nazionali di Lavoro, in Brindelli L., Leonardi S., Raitano M. (eds) Salari minimi contrattuali e bassi salari nelle imprese del terziario privato, Roma, Ediesse

Bordogna L. (2021) Enhancing the social partners and social dialogue in the new world of work: the case of Italy, in Vaughan-Whitehead D., Ghellab Y. and de Bustillo Llorente R.M. (eds) The new world of work, Cheltenham, Edward Elgar, 319–368.

Bordogna L. and Pedersini R. (2019) Relazioni industriali. L'esperienza italiana nel contesto internazionale, Bologna, Il Mulino.

Carrieri M. and Feltrin P. (2016) Al bivio. Lavoro, sindacato e rappresentanza nell'Italia d'oggi, Roma, Donzelli.

Cella G.P. (2008) Le culture sindacali nel secolo industriale, in Causarano P., Falossi L. and Giovannini P. (eds) Mondi operai, culture del lavoro e identità sindacali: il Novecento italiano, Roma, Ediesse, 49–62.

CISL (2019) Manifesto per gli Stati Uniti d'Europa, Roma. https://fitcisltrentino.com/2017/03/23/manifesto-cisl-per-gli-stati-uniti-deuropa/.

CNEL (2019) Notiziario dell'Archivio dei contratti, Bollettino, Roma, Consiglio Nazionale Economia e Lavoro.

CNEL (2020) XXI Rapporto sul mercato del lavoro e sulla contrattazione collettiva 2019, Roma, Consiglio Nazionale Economia e Lavoro.

CNEL (2021) XXII Rapporto sul mercato del lavoro e sulla contrattazione collettiva 2020, Roma, Consiglio Nazionale Economia e Lavoro.

CNEL-ISTAT (2016) Produttività, struttura e performance delle imprese esportatrici, mercato del lavoro e contrattazione integrativa. Report intermedio, Roma, Consiglio Nazionale dell'Economia e del Lavoro, Istituto Nazionale di Statistica.

Crouch C. and Pizzorno A. (1977) Conflitti in Europa: lotte di classe, sindacati e stato dopo il '68, Milano, Etas Libri.

De Sario B. and Galossi E. (eds) (2021) Migrazioni e sindacato, Roma, Ediesse.

De Sario B., Di Nunzio D. and Leonardi S. (2021) Azione sindacale e contrattazione collettiva per la tutela della salute e sicurezza sul lavoro nella fase 1 dell'emergenza da pandemia di Covid-19, Rivista giuridica del lavoro e della previdenza sociale, 1, 91–110.

Frangi L. and Barisione M. (2015) 'Are you a union member?' Determinants and trends of subjective union membership in Italian society (1972–2013), Transfer, 21 (4), 451–469.

Garnero A. (2017) The dog that barks doesn't bite: coverage and compliance of sectoral minimum wages in Italy, IZA Discussion Paper 10511, Bonn, Institute of Labour Economics.

INPS (2020) INPS tra emergenza e rilancio. XIX Rapporto annuale, Roma, Istituto Nazionale Previdenza Sociale.

IPSOS (2017) Global views on immigration and the refugee crisis, IPSOS, 14 September 2017. https://www.ipsos.com/en/global-views-immigration-and-refugee-crisis.

Leonardi S. (2018) Trade unions and collective bargaining in Italy during the crisis, in Lehndorff S., Dribbusch H. and Schulten T. (eds) Rough waters. European trade unions in a time of crisis, Brussels, ETUI, 87–115.

Leonardi S. and Carrieri M. (2020) Populism and trade union internationalism: the case of Italy, in Transfer, 26 (3), 273–288.

Leonardi S. and Pedersini R. (eds) (2018) Multi-employer bargaining under pressure: decentralisation trends in five European countries, Brussels, ETUI.

Mattina L. (2019) Il voto 'diviso' degli iscritti ai sindacati alle elezioni politiche del marzo 2018, Quaderni Rassegna Sindacale – Lavori, 20 (2): 7–26.

Meardi G. (2012) Constructing Uncertainty: Unions and Migrant Labour in Construction in Spain and the UK, Journal of Industrial Relations, 54(1): 5–21.

Morgan G. and Pulignano V. (2020) Solidarity at Work: Concepts, Levels and Challenges. Work, Employment and Society, 34(1): 18–34.

OECD (2019) Negotiating our way up. Collective bargaining in a changing world of work, Paris, OECD Publishing.

Pedersini R. (2019) Italy: institutionalisation and resilience in a changing economic and political environment, in T. Müller, K. Vandaele and J. Waddington (eds) Collective bargaining in Europe: towards an endgame, Brussels, ETUI, 337–359.

Pepe A., Iuso P. and Loreto F. (eds) (2003) La CGIL nel Novecento, Roma, Ediesse.

Prosser T. (2019) European labour movements in crisis, Manchester, Manchester University Press.

Regini M. (1991) Confini mobili: la costruzione dell'economia fra politica e società, Bologna, Il Mulino.

Rugiero S. (2019) Decarbonisation in the Italian energy sector: the role of social dialogue in achieving a just transition – the case of Enel, in Galgóczi B. (ed.) Towards a just transition: coal, cars and the world of work, Brussels, ETUI, 109–134.

Tassinari A. and Maccarrone V. (2017) The mobilisation of gig economy couriers in Italy: some lessons for the trade union movement, Transfer, 23 (3), 353–357.

Tassinari A. and Maccarrone V. (2020) Riders on the storm: workplace solidarity among gig economy couriers in Italy and the UK, Work, Employment and Society, 34 (1), 35–54.

Turone S. (1988) Storia del sindacato in Italia dal 1943 ad oggi, Bari, Laterza,

Turone S. (1990) Storia dell'Unione Italiana del lavoro, Milano, Franco Angeli.

Visser J. (2019) Trade unions in the balance, ILO ACTRAV Working Paper, Geneva, ILO.

Abbreviations

ARAN	Agenzia per la Rappresentanza Negoziale delle Pubbliche Amministrazioni (Agency for the representation of public administrations in collective bargaining)
CAF	Centro Assistenza Fiscale (Tax advice centre)
CGdL	Confederazione Generale del Lavoro (General confederation of labour)
CGIL	Confederazione Generale Italiana del Lavoro (Italian general confederation of labour)
CISAL	Confederazione Italiana Sindacati Autonomi Lavoratori (Italian confederation of independent workers' unions)
CISL	Confederazione Italiana Sindacati dei Lavoratori (Italian confederation of workers' unions)
CNEL	Consiglio Nazionale Economia e Lavoro (National council for the economy and labour)

CONFSAL	Confederazione Generale dei Sindacati Autonomi dei Lavoratori (General confederation of independent workers' unions)
DC	Democrazia Cristiana (Christian democracy)
INPS	Istituto Nazionale per la Protezione Sociale (National social security institute)
ISTAT	Istituto Nazionale di Statistica (National institute of statistics)
M5S	Movimento 5 Stelle (Five-star movement)
PCI	Partito Comunista Italiano (Italian communist party)
PDS	Partito Democratico della Sinistra (Democratic party of the left)
PSI	Partito Socialista Italiano (Italian socialist party)
RLS	Rappresentante Lavoratori per la Sicurezza (Health and safety workers' representative)
RSU	Rappresentanza Sindacale Unitaria (Joint trade union representation structure)
UIL	Unione Italiana del Lavoro (Italian labour union)
UGL	Unione Generale del Lavoro (General labour union)
USB	Unione Sindacale di Base (Rank-and-file workers' union)

Chapter 17

Latvia: Trade unions with the potential to escape marginalization

Elza Ungure

During the 1990s, a series of major social, political and economic transformations took place in Latvia as the former Soviet system and structures were reformed when the independent Republic of Latvia was re-established. Some trade unions split from Soviet institutions, some ceased their operations and others were newly established. In the context of these transformations, trade unions had to adjust their practices from arrangements in which the state was the dominant actor to a model of social partnership involving government, employers' representatives and other local and cross-border agents.

This transition proved to be challenging for unions. The struggle to adapt to the new circumstances, coupled with an often restrictive and rigid legislative framework, not to mention the relatively large scale of the informal sector, led to a decrease in membership and collective bargaining coverage (see Table 17.1). Another consequence was a heavy reliance on institutional power and external resources, in particular for funding, instead of organizational power and internal resources. Against this background, it would be fair to suggest that trade unions in Latvia have become 'marginalized' (Visser 2019: 59–61) since the 1990s.

Despite the somewhat grim outlook during the period 1990–2020, ongoing efforts of the social partners – trade unions and employers' organizations – to improve the legislative framework and alleviate pressure on the social partners and the members represented by them have paid off in recent years. Amendments to labour law, although minor, have proved important in facilitating the conclusion of a few industry-level collective agreements and the extension of collective agreements to whole industries. Recent positive developments also indicate the growing role of cross-border cooperation between trade unions and the Free Trade Union Confederation of Latvia (LBAS, *Latvijas Brīvo arodbiedrību savienība*) – the sole trade union confederation in Latvia – and partners within the EU institutional framework. Various forms of support from the European Trade Union Confederation (ETUC), the European Trade Union Institute (ETUI) and the European Trade Union Federations (ETUFs), as well as involvement in the European Semester may help LBAS and trade unions in general to position themselves as actors to be reckoned with, not only in national-level discussions on various aspects of industrial relations, but also in bipartite dialogue with employers' representatives and, perhaps in future, in social dialogue with the general public. These recent developments could be seen as a sign of potential trade union revitalization. Whether this opportunity will be seized by the unions remains to be seen because it would probably require some further changes in union practices.

Table 17.1 Principal characteristics of trade unionism in Latvia

	1995	**2000**	**2019**
Total trade union membership	225,000	175,000[a]	95,000[b]
Women as a proportion of total membership	60 %[e]	59 %[a]	65 %[f]
Gross union density	29 %	21 %[a]	12 %[b]
Net union density	n.a.	n.a.	n.a.
Number of confederations	1	1	1
Number of affiliated unions (federations)	n.a.	26[3]	20
Number of independent unions	n.a.	n.a.	n.a.
Collective bargaining coverage	n.a.	18 %[c]	14 %[d]
Principal level of collective bargaining	Company,	Company,	Company, industry
Days not worked due to industrial action per 1,000 workers	0	0	0

Note: [a] data for 2003; [b] data for 2018; [c] data for 2002; [d] data for 2016; [e] data for 1998; [f] data for 2015.

Source: Appendix A1, OECD.Stat (2020), ILOSTAT (2020), LBAS (2016a).

Historical background and principal features of the industrial relations system

When Latvia was a Soviet Socialist Republic (1940–1941 and 1944–1990), all companies and organizations had a union presence and all unions were grouped in industrial unions. Their principal organization was the Latvian Central Trade Union Council (Kurtyka 2006: 26). The vast majority of workers were trade union members (Stacenko 2014: 104). After the restoration of national independence in 1991, Latvia, which was the most industrialized of the three Baltic states during the Soviet period, with 90 per cent of its markets in the USSR, underwent severe social, political and economic transformations (Kurtyka 2006: 23). Trade unions split from the Soviet institutions and established the independent confederation LBAS (Kluinis and Pētersons 2006: 12–70).

After 1991 the political and economic climate was characterized by the implementation of neoliberal 'shock therapy' based on the Washington Consensus. This policy manifested itself in institutional, fiscal and budget reforms, coupled with the restructuring of large enterprises in all industries, with technical help from the International Monetary Fund (IMF) and the World Bank (Stacenko 2014: 89–90). Privatization was considered the best method for economic transformation, while the legal system was transformed in line with the principles of the Romano-Germanic legal system. Since then, under the Latvian legal system, 'soft law in general is used only as an auxiliary for the correct interpretation and application of the primary source' (ILO n.d.): laws and regulations. Therefore, collective agreements too can only cover issues delegated by law and cannot contradict the law. This narrows down the aspects of industrial relations that can be negotiated through collective bargaining. Thus, the focus of unions is more on national-level social dialogue. A bipartite system of voluntary social dialogue between trade unions and employers' representatives was legally established in the early 1990s and the tripartite dialogue system was introduced in 1993, with several tripartite councils which were merged to form a single main council, the National Tripartite Cooperation Council (NTSP, Na*cionālā trīspusējās sadarbības padome)* with thematic sub-councils in 1998 (Karnite 2021b).

During the transformation from a planned command economy to a market economy, industries were restructured, collective dismissals were imposed, many companies and agriculture collapsed, large companies were first replaced by a growing number of micro-enterprises and later also by small- and medium-sized companies (Kurtyka 2006: 23). 'It was', trade union representatives recall, 'a time of unfair competition, even "mafia influence" – everybody tried to get something, it was a "brutal free economy"' (ibid.: 23). This forced many enterprises into the informal economy, at least to some extent, and also led to a dramatic decline in trade union membership because of the dismissals and a growing number of new types of enterprises and industries without a union presence (ibid.: 26).

Since then, collective bargaining has typically been decentralized to company level (Kjellberg 2021). This means that bargaining coverage depends strongly on the capacities of employee representatives at company level. The system of employee representation at company level differs between unions. Larger unions often establish representative bodies in the form of workplace branches. If workplace branches unite a large number of members, they can establish branch units and are usually grouped under associate branches on territorial or other grounds. Unions also sometimes establish bodies to coordinate the operation of branches. Meanwhile in smaller unions, there are often no workplace and associate branches and the capacity for employee representation – including collective bargaining – at company level is limited. Additionally, even if union branches are present, they do not always necessarily have the capacity to undertake bargaining. Because larger unions are typically LBAS affiliates or associates this puts pressure on LBAS to support a large number of bargaining units, provide services to increase their expertise and also take into account the diverse needs of specific memberships for bargaining to be effective (Waddington and Hoffmann 2000).

Structure of trade unions and union democracy

The only trade union confederation in Latvia is LBAS. The number of LBAS affiliates has decreased over time from twenty-seven in 2002 to twenty-one in 2010 and to twenty in 2020, as some trade unions have been liquidated and others have left LBAS, either because they no longer meet the requirements for affiliation or association, or, presumably, based on their members' decision to leave in cases in which the unions in question have remained operational (see Table 17.2). LBAS offers two kinds of membership, depending on union size. A trade union can be an affiliate if it has at least 300 members in at least two companies, or it can be an associate if it has at least 100 members in at least two companies (ibid.: Section 3). There are thus smaller unions that are not LBAS affiliates or associates because unions outside a company can be established by at least fifty people, while company unions can be founded by at least fifteen people or at least a quarter of the employees (but no fewer than five). While mergers have taken place in which smaller trade unions have joined larger unions in order to consolidate resources and power (Romele 2017: 126) – which is also encouraged by LBAS (LBAS 2016b: Section 2.2) – specific information on them is difficult to find.

Table 17.2 LBAS affiliates by type, 2002, 2010 and 2020

Current affiliates, 2020	**Type**
Latvian Union of Education and Science Employees (LIZDA, *Latvijas Izglītības un zinātnes darbinieku arodbiedrība*)	Professional/craft
Latvian Railway and Transport Industry Union (LDzSA, *Latvijas Dzelzceļnieku un satiksmes nozares arodbiedrība*)	Industrial
Latvian Health and Social Care Employees Union (LVSADA, *Latvijas Veselības un sociālās aprūpes darbinieku arodbiedrība*)	Professional/craft
Latvian Public Service and Transport Workers Union (LAKRS, *Latvijas Sabiedrisko pakalpojumu un Transporta darbinieku arodbiedrība 'LAKRS'*)	Professional/craft
Latvian Federation of Civil Aviation Unions (*Latvijas Aviācijas darbinieku arodbiedrību federācija*)	Industrial
Latvian Nursing and Health Care Personnel Union (*Latvijas Ārstniecības un aprūpes darbinieku arodbiedrība*)	Professional/craft
Latvian Building Sector Union (LBNA, *Latvijas Būvniecības nozares arodbiedrība*)	Industrial
Latvian Road Workers Union (*Latvijas Ceļu darbinieku arodbiedrība*)	Professional/craft
Latvian Trade Union 'Energija' (*Latvijas arodbiedrība 'Enerģija'*)	Industrial
Latvian Interior Employees Union (*Latvijas Iekšlietu darbinieku arodbiedrība*)	Professional/craft
Latvian Industrial Workers Union (*Latvijas Industriālo nozaru arodbiedrība*)	Professional/craft
Latvian Cultural Sector Union (*Latvijas Kultūras darbinieku arodbiedrība*)	Professional/craft
Latvian Agriculture and Food Industry Workers Union (*Latvijas Lauksaimniecības un pārtikas nozaru arodbiedrība*)	Industrial
Latvian Forest Workers Union (*Latvijas Meža nozares arodbiedrība*)	Industrial

(*Continued*)

Table 17.2 Continued

Current affiliates, 2020	**Type**
Latvian Local Government Union (*Latvijas Pašvaldību darbinieku arodbiedrība*)	Professional/craft
Latvian Communication Workers Union (*Latvijas Sakaru darbinieku arodbiedrība*)	Professional/craft
Latvian Commerce Workers Union (*Latvijas Tirdzniecības darbinieku arodbiedrība*)	Professional/craft
Latvian Merchant Seafarers Union (*Latvijas Tirdzniecības flotes jūrnieku arodbiedrība*)	Professional/craft
Latvian Water Transport Union Federation (*Latvijas Ūdenstransporta federatīvā arodbiedrība*)	Industrial
Latvian Union of Employees of State Institutions, Self-governments and Finance Sector (LVIPUFDA, *Latvijas Valsts iestāžu, pašvaldību, uzņēmumu un finanšu darbinieku arodbiedrība*)	Professional/craft
Past affiliates, 2002, 2010	**Type**
Latvian Metalworkers Union (*Latvijas Metālistu arodbiedrība*) (affiliate in 2002 and 2010, liquidated in 2011)	Professional/craft
Latvian Associated Police Union (*Latvijas Apvienotā policistu arodbiedrība*) (affiliate in 2002 and 2010, not liquidated)	Professional/craft
Latvian Food Industry Union (*Latvijas Pārtikas rūpniecības arodbiedrība*) (affiliate in 2002, liquidated in 2004)	Industrial
Associated Trade Union 'Latvian Metal' (*Apvienotā arodbiedrība 'Latvijas Metāls'*) (affiliate in 2002, liquidated in 2008)	Industrial
Latvian Fishermen's Union (*Latvijas Zvejnieku arodbiedrība*) (affiliate in 2002, liquidated in 2006)	Professional/craft
Metallurgical Workers Union of Liepaja (*Liepājas Metalurgu arodbiedrība*) (affiliate in 2002, liquidated in 2015)	Professional/craft
Latvian Book Industry Trade Union (*Arodbiedrība 'Latvijas Grāmatrūpniecības Arodu savienība'*) (affiliate in 2002, not liquidated)	Industrial
Latvian Fisheries Workers' Union (*Latvijas Zivsaimniecības darbinieku arodbiedrība*) (affiliate in 2002, not liquidated)	Professional/craft
State Electrotechnical Factory (VEF) Employees' Trade Union (*VEF darbinieku arodbiedrība*) (affiliate in 2002, not liquidated)	Company

Source: Author's compilation based on LBAS (n.d.b, 2002, 2010) and data from legal information database 'Lursoft'.

Statistics on the number of trade unions or their membership are not collected nationally, but a review of LBAS affiliates suggests that the majority of members are in the public sector (see Table 17.2), including companies in which the state and local governments are large shareholders. The largest LBAS affiliates are the Latvian Union of Education and Science Employees (LIZDA, *Latvijas Izglītības un zinātnes darbinieku arodbiedrība*), with 1,100 workplace and regional branches and around 27,500 members, the Latvian Railway and Transport Industry Union (LDzSA, *Latvijas Dzelzceļnieku un satiksmes nozares arodbiedrība*), with around 11,000 members, the Latvian Health and Social Care Employees Union (LVSADA, *Latvijas Veselības un sociālās aprūpes darbinieku arodbiedrība*), with sixty-seven workplace and regional branches and around 10,000 members, and the Latvian Public Service and Transport Workers Union (LAKRS, *Latvijas Sabiedrisko pakalpojumu un Transporta darbinieku arodbiedrība*), with 219 workplace and regional branches (Ījabs 2021, Fulton 2020a). These four unions account for more than half of the 90,000 or so employees represented by LBAS affiliates.

LBAS represents employees at national level because its member unions cover the largest number of employees (Labour Law section 16). Representation mainly takes the form of tripartite social dialogue, but LBAS also represents its members in concluding collective agreements and other legal agreements with the state and municipal institutions, employers' organizations, the Latvian Association of Local and Regional Governments (LPS, *Latvijas Pašvaldību savienība*), as well as municipal governments (LBAS 2016b: Section 2.2.). Meanwhile employee interests at industry, professional/craft, and regional level are represented by LBAS affiliates, while unions that are not affiliates can be invited to participate (Karnite 2021b). Because of lower and more dispersed economic activity and the reduced presence of the public sector, employee and employer representation and social dialogue outside Riga are generally less developed (Stacenko 2014: 93).

LBAS' supreme decision-making body is the congress, which is convened at least once every five years (LBAS 2016b: Section 6). The delegates are elected by affiliates based on the number of members whose membership fee has been paid, and each associate is allowed to delegate a member as an advisor. The congress also elects the audit committee, consisting of five members from different affiliates for a term of five years (ibid.: Section 11). It is independent and reports only to the congress, while also submitting annual reports to the board and the council. Meetings of the audit committee take place at least once a year.

In-between congresses, the council is LBAS' decision-making body. The council is established after each congress and consists of delegates from all affiliates, proportional to the number of members, based on the principle that each affiliate elects one delegate and an additional one for every 2,000 members (ibid.: Section 8). The procedure for appointing delegates is determined by each affiliate autonomously. Council meetings are convened by the chair at least twice a year or at the request of at least one-third of council members.

The board is LBAS' executive body and comprises nine members: the chair and vice-chairs of LBAS and chairs of affiliates elected by the council. Only one board member can be elected from each affiliate (ibid.: Section 9). Chairs of affiliates not elected as board members can participate in board meetings as advisors. The board meetings are convened by the chair or vice-chairs or at the request of at least two board members and at least every two months. Other parties can be invited to participate in board meetings if their presence is relevant to the issues discussed. The board is different from other LBAS structures in that it is explicitly forbidden for a board member to be actively involved in political parties during their term of office.

LBAS also has regional structures, which implement congress, council and board decisions (ibid.: Section 12). Affiliates and associates are obliged to delegate representatives to industrial experts' councils and other councils, as well as to participate in industrial actions organized and supported by LBAS (ibid.: Section 2.2). Meanwhile LBAS affiliates have a right to delegate representatives to the administrative bodies of LBAS and NTSP and its sub-councils (LBAS 2016b: Section 4.1). Affiliates also have a right to participate in decision-making, to be involved in the management of properties, as well as to submit issues to be added to the agenda of the LBAS board, council and congress, and to participate in LBAS projects (ibid.: Section 4.1–4.2). No surveys by impartial third parties, however, have been carried out recently to assess the members' sense of involvement and the quality of relations between the confederation, industrial and regional unions and their affiliates. Overall, unions that are LBAS affiliates and associates are autonomous in their decision-making, although their operations must comply with LBAS statutes and any agreement concluded by LBAS.

Unionization

Official data are not collected on overall trade union membership and density, and LBAS receives data from its affiliates on a voluntary basis only, which raises issues of comparability and reliability (Karnite 2021a). The LBAS data do, nonetheless, provide a source for estimations of total union membership and density. These suggest that union density in Latvia has been decreasing since the restoration of independence and the concurrent socio-economic and political transformations, from 29 per cent in the 1990s, to 17 per cent in the 2000s, and 13 per cent in the 2010s and 2020s (see Appendix A1). Union density in the public sector is higher than the overall average. In 2011, it was estimated to account for 33 per cent, and in health care, social care and education even up to 60 per cent (Stacenko and Gude 2011: 170). While the specific figures are likely to have decreased since 2011, the pattern can be expected to have remained. There is no single reason or a simple explanation for the decline in union density over the past 30 years. Instead, a complex combination of socio-economic and political transformations has led to the decline.

First, Latvia's accession to the EU in 2004 and the Schengen Area in 2007 opened the door for external labour migration. This opportunity was seized by many low-paid manual workers and workers who had lost their jobs because of the structural changes in labour demand during the transition from a manufacturing to a service economy in the 1990s. Young people with no work experience who had difficulties entering the labour market also migrated in search of employment (LR LM 2007). Because this group of workers largely came from traditional union strongholds in the manufacturing and public sector, their migration to other EU states led to a decrease in union membership.

Furthermore, in the aftermath of the global financial crisis, major structural reforms took place within the public sector. In 2010, the central apparatus of ministries was reduced in size by 30 per cent and the number of state agencies was reduced by 50 per cent: several schools and hospitals were closed. Some 29 per cent of government officials, 14 per cent of education system workers, and 8 per cent of healthcare workers lost their jobs (European Economic and Social Committee 2013: 8). The reforms in the public sector – which generally has higher unionization rates – reportedly led to a marked decrease in union membership and also a decrease in collective bargaining coverage (ibid.: 13). Furthermore, working pensioners also experienced dismissal during the crisis. Because at the time they constituted a large share of union members, this also affected union membership (Stacenko 2012: 76–77; Stacenko 2014: 122–123).

Structural changes also took place in the private sector as employers' efforts to save their businesses and remain profitable, or at least to avoid losses in some cases led to intensified international competition and relocation of manufacturing (Stacenko 2012: 76–77; Stacenko 2014: 122–123). This translated into continuing external migration of labour, further decreasing union membership and union density. In other cases, private sector employers engaged in informal practices, effectively excluding the potential for unions to organize their employees. Unions do not endorse informal practices, but at the time they were perceived as necessary by the majority of workers. In 2011, for example, the informal economy was estimated to amount to 32 per cent of GDP and 67 per cent of workers reported being open to receiving 'envelope wages' (i.e. to be paid under the table) (Lejiņš 2011).

The global financial crisis also incentivized further 'individualization' of employment structures with an increasing number of small-scale forms of entrepreneurship, as witnessed by the growing number of self-employed and micro-enterprises. The number of self-employed increased from 49,000 (or 5 per cent of the working population) in 2011 to 69,000 or 8 per cent of the working population in 2016 (CSP 2020c), probably because some of those who had lost their jobs attempted to start their own business and others were looking for additional income. The number of micro-enterprise tax payers rose from 7,198 to 47,150 or from 1 to 6 per cent of the working population between 2011 and 2016 (Labklājības ministrija 2016). Micro-enterprise tax payer status was introduced in 2010 'to reduce the administrative and tax burden for micro-enterprises, especially in the period of commencement of economic activity, and also in [industries] with a low income potential' (Likumi.lv 2010: Section 1). Among other things, social security contributions are calculated on the basis of annual turnover, which for micro-enterprises is generally very small. Some used this novel form of taxation to launch new businesses, whereas others saw it as a means of restructuring existing business to take advantage of the benefits.

The plethora of self-employed people and micro-enterprises is another segment of the market outside the 'traditional' scope of trade unions in Latvia that is particularly difficult to reach, for several reasons. First, these small bodies often do not have enough members to form an individual union. Second, they are extremely diverse in terms of their activities or, often, combinations of activities, and their economic activities are individualistic in nature. This makes it more difficult to connect and unionize with others. Third, unlike other forms of employment, self-employment in Latvia is typically not regulated by labour law, but by civil law because the majority of self-employed workers do not conclude employment contracts, but service agreements and are not legally in an employment relationship but work as entrepreneurs (Bukovska et al. 2016: 15–16, 20). Because self-employment is regulated mainly by civil law the potential for trade union representation is extremely limited (ibid.: 15–16).

These developments, albeit anecdotal, signal that economic structures and the market are dynamic. Trade unions thus risk further alienation from an increasingly large market segment if they keep their focus only on the core workforce in more 'traditional' industrial relations – the public sector and large- and medium-sized companies – and do not adapt to transformations of the market and economy and fail to reach as yet uncharted 'territories'. The key challenge for unions, therefore, is to shift their focus from prioritizing the protection of their members' rights to the interests of emerging 'non-traditional' segments of the working population (Bukovska et al. 2016: 18). This shift is also relevant in the context of attracting younger members.

Union density among younger people is decreasing. In 2010, for example, only around 10 per cent of union members were under the age of 35, falling to 7 per cent by 2017 (Romele 2017: 136). It has been speculated that young people's unionization rate is low because of emigration, frequent company restructuring in the private sector, which can slow down the formation of unions and hinder bargaining potential, as well as a general lack of knowledge about unions among younger people (ibid.: 136). Although LBAS and its affiliates acknowledge the importance of generational renewal and attracting new members, and the objective of recruiting younger workers is frequently included in strategic planning documents, in practice, trade union organizing is not always systematic and reportedly more successful in companies where unions and employers work together as partners in an ongoing dialogue, which is rare (Vilde 2006: 6).

Union resources and expenditure

While specific data on union income and expenditure are not publicly available in Latvia, annual union reports are submitted and can be purchased from the legal information database 'Lursoft'. Generally, in the case of larger unions, workplace or associate branches collect membership fees and then pay a share to the union, determined by the union's statutes. Shares of unions' income are directed towards centralized saving funds, allocated to funds of workplace and associate branches and their structures, and used for the implementation of union objectives.

LBAS's statutes lay down that it should obtain income from affiliation and association fees, operational activities, donations, gifts and other, unspecified forms of income (LBAS 2016b: Section 14). LBAS receives monthly income from affiliates (3 per cent of their revenue from membership fees) and from associates (30 per cent of their income from membership fees) (ibid.: Section 5). A review of selected LBAS annual reports (see Table 17.3) shows that the dominant sources of income and objects of expenditure have changed over time.

Table 17.3 LBAS income and expenditure 2000, 2011 and 2019

Income[a]	**2000**[b] **(€)**	**Percentage of total**	**2011**[b] **(€)**	**Percentage of total**	**2019 (€)**	**Percentage of total**
Affiliation and association fees, enrolment fees, and other annual contributions	70,940	38.9	85,332	10.4	206,707	17.2
Donations and gifts	0	0.0	10,439	1.3	400	0.0
Grants, including from foreign funds	0	0.0	558,955	68.2	604,877	50.2
Income from economic activities	99,424	54.5	118,780	14.5	297,571	24.7
Other income	12,214	6.7	46,513	5.7	95,549	7.9
Total	182,579		820,018		1,205,104	
Expenditure[a]	**2000**[b] **(€)**	**Percentage of total**	**2011**[b] **(€)**	**Percentage of total**	**2019 (€)**	**Percentage of total**
Expenses for achieving objectives and targets defined in the LBAS statutes[c]	12,231	6.6	0	0.0	0	0.0
Payments to people	0	0.0	1,578	0.2	7,990	0.7

Table 17.3 Continued

Expenditure[a]	2000[b] (€)	Percentage of total	2011[b] (€)	Percentage of total	2019 (€)	Percentage of total
Material expenses	1,148	0.6	127	0.0	2,581	0.2
Wages	71,978	39.0	285,577	32.7	609,550	50.8
Social security contributions	18,640	10.1	65,393	7.5	141,889	11.8
Depreciation/ amortization of tangible and intangible assets	4,570	2.5	3,005	0.3	12,660	1.1
Other expenses	71,756	38.9	499,582	57.2	394,890	32.9
Taxes	4,115	2.2	17,391	2.0	29,687	2.5
Total	184,438		872,653		1,199,247	

Source: Author's elaboration based on data from LBAS annual reports accessed in the 'Lursoft' database.

Notes:
[a] Positions as defined in LBAS annual reports.
[b] Converted to euros based on an official exchange rate of LVL/EUR: 0.702804.
[c] Position only included in 2000 annual report.

In 2000, 54.5 per cent of LBAS income was generated from economic activities (presumably including but not limited to real estate, shares and loans) and 38.9 per cent from affiliation and association, as well as enrolment fees and other annual contributions of affiliates and associates. In 2011 and also in 2019, grants were the dominant source of income, accounting for 68.2 and 50.2 per cent, respectively, shifting income from economic activities and contributions by affiliates and associates to second and third positions. Although the unions publicly suggested that income had fallen because of falling membership of affiliates and associates, it must be noted that although income from affiliates and associates has indeed not been the dominant source of income for LBAS since the 2010s, the absolute figures in annual reports suggest that such income has, in fact, increased over time. Also LBAS' total income, even disregarding income from various grants, shows a positive trend.

As regards grants, funding from participation in EU projects such as 'Youth Guarantee', 'Framework of Actions on Youth Employment' and the Erasmus+ project 'Vocational education and training (VET) for employment' (LBAS 2016a: 16) has allowed LBAS to cover some of its more pressing issues, such as youth employment, relations – or the lack of them – between trade unions and young workers, as well as the fit – or lack of it – between VET and labour market demands. While grants are a great resource, enabling increased focus on particularly pressing subjects, the issues (as will be discussed in the following sections) have proven unresolvable through short-term projects. A more systematic approach, less reliant on external resources, is required.

LBAS expenditure, similarly to its revenue, also changed during the global financial crisis, but has since returned to its previous pattern. In 2000, wages and social security contributions jointly accounted for 49.1 per cent of total expenses, while 38.9 per cent was in the vague category of 'other expenses'. This probably included, among other things, credit commitments, loans and potentially also income allocation to internal funds and members' benefits. During the crisis, 'other expenses' became the dominant expenditure, accounting for 57.2 per cent of the total, while wages and social security contributions accounted for 40.2 per cent. In 2019, however, the proportion of wages and social security contributions surpassed this level, accounting for 62.7 per cent, while 'other expenses' made up 32.9 per cent. The large share of wages and social security contributions in LBAS' expenses can be explained by the fact that in its day-to-day activities LBAS relies heavily on paid union employees rather than on the active participation of union members. It must be noted nonetheless that LBAS' structure of income and expenditure is not necessarily indicative of all trade unions in Latvia. An evidence-based assessment of income would require extensive research in union annual reports.

Generally, union membership fees are defined by union statutes and typically amount to 1 per cent of members' monthly earnings (LBAS n.d.). Fees can either be covered directly by members or employers can withhold the agreed amount from union members' wages and transfer it to the union (Stacenko 2014: 108). In the case of industrial trade unions, around 60–90 per cent of revenue from membership fees remain at branch level, while around 10–30 per cent is transferred to industrial unions and national union centres (Mickeviča 2014: 12). In LBAS, affiliates must pay a monthly fee of 3 per cent and associates must pay a monthly fee of 30 per cent of monthly revenue from membership fees. The basis for calculation must not be lower than the annually defined amount of the minimum wage (LBAS 2016b: Section 5).

Unions suggest that grants have become an important resource for access to experts in various aspects of industrial relations, who can advise affiliates and associates about collective agreements and other legal questions, help prepare pre-trial warnings and creditor claims, lodge applications in the court, ensure efficient participation in national-level tripartite dialogue regarding legal act projects and other relevant initiatives, and educate branch officials regarding collective bargaining and recruitment process (Mickeviča 2014: 13; Romele 2017: 128). The funding has also proven useful for carrying out information campaigns promoting labour rights, occupational safety and health (OSH), and sustainability in the context of employment, as well as for celebrating examples of good industrial relations practice in Latvia and by extension promoting trade unions and unionization (LBAS 2016a: 60–63; Romele 2017: 134–136).

In addition to those related to direct representative and consultative functions expenses are also incurred for information campaigns and other forms of communication with the general public and members. In addition, trade unions provide benefits and services to members including, but not limited to, health insurance, Christmas gifts, professional training and lunch vouchers (Stacenko 2014: 145; Stacenko and Sloka 2014: 109).

Collective bargaining and unions at the workplace

In Latvia, as in other Baltic states, single employer bargaining at the company level is the predominant form of bargaining, although recent developments suggest the increasing importance of industry-level bargaining (Lulle and Ungure 2019). Generally, collective bargaining is conducted by trade unions, although labour law also allows non-union trusted representatives, who can be elected as employee representatives in companies with at least five employees, to conduct negotiations with employers. Compared with these trusted representatives unions are in a privileged position, for two reasons. First, labour law defines very specific conditions for the bargaining activities of trusted representatives. Non-union trusted representatives can initiate collective bargaining only if the employees have not joined or established a trade union (Likumi.lv 2001: Section 18). Furthermore, if there is one or more trade union and non-union trusted representatives in a company at the same time, each body must nominate representatives for the negotiations with the employer in proportion to the number of employees they represent and they must agree upon a joint bargaining position (Likumi.lv 2001: Section 10). The second reason why unions are in a privileged position is the numerical fact that the number of union representatives is significantly higher than the number of trusted representatives. In 2019, there were only around 1,000 trusted representatives, compared with almost 2,000 workplace and associate branches of LBAS affiliates alone (LBAS 2019b).

Statistical data on the presence of union and non-union employee representatives at companies are not collected nationally and the only indication as regards company- and firm-level representation structures comes from Eurofound's 2013 European Company Survey, which suggests than only 9 per cent of companies with at least ten employees had some form of employee representation (Fulton 2020c). The survey results also indicate that larger companies are more likely to have employee representation (31 per cent of companies with more than 250 employees and 22 per cent of companies with 59–249 employees) than those with smaller number of employees (6 per cent of companies with 10–49 employees) (ibid.).

Company size and sector are also influential in relation to bargaining coverage, which is distinctly higher in the public sector and in large- and medium-sized companies, whereas collective agreements are rarely concluded in small companies and micro-enterprises (Bukovska et al. 2016: 20). Although LBAS affiliates have always concluded a significant proportion of collective agreements, in the aftermath of the global financial crisis, LBAS data suggest that it has been a challenge to maintain collective agreements (Stacenko 2012: 76). Both the number of valid agreements and coverage are decreasing (see Table 17.4).

Table 17.4 Collective agreements in LBAS affiliate and associate organizations (data for end of year), 2001 and 2006–2016

	2001	2006	2007	2008	2009	2010	2011	2012	2013	2014	2015	2016
Number of valid collective agreements	2,287	2,426	2,007	1,921	1,712	1,460	1,310	1,307	1,339	1,284	1,268	1,152
Number of industry-level agreements	17	21										8
Number of company-level agreements	2,167	2,405										1,144
Number of people employed	935,600	1,030,900	1,057,400	1,054,900	908,500	850,700	861,600	857,600	893,900	884,600	896,100	893,300
Employees covered by collective agreement	203,374				176,075		101,647	136,064	121,150	119,484	116,278	
Collective bargaining coverage	21.7 %				19.4 %		11.8 %	15.9 %	13.6 %	13.5 %	13.0 %	

Source: Author's illustration based on data from ILO (n.d.), Fulton (2020b), Dārziņa (2010), Līne (2016: 107), LBAS surveys (2014, 2015, 2016) cited in Karnite (2021c), CSP (2020b).

An alternative source of data providing quite a different perspective are the sample survey data from the Central Statistical Bureau (CSP, *Centrālā statistikas pārvalde*), which have been collected and processed once every four years since 2010. CSP data suggest that the number of employees covered by collective agreements (i.e. bargaining coverage) is much higher than LBAS estimates (see Table 17.5). It is not clear what the source of these discrepancies might be and also what data might represent the actual situation and developments more accurately. This point attests to the dire need for reliable, official statistics on various indicators regarding collective bargaining.

Table 17.5 Collective agreements and coverage by collective agreements, 2010, 2014 and 2018

	2010	**% of total**	**2014**	**% of total**	**2018**	**% of total**
Number of employees	766,200		889,500		904,500	
Collective bargaining coverage (%)	32.9		32.4		27.1	
Number of employees covered by collective agreement	251,800		288,400		244,700	
Employees covered by company-level agreements	224,800	89.3	268,300	93.0	218,000	89.1
Employees covered by industry-level agreements	25,800	10.2	18,300	6.3	18,200	7.4
Employees covered by territorial/regional agreements	1,100	0.4	1,300	0.5	3,500	1.4
Employees covered by cross-industry agreements	0	0.0	500	0.2	5,100	2.1

Source: Author's illustration based on the data from CSP (2020a).

As a rule, bargaining coverage is higher if collective agreements are concluded at industry level because company-level agreements often cover a relatively small number of workers, especially in an economy dominated by small and micro-enterprises. In principle, the law provides for the possibility to extend agreements to cover a whole industry if, according to CSP data, the members of the signatory employers' association employ more than 50 per cent of the workers in the respective industry or if the turnover of their goods or volume of services amounts to more than 50 per cent of that in the whole industry (ibid.: Section 18, Part 4).

If these two conditions are met, the agreement can be extended to be binding for all employers of the respective industry and their employees, whether unionized or not. In practice, however, this rarely happens, as illustrated by the low number of industrial agreements more generally (see Tables 17.4 and 17.5).

The decreasing bargaining coverage can at least partially be attributed to the legal transformations in 2010, when the Law on Remuneration of Officials and Employees of State and Local Government Authorities entered into force, setting the terms for determining the monthly salary of officials of the state and local government authorities (Likumi.lv 2009b: Chapter III). Additional payments and bonuses, compensation, insurance, and reimbursement of expenses of officials is also determined by law and no other forms and amounts of remuneration and social guarantees can be provided by collective agreements, except for a modest selection of cases listed in the Law (Likumi.lv 2009b: Chapter II, Section 3).

Concluding collective agreements in the public sector has thus in many cases become redundant as the Law removes the right to collective bargaining on wages and monetary bonuses in most cases for employees of the state and local government authorities. As a result of the law coming into force, in 2010, only one out of fourteen ministries had a valid collective agreement and because of the Law its regulations were essentially not followed (Dārziņa 2010). Also, in almost all local governments and the majority of companies in which the state and local governments were large shareholders – the majority of which previously had valid agreements – the agreements were suspended (ibid.). Because the largest unions represent the public sector, these restrictions on wage bargaining have hindered the increase of bargaining coverage. While trade unions have been pushing for amendments to the Law, there have been no substantial improvements.

Additionally, although employers are not legally allowed to refuse collective bargaining they are generally not particularly keen on concluding collective agreements – even though since 2020, a warning or a fine ranging from 70 to 140 'fine units' (in 2020, one 'fine unit' equalled EUR 5) can be imposed on an employer refusing to participate in collective bargaining (Likumi.lv 2001: Section 160). The reluctance of employers to engage in collective bargaining can be explained partly by the fact that collective agreements set higher standards for the signatory parties, particularly regarding wages. Because the statutory minimum wage, which is determined annually by the government, is mostly well under the average wage level of any industry, employers who have concluded collective agreements sometimes put themselves at a competitive disadvantage compared with those employers who have not concluded agreements and are potentially involved in informal economic practices, choosing to pay above the minimum wage (envelope wages) and in consequence spending less on taxes (Helmane 2018).

Although company agreements are still much more common than industrial agreements and provide most of the coverage, in recent years, the government has become more open to the possibility of introducing legislative amendments to foster industrial agreements and their extension. In 2019, the Labour Law was amended and now provides that in industries with valid agreements defining a minimum wage level that is at least 50 per cent above the statutory minimum wage, a supplement to compensation for overtime work can be set at less than 100 per cent of the daily salary rate or a piecework salary as defined by the state. It cannot be less than 50 per cent of the daily wage, however (Likumi.lv 2001: Section 68). It is expected that this amendment will promote industrial agreements and a higher minimum wage, particularly in industries characterized by seasonal and, potentially, also project-based work (Helmane 2018).

As a result, industrial agreements were concluded in the construction industry and the glass fibre industry (LBNA 2019c; LDDK and LBAS 2020). Another agreement was concluded in the hospitality industry, but has not yet become binding (LDDK and LBAS 2020). In 2018, the Ministry of Finance signed a cooperation agreement with the Association of Hotels and Restaurants of Latvia and the Latvian Restaurant Society (*Latvijas Restorānu biedrība*) to foster the conclusion of an industrial agreement in the hospitality industry. The Ministry agreed to work towards reducing the VAT rate for the catering industry if the agreement manages to provide for an increase in the average wage in the sector, thereby curbing the extent of the informal economy (Finanšu ministrija 2018). Application of the reduced VAT rate is considered a precondition for the industrial agreement to become binding by its signatories, but so far it has not been met. Since 2018, there have also been negotiations on concluding an industrial agreement in the transport industry. Both industries are recognized by LAKRS as not meeting expectations as regards decent work (LAKRS 2020; Dābola n.d.). As of April 2022, however, neither of these agreements had been concluded. Extended agreements concluded before legislative amendments are still valid in the railway industry and in health care (Fulton 2020b).

Industrial conflict

Latvia is generally not a strike-prone country (see Appendix A1). Other forms of industrial conflict are more common (Stacenko 2014: 116). When industrial action happens, it is typically within the public sector. Three of the trade unions that have been more active than others in terms of mobilizing and organizing rallies, protests and pickets during and after the global financial crisis are LIZDA, LVSADA and LVIPUFDA, which represent workers in education, health and social care, and state institutions (Romele 2017: 129). All three unions mobilized for similar reasons, to demand increases in funding and income equality. LVSADA fought for an improved healthcare budget to guarantee accessibility and quality of services, minimize co-payments, and increase international and intersectoral wage competitiveness. LVIPUFDA was trying to ensure income equality in state institutions between different institutions and ranks and also territorially, between the centre and the periphery of the country. LIZDA attempted to eliminate income inequality in education and science, fought reductions in teachers' salaries and strove for a new model for teachers' remuneration, for a general increase in funding for science, and for improvements in the remuneration of higher education and science workers. They also implemented protest measures, feeling that education workers' perspective was being disregarded during the planning of education reforms.

Overall, letter and signature campaigns for different industrial relations causes are more popular and seem to have been more successful in terms of achieving goals than other forms of industrial action (ibid.: 129–130). One of the most successful letter campaigns was organized by LIZDA in 2011 against further reductions of teachers' salaries, as a result of which salaries remained unchanged (ibid.: 129). A successful petition campaign was organized by LBAS during the global financial crisis in response to the employers' initiative to cut overtime payments by 50 per cent purportedly in order to improve Latvia's competitiveness. LBAS' campaign 'Hands off the Labour Law' managed to gather around 20,000 signatures for a petition to reject the employers' proposal and ensured that the proposed legislative changes were not implemented (ibid.: 130).

Overall, there are two main reasons for the lack of strikes. First, the legislation regulating strikes is rather restrictive. The Law provides that 'the right to strike shall be exercised as a last resort if no agreement and reconciliation has been reached in the collective interest dispute' (Likumi.lv 2002: Section 3). The Strike Law also limits the strike possibilities of a significant part of the working population. The Law completely prohibits 'judges, prosecutors, police officers, employees of fire safety, fire-fighting and rescue services, border guards, employees of the state security institutions, warders and people serving in the national armed forces' from striking (Likumi.lv 1998: Section 16). It also states that in case of a strike a minimum level of services must be ensured in critical public services, including health care, public transport, electricity and gas production and supplies, communications, waste and waste water collection and treatment, and civil defence (ibid.: Section 17). The definition of 'minimum level' was left open for interpretation, thus limiting the potential for strikes in these industries because they may be deemed unlawful (Līne 2016: 91). Also, solidarity strikes are prohibited unless they are related to a collective agreement that has not been concluded or breaches of a binding agreement relevant to the particular industry or profession/craft (Likumi.lv 1998: Section 23), which might limit the potential to achieve a 'critical mass' for any strike to be effective.

Second, during a strike, striking employees do not get paid and the employer does not make social security payments for them either, unless a collective agreement provides for a different arrangement (Likumi.lv 2002: Section 28). Similar to other Eastern European countries, apart from Slovenia and Poland, revenues from membership fees in Latvia are typically not allocated to strike funds (Mickeviča 2014: 13). Although data on strike funds are not publicly available, the fact that unions have a right to use strike funds not only to support members in case of a strike but also to cover the cost of services, it is very likely that unions might not be able to guarantee sufficient funding to members during a strike (ibid.: 118–119). As a result, LBAS considers strikes as an extreme measure, preferring to pursue its aims through social dialogue (Romele 2017: 128–129) and different forms of industrial action.

Political relations

Latvian unions operate in a difficult political environment. Since 1990, there have been around twenty government coalitions, in most cases dominated by the centre-right pursuing a neoliberal economic agenda emphasizing privatization and individualization (Lulle and Ungure 2019). Furthermore, similar to other new EU member states in which trade unions used to be part of the socialist trade union system, during the 1990s trade unions in Latvia transitioned from a mode of conduct in which the state was the dominant actor to a model of social partnership. Within this framework it can be challenging to find a balance between political participation for the improvement of workers' situations and association with political parties, which, because of the historical context, can lead to public distrust and a further decrease in membership (Stacenko and Gude 2011: 170). This historical legacy coupled with the legislation restricting the freedom to bargain and to engage in industrial action means that the only option trade unions in Latvia have left to protect and represent their members' interests is social dialogue, tripartite social dialogue in particular.

The tripartite NTSP is the main platform for social dialogue and includes representatives from LBAS, the Employers' Confederation of Latvia (LDDK, *Latvijas Darba devēju konfederācija*), and the government. They engage in social dialogue on a range of issues, such as legislation and potential legal amendments regarding social security, the national budget, economic development, public health, general and vocational education, employment, professional classification, ratification of ILO conventions, and compliance of national legislation with EU legislation (LBAS 2011: 4). The NTSP's sub-council for vocational education and employment can establish industrial expert councils (Likumi.lv 2016) at the request of employers, trade unions, professional organizations, ministries and coordinators of industry experts' councils (Likumi.lv 2016). The purpose of sub-councils is to coordinate the actions of the actors involved in order to facilitate the development of human resources and vocational education corresponding to labour demand (Likumi.lv 1999: Section 12).

Trade unions can also exercise political influence through lobbying before the state presents an official opinion on any EU legislation to the Council of the EU because the official opinion must be coordinated with the social partners. The latter have a right to lobby not only national institutions but also EU institutions (Likumi.lv 2009a).

Together with the Ministry of Economics, LDDK, LPS and the Latvian Chamber of Commerce and Industry (LTRK, *Latvijas Tirdzniecības un rūpniecības kamera*), LBAS is the founder of the

Economic Council (*Tautsaimniecības padome*), which analyses and provides consultations on issues related to business policy with the aim of fostering national competitiveness, improving the business environment and promoting cross-cutting policies for the development of various forms of doing business (Ekonomikas ministrija 2020). The Economic Council collaborates with local and regional municipalities, researchers, employers and the government in seeking compromises and establishing common perspectives (Līne 2016: 104). LBAS also participates in the Labour Market Forecasting Consulting Council of the Ministry of Economics, the Training Commission of the Ministry of Welfare, and the Cooperation Council of the Career Development Support System (LBAS 2016a: 16), which was created to ensure the circulation of information between different agents concerning guidance on education and training in order to develop, promote and advise on career development support services and promote vocational education and continuing education (Euroguidance n.d.).

Also, in 2017, LBAS and LDDK launched a European Social Fund project with the aim of establishing collective agreements in the timber industry, chemicals, construction, transport and logistics, and telecommunications (LBAS 2019a). It is expected that collective agreements include terms encouraging employers' investments in employee skill improvement and lifelong learning, promoting gender equality and allowing the regular production of labour market forecasts to ensure timely adjustment of the labour supply to demand in terms of adequate education and skills and to adjust to the predictable disappearance of certain occupations and crafts (ibid.).

Typically, unions do not have an explicit working relationship with political parties, although there was an exceptional case regarding the trade union LABA, which is not an affiliate or an associate of LBAS and does not hide its links with the left-leaning alliance of political parties 'Saskaņa', previously 'Saskaņas centrs' (Latvijas TV raidījums 'De facto' 2013, Dragiļeva 2015, 'De facto' and Šņore 2017). Generally, LBAS as a trade union confederation attempts to conclude memorandums of cooperation with most political parties (DIENA 2010). Trade unions are also allowed to conclude agreements about issues relevant to their industry or profession/craft directly with political parties but this rarely happens (Zvirbulis 2017). Overall, LBAS and most of its affiliates and associates are cautious of becoming associated with any political party and for the most part retain political neutrality, remaining aloof from politics in order to best serve their members' interests (Šņore and 'De facto' 2015). The cautious union attitude towards involvement in politics is explained by the general public distrust in political parties stemming from the socialist past. This distrust has remained very high since the restoration of independence. In 2020, still only 6 per cent of the public expressed trust in political parties in a Eurobarometer survey (European Commission 2020: T31) and it has scarcely improved since then.

Societal power

Societal power seems to be the most untapped power resource for trade unions in Latvia. This is because information on labour rights and OSH is lacking in school curricula. This means that young people are not informed about employment relationships, including the role of trade unions (Romele 2017: 134). Trade unions are also poorly covered by public media (see Līne 2016) and have not managed to seize the opportunities provided by social media. For example, LBAS runs accounts on Twitter and Facebook, but the number of followers is quite modest at around 2,000 followers on each platform in 2021.

To mitigate the lack of public knowledge about unions, particularly among young people, in 2007 LBAS launched a competition 'A Pro' ('Profs') about labour rights and OSH targeted at vocational school pupils, running until 2013. In 2011 it was extended to include secondary school pupils under the name 'Smart: a game for those who learn' (*Smārts: spēle tiem, kuri mācas*). Training sessions on labour rights and OSH were held by LBAS at all education institutions that qualified for the semi-finals, and a training manual 'Becoming an Employee' was issued with the aim of providing pupils with the basic information necessary for entry into the labour market. After 2013, the contest was continued at secondary schools in Riga municipality and in 2015, 35 per cent of all secondary schools in Riga had become participants. This was interpreted by LBAS as a successful targeted information campaign (Romele 2017: 134, 135–136). These activities, however, do not seem to have translated into a substantial growth of union membership.

Preserving and acquiring societal power remains one of the biggest challenges for LBAS and unions in Latvia in general not only in terms of reaching young people – the new generation of workers and potential trade union members and officials – but also in terms of communication and cooperation with NGOs, which for the moment seems to be severely lacking. Furthermore, even in a research context it is difficult to find reliable data on the basis of which to assess trade unions' developments and achievements, as exemplified by the discussion above on the availability of statistics on collective bargaining. There is thus a dire need for open communication and engagement with the general public by the unions in order to accumulate the societal power necessary to maintain their representative function.

Trade union policies towards the European Union

While not all trade unions in Latvia have strong direct working relationships with international colleagues, some of the industrial unions, as well as LBAS, do. LBAS is the most active in terms of engagement with partners within the EU institutional framework.

LBAS became an ETUC member in 2003, one year before Latvia's accession to the EU in 2004. Since then LBAS has participated in ETUC congresses and working structures. In addition, LBAS has occasionally participated in demonstrations, campaigns and other events organized by the ETUC, particularly those particularly relevant to Latvia in the context of the global financial crisis. This includes the EU-wide initiative 'No to austerity measures, priority for jobs and growth' in 2010 and the campaign 'Enough is enough!' in 2012. Despite the relevance of the issues highlighted by these initiatives, the degree of mobilization was low among trade union members (Romele 2017: 130).

Overall, in relation to the EU institutions, LBAS values them mainly as a source of knowledge, exchange of expertise and finance. In particular, LBAS appreciates the potential for training and learning provided by the ETUC and the ETUI related to legislative matters and political initiatives, especially with regard to employment protection issues (interview with LBAS representative 2021). ETUI's training course 'European training for young trade union leaders' in particular has been highlighted by LBAS as a very useful resource, providing much needed knowledge and experience to local unions (ibid.). Some LBAS employees are now undergoing training to become future coaches, enabling them to pass on their knowledge and skills to other colleagues, internationally and locally (ibid.).

In relation to ETUFs, LBAS and industrial unions are most appreciative of the opportunity to access the texts of collective agreements concluded by others. This has improved the quality of collective agreements in Latvia (ibid.). Also, LBAS affiliates, the Forestry Workers Trade Union, the Latvian Building Sector Trade Union, the Communication Workers Trade Union and the Federation of Trade Unions in Civil Aviation have established good working relationships with the corresponding ETUFs. According to LBAS, support from the European Federation of Building and Woodworkers (EFBWW) and also from the ETUC for their demands for legislative changes regarding compensation for overtime work was crucial for achieving amendments and the conclusion of a collective agreement in the construction industry (ibid.).

Furthermore, in 2015/2016 LBAS started training for involvement in the European Semester and recalls first sensing a certain level of agency in the Semester in 2018/2019, when, after having highlighted the key challenges in the annual Semester report, LBAS received significant support from the European Commission representation in Latvia with regard to involving social partners in the preparation of the National Development Plan by the government. As a result of this LBAS received a draft plan for review in good time. Unfortunately, during the Covid-19 pandemic when the annual report for the European Semester was not prepared and instead a recovery resilience plan was drawn up, the government failed to involve the social partners in strategic planning and discussions. This left little time for the partners to review the plan (ibid.).

In parallel with cross-border relationships within the institutional structures of the EU, since 1999 Latvia has been a member of the Baltic Sea Trade Union Network (BASTUN). BASTUN deals with issues specific to the Baltic Sea region countries – the Baltic states (Latvia, Lithuania and Estonia), Poland, Germany, Russia, Norway, Sweden, Denmark and Finland. Historically, issues such as 'flexicurity', energy and climate policies, the impact of geopolitically relevant conflicts on trade unions, infringements of trade union rights, the potential for strengthening social dialogue and equal representation of all social partners, as well as labour migration (freedom of movement) with undesirable consequences, such as social dumping, have been analysed by BASTUN members (Ostrowski 2017: 18–19).

Latvia has adopted the EU directive on the establishment of EWCs and the Law on Informing and Consulting Employees of Community-scale Undertakings and Groups of Undertakings (Likumi.lv 2011) regulating the establishment and operation of EWCs. But while there are transnational companies operating in Latvia, no parent companies known to LBAS are locally based and so their EWCs are also based in other countries (interview with LBAS representative 2021). Overall, because only one LBAS employee is directly responsible for EU issues, there are not enough resources for full involvement in these issues and the ability to reach out to EWCs and EU institutions is very limited (ibid.).

Conclusions

The developments described in this chapter attest that trade unions in Latvia have experienced several significant social, political and economic transformations impacting their practices, affecting their power and challenging their representative role.

To sum up these developments, first, what has been described as the 'brutal free economy' of the 1990s forced many employers into informal economic practices that effectively rendered unionization unviable. This is because employees feared loss of employment and employers feared loss of business. Second, the legislative framework in Latvia is quite restrictive and rigid, leaving little to be negotiated through collective bargaining and regulated by collective agreements. This disincentivized employees from engagement in bargaining, even where unions were present. The legislation also limits the potential for industrial action – traditionally a fundamental source of union power – leaving employees asking what kind of power unions actually have. During the 1990s, the economy underwent a tertiarization, shifting the main focus from manufacturing to services. This not only changed the structure of labour demand but also led to increased unemployment in industries that are traditional union strongholds. This in turn is an important explanation of the fall in union density.

Shortly after the initial hostility towards the transition to a market economy had subsided to some degree around the turn of the century, trade unions faced yet another challenge. As Latvia became part of the EU and the Schengen Area, masses of workers migrated abroad in search of better employment, further reducing union membership. The process continued throughout the global financial crisis, which was accompanied by strict austerity measures, fostering the intensification of informal practices, legislative changes limiting the potential for collective bargaining in the public sector, as well as a significant reduction in the size of the public sector and lay-offs of working pensioners, both major segments of union membership until then.

These developments might have forced trade unions to either perish or to adjust their practices to the new and ever-changing conditions. To have achieved adjustment, unions would have had to operationalize and optimize internal resources; mobilize members for collective goals; provide systematic training to young people in industrial relations and unionism; actively recruit the new generation of workers as members; and develop links with NGOs. In this context access to grants served only as short-term fixes and potentially delayed the accumulation of organizational power by keeping unions' focus on themselves as one of the – in theory competing – social partners in negotiations with the state: that is, by prioritizing institutional power over organizational power.

More generously, it might be argued that grants may also have served to provide leeway for a more gradual shift towards union revitalization. Grants have allowed unions and LBAS to continue to operate under difficult and rapidly changing conditions, giving them time and opportunities for training and building experience within the EU institutional framework. They also enabled them to find and explore common ground with employers' representatives over mutually unfavourable legislation on industrial relations. In some respects in recent years the establishment of common ground has evolved into a partnership protecting both employer and trade union interests vis-à-vis the state. This has generated mutual benefits in the form of the growing number of industrial and extended agreements, which allow for a more individualized regulation of industrial relations. These recent developments provide a sense of potential for a scenario of revitalization and escaping marginalization, as theorized by Visser (2019: 68–70) for the future of trade unions in Latvia. It seems unlikely, however, that complete revitalization would be possible without a significant shift in terms of increasing the unions' associational and organizational power resources.

References

All links were checked on 28 February 2022.

Bukovska M. et al. (2016) The rise of the dual labour market: fighting precarious employment in the new member states through industrial relations (PRECARIR). Country report: Latvia, CELSI Research Report 16, Bratislava, Central European Labour Studies Institute.

CSP (2020a) DSS170. Darbinieku skaita sadalījums pa darbības veidiem pēc koplīguma veidiem oktobra beigās (tūkst. cilvēku). https://data.csb.gov.lv/pxweb/lv/sociala/sociala__dsamaksa__dsamaksa_strukt__dsamaksa_strukt/DSS170.px/

CSP (2020b) NBG070. Nodarbinātie pa vecuma grupām un pēc dzimuma. https://data.csb.gov.lv/pxweb/lv/sociala/sociala__nodarb__nodarb__ikgad/NBG070.px

CSP (2020c) NBG090. Nodarbinātie pēc statusa un dzimuma. https://data1.csb.gov.lv/pxweb/lv/sociala/sociala__nodarb__nodarb__ikgad/NBG090.px/

Dābola E. (n.d.) Ģenerālvienošanās ēdināšanas nozarē! https://lakrs.lv/?p=1658#more-1658

Dārziņa L. (2010) Darba koplīgumi – problēmas ne tikai krīzes spaidos. https://lvportals.lv/norises/213069-darba-kopligumi-problemas-ne-tikai-krizes-spaidos-2010

'De facto' and Šņore I. (2017) 'Saskaņai' pietuvinātā arodbiedrība mēģina izplesties Latvijas Pastā. https://www.lsm.lv/raksts/zinas/latvija/saskanai-pietuvinata-arodbiedriba-megina-izplesties-latvijas-pasta.a247309/

DIENA (2010) Tagad visi naski uz vienošanos. Diena, 28 July 2010. https://www.diena.lv/raksts/sodien-laikraksta/tagad-visi-naski-uz-vienosanos-744044

Dragiļeva O. (2015) Arī 'Rīgas namu pārvaldnieks' dāsni baro 'Saskaņai' lojālo arodbiedrību, LSM.lv, 18 January 2015. https://www.lsm.lv/raksts/zinas/zinu-analize/ari-rigas-namu-parvaldnieks-dasni-baro-saskanai-lojalo-arodbiedribu.a114210/

European Economic and Social Committee (2013) Pētījums par ekonomisko un sociālo situāciju Baltijas valstīs: Latvija: pētījums, Brussels, European Economic and Social Committee. https://www.eesc.europa.eu/resources/docs/qe-30-12-151-lv-c.pdf

Ekonomikas ministrija (2020) TSP nolikums. https://www.em.gov.lv/lv/Ministrija/sabiedribas_lidzdaliba/konsultativas_padomes/tautsaimniecibas_padome/tsp_nolikums/

Euro guidance (n.d.) Guidance System in Latvia. https://www.euroguidance.eu/guidance-system-in-latvia

European Commission (2020) Public opinion in the European Union: Standard Eurobarometer, 93 Summer 2020 Annex. https://europa.eu/eurobarometer/surveys/detail/2262

Finanšu ministrija (2018) FM un viesmīlības nozares uzņēmumi paraksta vienošanos par sadarbību. https://lvportals.lv/dienaskartiba/298865-fm-un-viesmilibas-nozares-uznemumi-paraksta-vienosanos-par-sadarbibu-2018

Fulton L. (2020a) Worker representation in Europe. National industrial relations: Trade Unions Latvia. http://www.worker-participation.eu/National-Industrial-Relations/Countries/Latvia/Trade-Unions

Fulton L. (2020b) Worker representation in Europe. National industrial relations: collective bargaining. Latvia. http://www.worker-participation.eu/National-Industrial-Relations/Countries/Latvia/Collective-Bargaining

Fulton L. (2020c) Worker representation in Europe. National industrial relations: workplace representation. Latvia. http://www.worker-participation.eu/National-Industrial-Relations/Countries/Latvia/Workplace-Representation

Helmane I. (2018) Ko paredz ģenerālvienošanās. https://lvportals.lv/skaidrojumi/294656-ko-paredz-generalvienosanas-2018

Ījabs I. (2021) Politiskā līdzdalība, vēlēšanu sistēma Latvijā. https://enciklopedija.lv/skirklis/25486-politisk%C4%81-l%C4%ABdzdal%C4%ABba,-v%C4%93l%C4%93%C5%A1anu-sist%C4%93ma-Latvij%C4%81

ILO (n.d.) National labour law profile: Latvia. https://www.ilo.org/ifpdial/information-resources/national-labour-law-profiles/WCMS_158912/lang--en/index.htm

ILOSTAT (2020) Days not worked per 1000 workers due to strikes and lockouts by economic activity (per 1000 workers). https://www.ilo.org/ilostat-files/Documents/Excel/INDICATOR/STR_DAYS_ECO_RT_A_EN.xlsx

Karnite R. (2021a) Working life in 2020. Latvia: Actors and institutions. https://www.eurofound.europa.eu/country/latvia#actors-and-institutions

Karnite R. (2021b) Working life in 2020. Latvia: background. https://www.eurofound.europa.eu/country/latvia#background

Karnite R. (2021c) Working life in 2020. Latvia: Collective bargaining. https://www.eurofound.europa.eu/country/latvia#collective-bargaining

Kjellberg A. (2021) The shifting role of unions in the social dialogue, European Journal of Workplace Innovation, 6 (2), 220–244. https://doi.org/10.46364/ejwi.v6i2.807

Kluinis A. and Pētersons R. (2006) Arodbiedrību gadsimts, Rīga: AGB.

Kurtyka M. (2006) Study on restructuring in new Member States. Latvia – Country dossier. http://erc-online.eu/wp-content/uploads/2014/04/2006-00887-EN.pdf

Labklājības ministrija (2016) Informatīvais ziņojums 'Par Mikrouzņēmumu nodokļa likuma praktiskās īstenošanas gaitu un rezultātiem, kā arī mazās saimnieciskās darbības veicēju sociālo nodrošinājumu'. http://tap.mk.gov.lv/doc/2016_10/LMZino_30082016.1900.docx

LAKRS (2020) Latvijas Sabiedrisko pakalpojumu un Transporta darbinieku arodbiedrības LAKRS atklātā vēstule. https://lakrs.lv/wp-content/uploads/2020/05/25052020_Nr_50_Atklata_vwstule.pdf

Latvijas TV raidījums 'De facto' (2013) 'Saskaņas centram' lojālā arodbiedrībā mēģina apvienot lielāko Rīgas uzņēmumu darbiniekus, Latvietis 245. http://laikraksts.com/raksti/raksts.php?KursRaksts=3214

LBAS (n.d.a) Arodbiedrības biedri. https://arodbiedribas.lv/mes/arodbiedribas-biedri/

LBAS (n.d.b) Dalīborganizācijas. https://arodbiedribas.lv/daliborganizacijas/

LBAS (2010) Dalīborganizācijas. https://web.archive.org/web/20100225062814/http://www.lbas.lv/lbas_str_daliborg.php

LBAS (2002) Dalīborganizācijas. https://web.archive.org/web/20020705230903/http://www.lbas.lv/daliborganizacijas.html

LBAS (2011) Sociālā dialoga un sociālo partneru definīcija. https://arodbiedribas.lv/wp-content/uploads/2019/11/sociala.dialoga.un_.socialo.partneru.definicija.tiesibu.aktos_29072011_gala.pdf

LBAS (2016a) Latvijas Brīvo arodbiedrību savienības darbības pārskats 2011–2016. https://arodbiedribas.lv/wp-content/uploads/2019/11/lbas_kongress2016_majas_lapai.pdf

LBAS (2016b) Latvijas Brīvo arodbiedrību savienības Statūti (jaunā redakcija). https://arodbiedribas.lv/mes/dokumenti/

LBAS (2019a) LBAS par Nacionālo attīstības plānu 2021–2027. https://www.pkc.gov.lv/sites/default/files/inline-files/LBAS%20par%20NAP2027.pdf

LBAS (2019b) Darba aizsardzības konferencē. https://arodbiedribas.lv/news/darba-aizsardzibas-konference/

LBNA (2019c) General Agreement, Rīga, Latvijas Būvniecības nozares arodbiedrība. https://lbna.lv/en/general-agreement

LDDK and LBAS (2020) Attīstot nozaru koplīgumu pārrunas. Online conference, 9 December 2020.

Lejiņš A. (2011) BSF 7. foruma: 'Arodbiedrību loma nabadzības samazināšanā, pilsoniskās sabiedrības veidošanā un darbinieku tiesiskajā aizsardzībā Latvijā' kopsavilkums (Rīga, 03.12.2010), Rīga, Brīvības un solidaritātes fonds. http://bsf-latvija.lv/lv/2011/03/04/bsf-7-forumakopsavilkums/

Likumi.lv (1998) Strike Law, Latvijas Vēstnesis, 130/131. https://likumi.lv/ta/en/en/id/48074-strike-law

Likumi.lv (1999) Vocational education law, Latvijas Vēstnesis 213/215. https://likumi.lv/ta/en/en/id/20244-vocational-education-law

Likumi.lv (2001) Labour law, Latvijas Vēstnesis, 105. https://likumi.lv/ta/en/en/id/26019-labour-law

Likumi.lv (2002) Labour dispute law, Latvijas Vēstnesis 149. https://likumi.lv/ta/en/en/id/67361-labour-dispute-law

Likumi.lv (2009a) Latvijas Republikas nacionālo pozīciju Eiropas Savienības jautājumos un ar tām saistīto instrukciju izstrādes un informācijas aprites kārtība, Latvijas Vēstnesis 21. https://likumi.lv/ta/id/187425-latvijas-republikas-nacionalo-poziciju-eiropas-savienibas-jautajumos-un-ar-tam-saistito-instrukciju-izstrades-un-informacijas

Likumi.lv (2009b) Law on remuneration of officials and employees of state and local government authorities, Latvijas Vēstnesis 199. https://likumi.lv/ta/en/en/id/202273-law-on-remuneration-of-officials-and-employees-of-state-and-local-government-authorities

Likumi.lv (2010) Micro-enterprise tax law, Latvijas Vēstnesis 131. https://likumi.lv/ta/en/en/id/215302-micro-enterprise-tax-law

Likumi.lv (2011) Law on informing and consulting employees of European Union-scale undertakings and European Union-scale groups of undertakings, Latvijas Vēstnesis 82. https://likumi.lv/ta/en/en/id/230721-law-on-informing-and-consulting-employees-of-european-union-scale-undertakings-and-european-union-scale-groups-of-undertakings

Likumi.lv (2016) Procedures for establishment, operation, and coordination of activities of sectoral expert councils, Latvijas Vēstnesis 141. https://likumi.lv/ta/en/en/id/283737-procedures-for-establishment-operation-and-coordination-of-activities-of-sectoral-expert-councils

Līne A. (2016) Latvijas arodbiedrību stratēģiskās vadīšanas pilnveide. Promocijas darbs doktora zinātniskā grāda iegūšanai vadībzinātnē

(Dr. adm.), Rīga, Latvijas Universitāte. https://dspace.lu.lv/dspace/bitstream/handle/7/34471/298-56266-Line_Antra_AugP040002.pdf?sequence=1&isAllowed=y

LR LM (2007) Darbaspēka ģeogrāfiskā mobilitāte, Riga, Latvijas Universitāte. https://www.lm.gov.lv/lv/media/3886/download

Lulle A. and Ungure E. (2019) Latvia: post-Soviet legacy and the impact of neoliberal ideology on collective bargaining, in Müller T., Vandaele K. and Waddington J. (eds) Collective bargaining in Europe: towards an endgame, Brussels, ETUI, 361–379. https://www.etui.org/sites/default/files/CB%20Vol%20II%20Chapter%2017.pdf

Mickeviča N. (2014) Arodbiedrību pakalpojumi Eiropas Savienības dalībvalstīs, Rīga, Latvijas Brīvo arodbiedrību savienība. https://arodbiedribas.lv/wp-content/uploads/2019/11/tu_services_mickevica_28_02_2014_final.pdf

OECD.Stat (2020) Trade unions and collective bargaining. https://stats.oecd.org/Index.aspx?DataSetCode=TUD

Ostrowski P. (2017) Europe 2020 and the Baltic Region, Warszawa, European Commission. https://www.opzz.org.pl/assets/opzz/media/files/684cc46e-33ed-45dd-acc7-b0383428d470/lv-en-arodbiedr-bu-sadarb-ba-baltijas-re-ion-un-eiropas-savien-bas-strat-ija-eiropa-2020.pdf

Romele L. (2017) From politics to schools: innovative union practices in Latvia, in Bernaciak M. and Kahancova M. (eds) Innovative union practices in Central-Eastern Europe, Brussels, ETUI, 125–138.

Stacenko S. (2012) Employment policies and industrial relations: research issues and practical applications, in Muravska T. and Prause G. (eds) European Integration and Baltic Sea Region Studies: University-Business Partnership through the Triple Helix Approach, Berlin, Berliner Wissenschafts Verlag, 63–79.

Stacenko S. (2014) Arodbiedrību loma sociālajā partnerībā publiskās pārvaldes lēmumu pieņemšanā. Promocijas darbs doktora zinātniskā grāda iegūšanai vadībzinātnes nozarē (Dr. adm.), Rīga, Latvijas Universitāte.

Stacenko S. and Gude I. (2011) Arodbiedrības un to nozīme mūsdienu sabiedrībā [Trade Unions and their role in Contemporary Society], in Ekonomika. Vadības zinātne, Latvijas Universitātes Raksti 766, 163–176.

Stacenko S. and Sloka B. (2014) Trade union practices in the EU and Latvia: experience for Eastern partnership countries, Baltic Journal of European Studies, 4 (2), 99–118.

Šņore I. and 'De facto' (2015) Līgums ar 'Saskaņu' draud sašķelt mediķu arodbiedrību, LSM.lv, 1 February 2015. https://www.lsm.lv/raksts/zinas/zinu-analize/ligums-ar-saskanu-draud-saskelt-mediku-arodbiedribu.a116091/

Vilde K. (2006) Cilvēks vēlas strādāt stabile darba vidē, Arodbiedrību avīze, 6 (8), 6. https://arodbiedribas.lv/wp-content/uploads/2019/11/arodbiedribuavize6_lv.pdf

Visser J. (2019) Trade unions in the balance: ILO ACTRAV Working Paper, Geneva, ILO. https://www.ilo.org/wcmsp5/groups/public/---ed_dialogue/---actrav/documents/publication/wcms_722482.pdf

Waddington J. and Hoffmann R. (eds) (2000) Trade Unions in Europe: facing challenges and searching for solutions, Brussels, ETUI.

Zvirbulis Ģ. (2017) Mediķu arodbiedrībai vairs nebūs līguma ar 'Saskaņu'. https://www.la.lv/mediku-arodbiedribai-vairs-nebus-liguma-ar-saskanu

Abbreviations

BASTUN	Baltic Sea Trade Union Network
CSP	Centrālā statistikas pārvalde (Central Statistical Bureau of Latvia)
ETUC	European Trade Union Confederation
ETUI	European Trade Union Institute
EU	European Union
EWCs	European Works Councils
FICIL	Ārvalstu investoru padome Latvijā (Foreign Investors' Council in Latvia)
ILO	International Labour Organization
IMF	International Monetary Fund
LAKRS	Latvijas Sabiedrisko pakalpojumu un Transporta darbinieku arodbiedrība 'LAKRS' (Latvian Trade Union of Public Service and Transport Workers 'LAKRS')
LBAS	Latvijas Brīvo arodbiedrību savienība (Free Trade Union Confederation of Latvia)
LBNA	Latvijas Būvniecības nozares arodbiedrība (Latvian Building Sector's Trade Union)

LDDK	Latvijas Darba devēju konfederācija (Employers' Confederation of Latvia)
LIZDA	Latvijas Izglītības un zinātnes darbinieku arodbiedrība (Trade Union of Education and Science Employees)
LPS	Latvijas Pašvaldību savienība (Latvian Association of Local and Regional Governments)
LTRK	Latvijas Tirdzniecības un rūpniecības kamera (Latvian Chamber of Commerce and Industry)
LVIPUFDA	Latvijas Valsts iestāžu, pašvaldību, uzņēmumu un finanšu darbinieku arodbiedrība (Trade Union of Employees of State Institutions, Self-Governments and the Finance Sector)
LVSADA	Latvijas Veselības un sociālās aprūpes darbinieku arodbiedrība (Latvian Trade Union of Health and Social Care Employees)
NTSP	Nacionālā trīspusējās sadarbības padome (National Tripartite Cooperation Council)
OSH	Occupational safety and health
USSR	Union of Soviet Socialist Republics
VET	Vocational education and training

Chapter 18

Lithuania: Trade unions still see light at the end of the tunnel

Inga Blažienė

Independent trade unions in Lithuania came into existence in the late 1980s when the country was regaining its independence and faced numerous unfavourable conditions. Large factories, which dominated during the Soviet era, collapsed, an unrestricted free market was seen as an absolute good, and trade unions for many decades had been established in most people's minds as an element of the Soviet system.[1] The image of unions and public trust in them were also undermined by conflicts among national confederations over distribution of the assets of the former Soviet trade unions. Structural changes taking place in the economy and social life, particularly growing inequality, also hindered the development of a trade union movement: new free market 'winners' did not want and had nothing to do with unions, while 'losers' were fully occupied with surviving and not losing their jobs during the market transformations of the 1990s.

As the structure of the economy changed, with manufacturing weakening and the service sector expanding, small and micro companies gradually replaced large companies, which were more favourable for trade unions. Declining union membership was further accelerated by Lithuania's accession to the European Union (EU). With the opening of the country's borders and opportunities for cross-border mobility, many employees opted to emigrate rather than to fight for better working

---

1 As there is little research on trade unions and industrial relations in Lithuania, this chapter is based primarily on interviews with union representatives, experts and researchers.

conditions. Attempts were made to compensate for low union representation among employees with a fairly strict legal framework. This did not provide the necessary protection for employees without appropriate enforcement, however. It also did a disservice to unions in that, at a time of tight regulation of employment relationships, there was nothing left to negotiate in collective agreements.

The issue of identity also prevented the trade unions from becoming strong players in the market: for many years, unions, or at least a considerable proportion of them, have identified themselves as a kind of 'last resort' institution, maintaining a kind of 'bellicose' rhetoric. In the context of improving living standards and rising educational qualifications among employees, trade unions often have little to offer or were unattractive to employees on higher earnings who were generally satisfied with their working conditions. All this is reflected in some of the indicators in Table 18.1: low union density, low collective bargaining coverage, the prevalence of company-level collective agreements, and largely non-existent strike activity. Nevertheless, despite all the unfavourable circumstances for the development of collective bargaining, there are some institutions that provide unions with a possibility to retain and even further develop a sufficiently important role in working life.

Table 18.1 Principal characteristics of trade unionism in Lithuania

	1995	2000	2019
Total trade union membership	400,000	184,000[b]	99,300[e]
Women as a proportion of total membership	n.a.	57 %[d]	54 %[f]
Gross union density	n.a.	n.a.	n.a.
Net union density	33 %	17 %[b]	7.4 %
Number of confederations	1[a]	3[b]	3
Number of affiliated unions (federations)	n.a.	48[d]	61
Number of independent unions	n.a.	n.a.	n.a.
Collective bargaining coverage	n.a.	15 %[c]	7 %[f]
Principal level of collective bargaining	Company level[a]		
Days not worked due to industrial action per 1,000 workers	n.a.	1	2

Note: Union and strike data related to the union confederations represented in the Tripartite Council of the Republic of Lithuania, and the affiliated industry-level and territorial unions of the two largest confederations. [a]1991; [b]2001; [c]2002; [d]2003; [e]2020; [f]2015.

Source: Appendix A1; Statistics Lithuania (2021).

Probably the most important institution or pillar that has supported a role for unions throughout the period since the mid-1990s and has allowed them to remain a sufficiently important player in determining working conditions is the Tripartite Council of the Republic of Lithuania (LRTT, *Lietuvos Respublikos trišalė taryba*), which was established in 1995. The LRTT is the main tripartite social dialogue institution in the country. All the most important labour market–related regulations and other decisions important for employees are discussed there. The second pillar, allowing unions to remain an important player in the social and political arena, is Lithuania's membership of the EU and the support of the European Commission (EC), the European Trade Union Confederation (ETUC) and other European institutions for national unions. The third pillar, which is often omitted but is nevertheless important, is the real estate managed by the main confederations, which for a long time was an important source of revenue. This ensured a degree of continuity and stability for their activities, even during periods of decreasing union membership.

These three pillars provide national and, to a certain extent, industry-level trade unions with some stability, a situation that is unlikely to change soon. In addition, it should be noted that unions do not stand still – recent developments show that:

- young people are joining;
- new ideas are emerging from within;
- unions are paying much more attention to publicizing their activities and ensuring visibility in society;
- unions are developing cooperation with NGOs;
- they are launching initiatives to protect the self-employed, platform workers and third-country nationals; and, importantly,
- they have recently greatly strengthened their position in the public sector by taking advantage of the favourable political situation.

Since 2018 national and industry-level collective agreements have been signed on a regular basis in the public sector and the number of union members has increased in this sector. All of these developments provide some reason to expect that Lithuanian trade unions might remain fairly important players and may indeed still see light at the end of the tunnel.

Historical background and principal features of the industrial relations system

The first trade union in Lithuania was established in 1892. The workers' movement of the late nineteenth and early twentieth century was generally quite well organized. During the Soviet period after 1940, unions were taken over by communists and nationalized, becoming part of the All-Union Central Council of Trade Unions (VPSCT, *Visasąjunginė profesinių sąjungų centro taryba*). In 1980, Lithuanian unions united twenty industries and had some 1,735,000 members. At the end of the 1980s, with the beginning of the National Revival in Lithuania, under the Reform Movement 'Sąjūdis', the 'Labora' club was established, which generated ideas for the renewal of trade unions. In 1989, the Trade Union Reform Movement (PSPS, *Profesinių sąjungų persitvarkymo sąjūdis*) and the Lithuanian Workers' Union (LDS, *Lietuvos darbininkų sąjunga*) were established; the latter changed its name in 2002 and became the current Lithuanian Trade Union 'Solidarumas' (LPS 'Solidarumas', *Lietuvos profesinė sąjunga 'Solidarumas'*) (Glovackas 2007 – see Figure 18.1).

After the restoration of Lithuanian independence, on 11 March 1990, a congress of Lithuanian trade unions took place, which established the Lithuanian Free Trade Union Confederation (LLPSK, *Lietuvos laisvųjų profesinių sąjungų konfederacija*) on the basis of the unions of the former Soviet Lithuania. The LLPSK inherited all rights of the former Soviet trade unions. Later, the Lithuanian Trade Union Centre (LPSC, *Lietuvos profesinių sąjungų centras*) was set up, based on this organization. Dissatisfied with the slow reform and the 'Soviet' past, some unions did not join this confederation and founded another, the Lithuanian Trade Union Unification (LPSS, *Lietuvos profesinių sąjungų susivienijimas*), in February 1992. These two organizations, the LPSC and LPSS, merged in 2002 to become the current Lithuanian Trade Union Confederation (LPSK, *Lietuvos profesinių sąjungų konfederacija*) (Glovackas 2007). The Lithuanian Labour Federation (LDF, *Lietuvos darbo federacija*), which was set up in 1919, was also re-established at the end of 1991. After long being the 'third most important' confederation of independent Lithuania, it has shrunk considerably and to some extent suspended its activities in recent years (see Figure 18.1).

Figure 18.1 Comparing trade union organizations in Lithuania, 2000 and 2020

Lithuanian Trade Union Centre, formerly Lithuanian Free Trade Union Confederation, est. 1990	→	Lithuanian Trade Union Confederation (LPSK)
Lithuanian Trade Union Unification, est. 1992		
Lithuanian Workers' Union, est. 1989	→	Lithuanian Trade Union 'Solidarumas' (LPS 'Solidarumas')
Lithuanian Labour Federation, est. 1919, restored 1991	→	Lithuanian Labour Federation (LDF)
Lithuanian Trade Union 'Sandrauga', est. 1999	→	Lithuanian Trade Union 'Sandrauga' (LPS 'Sandrauga')
Various independent trade unions, est. 1990–2000	→ →	Various independent trade unions
		General Trade Union of the Republic of Lithuania (RJPS), est. 2002
		Various independent trade unions
2000		2020

Source: Author's elaboration.

Disagreements between the confederations and their affiliates over the property of the former Soviet trade unions caused much long-term damage to the modern union movement. Quarrels resulted largely from inconsistent policy decisions on the use and redistribution of this property. Eventually, however, unions began to collaborate with each other, to support each other's initiatives and to coordinate positions. They thus turned from confrontational into relatively united and mutually supportive organizations. A major contributory factor in the increasing union collaboration was the establishment of the LRTT in 1995.

Structure of trade unions and union democracy

Nine criteria define the trade union confederations represented in the Tripartite Council. Among them are membership of international organizations, having members or representatives in different regions or industries, being active for at least three years and organizing at least 0.5 per cent of the workforce. In 2021 three confederations were considered representative according to the criteria defined in the Labour Code (DK, *Lietuvos Respublikos Darbo kodeksas*): the LPSK, LPS 'Solidarumas' and the Lithuanian Trade Union 'Sandrauga' (LPS 'Sandrauga', *Lietuvos profesinė sąjunga 'Sandrauga'*). The LPSK and the LPS 'Solidarumas' are the main confederations.[2] LPSK represents around 50,000 members (approximately 4 per cent of employees) and unites twenty-five industry-level unions today (LPSK 2021). LPS 'Solidarumas' represents around 20,000 members or approximately 1.5 per cent of Lithuanian employees and unites fifteen industry-level and twenty-one territorial affiliates (Solidarumas 2021). One more, smaller national trade union organization is the Lithuanian Trade Union 'Sandrauga' (LPS 'Sandrauga', *Lietuvos profesinė sąjunga 'Sandrauga'*), which was also represented in the LRTT until mid-2022. There is no reliable information about its membership, finances and structure. According to LPS 'Sandrauga' own reporting, this confederation provides free labour law consultations for its members, represents them in labour dispute commissions and courts, drafts collective agreements, and participates in collective bargaining (Sandrauga 2021).

Both the LPSK and the LPS 'Solidarumas' operate on a confederal basis; that is, they bring together industry-level trade unions, and in the case of LPS 'Solidarumas', territorial union organizations. The affiliates at industry-level and territorial unions are company-level trade unions. The LPSK incorporates a Women's Centre and a youth section, LPSK Youth. The mission of the LPSK is to recruit and protect Lithuanian employees and influence government institutions on labour and social issues. LPSK's largest industry-level affiliated unions are the Lithuanian

---

[2] As there have been no studies or research carried out in Lithuania on the country's trade unions, and the unions themselves often provide little publicly available information about their activities, internal structure, and other issues, this chapter focuses mainly on the two main confederations. Other union organisations are mentioned as far as possible.

Education and Science Trade Union (LŠMPS, *Lietuvos švietimo ir mokslo profesinė sąjunga*), the Lithuanian Nurses' Organization (LSSO, *Lietuvos slaugos specialistų organizacija*) and the Lithuanian Federation of Industrial Trade Unions (LPPSF, *Lietuvos pramonės profesinių sąjungų federacija*). LPS 'Solidarumas' also has a Women's Council and a youth structure, the Youth Group.

The union confederations' governing bodies are the congress (*suvažiavimas*), the council (*taryba*) and the management board (*valdyba*). Congresses are convened every four years. The council is a collegiate body that functions between congresses; meetings of the council are normally convened at least twice a year. Activities of the confederation between congresses and meetings of the council are organized by the management board. Management board meetings are usually convened at least once a month; the majority of the management board consists of the chairs of confederation affiliates: that is, the industry-level or territorial unions, or both. In addition to the collegiate governing bodies, the confederation has a chair; the LPSK also has a secretary-general. Thus, primary day-to-day management of the confederation is carried out by the chair and the management board, which deal with all day-to-day issues and take various ad hoc decisions (LPSK 2018; Solidarumas 2018).

Since 2002 one other national union confederation has been operating in Lithuania, the General Trade Union of the Republic of Lithuania (RJPS, *Respublikinė jungtinė profesinė sąjunga*). At the beginning of 2021 two previously independent industry-level unions affiliated to the RJPS: the Lithuanian Education Employees Trade Union (LŠDPS, *Lietuvos švietimo darbuotojų profesinė sąjunga*) and the National Unification of Officials Trade Unions (NPPSS, *Nacionalinis pareigūnų profesinių sąjungų susivienijimas*). The affiliation of these relatively large unions and RJPS's decision to become a member of the European Confederation of Independent Trade Unions (CESI, *Confédération Européenne des Syndicats Indépendants*) – not, properly speaking, a union confederation at the European level – enabled the RJPS to meet the established representativeness criteria. Since 1 July 2022 it has been a member of the LRTT.

There are a few other national and industry-level union organizations, not affiliated to the aforementioned peak-level confederations. The LDF is one of the oldest unions in Lithuania, and for a long time was the third most important union confederation, with representatives on the LRTT. Since mid-2010, its activities have declined significantly, however, as its membership has decreased. The union no longer meets the representativeness criteria and may no longer delegate members to the LRTT. Currently, LDF claims about 4,500 members. The 1 May Trade Union (G1PS, *Gegužės 1-osios profesinė sąjunga*) is small, comprising only a few hundred members, but it is active in the area of platform work. The Union of Lithuanian Doctors (LGS, *Lietuvos gydytojų sąjunga*) is large, uniting about 70 per cent of Lithuanian physicians and having about 7,000 members in industry-level trade unions. It is not affiliated to any national trade union confederation.

Affiliates of the confederations are duly registered industry-level or territorial unions that accept the statutes of the confederations and pursue goals and activities that do not contradict them. An organization may become a member of the LPSK if it meets certain requirements and has at least 1,000 members (LPSK 2018). An industry-level or territorial union may join LPS 'Solidarumas' if it has at least 100 members (Solidarumas 2018). Affiliated unions have the right to make demands or requests, submit proposals to the bodies of the confederation, ask confederal representatives questions and receive answers, participate in the adoption and implementation of resolutions at confederal level, receive information on confederation activities, and have access to its funds and assets. Affiliates may also participate in and support campaigns, rallies, pickets and strikes organized by the confederation.

In general, affiliated unions are required to respect resolutions of the congress, the council and the management board, as well as to pay fixed membership fees and other contributions, and to actively participate in the confederation's activities. Industry-level unions may exercise discretion within their industry; they usually have their own chairs and governing bodies, such as presidiums (*prezidiumas*), management boards or councils, as well as industry-level union congresses. Industry-level unions are completely autonomous; they are independent in making all decisions about their activities. Breakaways and mergers with other industry-level unions may be concluded without any interference from the confederation. Upon joining the confederation, industry-level unions undertake to stick to its statutes. The relationships between individual industrial-level unions are also different. As a rule, unions operating in the public sector cooperate more with each other, for example by coordinating their positions in signing a national collective agreement in the public sector, while industry-level unions in the private sector are more diverse and often operate more independently.

Industry-level and territorial unions comprise mainly company-level unions. The relationships between industry-level and company-level unions are diverse in both principal confederations. Some trade unions, such as the Lithuanian Trade Union of Food Producers (LMPS, *Lietuvos maistininkų profesinė sąjunga*), are more centralized and have strong working relationships and cooperation with the company-level unions. For example, LMPS (the industry-level union) is directly involved in company-level collective bargaining. There are also cases in which industry-level unions admit members directly to the industry-level and the company-level unions are only subdivisions of the industry-level union. Other industry-level unions are more decentralized and less involved in collective bargaining at company level. It is difficult to estimate the proportion of trade unions operating with these different relationships to industry-level unions in Lithuania, but it is likely that the majority are less centralized unions. If company-level unions need support in preparations or participation in collective bargaining, however, in most cases this is provided by industry-level or even confederation lawyers or other professionals. On the other hand, there are also very strong unions operating at company level in chemicals and oil, which have adequate teams of lawyers or other professionals.

According to the current DK, a company-level union can be set up if it has at least twenty members or its members account for at least 10 per cent of the total employees of the company, provided this is equivalent to three or more employees. Unionists have the right to join or set up an industry-level or territorial union, if there at least five company-level unions are involved. Industry-level and territorial unions may join national-level union organizations. There is no distinction between white-collar and blue-collar workers. Accordingly, unions claim to have no specific strategies for attracting members from different categories of employees. Normally, unions operating in companies unite all employees working there, while upper-level unions unite at the territorial or industry-level/branch level. In fact, no unions unite employees based on their occupational affiliation, the only exception being health care, in which there are some instances of different unions for doctors and nurses.

Unionization

Although Lithuanian law lays down that Lithuanian nationals with both working and legal capacity may become members of a trade union, there are only a few retired people, students or unemployed persons among union members, not to mention immigrants (Interviews, 2020). Data on union members are generally very scarce, however – there is actually no mechanism for verifying membership figures provided by the national unions. Furthermore, membership structure has always been dominated by the public sector; this trend is likely to continue and grow in the near future. Given that employment in the public sector has traditionally been dominated by women in Lithuania, their membership rates have usually been somewhat higher than those of men. Overall, trade union membership is decreasing, with union density falling from approximately 15 per cent in 2000 to approximately 8 per cent in 2020. After Lithuania's declaration of independence, trade unions lost a critical mass of members by 2000. This dramatic decline was mainly the result of economic restructuring, the fundamentally changed role of unions, their fragmentation, inter-union competition, and other processes taking place in the transition period, which were common to many post-Soviet countries. Although unions generally have seen a decline in membership in recent decades, the period between 2000 and 2020 can be divided into two sub-periods: 2000 to 2010, which was characterized by a steep decline in membership, and the period since 2010, marked by relative stability in membership.

During the period from 2000 to 2010 trade union membership continued to decline steadily, albeit at an increasingly slower pace. Overall, membership almost halved over this decade, from approximately 180,000 to 90,000. This decline was to some extent determined by large-scale emigration, which began after Lithuania's accession to the EU in 2004. In 2004–2006 annual net migration in Lithuania almost doubled compared with the pre-accession period. At the same time, unions lost approximately one-quarter of their members, falling from 158,000 in 2003 to 116,000 in 2006. The 2008–2009 financial and economic crisis also had a severe impact on union membership, although with a time lag.[3] Although there was a slight increase in membership in the crisis years, it fell by an annual average of 4–5 percentage points in 2010–2013.

The decade 2011–2020 can be considered a period of stabilization in union membership. This relative stability went together with relatively

3 The crisis hit Lithuania particularly hard: GDP, for example, fell by 15 per cent in 2009.

significant internal changes in union membership in the main confederations: some unionized industries grew; unions organizing in education, health care, social work, journalists and transport joined the confederations; other unions shrank or left the confederations (water transport, railways), and others merged (chemical and energy industry-level unions, education industry-level unions). Despite some internal changes, the total number of union members during this period fluctuated around 90,000 (Statistics Lithuania, 2021), and even increased at the end. This increase was probably influenced by industry and national collective bargaining in the public sector, which has intensified since 2018, encouraging more employees to join unions. A modest increase in membership and density was registered by Statistics Lithuania (SD, *Statistikos departamentas*) in 2019–2020. From the interviews with national trade union confederations, they expected that this increase will continue.

Union confederations posit increasing membership as one of their most important goals. They use various strategies and actions to achieve this goal. One of the most important strategies is union awareness raising through participation in various debates, actions, mass media and social media. This strategy has been of particular importance for LPSK since 2018, with the launch of various 'social events'. For instance, in recent years, LPSK representatives have travelled throughout the country with a 'tent', which is usually set up in the central squares of cities or towns, providing information to all interested persons on workers' rights, various issues related to work organization, working hours, and other labour law issues. They also organize career aptitude tests in the form of games, and run children's zones. Affiliated unions have also organized a number of campaigns and marches, and actively participated in various festivals, exhibitions, fairs, TV and radio programmes, and in social media. These activities are particularly focused on regional work and cooperation with NGOs and local media. Another direction is work with young people: unions hold meetings for young people, at which they present them with information about union activities and their labour rights. The main idea behind these events is not directly to persuade people to join unions, but to raise their visibility and public awareness of where to look for help in case of violations of their rights or other work-related problems.

In order to support employees and attract more members, LPS 'Solidarumas' often focuses on large, relatively low-wage industries, for example, retail workers in the private sector or nurses and social workers in the public sector, as well as industries undergoing restructuring, such as forestry, energy or road transport. Also, worth highlighting are activities of LPS 'Solidarumas' directed towards atypical employees, including third-country nationals such as long-distance drivers or self-employed tourist guides. Such activities contribute to improving the working conditions of these workers, but also the public visibility of the confederation. To attract more members from certain industries, especially workers who are more difficult to reach – for example, in retail, trade, carriers or truck drivers – and to be more efficient, LPS 'Solidarumas' often starts by admitting members directly to industry-level unions. Then it tries to identify industry-specific problems, enters into discussions with industry-level employers' organizations, and only then goes to companies and organizations with specific proposals on how the union could help to solve problems relevant to employees and improve working conditions, thus promoting the establishment of company-level unions. This approach is also used by other confederations.

In contrast to the confederal level, rather than attracting new members, industry-level union strategies and policies are focused more on retaining existing members, providing them with assistance, information and consultation, and on solving problems relevant to members in the industry. In pursuit of these objectives, unions often have their own experts to assist company-level unions in collective bargaining and drafting collective agreements, as well as to represent their members in labour dispute commissions (DGK, *darbo ginčų komisijos*) and courts. Nevertheless, there are also some examples of trade union strategies aimed at attracting new members, organizing and servicing direct membership in industry-level unions, and also 'invisible' or secret membership: the latter means that membership fees are paid by employees directly to the union to make it easier to penetrate certain companies, to facilitate the establishment of new company-level unions or simply to protect their members from unfavourable treatment by employers.

Freelancers and self-employed persons – for example journalists, platform workers or self-employed tour guides – account for a very small share of union members. This is partly because of the low union density in Lithuania. There are many non-unionized large, 'traditional' industries in which there are large numbers of non-unionized 'typical' employees. Unions are more focused on such industries or employees than on more difficult, 'atypical' industries and employees. On the other hand, these days there are some more active initiatives or attempts to join or seek help from unions on the part of 'atypical' employees. The largest union confederation, the LPSK, has for several years been considering the establishment of a kind of 'virtual union' which could be joined by members working in any industry or under any type of contract. This would include 'atypical' employees as well.

US-style organizing is not widespread in Lithuania. Industry-level unions usually have a very limited number of staff, who, as a rule, work for existing members rather than on recruiting new members. Some industry-level unions (LMPS, Lithuanian Federation of Forest and Wood Workers Trade Unions; LMPF, *Lietuvos miško ir miško pramonės darbuotojų profesinių sąjungų federacija*) have participated in the Baltic Organizing Academy (BOA) framework since the beginning of the 2010s to learn from the experiences of unions in Nordic countries. No significant breakthrough has been achieved in this area, however. The provision of services by unions as a strategy for attracting and retaining new members is also not common in Lithuania. There is no research on why trade union activity is low in the area of organizing or servicing, or both. It can be assumed that reasons include the absence of traditions and knowledge, as well as trade unions' low human and financial capacities.

Only a few examples of such union services can be identified, such as a qualification improvement system for union members and non-members, implemented by the Lithuanian Nurses' Organization or the social initiative 'Stop Poverty' carried out by LPS 'Solidarumas', involving union assistance for unemployed persons from disadvantaged groups searching for work in some regions. There are still some union leisure services that were 'popular' in the Soviet era, when union members enjoy preferential access to union-owned leisure facilities, for example at the seaside. Unions traditionally pay much attention to training for their members. Many stronger industrial unions organize training and educational events for members on computer literacy, labour law or negotiation. In most cases union members receive benefits at company level: unions operating in larger companies negotiate with employers on various advantages, such as payment for additional health care or other services. These negotiated benefits are usually available for all employees of the company, irrespective of union membership. Lately, however, negotiated benefits have increasingly been available only for union members.

In addition, unions understand that the labour market and jobs are changing and will continue to change. Therefore, unions need to prepare for and be open to these changes. These new forms of work will involve more and more activities and economic segments. There will also be a move to smaller and medium-sized sites from large sites, which is associated with transference from well-regulated employment relationships to weakly regulated civil relations. Being well aware of the inevitability of all this, unions at the same time strongly emphasize the need for joint European actions and initiatives in new and ever-changing conditions.

Union resources and expenditure

In Lithuania, as in many other post-Soviet countries, the main trade union confederations inherited real estate, which is now leased out and makes up a part of confederal income, in addition to membership fees. Such assets are at the disposal of the two main confederations, LPSK and LPS 'Solidarumas'. Furthermore, the share of membership fees for the two main confederations ranges from 0.10 euros (€) to €0.50 per member per month and amounts to only a modest share of revenue. Figure 18.2 shows the average income of all Lithuanian unions possessing or not possessing real estate. On average, membership fees amount to approximately 50 per cent of union revenues. At the same time, this share varies greatly both between the confederations and between unions at different levels within the confederations. Other confederations, such as LPS 'Sandrauga' or RJPS, did not inherit real estate, however, and therefore they claim that their main source of income is membership fees.

Figure 18.2 Revenues of Lithuanian trade unions, 2018–2020

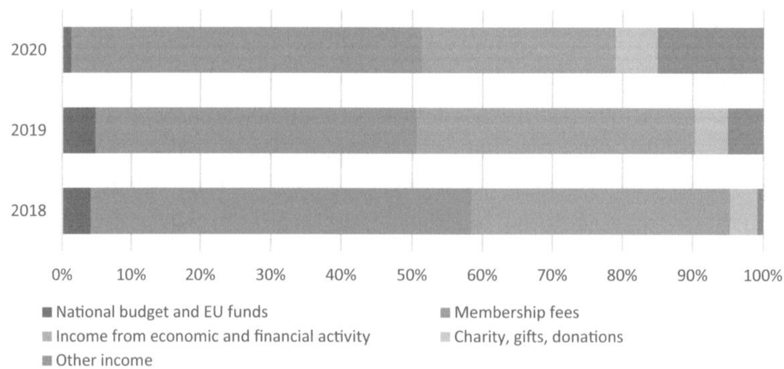

Source: Statistics Lithuania, 2021.

In addition, it is worth mentioning here the option available in Lithuania whereby once a year any resident of the country can transfer 0.6 per cent of their personal income tax liability to a union. This provides unions with additional income and thus strengthens their activities. Such transfers, however, do not represent a significant source of union revenues, less than 4–6 per cent (Figure 18.2). It should be stressed that membership fees are not the main source of revenues for LPSK and LPS 'Solidarumas', which to some extent makes them less dependent on membership fluctuations. They are still intent on boosting membership, however.

As confederations are not rich either in members or financial resources, staff numbers are also modest. According to the available information, at the end of 2020, the LPSK had seventeen employees and LPS 'Solidarumas' had twelve; these figures include both office and technical staff. The number of staff in industry-level unions is even lower: most industry-level unions declare only one or two employees.[4] There are larger industrial unions with more employees; the LŠMPS, for example, had ten staff members at the end of 2020. As a rule, national confederations have a president, vice-president(s), general secretary, public relations officer, international relations officer, lawyer, project manager, administrator and accountant. The staff of industry-level unions usually comprises a president and, in some cases, a vice-president(s) and an accountant. Some larger industry-level unions, for example the LŠMPS, also have lawyers among their staff. Trade unions based in some large enterprises, such as Achema and Orlen Lietuva, have lawyers as well.

Although there is no publicly available information on the structure of confederations and unions at different levels, interviews with union representatives suggest that, traditionally, union members pay between 0.8 and 1 per cent of their net wages to company-level unions. Some industrial unions, such as LSSO, have set a flat-rate membership fee, independent of their members' wages. As a rule, most of the membership fee remains within the company-level union. Although there is no reliable information, it can be assumed that about 70 per cent of income from members remains with the company-level union. In addition, sometimes company-level unions manage to have it stipulated in collective agreements that additional funds be allocated for union activities, but as a

---

4 See www.rekvizitai.lt

rule it is a very small amount, usually defined as a 'collective agreement administration fee'. It may be used for team building or similar activities at company level.

Union membership fees are usually transferred monthly by the company to the company union, or to the account of the industry-level union in industries in which company-level unions are not legal entities. There are also cases in which employees do not want the employer to know that they are union members, and so they pay their monthly fees directly. The share of funds transferred to industrial unions varies from one industry to another: often companies/enterprises transfer 25–30 per cent of collected membership fees to the industrial union. There are also more centralized industrial unions, usually those whose members join directly to industry-level unions. In this case, the industry level usually receives the whole membership fee.

The new Labour Code (DK) that came into effect in Lithuania on 1 July 2017 introduced, among other things, a provision on the application of collective agreements. Since the implementation of the new Labour Code collective agreements apply only to members of signatory unions, instead to all of the employees of the company. If trade union and employer agree on the application of an agreement to the whole workforce, this has to be approved by the general meeting of all employees. In practice, company-level collective agreements still more often apply to all employees of the company than to union members only, though the latter practice is also expanding. National collective agreements and several industry-level collective agreements that came into force in the public sector in 2018–2020, provided additional benefits for union members: additional holidays, extra days off for study and even more favourable pay conditions for union members. Although this practice has been widely used in the public sector in recent years, collective agreements have already appeared in the private sector with similar benefits for union members. According to the unions, these benefits have proved to be important for employees, and there has been a recent upsurge among public sector employees seeking union membership.

Regarding member benefits and services, mention should also be made of legal services, advice and representation of members before labour dispute commissions and courts, which are regularly provided to members by both industry-level and national unions. These unions provide, as far as possible, all legal and advisory services both to company-level unions and individual union members. Services for company-level unions include assistance in setting up and registering a union; advice and assistance in preparing for and participating in collective bargaining; drafting collective agreements; and support for unions during company restructuring or collective labour disputes. Services for individual members include legal advice on various employment issues, assistance in drawing up documents and representation before labour dispute commissions or courts. Certain social guarantees or advantages for unions and their members are also provided in some company-level collective agreements. These include extra days off for union members, free paid time-off to attend union events, and employer funding for union activities or collective agreement administration.

Collective bargaining and unions at the workplace

According to the 2017 Labour Code (DK), the rights to initiate collective bargaining for the conclusion or amendment of collective agreements, to participate in it, and to conclude collective agreements are assigned to employers, employers' organizations and trade unions. Employees may be represented in collective bargaining only by trade unions. Usually, company-level unions are affiliated to industry unions; they are allowed to engage in collective bargaining and to conclude collective agreements, while the main function of works councils is information and consultation.

Collective agreements can be concluded at the following five levels: national or cross-industry; territorial; industrial, including production, services and professions; employer or company; and workplace or plant. Information on collective agreements and their supplements concluded in 2018–2020 is provided in Table 18.2. At the end of 2019, 15 per cent of employees were covered by valid collective agreements, the majority of them in the public sector (MSSL 2019). This share should be assessed bearing in mind that not all collective agreements cover remuneration issues; some of them are declarative in nature and their contents primarily repeat the existing legal norms (Blažienė et al 2019: 377; Research Council 2015; ESTEP 2016). One of the reasons for this situation is the fairly strict regulation of all main employment and working conditions, including remuneration issues, by national legislation; thus, there is little room for manoeuvre for collective bargaining in the public sector.

Table 18.2 Number of collective agreements and their supplements, 2018–2020

	2018	2019	2020
National (public sector)-level collective agreements	1	1	1
Industry-level collective agreements	4	6	2
Territorial-level collective agreements	0	1	2
Company-level collective agreements	84	154	48

Source: MSSL (2021).

Although collective bargaining coverage is generally low, collective bargaining and collective agreements are usually in place in companies with unionized workers. According to representatives of LPSK, about 95 per cent of companies with active unions affiliated to the LPSK have collective bargaining. Company-level bargaining usually takes place in the public sector or related industries, such as education, health care, railways, culture, forestry, post and energy, and in large and medium-sized, more often multinational, private sector companies in food, alcohol, tobacco and other manufacturing. Parties to a company- or workplace-level collective agreement are the company-level union and the employer. In cases where more than one union operates at an enterprise, the enterprise's collective agreement may be concluded by a union and employer or by a joint union representation and the employer. If employees of the company are represented by the industry-level union, a company-level collective agreement might be concluded by the employer and industry-level union.

Although the company level remains the main collective bargaining level, a number of national and industry-level collective agreements were signed in the public sector in 2018–2020, incorporating some remuneration issues, among other things. These are national public sector collective agreements, alongside industry-level collective agreements in education, health care, civil service, social work and some other sectors. In most of the latter agreements there are provisions on additional rest/holiday days and/or better remuneration conditions, applicable only to union members of the signatory parties. This practice began with the introduction of the Labour Code that came into effect on 1 July 2017. The Labour Code introduced, among other things, fairly radical amendments to the provisions regulating industrial relations, including collective bargaining.

From 1 July onwards, the right to conduct collective bargaining is granted exclusively to unions, instead of unions and works councils, as in the old version of the Labour Code, and collective agreements apply only to members of signatory unions, unless agreed otherwise.

Since 2018 unions have increasingly used the opportunity provided by the Labour Code to establish more favourable working or remuneration conditions for their members. As this practice is relatively new, no specific impact assessments have yet been carried out. According to union representatives, the application of better remuneration and working conditions to union members yields positive results, as it helps to attract more members. Moreover, according to the unions, the practice of agreeing additional benefits for union members has been adopted not only by public sector institutions, but also by state and private sector companies.

Parties involved in collective bargaining at any level must comply with the favourability principle, which means that the working conditions guaranteed by law are the minimum permissible, but collective or individual subjects can agree additional guarantees and conditions that are more favourable to employees. To comply with the new Labour Code, no collective agreement, or any other local regulations on working conditions are considered valid if they put employees in a worse position than defined by the Labour Code, laws and other regulations. This means that not only the Labour Code and laws take precedence over collective agreements, but also resolutions of the government and regulations adopted by other national and municipal authorities (Blažienė et al. 2019).

In 2019–2020, about 70 per cent of collective agreements were signed in the public sector, and the rest in the private sector (MSSL 2019; MSSL 2021). The largest number of agreements were signed in education; other industries with high numbers of collective agreements are transport, social work and social care, water supply, health care, local government, and cultural organizations (mainly libraries). The main features of collective agreements are as follows:

- about half of agreements have been concluded for a term of four years, but there are a number of open-ended contracts, representing about one-quarter of all agreements;
- remuneration systems or certain remuneration provisions are established or mentioned in approximately 75 per cent of agreements;

- approximately 35 per cent of agreements contain provisions related to working arrangements, such as on-call time, individual working time, and flexible working hours;
- 25 per cent of collective agreements provide for overtime other than that set by the Labour Code; it is generally agreed that overtime should not exceed 200–280 hours per year;
- about 27 per cent of collective agreements contain provisions on the forms of work organization; teleworking, partial work and part-time work (MSSL 2019).

To sum up, there is still a lack of original qualitative provisions in collective agreements, for example on gender equality, stress and psychological violence in the work environment. References to the Labour Code are still very common; many agreements simply state that certain issues shall be settled in accordance with it.

Although collective bargaining coverage in the public sector has been increasing, in the private sector it remains low. Among the reasons for this is an incongruity between the respective structures of unions and employers' associations at the industrial level that to some extent prevents the parties from engaging in collective bargaining. Moreover, even with numerous organizations and associations representing the interests of employers in Lithuania – including six participating in social dialogue at the national level – employers' associations have been reluctant to take up the role of social partners or sign collective agreements, or claim that they do not have a mandate from their members to do so (Blažienė and Gruzevskis 2017).

There is no information on unions at the workplace in Lithuania. According to the Labour Code, works councils must be established when the employer's average number of employees is twenty or more, except where trade union operating at the workplace unite more than one-third of employees. Not all companies comply with this, however. According to the European Company Survey (Eurofound 2019a), the presence of a recognized body for employee representation in Lithuania is recorded in 44 per cent of establishments with ten or more employees; presumably this figure covers both the presence of a trade union and/or a works council at the establishment. The highest share of establishments with a recognized body for employee representation in 2019 was recorded in the industry sector, at 57 per cent, the lowest being in transport, at 29 per cent.

Industrial conflict

The right of employees to strike is put into law in the Constitution of the Republic of Lithuania. Before 2017, the right to call a strike was also given to works councils. Works councils, however, never initiated a single strike. Since the Labour Code of 2017, the right to call a strike has been granted only to unions. According to the Code, a strike is a stoppage of work by employees organized by a trade union to resolve a collective labour dispute on interests or to ensure compliance with a decision reached in resolving such a dispute. Two types of strike action are distinguished, based on duration. A warning strike is defined as a strike that lasts no more than two hours. A 'genuine strike' has no restrictions on duration.

Figure 18.3 Number of strikes and warning strikes, 2000–2019

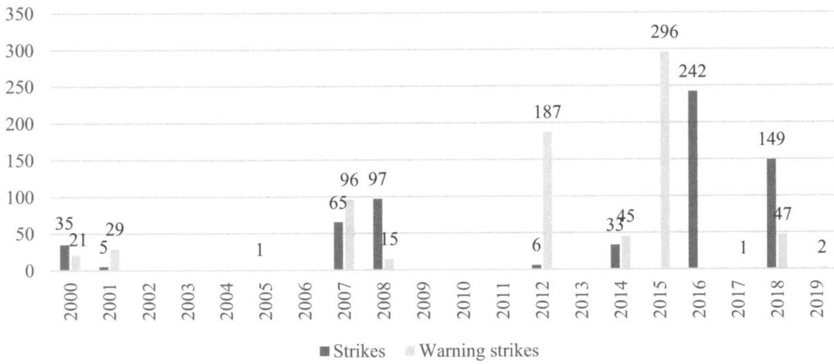

Source: Statistics Lithuania, 2020.

Figure 18.3 shows that strikes are rare in Lithuania, and if they occur, they are quite often warning strikes. Strikes are overwhelmingly held in education (more than 90 per cent). Strike dynamics are thus basically determined by collective bargaining developments in education; other strikes have been reported in transport and health care. There have been no strikes in other industries. According to unions, this situation is largely the result of the legal regulation of strikes, which is still restrictive, especially if valid collective agreements are in place. Several unfavourable precedents for unions and strike developments are also recorded. These involve cases in which employers went to court over the initiation of strikes and the court imposed provisional safeguards and suspended or postponed the strike or declared it illegal. Probably the most famous cases, with litigation lasting for several years, were the strikes held by the employees of UAB 'Švyturys-Utenos alus' and UAB 'Vilniaus viešasis transportas'. The limited spread of strikes can also be explained by the absence of a tradition of striking, limited union financial resources and the lack of strike funds. Few unions have a strike fund. The educational union, LŠMPS, for example, collects special strike fund fees from its members. If a strike is successful from the union perspective, an 'agreement to end the strike' may provide that the employer shall pay wages to the employees for the days of the strike.

The decision to call a strike at the company level requires approval by at least one-quarter of all union members. Calling a strike in an industry requires a relevant decision from the industry-level union. The employer or employers' association and the relevant member companies must be given written notice at least three working days before the beginning of a warning strike or at least five working days before the beginning of a full strike. Written notice of the beginning of an upcoming warning or full strike in enterprises or industries that provide 'urgent or vital services' to the public must be given to the employer or employers' association and the individual member companies at least ten working days in advance by sending them the decision of the union or union organization to declare the strike.

The following services are considered vital to the public: health care, electric power supply, water supply, heat and gas supply, sewage and waste disposal, civil aviation (including air traffic control), telecommunications, railway and urban public transport. In addition, the right to call a strike of emergency medical service employees and other employees (professional soldiers; police, customs, state boarder guard service officers; and judges) is limited by laws that prohibit them from calling a strike. The demands put forward by these employees are settled by bodies for the resolution of collective labour disputes on interests. While a collective agreement remains valid employees are prohibited from calling a strike regarding the requirements or terms of employment regulated in this agreement, if these terms are being adhered to. The latter restriction does not apply to collective labour disputes on interests, which arise and are not resolved in accordance with the procedure established by the Labour Code or by conducting collective bargaining on a collective agreement.

Based on the object of dispute and the subjects involved in the labour dispute, labour disputes in Lithuania are divided into: (i) labour disputes on rights (individual labour disputes on rights[5] and collective labour disputes on rights);[6] and (ii) collective labour disputes on interests.[7] On the subject of industrial conflict and labour disputes, the role of Labour Dispute Commissions (DGK), which started operating in 2013, must be mentioned. The Commissions greatly simplify the process of dealing with individual labour disputes, as previously court action was the only resort. Because of long and costly court proceedings, employees usually refrained from any actions to resolve conflict situations. Since 2013, the DGK have been operating on a tripartite basis, with the active participation of national confederations and industry-level unions in the activities of the Commissions; representatives of confederations and industry-level unions both act as members of the Commissions and represent the interests of their members in resolving specific disputes.

Political relations

Trade unions that started to operate during the 1990s – that is, after Lithuania regained its independence – initially had a fairly clear political affiliation, some of them being quite closely connected with the Social Democratic Party (LSDP, *Lietuvos socialdemokratų partija*) and others with the Christian Democrats (KD, *Krikščionys demokratai*). It was quite common for unions to have some cooperation agreements signed with one or other party. Since about the mid-2010s, however, these relationships have weakened: confederations now declare themselves to be

---

5 An individual labour dispute on rights is a disagreement between an employee or other participants in an employment relationship on one side, and the employer on the other side, arising from the conclusion, amendment, fulfilment or termination of an employment contract, or regarding non-fulfilment or improper fulfilment of labour law provisions in the labour relations between the employee and the employer.

6 A collective labour dispute on rights is a disagreement between employee representatives on one side, and the employer or employers' organisations on the other side, regarding non-fulfilment or improper fulfilment of labour law provisions or mutual agreements.

7 A collective labour dispute on interests is a disagreement between employee representatives on one side, and the employer or employers' organisations on the other side, arising from regulation of the mutual rights and obligations of the parties or the establishment of labour law provisions.

completely independent of any political party and are equally open to or critical towards any political party or its ideas. The confederations have no obligations or agreements with parties and describe such connections with political parties as 'working' relationships. This is because 'cooperation with political parties is weak due to the efforts of trade unions to maintain autonomy and the high risk of being subordinated to business interests that dominate the parties' (Lipajev 2020: 115). Instead of developing cooperation with parties, unions often try to act through individual politicians, usually with a history in trade unions, through whom they initiate the implementation of legal acts or individual legal provisions that are more favourable to unions.

The trade unions' relationships with politicians in power depend to a large extent on the latter's attitudes towards unionism and social dialogue in general. In periods when the ruling majority is made up of political parties that are more supportive of both the union movement and their role in the decision-making process, union standpoints are more visible, more and better agreements are made. For example, in 2016–2020, the government coalition was formed by the Lithuanian Farmers and Greens Union (LVŽS, *Lietuvos valstiečių ir žaliųjų sąjunga*), which positioned itself as a political party favouring social dialogue. As a result, social dialogue greatly improved and a number of union-favourable national- and industrial-level collective agreements were signed in the public sector during this period. This increased public awareness and the visibility of unions and encouraged more people to join. After the election of the President of Lithuania in 2019, meetings between the social partners and the President or his advisers have been organized on a regular basis to discuss issues relevant to the social partners.

Trade unions also use various other channels to influence national-level decision-making. The most important of these is the LRTT and other tripartite commissions and committees in which union confederations actively seek participation. The LRTT, together with specialized tripartite councils and commissions, and tripartite councils operating within local municipalities are the main scene of interaction between public authorities and social partners. The social partners in the LRTT discuss issues and present conclusions and proposals in the areas of labour, social and economic policy. Concerning these policy areas, the LRTT has the right to receive any information necessary for the work of the Council, to adopt decisions and submit conclusions and recommendations to the parties, and to conclude tripartite agreements. The

Council meets at least once a month to discuss projects, proposed legal acts and other matters in relation to labour, social and economic issues. Discussions at the Tripartite Council are sometimes very frank, but once consensus is reached it is usually successfully implemented in practice (Blažienė 2018).

To influence decisions adopted by the Parliament or the government, union confederations try to follow the work of both these institutions and participate, as necessary, in the meetings of commissions and committees at the parliament and the government, express their positions, meet with individual members of parliament, and participate in the meetings of parliamentary factions. Seeking to further increase their influence on decision-making processes, confederations adopted the practice of sending their representatives for voluntary service at the Parliament and in government, but this practice proved to be ineffective and was abandoned. One more important channel is the unions' participation in various task forces and working groups, aimed at developing, drafting or implementing national, industry-level or regional programmes and strategic documents. As a rule, representatives of confederations are members of all key task forces and working groups created by the government, ministries and other public institutions.

Societal power

In Lithuania, a significant part of society, particularly young people, are unaware of unions or what information they do have is very sketchy. The basics of industrial relations are generally not taught in secondary schools or higher education, and the achievements of unions, their good practices in defending employees or representing their interests are rarely covered in the mass media and public debate. At the same time, this provide the unions with an opportunity. Hence, unions should make an effort to raise awareness in society. One of the best strategies, with particular reference to the LPSK, for this purpose is participation in various debates and campaigns, and mass and social media. Unions have recently been fairly successful in this respect: in 2020 one union leader was among the top three most-cited leaders in Lithuania.

Trade union activities in society are strongly dependent on their relations with politicians in power, including reforms or other relevant decisions concerning unions. For example, in 2014–2016, a so-called 'new social model' was developed and debated, which included a new version of the Labour Code (DK). Dissatisfied with the attempts of government and business representatives to liberalize labour regulation, unions were very active in society and organized numerous rallies and protest actions during this period. Meanwhile, when the more pro-union LVŽS came to power in 2016–2020, the unions organized fewer campaigns and rallies, although they did not give up their annual campaigns, such as the May Day (1 May) or traditional union processions held on 7 October in commemoration of Decent Work Day.

Since the 1990s, trade unions have carried out various campaigns and events, targeted at achieving specific objectives. But since 2018, the unions, especially the LPSK, have frequently striven to hold 'festivals for the public': they organize concerts, processions and child zones; confederations and their affiliates set up tents in city squares where they distribute leaflets, inform about union activities, answer questions about rights and employment relations, and serve coffee. As a rule, unions avoid direct recruitment efforts during such events.

Trade unions traditionally cooperate, to a greater or lesser extent, with various NGOs working in poverty reduction, equal opportunities or the social integration of people with disabilities. They often participate and cooperate in various working groups and meetings, and share in the development and implementation of joint projects. Recently, as the issue of climate change continues to become more prominent, unions have established closer cooperation with various NGOs working in climate change mitigation. For example, the LPSK has maintained regular contact with the 'Fridays for the Future' unit in Lithuania and also in general try to include climate change issues in their agenda. Furthermore, the young, small but active and visible trade union G1PS encourages unions not only to cooperate with NGOs, but also to develop themselves and become organizations with a 'broader profile', focusing not only on labour market issues, but also on other issues relevant to employees, such as family, social and ecological issues (Lipajev 2020: 76). The unions often support various ecological or LGBT actions.

All confederations and most – though not all – of their affiliates have their own websites and Facebook accounts, where they regularly publish the most relevant information, write comments, discuss political decisions, and place notices on various campaigns, the texts of signed collective agreements or the fact that collective bargaining has been initiated.

Trade union policies towards the European Union

Since their establishment, trade unions have striven to maintain close relations with the international and EU movement, both at confederal and industrial level. Both the largest union confederations, LPSK and LPS 'Solidarumas', are affiliated to the International Trade Union Confederation (ITUC) and the ETUC, and participate in the activities of the European Trade Union Institute (ETUI), the Pan-European Regional Council (PERC), the European Trade Union Federations (ETUFs) and other European institutions and associations. They also closely cooperate with the International Labour Organization and the Baltic Sea Trade Union Network (BASTUN). Union representatives are present at the European Economic and Social Committee and industry-level social dialogue committees, as well as at several other European institutions.

As a rule, the confederations put great emphasis on international cooperation and liaison with EU umbrella organizations, union networks and union-friendly international organizations. This process usually involves all national-level union leaders, as well as the vast majority of industrial-level union leaders. In addition, the confederations have special staff members responsible for international cooperation, who coordinate and liaise both with union organizations from individual countries and with international union organizations.

According to the confederations, participation in the activities of the international and European organizations not only allows them to gain new experience and knowledge, but also has a positive impact on social dialogue in Lithuania. When particularly problematic situations arise, Lithuanian confederations often turn to international or European partners and receive their support and encouragement. The same refers to the European Semester: country-specific recommendations for Lithuania submitted for several years have repeatedly called for the promotion of social dialogue and the participation of social partners in social and economic policymaking. This provided trade unions with a stronger basis for negotiations with the government, increased their involvement in various working groups, and boosted cooperation with authorities and ministries.

RJPS (since 2021) is a member of the European association CESI, although it is rather sceptical about international collaboration. According to RJPS, union confederations, with their limited resources, should not devote much time to international organizations, as the 'benefits of such participation for ordinary members are questionable' (Lipajev 2020: 88).

Union confederations' participation in the European Semester process is not very significant at the national level. On one hand, in recent years, all key documents related to the European Semester have been drawn up exclusively by public institutions in Lithuania: social partners may only provide comments and suggestions to the prepared documents when they are published on the Parliament's website. The form in which opinions can be expressed and the time allocated are usually unsatisfactory or insufficient to make a substantial impact on the content of the documents. Sometimes trade union representatives are also included in various working groups on European Semester–related matters. On the other hand, confederations, employers' associations and civil society organizations do not have sufficient resources to make a significant contribution to the implementation of documents or planned measures (Eurofound 2019b).

Regarding trade unionists' expectations of the European institutions in general, including European trade union umbrella organizations, Lithuanian confederations and their affiliates frequently mention their desire for stricter regulations on various social issues. This refers to the European Social Model, the European Pillar of Social Rights and even the recently discussed European minimum wage. Union representatives have continually emphasized that many of Europe's declared social aspirations are extremely desirable, but that there is a lack of political will at the national level to put them into practice, and national unions lack the strength to enforce the implementation of the declared provisions in practice. According to the unions, stricter, more imperative regulation would greatly help them to achieve their goals at the national level (Gruževskis and Blažienė 2020).

In addition to organized cooperation at the European level, the main Lithuanian trade union organizations traditionally maintain close cooperation with unions from neighbouring countries, mainly with Baltic, Polish and Nordic unions. Unions of the Baltic Sea region have established BASTUN, which includes the Baltic and Nordic countries. Every year, the heads of the union confederations of the three Baltic states meet at the Council of the Baltic States. Lithuanian unions often coordinate joint actions and initiatives with the neighbouring Latvian and Estonian unions and there is ongoing bilateral cooperation with unions from the Nordic countries, Poland, Belarus, Ukraine and Georgia. According to union representatives, cross-border cooperation is not only a useful tool per se, but it is also important for increasing domestic cooperation of unions. Foreign experts and cooperating partners often strive to work with representatives of different national and industry-level unions operating in the country, and thus encourage internal collaboration among domestic unions.

Conclusions

Although the independent trade unions of Lithuania have faced many unfavourable circumstances throughout their existence, they have not only survived, but have also managed in some areas to secure or even expand their positions during the past few decades. These conditions include the LRTT, which ensures the participation of union confederations in key decision-making in the labour market and related areas. As the LRTT, as well as its functions, rights and responsibilities are laid down in Lithuanian legislation, its role is expected to remain significant in the future, irrespective of the ruling party. EU support for the development of social dialogue and active union cooperation with trade unions in Europe and neighbouring countries also strengthen Lithuanian unions.

The fact that membership fees are not the only source of revenues for the largest trade union confederations to a certain extent makes them less dependent on fluctuating membership and enables them to remain active at the national level. New unions, such as G1PS, may also play an important role, as they are focused on a completely new model of activity that is equally suitable for both traditional and new forms of employment.

Trade unions have also found some success in their significant and constantly growing role in the public sector. They recently achieved a breakthrough in the content and coverage of collective bargaining in the public sector and are likely to maintain it in the future. Unions expect that their success in the public sector will have a positive impact on collective bargaining in the private sector as well. According to the newest information from the Ministry of Social Security and Labour (MSSL, 2022), collective bargaining coverage in 2021 reached 25 per cent; the majority of covered employees work in the public sector.

Given all the aforementioned challenges that Lithuanian trade unions have overcome – the transformation of the economy after the collapse of the Soviet Union, growing inequality, the poor image of unions and low public trust in them, high emigration flows, strict regulation of employment relationships and often insufficient union flexibility in adapting to the new and changing labour environment – Visser's marginalization scenario should be rejected. After overcoming all these challenges Lithuanian unions were hardly likely to step back when they became significant actors in both national and European industrial relations systems. Recent trends have demonstrated some revitalization, although this involves mainly positive developments in public sector industrial relations. Thus the dualization scenario is more likely to prevail in future Lithuanian trade union development than the substitution scenario. In Lithuania, the dualist cleavage is likely remain, with strong and fairly powerful trade unions in the public sector, especially in education, health and social care, some parts of the civil service and municipal administrations. Company size is important: industrial relations remain weak or almost absent in small companies and more important in large companies, especially those with old industrial relations traditions (examples may be found in the food industry, electricity and water supply, and transport services).

This trend is further strengthened by the fact that, although platform work, as well as other new forms of employment are growing in Lithuania, as already mentioned the trade union confederations focus their attention and recruitment strategies not on the new, but rather on 'traditional', large industries (including social work, culture, civil service, retail trade).

References

All links were checked on 13 August 2021.

Blažienė I. and Gruževskis B. (2017) Lithuanian trade unions: from survival skills to innovative solutions, in Bernaciak M. and Kahancová M. (eds) Innovative union practices in Central-Eastern Europe, Brussels, ETUI, 111–124.

Blažienė I., Kasiliauskas N. and Guobaite-Kirsliene R. (2019) Lithuania: will new legislation increase the role of social dialogue and collective bargaining?, in Waddington J., Müller T. and Vandaele K. (eds) Collective bargaining in Europe: towards an endgame, Brussels, ETUI, 381–401.

Blažienė I. (2018) Peer country comments paper – Lithuania. Moving from the opposite side of the axis. Peer Review on 'The organisation, outcomes and effectiveness of social dialogue', Belgium, 23–24 October 2018. Mutual Learning Programme, Brussels, European Commission. https://ec.europa.eu/social/BlobServlet?docId=20418&langId=en

ESTEP (2016) Evaluation of results, efficiency and impact of the 2007–2013 measure to facilitate social dialogue in Lithuania, Summary of the final report, 19 April 2016, Vilnius.

Eurofound (2019a) European Company Survey, Dublin, Eurofound.

Eurofound (2019b) The involvement of social partners in national policy-making, Luxembourg, Publications Office of the European Union.

Glovackas S. (2007) History and structure of trade unions. [Manuscript]

Gruževskis B. and Blažienė I. (2020) Lithuanian trade unions in the Europeanization of industrial relations, Vilnius, Lithuanian Social Research Centre.

Interviews (2020) Interviews with leaders of national trade union organisations, conducted in 2019–2020.

Lipajev L. (2020) Lithuanian trade unions as political actors. Masters thesis in Contemporary European Politics, Kaunas. Vytautas Magnus University, Faculty of Political Science and Diplomacy, Department of Political Science. https://www.vdu.lt/cris/bitstream/20.500.12259/102280/4/leonid_lipajev_%20md.pdf

LPSK (2018) Statute of Lithuanian Trade Union Confederation.

LPSK (2021) Lithuanian Trade Union Confederation. www.lpsk.lt

MSSL (2019) Information on the collective agreements monitoring, Ministry of Social Security and Labour. https://socmin.lrv.lt/uploads/socmin/documents/files/veiklos-sritys/darbas/partneryste/Trisal-taryb-medziaga/ks%20monitor_2019%2012.pdf

MSSL (2021) Register of collective agreements. Ministry of Social Security and Labour. https://socmin.lrv.lt/lt/paslaugos/administracines-paslaugos/kolektyviniu-sutarciu-registras-ir-kolektyviniu-sutarciu-registravimo-tvarka

MSSL (2022) A quarter of employees are covered by collective agreements: benefits for employees and employers. Ministry of Social Security and Labour. https://socmin.lrv.lt/lt/naujienos/ketvirtadalis-salies-darbuotoju-dirba-pagal-kolektyvines-sutartis-naudinga-tiek-darbuotojams-tiek-darbdaviams

Research Council (2015) Research on collective agreements and their role in creating quality labour relations (2014–2015), Vilnius, Lithuanian Social Research Centre. http://www.dsti.lt/projects.php

Sandrauga (2021) Lithuanian Trade Union 'Sandrauga'. www.sandrauga.lt

Statistics Lithuania (2020). Labour Market in Lithuania (edition 2020). Strikes. https://osp.stat.gov.lt/darbo-rinka-lietuvoje-2020/darbo-uzmokes tis-darbo-sanaudos-ir-streikai/streikai

Statistics Lithuania (2021). Religious communities and membership organisations. https://osp.stat.gov.lt/religines-bendruomenes-ir-narystes-organi zacijos

Solidarumas (2018) Statute of Lithuanian Trade Union 'Solidarumas'. https://www.lps.lt/istatai/

Solidarumas (2021) Lithuanian Trade Union 'Solidarumas'. www.solidaru mas.lt

Abbreviations

G1PS	1 May Trade Union (G1PS, Gegužės 1-osios profesinė sąjunga)
LDF	Lithuanian Labour Federation (LDF, Lietuvos darbo federacija)
LGS	Union of Lithuanian Doctors (LGS, Lietuvos gydytojų sąjunga)
LLPSK	Lithuanian Free Trade Union Confederation (LLPSK, Lietuvos laisvųjų profesinių sąjungų konfederacija)
LMPF	Lithuanian Federation of Forest and Wood Workers Trade Unions (LMPF, Lietuvos miško ir miško pramonės darbuotojų profesinių sąjungų federacija)
LMPS	Lithuanian Trade Union of Food Producers (LMPS, Lietuvos maistininkų profesinė sąjunga)
LPPSF	Lithuanian Federation of Industrial Trade Unions (LPPSF, Lietuvos pramonės profesinių sąjungų federacija)
LPS 'Sandrauga'	Lithuanian Trade Union 'Sandrauga' (LPS 'Sandrauga', Lietuvos profesinė sąjunga 'Sandrauga')

LPS 'Solidarumas'	Lithuanian Trade Union 'Solidarumas' (Lietuvos profesinė sąjunga 'solidarumas')
LPSC	Lithuanian Trade Union Centre (LPSC, Lietuvos profesinių sąjungų centras)
LPSK	Lithuanian Trade Union Confederation (Lietuvos profesinių sąjungų konfederacija)
LPSS	Lithuanian Trade Union Unification (LPSS, Lietuvos profesinių sąjungų susivienijimas)
LRTT	Tripartite Council of the Republic of Lithuania (LRTT, Lietuvos Respublikos trišalė taryba)
LSDP	Social Democratic Party (LSDP, Lietuvos socialdemokratų partija)
LŠDPS	Lithuanian Education Employees Trade Union (LŠDPS, Lietuvos švietimo darbuotojų profesinė sąjunga)
LŠMPS	Lithuanian Education and Science Trade Union (LŠMPS, Lietuvos švietimo ir mokslo profesinė sąjunga)
LSSO	Lithuanian Nurses' Organization (LSSO, Lietuvos slaugos specialistų organizacija)
LVŽS	Lithuanian Farmers and Greens Union (LVŽS, Lietuvos valstiečių ir žaliųjų sąjunga)
NPPSS	National Unification of Officials Trade Unions (NPPSS, Nacionalinis pareigūnų profesinių sąjungų susivienijimas)
RJPS	General Trade Union of the Republic of Lithuania (RJPS, Respublikinė jungtinė profesinė sąjunga)
SD	Statistics Lithuania (SD, Statistikos departamentas)

Chapter 19

Trade unions in Luxembourg: Residual institutional strength and declining mobilization capacity

Adrien Thomas

Luxembourg has undergone far-reaching economic and demographic changes over the past four decades. The years of economic crisis and of the demise of the steel industry from 1975 to 1985 were followed by twenty 'splendid' years with annual average GDP growth of 5.3 per cent (Zahlen 2012). The main driver of economic growth during these years was Luxembourg's role as a financial hub, whose development was fuelled by lax financial and fiscal regulations (Pieretti et al. 2007; Zucman 2015). As a result of the growth of financial activities, the labour force considerably diversified, increasing from 154,000 in 1981 to more than 440,000 in 2020. Today, 46 per cent of jobs are filled by cross-border workers from neighbouring countries, 27 per cent by resident immigrants, with a large majority coming from other member states of the European Union (EU), and 27 per cent by native residents. Many of these migrant workers are attracted by the high net wages in Luxembourg, which result from the fact that income taxes and social security contributions are lower in Luxembourg than in the neighbouring countries (Zahlen 2008). While the recession of 2008 had fewer economic repercussions in Luxembourg than in most other EU member states, it led to tenser collective bargaining and national-level social dialogue. In addition, increasing social inequalities render the limits of Luxembourg's welfare state more and more apparent (Fusco et al. 2014).

In response to these labour market and economic changes, trade unions have focused on maintaining their political influence and the established institutions of social concertation. They have also striven to innovate and adapt their organizational structures, diversify their service offer and recruit the growing migrant workforce. The results of their efforts are mixed. The unions have managed to some extent to recruit new members and maintain a political consensus around the intrinsic value of 'social partnership'. The principal characteristics of Luxembourg's industrial relations system have not changed: unions as the sole negotiators of collective agreements at company and industry level, extension mechanisms for industry-level collective agreements and the intrinsic value attributed to social peace. The number of independent unions has diminished over the past two decades, so that today's union landscape is dominated by three larger confederations, with a limited number of independent unions (see Table 19.1). The unions have managed to retain, in the face of employer opposition, the automatic indexation of wages, whereby wages are adjusted to consumer price increases. The changing morphology of Luxembourg's economy, however, with the growth of the service sector, the rise in qualification levels and the increase in small and medium-sized companies, increasingly calls into question the established patterns of collective bargaining. Union density has been declining significantly, throwing doubt on unions' capacity to maintain the current collective bargaining coverage. In the near future, the contrast between the institutionalized involvement of unions in national policymaking and the declining unionization rates risks undermining union legitimacy.

Table 19.1 Principal characteristics of trade unionism in Luxembourg

	1980	2000	2019
Total trade union membership*	69,000	96,000**	123,000
Women as a proportion of total membership	n.a.	34 %***	n.a.
Gross union density	n.a.	n.a.	35 %
Net union density	50 %	43 %**	28 %
Number of confederations	4	3	3
Number of affiliated federations	n.a.	32	40
Number of independent unions	12	9	5
Collective bargaining coverage	60 %	60 %	57 %****
Principal level of collective bargaining	Company and industry		
Days not worked due to industrial action per 1,000 workers	n.a.	12	n.a

Note: *Union membership data does not include retired workers; **1998; ***2002; ****2018.

Source: Appendix A1.

Historical background and principal features of the industrial relations system

Luxembourg's trade unions have been historically divided along industrial and professional lines, as well as political and confessional cleavages. The modern labour movement in Luxembourg took shape between 1916 to 1921, a period characterized there, as in other European countries, by demands for democratization and social rights (Scuto 1990; Thomas 2012; Trausch 1974). Whereas up to the First World War unionization had been limited mainly to civil servants, white-collar workers and certain categories of blue-collar workers in small and medium-sized industries, mass unionism developed from 1916 onwards in the mining and steel industry (Kieffer 1993; Lentz 1992; Wehenkel 2009). In contrast to other European countries where the present-day union movement was the result of the slow aggregation of pre-existing unions, the modern union movement in Luxembourg was almost constructed from scratch, as a result of the social mobilization in the mines and steel factories between 1916 and 1921. The Federation of Miners and Metallurgists (*Berg- und Hüttenarbeiter-Verband*), which proclaimed its political neutrality, and the Luxembourg Federation of Metallurgists (*Luxemburger Metallarbeiterverband*), of socialist orientation, were both founded in 1916. The two federations merged in 1920 to form the Federation of Miners and Metal Workers (*Berg- und Metallindustriearbeiter-Verband*), which took the name Luxembourg Workers' Union (LAV, *Letzeburger Arbechter-Verband*) in 1944. In 1921, the Luxembourg Confederation of Christian Trade Unions (LCGB, *Lëtzebuerger Chrëschtleche Gewerkschaftsbond*) was founded with the support of the Catholic Church (Weber 1999).

The inter-war years saw isolated eruptions of working class militancy, such as the general strike of March 1921 or the strike wave of July 1936, but also the beginning of a process of institutionalization of industrial relations characterized by the introduction of works councils in 1919, the creation of professional chambers for blue- and white-collar workers in 1924 and the creation of a mediation body for the negotiation of collective agreements in 1936, which turned the state into a facilitator of collective bargaining and represented a departure from its previous laissez-faire approach (Adam and Zahlen 1999; Wey 2003). The basic principles of workers' representation introduced in the inter-war years are still relevant today: the representation of workers' interests in the workplace through unionized or non-unionized staff representatives and the negotiation of collective agreements at the company and industry levels by trade unions, with an active role for the state in the extension of collective agreements and as a mediator in case of industrial conflicts.

The political realignments and conflicts after the Second World War were reflected in the union movement when the newly founded Free Luxembourg Workers' Union (FLA, *Freie Letzeburger Arbechterverband*), led by the Communist Party, competed with the socialist-led LAV for hegemony over the working class (Majerus 1992). The 1950s continued to be characterized by competitive struggles between communist and socialist unionists and by large-scale strikes in the mines and steel factories (Scuto 1999). From the 1960s onwards, the institutionalization of industrial relations and the union movement deepened. This encompassed the marginalization of the FLA; the legislation on collective bargaining of 1965, which set criteria for unions' representativeness and excluded industry-level unions from negotiations; the creation of the Economic and Social Council in 1966; the law on codetermination within larger companies in 1974; and the introduction of the Tripartite Coordination Committee in 1977, which became the most emblematic institution of social partnership and union involvement in public policymaking. Under the auspices of the Tripartite Coordination Committee, Luxembourg's steel industry was restructured, with employment being cut from 25,000 workers in 1975 to 13,000 workers in 1985. This was carried out without any major confrontation with organized labour.

Faced with the decline of the steel industry and the transition to a service economy, unions tried to adapt their structures and to preserve their bargaining power. Starting in the 1970s, a steady process of centralization and realignment began. One key issue in the debate among unions was how to overcome the divide between blue- and white-collar workers. Indeed, up to 2009, the legislation established different labour regulations and social security regimes for blue- and white-collar workers. These legal differences resulted in separate collective agreements, different professional chambers and in unions that represented only white-collar workers (*employés privés*). In 1978, talks on a possible amalgamation were conducted between the LAV, the LCGB and the Federation of Private Sector Employees (FEP, *Fédération des Employés Privés*), founded in 1920 (Krier et al. 2016). While the LCGB rapidly pulled out, in 1979 the LAV merged with parts of the white-collar union FEP to form the Luxembourg Independent Trade Union Confederation (OGBL, *Onofhängege*

Gewerkschaftsbond Lëtzebuerg). Except for the Luxembourg Association of Bank and Insurance Employees (ALEBA, *Association Luxembourgeoise des Employés de Banque et Assurance*), the remaining independent unions representing white-collar employees gradually lost members as a consequence of infighting, split-offs and dissolutions. The social elections for the professional chambers document the gradual loss of relevance of these smaller unions. By the social elections of 1998 and 2003, the various splinter organizations resulting from the decomposition of the FEP had vanished into irrelevance.

Structure of trade unions and union democracy

The two main union confederations are the OGBL and the LCGB. The OGBL claimed 71,000 members in 2019 (of whom approximately 10,000 were retirees) and counts sixteen affiliated federations. The LCGB claimed 43,000 members (of whom approximately 5,000 were retirees) and counts fourteen affiliated federations. The OGBL is historically close to the Socialist Party, while the LCGB is close to the Christian Social Party. Relations between the OGBL and the LCGB have often been terse and competitive, because of ideological divides in the past, and because of struggles for influence and membership in the present. Both confederations are considered nationally representative by the authorities and are solely entitled to sign collective agreements in all sectors of the economy.

The notion of 'national representativeness' is important in the Luxembourg debate and reflects the legislator's aim to ensure that unions take into account broader considerations of national interest and competitiveness, and not just narrow company- or industry-specific considerations (Zahlen 2003). According to the 2004 law on union representativeness, only unions with a strong cross-industrial presence – which is measured by their having received at least 20 per cent of the votes in the election of the Chamber of Wage Earners (CSL, *Chambre des Salariés*) – can sign collective agreements. In addition, to accommodate the situation of ALEBA in finance, the legislator decided that unions with a particularly strong presence in an industry employing more than 10 per cent of the nation's workforce can sign agreements in that industry. Other unions have a more limited industrial role, such as the two railway unions, the National Federation of Luxembourg Railway and Transport Workers and Civil Servants (FNCTTFEL, *Fédération Nationale des Cheminots, Travailleurs du Transport, Fonctionnaires et Employés Luxembourgeois*) and the Christian Federation of Transport Personnel (SYPROLUX, *Fédération Chrétienne du Personnel des Transports*). While the FNCTTFEL integrated the OGBL 'on a provisional basis' in 2020, with a view to full absorption in 2024, SYPROLUX remains independent (see Table 19.2).

Table 19.2 Trade union confederations and independent unions in Luxembourg

Confederations	Organizing domain and main affiliates	Total members*
CGFP	Public sector (Fédération Générale des Universitaires au Service de l'État; Syndicat National des Enseignants; Syndicat Professionnel de la Force Publique; Association Générale des Cadres)	31,000
LCGB	Cross-industry (Fédération Services et Commerce; Fédération INDUSID; Fédération Construction et Artisanat; Fédération Transport; Fédération Banques et Assurances)	43,000
OGBL	Cross-industry (Syndicat Santé, Services Sociaux et Éducatifs; Syndicat Bâtiment, Artisanat du Bâtiment et Constructions Métalliques; Syndicat Commerce; Syndicat Services et Énergy)	71,000
Independent unions	**Organizing domain**	**Total members**
ALEBA	Banks and insurances	10,000
APESS	Teachers	n.a.
FGFC	Local government	5,000
FNCTTFEL	Railway workers, local government	5,000
SYPROLUX	Railway workers	1,600

Note: * self-declared membership data from 2019, including retired workers.

Source: Author's elaboration.

As regards the public sector, the General Public Sector Confederation (CGFP, *Confédération Générale de la Fonction Publique*) is considered representative. The CGFP counts 31,000 members but the number of pensioners among the membership is unknown.[1] The CGFP, which proclaims

[1] The CGFP did not answer requests for information on the number of retirees among its membership.

a strict political and ideological neutrality, negotiates agreements for civil and public servants (*fonctionnaires d'État* and *employés de l'État*) with the government. The Federation of Local Government (FGFC, *Fédération Générale de la Fonction Communale*) represents the employees of local administration and counts approximately 5,000 members.

The two nationally representative confederations OGBL and LCGB organize members according to workplace and on a geographical basis. Members are directly affiliated to the confederation and then assigned to an industry federation in line with their place of work or occupation and to a local branch, depending on where they live. According to their situation, members can also be affiliated to other structures, such as the OGBL's immigrant department or the LCGB's committee for Portuguese residents. Currently, the federations affiliated to the OGBL with the most members are the Health and Social Services Federation and the Construction Workers' Federation.[2] In the case of the LCGB, the largest affiliate is a heterogeneous conglomerate federation made up of private services, retail and hospitality. In both the OGBL and the LCGB, the formerly prevalent manufacturing industry federations have lost ground in comparison with the private and public service sector federations.

In both the OGBL and the LCGB the number of federations has increased over recent decades. The number of federations affiliated to the OGBL increased from twelve in 1980 to sixteen in 2020, through the addition of a federation for cleaning services in 1989, road transport in 2001 (after the integration of road transport workers previously organized in the FNCTTFEL), air transport in 2006 and railway workers in 2020 (following the 'provisional integration' of the FNCTTFEL into the OGBL). As regards the LCGB, it increased its number of federations from nine in 1999 to fourteen in 2020. Over the past two decades, the LCGB has merged its steel, metalworking and chemical industry federations into a single federation and has, similar to the OGBL, split up its formerly unified transport workers' federation into road, passenger, air and maritime transport. In addition, the LCGB has created several small new federations covering private security services, cleaning services, private school teachers, and vehicle repair and maintenance. In both the OGBL and the LCGB, the confederal leadership is in charge of creating and delimiting new federations.

---

2 Confederations do not, however, have reliable data on the evolution of the membership of their various federations.

The internal organization of the OGBL and the LCGB is similarly hierarchical. The two confederations hold a national convention every five years. In the case of the OGBL, the national congress, characterized as the 'supreme body' by its statutes, is composed of delegates of the industry federations, the local branches and specific structures, such as the immigrant department. The main governing body between congresses is the national committee, comprising mainly representatives of industry and local branches. Between the meetings of the national committee, a more limited leadership body meets, the executive committee, which delegates daily management to the executive bureau. In practice, decision-making power is concentrated in the executive bureau, with ten members in the case of the OGBL. The LCGB's coordination committee counts eleven members, among them a union chaplain tasked with acting as a link to the 'institutions of the Catholic Church' (LCGB 2014).

Although the OGBL elected a woman as president in 2019, women remain sorely underrepresented in union leadership bodies. Women make up as few as 15 per cent of the members of the OGBL's forty-member executive committee, representing the affiliated federations and local branches, and 21 per cent of the LCGB's 23-member executive committee. Some of the independent unions still have all-male leadership bodies, such as the union of local government FGFC and the teachers' union, the Association of Teachers of Secondary and Higher Education of the Grand Duchy of Luxembourg (APESS, Association des Professeurs de l'Enseignement Secondaire et Supérieur du Grand-Duché de Luxembourg) (Blond-Hanten 2021).

In both the OGBL and the LCGB, the president has traditionally had a strong influence on the confederation's policies, among other things because Luxembourg's neo-corporatist political system relies on negotiation partners that are able to commit the organizations they represent. The statutes of the LCGB, last modified in 2014, stress hierarchy and control in the organization of the union's apparatus and are particularly explicit as regards the authority of the confederation president: 'The National President chairs the union council, the central committee, the executive committee, the coordination committee and other LCGB meetings, and has the right to attend all other meetings' (LCGB 2014). In general, the full-time officials in charge of the affiliated federations are strongly present in the daily running of the OGBL and the LCGB: they are the interlocutors of political decision-makers and the media, more so than the unionized staff representatives in the companies.

The CGFP represents public servants. It is a conglomerate of sixty-five professional and craft associations regrouped in eleven 'federations', which represent either specific categories of public servants – such as teachers, police and army personnel – or broader categories, such as lower, middle and higher civil service. In comparison with the OGBL and the LCGB, the CGFP is much more loosely structured, and its confederal level is leaner. Its leadership bodies are an executive committee made up of seventeen members and an executive bureau counting five members, all men. The public authorities played a key role in the founding of the CGFP in 1967. At the time, the minister in charge of the public sector refused to continue negotiating with the dozens of small associations representing civil servants, which were at war over a general revision of wages for public servants and asked them to create a common organization (Confédération Générale de la Fonction Publique 2010; Jentgen 1981). Historically, the middle layers of the public service have made up the bulk of the CGFP's membership, with the higher categories providing the leadership of the organization (Kieffer 1992).

As the relevance of the political and confessional cleavages between the OGBL and the LCGB has become more and more questionable, with society's secularization and de-ideologization, the OGBL has been advocating the creation of a united confederation. The LCGB asserts, however, the value of pluralism and its relationship with the OGBL is notoriously tense, while the CGFP holds on to its autonomy in the name of protecting the distinct status of public servants, just as ALEBA upholds the value of its apolitical approach to labour relations. As a result, the representation of the two best-paid segments of Luxembourg's workforce, public servants and bank employees, to a large degree eludes the OGBL and the LCGB.

Unionization

Union density and unions' socio-political influence have been declining since the 1980s. Density decreased from 50 per cent in 1980 to 43 per cent in 1998, and stood at 28 per cent in 2019, although the absolute membership has increased almost continuously in a context of strong job creation. The OGBL, for instance, increased its membership from 39,000 in 1993 to 71,000 in 2019, although a stagnation or even a slight regression has set in over the past couple of years. The decline in union density is thus mainly due to the fact that the recruitment of new members has not kept pace with the strong job creation and diversification of the economy since 1985. Employment creation has been most vigorous in industries in which the presence of unions has traditionally been weak, such as business services and retail. Because union competition pushes each union to project an image of strength, these issues are not publicly acknowledged or discussed by the unions.

Union members are typically older than the average employee, frequently of intermediate qualifications and often employed in public administration, education, transport and manufacturing industry (Ries 2011). Luxembourg-born workers are also more likely to be unionized than foreign-born workers. While in 2010 the union membership rate was 53 per cent for Luxembourg-born workers, it was 35 per cent among Portuguese immigrants living in Luxembourg, 27 per cent among Belgian immigrants, 24 per cent among German immigrants and 19 per cent among French immigrants (Ries 2011). While some of the differences in the unionization rates can be attributed to the industries in which workers are employed or to workers' sociodemographic characteristics, it is still true that, even when these factors are taken into account, immigrants remain significantly less unionized than nationals (Fleury et al. 2011).

Given that residents of Luxembourg nationality only make up 27 per cent of Luxembourg's work force, migrant workers are strongly present among the membership of the OGBL and the LCGB. In the case of the OGBL, 31 per cent of the membership were of Luxembourg nationality and 69 per cent of foreign nationality in 2019. Twenty per cent of all members of the OGBL were French cross-border workers in 2019, 11 per cent Belgian cross-border workers and 10 per cent German cross-border workers, according to a former OGBL president (Interview, March 2020).

To address the internationalization of Luxembourg's labour market, trade unions have created specific organizational structures to integrate migrant workers. The OGBL and the LCGB thus set up immigrant departments and branches for cross-border workers in the 1980s (Thomas 2015). These structures take positions, from the perspective of migrant workers' interests, on issues such as social security entitlements, housing or education. They also undertake unionization drives in industries with a large immigrant population, such as construction and cleaning, where they also seek out foreign candidates ready to stand at the elections of workplace staff delegations. Furthermore, both the OGBL and the LCGB have built links in particular with the Portuguese community in Luxembourg, which is the largest migrant group, and its network of associations and ethnic media. This active representation of the interests of migrant workers also generates dilemmas and tensions within unions, namely relating to the unification of members' interests and to the limits of organizational diversification. The defence of migrant workers' interests may, for instance, render the unification of members' interests more difficult, as it moves unions away from a general representation of members' interests, giving rise to distributional and political conflicts among the membership. The creation of specific structures for migrant workers has also provoked debates over the degree of autonomy and integration of these structures, with representatives of cross-border workers' branches seeking to extend their autonomy, while immigrant workers residing in Luxembourg aim to deepen their integration into existing union structures (Thomas 2020).

Unionization strategies traditionally rely on the negotiation of collective agreements at company and industry level. Unions also try to gain new members and retain existing members by developing individual services. Unions have increasingly put into place individual counselling and support services since the 1990s, focusing in particular on labour law and social security issues. The counselling and support services of the OGBL and the LCGB, which employ, respectively, twenty-five and fifteen social counsellors, are accessible to all union members, but they may be particularly useful for immigrants without sufficient knowledge of Luxembourg's official languages (French, German and Luxembourgish), or who do not feel comfortable dealing with the public administration. Given that 15 per cent of Luxembourg's population is of Portuguese nationality, the unions have hired numerous Portuguese-speaking social counsellors and published information material in Portuguese. In addition, unions offer individual services not directly related to work and employment. The OGBL and the LCGB offer, for instance, a free leisure accident insurance and preferential rates for other insurances. The CGFP sells various kinds of insurance, ranging from life to car insurance, as well as consumer loans. The CGFP even launched an investment vehicle through which it invested the savings of its members, although it decided to shut it down because of the low-interest rate environment.

Union resources and expenditure

Membership dues are the trade unions' main resource, and the maintenance of the full-time apparatus is an important point of expenditure.

In parallel to their increasing institutionalization, unions have undergone a steady process of professionalization, with an increase in their number of full-time staffers. This increase is driven by the professionalization of individual member services and the growth in the number of full-time officials negotiating collective agreements, supporting unionized staff representatives in companies and coordinating the activities of the federations. The criteria determining whether a union can be considered representative include its organizational capacity, to be measured among other things by its capacity to fund full-time officials through members' dues (Castegnaro 2015). The OGBL today has over 120 employees, compared with the seventeen officials of its predecessor organization, the LAV, in 1978 (Auger 1980). The LCGB has fifty-four employees. Moreover, unions can rely on economic analyses and legal opinions produced by the CSL, which has eighty-five employees. The CGFP has a leaner internal organization, with twelve employees.

Trade union expenditure is financed mainly through members' dues, which make up over 90 per cent of unions' budgets, and through state subsidies for specific activities. The OGBL and the LCGB thus receive a subsidy from the Ministry of Labour for the functioning of their joint European secretariat. In addition, the OGBL and the CGFP have set up development cooperation structures that receive funding from the Ministry of Development Cooperation. Unions may also receive revenues from the lease of real estate and commercial activities. Because of the steady increase in membership, unions have to date not encountered difficulties in financing their activities.

The unions mainly collect flat-rate member dues. The OBGL and the LCGB both receive monthly membership dues of – in theory – 1 per cent of gross income, although this is capped at 20.4 and 19.4 euros, respectively. The members' dues are paid directly at the confederal level and then redistributed among the federations and local branches. This direct affiliation of members to the confederation gives control over union dues to the confederal level and contributes to the strong centralization of the OGBL and the LCGB. In the case of the CGFP, each professional association affiliated to the confederation collects its own dues and transfers a share of them to the confederate level (3 euros per month in 2020).

To preserve their liberty of action, the major unions do not have legal personality, they are de facto associations (Putz 2014). To be able to own financial and property assets, however, the OGBL, the LCGB and the FNCTTFEL have created distinct structures to manage their financial participation in companies and real estate holdings, which are mostly a legacy of the numerous consumer cooperatives and 'People's Houses' (*Maisons du Peuple*) set up during the 1920s and 1930s. While formally independent of the unions, these structures are run by former and current union leaders. The OGBL has two such structures: the Maison du Peuple, with assets of 3.5 million euros in 2018, and the Centrale du LAV, which has not published its recent balance sheets. The LCGB's Luxmill possesses real estate of a total value of 26.9 million euros (financed through a bank loan of 19.2 million euros), and the FNCTTFEL's Coopérative Casino syndical possesses real estate valued at 7.2 million euros.

Participation in commercial ventures can also turn into a liability for unions. Currently, the OGBL and the FNCTTFEL own 61 and 17 per cent, respectively, of the media group Editpress, via the Centrale du LAV and the Coopérative Casino syndical. The group publishes the daily newspaper *Tageblatt* and operates a printing press. Editpress is also a co-shareholder of the companies publishing the dailies *Le Quotidien* and *L'Essentiel*, and the weekly *Revue*. Because of the erosion of print media, Editpress has in recent years accumulated considerable losses and debt, leading to the closure of the weekly newspaper *Le Jeudi* in 2019. The restructuring and consolidation of the group, which had a total debt of 15.8 million euros in 2018, has become a pressing concern and confronts the involved unions with difficult choices.

Collective bargaining and unions at the workplace

Traditionally, collective bargaining in Luxembourg has been most developed in manufacturing and in the public sector. Since the 2000s, however, unions have increasingly been negotiating collective agreements in the private service sector. When it comes to negotiating collective agreements and mobilizing workers, unions rely mainly on the staff representation bodies in companies. Luxembourg knows no equivalent of the union delegate or the company union section, as exist for instance in France. Unions may, however, submit lists during the election of the staff delegations and almost half of the elected staff representatives are elected from such lists (see Table 19.3).

Under Luxembourg labour law, private sector companies with at least fifteen workers have to hold elections every five years for a staff representation body tasked with 'safeguarding and defending employees' interests'. While in the 2008 elections, 53 per cent of the elected representatives were candidates put forward by unions, the number of unionized workers' representatives dropped to 43 per cent in 2019,[3] according to the labour inspectorate in charge of supervising the elections. In companies with more than 100 employees, 66 per cent of workers' representatives are unionized, while only 23 per cent are unionized in companies with fewer than 100 employees. The new law on social dialogue of 2015 lowered the threshold for the designation of full-time workers' representatives at the company level from 500 to 250 workers. This reform, which was strongly advocated by the OGBL, has created numerous additional full-time representatives in medium-sized companies, further contributing to the professionalization of union work. No staff representations are elected in the public administration.

Table 19.3 Elected staff representatives at the company level, 2008, 2013 and 2019

	2008 (%)	2013 (%)	2019 (%)
Non-union representatives	47	51	57
OGBL representatives	31	29	24
LCGB representatives	15	14	14
Other union representatives	7	6	5

Source: Press articles and Inspectorate of Labour and Mines. Prior to 2019, when the results of the social elections were for the first time collected in digital form by the labour inspectorate, the aggregated results of the elections of staff representatives were notoriously contested, with the labour inspectorate, union confederations and independent unions often putting forward significantly different results.

The OGBL and the LCGB, considered nationally representative, have a monopoly on the negotiation of collective agreements in the private sector, whether at company or industry level. While the ALEBA still benefits from industry-level representativeness in the financial sector, its position is eroding, and its strongholds are nowadays mainly the small and medium-sized banks. In the aftermath of the global financial crisis of 2008, labour–management relations in many banks became more difficult in a context of cost-cutting, digitalization and tightened banking regulations (Kirov and Thill 2018). The introduction in 2015 of the

[3] The workplace and CSL elections that should both have taken place in November 2018 were postponed to 2019 to avoid an overlap with the general elections held in October 2018.

automatic exchange of information to reduce tax evasion put further pressure on Luxembourg-based private banking activities. These developments strained the ALEBA's non-conflictual approach to interest representation. In addition, in the run-up to the 2019 social elections, opaque and acrimonious internal conflicts led to the firing of several union officials and the abrupt resignation of the president of ALEBA.

While unionized employee representatives from the relevant companies or industries participate in the negotiation of collective agreements, these are led mainly by full-time union officials. At the end of the negotiation process, collective agreements are usually ratified by a meeting of the unionized employee representatives from the company or industry concerned. To be recognized by the authorities, collective agreements in the private sector may be signed only by the OGBL and the LCGB confederations. Most collective agreements are negotiated at the company and industry level, with hardly any bargaining at cross-sector level.

The overall coverage rate of collective agreements has remained stable at approximately 60 per cent since the 1980s. This remarkable stability is due to the unions' ability to negotiate new collective agreements at the company level and to the extension of a number of industry-level collective agreements. The declaration of general interest by the Ministry of Labour makes it possible to render collective agreements compulsory for a given industry (Thomas et al. 2019). The bargaining power of unions differs, however, strongly depending on industry. In 2018, at the industry level, the coverage rate of collective agreements varied from 75 per cent of workers in health and social work and 64 per cent in manufacturing to 21 per cent in hospitality and 14 per cent in professional, scientific and technical activities, according to the Structure of Earnings Survey. The government also influences wage bargaining indirectly through the indexation of wages, which was introduced for public servants in 1921 and gradually extended to the general economy in 1965 and 1975, and the setting of the statutory minimum wage introduced in 1944, increases in which influence the wage raises negotiated in collective agreements.

The existing collective agreements at the industry level are mainly either long-established, such as in banking or construction, or the result of a shared interest between employers and unions to cut out competition over wages, such as in security or hospitals. Unions have hardly negotiated any new such collective agreements at the industry level over the past decade. In retail, for instance, unions ended up negotiating agreements at the company level because they did not succeed in negotiating an agreement at the industry level. In finance, because of outsourcing of IT services and back-office functions by many banks, employment has increased among so-called 'financial sector professionals' (*professionnels du secteur financier*) not covered by the banking collective agreement. Unions are also hardly represented among the Big Four accounting firms Deloitte, Ernst & Young, KPMG and PwC, which are heavily present in Luxembourg. At the company level, a substantial number of collective agreements are negotiated in manufacturing, retail and transport, while agreements are very rarely concluded in hospitality and business support activities.

Several recently signed collective agreements contain only limited extra-legal advantages or seem to be caught in a process of gradual hollowing out. For instance, in banking, the multi-annual collective agreements concluded in 2014 and 2018 did not contain any linear pay increases. In addition, the number of bank employees considered to be senior executives (*cadres supérieurs*) – and thus not covered by the collective agreement – has increased. Unions in banking claim that approximately one-third of all bank employees are wrongly categorized as senior executives. Classified as senior executives, these employees are not entitled, for instance, to paid overtime or supplementary holidays.

As a general rule, in recent years trade union bargaining power has been strongest in the segments of the economy directly or indirectly controlled or funded by the state, as witnessed by the advantageous collective agreement for the social sector negotiated by the OGBL in 2017 and by the favourable wage agreement in the public service negotiated by the CGFP in 2018. In manufacturing and private services, unions have encountered more difficulties in mobilizing their members and achieving favourable bargaining outcomes. In 2019, the OGBL developed, with a degree of success, innovative mobilizing tactics during the negotiation of a collective agreement with a major retailer in Luxembourg, the Cactus group. The union put pressure on Cactus through public campaigning and by targeting the company's weak spots, such as its dependence on the truck drivers supplying local supermarkets. Such attempts at developing organizing practices, however, are for the present mainly the product of individual initiatives within the confederations, and there is no systematic approach to organizing by central leaderships. In general, non-standard workers and platform workers are a blind spot of union recruitment.

Industrial conflict

Luxembourg's strike legislation is highly restrictive, and strikes are rare. While France and Italy inscribed the right to strike in their constitutions after the Second World War, Luxembourg's Council of State opposed this. Only in 2007 were strikes mentioned in the constitution, albeit in an implicit and restrictive form: 'The law [...] organizes the right to strike'. The driving force of Luxembourg's economy, banking, has thus far known only one industry-wide strike, in July 1991. The generally low level of strike activity is due to a combination of different factors: the restrictive legal framework, the high threshold for strikes set by unions themselves, and, finally, the consensus orientation of industrial relations that results from the 'ideology of social partnership' that historically has permeated Luxembourg, like other small countries in Western Europe (Katzenstein 1985).

Strike action is possible only after the referral of the litigious issue to the government-appointed National Conciliation Office (*Office National de la Conciliation*) and the formal drafting of a statement of 'non-conciliation'. Legal experts have raised the question of whether Luxembourg's strike legislation conforms with international norms, although unions have never tried to challenge it in court (Castegnaro and Arcanger 2010; Putz 2014). This restrictive legal framework pre-structures interactions between employers and workers' representatives, and tends to impede strike action by making the recourse to industrial action potentially costlier, in particular spontaneous and solidarity strikes.

Both the OGBL and the LCGB pay out strike benefits when their members engage in a strike called by the union; the CGFP does not have a strike fund and does not pay out benefits to strikers. OGBL and LCGB statutes stipulate, however, that at least 75 per cent of their members in the relevant company or industry have to vote in favour of a strike in a secret ballot, which sets a high threshold for engaging in industrial action. Unions consider this high threshold to be a safeguard against premature industrial action. Historically, Luxembourg unions have been very cautious in calling strikes since the failed general strike of March 1921, which led to numerous dismissals of union activists and membership losses (Scuto 1990). The March 1921 strike left a lasting imprint of distrust towards spontaneous industrial action on the labour movement.

In addition, public discourse in Luxembourg is underlain by a normative conception of industrial relations, valuing social peace and political stability as intrinsic values. In Luxembourg, as in Belgium and the Netherlands (Conway and Romijn 2007), proportional political representation and multi-party coalitions have shaped political systems in which compromise rather than conflict has been the defining characteristic. If a degree of social conflict is accepted, the dominant thinking is that it needs to be channelled and organized. Because of Luxembourg's strategic vulnerability as a small country dependent on foreign investments, social peace is also presented by the government as a crucial factor in the country's economic viability.

In a context of dwindling unionization rates and tougher employer resistance since the financial crisis of 2008, unions' ability to mobilize their members for industrial action has diminished. Over the past decade, several union attempts to organize strikes have failed. These failures have occurred both in strongly unionized companies and industries – such as the steel producer Arcelor-Mittal or among teachers in 2013 – in which unions have not managed to gather sufficient votes among their membership to call for strikes, and in weakly organized industries, such as cleaning in 2014–2015. Moreover, unions have encountered difficulties mobilizing their members on crucial cross-industrial issues, such as the 'modulation' (in fact, a temporary suspension) of the wage indexation mechanism in 2011 and the reform of the pension system in 2012. In other instances, in relation to industry-specific concerns, unions have been more successful in mobilizing workers. In 2013, unions conducted a successful mobilization in the construction industry to prevent a flexibilization of working time. In 2018, an 11-day strike by retirement home workers lead to a successful outcome for the mobilized workers. In general, unions have been very careful in choosing their battles, considering strikes as a last resort, and, in case of doubt, have shrunk back from large-scale confrontations. For instance, during the economic downturn triggered by the Covid-19 pandemic, numerous companies have cut jobs without facing any meaningful industrial action, in particular Arcelor-Mittal, the air company Luxair, the publishing company Saint-Paul or the glass manufacturer Guardian Luxguard.

Political relations

The main private sector confederations OGBL and LCGB retain strong links with the two main political parties that have shaped politics in Luxembourg since the Second World War. The OGBL is close to the

Social Democrats and the LCGB to the Christian Democrats. Up to the 1990s, dual careers as trade union leaders and politicians were frequent, and most governments featured at least one prominent union leader as minister, typically as minister of labour. Since the 2000s, there has been a gradual distancing, with relations becoming less organic and occasional divergences being publicly voiced. In contrast to the OGBL and the LCGB, the CGFP and ALEBA highlight their political and ideological neutrality.

Both Luxembourg's Christian Democrats, who were almost continuously in power from 1945 to 2013, and their junior partner, the pragmatic Social Democrats, have been pivotal supporters of social concertation and partnership. This reflects these political currents' scepticism as regards the capacity of liberal and individualistic societies to maintain social cohesion (Streeck 2006). The Tripartite Coordination Committee has come to be considered as the cornerstone of social concertation in Luxembourg. After playing a key role in the restructuring of the steel industry, the focus of the Tripartite Coordination Committee gradually shifted in the 1990s and 2000s to issues of national competitiveness and the implementation of the European Employment Strategy. Since the economic crisis of 2008, national-level social dialogue and consultation processes have become increasingly conflict-ridden, however.

The difficulty of achieving a consensus in the tripartite format has led governments to engage in bipartite rather than tripartite negotiations. In addition, the formerly dominant Christian Democrats, who were strong backers of corporatist forms of governance, were not part of the governments formed in 2013 and 2018 by the centre-right Democratic Party, the Social Democrats and the Green Party. Neither the Democratic Party nor the Green Party maintain any organic links with unions, although, for the time being, they do not openly question the key pillars of the traditional industrial relations system, comprising unions as sole negotiators of collective agreements, the wage indexation mechanism and the intrinsic value of structured social dialogue.

Since the economic and financial crisis of 2008, employer organizations have increasingly been distancing themselves from social partnership and have reasserted their freedom to regulate wages and working time either unilaterally or at the workplace level. A new generation of leaders of employer organizations have taken a more confrontational attitude towards unions and portray tripartite social dialogue as a tiresome burden from the past. While Luxembourg's employer organizations were led for over a century by steel executives accustomed to dealing with unions, this has changed in recent years. In 2019, the long-serving Michel Wurth, a board member of Arcelor-Mittal, stepped down from his position as president of the two main employer organizations, the Chamber of Commerce and the Union of Luxembourg Enterprises (UEL, *Union des Entreprises Luxembourgeoises*). Documenting the loss of influence of manufacturing, Luc Frieden, chair of the board of directors of the Chinese-owned bank Banque Internationale à Luxembourg, became head of the Chamber of Commerce, and Nicolas Buck, owner of a small company providing services to investment funds, was elected president of the UEL.

An indirect means of trade union participation in national politics are the professional chambers consulted by the government and the parliament on proposed legislation and regulations relevant to the categories they represent. At their creation in 1924, the professional chambers – which are elected every five years by all workers – were intended by the government to act as a counterweight to unions (Putz 2014; Wey 2003). The chambers never played that role, however, as unions were always hegemonic in the chambers of blue- and white-collar workers, which merged in 2009 to form the CSL, to which all employees in the private sector are automatically affiliated. Unions are nonetheless still careful to prevent the CSL from gaining autonomy. Emblematic of this is the fact that the current president of the OGBL is at the same time president of the CSL, leaving hardly any room for autonomous expression by the CSL. When elections were held in 2019 to determine the new composition of the professional chamber, the participation rate continued its downward trajectory, at 33 per cent, down from 36 per cent in 2013. The participation rate of non-nationals, both immigrants living in Luxembourg and cross-border workers, is significantly lower than that of nationals. The steady decline of the participation rate calls into question the traditional function of voting for the CSL as an indicator of non-unionized workers' support for the established unions. Public servants are affiliated to the Chamber of Civil Servants and Public Employees (*CHFEP, Chambre des fonctionnaires et employés publics*), created in 1964. Women are underrepresented in both professional chambers: roughly one-third of the elected members of the CSL are women and as few as one-fifth of the members of the CHFEP (Blond-Hanten 2021).

In general, the unions' political influence has diminished with the internationalization of Luxembourg's labour market. Today a majority of the OGBL and LCGB membership are migrant workers who do not have the right to vote at national elections, whereas CGFP's membership is largely made up of nationals. The fact that the workforce in manufacturing and the private service sector is made up mainly of immigrants and cross-border workers renders the working class even more 'invisible' in Luxembourg than in other Western European countries (Raphael 2019). During the legislative election of 2018, the main parties did not have a single manual worker on their lists, and only 7 per cent of all surveyed voters self-identified as working class, according to a post-election survey for the University of Luxembourg. The fact that many Luxembourg nationals, who are the only ones to vote in the legislative elections, work in the public sector confers a strong political influence on the CGFP. The CGFP is not shy in using its political clout whenever it judges that public servants' core interests are at stake: wages and working conditions in the public service and requirements in terms of nationality and language proficiency for public servants.

Societal power

The capacity of trade unions to pursue their objectives also depends on their societal power, their ability to influence broader debates in society. From the 1920s to the 1960s, unions primarily conceived their role as that of labour market bargainers. The division of work was well established: unions focused on labour market issues and their sister parties dealt with broader political issues. From the 1960s onwards, unions started to conceive their role more broadly as societal actors. In recent years, the OGBL and the LCGB have increasingly engaged with environmental and social non-governmental organizations (NGOs) over a range of issues, such as free trade agreements and climate policies.

Historically, unions' local branches had a mission to engage with local communities. The unions linked to the Social Democrats were engaged in the construction of a counter-society through consumer cooperatives, local libraries and further education (Fayot 1979). In this perspective, local union branches had an important role. Over time, the vitality of these branches has steadily declined. Fewer workers live close to their place of work and the consumer cooperatives and local libraries previously run by local branches have disappeared. Local branches have moreover been unwilling to open themselves up to migrant workers, largely because the older and locally well-established union members in charge of these branches have been unwilling to make room for newcomers (Thomas 2015). In turn, they have become overaged structures, whose sole activity is often to organize an annual general assembly and an occasional excursion.

While the decline of local branches has made it impossible for unions to use them as a vector for pursuing broader political, social and cultural goals, unions have engaged with NGOs, mainly through peak-level coalitions. In keeping with Luxembourg unions' centralized organizational structures and bureaucratic culture, these coalitions mainly involve the unions' leaderships, with limited involvement of the rank-and-file. Societal engagement is mostly the domain of the OGBL and the LCGB. The more corporatist-minded CGFP and the independent unions ALEBA, SYPROLUX and APESS mainly stick to work-related issues and do not have a tradition of broader societal involvement.

The OGBL and the LCGB have built coalitions with environmental and social NGOs, joining, for instance, the 'Stop TTIP and CETA' coalition contesting the negotiation of free trade agreements between the EU and the United States and Canada (the Transatlantic Trade and Investment Partnership and the Comprehensive Economic and Trade Agreement). They have been actively involved in lobbying political decision-makers and in street demonstrations. Trade union participation in the coalition has undoubtedly contributed to the vitality of the discussion on trade agreements in Luxembourg and represents a broadening of trade union scope.

Unions have also engaged with Luxembourg's branch of the Fridays for Future movement. Unions have, however, had trouble developing a coherent policy on decarbonization. While the OGBL and the LCGB at confederal level take general positions in favour of ambitious climate policies, they do not necessarily enact them at the company or industry level, which leads to policy incoherencies. There is thus a gap between the principled positions adopted by union confederations and the concrete climate strategies pursued at company and industry level. During the debate on the most recent reform of the EU Emissions Trading System between 2014 and 2017, many union representatives of the steel industry paid lip service to the need for climate protection, while concentrating on buying time and minimizing regulation (Thomas 2021). This kind of ambivalent positioning will prove more and more difficult to sustain with the growing societal acknowledgement of the need for deep decarbonization and increasing pressure from non-state actors for tighter climate regulations.

Trade union policies towards the European Union

As Luxembourg was a founding member of the European Coal and Steel Community and the European Community, the unions were confronted early on with the effects of Europeanization. In line with the historical attitudes of Social Democracy and Christian Democracy in favour of European unification, the OGBL and the LCGB have generally advocated stronger European integration. With the EU's adoption of fiscal austerity policies after the financial and economic crisis of 2008 and the European Commission's recommendations to abolish Luxembourg's wage indexation mechanism, put forward in the context of the European Semester, unions increasingly became more critical towards EU policies.

Given the strong presence of migrant workers in Luxembourg, the most important impact of European unification on trade union policies has arguably been in the domain of free movement of labour. Although historically the trade unions advocated labour market protectionism, they rapidly came to accept during the 1950s the implementation of freedom of movement of workers, considering it inevitable. Since the 2000s, the unions have come to use the growing body of European law and the judgements of the European Court of Justice in the domains of freedom of movement and the coordination of social security systems as a legal infrastructure to offer advice and support services to migrant workers. Unions use the provisions on freedom of movement to advocate and mobilize on behalf of migrant workers. The principles of equality of treatment as regards employment, working conditions, and tax and social benefits have thus become a resource for legitimizing union demands concerning migrant workers. For instance, in 2011, the unions heavily relied on the notions of equality of treatment and non-discrimination when acting in defence of migrant workers' right to access certain social benefits, which was being called into question by government austerity policies (Thomas 2016).

During the extended post-war boom, the immigration policy of successive Luxembourg governments was based on labour agreements, first with Italy and then with Portugal. In response, the LAV and the OGBL signed agreements with Italian and Portuguese unions foreseeing aid and assistance to migrant workers, in particular on social security issues. In the case of cross-border workers, international union collaboration is also well developed. The LCGB, for instance, has concluded a dual membership agreement with the Belgian Confederation of Christian Trade Unions (CSC, *Confédération des Syndicats Chrétiens*). Belgian cross-border workers can be a member of both the LCGB and the CSC, and benefit from the services offered by the two unions.

While trade unions have in general advocated stronger integration of social policies within the EU, they did not challenge Luxembourg's transformation from a centre of steel production into an offshore financial hub in the 1980s and 1990s. None of the measures to rein in the financial sector taken by Luxembourg's governments in recent years under pressure from the EU and the OECD had been advocated by unions: automatic exchange of information, prevention of money laundering and measures against aggressive 'tax planning'. This is certainly because of the logic of competitive corporatism to which the unions subscribe, but also the fact that the tax revenues generated by the financial hub have been used in part to fund welfare policies and ensure a degree of social cohesion. Unions have thus focused on wage increases and welfare provisions for workers in Luxembourg, without raising broader questions concerning transnational fiscal justice and the negative consequences of fiscal evasion for neighbouring countries.

Luxembourg's trade unions have played an active role as affiliates of EU structures, including the European Trade Union Confederation (ETUC) and interregional structures. They were among the founding members of the ETUC and a former leader of the LAV, Mathias Hinterscheid, served as the ETUC's general secretary from 1976 to 1991 (Degryse 2013). The two ETUC affiliates in Luxembourg, the OGBL and the LCGB, have a joint European secretariat to follow EU policies and to participate in the ETUC's working groups and committees. The first interregional trade union council in Europe was created between Luxembourg, Saarland (Germany) and Lorraine (France) in 1976. The two interregional councils in which Luxembourg unions participate have joined together in a 'Platform of the Greater Region', which aims to represent workers' views at executive summits of the Greater Region (made up of Luxembourg, Lorraine in France, Saarland and Rhineland-Palatinate in Germany, and the Walloon region in Belgium). The platform also coordinates the activities of union representatives within the Economic and Social Council of the Greater Region. Luxembourg unions, along with German, Belgian and Dutch unions, also participated in the pioneering 'Doorn declaration' (Dufresne 2011). This initiative, now defunct, aimed to achieve closer cross-border coordination of collective agreements within the Economic and Monetary Union. The public servants union CGFP is affiliated to the European Confederation of Independent Trade Unions (CESI). The CGFP's president, Romain Wolff, was elected president of the CESI in 2012.

Despite the numerous attempts at closer coordination, the unions are still struggling to develop cross-border solidarities and collective action. All too often, cross-border cooperation between unions remains circumscribed at the institutional level, without rank-and-file involvement (Thomas 2015).

Conclusions

The main drivers of change in the case of Luxembourg are similar to those in other Western European countries (Raphael 2019), first and foremost the relative decline of the industrial sector in overall employment, the effects of automation and mechanization, and the rise of the private service sector. In Luxembourg, the magnitude of change has been amplified by the rapid growth of financial activities, dramatically changing the composition of Luxembourg's labour force. The powerful employment creation linked to the long period of high GDP growth that started in the second half of the 1980s, the increase in workers' qualification levels and the creation of numerous small and medium-sized companies have confronted unions with the limits of unionization strategies built on the negotiation of collective agreements and service provision. Industries with no established tradition of collective bargaining and with a weak union presence, such as business services and retail, have grown most strongly. Sustained immigration and the rise of cross-border work represent an additional challenge to unions as many new workers are not familiar with Luxembourg's industrial relations system.

Unions still have important organizational and institutional resources that give them substantial residual strength. They maintain significant collective bargaining coverage, are efficient at providing services and have developed solid links with the most numerous migrant group (the Portuguese) and with cross-border workers. Important building blocks of Luxembourg's industrial relations system – the minimum wage and collective bargaining mechanisms – have been preserved over the financial and economic crisis of 2008 or lightly modulated, as seen in the wage indexation system. Unions have increased their absolute membership and continue to be solely entitled to negotiate collective agreements. Political support for an industrial relations culture favouring consensus and the search for negotiated outcomes remains widespread among the political parties represented in Parliament.

But the balance sheet of (neo)corporatism is ambiguous: while it has ensured a degree of political influence for unions, it has also reinforced their centralized and bureaucratic culture. Their integration into a myriad of commissions, boards and committees tends to cut union leaders off from their constituencies and to nourish an overly pragmatic approach to policy issues. In addition, unions' capacity to engender and organize social conflict has atrophied in the absence of large-scale social conflicts and strikes. This, in conjunction with a lack of interest in programmatic and theoretical perspectives, makes it more difficult for unions to question their established routines and build links with new actors. As a result, unions are struggling to develop policy responses to key issues such as the pressing need for decarbonization of the economy and the challenges of digitalization. Unions have also not developed a critical outlook on a core issue of Luxembourg's political economy, the country's responsibility as a financial centre amidst the international surge of tax avoidance strategies.

Given this mixed balance sheet, what does the future hold for Luxembourg's unions? The four scenarios for future union development spelled out by Dutch labour sociologist Jelle Visser provide useful reference points: marginalization, substitution, dualization or revitalization (Visser 2019). In the absence of a revitalization of their outlook and organizational practices, a gradual marginalization as a result of decreasing unionization rates is a distinct risk for Luxembourg's unions. This marginalization may, in turn, lead to an incremental dualization of union representation and policies, limiting unions' influence to the well-organized segments of the economy. While the era of social partnership has accustomed unions to think of themselves as having a broad socio-political mandate, marginalization and dualization would condemn them to a future as one special interest group among many.

References

Adam F. and Zahlen P. (1999) Relations sociales, droit du travail et salaires: intérêts économiques et paix sociale, in Weides R. (ed.) L'économie luxembourgeoise au 20e siècle, Esch-sur-Alzette, Editpress, 124–173.

Auger J. (1980) Syndicalisme des autres, syndicats d'Europe, Paris, Editions Ouvrières.

Blond-Hanten C. (2021) The 'degressive' involvement of social partners in the implementation of gender equality in Luxembourg, paper presented at the Annual Congress of the Swiss Political Science Association.

Castegnaro G. (2015) Relations collectives de travail au Luxembourg, Luxembourg, Legitech.

Castegnaro G. and Arcanger N. (2010) Le droit de grève au Luxembourg, Les Cahiers du Droit Luxembourgeois, n°10.

CGFP (2010) Cents ans de mouvement syndical dans la fonction publique 1909–2009, Luxembourg, CGFP.

Conway M. and Romijn P. (2007) Belgium and the Netherlands, in Gerwarth R. (ed.) Twisted paths: Europe 1914–1945, Oxford, Oxford University Press, 84–110.

Degryse C. (2013) 1973–2013. Forty years of history of the European Trade Union Confederation, Brussels, ETUI.

Dufresne A. (2011) Le salaire, un enjeu pour l'euro-syndicalisme. Histoire de la coordination des conventions collectives nationales, Nancy, Presses Universitaires de Nancy.

Fayot B. (1979) Sozialismus in Luxemburg, Luxembourg, Centre de Recherches et d'Études Socialistes.

Fleury C., Maas R. and Thomas A. (2011) Les immigrants et les syndicats, Working Papers 2011–63, Esch-sur-Alzette, CEPS/INSTEAD.

Fusco A. et al. (2014) Luxembourg: has inequality grown enough to matter? in Nolan B., Salverda W., Checchi D., Marx I., McKnight A., Tóth I.G. and van de Werfhorst H. (eds) Changing inequalities and societal impacts in rich countries: thirty countries experiences, Oxford, Oxford University Press, 437–458.

Jentgen C. (1981) L'association générale des fonctionnaires de l'État (A.G.F.). De l'origine des syndicats au mouvement syndical de la fonction publique, Hémecht, 33 (3), 325–351.

Katzenstein P.J. (1985) Small states in world markets: industrial policy in Europe, Ithaca, NY, Cornell University Press.

Kieffer M. (1992) Luxembourg, in Campbell J. (ed.) European Labor Unions, Westport, CT, Greenwood Press, 271–290.

Kieffer M. (1993) Les employés et fonctionnaires des années 1880 à 1921: un aspect de la constitution de la société contemporaine au Luxembourg, in Dostert P. (ed.) Le Luxembourg en Lotharingie. Mélanges Paul Margue, Luxembourg, Editions Saint-Paul, 277–320.

Kirov V.N. and Thill P. (2018) The impact of crisis and restructuring on employment relations in banking: the cases of France, Luxembourg and Romania, European Journal of Industrial Relations, 24 (3), 297–313.

Krier F., Maas J., Sauer A. and Scuto D. (eds) (2016) 100 Joer fräi Gewerkschaften (1916–2016): contributions à l'histoire du mouvement syndical luxembourgeois, Esch-sur-Alzette, Le Phare.

LCGB (2014) Statuts, https://lcgb.lu/files/2016/10/Statuts-LCGB-FR.pdf [Accessed 20.01.2021]

Lentz M. et al. (eds) (1992) 75 Joër fräi Gewerkschaften: contributions à l'histoire du mouvement syndical luxembourgeois, Esch-sur-Alzette, OGBL.

Majerus J.M. (1992) La vie syndicale au lendemain de la Seconde Guerre mondiale, in Lentz M. et al. (eds), 75 Joër fräi Gewerkschaften: contributions à l'histoire du mouvement syndical luxembourgeois. Esch-sur-Alzette, OGBL, 263–281.

Pieretti P., Bourgain A. and Courtin P. (2007) Place financière au Luxembourg: analyse des sources de ses avantages compétitifs et de sa dynamique, Bruxelles, De Boeck.

Putz J.L. (2014) Aux origines du droit du travail: éléments de réflexion sur la genèse et sur l'état actuel du droit du travail luxembourgeois, Luxembourg, Promoculture-Larcier.

Raphael L. (2019) Jenseits von Kohle und Stahl – Eine Gesellschaftsgeschichte Westeuropas nach dem Boom, Berlin, Suhrkamp Verlag.

Ries J. (2011) Regards sur la syndicalisation au Luxembourg, Luxembourg, Statec.

Scuto D. (1990) Sous le signe de la grande grève de mars 1921. Les années sans pareilles du mouvement ouvrier luxembourgeois (1918–1923), Esch-sur-Alzette, Editpress.

Scuto D. (1999) L'âge d'or du syndicalisme ouvrier: l'évolution du monde syndical et de la question sociale dans les années cinquante, in Wey C. (ed.) Le Luxembourg des années 50: une société de petite dimension entre tradition et modernité, Luxembourg, Musée d'histoire de la ville de Luxembourg, 123–147.

Streeck W. (2006) The study of organised interests: before 'The Century' and after, in Streeck W. and Crouch C. (eds) The diversity of democracy: corporatism, social order and political conflict, Cheltenham, Edward Elgar, 3–45.

Thomas A. (2012) Une mosaïque incomplète. La littérature sur le syndicalisme et les relations professionnelles au Luxembourg, Hémecht, 64 (4), 132–153.

Thomas A. (2015) Les frontières de la solidarité. Les syndicats et les immigrés au cœur de l'Europe, Rennes, Presses universitaires de Rennes.

Thomas A. (2016) Degrees of inclusion: free movement of labour and the unionisation of migrant workers in the European Union, Journal of Common Market Studies, 54 (2), 408–425.

Thomas A. (2020) Cross-border labour markets and the role of trade unions in representing migrant workers' interests, Journal of Industrial Relations, 62 (2), 235–255.

Thomas A. (2021) 'Heart of steel': how trade unions lobby the European Union over emissions trading, Environmental Politics, 30 (7), 1217–1236.

Thomas A., Kirov V and Thill P. (2019) Luxembourg: an instance of eroding stability?, in Müller T., Vandaele K. and Waddington J. (eds) Collective bargaining in Europe: towards an endgame, Brussels, ETUI, 403–421.

Trausch G. (1974) Contributions à l'histoire sociale de la question du Luxembourg 1914–1922, Hémecht, 26 (1), 5–118.

Visser J. (2019) Trade unions in the balance, ILO ACTRAV Working Paper, Geneva, ILO.

Weber R. (ed.) (1999) 75 Joer Chrëschtlech Gewerkschaftsbewegung, Luxembourg, Imprimerie Saint-Paul.

Wehenkel H. (2009) Sternstunden der Luxemburger Gewerkschaftsbewegung, in Arendt M. et al. (eds) 100 Joer FNCTTFEL Landesverband: 1919–2009, Luxembourg, Landesverband, 7–21.

Wey C. (2003) De l'émergence du soi-disant modèle social luxembourgeois 1880–1940, in Allegrezza S., Hirsch M. and von Kunitzki N. (eds) L'histoire, le présent et l'avenir du modèle luxembourgeois, Luxembourg, Institut d'études européennes et internationales du Luxembourg, 3–18.

Zahlen P. (2003) La création du modèle luxembourgeois après la Deuxième guerre mondial: continuités et discontinuités, in Allegrezza S., Hirsch M. and von Kunitzki N. (eds) L'histoire, le présent et l'avenir du modèle luxembourgeois, Luxembourg, Institut d'études européennes et internationales du Luxembourg.

Zahlen P. (2008) Arbeitsmarktpolitik, in Lorig W.H. and Hirsch M. (eds) Das politische System Luxemburgs. Eine Einführung, Wiesbaden, VS Verlag für Sozialwissenschaften.

Zahlen P. (2012) L'évolution économique globale du Luxembourg sur la longue durée, Luxembourg, Statec.

Zucman G. (2015) The hidden wealth of nations: the scourge of tax havens, Chicago, University of Chicago Press.

Abbreviations

ALEBA Association Luxembourgeoise des Employés de Banque et Assurance (Luxembourg Association of Bank and Insurance Employees)

APESS Association des Professeurs de l'Enseignement Secondaire et Supérieur du Grand-Duché de Luxembourg (Association of Teachers of Secondary and Higher Education of the Grand Duchy of Luxembourg)

CESI Confédération Européenne des Syndicats Indépendants (European Confederation of Independent Trade Unions)

CGFP Confédération Générale de la Fonction Publique (General Public Sector Confederation)

CHFEP Chambre des Fonctionnaires et Employés Publics (Chamber of Civil Servants and Public Employees)

CSC Confédération des Syndicats Chrétiens (Confederation of Christian Trade Unions)

CSL Chambre des Salariés (Chamber of Wage Earners)

EU European Union

ETUC European Trade Union Confederation

FEP Fédération des Employés Privés (Federation of Private Sector Employees)

FGFC Fédération Générale de la Fonction Communale (Federation of Local Government)

FLA Freie Letzeburger Arbechterverband (Free Luxembourg Workers' Union)

FNCTTFEL	Fédération Nationale des Cheminots, Travailleurs du Transport, Fonctionnaires et Employés Luxembourgeois (National Federation of Luxembourg Railway and Transport Workers and Civil Servants)
LAV	Letzeburger Arbechter-Verband (Luxembourg Workers' Union)
LCGB	Lëtzebuerger Chrëschtleche Gewerkschaftsbond (Luxembourg Confederation of Christian Trade Unions)
NGO	Non-governmental organization
OECD	Organization for Economic Co-operation and Development
OGBL	Onofhängege Gewerkschaftsbond Lëtzebuerg (Luxembourg Independent Trade Union Confederation)
SYPROLUX	Fédération Chrétienne du Personnel des Transports (Christian Federation of Transport Personnel)
UEL	Union des Entreprises Luxembourgeoises (Union of Luxembourg Enterprises)

Chapter 20

Malta: Trade union resilience in a changing environment

Manwel Debono and Luke Anthony Fiorini

Malta's trade union movement appears healthier than the movements in several other member states of the European Union (EU). Total union membership has more than doubled since 1980, although the rate of increase has slowed considerably over the past twenty years (see Table 20.1). Despite shrinking unionization rates and collective bargaining coverage, trade unions still officially represent around 45 per cent of workers, while collective bargaining coverage is around 50 per cent. It is noteworthy that collective agreements in the private sector are signed only at company level and there are no 'erga omnes' extension provisions. Conversely, the public service has two tiers of collective bargaining: a general agreement covering all employees is complemented by a number of agreements at the industry level.

Union membership is becoming more varied. The female share of union membership has increased substantially since 1980, and the proportion of foreign members appears to have grown, too. This increasing heterogeneity is not sufficiently reflected in union leadership, however, which is still largely composed of Maltese men. Furthermore, union structures do not necessarily give sufficient attention to the interests of the new types of members. The Covid-19 pandemic has accentuated the plight of several adversely hit groups of workers, including foreigners, which has prompted unions to take public stands to protect the rights of these workers.

There are three peak trade union organizations in Malta, namely the General Workers Union (GWU), which is by far the largest; the Confederation of Malta Trade Unions (CMTU), which includes the second largest union in Malta, the Union of United Workers (now *Union Ħaddiema Magħqudin* – Voice of the Workers, UĦM); and the more recently set up umbrella organization *Forum Unions Maltin* (For.U.M.).

Adopting Hyman's (2001) model of trade unions' strategic orientation, Maltese unions are particularly oriented towards the market and society. Because of Malta's colonial past, unions have their roots in the confrontational British industrial relations tradition and invest most of their energies in representing their members' interests in relation to employers, often through collective bargaining. Over the years, there has been a marked change in their strategies, however, moving away from industrial action and rather emphasizing dialogue and cooperation. Concurrently, the trade union movement, in particular peak union organizations, is strongly involved in promoting social integration and social conditions more generally. Successive governments have facilitated unions' participation in tripartite institutions and generally pay adequate attention to social dialogue. EU membership has strengthened union involvement at the level of national policy. Trade unions have been involved in a number of important social agreements, one of which resulted in the setting up of the Cost of Living Allowance (COLA) mechanism, which has contributed to maintaining industrial calm over the past thirty years.

The rather traditional set up and structures of most unions may make their efforts to reinvent themselves less evident. This chapter indicates that, despite some adversity, the trade union movement has managed to retain its influence and status as a key stakeholder in Maltese society.[1]

1 The authors wish to thank the following stakeholders who generously contributed considerable information towards this chapter: Josef Bugeja and Kevin Camilleri representing GWU, Josef Vella representing UĦM – Voice of the Workers; Marco Bonnici, Colin Galea, and Chris Attard representing For.U.M.

Table 20.1 Principal characteristics of trade unionism in Malta

	1980	2000	2019
Total trade union membership	39,238	86,047	101,801
Women as a proportion of total membership	n.a.	24 %	41 %
Gross union density	n.a.	n.a.	n.a.
Net union density*******	53 %*	60 %	45 %****
Number of confederations********	2	2	3
Number of affiliated unions (federations)********	7**	11***	25
Number of independent unions	7**	22***	7
Collective bargaining coverage	n.a.	57 %***	50 %*****
Principal level of collective bargaining	Company		
Days not worked due to industrial action per 1,000 workers	n.a.	38	0******

Note: *1983; **1985; ***2002; ****2018; *****2016; ******2017; *******Official statistics reported in this table may overestimate real membership data (see the section on 'Unionization'); ********Includes the three peak trade union organizations, namely the GWU, the CMTU and For.U.M in 1980 and 2000 and Includes unions affiliated with CMTU, For.U.M., GWU and UĦM in 2019.

Source: Appendix A1; Baldacchino (1990); Baldacchino et al. (2003).

Historical background and principal features of the industrial relations system

The industrial relations system in Malta was formed on the British model. The first trade unions were set up in the nineteenth century, when the country was a colony of the British Empire. Unionism remained ineffective for several decades, however, because of 'the inexistence of any institutional machinery for negotiation' (Baldacchino 1988: 68). The industrial relations scenario changed momentously in 1943, when the GWU was set up to protect the rights of the employees working at HM Dockyard Malta (later, Malta Drydocks Corporation and Malta Shipyards Limited) on British war ships, who were faced with mass redundancies because of the imminent end of the Second World War (Baldacchino 1988). The GWU quickly became the largest union in the country and within two years, it represented a quarter of all the workers in Malta (Baldacchino 2021). By aligning itself with the centre-left Malta Labour

Party (now *Partit Laburista*, PL), one of Malta's two major political parties, the union contributed towards the enactment of employment legislation, including the first rudimentary industrial relations framework. The CMTU was established in 1959 with the intention of 'coordinating and rationalizing … trade union activities' (Zammit et al. 2015: 188), but the GWU refused to join it.[2] The CMTU became the second major union block in the country, spearheaded by the UĦM. As will be discussed in the next section, the growth of the CMTU was in part a reaction to the GWU's close relationship with the PL. While the adversarial relations between the two blocks have often been criticized as unhelpful to the cause of the workers, it has also led to innovative ideas that have facilitated the unions' adaptation to a changing society.

The For.U.M. was set up in 2004 to protect the interests of a number of unions that were not affiliated to GWU or CMTU and that felt the need for representation at a national level. This umbrella organization constitutes the third union block and represents the last major addition to the current union structure in Malta.

The current industrial relations system is difficult to categorize (Debono 2018), as it is composed of a mosaic of elements reflecting both the British industrial relations traditions, as well as continental models. Over the years, unions have been very active at company level, negotiating collective agreements and protecting their members' rights. Shop stewards are the main union representatives at workplaces. Traditionally, employment legislation only provided for the basic conditions of employment, and working conditions were often improved through collective agreements. The legacy of British colonial rule gradually lost some of its strength, however. Over time, especially since Malta embarked on the process of joining the EU (which it did in 2004), through government facilitation, unions increased their voice at policy level and became closely involved in tripartite concertation. At the same time, industrial relations at company level started shifting away from confrontation, as evidenced by a decrease in industrial conflict.

Structure of trade unions and union democracy

The Registrar of Trade Unions (RTU) listed thirty-two trade unions in 2019 (DIER n.d.b). 'The dominant rationale for union organization

---

2 Despite its name, CMTU's affiliates are trade unions, not federations.

in Malta, and in true British tradition, remains the trade or employment class or profession' (Debono and Baldacchino 2019: 426). Indeed, apart from the two general unions, which represent workers from all industries and companies, the GWU and UĦM (which forms part of CMTU), most unions may be categorized as professional unions, often covering a specific profession or class of workers within a particular organization. Out of the current unions, only about half existed in 1993. Smaller unions often have a shorter lifetime than larger ones. While some of the newer unions splintered off from larger ones, there does not appear to be a general trend towards fragmentation in unions.

There are three union blocks in Malta, namely the GWU, the CMTU and the For.U.M., together with a small number of independent unions. The GWU is by far the largest union and accounts for around half (51 per cent) of all union membership on the island (DIER n.d.b). While it is essentially a union, the GWU also functions as a federation or confederation. It has other unions and associations affiliated with it, namely the Police Officers Union, the Open Market Sellers, the Community Workers' Union, the Malta Football Players Association and a taxi association. A union representing the armed forces, which was previously affiliated to the GWU, was eventually incorporated in the GWU. Affiliate members benefit from the GWU's strength, as well as being able to make use of its resources. Because of its size and importance, the GWU has been granted the privileges and status of a peak trade union organization, both nationally, and at EU and international levels. The GWU covers all types of workers and industries. Having its roots in the dockyard, however, the GWU has traditionally been strongest among blue-collar workers and has throughout its history been linked to the PL. The union comprises twelve sections, eight of which represent different industries and are headed by section secretaries. There are also a youth section, a pensioners association, an international section, and a CGIL-GWU trade union contact point. Section secretaries can carry out collective bargaining in their own industries autonomously, within the aims and values of the organization, but involve the Union's National Council when bargaining decisions may have wider implications (GWU 2020). This indicates a strong level of autonomy for individual sections during bargaining, though they form part of the same trade union and ultimately have to follow union policies.

The CMTU currently has seven autonomous affiliate unions that together represent around 31 per cent of all unionized workers (DIER n.d.b). Like the GWU, the CMTU covers all industries and occupations. It has traditionally been strongest among white-collar workers, however. While it has never had any formal political affiliation, the confederation arguably leans towards the centre-right Nationalist Party (Partit Nazzjonalista – PN).[3] Representing around 83 per cent of the members of CMTU or 25 per cent of all unionized persons, the UĦM is by far the largest and most powerful union within CMTU. The union traces its roots to the Malta Government Clerical Union, set up in 1966. Over the years, the union has transformed itself. It widened its scope, increased its membership, and eventually adopted its current statute and name in 2015. A change in the method of appointment of high officials as part of this revitalization process, increased the number of women and highly qualified union managers. The union has four pillars: the first is the traditional union, which has seven sections representing different parts of the economy, as well as sections representing young people and pensioners. The other pillars consist of affiliated unions; affiliated associations (e.g. Malta Environmental Health Officers Association); and affiliated cooperatives (e.g. Ports Foremen Cooperative Limited). The concept of four pillars emerged from the different needs of entities that did not fit under the traditional union sections. Affiliated groups benefit from the UĦM's knowhow, as well as access to its resources.

For.U.M. is the smallest and newest trade union block. It was established in 2004 in response to the fact that a number of unions that were not part of an existing peak trade union organization were being excluded from national-level discussions. For.U.M.'s request to participate in national-level debate was met with substantial resistance from nearly all members of the Malta Council for Economic and Social Development (MCESD)[4] (The Malta Independent 2011). The reasons for such resistance varied and appear to have included fear on the part of employers' associations of overrepresentation of trade unions and inter-union rivalries (Rizzo 2010). It was not until 2012 that it was allowed to form part of the MCESD, by which time it had already been admitted to the ETUC in 2011 (Debono 2012). Unions within For.U.M remain autonomous.

---

3 While extreme-right wing parties are not represented in parliament, the country has also experienced the international wave of populist nationalism, which is reflected in politics, and which translates into negative sentiments towards foreigners. Trade unions in Malta generally oppose such sentiments and are becoming more vociferous against the exploitation of foreign workers.

4 MCESD is Malta's highest organ for tripartite concertation.

The purpose of this umbrella organization is to provide unions with access to national and international bodies they may not otherwise have access to, while also providing unions with the possibility to aid each other (e.g. during collective bargaining, if necessary), as well as a forum to discuss and possibly reach common positions on national-level concerns. For.U.M. has grown from eight to fourteen union affiliates, representing around 15 per cent of all union membership. The affiliates of For.U.M. are mainly unions of professional workers, hailing from a wide spectrum of industries, allowing For.U.M. to take an informed position on various national-level concerns. The Malta Union of Teachers (MUT) is its largest affiliate, representing around 64 per cent of all the unionized members of For.U.M. (DIER n.d.b).

After the setting up of For.U.M., the most prominent change in the main union blocks took place when the MUT withdrew its membership from the CMTU in 2008 following disagreements about the government's decision to increase water and electricity rates (Baldacchino 2009; Times of Malta 2008). This resulted in a significant drop in CMTU membership. When MUT joined For.U.M. in 2009, it not only strengthened the latter in terms of members, but also moved it away from the CMTU and closer to the GWU. Indeed, in 2012, For.U.M. and GWU pledged to strengthen cooperation between them (Times of Malta 2012).

The friction between the two largest union blocks – namely, the GWU and the CMTU – has been a constant feature of the industrial relations landscape. Despite this, there have been a few instances in which they have joined forces. In a rare show of force, in November 2008, twenty trade unions participated in a historic demonstration against the government's proposals to increase utility tariffs (Debono 2009). More recently, a package of measures to assist the economy during the 2020 pandemic was approved by all social partners represented on the MCESD, including both the GWU and CMTU (The Malta Independent 2020). The deep division and strained relationship between the GWU and CMTU is evident in the fact that, despite interventions by the British Trade Union Congress and the European Trade Union Confederation (ETUC), the blocks did not agree 'to establish a consensual code of practice and dispute resolution mechanism' (Rizzo 2006: para. 9). It is evident that the level of trust required for such cooperation does not exist. In 2014, a National Forum of Trade Unions was set up by the President of Malta and the Centre for Labour Studies, within the University of Malta, with the aim of strengthening the unity of trade unions. While several activities were carried out by the Forum towards this aim, the trust gap between union blocks hardly appears to have been affected.

Competition among unions is apparent not only at the level of peak organizations, but also between individual unions. The reasons for such competition vary and include: clash of leaders' personalities, differing political allegiances, demonstrations of power, and perhaps most importantly, competition for members and for the right to carry out collective bargaining. Over the years, several conflicts between unions developed over the right to carry out collective bargaining in specific places of work. For example, the disagreement between the MUT and the University of Malta Academic Staff Association over the right of sole representation of academic staff at the University of Malta took three years to be settled (Baldacchino 2007). Over the years, high inter-union conflict became a concern to the Malta Employers Association (MEA 2015), a major employers' association, as it was harming companies by disrupting collective bargaining. Eventually, the Recognition of Trade Unions Regulations (2016) was enacted to prevent disputes over union recognition.

Political relations

The continuous dominance of the GWU in the sphere of industrial relations since it was set up in 1943 makes it an obvious starting point for an examination of relations between unionism and the polity. The GWU emerged at the dockyard as a reaction to the precarious conditions workers experienced as a result of British colonial policies. Ever since its early days, the history of the GWU has been intertwined with that of the PL. Such links, which 'fluctuated in both intensity and form over time' (Baldacchino 2009: 7), were facilitated by the fact that both organizations relied on the support of workers hailing from the same social background. Indeed, dockyard workers not only constituted the most militant section of the GWU, but also formed the backbone of the PL (Zammit 2003). While the formal ties between the GWU and the PL were already apparent in the social pact that the two organizations agreed in 1946, their relationship reached its full strength between 1978 and 1992, when the organizations were united by statute. This 'marriage' resulted in the GWU being represented in the cabinet of the Labour government. Whether one focuses on the vigorous support that the GWU provided to Labour government policies (e.g. Zammit 2003) or the need of subsequent governments to accommodate the GWU's demands in order to avoid serious damage (Baldacchino 2021), there is no doubt that the GWU was a major contributor to the development of industrial policy and legislation. The GWU's sustained close relationship with the PL inevitably led to strong conflicts with governments formed by the centre-right PN, Malta's other major political party. When the GWU ordered a strike by the dock mooring men, it not only led to what has been described as probably the most economically damaging dispute since the country's independence, but also contributed to the downfall of the Nationalist government in 1971 (Baldacchino 2021). More recently, the GWU's campaign against precarious employment led to several legal and policy changes meant to reduce such problems, and also contributed to bringing down the Nationalist government in 2013 (Debono and Marmara 2017). The strained relations between the GWU and the Nationalist government culminated in 1999, when 'the police intervened in the course of an industrial dispute at Malta's international airport. The union's officials were arrested, subsequently arraigned in court and charged with "criminal offences"' for damaging state property (Zammit 2003: 83). Subsequently, in 2006, the GWU lost a significant source of revenue when a Nationalist government did not renew the union's subsidiary's (Cargo Handling Co. Ltd.) contract to handle cargo in Maltese ports (Debono and Farrugia 2006). This company had acted as the sole operator of cargo handling at the ports for decades. Besides, while the dockyard's closure in 2008 by the Nationalist government was caused by its long-term financial losses, it has also been viewed as the party's 'sweet revenge' on the union (Baldacchino 2021). Since the PL returned to government in 2013, the union's sources of revenue appear to have broadened (e.g. Briguglio 2018; Camilleri 2016).

Relations between the Labour government and the affiliates of the CMTU 'progressively deteriorated' in the 1970s and 1980s (Zammit 2003: 77), and this increased the rivalry between the GWU and the smaller unions. During this period, the PN, in opposition, encouraged workers to leave the GWU and join the so-called free trade unions (who were not formally affiliated to any political party) (Zammit 2003). Such conflict and politicization of union membership increased the class consciousness of white-collar workers, which fuelled the growth of the second largest union, the UĦM, emerging from a number of mergers of smaller unions (Zammit 2003). While 'the CMTU and its affiliated trade unions profess no formal political allegiance … their official policies often converge with those of the Nationalist Party, thus reflecting the social background of most of their members' (Zammit 2003: 84–85).

Because of its size, the UĦM holds a dominant position within the CMTU. Besides, unlike the other unions within the CMTU, the UĦM sought and obtained direct representation on the MCESD. The union has contributed substantially to social dialogue and government policy over the years. For instance, in 2012 the UĦM proposed an employment policy 'meant to improve the flexibility and productivity of the Maltese labour market; this was endorsed by the major social partners and political parties before the 2013 general election, and later adopted by the new Labour government' (Debono 2016: 176). It is interesting to note that, like its rival the GWU, the UĦM also won contracts relating to active labour market policies under the new Labour government formed in 2013 (Dalli 2016).

Over the past three decades, there has been something of a departure from the British model of industrial relations to a more continental one: the 'traditionally polarised relationship between employers and trade unions' has given way to 'a pattern of corporate, tripartite, bargaining at the national level based on social partnership' (Zammit 2003: 68). This was partly brought about by a growing realization that industrial action might scare away private business and thus harm employees. But it was also facilitated by successive government policies. In line with its electoral manifesto, the Nationalist government set up the Malta Council for Economic Development in 1990 (later renamed the MCESD) as a forum for tripartite consultation. According to Zammit (2003: 114–115), setting up this structure 'entailed a departure from the state centralized and divide-and-rule policies of the previous era; as well as from the informal and ad hoc dealings that often characterize social relations among actors in a small state society'. During this period, the GWU was involved in a harsh confrontation with the Nationalist government over the latter's income's policy, which inadvertently led to the closure of the Hotel Phoenicia (a historic luxury hotel) and the dismissal of all its employees (Rizzo 2003). Such a disastrous outcome of industrial action led to a negotiated agreement in 1990 within the MCESD on a national incomes policy, consisting of a mandatory annual allowance (COLA) based on an official cost of living index. This agreement was a watershed moment that greatly boosted the standing of social dialogue in Malta. An era of more conciliatory industrial relations commenced. Since the 1990s, 'manifest unilateralism has tended to be used infrequently, as a last resort in cases of lack of consensus among social partners' (Debono 2016: 6). Over the years, it has become customary for the government to carry out annual pre-budget consultations within the MCESD, which shape government policy and strategy, and increase industrial peace. The country's EU accession process and eventual EU membership in 2004, also helped to strengthen the culture of social dialogue in Malta, especially by enabling government and social partners to learn from their participation in social dialogue at EU level. Apart from the MCESD, the main social partners are also represented on other tripartite fora, including the Employment Relations Board, a tripartite body consulted by government on labour legislation. Besides, union officials are appointed to the boards of influential public sector organizations, authorities and other entities, such as the Occupational Health and Safety Authority, and Jobsplus, Malta's public employment service organization.

Unionization

The Employment and Industrial Relations Act (EIRA 2002) requires unions to keep an up-to-date record of their members and annually submit their membership numbers to the RTU. The RTU has the power to inspect such records and to cancel a union's registration if it is not in conformity with EIRA (2002). This system provides for an official public count of union membership, although – as will be explained below – its reliability has been questioned.

According to these official figures, the raw number of union members increased considerably from 44,760 in 1980 to 101,801 in 2019 (DIER n.d.b.). While there is a clear upward trajectory in membership figures, its magnitude has declined considerably over the past twenty years. Whereas membership more than doubled between 1980 and 2000, it only increased by 8 per cent between 2000 and 2019. These membership figures include the pensioners' sections of the GWU and the UĦM, which total 11,548, or 11 per cent of all union membership in Malta. The smaller unions do not provide a count of their pensioner members. It should also be noted that in 1999 (the first time both the GWU and the UĦM reported on their pensioners' sections), there were 6,033 registered pensioners, representing 6 per cent of all union members. Thus, the number of pensioners has increased both in absolute terms and as a proportion of total membership over the past twenty years. This reflects the ageing population, but also the relatively low growth of younger members, a phenomenon that will be further discussed below. The declining growth of union membership has coincided with strong growth of around 75 per cent of total employment over the past twenty years (Eurostat 2020).

Official union membership data might be inflated (see Debono 2006) and thus also union density. Besides, the reliability of union density figures is also affected by such things as: the inclusion or otherwise of pensioners when counting union members; the inclusion or otherwise of self-employed persons, and persons who are (or were) legally prohibited from joining unions; and perhaps more significantly, which data source (Labour Force Survey or employment records kept by the Public Employment Service [PES]) is used to represent the workforce. Having said that, there was a clear increase in union density between the 1980s and the early 2000s. At its peak, density reached over 60 per cent (Baldacchino and Debono 2009). The trend has been reversed over recent years. Membership levels have not kept pace with the growth of the labour force, fuelled by a growing number of female and foreign workers. Thus, in June 2019, union density was about 40 per cent. This figure is based on the official records of union members, excluding pensioners, as a ratio of all employees as listed in PES records. One should note that data gathered in 2014 from a representative survey of workers revealed that just over a third of all employees (33.8 per cent) are union members (Debono 2018). These lower figures reflect methodological differences in data capture, but also point towards the possible inflation of official membership figures mentioned earlier.

Public sector employees are significantly more likely to be unionized than their peers in the private sector (55 and 22 per cent, respectively) (Debono 2018). Within the private sector, unionization tends to be strong in the secondary, and weak in the primary and tertiary sectors. Indeed, 'there are no collective agreements in the primary sector, which is characterized by self-employed persons and family-owned micro enterprises. For the same reason, hardly any wholesale and retail employees are covered by collective agreements' (Debono and Baldacchino 2019: 429). The programme of economic liberalization that started around thirty years ago and the economic expansion that has gathered momentum over the past decade resulted in the expansion of industries, such as financial services, insurance, IT, teaching English as a foreign language, electronic gaming and others, which the unions have found difficult to infiltrate and organize (Baldacchino 2021).

Workers on typical working contracts are more likely to be unionized than those in atypical jobs. Thus, while 38 per cent of all full-time employees are unionized, the figure drops to 9.5 per cent among part-timers (Debono 2018). Besides, while 35.8 per cent of employees on indefinite contracts are unionized, the figure drops to 24.4 per cent among those on definite contracts (Debono 2018). Some atypical workers, in particular, part-timers, 'might view trade union membership less favourably as they might be more likely to perceive their job as a transient income-generating activity rather than a "career" which requires long-term protection' (Debono 2018: 55). Platform workers are a recent development in the country and have become conspicuous in industries such as taxis and food delivery. The GWU has been proactive in attempting to unionize such workers, while increasing social awareness about their challenges. In 2020, the GWU had around 800 members with such work arrangements in the taxi industry who do not have adequate legal protection.

Official data started separating union membership figures by gender in the early 1990s. The proportion of women rose from 18 per cent of all membership in 1994 to 41 per cent in 2019. This trend is markedly stronger than the growth of women in the labour market. Indeed, while in 1997, around 30 per cent of all workers were women, this figure expanded to around 41 per cent in 2019, thanks to cultural change, and government educational and employment policies (DIER n.d.b). The rise of women in the labour market has been characterized by younger and more highly qualified women, often entering white-collar occupations. This in turn has been reflected in the rise of professional unions, which have grown at a faster rate than the general unions. Thus, while in 1980, the GWU and the UĦM represented 85 per cent of all union members, in 2019 they represented 76 per cent, 9 percentage points fewer (DIER n.d.b). The growth of professional unions has benefitted For.U.M. which, while still being the smallest peak organization, has gained ground with regard to its membership ratio in comparison with the GWU and the CMTU. The largest non-general unions, namely the MUT, the Malta Union of Midwives and Nurses, the Malta Union of Bank Employees, and the Union of Professional Educators, have all substantially more female than male members, contrary to the general unions, and unions representing manual or other lower qualified workers. Women who have invested more in their education are more likely to be unionized than those who have invested less (Debono 2018). It should be noted that despite the increasing membership density of women, they are still largely under-represented in high union positions (Debono 2018).

Age is positively related to union membership. The least unionized employees are in the 15–24 age bracket, while the most unionized are in the 45–64 bracket (23.5 and 38.6 per cent, respectively) (Debono 2018). 'When compared to their older peers, younger employees may be less willing, or aware of the possibility of defending their rights through unions' (Debono 2018: 55). Notably, younger persons are more likely than older ones to join non-unionized companies operating in the services industry.

Migration has increased substantially over the past decade. The GWU has been proactive in trying to increase its membership among migrants and estimates that more than 4,000 of its members are third-country nationals. Interpreters were necessary for the first time at a recent GWU congress because of the increase in foreign shop stewards. Furthermore, in view of the GWU's relationship with the Confederazione Generale Italiana del Lavoro (CGIL, see the section on 'Trade union policies towards the European Union'), all public communication is now published in Maltese, English and Italian.

Union resources and expenditure

Trade union financial data is not publicly available, and so the information reported in this section is incomplete. Besides, it is worth noting that there are no strike funds or strike benefits in Malta.

The GWU affirms that its income has increased over the past two decades. The GWU's major source of funding is membership fees. Such income has increased because of rising membership and membership fee levels. In 2009 the GWU raised its annual membership fee for the first time for twenty years, from €30 to €40 (ToM 2009). In 2021 the annual fee stood at €54. The GWU justifies this fee on the basis of the services it offers members at no added cost, such as access to legal services. Furthermore, the GWU has consciously moved away from a model under which it provides members solely with services related to industrial relations. The union has invested in turning its website into an interactive portal and has developed a mobile application. These allow members to read the union's news publications, book appointments with section secretaries and access other services, while also providing them with access to a range of discounts in partner outlets, which are meant to improve the members' quality of life, such as supermarkets and providers of health and education-related services. Over the years, the GWU has also diversified its business and currently derives revenue from the renting of buildings, the organization of courses, and from public and private tenders. The GWU also has several subsidiaries, among them an English language school and a training and recruitment firm.

The CMTU's revenue derives from the affiliation fees of its affiliate unions; the amount contributed by each union thus depends on its membership. Financial data is not made public. The CMTU limits its expenditure by making use of its affiliate members' resources. Like the GWU, the UĦM's primary source of income is membership fees. The union, which has thirty-five employees, also has two subsidiary companies, one which provides educational services and another one which is more commercial and whose activities include selling household products. In terms of services, apart from collective bargaining, the UĦM offers its members complementary legal services, the opportunity to make individual claims, and the ability to obtain fuel at reduced prices from select fuel stations.

Similar to the CMTU, For.U.M. derives its income from the affiliation fees of its affiliate unions. Each union is required to pay the same basic amount, as well as a fee calculated on the basis of membership. Affiliate unions in turn derive their income from membership. Consequently, while financial data is not published publicly, For.U.M.'s income has increased over time and has kept up with increased expenditure. This is because of both the increase in the number of affiliate unions that have joined For.U.M. over time, as well as the growing number of members joining many of its affiliates. For.U.M. attributes strong membership growth among its affiliate unions to the expansion of the white-collar professions it represents. For.U.M. expenditure is kept in check by using the resources of the larger affiliate unions; for example, meetings are held at the MUMN and MUT headquarters. For.U.M.'s administrative staff is limited to five individuals, who also hold positions in their original parent unions.

A couple of local schemes also assist in the funding of trade unions. Individual unions and confederations can apply for a Civil Society Fund capped at an annual €6,000 per organization, which aims to facilitate organizations' affiliation and participation in European bodies, as well as in training related to EU policies and programmes. A separate Civil Society Fund also provides funds to three union organizations, the GWU, the UĦM and For.U.M., as well as three employer associations. It was reported that each organization received €58,000 per year in 2018 and 2019, meant to cover 80 per cent of the costs of participating in local and

European fora (Borg 2020; The Malta Independent 2019). Furthermore, each confederation is provided with a full-time worker paid by the government to aid with administrative work.

Finally, unions also benefit from EU funds, obtained following applications to carry out specific projects and are often financed through the European Social Fund. Examples include a UĦM project to increase workers' knowledge of and participation in social dialogue (€323,830), a CMTU project to improve social partners', civil society's and the general public's awareness of policy issues (€67,207), and a GWU project to provide training to shop stewards (€4,761) (European Union Funds Malta, 2017).

Collective bargaining and unions at the workplace

Collective bargaining has been instrumental in improving working conditions. While EIRA (2002) and related regulations guarantee basic conditions, which have been aligned with EU directives, collective bargaining is the main tool that brings added benefits to workers. 'The terms of a collective agreement normally follow a standard pattern and cover both procedural aspects, relating to union recognition and dispute resolution and substantive issues, relating to wages and other the conditions of employment' (Zammit et al. 2015: 245).

Collective bargaining within the private sector is carried out at enterprise level. Normally this consists of one union negotiating with one employer. To register a trade union, a minimum number of seven members is required. In order to be granted recognition to carry out collective bargaining in an enterprise, however, a trade union's membership must account for more than 50 per cent of employees. Employers' associations are not directly involved in collective bargaining, although they may be consulted by their members throughout the process. Collective agreements in the private sector generally last three years, but they remain active until the next agreement is signed. Industrial or multi-employer bargaining does not exist. Enterprise-level collective bargaining is preferred by both unions and employers to higher level bargaining as it gives them the opportunity to adapt the agreement to the specific circumstances of the workplace and its employees.

The process of collective bargaining in the public sector is more complex than in the private sector and takes place at two different levels.

Public service employees are covered by a general collective agreement signed by the government and seven unions. This is complemented by a number of lower-level industrial agreements. Other organizations within the public sector sign enterprise-level agreements. All agreements in the public sector are coordinated by the Industrial Relations Unit, which aims to ensure sustainable outcomes based on harmonious industrial relations across the public sector. Collective agreements in the public sector tend to last longer than three years, with the 2017 agreement for public service employees spanning a record eight years (Office of the Prime Minister 2017). The scope of agreements in the public service is narrower than in the private sector, as many employment conditions are regulated by the Public Service Management Code.

Based on the British tradition, shop stewards act as union representatives within enterprises, and play a vital role in collective bargaining. They recruit members, mobilize them, understand and relay the members' needs to the union, and take part in collective bargaining negotiations. Shop stewards also provide the recruitment pool from which higher union officials are normally elected (MEA 2015). Research carried out in Malta shows the importance of shop stewards to increasing union membership (Debono 2015). Indeed, it is reasonable to argue that the decline of trade union density is at least partly because of unions' inability to establish shop stewards in particular employment sectors and firms. Little, if any research exists on shop stewards in Malta. Their performance has been subject to criticism by employers, however, who assert that increasing numbers of shop stewards are taking up the role 'because of personal grudges against the company' or do not have the necessary training to perform such a role properly (MEA 2015: 10). Aware of these issues, some unions do carry out training to improve their shop stewards' knowledge and skills.

An average of forty-five agreements were registered at the Department of Industrial and Employment Relations (DIER n.d.a) annually between 2001 and 2018. These consist of new collective agreements, renewals or extensions, side agreements, addenda and amendments. It is estimated that about 56 per cent of all employees were covered by collective agreements in 2014 (Debono 2015). While nearly all workers in the public sector are covered by collective agreements, the figure drops to over a third of those working in the private sector. Workers are also more likely to be covered by a collective agreement if they have a higher level of education, work full-time, or in a large organization. Collective bargaining coverage appears to be decreasing, in line with falling membership density. Several of the industries that have grown in strength in recent years, such as financial services, ICT and iGaming, tend to be non-unionized, while the number of medium and large companies in highly unionized industries has shrunk. For example, the number of companies with more than fifty workers in manufacturing decreased from eighty-five to seventy-four between 2001 and 2019 (National Statistics Office 2010, 2020).

While the content of collective agreements has not changed dramatically over the past decade, some new topics have emerged. For example, to curb sick leave absenteeism, some collective agreements now feature an allowance for attendance, which is gradually lost when workers' absenteeism exceeds predefined annual benchmarks.[5] Another more recent clause included in the majority of agreements concerns the accumulation of sick leave, whereby workers can utilize the unused sick leave of previous years in case of some major medical event. As the number of working women has increased, clauses on flexibility and work–life balance have become more common in collective agreements. Furthermore, with the growth of health and safety issues, clauses related to this topic have become more prevalent. The UĦM also notes that topics related to skills development and the development of specialist positions have become increasingly common. Some collective agreements have also started to include clauses on setting up third-pillar pension schemes, which are still relatively rare.

Workers receive mandatory wage increases based on an annual average inflation rate as determined by the Retail Price Index. This mechanism, which was agreed by the government and the social partners in 1990, establishes the mandatory COLA, which is granted as a flat rate to all employees, irrespective of how much they earn (Debono and Farrugia 2013; Vella 2014). Employer associations and the European Commission have over the years pressured the Maltese government to review the COLA mechanism to better reflect labour productivity and competitiveness (Council of the European Union 2011; Malta Chamber of Commerce, Enterprise and Industry 2014; MEA 2014). While unions have often defended COLA, the UĦM recently stated that it is time to discuss whether COLA should continue to be used, or perhaps should be replaced by a living wage (Galea 2019). To date, however, the

5 Administrative methods aimed at reducing absenteeism may result in counterproductive behaviour, such as workers attending work while ill (Fiorini et al. 2018).

government has resisted such calls, arguing that the COLA system has helped to reduce industrial action (Ministry for Finance of Malta 2013).

Malta also has a national minimum wage, complemented by a series of wage regulation orders setting minimum terms, including wages in specific industries. The national minimum wage was introduced in 1974 (Vella 2014) and is revised annually through COLA. One criticism is that it is not sufficient to guarantee a decent standard of living (Caritas 2019). While the government has been reluctant to change the existing mechanism, in 2017 it reached a rare agreement with both trade unions and employers' associations to increase the wages of workers on minimum wage who work with the same employer for more than a year, with gradual increases after the first and second years of work.

In recent years, the general trade unions have complained about the unfairness of non-unionized workers benefiting from the gains made through collective bargaining. The GWU pushed forward the idea of mandatory union membership for all workers, with the possibility of non-enrolment by paying an amount of money into a union fund.[6] According to the union, their proposal 'would boost the fight against precarious employment and exploitation in sectors where unionization is very low or non-exist[ent], such as in construction and tourism' (Micallef 2019). On its part, the UĦM believes that compulsory membership for all workers may not be feasible with the unions' current resources, which might be insufficient to provide adequate services after a sudden substantial increase in members. Thus, the UĦM proposes that the system be introduced gradually, with membership first being made compulsory for more vulnerable workers. Presumably, the two unions believe that compulsory union membership would significantly strengthen their membership numbers and enable them to influence a wider range of companies and sectors. The idea of compulsory membership has come up against strong resistance from employers, however, who have labelled it 'unconstitutional'.[7] On the other hand, the Labour government has agreed in principle with the idea and claims to be studying it (Pace 2019).

---

6 No further information about such a fund is available.

7 Compulsory union membership may also infringe the ILO convention on Freedom of Association and Protection of the Right to Organise Convention (No. 87) 1948, and Article 11 of the European Convention on Human Rights.

Industrial conflict

Trade unions have traditionally shown their strength through industrial action. While, as already noted, general strikes and public demonstrations have been used over the years, they are uncommon. As will be discussed in this section, industrial action is nowadays being resorted to less frequently, especially in the private sector.

Industrial action is regulated by EIRA (2002), which provides immunity to trade unions and employers' associations in relation to industrial action, protects sympathy strikers from liability, and allows peaceful picketing. The law also prohibits certain categories of workers from carrying out industrial action, such as members of the disciplined forces, and other employees carrying out essential services. Strike legislation has been described as 'fairly lax' (Debono and Baldacchino 2019: 430) and the legality or otherwise of strikes has often been unclear, leading to contestation (Zammit et al. 2015). The lack of legal precision has over the years resulted in several disputes over the legality or otherwise of industrial action. Law courts have helped to clarify some aspects relating to strikes. The following are two examples of this.

The first example concerns what constitutes a 'trade dispute'. The UĦM vigorously opposed the increases in utility prices announced as part of the 1998 government budget and carried out industrial action across the public sector. The Freeport Terminal Company, then owned by the government, sued the UĦM for damages, contending that 'since no trade dispute existed with the UĦM and that the collective agreement had been honoured, the industrial actions taken by the union at the Freeport were illegal and abusive' (Zammit et al. 2015: 274). In 2001, however, 'the Court of Appeal ruled that unions had a right to strike on budget measures, given that these affected the conditions of employment … [This] demarcated an area of industrial relations that was previously untested' (Zammit et al. 2015: 275).

The second example concerns whether union action may be carried out lawfully in relation to issues of recognition. Disagreement between the UĦM and the GWU in the late 1990s concerning who had the right to represent the workers at Malta International Airport (MIA) led the GWU to order industrial action at the company. MIA tried to stop such industrial action by stating that it was illegal because there was no 'trade dispute' at the company according to law. The dispute was eventually resolved in 2000, with the two unions agreeing to jointly negotiate the collective agreement. Subsequently, the International Labour Organization (ILO) ruled that the GWU's actions were not subject to immunity as they were not covered under existing laws. The ILO also 'recommended the government to amend industrial and labour legislation to clearly define trade union recognition as legitimate subject for trade dispute, something that the government acted upon following the enactment of EIRA in 2002' (Zammit et al. 2015: 277).

'The ability to carry out industrial action … has traditionally been a major source of union strength' (Debono and Baldacchino 2019: 430). Over the years, industrial action has been instrumental in bringing about political and social change. For many years until its closure in 2010, the dockyard remained a central hub of both industrial and political activism. Industrial conflict peaked in 1970–1971, when a seven-month long strike ordered by the GWU crippled the dockyard, and was probably the most economically damaging industrial action since independence (Baldacchino 2021). Strikes remained frequent in both the 1970s and 1980s, however. The longest industrial action ever registered started in 1977 when a strike ordered by the Medical Association of Malta (a member of CMTU) resulted in a government-imposed lock-out. The dispute was only resolved after ten years, when the PN came to power in 1987 (Baldacchino 2021).

Over the years, industrial disputes and strikes have trended downwards and 'Malta has enjoyed an atmosphere of relative industrial peace and stability' (Zammit et al. 2015: 262). Indeed, trade unions became increasingly reluctant to resort to industrial action, especially full-blown strikes in the private sector, for fear of scaring away foreign companies. DIER stopped collecting strike data in 2018, which might also indicate their reduced role.[8] A few high-profile cases of industrial action resulting in the closure of private companies highlighted the dangers and increased social partners' propensity to work together to find amicable solutions. The global financial crisis of 2008, and more recently the Covid-19 pandemic, reinforced the importance of solving industrial disputes without resorting to industrial action. During the pandemic, the law courts also intervened to stop industrial action in the health care sector on the basis

8 Official strike statistics exclude partial industrial action such as work-to-rule (Zammit et al. 2015).

that it would endanger public health, which points to the increased difficulty of trade unions availing themselves of such rights.

Despite this, some industrial action has continued to be registered in recent years, especially in the public sector, where unions have more leverage to realize their demands. It is interesting to note that industrial action in the public sector often concerns professional workers rather than the blue-collar workers historically associated with industrial action (Baldacchino 2021).

The Director of the DIER often investigates 'trade disputes' before they are officially registered (Debono and Baldacchino 2019). Between 2000 and 2019, the Director was involved in about fifty-seven annual mediation/conciliation interventions (DIER n.d.a). There has been a decreasing trend of interventions, which could reflect the overall reduction in industrial conflicts. Around 80 per cent of interventions resulted in agreement between the parties. When agreement cannot be reached, the case might be referred to the industrial tribunal. An average of seven cases were decided by the industrial tribunal annually between 2000 and 2019.

Societal power

Despite losing ground in terms of unionization rate and collective bargaining coverage, and irrespective of the decline of industrial conflict over the years, trade unions maintain strong societal power. They do not appear to be suffering from a crisis of legitimacy (Debono 2019; Zammit and Rizzo 2003), and are viewed as an important societal institution, countering the power of employers and serving as a powerful lobby group to government.

The public campaigns organized by the large unions over the years yielded significant social changes. The campaign against precarious employment spearheaded by the GWU in the wake of the 2008 international economic recession is an interesting case. Despite the employers' attempts at minimizing the problem, unions managed to give prominence to the issue, and to turn the then unknown idea of precariousness into a popular term commonly referred to in Maltese mass media, among other things (Debono and Marmara 2017). During the Malta Presidency of the EU in 2017, the GWU lobbied the government, the EU Commission and the ETUC to update the regulations on posted workers, so that the latter would be provided with the same employment rights and health and safety rights as other workers.

Related to this topic, unions have also campaigned for equal pay for equal work. Through a combination of industrial and legal action, various unions have been successful in ensuring that sub-contracted workers at government entities received the same remuneration as other employees carrying out the same work. Similar successes have also been achieved at public-private institutions where employees employed by the private entity were initially paid less than their publicly employed counterparts (Cordina 2020). Unions are currently working with stakeholders to close loopholes in the law which allow for individuals to be paid differently when working for different employers within the same workplace.

Unions have proactively worked with other organizations to tackle a wide variety of issues. For example, the UĦM aided the development of cooperatives by providing them with guidance on contracts, assisting them in dealing with regulators, and acting as a pressure group on government. The GWU in collaboration with the UN's Refugee Agency developed a series of videos on working rights and integration, targeting third-country nationals (with subtitles in various languages). The production of these videos, coupled with talks held with third-country national communities, which aimed at informing unions about migrants' plight, as well as explaining Maltese employment laws and the benefits of trade union membership, may have aided the GWU in unionizing some migrant workers (see the section on 'Unionization').

In recent years, For.U.M. has lobbied for the 'right to disconnect', which refers to employees' right to refrain from engaging in work tasks and being contacted on work matters outside their working hours. This is of particular importance to union members who are professionals. This resulted in a meeting organized within the Malta–EU Steering and Action Committee (MEUSAC). Subsequently, unions took up the topic at EU level with a Maltese Member of the European Parliament who has pushed for EU regulation on the matter. National discussion on this topic is ongoing, with the MEA arguing that legislation should not be introduced prior to the adoption of a related EU directive (Meilak 2021). For.U.M. also collaborates with the MEA by organizing an annual seminar on themes of common interest.

Union press releases and conferences, industrial threats and actions, and collective agreements are often reported prominently on national media. The opinions of union leaders are often sought when industrial or sectoral issues affecting workers emerge, and their public views are expected in relation to government policies and actions. For example, their opinions on the annual government budget have become an important tradition. The government publishes a pre-budget document and social partners and civil society are expected to give their feedback. Trade unions' feedback is normally given prominence by the media and is taken into consideration by government.

The impact on the media of the general unions, especially the GWU, however, is much greater than that of the smaller unions. The GWU has been influencing public opinion since the 1960s through its two national newspapers, the daily *L-Orizzont* and weekly *It-Torċa*. These newspapers have a large readership, especially among the Labour leaning population. More recently, the GWU has also launched the IT portal iNews. The GWU's voice is given prominence on the PL media platforms, such as One TV, the Party's television station. On the other hand, while the second largest union, the UĦM, does not have its own newspaper, it is given ample media space, especially on the PN media, such as the newspaper *In-Nazzjon* and Net News. The advance of digitalization, the growth of social media, especially Facebook, may have started to erode this traditional difference between the large and small unions, however, because it is now easier for smaller unions to publish and propagate their views.

Eurobarometer Surveys between 2005 and 2019 indicate a consistent positive opinion of trade unions among the majority of the public. Besides, while results vary from year to year, there appears to have been an improvement over the surveyed years. As can be seen from Figure 20.1, while public opinion on unions in Malta was nearly always higher than the EU average, the gap between the two has widened in recent years.

Figure 20.1 Positive public opinion on trade unions, 2005–2019

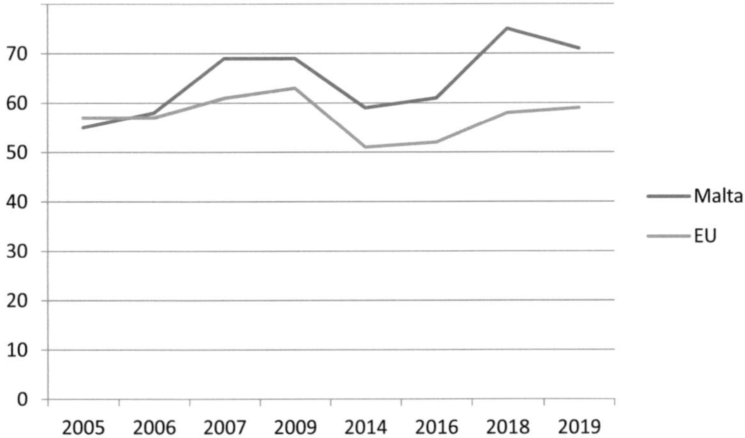

Note: The question asked was: Could you please tell me for each of the following, whether the term brings to mind something very positive, fairly positive, fairly negative or very negative – Trade union.
Source: European Commission (2005, 2007a, 2007b, 2010, 2014, 2016, 2018, 2019).

Such a trend was replicated in a recent study carried out among a representative sample of Maltese working-age people, which found that respondents have an overall positive opinion of unions (Debono 2019). Over two-thirds of adults (70.9 per cent) think that unions play an important role in protecting workers' rights. Unions are viewed as playing a major role in seeking unity among workers (68.4 per cent). Besides that, people appreciate union contributions to national debates (69 per cent) (Debono 2019). Despite such overall positive views of unions, there appears to have been some erosion of confidence towards unions among their members during the new millennium. While a survey carried out in 1999 found that 89.7 per cent of union members believed that unions were needed by society (Zammit and Rizzo 2003), the levels of confidence expressed by union members about the role of unions never reached 80 per cent among Debono's (2019) respondents and varied according to the type of role being examined. Attitudes towards unions also vary considerably depending on demographic status. Thus, a section of the working population, especially 'women, those who were never unionized, those not covered by a collective agreement, those who have never sought help from trade unions and those employed in small organizations' (Debono 2019: 1,011) are less likely to have clear opinions about unions.

Trade union policies towards the European Union

The three trade union peak organizations, namely the GWU, the CMTU and For.U.M., are affiliate members of the ETUC. All three organizations benefit from this affiliation by being involved in European issues. Resources preclude Maltese organizations from participating at a European level to the same degree as unions hailing from larger countries and must often be selective with regards to which ETUC meetings they participate in. It is worthwhile noting that not all topics discussed within the ETUC are directly applicable to Maltese industrial relations. The GWU is the only Maltese affiliate member of the International Trade Union Confederation (ITUC). Insufficient resources, however, prevent the GWU from participating in the ITUC to the desired degree.

The GWU, the CMTU, the UĦM, and For.U.M. are involved in the European Semester, along with other social partners, through the MCESD. While it was reported that the MCESD used to take a reactive approach to the European Semester, whereby reports on EU activity were discussed among the social partners, the approach is now more proactive, with the national agenda formulated around the European Semester. While in general, they feel that they are contributing positively to the European Semester, some union representatives believe that there is still much room for progress because of social partners' limited capacity. Further interaction on EU matters occurs through the Malta–EU Steering and Action Committee (MEUSAC), which aims to facilitate consultation on EU policy and legislation, as well as transposition of EU directives. The Core Group of MEUSAC includes representatives of government, the national parliament, social partners, civil society representatives and EU-related entities. Among its members representing workers are the CMTU, GWU, For.U.M. and the UĦM Voice of the Workers. The Core Group meets regularly, and joint meetings are sometimes organized between the MEUSAC Core Group and the MCESD (MEUSAC 2020). The Employment Relations Board, which also includes representatives of employers and employees, also meets regularly to discuss EU developments which may impact upon Malta. For example, discussions were recently held regarding the proposed EU Directive to ensure that workers are protected by adequate minimum wages.

The UĦM and the GWU also contribute to European Semester discussions via their representation of workers in Malta within the European Economic and Social Committee (EESC), the European equivalent of the MCESD (EESC n.d.). For.U.M.'s exclusion from this body has created some friction between the federations; For.U.M. representatives believe that while the union representatives within this body represent all unions in Malta, no communications on EESC developments occurs between For.U.M. and those that are party to EESC meetings.

Maltese unions are also active within the European Trade Union Federations (ETUFs) and other European groups they form part of. A case in point is the GWU's affiliation with the European Transport Workers' Federation and the International Transport Workers' Federation. Primarily, the interaction between these entities has concerned maritime workers and their lack of rights when working in international waters. The GWU has been pushing for such workers, who are usually third-country nationals working on Maltese-flagged boats to be granted the same rights as workers in Malta. This is an ongoing issue. The partnership between the GWU and these international bodies has also been active in discussing their concerns with government in the aviation sector, when Ryanair set up a subsidiary in Malta (Malta Air) and planned to transfer workers from around the EU to contracts with this new subsidiary (ETF 2019).

Maltese organizations also contribute to EU policy by means of their representation on boards of EU agencies. For.U.M. and the GWU are represented on the European Agency for Safety and Health at Work (EU-OSHA) Management Board, whereas For.U.M. provides an alternative member to the EU-OSHA Executive Board of the Management Board. For.U.M. is present on the Management Board of the European Centre for the Development of Vocational Training, with the GWU providing an alternative member representing the interests of workers (CEDEFOP 2019).

The GWU has also forged its own cross-border relationships. Of primary interest is its relationship with the CGIL, the largest Italian confederation. Malta has experienced a substantial influx of foreign workers over the past few years, with the largest group coming from Italy. The exponential increase of Italian workers and their growing needs led the GWU to reach an agreement with CGIL to offer the latter's members in Malta a contact point that provides them services, assistance and representation, as needed (CGIL 2019).

Conclusions

The idiosyncratic development of trade unionism in Malta needs to be understood in relation to the country's colonial past and its socio-economic, geographic and political context. Many of the current challenges faced by unions have been created or intensified by the country's recent strong economic growth, which led to changing employment in industries, an increasingly heterogeneous workforce, growing numbers of people at risk of poverty, and stresses on the quality of life and on environmental sustainability. The complexity of this situation has been further compounded by growing challenges to the rule of law and the pandemic's shock on the economy and social life. While several of these challenges are being tackled by unions, others, including the move towards a carbon-reduced economy, are still not sufficiently high on their agenda.

Maltese unions have been feeling the pressures of the megatrend of diminishing union influence across the Western world, including difficulties penetrating growing industries in private services, ageing union membership, and the shrinking unionization rate and collective bargaining coverage. But the union movement remains strong, as indicated by the raw membership figures, which are still increasing. Besides, the reduction of strikes does not appear to derive from the unions' inability to organize workers but is rather a strategic decision based on a preference for dialogue over confrontation. In order not to jeopardize their strategic social relevance, unions need to be particularly careful about their revenue streams, which in recent years have become more diversified.

It is clear that unions' reach and impact are not consistent across all categories of workers. Indeed, research 'portrays a rather traditionally-oriented trade union movement in Malta, which appears not to be particularly effective in attracting and retaining younger workers, part-time workers, workers on definite contracts and those in the private sector, especially in smaller organizations' (Debono 2018: 56). Despite this and their limited resources, unions constantly strive to assist vulnerable workers, as can be seen from their campaigns against precariousness, including the recent endeavours to protect platform workers, and the fledgling efforts to increase the representation of migrant workers.

While retaining their core function of collective bargaining, the larger and better organized trade unions, on their own or through their umbrella organizations, have increased their influence on the national agenda. They contribute to policy debate that affects not only their members but also the larger society. Over the years, trade unions have also shaped government policy through a variety of other social actions, such as public demonstrations and campaigns.

As shown in this chapter, the trade union movement in Malta has been resilient in the face of emerging challenges. None of Visser's (2019) four scenarios appear to depict well the likely future trends of the movement. The more successful unions will be those that manage to adapt their strategies to the emerging challenges and needs. Several union leaders are willing to seek creative avenues in terms of helping workers in general and boosting their membership numbers. Efforts are under way to expand membership beyond their traditional base, focusing on previously non-unionized industries and occupational groups. Higher participation of women and more highly educated people is particularly visible, while efforts to increase representation of migrant workers are also on the increase. There is currently even a bold attempt by the GWU and the UĦM to increase union membership through government intervention. Cooperation and alliances with other organizations both nationally and internationally are also increasingly common; though, unfortunately, cooperation between the two major union blocks themselves is very rare.

Despite the fact that 'the traditional cadre of union members is set to continue declining in the coming years due to economic, organizational and demographic trends' (Debono 2018: 56), with potential further reductions in membership rates and collective bargaining coverage, the unions' efforts, coupled with a generally favourable public opinion and supportive political class, and even cooperation with employers' associations on aspects of common interest, augur well for the future of the trade union movement. Whether these and other efforts will lead to the movement's revitalization is still difficult to predict.

References

All links were checked on 17 May 2021.

Baldacchino G. (1988) The industrialization of Malta: a historical analysis of the formation, control and response of labour, Malta, New Economics Society, 60–87.

Baldacchino G. (1990) A review of Maltese trade unionism: analysis based on the annual reports of the registrar of trade unions, Economic and Social Studies 5, 64–82.

Baldacchino G. (2007) Industrial Tribunal rules on union representation at University of Malta. https://www.eurofound.europa.eu/publications/article/2007/industrial-tribunal-rules-on-union-representation-at-university-of-malta

Baldacchino G. (2009) Trade unions in Malta, Report 110, Brussels, ETUI.

Baldacchino G. (2021) Unwept, unhonoured and unsung: the decline of UK-style industrial relations in Malta, in Debono M. and Baldacchino G. (eds) Working life and the transformation of Malta 1960–2020, Malta, Malta University Press, 129–144.

Baldacchino G. and Debono M. (2009) Trade union density in Malta from 1953 to 2008. https://www.eurofound.europa.eu/publications/article/2009/trade-union-density-in-malta-from-1953-to-2008

Baldacchino G., Rizzo R. and Zammit E.L. (2003) Evolving industrial relations in Malta, Malta, Agenda.

Borg J. (2020) Construction lobby hoovers up €240,000 in government funds, Times of Malta, 18 May 2020. https://timesofmalta.com/articles/view/240000-in-government-funds-for-developers-association.792788

Briguglio M. (2018) Workers for partisan needs, Times of Malta, 4 June 2018. https://www.timesofmalta.com/articles/view/20180604/opinion/workers-for-partisan-needs-michaelbriguglio.680819

Camilleri, I. (2016) Transport Malta pays €122,000 for unused building, Times of Malta, 20 January 2016. https://timesofmalta.com/articles/view/transport-malta-pays-122000-for-unused-building.599400

Caritas (2019) A minimum budget for a decent living. Research on three low-income household categories, Caritas, 20 February 2019. https://www.caritas.eu/a-minimum-budget-for-a-decent-living/

CEDEFOP (2019) Management board members. https://www.cedefop.europa.eu/en/about-cedefop/who-we-are/management-board?search=malta

CGIL (2019) Cgil e Gwu, il 30 novembre a Malta inaugurazione contact point con Landini, 26 November 2019. http://www.cgil.it/cgil-e-gwu-il-30-novembre-a-malta-inaugurazione-contact-point/

Cordina J.P. (2020) Unequal pay for equal work dispute with steward health care resolved – UHM, Newsbook, 19 November 2020. https://newsbook.com.mt/en/unequal-pay-for-equal-work-dispute-with-steward-health-care-resolved-uhm/

Council of the European Union (2011) Council Recommendation of 12 July 2011 on the National Reform Programme 2011 of Malta and delivering a Council opinion on the updated Stability Programme of Malta 2011–2014, Official Journal of the European Union, C 215, 27 June 2011, 10–13.

Dalli M. (2016) Unions rake in millions from unemployment schemes, Maltatoday, 30 November 2016. https://www.maltatoday.com.mt/news/national/72126/unions_rake_in_millions_from_unemployment_schemes#.X5VMj-0o82w

Debono J. (2012) A trade unionist for life – John Bencini, Maltatoday, 22 April 2012. https://www.maltatoday.com.mt/news/interview/17630/a-trade-unionist-for-life-john-bencini-20120421#.X6Wb8iySk2w

Debono M. (2006) Reported increase in union membership called into question. https://www.eurofound.europa.eu/publications/article/2006/reported-increase-in-union-membership-called-into-question.

Debono M. (2009) Social partners protest against new energy tariffs. https://www.eurofound.europa.eu/publications/article/2009/social-partners-protest-against-new-energy-tariffs.

Debono M. (2015) National survey on trade unions in Malta, Malta, President's Foundation for the Wellbeing of Society and Centre for Labour Studies.

Debono M. (2016) The role of social partners in the design and implementation of policies and reforms – Malta, Luxembourg, Publications Offices of European Union.

Debono M. (2018) An analysis of trade union membership in Malta, Xjenza Online, 6, 46–58. https://doi.org/10.7423/XJENZA.2018.1.06

Debono M. (2019) Attitudes towards trade unions in Malta, Economic and Industrial Democracy, 40 (4), 997–1017.

Debono M. and Baldacchino G. (2019) Malta: moving away from confrontation, in Muller T., Vandaele K. and Waddington J. (eds) Collective bargaining in Europe: towards an endgame, Brussels, ETUI, 423–444.

Debono M. and Farrugia C. (2006) Union dispute in the wake of ports restructuring. https://www.eurofound.europa.eu/publications/article/2006/union-dispute-in-the-wake-of-ports-restructuring

Debono M. and Farrugia C. (2013) Malta: annual update on pay 2012 – Questionnaire. https://www.eurofound.europa.eu/publications/report/2013/malta-annual-update-on-pay-2012-questionnaire.

Debono M. and Marmara V. (2017) Perceived precarious employment in Malta, E-Journal for International and Comparative Labour Studies, 6 (2), 62–81. http://ejcls.adapt.it/index.php/ejcls_adapt/article/view/424.

DIER (n.d.a) Annual Reports. https://dier.gov.mt/en/About-DIER/Archives/DIER%20Annual%20Reports/Pages/DIER%20Annual%20Reports.aspx

DIER (n.d.b) Reports by the Registrar of Trade Unions, Malta, Department for Industrial and Employment Relations. https://dier.gov.mt/en/About-DIER/Archives/Reports%20by%20the%20Registrar%20of%20Trade%20Unions/Pages/Reports-by-the-Registrar-of-Trade-Unions.aspx

EESC (n.d.) Members and CCMI delegates. https://www.eesc.europa.eu/en/members-groups/members/members-and-ccmi-delegates

ETF (2019) As Ryanair plans move to Malta, international transport unions meet Maltese government, 4 July 2019. https://www.etf-europe.org/as-ryanair-plans-move-to-malta-international-transport-unions-meet-maltese-government/

European Commission (2005) Eurobarometer 63 – Public Opinion in the European Union. https://europa.eu/eurobarometer/surveys/detail/505

European Commission (2007a) Eurobarometer 65 – Public Opinion in the European Union. https://europa.eu/eurobarometer/surveys/detail/583

European Commission (2007b) Eurobarometer 67 – Public Opinion in the European Union. https://europa.eu/eurobarometer/surveys/detail/617

European Commission (2010) Eurobarometer 72 – Public Opinion in the European Union. https://europa.eu/eurobarometer/surveys/detail/831

European Commission (2014) Eurobarometer 82 – Public Opinion in the European Union. https://europa.eu/eurobarometer/surveys/detail/2041

European Commission. (2016) Eurobarometer 85 – Public Opinion in the European Union. https://europa.eu/eurobarometer/surveys/detail/2130

European Commission (2018) Eurobarometer 90 – Public Opinion in the European Union. https://europa.eu/eurobarometer/surveys/detail/2215

European Commission (2019) Eurobarometer 91 – Public Opinion in the European Union. https://europa.eu/eurobarometer/surveys/detail/2253

Eurostat (2020) Database. https://ec.europa.eu/eurostat/data/database

Fiorini L.A., Griffiths A. and Houdmont J. (2018) Reasons for presenteeism in nurses working in geriatric settings: a qualitative study, Journal of Hospital Administration, 7 (4), 9–16.

Galea A. (2019) The time has come to discuss whether the COLA mechanism should be used or not – UHM CEO, The Malta Independent, 13 October 2019. https://www.independent.com.mt/articles/2019-10-13/local-news/The-time-has-come-to-discuss-whether-the-COLA-mechanism-should-be-used-or-not-UHM-CEO-6736214708

GWU (2020) Struttura. https://gwu.org.mt/kompozizzjoni-organizzattiva/

Hyman R. (2001) Understanding European trade unionism: between market, class and society, London, Sage.

Malta Chamber of Commerce, Enterprise and Industry (2014) Economic Vision for Malta 2014–2020, Valetta, Malta Chamber of Commerce, Enterprise and Industry.

The Malta Independent (2011) Forum Place on MCESD 'blocked' by six members, 2 July 2011. https://www.independent.com.mt/articles/2011-07-02/news/forum-place-on-mcesd-blocked-by-six-members-294983/

The Malta Independent (2019) €348,000 in aid given to six organisations, 11 October 2019. https://www.independent.com.mt/articles/2019-10-11/local-news/348-000-in-aid-given-to-six-organisations-673214647

The Malta Independent (2020) Watch: new economic measures – government to pay €800 per month for employees of worst hit sectors, 24 March 2020. https://www.independent.com.mt/articles/2020-03-24/local-news/Live-Coronavirus-Prime-Minister-Robert-Abela-announces-new-economic-measures-6736221239

MEA (2014) Proposals for national budget 2015. https://www.maltaemployers.com/Portals/22/Proposals%20for%20National%20Budget%202015.pdf

MEA (2015) The state of social dialogue and industrial relations in Malta. https://www.maltaemployers.com/loadfile/f3a55822-c043-41ae-aa74-d0e5c9f8d847

Meilak N. (2021) Malta Employers' Association hits out at premature 'right to disconnect' laws, Malta Today, 15 February 2021. https://www.maltatoday.com.mt/news/national/107741/malta_employers_association_hits_out_at_premature_right_to_disconnect_laws#.YGHx17Dis2w

MEUSAC (2020) Consultation. https://meusac.gov.mt/consultation/

Micallef K. (2019) GWU's planned mandatory union membership allows paid opt-out, Times of Malta, 22 August 2019. https://timesofmalta.com/articles/view/gwus-planned-mandatory-union-membership-allows-paid-opt-out.730165

Ministry for Finance of Malta (2013) Malta's National Reform Programme under the Europe 2020 Strategy, Valletta, Policy Development Directorate, Ministry for Finance. https://mfin.gov.mt/en/home/popular_topics/Documents/National%20Reform%20Programme/2013/National%20Reform%20Programme%202013.pdf

National Statistics Office (2010) Business demographics: 2001–2009, News Release, 13 August 2010. https://nso.gov.mt/en/News_Releases/Archived_News_Releases/Documents/2010/News2010_152.pdf

National Statistics Office (2020) Registered business units: 2019, News Release, 4 May 2020. https://nso.gov.mt/en/News_Releases/Documents/2020/05/News2020_072.pdf

Office of the Prime Minister (2017) New collective agreement for Public Service is the first of its kind. Valetta, Office of the Prime Minister.https://publicservice.gov.mt/en/Pages/News/2017/20170420_FtehimKollettiv.aspx

Pace Y. (2019) Mandatory employee union membership being studied by government, Maltatoday, 19 August 2019. https://www.maltatoday.com.mt/news/national/96952/mandatory_employee_union_membership_being_studied_by_government_#.X4Q7Mu2xXt5

Rizzo S. (2003) Flashpoints in local industrial relations in the 1990s, in Baldacchino G., Rizzo S. and Zammit E. (eds) Evolving industrial relations in Malta, Malta, Agenda, 28–64.

Rizzo S. (2006) No agreement on proposal to form trade union council. https://www.eurofound.europa.eu/publications/article/2006/no-agreement-on-proposal-to-form-trade-union-council

Rizzo S. (2010) FORUM requests representation on Malta Council for Economic and Social Development. https://www.eurofound.europa.eu/sr/publications/article/2010/forum-requests-representation-on-malta-council-for-economic-and-social-development

Times of Malta (2008) MUT leaves CMTU, 13 December 2008. https://timesofmalta.com/articles/view/mut-leaves-cmtu.237068

Times of Malta (2009) GWU delegates agree fee increase, 5 October 2009. https://timesofmalta.com/articles/view/gwu-delegates-agree-fee-increase.276174

Times of Malta (2012) GWU and Forum pledge collaboration, 22 March 2012. https://timesofmalta.com/articles/view/GWU-and-Forum-pledge-collaboration.412177

Vella M. (2014) The effect of minimum wage on employment in Malta, Bank of Valletta Review, (49), 1–20.

Visser L. (2019) Trade Unions in the balance. ILO ACTRAV Working Paper. Geneva, ILO.

Zammit E.L. (2003) The social partners, dialogue & industrial relations in Malta, in Baldacchino G., Rizzo S. and Zammit E. (eds), Evolving industrial relations in Malta, Malta, Agenda, 65–128.

Zammit E.L. and Rizzo S. (2003) The perceptions of trade unions by their members: a survey report on trade unions in Malta, in Baldacchino G., Rizzo S. and Zammit E.L. (eds) Evolving Industrial Relations in Malta, Malta, Agenda, 129–155.

Zammit E., Debono M. and Brincat M. (2015) Malta, in Blanpain R. and M. Colucci (eds) International Encyclopaedia for Labour Law and Industrial Relations, The Hague, Kluwer Law International.

Abbreviations

CEDEFOP	European Centre for the Development of Vocational Training
CGIL	Confederazione Generale Italiana del Lavoro (Italian General Confederation of Labour)
CMTU	Confederation of Malta Trade Unions
COLA	Cost of living allowance
DIER	Department of Industrial and Employment Relations
EESC	European Economic and Social Committee
EIRA	Employment and Industrial Relations Act
ETUC	European Trade Union Confederation
ETUFs	European Trade Union Federations
EU	European Union
EU-OSHA	European Agency for Safety and Health at Work
For.U.M.	Forum Unions Maltin (Forum of Maltese Unions)
GWU	General Workers Union
ILO	International Labour Organization
ITUC	International Trade Union Confederation
MCESD	Malta Council for Economic and Social Development

MEA	Malta Employers Association
MEUSAC	Malta–EU Steering and Action Committee
MIA	Malta International Airport
MUT	Malta Union of Teachers
PES	Public Employment Service
PL	Partit Laburista (Labour Party)
PN	Partit Nazzjonalista (Nationalist Party)
RTU	Registrar of Trade Unions
ToM	Times of Malta
UĦM	Union Ħaddiema Magħqudin – Voice of the Workers (Union of United Workers – Voice of the Workers).

Chapter 21

Trade unions in the Netherlands: Erosion of their power base in the stable Polder Model

Paul de Beer and Lisa Berntsen

Trade unions in the Netherlands are characterized by a strong institutional embeddedness, but their power base has been eroding. Since the Second World War, close cooperation between unions, employers' associations and the government has been one of the defining characteristics of the Dutch 'Polder' system of industrial relations. As a consequence, unions have a strong influence on government policies, albeit at the price of accepting compromises that are not always understood by their rank and file. Moreover, unions are strongly represented at the industry level, the main level of collective bargaining, which covers approximately three-quarters of all employees and two-thirds of all employed persons (including self-employed). Often, affiliates of the three national confederations, the Confederation of Dutch Trade Unions (FNV, Federatie Nederlandse Vakbeweging), the Christian National Confederation (CNV, Christelijk Nationaal Vakverbond) and the Confederation for Professionals (VCP, Vakcentrale voor Professionals), cooperate in collective bargaining, although recently an increasing number of collective agreements have not been signed by FNV affiliates, or have been signed only by small independent or in some cases 'yellow' unions. Because the FNV confederation organizes the lion share of union members, most attention in this chapter will be paid to FNV, and much less to the other confederations and the independent unions.

Table 21.1 Principal characteristics of trade unionism in the Netherlands

	1980	2000	2019
Total trade union membership	1,717,000	1,913,000	1,602,000
Women as a proportion of total membership	14 %	31 %	39 %
Gross union density	39 %	27 %	21 %
Net union density	35 %	22 %	15 %
Number of confederations	3	3	3
Number of affiliated unions (federations)*	27	25	19
Number of independent unions	n.a.	n.a.	n.a.
Collective bargaining coverage	85 %	82 %	76 %
Principal level of collective bargaining	industry	industry	industry
Days not worked due to industrial action per 1,000 workers	12	1	54

Notes: * This number includes only affiliates of the two largest confederations, FNV and CNV.

Source: Appendix A1, CBS (Statline), FNV, CNV.

Whereas the unions' institutional position is relatively stable, their power base is weakening, mainly because of the secular decline of union density, which has halved since the 1980s and currently stands at about 15 per cent of all employees (see Table 21.1). Moreover, because of membership ageing and the underrepresentation of young, flexible and migrant workers, union membership reflects the composition of the labour force less and less. New union strategies, in particular organizing, although successful in some industries, have not reversed the downward unionization trend. Employer strategies to circumvent collective agreements are also undermining the unions' power base, for example by hiring agency workers or solo self-employed or by negotiating an agreement on terms of employment with the works council instead of bargaining with the unions. The unions' political base has also weakened because all formal ties with political parties have been severed and dominant government policies have turned in a neoliberal direction since the 1990s. Hence, the argument running through this chapter is that, despite their strong institutional embeddedness and stable formal position, the unions' power base has weakened and, consequently, they find it increasingly difficult to achieve their goals. In the longer run, this may also weaken their institutional base, which could ultimately result in marginalization.

Historical background and principal features of the industrial relations system

The Dutch industrial relations system, which today is often named the 'Polder model',[1] finds its origins in the inter-war period, when a number of important laws were enacted that still constitute the core of the current system, in particular the Act on Collective Labour Agreements (1927) and the Act on the Mandatory Extension of Collective Labour Agreements (1937). The system came to full bloom after the Second World War. Immediately after the war, the Labour Foundation (StvdA, *Stichting van de Arbeid*) was formed by the central employers' associations and the trade union confederations. The Foundation did not attain the central role in economic governance that the founders intended, but it nevertheless played a crucial role in the 'guided wage policy' that was in force until the early 1960s. Only after 1963, and formally after 1970, did collective bargaining become 'free', although the government still regularly intervened until 1981.

In 1950 the tripartite Socio-Economic Council (SER, *Sociaal-Economische Raad*) was established, composed of an equal number of union and employers' representatives and independent Crown members, who are mostly academics, appointed by the government. This became the most important government advisory body on socio-economic policies. Both the Labour Foundation and the Socio-Economic Council reflect the long-standing tradition of consulting and consensus-seeking, in which collective actors, despite their different ideologies or religion, acknowledge that they have to cooperate in order to build and maintain a prosperous and relatively egalitarian society.

In the post-war period, this resulted in the so-called 'pillarization' of Dutch society. Society was divided into three 'pillars' (Catholic, Protestant and socialist, although sometimes a fourth 'neutral' pillar is distinguished), each with its own political parties, newspapers, broadcasting companies, schools, sports clubs and also trade unions. Despite the sharp dividing lines between the pillars, the respective leaderships were willing to cooperate and seek compromises across pillars to govern the country. This was also reflected in the positions taken by the union

---

1 After the parts of the country that lie below sea level and are protected by dykes that have been built through the cooperation and joint effort of diverse societal groups.

confederations and their affiliates, which were willing to cooperate with each other despite their ideological differences.

In the course of the 1960s the pillars started to crumble, which led, among other things, to talks about closer cooperation between the confederations, ultimately resulting in a merger of the socialist and the Catholic confederations into the FNV. Depillarization also led to a more conflictual and polarized period in terms of relations between unions and employers during the 1970s. The 1982 Wassenaar Agreement marked the return to a phase of more consensual relations between the social partners. It was followed by a long series of bipartite and tripartite national agreements and social pacts, which have become typical of the Polder model.

The system of industrial relations has long been characterized by a high collective bargaining coverage rate of around 75–85 per cent of all employees. This high coverage is mainly the result of high employer density: approximately 80 per cent of all employees work for an employer who is a member of an employer association, most of which conclude collective agreements that apply to all their employees. Bargaining takes place primarily at the industry level, and the extension of collective agreements at this level further explains the high coverage. Since the Wassenaar Agreement and in particular since the New Course agreement of 1993, however, industry collective agreements increasingly leave room for individual employers to deviate from the agreement, mostly after consulting the works council.

Structure of trade unions and union democracy

Faced with declining union membership and weakening political influence, the three main union confederations, FNV, CNV and VCP, have all undergone organizational changes in recent years. Since the 1990s, there has been a series of mergers, especially in the largest confederation, FNV. As a consequence, two affiliates, *FNV Bondgenoten*, which resulted from a merger or amalgamation of a number of private sector unions in 1998, and *AbvaKabo FNV*, the largest public sector union, became by far the largest affiliates within FNV, representing about two-thirds of its membership. In 2015, these two affiliates, together with the construction workers' union (*FNV Bouw*) and a few smaller affiliates, amalgamated with the confederation to form one big union (see Figure 21.1). This undivided FNV includes twenty-three sectors (including separate sectors for women, young people and seniors). Eleven smaller FNV affiliates (most of them representing specific occupations, such as teachers, journalists and police officers) did not merge into the undivided FNV but remained independent, out of fear of losing their identity. As a result FNV now has individual members as well as (industry) unions as affiliates, making it a union *and* a confederation at the same time (de Beer and Keune 2018).

Figure 21.1 Structure of FNV

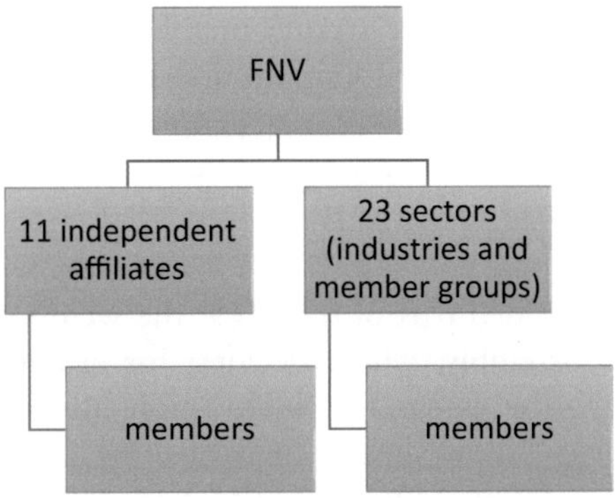

Source: https://www.fnv.nl/over-de-fnv/wie-we-zijn/ledenparlement.

This merger was the outcome of the internal governance struggles created by the crisis within FNV that occurred in 2011 when *FNV Bondgenoten* and *AbvaKabo FNV* refused to accept the pension agreement reached between the unions, the employers' associations and the government (de Beer 2013). The agreement boiled down to a transition from a defined-benefit to a defined-contribution scheme, which was decried by its adversaries as a 'casino pension'. The internal crisis was also fuelled by the dominance of the two affiliates that represented the large majority of FNV membership and the tension between two opposing currents within FNV advocating different union strategies. On one hand, one group, strongly represented in the two largest affiliates, pleaded for a more activist strategy, for instance, through organizing activities (see below), while another group, including the majority of the confederation's executive committee, favoured a more consensual approach to maintain good relations with the employers and the government. Although the merger did not resolve the tension between these two currents, it became less overt because the major protagonists in the conflict, the presidents of the confederation and the two largest affiliates, resigned.

Within the amalgamated FNV, which currently has just under 1 million members, a members' assembly is the main decision-making body: they determine long-term union strategies, control the FNV board and have a deciding vote on board proposals. The assembly consists of 103 elected or assigned (unpaid) union members from both the undivided FNV and the independent affiliates. Each of the twenty-three sectors has one or more representatives in the members' assembly. The number of representatives depends on the sector's membership size: education, for instance, has eight seats; the self-employed sector one; the sector 'seniors' has eighteen seats; and the sector 'young people' has one seat.[2] The assembly meets every month. There are no public minutes from the members' assembly meetings and only the discussion headlines are published on the FNV website.

Within the undivided part of the FNV, the sectors are subordinated to the members' assembly, which decides, for example, on collective bargaining policy. The extent to which union officials at the sectoral (industry) level can follow their own bargaining course varies. FNV's 'independent' affiliates have more room to manoeuvre, despite their formal subordination to the member assembly's decisions.

Also, within the second largest, but much smaller Christian confederation, CNV, affiliates merged to strengthen their position in the face of declining membership rates. In 2015, the public sector unions merged into *CNV Connectief* (c. 100,000 members),[3] and in 2010 the manufacturing, construction and transport unions merged into *CNV Vakmensen*, which subsequently merged with the union of artists in 2011 and with the services union in 2016, although these were actually more like acquisitions. It now has approximately 140,000 members. These two unions now account for the large majority of CNV membership. This has not led to (overt) tensions comparable to those in FNV, however. CNV's highest decision-making body is the General Assembly, consisting of representatives of the affiliates, in proportion to their membership, which convenes

---

2 See https://www.fnv.nl/over-de-fnv/wie-we-zijn/ledenparlement

3 The unions CNV Onderwijs (education), Overheid (public sector), Zorg & Welzijn (health and well-being) and Publieke Diensten (public services) still exist under the CNV Connectief umbrella.

twice a year. Each affiliate delegates a representative to the general board, which also includes the executive committee appointed by the General Assembly for a period of four years (CNV 2011). In 2012, the General Christian Police Union (ACP, *Algemene Christelijke Politiebond*), dissatisfied with the confederation's overall course, decided to leave CNV, which currently has a membership of approximately 240,000.

The smallest union confederation, MHP (*Vakcentrale voor Middelbaar en Hoger Personeel*), which organized mainly middle and senior staff, experienced the departure of its largest affiliate, De Unie, in 2013 because it disagreed with the course of the confederation. This meant that MHP lost almost half of its members. In 2015, MHP together with ACP formed a new confederation under the name of the Confederation for Professionals (VCP). VCP now has over fifty mostly small affiliates, including De Unie, that joined VCP in 2017, and it has a total of 160,000 members.

Meanwhile, the Netherlands has seen an increase in the number of independent unions. These are mainly affiliates that have left a union confederation because of a policy disagreement, not newly established independent unions. The total membership of independent unions has increased by half over the past twenty years (de Beer and Keune 2018: 253). Independent unions often organize specific occupational groups, such as civil servants or train operators. Next to these independent unions, there is probably an increasing number of 'yellow unions', which are largely dependent on (funding from) employers. An interesting, yet controversial example is the Alternative to Union (AVV, *Alternatief voor Vakbond*), which claims to represent groups of workers, such as young people, flexible workers and self-employed, that established unions represent only inadequately. Although AVV has only a small number of members – approximately 700 – they claim to be more representative than other unions because they gauge the opinion of the employees of a company via workforce surveys. Because they are financially almost completely dependent on the contributions of the employers or employers' associations with which they conclude a collective agreement, their independence has been questioned by the established unions (Delhaas and Davidson 2020).

Both CNV and FNV have specific union bodies for young people (CNV Jongeren with 1,400 members and FNV Jong with 8,000 members), although youth membership is generally low in both unions (less than 5 per cent of total membership is under the age of 25). The youth section in CNV was established in 1955 as an independent union body within the confederation. The need for a specific youth section in FNV has been subject to internal debates over the years. In the 1990s, the FNV youth section was dissolved, because of the small membership and the internal strategy to represent youth interests primarily via the sectors. In 2011, the youth section was re-established, after AVV criticized established unions for neglecting the interests of young people (Keune and Tros 2014). Through the use of social media, lobbying and issue-based alliances, FNV Jong has put youth issues on the FNV's agenda and has had some public influence (Vandaele 2013), especially during the FNV Young and United youth wage campaign in 2015–2016 (see below).

Unionization

Total union membership increased continuously from 805,000 in 1945 to 1,792,000 in 1979, then dropped slightly until 1984, to rise again to its peak of 1,923,000 in 2002. After that, membership declined by more than 300,000 (–17 per cent) to 1,602,000 in 2019, the lowest number in almost half a century. Although membership peaked in 2002, the net union density rate had already reached its highest point in 1975 with 33.6 per cent and subsequently declined steadily, with a brief intermission between 1990 and 1994 – the term of the popular FNV chairman Johan Stekelenburg. In 2019, net union density stood at 15.4 per cent, less than half the density rate of 1975.

As in many countries, union density varies strongly between industries. It is highest in public administration, education, manufacturing, construction and transport, and lowest in financial services, retail and wholesale, and hospitality (see Table 21.2). Union density has declined in all industries, however, and most dramatically in some more highly organized industries. From 2007 to 2018, union density fell by 11 to 12 percentage points in, for instance, construction, transport and public administration and by 8 points in manufacturing, whereas it declined by 3 to 4 percentage points in retail and wholesale, education and health care (TNO/CBS, microdata NEA 2007 and 2018).

The basic explanation for the decline of union membership is that each new (younger) generation is joining a union less often than the previous generation. This is illustrated by the membership rates presented in Table 21.2. The table shows that union density increases with age and declines over time. If one compares the union density of specific age groups in 2009 with the next – 10 years older – age group in 2018, one notices little change in union density over time within cohorts, but overall density decreases as older cohorts are replaced by younger cohorts. This tendency contributes to the ageing of union membership, because the difference in membership rates between older and younger workers is increasing. Moreover, an increasing share of union membership consists of retirees.

The declining trend in union membership can only partly be explained by the growth of the labour market segments with a low union density, such as business and consumer services, and atypical contracts, such as fixed-term contracts, agency work, on-call work or solo self-employment, because membership is also declining within segments with a higher union density. Because union density among part-time workers and female workers – largely overlapping groups – is only slightly lower than among full-time workers and male workers (see Table 21.2), the growth of part-time and female employment does not explain the decline of union membership, either.

A recent time series analysis revealed that union decline is partly explained by the long process of wage 'moderation' (de Beer and Berntsen 2019). Each percentage point increase of contractual wages boosts membership by about 0.16 per cent. Apparently, employees are more likely to join a union when they see that it has been able to raise wages. Interestingly, a reduction in public expenditure on social benefits as a percentage of GDP by 1 percentage point increases union membership by 0.94 per cent. Apparently, (potential) union members perceive unions as a shield against the risk of unemployment and therefore as a substitute for state protection.

Table 21.2 Net union density rate by member categories, 2009 and 2018/2019

	2009 (%)	**2018/2019 (%)**
Total	24	18
Gender		
Male	28	20
Female	19	17
Age		
less than 25	10	6
25 to 35	17	13
35 to 45	21	17
45 to 55	30	22
55 to 65	40	31
Educational attainment		
Low	24	18
Intermediate	24	20
High	23	17
Working time		
Full-time	26	20
Part-time	20	17
Contract type		
Permanent	26	21
Flexible	13	9
Sector		
Agriculture	14	12
Manufacturing	28	22
Construction	34	25
Retail, wholesale	12	9
Transport, logistics	37	28
Hospitality	12	9
Information, communication	15	7
Financial services	15	9
Business services	15	10
Public administration	40	34
Education	35	32
Health care, social services	24	22
Culture, sports, recreation	19	16

Table 21.2 Continued

	2009 (%)	2018/2019 (%)
Unemployed/disabled	n.a.	9
Pensioners	n.a.	8

Note: Employees only, except unemployed, disabled and pensioners.

Source: TNO/CBS (NEA 2009 and 2018), except unemployed and disabled: AIAS-HSI (WWM 2019) and pensioners: CBS (Statline 2019).

Although the unions' institutional position does not directly depend on membership or their capacity to mobilize, the continuous decline in membership undermines representative legitimacy and has led unions to explore new strategies to halt this decline, stimulate member engagement and revitalize their organization. Initiatives focus particularly on attracting and engaging new and underrepresented groups of workers, such as women, young workers, self-employed workers and (im)migrant workers (Kloosterboer 2007). Membership growth is high on the FNV agenda: FNV launched an organization-wide membership plan in 2020 to strengthen membership recruitment and retention, putting particular emphasis on attracting and engaging young members. FNV has further introduced organizing methods to extend representation of underrepresented groups. CNV, on the other hand, experiments with member and non-member engagements to enhance its representativeness.

FNV commenced its organizing efforts after the 2005 FNV Congress established worker engagement and representation of underrepresented groups as crucial issues. Some of the assertive organizing techniques diverge from the consensus-based action repertoire characteristic of the social partnership tradition. The outcomes in the form of extended regulation via collective agreements and representation of workers, however, have enhanced the unions' institutional power base (Connolly et al. 2017; Knotter 2017). While organizing was introduced to attract and engage a new membership base, its tactics and narrative have also stimulated internal reflection and debate on union purpose and identity (Connolly et al. 2017). It has, for example, led to organizational changes: an organizing department, established in 2009 within FNV Bondgenoten, was continued as an internal department in the amalgamated FNV, employing around 100 organizers (Tamminga 2017: 89). The scope of organizing compared with servicing and partnership – the latter with employers and the state – remains small, as FNV has a total of around 2,000 paid employees. Still, organizing has led to changed and qualitatively different social relationships within FNV's overall social dialogue repertoire (Connolly et al. 2017: 332). At the same time, organizing is not uncontested in FNV: it is labour-intensive, especially when one compares the ratios of organizers versus union officers (*bestuurders*) to the number of members, and campaigns in low-member and low-wage sectors have been cross-financed by more affluent sectors of FNV, such as manufacturing and construction.

The first organizing drive in the Netherlands was the 'Clean Enough' (*Schoon genoeg*) campaign by FNV Bondgenoten in 2007, modelled on the American Service Employees International Union's successful 'Justice for Janitors' campaign. The 'Clean Enough' campaign combined grassroots organizing, direct action – including prolonged strike action in 2010 and 2012 – and broad coalition formation to pressure employers and contractors to improve pay and working conditions in cleaning. FNV Bondgenoten officials were trained by American colleagues in organizing techniques, including methods of identifying workplace leaders, (re)building workplace collectives and activating members. Inspiration for public actions during the campaign was taken from exemplary campaigns in the United States and Britain (Connolly et al. 2017). FNV mobilized a significant share of cleaners, despite the fragmented nature of their employment and workplaces. This resulted in collective agreements with better wages and working conditions, and increased membership and mobilizing capacity in the sector. The increase in union membership among cleaners was highest in the first few years of the campaign, but levelled off subsequently.

Other organizing campaigns were conducted in care in 2011–2017; in supermarket distribution centres in 2009–2013; and at the national airport Schiphol since 2013, which is still ongoing. The Schiphol campaign has organized workers based on the shared geographical location of their work, instead of their specific job or organization. The organizing activities have led to various types of industrial action, including work stoppages of security personnel, freight handlers, ground stewards at KLM and cabin crew at Ryanair, and to an increase in passive and active membership among various types of jobs at Schiphol airport (de Beer and van der Valk 2020).

Organizing also contributes to union renewal. The fact that it brings in a new cohort of officials and organizers, equipped with different toolboxes of union tactics, shifts the focus, at least in part, towards social movement unionism (Connolly et al. 2017: 330). The question is, how new methods of operation are incorporated and structurally embedded within conventional union practices. One way to bridge organizing and partnership practices could be found in what Mundlak (2020) has called 'integrative innovations'. One example is the cleaners' assembly, established during the cleaners' campaign. This is a representative body of elected cleaners and an elected president who joins the negotiating team at industry-level negotiations. The cleaners' assembly functions independently of the FNV's organizing team as a democratic instrument to build worker participation from the ground up. Mundlak, however, points to the difficulty for the assembly of continuing on its own without the organizing division's support, now that the industry's campaign has come to a close (Mundlak 2020: 189).

While migrants and ethnic minority workers are underrepresented in unions' membership base (Kranendonk and de Beer 2016), FNV has attracted migrant members via a number of campaigns (Roosblad and Berntsen 2017). The exact number of migrant members is unknown, because their nationality is not recorded. The cleaners' campaign mentioned above organized many ethnic minority workers in the industry. With campaigns for equal pay for equal work at the same workplace, FNV fights the underpayment and poor working conditions of mobile/migrant European Union (EU) workers. Although, on occasion, FNV has mobilized EU migrant workers, including posted workers, retaining their membership has proved challenging (Berntsen and Lillie 2016). Specifically, advances were made with a short-term cross-industrial initiative within FNV informing Polish workers, mainly in agriculture and meat-processing, about their rights in the Netherlands in 2013–2015. The idea behind this initiative, called the 'Polish brigade' (*Poolse brigade*) was to improve union accessibility for migrants with flexible jobs. Advances have also been made in activating Polish union members; for example, in 2014 the first group of Polish shop floor representatives finished an FNV training course. Still, the overall number of Polish union members remains small. With the 'Matter of Civilization' (*Kwestie van beschaving*) campaign since 2019, FNV has raised public awareness of the precarious conditions of migrant workers coming from other member states within the EU. The campaign has brought together an active group of migrant workers who publicly share their experiences. For instance, they shared the problematic coupling of work and housing practices by temporary agency firms, which have become poignantly visible during the Covid-19 pandemic.[4] The membership and engagement of EU migrants have been developed particularly by FNV officials with Polish and Romanian backgrounds. This is part of several – though not all successful – initiatives by FNV since the 1990s to increase its organizational diversity. Despite these initiatives, migrant and ethnic minority workers remain underrepresented, especially in more senior staff positions (Roosblad 2013).

The increasing proportion of solo self-employed persons (zzp, *zelfstandigen zonder personeel*) in the workforce has led unions to focus more on this group. Self-employed workers and freelancers have always been able to join unions, such as the Union for Journalists (Nederlandse Vereniging van Journalisten) and the Union for Creative Professions (Kunstenbond). In 2000, FNV established the first union for self-employed workers with FNV Zelfstandige Bondgenoten, which later became FNV ZZP and joined the undivided FNV in 2015. Although relatively small in size, with around 10,000 members in 2017,[5] FNV ZZP sets itself clear membership goals: in the period 2017–2022 it aims to recruit 15,000 new members (FNV 2016a: 5).

FNV has also developed activities involving workers in the platform economy. Freelance food delivery riders organized themselves in the Riders Union, which later became integrated as a section within FNV as the FNV Riders Union. When Deliveroo changed the employment contracts of delivery workers into freelance contracts, FNV successfully challenged this change of employment status before the court, which ruled that the delivery workers should be considered employees of Deliveroo. While the FNV Riders Unions was relatively active initially, with well-covered protest actions by the media, it is more or less dormant now. This is again indicative of the difficulties unions face embedding new initiatives in established union structures. On the other hand, unions' engagement with platform food delivery services may be informed by attempts to regulate the platform economy in general, and not so much by the desire to build up a membership base among platform workers (Vandaele 2020).

---

4 See https://kwestievanbeschaving.nl/english/

5 See https://fnvzzp.nl/nieuws/2017/01/fnv-zelfstandigen-nu-integraal-onderdeel-van-fnv

CNV does not use organizing to strengthen its position, because it does not fit well with its more consensual approach. Instead, CNV aims to create more engagement between members and non-members to become a more representative organization, even if that means having fewer members (van der Valk 2020). One initiative aimed at promoting such engagement is the CNV project 'James career counselling', available to both CNV members and non-members. Membership recruitment is not one of its objectives, but the project does actively approach people on the shop floor, especially in cases of upcoming bankruptcy, to encourage workers to think about career development (van der Valk 2020). The 'Try the Union' (*Probeer de Bond*) initiative of CNV Vakmensen aims to attract young members by informing students in vocational education about unionism and offering free union membership to students.[6] It aims to recruit 5,000 to 6,000 non-paying members each year, of whom 20–30 per cent become paying union members after finishing their studies. The plan is to extend the programme to universities of applied sciences (de Beer and van der Valk 2020).

Union resources and expenditure

Trade unions' main sources of funding are membership fees, employer contributions when concluding collective agreements, income from social and pension funds, and, for the well-endowed unions such as FNV, returns on investments.[7] There is no state funding of unions, although particular activities, such as training and support for unions in developing countries, receive some government subsidies. In general, unions are relatively well-endowed. How financially solid they are is not exactly clear, however, because no annual accounts are published. Recently, financial details were leaked to the press, indicating that FNV's wealth totals some 739 million euros (€), of which €67 million is allocated to the strike fund (Kuijpers and Van Keken 2020). The financial reserves are mostly brought in by wealthy affiliates, such as FNV Bondgenoten and FNV Bouw. Within FNV, these wealthy affiliates helped finance less well-off

---

6 See https://www.cnvvakmensen.nl/probeerdebond

7 In 2019, FNV's return on investments was €73.7 million; in 2018 FNV made a loss of €21.6 million (Kuijpers and Van Keken 2020).

affiliates through ‘cross-subsidies’. Also, financial reserves are earmarked to fund incidental costs or expenditures.

Even though the unions are well resourced, their position is under strain because of declining union income, as membership contributions diminish and employer contributions tail off because fewer collective agreements are concluded.[8] The extent to which the unions’ financial position is under pressure is not known. Since the 2015 merger, FNV has not published a public annual report.[9] Annual financial reports are not shared by CNV either. Despite FNV’s well-endowed strike fund and financial buffer against investment risks, its financial solidity is precarious. In 2015, the members’ assembly questioned the use of financial reserves for incidental costs or structural expenditure (*Het Financieele Dagblad*, 22 January 2016). For FNV, annual structural deficits of €24 million, mainly because of declining membership fees, led to the announcement of restructuring in 2019, including a plan to cut about 20 per cent of staff. According to the leadership, structural expenditure should be financed from structural revenues (*De Volkskrant*, 21 May 2019). The restructuring plans were put on hold after internal protests, however, leaving the issue of financial solidity unresolved (De Vries 2019).

For most collective agreements signed, the unions receive an employer contribution per employee. This arrangement dates back to 1966, when it was signed off by the General Employers Association (AWVN, Algemene Werkgeversvereniging Nederland), and the predecessors of FNV, CNV Vakmensen and De Unie. In 2020, the AWVN determined the contribution at €21.43 per employee when a new collective agreement is concluded.[10] Although this money cannot be used to fund strike activities, it can be used for union officials’ salaries. The Foundation Industrial Unions Fund (FIB, Stichting Fonds Industriële Bonden) distributes the money to the signing unions, after employers indicate the number of employees covered by the collective agreement, based on a ratio determined by the unions. In recent years, an increasing number of collective agreements have been concluded without FNV as signatory party. According to the Ministry of Social Affairs and Employment, in the period 2013–2018, 40 per cent of

---

8 Where the established unions miss out on these employer contributions, these contributions benefit the smaller, new, ‘yellow’ unions that do sign these agreements.

9 Independent unions in FNV do publish annual reports online, such as FNV Horeca.

10 See https://www.awvn.nl/nieuws/awvn-werkgeversbijdrageregeling-werkgeversbijdrage-2020/

employees were covered by a newly closed collective agreement not signed by FNV.[11] FNV's stance of refraining from signing 'bad' collective agreements directly infringes on an important source of income.[12] Around 20 per cent of FNV's income is derived from employer fees (Jansma 2019).

CNV derives 27 per cent of its income from employer contributions, De Unie 19 per cent (Jansma 2019). For AVV, employer contributions and structural fees from social funds are its main sources of income. AVV estimates that less than 3 per cent of its total income originates from membership contributions. Structural fees from social funds (67 per cent), employer contributions (16 per cent) and project fees from social funds (12 per cent) are more important sources of income.[13] This has raised questions about AVV's independence (Jansma 2019; Julen 2020).

As already mentioned, unions are not publicly financed but they obtain government subsidies for particular activities. The CNV youth union, which is an independent union body under the CNV umbrella, attracts external funding, for instance, through collaborative projects with municipalities, operating on a project basis. International activities, such as support for unions in developing countries, are often subsidized by the Ministry of Foreign Affairs. Unions also attract income from attendance fees (*vacatiegelden*), for instance when union employees are on the board of a pension or sectoral fund. For AVV, 2.3 per cent of its annual income is derived from attendance fees.[14]

The monthly membership contributions for FNV and CNV are similar, differing by income category, whereas CNV membership contributions also differ by industry (see Table 21.3). Both unions grant free membership in exceptional cases. FNV offered free membership for a year during the Young & United youth wage campaign. CNV Vakmensen has a free membership option for young people in vocational education, part of the 'Try the Union' project mentioned above. CNV offers young people, working or studying, a reduced membership rate of €1.50; FNV has a youth rate for students in full-time education of €2.08.

---

11 By comparison, only 13 per cent of employees in the same period were covered by a collective agreement not signed by CNV; Ministerie van SZW (2019) in de rapportage Cao-afspraken 2018, p. 141.

12 In 2018, 20 collective agreements were concluded without FNV, amounting to a possible €15 million loss of revenues; estimation by De Waard, Peter (2018) 'Waarom betalen niet-leden ook vakbondscontributie?' *De Volkskrant* 11 July 2018.

13 According to the 2020 budget.

14 According to the 2020 budget.

Table 21.3 Monthly membership fees of FNV and CNV (in Euro), 2020

FNV membership fees	
full-time students	2.08
income < € 826.00; unemployed or retired	8.62
income between € 826.00 and € 1,653.60	12.93
regular membership	17.25
CNV membership fees	
CNV membership fees	
CNV Vakmensen	
income below € 1,051	5.34
income between € 1,051 and € 1,578	12.76
income between € 1,578 and € 2,630	17.10
income above € 2,630	19.26
CNV Connectief	
income less than half minimum wage	9.95
income less than minimum wage; workers below 26 years old in education	12.95
regular membership	17.50
CNV Jongeren	1.50

Source: CNV and FNV.

The unions offer their members similar benefits and services, providing legal advice on work and income, assistance with filing tax returns, career counselling, help in case of occupational disease, and reductions on various products and services, such as insurance, education or mobile phone subscriptions. FNV and CNV also offer their members discount health insurance, although FNV cancelled this in 2019, because no new agreement could be reached that satisfied both FNV and the health insurance company.

Collective bargaining and unions at the workplace

Collective bargaining takes place both at company and industry level. Although there are more company level than industry (multi-employer) agreements (475 versus 176), the vast majority (91 per cent) of employees covered by a collective agreement are covered by an industry agreement. Industry agreements can be either standard, minimum or framework agreements. A standard agreement prescribes all terms of employment; a minimum agreement formulates only a basic level, which means that the employer can deviate from the agreement if it is more favourable to the employees; and a framework agreement leaves room to deviate from the standard if the employer and the works council agree on this.

Almost all collective agreements are concluded with one or more affiliates of the three confederations. Sometimes, one or more independent unions sign the agreement, too. Increasingly, collective agreements are not signed by affiliates of all three confederations. In particular, the largest union, FNV, refuses to undersign agreements that do not meet their minimum standards. Sometimes, collective agreements are signed only by a very small independent or 'yellow' union.

Although bargaining coverage is high and relatively stable, it has declined somewhat in recent years. Probably more important is the increased circumvention of collective agreements by employers. The manoeuvres they employ for this purpose include hiring solo self-employed workers who are not covered by a collective agreement, or agency workers who are covered by a 'cheaper' collective agreement, or outsourcing services – for instance, cleaning or catering – to an industry with a collective agreement with less generous terms of employment. This erodes the effective scope of collective agreements, even though bargaining coverage remains stable.

There are no recent studies of the wage-effect of collective bargaining. The Bureau for Economic Policy Analysis (CPB 2016) concluded that mandatory extension raises wages on average by 2 per cent, varying between 4 per cent in a boom (2007) and zero in an economic slump (2011). The CPB compares wages under mandatory extension with the hypothetical situation that all employees are directly covered by a collective agreement, in which case extension makes little sense. An alternative reading of the CPB analysis is that mandatory extension lowers wages by 2 to 4 per cent compared with a situation in which the employees who are subject to extension are not covered by a collective agreement (De Beer 2016). There is thus little evidence of a positive mark-up effect of collective bargaining. There are no studies of the non-wage effects of collective bargaining, though it is probably beneficial for secondary terms of employment, such as pension schemes and training facilities, for instance, through industrial training funds.

Another indicator of the impact of collective bargaining on wages is the difference between the evolution of contractual wages and earnings over time. Figure 21.2 shows index figures of real contractual wages and real earnings – that is, after correcting for consumer price increases – since 1970. Real contractual wages have been virtually stable since 1979! This means that unions have, overall, only managed to adjust wages to inflation and have not realized any real wage increase over the past forty years. In the same period, real earnings increased by 18 per cent, which points to a positive wage drift of, on average, 0.5 per cent per year. This prolonged period of wage moderation has been heralded both as the 'secret' of the Polder Model and the engine of strong job growth (Visser and Hemerijck 1996) and as a drag on innovation and productivity growth (Becker 2005).

Since 1999, FNV has striven for a stronger increase in the lowest contractual wages than the average pay rise. In 2010, a wage floor target of 1.3 times the minimum wage was formulated (FNV 2010: 5). Nevertheless, Figure 21.3 shows that the opposite happened. Since 1990, the lowest contractual wages have declined in real terms and the gap between the lowest contractual wages and the minimum wage narrowed from 12 per cent on average in 1993 to only 2 per cent in 2018. In more than half of collective agreements, weighted by the number of employees, the lowest wage is now equal to, or even lower than, the mandatory minimum wage. As a consequence, half a century after its introduction in 1969, the minimum wage is increasingly becoming the actual wage floor. Given that the minimum wage strongly lagged behind contractual wages from 1983 to 1996, because the government refrained from regular indexation, the relative level of this wage floor has plummeted, however.

Figure 21.2 Evolution of real contractual wages and real earnings since 1970

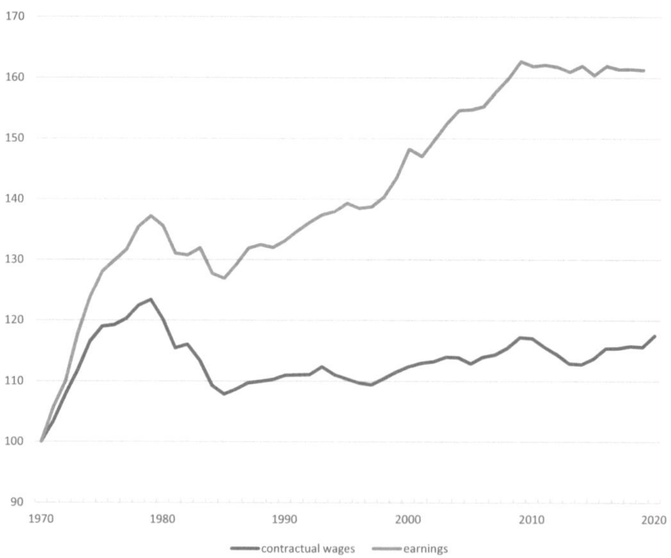

Note: 1970= 100. Authors' calculations.
Source: CBS (Statline).

Figure 21.3 Evolution of real minimum wage, real lowest contractual wage and real average contractual wage since 1980

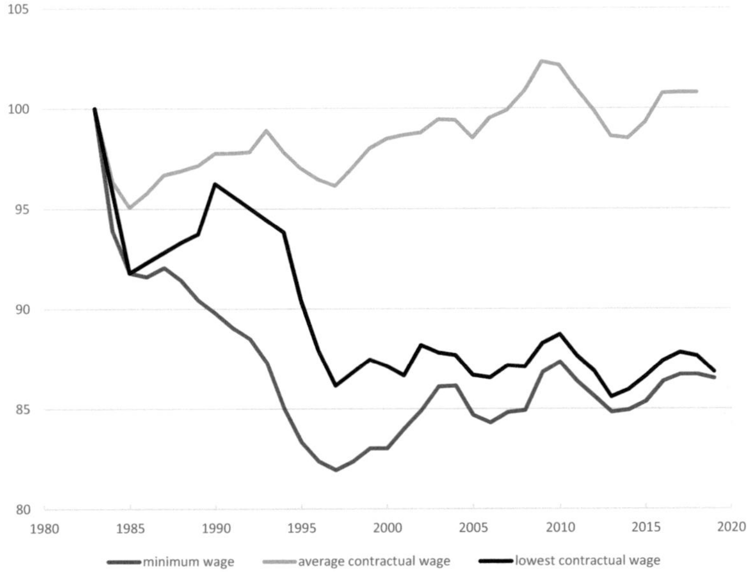

Note: 1983= 100. Authors' calculations from de Beer, Been and Salverda (2017).
Source: CBS (Statline), Ministry of Social Affairs and Employment.

Of course, wages are only one component of collective bargaining. It is possible that improvements in other terms of employment have compensated for wage losses. Quantitative indicators cannot trace these other terms of employment over time, but in any case it seems unlikely that they could fully compensate wage losses. Pension contributions, the most important non-wage component in terms of 'costs', have increased strongly in recent decades. Because the employer usually pays two-thirds of pension contributions, actual wage 'costs' have increased more than contractual wages. Even if these pension contributions are taken into account, however, total wage 'costs' have declined, from 58 per cent of GDP in 1980 to 48 per cent in 2018.

Special perks for union members in collective agreements, although legally not forbidden, are rare. Unions seem to fear that such perks might harm unions' legitimacy as representatives of all employees and may also jeopardize the quasi-automatic mandatory extension of collective agreements to all companies in an industry, although perks for union members are excluded from such extension. Special measures for union members, however, such as special support or additional severance pay, are not uncommon in the 'social plans' that are often concluded between unions and companies in cases of mass redundancy.

The presence of unions on the shop floor has always been weak in the Netherlands. When the Labour Foundation was established in 1945, the unions accepted that they would play no role whatsoever at the workplace in exchange for a prominent role at the national and industry levels. In 1950, the Act on Works Councils established works councils as workers' representative body at the company level. Although works council competences were extended in 1979, most councils still do not exert a significant influence on company strategy. The unions usually nominate candidates for works council elections, but an increasing number of members are independent and do not represent a union.

Occasionally, individual companies negotiate with their works council on a collective agreement. Legally, this is not a collective labour agreement – which can only be concluded by a trade union – and instead is called a 'terms of employment regulation', which cannot be enforced on all employees. Nevertheless, some companies find this an attractive alternative to bargaining with the unions. In an increasing number of cases, industry collective agreements allow companies to deviate from particular clauses after consulting the works council, even if these are detrimental to the employees. Several industry agreements distinguish between mandatory clauses and terms of employment that can be negotiated with the works council at the company level.

Industrial conflict

Dutch workers have never been very strike prone. In rankings of the countries with the largest numbers of days lost due to industrial conflict, the Netherlands always shows up somewhere near the bottom. This is probably because of its strong consensual tradition and the division of unions as a consequence of pillarization. Despite ideological differences, union leaderships have traditionally been characterized by their willingness to deliberate and seek compromises. Figure 21.4 shows that the number of strikes declined substantially after the 1970s. Since the 1980s, the annual number of strikes has hovered between twenty and twenty-five. The numbers of day lost per 1,000 workers varies strongly, reaching an all-time low in the first decade of the twenty-first century but increasing strongly in recent years. On average, forty-three days were lost per 1,000 workers in the period 2017–2019, a figure comparable to the 1970s. The share of workers that participated in strikes was even higher than at any time since the 1960s.

Figure 21.4 Number of strikes, days not worked due to industrial action (per 1,000 employees) and workers involved, averages per decade

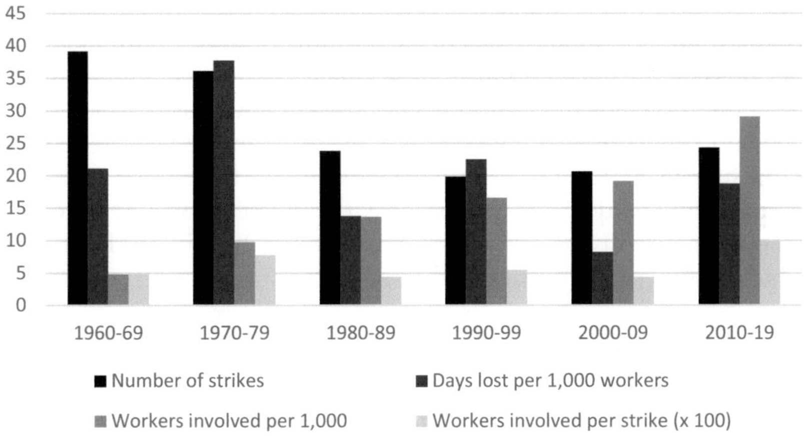

Note: Authors' calculation.
Source: CBS.

These strikes took place mainly in the public sector, in particular in education and health care, in which a number of 24-hour strikes were declared. This was because of increased dissatisfaction in the public sector with the fact that wages lagged behind the private sector as a consequence of 'austerity' policies. Another general trend in industrial action is that most strikes are relatively brief but involve a large proportion of the workforce. The average number of workers participating in a strike tripled from about 1,000 in the 1970s to almost 3,000 in the 2010s. This is partly explained by the shift to the public sector, where bargaining units are relatively large.

Union members usually receive strike benefit from their union. FNV pays an average strike benefit of €75.44 per day (€64 for the first five days, €87 after that).[15] Whereas in the past each affiliate had its own strike fund, currently FNV has one central strike fund, which amounts to €67 million.[16] If a strike is declared in a particular industry, the strikers will receive a benefit only if the confederation board approves the strike. CNV Vakmensen pays a similar amount.[17]

Unions also organize other forms of industrial action, such as rallies, work to rule actions and petitions. No statistics are available about such actions, so it is difficult to determine whether their frequency and size vary over time. Although general strikes are virtually absent in the Netherlands, the unions sometimes organize large demonstrations to put pressure on the government. The largest post-war union-organized demonstration took place on 2 October 2004 in Amsterdam, when about 300,000 people demonstrated against the government plan to abolish early retirement schemes. Later demonstrations have never attracted over 100,000 participants. For example, the largest union rally of recent years was a demonstration by teachers in October 2017 in The Hague, in which 60,000 people participated.

Political relations

In the past, relatively strong institutional ties existed between the union confederations and political parties, as part of the pillarized society. The breakdown of pillarization in the 1960s and 1970s also meant that the ties between the confederations and the political parties were loosened. Nevertheless, informal contacts and consultations between them continued to play an important role. Although not visible to the outside observer, there is ample anecdotal evidence that confederations and political parties often consult each other and align their stances with regard to important political issues. Nowadays, CNV maintains most contact with the Christian Democratic Appeal (CDA, Christen-Democratisch Appèl), whereas FNV has links with the social democratic Labour Party (PvdA, Partij van de Arbeid), as well as with the more radical left-wing Socialist Party (Socialistische Partij) and the Green Party (GroenLinks).

---

15 See https://www.fnv.nl/werk-inkomen/staken/stakingsuitkering

16 See https://www.vn.nl/fnv-transparant/. This is less than 10 % of total equity of FNV, which amounts to €739 million.

17 See https://www.cnvvakmensen.nl/diensten/kennisbank/stakingsuitkering

A recent example is the coordination between FNV, on one hand, and the PvdA and GroenLinks, on the other, during the negotiations between the confederations, the employers and the government about pension system reform in 2019. Because the centre-left government needed the support of the two left-wing parties to attain a majority in the Senate, the tuning between the confederations and those parties was an important precondition for passing the pension reform in Parliament.

Another indication that there are still important informal ties between the confederations and political parties is the significant number of former union officials who have become politicians in one of these parties. The best known example is Wim Kok, the former FNV chairman (1976–1985) who became leader of the PvdA in 1986 and later prime minister (1994–2002). More recent examples include former FNV chair Agnes Jongerius, who is now a member of the European Parliament for the PvdA, former CNV vice-chair Aart Jan de Geus, who became Minister of Social Affairs and Employment for the CDA, and former chair of Young-CNV Jesse Klaver, who is now leader of the Parliamentary group of GroenLinks.

The confederations also play an important role in the (neo-)corporatist Polder model, in which regular consultation of the confederations – usually together with the employers' associations – by the government about important socio-economic issues takes place in various forms. The tripartite Socio-Economic Council is one of the government's most influential advisory bodies. The bipartite Labour Foundation is not only an important body for national-level discussions between the social partners, but also acts as a representative of their common interests vis-à-vis the government. Many social pacts concluded since the 1982 Wassenaar Agreement have been the outcome of negotiations between the Labour Foundation and the government. Finally, there is also ample informal consulting between union and government officials. The key players in the Polder model – union officials, employers' representatives and ministers – know each other's phone numbers and will not hesitate to call or text if they want to discuss a pressing issue. As a consequence, important changes in socio-economic policy never pass Parliament unless they have been extensively discussed with the social partners and only rarely without the consent of the confederations.

Populist right-wing parties have enjoyed increasing success in the Netherlands in recent decades, including the Freedom Party (PVV, *Partij voor de Vrijheid*) and, more recently, the Forum for Democracy

(FvD, *Forum voor Democratie*). Whereas the confederations were quite outspoken against racism and xenophobia during the 1980s and 1990s, in recent decades they have been rather silent on these issues. There is an internal debate on whether FNV should publicly denounce the ideas of PVV and FvD (*Trouw*, 20 April 2019). The call from Geert Wilders of the PVV for 'fewer Moroccans' in Dutch society during the 2014 municipal election campaign was an exception, as confederations publicly denounced this statement for its racist and discriminatory message (Roosblad and Berntsen 2017: 187). Earlier, when anti-Islam discourse intensified after the murder of filmmaker Theo van Gogh in 2004, FNV started the 'Shop Floor Dialogue' project: workplace meetings to stimulate dialogue between workers from various background (ibid.).

Societal power

Public trust in Dutch trade unions has been relatively high and stable, with average percentages fluctuating between 60 and 70 per cent. The high degree of trust in unions does not translate into stable membership numbers, however. While public campaigning is not one of the prime instruments used by the confederations, it is gaining importance. When 300,000 people protested against government plans to abolish early retirement schemes in 2004 (see above), this was unprecedented. Other examples are the general publicity campaigns for union work, such as the FNV campaign 'This is how the Netherlands works' (*Zo werkt Nederland*). In the cleaners' campaign, and more recently in the Young & United campaign against youth wages, it was considered important to gain targeted support from the general public.

Obtaining sympathy and support from the general public was an important element in the cleaners' campaign, for instance, via 'inverse-strike' actions such as cleaning premises extra-thoroughly (Mundlak 2020: 201). Public support for the cleaners' demands was especially important to compensate for the cleaners' structurally weak power position. Many of them work via temporary work agencies or subcontractors on small contracts, which are easily discontinued by employers.

In the FNV's Young & United youth wage campaign, young people were the face of the campaign. Via various media outlets, young people shared the difficulties they experience in sustaining themselves with low youth wages. The campaign appealed to the broader public with its slogan 'half wage for adult work'. One of the public statements made at the start of the campaign was a young stock clerk taking off half his business suit in front of the Ahold supermarkets' shareholders meeting to symbolize the fact that youth wages are only half a full wage. Such creative actions attracted the media attention needed to raise public support for the abolition of youth wages. In only a few months 130,000 signatories were collected to abolish youth wages. Even municipalities and large companies issued their support for the abolition of youth wages (Berntsen 2019).

Confederations on occasion build coalitions with NGOs or social movements, although this was more common in the past. Recent examples are the coalition in health care 'Save the health care sector' (*Red de zorg*) and the campaign to increase the minimum wage to €14 per hour. The 'for 14' claim is supported by various municipalities.[18] In care, FNV initiated a petition (*volkspetitie*), which obtained 700,000 signatures in six weeks, calling upon the secretary of state to stop budget cuts in the sector. CNV supported this, as did various organizations and prominent people. Recently, a coalition was formed with the grassroots initiative in primary education called 'Primary education in action' (*PO in actie*). When *PO in actie*, fighting for higher wages and reduced work pressure for schoolteachers, gathered support from 40,000 teachers within a few months in 2017, the unions decided to join forces with them. Together they called for a strike and in October 2017, 60,000 teachers protested in The Hague. This yielded extra government investments in the sector.

FNV and CNV and their affiliates are present on the common social media platforms, such as Facebook, LinkedIn, Twitter and Instagram. FNV has over 40,000 likes on Facebook, 16,000 followers on Twitter, almost 10,000 followers on LinkedIn, and almost 4,000 followers on Instagram. CNV has almost 3,000 likes on Facebook, 6,000 followers on Twitter, almost 4,000 followers on LinkedIn and 200 followers on Instagram.[19] FNV Young & United has gathered almost 30,000 likes on Facebook, a number unequalled on the other social media channels. The social media presence of the youth branch of CNV on Facebook outweighs that of the CNV confederation. CNV presence on Twitter is more developed than on Instagram compared with that of FNV.

---

18 See https://www.fnv.nl/nieuwsbericht/algemeen-nieuws/2020/06/volgende-gemeente-steunt-fnv-bij-pleidooi-voor-hog

19 Likes and followers as of 7 July 2020.

Trade union policies towards the European Union

Dutch confederations have been deeply involved in international and EU bodies from the outset. Over recent years, the European domain has been gaining in importance. The still prominent position of Dutch confederations at the international level was, for instance, reflected in the election of FNV official Catelene Passchier as president of the Workers' Group of the International Labour Organization in 2017. Compared with FNV, CNV invests fewer resources in EU work (Gumbrell-McCormick and Hyman 2013: 165). CNV, FNV and VCP are all members of the European Trade Union Confederation (ETUC). CNV is also part of the European Union of Christian Democratic Workers (EUCDW) via EUCDW-Netherlands. FNV and CNV affiliates are members of the European Trade Union Federations (ETUF) at industry level.

Dutch confederations are involved in several cross-border union initiatives. A well-known example is participation in the Doorn group,[20] an initiative of cross-border union cooperation to coordinate collective bargaining policy between unions in the Netherlands, Germany, Belgium and Luxembourg. In the border regions, there are Inter-regional Trade Union Councils (IVR, *Interregionale VakbondsRaad*) in which unions from each side of the border participate to advocate for the rights and interests of border workers and encourage cross-border mobility for work. The IVR collaborate with public employment agencies and employers within the European jobs network EURES (FNV 2014: 37).

The confederations' stance towards the European project is generally favourable. Regarding the imposed transitional restrictions in the Netherlands following Eastern European enlargement in 2004, they were initially divided: FNV opposed transitional measures, because it might encourage irregular employment; while CNV supported restrictions to cushion the impact of labour inflows. When it came to the Dutch vote on the Constitutional Treaty in June 2005, which resulted in a 62 per cent 'no' vote, FNV urged its members to vote 'yes', because it saw the European Constitution as a step forward, but it did not actively engage in the campaign (Gumbrell-McCormick and Hyman 2013: 175). More recently, FNV adopts a more critical stance calling for a Europe with a strong social dimension. This is for instance echoed in FNV's 2014 vision document on Europe titled 'FNV on the move towards a social

20 Named after the Dutch town where the first meeting took place in 1998.

Europe'. In this, FNV calls for, among other things, European social (minimum) norms and cross-border inspections to halt social dumping practices (FNV 2014). Similar calls have been made at the industrial level. In 2016, FNV and the European Transport Union urged the Dutch government, then with the EU presidency, to create European regulations for fair road transport (FNV 2016b).

Conclusions

Dutch unions are characterized by a stable formal position, but a crumbling power base. On one hand, unions still play a crucial role in determining the terms of employment for three out of four employees, through collective bargaining with the employers, and by influencing government policies via national-level consulting mechanisms. On the other hand, unions are gradually losing ground in achieving their ultimate goals, as illustrated by, among other things, the stagnation of real negotiated wages, the steady decline of the wage share in GDP, the dominance of neoliberal government policies, the retreat of the standard employment relationship and companies' increasing evasion of collective agreements. The secular decline of union density and the growing power of capital compared with labour are important driving forces behind these trends.

To conclude, we briefly discuss which of Visser's (2019) four possible futures for the unions seems to be most likely for the Dutch unions. To start with Visser's last scenario, there are no signs of an upcoming *revitalization* of the unions. Even though union officials regularly express their confidence that they will succeed in reclaiming some of the lost terrain, all attempts to revitalize them have not yet yielded tangible results. Even new activities and campaigns that are generally considered successful, such as organizing activities among cleaners or the campaign to abolish the youth minimum wage, have not left a noticeable mark on the unions' structural position, as measured for example by the union density rate or the wage share in GDP. Of course, it is imaginable that further erosion of union power will incentivize unions to become more active in the future, with activities that will have more lasting impact, but up till now this is wishful thinking.

The *substitution* scenario is recurrently suggested by critics of the current union movement, who claim that the unions are twentieth-century institutions that are not adapted to the challenges of the twenty-first century. It is far from clear, however, which organizations could take over the unions' role. In some companies, works councils negotiate terms of employment with management, but there are just as many doubts about the legitimacy and representativeness of works councils as about the unions. Moreover, works councils are largely absent in small companies and at the industry level. Some new unions, which are not based on the traditional member model, such as AVV, claim to better represent the interests of all workers, because they base their demands on surveys of the entire staff of a company or industry. Because these small unions are financially fully dependent on the employers' contribution, however, their independence is questionable, to say the least.

Even though substitution of the unions' role by other organizations does not seem to be a likely future, a more realistic option is that unions will increasingly cooperate or even form coalitions with other NGOs, as they have done quite often in the past, mostly in joint campaigns for reform of government policies. Such joint campaigns, however, usually address issues that lie outside unions' core activity of negotiating terms of employment with employers. Therefore, these kinds of cooperation do not interfere with the unions' dominant role in collective bargaining and it is unclear how this might structurally strengthen their position.

Even though collective bargaining coverage is still around 75 per cent, some tendencies seem to point to a *dualization* of industrial relations. That is to say, an increasing share of the labour force is not covered (anymore) by collective agreements that are concluded by the largest union, FNV. From the latter's perspective, labour market dualization might already be a fact.

In the private service sector, unions play a marginal role, particularly in retail, wholesale and hospitality, where union density is low, the terms of employment unfavourable and the share of non-standard employment large and increasing. On the other hand, the unions remain relatively strong in manufacturing, transport, education, health care and public administration, industries that are characterized by higher union density rates and relatively good terms of employment. Although there are thus clear signs of dualization, it is not very likely that the unions will disappear completely from the industries in which they are relatively weak, which is a testament to FNV organizing efforts to rebuild union power in some of these low-wage sectors. Most employers – and especially the employers' associations at the industry level – still endorse the importance of collective agreements concluded with the 'traditional' unions. The weakening of the unions makes collective bargaining even more attractive for them, because they can realize more of their preferences, while maintaining the legitimacy vis-à-vis their employees of an agreement signed by one or several unions. Thus, despite clear dualization tendencies, it is not likely that in the future the unions will be fully absent from a substantial part of the labour market.

Finally, there is the marginalization scenario. If we extrapolate the trends of the past two decades, marginalization seems the most likely scenario for the Dutch unions. To date, there have been no indications that the union density rate has bottomed out, and trends such as globalization, technological progress and migration will most likely continue to weaken the unions' position vis-à-vis employers. The unions' formal position is still strong and stable, however. The 2019 agreement between the unions, the employers and the government on a profound pension reform underlines that the unions still play a pivotal role in realizing important policy changes. Arguably, however, they can continue to play this role only as long as the employers and the government are willing to allow it. As the erosion of union membership and power continues, ultimately a point may be reached at which the employers and the government no longer need the unions to secure societal and political support for their aims. If that happens, their formal position may be endangered, too.

By and large, this implies that Dutch unions are on the road to potential marginalization in the future. Unless, of course, something unexpected happens that changes the downward slope on which the unions currently find themselves into an upward slope.

References

Becker U. (2005) An example of competitive corporatism? The Dutch political economy 1983–2004 in critical examination, Journal of European Public Policy, 12(6), 1078–1102.

Berntsen L. (2019) Vakbonden En Jongeren Belgische Inspiratie Voor de Nederlandse Vakbeweging, Amsterdam, De Burcht.

Berntsen L. and Lillie N. (2016) Hyper-mobile migrant workers and Dutch trade union representation strategies at the Eemshaven construction sites, Economic and Industrial Democracy, 37(1), 171–187. DOI: 10.1177/0143831X14537357.

CNV (2011) Statuten CNV, Utrecht, CNV.

Connolly H., Marino S. and Martinez Lucio M. (2017) 'Justice for Janitors' goes Dutch: the limits and possibilities of unions' adoption of organizing in a context of regulated social partnership, Work, Employment and Society, 31(2), 319–335. DOI: 10.1177/0950017016677943.

CPB (2016) What are the wage effects of extending collective labour agreements? Evidence from the Netherlands, CPB Background Document, The Hague, CPB Netherlands Bureau for Economic Policy Analysis.

de Beer P. (2013) Dutch trade union confederation in crisis, Transfer: European Review of Labour and Research, 19(1), 129–132. DOI: 10.1177/1024258912471265.

de Beer P. and Berntsen L. (2019) Vakbondslidmaatschap onder druk in Nederland, maar niet in België, Tijdschrift voor Arbeidsvraagstukken, 35(3), 255–274.

de Beer P. and Keune M. (2018) Dutch unions in a time of crisis, in Lehndorff S., Dribbusch H. and Schulten T. (eds) Rough Waters – European Trade Unions in a Time of Crises, Brussels, ETUI, 235–258.

de Beer P. and van der Valk P. (2020) Effectief Vakbondswerk? Een Verkennend Onderzoek Naar Factoren Die de Effectiviteit van Vakbondsactiviteiten Beïnvloeden, Amsterdam, De Burcht.

Delhaas R. and Davidson D. (2020) Cao in de uitverkoop, Argos. https://www.vpro.nl/argos/lees/nieuws/2020/cao-in-de-uitverkoop.html

de Vries (2019) Directie FNV trekt reorganisatieplan in, gaat in gesprek met vakbondspersoneel, De Volkskrant, 21 May 2019.

de Waard P. (2018) Waarom betalen niet-leden ook vakbondscontributie? De Volkskrant 11 July 2018.

Financieel Dagblad 22 January 2016, FNV is voorlopig nog niet uit de financiële problemen.

FNV (2010) Accent op werk en eerlijk delen, Arbeidsvoorwaardennota 2010, Amsterdam, FNV.

FNV (2014) FNV in Beweging Voor Een Socialer Europa, Utrecht, FNV.

FNV (2016a) 07.05 Verenigingsplan FNV En FNV Zelfstandigen, FNV.

FNV (2016b) Visie Op Eerlijk Vervoer: In Heel Europa, Utrecht, FNV.

Gumbrell-McCormick R. and Hyman R. (2013) Trade Unions in Western Europe: Hard Times, Hard Choices, Oxford, Oxford University Press.

Jansma (2019) Vakbonden krijgen geld van werkgevers: wat betekent dat voor hun onafhankelijkheid?, NOS, 17 July 2019.

Julen (2020) Frictie bij bonden teistert cao-onderhandelingen technische groothandels, Trouw 29, January 2020.

Keune M. and Tros F. (2014) Country report: The Netherlands, Adapt special bulletin, No. 4/2014, Modena, Adapt/YOUnion - Union for Youth.

Kloosterboer D. (2007) Innovative Trade Union Strategies, Utrecht, FNV.

Knotter A. (2017) Justice for Janitors Goes Dutch. Precarious Labour and Trade Union Response in the Cleaning Industry (1988–2012): A Transnational History, International Review for Social History, 62(1), 1–35.

Kranendonk M. and de Beer P. (2016) What Explains the Union Membership Gap between Migrants and Natives?, British Journal of Industrial Relations, 54(4), 846–869. DOI: 10.1111/bjir.12192.

Kuijpers D. and Van Keken K. (2020) Vakbond FNV niet transparent over inkomen eigen bestuurders, Vrij Nederland, 11 June 2020.

Ministerie van SZW (2019) Cao-afspraken 2018, The Hague, Ministry of Social Affairs and Employment.

Mundlak G. (2020) Organizing Matters: Two Logics of Trade Union Representation. GraphiCommunicator, Cheltenham, UK, Northampton, MA, USA, Edward Elgar Publishing. DOI: 10.1353/ecs.2017.0006.

Roosblad J. (2013) Trade unions and the representation of migrant and ethnic minority workers: challenges in deteriorating industrial relations, in Van Heelsum A. and Garces-Mascarenas B. (eds) Filling in Penninx's Heuristic Model, Amsterdam, Amsterdam University Press, 91–109.

Roosblad J. and Berntsen L. (2017) The Netherlands: Finding common ground in an increasingly fragmented workforce, in Marino S., Roosblad J. and Penninx R. (eds) Trade Unions and Migrant Workers: New Contexts and Challenges in Europe, Cheltenham, UK, Northampton, MA, USA, Edward Elgar Publishing, 178–199.

Tamminga M. (2017) De Vuist van de Vakbond: Een Recente Geschiedenis, Amsterdam, Antwerpen, De Bezige Bij.

Trouw (2019) Tweestrijd binnen de FNV: moet de bond zich uitspreken tegen FvD en PVV of niet? 20 April 2019.

van der Valk P. (2020) Factoren Die Vakbondswerk Beïnvloeden: Een Verkennend Onderzoek, Amsterdam, De Burcht.

Vandaele K. (2013) Union responses to young workers since the Great Recession in Ireland, the Netherlands and Sweden: are youth structures reorienting the union agenda? Transfer, 19(3), 381–397.

Vandaele K. (2020) From street protest to 'improvisational unionism': platform-based food delivery couriers in Belgium and the Netherlands, Friedricht-Ebert-Stiftung.

Visser J. (2019) Trade Unions in the Balance, ILO ACTRAV Working Paper, Geneva, ILO.

Visser J. and Hemerijck A. (1996) A Dutch miracle, Amsterdam, Amsterdam University Press.

Abbreviations

ACP Algemene Christelijke Politiebond (General Christian Police Union)

AVV Alternatief Voor Vakbond (Alternative for Trade Union)

AWVN Algemene Werkgeversvereniging Nederland (General Employers Association)

CDA Christen-Democratisch Appèl (Christian Democratic Appeal)

CNV Christelijk Nationaal Vakverbond (Christian National Confederation)

EU European Union

FIB Stichting Fonds Industriële Bonden (Foundation Industrial Unions Fund)

FNV Federatie Nederlandse Vakbeweging (Federation of Dutch Trade Unions)

FvD *Forum voor Democratie* (Forum for Democracy)

IVR Interregionale VakbondsRaad (Inter-regional Trade Union Councils)

MHP Vakcentrale voor Middelbaar en Hoger Personeel (Confederation for Middle and Senior Staff)

PvdA Socialistische Partij (Socialist Party)

PVV Partij voor de Vrijheid (Freedom Party)

SER Sociaal-Economische Raad (Social-Economic Council)

StvdA Stichting van de Arbeid (Labour Foundation)

VCP Vakcentrale voor Professionals (Confederation for Professionals)

zzp zelfstandigen zonder personeel (solo self-employed persons)

Chapter 22

Poland: Trade unions developing after a decline

Jan Czarzasty and Adam Mrozowicki

Polish trade unionism, on one hand, is typical of Central and Eastern Europe (CEE), where by and large unions are institutionally weak and have experienced a sharp decline in membership since the end of state socialism (Crowley 2004; Ost 2005). Over the past ten years, however, Poland's trade unions, in the tradition of the Solidarity movement and with extensive international links and pioneering union organizing in the early 2000s, have managed to develop a range of innovative practices to counteract their decline. Remarkably, such practices unfolded in Poland earlier and more extensively than in other CEE countries (Bernaciak and Kahancová 2017).

This chapter explores the contemporary situation of trade unions in Poland and addresses the positive and negative aspects of trade union attempts to re-establish their position after decades of decline, following the systemic transformation after 1989. The diagnosis is mixed: some positive changes, mainly in terms of increased union capacity to define social problems and influence public opinion, alongside continuous, albeit slowing, decline in membership, the return of inter-union, politically driven conflicts and limited advances in collective bargaining. It has been argued that Polish unions pursue a 'logic of influence' (Schmitter and Streeck 1981) based on their 'societal resources' (Schmalz et al. 2018) and, to lesser degree, ad hoc political coalitions rather than a 'logic of membership' aimed at increasing membership numbers, diversity and internal solidarity, in particular with and among peripheral segments of the workforce, such as precarious workers.

Table 22.1 Principal characteristics of trade unionism in Poland

	1981	**2000**	**2018**
Total trade union membership	12,500,000	2,603,000	1,500,000
Women as a proportion of total membership	48 %	43 %***	56 %*****
Gross union density	65 %*	20 %	11 %
Net union density	65 %*	20 %	13 %******
Number of confederations	2	2	3
Number of affiliated unions (federations)	23**	106****	131
Number of independent unions	0	n.a.	± 2,175 [8]
Collective bargaining coverage	n.a.	25 %	17 %*******
Principal level of collective bargaining	Industry	Company	Company
Days not worked due to industrial action per 1,000 workers	n.a.	8	<1

Note: *1980; **1975; ***2003; ****2002; *****2017; ******2019; *******2015; Gross union density expresses trade union membership as a proportion of the employed labour force, including the unemployed. We calculated gross union density taking into account the number of employees provided by Eurostat's Labour Force Survey (LFS) and the number of unemployed provided by Statistics Poland for 2000 and 2018. Given that in 1981 official unemployment did not exist, gross and net union density are equal; Solidarity (NSZZ Solidarność) is considered a confederation despite being, technically, a unitary union.

Source: Appendix A1; Total trade union membership for 2018 is estimated based on Statistics Poland (GUS 2019); Gross union density for 1980 and union density for all years is estimated based on Public Opinion Research Centre surveys (Feliksiak 2017; Wenzel 2009); The sources for the number of affiliated unions are official OPZZ data and the FZZ website for 2018 (all nationwide affiliates are counted as federations); The number of independent unions for 2019 is based on administrative data from GUS (2019), authors' calculations.

The basic features of Polish trade unions are documented in Table 22.1. In relation to the meaning and identity of trade unionism (Hyman 2001), the nationally representative confederations – the Independent Self-Governing Trade Union 'Solidarity' (NSZZ Solidarność, *Niezależny Samorządny Związek Zawodowy 'Solidarność'*),[1] the All-Poland Alliance of Trade Unions (OPZZ, *Ogólnopolskie Porozumienie Związków Zawodowych*), and the Trade Unions Forum (FZZ, *Forum Związków*

1 Formally, NSZZ Solidarność is a general workers union (unitary). It is often referred to as a 'confederation', however, especially when discussed alongside two other major organizations (OPZZ and FZZ), which are indeed trade union confederations.

Zawodowych) – represent a mixture of market and society identities. On one hand, they aspire to play the role of social partner, influencing economic affairs and policymaking through social dialogue and tripartite institutions. On the other, because of their organizational and institutional weakness they are restricted to the role of representatives of workers' voice at the company level (market/business unionism) (Figure 22.1). We can also observe some rather marginal unions – such as the All-Poland Trade Union Workers' Initiative (OZZ IP, *Ogólnopolski Związek Zawodowy Inicjatywa Pracownicza*) or the Confederation of Labour (KP, *Konfederacja Pracy*), affiliated to OPZZ – leaning on class-oriented unionism. This type of radical political unionism is exceptional in CEE (Mrozowicki and Maciejewska 2017).

Figure 22.1 The identity of Polish trade unionism

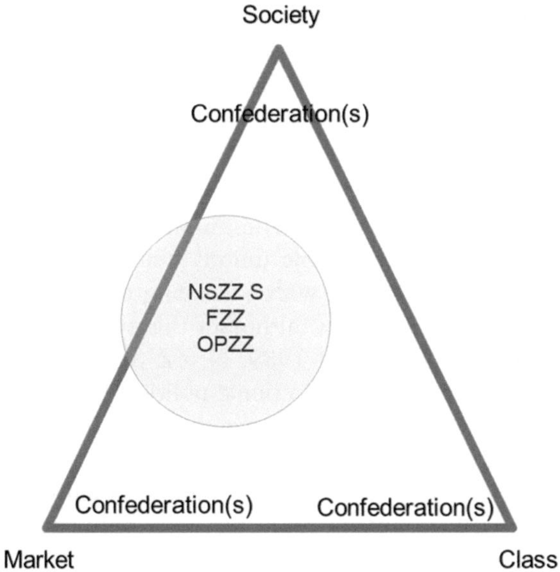

Source: Authors' elaboration based on Hyman (2001).

Historical background and principal features of the industrial relations system

The current shape of industrial relations in Poland can largely be explained in terms of its complicated past, mirroring Poland's modern history, with all its twists and discontinuities. Trade union history in the country dates back to the late nineteenth century when the first socialist, Christian and nationalist unions and workers' associations were formed (Hojka 2006). Employers' organizations emerged in the early 1920s. The trade union movement in the Second Republic of Poland (1918–1939) was divided along confessional, ideological and political lines. In 1938, some 1 million workers were unionized, around 8–10 per cent of the total workforce (Hauner 1986: 99).

The Second World War and the introduction of state socialism in 1944 meant a break with pre-war traditions. In 1949, the trade union movement was centralized under the Association of Trade Unions (ZZZ, *Zrzeszenie Związków Zawodowych*) and subordinated to the Polish United Workers' Party (PZPR, *Polska Zjednoczona Partia Robotnicza*). Workers' protests involving economic issues; political and national independence from the USSR; and industrial democracy, rights of association and workers' self-government demands took place in 1956, 1970, 1976 and 1980. The latter protests led to the emergence of NSZZ Solidarność in 1980, which was the first independent trade union and the largest mass civil society movement in the communist bloc, comprising some 9.5 million people.

Following the rise of independent unions, the Leninist model of industrial relations collapsed. Trade unions were no longer part of the party-state bureaucracy charged with overseeing workers and serving as a workplace-level welfare agency, although this system continued elsewhere in the Eastern Bloc until 1989. NSZZ Solidarność was a massive social movement and an institutional political representation of the entire society over against the undemocratic government. The crushing of the movement by a military junta in 1981 did not result in a return to the 'old ways', however. The short-lived union pluralism was replaced by a peculiar model, seemingly 'monistic', with only one formal union confederation, but accompanied by the continuous underground operations of the delegalized NSZZ Solidarność. The new, official confederation OPZZ emerged as a pyramid, whose base comprised strong, very much self-steering workplace unions, relatively weak industrial structures and a senior leadership with political influence, as they were part of the ruling elite. In institutional terms, however, they were not able to exert firm control over the lower layers of the organization.

The legacy of state socialism for Polish industrial relations is twofold. On one hand, Polish industrial relations still struggle with the burden of the authoritarian socialism era, in common with all CEE EU Member States. On the other, the post-communist legacy in Poland differs from other CEE Member States because of the unique experience of NSZZ Solidarność in 1980–1981. The tradition of workers' protests under state socialism also provides something of a repertoire for trade unions in contemporary Poland. This tradition is manifested in the intersection of economic demands with political demands and attempts to create stronger links between civil society organizations and social movements and trade unions (Mrozowicki and Kajta 2018; Mrozowicki and Maciejewska 2017).

The two big 'historical' unions sat on opposite sides during the 'Roundtable' talks in early 1989, a milestone on the way to democracy: OPZZ was in the government camp, while NSZZ Solidarność formed the core of the opposition. These negotiations had wide-ranging consequences for the future of industrial relations. First, the idea of 'union elections' at the workplace, promoted by OPZZ, failed in the face of NSZZ Solidarność opposition. Subsequently, so-called competitive pluralism emerged and lasting fragmentation and internal conflicts split the union movement (Gardawski 2003). The accords agreed by the unions in 1989 shaped the legal environment, which allows for the existence of an unlimited number of unions at workplace level by setting very low thresholds for recognition and representativeness criteria. Second, the crucial political role of trade unions at the time, especially of NSZZ Solidarność, as the cornerstone of the entire anti-communist opposition, contributed to the demobilization of labour and established a cleavage between the two major confederations for decades. Political and institutional factors disempowered trade unions in the context of massive economic restructuring, liquidation and privatization of state-owned companies, and a rapidly growing number of small and micro-enterprises. As result, deunionization proceeded swiftly, and during the 1990s union density fell by half from almost 50 per cent to about 25 per cent (Table 22.2).

Both major confederations remained active in politics on opposite sides of the barricade known as the 'post-communist divide' (Grabowska 2004). Their political entanglement paved the way for foundation of another national confederation, FZZ positioning itself as 'apolitical' in 2002. The political scene was split by historically determined loyalties and interests. A moderating role in national industrial relations was played by the Tripartite Commission on Social and Economic Affairs (TK,

Trójstronna Komisja ds. Społeczno-Gospodarczych) established in 1994. Its main statutory function was to maintain social peace. Regardless of the existence of the Tripartite Commission, the company is the principal level of collective bargaining in Poland. Collective bargaining coverage is low, sectoral collective agreements are very rare and tripartite institutions are 'illusory' (Ost 2011).

The 'post-communist divide' started to fade in 2005, and vanished after 2007, with the election of the centre-right coalition government of the Civic Platform (PO, *Platforma Obywatelska*) and Polish Peasant's Party (PSL, *Polskie Stronnictwo Ludowe*), led by Donald Tusk. This was particularly the case when it came to relationships between central government and trade unions. The first (2007–2011) and second (2011–2013) Tusk cabinets came to treat the increasingly weak trade union movement as a lower ranking stakeholder, treatment it also applied to employers' organizations. It reoriented its policies towards global financial markets, especially after 2009. The changed preferences were manifest in the crisis in social dialogue that led to the demise of the Tripartite Commission in 2013.

The restoration of tripartism with the establishment of a new central tripartite body, the Social Dialogue Council (RDS, *Rada Dialogu Społecznego*) in 2015, coincided with the ascent to power of the Law and Justice (PiS, *Prawo i Sprawiedliwość*) party. Early hopes for a revival of social dialogue diminished relatively quickly, with RDS being sidelined. While NSZZ Solidarność and the PiS government initially developed a 'special relationship', union influence on policymaking seems to have deteriorated, also because the government eagerly 'hijacked' the union agenda.

Structure of trade unions and union democracy

A basic feature of Polish trade unionism is its long-standing fragmentation into three large nationally representative confederations: NSZZ Solidarność, OPZZ and FZZ, along with a number of small autonomous unions. The total number of active unions in Poland was 12,500 in 2018 (GUS 2019), of which 82.6 per cent (10,325) were affiliated to NSZZ Solidarność, OPZZ or FZZ, and 17.4 per cent (2,175) were unaffiliated. The three confederations covered about 87.5 per cent of all unionized workers, while autonomous unions represented the remaining 12.5 per cent of the unionized workforce in 2018 (GUS 2019, own calculation).

NSZZ Solidarność, OPZZ and FZZ are all-grades multi-sector confederations, organizing workers across industries.[2] To be nationally representative, under Polish law, they must have more than 300,000 members across at least half of all industries specified by the Polish Classification of (Economic) Activity. Following the emergence of FZZ in 2002, the landscape of trade unionism at the national level has remained fairly stable with no major amalgamations or acquisitions, despite a gradual consolidation trend. The total number of autonomous unions, the latter understood as those not affiliated to one of the three nationally representative confederations, decreased from 2,700 in 2014, when they comprised 21 per cent of total active unions, to 2,175 in 2018, when they comprised 17.4 per cent of active unions (GUS 2015, authors' calculations).[3]

The legal environment weakens Polish unions' organizational power. First, the Trade Union Act makes it difficult to organize workers in companies with fewer than ten employees, the minimum threshold for establishing a basic trade union organization at company level. Nearly 96 per cent of all economic entities have fewer than ten staff and micro-firms account for around 40 per cent of all employees. Second, legislation supports the decentralization of union structures because company-level unions are 'separate legal entities that retain significant autonomy vis-à-vis union federations and confederations' (Gardawski and Meardi 2010: 17). Annex 22.2 illustrates the various types of trade union structures in Poland and the relations between them.

The main divide within the trade union movement is historical and political. NSZZ Solidarność, established in 1980 in the wake of workers' economic and political protests against the communist authorities, has retained its identity as a right-leaning, Christian-democratic trade union. OPZZ was established in 1984 as the successor of the official Association of Trade Unions (ZZZ, *Zrzeszenie Związków Zawodowych*). The conflict over NSZZ Solidarność property confiscated by the communist

---

2 In naming trade union types, we refer to the vocabulary developed in earlier ETUI reports. The most often mentioned types include: (1) all-grades multi-sector union – 'a union organizing all white-collar and blue-collar occupations within several sectors'; (2) general all-grades union – 'a union with a broad membership base (traditionally un- and semi-skilled workers) without clear sectoral boundaries.' In addition, we also distinguish 'craft unions' (union of blue-collar craft(s)) and various types of white-collar unions (multi-sector, single sector, general) (Ebbinghaus and Visser 2000: 13).

3 This trend is discussed in the next section.

authorities during Martial Law in 1981 and handed over to OPZZ, as well as the divergent political identities of the two largest confederations long set the scene for Polish unionism.[4] The third and youngest trade union confederation, FZZ, was established in 2002 as a politically neutral organization. Professional unions, which were either established after 1989 or broke away from OPZZ and NSZZ Solidarność, comprise a large share of FZZ affiliated unions.

The three largest, nationally representative confederations differ in terms of their internal structures.[5] OPZZ is a confederation with seventy-eight affiliates, mostly professional union federations, industrial unions and general unions. OPZZ affiliates are grouped into seven 'branches' or industry structures, whose activities are coordinated by the Council of Branches: (1) mining and energy; (2) manufacturing; (3) education and science; (4) public services; (5) construction and timber; (6) transport; (7) commerce, services, culture and art. There are also sixteen regional structures in 'voivodships', regional administrative units in Poland. OPZZ is governed by a National Congress, the main 'legislative body'; a Council, the 'legislative' body acting between Congresses; a Presidium, the 'executive' and 'legislative' body; and an Audit Committee, elected for a four-year term (Gardawski and Meardi 2010: 39). The Council consists of the representatives of branch structures, regional structures and the Presidium. Historically, the role of branch structures in OPZZ has been more important than territorial ones and it remains a decentralized confederation, in which control of the presidium over affiliates is limited (Czarzasty et al. 2014).

NSZZ Solidarność is the largest national-level trade union organization at the time of writing. NSZZ Solidarność is a unitary trade union in which 'company-level union organizations do not have separate legal status', but all have the same statutes and name (Gardawski and Meardi 2010: 34). Compared with OPZZ, NSZZ Solidarność is much more centralized and its organization is based on a hierarchy of company-level union organizations, inter-company union organizations and regional branches (Gardawski and Meardi 2010: 41). The union consists of thirty-eight 'regions' or territorial structures and fourteen branch

---

4 The issue of union property was eventually resolved only in the mid-2000s and was one reason for the successful blocking of OPZZ's application to ETUC by NSZZ Solidarność (Mrozowicki 2017).

5 This part is an updated summary of our earlier report (Gardawski and Meardi 2010).

secretariats: (1) energy and mine workers; (2) metalworkers; (3) food industry workers; (4) science and education workers; (5) rural workers; (6) construction workers; (7) chemical workers; (8) postal workers; (9) transport workers; (10) public services workers; (11) media and entertainment workers; (12) banks, commerce and insurance workers; (13) natural resources, environmental protection and forestry workers; and (14) pensioners. Most 'secretariats' are divided into 'sections'. The main decision-making body is the National Congress of Delegates (*Krajowy Zjazd Delegatów*), elected by the delegates to regional assemblies. The executive power at the national level lies in the National Commission (*Komisja Krajowa*), which comprises regional leaders, leaders of branch secretariats and members elected by the National Congress of Delegates. The executive bodies, company committees, Regional Boards, Secretariat Councils and National Commission are elected for five-year terms.

The youngest and smallest nationally representative confederation is FZZ. The main strategic reason for consolidating initially seventeen independent and breakaway unions into FZZ in 2002 was the Act on Tripartite Commission of 2001 which established the criteria for national-level representativeness at 300,000 members. This threshold was attainable for any professional or industrial union. The confederation consists of fifty-four unitary unions and union federations of all types, with its strongest representation of workers in public services, health care, education, transport and state security. The main reason for the growing number of affiliates was the tendency of the new confederation to attract not only formerly independent unions seeking leverage in joining a nationally representative organization, but also those previously affiliated to OPZZ.

FZZ also has sixteen voivodship (regional) boards to which sixty-six smaller unions are directly affiliated. Of the three confederations FZZ is the most decentralized. It does not currently have branch structures allowing the organization of affiliates in particular industries: these were abandoned in 2009 because of a lack of resources. The highest statutory body of the confederation is the national Congress (*Kongres*), which elects the Main Union Board (*Zarząd Główny*), the Presidium and the National Audit Committee for a four-year term. Congress delegates are elected by member organizations on the basis of three delegates per organization plus one additional delegate per 10,000 members. Member organizations also have the right to one seat on the Union Board.

The three nationally representative confederations developed special structures to make them more inclusive towards special groups of members. In the case of OPZZ, the special commissions involve young people and women. Since 2009 there has also been an ombudsman for the rights of LGBT+ employees. In NSZZ Solidarność, there are the National Section of Young People and the National Section of Women. FZZ also has a Youth Commission. The unionization of young people in Poland, however, remains relatively low: 4 per cent of people aged 18–24 in 2017 compared with 11 per cent of the general working population (Feliksiak 2017). Similarly, despite bottom-up mobilization of women in many industries – such as health care, education and retail – the leadership of the main trade union confederations is predominantly male. There were only seven women out of 104 National Commission members of NSZZ Solidarność in the 2018–2023 term; eighteen women out of seventy-seven members of the OPZZ council in the 2018–2022 term; and twenty-five women out of seventy-five members of the Main Union Board of FZZ in the 2018–2022 term. Notably, FZZ's President for the 2018–2022 term is a woman. Nevertheless, no quotas have been introduced in the major confederations, and indeed, to the knowledge of the authors, in any Polish trade unions with regard to female representation on union boards.

There is little information on the organizational structures of trade unions not affiliated to NSZZ Solidarność, OPZZ or FZZ. Earlier research suggests that they include all types of unions in terms of organizational levels – company unions, inter-company unions, unitary unions and federations – and coverage (general, all grades and single grades, craft, blue-collar white-collar unions). A good example of 'competitive pluralism' (Gardawski 2003) is the situation at Polish Post (Poczta Polska), where eighty-seven trade unions operate in 2021. In 2014 more than one trade union operated in only 23 per cent of unionized companies and in just 1 per cent of companies there were more than five unions (GUS 2015: 11). Competitive pluralism often involves the emergence of yellow unions. There are also examples of successful new radical unions, such as the anarcho-syndicalist Workers' Initiative (OZZ IP, *Ogólnopolski Związek Zawodowy 'Inicjatywa Pracownicza'*), established in 2001 and experiencing membership growth from 700 in 2018 to 3,500 in 2020. Thanks to peer-group and community-based method of organizing – in the so-called milieu committees – OZZ IP managed to enter industries in which larger confederations had found it difficult to organize workers, such as NGOs, art or logistics, including a committee in Amazon (Mrozowicki and Maciejewska 2017).

Unionization

In assessing unionization trends, it should be noted that administrative data on trade union membership was not collected for twenty-five years between 1989 and 2014 (GUS 2015).[6] The Public Opinion Research Centre (CBOS, *Centrum Badania Opinii Społecznej*) surveys provide a reliable and comparable source of longitudinal data on trade union membership and density in Poland, also partially used by the ICTWSS database (Gardawski et al. 2010; Visser 2019a; Wenzel 2009). Furthermore, two waves of administrative data (2014 and 2018) were collected by Statistics Poland (GUS, *Główny Urząd Statystyczny*). It is also possible to make use of self-reported union data which, however, do not cover independent unions and suffer from reliability problems.[7] Table 22.2 presents trends in union density based on CBOS surveys.

Table 22.2 Union density, 1980–2019

Year	**1980**	**1987**	**1991**	**2000**	**2002**	**2007**	**2008**	**2010**	**2013**	**2015**	**2017**	**2019**
Trade union density	65 %	38 %	28 %	20 %	18 %	14 %	16 %	15 %	10 %	11 %	11 %	13 %

Note: statistical error is +/- 3 per cent.

Source: CBOS surveys compiled in: Wenzel (2009: 540); Gardawski and Meardi (2010: 54); Badora (2019); Feliksiak (2013).

In 2018, NSZZ Solidarność claimed to have 557,749 members and 7,200 affiliated unions (Adamczyk et al. 2018: 44). This indicates a decline of over 1.6 million members since 1991, when there were 2,246,119 members and almost 10,000 unions, as there were 16,992 affiliates in 1992 (Gardawski and Meardi 2010: 42). The reasons for membership

6 This is why OECD statistics do not represent 'administrative data' despite being labelled as such.

7 As trade union membership is related to membership fees, for instance in confederal structures at the European level, some trade unions quote lower number of members than they actually have.

decline include restructuring, company closures, union political involvement and NSZZ Solidarność's conditional support for painful market reforms (Gardawski et al. 1999; Ost 2005). OPZZ suffered from major schisms during the 1990s: between 1985 and 2000 it lost 131 affiliated unions and over 4.2 million members for similar reasons to Solidarność. After 2000 the decline of OPZZ slowed down: in 2018 it claimed to have 541,167 members, 4,532 company organizations and seventy-eight affiliates.[8] The decrease in membership in NSZZ Solidarność in 1991–2018 was slower than that of OPZZ. This can be considered the result of its more centralized, territory-based structure, stronger union identity as a social movement and relatively early development of union organizing strategies that emerged earlier than in other CEE countries and helped to organize workers in some parts of the new private sector (Czarzasty et al. 2014). FZZ claimed 306,141 members in 2018, a decline from the 371,033 members it claimed in 2002 (Czarzasty 2019b; Gardawski et al. 2012a, 2012b).[9] The estimated number of members of autonomous unions was 187,000 in 2018 or 12 per cent of total union membership (GUS 2019); in 2008 total membership was estimated at 500,000 or 20 per cent of the total, while in 2014 administrative data suggest that total membership was 272,000 or 14 per cent of the total. The relative decrease in the number of workers in autonomous unions is not reflected in the growth of large, nationally representative unions. Thus, smaller organizations that are unable to serve workers' needs disappear rather than join larger unions.

Figure 22.2 provides an overview of the development of union membership in the largest confederations based on original primary data collected by authors for the purpose of a study (Gardawski and Meardi 2010) and continued in the ICTWSS 6.0 database (Visser 2019a). According to the most recent data (as of 2018, see Annex 22.1), the total number of union members in 2018 can be estimated at 1,592,000. A slightly lower, but similar figure is based on administrative data collected by Statistics Poland: 1,500,000 union members (GUS 2019). It can be assumed that union density in Poland in 2018 was between 11.4 and 12.2 per cent of employees, of which there were 13,130,000 in 2018 (Eurostat LFS).

---

8 OPZZ self-reported data provided to the authors by the union.

9 We have not received up-to-date self-reported data from FZZ. The data source is the Court decision of 7 December 2018 confirming that it meets the criteria of representativeness, http://www.kadra.org.pl/wp-content/uploads/2018/12/Skan_20181218-1012.pdf (accessed on 22 August 2020).

Figure 22.2 Trade union membership (in thousands), 1980–2018

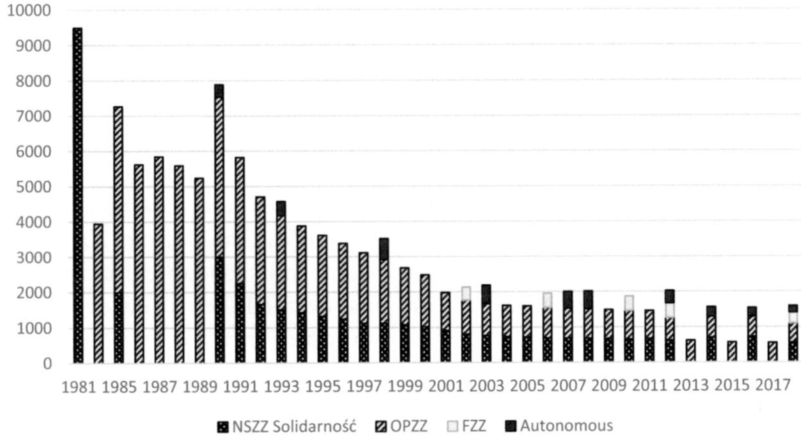

Source: Self-reported data collected by Gardawski and Meardi (2010); Gardawski et al. (2012b); Visser (2019b). Autonomous unions: survey data by Visser except for 2018 (GUS 2019). For detailed data, see table in Annex 1.

Whatever data are used, it is clear that Polish trade unionism has suffered a marked membership decline since 1990. This decline has occurred at an uneven pace: the sharpest deunionization was observed during the 1990s, and then slowed during the 2000s, while thereafter membership occasionally grew. In addition to the reasons for deunionization mentioned above, trade unions also suffered identity problems: NSZZ Solidarność because of its legacy as both anti-communist movement and trade union (Ost 2005) and OPZZ because of its old role as 'welfare agency' at the workplace level, a function now difficult to perform as a result of lost resources. The privatization of workers' strategies (Mrozowicki 2011), the availability of migration as an alternative to organizing, in particular after EU enlargement in 2004 (Meardi 2007) and the difficulties trade unions faced in expanding into the private sector and new categories of workers, such as precarious employees with civil-law contracts (Trappmann 2011) are further reasons for the downward trend of the 2000s.

Additional factors contributing to low unionization include the Trade Union Act of 1991, which made the unionization of the self-employed, civil-law workers and workers in small and micro-firms difficult.[10] Until January 2019 trade union membership was open to employees only. An employee was defined narrowly as a hired (paid) worker employed according to Labour Code regulations. Trade unions made use of legal and political means to extend the notion of worker to those with civil-law contracts and the dependent self-employed. One such was a complaint to the International Labour Organization by NSZZ Solidarność in 2011 on Poland's violation of ILO Convention No. 87 and a motion filed at the Constitutional Tribunal of Poland by OPZZ in 2012. In 2012, the ILO advised the Polish government to change its labour legislation and in June 2015 the Constitutional Tribunal deemed the narrow definition of 'worker' unconstitutional. It took four more years to change the Trade Union Act and extend eligibility for union membership to all 'persons performing paid work.'[11]

As of 2021, according to CBOS survey data, membership losses have slowed further of late. This can partly be explained by trade union strategies aimed at increasing their associational, institutional and societal power (Czarzasty and Mrozowicki 2018). These strategies include: (i) US-inspired union organizing in private sector companies led since the late 1990s by NSZZ Solidarność and the Confederation of Labour affiliated to OPZZ (Gardawski 2001; Mrozowicki 2014); (ii) collective mobilization through street protests and public campaigns in the 2010s against junk contracts, rises in the retirement age and Sunday working, which increased union visibility and led to expected legislative reforms; (iii) legal pressure on the Polish government to change the Trade Union Act in order to extend the definition of workers eligible for union membership; (iv) coalition-building with social movements, which included left-wing movements in the case of OPZZ and some FZZ affiliates (Kubisa 2014), but right-wing movements in the case of NSZZ Solidarność, such as *Gazeta Polska* newspaper clubs, and political parties (Law and Justice) (Mrozowicki and Kajta 2018); (v) grassroots organizing of various new categories of mostly precarious and temporary

---

[10] It should be noted that certain categories of employees have limited rights to join or establish trade unions according to Polish regulations (see Gardawski and Meardi 2010: 68).

[11] The amendments to the Trade Union Act in 2018, besides extending the definition of those eligible for membership to those performing paid work, also enabled the unemployed, unpaid trainees and volunteers to join trade unions.

workers in industries such as logistics, art, NGOs, and live performance; and (vi) attempts to organize Ukrainian migrant workers led by OPZZ, which created the first separate union of Ukrainian migrants in 2016, the Intercompany Union of Ukrainian Workers (*Międzyzakładowy Związek Zawodowy Pracowników Ukraińskich w Polsce*).

Recent survey and administrative data on union membership provide information on the sectoral, industrial and demographic structure of contemporary trade union membership. Polish trade unions are more feminized than in the past: in 1991, 23 per cent of men and 15 per cent of women (aged 18+) were trade union members. In 2017, the union density of working men was 9 per cent and that of working women 13 per cent (Feliksiak 2017). The feminization of union membership can be linked to the concentration of women in public services, where the large trade unions are predominantly based, and the decline of male-dominated industries, such as mining, shipbuilding and steel. As in other countries (Visser 2019b), the fact that members are growing older is a challenge for unions in Poland: in 2007, the average union member was 43 years old (Gardawski et al. 2012a: 57), but by 2019, they were 47 years old, compared with an average of 41 years of age for non-unionized workers (Badora 2019). According to administrative data, 8.7 per cent of union members (130,500 people) were pensioners in 2018 (GUS 2019).

In 2019, unions were present in the following occupations: technicians and mid-ranked specialists, such as nurses and police officers, 25 per cent; administrative workers, 20 per cent; skilled blue-collar workers, 20 per cent; professionals with university degrees, 15 per cent; management, 8 per cent; retail and private service workers, 6 per cent; pensioners, 5 per cent; and unskilled workers, 1 per cent (Badora 2019). Union density among university graduates was 13 per cent in 2017 compared with 11 per cent in the case of those with a secondary education and 9 per cent among those with a basic vocational education. It is clear that the unionization of white-collar workers in the public sector and the deunionization of blue-collar workers, in particular in the private sector, are long-term trends (Gardawski et al. 2010: 58). A similar tendency was noted for forty-nine countries by Visser (2019b: 28).

Figure 22.3 Company-level trade union membership and density by industry (%), 2014

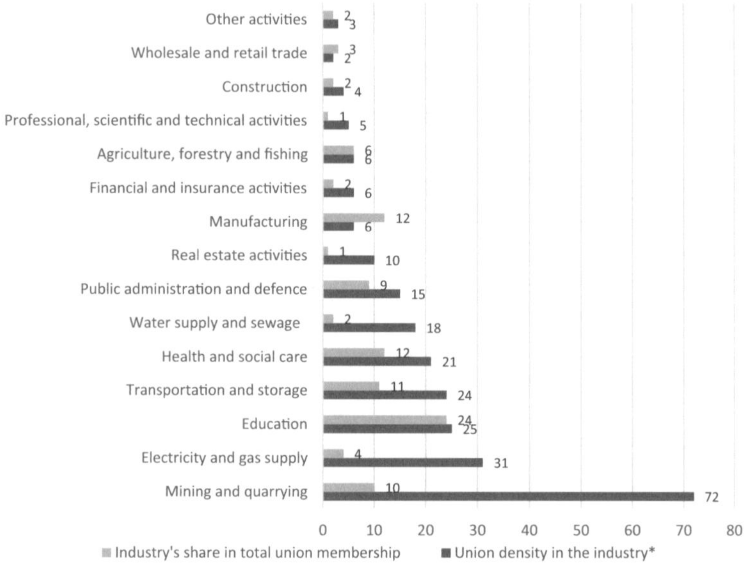

Note: Union density calculated for the number of workers in companies employing more than nine people.
Source: GUS (2015: 6), administrative data.

In 2014, the highest percentage of company-level trade union members were employed in education, at 24 per cent; followed by manufacturing, 12 per cent; health and social care, 12 per cent; transportation and storage, 11 per cent; mining and quarrying, 10 per cent; and public administration and defence, 9 per cent (Figure 22.4). Industrial trade union density data reveals the highest density in 2014 in mining and quarrying, at 72 per cent; followed by gas and electricity supply, 31 per cent; education, 25 per cent; transportation, 24 per cent; and health care, 18 per cent. In manufacturing, which used to be a trade union stronghold, only 6 per cent of workers were unionized, a similar share to newly organized industries, such as real estate, financial and insurance activities.

Also in 2014, 86 per cent of all unionized companies employed more than fifty workers, including 31 per cent that employed over 250 workers (GUS 2015: 11). The majority of unionized companies – 62 per cent – operated in the public sector (ibid). Unionization rates in genuinely private firms are very low, at 2 per cent (Feliksiak 2017). Finally, the majority of trade union members in 2018 were employed on employment contracts; only 0.1 per cent had civil-law contracts (GUS 2019: 4). These data confirm that Polish unions have not yet been able to expand their activities to the most precarious segments of the workforce.

Union resources and expenditure

The main sources of income as reported by the unions are: membership dues, voluntary contributions, business activities, property rights and occasional financing, such as donations, legacies and grants. EU grants, in particular from operational programmes financed by the European Social Fund – most recently the Operational Programme Knowledge, Education and Development (POWER) – have been important, but the sums are difficult to estimate precisely.

As outlined in the statutes of NSZZ Solidarność, its sources of income are as follows: (i) membership dues; (ii) contributions by members and organizational units to specific causes; (iii) donations and subsidies; (iv) profits made by entities legally linked to the union and conducting business operations; (v) lease and rent of real estate and other real assets, as well as rights and licences and other intangible fixed assets of the union and its organizational units; (vi) awards; and (vii) public fundraising. It is worth examining NSZZ Solidarność's internal regulations more closely, as it is a general workers' organization. The structure of its income may serve to characterize the finances of such unions, regardless of size and scale of operations.

In the case of NSZZ Solidarność, 60 per cent of funding from membership dues remains with company-level trade union organizations, 25 per cent is allocated to regional structures and 10 per cent goes to the national central structure, of which only 2 per cent is given to branch trade union structures. In OPZZ and FZZ, the distribution of membership fees is diversified, with a small share going to national-level structures and most remaining at the level of company and union federations., It must be stressed that the relative importance of membership decline and thus the decreasing income from membership dues is greater for smaller unions, with little or no fixed assets, particularly real estate.

Trade union dues can be deducted from wages by an employer in agreement with the company-level union organization and the employee. This practice, once widespread in large companies, has declined markedly as trade unions are now reluctant to provide employers with a list of their members. As a result, membership fees are to an increasing extent collected directly from union members.

Collective bargaining and unions at the workplace

The collective bargaining system in Poland is concentrated at the enterprise level. The dominant type of collective agreement is thus the single-employer agreement (Czarzasty 2019a). Supra-enterprise bargaining is virtually absent with a very low number of multi-employer collective agreements. As of 2020 there are sixty-one multi-employer collective agreements, covering 200,000 employees, largely in the public sector.

By 2018, 9,908 single-employer collective agreements had been registered for slightly more than 1.8 million workers, of whom roughly 1 million were employed in the public sector, and approximately 800,000 in the private sector. Based on all the available figures, including those on single- and multi-employer collective bargaining, we estimate collective bargaining coverage to be no more than 20 per cent.

Table 22.3 Single-employer collective agreements registered annually, 2004–2018

Year	Number of new agreements	Additional protocols to existing agreements	Accords on application of agreements	Number of employees covered by new agreements
2004	328	2,193	21	166,661
2005	220	1,792	12	119,601
2006	177	1,646	6	68,000
2007	168	1,961	15	121,454
2008	155	1,732	4	62,802
2009	123	1,688	2	62,572
2010	130	1,396	1	172,425
2011	136	1,291	3	49,407
2012	92	1,265	3	61,109
2013	109	1,131	1	43,800
2014	88	1,030	1	43,576
2015	69	909	0	101,473
2016	79	896	–	38,227
2017	50	845	–	28,230
2018	54	945	–	21,067

Note: all figures in rows reported annually; *protokół dodatkowy do układu zbiorowego* (additional protocol to existing collective agreements) is a formal amendment to a collective agreement; the parties are required to notify the labour inspectorate of its conclusion.

Source: National Labour Inspectorate (PIP) annual reports.

To a large extent the weakness of collective bargaining in Poland can be explained by the peculiarities of the legal system, which discourage employers and employees from entering into negotiations. Clause 3 of the Labour Code, for example, defines 'employer' as 'an organizational unit, even if it has no legal personality, or an individual, provided they employ employees'. It does not matter whether such an 'employer' has any ownership rights. In large corporations this is a significant problem, as an establishment represented by its senior manager could be acting as employer for the purpose of bargaining. It is also a problem in the public sector, especially in local government, as the person actually in control of financial resources, such as the head of a municipality, cannot be addressed directly by trade unions during any industrial dispute. For example, pay demands from public school teachers must be presented to the head teacher (the formal employer), although they do not have any authority to make decisions on raising wages, so the demands are passed forward. For trade unions this undermines the legitimacy of their negotiating partner, and the credibility of agreements because they cannot speak directly to the entity with the real control of resources.

Employers are not fond of collective bargaining. Regarding the single-employer bargaining level there are a number of considerations that contribute to this. First, given that often there are no unions at all, the absence of a party with whom the employer could enter into negotiations. Second, if there is a union, it is often weak and its voice can simply be disregarded. Finally, there may be a situation of competitive pluralism with a number of active unions. As far as the industry level is concerned, employer organizations stay away from supra-enterprise collective bargaining because they fear their members might be inclined to withdraw. Paradoxically, however, the inability of employer organizations to aggregate and effectively represent the collective interests of their constituency is a major factor discouraging potential member companies from joining.

Two major principles of collective bargaining are laid down by law: first, 'freedom of contract', except for provisions threatening the rights of third parties; and second, 'favourability', which means that collective agreements cannot introduce less favourable provisions for employees than those secured by law. In addition, Polish law allows for no 'closed-shop' type of arrangements, so collective agreements apply to all employees. This encourages free-riding and demotivates employees from joining trade unions.

The quality of bargaining, in terms of the content of agreements, has been poor. According to the National Labour Inspectorate (PIP, *Państwowa Inspekcja Pracy*) collective agreements usually stick to the letter of the law and rarely contain any clauses surpassing the legal minimum. Screening PIP reports shows that the most common topics of collective agreements are: employers' and employees' mutual obligations and entitlements, pay structure, conventional pay, flexible elements of pay including bonuses, performance bonuses, seniority bonuses, working time, death allowances and rules on determination, workplace safety rules and regulations, holidays and other forms of leave (Czarzasty 2020).

Importantly, pay is also the subject of the central-level tripartite negotiations, but this is limited by law to the national minimum wage. The RDS determines the minimum wage level annually, on the basis of the government's proposal. The decision must be made unanimously by the social partners and the government. Only if the RDS fails to reach a consensus does the government take the decision unilaterally, although a minimum wage determined this way cannot be lower than the original proposal.

As already indicated, Poland's industrial relations system is highly decentralized, with company-level bargaining dominant. Basic company-level trade union organizations (*zakładowe organizacje związkowe*) constitute the main channel of workplace employee representation. Works councils (*rady pracowników*) have been in existence since 2006, which formally makes the system of worker representation dual channel. Works councils can be established by any employer with at least fifty employees. In order to establish a works council, at least 10 per cent of employees need to request the election (general ballot) of such a body. In unionized workplaces, unions have generally managed to maintain control over works councils. Works councils, however, have largely failed as a viable institution and their incidence is continuously decreasing. This decline does not matter as far as collective bargaining is concerned, because the law guarantees unions a monopoly in negotiations on behalf of employees.

Industrial conflict

There were three main peaks of strike activity in Poland in the period 1989–2019: in 1992–1993, 2008 and 2019. In each case, education was the main sector in which strikes took place, accounting for 84 per cent of strikes registered in 1992, 56 per cent in 1993, 99 per cent of strikes in

2008 and 98 per cent in 2019 (ILO 2020). Teachers' financial demands, such as wage increases, were almost never achieved: in particular, the largest strikes in 1993 and 2019 failed in this respect. Indirectly, however, the capacity of this occupational group to mobilize collectively might be considered one of the reasons for the preservation of the Teachers Charter (*Karta Nauczyciela*), which guarantees certain financial and non-financial benefits for teachers in state schools.

Other industries in which strikes took place include manufacturing (accounting for 61 per cent of strikes in 1991 and 10 per cent in 1992; in absolute figures this comprised 674 strikes, the highest ever in this sector since 1989), public administration and community services, as well as transport, health care and social work. Since the early 2000s, there has been a clear shift from strikes in manufacturing towards strikes in public services. This also indicates the growing associational power of white-collar workers and professionals compared with other groups. Some successes were noted in terms of wage increases as a result of strikes, among others – in the late 2000s – in health care, particularly among doctors and, to lesser degree, nurses. In other industries, collective mobilization of miners' trade unions could partially account for their capacity to block successive governments' attempts to restructure the industry; the current date of closing all black-coal mines for environmental reasons has been negotiated between the unions and the government for the year 2049, with employment guarantees and payments secured.

Figure 22.4 Number of strikes, 1989–2019

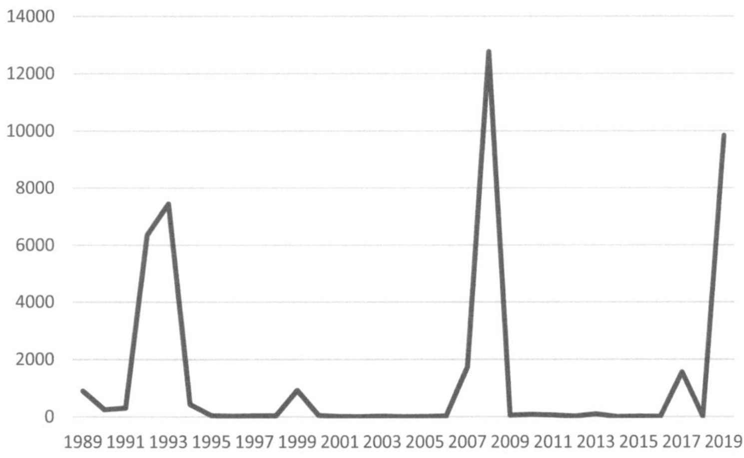

Source: ILOSTAT, authors' elaboration.

The strike waves indicate important moments in the history of change in Poland after 1989: the first phase of privatization, closures and restructuring in 1989–1993; the second phase of privatization and the liberalization of public services in 1999–2001; post-EU accession economic development marked by the rising structural power of workers resulting, among other things, from emigration in 2006–2008; and, finally, the impact of the Law and Justice government after the elections in 2015, with a favourable labour market situation and improved worker bargaining power, as well as growing political conflicts.

It should be remembered that during some periods characterized by relatively low strike rates, the number of individual grievances remained relatively high. The changes in the number of grievances and collective disputes registered by the National Labour Inspectorate (PIP, *Państwowa Inspekcja Pracy*) in 2010–2019 is presented in Table 22.4 and demonstrates a slow upward trend. The high number of collective disputes registered in 2015 and 2017 is largely accounted for by upcoming teachers' strikes, as the registration of a collective dispute is the first legally required step in organizing a strike.

Table 22.4 Number of grievances and collective disputes registered by the NLI, 2010–2019

	2010	**2011**	**2012**	**2013**	**2014**	**2015**	**2016**	**2017**	**2018**
Number of grievances (000s)	42.7	41.7	44.3	44.1	41.7	43.7	44.2	50.5	54.1
Number of collective disputes	342	365	301	284	254	1,202	242	9,492	354

Source: National Labour Inspectorate reports, https://www.pip.gov.pl/pl/o-urzedzie/sprawozdania-z-dzialalnosci

Following the economic slowdown after 2008, Polish trade unions resorted more to political instruments based on social campaigns, such as political coalitions and street protests outside the workplace. The campaigns concerned, among other things, opposition to the expansion of precarious employment, to increasing the retirement age and to the flexibilization of working time. The peak of street protests was in 2013, when the first post-1989 general strike took place in Silesia involving 85,000 workers during March 2013, followed by days of protests in

Warsaw. The latter included the largest post-1989 trade union demonstration in Warsaw in September 2013 in which over 100,000 workers participated. Because political strikes are banned in Polish law, the general strike was a way to mobilize workers against the crisis of social dialogue with the government. The pressure worked, leading to reforms of the Tripartite Commission, which was transformed into the Social Dialogue Council in 2015 and granted broader prerogatives. After 2015, under the Law and Justice (PiS) government, the largest mobilization of workers was observed, again in education, when the Polish Teachers' Union (ZNP, *Związek Nauczycielstwa Polskiego*) organized a large-scale strike in March 2017 against education system reforms, and then another nationwide strike demanding wage increases in April 2019.

Polish unions are among the least strike prone in Europe (Vandaele 2018). This can be explained by their limited associational and organizational power, the expansion of non-standard and precarious employment, workers' preference for 'exit' via migration (Meardi 2007) and individualistic coping strategies (Mrozowicki 2011). In addition, unions' strike funds have been weakened by the erosion of their memberships. Employees in Poland retain the right to social insurance benefits during a legal strike, but employers are not obliged to pay them. Consequently, the shift towards street protests, social campaigns and political lobbying can also be explained by the limited union resources available to support workers undertaking more classical forms of industrial action.

Political relations

Polish trade union relations with political parties have a long and rather turbulent history.[12] In 1989, NSZZ Solidarność was the driving force behind the transition to democracy and became a cradle for a wide spectrum of parties commonly regarded as stemming from the Solidarność movement until roughly 2005. Between 1997 and 2001 the political representation of the confederation, Solidarity Electoral Action (AWS, *Akcja Wyborcza Solidarność*), led the coalition government. This ended in a disastrous electoral defeat, which contributed to NSZZ

12 This part of the chapter is based on our earlier papers (Gardawski and Meardi 2010; Mrozowicki, Kajta 2018).

Solidarność's official distancing from any involvement in high-level politics. OPZZ, in turn, until 2005 remained close to the post-communist Democratic Left Alliance (SLD, *Sojusz Lewicy Demokratycznej*), being one of the founders of SLD as a coalition in 1993, although later it gradually loosened ties. FZZ from its outset in 2002 has accentuated its 'apolitical' profile, aimed at attracting organizations disillusioned with union political entanglements.

In early 2010s industrial relations scholars in Poland started to talk about the increasing cooperation between NSZZ Solidarność, OPZZ and FZZ. This was brought about, among other things, by the effects of economic slowdown, closer collaboration within the ETUC and European Sectoral Social Dialogue Committees and, crucially, the ostentatious contempt exhibited by the liberal-conservative PO-PSL government for tripartite social dialogue (Gardawski et al. 2012a). Despite initial hopes of a revival of social dialogue following the Social Dialogue Council reform in 2015, the situation after the PiS's absolute victory in the parliamentary and presidential elections in 2015 meant that the government did not need to form alliances with unions to pursue ambitious reforms, whether it be of the judicial system, pensions or education.

Since 2015, NSZZ Solidarność and PiS have cooperated closely. The union has maintained ties to PiS since 2005. During the course of the presidential campaigns in 2015, the PiS candidate and the current president, Andrzej Duda, concluded an agreement with NSZZ Solidarność in which the union was promised support for its social policy preferences in exchange for its electoral support. A similar agreement was also concluded between the union and President Duda in the 2020 campaign. In 2015, a number of NSZZ Solidarność representatives assumed government offices in the Ministry of Family, Labour and Social Policy (MRPiPS, *Ministerstwo Rodziny, Pracy i Polityki Społecznej*). OPZZ and FZZ, while being part of the Social Dialogue Council, do not enjoy comparable opportunities for political influence.

Although Polish trade unions have officially distanced themselves from politics, their leadership also recognizes the need to influence labour policies through cooperation with parliamentary forces, which leads to unavoidable tensions. On one hand, PiS social policies fulfil some of the unions' goals, including better regulation of civil-law contracts, income support for families and lowering the retirement age back to 60 years for women and 65 years for men, from the 67 years implemented by the PO-PSL government in 2013. On the other hand, both NSZZ Solidarność and, in different ways, OPZZ and FZZ, have to cope with a situation in which the government, while meeting some of their wishes, at the same time suppresses protests in other areas of social life and tries relentlessly to increase political control over the media, courts and education. Moreover, most of the opposition parties, perhaps except for the Left (*Lewica*) coalition, have not expressed any significant interest in cooperating with the unions.

Societal power

During the past decade Polish trade unions, similarly to their counterparts elsewhere in CEE (Bernaciak and Kahancová 2017) have begun to look for substitutes to mitigate their declining associational and institutional power. In this context, they have also started to rebuild their 'societal power resources', defined as 'the latitude for action arising from viable cooperation contexts with other social groups and organizations, and society's support for trade union demands' (Schmalz et al. 2018: 122).

In 2010–2020, trade unions were involved in several campaigns aimed at mobilizing public support. They included collecting signatures to organize referenda on the topics such as increasing the minimum wage to 50 per cent of the national average (2011) and returning the retirement age to 60/65 (2012), as well as traditional and new media campaigns aimed at stopping the expansion of civil-law, 'junk' contracts (2010–2015), banning Sunday trading and national holidays (2008–2017) and increasing wages in education (2019). As argued earlier, at least some of trade union demands raised in the course of campaigns during the 2010s were implemented by PiS after 2015.

During the 2010s trade union social campaigns became increasingly based on internet tools, trade union websites, social media and online petitions. One reason for shifting trade union activities from traditional media to new ones has been the negative picture of trade unionism presented in the mainstream media (Ostrowski 2017; Zioło-Pużuk 2019).

The trade union presence in social media is uneven. As of August 2020, for example, the small radical trade union Workers' Initiative had more followers (9,754 people) on Facebook than NSZZ Solidarność (9,139), FZZ (3,862) and OPZZ (573). Yet, large trade unions still publish in traditional outlets, which also have electronic versions, websites and social media profiles. NSZZ Solidarność, for example, publishes *Tygodnik*

Solidarność ('Solidarity Weekly') in 20,000 copies. Simultaneously, there are examples of trade union campaigns which have successfully mobilized broad support for union positions and were used to communicate trade union demands, for instance the ZNP-led teachers' strike, 'Protest with an Exclamation Mark', in 2019, which involved 40,350 people.

Regardless of the rather negative image of unions in the media, according to CBOS survey data, at the national level trade union activities enjoy at least moderate, and relatively stable, public support. In 2019, 38 per cent of respondents agreed with the statement that trade union activities are good for the country, 21 per cent expressed the opposite view and 41 per cent chose 'difficult to say' (Badora 2019). Although support for unions in this survey was the highest since 1994, a large share of respondents declared that they had no opinion about them. Support for union activities was the highest among the youngest interviewees: 40 per cent said that trade unions are effective in defending workers' interests compared with 27 per cent in the general population. This positive image was qualified by the fact that 40 per cent of the youngest workers had no opinion on unions' effectiveness in the workplace. The fact that young workers indicate relatively high support for trade unions while being reluctant to join one requires further research.

Trade union policies towards the European Union

Polish trade unions were involved at the EU level long before the 2004 enlargement and even prior to the opening of the accession process. NSZZ Solidarność was admitted to the ETUC in 1996, having been an observer since 1991. OPZZ joined the ETUC in 2006, following the final settlement made with other trade unions and facilitated by the law regarding the division of property inherited by OPZZ from CRZZ and the issue of compensation for the property of NSZZ Solidarność confiscated by the communist government in 1981. FZZ joined the ETUC in 2012, having previously been a member of the European Confederation of Independent Trade Unions. All nationally representative confederations supported Poland's accession to the EU in 2004. NSZZ Solidarność, thanks to its contacts and membership of the ETUC, was involved in the accession process through various consultative bodies, such as the European Integration Commission and the Joint Consultative Committee, a tripartite structure set up by the EU's European Economic and Social Committee (Mrozowicki 2017: 204).

Polish trade unions have been active in recent years in the context of divisive EU-level issues, such as revisions of the Posted Workers Directive, the Mobility Package and the European minimum wage. They also supported the Proposal for a Directive on adequate minimum wages in the European Union. In most cases Polish unions have remained loyal to the official ETUC line, but their support could not be described as unconditional (Adamczyk 2018). In 2018, Polish unions, along with other organizations from Visegrad countries, expressed their support for the amendment of the Posted Workers Directive. Also in 2018 NSZZ Solidarność and OPZZ, along with CMKOS (Czechia) expressed support for the optional legal framework (OLF) for transnational company agreements (TCA) in a joint statement to the ETUC.[13] The ETUC action programme adopted at the Vienna Congress in 2019, however, includes only a declaration that the ETUC will seek to conclude some kind of tripartite framework agreement on the status of TCAs, although the OLF is mentioned (Czarzasty et al. 2020). In November 2019, at the initiative of NSZZ Solidarność, twenty-four ETUC affiliates from CEE and the Balkans sent a letter to the ETUC General Secretary expressing support for the idea of a EU directive on minimum wages and the promotion of collective bargaining.

Nevertheless, the position of Polish unions in the ETUC, like all unions from CEE, is still relatively weak. At the ETUC Congress in Vienna in 2019 there were seventy delegates from the region, less than 18 per cent of participants. There are noticeable disparities in positions of power held by Polish and other CEE member organizations compared with those held by representatives from 'old' EU countries (Czarzasty et al. 2020). Polish unions, in line with their counterparts from CEE – with the exception of Slovenia – tend to acknowledge the existence of an 'East–West' divide. On some issues – such as the relocation of companies from the old to the new Member States – the gap is evident, while in other areas, more complicated lines of division cut across the 'West', such as the Nordic unions' resistance to a European minimum wage, or, for the matter, across the 'East', exemplified by Slovenian unions' preference for national industrial relations institutions in contrast to the strong enthusiasm for EU-level institutions in some other CEE countries (Czarzasty 2020).

---

[13] Letter from OPZZ, FZZ, NSZZ Solidarność to the General Secretary of ETUC of 6 December 2018.

Data from NSZZ Solidarność suggests that Polish union delegates are present in about 180 EWCs. The only known case of an EWC regulated by Polish law is the one at Arctic Paper, which has transferred its headquarters to Poland. Polish unions are affiliated to most, but not all European Trade Union Federations (ETUFs). The affiliates from Poland include national federations, autonomous national-level unions and, in one case, a non-union member organization, a journalists' syndicate. In all but one case – ZZPR RP – unions are affiliated to the big three national-level confederations.

Besides the formal links with the European Union and the ETUC, there are also forms of cross-border cooperation between trade unions at the regional level and within multinational companies. With regard to the former, a good example is the Interregional Trade Union Council 'Viadrina' (MRZZ 'Viadrina', *Międzyregionalna Rada Związków Zawodowych 'Viadrina'*), established in 1996 to foster information exchange and joint seminars between the German Trade Union Confederation (DGB, *Deutscher Gewerkschaftsbund*), NSZZ Solidarność, the Zielona Góra Region and, since 2016, OPZZ (Lubuskie Voivodship). At the company level, there are interesting cases of transnational union pressure. An example of the latter are the joint protests of Amazon workers in France, Italy, Spain and Poland in 2020 demanding better health protection measures during the Covid-19 pandemic, a reduced workload and pay increases. Finally, there are international projects supporting trade union organizing, such as the Central European Organising Centre (COZZ, *Centrum Organizowania Związków Zawodowych*), financially supported by Uni Global Union and pursuing trade union development in Poland, Czechia, Slovakia and Hungary.

Conclusions

Visser (2019b) presents four scenarios for the future of trade unions: marginalization, dualization, substitution and revitalization. Our chapter does not give a definitive answer regarding which of these is the most likely in Poland. Following a long period of marginalization after 1989, the decline in union density slowed down during the mid-2000s. We argue that this was largely because of a rise in union membership in public services and among white-collar professionals, partially as result of successive waves of collective mobilization, and to some extent as a result of trade unions backing off from party politics and even occasionally standing together against government policies, particularly during 2011–2015. Despite successful organizing efforts in some private sector companies, trade union revitalization, concerning which hopes were strong ten years ago (Czarzasty and Mrozowicki 2014), is still not in sight. Trade union density in the private sector remains at a microscopic 2 per cent of employees. This indicates a real danger of dualization, leading to the disappearance of collective labour relations from the majority of private sector companies.

Despite some hopes linked to a 'new opening' in social dialogue with the establishment of RDS in 2015, union influence over government policies through tripartite bodies has not grown. The 'illusory corporatism' claim thus still seems valid. Since 2015, some trade union policies have been introduced into Polish law by the PiS government. The origins of these policies in workers' mobilization and/or union pressure is hardly mentioned in the media and credit for their implementation is allotted mainly to the governing party. In the context of the growing challenges to liberal democracy in some CEE countries, Poland included, there is also a danger of a replacement of trade unions by right-wing populist governments offering workers social and economic benefits in exchange for their support for their broader political agenda.

The outbreak of Covid-19 and subsequent socio-economic crisis has not helped to bolster trade unions in Poland. Organized labour – and employers' organizations – played a marginal role in designing and introducing anti-crisis policy measures in 2020. The government acted unilaterally, and its disregard for tripartite social dialogue is best exemplified by a clause in the anti-crisis legislation of March 2020, by virtue of which the prime minister can dismiss any member of the Social Dialogue Council if they commit an act deemed to constitute 'misappropriation of the Council's activities'. All national-level social partners protested against the new regulations, so the President of Poland asked the Constitutional Court to review their legality.

Some anti-crisis measures – such as furlough payments for workers whose working time was reduced or who were left idle because of the suspension of company operations (downtime) for economic reasons; the possibility of extending the working time calculation period from four to twelve months; or changing some parts of employment contracts, for example holiday pay – required agreement with company trade unions or employee representatives. Between March 2020 and February 2021, 27,400 such agreements were registered by the National Labour

Inspectorate. It is not clear, however, how many of these agreements were actually signed by trade unions.

Potential areas of trade union innovation in the future could include the issues of green transition and digitalization. As far as green transition is concerned, the situation is complicated. NSZZ Solidarność is most critical of the current direction of the transformation, claiming it poses a threat to the national economy by making it overly dependent on external (imported) energy resources (NSZZ Solidarność 2020). All confederations emphasize the need for a 'just transition', combining environmental goals and job creation, as exemplified by the joint statement of the Polish and German trade unions before the United Nations Climate Change Conference in Katowice in 2018 (DGB 2018).

As for digitalization, trade unions are virtually absent from the platform and gig economy in Poland. To date, their actions have been limited to issuing statements regarding the need for protection of workers' and social rights in the gig economy. OPZZ, together with the Friedrich Ebert Foundation (FES), has published a guide for workers in the platform economy (Rogalewski 2020). The Covid-19 pandemic accelerated attempts to regulate remote working in the Labour Code. The negotiations between trade unions and employers' organizations in the RDS on this topic have dragged on since March 2020. The amendment to Labour Code was eventually passed in January 2023. It seems important that trade unions were consulted on this issue within the RDS.

References

All links were checked on 20 June 2021.

Adamczyk S. (2018) Inside the trade union family: the 'two worlds' within the European Trade Union Confederation, European Journal of Industrial Relations, 24 (2), 179–192.

Adamczyk S., Surdykowska B. and Szymański M. (2018) Przewodnik po dialogu społecznym, Warsaw, Centrum Partnerstwa Spolecznego 'Dialog'.

Badora B. (2019) Związki zawodowe w Polsce, Komunikat Z Badan 138/ 2019, Warsaw, Centrum Badania Opinii Spolecznej (CBOS).

Bernaciak M. and Kahancová M. (2017) Introduction: innovation against all odds?, in Bernaciak M. and Kahancová M. (eds) Innovative union practices in Central and Eastern Europe, Brussels, ETUI, 7–20.

Crowley S. (2004) Explaining labor weakness in post-communist Europe: historical legacies and comparative perspective, East European Politics and Societies, 18 (3), 394–429.

Czarzasty J. (2019a) Collective bargaining in Poland: a near- death experience, in Müller T., Vandaele K. and Waddington J. (eds) Collective bargaining in Europe: towards an endgame, Brussels, ETUI, 465–481.

Czarzasty J. (2019b) Poland: latest working life developments Q4 2018, Dublin, Eurofound.

Czarzasty J. (2020) Articulation of the trade unions' strategies on the upward convergence of social standards in the enlarged European Union – the voice of CEE countries, Comparative Report, Warsaw, Institute of Public Affairs.

Czarzasty J. and Mrozowicki A. (2014) Organizowanie związków zawodowych w Europie. Badanie i praktyka społeczna, Warsaw, Wydawnictwo Naukowe 'Scholar'.

Czarzasty J. and Mrozowicki A. (2018) Industrial relations in Poland: historical background, institutional evolution and research trends, Employee Relations, 40 (4), 674–691.

Czarzasty J., Adamczyk S. and Surdykowska B. (2020) Looking for European solutions. Trade unions in Central and Eastern Europe striving for cross-border solidarity, Transfer, 26 (3), 307–323.

Czarzasty J., Gajewska K. and Mrozowicki A. (2014) Institutions and strategies: trends and obstacles to recruiting workers into trade unions in Poland, British Journal of Industrial Relations, 52 (1), 112–135.

DGB (2018) Joint Declaration by the Polish and German Trade Union Confederations: Shaping a Fair Change – Creating Decent Work and Ensuring Climate Action. https://www.dgb.de/downloadcenter/++co++7f5ac0d4-bda2-11e8-a618-52540088cada

Ebbinghaus B. and Visser J. (2000) Trade unions in Western Europe since 1945, London, MacMillan Reference Ltd.

Feliksiak M. (2013) Członkostwo w związkach zawodowych i opinie o ich działalności, Report BS/62/2013, Warsaw, Centrum Badania Opinii Spolecznej. http://www.cbos.pl/SPISKOM.POL/2013/K_062_13.PDF

Feliksiak M. (2017) Działalność związków zawodowych w Polsce, Komunikat zBadan 87/2017, Warsaw, Centrum Badania Opinii Spolecznej. https://www.cbos.pl/SPISKOM.POL/2017/K_087_17.PDF

Gardawski J. (2001) Związki zawodowe na rozdrożu, Warsaw, Instytut spraw publicznych.

Gardawski J. (2003) Konfliktowy pluralizm polskich związków zawodowych, Warsaw, Friedrich Ebert Foundation.

Gardawski J. and Meardi G. (2010) Keep trying? Polish failures and half-successes in social pacting, in Pochet P., Keune M. and Natali D. (eds) After the Euro and enlargement: social pacts in the EU, Brussels, ETUI, 371–394.

Gardawski J., Gąciarz B., Mokrzyszewski J. and Panków W. (1999) Rozpad bastionu? Związki zawodowe w gospodarce prywatyzowanej, Warsaw, Instytut spraw publicznych.

Gardawski J., Mrozowicki A. and Czarzasty J. (2012a) Trade unions in Poland, Brussels, ETUI.

Gardawski J., Mrozowicki A. and Czarzasty J. (2012b) Historia i teraźniejszość związków zawodowych w Polsce, Dialog, 34 (3), 3–30. http://cps-dialog.gov.pl/images/zdjecia/analiza_historia_i_terazniejszosc_zwiazkow_zawodowych.pdf

Grabowska M. (2004) Podział postkomunistyczny: społeczne podstawy polityki w Polsce po 1989 roku, Warsaw, Scholar.

GUS (2015) Związki zawodowe w Polsce w 2014 r., Notatka informacyjna, 13 July 2015. https://stat.gov.pl/download/gfx/portalinformacyjny/pl/defaultaktualnosci/5490/10/1/1/notatka_zz_1007_ost.pdf

GUS (2019) Partnerzy dialogu społecznego – związki zawodowe i organizacje pracodawców – wyniki wstępne, 27 August 2019.

Hauner M. (1986) Human Resources, in Kaser M.C. and Radice E.A. (eds) The economic history of Eastern Europe 1919–1975, Oxford, Clarendon Press.

Hojka Z. (2006) Polski ruch zawodowy w województwie śląskim (1922–1939), Katowice, Wydawnictwo Uniwersytetu Śląskiego.

Hyman R. (2001) Understanding European trade unionism: between market, class and society, London, Sage Publications.

ILO (2020) Statistics on work stoppages. https://ilostat.ilo.org/topics/work-stoppages/

Kubisa J. (2014) Bunt białych czepków. Analiza działalności związkowej pielęgniarek i położnych, Warsaw, Wydawn, Naukowe Scholar.

Meardi G. (2007) More voice after more exit? Unstable industrial relations in Central and Eastern Europe, Industrial Relations Journal, 38 (6), 503–523.

Mrozowicki A. (2011) Coping with social change: life strategies of workers in Poland's new capitalism, Leuven, Leuven University Press.

Mrozowicki A. (2014) Varieties of trade union organizing in Central and Eastern Europe: a comparison of the retail and automotive sectors, European Journal of Industrial Relations, 20 (4), 297–315.

Mrozowicki A. (2017) Polish pathways to the European Trade Union Confederation, in Ciampani A. and Tilly P. (eds) National trade unions and the ETUC: a history of unity and diversity, Brussels, ETUI, 195–210.

Mrozowicki A. and Kajta J. (2018) Rechtspopulismus in Polen, in Becker K., Dörre K. and Reif-Spirek P. (eds) Arbeiterbewegung von rechts?: Ungleichheit – Verteilungskämpfe – populistische Revolte, Frankfurt am Main, Campus Verlag, 257–270.

Mrozowicki A. and Maciejewska M. (2017) 'The practice anticipates our reflections' – radical unions in Poland, Transfer, 23 (1), 67–77.

NSZZ 'Solidarność' (2020) Stanowisko Prezydium KK i zespołu DS. polityki klimatycznej NSZZ 'Solidarność' [Position of the Presidium of the National Commission and the climate policy committee of NSZZ Solidarność], 9 October 2020. http://www.solidkwbbel.pl/aktualnosci/372-stanowisko-prezydium-kk-i-zespolu-ds-polityki-klimatycznej-nszz-solidarnosc

OPZZ (2018) Wspólne oświadczenie polskich i niemieckich konfederacji związków zawodowych ws. polityki klimatycznej, News, 25 September 2018. https://www.opzz.org.pl/aktualnosci/swiat/wspolne-oswiadczenie-polskich-i-niemieckich-konfederacji-zwiazkow-zawodowych-ws-polityki-klimatycznej

Ost D. (2005) The defeat of solidarity. Anger and politics in postcommunist Europe, London, Cornell University Press.

Ost D. (2011) 'Ilusory corporatism' ten years later, Warsaw Forum of Economic Sociology, 2:1 (3), 19–49.

Ostrowski P. (2017) W poszukiwaniu przyczyn erozji i marginalizacji polskich związków zawodowych: element rekonstrukcji dyskursu, Władza sądzenia, 11, 89–100. http://wladzasadzenia.pl/2017/11/w-poszukiwaniu-przyczyn-erozji-i-marginalizacji-polskich-zwiazkow-zawodowych-element-rekonstrukcji-dyskursu.pdf

Rogalewski A. (2020) Cyfryzacja i praca platformowa. Informator dla pracowników, Warsaw, Friedrich-Ebert-Stiftung. http://library.fes.de/pdf-files/bueros/warschau/16035.pdf

Schmalz S., Ludwig C. and Webster E. (2018) The power resources approach: developments and challenges, Global Labour Journal, 9 (2), 113–134.

Schmitter P. and Streeck W. (1981) The organisation of business interests, Berlin, Wissenschaftszentrum Berlin. https://pure.mpg.de/pubman/faces/ViewItemOverviewPage.jsp?itemId=item_1235969_2.

Trappmann V. (2011) Precarious employment in Poland – a legacy of transition or an effect of European integration?, Emecon, 2 (1), 1–22.

Vandaele K. (2018) Strikes – Map of Europe. https://www.etui.org/Services/Strikes-Map-of-Europe

Visser J. (2019a) ICTWSS Database. version 6.0. https://www.ictwss.org/downloads

Visser J. (2019b) Trade Unions in the balance, ILO ACTRAV Working Paper, Geneva, ILO.

Wenzel M. (2009) Związki zawodowe w badaniach CBOS 1980–2008', in Gardawski J. (ed.) Polacy pracujący a kryzys fordyzmu, Warsaw, Wydawnictwo Naukowe Scholar, 533–550.

Zioło-Pużuk K. (2019) Niezniszczalna siła stereotypu. Obraz związków zawodowych w mediach na przykładzie relacji z demonstracji 22 września 2018 roku, Prakseologia, 161, 187–208.

Abbreviations

NSZZ Niezależny Samorządny Związek Zawodowy (Independent Self-governing Trade Union)

OPZZ Ogólnopolskie Porozumienie Związków Zawodowych (All-Poland Alliance of Trade Unions)

FZZ Forum Związków Zawodowych (Trade Union Forum)

PO Platforma Obywatelska (Civic Platform)

PiS Prawo i Sprawiedliwość (Law and Justice)

RDS Rada Dialogu Społecznego (Social Dialogue Council)

SLD Sojusz Lewicy Demokratycznej (Democratic Left Alliance)

Annex 22.1

Trade union membership in Poland, 1981–2018

	NSZZ Solidarność	OPZZ	FZZ	Autonomous
1981	9,500,000			
1984	n.a.	3,948,189		
1985	2,000,000	5,274,491		
1986	n.a.	5,624,427		
1987	n.a.	5,843,321		
1988	n.a.	5,589,732		
1989	n.a.	5,236,072		
1990	3 000,000	4,538,276		350,000
1991	2,246,119	3,576,110		n.a.
1992	1,660,761	3,042,021		n.a.
1993	1,507,084	2,667,032		400,000
1994	1,422,764	2,457,873		n.a.
1995	1,312,050	2,300,687		n.a.
1996	1,233,209	2,153,444		n.a.
1997	1,118,229	2,001,050		n.a.
1998	1,113,440	1,803,468		600,000
1999	1,075,045	1,603,837		n.a.
2000	1,018,439	1,461,685		n.a.
2001	910,398	1,067,873		n.a.
2002	800,906	961,565	371,000	n.a.
2003	759,336	902,853	n.a.	521,000
2004	730,919	881,888	n.a.	n.a.
2005	721,356	874,086	n.a.	n.a.
2006	690,042	859,661	402,900	n.a.
2007	685,329	846,872	n.a.	470,000

	NSZZ Solidarność	OPZZ	FZZ	Autonomous
2008	679,975	833,633	n.a.	500,000
2009	667,572	821,712	n.a.	n.a.
2010	648,868	810,489	407,800	n.a.
2011	667,500	792,503	n.a.	n.a.
2012	622,577	639,458	408,100	350,000
2013	n.a.	618,253	n.a.	n.a.
2014	700,000	589,219	n.a.	272,000
2015	n.a.	565,712	n.a.	n.a.
2016	722,000	564,843	n.a.	250,000
2017	n.a.	552,923	n.a.	n.a.
2018	558,749	541,167	306,141	195,000

Note: Membership includes active members only except for 1984–2001 in the case of OPZZ, when data also includes pensioners; grey area: not applicable (the union(s) did not yet exist).

Source: Self-reported data collected by Gardawski et al. (2010, 2012a,b), authors and Visser (2019a). NSZZ Solidarność data for 1981: Gardawski et al. (2010), for 1985: survey data; for 2014 and 2016 – the union websites quoted by Visser (2019). Autonomous unions: survey data extrapolated by Visser except for 2014 and 2018, for which it is based on administrative data (GUS 2015, 2019).

Annex 22.2

Types of trade union structure in Poland

Trade union type	Description
Company-level trade union organization	Basic trade union organization covering one enterprise of one employer
Departmental trade union organization	Lower-level trade union structure within a (usually nationwide) company-level trade union

Trade union type	Description
Supra-company trade union / nationwide trade union	Trade union covering more than one employer – unitary trade unions, inter-company trade unions, federations and confederations. Supra-company trade unions are synonymous with nationwide trade unions. They can be single-sector or multi-sector trade unions
Unitary trade union	Supra-company trade union in which company-level union organizations do not have a separate legal status. The unitary union is considered a single legal entity on Polish territory. It encompasses company-level unions with the same statutes and name
Inter-company trade union organization	Trade union organization that covers at least two enterprises belonging to two different employers
Trade union federation	Supra-company (nationwide) trade union that associates company-level trade unions
Trade union confederation	Supra-company (nationwide) organization to which company-level trade unions and trade union federations are affiliated

Source: Gardawski et al. (2010: 75).

Chapter 23

Trade unions in Portugal: Between Marginalization and revitalization

Maria da Paz Campos Lima and Reinhard Naumann

This chapter scrutinizes trends and critical challenges of Portuguese trade unionism with an emphasis on the past two decades (see Table 23.1). It discusses changes in trade unions' organizational and mobilization power, in their institutional power in collective bargaining and tripartite concertation, and in their relations with social movements (Lehndorff et al. 2017). This retrospective analysis also focuses on trade union identities, strategies and orientations (Hyman 2001) and how they have framed their priorities and responses. This analysis provides some elements for the debate on what the future of unions in Portugal may be, taking into account the 'four possible futures' for the next couple of decades suggested by Visser (2019): gradual marginalization; dualization of union representation and policies; replacement; and revitalization.

The analysis shows that the continued neoliberal reconfiguration of the labour market and collective bargaining institutions, and the lasting effects of austerity policies have eroded union power in Portugal (Campos Lima 2020; Teles et al. 2020) and that unions are struggling to find adequate answers to the challenges. This suggests a trend towards de facto marginalization and the risks of intensifying dualization within the labour market. On the other hand, there have been some important cases of unity in action that allowed unions to regain the initiative in collective bargaining, as well as some important efforts to integrate precarious workers into the regular workforce in the public administration and mobilize platform workers. These steps counteract marginalization and dualization and foreshadow possible revitalization. In addition, we argue that unions retain a considerable capacity for mobilizing workers, as was evident during the anti-austerity protests organized by unions and new social movements linked to precarious workers. Cooperation with these movements holds great potential for the political struggle for a progressive labour agenda and for strengthening unions' societal power.

Table 23.1 Principal characteristics of trade unionism in Portugal

	1980	2000	2019
Total trade union membership	1,460,000	812,000	615,000
Women as a proportion of total membership	n.a.	41 %*	42 %**
Gross union density	60 %***	21 %****	15 %*****
Net union density	n.a.	n.a.	n.a.
Number of confederations	2	3	3
Number of affiliated unions (federations)	234 CGTP: 200 UGT: 33	173 CGTP: 107 UGT: 58 USI: 8	143 CGTP: 79 UGT: 50 USI: 14
Number of independent unions	143	195	233
Collective bargaining coverage	n.a	78.3 %	73.6 %******
Principal level of collective bargaining		Industry	
Days not worked due to industrial action per 1,000 workers	382******	41	56

Note: *2002; **2014; ***1979; ****2002; *****2016; ******1986; ******2018.

Source: Appendix A1. Union membership for 2019 is based on the authors' own research; for Collective bargaining coverage - Adjusted coverage OECD/AIAS (2021).

Historical background and principal features of the industrial relations system

Present-day Portuguese industrial relations were initiated by the 25 April 1974 democratic revolution, which overthrew the longest lasting authoritarian corporatist regime in Europe (Schmitter 1999). Restoring free unions and building industrial relations institutions was implemented alongside the unprecedented mobilization of workers and challenges to capitalist ownership and control leading to the nationalization of key sectors and companies (Barreto and Naumann 1998).

The Constitution of 1976 laid the foundations of the industrial relations regime. It included trade union freedom of organization; their exclusive prerogative of collective bargaining; extensive rights to strike and prohibition of lockout; consultation rights in relation to labour legislation, and economic and social policies; and rights of participation in the management of social security institutions. On the other hand, the Constitution recognized the *Comissões de Trabalhadores* (works councils), the direct company-based employee representative bodies that emerged during the revolution (Stoleroff 2016). Broadly considered, all these rights and prerogatives prevailed during the course of subsequent revisions of the Constitution. The 1976 Law on Unions (*Lei Sindical*) established the freedom of trade unions to decide their organizational forms, at all levels, including the confederal level, while the 1977 Law on Strikes (*Lei da Greve*) gave unions almost the exclusive prerogative of industrial action. Basically, the provisions set by these two laws were integrated in subsequent legislative reforms and prevail even today.

The trade union confederations were formally established in the end of the 1970s. During the revolutionary period 1974–1975, the previously semi-clandestine Intersindical functioned as a confederal structure and held its inaugural Congress I at the peak of the revolution, during the summer of 1975. Amid tensions within the trade union movement, Intersindical convened the so-called 'Congress of All Trade Unions' in January 1977 and constituted itself as the General Confederation of Portuguese Workers (CGTP-IN, *Confederação Geral dos Trabalhadores Portugueses – Intersindical Nacional*). This operation was meant to avert the organizational division of the trade union movement, but the contradictions between the advocates of class unionism, who had the majority in the CGTP, and social-liberal forces proved to be irreconcilable, Thus, in 1978 the General Union of Workers (UGT, *União Geral de Trabalhadores*) was created, challenging the hegemony of the CGTP. The creation of the UGT was supported by unions in the services sector (banking, insurance, administrative staff) and by 'parallel unions' created and expanded from 1976 onwards. UGT's creation changed the balance of forces within the union movement, although CGTP retained stronger organizational power (Barreto 1991; Barreto and Naumann 1998).

The Collective Bargaining Act of 1979 (*Lei dos Instrumentos de Regulamentação Coletiva*) established the foundations of the collective bargaining regime. These include: the favourability principle (*favor laboratoris*), most favourable treatment of workers; the rule that an agreement can be ended only by joint decision of the signatory parties and no party can withdraw unilaterally; and the extension of agreements by ministerial order. The Collective Bargaining Act did not establish any criterion of representativeness for unions or employers' organizations to sign collective agreements or to request extension orders. Industry-level agreements have always covered the large majority of workers, which remains a characteristic of Portuguese industrial relations.

Industrial relations in Portugal have been marked by the strong role of the state, establishing substantive and procedural rules through detailed labour legislation. State intervention has remained central. Since 1984, tripartite concertation has played an important role in income and labour and social policies. CGTP's and UGT's strategies have diverged profoundly at the macro-concertation level, although with occasional convergence on important themes (Campos Lima and Naumann 2011; de Almeida et al. 2017).

After the turn of the century, increasing exposure to international shocks and integration in the euro zone accentuated the pressure to neoliberal policies (Baccaro and Howell 2017). The 2003 Labour Code, an initiative of the centre-right coalition comprising the Social Democratic Party (PSD, *Partido Social Democrata*) and the Democratic and Social Centre Party (CDS, *Partido do Centro Democrático e Social*) reversed the favourability principle and allowed unilateral withdrawal from collective agreements. Notwithstanding some gradual changes, these radical changes made to power relations between employers and unions were never reversed. The revision of the Labour Code in 2009, carried out by the Socialist Party (PS, *Partido Socialista*) government, introduced a mitigated version of the favourability principle for some topics, while concurrently facilitating unilateral withdrawal from collective agreements (Campos Lima 2019; Naumann 2014).

The 2008 international financial crisis and the following austerity/neoliberal programme (2011–2014) implemented by the centre-right coalition PSD/CDS under the shadow of the so-called Troika, prolonged and intensified the economic recession in the country and deregulated further the labour market and collective bargaining institutions. This combination weakened the unions significantly (Campos Lima 2019; Cruces et al. 2015; ILO 2018; Távora and González 2016).

In 2015, the unprecedented alliance of the left-wing parties began to turn the page on austerity. The alliance comprised the PS, the Left Bloc (BE, *Bloco de Esquerda*), the Communist Party (PCP, *Partido Comunista Português*) and the Greens (PEV, *Partido Ecologista 'Os Verdes'*) and allowed the PS to form a minority government (2015–2019). This opened up opportunities to implement pro-labour policies and to start to eliminate the Troika legacy. The limited scope of the left alliance and the complexity of the political exchange between left-wing parliamentary agreements and tripartite concertation, however, hindered the full use of this window of opportunity (Branco et al. 2019; Campos Lima 2020; Teles et al. 2020). The discontinuation of the left-wing alliance after the general elections in late 2019 (won by the PS) put further limitations on the implementation of progressive labour policies. These limitations have been amplified by the Covid-19 pandemic, which laid bare the cumulative impact of the Troika's legacy and the high vulnerability of collective bargaining and trade unionism in Portugal.

Structure of unions and union democracy

CGTP and UGT are the only authentic cross-sector confederations and are recognized by the government and by employers as social partners at national level. ICTWSS estimates that CGTP's affiliates have 400,000 members and that UGT's affiliates organize 160,000 (2016). The disagreements in terms of ideology, strategy, organization and practice that originated the split of the Portuguese trade union movement into two confederations persist today.

During the late 1990s and the first decade of 2000s, CGTP opened up, to a certain extent, towards tripartite concertation, as well as towards convergence with UGT around specific topics (Campos Lima and Naumann 2011). Nonetheless, the steps taken did not result in the approximation between the two confederations towards strategic cooperation. A decade later a generational change at UGT improved the conditions for a better inter-confederal relationship. Meanwhile, however, CGTP had begun a reorientation towards its prior strict class struggle strategy and was less receptive to a rapprochement. Irrespective of this distance, occasional convergences have been possible around specific policies in tripartite concertation and industrial action, such as those that occurred during the Troika intervention.

The overall number of unions has stayed at a constantly high level, 376 in 2020 compared with 377 in 1980, but behind this continuity important structural changes have taken place.[1] Three major factors can be identified in these developments.

First, in 1996, CGTP launched a profound restructuring process that resulted in numerous mergers of single unions and the creation of a grid of 'vertical' structures at industry level. This comprised national federations with regional member unions, and integrated national unions, as well as regional structures, *uniões*.[2] This ongoing restructuring process with numerous mergers of unions and federations has been promoted and coordinated by the confederation. Unions in financial difficulties draft intervention plans for recovery jointly with the confederation. Besides the vertical federations in manufacturing and services, there are also some important occupational trade unions, such as the Teachers' Union Federation (FENPROF, *Federação Nacional dos Professores*) and the National Union of Nurses (SEP, *Sindicato dos Enfermeiros Portugueses*). The restructuring process in CGTP has resulted in a drastic reduction in the number of unions, from 200 in 1996 to seventy-nine in 2020. CGTP's affiliated unions have on average about 5,000 members each. During the same period, the number of federations was brought down from eighteen to ten. At present (2020), approximately two-thirds of CGTP affiliated unions and seven of its ten affiliated federations have an industrial domain, while about one-third of the unions and federations organize occupational groups, such as teachers and physicians, or have mixed domains, for instance commerce, services and administrative workers. CGTP's process of restructuring and rationalization has reduced the total number of existing unions by one-third. The creation of new unions outside this confederation, however, has resulted in the continuity of a very high number of existing unions in Portugal.

Second, after its Congress I in 1979, the number of UGT-affiliated unions increased markedly from thirty-three to fifty-eight in 2000 and decreased during the following two decades to fifty. Half of UGT-affiliated unions organize specific occupational groups, one-third have a 'vertical' industrial structure and the rest have a mixed domain. UGT's

1 Data DGERT/MTSSS.

2 Data and other info about CGTP restructuring are drawn from the Reports on Activities between 1999 (VIII Congress) and 2020 (XIV Congress). See references at the end of the chapter.

structure is the result of a continuous effort to win or create new member unions, some of them of short duration. UGT has not intervened in the same way as CGTP in the structure of its affiliates. UGT's structuring measures have basically taken the form of aggregating the existing organizations in regional structures similar to the 'uniões' existing at CGTP and in federations with varying domains.[3]

Third, a consequence of the fragmentation of the Portuguese trade union structure is the creation of numerous unions outside confederal structures. Three-quarters of the 121 new unions constituted between 1980 and 2020 did not join a confederation. Many of them organize specific occupational groups, such as nurses, social workers, members of civil protection and drivers. With few exceptions, such as the long-standing Union of Journalists (SJ, *Sindicato dos Jornalistas*) – which has a membership in the thousands – most of these 247 non-affiliated unions have an average of around 300 members and thus do not have quantitative weight in the respective domains, independently of being craft, professional or industry. The major driver for the continuous proliferation of unions, often extremely fragile or only existing on paper, is the increasing difficulty faced by existing trade unions in achieving positive results in their negotiations with employers and government. Union decision-making and communication as reflected in democracy, transparency and participation, and their general practices do not seem to be on a par with the challenge of responding to the widespread discontent among workers. Ideological reasons are certainly not the major factor for setting up new unions because the existing unions and confederations cover the whole spectrum of relevant ideologies in society.

The result of the diverging structural processes in the different segments of the trade union movement is a strongly fragmented general structure (376 unions with an average of 1,800 members), with extreme imbalances between a few larger organizations with tens of thousands of members and a large number of organizations with some tens or hundreds of members.

Relations between the two confederations and their respective member organizations differ. The CGTP has a strong coordinating and

---

[3] Data and other information about UGT's structures drawn from the Reports of Activities since 2000 (VIII Congress) until 2017 (XIII Congress). See references at the end of the chapter.

steering role in its affiliates' organizational work and in collective bargaining, in contrast to UGT's more restrained role in relation to its member organizations. CGTP and UGT are the exclusive trade union protagonists in tripartite concertation, which is of major importance not only for national macro-negotiations, but also in relation to their affiliates' access to information and consultation at industrial and occupational level. From this perspective access to the CPCS strengthens the power position of both confederations vis-à-vis their members.

The diversity of the numerous unions is mirrored by significant differences in the relations between unions and their members. One relevant manifestation of this variety is voter turnout at internal elections. In a sample of ballots at nineteen unions (twelve CGTP, four UGT, three non-affiliated), with a total of 244,000 members at the election date (2003–2008), total average turnout was 42.4 per cent, with variations between 21 and 76 per cent (IRR 2010). While these figures suggest, despite variations, a considerable interest on the part of members in trade union life, there are reasons to imagine that the general average of participation in internal union elections might be considerably lower than in this sample of relatively large organizations belonging to the small group of unions that publish their election results.

Unionization

Based on the figures provided by the OECD/AIAS ICTWSS database (OECD and AIAS 2021) and our own data (IRR 2010) it is estimated that the total number of trade union members decreased from approximately 1.5 million in 1980 to 800,000 in 2000, a reduction of 47 per cent, and to 670,000 in 2018, a further 16 per cent decline. The very high number of unionized workers in 1980 was the result of a set of exceptional factors.[4] In this perspective, the huge loss of members between 1980 and 2000 can be interpreted partly as the result of the ending of the extraordinary political circumstances that favoured unionization and of the deindustrialization, deregulation and privatization that began in the 1990s. It is estimated that the present total union membership is

4 Under the dictatorship, membership of corporatist unions was mandatory. After the 1974 revolution the free unions 'inherited' their members. Another exceptional factor was the enthusiastic political mobilization in Portuguese society during the revolution, which was still noticeable in the following years.

670,000 in 2018, 460,000 in the private sector and 210,000 in public administration.[5] These absolute numbers correspond to an overall union density of 19 per cent, 16 per cent in the private sector and 31 per cent in public administration.

Since 2010, the administrative data of Relatório Único (RU) provided by the Ministry of Labour Solidarity and Social Security (MTSSS, *Ministério do Trabalho, Solidariedade e Segurança Social*), concerning all private and state-owned companies, includes information about trade union membership provided by employers. Union members who pay their fees without the involvement of their companies are not captured by this survey. Irrespective of the abovementioned limitations, the RU data on trade union membership provides valid information for accessing the general trends in the evolution of union density (Table 23.2). The key points are: unions lost a considerable proportion of their membership in seven consecutive years (2011–2017), with an upturn in the last year of the observed period (2018). The losses were highest in the first four years (2011–2014) when the euro-zone crisis, combined with the anti-union policies of the Troika and the Portuguese right-wing government, damaged the foundations of social and labour rights. The annual decreases summed up to a total of 21.7 per cent over the period 2011–2018,[6] representing a huge loss in a short period of time.

Table 23.2 Trade union density in the private sector, 2011–2018

	2011	**2012**	**2013**	**2014**	**2015**	**2016**	**2017**	**2018**
Rate of change (%)	–7.3	–4.6	–3.1	–4.2	–1.3	–1.8	–4.1	2.6

Source: Authors' calculations based on Relatório Único (RU) and Quadros de Pessoal/ Ministry of Labour, Solidarity and Social Security.

Despite the limitations of this source, which underestimates density rates and must for that reason be understood as providing minimum values, numbers regarding the change of density between 2010 and 2018 at industry level can be considered much closer to real developments.

5 Estimate of union membership in public administration based on official data (Balanços Sociais); sample of public institutions covering approximately 30 per cent of the public administration (2015).

6 The figure of 21.7 per cent is calculated on the basis of the union membership numbers provided by the RU and the annual number of employees provided by Quadros de Pessoal/ Ministry of Labour, Solidarity and Social Security (MTSSS).

Table 23.3 Trade union density at industry level, 2010–2018

	Minimum value of union density based on RU In 2018 (%)	**Change in union density RU 2010–2018 (%)**
Mining and quarrying	10.6	−1.3
Manufacturing	7.3	–4.4
Electricity, gas, steam and air-conditioning supply	49.0	–7.8
Water supply, sewerage, waste management and remediation	12.4	−2.1
Construction	2.0	–0.9
Wholesale and retail trade, repair of motor vehicles and motorcycles	3.6	−1.3
Transportation and storage	24.7	–7.1
Accommodation and food service activities	3.4	–4.9
Information and communication activities	7.4	–8.0
Financial and insurance activities	46.9	–17.1
Real estate activities	1.4	–0.1
Consultancy, scientific, technical and similar activities	2.0	–0.4
Administrative and support service activities	4.8	+0.1
Public administration and defence, compulsory social security	13.6	–0.8
Education	5.1	+0.5
Human health activities and social support	9.8	0
Arts, entertainment, sports and recreation	6.7	–5.0
Other services	5.2	–2.8

Source: Authors' calculations with basis on data provided by GEP/MTSSS (2021).

The most striking results of this exercise are the high losses in the three high-density industries, 'financial and insurance activities', 'electricity, gas, steam and air-conditioning supply', and 'transportation and storage', and the very low density in large industries such as 'construction' and 'accommodation and food service activities'. The low average density in manufacturing is another important feature.

Based on the RU figures and our own estimates it is reasonable to assume that the largest absolute numbers of employed union members are in 'manufacturing' (~90,000), 'transportation and storage' (~70,000), 'financial and insurance activities' (~45,000), 'administrative and support service activities'

(~55,000) and 'human health activities and social support' (~50,000). Approximately two-thirds of all union members in the private sector work in these five industries.

In conclusion, since 1980 Portuguese trade unions might have lost more than half of their membership. In the first period, the 1980s, this was because the exceptionally favourable political context of the revolution (1974–1975) was vanishing and in the 1990s because economic liberalization and privatization undermined union power and strongholds. In the new millennium, severe adversities such as the amendments to the Labour Code (2003) and the Troika intervention (2011–2014) promoted further membership losses.

In the debate about membership losses the official union discourse tends to focus on contextual factors that are beyond reach of trade union action or that unions can influence only indirectly and/or partially. The question remains, however, what can the unions do to reverse the negative trend in membership? How can unions improve their organization, communication with workers, ways of mobilization and their cooperation with other unions and with other forces in society in a way that allows them to return to a path of growing membership and influence?

In Portugal, the most prominent case of a focus of union action and internal (not external) discourse on the unions' responsibility for strengthening their organization is the restructuring process launched by CGTP in 1996. CGTP's comprehensive organization programme combines restructuring of the basic unions and federations; rationalization and increasing efficiency of operations in the field, including a reduction of the administrative workforce and putting finances in order; recruitment and training of cadres, shop stewards and workplace leaders; and systematic membership recruitment in one integrated approach to organized union work.[7] In the course of its restructuring effort CGTP is running a permanent organizing campaign, with particular attention to women and young workers. During the first ten years this effort enjoyed considerable success and CGTP was able to obtain many new members, about 60 per cent of them women.[8] There are strong indicators, however,

---

7 CGTP designates this approach 'integrated trade union action' (*acção sindical integrada*). See CGTP (2020) Report of Activities 2016–2020, p. 11.

8 CGTP Congress Activity Reports indicate that new members decreased from 223,000 (1999–2003) to 115,000 (2016–2019). The share of women among new members has remained at a constant 60 per cent in contrast to only 42 per cent of total membership

that after the initial period of gains and stabilization (1996 until 2005/2010) membership losses have been substantial. It would be of considerable interest to understand whether this recent trend is the result of fatigue within the organization after a long period of intense mobilization under adverse conditions or whether there are other reasons for the decreasing success of the confederation's organizing effort.

Union resources and expenditure

Trade union income in Portugal is largely based on membership fees that represent in general 1 per cent of workers' wages (basic rates). Each confederation regulates internally the fees to be paid by individual unions to the federations (by industry or occupation), to the regional structures (*uniões*) and to the confederation itself.

During the first decade of its restructuring, CGTP published the sum of its affiliates' income from membership fees, which rose from 23 million euros (€) in 1995 to €39 million in 2006. The huge increase of €16 million resulted from the various elements of the restructuring process, membership recruitment and organizational improvement of affiliates, and from the entry of four teachers' unions, whose membership fees totalled €9.4 million in 2002. After stopping publishing data about membership fees received by its affiliates, CGTP began to publish the value of the fees paid by member unions to the confederation. CGTP's income from this source decreased from €2.5 million in 2007 to €2.0 million in 2019. Membership fees represent approximately 70 per cent of the confederation's income.[9]

---

in 1998. The share of young workers among new members decreased constantly from 34 per cent (1999–2003) to 14 per cent (2016–2019). CGTP's organizing campaign includes a systematic effort to elect shop stewards (*delegados sindicais*) at workplace level. The newly elected shop stewards at CGTP unions (1999–2004: 14,934; 2016–2020: 12,745) revealed an increase in the share of women from 54 per cent to 65 per cent between the two periods. The share of youngsters among shop stewards reached 17 per cent (1999–2003), but then it fell constantly and finally dropped to 3 per cent (2016–2019). The share of women at the level of single union leaderships (2016–2019: 38 per cent) has lagged behind their enormous gains among members and shop stewards. The share of young workers at the leadership level has been in line with the trends at membership and shop steward level: a brief increase to 7 per cent (2004–2007) followed by a drop to very low shares (2016–2019: 3 per cent).

9 All figures are based on data regarding CGTP finances, published in its Activity Reports presented at the Congresses in 2004, 2008, 2012, 2016 and 2020, and on authors' own calculations.

According to journalistic research UGT's total income in 2012–2013 and 2016–2017 was close to €1.8 million. The share of its affiliates' fees represented approximately 55 per cent of total income (€1.0 million) (Suspiro 2019).

Collective bargaining and unions at the workplace

The 1979 Collective Bargaining Law institutionalized three types of legally binding agreements without articulation: at the industry level or professional/occupational agreements between unions and employers' associations (CCT, *Contrato Coletivo de Trabalho*); agreements between unions and a group of companies not represented by an employers' association (ACT, *Acordo Coletivo de Trabalho*); and single employer agreements (AE, *Acordo de Empresa*). The lower-level ACT or AE agreements prevailed over industry-level agreements. This law did not provide for an effective resolution of conflicts over the implementation at company level of competing industrial agreements. Nevertheless, it gave the most representative union – among the workers potentially covered – the prerogative of deciding which *globally more favourable agreement* should apply in the company. At the same time, it stipulated that in the absence of an opinion from the union, the decision rested with the majority of workers. Moreover, respect for the favourability principle helped to resolve conflicts and ensure progressive labour standards.

The 2003 Labour Code introduced radical changes, eliminating the favourability principle and making it possible to terminate agreements at the unilateral request of one of the signatory parties. Moreover, it eliminated the prerogative of the most representative union to decide which agreement was to apply at company level in the case of competition. These rules also started to apply in the case of competition between extensions, a highly contentious issue in the case of 'parallel agreements', which brought CGTP and UGT into competition (Costa 1992; Leite and Almeida 1992; Moura 1984). Because unions could sign agreements independently of their representativeness, agreements between employers' associations and minority unions could easily be extended, to the detriment of the most representative unions. The pace of renewal of agreements became a major issue in the context of the unions' struggle to defend progressive achievements and of the employers' pressure for far-reaching alterations of agreements concluded during the years following the revolution. Last but not least, the Labour Code allowed each non-unionized worker to choose individually the agreement to apply, in the case of competing agreements at company level.

The 2009 Labour Code limited the after-effect period of terminated agreements and removed previous obstacles to unilateral termination. This paved the way for the cancellation of several industry-level agreements, initially affecting mainly CGTP unions in manufacturing and spreading later to services and targeting also UGT unions (Campos Lima 2019; Naumann 2014). On the other hand, it enabled workers to retain basic rights after the expiry of agreements, such as remuneration, category, working time duration and certain social protection schemes. It also partially reinstated the favourability principle, forbidding some specific norms of labour law to be derogated *in pejus* (to the detriment of the workers) by collective agreements. The 2009 Labour Code also enabled non-union workers representation structures to conclude collective agreements in companies with at least 500 workers, when authorized by the unions.

The austerity and neoliberal measures oriented towards so-called 'internal devaluation' required by the Memorandum of Understanding (MoU) with the Troika were implemented by the centre-right coalition PSD/CDS (2011–2014). This had a major impact, weakening union bargaining power. This facilitated dismissals, reduced unemployment protection, froze the minimum wage, and reconfigured collective bargaining institutions (Campos Lima 2019; Cruces et al. 2015; Távora and González 2016). The *de facto* suspension of extension ordinances and the legal restrictions on extension dependent on the representativeness of employer associations, in combination with the economic crisis, reduced the number of industrial agreements negotiated and a sharp fall in collective bargaining coverage (Schulten et al. 2015). Instead of the decentralization proclaimed by the MoU, the country experienced the temporary collapse of industry collective bargaining for three successive years. 'A down-to-earth analysis demonstrates that the Memorandum was designed to weaken the Portuguese system of social dialogue at all levels, in particular collective bargaining at sector or branch level' (Naumann 2017: 195).

From 2002 to 2018, the evolution of the distribution of workers covered by collective agreements at industry level (CCT, 92 per cent), encompassing groups of companies (ACT, 4 per cent), and at single company level (AE, 4 per cent), remained almost constant. Unions, in particular those affiliated to CGTP, however, have over the years engaged in other forms of company negotiation, *cadernos reivindicativos*, leading to ad hoc agreements, as a strategy to respond to industrial bargaining blockages or poor outcomes and also to respond to employers' reluctance to sign legally binding company agreements. The works councils have also frequently been involved in the negotiation of this type of agreement (Barreto and Naumann 1998; Távora and González 2016).

The most obvious explanation for the low incidence of company bargaining negotiations is the structural lack of organization/representation of workers at the company level in all its forms, including union delegates, works councils and workers' representatives for safety and health, despite the legislation protecting these forms of representation. The predominance of micro-enterprises, the precariousness of labour relations and the dynamics of externalization have certainly contributed to the persistence of the problem. On the other hand, it also reflects the unions' lack of resources and their strategic visions and priorities in terms of organization and locus of action. This influences not only their ability to negotiate at the company level, but also their ability to control the implementation of industry-wide agreements (Stoleroff 2016).

Since 2015 the new left-wing political cycle has opened opportunities for improving union influence in collective bargaining, but it has also revealed deadlocks and emerging challenges (Figure 23.1). The partial reversal of austerity policies removed nominal wage cuts in the public sector and enabled a regular and significant increase in the statutory minimum wage (GEP/MTSSS 2019). This helped to generate a new climate, favouring a certain recovery of wage bargaining dynamics and coverage. Since 2017 this has been boosted by new rules favouring the extension of agreements and by the bipartite commitment to suspend for 18 months any unilateral requests for termination of agreements.

Figure 23.1 Coverage rates of valid agreements and of updated/new agreements, 2002–2018

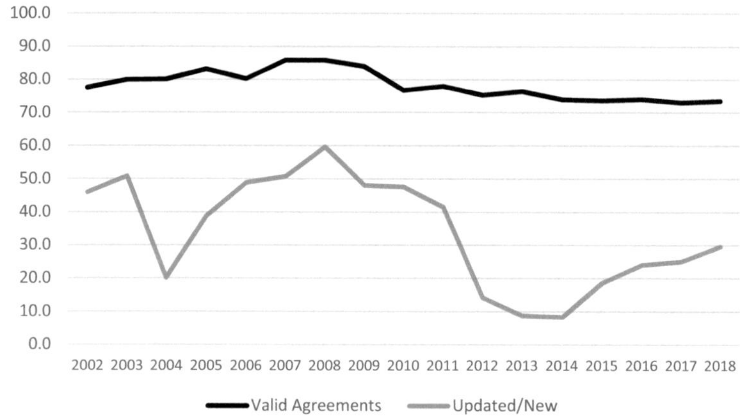

Note: The coverage of valid agreements corresponds to the concept of adjusted coverage, as a proportion of all wage workers, excluding those in public administration.
Source: Ministry of Labour, Solidarity and Social Security, DGERT and GEP/Quadros de Pessoal DGERT/MTSSS (2020).

Among the most severe problems in collective bargaining are the multiple divisions between trade unions along the lines of confederal affiliation, political orientation, regional origin and/or professional groups. During the term of the PS government, supported by the left, unions in private security (2017) and industrial cleaning (2019) were able to overcome their disputes and form powerful union coalitions that achieved major successes in collective agreements.[10] Both cases offer important lessons in terms of union bargaining strategies; their communication with workers in their industries; their mobilization of all available power resources, including contacts with international companies via UNI Europa; their relationships with each other; and their capacity to introduce innovative solutions into negotiations. Three trade union organizations were the major protagonists in these cases: the Service Workers' Union (STAD, Sindicato *dos Trabalhadores de Serviços de Portaria, Vigilância, Limpeza e Domésticas*),

10 The two sectors employ together approximately 8 per cent of all workers covered by collective agreements in the private sector.

affiliated to CGTP; the Federation of Service Unions (FETESE, *Federação dos Sindicatos da Industria e dos Serviços*); and the Energy and Manufacturing Union (SINDEL, *Sindicato Nacional da Industria e da Energia*) (Naumann 2020).

The debate about the amendment of the Labour Code in 2019 made clear that the PS government and employers' confederations were not willing to comply with the unions' demands, supported by the left-wing parties BE, PCP and PEV, for full reinstatement of the favourability principle and for the reversal of provisions allowing the unilateral termination of agreements. Instead, the approved amendment (Law 39/2019 of 4 September) reinforced the mechanisms of arbitration and mediation in collective bargaining and expanded the scope of rights that workers retain when agreements expire, adding parental rights and rights to health and safety at work. On the other hand, this amendment introduced two potentially disruptive measures: the termination of collective agreements in the event of the extinction of one of the signatory organizations, increasing the opportunities for employers to withdraw from collective bargaining regulations; and the introduction of company referenda by employers' initiative as a possible alternative to collective agreements. This last measure establishes that 'working time accounts' can be decided by collective bargaining or by 'group agreements', the latter based on employers' direct consultation of workers through referendum, without the mediation (consultation or negotiation) of unions or representative structures of workers. Trade unions and workers' representative structures, or, in their absence, labour inspectors, have a role only in overseeing these referenda (Campos Lima 2020).

After a promising first quarter, the positive dynamic of recovery in collective bargaining was interrupted in 2020 when the Covid-19 pandemic emerged. The number of workers covered by the wage updates agreed in 2020 fell by 46 per cent in relation to 2019, encompassing only about 394,277 workers, a number close to that observed in the worst years of the Troika. In response to this crisis, the government launched an exceptional measure (Law No. 11/2021 of 9 March) suspending the deadlines associated with the survival and expiry of collective agreements for a period of 24 months. This measure was welcomed by the unions, with CGTP demanding that unilateral termination of agreements to be definitively revoked, and heavily criticized by the employers' confederations.

Industrial conflict

The Portuguese Constitution guarantees the right to strike, grants unions the prerogative to call for strikes and prohibits lockouts. Exceptionally, workers are entitled to call a strike at company level, provided unions are not represented. Limitations to strike action include the provision of minimum services in certain activities;[11] a notice period of five days in general and of ten days in the case of activities responding to imperative social needs; and civil requisition in situations of national emergency in essential services of public interest (Campos Lima 2019).

Portugal has no tradition of strike funds. The possibility of extending the duration of strikes depends on the capacity of the workers involved to withstand the conflict. One-day strikes are common, although they can be prolonged depending on the sector of activity or the company and the issues at stake (Costa et al. 2015). Since the second half of the 1980s a downward trend in strikes has been observed in the private sector and in state-owned companies, measured by various indicators, such as the number of strikes, workers involved and working days lost (Figures 23.2 and 23.3).

This downward trend reflects several problems. Declining union density has undermined capacity to organize strikes. The processes of deindustrialization, privatization, restructuring and downsizing have eroded strongholds of union organization, strongly impacting strike action in manufacturing. In addition, the expansion of temporary work contracts has exposed workers to greater risks in the event of participation in strikes, including the non-renewal of their contracts. Moreover, competition in collective bargaining between unions has made the organization of sectoral strikes, with a focus on negotiations at the industry level, increasingly complex and less effective.

---

[11] These include: postal services and telecommunications; medical services and public health; power supply, mines and fuel; water supply; firefighting; public transport of cattle, public perishable foods and essential goods.

Figure 23.2 Workers participating in strikes and days not worked due to industrial action, 1986–2019

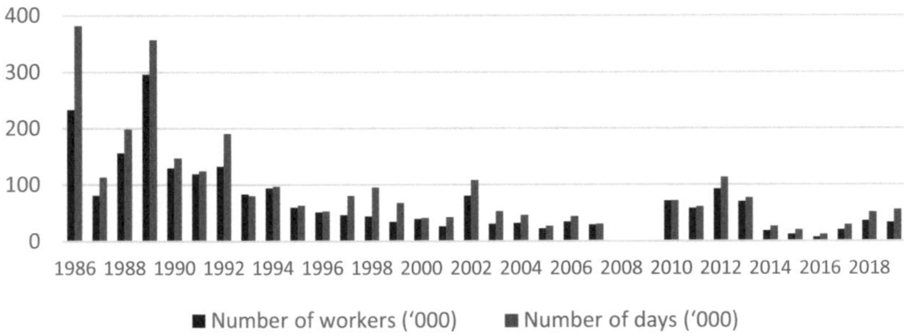

Note: Excluding public administration. Data for the years 2008 and 2009 was not published.
Source: GEE/METD| DGERT/MTSSS; Pordata.

Figure 23.3 Number of strikes, 1986–2019

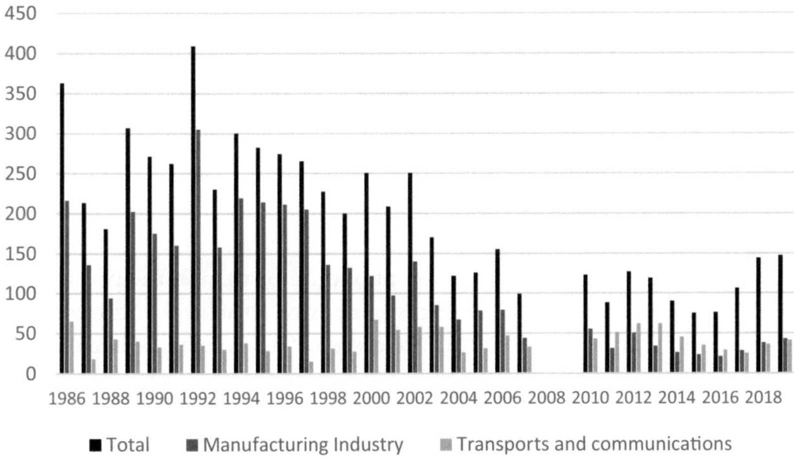

Note: Excluding public administration. Data for the years 2008 and 2009 was not published.
Source: GEE/METD| DGERT/MTSSS; Pordata.

Within the broad downward trend, most of the upturns coincided with the participation of workers in general strikes, the majority of which involved struggles against the negative changes in labour legislation and, more recently, against austerity policies. This pattern started with the wave initiated by the 1988 general strike, the first called jointly by CGTP and UGT, and continued to the most recent wave initiated in 2010 by the general strike called by the two confederations against austerity policies (see Table 23.4).

Table 23.4 General strikes in Portugal, 1988–2020

General strikes	Trade union confederations involved	Motive
1988	CGTP and UGT	Revision of labour law
2002	CGTP	Idem
2007	CGTP	Idem
2010	CGTP and UGT	Austerity package
2011	CGTP and UGT	Idem
2012, 22 March	CGTP	Revision of labour law
2012, 14 November	CGTP and 14 unions and 4 federations affiliated of UGT	Austerity package/joining ETUC European protest
2013, 27 June	CGTP and UGT	Austerity package

Source: Campos Lima and Martin Artiles (2014).

There is more job security in the public sector than in the private sector and unions are stronger in terms of density, structures and resources. Participation in strikes in the public sector has generally been much greater and more centralized than in the private sector (Costa et al. 2015).

Since 2010 austerity measures in the public sector have triggered a wave of strikes organized by public sector unions. Protests against such measures were one of the main reasons for the convergence between UGT and CGTP in three general strikes. In the past decade, worker mobilization has been more widespread in the public sector than in the private sector (Figure 23.4). The year 2012, when unions staged two general strikes against austerity and Labour Code amendments, is an exception, with equal participation of private and public sector workers. After strong strike activity during the Troika years (2010–2013) participation dropped sharply during the first years of recovery (2015–2016). In 2017 strike action peaked in public administration, but in general conflict settled at a low level.

Figure 23.4 Number of workers participating in strikes in the private and public sectors (thousands), 2012–2019

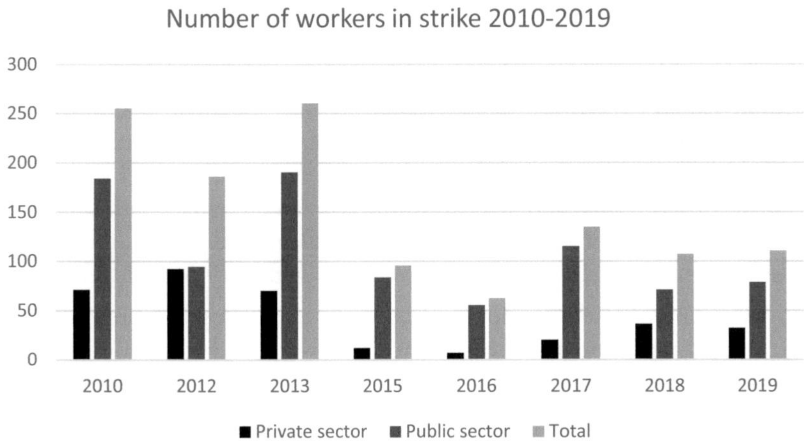

Note: Comparable data missing for the public sector in 2011 and 2014.
Source: Data for private sector based information from DGERT/MTSSS; for public sector based on DGAEP. https://www.dgaep.gov.pt/index.cfm?OBJID=e61955ea-6194-44bc-a938-b6dcbbec5902

During the first term – 2015–2019 – of the PS-minority government after the Troika years, a wave of strikes focusing on wage increases and career upgrades culminated in two public sector general strikes called by CGTP unions in 2017 and two called jointly by CGTP and UGT unions in 2018 and 2019 (Campos Lima 2020).

Since 2016, strikes at large private sector companies illustrate the intensification of social conflict and the emergence of new challenges (Costa et al. 2020; Fonseca 2019). CGTP- and UGT-affiliated unions and independent unions united in the strike at Portugal Telecom against the transfer of workers to the Altice Group, which had acquired the utility. A similar mobilization occurred at CTT postal services – privatized as a consequence of MoU conditionalities – against the reduction of 800 jobs and in pursuit of renationalization and compliance with the company agreement. Industrial action at the Volkswagen/Autoeuropa car assembly plant against plans to introduce mandatory Saturday working with three shifts, divided CGTP and UGT unions and the works council, while twice a majority of workers voted to continue the strike and rejected the 'pre-agreement' between the management and the works council. Last but not least, at the end of 2018 the dockworkers at the port of Setúbal staged a one-month strike demanding a collective agreement and the integration of precarious workers, who constituted 90 per cent of the workers at the port, into the regular workforce. Organized by the dockworkers' independent union the Loggers and Logistics Activity Union (SEAL, *Sindicato dos Estivadores e da Actividade Logística*) the strike paralysed the strategic port. Also, since 2016, CGTP unions and non-affiliated unions have organized various strikes of workers at the call centres of electricity and telecommunications companies, culminating, in the last quarter of 2019, with industry and national strikes demanding workers' integration into the companies to which they provide services.

In contrast, newly formed trade unions, distancing themselves from the bargaining strategies of established unions, launched various strikes, breaking with the conventional strike patterns and raising new challenges (Costa 2019; Fonseca 2019). That was the case with nurses' 'surgical' *intermittent* strikes, staged in 2018 and 2019, called by the Nurses Democratic Union of Portugal (SINDEPOR, *Sindicato Democrático dos Enfermeiros de Portugal*), affiliated to UGT, and by the independent Portuguese Nurses Union Association (ASPE, *Associação Sindical Portuguesa dos Enfermeiros*), two unions created in 2017. The same applies to the fuel-tanker drivers' *indefinite* strikes staged in 2019 by the independent Hazardous Material Driver's Union (SNMMP, *Sindicato* Nacional de Motoristas de Matérias Perigosas), created at the end of 2018. These conflicts encompassed specific categories of workers in positions of strategic power, 'surgical nurses' in the Public Health Service and 'oil tanker drivers' in the transport sector, whose highly disruptive strikes, in the first case, cancelled surgery in the operating theatres of public hospitals and, in the second case, interrupted the supply of fuel to stations, hospitals and airports. Last but not least, the 'surgical' strike was supported by strike funds based on crowdfunding, an unprecedented funding operation that raised serious doubts regarding the transparency and independence of the strike movement. In both cases the government enacted a civil requisition and other measures to end the strikes.

In the context of the Covid-19 pandemic, between 18 March and 2 May 2020, the 'state of emergency' suspended the constitutional right to strike 'as it may compromise the functioning of critical infrastructures or health care units, as well as in economic sectors vital to the production and supply of essential goods and services to the population' (Decree of the President of the Republic no. 14-A / 2020, Article 4). This suspension did not continue throughout the long period of the state of emergency between November 2020 and April 2021. During the second and third quarters of 2020, strike notices in the public and private sectors decreased dramatically. When the economy reopened, strike notices reached higher levels than in the first quarter.

Political relations

The political orientations of CGTP and UGT are historically linked to the period of their formation and the transition to democracy. CGTP's predecessor Intersindical was based on the broad anti-fascist alliance in the final years of the dictatorship between union leaders linked predominantly to the clandestine PCP and to Catholic progressive and socialist tendencies, some of which would join the PS or other left-wing parties. The coalition that constituted the CGTP in 1977 gathered the larger part of the old alliance, but the breakaway of an important part of unions and militants who were close to the PS and to the liberal-conservative PSD put an end to the organizational unity of the labour movement (Barreto and Naumann 1998). CGTP's anti-capitalist orientation, articulating 'society and class', focused on organizational power and mobilization at all levels. UGT, on the other hand, followed a consensus-building approach, articulating 'society and market' and focusing on gaining institutional power at sectoral and macro-concertation level (Hyman 2001).

The creation of the CPCS in 1984 and the institutionalization of tripartite concertation in the following decade granted trade union confederations and employer confederations institutional power at the macro political level (Campos Lima and Naumann 2011). Paradoxically, this period coincided with trends towards 'competitive corporatism' (Rhodes 1998). The policies of liberalization and privatization implemented by the centre-right PSD governments between 1985 and 1995 shifted power relations in favour of employers and weakened unions' organizational and mobilization power (Lehndorff et al. 2017).

Between 1986 and 1997, tripartite concertation, with a focus on wage moderation, constituted the reference for wage bargaining increases. CGTP and UGT diverged markedly on this issue, the former refusing to sign any agreement including wage moderation, and the latter emerging as a key protagonist of concession bargaining. In a later phase of concertation marked by simultaneous negotiations on specific issues, but not wage moderation, the two confederations converged to sign in 2006 the tripartite agreement increasing the statutory minimum wage for the period 2007–2011 at an annual rate of about 5.3 per cent. Previously, CGTP and UGT had agreed tripartite agreements on vocational training and health and safety at work (two in 1991 and two in 2001), which helped unions to push forward the collective bargaining agenda around these topics, although with uneven results in collective agreements. The agreements signed in 2001 contributed also to setting up tripartite institutions dealing with vocational training and active labour market policies.

The positions of CGTP and UGT differed substantially regarding the tripartite agreements with an impact on the revision of the labour legislation. The contentious and critical topics have been as follows: working time flexibilization in various forms, since the tripartite agreements in the 1990s; and employment protection, dismissals regime and legal framework for collective bargaining since the 2008 tripartite agreement until the present (Campos Lima 2020; Campos Lima and Naumann 2011). While UGT signed all the tripartite agreements on these issues, CGTP opposed them without exception. The content of the tripartite agreements on these topics influenced labour legislation and consequently also the employers' and trade unions' strategies in collective bargaining.

An important part of the legislative measures reconfiguring labour market and collective bargaining institutions in a neoliberal direction has been sanctioned by tripartite agreements, not subscribed to by the CGTP. The extreme case was the 2012 tripartite agreement under the shadow of the Troika, which reflected the centre-right PSD/CDS government's strategy of intensifying the 'governmentalization' of tripartite concertation (Almeida et al. 2017). This anti-labour tripartite agreement legitimized not only the impositions of the MoU, but also other austerity and liberalization measures 'beyond the Troika' (Leite et al. 2014). UGT signed the agreement in the face of the government's threat to increase working time in the private sector if they did not sign and the promise (not kept) that any future labour changes would be discussed in social concertation. CGTP opposition to the proposed measures was one of the central reasons for the two general strikes this confederation organized in 2012 (Campos Lima and Abrantes 2016).

Along the way, the intervention of the Constitutional Court, called for by left-wing opposition parties and demanded by CGTP and, in part, by UGT, halted or reversed some significant austerity and neoliberal measures by stopping cuts in Christmas and holiday bonuses, reversing various amendments to the Labour Code, prohibiting certain wage cuts in the public sector, and overturning the government's blockade of collective agreements signed in local administrations (Campos Lima and Abrantes 2016).

In 2015, the political context of tripartite concertation changed substantially when the left-wing parties gained the majority in the parliament. The PS needed the support of the left-wing parties and to this end signed separate parliamentary agreements with the Left Block, the Communist Party and the Greens. These agreements set out the following conditions for support: reversal of the exceptional measures under the Troika in the public sector, in particular nominal wage cuts; regular and significant minimum wage increases during the 2015–2019 term of office; and measures to combat precarious work. Subsequently, the government submitted the proposed measures to tripartite rounds, but also additional ones in line with employer confederations' concerns, not agreed with left-wing parties.

During this mandate, the PS government and the social partners, with the exception of CGTP, signed two tripartite agreements covering a wide range of issues. The first, the Tripartite Commitment to a Medium-Term Consultation Agreement (CES 2017), defined the increase in the minimum wage and the priorities for a future social pact and included a bipartite agreement signed by employers and UGT that suspended for eighteen months any requests for the termination of collective agreements. CGTP opposed the agreement, arguing against the reduction of employers' social security contributions in return for the minimum wage increase and demanding the definitive reversal of legislation allowing unilateral termination of agreements, as well as re-establishment of the favourability principle.

The second tripartite agreement, the Agreement to Combat Precariousness and Reduce the Segmentation of Labour and Promote Greater Dynamism in Collective Bargaining (CES 2018), laid down significant changes in the Labour Code, introduced a year later by Law 93/2019. This tripartite agreement included, in addition to the measures stemming from the left-wing parties, commitments to combat precarious work; some new measures reflecting employers' expectations, such as extending the probationary period when hiring long-term unemployed and first-time workers; the facilitation of very short-term employment contracts; the expiry of collective agreements in the event of the termination of a signatory organization; and company referenda on working time accounts.

Societal power

Since the revolution, campaigning in the public sphere by workers and citizens beyond their own affiliates has been standard union practice, traditionally more pronounced within CGTP than in UGT. Over the years, these campaigns have covered a wide range of topics: the reduction of working time and work–life balance; labour and social rights; employment quality and job security, gender equality and youth rights of integration in the labour market; and the quality of public services and against the privatization and the liberalization of the economy. In the health care and education sectors the unions often articulated their labour specific demands with campaigns to improve the quality of response of public services. In some cases, these union initiatives included alliances or ad hoc partnerships with other types of organization (mostly NGOs), and more recently with new social movements.

Before the cycle of mobilization against austerity under the Troika, Portugal registered extremely low levels in the European Social Survey indicator of citizens 'participation in demonstrations', with around 3.4 per cent of the population participating (2006–2011). Irrespective of its limitations, this indicator shows that there was an increase in citizen mobilization in the period 2012–2015, in Portugal reaching 7 per cent on average and in Spain 25 per cent (compared with 17 per cent in the previous period). Both in Portugal and Spain the increase in mobilization was concurrent with the participation of mostly left-oriented people; curiously, the evolution of the proportion of protestors who were members of a trade union showed a much higher level in Portugal than in Spain (Campos Lima and Artiles 2018).

On 12 March 2011, the newly formed social movement Struggling Generation (*Geração à Rasca*) organized a mass demonstration against austerity and precarious work, mobilizing more than 300,000 people in all parts of Portugal. This extraordinary event, the largest of its kind since the 1974 'Revolution of the Carnations' and organized without public support from political parties or trade unions, set the pace for the cycle of mobilization against austerity (Baumgarten 2013). This protest was succeeded by a demonstration jointly organized by the CGTP and by the movement *Que se Lixe a Troika* (Screw the Troika!) on 14 November 2012, the day of a general strike against austerity called by CGTP and eighteen UGT affiliates joining the European Trade Union Confederation's (ETUC) European protest.

Table 23.5 Mass demonstrations against austerity called by unions and social movements, 2011–2013

Year	Date	Initiative of the call
2011	12 March	Geração à Rasca (Desperate generation)
	1 October	CGTP
	15 October	M12M (Movement 12 March)
	24 November	M15M (Movement 15 October)
2012	11 February	CGTP
	15 September	Que se Lixe a Troika (Screw the Troika!)
	29 September	CGTP
	14 November	European protest – CGTP and Que se Lixe a Troika
2013	2 March	Que se Lixe a Troika with support of CGTP
	19 October	CGTP and Que se Lixe a Troika
	26 October	Que se Lixe a Troika
	1 November	CGTP

Source: Campos Lima and Martin Artiles (2014).

Various studies highlight convergence and divergence, complementarities and competition between social movements and unions, scrutinizing the overlapping and distinctive agendas, the distinctive styles of organizing and networking, and strategic orientations (Campos Lima and Artiles 2011; Costa 2017; Estanque et al. 2013). Objectively, they both contributed to the visibility and prestige of a progressive agenda against neoliberalism and austerity that impacted public opinion and the left turn in the general elections in 2015.

Moreover, the active intervention of social movements against precariousness in the 2010–2014 cycle of mobilization was translated into forms of flexible organization that consolidated during the following left political cycle (2015–2019), pushing the agenda to combat precariousness. The Association for Combatting Precariousness–Inflexible Precarious, hereafter called 'Inflexible Precarious', is one of the best examples. They combined the characteristics of a protest movement with a strategy to influence institutional developments. Their active intervention helped to push further various measures to combat bogus self-employment and to improve the social and labour rights of temporary and self-employed workers. In these policy domains, in conjunction with the specific parliamentary agreements between the PS and the left leaning parties BE, PCP and PEV, the left cycle constituted an unprecedented political opportunity to improve complementarity and convergent actions of unions and social movements and enlarge the scope of their intervention.

An example of the complementarity of the actions of unions and social movements, although without alliances, was their intervention in relation to the 'Extraordinary Programme for the Regularization of Precarious Employment Contracts in the Public Administration' (PREVPAP), a government initiative focused on regularizing the situation of workers without a 'proper legal employment relationship'. Unions took part in this process in the context of Bipartite Evaluation Committees with competences for examining workers' requests. They were engaged in defining evaluation criteria for workers' integration and participated in the decisions for their integration into the respective services. The 'Inflexible Precarious' and the platform *Precários do Estado* (Precarious of the State), an alliance of action groups in the public sector from very diverse professional backgrounds, played an important role by monitoring and pushing the process under the motto 'nobody left behind'. These movements cooperated with unions and works councils in the promotion of inclusive and effective solutions. Furthermore, CGTP and 'Inflexible Precarious' converged in their criticism against some measures to amend the Labour Code in 2019, focusing on precariousness (Campos Lima and Perista 2020). In addition, social movements of precarious workers often supported union actions or campaigns.

In connection with the pandemic crisis, trade unions strengthened the use of social media to inform, organize, mobilize and campaign. Unions and social movements participated in debates about topics of common interest, such as the widespread use of telework, compulsory for long periods during the pandemic crisis, and its implications; and about the responses to the vulnerability of workers in precarious or non-standard employment contracts, including electronic platform workers (Uber and Glovo, for example). Trade unions have been engaged in initiatives to organize platform workers, with considerable success in the area of call centres, but with serious difficulties in food delivery (Boavida et al. 2021).

Trade union policies towards the European Union

CGTP and UGT are both affiliates of the ETUC. UGT has been a member since the early days of its existence and a founding member of the International Trade Union Confederation (ITUC). Affiliates of the confederations are themselves affiliates of the respective European Trade Union Federations (ETUFs) and its strategy and practice are in the mainstream of the ETUC and ITUC. CGTP joined the ETUC much later, in 1995, initially because of its scepticism in relation to European integration and its rejection of the class-conciliatory orientation of the dominant forces inside the ETUC, and later because the UGT did not agree with CGTP's affiliation. In the early years of its entry to the ETUC, CGTP took 'an abstentionist and critical stance towards the political documents' of the ETUC (Costa 2006). This attitude has since developed into a more proactive and critical position with more developed arguments.

At its most recent Congress in 2020, CGTP's leadership questioned in its Report on Activities the increasing impositions in the context of the Economic and Monetary Union, the Euro Area, the Budgetary Treaty, European Governance, European Semester, and EU Banking Union for their central role in the offensive against workers' and people's rights and against the sovereignty of Member States. In this context CGTP sought - as pointed in this confederation XIV Congress Activity Report (CGTP-IN 2020) -, to make a contribution on the basis of its principles to the development of a firm and coherent perspective of intervention and struggle against policies of exploitation and impoverishment and for a sovereign and left-wing policy for Portugal and for a 'Europe of Workers and Peoples'.

UGT has a basically positive view on the European Union and agrees with the central position of the ETUC. In its report to the XIII Congress (2017), the leadership highlights UGT's intervention for a 'fairer and more solidary model of economic and social development … namely with the ETUC and the ITUC, … for more balanced policies, for workers' rights and for an improvement in working and living conditions, for the fight against poverty and inequality and strengthening for the reinforcement of social cohesion' (UGT 2017: 11, XIII Congress Report). UGT considers that a more Social Europe and the improvement of the Social Model requires rebalancing EU policies, particularly within the framework of the European Semester.

Several UGT member unions immediately after their creation joined the respective ETUFs. The entry of CGTP's affiliates to the ETUFs occurred later. Today, twenty-two Portuguese unions are represented on eight ETUFs, eleven of them affiliated to UGT, eight to CGTP and three are non-affiliated.[12] Most of these Portuguese affiliates are effectively representative in their domains. The National Federation of Trade Unions of Public and Social Service Workers (FNSTFPS, *Federação Nacional dos Sindicatos dos Trabalhadores em Funções Públicas e Sociais*) and the Federation of Transport and Communication Trade Unions (FECTRANS, *Federação dos Sindicatos de Transportes e Comunicações*) have close ties to the World Federation of Trade Unions (WFTU 2016).

The outcome of CGTP's internal debate about its accession to the ITUC revealed the persistent political reservations of the dominant forces inside this confederation against affiliation at international level. CGTP had been invited to be part of the group of founding members of the new global confederation in 2006, but after some internal controversy CGTP decided not to affiliate to the ITUC and to maintain equidistant relations with both it and the WFTU.

At the level of European works councils, Costa and Araújo (2013) report that in 2004–2006, according to the European Works Councils Database, 201 Portuguese representatives had been elected/appointed in 163 EWCs in 163 multinational companies. In 2011, Costa and Costa (2017: 120–121) noted 112 companies in the metal and chemical industries and in financial services operating in Portugal that had Portuguese representatives on their EWCs. CGTP and UGT represent Portugal at the EESC, each with two members. Furthermore, both confederations participate in three Interregional Trade Union Councils (IRTUCs) with Portuguese and Spanish participation: namely, North of Portugal-Galiza, Northeast Portugal and León, and Alentejo-Estremadura and Algarve-Andulcia (CGTP 2012).

Conclusions

After the revolution of 1974–1975, trade unions were on the offensive and created powerful organizations and a framework of collective agreements with high regulatory capacity, supported by very favourable constitutional and legal provisions. This golden age of Portuguese trade unionism ended in the late 1980s. Since then, unions have been on the

12 The following federations could be identified with CGTP- and/or UGT affiliates among their members: EFBWW/FETBB, IndustriAll, EPSU, ETF, ETUCE/CSEE, and UNI-EUROPA.

defensive. They have been losing members and power almost constantly; labour legislation has been modified to the workers' and unions' disadvantage; and collective bargaining has lost much of its regulatory capacity. As for trade union resistance to this negative long-term trend, two aspects stand out: CGTP's broad organizational and political offensive in the late 1990s/early 2000s and UGT's recent openness to better interconfederal relations. The most harmful attacks against workers' rights and trade unions were carried out by right-wing governments (2001–2004 and 2011–2015).

At present, there are strong indicators to support Visser's negative scenario of marginalization, with some elements of revitalization. The loss of power resources makes unions less important in shaping the labour market in a context of growing precariousness. Attempts by some governments to promote other actors than unions in labour relations have not succeeded, and the emergence of new social movements in defence of precarious workers has been a positive stimulus for trade unions and their standing in society. Therefore, we suppose that the risk of replacement is relatively low. Last but not least, the interaction between unions and social movements during the cycle of mobilizations (2010–2014) and the joint action of CGTP and UGT on different occasions, including general strikes, represent experiential capital that may help in revitalizing trade union strategies.

The deregulation of collective bargaining and of labour market institutions, and the persistent effects of internal devaluation have favoured the proliferation of low-wage jobs and precarious work, including bogus self-employment, intensifying the trend towards dualization. Against this trend, the trade unions have generally followed an inclusive approach, favouring comprehensive collective agreements and their extension to all workers, and participating in significant actions in an effort to integrate precarious workers in regular labour contracts.

Marginalization of unions, on the other hand, may occur even when they formally preserve their prerogatives and through processes of institutional conversion (Baccaro and Howell 2017). The institutional framework of tripartite concertation and social partners' prerogatives did not change for decades, but the modus operandi did: wage moderation and legitimation of government policies in the first decade, real exchange in the exceptional periods of 1997–2001 and 2005–2009, pure political legitimation in the shadow of the Troika, and most recently, the use of tripartism in an attempt to postpone progressive legislative measures.

Marginalization might also take the form of maintaining the formalities of collective negotiations while they are in fact stripped of their regulatory capacity (employers reduce collective bargaining to very low wage increases and governments block wage bargaining in the public sector).

What can be done to avoid these negative scenarios and explore the potential of recent experiences to open the way to revitalization? The present political power relations (with a left-wing majority in parliament since 2015) create a favourable context for an offensive to promote workers' and unions' rights, but the unions have not been able to take full advantage of this situation. It is crucial that unions improve their capacity to make use of political possibilities to push their agenda and to prepare for highly probable attacks in the future. At the same time, it is important that unions continue their efforts in consolidating and extending their organizational capacities in terms of members, activists and effective structures.

Furthermore, in view of the greatly diminished power base of the trade union movement as a whole, cooperation between the confederations CGTP and UGT is clearly key to strengthening the unions' position in collective bargaining and social concertation, improving their standing among workers and increasing their influence in politics and society. Renewal requires innovation, innovation implies risks, and unions will avoid risks in an overly hostile environment. More cooperative inter-union relations would reduce hostility and thus contribute to better conditions for rejuvenation and the search for innovative responses to the challenges of digitalization, instability of labour relations and other things. Better enmeshing with social movements would further improve mutual capacities to deal with the new challenges.

References

All links were checked on 1 July 2021.

Almeida J.R., da Silva M.C., Ferreira A.C. and Costa H.A. (2017) A concertação social em tempos de crise, in da Silva M.C., Hespanha P. and Caldas J.C. (eds) Trabalho e politicas de emprego – um retrocesso evitável, Coimbra, Actual Editora, 301–361.

Baccaro L. and Howell C. (2017) Trajectories of neoliberal transformation: European industrial relations since the 1970s, Cambridge, Cambridge University Press.

Barreto J. (1991) A formação das centrais sindicais e do sindicalismo contemporâneo em Portugal (1968–199O), PhD thesis, Lisbon, Instituto de ciências sociais da Universidade de Lisboa.

Barreto J. and Naumann R. (1998) Portugal: industrial relations under democracy, in Hyman R. and Ferner A. (eds) Changing industrial relations in Europe, 2nd edn, Oxford, Blackwell, 395–425.

Baumgarten B. (2013) Geração à Rasca and beyond: mobilizations in Portugal after 12 March 2011, Current Sociology, 61 (4), 457–473.

Boavida N., Moniz A., Naumann R., Roque I. and Azevedo R. (2021) Case studies on digital labour platforms in Portugal: 2nd National Report of Project Crowdwork, Lisbon, CICS.NOVA of Universidade Nova de Lisboa. https://drive.google.com/file/d/1MY7EcPT9Hb4fqE-jkxlXSxYitmfCjQjn/view?usp=sharing

Branco R., Cardoso D., Guillén A.M., Sacchi S. and Balbona D.L. (2019) Here to stay? Reversals of structural reforms in Southern Europe as the crisis wanes, South European Society and Politics, 24 (2), 205–232.

Campos Lima M.P. (2019) Portugal: reforms and the turn to neoliberal austerity, in Müller T., Vandaele K. and Waddington J. (eds) Collective bargaining in Europe: towards an endgame, Brussels, ETUI, 483–504.

Campos Lima M.P. (2020) Reconfiguring labour market and collective bargaining institutions in Portugal: turning the page on internal devaluation? in Santos A.C. and Teles N. (eds) Financialisation in the European periphery: work and social reproduction in Portugal, London, Routledge.

Campos Lima M.P. and Abrantes M. (2016) DIADSE – dialogue for advancing social Europe: Country report Portugal, Amsterdam, University of Amsterdam. http://www.cesis.org/admin/modulo_projects/upload/files/DIADSE_Portugal%20Report.pdf

Campos Lima M.P. and Martin Artíles A. (2011) Crisis and trade union challenges in Portugal and Spain: between general strikes and social pacts, Transfer, 17 (3), 387–402.

Campos Lima M.P. and Martin Artíles A. (2014) Descontentamento na Europa em tempos de austeridade: Daaçao coletiva à participaçao individual no protesto social, Revista Critica de Ciencias Sociais, 103, 137–172.

Campos Lima M.P. and Martin Artíles A. (2018) Social protests, discontent and politics in southern and eastern Europe: trends, patterns and polarisation, Transfer, 24 (2), 195–215.

Campos Lima M.P. and Naumann R. (2011) Portugal: from broad strategic pacts to policy-specific agreements, in Avdagic S., Rhodes M. and Visser J. (eds) Social Pacts in Europe: emergence, evolution, and institutionalization, Oxford, Oxford University Press, 147–174.

Campos Lima M.P. and Perísta H. (2020) NEWEFIN project. New employment forms and challenges to industrial relations: country report Portugal, Amsterdam, University of Amsterdam. https://aias-hsi.uva.nl/en/projects-a-z/newefin/drafts-country-reports/newefin-drafts-country-reports.html

CES (2008) Acordo tripartido para um novo sistema de regulação das relações laborais, das políticas de emprego e da proteção social em Portugal, Lisbon, Comissão Permanente de Concertação Social – Conselho Económico e Social.

CES (2011) Acordo tripartido – Compromisso para o crescimento, competitividade e emprego, Lisbon, Comissão Permanente de Concertação Social – Conselho Económico e Social.

CES (2012) Acordo tripartido para a competitividade e o emprego, Lisbon, Comissão Permanente de Concertação Social – Conselho Económico e Social.

CES (2017) Compromisso Tripartido para um acordo de concertação de Médio Prazo, Lisbon, Comissão Permanente de Concertação Social – Conselho Económico e Social.

CES (2018) Acordo para Combater a precariedade e reduzir a segmentação laboral e promover um maior dinamismo da negociação coletiva, Lisbon, Comissão Permanente de Concertação Social – Conselho Económico e Social.

CGTP-IN, Reports on Activities presented at the Congresses 1999, 2004, 2008, 2012, 2016 and 2020, Lisbon, Confederação Geral dos Trabalhadores Portugueses – Intersindical Nacional.

GGTP-IN (2020), XIV Congress Activity Report.

Costa H.A. (2006) Portuguese trade unions and European integration – lessons from a dual vision, Lusotopie, XIII (1), 7–35. https://journals.openedition.org/lusotopie/1446?lang=en#tocto2n4

Costa H.A. (2017) Sindicalismo e atores sociolaborais em contexto de austeridade: do voluntarismo dos protestos ao receio das alianças, Análise Social, 52 (224), 662–688.

Costa H.A. (2019) Is the strike still a right? The case of the Portuguese nurses' surgical strike, International Union Rights, 26 (1), 16–17.

Costa H.A. and Araujo P. (2013) Os conselhos de empresa europeus: entre a responsabilidade social da empresa e a participação laboral, CESCONTEXTO Estudos 1, Coimbra, Centro de Estudos Sociais – Universidade de Coimbra. https://www.ces.uc.pt/publicacoes/cescontexto/ficheiros/cescontexto_estudos_i.pdf

Costa H.A., Dias H. and Soeiro J. (2015) Strikes and austerity in Portugal: perspectives, expression and recomposition, RCCS Annual Review, (7), 45–73. http://doi.org/10.4000/ rccsar.596

Costa H.A., Estanque E., Fonseca D. and Silva M.C. (2020) Poderes Sindicais em Debate: Desafios e oportunidades na Autoeuropa, TAP e PT/Altice, Coimbra, Almedina.

Cruces J., Álvarez I., Trillo F. and Leonardi S. (2015) Impact of the euro crisis on wages and collective bargaining in southern Europe: a comparison of Italy, Portugal and Spain, in Van Gyes G. and Schulten T. (eds) Wage bargaining under the new European economic governance: alternative strategies for inclusive growth, Brussels, ETUI, 93–137.

DGERT/MTSSS (2020) Relatório sobre regulamentação coletiva de trabalho publicada no ano 2019, Lisbon, Direção Geral de Emprego e das Relações de Trabalho, Trabalho, Solidariedade e Segurança Social.

Estanque E., Costa H. and Soeiro J. (2013) The new global cycle of protest and the Portuguese case, Journal of Social Science Education, 12 (1), 31–40.

Fonseca D. (2019) Mais é menos? Dos novos sindicatos e outras questões, Le Monde Diplomatique, [Portuguese edition], 30 June 2019.

GEP/MTSSS (2019) Salário Mínimo Nacional 45 Anos depois – Balanço e Perspetivas Atuais Sobre Emprego e Salários em Portugal, Lisbon, Gabinete de Estratégia e Planeamento – Ministério do Trabalho, Solidariedade e Segurança Social.

GEP/MTSSS (2021), Relatório Único - Quadros de Pessoal, Gabinete de Estratégia e Planeamento/Ministério do Trabalho, Solidariedade e Segurança Social, unpublished.

Hyman R. (2001) Understanding European trade unionism: between market, class and society, London, Sage.

ILO (2018) Decent work in Portugal 2008–2018: from crisis to recovery, Geneva, ILO.

IRR (2010) Base de dados dos sindicatos portugueses [Database of Portuguese trade unions], compiled by the Instituto Ruben Rolo. https://institutorubenrolo.pt/docs/IRR_Base_de_Dados_Front.pdf

Lehndorff S., Dribbusch H. and Schulten T. (2017) European unions in a time of crisis – an overview, in Lehndorff S., Dribbusch H. and Schulten T. (eds) Rough waters – European unions in a time of crisis, Brussels, ETUI, 7–35.

Leite J. and Almeida F.J.C. (1992) Legislação do Trabalho, Coimbra, Coimbra Editora.

Leite J., Costa H., Silva M.C. and Almeida J.R. (2014) Austeridade, reformas laborais e desvalorização do trabalho, in Reis J. (ed.) A economia política do retrocesso, Coimbra, Almedina, 127–188.

Moura J.B. (1984) A convenção colectiva entre as fontes do direito do trabalho, Coimbra, Livraria Almedina.

Naumann R. (2014) Collective bargaining in Portugal: Study on the survival of contracts that are expired but not renewed (sobrevigência), Final Report, ICF CHK, European Commission, DG Employment, Social Affairs and Inclusion.

Naumann R. (2017) El papel de los actores sociales en las cambiantes relaciones de poder entre trabajo y capital en Portugal, ARXIUS de Ciencias sociales, (36–37), 191–206.

Naumann R. (2020) 'It was a process with many stones in its path', unpublished document presented at the Online Workshop 'Making collective bargaining in Europe more dynamic' on 18–19 June 2020, Friedrich Ebert Foundation in Portugal.

OECD and AIAS (2021) OECD/AIAS ICTWSS database, Version 09/2021. https://www.oecd.org/employment/ictwss-database.htm

Rhodes M. (1998) Globalization, labour markets and welfare states: a future of 'competitive corporatism'?, in Rhodes M. and Mény Y. (eds) The future of European welfare, London, Palgrave Macmillan, 178–203.

Schulten T., Eldring L. and Naumann R. (2015) The role of extension for the strength and stability of collective bargaining in Europe, in Van Gyes G. and Schulten T. (eds) Wage bargaining under the new European economic governance: alternative strategies for inclusive growth, Brussels, ETUI, 361–401.

Schmitter P.C. (1999) Portugal: do autoritarismo à democracia, Lisbon, Imprensa de Ciências Sociais.

Stoleroff A. (2016) The Portuguese labour movement and industrial democracy: from workplace revolution to a precarious quest for economic justice, Transfer, 22 (1), 101–119.

Suspiro A. (2019) Outros poderes. Como resiste a UGT à crise do sindicalismo?, Observador, 26 December 2019. https://observador.pt/especiais/outros-poderes-como-resiste-a-ugt-a-crise-do-sindicalismo/

Távora I. and González P. (2016) The reform of joint regulation and labour market policy during the current crisis: national report on Portugal, in Koukiadaki A., Távora I. and Martínez Lucio M. (eds) Joint regulation and labour market policy in Europe during the crisis, Brussels, ETUI, 321–393.

Teles N., Caldas J.C. and Martins D. (2020) Financialisation, labour and structural change: the case of Portuguese internal devaluation, in Santos A.C. and Teles N. (eds) Financialisation in the European periphery: work and social reproduction in Portugal, London, Routledge, 127–162.

UGT, União Geral de Trabalhadores: Reports on Activities presented at the Congresses 2000, 2004, 2009, 2013 and 2017.

Visser J. (2019) Unions in the balance, ILO ACTRAV Working Paper, Geneva, ILO.

WFTU (2016) Report of Action 2011–2016, 17th World Trade Union Congress, Durban, South Africa. http://www.wftucentral.org/download/documents/documents%20en/WFTU_Report-of-Action-2011-2016_EN_web.pdf

Abbreviations

ACT Acordo coletivo de trabalho (Collective labour agreement)
AE Acordos de Empresa (Single employer agreements)
ASPE Associação Sindical Portuguesa dos Enfermeiros (Nurses Democratic Union of Portugal)
BE Bloco de Esquerda (Left Bloc)
CCT Contrato coletivo de trabalho (Collective labour contract)
CDS-PP Centro Democrático e Social – Partido Popular (Democratic and Social Centre Party)

CGTP-IN	Confederação Geral dos Trabalhadores Portugueses – Intersindical Nacional (General Confederation of Portuguese Workers – Inter-Union National)
CIP	Confederação Empresarial de Portugal (Confederation of Portuguese Business)
CPCS	Comissão Permanente de Concertação Social (Standing Committee for Social Concertation)
CTT	Correios de Portugal (Post of Portugal)
DGAEP	Direção-Geral da Administração e do Emprego Público (Directorate-General for Administration and Public Employment)
DGERT	Direção-Geral do Emprego e das Relações de Trabalho (Directorate-General for Employment and Labour Relations)
EESC	European Economic and Social Committee
EFBWW	European Federation of Building and Woodworkers
EPSU	European Federation of Public Service Unions
ETF	European Transport Workers' Federation
ETUC	European Trade Union Confederation
ETUCE	European Trade Union Committee for Education
ETUF	European Trade Union Federation
EWC	European Works Council
FECTRANS	Federação dos Sindicatos de Transportes e Comunicações (Federation of Transport and Communication Trade Unions)
FENPROF	Federação Nacional dos Professores (Teachers' Union Federation)
FETESE	Federação dos Sindicatos da Indústria e dos Serviços (Federation of Manufacturing and Service Unions)
FNSTFPS	Federação Nacional dos Sindicatos dos Trabalhadores em Funções Públicas e Sociais (National Federation of Trade Unions of Public and Social Service Workers)
GEE	Gabinete de Estratégia e Estudos (Strategy and Research Office)
GEP	Gabinete de Estratégia e Planeamento (Strategy and Planning Office)

ICTWSS	Institutional Characteristics of Trade Unions, Wage Setting, State Intervention and Social Pacts (database)
IndustriAll	European Trade Union.
IRR	Instituto Ruben Rolo (Institute Ruben Rolo)
IRTUC	Interregional Trade Union Councils
ITUC	International Trade Union Confederation
M12M	Movimento 12 de Março (Movement 12 March)
M15M	Movimento 15 de Outubro (Movement 15 October)
METD	Ministério da Economia e da Transição Digital (Ministry of Economy and Digital Transition)
MoU	Memorandum of Understanding on Specific Economic Policy Conditionality
MTSSS	Ministério do Trabalho, Solidariedade e Segurança Social (Ministry of Labour, Solidarity and Social Security)
PCP	Partido Comunista Português (Portuguese Communist Party)
PS	Partido Socialista (Socialist Party)
PEV	Partido Ecologista 'Os Verdes' (Greens Party)
	Pordata Base de Dados de Portugal Contemporâneo (Contemporary Portugal Database)
PREVPAP	Programa de Regularização Extraordinária dos Vínculos Precários na Administração Pública (Extraordinary Programme for the Regularization of Precarious Employment Contracts in the Public Administration)
PSD	Partido Social Democrata (Social Democratic Party)
RU	Relatório Único (Single Report)
SEAL	Sindicato dos Estivadores e da Actividade Logística (Union of Dockworkers' and Logistics Activity)
SEP	Sindicato dos Enfermeiros Portugueses (Union of Portuguese Nurses)
SINDEL	Sindicato Nacional da Industria e da Energia (National Manufacturing and Energy Union)
SINDEPOR	Sindicato Democrático dos Enfermeiros de Portugal (Democratic Union of the Nurses of Portugal)
SJ	Sindicato dos Jornalistas (Union of Journalists)

SNMMP	Sindicato Nacional de Motoristas de Matérias Perigosas (National Union of Hazardous Material Driver)
STAD	Sindicato dos Trabalhadores de Serviços de Portaria, Vigilância, Limpeza, Domésticas e Actividades Diversas (Trade Union of the Workers of Gatekeepers, Private Security, Cleaning, Housekeeping and Other Activities)
UGT	União Geral de Trabalhadores (General Union of Workers)
UNI-Europa	Union Network International – Europa
USI	União dos Sindicatos Independentes (Confederation of Independent Unions)
WFTU	World Federation of Trade Unions

Chapter 24

Trade unions in Romania: Walking the thin line between politics and the market

Ștefan Guga and Aurora Trif

Trade unions in Romania have been fighting a losing battle over recent decades. Union density, militancy and overall influence in society have declined massively in comparison with the 1990s (Table 24.1) as unions have struggled to keep up with the structural transformation of the Romanian economy. Restructuring and privatization have crippled previously strong unions in manufacturing and services, with few unions surviving to this day in a position of relative strength. With five national confederations and over a hundred industry federations, fragmentation remains an important issue, whose implications have been made worse by dwindling overall membership. The same goes for long-standing tensions within the union hierarchy, as well as between public- and private-sector unions.

Union density has remained high only in the public sector, with only islands of activity persisting in the private sector. Relatively strong company unions and industry federations have survived in industries such as automotive and banking, while in commerce or IT new unions have managed to establish a fairly solid foothold (Trif 2016). These latter cases are exceptional, however, and not enough reason for optimism.

The hostility of foreign companies and the loss of unions' political clout led to the adoption in 2011 of restrictive legislation on collective bargaining, crippling unions at the industry level and severely curtailing opportunities for unionization in small companies (Trif 2016). While collective bargaining is widely regarded as the only legitimate purpose of company and industry-level unions, the legal restrictions introduced in 2011 made it impossible for many unions to pursue it, resulting in a dramatic decline in collective bargaining coverage (Table 24.1).

At the national level, we have a classic case of 'illusory corporatism' (Ost 2000, 2011), with political forays of confederations yielding increasingly less tangible results at the expense of dwindling legitimacy. The primarily consultative nature of the otherwise extensive institutional framework of social dialogue and the diminishing threat constituted by weak trade union organizations have rendered the once paramount relationship between unions and the government largely devoid of substance "(Trif 2016)."

While an overall decline in membership and militancy is the dominant tendency, there is also a cyclical character to union activity. Just as in the late 2000s, labour shortages determined by strong economic growth and massive emigration have in recent years led to a return of proactive union action, although in comparison with the previous decade this time around overt militancy has been far smaller in terms of both scale and effectiveness. The pandemic-induced economic crisis at the beginning of the 2020s brings yet another swing of the pendulum in the direction of defensive action. History shows that unionism in Romania has not fared well in such periods.

Although revitalization is the only way forward, a strategic reorientation in this direction would have to contend with hostile employers with a dominant presence in the public sphere, indifferent or similarly hostile political parties, and widespread apathy and suspicion on the part of the general public. Moreover, unions would also have to deal with long-standing internal problems. These include an ageing membership, fragmentation and infighting, limited legitimacy of leaders, and dwindling financial and organizational resources. Tackling all these challenges would require a mammoth effort, and as yet no concerted response is in sight.

Table 24.1 Principal characteristics of trade unionism in Romania

	1995	2000	2019
Total union membership*	±4,000,000	±2,500,000	±1,350,000
Women as a proportion of total membership*	55 %	58 %	>60 %
Gross union density	38 %	26 %	16 %
Net union density	42 %	29 %	16 %
Number of confederations	5	5	5
Number of affiliated unions (federations)**	>200	>200	127
Number of independent unions	n.a.	n.a.	n.a.
Collective bargaining coverage***	100 %	100 %	20 %
Principal level of collective bargaining	company/ national	company/ national	company
Days not worked due to industrial action per 1,000 workers	n.a.	1,543	n.a.

Notes: *All data estimated using Appendix A1 corroborated by historical trends and information published by the Romanian Ministry of Labour. For example, there is no data on the share of women in trade union membership later than 2003, but correctly identifies a previous tendency for this share to grow. It can be assumed this is because of two tendencies: (i) deindustrialization has primarily affected the male workforce; (ii) unions retrenched towards the public sector. **Data for 2019: documents submitted by confederations to the Romanian Ministry of Labour. Figures for 1995 and 2000 are rough estimates based on historical trends; ***Collective bargaining coverage calculated just for employees, which are the only ones legally entitled to collective bargaining; ****Data on days not worked due to industrial action is generally unavailable. The 2000 figure comes from ILOSTAT and its reliability cannot be assessed.

Source: Appendix A1; Romanian Labour Inspectorate.

Historical background and principal features of the industrial relations system

A trade union movement began to develop in Romania at the end of the nineteenth century and eventually established the Social Democratic Party, only to see its position erode in the interwar period, culminating with a ban on unions in 1938, when the Royal dictatorship was established (Burloiu 1997). Post-war legal arrangements were aimed at expanding unionization. Union membership became mandatory if one wanted access to certain benefits and avoid being regarded as an opponent of the new regime. Union membership increased from 30 per cent in 1945 (519,000 members) to 89 per cent of the industrial labour force in 1954, reaching almost 100 per cent after 1969 (Trif 2004). A single confederation including all unions was created in 1966, named the General Unions Confederation of Romania (UGSR, *Uniunea Generală a Sindicatelor din România*), which functioned by and large as an instrument of party control over industrial labour and had no distinct identity, authority or legitimacy deriving from their members (Trif 2004).

Similar to unions in other CEE countries, after 1989 most Romanian unions were eager to distance themselves from communism, which was an important factor in their acceptance of reforms aimed at transforming centrally planned economies into market economies (Ost 2009). The new governments in the region often asked for union support to introduce reforms leading to massive job losses and a severe decline in union density during the 1990s (Bohle and Greskovits 2012). Like their regional peers, unions in Romania expected that these reforms would eventually prove to be for the better.

In exchange for their acquiescence, Romanian governments accepted unions' demands for a favourable institutional setting. The laws adopted during the 1990s strengthened the position of unions against potentially more radical workers' actions and supported the development of bipartite collective bargaining and tripartite consultation (Bush 1993). The favourability principle – the rule according to which lower-level collective bargaining can only improve on the conditions set at higher levels – was established in law (Trif and Paolucci 2019), together with statutory extension of collective agreements at cross-industrial, industrial and company levels, which remained in place until 2011. Many company-level unions relied on the provisions of multi-employer collective agreements, because only strong unions from large companies were able to improve significantly on the standards established at the industry or national level.

The Romanian union movement is situated between labour market and society in Hyman's (2001) triangle of union identity. On one hand, the general orientation of unions since the 1990s has been the pursuit of collective bargaining, while eschewing broader social and economic issues. A business unionism strategy was actively pursued during the 1990s as a means to establish some distance from the state-socialist UGSR and re-establish legitimacy for unionism as such. It was broadly believed that a market economy was the basis on which a modern unionism should be built. As a consequence, union officials rejected the pursuit of broader class-based goals and regularly decried unions' political involvement. On the other hand, the post-1989 Romanian legal framework granted increasingly broad formal prerogatives to social dialogue, with unions being involved in much more than the narrow regulation of labour relations. Broadly speaking, this orientation towards society has remained the prerogative of national confederations, while industry- and especially company-level organizations are typically interested strictly in collective bargaining. This has remained a source of tensions up to the present.

Summing up, Romanian unions have been facing major challenges since the early 1990s. They supported the change towards what was hoped to be a more efficient economic system that in the long term would improve workers' livelihoods, while having to protect workers' interests in the short and medium terms. During this time, Romanian unions faced constant problems of survival and legitimization (Trif and Paolucci 2019). The once vital conundrum of collective bargaining versus political involvement was eventually resolved by fiat, as the union movement lost most of its previously massive political clout. By the time this happened, the union movement was left fragmented and with limited internal resources.

Structure of unions and union democracy

Post-1989 legislation defined unions as independent professional organizations, constituted from employees working in the same workplace or based on their profession, aiming to defend and promote their members' professional, social and economic interests. The situation in the early 1990s was nonetheless far from clear in this regard. The workers who protested most visibly for non-occupational reasons, the miners, were just the tip of the iceberg when it came to workers using collective action to make demands outside the standard scope of collective bargaining. Legislation adopted in the early 1990s aimed to curb any political involvement on the part of workers' organizations by strictly limiting the scope of organization, bargaining and collective action.

Current legal provisions require a minimum of fifteen employees to form a union; two unions from the same industry can form a federation if they have at least sixty members combined; and two federations can form a confederation. This legal framework contributed to the development of a decentralized and fragmented union movement, with a constant tug of war between different union levels over the control of resources.

Table 24.2 Trade union confederations in Romania, 2019–2020

	BNS	CNSLR-Frăția	Cartel Alfa	CSDR	Meridian
Membership	259,400	304,800	258,100	256,000	254,300
Federations	29	14	39	16	29
Public sector share	32 %	76 %	60 %	76 %	24 %
Dominant sector(s) (% of members)	Manufacturing (18 %), construction (13 %), transportation (12 %), public services (9 %)	Health care (33 %), education (24 %)	Police (17 %), manufacturing (16 %), public administration (15 %), healthcare (11 %)	Education (68 %)	Agriculture (50 %)

Source: Confederations' representativeness dossiers (2020 for Meridian and CNSLR, 2019 for BNS and Cartel Alfa, 2016 for CSDR).

Union fragmentation is common in CEE, initially engendered by the division between the old reformed unions and newly established organizations. In Romania, the reformed union ended up merging with the largest new organization in 1993 to create the National Romanian Free Trade Union Confederation–Brotherhood (CNSLR-Frăția, *Confederația Națională a Sindicatelor Libere din România-Frăția*). Today, over three-quarters of the CNSLR constituency come from the public sector, the largest federation in health care representing around a third of its total membership (Table 24.2). There are four other important confederations: (i) the National Trade Union Bloc (BNS, *Blocul National Sindical*), representing primarily the public sector (32 per cent of members), manufacturing (18 per cent) and construction (13 per cent); (ii) the Romanian Democratic Trade Union Confederation (CSDR, *Confederatia Sindicatelor Democratice din România*), created in 1994 as a result of a split from CNSLR-Frăția, representing primarily the public sector (over three-quarters of CSDR members, with over two-thirds-coming from a single federation in education; 13 per cent of CSDR members are from the manufacturing sector); (iii) the National Trade Union Confederation Cartel Alfa (*Confederatia Nationala a Sindicatelor Cartel Alfa*), representing primarily the public sector (60 per cent of members) and manufacturing (16 per cent of members); and (iv) The Meridian National Trade Union Confederation (*Confederatia Sindicala Nationala Meridian*), whose members come primarily from agriculture and forestry (50 per cent) and the public sector (24 per cent). Potential mergers between these confederations have been discussed several times during recent decades, but they have so far proved inconclusive. The decline in membership figures has rendered the problem of fragmentation even more acute, as confederations struggle to maintain representativeness.

Since 1989, confederations have mainly been intent on influencing the adoption of new legislation on employees via participation in tripartite social dialogue bodies, political lobbying and, until 2011, through cross-industrial collective bargaining at national level. They also offer legal assistance to their members and support federations in collective bargaining when needed. Because minimum labour standards have degraded and the legal framework is often ignored in practice, the benefits for employees at company level have become less visible over the years (Trif and Paolucci 2019).

Union federations are constituted from company unions from the same industry. As only two company unions are required to form a federation, they are often fragmented and competing. Federations generally deal with industry-specific labour legislation, collective bargaining and professional training. They are oftentimes called upon to support company-level unions, especially when the latter do not have a strong footing. The 2011 legislation stipulated that an industry-level agreement can be extended to cover all employers and workers only if both trade unions and employers' associations signing it covered at least 50 per cent of all employees in the respective industry. In effect this represents a de facto block on industry-level bargaining, because unionization is far below this threshold in almost all private-sector industries and the vast majority of private-sector employers remained unorganized. Indeed, through such legal provisions, employers were in fact given additional incentives not to organize. Union federations, on the other hand, were left with severely diminished room for manoeuvre and faced renewed legitimation problems. Some federations merged in response, while others diminished in importance and some even disappeared altogether (Guga and Constantin 2015).

Although formally significant, the virtual disappearance of industry-level agreements has had a limited impact on company unions, because these agreements established only minimal terms and conditions and were often similar to those set by national-level agreements (Trif 2004). While the 2011 legislative change, introduced by the right-wing party then in power, aimed explicitly at the decentralization of collective bargaining, company unions were tasked with negotiating effective wage levels and employment conditions even before that. Nevertheless, cross-industrial and industry-wide agreements covered at least wage indexation, contingent on workers' qualifications, and often pay increases were linked to inflation, while the company-level bargaining agenda began with a blank canvas after 2011. Company-level union representatives in metallurgy, for example, reported that they realized the importance of cross-sectoral and industry-wide agreements only after they had ceased to exist (Trif and Paoluci 2019).

Company unions are constituted from employees working in the same enterprise. One or more unions may operate in the same enterprise. Since 2011, only those covering more than 50 per cent of the labour force are eligible to negotiate collective agreements, while before the adoption of the Social Dialogue Act (LDS, *Legea Dialogului Social*) this threshold was 33 per cent (Trif and Paolucci 2019).[1] While this change has reduced fragmentation and has strengthened the position of already powerful organizations, it has undermined the role of unions that cover less than 50 per cent of the labour force and has made unionization more difficult. Apart from concluding and monitoring the implementation of collective agreements, company unions deal with individual issues for their members, depending on their own statutes and resources.

Unionization

Union membership has declined since the early 1990s, although the scarce and unreliable data makes it difficult to develop an accurate picture of the year-by-year rate of decline. The data in the ICTWSS database is fragmentary (Figure 24.1) and pre-2011 information is unreliable. The legislation adopted in 2011 introduced transparency criteria for federations and confederations, forcing them to provide proof of membership

---

1 The LDS received a major amendment coming into force in January 2023. Among other things, this included a reduction of the company-level representativenes threshold to 35%. While the legal changes appear substantial at face value, it is uncertain whether they will have major consequences for the functioning of trade unions and collective bargaining in Romania. It is clear that any impact would take some time to materialize, whcih means that future research is needed to address this question.

figures when demanding representativeness. Before that, membership seemed to fluctuate significantly as union organizations sometimes tried to appear stronger than they actually were in order to improve their bargaining position, while on other occasions they communicated lower membership figures in order to reduce the financial impact of membership in higher union bodies. While this latter issue remains relevant today, we can be certain that since 2011 official figures on union membership have been much closer to reality than previous ones.

Figure 24.1 Union membership and density, 1993–2019

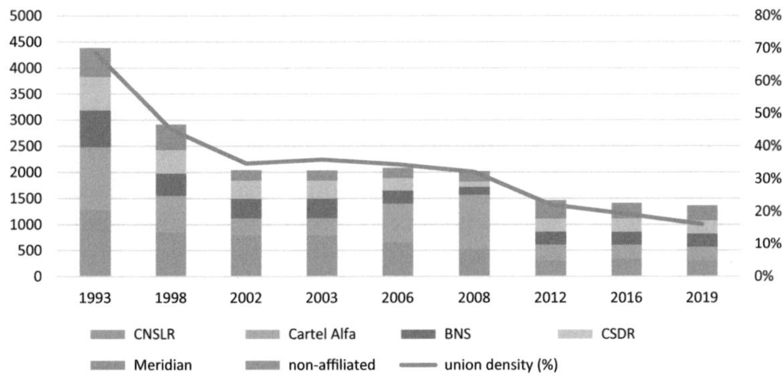

Source: Appendix A1 for 1993–2008, Romanian Ministry of Labour for 2012–2019. Number of non-affiliated members estimated at 30,000, based on Appendix A1.

Figure 24.1 shows a strong decline in membership throughout the 1990s, from over 4 million members in 1993 to around 2 million in 2002. This can be attributed unambiguously to profound economic transformations and especially to the massive decline in employment in union strongholds across manufacturing, services and mining. While overall employment has declined as well, the halving of union density (from 68.7 to 34.7 per cent) clearly indicates that unionized industries were disproportionately affected by the transformation of the Romanian economy. Union membership and density remained somewhat stable during the 2000s, even though major economic transformations continued apace. This puzzling trend is probably explained by the decreasing reliability of official membership information (Guga and Constantin 2015). The major decline in membership between 2008 and 2012, from approximately 2 million to less than 1 million and a half, can to an important extent be attributed to the transparency regulations introduced in 2011 and is not simply a consequence of the economic crisis.[2]

During the past decade, union membership has declined slowly (by 7 per cent between 2012 and 2019), while the shrinking of union density has been much more severe (from 22.1 to 16.1 per cent – a decline of 6 percentage points, an effective decline of approximately 28 per cent) (Figure 24.1). This shows that unions have been unsuccessful in increasing their membership during times of significant economic and employment growth, remaining entrenched in their traditional strongholds: the public sector and large state-owned or formerly state-owned enterprises. This is typical of the past two decades: while the economy became increasingly privatized and increasingly dominated by foreign capital, unions have remained largely on the defensive, counting on their shrinking traditional membership while making very limited inroads into the more dynamic segments of the economy.

The public sector has remained the only heavily unionized part of the economy, with a union density of more than 75 per cent. Today, over half of union members come from the public sector, especially from education, public administration, health care and policing (Tables 24.3 and 24.4). While the public sector comprises less than a fifth of total employment and more than half of union members, manufacturing employment represents almost a quarter of the total but has only 9 per cent of total union membership (Table 24.5). It is thus in manufacturing that the impact of economic transformation on union membership has been felt the most. On one hand, most of the former state-owned industrial giants were privatized, severely shrunk or closed for good. Those that have survived are likely to be unionized, although over the years few have flourished while maintaining a strong union presence. The most significant outlier in this regard is the Dacia union, which has around a half of all union members in the country's burgeoning automotive industry (Adăscăliței and Guga 2017). On the other hand, although manufacturing has been revitalized by substantial inflows of foreign direct

---

2 There are still are several obstacles when it comes to assessing the exact number of union members. Company level organisations might intentionally underreport their membership levels in order to hold on to a larger part of membership fees. The exact extent of this and its implications for overall membership levels are impossible to assess.

investment, greenfield manufacturing sites are generally non-unionized and, where unions do exist, they are typically weak.

The private service sector has few unionized industries. Banking is fairly typical, with several formerly state-owned banks still having strong unions (Guga and Spatari 2020). Commerce is the exact opposite: very large multinational retail chains and wholesalers are unionized, while that is rarely the case for small and dispersed local companies (Guga and Spatari 2019). The discrepancy in relation to other industries is even higher if we consider that multinational commerce operations are typically greenfield. Commerce in Romania has thus been one of the very few areas to see successful unionization campaigns during the past two decades. A similar, albeit smaller-scale, example is IT, where a relatively strong multi-employer union started to emerge in the second half of the 2000s (Trif 2016). Outside these industries, recruitment campaigns in the private sector have been rare and in recent years have aimed rather at conserving membership numbers in a context of high labour turnover than at boosting union strength (Guga and Spatari 2020). In many growing companies with a strong union presence, unions continue to count on the assumption that new employees consider union membership as customary.

Although no reliable statistical evidence is available, given the sector- and industry-specific concentration of membership, it is a safe guess that the majority of union members are female (72 per cent of public sector employees are women). According to ICTWSS, 57.5 per cent of union members were female already at the beginning of the 2000s, which most likely means that today female membership is at well over 60 per cent.

Table 24.3 Union membership by sector, 2019*

Sector	Members	Percentage of total trade union members	Percentage of total employment
Public	724,755	54.4	19.3
Manufacturing	120,008	9.0	23.0
Agriculture	118,935	8.9	2.4
Energy	66,842	5.0	1.8
Other services	66,327	5.0	39.8
Transportation	65,687	4.9	5.4
Construction	39,515	3.0	8.0
Mining	15,706	1.2	0.3
Other	113,631	15.7	–

Table 24.4 Union membership in the public sector, 2019*

Industry	Members	Percentage of total trade union members	Percentage of total employment
Education	263,690	19.8	7.1
Administration	151,142	11.4	–
Health care	144,772	10.9	8.0
Police	87,136	6.5	–
Services	52,972	4.0	–
Culture/media	11,439	0.9	–
Other	13,604	1.0	–

Table 24.5 Union membership in manufacturing, 2019*

Industry	Members	Percentage of total	Percentage of total employment
Automotive	39,721	3.0	3.6
Metallurgy	17,693	1.3	0.6
Food	14,536	1.1	3.7
Chemical	14,242	1.1	1.8
Multiple	12,800	1.0	–
Textiles	11,930	0.9	2.8
Machine building	4,014	0.3	–
Cement	2,859	0.2	–
Electronics	2,213	0.2	–

Note: *Data correspond to 2019–2020 for four confederations and 2016 for the fifth.

Source: Compiled from union confederation files from the Romanian Ministry of Labour. Employment figures for October 2019 published by the National Institute of Statistics.

Traditionally, unions in Romania have been organizations of employees. The legal framework does not allow for unions of non-employees (e.g. self-employed and retired workers) and unions have never contested this. Union membership is usually renounced once an employee leaves a company, regardless of the reason. Some company unions continue to provide minimum legal assistance to early retirees seeking to revise their pension calculation, but generally unions focus strictly on employees' interests. At national level, confederations seek to achieve higher benefits for pensioners in order to improve the future welfare of their current members, many of whom are approaching retirement. Union success in improving pensions has been limited and some confederations have actually opposed pension increases in the belief that they would constitute too high of a burden on the state budget and could thus harm the interests of employees who on this understanding would likely have to bear the burden of higher taxes.

The fact that the majority of union members are approaching retirement age represents an existential threat for many union organizations, to which they have no clear answer. At national level, there has been no palpable attempt to expand the membership beyond the confines of the standard employment relationship. Workers with temporary contracts are often not interested in joining a union and it is not unusual for company unions to prefer to focus on employees with permanent labour contracts. Some strong unions occasionally demand from employers that they hire their workers on a permanent basis (Guga 2017). In companies with a high share of both permanent and temporary employees, the former often see the latter as a threat, while some union officials might not consider it worthwhile spending resources on defending the interests of temporary workers who are bound to lose their union membership sooner rather than later (Trif 2016). More generally, unions have been largely unable to respond to the growth of atypical employment during the past decade, while employers have constantly pushed for increased flexibility. Platform work and workers from abroad are new phenomena on the Romanian labour market that are very likely to grow significantly in the future. The construction workers' federation FGS Familia has historically been interested in the question of migration, first in the case of Romanian construction workers abroad and more recently for foreign workers coming to Romania (Trif 2016). Apart from such rare exceptions, unions have so far shown little more than modest academic interest in these issues. Public discourse on immigration is dominated by employers' concerns about labour shortages caused by mass emigration.

Union resources and expenditure

Unions in Romania can count on three sources of funding: membership fees collected at the company level; income resulting from administering ex-UGSR real estate granted to confederations in the 1990s; and EU funding, which for many years has been an important source of income, particularly for confederations.

Membership fees are typically calculated as 1 per cent of the gross base wage. Few unions opt for a fixed monthly sum, usually to reduce the financial burden on their members and attract new members or prevent membership loss. There are cases where the difference between the two types of fees has over the years become very large because of rapid wage growth, with union leaders finding it difficult to increase fixed-sum fees.

Membership fees have often been an object of controversy. The legal changes adopted at the beginning of the 2010s removed employers' obligation to automatically withhold fees from union members' pay and transfer the money to the unions based on membership lists. Employers and the government argued that this latter procedure put an unnecessary and illegitimate burden on employers, while not allowing members to be in full control of their remuneration. For unions, the changes required major logistical efforts and involved the risk of massive membership loss. The changes were eventually overturned in 2016 and fee collection has since remained a task for the employer to handle on behalf of the union. While this is definitely the more stress-free option for union officials, it comes at a price, because employers are always fully informed of the number and identity of union members and can use this information to counter union action.

Company unions use the membership fees to cover regular and exceptional expenses. Only large unions have sufficient finances to hire full-time staff, although in some situations this is made possible by agreeing with the employer to pay the wages of one or several union officials. Other regular expenses include gifts in kind to their members once or several times per year (for Christmas, for example). Some unions organize social events for their members, which they have to finance independently. Exceptional expenditure such as legal fees also have to be paid from the standard union budget.

Company unions transfer a part of their income from membership fees to federations, which in turn transfer a part of the funds to confederations. The funding of higher union bodies thus depends on membership figures reported by lower-level organizations. In a context of dwindling membership, this is a major source of tensions between unions across the three levels, with cash-strapped company unions and federations underreporting their membership numbers in order to pay lower fees to umbrella organizations. On occasion, officials end up agreeing on a fixed membership figure in order not to escalate these tensions. Although such agreements have successfully ameliorated the climate of mutual suspicion among union leaders, they cannot provide a solution to the major funding problems affecting many organizations. As a result, some company unions have been forced to cut back on otherwise vital expenditure such as legal counselling or employing full-time staff. Federations have been hit hardest, because they could not forgo paying staff and some have to cover expenses related to maintaining an office. As a consequence, many federations ended up permanently functioning with a skeleton staff of just one or two officials.

Figure 24.2 Employees and annual income for Confederation 1, 2006–2019

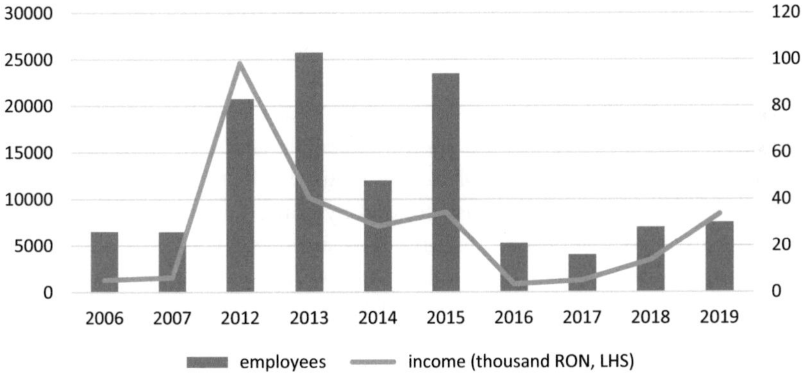

Source: Annual financial filings published by the Romanian Ministry of Finance.

Figure 24.3 Employees and annual income for Confederation 2, 2006–2019

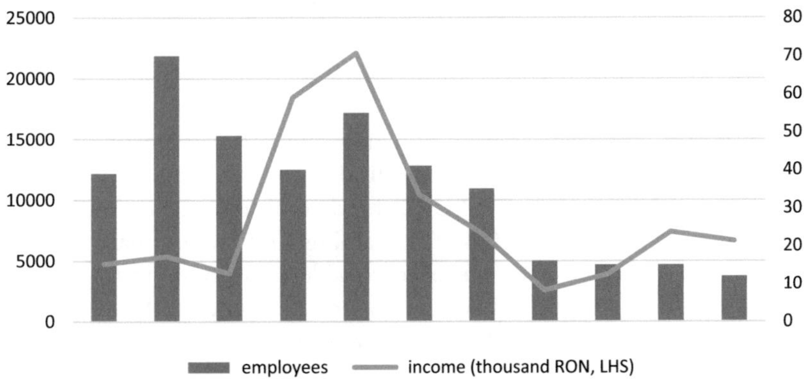

Source: Annual financial filings published by the Romanian Ministry of Finance.

Confederations have also been impacted by reduced funding from membership fees, but in contrast to lower-level organizations they have been able to access other sources of funding. Historically, confederations have administered vast real estate portfolios, including hotels and various types of recreational venue. These have been an important source of controversy, fuelling accusations of corruption and incompetence in handling such allegedly highly valuable assets.[3]

Some unions have compensated for dwindling financial resources from traditional sources by accessing EU funding. Given the high level of expertise and resources required to implement EU-funded projects, this has typically been a perquisite for confederations, or of federations willing and able to dedicate considerable resources to this task. Unions accessed a total of approximately 150 million euros between 2007 and 2015 from the Operational Sectoral Programme Human Resources Development (POSDRU, *Programul Operațional Sectorial Dezvoltarea Resurselor Umane*), financed primarily from the European Social Fund. Around a third of this sum was accessed by confederations, with the rest going mostly to federations. Figures 24.2 and 24.3 show the activity of two confederations that accessed a total of approximately 40 million RON (approximately €8.2 million) of POSDRU funding (and approximately 120 million RON [approximately €24.6 million] total funding, if we consider their member organizations; data published by the Ministry of European Funds). The most striking aspect is probably the growth of income by a factor of 16 for Confederation One between 2007 and 2012 and by a factor of 3.4 for Confederation Two. Accessing POSDRU funds was notoriously complex and required substantial additional staffing, which is visible in the case of both confederations. Once the programme ended, the two confederations reverted to low levels of income and staffing.

POSDRU was dedicated to 'human resource development' and was not a programme designed specifically for unions. Employee organizations wanting to access POSDRU funds typically had to implement projects dealing with professional training and career management. Since this has traditionally not been considered a union prerogative, it raised significant suspicions on the part of the rank-and-file and from company unions. Union officials involved in EU-funded projects were

3 For just one out of countless examples, see Digi24 (2016).

accused of betraying their members' interests and giving up on the bread and butter of union activity in favour of such highly lucrative alternatives. Involvement in accessing EU funds further harmed the unions at a national level, with regular media articles highlighting the disproportionately high personal incomes of high-level union officials. The fact that confederations appeared to prosper financially and organizationally at a time when the rank-and-file and company unions were dealing with the aftermath of severe austerity and changes to labour laws further contributed to the perception of corruption surrounding unions' usage of EU funds.[4] Furthermore, some organizations did not manage their projects adequately and ended up being crippled financially. Some ended up effectively dissolving as a result of botched EU-funded projects, while others have remained massively debt-ridden ever since.

Collective bargaining and unions at the workplace

The legal changes introduced by the 2003 new Labour Code, as well as those associated with EU accession in 2007, were aimed generally at strengthening the role of collective bargaining in regulating terms and conditions of employment. By comparison, the legal changes introduced in 2011 sought to reverse previous advances and weaken collective bargaining (Trif 2016). The result was a rapid decentralization of collective bargaining and a massive decline in coverage. In the realm of social dialogue, the Romanian Economic and Social Council (CES, *Consiliul Economic și Social*), the tripartite forum in which union confederations had a statutory right to be consulted by the government on key legislative issues, was replaced by a weaker tripartite body established under the LDS provisions. All these were compounded by amendments to the Labour Code that made it easier for employers to dismiss employees, including union officials, as well as to increase workloads unilaterally and impose flexible working time arrangements (Trif and Paolucci 2019).

Take the example of industry-level collective bargaining. In 1998, twelve industries were covered by collective agreements, comprising 42.6 per cent of the total labour force (Trif 2004). The number declined in the 2000s, but in 2011 industry-level contracts were still a salient part of the collective bargaining landscape. Since then, they have largely disappeared

---

4 For a recent example, see Jurnalul.ro (2021).

because of extremely restrictive legal conditions: only seven industry-level agreements have been signed since the adoption of the LDS, all in the public sector. The prohibition of cross-industrial collective bargaining and the removal of the extension mechanism at the industrial level led to a decline in bargaining coverage from almost 98 per cent in 2010 to 35 per cent in subsequent years (Visser 2019a). Many employers have taken advantage of deregulation to undermine multi-employer arrangements and reduce joint regulations at company level.

The erga omnes mechanism is still in place at the company level, where generally speaking the actual terms and conditions of employment are set (Trif 2016). This means that all employees of a company are covered by the provisions of the company-level collective agreement signed for that respective company, independent of whether or not they are union members. Nevertheless, the LDS makes it far more difficult for unions to negotiate agreements at company level. Since 2011, it has no longer been possible to unionize workers in companies with fewer than fifteen employees (Trif and Paolucci 2019), while the representativeness threshold was raised from 33 to 50 per cent. The 2011 legislation also introduced the possibility for collective agreements to be negotiated and signed by individual employee representatives elected for the purpose, allowing many private-sector companies to maintain the appearance of collective bargaining without having to deal with a unionized labour force. This is more than just a convenient PR move for companies because the new law makes negotiations mandatory (but not the signing of an actual agreement) for companies with over twenty-one employees. In 2017, 92.4 per cent of new collective agreements at the company level were signed by such employee representatives, with only 7.6 per cent signed by representative unions. A few unions have managed to improve their position despite the dire legal framework (Trif and Paolucci 2019).

Industrial conflict

No one would contest that the strong history of militancy of the Romanian union movement during the 1990s is today dead and buried. With the Great Recession at the end of the 2000s, strikes became so rare that state authorities considered it unproblematic to stop reporting on them entirely. In effect, no official data on strikes are available starting with 2010. This is probably tied to the authorities' attempts to curb trade union strength by pushing the question of strike action outside the purview of public debate and preventing criticism of the new legal restrictions.

All this notwithstanding, strikes were in any case virtually extinct by the end of the 2000s. Between 2000 and 2009 fewer than eight legal work stoppages occurred per year on average, a far cry from the annual average above thirty-three between 1992 and 1999. During the 1990s, strikes had shifted from offensive in the first couple of years after December 1989 to defensive, in reaction to ongoing economic problems (Bush 1993). The peak registered in 1998 and 1999 came in response to the government's new policy of privatization at all costs and the ensuing massive economic crisis. The significant drop in strike activity at the beginning of the 2000s can be attributed to several factors: the successful government crackdown on the most militant strikers, the passing of the severe economic downturn of 1998–1999 and the election of a new social democratic government that maintained close links to union confederations (Varga and Freyberg-Inan 2015).

Over the years, fewer and fewer unions have been organizationally prepared to organize strikes. A clear indication of this is the rarity of pre-emptively setting up a strike fund. Very few unions still do this, partly because of the risks associated with putting an additional financial burden on their members, and partly because officials believe it is not necessary. For most of the 2000s, strikes remained defensive, reacting to privatizations, closures and restructuring. This changed in the second half of the decade, once economic growth picked up pace and the impact of post-privatization restructuring was fully absorbed. With high-profile, offensive strikes in new multinational companies, 2007 and 2008 were entirely atypical for the post-1989 period. This renewed offensive impetus was cut short by the economic crisis and austerity that followed. Until the second half of the 2010s, strikes remained virtually extinct, with offensive movements reappearing only in 2018–2019, when a handful of drawn-out conflicts seemed to indicate a revival similar to 2007–2008. This time, however, strikes were not only far fewer in number, but also occurred in relatively small manufacturing companies, while in 2007–2008 they were prevalent among the largest industrial operations in the country. The pandemic-induced economic turmoil has most likely put an end to any resurgence of union militancy.

Union officials regularly blame the lack of strike activity on legal restrictions. Indeed, striking is highly regulated: unions can strike only if a collective agreement is not in force and even then only after a protracted bureaucratic process. The largest part of these restrictions have nonetheless been in place since the early 1990s, being aimed initially at containing what appeared to be uncontrollable workers' militancy (Bush 1993).[5] The rarity of strikes has more to do with a general decline in militancy and a loss of organizational strength on the part of unionized workers. This is obvious when looking at the number of collective labour disputes, which declined by approximately 75 per cent in the 2010s compared with the previous decade. In Romania, collective labour disputes are legal procedures that unions can start if they do not reach an agreement during collective bargaining. This is voluntary and remains a key union prerogative. Because an open dispute is a legal prerequisite for a legal strike, it is usually perceived as a clear strike threat; more militant unions regularly open collective labour disputes during bargaining. The data in Figure 24.4 shows that unions proved largely unable to mount effective defensive opposition during the years of crisis and austerity (2009–2014) and have not managed to recover during times of economic boom (2015–2019). Overall, the data also shows that union militancy has been declining more or less constantly since the end of the 1990s.

Figure 24.4 Number of collective labour disputes, 1992–2019

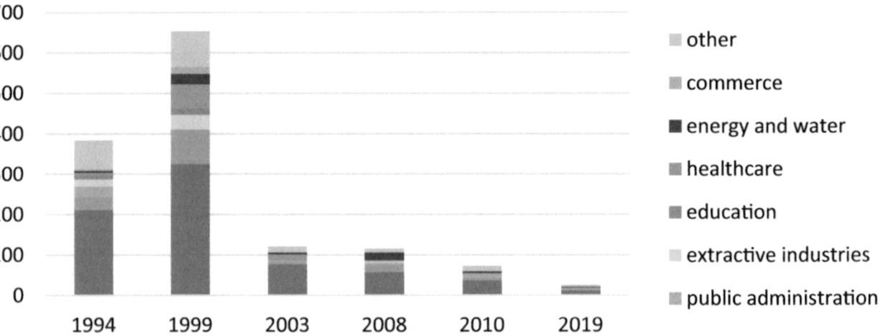

Source: National Institute of Statistics, Romanian Ministry of Labour.

By far the most numerically substantial decline has occurred in manufacturing (Figure 24.6), where only eleven disputes were registered in 2019, compared with thirty-seven in 2010, seventy-seven in 2003 and

5 On additional restrictions introduced in 2011, see Trif and Paolucci (2019: 511–512).

over 300 in 1999. As discussed in previous sections, this is because of the profound transformation of manufacturing over the past two decades. Foreign capital has been largely anti-union, and unionization in greenfield plants has proved extremely difficult. At the same time, older union strongholds have been privatized, restructured or simply shut down and, as a consequence, many manufacturing unions have disappeared or ended up counting on ageing members who are much less willing to take risks. A small number of disputes still occur in transportation and construction, as well as in the public sector, but in absolute terms they are also far fewer and less effective than in previous decades. The number of participants has also declined severely: just over 30,000 employees were involved in collective disputes in 2019, compared with nine times more in 2008 and over fifty times more in 1998–1999.

Figure 24.5 Collective labour disputes by industry, 1994–2019

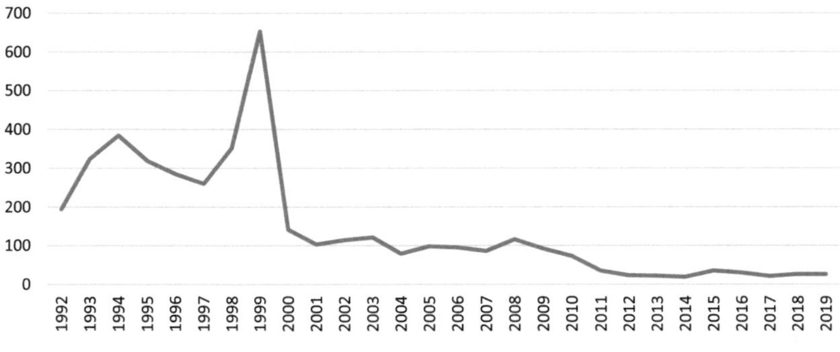

Source: National Institute of Statistics, Romanian Ministry of Labour.

Public protests are a part of a union repertoire that has survived somewhat better than strike action proper, even though here too there has been a clear decline. Mass gatherings and marches organized especially in Bucharest were a staple feature of the 1990s, but largely disappeared once mass privatization, restructuring and stronger state control kicked in (Varga and Freyberg-Inan 2015). Exceptionally, some large unions still occasionally organize public protests to pressure the government into adopting a certain policy, such as changes to the Labour Code (Adăscăliței and Guga 2017). Though still very rare, a more common occurrence is for private-sector company unions to organize local protests in public space instead of actual work stoppages.

Protests in public space function as an alternative to open contestation in the workplace, which has become practically extinct (Guga et al. 2018: 64–66). Protests are easier to organize and involve much lower risk, but they are also far less effective, especially because protest activity has become less contentious over time. Most protests take place in spaces designated by the authorities, rarely disrupt traffic and thus largely fail to draw significant attention. This lack of effectiveness is also related to the typically small size of these gatherings. While many union organizations find it difficult to convince the rank-and-file to participate, the most serious obstacle is the lack of funding for transportation and food. The vicious circle linking lack of resources and lack of effectiveness has pushed federations and confederations towards slowly giving up on street protests as well.

Political relations

The union movement today seems politically isolated, with no political allegiance at the national level and no political relevance at the local level. The only potential direct link with politics that may have survived is for unions in the public sector, where wage policy has historically depended on which party was in power. Apart from this, unions in general are left with participation in tripartite social dialogue structures, which remains a highly ineffective and frustrating experience (Guga and Constantin 2015).

From the second half of the 1990s until the late 2010s, union confederations were unofficially linked to the Social Democratic Party (PSD, *Partidul Social-Democrat*). During the first half of the 1990s, confederations turned to supporting the right-wing opposition coalition that promised economic reform and mass privatization. The economic collapse that followed the implementation of this policy made unions turn once more to the Social Democrats, who returned to power in 2000. The first half of the 2000s was probably the most fruitful period for unions' political forays, the pinnacle being the adoption of an ostensibly favourable Labour Code in 2003. By the end of the decade, however, the situation had totally reversed: right-wing parties were again in power and managed to push through not only a new employer-friendly Labour Code, but also a total overhaul of the legislation on collective bargaining and social dialogue. The Social Democrats, who returned to power in 2012, again succeeded in securing the unions' allegiance by promising to roll back these legal changes. But because several subsequent Social Democratic governments have refused to budge on what unions consider a vital objective (the 2011 legislation is still in place), high-level union officials eventually understood that political alliances were no longer a useful tool for their organizations.

This realization did not matter much, especially because the unions had already become politically isolated. The recent agreements with the Social Democrats were never going to pay off, because employers had by then gained massive political clout and unions' reactions to the austerity of the early 2010s proved they were no longer a real threat to the government (Guga and Constantin 2015). The consequences for unions in general and for union confederations in particular were much more serious than missing out on legislative change, however. For many years, confederation leaders had made deals with politicians without consulting with the rank-and-file on whether this was the best way to make things happen. Starting with the early 1990s, an explicitly anti-political stance became dominant among the rank-and-file and the lower-level union organizations. This was motivated by the perceived inherent corruption of politicians and politics as such. 'We don't do politics!' was a staple slogan of the union movement at the grassroots. Confederations and their leaders appeared to systematically break such vows by sealing deals with parties and, above all, by jumping ship and joining political organizations (Guga 2017). This continues to be a source of tension within the union movement. Plenty of company-level and federation officials still believe confederations have betrayed the cause by allying with political parties and that the much sought-after legal changes could have been achieved in other ways.

Social dialogue has been another important source of frustration with politics and the state in general. Legislation formally provides ample opportunities for unions to have a say in local, regional and national political decision-making. Commissions for social dialogue are organized at local, county and ministry levels, providing unions and employers' associations with the possibility of influencing decisions on relevant policies. Added to these, the CES and the National Tripartite Council for Social Dialogue are high-level bodies tasked with consulting unions and employers on the activities of the parliament and the government. Though comprehensive in theory, in practice this institutional setup has little real significance for union members' interests (Guga and Constantin 2015). There are several reasons for this. First, all social dialogue structures have a purely consultative role, which allows the authorities to ignore the unions' views without any formal penalties. Second, the diminishing strength of the union movement as a whole means that unions constitute less and less of a threat to the authorities, which suffer little or no collateral damage from disregarding union positions in social dialogue structures. Third, the most capable employers' associations have found alternative informal channels to influence government decisions, leaving unions to deal with the formalism of social dialogue and countering union action behind the curtains.

Arguably, the only instance in which unions have maintained an input at national level is the government's wage policy. During the past decade, minimum wage increases have become the single most important labour-friendly measure. While confederations are officially consulted in the National Tripartite Council for Social Dialogue on the minimum wage, the timing and magnitude of increases are established arbitrarily by the government. The wage situation in the public sector is similar. Legally, wage levels in the public sector fall outside the scope of collective bargaining, which means that unions can pressure the government only through the ministry-level social dialogue structures or via informal channels. While healthcare unions have become more militant in recent years in pursuit of their objectives, the perception that the public sector union leadership is too close to the government is still pervasive. With this comes the idea that those in power use public sector employees as an electoral mass, with the help of public sector unions. Furthermore, many union officials in the private sector consider that public sector unions act against the interest of private-sector employees, pursuing their objectives in utter disregard of the latter (Guga and Constantin 2015). More specifically, because the confederations are dominated by public sector federations, many consider that they use up the little political influence they still have to serve the interests of public sector employees, while sacrificing those of private-sector members.

The repeated failure of agreements with political parties and the constant inadequacy of social dialogue have created legitimacy problems for union confederations. Many union members, company union officials and even federation officials regard the ineffectiveness of formal and informal confederate actions as evidence of long-standing historical shady dealings with politics. Few see the organizational-cum-institutional vicious circle at work in the loss of both the strength and influence of unions on the political scene.

Societal power

The unions' public image is no better today than it has been for the past two decades. It is not necessarily worse either: it reflects how unions have lost much of their once quite salient presence in the public sphere. At local level, however, some unions have remained a powerful public force. The case of the Dacia union might indeed be the only example in this regard, facilitated by an exceptional situation: the comparatively large size of the union in a geographic area in which the employer is by far the most dominant economic actor. Nationally, the unions' public presence is largely limited to occasional controversies surrounding the minimum wage or other, predominantly income-related policies. The largely employer-friendly media continues to put pressure on the union movement by regularly highlighting the relatively high incomes of high-level union officials and their alleged corruption (Jurnalul.ro 2021).

These tactics became common from around 2010, when the right-wing party then in power launched a public campaign to discredit unions by accusing confederation officials of corruption and preventing unions from rallying support against austerity and employer-friendly legal changes. Such accusations were definitely not new – indeed, they had been common for many years – but this time around they were systematic and documented. Some confederation officials ended up in prison following the ensuing official investigations. The long-standing history of political ventures on the part of confederation officials, the often inefficient or suspicious management of real estate portfolios, unions' involvement in accessing significant EU funding, and the de facto permanent mandate that most high-level union officials appear to enjoy are points of criticism that still weigh heavily in defining the overall negative public image of unions. Employers and politicians rarely miss an opportunity to draw attention to these issues when they want to prevent or mitigate union opposition.

The difficulty of regaining some public support cannot be underestimated. Regardless of the unions' own problems, employers have gained a very strong grip over the public sphere during the past decade. Wage demands of whatever kind are routinely denounced as morally questionable and economically unfeasible (Guga 2020), social safety nets are always portrayed as promoting indolence, and the need to curtail employees' bargaining power by boosting labour supply through workfare and immigration is considered entirely unproblematic. In such a context, even the best organized unions would be fighting a huge uphill battle. This stands in stark contrast to the pre-2010 period, when public discourse was much more balanced, and unions could compete with employers in influencing the general public.

There are few allies on whom unions can count outside their own ranks. Romanian academia has ignored the labour question for decades (Varga 2011), which means that alternative discourses to those of employers are hard to come by and unions are generally starved of expertise. The same goes for other civil society organizations, which are very rarely interested in labour issues. Likewise, union protests have typically remained separate from the otherwise frequent popular protests occurring in large cities over the past decade. As far as the more recent period is concerned, this makes sense from a strategic point of view, as unions might not have wanted to become associated with protests harbouring an implicit right-wing agenda against governments that explicitly favoured growth in minimum and public sector wages. The protests of the first half of the decade, on the other hand, were much more diverse, turning first against austerity and then against the potential environmental disaster associated with the planned opening of a large goldmine in the northwest of the country. Unions did not attempt to rally themselves to these causes and have generally been reluctant to seek broader-based solidarity.

Somewhat paradoxically, the 2011 legal changes made things worse in this regard. One of the innovations at the time was to turn the CES into an institution of so-called 'civic dialogue', replacing the standard tripartite structure of unions, employers and government with unions, employers and representatives of 'civil society' (namely, select NGOs). Many confederation officials regarded the move as sabotage of the Social and Economic Council, whose capacity to influence political decisions was curtailed with the exit of government representatives. Moreover, the entry of NGOs into territory over which unions and employers' associations had held a monopoly for more than two decades was perceived as a threat, highlighting potential future encroachment on their prerogatives.

Trade union policies towards the European Union

In line with the dominant public opinion in Romania, union members and officials have a positive view of the EU.[6] With the benefit of

6 According to the Standard Eurobarometer 91 (June 2019), 60 per cent of Romanian respondents had a positive view of the EU compared with an EU average of 45 per cent.

hindsight, we could nonetheless say that the implications of the January 2007 EU accession have been rather ambivalent for the Romanian union movement. Take the all-important example of labour law. On one hand, the pre-accession negotiations catalysed what is arguably unions' most important victory of the past three decades, the 2003 Labour Code. On the other hand, when the government forced through massive changes to labour legislation in 2011 the unions looked in vain for allies in Brussels, a point made clear by the European Commission's explicit support for the new legal arrangements (Trif 2016). Access to EU funding is another important subject: while it secured relative financial prosperity for confederations, it also sapped their already limited legitimacy.

With one exception (Meridian), all confederations are members of ITUC and ETUC. At the European level, the agenda being pursued is ostensibly that of convergence in living standards and working conditions, although there is no definite strategy on how this can actually be achieved. The European Semester has recently begun to stress the need to improve social dialogue, although it is far from clear how much this comes as a result of union influence and how much that of employers' associations.[7] In any case, as long as the recommendation remains so vague, it is unclear what is meant by 'improvement'. Moreover, the European Semester reports regularly criticized the wage policies of Social Democratic governments during the second half of the 2010s. While wage rises in the public sector were criticized unequivocally, the recommendation to make minimum wage increases less arbitrary and more transparent is not necessarily favourable to unions (see also Jordan et al. 2020: 9). The main point of contention is not that minimum wage increases are the result of arbitrary decisions, but rather what kind of mechanism should be put in place. Indeed, following up on such critiques of the minimum wage policy the current government has argued for the need for 'objectivity' in order to limit wage increases.

As far as the federations are concerned, many private-sector organizations are members of their corresponding European federations: EPSU has nine Romanian affiliates; IndustriAll six; ETF seven; the EFBW, EFFAT and ETUCE each have three. A few federation officials have given up on their European affiliation in frustration with what they perceive as

---

7 Shifting from their previous positions, the major representatives of foreign capital in Romania have begun to stress the need for more effective social dialogue, especially at the national level. Previously, they had preferred to rely solely on informal lobbying, while attempting to undermine social dialogue institutions.

a lack of effectiveness of European organizations and the inferior position in which they find themselves in relation to their Western counterparts.[8] Informal discussions with federation officials suggest that the idea of convergence is not really supported by Western unions, either because they are not interested or because they believe it is in fact contrary to their interests.

The picture is somewhat similar at the company level. With foreign capital dominating the private sector and given the strong presence of Western European multinational corporations, many union officials have become used to participation in European Works Councils (EWC). One novelty brought by EWC participation is the process of information and consultation, to which Romanian unions have not been accustomed locally. EWCs also offer Romanian employee representatives an opportunity to come into contact with corporate management, which is all the more important given that local management often insists its hands are tied when it comes to strategic decisions. The boosting of transnational solidarity by EWCs is nonetheless limited. Similar to the rare critics at the federation level, some Romanian union officials criticize the unwillingness of EWCs to approach the question of wage and living standard gaps head on, even at the limited level of simple information and consultation, indicating that their Western European peers are not interested in or sometimes even try to block such attempts. Moreover, the effectiveness of EWC participation is objectively limited for Romanian employee representatives, because restructuring in multinationals (the main reason for triggering EWC information and consultation) may not directly affect low-cost subsidiaries in Romania.

Conclusions

The challenges currently facing the Romanian union movement are likely to linger long into the future. Membership decline over the past decade has been much slower than previously, but it nonetheless poses an existential threat to many organizations. Most union officials attribute their current troubles to the 2011 legislation, but the priority goal

---

8 Giving up on affiliation to EU federations undoubtedly also has a financial underpinning because cash-strapped unions can experience significant problems in paying affiliation fees to national or European umbrella organisations.

of rolling back these changes has proved illusory. It should now be clear that this will not happen without strong union pressure, which cannot be achieved without an organizational overhaul and a major reversal of past and present trends.

Overall, unions have failed to gather popular support to their causes and have in fact become increasingly isolated. The loss of membership and history of public controversy have played an important part in this. Moreover, the concentration of union members in the public sector has made many private-sector employees even more reticent towards existing union structures, which are often perceived as serving interests opposite to those of private-sector employees. Member recruiting and unionization are much more difficult in such a context and high-level union officials routinely highlight the need to reshape the image of the union movement as a whole. Here too we are dealing with a vicious circle.

At company and industry levels, the situation has historically shifted with the economic cycle, with all but the strongest union organizations highly dependent on the employees' marketplace bargaining power. The slight revivals in union militancy in the late 2000s and 2010s were to a great extent due to tightening labour markets in a context of strong economic growth and mass emigration. The Covid-19 pandemic has likely reversed this dramatically and unions are bound to go on the defensive and try to limit the damage to their organizational strength. With so many employees once again fearing for their jobs, unionization, recruiting and supporting strong demands are likely to prove much more difficult.

In the long run, demographics is one of the major factors working against unions. Since the mid-1990s, unions have not kept pace with the rhythm and direction of economic transformation. They have retrenched in their strongholds in the public sector and in manufacturing, counting on an increasingly ageing membership. Unionization in new private-sector companies in services and manufacturing has been very rare. In such a context we can expect that many unions in the private sector will disappear due to 'natural causes' during the next decade or so. To be sure, these would be the unions already strongly affected by economic and legal changes, while those maintaining a relatively stable membership (in industries such as commerce and banking, as well as in a handful of large manufacturing companies) will continue. At company and industry levels, where objectively possible and agreed upon by leaders, the disappearance of smaller organizations will occur through absorption by larger ones, which will ease some of the pressure on larger organizations.

Two additional questions concerning demographic change and membership decline loom large. The first concerns the future of confederations. Since 2011, confederations have secured their representativeness with a minimum number of members and while making considerable efforts in keeping their membership figures stable, which has also involved trying to attract federations from other confederations. For the reasons discussed above, the existence of five representative confederations is not feasible in the long run and it remains to be seen when and how consolidation will take place at the national level. The five confederations have existed for so long and the history of attempted mergers is so convoluted that the circumstances in which one or several disappear from the scene are impossible to foresee.

The second question applies to the entire union movement, at company, industry and national levels, as well as for weak and strong organizations. Demographic change will sooner or later force a change of leadership. This is a major conundrum in a context in which the leadership of most organizations has not changed for decades. Preparing a new generation of union officials and ensuring a transparent and democratic transition is going to be a novelty in the history of many unions.

In Visser's (2019b: 59–71) terms, we can expect that the historical trend towards marginalization will continue, although a lot of the damage has already been done. Public sector unions will probably remain strong despite the threat of austerity brought about once again by Covid-19, while survival is also unlikely to become a problem in the foreseeable future for strong private-sector unions. Because the latter are few in number and concentrated in large enterprises, we can expect marginalization to go hand in hand with dualization between public and private sector, large and small enterprises, and standard and non-standard employment relationships.[9] Substitution is also already well under way following the 2011 legal changes that allowed individual employee representatives to sign collective agreements. As for revitalization, no one would deny it is necessary on a large scale, but it is difficult to fathom how it can actually be achieved. A reversal of the above trends would be necessary, but unions have so far been fighting a losing battle simply trying to prevent them from deepening. Reaching out to younger employees in non-unionized companies and industries would require massive additional

---

9 Data presented by Visser (2019b: 64) on union density by enterprise size are questionable when it comes to Romania, because from a legal point of view at least fifteen employees from the same enterprise are needed in order to create a union.

resources and a radical shift in strategy. Developments in the commerce and IT sectors show that this is nonetheless possible when local leaders focus their efforts on organizing workers (Trif 2016). The same goes for precarious workers, although here legal restrictions are also a major problem, because Romanian legislation defines trade unions as organizations of employees. Government hostility and a public sphere pervaded by right-wing ideology are additional major headwinds to which unions have not found proper responses yet.

In such a context, it is understandable that the majority of unions do not plan far in advance and are focused primarily on immediate bread-and-butter issues, above all, wages. Major strategic issues such as the digital transformation of economic activity or the question of global warming and the need for a green transition for the Romanian economy usually do not figure on their agenda. Because existing problems are bound to be exacerbated by the Covid-19 pandemic in the short term, and by ongoing economic and organizational transformation in the medium term, there is little indication that things will change for the better.

References

Adăscăliței D. and Guga Ș. (2017) Negotiating agency and structure: trade union organizing strategies in a hostile environment, Economic and Industrial Democracy, 38 (3), 473–494.

Bohle D. and Greskovits B. (2012) Capitalist diversity on Europe's periphery, Ithaca, Cornell University Press.

Burloiu P. (1997) Managementul resurselor umane: tratare globala interdisciplinara, Bucharest, Lumina Lex.

Bush L.S. (1993) Collective labor disputes in post-Ceausescu Romania, Cornell International Law Journal, 26 (2), 373–420.

Digi24 (2016) România furată: Pețitorii averii sindicatelor, 1 November 2016. https://www.digi24.ro/special/campanii-digi24/romania-furata/romania-furata-petitorii-averii-sindicatelor-603973.

Guga Ș. (2017) Low-cost Fordism? The antinomies of class in the Romanian automobile industry, 1989–2016, PhD dissertation, Budapest, Central European University.

Guga Ș. (2020) The question of productivity: controversies and clarifications, Bucharest, Friedrich-Ebert-Stiftung.

Guga Ș. and Constantin C. (2015) Analiza impactului legislației dialogului social adoptate în 2011. Cercetare sociologică și juridică, Bucharest, Asociația Conect.

Guga Ș. and Spatari M. (2019) Sectorul comerț în România: un bilanț după trei decenii de transformări, Bucharest, Friedrich-Ebert-Stiftung.

Guga Ș. and Spatari M. (2020) Back to bargaining in banking: how digitalisation plays Romanian trade unions an upper hand, Berlin, Friedrich-Ebert-Stiftung.

Guga Ș., Spatari M. and Chelaru D. (2018) Situația salariaților din România, Bucharest, Syndex.

Hyman R. (2001) Understanding European trade unionism: between market, class and society, London, Sage.

Jordan J., Maccarrone V. and Erne R. (2020) Towards a socialization of the EU's new economic governance regime? EU labour policy interventions in Germany, Ireland, Italy and Romania (2009–2019), British Journal of Industrial Relations, 59 (1), 191–213.

Jurnalul.ro (2021) Cel mai bogat lider de sindicat, plătit cu 13000 de euro/ lună, 1 February 2021. https://jurnalul.ro/bani-afaceri/economia/cel-mai-bogat-lider-de-sindicat-platit-cu-13-000-de-euro-luna-865589.html

Ost D. (2000) 'Illusory Corporatism' in Eastern Europe: neoliberal tripartism and postcommunist class identities, Politics & Society, 28 (4), 503–530.

Ost D. (2009) The consequences of postcommunism: trade unions in eastern Europe's future, East European Politics and Societies, 23 (1), 13–33.

Ost D. (2011) Illusory corporatism ten years later, Warsaw Forum of Economic Sociology, 2 (1), 19–49.

Trif A. and Paolucci V. (2019) Romania: from legal support to frontal assault, in Müller T., Vandaele K. and Waddington J. (eds) Collective bargaining in Europe: towards and endgame, Volume III, Brussels, ETUI, 505–523.

Trif A. (2004) Overview of industrial relations in Romania, South-East Europe Review for Labour and Social Affairs, 7 (2), 43–64.

Trif A. (2016) The rise of the dual labour market: fighting precarious employment in the new member states through industrial relations: country report Romania, Research project VS/2014/0534, European Commission.

Varga M. (2011) An anatomy of 'collective anti-collectivism': labor sociology in Ukraine and Romania, Global Labour Journal, 2(1), 43–63.

Varga M. and Freyberg-Inan A. (2015) Post-communist state measures to thwart organized labor: the case of Romania, Economic and Industrial Democracy, 36 (4), 677–699.

Visser J. (2019a) ICTWSS Database, version 6.1, Amsterdam, Institute for Advanced Labour Studies.

Visser J. (2019b) Trade unions in the balance, ILO ACTRAV Working Paper, Geneva, ILO.

Abbreviations

BNS	Blocul Național Sindical (*National Trade Union Bloc*)
CES	Consiliul Economic și Social (*Economic and Social Council*)
CNSLR-Frăția	Confederația Națională a Sindicatelor Libere din România-Frăția (*National Romanian Free Trade Union Confederation–Brotherhood*)
CSDR	Confederatia Sindicatelor Democratice din România (*Romanian Democratic Trade Union Confederation*)
EWC	European Works Council
LDS	Legea Dialogului Social (*Social Dialogue Act*)
POSDRU	Programul Operațional Sectorial Dezvoltarea Resurselor Umane (*Operational Sectoral Programme Human Resources Development*)
PSD	Partidul Social-Democrat (*The Social Democratic Party*)
UGSR	Uniunea Generală a Sindicatelor din România (*General Unions Confederation of Romania*)

Chapter 25

Trade unions in Slovakia: From politics to bread-and-butter unionism

Marta Kahancová and Monika Uhlerová

Trade unions in Slovakia have been a stable part of economic and political developments since the transition from state socialism to democracy and a market economy after 1989. Although the unions are often associated with the country's socialist past, the current landscape encompasses unions with a history in the former regime, as well as unions newly established in the transition period after 1989 or in the years shortly before the 2020 Covid-19 pandemic. Unions whose existence dates back to state socialism were often seen as the 'extended hand of the communist party' before 1989. Nevertheless, unions did support democracy-building after 1989, including the establishment of independent interest representation and collective bargaining. Legislation on collective bargaining was among the first regulations adopted after the 1989 regime change. The former unitary structure of trade unions was gradually transformed, leading to the emergence of the current, more fragmented landscape.

While today unions are established as genuine representatives of workers' interests at enterprise and industrial levels, their institutional powers are strongly entrenched in legal regulations. At the same time, unions often face criticism for being subordinated to party politics and business interests.

The combination of economic growth, derived from market liberalization and labour market deregulation from the early 1990s, with the persistence of coordinated industrial relations and firmly established trade union structures, make Slovakia an interesting case for analysing union structures and their transformation. Slovakia constitutes a case of marked and wide-ranging change during a period characterized by economic and political transition, labour market liberalization, Slovakia's European Union (EU) and European Monetary Union (EMU) membership, domestic political cycles and crisis conditions after 2008, as well as the 2020–2021 Covid-19 crisis. This chapter aims to account for these trends by summarizing key elements in trade union development in Slovakia, including changes to organizational structure, membership and the scope of union activities.

The chapter presents the following arguments. First, trade unions' strong institutional embeddedness during the early 1990s, through legally entrenched representativeness criteria, bargaining rights and participation in national tripartism, opened trade union access to policy-making, which is still maintained and practiced today. Nevertheless, this policy influence has been gradually weakening because of changes to legally defined representativeness criteria and the weakening impact of tripartism. In conditions of eroding institutional resources and declining membership unions sought political support and legislative entrenchment of the regulation of working conditions (see Table 25.1). This trend has had a contested impact on unions and collective bargaining, which is gradually being replaced by legal regulation (Kahancová 2015).

Second, while the transformation from state socialism to a market economy after 1989 did not undermine trade union hierarchy, recent years have seen fragmentation of unionism. While unions that have existed for decades continue to focus on traditional modes of action, collective bargaining and social pacts with incumbent governments, new unions emerged dissatisfied with the results achieved through bargaining and are now seeking other kinds of action. The latter group of 'new' unions is more radical and uses the public arena for their actions, including protests, demonstrations and petitions. Such action became increasingly important among public-sector trade unions, especially in response to 'austerity' measures in the post-crisis years (Kahancová and Sedláková 2020). While such new types of action strengthen union resources at a time of a general decline in union membership, they also undermine the traditional pillars of industrial relations, most importantly, coordinated bargaining and wage setting above the enterprise level.

Since the onset of the Covid-2019 pandemic and changes in the government, traditional unions, organized under the Confederation of Trade Unions of the Slovak Republic (KOZ SR, *Konfederácia odborových zväzov SR*), also changed their strategy to focus more on public campaigns/

protest actions and simultaneously on company-level trade union work. This trend is referred to throughout the chapter as a return to 'bread-and-butter unionism', which means that union strategies focus on workers and their support, rather than on political support, especially when dependent on a single political party.

Third, this chapter analyses the reasons behind union fragmentation not only in terms of new strategies and actions, and bargaining contrasted to activism and lobbying, but also in terms of changing union structures. Several of the new unions that have become very vocal in the past two decades are professional unions, representing the interests of a narrowly defined profession, which creates a comparative advantage for these unions in identifying their members' shared interests. This is more difficult in unions representing a broader and more diversified workforce. In turn, union fragmentation is driven by professional diversification and the diversification between prioritized levels for union action, such as national tripartism or company-level activities. Another line of fragmentation is the ways unions represent and serve their members. KOZ SR has for years been the only representative union confederation in national tripartism. While KOZ SR remains committed to its traditional strategies in social dialogue and bargaining,[1] recently it has also begun to engage in public protests/campaigns and workplace unionism. The newly established trade union confederation Joint Trade Unions of Slovakia (SOS, *Spoločné odbory Slovenska*) presents itself as a think tank, representing several so-called 'modern' professional and company-level unions that emerged by breaking away from the long-established unions in their industries or establishments.

1 KOZ SR itself does not engage in collective bargaining, but its affiliated union federations bargain at industry level.

Table 25.1 Principal characteristics of trade unionism in Slovakia

	1990	2000	2020
Total trade union membership in KOZ SR	2,443,997	702,419	239,632
Proportion of women in total membership	n.a.	42 %*	46 %**
Gross union density	n.a.	32 %	12 %
Net union density	n.a.	32 %	12 %
Number of confederations	2***	1	2
Number of affiliated unions (federations)	39	38	25
Number of independent unions[7]	2	2	3
Collective bargaining coverage	n.a.	51 %	26 %****
Principal level of collective bargaining	Industry	Alternating between Company, multi-employer, sector	Company (wage bargaining), multi-employer and/or sector
Days not worked bs of industrial action per 1,000 workers	n.a.	0	0*****

Note: *2002; **2016; ***The Confederation of Arts and Culture (Konfederácia umenia a kultúry), ceased to exist in 1994; ****2019; *****2017.

Source: Appendix 1; Internal data from KOZ SR.

Historical background and principal features of the industrial relations system

The Slovak labour movement developed within the larger territory of the Austro-Hungarian Empire (Docherty and van der Velden 2012). The number of union members in Czechoslovakia, established in 1918, peaked in 1928, when 583 unions organized 1,738,300 members (ibid.). Union plurality ceased to exist in 1938 because of the unions' role as a democratic opposition in an increasingly authoritarian state as Slovakia became subordinated to Nazi Germany (Šumichrast 2018). Unions merged with other professional organizations in 1940 to raise the foundations of the 1942 Slovak Working Commonwealth (*Slovenská pracujúca pospolitosť*), an organization serving to increase general labour productivity (Roháček 2017). This organization laid the foundations of centrally coordinated unionism in 1945 by forming the Central Council of Trade Unions (ÚRO, *Ústredná rada odborov*), later transformed into the Revolutionary Trade Union Movement (ROH, *Revolučné odborové hnutie*). ROH became fully subordinated to the ruling Communist Party (Drahokoupil and Kahancová 2019).

The main characteristic of trade unions under state socialism in Czechoslovakia was their highly unified and centralized structure; its activities were standardized and subordinated to political power (Myant 2010). This framed unions as 'an extended hand of the Communist Party' (Malová 1997; Uhlerová 2012). Unions were not able to represent workers' interests independently and negotiations about employment relations, such as pay, were beyond the unions' scope of influence. Trade unions had formal powers over health and safety issues at the workplace and ensured compliance with legislation. In addition, trade unions often signed agreements with management at the establishment level to encourage higher productivity, with promised individual benefits in return (Drahokoupil and Kahancová 2019; Myant 2010). With this special position in society, trade unions enjoyed almost universal membership (Myant 2010). Their roles and membership structure changed during the period of economic and political transition after 1989.

Structure of trade unions and union democracy

The structure of Slovak trade unions is relatively transparent and not particularly fragmented, although fragmentation has increased in the past decade. Unions' current structure, position and power resources are to a large extent influenced by legally defined representativeness criteria. A 2021 legislative change to the Labour Code (ZP, *Zákonník práce*) and the Act on Tripartite Consultations (*Zákon o trojstranných konzultáciách na celoštátnej úrovni*, No. 103/2007) also opens national tripartism to unions not meeting the threshold of 100,000 members, thereby forcing union pluralism into tripartism.[2]

---

2 The government that took office in March 2020, after growing hostility between the Ministry of Labour, Social Affairs and Family (MPSVaR, *Ministerstvo práce, sociálnych vecí a rodiny*) and KOZ SR following minimum wage negotiations in the aftermath of the Covid-19 pandemic in 2020, proposed an adjustment of the representativeness criteria to allow smaller unions to enter tripartite structures and thereby challenge KOZ SR's monopoly power in national tripartism. The recommendation for trade union representativeness was the approval by 20 per cent of all workers, including non-unionists (Košč 2020).

KOZ SR is a confederation of twenty-five independent trade unions, whose position and powers are governed by their own statutes. In 2020, KOZ SR represented sixteen union federations in manufacturing and nine industrial union federations in services, from both the private and public sectors (KOZ SR website). At the same time, until the 2021 legislative change, KOZ SR was the only recognized trade union confederation that meets the legally defined representativeness criteria for representing workers' interests in national tripartism.[3]

KOZ SR acts on the basis of individual trade unions' decisions adopted through bodies composed of representatives of affiliated trade unions. KOZ SR's supreme body is a Congress convened every four years. Congress delegates are nominated by individual trade unions based on membership base. The Congress elects the President and Vice-President and members of the KOZ SR Board and Revision Commission. The Board is KOZ SR's statutory body. The President and Vice-President have limited competences: they represent KOZ SR externally, while the Vice-President coordinates tripartite social dialogue at the national level and collective bargaining in the public sector. The activities of the President and Vice-President are governed by decisions taken by KOZ SR bodies and de facto affiliated trade unions. The Board of Trade Union Chairs is a body in which each affiliated trade union is represented by its chair. It adopts decisions predominantly on conceptual and thematic issues. In the period between Congresses the KOZ SR Assembly, which meets twice a year, is the supreme body composed of delegates representing unions according to the size of their membership base. Decision-making in individual bodies is based on majority voting, respecting the 'one vote for one delegate/member' principle. For decisions on financial, staff and pressure-related activities voted on by the KOZ SR Assembly, however, the 'more members, more votes' principle applies with the consequence that larger trade unions have more influence. This structure and decision-making process is bottom-up and democratic. The implementation of decisions of KOZ SR members, however, is not enforceable or subject to sanctions. This complicates the implementation of decisions and decreases KOZ SR's efficiency and dynamism.

---

3 The Act on Tripartite Consultations of 2007 (No. 106/2007, *Zákon o trojstranných konzultáciách na celoštátnej úrovni*) stipulates that union (con)federations jointly organizing at least 100,000 members, and employers' associations representing at least 100,000 employees working in member companies, meet the representativeness criteria and are entitled to participate in national tripartite social dialogue.

KOZ SR's power resources are predominantly derived from entrenched representativeness and access to tripartism. The power resources of the SOS confederation are currently under development, possibly building on distinct strategies and the services approach to members rather than engagement in coordinated bargaining and tripartite social dialogue.

Apart from KOZ SR, there are other trade unions with smaller membership bases (see Table 25.1). Some new unions emerged in the aftermath of the 2008–2009 financial and economic crisis, particularly after the government's efforts to rationalize public spending and to 'freeze' public-sector wages (Kahancová et al. 2019). Such austerity measures fuelled the fragmentation of public-sector unions in health care and education. In June 2012, New Education Trade Unions (NŠO, *Nové školské odbory*) emerged. In March 2012, the Trade Union of Nurses and Midwifes (OZSaPA, *Odborové združenie sestier a pôrodných asistentiek*) was established. These new unions emerged in response to dissatisfaction with how 'old' trade unions protected workers' interests and the lack of union democracy. Both NŠO and OZSaPA were founding members of the new union confederation SOS in 2018. In addition, two independent unions were established even earlier: the Trade Union Federation of Medical Doctors (LOZ, *Lekárske odborové združenie*), which was a KOZ SR member until 2004, and the Independent Christian Trade Unions of Slovakia (NKOS, *Nezávislé kresťanské odbory Slovenska*). NKOS operates in education and culture and its membership base is estimated at several dozens.[4] Both LOZ and NKOS participate in collective bargaining at establishment and industrial levels: LOZ in health care/hospitals, and NKOS in public services (with particular interests in the education subsector).

Some of these new, or independent, trade unions formed a new confederation, the Joint Trade Unions of Slovakia (SOS, *Spoločné odbory Slovenska*), in 2018. SOS currently organizes six trade unions: Modern Trade Unions AIOS (AIOS, *Moderné odbory AIOS*); Modern Trade Unions Volkswagen (MOV, *Moderné odbory Volkswagen*); Trade Union Federation of Nurses and Midwives (OZSaPA, *Odborové združenie sestier a pôrodných asistentiek*); New Trade Union of the Police (NOZP, *Nový odborový zväz polície*); New School Trade Unions (NŠO, *Nové školské odbory*) and the JAVYS trade union (ZO JAVYS, *Základná organizácia JAVYS*). SOS also organizes three collaborating trade unions and

[4] This estimate by the authors is based on NKOS's annual income of €2,563, stated in the 2019 annual report.

its membership is estimated at 20,000 (unofficial data). SOS is present mainly in the automotive and related industries, in information technology, trade and services, education, social services, police, and public and state administration. The membership base of trade unions affiliated to SOS comes partially from the breakaway of organizations originally affiliated to KOZ SR and also from members' desire to support trade union pluralism beyond KOZ SR. SOS frames its existence around the distinctions between 'modern' and 'traditional', 'old' and 'new', 'non-party' and 'partisan', and 'political' and 'bread-and-butter' unionism. Data on SOS are not as extensive as those provided for KOZ SR.

SOS emerged from the fragmentation process within the largest industrial union federation, the Metalworkers' Union (OZ KOVO, *Odborový zväz KOVO*), an affiliate of KOZ SR. The base organization of the industrial OZ KOVO within the largest automotive producer Volkswagen, allied to the personal ambition of some union representatives to build a competitive confederation over against KOZ SR, motivated the split from OZ KOVO and KOZ SR and the formation of MOV and SOS. Nevertheless, currently SOS lacks internal capacities to strengthen its activities. SOS has remained inactive at the national level since its establishment in 2018: it is not a member of the tripartite committee, does not comment on legislation, and is not involved in international trade union structures. The activities of some affiliates, particularly MOV, include establishment-level collective bargaining and member recruitment. SOS's ambitions were based on the strong leadership of a single person, although that person has now ceased active participation in union affairs.

Other, smaller unions developed their associational power by representing specific groups of workers with a relatively strong structural position within the labour market, including medical doctors (LOZ) and teachers (NKOS). In the case of medical doctors, LOZ is the only vocal union representing their interests besides the all-encompassing Slovak Trade Union of Healthcare and Social Services Employees (SOZZaSS, *Slovenský odborový zväz zamestnancov zdravotníctva a sociálnych služieb*), affiliated to KOZ SR. In the case of teachers, the union landscape is more fragmented despite representing a relatively unified workforce with clearly defined interests. Teachers are represented by several fragmented and competing unions, including OZPŠaV (affiliated to KOZ SR), the New Education Trade Union (NŠO, *Nové školské odbory*) and several non-union initiatives, such as the Initiative of Slovak Teachers (ISU, *Iniciatíva slovenských učiteľov*) and the Initiative of Bratislava Teachers (IBU, Iniciatíva bratislavských učiteľov). Since 2016, they have organized strikes and protest actions and, in consequence, have partly taken over the union agenda and teachers' demands.

Unionization

Trade union membership has been declining steadily since the early 1990s and this trend has not yet been reversed (Uhlerová 2015). Several recruitment strategies have been implemented in an attempt to reverse membership decline. Examples of these strategies include regular workshops targeting young people, some with support from the Friedrich-Ebert-Stiftung (FES), at what innovative recruitment strategies were presented and discussed. Unions also established a Trade Unions' Customer Centre (KCO, *Klientské centrum odborov*) after obtaining funding to stabilize social dialogue. The Customer Centre is operated by KOZ SR and provides legal service to all individuals in need, thereby raising awareness of trade union activities.

In 2017 trade unions affiliated to KOZ SR organized almost 245,000 members, 38.8 per cent of whom are women and 6.1 per cent are young members below 35 years of age. In 2020 the twenty-five trade unions affiliated to KOZ SR comprised 4,850 company-level trade unions, 63.7 per cent of which are led by women. At the national level only 32 per cent of trade union leaders are women. Neither KOZ SR nor its affiliated unions have defined quotas for the representation of young people or women in decision-making bodies.

In terms of sectoral variation, unions are present in both industry and services, as well as in the public and private sectors.[5] Detailed data on the unionization rates of KOZ SR affiliates are available in Table 25.2. The largest union federation OZ KOVO also organizes workers in several related industries, including transport and retail, education, and public services. Industrial wage bargaining is practiced only in the metal, steel and chemical industries and in the public sector. At the same time, industry-level bargaining on wages has disappeared in commerce and banking, where bargaining remains decentralized to the establishment level (Kahancová et al. 2017). This suggests a weakening role of unions in industry bargaining and the reorientation of their activities to the establishment level and also to the national level (often via membership of KOZ SR).

---

5 Union density reached 15.4 per cent in the private sector and 65.3 per cent in the public sector in 2019 (Košč 2020).

Table 25.2 KOZ SR membership structure by sectoral union federations, 2011–2019

Union federation	2011	2012	2013	2014	2015	2016	2017	2018	2019
Union Federation of Workers in Mines, Geology and Oil Industry (*OZ pracovníkov baní, geológie a naftového priemyslu SR*)	4,710	4,529	4,106	4,011	3,811	3,498	3,325	3,387	3,367
Energy-technology Trade Union Federation (*Energeticko-Chemický OZ*)	13,340	13,125	13,055	13,005	12,865	12,372	11,646	11,389	11,162
Metalworkers' Union Federation (OZ KOVO)	69,518	69,548	69,982	70,011	69,486	70,037	70,051	70,251	71,014
Integrated Trade Union Federation (*Integrovaný odborový zväz*)	14,186	13,610	12,095	11,102	10,159	10,047	10,069	10,074	10,084
Federation of Unionists in Nuclear Power (*Združenie odborárov jadrovej energetiky*)	4,566	4,308	4,200	3,896	2,556	2,431	2,323	2,376	2,301
Slovak Trade Union Federation of Glass Industry (*SOZ sklárskeho priemyslu*)*	2,585	2,560	2,521	2,446	2,258	x	x	x	x
Trade Union Federation of Railway Workers (*Odborové združenie železničiarov*)	20,546	17,197	15,887	14,458	13,803	13,449	12,824	12,202	11,879
Trade Union Federation of Postal Services and Logistics (*OZ pôšt a logistiky*)**	3,682	3,908	3,638	2,971	2,690	2,676	2,692	2,168	2,064
Public Sector Union (SLOVES)	26,276	25,151	24,076	22,546	21,713	21,196	21,087	21,296	21,589
Trade Union Federation of Workers in Banking and Insurance (*OZ pracovníkov peňažníctva a poisťovníctva*)	4,584	4,709	4,548	4,470	4,465	4,456	4,612	4,798	4,934
Slovak Trade Union Federation of Defence Workers (*SOZ zamestnancov obrany*)	2,796	2,619	2,291	2,056	2,006	1,971	2,318	2,372	2,384
Trade Union Federation of Firefighters (*OZ hasičov*)	1,242	1,253	1,186	1,179	1,258	1,258	1,232	1,146	1,095
Trade Union Federation of Justice in Slovakia (*OZ justície v SR*)	2,589	2,653	2,571	2,582	2,697	2,535	2,577	2,708	2,759

Union federation	**2011**	**2012**	**2013**	**2014**	**2015**	**2016**	**2017**	**2018**	**2019**
Trade Union Federation of Workers in Water Transport (*OZ pracovníkov vodnej dopravy*)	127	123	76	56	56	50	42	27	19
Trade Union Federation of Slovakian Agricultural Workers (*OZ pracovníkov poľnohospodárstva na Slovensku*)	4,465	4,170	2,426	1,877	1,868	1,687	1,551	1,382	1,321
Trade Union Federation of Wood Processing Industry, Forestry and Water Management (*OZ Drevo, lesy, voda*)	14,029	13,246	12,385	11,724	11,656	11,271	10,859	10,948	10,591
Trade Union Federation of Slovakian Food Processing Workers (*OZ potravinárov SR*)	2,630	2,630	2,120	1,911	1,911	1,958	1,944	2,082	2,404
Slovak Trade Union Federation of Polygraphy Workers (*SOZ pracovníkov polygrafie*)	174	171	172	128	128	128	126	126	126
Trade union federation of Commerce and Tourism Workers (*OZ pracovníkov obchodu a cestovného ruchu*)	11,212	10,494	9,932	9,393	9,295	8,989	8,782	8,316	8,122
Trade Union Federation of Prison and Judicial Guard Corps (*OZ Zboru väzenskej a justičnej stráže*)	1,352	1,397	1,314	1,306	1,293	1,264	902	945	1,029
Trade Union Federation of Healthcare and Social Services (*SOZ zdravotníctva a sociálnych služieb*)	24,041	23,051	21,460	20,140	19,045	19,101	18,703	18,380	17,767
Trade Union Federation of Education and Science Workers (*OZ pracovníkov školstva a vedy na Slovensku*)	54,405	53,048	50,529	48,792	48,484	46,269	45,336	44,858	44,938
Trade Union Federation of police in Slovak Republic (OZ polície v SR)	8,721	8,763	8,533	8,675	8,555	8,588	8,835	9,115	9,625

(*Continued*)

Table 25.2 Continued

Union federation	2011	2012	2013	2014	2015	2016	2017	2018	2019
Trade Union Federation of physical Education and Sports Workers (*OZ pracovníkov telesnej výchovy a športu na Slovensku*)***	31	23	18	15	17	15	15	x	x
Trade Union Federation of Workers at the Slovak Academy of Sciences (*OZ pracovníkov SAV*)	1,213	966	935	934	936	936	938	800	815
Slovak Trade Union Federation of Free Professions (*SOZ slobodných povolaní*)****	431	423	383	377	x	x	x	x	x
Gas Industry Trade Union Federation (*Plynárenský odborový zväz*)	2,150	2,180	2,145	1,924	1,845	1,710	1,605	1,585	1,525
Slovak Trade Union Federation of Postal Services and Telecommunications (*SOZ pôšt a telekomunikácií*)	315	304	327	319	449	437	429	379	363
Total members	**295,916**	**286,159**	**272,911**	**262,304**	**255,305**	**248,329**	**244,823**	**243,110**	**243,277**

Note: *Merged with OZ KOVO on 31/10/2015; **Joined KOZ SR on 30 March 2011; ***Ceased activities on 31 December 2018; ****Ended membership of KOZ SR on 31/1/2015.

Source: KOZ SR Internal statistics from 2020.

Unionization rates have been largely unaffected by the emergence of new worker cohorts in the labour market. This is because Slovakia has a stable industrial structure, in which work-related migration and the emergence of new forms of work, such as platform work, are not yet extensive. Rather, unions are concerned about the 'brain drain' of Slovak workers and subsequent labour shortages in sectors such as health care (Kaminska and Kahancová 2011). Workers in new labour market situations, including migrants, agency workers or platform workers, do not tend to organize in unions, although research indicates that they are interested in doing so (Sedláková 2018). Still, the emergence of alternative and often precarious forms of work has fuelled a remarkable shift in union policies. Initially, unions did not target new types of workers in their recruitment activities, claiming that such workers lack commitment to a particular industry or employer and are therefore hard to organize in established industrial union structures (Kahancová 2015). Nevertheless, the attitude of unions towards such workers changed after a leadership change within relevant industrial unions, particularly OZ KOVO. While workers without a stable job in general do not tend to organize and unions acknowledge this difficulty, they increasingly focus on representing such workers even without organizing them. This approach is accompanied by an in-depth understanding of precarity from a union perspective and attempts to transform the challenges arising from precarity into opportunities for union action (Kahancová 2015; Trif et al. 2021).

While unions in the long run have failed to organize the bogus self-employed, the abovementioned example of acting on behalf of workers without organizing them includes a case in which unions successfully influenced a change in the Labour Code's definition of dependent employment. The aim was to reduce the number of bogus self-employed and shift these workers into regular employment relationships. Without effective enforcement of this legislation and monitoring work status at establishment level, however, this effort has not been widely successful. A further trade union aimed at limiting precarious work was the legislative proposal introduced by the Integrated Trade Union (IOZ, *Integrovaný odborový zväz*) to regulate the conditions of public procurement, under which tender applicants must prove that a certain percentage of employees are subject to a collective agreement and that obligations have been fulfilled. This proposal was not accepted.

KOZ SR underwent significant internal reorganization in 2012, slimming down considerably. Instead of several vice-presidents, all their functions were integrated under a single vice-president. The confederation still faces a lack of internal analytical and research capacities. Smaller unions, from among both KOZ SR affiliates and independent unions, are also poorly equipped in terms of professional staff and analytical capacities, often depending on voluntary work by their leaders. In addition, KOZ SR lacks capacities for strengthening its regional union structures and has delegated the selection of its regional representatives to its member federations.

Union resources and expenditure

The main source of income is membership fees, charged as a percentage of workers' wages (usually 1 per cent of the net wage). KOZ SR has detailed internal statistics on membership and income from membership fees. Figure 25.1 shows that although membership has been declining since 1990, KOZ SR's overall income has remained stable and the proportion of membership fees per member has actually been increasing.[6] A slight decline occurred after 2009, when the financial and economic crisis resulted in wage stagnation and thus a stagnation in membership fees that are collected as a percentage of wages, while the overall number of union members continued to decline.

Figure 25.1 KOZ SR membership and income from membership fees, 1990–2020

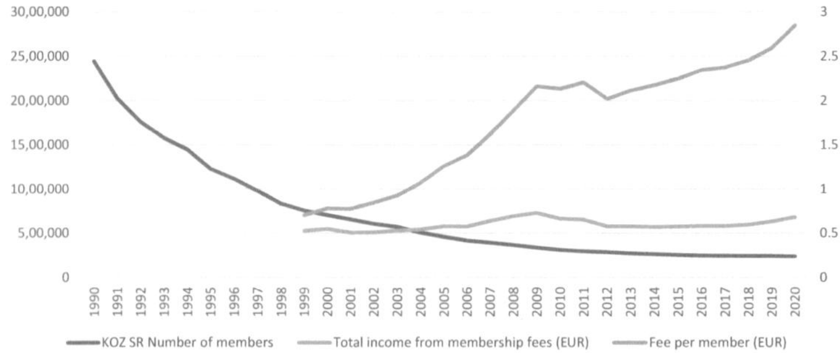

Note: Number of members as per 30 September of respective years. Conversion from SKK to EUR for 1999– 2008 based on the average annual exchange rate of the Slovak National Bank. Data for 2020 are an estimate.
Source: Authors' compilation based on internal statistics of KOZ SR from 2020.

---

6 KOZ SR's income from members was in the range €526.624.00 in 1999, €570.590.00 in 2014 and €682.968.00 in 2020 (source: internal statistics of KOZ SR).

The largest proportion of union revenues comes from membership fees (see Table 25.3). Other income of trade unions affiliated to KOZ SR comes from property operated by a limited company United Property Fund (JMF, *Jednotný majetkový fond*). The JMF was established in 1993 in order to operate property that trade unions inherited from ROH in the form of hotels, buildings and recreation facilities. JMF operates eleven hotels in Slovakia, as well as other property. KOZ SR has no share in JMF properties, does not participate in its decision-making and does not benefit from these assets. Trade unions affiliated to KOZ SR participate in asset management and revenue sharing. This structure demonstrates a unique phenomenon: while trade unions' political power is concentrated in KOZ SR, economic power is decentralized among KOZ SR members.

Table 25.3 Membership fees as a proportion of overall income for KOZ SR affiliated unions, 2014–2020

Year	Total income (EUR)	Income in membership fees (EUR)	Income from membership fees on total income (EUR) (%)
2014	724,029.34	570,590.41	79
2015	687,572.25	574,374.14	84
2016	614,251.17	582,802.84	95
2017	619,079.35	581,159.91	94
2018	617,810.21	596,659.90	97
2019	632,039.07	631,087.83	>99
2020	–	682,968.00	–

Source: KOZ SR internal statistics from 2020.

Each trade union has its own organizational system, institutions and decision-making, as well as membership fee collection and distribution. In general, the company-level trade union is the founding/base organizational unit. At company level, union membership contributions are collected, between 25 and 40 per cent of which are paid to the industrial trade union federation. The industrial unions then pay 3.8 per cent of their membership fee income to KOZ SR. In general, the largest proportion of membership contributions is managed by the company-level trade unions. While this principle of bottom-up union funding allows the stable operation of base union organizations at the workplace level and motivates the establishment of new ones, it also impedes the professionalization and capacity-building efforts of peak-level trade unions,

To sum up, in conditions of declining union membership, the unions have managed to sustain a stable income at national level. At the same time, unions' economic power resources have remained decentralized and concentrated within workplace unions and industrial union federations.

Collective bargaining and unions at the workplace

Collective bargaining in Slovakia is in the hands of trade unions, although the coverage of bargaining has been declining steadily (Kahancová et al. 2019). Act No. 2/1991 on collective bargaining stipulated that collective agreements can be negotiated and concluded by employers and union representatives, and authorized through union statutes or internal union regulations. In cases in which more than one union operates at a workplace, the unions need to agree on the negotiating provisions. For higher-level collective agreements, employers may conclude an agreement with unions representing the largest number of employees of member companies. Information on negotiations and approval procedures within employers' organizations is limited and not publicly accessible. These procedures are stipulated in internal regulations accessible only to members. At the establishment level, union representatives serve as negotiators and oversee the implementation of collective agreements. Union representatives, unlike works councils or work trustees, have the right to call a strike after a majority vote in a secret ballot.

At the industry level, unions usually appoint a chief negotiator. For instance, OZ KOVO, the metalworkers' union, approves a chief negotiator and the overall strategy in collective bargaining through its Presidency of the Council of the Trade Union Federation (*Predsedníctvo rady odborového zväzu*). The Council acts as the union's statutory and executive body. The internal appointments mechanism in many cases is specific to the union's constitution and studies accurately describing appointment procedures, for example by voting or only by formal approval, are almost non-existent. The depth of collective bargaining is thus less pronounced at the industry level that at the establishment level. Union representatives who conclude collective agreements with an industrial or higher-level employer organization may be, and in most cases are, professionals employed by industry-level unions. In some cases, a representative of the higher-level union also serves as a representative of an establishment-level union, as in banking, although industrial wage bargaining has ceased to exist in that sector (Kahancová et al. 2017).

Unions have actively supported the application of extensions to collective agreements. Some extension arrangements have been legislatively stipulated since 2011 in the construction, chemical, steel and mechanical engineering industries. After changes in government, *erga omnes* extensions have been repeatedly introduced into or removed from legislation. The current legislation stipulates that a representative collective agreement, covering the largest share of the workforce in the industry, can be extended to other employers after a committee decision under the control of the Ministry of Labour, Social Affairs and Family (MPSVR, *Ministerstvo práce, sociálnych vecí a rodiny*). Rather than free-riding in bargaining, unions are concerned with legal regulation, which is perceived as the most important coercive regulation. With the weakening of unions' associational power and insecurity in bargaining trends and coverage, unions increasingly advocate legal regulation, which has tended to replace collective bargaining. For example, wage increases for doctors and other healthcare staff, which has been a highly debated topic for years, are now legally stipulated and no longer subject to industrial bargaining. Besides union efforts concentrated on legislative changes at the national level, another important trend can be observed: namely, the growing role of a minimum wage as a regulatory tool to decrease wage inequalities. Because unions have been able to introduce an automatic legal mechanism for minimum wage setting, they remain committed to using this tool and refrain from other wage setting strategies (Martišková et al. 2021).

Since 2004 KOZ SR has bargained with representative organizations of the government and state, the regional self-governments (SK 8) and municipalities (Association of Towns and Communities of Slovakia – ZMOS, *Združenie miest a obcí Slovenska*), concluding higher-level collective agreements for the public and state sector representing more than 360,000 employees.[7] This approach was adopted in line with the fact that KOZ SR covers several national public-sector trade unions, which would have to negotiate collective agreements separately with the government, as all benefits and wage rises increase budget expenditures. Therefore, coordinated bargaining for public and state employees is more effective. In 2018, KOZ SR participated in the modification of the remuneration system for public servants, in order to eliminate the fall of wage tariffs below the statutory minimum wage.

---

7 The mandate to engage in this kind of bargaining is anchored in the Act on Collective Bargaining (No. 2/1991).

Some subsections of public services and state administration developed an additional bargaining round with upward derogations possible from higher-level collective agreements. This applies to police officers, firefighters and prison guards in their bargaining with the Ministry of Interior Affairs.

In addition to bargaining, unions at the workplace are concerned with member recruitment, occupational safety and health, and members' services. Trade unions are also perceived as a potentially relevant stakeholder in cooperating with labour inspectorates in tackling undeclared work and reporting cases of abuse at the workplace. A recent study also showed that trade union potential in supporting non-standard and vulnerable groups of workers, such as workers returning to work after absence because of chronic illness, is increasing (Holubová et al. 2021).

Industrial conflict

CEE countries are known for labour quiescence, arising in part from trade unions' restricted mobilizing capacity (Bohle and Greskovits 2012). Several factors influence the low strike activity in Slovakia: the legislative framework, the economic consequences for employees on strike, psychological and behavioural factors, the lack of a strike tradition as a stable part of political culture, low support of elites, and limited financial support from trade unions to striking workers.

Nevertheless, the past decade has seen several substantial strike actions. In November 2012, OZPŠaV, a KOZ SR affiliate, organized one of the largest teachers' strikes in Slovakia, lasting for three days. The strike was supported by 73 per cent of primary education workers, more than 63 per cent of secondary education workers and about 5 per cent of higher education employees. Teachers demanded a 10 per cent pay rise and an adjustment to the remuneration system to make teachers' salaries between 1.2 and 2.0 times the average wage in the national economy. The protest was accompanied by tactical errors and poor communication between professional trade unionists, strike committee members and teachers. The inappropriate timing of the strike in the run-up to Christmas caused many schools to give up after the first day, another after two or three days. During the strike period, employees were not paid and had to bear their own health insurance costs, which deterred many from prolonged protest. Trade unionists then relied on negotiating with government officials. The strike was officially terminated after three days, and the government offered the trade unions an annual 5 per cent pay rise between 2013 and 2015. Some dissatisfied teachers established the non-trade union Initiative of Slovak Teachers (ISU, *Iniciatíva slovenských učiteľov*), which carried on the street protests and rallies. ISU organized various protests in the following period, directed against the activities of the OZPŠaV, as well as against the government. These protests were fruitless, however, as the government officially negotiates only with trade unions.

In 2017, KOZ SR called for a complex change to the remuneration system of public-sector workers. The key requirement was a change in pay rates, which previously had been increased only based on rises laid down in collective agreements. The minimum wage grew faster than developments in collective agreements, however. As a consequence, the pay of many public-sector workers fell below the minimum wage in 2004. The government reacted to the demand for changes in pay only half-heartedly, however, which is why trade unions affiliated to KOZ SR organized several protests in three large Slovak cities at the end of 2017. During the spring of 2018, the government responded to increasing pressure from trade unions and the media by bringing forward new legislation to address these systemic shortcomings in public pay. Subsequently, in collective agreements, KOZ SR negotiated a 10 per cent increase in the salaries of civil and public servants in 2019 and also in 2020. Several favourable factors underpinned this success: pressure from trade unions, media interest and coverage, favourable economic results and economic growth, political partnership with the ruling party, and the unions' proficiency in handling the issue.

In August 2020 after the negotiations on the minimum wage for 2021 and conflicts with the Minister of Labour, KOZ SR representatives left the tripartite Economic and Social Council of the Slovak Republic (HSR SR, *Hospodárska a sociálna rada SR*) and decided not to participate in national social dialogue. This action led to several protests by KOZ SR in autumn 2020. Rallies in six Slovak cities and in front of the Ministry of Labour, Government Offices and Parliament criticized the government's proposals to reduce social and wage standards and legislative changes connected to minimum wages, the Labour Code and tripartism. The government adopted legislation that affects the functioning of trade unions at the workplace and in tripartite structures.

Therefore, in November 2020 KOZ SR launched a petition to call a referendum to protect workers' rights and preserve the status of trade unions in Slovakia. This is not the first time that KOZ SR has chosen a petition as a tool for promoting its interests. In 2003, the trade unions also launched a petition to trigger a referendum on shortening the parliamentary term of the then government of Mikuláš Dzurinda from four to two years. The petition was also supported by a number of opposition parties. In general, trade unions do not resort to petitions to defend their interests. In 2003, because of the distribution of seats between the political parties, the petition became not only political but also a partisan action, which poses a big risk for the unions. Unlike the 2003 petition, in 2020 the unions opted for an instrument expressing civic attitudes in the form of direct democracy, targeted at specific government measures and without the participation or direct support of political actors. While these steps may eliminate the risk of politicizing trade union activities and the presence of party interests, at the same time they support the argument put forward in this chapter on unions turning away from political unionism and returning to bread-and-butter unionism.

The impossibility of pursuing union interests through tripartite structures led KOZ SR to use various means of exerting pressure, including protest rallies, social media campaigns, petitions and complaints to the General Prosecutor's Office (GP, *Generálna prokuratúra*) to review the procedures of the Minister of Labour in relation to minimum wages and tripartism. Complaints and initiatives have also been addressed to the European Commission, the European Trade Union Confederation (ETUC), the International Trade Union Confederation and the International Labour Organization (ILO).

With its decision to leave HSR SR, KOZ SR has not achieved a fundamental change in its position and legislation. Past experience and knowledge would suggest that it is more effective for trade unions to participate in tripartite social dialogue. If they do not participate, unions need to identify complementary tools to achieve their interests, which is more challenging in financial and organizational terms, as well as in terms of personnel and time. In 2021, union participation in tripartite social dialogue resumed, and the new prime minister Eduard Heger promised regular and closer interactions between the government and unions, even beyond tripartism.

Political relations

Since its establishment, KOZ SR has focused, in general, on three main issues: defining its attitude to political parties and movements; defining its position on the HSR SR and the national tripartite council; and membership decline. In the first years of its democratic existence, KOZ SR focused mainly on building structures to meet the new conditions of democracy, and acquiring property and assets from the former ROH. Because of the negative 'legacy' of the former regime, KOZ SR was committed to political and party neutrality. Political relations underwent an important turning point in 1998, when unions affiliated to KOZ SR started to engage actively in election campaigns in order to mobilize their members to participate in parliamentary elections in the hope of a political outcome that would facilitate a stronger role for unions to promote their members' interests (Uhlerová 2015). During 1998, KOZ SR considered four options for participation in the election campaign: to maintain neutrality and passivity; to actively promote pluralistic and socially sensitive election outcomes; to communicate its electoral preferences; and to create a political party. Having considered all the hazards, particularly the loss of credible trade union independence, entering into competition with some political parties and financial risks, the confederation chose the second option. After evaluating the priorities of various political parties, the confederation did not declare open support for one of them, thereby protecting itself from the fallout of potential electoral failures (Uhlerová 2015: 69).

The main reason for KOZ SR's active participation in election campaigns was to contribute to changing Slovakia's mode of governance and thus strengthen its own position in society and in social dialogue institutions. At that time, the government was formed by the Movement for Democratic Slovakia (HZDS, *Hnutie za demokratické Slovensko*). This is considered to have been a period of failure of democracy. Trade unions were in conflict with the government, and social dialogue at national level was not functioning. After the election, the newly established government of Mikuláš Dzurinda (SDK, *Slovenská demokratická koalícia*) acknowledged the unions' active participation in political change by adopting the Tripartite Act (*Zákon o hospodárskom a sociálnom partnerstve*, No. 106/1999) in 1999. This event marked the legal anchoring of tripartism in Slovakia.

After the 2002 elections, government policy became hostile towards corporatism, which motivated unions to try to promote their interests with political support. As a result of growing tensions between the incumbent government, unions organized protests and rallies, during which convergence of the unions' interests with priorities of the Social Democratic Party SMER (SMER, *Sociálna demokracia*), then in opposition, crystalized. KOZ SR started actively cooperating with SMER after 2003 after recognizing a joint interest in calling a referendum to organize new elections before the end of the regular parliamentary term. Because several political parties joined this petition initiative, it is considered a political action, not resulting directly from trade union pressure. As a result, a referendum was organized in 2004 but did not yield a parliamentary change as it did not meet the condition of an absolute majority of eligible voters participating in the referendum.

The broader discourse on the relationship between unions and political parties continued after 2005 when KOZ SR and SMER signed a cooperation agreement. KOZ SR justified its strategic alliance with SMER as an effort to strengthen the trade unions' position in tripartism and secure enforcement of legislation to improve workers' rights and working conditions. At the same time, such political alliances also create risks for unions: namely, labelling unions political organizations. This is especially sensitive in a post-socialist country, where unions already face the historical legacy of subordination to the ruling party. At the same time, KOZ SR faced the challenge that political failure would also be considered a trade union failure.

SMER was the governing party between 2006 and 2020 (with the exception of a short break between 2010 and 2012). SMER's policies and suspicions of its links to the oligarchy and business increased the negative public perception of SMER and indirectly that of KOZ SR. To reach the electorate, SMER has recently flirted with conservative and nationalist issues, which conflict with social democracy.

Before the parliamentary elections in February 2020, KOZ SR changed its attitude to engagement in political exchange and elections. Instead of supporting a single party, KOZ SR prepared its own analysis of party election programmes and made it available to its members and the general public as a comprehensive view of selected areas from the perspective of trade union priorities. KOZ SR also negotiated with selected political parties to integrate key union priorities into their programmes. This approach demonstrates the effort made within KOZ SR to loosen ties with a single political party and to seek broader political support for union goals. In parallel with attempts to strengthen these external ties, the political views and preferences of workers and KOZ SR members have never been homogenous and continue to differ also after the 2020 elections.

After the 2020 elections, trade unions faced hostility from the new government regarding tripartism, and gradually lost their influence. To illustrate, despite a mechanism for setting minimum wages adopted in legislation in 2019, the current government preferred to re-open negotiations, which caused KOZ SR to walk out from a tripartite meeting (Kahancová 2021). This indicates KOZ SR's reliance on other ways of achieving their goals and interests, specifically through lobbying and campaigns, which also tests the unions' mobilization skills and capacities. While the pandemic has significantly limited union possibilities to organize such activities, it is an opportunity for unions to focus on strengthening their influence and organizational, personnel, professional and international capacities by focusing on 'bread-and-butter' unionism rather than on political support.

Societal power

Despite union fragmentation and a declining union capacity to represent their members' interests, union resources are not completely depleted (Kahancová 2015). Unions are able to mobilize relevant worker groups and gain public profile by raising demands in protests and rallies. The most recent evidence of such actions are the public rallies organized by KOZ SR in September 2020, after the minimum wage for 2021 had been approved at a level different from that stipulated by legal regulations (Kahancová 2021). While the unions aimed at a legal commitment, derived from an automatic minimum wage setting mechanism, to 60 per cent of the average wage from two years previously, the Ministry of Labour and the employers proposed an adjustment because of the Covid-19 crisis and continued negotiations without union involvement to adopt a minimum wage for 2021 at a lower level of 57 per cent of the average wage. In addition, the Ministry responded to the unions' walkout from the tripartite negotiations by revisiting the Act on Tripartism (*Zákon o trojstranných konzultáciách na celoštátnej úrovni*, No. 103/2007), including changes in setting representativeness criteria for unions, as well as opening tripartism up to actors other than the social partners. The unions responded to these proposals by notifying the ETUC and the ILO and by organizing protest actions in several major cities in order to defend workers' rights and their commitment to existing legal regulations, despite the Covid-19 pandemic and related labour market changes.

Despite the abovementioned mobilization of societal resources, relations between unions and other civil society actors are fairly underdeveloped because of the differing scope of their activities. An exception is the emerging cooperation between unions and professional associations, visible mainly in public services, particularly health care and education. In health care, the Nurses and Midwives' Trade Union (OZSaPA, *Odborový zväz sestier a pôrodných asistentiek*), established in 2012, has cooperated closely with the Chamber of Nurses and Midwives (SKSaPA, *Slovenská komora sestier a pôrodných asistentiek*) in all public actions, including protests, a hunger strike, lobbying and a resignation campaign among hospital nurses in an effort to improve their working conditions. OZSaPA and SKSaPA acted jointly in these events, thus raising concerns about the relationship between the activities of a union and of a professional association. Experts, for example, asked whether non-union actors, including professional associations, are in a position to adopt priorities and strategies that have traditionally been part of the trade union agenda (Kahancová and Sedláková 2020).

Another recent phenomenon, partly accelerated by the current government's proposal to open up national social dialogue to non-union actors, is the growing importance of NGOs active in defending labour rights. Such NGOs, including The Working Poor (*Pracujúca chudoba*), closely interact with trade unions and offer services to individual workers, engage in lobbying, and develop direct relationships with politically important actors. In this way, NGOs complement trade union activities. Nevertheless, the similarity between topics addressed by NGOs and those on the trade union agenda also raises the question of competition with trade unions. NGO agendas often overlap with those of trade unions, but while NGOs tend to be respected in the media and public opinion, trade unions often face public criticism for similar arguments. The key difference is societal trust towards these NGOs, Many NGOs were established only recently, while the public still regards trade unions as organizations of the pre-1989 regime, or at least associates them with SMER, which led the Slovak government for most of the period 2006–2020.

Trade union policies towards the European Union

A survey implemented within the project Enhancing the Effectiveness of Social Dialogue Articulation in Europe (EESDA) in 2018–2019 shows that not all Slovak unions are engaged in European trade union and social dialogues. The findings show that a lack of involvement may be due to financial resources, capacity constraints and language barriers (Kahancová 2019). Additional interview data show that the most common barriers to participation include the lack of internal capacity and financial resources.

Representatives of those Slovak unions that are involved in EU-level structures emphasize skills and working conditions as the topics that they would expect to be addressed within EU-level social dialogue structures and trade union initiatives. At the same time, they indicated that topics are either discussed appropriately, given their importance, or that an even higher frequency of discussion would be appreciated. Furthermore, the EESDA survey showed that trade unions prioritize binding agreements and legislation, such as Directives and Autonomous agreements, at EU level over soft, non-binding outcomes. Slovak unions claim that binding outcomes at the EU level equip them with more bargaining power in domestic conditions, against the government and employers in national tripartism, in the adoption of legislation, or in industry-specific collective bargaining. Some industrial unions (all KOZ SR affiliates) are also members of EU-level sectoral trade union organizations and thereby linked to EU-level sectoral social dialogue developments. For example, the Metalworkers' Union OZ KOVO and the Integrated Trade Union (IOZ, *Integrovaný odborový zväz*) are both affiliates of IndustriAll. IOZ is also a member of the European Federation of Building and Woodworkers (EFBWW), and the Slovak Trade Union Federation of Health Care and Social Work (SOZZaSS, *Slovenský odborový zväz zdravotníctva a sociálnych služieb*) is a member of the European Public Services Union (EPSU). Smaller unions that are vocal on the Slovak trade union scene, although remaining outside KOZ SR, include the Independent Christian Trade Unions of Slovakia (NKOS, *Nezávislé kresťanské odbory Slovenska*) and the Medical Doctors' Trade Union Federation (LOZ, *Lekárske odborové združenie*), which have developed international ties outside the dominant EU-level union structures, mostly via national and regional contacts.

Besides direct participation in EU-level trade union organizations and social dialogue structures, Slovak unions have developed close cooperation with their Czech counterparts and other unions in the region and beyond. Slovak unions belong to the core group of CEE unions actively promoting the European minimum wage together with Polish unions and have managed to incorporate this issue in ETUC's agenda (Adamczyk 2018; Sedláková 2019). At the same time, Slovak unions have criticized the perceived duality in ETUC policies vis-à-vis the 'old' and the 'new' EU Member States (Adamczyk 2018).

Conclusions

Similar to other post-Socialist countries, the fall of state socialism left trade unions in Slovakia without relevant tradition of collective action. Unions entered the period of economic, social and political transformation in the 1990s with no experience of collective bargaining, no independent identity, little heritage of collective militancy and limited experience representing workers' interests. At the same time, trade unions inherited substantial apparatus and property that gave them the potential to assert independence and develop influence in workers' representation and policymaking (Drahokoupil and Kahancová 2019). Despite these mixed influences from the past, trade unions managed to re-establish themselves in the face of transition challenges, organizational fragmentation, emergence of new unions and the changing course of union action away from political unionism. The transition years were followed by a decade of economic growth, labour market flexibilization and deregulation, as well as two notable crises, the 2008–2009 financial crisis and the Covid-19 pandemic since 2020. These crises have intensified the challenges facing Slovak unions, but have also yielded new opportunities for unions to position themselves independently from their political allies, focusing on core union activities or 'bread-and-butter unionism'. In response to the Covid-19 pandemic, KOZ SR elaborated a strategy called the 'Post-Covid 10' for remedies and priorities for workers. These include shortening working time, fair minimum wages for all, and increased focus on education and training in government policies.

The main resource for trade union legitimacy is legal regulation, stipulating union rights in codetermination, information and collective bargaining. Unions also developed an image of political subordination, especially under the rule of the political party SMER. Recent years have seen a departure from cooperation with SMER, stricter rules for union representatives and a forced union fragmentation in tripartism from 2021. This, in turn, has pushed trade unions to a position in which they constantly have to re-establish themselves as legitimate organizations capable of representing their members and the wider labour force, independently of political support, engaging in social dialogue and delivering feasible collective bargaining outcomes. Facing this challenge, unions operating in an environment hostile to collective interest representation are focusing most of their capacities for action in two areas.

First, at the national level, unions seek to influence legislation as the strongest mechanism to address workers' interests (Martišková et al. 2021). This strategy brought union success under the pro-labour government of SMER between 2006–2010 and 2012–2020. As the government increasingly responds to business interests, however, trade union political resources remain contested. Unions have realized this threat and therefore are increasingly attempting to diversify their political resources, or even to retreat from political unionism. Instead, unions are looking for a more balanced mix of policies and resources in order to reduce their political dependence. Resources that would probably strengthen trade union legitimacy and structural power include organizing new members from more flexible and precarious parts of the labour market, developing strong international contacts with European and international trade union organizations, a more pro-active engagement in domestic socio-economic developments, and an active role in EU-wide debates within sectoral social dialogue committees and beyond.

Second, at the industrial and establishment levels, unions consider collective bargaining and monitoring employer's legislative compliance as their main functions. Despite variations in bargaining procedures and outcomes, the industrial principle still plays an important role in union structures and collective bargaining.

A major challenge facing trade unions is the decline in organizational capacities driven by membership decline. Trade unions face difficulties in recruiting young members and members from among precarious employees in segmented labour markets. KOZ SR estimates that precarious workers comprise 15 per cent of all union members (Kahancová 2013). Besides membership decline, trade unions are worried about the declining coverage of collective agreements. In this light, trade unions welcomed the legislative change to support *erga omnes* extensions to higher-level collective agreements.

Recent years have seen fragmentation between unions focused on traditional modes of action, such as industrial collective bargaining and tripartite social dialogue, and 'new' unions, particularly in the public sector, whose actions focus on protests, demonstrations, petitions and campaigns to influence public opinion. While such new types of action strengthen union resources, at the same time they undermine the traditional pillars of industrial relations, most importantly coordinated bargaining and solidarity wage setting.

Finally, trade unions in Slovakia increasingly recognize the need to adjust their internal structures to meet the above challenges. This includes the incorporation of young trade union professionals with international education in industrial trade union structures. Slovak trade unions need to modify their internal structures to ensure that decision-making structures and processes are more dynamic, efficient and acknowledge the use of digital technologies and innovative communication methods. Trade unions need to attract young people, strengthen their professional capacities and connection to research institutions, link with international structures, and eliminate the risk of political influence on union activities.

Currently, personal inertia prevails in trade union management at all levels, which hinders essential transformation and generational replacement, a necessary element in union revitalization. Slovak trade unions recognize opportunities for increasing their membership base with workers in non-standard employment forms, including agency workers, platform workers, domestic workers, migrant workers, students and the unemployed.

The structure of unions, however, is built mainly on the principle of so-called 'traditional' areas and professions grouped in individual trade unions, which is typical of an industrial or post-industrial era. In this scenario, the increased rivalry of union organizations is likely to be typified by the presence of several trade unions with varying or no affiliation to the same workplace, and the establishment of new forms of articulation of workers' interests via non-union actors.

Evaluating the trajectory for Slovak trade unions in light of Visser's (2019) different scenarios of union development, it can be argued that if trade unions in Slovakia do not undergo the necessary personnel, leadership, programme and content revitalization accompanied by a minimal dependence on political and economic changes in the country, the scenario of gradual marginalization of trade unions seems likely. This scenario may be transformed into other scenarios as a related phase, namely, the dualization of trade unions and their policies, or the replacement of trade unions by other forms of workers' interest representation by civil society actors (cf. Visser 2019).

For revitalization, it will be necessary for unions to adapt their internal structures to face new challenges, including labour market changes, digitalization, climate change, economic transformation, post-Covid challenges and demographic changes. The trade unions' approach to communications and policymaking should be more pro-active. Trade unions should become agenda setters and influencers, with clear and attractive communications, and attractive marketing. Unions should also open and influence public debates. Decision-making structures and processes need to be more dynamic, streamlined and adapted to the challenges of the modern digital age. To represent the full breadth of the Slovak labour force, unions need to organize new types and forms of work; adapt innovative forms of communication; reach more young people, and other social or marginalized social groups; strengthen professional and leadership capacities; and increase connectivity with research institutions and international affiliation structures, to eliminate the risk of politicization and the penetration of party interests into union activities.

References

All links were checked on 6 July 2021.

Adamczyk S. (2018) Inside the trade union family: the 'two worlds' within the European Trade Union Confederation, European Journal of Industrial Relations, 24 (2), 179–192.

Bohle D. and Greskovits B. (2012) Capitalist diversity on Europe's periphery, Ithaca, Cornell University Press.

Docherty J.C. and van der Velden S. (2012) Historical dictionary of organized labor, 3rd edn, Lanham, Scarecrow Press.

Drahokoupil J. and Kahancová M. (2019) Worker participation in Czechia and Slovakia, in Berger S., Pries L. and Wannöffel M. (eds) Palgrave Handbook of workers' participation at plant level, Basingstoke, Palgrave Macmillan, 301–322.

Holubová B., Kahancová M., Sedláková M. and Šumichrast A. (2021) Return to work practice in Slovakia: matching best practice with the scope of social partner activity, in Akgüç, M. (ed.) Continuing at work. Long-term illness, return to work schemes and the role of industrial relations, Brussels: ETUI, 143–162.

Kahancová M. (2013) The demise of social partnership or a balanced recovery? The crisis and collective bargaining in Slovakia, Transfer, 19 (2), 171–183.

Kahancová M. (2015) Central and Eastern European trade unions after the EU enlargement: successes and failures for capacity building, Transfer, 21 (3), 343–357.

Kahancová M. (2021) Articulation of trade union strategies on upward convergence of social standards in the enlarged EU: the case of Slovakia, Policy Brief 17/2021, Bratislava, Central European Labour Studies Institute (CELSI).

Kahancová M. and Sedláková M. (2020) Erosion of bargaining in the world of vital actors: industrial relations in the aftermath of public sector reforms in Slovakia, in Keune M., Ramos Martín N.E. and Mailand M. (eds) Working under pressure: employment, job quality and labour relations in Europe's public sector since the crisis, Brussels, ETUI, 253–286.

Kahancová M., Martišková M. and Sedláková M. (2017) Negotiating wage inequality in Slovakia, Research Report 21/2017, Bratislava, Central European Labour Studies Institute (CELSI).

Kahancová M., Martišková M. and Sedláková M. (2019) Slovakia: between coordination and fragmentation, in Müller T., Vandaele K. and Waddington J. (eds) Collective bargaining in Europe: towards an endgame, Brussels, ETUI, 525–544.

Kaminska M.E. and Kahancová M. (2011) Emigration and labour shortages: an opportunity for trade unions in the New Member States?, European Journal of Industrial Relations, 17 (2), 189–203.

Košč J. (2020) Naozaj odbory nie sú reprezentatívne? [Are trade unions really not representative?], Pole – Kultúrno-spoločenský magazín, 10 September 2020. https://new,poleblog,sk/naozaj-odbory-nie-su-reprezentativne/

Malová D. (1997) Reprezentácia záujmov od prevodových pák ku štátnestraníckemu korporatizmu? [The development of interest representation: from 'transmission belts' to 'party-state corporatism'?], in Szomolányi, S. (ed.) Slovensko: problémy konsolidácie demokracie [Slovakia: Problems of Consolidation of Democracy], Bratislava: Friedrich Ebert Stiftung and the Slovak Political Science Association.

Martišková M., Kahancová M. and Kostolný J. (2021) Negotiating wage (in)equality: changing union strategies in high-wage and low-wage sectors in Czechia and Slovakia, Transfer, 27 (1), 75–96.

Myant M. (2010) Trade unions in the Czech Republic, Brussels, ETUI.

Roháček P. (2017) Korporativizmus v podmienkach vojnovej Slovenskej republiky (1939–1945) [Corporatism in conditions of the Slovak republic during the war (1939–1945)], Právne noviny, 24 August 2017. https://www,pravnenoviny,sk/korporativizmus-v-podmienkach-vojnovej-slovenskej-republiky-1939–1945

Sedláková M. (2019) Industrial relations and social dialogue in the age of collaborative economy (IRSDACE), National report: Slovakia, Research Report 28/2018, Bratislava, Central European Labour Studies Institute (CELSI).

Šumichrast A. (2018) Transformácia či zánik? Vývoj odborov v Slovenskom štáte (1939–1945) v kontexte vybraných európskych diktatúr [Transformation or extirpation? Development of trade unions in the Slovak state (1939–1945) in the context of selected European dictatorships], Studia historica Brunensia, 65 (2), 85–102.

Trif A., Paolucci V., Kahancová M. and Koukiadaki A. (2021) Power resources and successful trade union actions that address precarity in adverse contexts: The case of Central and Eastern Europe, in Human relations, first published online, 15 May 2021.

Uhlerová M. (2012) Inštitucionalizovaný sociálny dialóg a jeho dosahy na postavenie odborov v post-komunistických krajinách strednej Európy (prípadová štúdia Slovenska) [Institutionalized social dialogue and its impact on trade union position in post-communist countries of Central Europe (Case study of Slovakia)], in Politické vedy, 15 (1), 8–51.

Uhlerová M. (2015) Trade unions politics in Slovakia after 1989, Banská Bystrica, Vydavateľstvo Univerzity Mateja Bela – Belianum.

Visser, J. (2019) Trade unions in the balance. Working paper, Geneva: International Labour Organization.

Abbreviations

AIOS	Moderné obdory AIOS (Modern Trade Unions AIOS)
GP	Generálna prokuratúra (General Prosecutor's Office)
HSR SR	Hospodárska a socilálna rada SR (Economic and Social Council of the Slovak Republic)
ICTWSS	Institutional Characteristics of Trade Unions, Wage Setting, State Intervention and Social Pacts (database)
IBU	Iniciatíva bratislavských učiteľov (Initiative of Bratislava Teachers)
IOZ	Integrovaný odborový zväz (Integrated Trade Union)
ISU	Iniciatíva slovenských učiteľov (Initiative of Slovak Teachers)
JMF	Jednotný majetkový fond (United Property Fund)
KCO	Klientské centrum odborov (Trade Unions' Customer Centre)
KOZ SR	Konfederácia odborových zväzov SR (Confederation of Trade Unions of the Slovak Republic)
KUK	Konfederácia umenia a kultúry (Confederation of Arts and Culture)
LOZ	Lekárske odborové združenie (Trade Union Federation of Medical Doctors)
MOV	Moderné odbory Volkswagen (Modern Trade Unions Volkswagen)
MPSVR	Ministerstvo práce, sociálnych vecí a rodiny (Ministry of Labour, Social Affairs and Family)
NKOS	Nezávislé kresťanské odbory Slovenska (Independent Christian Trade Unions of Slovakia)
NŠO	Nové školské odbory (New Education Trade Unions)
OZ KOVO	Odborový zväz KOVO (Metalworkers' Union)
OZPŠaV	Odborový zväz pracovníkov školstva a vedy na Slovensku (*Trade Union* of Workers in *Education* and Science of Slovakia)

OZSaPA	Odborové združenie sestier a pôrodných asistentiek (Trade Union of Nurses and Midwifes)
ROH	Revolučné odborové hnutie (Revolutionary Trade Union Movement)
SKSaPA	Slovenská komora sestier a pôrodných asistentiek (Chamber of Nurses and Midwives)
SLOVES	Slovenský odborový zväz verejnej správy a kultúry (Public Sector Union)
SOS	Spoločné odbory Slovenska (Joint Trade Unions of Slovakia)
SOZZaSS	Slovenský odborový zväz zamestnancov zdravotníctva a sociálnych služieb (Slovak Trade Union of Healthcare and Social Services Employees)
ÚRO	Ústredná rada odborov (Central Council of Trade Unions)
ZO JAVYS	Základná organizácia JAVYS (Trade Union JAVYS)
ZMOS	Združenie miest a obcí Slovenska (Association of Towns and Communities of Slovakia)
ZP	Zákonník práce (Labour Code)

Chapter 26

Slovenia: From strong trade union movement to uneven de-unionization

Miroslav Stanojević, Andreja Poje and Živa Broder

During the past 30 years the development of industrial relations in Slovenia has been marked by two important turning points: first, the change of political system in the early 1990s and, second, Slovenia joining the EU in 2004. The huge change in the political system was followed by the formation of neo-corporatist industrial relations (Bohle and Greskovits 2007, 2012; Feldmann 2006); while the second turning point, EU accession, triggered the partial dismantling or liberalization of this system (Feldman 2016; Guardiancich 2016).

This chapter shows that, following the first turning point all processes seemed to be helping to shape and stabilize the strength of trade unions. In this period during the 1990s, trade union density in Slovenia stabilized at 40 per cent. After the second turning point, however, the trends of the 1990s went into reverse, leading to a sharp decline in union density.

Only at first glance is the intensity of this latest significant change reminiscent of the change seen during the late 1980s and early 1990s. While a massive decline in union membership characterized both turning points, the first (new political system) led to a huge drop in union density, from nearly complete unionization during the socialist period to 50 per cent in the decade 1985–1995. The second turning point pushed the density rate further down, from just above 40 to 20 per cent in a little more than a decade (2003–2015) (see Table 26.1). Direct comparison of these two contractions suggests that the decline in union membership in Slovenia following the first turning point was much sharper. This chapter shows, however, that a direct comparison of quantitative data is misleading and that indeed the decline after the second point in time was much more intense (and dramatic) than the drop observed during the early 1990s. The chapter argues that the fall in union membership in the early 1990s was not accompanied by the weakening of trade unions. In fact, the situation was then precisely the opposite: new, autonomous trade unions were established, boasting large-scale membership and considerable mobilization potential. Following the second turning point when Slovenia joined the EU in 2004 and Economic and Monetary Union (EMU) in 2007 and during the pre-crisis period of the economic boom (2004–2008), independent trade unions in Slovenia started to lose members and mobilizing potential. The first juncture was followed by a period of stabilizing the institutional framework for social partnership within which powerful trade unions exercised strong influence over public policies. After the second turning point, however, their influence within that same institutional framework has constantly diminished, despite occasional strikes and mass protests. Thus, the key questions addressed in this chapter are: what explains the considerable power held by trade unions in Slovenia during the 1990s and why have unions incurred such dramatic losses in the past fifteen years?

Table 26.1 Principal characteristics of trade unionism in Slovenia

	1992	2000	2019
Total trade union membership (1)	619,115	400,608	218,572
Women as a proportion of total membership	43 %	51 %	61 %
Gross union density	60 %	42 %	21 %
Net union density	66 %	47 %	24 %
Number of confederations	4	7	7
Number of affiliated unions (federations)	n.a.	n.a.	67
Number of independent unions	n.a.	n.a.	15
Collective bargaining coverage	100 %	100 %	79 % (2)
Principal level of collective bargaining	–	central	central in public sector; industrial in private sector
Days not worked due to industrial action per 1,000 workers	189	n.a.	n.a.

Notes: (1) Share of labour force based on density rates calculated from public opinion surveys. Labour force in 1993: 931,000; 2000: 963,000; and 2019: 1,032,000.

Source: Appendix A1; SORS 1994 and 2001;(2) Stanojević and Poje (2019).

Historical background and principal features of the industrial relations system

Similar to other 'real-socialist' countries at the time, trade unions in the former Yugoslavia were subordinated to the communist party. But Yugoslav socialism had a special feature that distinguished it from other 'real socialisms', the legally protected institution of workers' councils. Workers elected as representatives on these councils competed with official trade unions, frequently taking over traditional trade union roles in companies that the official unions were unable to fulfil. The most critical issue was work stoppages. Members of workers' councils were usually more in favour of strikes than union representatives (Arzenšek 1984).

In the early stages of the transition to a 'market economy', when new legislation began to limit the power of the workers' councils, the trade unions took over the functions the councils previously performed. This was an early stage in the emergence of autonomous trade unions. In fact, the decline in trade union density (which had dropped to 70 per cent in the late 1980s) was counterbalanced by an increase – not a decline – in unions' (mobilizing) power. Within companies, union organizations were transformed into the main employee representation bodies. Simultaneously, the workers' councils survived as works councils, a 'new old body' that referred closely to the German model (see Chapter 12). The result was a dual system of interest representation in which unions had a leading role.

The emergence of autonomous trade unions coincided with the pluralization of the trade union scene, which forced unions to compete with each other for members. By adopting workers' councils (and councillors), as well as the infrastructural and organizational resources inherited from socialism, trade unions were able to adjust their policies relatively efficiently to meet workers' demands. Accordingly, trade unions preserved their massive memberships even between 1990 and 1992, when the transformation depression in Slovenia was at its deepest.

Trade union power was concentrated in manufacturing industry, especially in its export sector. At the time, blue-collar workers prevailed among union members, mainly in the affiliates of the 'old', reformed confederation of trade unions, the Association of Free Trade Unions of Slovenia (ZSSS, *Zveza svobodnih sindikatov Slovenije*).

During the 1990s, the robust export sector chiefly relied on Western markets, much like today. This key aspect of the Slovenian economy was shaped in the decades after the Second World War, within the framework of the comparably open and reform-oriented Yugoslav socialism. The export sector was also a stronghold of the long-standing market-oriented reformist coalitions of export company managers and a reformist faction of the political elite. These inherited coalitions crucially impacted the first stage of Slovenia's transition during the 1990s.

Throughout the process that led to the country's independence in 1991 and in the immediate post-independence period in the early 1990s, Slovenia experienced a transformation depression because it had lost the Yugoslav market. In 1991, GDP fell by 9 per cent and then by a further 5.5 per cent in 1992; the unemployment rate rose from a low level to 9 per cent between 1992 and 1994. By 1992, the annual inflation rate had reached 200 per cent (Silva-Jauregui 2004: 116, 119, 125). It was in these circumstances that, in spring 1992, the first, centre-right coalition government announced a wage freeze. The goal was to curb skyrocketing inflation. The trade unions were resolutely opposed, organizing a general, several-hours-long warning strike. This impressive manifestation of union power led to the intended wage freeze being called off. The centre-right coalition government soon collapsed.

In December 1992, the centre-left party Liberal Democracy of Slovenia (LDS in Slovenian) won the elections. It remained in power for the next twelve years, leading generally unstable and weak coalition governments during the entire EU accession process. As early as 1993, during the term of the first LDS government, Slovenia started to grow economically by successfully replacing the Yugoslav with a European market based on a successful export sector. This growth continued more or less unabated until 2009, when the global economic crisis struck.

With regard to economic growth, the first LDS government also had to confront the dual problems of high inflation and rising unemployment, which the government could not resolve without the support of strong unions. Including the trade unions in policymaking was therefore imperative. This inclusion was institutionalized when the Economic and Social Council of the Republic of Slovenia (ESS, *Ekonomsko-socialni svet*) was established in 1994. At the time, Slovenian workers' and employers' organizations were highly centralized. On the union side, most industrial trade unions were included in the 'old, reformed' ZSSS. On the employer side, the Chamber of Commerce and Industry (GZS, *Gospodarska zbornica Slovenije*), membership of which was compulsory, was the most important interest organization. In 1990, these social partners concluded two collective agreements, one for the 'private' and the other for the public sector. Because of the Chamber's obligatory membership and key role as representative of the employers in collective bargaining, bargaining coverage was almost 100 per cent at the time.

The key actors in this system had opposing or at least different priorities. The government and the employers focused primarily on curbing inflation and making the national economy more competitive. The trade unions' priority was protecting workers' interests by regulating wages, preserving jobs, finding solutions to the problem of redundant workers and defending the worker-friendly pension system: in short, the preservation of the welfare state. The one priority shared by all these actors, which partly enabled the integration of their diverse interests, was the EU accession process.

During the mid-1990s and in the context of revived economic growth, the first LDS government boosted growth and competitiveness even further by gradually curbing inflation through wage restraint, in combination with an incremental currency devaluation. The highly centralized collective bargaining system, with its high coverage rate, offered an opportunity to implement the demanded wage (restraint) policies. The government, however, still needed the consent of the trade unions to introduce such policies. The cost of this consent was to accept the unions' systematic influence on employment relations and the wider system of social protection, which was aimed at retaining the main traits of the welfare system. The result of this (political) exchange was ten years of the Slovenian 'success story'. The robust economic growth seen in the 1990s was accompanied by the gradual marketization of the economy, but without undermining the foundations of the welfare system.

During the first decade of the 2000s, Slovenia experienced several important changes. In 2004, the country joined the EU, which meant that the one common priority of all industrial relations actors literally vanished overnight. In the same year, a centre-right coalition came to power, bringing the twelve-year rule of the centre-left to an end. The new government immediately launched neoliberal reforms, intending to introduce a flat-rate tax. Massive resistance on the part of the trade unions in autumn 2005, however, forced the government to shelve the plan. The second key aspect of the government's planned systemic changes was to launch a new privatization wave. This soon turned into a large and convoluted process, strongly supported by an influx of cheap money into the new EU member states. Many company managers took over their respective companies using cheap loans that, unfortunately, were paid back from the privatized companies' resources, to the detriment of their employees. During the economic crisis in 2009–2013, privatization made possible another form of ownership, as a series of bankruptcies ushered in the rapid internationalization of the Slovenian economy. These developments further exacerbated changes in the industrial relations regime.

Before the abovementioned changes, Slovenia had accelerated preparations for joining EMU. Accordingly, before the formal introduction of the euro in 2007 it was embedded in a 'hard currency regime'. From then on, the policy of incremental currency devaluation, which in combination with the centralized wage restraint policy had made the Slovenian economy more competitive, could no longer be pursued. The incremental devaluation was instantly substituted by pressures for 'internal devaluation' (Streeck 2014), increasing labour market flexibility and cutting public spending. Because of the inherited institutions of social partnership and trade union opposition, any immediate flexibilization of the labour market and austerity measures were not (yet) possible. The first palpable form of 'internal devaluation' (rather, the first functional substitute for more labour market flexibility and the austerity measures that were introduced later) was the introduction of stricter working regimes, leading to an intensification of work (see European Foundation for the Improvement of Living and Working Conditions 2007 and subsequent EFWC studies).

In 2009, only two years after formally entering the euro zone, the Slovenian economy was hit by the global financial crisis. The sharp drop in European market demand drastically affected the export sector; next came the collapse of the construction industry, which had experienced extreme investment activity before the crisis. The first wave of the crisis was followed by a lull, before it turned into a fairly serious financial and sovereign debt crisis in 2012 and 2013.

The pre-crisis pressure for 'internal devaluation', to which (over-indebted) companies responded by intensifying work, was complemented by increasingly radical austerity policies to cope with the deepening crisis in 2009–2013. The government tried to implement these policies with various forms of short-term interventions and more long-term-oriented structural reforms, which focused primarily on the pension system and the liberalization and deregulation of the labour market. The evidence presented below shows that this environment was extremely detrimental to the trade unions.

Structure of trade unions and union democracy

The pluralization of the political system which started in the late 1980s reached a qualitative turning point in 1990, when the first multi-party parliamentary elections were held. This huge systemic change showed that the Slovenian electorate was equally divided between a conservative camp and a liberal and social-democratic camp (Fink-Hafner and Krašovec 2004: 15).

This early ideological and political split framed the abrupt reorganization and pluralization of the trade union scene. At the beginning of the process, trade unions were influenced by powerful political polarization, peaking in the political conflict between ZSSS and the Confederation of New Trade Unions – Independence (KNSS-Neodvisnost, *Konfederacija novih sindikatov Slovenije*). KNSS-Neodvisnost was closely related to the new, anti-communist Social Democratic Party (SDS, *Social demokratska stranka*, later renamed the Slovenian Democratic Party), which positioned itself as a centre-right party. The opposite pole was occupied by the 'reformed old ZSSS' associated with the United List of Social Democrats (ZLSD, *Združena lista socialnih demokratov*), the reformed communists (today the SD, Social Democrats). Because both ZSSS and KNSS-Neodvisnost were strong trade unions, their respective affiliations with various competing political camps accentuated powerful ideological and political splits within the trade union movement.

During the decade dominated by the centre-left coalitions (1992–2004), when the trade unions concentrated on collective bargaining and co-shaping the industrial relations system in line with the model of a social market economy, the previous ideological splits (especially between ZSSS and KNSS-Neodvisnost) virtually disappeared. The interest-based differences among various segments of the labour force increasingly replaced the former ideological conflicts and personal grudges. As a result, the interest-based fragmentation, until then obscured by ideological and political splits, became a distinct characteristic of the trade union movement. Regarding important systemic issues, such as the reform of health care, the pension system and the labour market, the trade unions cooperated and opposed the privatization and/or dismantling of well-functioning systems.

Today, there are seven trade union confederations: the Association of Free Trade Unions of Slovenia (ZSSS), the Confederation of Public Sector Trade Unions (KSJS, *Konfederacija sindikatov javnega sektorja*), the Confederation of Trade Unions of Slovenia PERGAM (KSS PERGAM, *Konfederacija sindikatov Slovenije PERGAM*), the Confederation of New Trade Unions of Slovenia Neodvisnost (KNSS-Neodvisnost), the Confederation of Trade Unions 90 of Slovenia (KS-90, *Konfederacija sindikatov 90 Slovenije*), the Slovenian Association of Trade Unions *Alternativa*, and the Association of Workers Unions of Slovenia *Solidarnost.* ZSSS, KNSS-Neodvisnost, PERGAM and KS-90 were formed at the beginning of the transition, while Alternativa, Solidarnost and the KSJS appeared later, after 2000.

ZSSS and KSJS, and two smaller organizations (KSS Pergam and KNSS Neodvisnost) represent almost 90 per cent of all union members in Slovenia. The remaining, less than 10 per cent of union members (around 24,000 workers) are mainly members of autonomous company trade unions and/or smaller autonomous industrial or occupational unions of white-collar workers, such as FIDES, the trade union of medical doctors, and two smaller confederations (Alternativa and Solidarnost).

ZSSS is the largest and most influential trade union confederation. It consists of twenty-two affiliates representing members in the private and public sectors. ZSSS is the only confederation with a regionally organized structure. It was founded in Ljubljana on 7 April 1990 and is the successor to the former Association of the Trade Unions of Slovenia (ZSS, *Zveza sindikatov Slovenije*). Before the founding congress, the former association had to cope with a serious internal crisis after the secession of certain regional and industrial affiliates that formed independent organizations. This secession was partly because of internal splits over interests within the old ZSS, compounded by interpersonal conflicts among prospective leaders of the emerging ZSSS.

During the 1990s, ZSSS accounted for more than 50 per cent of union membership in Slovenia. Like most other trade unions, ZSSS has experienced a loss in membership in the past fifteen years. Data suggest that ZSSS has been losing members more rapidly than other trade union organizations, especially public sector unions, meaning its share in total union membership has gradually decreased in the past decade and a half. According to a public opinion survey conducted in 2009, ZSSS had 155,000 members. The largest affiliate is the Trade Union of Metal and Electrical Workers of Slovenia (SKEI, *Sindikat kovinske in elektroindustrije Slovenije*). In 2009, SKEI had almost 40,000 members (Interview with Jerkič, the President of SKEI), accounting for around one-quarter of the entire ZSSS membership. Recent estimations of ZSSS in 2019 put its membership at some 130,000; membership had begun to rise again following the 2008–2013 crisis (Nared 2019). In 2015, ZSSS was still the biggest confederation, representing approximately 40 per cent of all trade union members in Slovenia (opinion survey data).

In the early stages of the transition, ZSSS had a significant head start over new trade unions because of its inherited organizational infrastructure and other resources shaped or accumulated during the 'real-socialist' regime. Although significant, this advantage could not in itself guarantee survival. The key factor in ZSSS' endurance was its early focus on worker protection. This was in part an intrinsic goal and in part triggered by growing trade union competition. During this period practically the entire workforce was affected by the lost Yugoslav market, but ZSSS' endeavours to safeguard workers' protection and limit unemployment successfully transformed the uncertainty that had engulfed the labour force into a truly impressive mobilizing power. The real extent of this power was first shown to the political elite in early spring 1992, when ZSSS organized a country-wide strike against the salary freeze announced by the government.

KSJS (Confederation of Public Sector Trade Unions of Slovenia) is the second-largest trade union confederation. In 2008–2009, it had approximately 60–70,000 members spread across seven national industrial trade unions (public opinion survey 2008; data from KSJS head office 2009). This means that it represented almost a quarter of all trade union members (Broder 2016: 46–47). The largest affiliates were the Education, Science and Culture Trade Union of Slovenia (SVIZ, *Sindikat vzgoje, izobraževanja, znanosti in culture Slovenije*) and the Trade Union of Health and Social Services of Slovenia (ZSVS, *Sindikat zdravstva in socialnega varstva Slovenije*). With almost 40,000 members, SVIZ was comparable to SKEI, the key industrial trade union within ZSSS. ZSVS then had 18,000 members (SJM 2008; KSJS 2009).

KSJS was established in early 2006 when SVIZ joined with some other (smaller) public sector trade unions and formed a new confederation. This most important union merger since 1990 came just a few months after a huge union protest in Ljubljana in 2005 when all trade unions came together to oppose the neoliberal reforms planned by the then centre-right government. At that time, the government also announced the formation of a new, unified payment system for employees in the public sector. This announcement precipitated the establishment of the new public sector confederation.

The third-largest trade union confederation, with approximately 20,000 members, is KSS Pergam. It was established in June 1991; before then, it was part of ZSSS.

Table 26.2 Key trade union associations, main affiliates, and number of members, 2008

	Number of affiliates	Number of members	Regional structure
ZSSS	22	150,000–160,000[a]	Yes
SKEI – TU of Metal and Electrical Workers of Slovenia		38,000[a]	
KNG		11,000[a]	
KSJS	7	60,000–70,000[a]	No
SVIZ – Education, Science and Culture Trade Union of Slovenia		40,000[a]	
ZSVS – Trade Union of Health and Social Services of Slovenia		18,000[a]	
KSS PERGAM		20,000[b]	No

Notes: [a]The data on membership distribution across the main trade union confederations are based on data collected through public opinion surveys in 2008, before the global financial crisis struck.

[b] Data based on their own reporting.

While ZSSS remains anchored in traditional industries and is still an organization of blue-collar workers, KSJS advocates a powerful role for the public sector in society and the protection of public sector employees. ZSSS includes company trade unions networked in broader sectoral and territorial organizations. ZSSS is a relatively centralized organization, but the leaders of affiliated industrial unions have strong influence within the confederation. Its leadership consists of a chair, a secretary-general, executive secretaries, and three vice-chairs (representatives of the industrial, service and public sectors). The Presidency, composed of all industrial trade unions, is the most important decision-making body.

KSJS is organized by sector. Its membership is organized formally at the level of agencies within the public sector, for example, education and health care. Industrial organizations retain considerable autonomy; their members identify more strongly with industrial unions than with the confederation. The KSJS leadership partly overlaps with that of the Education, Science and Culture Trade Union of Slovenia (SVIZ), which is by far the largest affiliate, representing approximately two-thirds of KSJS membership. The head office of KSJS is located on the premises of the SVIZ. KSJS regularly cooperates with other confederations and industrial trade unions, although tensions occasionally arise, mainly regarding representation and wage imbalances in the public sector.

While ZSSS' sectoral trade unions are representative in almost all industries in the private sector and negotiate the majority of the twenty-six collective agreements, KSS Pergam was the sole representative union organization in the graphic, paper, publishing, newspaper and information industries. It recently expanded its operations to the public sector and other parts of the private sector. Since 2000, it has also represented workers in health care, road infrastructure, compulsory social security, centres for social work, veterinary activities, university education, air traffic, and various professionals, such as laboratory technicians, medical biochemists, pilots, pharmacists, radiologists and university teachers.

One advantage of ZSSS compared with other confederations is its region-based structure, which simplifies interaction with its members across all regions of Slovenia. At the moment, it has eight regional organizations, fifty-eight regular employees and three employees under contract. By contrast, KSJS has two regular employees; SVIZ, its largest affiliate, has twelve employees; while KSS Pergam has seven employees.

Overall, opinion survey data suggest that the expansion of confederations, which culminated in 2006 with the foundation of KSJS, was concurrent with a latent, yet indicative counter trend: interest-based fragmentation, which persisted and even strengthened under the formal trend of mergers. According to public opinion survey data from 2008, approximately 20 per cent of participants who were formally included in confederations through industrial trade unions identified primarily with their company trade unions. As regards ZSSS, in 2015 around one-quarter of its members chiefly identified with the Trade Union of Metal and Electrical Workers of Slovenia (SKEI), the biggest ZSSS affiliate (Broder 2016: 47). In short, formally speaking, trade union membership is concentrated in the two largest confederations, with blue-collar workers covered by ZSSS and white-collar workers by KSJS. Within the framework of this formal membership concentration, however, another trend is apparent: interest-based fragmentation, combined with a number of smaller trade unions outside the large confederations.

Unionization

In the late 1980s and early 1990s the Slovenian trade union scene became pluralized. This change was characterized by a massive decline in membership. Both trends were comparable to those in other 'post-communist' countries. One feature that sets Slovenia apart, however, was the early de-politicization of the entire trade union movement and the consolidation of membership in the mid-1990s, when trade union density had stabilized at around 40 per cent.

Since 2005, public opinion surveys have recorded a new, relatively steep drop in unionization. According to a 2005 survey, the unionization rate was 37.1 per cent, but only three years later, it had decreased to 26.6 per cent and, after the crisis, in 2015 it was just 19.9 per cent (see Table 26.3).

Table 26.3 Trade union density rates in Slovenia, 1991–2008

1991/2	**1995/1**	**1996/1**	**1997/3**	**1998/1**	**1999/4**	**2000/1**	**2001/2**	**2002/1**
66.5 %	50.4 %	48.8 %	44.1 %	42.7 %	40.4 %	41.6 %	40.8 %	44.6 %
2003/1	**2005/1**	**2006/1**	**2008/2**	**2015/1**	**2016/2**	**2017**	**2018/2**	**2019/2**
43.7 %	37.1 %	31.4 %	26.6 %	19.9 %	21.8 %	20.2 %	19.6 %	21.2 %

Source: SJM – Slovene Public Opinion Surveys 1991–2019.

The public opinion survey data and conversations with representatives of the two largest confederations in 2009 lead us to conclude that, after Slovenia joined the EU and as early as during the pre-crisis period, trade unions experienced the most dramatic decline in their memberships, causing their restructuring.

To sum up, the overall membership of autonomous trade unions in Slovenia stabilized during the economic growth of the 1990s. During the period of extraordinary economic performance preceding the crisis, however, approximately fifteen years ago, they began to experience sharp drops in membership, from 43.7 per cent in 2003, the level it reached in the second half of the 1990s, to 26.6 per cent in 2008, even before the outbreak of the economic crisis. This means a decline of 17 percentage points within only five years or, in absolute numbers, a fall from roughly 420,000 to 280,000 members. Put differently, between 2003 and 2008, Slovenian trade unions lost one-third of their membership. These aggregate figures mask important membership developments as regard gender, age, education and industry, which will be tackled in the remainder of this section.

From 1991, when Slovenia gained its independence, to 2008, trade union membership was gender-balanced, but this changed in 2009 (see Figure 26.1). The rise in the number of women coincided with the rise in the share of members with a college and university education, and the more agile trade union activity in the public sector, primarily in various areas of education.

Figure 26.1 Gender structure of union membership, 1991–2019

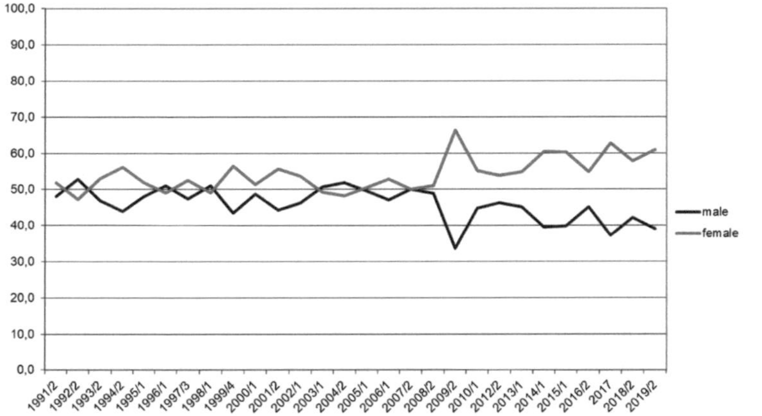

Source: FDV-CJMMK, SJM – Slovenian public opinion, 1991–2019.

A look at the age structure shows that generational renewal slowed down during the period 2003–2007, and practically stopped at the beginning of the economic crisis. There was a continuous fall in the share of younger members between 2009 and 2015 (see Figure 26.2). In 1991, almost one-quarter of all union members were below 30 years of age, and only slightly more than 1 per cent were older than 60. If we observe these two border age groups over the years, it becomes obvious that the share of the youngest members sharply declined, so that in 2015 they accounted for just 2 per cent of membership, while the share of older members increased to slightly over 14 per cent. Overall, the figures illustrate that the inflow of new members, especially younger ones, was (and continues to be) critically weak.

Figure 26.2 Age structure of union membership, 1991–2019

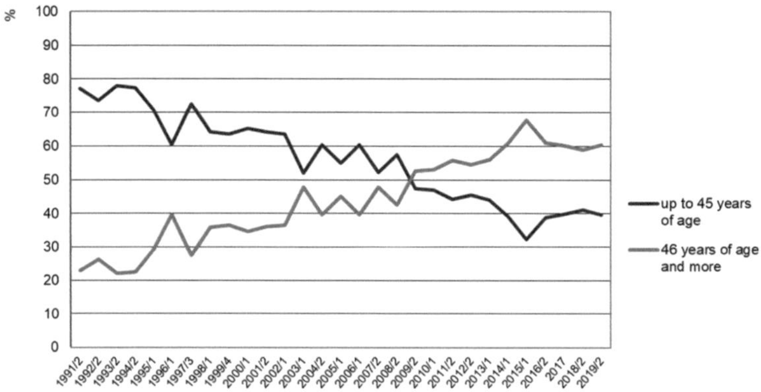

Source: FDV-CJMMK, SJM – Slovenian public opinion, 1991–2019.

Figure 26.3 shows the fluctuation in the proportion of members with elementary and vocational education levels, on one hand, and members with secondary, college and university education levels, on the other. During the period following Slovenia's independence, almost 60 per cent of union members had lower educational levels; of those, half had completed elementary education. Their share dropped steadily in the subsequent period, with smaller or larger deviations, reaching its lowest point in 2017–2018. As regards those with secondary, college or university educational levels, the situation was exactly the opposite. The initial 42 per cent share gradually increased, with occasional oscillations, and accounts for well over one-half of members. The 2015 survey shows that slightly more than 30 per cent of union members were university graduates. Surveys conducted after 2015 reveal that their share increased to 40 per cent, making them the largest group. With regard to members who have completed only elementary education, smaller oscillations were observed, but over the past five years their share has been steady at around 10 per cent.

Figure 26.3 Share of union members with elementary, secondary and university education levels, 1991–2019

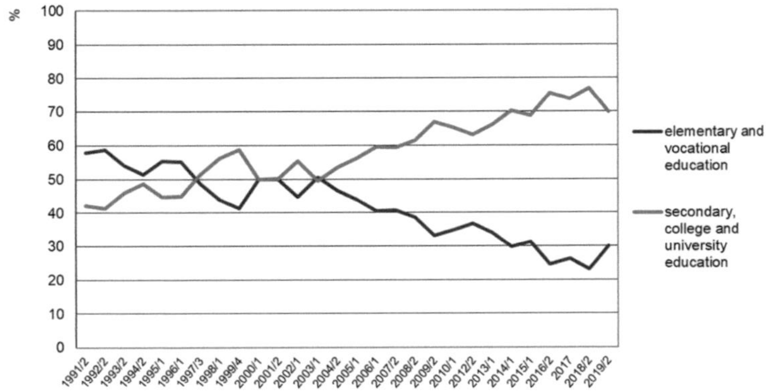

Source: FDV-CJMMK, SJM – Slovenian public opinion, 1991–2019.

The changes in the proportion of members with elementary and university education levels are generally connected to changes in the total population: the percentage of college or university graduates has increased somewhat over the years, while the percentage of people who have only completed elementary education has decreased. These trends are not as conspicuous among the general population as they are among trade union members.

The changes in employment across sectors have been gradual. At the beginning of the transition in 1991, the industrial sector had the highest number of workers, almost half of the total workforce (45.1 per cent), but then the services sector pulled ahead. But despite the rise in employment in services, the industrial sector's share in total employment in Slovenia remains comparatively high. Even during the period 2009–2013, when the pressure of the crisis was high, it never dropped below 30 per cent, and after the crisis it bounced back to almost the pre-crisis level (34.1 per cent). (Ignjatović 2010: 145; LFS data).

During the past three decades, trade union density in the public sector has been relatively stable; a significant decline was observed between 2005 and 2007 (after Slovenia joined the EU, when the first right-wing government was in power), and then again from 2013 to 2015, when the crisis was coming to an end. Throughout the past thirty years, trade union density in the public sector has constantly exceeded the density rate in the 'real economy' (privately and publicly owned companies). Before the second turning point in 2003, the density rate in the public sector was 69 per cent compared with 45 per cent in the 'real' sector. Ten years later, in 2015, union density in the public sector had fallen to 42 per cent, and to 13 per cent in the 'real' sector (Slovenian public opinion surveys, 1991–2019).

Analysis of the longitudinal data collected through the CRANET research (2004, 2008 and 2015) reveals that the de-unionization trend is not uniform across all sectors and that discrepancies have grown in the past decade, covered by the study, that is, during the 2009–2013 crisis and afterwards. The gap between the industrial sector and private sector services widened significantly; de-unionization in private sector services is much more intense than in the industrial sector.

In both cases, de-unionization is related to the rising number of non-standard employment arrangements: between 1991 and 2014 the number of fixed-term and part-time jobs doubled. In 2014, the total share of employees in various flexible work arrangements was 32 per cent. Fixed-term employment, for instance, reached a historical peak with a share of approximately 14 per cent during the period of economic growth preceding the crisis (MDDSZ 2013).

In the decade 2004–2015 non-standard employment arrangements became widespread across private sector services. This sector saw extreme numerical flexibility: serious limits on the number of standard employment arrangements, on one hand, and a conspicuous wave of new, mainly non-standard employment, on the other. Full-time employees in this sector are exposed to intense double pressure: the threat of losing one's job is compounded by the push for competitiveness generated by non-standard employment arrangements. This strong dual pressure corresponds to the low union density and/or the absence of trade unions in private sector services. In such circumstances, employees' bargaining position is weak (Stanojević and Čehovin Zajc 2017).

During the same period, the general de-unionization trend in the industrial sector was less intense. There are only a few de-unionized organizations with 100 or more employees. In most organizations in the industrial sector, union density before the crisis was more than 50 per cent, with the rate falling after the crisis.

In 2019, employers in sectors confronted by a shortage of new employees as a result of the record low unemployment rate, low wages and tough working conditions lobbied the government to relax the entry requirements for migrant workers, not only from the countries of the former Yugoslavia, but other countries as well. The recruitment of such employees to trade unions is harder to achieve, but some unions have still been quite successful in this regard.

More generally, in the face of declining membership, the largest trade unions set about formulating policies and initiatives aimed at recruiting new members from the ranks of young and precarious employees, and from within the industries with low union density. ZSSS, for instance, adopted guidelines for a strategy for organizing workers in trade unions (Vrhovec 2014). A task force was established that focuses exclusively on recruitment. In addition, new trade unions were established: Mladi+ ('Young+') and a trade union for precarious workers.[1]

Young activists, members of Mladi+, emphasize that the key strategy for attracting members was a personal approach because the most common answer to the question of why one was not a union member was 'because nobody has asked or invited me'. Social media (Facebook and Instagram) activities are also significant for recruiting young members. According to ZSSS, such an active approach, both through (social) media and in person, and endeavours to improve union members' situation at all levels (company, industry, national), has increased trust in trade unions and led to membership growth in the past two years.

Union resources and expenditure

The Representativeness of Trade Unions Act (U.l. RS, No. 13/93) stipulates that representative trade unions should be financed mainly from membership fees. They may also make use of donations and similar sources, such as donor funds, interest payments, sponsorship of individual campaigns and humanitarian aid.

The ZSSS statutes stipulate that it is a non-profit trade union organization, financing its activities through membership fees, project income and other revenues. ZSSS does not levy a fee but receives a certain percentage of its industrial affiliates' membership fees. The fee that individual members pay to their industrial trade union is 1 per cent of the gross wage. As defined in the Funding Rules adopted by the presidency

1 See: https://www.mladiplus.si/ and https://www.zsss.si/tag/sindikat-prekarcev/

of ZSSS, the industrial affiliates then pay 9 per cent of this income from membership fees to ZSSS. Similarly, the statutes of KSJS lay down that the confederation should be financed primarily from membership fees paid by affiliated trade unions. It is dependent on the number of union members. SVIZ's rule book lays down that the monthly membership fee for employed members shall amount to 0.6 per cent of their gross wage (SVIZ 2005).

According to the latest data from ZSSS, KSJS and KSS Pergam, the overwhelming bulk of the unions' income comes from membership fees. Operating income, which includes membership fees, services provided to industrial trade unions (13 per cent), EU funds (7 per cent), and the union's newspaper *Delavska enotnost* (5 per cent) amounted to 97 per cent of ZSSS' total income. By contrast, other income and financial income formed only a minor part (1.8 and 1 per cent) of total income. After 2017, total income increased until the Covid-19 year 2020, for which data are not yet available. Income and profits are used to implement ZSSS' five-year programme. Staff pay accounts for most of total expenditure. In 2019, ZSSS spent 71 per cent of its operating expenses to pay staff, including regional structures. Events and union actions, such as demonstrations and referenda, are co-financed by industrial trade unions. The unions have adapted to falling membership by finding new sources of revenues (among others, through increased participation in EU and national projects), cutting material costs and the cost of unnecessary goods and services, and by not replacing employees who are not crucial for member support and implementation of programmes. They have not cut member services.

Collective bargaining and trade unions at the workplace

CRANET data covering the decade 2004–2014 clearly reveal a significant decline in collective employment regimes in Slovenian companies. At the start of the decade, union density in most companies exceeded 50 per cent; at the end of the period companies with density rates below 50 per cent prevailed. The decline was most intensive in the private service sector, where precarious workers with transferable skills are concentrated, and less intensive in the industrial and public sector. The result of the process was that unions in industrial companies, with workers with non-transferable skills, started to change gradually into representative bodies of these segments of workforce (Stanojević and Čehovin Zajc 2017). According to CRANET data from 2015, in 60.1 per cent of Slovenian companies with 100 and more employees, density rates were below 50 per cent; in 14.2 per cent of companies workers are not unionized. The share of non-unionized companies is lowest in industry (8.2 per cent) and the public sector (10.0 per cent), and highest in private sector services (30.6 per cent).

The collective representation of workers' interests at the company level in Slovenia is usually dual: works councils are also present in most unionized companies by rule. Works councils are present in 69.2 per cent of companies in industry, and approximately in every second company or organization from market and public sector (Stanojević and Čehovin Zajc 2019: 670–671). In almost 80 per cent of Slovenian companies, unions are involved in bottom-up communication with managers; works councils are involved in this type of communication in less than 60 per cent of companies. Accordingly, unions, which are exclusive negotiators representing employees in collective bargaining at company level, are obviously the more active and relevant workers' representation body in Slovenian companies (ibid.: 673).

During the period of Slovenia's accession to the EU, highly centralized collective bargaining was the key instrument for ensuring wage restraint. As shown earlier, during the 1990s wage restraint was the main subject of (macro) political exchange between the social partners within the then system of (competitive) neo-corporatism (see Rhodes 1997). Upon entering the EU and the euro zone, the collective bargaining system began to change. After 2006, the previous, almost 100 per cent collective bargaining coverage decreased. In 2019, it was approximately 70 per cent (Stanojević and Poje 2019). This decline was caused by the changed membership status of the Chamber of Commerce and Industry, which shifted from mandatory to voluntary. It has been demonstrated above that unions also started to lose members in this period. These shifts occurred amid Slovenia's accession to the euro zone and the associated exposure of the Slovenian economy to greater competitive pressures. Another aggravating factor was the prolonged financial and economic crisis, causing a double dip recession (2009–2013).

These far-reaching shifts, however, did not lead to a corresponding decrease in collective bargaining coverage. A crucial factor that ensured high levels of bargaining coverage was the introduction of the extension mechanism, which has operated as a functional substitute for the previous role played by the Chamber of Commerce and Industry. A temporary halt to this mechanism occurred when the global crisis struck Slovenia, but after the crisis the previous high levels of bargaining coverage were restored (Stanojević and Poje 2019: 554).

Slovenia's EU accession triggered a decentralization of collective bargaining in the private sector. In the public sector, centralized bargaining structures were preserved, however, and indeed legally protected with the introduction of a unified payment system in 2008, just before the start of the economic crisis. Accordingly, collective bargaining for the entire public sector could take place exclusively within the parameters of this framework.

In the private sector, the centralized system of collective bargaining encountered obstacles immediately after the country joined the EU. In 2005 employers withdrew from the general collective agreement for the private sector. In the context of economic overheating and rising inflation ahead of the oncoming global crisis, there were attempts to re-centralize the system, but after the crisis central bargaining for the entire private sector was ultimately abandoned. Today, collective bargaining in the private sector takes place at the industry level.

As a consequence, there is a significant difference between the public and private sectors in terms of the level of internal, intra-sectoral coordination of collective bargaining. While coordination is relatively extensive in the public sector, in the private sector, where collective bargaining is decentralized, coordination is weaker. Furthermore, during the past fifteen years, wage-setting in the private sector has been fragmented. The common denominator of this growing fragmentation of wage models is an increase in wage flexibilization. Analysis of collective agreements suggests that there have also been deviations from legal standards with regard to the regulation of working time, particularly overtime work regulation (Stanojević and Poje 2019: 557).

Before the 2009–2013 crisis, the law allowed certain deviations from the favourability principle. After the crisis, these options were legally expanded, enabling greater flexibility in wages, working hours and employment regimes. In a bid to stay competitive, companies exploited gaps in the system: that is, various options were adopted that enabled them to lower standards and ensure more flexible work and employment relations within an otherwise formally well-organized and unified system. It seems the relatively intense de-unionization and the resulting decline in union power over the past fifteen years have contributed to weaken the regulatory capacity of the collective bargaining system. The result of the legal options allowing for deviations from the favourability principle, combined with the unions' declining bargaining power, favoured a gradual but significant increase in concession bargaining.

As regards wages, the main union focus was on ensuring decent pay for workers, first by establishing a new payment system in the private sector and second by ensuring an adequate statutory minimum wage for low-wage earners. The later will be dealt with in detail in the section on the unions' societal power. As regards the former, unions in the private sector, for several years, have been calling on employers' associations to introduce a new wage model to establish a more realistic price of work and harmonize definitions across different sectors. The present system rests on a wage system dating from the 1990s, which is based on low base wages and is supplemented with various add-ons (extra payments for distribution of working time and unpleasant working conditions as well as payment for years of service). This makes it very complex and opens up possibilities for anomalies. Similarly, when negotiating collective agreements at industry level, trade unions have tried to achieve decent pay for work done and for the regular adjustment of wages with both inflation and productivity growth, following the guidelines of the European Trade Union Confederation (ETUC) (ZSSS 2017: 18–19). During the past fifteen years, they have also worked to reduce the tax burden on wages in order to increase the net salaries of the low and middle class, and to relieve the pressures on the 'Christmas bonus' and other performance and vacation bonuses (ibid.: 18).

Industrial conflict

Data on strikes are difficult to obtain. During the past thirty years, Slovenia has faced two large strike waves. The first, which first broke out across the former Yugoslavia in 1987, occurred in the period of disassociation from the Yugoslav federation (1988–1992). In Slovenia, this wave abated in 1991, when the country was striving for independence, but resumed in 1992 once independence had been achieved as a new, sovereign state and when the transformation depression had reached its bottom. In 1992, there were almost 200 strikes with an average of 372 strikers per strike. The number of working days lost per 1,000 workers was 189 (Stanojević and Vrhovec 2001). The strike wave mainly swept over the labour-intensive economic industries: that is, industries most affected by disintegration of the Yugoslav market. It culminated in spring 1992 with a general warning strike organized by ZSSS.

The second wave of strikes broke out when the global crisis reached Slovenia in 2009. The growing dissatisfaction of workers with poor wages and working conditions literally exploded as a large spontaneous strike at Gorenje, an industrial company which produces household appliances and was the second biggest Slovenian exporter. In November 2009, under this pressure from below, unions organized a large-scale protest demanding higher minimum wages and rejecting the government's proposals to reform the pension system. The resistance continued and both demands were eventually met (Poje 2019; Vrhovec 2010).

In the meantime, during the second half of the 1990s, when strikes in the industrial sector had waned, another wave of less intense strikes engulfed the public sector. It was triggered by demands put forward by FIDES, the trade union of medical doctors, just before the 1996 elections.

Since the late 1990s, strikes have abated but public protests, generally organized by ZSSS, have grown in number. The most important was the large autumn rally in 2005 that attracted roughly 40,000 participants, mostly workers opposed to the government's attempt to radicalize the already strong trend of neoliberal reforms. The largest union protest in the history of Slovenia was held in November 2007 under the slogan 'United for higher wages'. In April 2008, the ETUC and ZSSS organized a pan-European rally under the slogan 'European workers demand higher wages'.

Political relations

The unions' relations with political actors are determined mainly by two factors: their links to political parties and their involvement in corporatist political decision-making bodies. Regarding the former, union confederations had distanced themselves from political parties by the second half of the 1990s and dropped the previous practice of mutual disqualifications based on political and ideological affiliation.

During the first period of the transition, from 1992 to 2004, diverse coalition governments led by the centre-left LDS were willing to cooperate with trade unions. Confronted by union power, on one hand, and the problems caused by inflation and the need to boost economic growth, on the other, the LDS saw cooperation with the trade unions and their inclusion in the policymaking process as a rational solution. Accordingly, the system of political exchange was institutionalized, or put differently, neo-corporatist regulatory mechanisms were established. In exchange for supporting wage restraint policies, unions were given an opportunity to influence social policies. The result was the quite unconventional and relatively successful 'post-communist' variant of a social market economy during the 1990s.

The regime of neo-corporatist regulation began to change visibly some fifteen years ago, prior to the outbreak of the 2009–2013 crisis, when Slovenia was preparing to join the EU and the euro zone. Deregulation of wage policy, by shifting collective bargaining to the industry level was the first response to the new context. The political shift to the right, which had started in 2004, foreshadowed more radical neoliberal reforms. It was followed by a structural reform to ensure a permanent 'internal devaluation', which in the crisis period was reinforced by every government, both 'left' and 'right'. These changes worsened the prospects for maintaining the previous practice of systematic political exchanges.

In the crisis period (2009–2013), three governments came to power in Slovenia, representing the centre-left, (2008–2012), the centre-right (2012–2013) and the centre. The last one operated as an approximation of the international Troika consisting of the European Commission, the European Central Bank and the International Monetary Fund. At the time, unions were involved in social dialogue with centre-left as well as centre-right governments. The dialogue developed into a huge political conflict with the centre-left government, however. Later, in the context of the prolonged crisis, it was renewed on a more cooperative basis with the centre-right government. In both cases the focus of dialogue was on pension and labour market reforms, which the unions accepted (Stanojević and Krašovec, 2022).

A comparison of the political exchanges during the 1990s and those taking place in the EU context (and in the 2009–2013 crisis) shows that the main subject of exchange in both periods was the welfare system. Because Slovenia is embedded in the euro zone, it engages in competition using 'internal devaluation' to curb the cost of the welfare system. In this setting, the unions' negotiating position is weak. The most they can hope to obtain in exchange for their approval of welfare cuts is a slowing down of the process. Therefore, in the new context, political exchanges, if they still exist at all, are reduced to concession bargaining.

Furthermore, the unions are formally involved in various corporatist political decision-making bodies. One of the most important is the tripartite Economic and Social Council (ESS, *Ekonomsko-socialni svet*) on which all three major confederations are represented. Following the establishment of the ESS in 1994, the ZSSS leadership regularly participated in dialogue. The embeddedness of ZSSS in the work of the ESS is an important external source of the power of its centre, despite sporadic marginalization of the ESS's operations and role. This not only legitimates ZSSS' role in society but induces and reinforces the internal integration and centralization of the entire confederation. Following the merger of public sector unions to form KSJS in 2006, the new confederation also became a full member of the ESS. Before then, the scattered public sector trade unions were not represented. Involvement in the ESS is important for the unions because this is where all social and economic issues are discussed and negotiated: pensions, invalidity benefits, social benefits, employment and labour relations, public finances, including taxation and prices.

In addition, ZSSS and KSJS have representatives on the National Council of the Republic of Slovenia. A critical instrument wielded by the Council is its veto on laws. In 2019, by using a veto, unions successfully prevented the adoption of a law that would have removed the allowance for work activity and endangered the most vulnerable employees. In addition to these policymaking bodies, the unions are also represented on governing and administrative bodies of welfare state institutions, such as the Administrative Boards of the Pension and Disability Insurance Institute of Slovenia (ZPIZ) and of the Health Insurance Institute of Slovenia (ZZZS), the board of the Employment Service of Slovenia, the supervisory board and the Committee of Compulsory Supplementary Pension Insurance (ODPZ), and the Economic and Social Expert Committee at the Slovenian State Holding company.

Societal power

In addition to their representation in various corporative political decision-making bodies, unions' societal power also stems from their active cooperation with civil society and non-governmental organizations (NGOs), which is crucial for ZSSS and KSJS. This cooperation bore fruit, for instance, when opposing the EU-USA Transatlantic Trade and Investment Partnership (TTIP) and the EU-Canada Economic and

Trade Agreement (CETA), as well as in referenda on mini-jobs and the pension reform in 2013. Other areas of joint activities include issues such as the demographic fund, long-term care, violence at the workplace, equal pay for equal work and work–life balance.

One of the most successful public campaigns conducted by the unions in cooperation with civil society and NGOs are the various initiatives to turn the minimum wage into a living wage by ensuring that the statutory minimum wage reflects the minimum cost of living. The unions' fight for an adequate minimum wage has a long history. The statutory minimum wage was re-introduced in 1995 on the unions' initiative and based on a tripartite agreement. Since then until 2015 its definition has remained unchanged.

After the Second World War, a guaranteed personal income – the so-called guaranteed wage – was established. The critical problem with the guaranteed wage and the reason for the unions' demand for the introduction of a statutory minimum wage was the link between social transfers and the guaranteed wage. The government did not adjust the guaranteed wage for inflation, intending to curb the costs of social transfers in times of high inflation, consequently reducing its real value dramatically. The introduction of the statutory minimum wage thus ensured a higher minimum wage at a more decent level, while at the same time, not affecting increases in social transfers, which remained tied to the guaranteed wage (Poje 2019). The unions argued that a minimum wage is payment for work and not a social transfer paid by the state to people who cannot work, and as such, it has to be set high enough to enable a decent standard of living.

The unions achieved a major breakthrough on the way to an adequate minimum wage in 2010 when, as a consequence of a large-scale campaign involving a series of protests and strikes, complemented by large demonstrations to put pressure in the government, they achieved an increase of the statutory minimum wage by 23 per cent. Furthermore, the new minimum wage law (ZminP in Slovenian) stipulated that the minimum wage should be adjusted annually at least to inflation. The next step was taken in 2015 when the unions successfully campaigned for a change to the minimum wage legislation in order to exclude from the calculation of the minimum wage payments for night, Sunday and holiday work (Poje 2019). This campaign once again involved a series of public events to raise public awareness. The unions also collected almost 30,000 signatures to demonstrate broad public support. In 2018, the aspiration to a living wage ensuring a decent standard of living was realized with another change to the minimum wage legislation, which excluded all extra payments from the minimum wage definition by 2020 and set the statutory minimum wage at 20 per cent above the minimum cost of living from 2021 onwards (Poje 2019). The unions' fight for a living wage illustrates how public campaigns are increasingly integrated into their repertoire of action for achieving their objectives. This also includes the increased use of modern means of communication through publications on websites, Facebook, Instagram and other media.

Trade union policies towards the European Union

Slovenian trade unions have always considered it essential to connect with other trade unions from Europe and the former Yugoslavia. The key is the idea of solidarity, that they will be more successful with the right information, including on best practices. International cooperation provides an advantage in negotiations with the government and employers (Vrhovec 2019).

Since 1999, ZSSS has been the only full member of the ETUC from Slovenia. Its representatives can influence the ETUC's standpoints, policies and decisions, while its membership also carries the responsibility for implementing policies agreed at European level. The ZSSS representatives participate in the ETUC's permanent committees, working groups and pan-European projects. They participate in negotiating groups in the context of the European social dialogue and cooperate with the European Trade Union Institute (ETUI), the European trade union research centre.

ZSSS affiliates consider it important to raise the European trade union federations' (ETUFs) awareness that trade unions from smaller EU states have fewer members and human and financial resources for international cooperation, and thus less capacity to influence EU policies. These trade unions often need the professional assistance of the European Federations in various areas such as collective bargaining, training, organizing, the exchange of experience, works councils, and labour and social protection of workers to prevent social dumping. For this purpose, it would be helpful for the affiliates of the Slovenian confederations to be regularly informed about the activities of the European federations, even if they are not members of the respective ETUFs.

ZSSS expects the ETUC to inform its members in a timely and regular manner on developments at European level. It strives for better assistance with interpreting EU directives' provisions and greater engagement by the ETUC in introducing and implementing minimum standards at EU level. ZSSS leadership say they would like to see greater and more active inclusion in implementing projects financed by the European Commission and emphasize that the ETUC should pay more attention to individual regions' specificities when implementing policies, for instance the Balkans. ZSSS is acutely aware of fractions within the ETUC which weaken its capacity to act and pose obstacles to enhancing workers' and social rights because positions on specific issues are sometimes diametrically opposed, depending on the prevailing national tradition and union practices. It also points out that the ETUC is an organization of equal members, not merely accountable to the Brussels leadership.

ZSSS participates in efficient cross-border cooperation within the framework of the Interregional Trade Union Council of Friuli-Julian Province (Italy) and Slovenia. ZSSS has also established the Interregional Trade Union Council of Austrian Carinthia and Styria and Slovenian Upper Carniola, Styria and Carinthia. Members of ZSSS participate in the regional Solidarnost Council which brings together trade unions from the territories of former Yugoslavia. It works closely with the Friedrich-Ebert-Stiftung Zagreb, and its Belgrade-based regional project for labour relations and social dialogue. The cooperation of trade unions in such councils is crucial in the light of workers' free movement, and it is useful to compare labour legislation and collective agreements, and to exchange experiences.

Moreover, ZSSS has representatives on the management board of EUROFOUND, the management board of CEDEFOP, the advisory boards of the Advisory Committee for Vocational Training (ACVT), the Advisory Committee on the Free Movement of Workers (ACFMW), the Advisory Committee for Safety and Health at Work (ACSH), the European Social Fund, and the European Agency for Safety and Health at Work (EU-OSHA). Representatives of all three trade union confederations (ZSSS, KSJS, KSS Pergam) are also members of the ECOSOC[2] (European Economic and Social Committee). Furthermore, all three

2 This is part of civil society dialogue: social partners' interests are harmonised with NGOs' interests. The social dialogue is a part of a wider civil dialogue.

confederations cooperate with the ILO, drawing on its expertise and actively participating in various seminars and conferences.

Conclusions

Analysis of developments during the past thirty years yields five distinct processes that have shaped the Slovenian trade union movement. First, despite the high 'market share' of one confederation, the composition of trade unions and relationships among various key unions have changed. After the early ideological/political splits, trade unions depoliticized their activities and became more stable. Throughout the past thirty years, the biggest organization has been ZSSS, a confederation of blue-collar workers, traditionally firmly anchored in manufacturing industry, especially its export sector. After the second turning point of industrial relations marked by EU accession in 2004, several larger public sector trade union organizations formed KSJS as the second biggest confederation in 2006. The third-largest confederation is PERGAM. The relationship between the confederations and their affiliates changed from one characterized by ideological splits to one characterized by interest-based fragmentation, a new phenomenon in Slovenian industrial relations since joining the EU.

Second, the relatively high union density of around 40 per cent in the 1990s began to plummet after Slovenia joined the EU, along with an abrupt change in the composition of union membership as regards gender, age and education. The recruitment of young people slowed down during the years of economic growth preceding the global crisis and practically came to a standstill after the beginning of the crisis. The share of union members with an elementary level of education has been declining more rapidly than the share of such individuals in the general population; at the same time, the share of members with higher/college education is increasing more rapidly than the share of such individuals in the general population. Both trends were conspicuous after the second juncture and related to the changes in relationships among union members within the 'real economy' and the public sector.

After the second turning point, unionization in the public sector was quite stable, while the 'real economic sector' witnessed de-unionization, with the trend being most pronounced in the sub-sector of private services. As regards the market sector, the de-unionization trend is most pronounced in the catering industry, followed by retail (where to some degree it has reversed recently). In certain industries that were seriously affected by the 2009–2013 crisis, the number of union members dropped during the crisis and then stabilized. Membership within the industrial sector is stable; after the second juncture (and the crisis), in companies with 100 plus workers slightly less than half of the employees remain unionized.

Third, after EU accession, the historically highly centralized system of collective bargaining in the private sector was decentralized and transposed to the industry level, as well as partly deregulated. In the public sector, however, the high level of centralization has been preserved and revived. In the 'real economic sector', decentralization to the industrial level allowed, despite the high collective bargaining coverage, deviations from the favourability principle and led to a gradual decline in the regulatory capacity of the entire collective bargaining system.

Fourth, industrial relations became less conflictual. In the years preceding the disintegration of the former Yugoslavia there was a strong wave of worker strikes, which resumed in 1992, soon after the country gained its independence. The strike movement abated in the mid-1990s, renewed as a second strike wave in 2009, at the beginning of the economic crisis. In the meantime and after the second wave, strikes were substituted by massive public protests in the unions' repertoire of action.

Fifth, during the 1990s trade unions in Slovenia had a conspicuous influence on the shaping of public policies – comparable to that seen in some Western countries after the Second World War. In the past fifteen years, namely after the second turning point, their influence has been decreasing.

In short, analysis of the trade union landscape during the past thirty years illustrates that there was a strong trade union movement during the 1990s. After Slovenia joined the EU and EMU, a crisis developed that led to a sharp drop in membership and a weakening of its social influence. The process has been uneven, moving towards dualization (Visser 2019) of the entire trade union scene. The workforce segments in the industrial and public sectors are still relatively well unionized, but weak unionization and de-unionization have occurred as the prevailing feature of private sector services.

This raises two key questions: first, what explains the strength of the trade unions in Slovenia during the 1990s? Second, why has the strong

Slovenian trade union movement suffered such dramatic membership losses in the past fifteen years? Concerning the first question, this chapter suggests that one explanation is the heritage of the former self-management regime in which workers had a voice within companies. When the changes made to the 'market economy' began to stifle this voice, the trade unions managed successfully to translate the voice of workers into the voice of trade unions, demanding preservation of the welfare system, protection of workers and those who lost their jobs when the Yugoslav market disintegrated. These focused policies gave rise to autonomous trade unions in the 1990s, in which the majority of members were industrial workers. The autonomous union movement of industrial workers began to take part in neo-corporatist political exchanges, which ensured economic growth in the 1990s while preserving the features of the welfare state.

After EU accession, these framework conditions changed dramatically, leading to a drop in membership. First, the decrease in the number of industrial workers reflected the shrinking of the industrial trade union base, although the intensity of this decline was greater than demographic changes. Second, once the Slovenian economy was fully integrated into the European single market, pressure on workers was systematically escalated. After joining the EMU, the export sector was left without its previous incentive (incremental devaluation), which when combined with the wage restraint policies provided a competitive edge. Because of this change, neo-corporatist exchanges immediately became less important.

The country's joining of the euro zone triggered a need in the export sector to substitute the former incremental devaluation with an 'internal devaluation'. In the initial period, however, the tradition of social-partnership regulation was still strong and 'internal devaluation' was still not on the agenda (flexibilization of the labour market, liberalization of dismissal regimes, limits on public sector expenditure and the like). Therefore, work *intensification* was the earliest form of 'internal devaluation' in Slovenia.

Before the crisis, gradual changes in work regimes were compounded by the second wave of privatization and corresponding reorganizations, including outsourcing and an increase in non-standard employment arrangements. These pressures, which during the crisis period were combined with structural reforms, resulted in abrupt de-unionization and the liberalization of the entire system of industrial relations dating from the 1990s, along with other changes.

References

Arzenšek V. (1984) Struktura in pokret (Structure and movement), Beograd, Institut društvenih nauka, Univerzitet u Beogradu.

Bohle D. and Greskovits B. (2007) Neoliberalism, embedded neoliberalism and neocorporatism: towards transnational capitalism in Central-Eastern Europe, West European Politics, 30 (3), 443–466.

Bohle D. and Greskovits B. (2012) Capitalist diversity on Europe's periphery, Ithaca, NY., Cornell University Press.

Broder Ž. (2016) Sindikalno gibanje v Slovenij i od osamosvojitve do danes, Magistrsko delo, Ljubljana, Univerza v Ljubljani.

Cranet (2004, 2008, 2015) Upravljanje človeških virov, Slovenske raziskave, Ljubljana, Fakulteta za družbene vede.

European Foundation for the Improvement of Living and Working Conditions (2007) Fourth European working conditions survey, Luxembourg, Office for Official Publications of the European Communities.

Feldmann M. (2006) Emerging varieties of capitalism in transition countries: industrial relations and wage bargaining in Estonia and Slovenia, Comparative Political Studies, 39 (7), 829–854.

Feldmann M. (2016) Crisis and opportunity: varieties of capitalism and varieties of crisis responses in Estonia and Slovenia, European Journal of Industrial Relations, 23 (1), 33–46. http://dx.doi.org/10.1177/0959680116672280

Fink-Hafner D. and Krašovec A. (2004) Ideološko-politične cepitve v slovenski strankarski areni po letu 1989 (Ideological and political splits in the Slovenian political party arena after 1989), Mednarodna konferenca 'Razvoj političnega pluralizma in strankarskih aren v Sloveniji in Bosni in Hercegovini v obdobju 1989–2003' [international conference 'The development of political pluralism and political parties arena in Slovenia and Bosnia-Herzegovina during the period 1989–2003'].

Guardiancich I. (2016) Slovenia: the end of a success story, Europe-Asia Studies, 68 (2), 205–231.

Ignjatović M. (2010) Slovenski trg delovne sile – med ekonomsko učinkovitostjo in socialno pravičnostjo (varnostjo) [Slovenian labour market between economic efficiency and social justice], in Vehovar U. (ed.) Neosocialna Slovenija? Koper, Univerzitetna Založba Annales, 141–160.

MDDSZ (2013) Za dostojno delo 2013 [For Decent Work], Ljubljana.

Nared M. (2019) Sindikati po hudem osipu spet bolj privlačni za delavce [Trade unions, after a severe decline, are more attractive to workers again], STA, 27 May 2019. https://www.sta.si/2640065/sindikati-po-hudem-osipu-spet-bolj-privlacni-za-delavce

Poje A. (2019) The introduction of a 'monthly living wage' in Slovenia, Transfer, 25 (3), 335–350.

Rhodes M. (1997) Globalisation, labour markets and welfare states: a future of 'competitive corporatism'? in Rhodes M. and Mény Y. (eds) The future of European welfare: a new social contract? London, Macmillan, 178–203.

Silva-Jauregui C. (2004) Macroeconomic stabilization and sustainable growth, in Mrak M., Rojec M. and Silva-Jauregui C. (eds) Slovenia, from Yugoslavia to the European Union, Washington, D.C., The World Bank, 115–131.

SORS – Statistical Office of the Republic of Slovenia (1994) Statistični letopis 1994 [Statistical Yearbook 1994], SURS, SiStat portal.

SORS – Statistical Office of the Republic of Slovenia (2001) Statistični letopis 2001 [Statistical Yearbook 2001], SURS, SiStat portal.

Stanojević M. and Čehovin Zajc J. (2017) Kadrovske politike v pogojih demontaže kolektivnih delovnih razmerij, in Kohont A. and Stanojevic M. (eds) Razpotja in prelomi: spremembe na pdročju menedžmenta človeških virov v Sloveniji, Ljubljana, Založba FDV, 133–162.

Stanojević M. and Čehovin Zajc J. (2019) The crisis of the collective employment relations systems: five countries compared, Teorija in Praksa, 56 (2), 660–680.

Stanojević M. and Krašovec A. (2022) The crisis and the changing nature of political exchange in Slovenia, in Ebbinghaus B. and Weishaupt T. J. (eds) The Role of Social Partners in Managing Europe's Great Recession, London, Routledge, 212–234.

Stanojević M. and Poje A. (2019) Slovenia: organised decentralisation in the private sector and centralisation in the public sector, in Muller T., Vandaele K. and Waddington J. (eds) Collective bargaining in Europe: towards an endgame, Brussels, ETUI, 545–562.

Stanojevic M. and Vrhovec P. (2001) Industrial conflict in Slovenia, SEER, 4 (1), 29–37.

Streeck W. (2014) Buying time: the delayed crisis of democratic capitalism, London, Verso.

SVIZ (2005) Pravilnik o članarini [Rules on membership fees], Ljubljana, Glavni odbor SVIZ Slovenije.

Visser J. (2019) Trade unions in the balance, ILO ACTRAV Working paper, Geneva, ILO.

Vrhovec P. (2014) Podlage za strategijo organiziranja in včlanjevanja delavcev v sindikate v Zvezi Svobodnih sindikatov Slovenije [The basis for the strategy of organizing and recruiting workers' in the trade unions, members of the Association of Free Trade Unions of Slovenia], ZSSS, 11 April 2014.

Vrhovec P. (2010) 20 let Zveze svobodnih sindikatov Slovenije [20 years of the Association of Free Trade Unions of Slovenia], Ljubljana, ZSSS.

Vrhovec P. (2019) Intervju s Pavletom Vrhovcem: „Skupaj smo močnejši – tudi na mednarodnem odru" [Interview with Pavle Vrhovec: „Together we are stronger – also on international stage"], Ljubljana, ZSSS, 31 May 2019. https://www.zsss.si/intervju-s-pavletom-vrhovcem-315/

ZSSS (2017) Poročilo o delu Zveze Svobodnih sindikatov Slovenije med 6. in 8. kongresom [Report on the work of the Association of Free Trade Unions of Slovenia between the 6th and 8th Congress], Ljubljana, ZSSS.

Interviews

Lidija Jerkič, President of the SKEI (9 April 2009)

Dušan Semolič, president of the ZSSS (31 March 2009)

Branimir Štrukelj, president of the KSJS and general secretary of the ESTUS (17 April 2009)

Pavle Vrhovec, executive secretary of the ZSSS (31 March 2009)

Data sets

Slovene Public Opinion Surveys 1991–2019, Ljubljana, University of Ljubljana, Faculty of Social Sciences, Public Opinion and Mass Communication Research Centre.

Abbreviations

ESS	Economic and Social Council (*Ekonomsko-socialni Svet*)

KNSS	Independence, Confederation of New Slovenian Trade Unions (*Konfederacija novih sindikatov Slovenije*)
KS-90	Trade Union Confederation 90 (*Konfederacija sindikatov 90*)
KSJS	Public Sector Trade Unions (*Konfederacija sindikatov javnega sektorja*)
KSS PERGAM	Confederation of Trade Unions of Slovenia PERGAM (Trade unions in paper and graphic industry) (*Konfederacija sindikatov Slovenije Pergam*)
LDS	Liberal Democrats of Slovenia (*Liberalna demokracija Slovenije*)
SD	Social Democrats (*Socialni demokrati*)
SDS	Social Democratic party of Slovenia, now the Slovenian Democratic Party (*Socialdemokratska stranka Slovenije*, now: *Slovenska demokratska stranka*)
SKEI	Trade Unions in Metal and Electrical Industry (*Sindikat kovinarstva in elektro industrije*)
SVIZ	Education, Science and Culture Trade Union of Slovenia (*Sindikat vzgoje, izobraževanja in znanosti Slovenije*)
ZLSD	Associated List of Social Democrats, now the Social Democrats (*Združena lista socialnih demokratov*, now: *Socialni demokrati*)
ZSSS	Association of Free Trade Unions of Slovenia (*Zveza svobodnih sindikatov Slovenije*)
ZSVS	Trade Union of Health and Social Services of Slovenia (*Sindikat zdravstva in socialnega varstva Slovenije*)

Chapter 27

Spain: Boundaries, roles and changes in trade unionism

Carlos J. Fernández Rodríguez, Rafael Ibáñez Rojo and Miguel Martínez Lucio

Independent trade unions in Spain emerged in the mid to late twentieth century through struggle during the last years of the Franco dictatorship. The need to consolidate a social state and a democratic system of collective regulation was being pursued, just as deregulation, privatization and globalization through marketization were *de rigueur* among political and economic elites (Martínez Lucio and Mustchin 2019). Trade unions were caught between the tensions of delivering social change and justice, while also ensuring economic stability and gains for their members. The balance here, however, varies according to particular trade unions' points of view (Hyman 2001). In this chapter we highlight that Spain is undergoing fragmentation beyond the labour market and the sphere of work, but also in terms of trade unions' very activities, although there are signs of innovation and change, with new voices and actors emerging. The constant need to sustain a decentralized and partial state role, as well as a slightly decreasing influence within industry means that relations with the state and employers are fundamentally constrained or limited to specific activities.

Table 27.1 Principal characteristics of trade unionism in Spain

	1980	2000	2019
Total trade union membership	1,110,000	2,263,0000	2,471,000
Women as a proportion of total membership	n.a.	n.a.	n.a.
Gross union density	13 %	18 %	15 %
Net union density	13 %	18 %	13 %
Number of confederations	6	6	6
Number of affiliated unions (federations)*	20	11	7
Number of independent unions**	n.a.	n.a.	n.a.
Collective bargaining coverage	83 %	85 %	80 %***
Principal level of collective bargaining	various		
Days not worked due to industrial action per 1,000 workers	n.a.	314	50

Note: *Average for CCOO and UGT. Data are calculated as the average for each decade (1991–2000; 2001–2010; 2011–2019); **It is difficult to provide an exact number due to bureaucratic issues; ***2018.

Source: Appendix A1.

Historical background and principal features of the industrial relations system

Since the political transition to democracy in the 1970s, the Spanish system of industrial relations has been seen to be a relatively stable and relatively institutionalized model of joint regulation (Köhler 2001), although this has become increasingly challenged by social and political developments (Köhler 2018; Köhler and Calleja Jiménez 2015, 2018). In formal terms, trade union density has tended to be about one-fifth of the workforce; participation in works councils and trade unions representative elections has been about two-thirds to four-fifths roughly speaking; and collective bargaining coverage has also tended to be four-fifths (see Table 27.1). One could argue that 'on paper' the system of industrial relations appears to be fairly well coordinated. Indeed, the degree of state influence over the trade union movement has varied considerably: however, the number of bipartite and tripartite agreements on a range of issues suggests that one should not discount or trivialize the influence of the trade union movement in political terms (Guillén Rodríguez and Gutiérrez Palacios 2008). Given Spain's history country and the legacy of right-wing dictatorship, one needs to appreciate these significant institutional traits.

The historical legacy and the nature of neoliberal policymaking since the 1980s, among governments of both left and right, mean that the Spanish system of industrial relations is in many respects contradictory. First, the emergence of the new democratic system in the late 1970s took place in the context of an attempt to divide the organizations of the working class. This undermined the possibility of a more coherent and unified workers' voice. The support of other trade unions, which have a broader historical legacy, led to a competitive system of trade union representation (Baylos 1988).

During the 1970s and 1980s, the tensions between the Workers Commissions (CCOO, *Comisiones Obreras*) and the social democratic General Union of Workers (UGT, *Unión General de Trabajadores*) played a decisive and divisive role in labour movement politics, although levels of coordination developed during the late 1980s and onwards. This tension was also reflected in different forms of trade union structures and decision-making. The impact of the politics of the early years of democracy was to fragment worker politics and interests, which, in turn, led to the relationship between the UGT and CCOO restricting the access of other, more radical unions in the anarchist union tradition and, more recently, those of a more autonomous nature (Fernández Rodríguez et al. 2014).

Second, while the two major confederations have had a complex relationship, there is a greater degree of coordination, and their relations with the state – as discussed later – were such that they created momentary but uneven levels of influence. For example, during the 1980s and 1990s there were significant social pacts that created a form of neo-corporatism, although this tended to decline in significance with the global financial crisis of 2008 (González Begega and Luque Balbona 2014). Third, this process of 'institutionalization' took place during a shift in Spanish economic policy, as it turned towards monetarist and neoliberal approaches, pursuing deindustrialization and privatization from the early 1980s onwards (Smith 1998). While the socialist governments tended to be more socially oriented than governments on the right, aspects of neoliberalism, such as privatization, marketization and promotion of multinational corporations, formed a common narrative. This has limited the dialogue between labour and the state, reducing it to palliative social measures. The state has constrained the influence of organized labour. While the system was 'democratizing' and developing, a more socially oriented state emerged, which concurrently was deregulating labour markets and pursuing neoliberal policies. This constrained the institutionalization of trade unions and their influence (Martínez Lucio 1998). It also generated a common ground between the two main trade union confederations as they found themselves from the late 1980s onwards without clear and sympathetic political allies, given the decline of socialist ideals with the Socialist Party (PSOE, *Partido Socialista Obrero Español*) and the failure of the parties to its left to have any electoral impact.

Fourth, the system of collective bargaining, while formally extensive, emphasized the most representative trade unions, according to trade union/works council electoral results, thereby limiting the influence of minority trade unions in most cases beyond autonomous regions with other influential union confederations. Thus, the relations between the two major confederations determine the content of collective bargaining demands, although the role of the employer and the state in these circumstances has become increasingly less supportive over time. Finally, what was a highly mobilizing tradition in the 1970s and early 1980s was undermined by the impact of neoliberal social democratic interventions in the 1980s (Sola 2013).

Structure of trade unions and union democracy

The general structure of the trade union movement is organized around a series of competing confederations, each with a particular political or social identity. The core of the system of Spanish industrial relations has been fundamentally dominated by CCOO and the UGT, although there are some regional exceptions, such as the Basque Country, where the dominant unions have included the Basque Workers' Solidarity (ELA, *Eusko Langileen Alkartasuna*) and the Nationalist Workers' Committees (LAB, *Langile Abertzaleen Batzordeak*), and Galicia, where the Galician Unions Confederacy (CIG, *Confederación Intersindical Galega*) has also played a role. The dominance of the two main confederations has been consistent since the late 1970s. The system of trade union workplace elections determines which is the most representative trade union and therefore those who can negotiate at various levels on behalf of the workforce.

Table 27.2 Trade union elections in Spain, 1978–2019

Year	Total representatives	CCOO		UGT		Others		Not affiliated	
		Number	Percentage	Number	Percentage	Number	Percentage	Number	Percentage
1978	193,112	66,540	34.5	41,897	21.7	25,953	13.4	58,725	30.4
1982	140,770	47,016	33.4	51,672	36.7	25,058	17.8	17,024	12.1
1986	175,363	59,230	33.8	69,427	39.6	33,998	19.4	12,708	7.2
1990	237,261	87,730	36.9	99,737	42.0	41,387	17.4	8,407	3.5
1995	204,586	77,348	37.8	96,770	37.2	57,006	21.9	8,969	3.1
2003	283,075	110,208	38.9	103,805	36.7	69,062	24.4	–	–
2007	312,017	122,079	39.1	114,973	36.8	74,965	24.0	–	–
2012	303,622	113,721	37.5	107,459	35.4	75,788	24.9	6,654	2.2
2015	259,282	93,662	36.1	85,254	32.9	73,956	28.5	6,410	2.5
2019	269,538	96,249	35.7	88,198	32.7	78,798	29.2	6,293	2.3

Source: Beneyto Calatayud (2018) and CCOO.

Alongside the national and regional/autonomous state confederations (Basque Country, Navarra, and Galicia), which are seen as 'representative' at these levels of the state, there were also a wide range of smaller unions in the last trade union elections. There are 57,499 representatives from these trade unions, approximately 22.1 per cent of the total. This degree of fragmentation constitutes a curious space in which there is a range of new and older organizations, ranging from more radically left-oriented unions to more company-oriented unions. The exceptions to this are the Workers' Trade Union (USO, *Unión Sindical Obrera*), which represents 3.9 per cent of representatives, and the anarcho-syndicalist General Confederation of Labour (CGT, *Confederación General del Trabajo*) representing 1.9 per cent (which emerged from the original anarcho-syndicalist National Confederation of Labour – CNT, *Confederación Nacional De Trabajo*). The remaining trade unions are, in the main, company-based unions, or specific trade unions representing certain public sector professional occupations (Jódar et al. 2018). With the exception of the Basque Country, however, the dominance of the two main confederations extends to all sectors and regional contexts: they also have elected representatives at 75 per cent of firms with under 500 workers and at 80 per cent of firms with between six and fifty workers. The Catalan national question created tensions within some trade unions, especially the CCOO, but it did not challenge the position of the two majority confederations in Catalonia. Company-based and minority unions account, however, for 30 per cent of representatives in firms with more than 500 workers.

The issue of fragmentation also extends to the internal life of trade unions. In the larger confederations, for example, historically there have been tensions between the representatives of larger nationwide firms and others. There are also tensions between the industrial and regional structures of the confederations. The regional structures, in which the industrial federations are also present, create a space that allows for a focus on local regional policy and unionization, but they also give rise to friction. In some regions, the dominance of the public sector federations means that, although present within the confederation, the voice of retail workers, for example, may not carry much influence. Furthermore, the state-level and national-level elements bring to the fore the sectoral federations. At the local level of collective bargaining, however, the territorial organizations of the confederations are lead players in the local application or development of local agreements, within the structure of the national agreements, as well as the organization of trade union electoral strategy for smaller firms and firms that are more difficult to organize. It should be borne in mind that, as with various other southern European trade union movements, the structure and presence of the main Spanish unions are both local and regional, by virtue of certain social and administrative centres, although in many cases these are less engaged in new struggles and labour market issues than organizations in the 1980s (Martínez Lucio and Connolly 2012).

In terms of the trade union movement's industrial structure, most of the larger trade confederations have a dual structure, balancing the industrial with the territorial. The dual structure of national industrial federations and regional organizations makes it possible to represent the broad sectoral level and the regional level in a form of matrix structure. The financial weakening of some structures and industries' mutating boundaries through economic change, however, have done much to bring about a major shift to a larger number of broad sectoral federations at the national and local levels within the main confederations. This has been accomplished by ongoing mergers that make possible resource sharing and a degree of internal staff restructuring. The UGT, for example, has reduced its organization to three main federations, each with its own specialist areas: the Federation of Public Services Employees (FeSP, *Federación de Empleados de Servicios Públicos*), Federation of Services, Mobility, and Consumption (FeSMC, *Federación de Servicios Movilidad y Consumo*) and the Federation of Industry, Construction, and Agriculture (FICA, *Federación de Industria, Construcción y Agro*). There are also two independent entities that are associated with UGT in specific sectors: UPA (*Agricultura y Ganadería*) and UPTA (*Profesionales Autónomos*). CCOO is organized internally as follows: the Federation of Industry (FI, *Federación de Industria*); the Federation of Construction and Services (FCS, *Federación de Construcción y Servicios*); the Federation of Education (FE, *Federación de Educación*); the Federation of Citizen Services (FSC, *Federación de Servicios a la Ciudadanía*); the Federation of Services (FS, *Federación de Servicios*); and the Federation of Health (FSS, *Federación de Sanidad y Sectores Sociosanitarios*). Overall, the number of industrial federations has fallen in the wake of mergers, albeit at different rates. Both the main confederations also have a federation for pensioners. To a certain extent, the differences between the UGT and the CCOO reflect not only the different ways in which internal politics have shaped developments, but also the ways they approach the economy, as can also be seen by the different types of terminology. The CGT maintains a more fragmented and classical internal structure, with ten industrial federations. USO has reorganized around five federations: the Federation of Industry (FI-USO, *Federación de Industria*), Federation of Services (FS-USO, *Federación de Servicios*), the Federation of Public Employees (FEP-USO, *Federación de Empleados Públicos*), the Federation of Education (FE-USO, *Federación de Enseñanza*) and the Federation of Private Security (FTSP-USO, *Federación de Seguridad Privada*). Another significant union is the Civil Servants' Independent Trade Union (CSIF, *Central Sindical Independiente y de Funcionarios*), which exclusively represents civil servants. While its organization covers different regions and areas where the public sector operates (health, education, general administration), it is relatively highly centralized.

The labour relations system that resulted from Spain's political transition towards democracy is based on two main channels through which workers' interests can be protected: the election-based channel, dependent on trade union elections, and the member-based channel. Alongside the generally applicable collective bargaining, this scheme constitutes the basic framework of the Spanish model of labour relations (Lahera 2018).

At the enterprise level, trade union elections result in the formation of a unitary representative body (works council), comprising union delegates chosen in accordance with the size of the company. As a consequence the negotiating body is not the corresponding union branch but the works council, although there is often much union–works council collaboration, with the former normally dominating the latter, especially unions that are in a majority position. In this sense, the leading role of trade unions in social concertation outside companies has run parallel to a certain lack of institutional leverage within the corporate sphere: much depends on the power levels of trade union branches and/or the manner in which different trade unions coordinate within works councils.

Workers' participation in elections is remarkable: around two-thirds of employees in companies with elections exercise their right to vote (Jódar et al. 2018). The system of trade union elections, however, together with the overall effectiveness of collective agreements, probably discourages workers from joining trade unions. From the workers' point of view, elections may involve them only as a voter rather than as a union member. Because membership does not have an overall impact on labour conditions, trade unions tend to suffer the same kind of criticisms as the political class more generally.

Regarding UGT, the service model of unionism, its less horizontal nature and greater focus on technical issues lend themselves to a slightly more centralized approach. CCOO historically has also experienced tensions between a leadership that has to some extent increasingly been integrated in national decision-making and a logic of action often far removed from the union's mobilizing foundations. One curious democratic feature of UGT and CCOO, and indeed other unions, is that the election of new leadership cohorts tends to lead to turnover in the personnel in a variety of key posts at the strategic level of the union.

In recent years, unions, because of their need to adapt rather than as a political preference, have reoriented themselves back towards attaining greater leverage and a focus on activity in the workplace. There have also been reforms within CCOO, especially regarding internal union democracy. As a result of the recent relative delegitimization of the institutional scheme inherited from the post-Francoist transition, unions – particularly the two main confederations – have increasingly reflected on the costs of their engagement with the state. The dominant perception is that the institutional framework developed by the two main confederations has been increasingly unable to adapt to the new economic and social context. This is due in part to the difficulties of systematically incorporating a range of new dynamics introduced by immigration, gender equality and the younger generations, despite a number of new initiatives. Highly symptomatic of this contradiction was the 15M/'indignados' movement (see below). An image was presented of a 'two-party state' and the dominance of a highly institutionalized industrial relations system dominated by two confederations. A catchphrase emerged, 'they don't represent us', aimed at both the political parties and the union confederations (Sampedro and Lobera 2014). The social and discursive legitimacy achieved by 15M, together with its political distance (at least at first) with regard to the two main union confederations, was a turning point for the future development of trade unionism in Spain, as much social space and identity needed to be re-addressed. Despite the slowness of changes due to bureaucratic inertia, it seems indisputable that in recent years Spanish trade unionism has been trying to regain the initiative in the workplace, while trying to put some distance between itself and institutional relations with the state.

A further challenge to trade unionism, both its development and its renewal, emerges from the fragmented nature of Spanish firms (Jódar et al. 2018). There is an increasingly large group of small firms without trade union representation and the organizational culture of paternalism has not only continued but also, in some cases, re-emerged in key parts of the Spanish employer class. This is noticeable in the greater use of legal and consultancy firms that advise on how to limit the effect of unions and joint regulation (Fernández Rodriguez et al. 2016a, 2016b). Another problem is that more and more workers are employed in large firms without a clear organizational structure that might correspond to the structure of trade union elections (Cruz Villalón 2017).

Unionization

According to data obtained by the unions and various surveys, the evolution of union density in Spain has not suffered abrupt disruptions in recent decades. Union density has gone through significant changes influenced by the economic cycle. The period after 1988, the year of the most successful general strike in the history of Spanish democracy held on 14 December 1988 to protest against labour market reforms and new forms of contracts, marked a key development, as the two main confederations started to coordinate more systematically in opposition to the economic 'modernization' and liberalization adopted by the PSOE governments. From then on, union density remained stable, and generally speaking between one-fifth and one-sixth of the workforce has been unionized. There were moments of occasional stability. The Spanish economy went through a period of relatively high levels of employment creation, partly because of high rates of temporary contracts. Figure 27.1 outlines some of these developments across time.

Figure 27.1 Total membership and union density in Spain, 1980–2018

Source: Appendix A1.

Figure 27.2 Trade union membership of CCOO and UGT (in thousands), 1981–2018

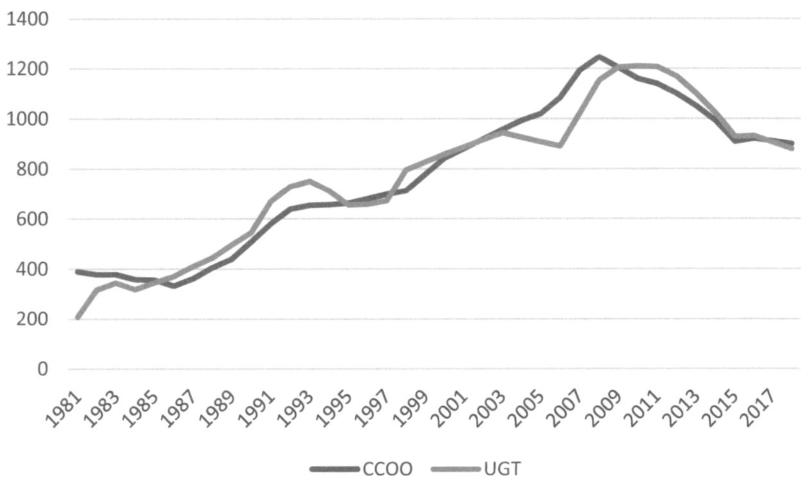

Source: Appendix A1.

This evolution of trade union density masks highly significant changes regarding membership levels, linked closely to the acute cycles of employment creation and destruction that characterize the Spanish economy. For instance, the number of CCOO members grew from around 400,000 in 1988 to over 1,100,000 in 2008, before falling once more below 900,000 in the current crisis (Vidal et al. 2016). In a similar way, UGT, according to internal data, experienced a membership decline from more than 1,200,000 in 2010 to 928,000 in 2015, albeit with a slight recovery in the following years.[1] Figure 27.2 outlines the membership levels of CCOO and UGT in more detail.

The main features of the socio-demographic composition of union affiliation in Spain are as follows. By gender, according to data from the last Quality of Life at Work Survey (ECVT), carried out in 2010, the union density rate among women was 16.8 per cent, 4 percentage points below that of their male peers. Even though the specific weight of women within trade unions has grown significantly, from 19.8 per cent in 1980 to 40.7 per cent in 2010 – close to the European Union average – this membership rate has still not translated into stronger leverage within unions: the percentage of female representatives in union congresses was much lower although this has been changing: UGT (19 per cent) and CCOO (23 per cent) (Torns and Recio 2011). The data from an European Trade Union Confederation (ETUC) survey carried out in 2006 show this same trend, according to which women constituted more than one-third of overall membership, thus closing the gap with the male membership rate as a result of their labour market participation. Furthermore, the data reflected no significant differences between trade unions regarding female participation, although UGT seems to have lower figures (Sechi 2007). Many trade unions have introduced various mechanisms to promote women's involvement. UGT has a compulsory gender quota for the regional and federation levels, and policies to boost youth participation. CCOO also has very detailed gender quotas, which are a core part of their organizational values and are also included in their rules and procedures.

The most remarkable feature of trade union membership is the low numbers of young members. Although people under 35 years of age represent more than 27 per cent of overall employment, they constitute only

---

1 UGT's affiliation data available at: https://www.ugt.es/portal-de-transparencia/C%C3%B3mo%20Somos

19 per cent of membership. According to the 2010 survey, the membership rate among the youngest workers, 16–24 years of age, was 7.2 per cent, which is low compared with the 25.1 per cent of workers over 45 years of age. The data provided by CCOO in its report (Vidal et al. 2016) give an idea of the problem of membership ageing that the two main unions are facing in Spain at present.

In 2013, members were distributed as follows: people 30 or under, 5.7 per cent; 31–40 year-olds, 25.7 per cent; 41–50 year-olds, 31.4 per cent; 51–60 year-olds, 28.0 per cent, and people over 60, 8.7 per cent. In terms of nationality, the rate for migrants is three times lower than that of native workers, at 6.6 per cent against 20.3 per cent, again according to the last 2010 ECVT (ibid). In part these changes in trade union coverage reflect the changing nature of the labour market, in which we see a larger peripheral workforce using non-standard contracts over the past few decades and a concentration of women, migrants and young workers in such areas. As an example, the temporary employment rate was 14 per cent in 1987 but rose to 34 per cent by 2007: the figures currently remain well over 25 per cent, one of the highest percentages in Europe. In terms of the distribution of membership across the different industrial sectors we see that industry, transport, financial services, media and information, public administration at various levels, education and health are the main areas, with between a quarter and a third of membership.

Table 27.3 Union density by industry, 2010

Economic segment	**Union density (%)**
Agriculture, animal husbandry, fishing industry	17.7
Industry – manufacturing sector	20.4
Construction	9.5
Trade; engine repairing	8.9
Transport and storage	21.7
Hotel industry	8.3
ICT industry. finance and insurance	22.0
Private administration and professional activities	9.9
Public administration and army forces	33.0
Education	24.8
Health and social services	22.2
Art, leisure and other services	9.5
Domestic service	1.5

Source: Spanish Quality of Life at Work Survey (2010).

In terms of these changes in overall trade union density in Spain, an emerging school of thought presents the following explanation. In the late 1970s, after the dictatorship, trade union membership increased. These higher membership levels were not sustainable, however, nor was a culture of progressive extension. This was partly because of deindustrialization and the political stigmatizing of trade unionism, which was considered peripheral to the aims of the Socialist government under Felipe González, 1982–1996. There was a time when, after the early democratic transition, it was believed that trade unions would decline and fall to a lower rate of membership. By the mid-1990s, however, a degree of stability had been achieved through a range of institutional responses and a focusing of trade union strategies that ensured membership of one-fifth of the workforce (Jordana 1996). The number of votes cast in trade union elections – as discussed earlier – was consistently high. These elections, which are held every four years, act as a de facto form of organization, to some extent, as the unions have to address and seek workers' votes, establishing their identities and policies from those of the other unions (Martínez Lucio 2017). It has been argued that CCOO's public and social campaigning has drawn attention to a range of issues and agendas beyond immediate, traditional workplace issues (Barranco and Molina 2019). Furthermore, the focus on reconnecting with workers has also been a major factor in the development of a more professional and informational role for trade unions in terms of how they collate data and maintain membership information (Martínez Lucio and Hamann 2007: 207). A range of organizational structures are increasingly entrusted with broader issues of membership and services that run alongside the national-level 'secretariats' for migration, women, and young people, for example. Trade unions have been addressing the question of equality more broadly and engaging with a range of struggles in new ways through networks of activists around lesbian, gay, transexual and bisexual workers, for example.

Trade unions began to expand their focus on aspects of collective bargaining such as health and safety, working conditions, equality, and other factors. This mirrored a national political effort to raise workers' social concerns in discussions with the state (Köhler and Calleja Jiménez 2012). There is also the ongoing provision of a range of legal and support services, which has allowed trade unions to be serve as a major focal point in their relations with workers. There has been a deliberate strategy to establish an active servicing role, even with new groups of workers, such as migrants (Martínez Lucio et al. 2013). The use of community centres tied to local trade union structures has been a key point of reference for engaging workers in terms of their needs for social and legal information, although these structures are not always campaigning structures that create active participation from marginalized workers (Martínez Lucio and Connolly 2012). This issue has been raised in relation to how learning and training strategies have been developed by the main trade unions through the use of state funding. This has been important in terms of raising the unions' visibility and role, but it has also been fraught because of the problems of working in a context of fragmented employer structures, and stigmatization of the role of trade unions because of problems of transparency (Rigby 2002; Rigby and Ponce Sanz 2016).

Attempts to boost membership, and trade union profiles more generally, have been the subject of much discussion. Below, we shall address the general disconnect perceived by many between trade unions and society (Köhler and Calleja Jiménez 2015). But there is also a school of thought that argues that trade unions have generally been caught between an uninterested state, confining the unions' room to manoeuvre to certain roles, and a declining social presence (Martínez Lucio and Hamann 2007). In an exhaustive study of trade union renewal in the main confederations, Calleja Jiménez (2016) argued that opinion polls since 2010 have pointed to a general dissatisfaction with unions affiliated to the confederations because of their inability to achieve systematic organization in smaller firms, and a general reliance on the state in some respects. He also argues that the presence of specific groups of workers, especially young workers, and their influence inside the trade union movement is variable (Calleja Jiménez 2016 – see also Fernández Rodríguez et al. 2015), possibly contributing to a crisis of representation linked to the 15M *indignados* movement. There also seems to be a strategic disconnect between the social, political and economic roles of the main trade unions and a failure to engage with broader constituencies of academics and debates on change (Calleja Jiménez 2016). Even so, there has been more research by, for example, CCOO's First of May Foundation (Fundación Primero de Mayo), which is focused on such activities. For others, the onus has been on new forms of worker voice and social movements that have acted more directly and have managed to use more participative structures, such as the assembly in sectors such as agriculture (Roca Martínez and Díaz Parra 2012). There has been an extensive development in resisting austerity measures, marked by new forms of direct action by a range of radical and independent worker structures (Las Heras and Ribera Almandoz 2017). These new forms of collective identity and flexible forms of organization have experienced some success (López-Andreu 2020).

Union resources and expenditure

The financial model of trade unions in Spain has long been a challenge because of the complexity and opacity of union accounts. The basic scheme of union financing is quite simple. Union contributions from members are the main source of income. At present, according to trade union sources, union dues constitute around 80 to 90 per cent of overall union income (Beneyto 2012; Mejías García 2017). In accordance with various regulations, trade unions also receive public funding through two further channels: (i) budgets established in accordance with their representativeness, determined by trade union elections, and linked to the employer; and (ii) subsidies as compensation for costs arising from their participation, together with employers' organizations, in the various advisory bodies. This public funding is more complex because there are also sources of income from both the regional/*autonomia* and national levels.

Nevertheless, some recent controversies have resulted from other sources of indirect income, specifically 'purpose-determined' funds, such as the funds aimed at workers' training. Information on these funds is ostensibly openly available on the relevant websites, but given how highly decentralized this network of subsidized activities is and how complex it is to monitor them, not all the activities directly managed by unions appear on these sites.

Historically, there has been a high degree of state subsidy or transfer of resources from the state to trade unions as part of the historic settlement that was deemed morally essential, given the almost physical destruction of trade unions and their structures by the Francoist dictatorship, and the expropriation of many of their assets by the dictatorship during and after the Spanish Civil War. In addition, the state-organized trade union *Organización Sindical Obrera* had extensive assets that were in part passed onto the free trade union movement after the dictatorship came to an end, although whether this constituted sufficient compensation is debatable. To this extent, the Spanish state owed and, for some, still owes, an extensive debt to the trade union movement, even the transfer of assets. The debate on financing and support remains active (Ortíz Vargas 2011).

Each trade union has its own approach to the collection of membership fees. Here the focus is on the rules and procedures of UGT and CCOO. At CCOO the confederation is responsible for setting membership fees and distributing them proportionally among the federations. In the UGT it is different: federations set the fees and collect them, and there is a subsequent redistribution, laid down in their statutes, with funds channelled to legal services, the confederation and so on.

Collective bargaining and unions in the workplace

The Spanish collective bargaining system can be understood as a mixed system, in which bargaining occurs at national, industrial, provincial and company levels (Fernández Rodríguez et al. 2019). In theory, all agreements have to defer to and not go beyond standards set at a higher level, although recent reforms yielded new rules that apply in exceptional circumstances. The evolution of negotiations depends on the respective industry: for instance, in chemicals or financial services, agreements are reached at the national level, then further arrangements are made at the company level. Meanwhile, in construction most discussions take place at the provincial level, although other levels are involved. Company agreements have tended to improve on content agreed at higher levels, but this usually happens only in large firms (Fernández Rodríguez et al. 2019).

The key actors in the Spanish collective bargaining system are unions, employers' associations and later, in a lesser role, the state. At the national level, representative unions and employers' associations, and, at the company level, works councils and firm representatives are entitled to bargain collectively. National agreements between employers and majority representative unions establish not only a framework of basic conditions – especially those related to wage increases – but also other issues (Guillén Rodríguez et al. 2008).

In some industries, there is a significant national industry-level agreement that sets minimum pay and working conditions. The industry-level affiliates of the main confederations tend to play a pivotal role in this sphere of collective bargaining. Coordination is becoming an issue in industries in which there may be national-level and industry-level agreements for specific parts of that industry, creating complex structures and challenging union coordination. There may be agreements (*pactos de aplicación*) that, in the main, apply to the superior levels of agreements, as opposed to classic collective agreements that merely extend the main content of the superior agreement. Collective bargaining occurs at all levels (company, provincial, industrial or national), but since 2012 company-level agreements have been 'favoured' by legislation (Fernández Rodríguez et al. 2016a). Within the union movement, key federations, such as in the metal and chemicals industries, have a strong general influence on proceedings, affecting the way demands and overarching policies are framed in relation to collective bargaining and employment policy. In view of the imposition of financial austerity in recent years, for example, sustaining employment has become a key factor in informal mediation (Fernández Rodríguez et al. 2016a).

The Spanish collective bargaining system was subject to significant reforms during the 2010s, linked to the financial austerity policies aimed at bringing the economic crisis of 2008–2013 to an end. The recent collective bargaining reforms introduced lower dismissal costs and new prerogatives for employers, but there were two key changes (Meardi 2014). First, company-level agreements are given absolute precedence over multi-employer agreements, including employers' prerogatives to reduce wages without union consent, subject to arbitration. Second, the duration of collective agreements has been reduced from an indefinite period, with no renegotiation, to a maximum of two years, after which all established rights from previous agreements terminate until a new agreement is signed.

As a result, company agreements can have precedence in key areas, irrespective of matters already addressed in industry-level agreements. In addition, companies in financial difficulties are in some cases able to suspend many of the agreed terms and conditions (Fernández Rodríguez et al. 2016b).

In terms of challenges to the coordination between levels of collective bargaining, major issues with regard to the traditions of labour relations and regulation include ongoing deindustrialization, outsourcing and offshoring (see Fernández Rodríguez et al, 2019). The car industry is a classic case of outsourcing and complex supply chains, curtailing the reach of unions beyond minimal conditions established at higher levels in the components sector (Las Heras and Ribera Almandoz 2017; Las Heras 2018). These spaces and gaps mean that the so-called 'articulation' or 'coordination' of bargaining (Molina 2007) has now become further challenged: there are also concerns about the adoption of a fragmented UK or

US model of company-based and disconnected bargaining (Waddington 2019). Nevertheless, trade unions continue to work through their respective branches within workplaces and collective forms of representation – where relevant – such as works councils to which they are elected.

The deep financial and economic crisis that followed the recession of 2008 put unions under tremendous stress. First, within southern Europe the impact of austerity measures and the neoliberal policy aspects of the EU have supported national attempts to weaken the role of joint regulation and union influence. Second, while differences in terms and conditions of employment have been established in various sectors – with the public sector tending towards a more centralized model and with certain key industries, such as chemicals, having a strong tradition of coordinated bargaining led at industry-level – there are signs of greater fragmentation. In some areas, such as retailing, this has resulted from the presence of a series of local provincial agreements that make for a complex pattern of regulation that, in the current circumstances, undermines attempts at coordination and tests coordination across the industry. Third, trade union legitimacy has been challenged for various reasons beyond the fact that the legal framework is less supportive and political exchanges with the government on social issues have been less fruitful in an age of financial austerity and right-wing policies. A neoliberal challenge to the role of unions that has been developing since the mid-2010s within the Spanish Right and related media has crystallized into a body of recent legislation allowing firms to opt out of agreements in particular circumstances (Fernández Rodríguez and Martínez Lucio 2013). This has had the curious effect of creating resource-based issues for unions, which must monitor an ever-wider range of management behaviour and actions that focus on either bypassing, or not implementing collective agreements. In some cases, it has forced majority unions to face criticisms from smaller, more radical unions, especially when terms and conditions of work have been agreed that are problematic because of the need to sustain levels of employment, or the process of collective bargaining itself. The new social movements and new left that have emerged since the early 2010s have been critical of the more institutionalist roles of the unions, and their perceived distance from younger workers and their precarious labour market conditions. This has created a new form of mobilization alongside the relatively institutionalized forms of industrial relations. This situation is comparable to the early years of the democratic system in the 1970s and 1980s, albeit without the full scope of that period.

The aim of the larger, more institutionalized unions has been to sustain the processes of collective bargaining even if the content appears to be deteriorating, so that, in the longer term, there is a basis for negotiation in the context of an upturn in events. Increasing precariousness in the labour market and policies of deregulation in terms of workers' rights, underpinned by what Rocha (2014) sees as a more challenging and less supportive climate of industrial relations in Spain, are an issue. There are also growing developments in direct forms of participation at work, although their impact is still a matter of judgement (González Menéndez 2011).

Because of the Covid-19 pandemic, there has been an important shift in Spanish politics towards the use of new measures for tackling the crisis, such as basic incomes. While these initiatives emerged at the turn of the millennium and have been supported by certain social scientists (Raventós and Casassas 2003), Spanish unions have traditionally been less enthusiastic. The depth of the crisis and the pandemic, however, have given rise to a very problematic situation, and the PSOE-Podemos government in 2020 responded with a number of important measures. There has been a wide use of ERTE (*Expediente Temporal de Regulación de Empleo*), a temporary redundancy benefit supported by the state, and especially – and as a novelty – initiatives such as the *Ingreso Mínimo Vital* (Vital Minimum Income) and austerity-based reforms have been increasingly reviewed.

Industrial conflict

In the early years of democracy, Spain was actively involved in the then generally increasing cycle of industrial conflict which marked the crisis of the 1970s: for example, approximately 6 million workers were involved in strikes and approximately 20 million working days were lost in 1978. The number of activists and the intensity of the conflicts which took place during the late 1970s have not recurred. According to the official government statistics on strikes and lockouts there has been a noticeable decline in strikes. In the late 1980s there were on average 1,163 strikes a year, with 1,503,937 participants and 4,458,305 working days lost. During the early to mid-2010s there were 809 strikes, 271,191 participants and 721,730 working days lost annually (Luque Balbona and González Begega 2017: 100). Despite some specific upturns, the trend since the early 1980s has been one of decline regarding the number of strikes and their intensity. The decline in the level of unrest, however, has not been reflected in a decrease in the number of strikes. What has fallen dramatically is the number of strikers and the days not worked because of strikes. Nevertheless, the systematic resort to strikes has remained important. As for the distribution of strikes, the intensity of conflict is still higher in the manufacturing sector, which during 2010–2016 accounted for more than 40 per cent of the strikes, although less than 30 per cent of the strikers (Lacalle 2015, 2019). Beyond these overall trends, the dynamics of industrial conflict in Spain in recent years have gone through an array of changes, some of which result from domestic specificities, but others are a consequence of global dynamics in which the repertoire of protest has been transformed within the developed economies. In the first place, and in line with other European countries, there has been a steady growth in the number of conflicts taking the form of demonstrations, which increased from 3,000 a year in the period before the crisis to 45,000 in 2013. More than 30 per cent of these demonstrations were linked to labour issues (Luque Balbona and González Begega 2017).

The resort to general strikes has been a feature of Spanish industrial relations, although their remit and length are usually quite short as they are used strategically in relation to a range of social issues (Hamann et al. 2016). Curiously, they form part of the fabric of industrial relations in terms of relations between the state and trade unions. In some senses the general strike is not just an economic weapon but an important and direct form of communication, although a study of trade unions and resort to strikes in Spain and Italy shows that trade unions are not able to effectively extend and frame their mobilization as strategically as they might like (Molina and Barranco 2016). This dynamic of short but large-scale general strikes has nevertheless been central, and to some extent more successful, in certain key autonomous states within Spain, as can be seen in recent years in the Basque Country (Gorosarri and Sauviat 2016). There is an emerging critical view of how the larger unions have been responding to questions of financial austerity and the forms of collective action they have taken, which have been criticized as not extensive enough (Roca and Las Heras 2020)

Diverse forms of worker conflict and action have also been seen in recent years. Some of these developments echo the direct forms of action, assemblyism and workplace occupations of the early years of the political transition (see Colectivo de Estudios por la Autonomía Obrera 1977). Yet, such forms of direct action have remained a salient part of the labour movement's repertoire, especially to the left of the main confederations. Sit-ins in the Lecta Group paper mills in France and Spain (Cantabria) in 2010, prompted by the employer's attempts to restructure and close sites, brought regional government action in relation to political support. Occupations are an important part of the repertoire of worker representatives, also transmitting a political message to political interests and institutions (Martínez Lucio 2011). New forms of direct action and worker organization have intensified, highlighting the more diverse approach to the use of workplace and non-workplace spaces (Fernández Rodríguez et al. 2015). In the telecommunications industry, in the past few years, a range of initiatives have been led by the rank and file, and by workers, using assembly-based forms of decision-making and involving a broader range of worker organizations (López-Andreu 2020). Within the taxi industry, the emergence of companies such as Uber has, relative to other European countries, led to a greater number of large-scale protests (*El País* 2019). In addition, the 'feminist strike' of 8 March 2019 in Spain was one of the largest, led by a wide range of groups and networks and engaging new forms of social media communication and organization (Fernández Rincón 2019). Indeed, there has been a new wave of literature and research on the role of minority radical unions that have been at the heart of a range of boycotts, demonstrations and short stoppages in the 'gig economy' (Rodríguez Fernández 2018), and resort to the courts to seek changes to the status of workers in such industries has been key, particularly employers' imposition of bogus self-employment.

While these initiatives are distant in form and content from the experiences of self-management with its anarcho-syndicalist traditions (Dolgoff 1974), they are nevertheless, in some cases, inspired by the democratic memory and culture of such historical forebears. The political changes brought by the 15M movement in 2011, and the new networks and movements tied to it with regard to work-related issues, have been the impetus for many developments in terms of new forms of boycott, public protest and occupations (Gorosarri and Sauviat 2016). This has had an impact on certain aspects of the more established and 'majority' labour movement, however, which has to some extent been expanding its remit of interests and campaigning regarding non-standard work issues for some time (Barranco and Molina 2019). Employers have responded to such developments in some cases by means of aspects of labour legislation that predate the democratic system. This has also become common in limiting local conflicts (Alonso et al. forthcoming).

Political relations

Trade unions have historically always had strong links to the political sphere in Spain. UGT has been linked to the social democratic PSOE and CNT has been part of the anarcho-syndicalist tradition. The emergence of CCOO during the latter years of Francoism and the political transition of the 1970s, countered the social democratic and anarcho-syndicalist hold on trade union politics, although the Communist Party of Spain (PCE, Partido Comunista de España) had significant political influence within it. Until the 1970s, the influence of key parties of the left within the trade unions was significant. The establishment of a more market-facing social democratic tradition since the early 1980s, the decline of PCE influence, and the continuing weaknesses of the anarchist tradition in contrast to the early twentieth century meant that trade unions found themselves with declining direct political influence. The ongoing tensions in the 'socialist family' between the PSOE and UGT; the tensions between CCOO and factions of the PCE and the CCOO-led United Left (IU, Izquierda Unida); the differences and divisions inside the anarcho-syndicalist union tradition; and the issues across the left in the Basque Country in relation to different unions, all led to a growing distance or tensions in relations between political actors and trade unions. There is also an increasing tendency for trade unions to don the mantel of the political and to mobilize and/or negotiate directly with the state (Martínez Lucio 1998). In some cases, organizations such as CCOO had to adopt the mantle of the 'left' during the 1980s, especially through its 'socio-political' identity (Martínez Lucio 1990). The emergence of Podemos and its increasingly significant influence since 2010 initially gave rise to tensions. Over time more dialogue and accommodation have emerged between specific trade unions and Podemos (interviews by authors).

There is a lively debate on the relations between the state and trade unions in Spain, which suggests there are various ways of understanding these dimensions. Relations between the three main actors in terms of tripartism and bipartism have been intriguing (Guillén Rodríguez and Gutiérrez Palacios 2008). A key role has been played by specific agreements and dialogue in terms of 'democratic consolidation' (Linz and Stepan 1996). This has been achieved through flexible but largely continuous neo-corporatist dialogue covering a range of employment and social issues (Guillén et al. 2008; González Begega et al. 2015; Molina and Rhodes 2011), although constraints have been placed on deepening these roles by governments determined to impose flexible labour markets (Martínez Lucio 1998) and an employer class intent on the individualization of work and fragmentation (Martínez Lucio 1991): for a broader discussion of constraints emerging from various dimensions especially in the economic realm (see Pérez, 2010). These relations have provided an important framework that has underpinned and supported a relative degree of coordination in terms of collective bargaining (Hamann 2012; Molina 2005, 2006). Since 2010, during a period of austerity and crisis and neoliberal-inspired labour reforms, short, but extensive, general strikes generated a degree of dialogue between trade unions and the state (González Begega et al. 2015), although a pattern of relatively contingent and unstable relations prevailed (Hamann 2013). The system in effect 'goes down' at certain moments, to use a computing term, but it has an ability to 'reboot' and revert to negotiation quite swiftly. Whether it is coherent and systematic is another matter, however (Martínez Lucio 1998, 2017). In addition, trade union representatives are present in various state agencies and fora regarding migration, health and safety, training, and other matters. In the regional autonomous state of Aragón, in north-east Spain, there has been an attempt to reinforce social dialogue by launching different institutional settings, such as a regional employment service (INAEM) and a mediation and arbitration service (SAMA). According to trade unions, employers' associations and Aragón's government, there has been a common effort whose outcome has been stability and industrial peace, which has pushed the regional economy forward (Pérez Ortiz et al. 2018). Much depends on the political profile of the region. Employers have also intensified their questioning of certain forms of workers' rights in some sectors and regions with a dependence on more precarious labour markets.

Whether this system of social dialogue is as structurally embedded as it first appears is another matter (Martínez Lucio 1987; Roca Jusmet, 1991). The system has not been as tightly articulated as imagined and remains fragmented in certain respects (Molina 2007). Even during key moments of trade union influence, there has been ongoing labour market reform and segmentation, which the labour movement has found difficult to reverse (Sola 2013). The institutional role of trade unions in the process of change has not been extensive, and mainly conjunctural, but much depends on the comparative reference point, and more direct forms of unilateral state action in southern Europe have been apparent (Molina 2014).

Societal power

There has been a socio-political identity and a community dimension to trade unions in Spain, especially to the left of mainstream social democracy, although this has changed in character and content (Martínez Lucio 1987, 1998). This has typically been linked to a strong social and community presence through the use of local centres or offices. It has also engaged in local social struggles. In the case of the CCOO, the notion that it is fundamentally a socio-political union has been key to its identity (Baranco and Molina 2019). Baranco and Molina (2019) argue that such public union campaigning has not fallen away but remains a key part of the public discourse and activities of key confederations such as CCOO, as it moves towards engaging with a broader set of issues concerning young workers and women in the labour market. To this extent, there has historically been a strong degree of social engagement and social presence within the trade union movement, often involving the local structures of the social democratic elements of the movement. Much has been said in terms of coalition-building and the role trade unions play in building bridges with social movements and non-government organizations (Heery et al. 2012). The Spanish experience of the 1960s through to the 1980s, especially the strong links with neighbourhood associations and welfare struggles – above all during the building of social infrastructure and welfare institutions by the state in that period – exemplifies this tradition. Some of the traditions of engaging locally with social and marginalized groups continued, with such initiatives as the establishment of information and support strategies for migrant communities from the 1990s. Although some aspects of these were institutionally supported by the state, they represented some of the more active initiatives of migrant support (Connolly et al. 2019). Smaller confederations, such as the CNT and the CGT, also engaged directly with new sets of workers around campaigns and occupations that highlighted their social vulnerability.

There is an argument that the steady institutionalization of trade unions and their proximity to the state led to a distancing from these 'socio-political' aspects. In 2011, the 15M movement represented a broad patchwork of progressive and radical interests, and groups of individuals who were closely concerned with the increasing precariousness of workers, the lack of social housing and ongoing corruption at state level (Morell 2012; Tormey and Feenstra 2015). This movement, which, in large part, transformed into Podemos, was critical of the larger trade unions, seeing them as having reneged on their social identities and historical presence within civil society (Köhler and Calleja Jiménez 2015, 2018). One could argue that the undermining of CCOO's socio-political identity has deeper origins, related to the nature of the transition (Martínez Lucio 1987, 1990). While generally true – in the sense that the trade union movement, particularly CCOO, recognized that it had been caught unawares by the possibilities of new social developments – there are those who argue that one cannot underestimate the broader social agendas that have emerged in the case of CCOO (Barranco and Molina 2019). Although many social initiatives were structurally institutional and reliant on the state for institutional resources (Martínez Lucio and Connolly 2012), trade unions have, to some extent, been extending their interests as a result of certain membership changes (Köhler and Calleja Jiménez 2012). There are also new voices and constituencies within established trade unions that are engaged in various social struggles and broader campaigning, although this is to some extent peculiar to CCOO, which has been less critical of new social movements than UGT (interview by authors).

Broadly speaking, since the 1990s the mass media, which has drifted to the right, has been less concerned with the trade union movement, with less reporting on industrial relations. Press hostility has been more apparent since the turn of the millennium, however, spotlighting what they consider to be 'rigid' labour market practices in line with the increasingly neoliberal – and even alt-right – influences within the Spanish right (Fernández Rodríguez and Martínez Lucio 2013).

Trade union policies towards the European Union

The main Spanish confederations actively engaged with the EU, partly because of the importance of Europe for the integration and stability of the political and economic system. There are competing opinions, however, concerning the cost to the Spanish economy of the neoliberalization that has accompanied this development, particularly in employment policies (Keune and Serrano Pascual 2014). The early integration of Spanish trade unions into the ETUC did not initially include CCOO: its exclusion was mainly the result of a veto by the German DGB (German Trade Union Confederation) arising from CCOO's political identity (Sigfrido and Ramírez Pérez 2017). Since then, the two main confederations have been significant partners within the European systems of trade union representation and related aspects of the European Commission's work. Support for the social dimension and the European social agenda has been a major part of the discourse of confederations such as CCOO, UGT and USO, although the social dimension remains largely a set of minimum standards and has not led to a more expansive approach to the welfare state.

European institutional access has played a part in improving relations between the two main confederations and, to some extent, could be argued to have reinforced their virtual duopoly of representation at the national level. In addition, the main federations of these trade unions have been relatively active within industrial European-level organizations. The main Spanish federations have been a clear presence in leading European-level campaigns and mobilizations, despite a range of structural barriers, pushing for a greater degree of social focus within the EU than some of the more powerful and established trade unions (Prosser 2019: 71–87). There has therefore been active engagement with certain European trade union federations, such as UNI-Europa. This is largely because of the highly internationalized nature of the Spanish economy and the presence of key multinationals, which have created a dynamic of engagement with EU institutions. The main Spanish trade unions have been active agents in the pursuit and development of European works councils. There have been national-level training and engagement programmes for workplace representatives that have mirrored those in various other key European countries. In the case of Banco Santander and Iberia, the national representative trade unions have led a range of internationalizing initiatives and campaigns around specific sets of work-related issues. But while confederations such as CCOO and UGT have had fairly close relations with some of their Portuguese and Italian partners, a coherent southern European voice has been lacking. The inability to construct a more organized southern European axis of interest and representation to replicate that of, say, the Nordic countries and to counter neoliberal EU policies and the activities of the Troika has been an important factor. While the debate on solidarity funds to tackle Covid-19 has seen some degree of dialogue, no clear common position has emerged among Spanish, Italian, Greek and Portuguese trade unions.

Conclusions

The debate on Spanish industrial relations, and on trade unions especially, always needs to be located within a historical context. The trade unions have emerged through struggle since the dictatorship – or during its final years – and have had to consolidate institutionally, while also working to establish a system of rights and regulation at a time when the post-Second World War model of social democratic consensus was in decline. The need to consolidate a social state and a democratic system of collective regulation was being pursued just as deregulation, privatization and globalization through marketization were de rigueur among the political and economic elites (Martínez Lucio 2016). Efforts to ensure a basic set of minimums constitutionally and socially constituted a political project that was balanced by a fundamental transformation of the national economic system. Attempting to judge Spanish trade unions and their strategies without understanding these tensions and contextual factors is ill-advised. Trade unions are caught between the tensions of delivering social change and justice, while also ensuring economic stability and gains for their members, although the balance here varies depending on the trade union in question (Hyman 2001). Balancing different spheres of engagement is key to the development of trade union strategies (Martínez Lucio and Mustchin 2019).

This chapter underlines that we are seeing fragmentation not purely in terms of the labour market and the sphere of work, but also in trade union activities. Given the historical circumstances and the uneven manner in which regulation has evolved, it would be naïve to underestimate some aspects of the unions' formal achievements in terms of their social pacts with the state and the extent of collective bargaining. This should be understood especially in the context of a state that has been caught between a neoliberal approach and social demands or pressures (Martínez Lucio 2016).

This curious 'balancing act' has been increasingly challenged, however. The instability of trade union relations with the state in terms of policymaking, and the ongoing fragmentation of Spain's social and labour market infrastructure, mean that the institutional infrastructure of worker representation is being seriously tested (Köhler 2018). One could argue that the signs of this social and regulatory fragmentation and change were visible during the 1980s and 1990s (Martínez Lucio 1998). The partial consensus that enveloped industrial relations in the 1980s and 1990s, itself not without its uncertainties and differences, is increasingly being severely tested. What is more, the fabric of worker representation has changed, with new sets of voices and social movements impinging on questions of work and employment. To some extent, this complexity is nothing new, given the social and community origins of many trade union practices. The formal renewal strategies of the majority trade unions, coupled with their institutionalized approach to re-engaging workers, and the more direct and ensemble forms of worker action emerging in a new range of sectors, suggest that we are seeing different patterns and spaces of development in worker representation (Köhler and Callejo Jiménez 2018).

As various firms and their managements continue to drift from the established customs of collective industrial relations; as more groups of workers exist on the periphery of 'organized' employment relations; and as working conditions continue to deteriorate in general; new challenges will emerge for trade unions as they seek to impose minimum conditions and seek ways to influence the state and capital to respect agreed standards. Another challenge will be to coordinate across the ever-expanding interests, voices and organizations that populate industrial relations.

Visser (2019) has argued that trade unions face four scenarios: *marginalization*, in which unions are effectively replaced and become ever weaker; *dualization*, in which unions represent a core and relatively stable workforce alongside a largely unorganized workforce; *substitution*, in which trade unions are replaced by alternative forms of social and non-governmental organizations; and *revitalization*, in which unions reconnect with new worker constituencies and develop a panoply of innovative strategies. In our view, the current degree of fragmentation in the world of work means that we cannot foresee the outcome. While in aspirational terms all trade unions seek – rhetorically at least – some form of *revitalization*, it is our view that the Spanish trade union movement will be balanced between two options. The first will be *dualization*, whereby, in various established workplaces, the 'business' of collective regulation will continue in some form, while beyond those spaces we are likely to see a *substitution* effect as other voices and movements organize and engage in a more direct participatory form of representation and protest. Needless to say, the links between worker actors in these two spheres will be broad, but the reality is that we will perhaps see two systems of industrial relations emerging, side by side. Granted, one could argue that *substitution* and *dualization,* assuming the conditions of core workers are improved, as in substitution, or sustained to certain extent, as in dualization, could be viewed as a form of *revitalization*. Nevertheless, we believe that two systems of regulation will emerge and develop alongside each other. This conforms to the view that a range of actors and players are emerging within the framework of industrial relations, to the extent that we may have to widen our view of the politics of work and employment (Alberti and Però 2018; Heery and Frege 2006). Much may also depend on how the political sphere in Spain develops in relation to the new progressive politics that have emerged since 2010; whether the political sphere can sustain itself in the face of the neoliberal, even xenophobic political milieu that has emerged; and the extent to which weakening the trade union movement becomes a political priority. History suggests, however, that the trade unions are not incapable of broader social engagement and identities (Martínez Lucio 1990).

References

All links were checked on 16 August 2021.

Alberti G. and Però D. (2018) Migrating industrial relations: migrant workers' initiative within and outside trade unions?, British Journal of Industrial Relations, 56 (4), 693–715.

Alonso L.E., Fernández Rodríguez C.J. and Ibáñez Rojo R. (2022, forthcoming) El acoso sindical en el trabajo: dos análisis de caso, in Moreno Pestaña J.L. and Costa Delgado J. (eds) Todo lo que entró en crisis?, Madrid, Akal.

Barranco O. and Molina O. (2019) Continuity and change in trade union frames: evidence from general strikes in Spain, Economic and Industrial Democracy. https://doi.org/10.1177/0143831X19857791

Baylos A. (1988) Institucionalización sindical y prácticas neocorporativas. El caso español (1977–1987), Revista de Trabajo, 91, 9–22.

Beneyto P.J. (2012) Sobre la legitimidad del sindicalismo. Derechos y fuentes de financiación en España y la Unión Europea, Madrid, Fundación 1º de Mayo.

Beneyto Calatayud P.J. (2018) Representación sindical en la Unión Europea y España: estructura, cobertura y nuevos retos, Acciones e Investigaciones sociales, 38, 37–62.

Calleja Jiménez J.P. (2016) Estrategias de revitalización de los sindicatos españoles, doctoral thesis, University of Valéncia.

Colectivo de Estudios por la autonomía obrera (1977) Luchas autónomas en la transición democrática, volumes I and II, Madrid, Zero.

Connolly H., Marino S. and Lucio M.M. (2019) The Politics of Social Inclusion and Labor Representation. New York: Cornell University Press.

Cruz Villalón J. (2017) Una propuesta de revisión de las reglas sobre representación de los trabajadores en la empresa, in Cruz Villalón J., Remedios Menéndez M. and Nogueira Guastavino M. (eds) Representación y representatividad colectiva en las relaciones laborales: libro homenaje a Ricardo Escudero Rodríguez, Madrid, Bomarzo, 147–175.

Dolgoff S. (ed.) (1974) The anarchist collectives: workers' self-management in the Spanish revolution, 1936–1939, Montreal, Black Rose Books.

El País (2019) Madrid taxi drivers intensify their protest against ride-hailing apps, El País, 28 January 2019. https://english.elpais.com/elpais/2019/01/28/inenglish/1548662803_560309.html

Fernández Rincón A.R. (2019) Activismo, co-creación e igualdad de género: la comunicación digital en la huelga feminista del 8M, Dígitos, 5, 56–74.

Fernández Rodríguez C.J. and Martínez Lucio M. (2013) Narratives, myths and prejudice in understanding employment systems: the case of rigidities, dismissals and flexibility in Spain, Economic and Industrial Democracy, 34 (2), 313–336.

Fernández Rodríguez C.J., Ibañez Rojo R. and Martínez Lucio M. (2014) Radical trade unionism in Spain: the re-invention and re-imagination of autonomy and democracy within and around the union movement during the past century, in Connolly H., Kretsos L. and Phelan C. (eds) Radical unions in Europe and the future of collective interest representation, Oxford, Peter Lang, 111–135.

Fernández Rodríguez C.J., Ibáñez Rojo R. and Martínez Lucio M. (2016a) The reform of collective bargaining in the Spanish metal and chemicals sectors (2008–2015): the ironies and risks of de-regulating employment regulation, in Koukidaki A., Tavora I. and Martínez Lucio M. (eds) Joint regulation and labour market policy in Europe during the crisis, Brussels, ETUI, 499–553.

Fernández Rodríguez C.J., Ibáñez Rojo R. and Martínez Lucio M. (2016b) Austerity and collective bargaining in Spain: the political and dysfunctional nature of neoliberal deregulation, European Journal of Industrial Relations, 22 (3), 267–280.

Fernández Rodríguez C.J., Ibáñez Rojo R., López Calle P. and Martínez Lucio M. (2015) Young workers and unions in Spain: a failed meeting?, in Hodder A. and Kretsos L. (eds) Young workers and trade unions: a global view, Basingstoke, Palgrave MacMillan, 142–161.

Fernández Rodríguez C.J., Ibáñez Rojo R. and Martínez Lucio M. (2019) Challenges and continuities within Spanish collective bargaining in a context of fragmentation and neoliberal reform, in Müller T., Vandaele K. and Waddington J. (eds) Collective bargaining in Europe: towards an endgame, Brussels, ETUI, 563–582.

González Begega S. and Luque Balbona D. (2014) ¿Adiós al corporatismo competitivo en España? Pactos sociales y conflicto en la crisis económica, Revista Española de Investigaciones Sociológicas, 148, 79–102.

González Begega S., Luque Balbona, D. and Guillén Rodríguez A.M. (2015) Gobiernos y sindicatos ante la reforma del estado del bienestar. ¿Ruptura del diálogo social en la periferia de la eurozona?, Revista de economía crítica, 20, 102–119.

González Menéndez M.C. (2011) The determinants of workplace direct participation: evidence from a regional survey, Work, Employment and Society, 25 (3), 397–416.

Gorosarri M. and Sauviat L. (2016) The uneven development of (mass) strikes in France and Spain, Workers of the World, 1 (8), 39–55. https://duepublico2.uni-due.de/servlets/MCRFileNodeServlet/duepublico_derivate_00042551/gorosarri_sauviat_workers_8_2016.pdf.

Guillén Rodríguez A. and Gutiérrez Palacios R. (2008) Treinta años de pactos sociales en España: un balance, Cuadernos de Información económica, 203, 173–180.

Hamann K. (2012) The politics of industrial relations: labour unions in Spain, London, Routledge.

Hamann K. (2013) The relationship between unions and Zapatero's government: from social pacts to general strike, in Field B. and Botti A. (eds) Politics and society in contemporary Spain, New York, Palgrave Macmillan, 123–141.

Hamann K., Johnston A. and Kelly J. (2016) The electoral effects of general strikes in Western Europe, Comparative Politics, 49 (1), 63–82.

Heery E. and Frege C. (2006) New actors in industrial relations, British Journal of Industrial Relations, 44 (4), 601–604.

Heery E., Williams S. and Abbott B. (2012) Civil society organizations and trade unions: cooperation, conflict, indifference, Work, Employment and Society, 26 (1), 145–160.

Hyman R. (2001) Understanding European trade unionism: between market, class and society, London, Sage.

Jódar P., Alós R., Beneyto P. and Vidal S. (2018) La representación sindical en España: cobertura y límites, Cuadernos de Relaciones Laborales, 36 (1), 15–34.

Jordana J. (1996) Reconsidering union membership in Spain, 1977–1994: halting decline in a context of democratic consolidation, Industrial Relations Journal, 27 (3), 211–224.

Keune M. and Serrano Pascual A. (eds) (2014) Deconstructing flexicurity and developing alternative approaches: towards new concepts and approaches for employment and social policy, Abingdon, Routledge.

Köhler H.D. (2001) El movimiento sindical en España, Madrid, Fundamentos.

Köhler H.D. (2018) Industrial relations in Spain – strong conflicts, weak actors and fragmented institutions, Employee Relations, 40 (4), 725–743.

Köhler H.D. and Calleja Jiménez J.P. (2012) Transformations in Spanish trade union membership, Industrial Relations Journal, 43 (3), 281–292.

Köhler H.D. and Calleja Jiménez J. (2015) 'They don't represent us!': Opportunities for a social movement unionism strategy in Spain, Relations Industrielles/Industrial Relations, 70 (2), 240–261.

Köhler H.D. and Calleja Jiménez J. (2018) Spain: a peripheral economy and a vulnerable trade union movement, in Lehndorff S., Dribbusch H. and Schulten T. (eds) Rough waters: European trade unions in a time of crisis, Brussels, ETUI.

Lacalle D. (2015) Conflictividad y crisis. España 2008–2013, Madrid, El Viejo Topo.

Lacalle D. (2019) IND-195 – La evolución de la conflictividad desde los inicios de la recuperación (2014–2018), Fundación de Investigaciones Marxistas. http://www.fim.org.es/02_02.php?id_publicacion=497

Lahera Forteza J. (2018) Representación y representatividad sindical: puntos críticos y propuesta de reforma, Papeles de Economía Española, 156, 18–27.

Las Heras J. (2018) Unions as 'managers of precariousness': the entrenchment of micro-corporatism in the Spanish automotive industry and its drawbacks, Employee Relations, 40 (6), 1054–1071.

Las Heras J. and Ribera Almandoz O. (2017) When corporatism fails: trade union strategies and grassroots resistance to the Spanish economic crisis, Journal of Labor and Society, 20 (4), 449–466.

Linz J.J. and Stepan A.C. (1996) Toward consolidated democracies, Journal of Democracy, 7 (2), 14–33.

López-Andreu M. (2020) Breaking fragmentation through mobilization: the development of a collective identity during Movistar's contractors' and technicians' strike in Spain, Work, Employment and Society, 34 (4), 661–677.

Luque Balbona D. and González Begega S. (2017) Declive de las huelgas y cambios en el repertorio de protesta en España, Arxius de sociologia, 36–37, 97–109.

Martínez Lucio M. (1987) El sindicalismo madrileño en un contexto de cambio, Alfoz: Madrid, territorio, economía y sociedad, 36–37, 44–50.

Martínez Lucio M. (1990) Trade unions and communism in Spain: the role of the CCOO in the political projects of the left, Journal of Communist Studies, 6 (4), 80–99.

Martínez Lucio M. (1991) Employer identity and the politics of the labour market in Spain, West European Politics, 14 (1), 41–55.

Martínez Lucio M. (1998) Spain: regulating employment and social fragmentation, in Ferner A. and Hyman R. (eds) Changing industrial relations in Europe, 2nd edn, Oxford, Blackwell, 426–458.

Martínez Lucio M. (2011) From action to communication? Explaining the changing context of worker occupations as direct forms of action with reference to the case of contemporary Spain, Employee Relations, 33 (6), 654–669.

Martínez Lucio M. (2016) Incertidumbre, indecisión y neoliberalismo emergente. El papel dual y complejo del Estado español en las relaciones laborales y de empleo, Sociología de Trabajo, 87, 68–88.

Martínez Lucio M. (2017) Organising without knowing it? The curious case of para-organising-style campaigns in southern Europe and the case of trade union elections in Spain, Transfer, 23 (1), 89–94.

Martínez Lucio M. and Connolly H. (2012) Transformation and continuities in urban struggles: urban politics, trade unions and migration in Spain, Urban Studies, 49 (3), 669–684.

Martínez Lucio M. and Hamann K. (2007) Trade union revitalisation in Spain, in Phelan C. (ed.) Trade union revitalisation: trends and prospects in 34 countries, Oxford, Peter Lang, 61–78.

Martínez Lucio M., Marino S. and Connolly H. (2013) Broadening and reimagining regulation: trade unions, 'active servicing' and immigration in Spain since the early 1990s, Journal of Industrial Relations, 55 (2), 190–211.

Martínez Lucio M. and Mustchin S. (2019) The politics and diversity of worker representation: the increasing fluidity and challenge of representation, in Gall G. (ed.) The handbook of the politics of labour, work and employment, Cheltenham, Edward Elgar Publishing, 144–160.

Meardi G (2014) Employment relations under external pressure: Italian and Spanish reforms in 2010–12, in Hauptmeier M. and Vidal M. (eds) Comparative political economy of work, Basingstoke, Palgrave Macmillan, pp. 332–350.

Mejías García A. (2017) La falacia de las subvenciones sindicales, Arxius de sociologia, 36–37, 143–150.

Molina O. (2005) Political exchange and bargaining reform in Italy and Spain, European Journal of Industrial Relations, 11 (1), 7–26.

Molina O. (2006) Trade union strategies and change in neo-corporatist concertation: a new century of political exchange? West European Politics, 29 (4), 640–664.

Molina O. (2007) State and regulation of industrial relations in Spain: old wine in a new governance bottle?, South European Society & Politics, 12 (4), 461–479.

Molina O. (2014) Self-regulation and the state in industrial relations in Southern Europe: back to the future?, European Journal of Industrial Relations, 20 (1), 21–36.

Molina O. and Barranco O. (2016) Trade union strategies to enhance strike effectiveness in Italy and Spain, Transfer, 22 (3), 383–399.

Molina O. and Rhodes M. (2011) Spain: from tripartite to bipartite pacts, in Avdagic S., Rhodes M. and Visser J. (eds) Social pacts in Europe: emergence, evolution, and institutionalization, Oxford, Oxford University Press, 174–202.

Morell M.F. (2012) The free culture and 15M movements in Spain: composition, social networks and synergies, Social Movement Studies, 11 (3–4), 386–392.

Ortíz Vargas F.J. (2011) Legitimidad y financiación de los sindicatos considerados 'más representativos' en España, CNT, 10 May 2011. https://fcs-villaverde.cnt.es/wp-content/uploads/2016/07/spcc-formacion-material-legitimidad-y-financiacion-sindicatos.pdf

Pérez, S.A. (2010) Social pacts in Spain: from post-EMU boom to bust in Pochet, P., Keune, M., and Natali, D. (eds) After the euro and enlargement: social pacts in the EU Brussels: ETUI, 161–190

Pérez Ortiz L., Fernández Rodríguez C.J., Ibáñez Rojo R., Ferrer Sais A., Alonso L.E. and Ruesga S. (2018) Un análisis sobre el diálogo social en la perspectiva regional, Revista de derecho de la seguridad social, Revista de Derecho de la Seguridad Social. Laborum, 14, 257–281.

Prosser T. (2019) European labour movements in crisis: from indecision to indifference, Manchester, Manchester University Press.

Raventós D. and Casassas D. (2003) La renta básica y el poder de negociación de 'los que viven con permiso de otros', Revista Internacional de Sociología, 61 (34), 187–201.

Rigby M. (2002) Spanish trade unions and the provision of continuous training: partnership at a distance, Employee Relations, 24 (5), 500–515.

Rigby M. and Ponce Sanz Y. (2016) International briefing 34: training and development in Spain, International Journal of Training and Development, 20 (4), 302–314.

Roca B. and Las Heras J. (2020) Trade unions as retaining walls against political change: a Gramscian approach to remunicipalisation policies in a Spanish City, Capital & Class, 44 (1), 3–25.

Roca Jusmet J. (1991) La concertación social, in Miguélez F. and Prieto C. (eds) Las Relaciones Laborales en España, Madrid, Siglo XXI, 361–377.

Roca Martínez B. and Díaz Parra I. (2012) De la tierra a los supermercados: el SAT como ejemplo de particularismo militante y de renovación sindical, Anuario del conflicto social, 2, 855–875.

Rocha F. (2014) Crisis and austerity policies in Spain: towards an authoritarian model of industrial relations, in Rocha F (ed.) The new EU economic governance and its impact on the national collective bargaining systems, Madrid, Fundacion 1° de Mayo, 175–206.

Rodríguez Fernández M.L. (2018) Sindicalismo y negociación colectiva 4.0, Temas laborales: Revista andaluza de trabajo y bienestar social, 144, 27–42.

Sampedro V. and Lobera J. (2014) The Spanish 15-M Movement: a consensual dissent?, Journal of Spanish Cultural Studies, 15 (1–2), 61–80. https://doi.org/10.1080/14636204.2014.938466

Sechi C. (2007) Women in trade unions in Europe: bridging the gaps, Brussels, ETUC.

Sigfrido M. and Ramírez Pérez S.M. (2017) Iberian trade unions and the ETUC: from the periphery to the centre, in Ciampani A. and Tilly P. (eds) National trade unions and the ETUC: a history of unity and diversity, Brussels, ETUI, 139–160.

Smith W.R. (1998) The left's dirty job: the politics of industrial restructuring in France and Spain, Pittsburgh, University of Pittsburgh Press.

Sola J. (2013) La desregulación laboral en España (1984–1997): recursos de poder y remercantilización del trabajo, Madrid, Universidad Complutense de Madrid.

Spanish Quality of Life at Work Survey (2010) https://www.mites.gob.es/estadisticas/ecvt/welcome.htm.

Tormey S. and Feenstra R.A. (2015) Reinventing the political party in Spain: the case of 15M and the Spanish mobilisations, Policy Studies, 36 (6), 590–606.

Torns T. and Recio C. (2011) Las mujeres y el sindicalismo: avances y retos ante las transformaciones laborales y sociales, Gaceta sindical: reflexión y debate, 16, 241–258.

Vidal S., Alós R., Beneyto P.J. and Jódar P. (2016) La afiliación a CC.OO: evolución, estructuras y trayectorias, Informes 123, Madrid, Fundación 1º de Mayo.

Visser J. (2019) Can unions revitalize themselves?, International Journal of Labour Research, 9 (1/2), 17–48.

Waddington J. (2019) United Kingdom: a long-term assault on collective bargaining, in Müller T., Vandaele K. and Waddington J. (eds.) Collective bargaining in Europe: towards an endgame, Brussels, ETUI, 605–624.

Abbreviations

CCOO Comisiones Obreras (Workers' Commissions)

CEOE Confederación Española de Organizacionez Organizaciones Empresariales (Spanish Confederation of Employers Organizations)

CGT Confederación General de Trabajadores (General Confederation of Labour)

CIG Confederación Intersindical Galega (Galician Unions Confederacy)

CNT Confederación Nacional de Trabajadores (National Confederation of Labour)

CSIF Central Sindical Independiente y de Funcionarios (Civil Servants' Independent Trade Union)

ECVT Encuesta de Calidad de Vida en el Trabajo (Quality of Life at Work Survey)

ELA Eusko Langileen Alkartasuna (Basque Workers' Solidarity)

ETUC European Trade Union Confederation

IU Izquierda Unida (United Left)

LAB Langile Abertzaleen Batzordeak (Nationalist Workers' Committees)

PCE Partido Comunista de España (Spanish Communist Party)

PSOE Partido Socialista Obrero Español (Spanish Socialist Workers Party)

UGT Unión General de Trabajadores (General Union of Workers)

USO Unión Sindical Obrera (Workers' Trade Union)

Chapter 28

Trade unions in Sweden: still high union density, but widening gaps by social category and national origin

Anders Kjellberg

Swedish industrial relations are considered to be peaceful with a high membership density among both trade unions and employers' associations. Seven out of ten employees are union members, and nine out of ten employees work at employers affiliated to an employers' association. This high union density is promoted by several factors. First, as in Denmark and Finland, there is the presence of state-supported union unemployment funds, commonly known as the 'Ghent system'. Second, the partly centralized and partly decentralized industrial relations system prevents fragmentary collective bargaining coverage, while the extensive network of shop stewards and 'union clubs' facilitates recruitment. Sweden has a single-channel system of union representation that relies on industry agreements in a multi-tier bargaining system. Third, there is a high organizational rate among employers' associations, which conclude basic agreements and other compromises with the unions. Fourth, the socially segregated union structure, with separate national unions and confederations for blue-collar workers, academics and other white-collar workers, promote cohesion within each group. Fifth, the dominance of self-regulation via collective agreements over state regulation means that unions have a clear role (Kjellberg 2017). One prominent aspect of this self-regulation is that, despite the absence of extension mechanisms, 90 per cent of employees are covered by collective agreements. This is also facilitated by the high organizational rate of employers' associations, mentioned above (see Table 28.1). The closest Swedish equivalent to an extension mechanism is, as in Denmark, the permissibility of strikes and sympathy strikes against non-organized employers who refuse to conclude a collective agreement. Another aspect of Swedish self-regulation is the absence of statutory minimum wages. Sixth, we might mention the relative absence of anti-union legislation, including on industrial action. And finally, long periods of social democratic government (1932–1976, 1982–1990, 1994–2006 and 2014–2022) have been driven the expansion of the welfare state, and the extensive pro-labour legislation introduced during the 1970s. Although breaking with the principle of self-regulation, the laws on codetermination and employment protection extended the area of workplace negotiations to new issues. Likewise, the law on shop stewards strengthened unions at workplace level.

Table 28.1 Principal characteristics of trade unionism in Sweden

	1980	2000	2020
Total trade union membership	3,512,600	3,846,700	3,713,600
Women as a proportion of active membership	46 %	52 %	53 %
Gross union density	83 %	88 %	68 %
Net union density	82 %	81 %	64 %
Net union density (labour force surveys)	81 % (1990)	81 %	69 %**
Number of confederations	3	3	3
Number of affiliated unions (federations)	71	61	48
Number of independent unions	7	7	5
Collective bargaining coverage	90 %	88 %	90 %
Principal level of collective bargaining	Cross-industry	Industry	Industry
Days not worked due to industrial action per 1,000 workers**	1,131	0	0

Note: *4.2 million days were not worked in the 'Great Conflict' of 1980. There was no large bargaining round in 2000. ** 70 % in 2021.

Source: Kjellberg (2022a, 2022b); Hällberg and Kjellström (2020).

Although union density is still among the highest in the world, based on the labour force surveys, it declined from 81 per cent in 2000 to 68 per cent in 2019, but turned upwards, for the first time since the mid-1990s, to 69 per cent in 2020 (Labour Force Surveys; Figure 28.2). As in Denmark and Finland, the remodelling of the Ghent system played a conspicuous role in the deterioration of union density, by considerably raising unemployment fund membership fees in Sweden in 2007–2013 when the centre-right government was in power. Because of the linkage of fees to unemployment among the members of each fund, blue-collar workers were particularly hard hit as their unemployment levels tend to be higher than those of white-collar workers. The result was a growing gap between white-collar and blue-collar union density. A further contributory factor to the blue-collar/white-collar divergence is the higher frequency of supplementary union income insurance available to white-collar workers. This is particularly attractive because white-collar workers' incomes are generally higher. The declining share of blue-collar workers in the labour force, combined with the growing gap between white-collar and blue-collar union density, has resulted in a power shift within the union movement from blue-collar to white-collar unions. Another difference in union density rates has emerged since 2006: union density is higher among domestic-born workers (71 per cent) than foreign-born workers (59 per cent). Many of the latter arrived as refugees during the 2010s from non-European countries with weak union traditions and several have fixed-term jobs in low-density industries, such as cleaning and restaurants.

Historical background and principal features of the industrial relations system

Until the 1930s Sweden was among the countries with the highest frequency of strikes and lockouts in the world. This changed during that decade, when a long period of social democratic government began. State-supported union unemployment funds, known as the 'Ghent system', were introduced in 1935. Although it was not obligatory for members of the unemployment funds to join the 'corresponding' trade union, direct affiliation to the funds did not become common until the economic boom of the late 1980s. Then, white-collar workers opted for direct affiliation, a practice that later spread to blue-collar workers and public sector employees. The Saltsjöbaden Agreement was concluded in 1938 between the blue-collar Swedish Trade Union Confederation (LO, *Landsorganisationen*, founded in 1898) and the Swedish Employers' Confederation (SAF, *Svenska Arbetsgivareföreningen*, founded in 1902). The agreement radically improved relations between the two sides of industry, manifested in the 'spirit of Saltsjöbaden' and the considerably reduced frequency of strikes and lockouts. Confrontation was replaced by a cooperative relationship between unions and employers. The centralization of LO in 1941 abolished balloting, thereby making it more difficult to start strikes in an effort to restrain more militant members.

There was space only for *representative* union democracy from then on, as union executive committees made decisions on industrial action. Also, the Law on Rights of Association and Negotiation (*Lag om förenings- och förhandlingsrätt*) of 1936 paved the way for union rights among private sector white-collar workers.

On the initiative of the employers, collective agreements were concluded at peak level from the 1950s onwards, supplemented by agreements at industry and workplace levels. With the growth of trade unions in the public sector and white-collar cartels, collective bargaining from the 1970s became quite complicated and the LO-SAF axis lost its privileged position. That also prevented SAF from transforming the 'Great Conflict' of 1980 into an 'investment for the future' aimed at stopping the wage-price spiral. Ten years later SAF changed strategy, however, and refused to participate in centralized wage negotiations. The ambition was to achieve completely decentralized and individualized wage setting arrangements. To prevent such a profound shift the largest trade unions in manufacturing formed a common cross-collar and cross-confederal front. This was extended to 'Unions in Manufacturing' (FI, *Facken inom industrin*) in 1996.

Under threat of state intervention to scale down wage increases, before Sweden joined the European Economic and Monetary Union (EMU), the 'Industry Agreement' (*Industriavtalet*) was signed in 1997. This agreement is the result of close cooperation between the blue-collar and white-collar unions in manufacturing and their negotiations with the employers. Sweden ultimately declined to join EMU, but a new form of coordinated bargaining was established. The 'Industry Agreement' involves blue-collar and white-collar unions cooperating closely when setting the benchmark for wage increases, known as the 'industry norm', in negotiations with employers at industry level. Under pressure from the Social Democratic government, the Industry Agreement was considered necessary, also by the labour market parties themselves, to maintain Swedish competitiveness by letting manufacturing set the 'industry norm' for the whole labour market (Kjellberg 2019). In this context, it is worth mentioning that large transnational companies, such as ABB, Electrolux, Ericsson and Volvo, dominate the Swedish economy. Another reason for agreeing to wage moderation was the unions' fear that the employers would accelerate the relocation of production to other countries.[1] All in

1 In 2018, 84 per cent of the employees working for the 80 largest Swedish-owned manufacturing groups were employed abroad (Kjellberg 2021c).

all, the spirit of cooperation was restored after being eroded during the 1970s wave of union-friendly legislation.

Structure of trade unions and union democracy

Sweden has the most class-based union structure in the world. Common to other Nordic countries is the division into three confederations: the blue-collar LO, the Swedish Confederation of Professional Employees (TCO, *Tjänstemännens Centralorganisation*, founded in 1944) and the Swedish Confederation of Professional Associations (Saco, *Sveriges Akademikers Centralorganisation*, founded in 1947).[2] The strong dominance of blue-collar unions in LO-Sweden is partly related to the broad Swedish definition of blue-collar workers or *arbetare* (Kjellberg 2014). For instance, practical nurses and health care assistants, organized in the LO-affiliated union Municipal Workers' Union (*Kommunal*), but also most restaurant employees and sales employees are, in official statistics, included under *arbetare*. TCO-affiliated unions represent 1.1 million active members, which is slightly fewer than the figure for LO affiliates (1.2 million). The most important independent union is the Association of Managerial and Professional Staff, *Ledarna* (managers and supervisors). *Ledarna* was expelled from TCO in 1997 as a result of a demarcation conflict arising from the union's ambition to recruit all managers. There are some other independent unions, although they are smaller, such as the Dock Workers' Union (*Hamnarbetarförbundet*), a breakaway from Transport (*Transportarbetareförbundet*), and the 'syndicalist' Swedish Central Organization of Workers (SAC, *Sveriges Arbetares Centralorganisation*), a general union founded after the LO defeat in the great 1909 strike/lockout. Both these unions consider ballots and local decision-making to be essential for union democracy.

Apart from the *Ledarna* case, because of the generally rising educational requirements, there is also intense membership competition between the large 'vertical' TCO unions (*Unionen*, *Vision* and *Fackförbundet ST* [Union of Civil Servants]), which organize all kinds of white-collar workers from the lowest to the highest grades, and the professional unions affiliated to Saco. *Unionen* has nevertheless expanded

---

2 This pattern is most pronounced in Sweden, in particular since LO-Denmark merged with the white-collar confederation corresponding to TCO.

much more than any other union during the past ten years. Conflicts about membership domains between other unions are muted, however. In fact, several unions affiliated to different confederations cooperate for bargaining purposes in different 'constellations' or alliances. Thus, the constellation, 'Unions in Manufacturing' (FI, *Facken inom industrin*) comprises the LO affiliates IF Metall, *GS-Facket* (graphical and wood workers) and *Livs* (food workers). The '6F Alliance' consists of five LO affiliates organizing building workers (*Byggnads*), painters (*Målarna*), electricians (*Elektrikerna*), maintenance workers (*Fastighets*) and communication workers (*Seko*). The 'Academic Alliance' (*AkademikerAlliansen*) is the negotiation council for Saco unions in local government. Other constellations are the Teachers' Collaboration Council (LS, *Lärarnas Samverkansråd*), the Public Employees` Negotiation Council (OFR, *Offentliganställdas Förhandlingsråd*), the alliance of the private sector white-collar unions (PTK, *Förhandlings- och Samverkansrådet PTK*) and the bargaining cartel of central government Saco unions (Saco-S). Finally, also the Swedish Teachers' Union (*Lärarförbundet*), affiliated to TCO, and the National Union of Teachers in Sweden (LR, *Lärarnas Riksförbund*) cooperate in collective bargaining in the joint Teachers' Collaboration Council. Those unions merged in 1 January 2023 into the Swedish Teachers' Union (*Sveriges Lärare*) (Kjellberg 2021c).

LO has the authority to adjudicate on demarcation conflicts, but not to decide about mergers. Thus, all mergers were initiated by the trade unions concerned. Although no merger has taken place between a blue-collar and white-collar union, the number of LO unions has decreased from eighteen in 2000 to fourteen in 2021 (Kjellberg 2005, 2022b). Of them only three (electricians, painters, and musicians) are occupational unions, comprising just 3 per cent of LO represented members. The unions organizing electricians and painters, respectively, are the only craft unions in Sweden. Every third union member in 2020 was represented by an occupational or professional union compared with fewer than every fifth member in 1980 in Sweden. The growth of employees with a higher education is the main explanation of this. The increasing membership share of occupational and professional unions in TCO has turned into its opposite due to the rapid growth of *Unionen*. This union surpassed *Kommunal* (LO) as Sweden's largest union in 2015. Finally, all Saco affiliates are professional unions. Almost all of them can be considered 'multi-professional' because of mergers and the broader scope of recruitment. In fact, one of them, SRAT, contains so many small professions that it might be labelled a 'general union of professions'.

Figure 28.1 provides an overview of union mergers in Sweden since 2000. The largest of them is the founding of *Unionen* in 2008 by a merger of the TCO union of white-collar workers in manufacturing (Sif, *Svenska Industritjänstemannaförbundet*) and that in commerce and other private services (HTF, *Handelstjänstemannaförbundet*). An important reason for this was to prevent the employers from playing off the members of the two unions against each other when jobs were outsourced from manufacturing to services. The decreasing number of manufacturing workers in the labour force in 2006 caused the LO unions *Metall* and *Industrifacket* (the Industrial Union) to merge into *Industrifacket Metall* (IF Metall). Instead of competing for the same category of members the Saco unions *Jusek* (recruiting lawyers, economists and other professions) and *Civilekonomerna* (economists) merged on 1 January 2020 to form *Akavia*, the eighth largest Swedish union. Mergers are often aimed at compensating for declining membership, making it possible to act more effectively with sparse resources, strengthen the ability to influence public opinion, increase visibility in media and avoid membership competition. Name changes are part of branding strategies. Unions have abandoned names containing *tjänstemän* (white-collar workers) and *arbetare* (blue-collar workers) and have adopted new names, such as *Unionen*, *Vision* and *IF Metall*. Lastly, since 2000 only one breakaway has occurred: maritime officers from *Ledarna* became a Saco union in 2016.

Figure 28.1 Mergers in Swedish unionism, 2000–2020

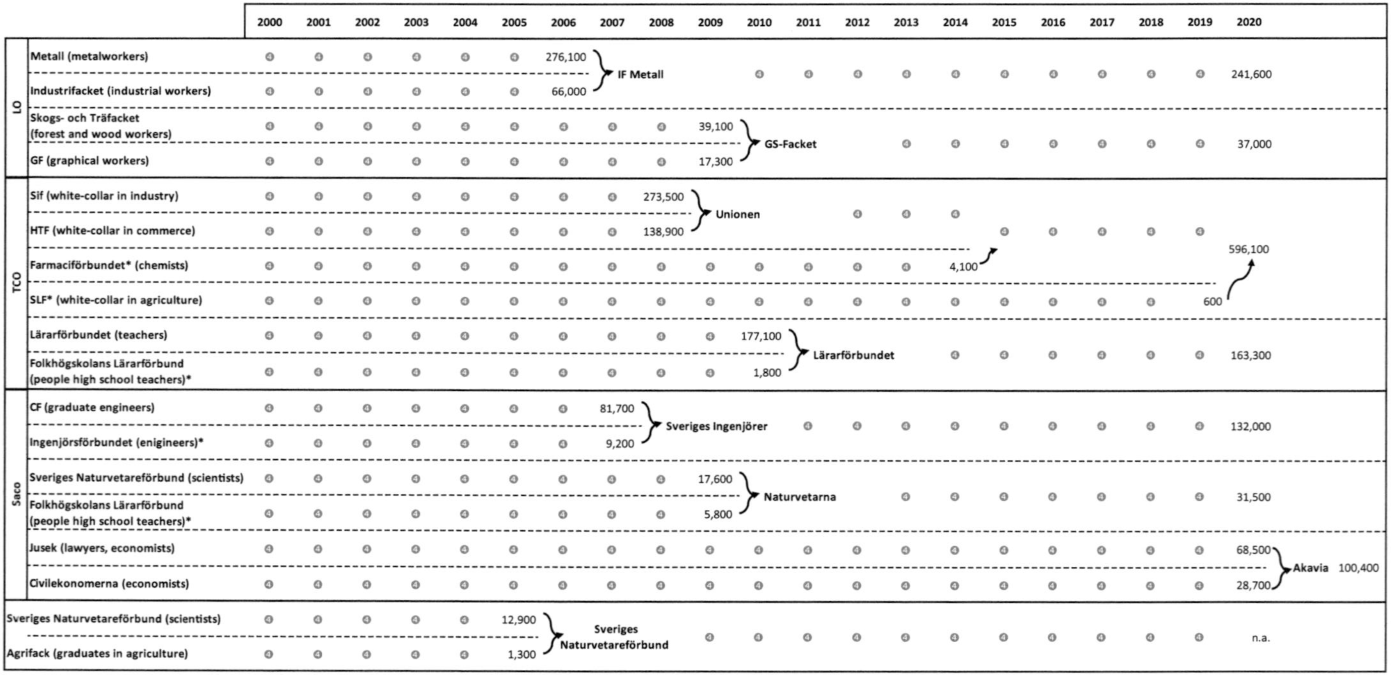

Note: * Acquisition.
Source: Kjellberg (2022b).

Table 28.2 lists the twenty largest unions based on their active membership. The table also provides information about their share of female members and organizing domain and constellation. The four largest LO unions – *Kommunal, IF Metall, Handels* and *Byggnads* – account for 78 per cent of all LO members. In 2020, the LO union *IF Metall* had 241,600 active members, and together with the other LO unions in the constellation 'FI', this makes up a quarter of LO-affiliated members. Although this is less than the half million *Kommunal* members (42 per cent), it is more than the '6F Alliance', which together represents 16 per cent. Among the remaining LO-affiliated unions *Handels* (commercial employees), *Transport,* HRF (hotel and restaurant workers) and *Pappers* (paper workers) account for another 18 per cent. To understand the strength of *IF Metall,* it should be observed that the cross-collar and cross-confederal Unions in Manufacturing, to which *IF Metall* belongs, includes Sweden's largest union, *Unionen* (596,100 members, TCO) and the largest Saco union, the Association of Graduate Engineers (*Sveriges Ingenjörer,* 132,000 members). That totals 1,029,500 members, or a third of Swedish unionists. All three unions were founded by mergers in the new millennium: *IF Metall* (2006), *Sveriges Ingenjörer* (2007) and *Unionen* (2008). *Unionen* organizes more than half of the TCO-affiliated membership. Together with *Lärarförbundet* (163,300 teachers), *Vision* (143,100 municipal employees) and *Vårdförbundet* (92,400 nurses), the four largest TCO unions comprise almost 90 per cent of all TCO-affiliated members. Within Saco (561,300 members) the four largest unions – *Sveriges Ingenjörer* (132,000 graduate engineers), *Akavia* (100,400 lawyers and economists), LR (64,600 teachers) and *Akademikerförbundet SSR* (59,400 social workers and the like) – represent two-thirds of all active Saco-affiliated members. Not even the large vertical and heterogeneous unions contain special sections or associations representing different groups, but the independent and multi-occupational union *Ledarna* functions similarly to the multi-professional Saco-affiliated union SRAT.

Table 28.2 The twenty largest national unions by confederation, 31 December 2020

Confederation	Union	Industry	Constellation	Active members	Female share (%)
LO	Kommunal	Municipal and private services	none	518,800	78
	IF Metall	Metal, chemical	FI	241,600	19
	Handels	Retail and wholesale	none	129,300	62
	Byggnads	Construction	6F	76,000	2
	Seko	Railways, post	6F	70,900	25
	Transport	Transport	none	48,800	17
	GS-facket	Graphics, wood	FI	37,000	18
	Hotell & Restaurang	Hospitality	None	26,500	57
TCO	Unionen	Manufacturing and services	FI, PTK	596,300	44
	Lärarförbundet	Teachers	OFR, PTK, LS	163,300	84
	Vision	Municipal and private services	OFR	143,100	72
	Vårdförbundet	Nurses, midwifes and biomedical analysts	OFR, PTK	92,400	89
	Fackförbundet ST	Civil servants	OFR	67,100	62
Saco	Sveriges Ingenjörer	Graduate engineers	FI, PTK, Akad., Saco-S	132,400	28
	Akavia	Lawyers, economists	PTK, Akad., Saco-S	100,400	58
	Lärarnas Riksförbund	Teachers	OFR, PTK, LS, Saco-S	64,600	70
	Akademikerförbundet SSR	Social workers, HR personnel	OFR, PTK, Saco-S	59,400	81
	Läkarförbundet	Swedish Medical Association	OFR, PTK, Saco-S	38,400	54
	Naturvetarna	University graduates in natural sciences	PTK, Saco-S, Akad.	31,500	64
Independent unions	Ledarna	Supervisors/ managers	PTK, OFR	95,800	33

Note: Unemployed included. Pensioners and students excluded.

Source: Kjellberg (2022b).

At large and middle-sized workplaces it is common that the union members are represented by a 'union club' (*fackklubb*, in engineering called a 'workshop club', *verkstadsklubb*), or more correctly, one club for each of the national unions with sufficient members willing to be elected club president, cashier or other posts. For example, at the Södertälje plant of the German-owned truck manufacturer Scania there is an *IF Metall* club, a *Unionen* club and a local Saco association for graduate engineers, economists and other university graduates. Also *Ledarna* has a local association at Scania. As the headquarters of the company and the research department are also located at Södertälje, there is a very large number of white-collar workers, which explains why the *Unionen* club has about eight full-time officials paid by the company. According to law, union representatives have the right to paid time off for union work at their workplace, the scope and timing of which are decided in local negotiations. At workplaces that do not meet the conditions for establishing union clubs (usually because of their small size and too few members) the union at best might have one or two workplace representatives (*arbetsplatsombud*), assisted by union officials (*ombudsmän*) from the regional union branch. The regional safety representatives obtain more than €10 million per year from the state for their work in small companies without their own safety representatives.

Representative democracy is a characteristic feature of the Swedish trade union movement. For example, LO's highest decision-making body is the Congress (*LO-kongressen*), which elects the Executive Council (*LOs styrelse*) and the general council (*Representantskapet*), the highest level decision-making body between Congresses. The 300 delegates to the LO Congress are appointed by the affiliated unions according to size. Similarly, the 300 delegates to the IF Metall Congress are elected by the local union branches, more precisely by their general councils, which, in turn, are elected by union clubs. No LO-affiliated union holds ballots among its members during the bargaining process. Assemblies of elected representatives take all decisions. The TCO unions of nurses and teachers sometimes arrange advisory ballots. In October 2021 a number of large journalists' clubs demanded in motions to the congress of the Union of Journalists (*Journalistförbundet*, also TCO) a ballot on whether the union should sign the new basic agreement between the Bargaining and Cooperation Council PTK, to which the union is affiliated, and the employer confederation SN. If at least 50 per cent of the members vote, then the ballot will be decision-making; otherwise, it is only advisory.

Finally, Saco unions elect delegates to the Saco congress, which appoints the executive council of the confederation.

Unionization

Swedish trade unions had 3.7 million members in 2020, including students and pensioners. This is a decrease of 3 per cent since 2000. Net union membership, excluding pensioners and students but including the unemployed, has declined from 3.2 million in 2000 to 3.1 million members in 2020. In contrast to non-Ghent countries members retain their membership in case of unemployment. Unions seldom provide information on how many of their members are unemployed, however. Membership development differs between union confederations, however (see Figure 28.2). Since 2000 LO affiliates have lost 511,000 active members, while TCO affiliates have increased by 98,600 and Saco

Figure 28.2 Total membership per union confederation, comparing 2000 with 2020

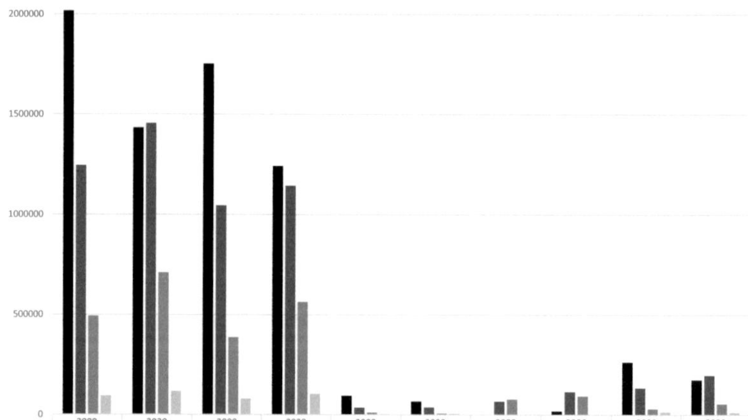

	Total membership		Active membership		Unemployed		Students		Pensioners	
	2000	2020	2000	2020	2000	2020	2000	2020	2000	2020
LO	2016200	1432900	1753100	1241800	94600	65700	1000	17000	262100	174100
TCO	1244600	1454700	1045500	1144100	35000	36800	66200	114200	132900	196400
Saco	492700	709400	386200	562700	10900	6300	76700	92900	29800	53800
Independent unions	93700	116600	78900	104300	4000	5400	100	1000	14700	11300

LO TCO Saco Independent unions

Note: Unemployed included in active members. Unemployed in LO, TCO and independent unions calculated from the rate of unemployment in their unemployment funds. Saco: statistics from the unemployment fund of academics.
Source: Data obtained from trade unions.

affiliates by 206,000. LO's 'market share' dropped from 54 per cent in 2000 to 41 per cent in 2020, while TCO increased its share from 32 to 37 per cent and Saco from 11 to 18 per cent in the same period. Two-thirds of employed union members were white-collar workers in 2020. The growing share of white-collar workers in the labour force, combined since 2007 with the larger drop in blue-collar union density, considerably reduced LO's share of active union members, including the unemployed, between 2000 and 2020.

TCO and Saco together exceeded LO in 2008. The total number of members represented by TCO for the first time surpassed that of LO in 2019, but LO affiliates still have more active members. In other words, TCO pensioners and students are together now more numerous than those in LO. Also, TCO-affiliated unions recruit more students than Saco affiliates today, reflecting the intense competition between the two white-collar confederations on university campuses. Lastly, although the independent unions have seen some growth in their active and passive memberships, their 'market share' has remained at around 3 per cent. In general, 40 per cent of union members were employed in the public sector in 2000 and 36 per cent in 2020. In Saco this accounts for as much as 54 per cent of its members, but in the independent unions (dominated by *Ledarna*) the figure is only 22 per cent (see Table 28.3). The decline is explained by the transformation of many public authorities into companies, privatizations and outsourcing. The growing share of union members represented by Saco affiliates has a positive impact on the average public sector share.

Table 28.3 Public sector share of active members per union confederation, 2000–2020

	LO (%)	TCO (%)	Saco (%)	Independent (%)	Total (%)
2000	33	48	65	7	40
2010	32	44	57	13	39
2020	30	35	54	22	36

Note: Employees in companies owned by central or local government are classified as private sector employees. Active members include unemployed. Saco excluding the union of military reserve officers. Saco excluding self-employed in 2000.

Source: Kjellberg (2022b).

Although union density is still high today, it has declined considerably since 2000: from 81 to 69 per cent in 2020 (see Figure 28.3). In a 'Ghent' country such as Sweden, the number of union members and density usually increase in recessions, but the global financial crisis of 2007–2008 had no such effects as the crisis occurred during the period (2007–2013) in which the centre-right government substantially raised the membership fees for unemployment funds and abolished tax reductions for union fees (25 per cent) and fund fees (40 per cent) (Kjellberg 2011; Kjellberg and Ibsen 2016). During 2007 and 2008 the unions lost 245,000 active members (180,000 from LO affiliates) and the union unemployment funds about 400,000 members, in particular during 2007. Union density declined from 77 to 71 per cent in the short period from 2006 to 2008.

The fees for blue-collar workers were hardest hit; total fees for membership of both a trade union and the corresponding unemployment fund could be very high. This is the main explanation for the increasing divergence between blue-collar and white-collar union density during the period when fund contributions were hiked (2007–2013). Union density was 77 per cent among both blue-collar and white-collar workers in 2006, but by 2020 the respective figures were only 61 per cent among blue-collar workers and 73 per cent among white-collar workers. Furthermore, union insurance provide supplementary unemployment benefits in addition to those from unemployment funds. Access to these supplementary benefits presupposes membership of both a union and an unemployment fund, and also that the wage is above the ceiling of the fund insurance. The higher wage is, the more a union member will obtain from supplementary income insurance. Such union income insurance is more common among and more favourable for white-collar workers, which explains the exceptional membership growth in the private sector white-collar *Unionen*.

When unemployment rose rapidly during the Covid-19 pandemic and the government made unemployment insurance more generous, the Ghent effect broke through with great force: people joined unions and particularly unemployment funds on a massive scale. During March and April 2020, the number of active union members increased by about 58,000 (Kjellberg 2020). The union unemployment funds grew three times more or by 177,600 persons. In all, the number of union members grew by 69,900 in 2020, of which LO affiliates accounted for 19,000, TCO affiliates 34,300 and Saco affiliates 14,800. As a result of the changed mode of calculation in the Building Workers' Union, however, real union growth was 75,100, of which LO affiliates contributed 24,200. Union density among white-collar and blue-collar workers increased by 1 percentage point in 2020.

Figure 28.3 Net union density for all employees, blue-collar and white-collar workers, 2000–2020

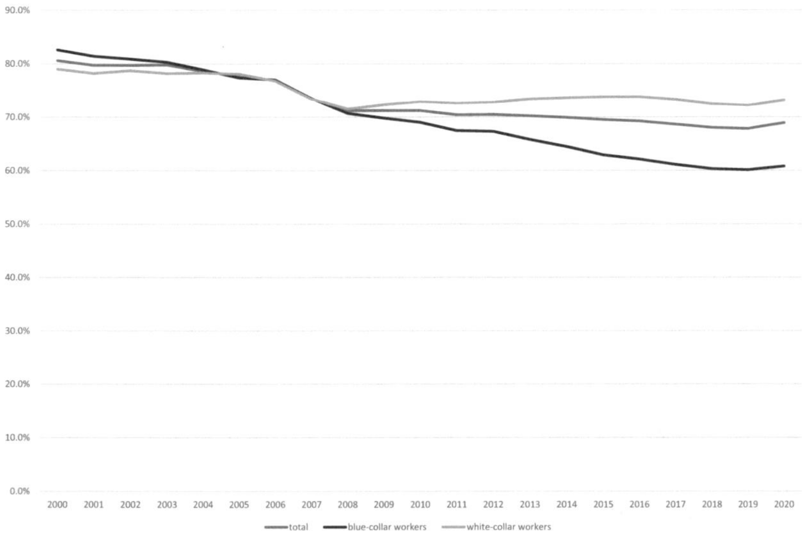

Note: Employees aged 16– 64 years, excluding employed full- time students.
Source: Labour force surveys.

The overall female share of active members was about the same in 2000 and 2020 (52/53 per cent), but increased in Saco affiliates, from 48 to 56 per cent, reflecting the feminization of higher education, and decreased from 63 to 58 per cent in TCO; the percentage has remained stable in LO (48 per cent). Furthermore, young people are overrepresented among blue-collar workers and in the most insecure employment forms, such as hospitality. Half of employees aged 16–24 have a fix-termed job compared with about 33 per cent during the early 1990s as legislative amendments in the early 2000s made it easier for employers to hire workers on a fixed-time basis and in the most insecure forms. Seven out of ten employees in the same age group are blue-collar workers. Often in low-paid jobs in private sector services, they have a limited capacity to pay contributions to unions and unemployment funds. Therefore, the sharply raised contributions to unemployment funds from 2007 hit the youngest workers hardest. Between 2006 and 2008 their union density dropped from 46 to 36 per cent and has remained almost unchanged ever since.

Apart from young people, immigrants are also overrepresented among blue-collar workers. The overall share of foreign-born members increased between 2003 and 2020 from 11 to 18 per cent. Growth in specific unions was as follows: from 14 to 26 per cent in LO (reflecting the growing share of blue-collar workers born abroad); from 7 to 15 per cent in TCO; from 8 to 15 per cent in Saco; and from 6 per cent in 2005 to 11 per cent in 2020 in the independent unions. While the unionization rate of domestic- and foreign-born blue-collar workers in 2006 was the same (77 per cent), this has changed today: 64 per cent of domestic-born blue-collar workers were unionized by 2020 but only 52 per cent of foreign-born blue-collar. Union density among foreign-born blue-collar workers has fallen twice as much as among native-born since 2006, and three times more between 2013 and 2018, when 375,000 refugees arrived in Sweden and increased their share of employees. In contrast to most other countries, asylum seekers have the right to work during the application process. Their low rate of unionization is also influenced by the fact that the large majority arriving in the past ten to fifteen years are from non-European countries with a limited knowledge of unions and collective agreements in general and of the Swedish labour market in particular. Furthermore, foreign-born blue-collar workers are overrepresented in private services such as hospitality and cleaning. These industries are characterized by small companies with no collective agreements and with a low union density in general (Frödin and Kjellberg 2018, 2020).

A range of strategies have been employed to address membership decline. Responding to sharp membership losses in 2007 and 2008, TCO launched the project 'The Value of Union Membership', which continued under the name 'The Union Is Changing Now'. The target group was the growing category of academics, whom TCO wanted to recruit as successfully as Saco. TCO also campaigned for 'the value of collective agreements'. Suffering even larger membership losses, before 2007 LO had implemented a strategy of contacting non-members at their workplaces and supported shop stewards in this task. For the LO unions recruitment is obstructed by the large proportion of blue-collar workers with fixed-term jobs (21 per cent in 2020), part-time employees (32 per cent in 2020), young workers or workers born abroad (29 per cent in 2020), or a combination of these structural features. Despite the recruitment of very large numbers of members, for example in restaurants, union density may remain the same or even decline because of high labour turnover. For many years representatives of LO-affiliated unions have visited schools to inform pupils about trade unions and collective agreements. These unions also offer student membership. During summers, unions support holiday-working young people. Within LO *Kommunal* prioritizes the recruitment of workplace union representatives and offers them union education to teach them how to recruit new members. The Commercial Employees' Unions (also LO) in a campaign to persuade members to pay their fees by autogiro gave them a one-month free membership.

Saco unions have always recruited students at universities. Students pay a reduced membership fee. Young professionals dissatisfied with their employment conditions before the Second World War founded several Saco unions. Successfully competing at university campuses, TCO unions today have more student members than Saco unions. Nevertheless, because of the difficulties involved in recruiting students at campuses during the Covid-19 pandemic the number of student members decreased in 2020. Furthermore, particularly white-collar unions, not the least *Unionen*, have recruited a fair number of members by introducing union income insurance, providing additional unemployment benefits, often followed up by media campaigns. These are especially attractive to white-collar workers as their incomes are often considerably above the unemployment insurance ceiling. The fact that membership of both unions and unemployment funds is required to obtain entitlement to income insurance benefits has partly restored the Ghent system's weakened recruitment capacity. Unions also offer other types of insurance, such as accident insurance. Finally, unions also provide individual advice at easily accessible union call centres. LO and TCO have long had a common centre for legal aid.

Union resources and expenditure

Most union funding comes from membership fees but rising financial asset values also play an important role. This applies to both blue-collar and white-collar unions. Finances are controlled from headquarters in all trade unions. LO's confederal income was €95 million in 2018, of which affiliated unions contributed almost 28 per cent or €26 million. €68 million were state subsidies and revenues from an insurance company owned together with PTK and SN administering collectively agreed insurances. The cost of the 346 employees, 211 of whom are employed at hotel and conference facilities in Sweden and Italy (the latter to make it possible to meet in a non-Nordic climate), was €29 million. All in all, the costs were €94 million and the result was thus a €1 million surplus. Assets were valued at €425 million (in reality worth about €470 million). Including financial revenues and taxes in 2018 LO had a surplus of €27 million. An investigation of union finances in 2010–2015 shows that six of the ten largest trade unions had deficits in their operating activities, but that these were covered by capital gains from financial assets (Arbetet 3/2 2017). Without rising stock prices, these unions would have overall deficits in their finances. Instead, they expanded their conflict funds. The ten largest unions did this, on average, by 5 per cent per year in 2010–2015. Fear of losing members explains why unions hesitate to raise membership contributions, but sometimes it is necessary. The Hotel & Restaurant Workers' Union (HRF, *Hotell- och Restauranganställdas Förbund*), for example, raised membership contributions in 2021 in response to membership losses and the increased need to support members during the pandemic. To avoid raising membership fees, since long before the year 2000, unions have cut staff at headquarters and merged regions into larger units. Most unions with special associations for sub-groups have abolished them. Saving money is a prominent motive for mergers. When *Unionen* was founded in 2008, its staff was supposed to be cut from 902 to 675 (Lag & Avtal 18 August 2008), but the real reduction was smaller as the number of employees was still around 750 at the end of 2009. At the same time, it was decided that at least 85 per of operating costs should be financed by membership fees and the remaining 15 per cent by capital revenues.

The fees of LO unions are higher than those of white-collar unions. This is partly because LO unions include more insurance in their fees, and in a few cases also the fees of the unemployment fund than white-collar unions do. For instance, *IF Metall* membership includes compulsory membership of the unemployment fund. Consequently, the fund fee is included in the union fee, which is calculated as a percentage of the monthly wage, ranging from about €23 to €63 in 2021. In 2019 *IF Metall* expenditure of €102 million included €54 million for union activities, €10 million for various forms of insurance, including income insurance introduced in July 2019, €31 million for the unemployment fund and the LO fee of €5 million. The €91 million revenues included €84 million in membership fees, €3 million in state subsidies and €5 million in revenues from services to related organizations. That means that expenditure exceeded revenue by about €10 million, a deficit covered by a €43 million surplus from financial assets. The value of the conflict fund was €1.1 billion. To attract more members from January 2015 *IF Metall* lowered the membership fee, but despite continued membership losses revenue increased because of rising wages: the fee is, on average, 1.56 per cent of the wage in 2021. *IF Metall* members who are sick, unemployed or pensioners pay a reduced fee. Student membership is free. Lastly, *IF Metall* headquarters employed 138 persons in 2019, while the thirty-five local branches employed 180 local union officers (*lokalombudsmän*) and another 250 office employees.

In *Unionen*, in 2020, the 596,000 active members, of whom 10,500 are self-employed, paid about €150 million in contributions (being non-active, students and pensioners pay a reduced fee). Other revenues amounted to €3 million. Total expenditure for the 1,050 employees at central and regional level – this number had grown by 300 (+40 per cent) since 2008 and the number of members by 48 per cent – union education, union magazine, fees to PTK and TCO, and other expenses (in total €205 million) exceeded income by more than €52 million. About a half of the 1,050 union officers and other personnel employed by *Unionen* worked at the headquarters in Stockholm and about the same number at the eighteen regional offices. A surplus in the conflict fund, invested in financial assets and real estate, covered the deficit arising from union activities and insurances. The nominal value of the conflict fund in 2020 was €900 million (according to a decision of the union congress), but total assets were much larger as the market value of the financial assets exceeded their nominal value by another €900 million (Annual Report 2020). In 2021 the *Unionen* membership fee, excluding the fee for the unemployment fund, varied from €5 to €25 a month, depending on the wage.

Collective bargaining and unions at the workplace

In contrast to Finland and Denmark, there is no tradition of tripartite wage agreements in Sweden. In some matters, however, there are tripartite deals: in 2020 there was an agreement on the system for short-term layoffs, based on a previous proposal on short-term jobs; and in 2018 there was a tripartite declaration of intent on the introduction of establishment jobs based on a previous agreement between LO, as the initiator, *Unionen* and the Confederation of Swedish Enterprise. The state subsidizes these jobs intended for newly arrived immigrants. The power shift between the union confederations, with a weaker LO, was clearly manifested in December 2020 when a new private-sector basic agreement on employment protection, skill development and conversion was signed by the white-collar Bargaining and Cooperation Council PTK (*Förhandlings- och samverkansrådet PTK* founded in 1973) and the Confederation of Swedish Enterprise (SN, *Svenskt Näringsliv*, the successor of SAF), but not by LO, because of internal disagreements (Kjellberg 2021b). Not until a year later, in November 2021, did LO, after many internal discussions, sign the agreement. Like the traditional basic agreement, the 1938 Saltsjöbaden Agreement, the basic agreement of 2020 (finally signed in 2022) came about under threat of legislation from the Social Democratic-led government, although specifically under pressure from two neoliberal parties on which the government depended. The agreement will be followed up by a revised law on employment protection, unemployment funds regulated by collective agreement and considerably improved prospects for skill development and conversion. The outcome is considered a victory for the principle of self-regulation.

Union confederations do not negotiate wages, but they conclude agreements with the Confederation of Swedish Enterprise on conversion, pensions, insurance and agency workers.[3] Affiliated confederation unions are involved in bargaining councils or bargaining cartels. The PTK comprises private sector members of unions affiliated to TCO, Saco and *Ledarna*, and concludes agreements on conversion, pensions and insurances. The Public Employees' Negotiation Council (OFR, *Offentliganställdas Förhandlingsråd*) negotiates about pensions, insurance, conversion, working environment, wage statistics and development of the public sector, and represents fourteen white-collar unions with members in the public sector. Saco-S is a bargaining cartel (negotiations on wages) for 'Academics in the state'. The Alliance of Academics (*AkademikerAlliansen*) coordinates negotiations for sixteen Saco unions in municipalities, regions and municipal companies.

In contrast to TCO and Saco, LO coordinates its affiliates during bargaining rounds. In the 2020 round, *Kommunal* and some other unions left the internal LO coordination. There are tensions between *IF Metall*, representing the 'industry norm', the wage-leading role of export industry, and low-wage LO unions, such as *Kommunal*. The five, mainly male-dominated 'LO home market unions', among them the Building Workers' Union (*Byggnads*), constitute the 6F Alliance and are those most critical of the industry norm. The norm, also called the 'mark', is a specified wage increase set by the unions and employers' associations in manufacturing (Table 28.4), which guides wage formation for the entire Swedish labour market, regardless of industry and whether an agreement contains precise figures for wage increases or is 'figureless', like some white-collar agreements (Kjellberg 2019). 'Figureless' agreements contain no wage increase: instead, wage formation is decentralized to workplace level.

3 LO negotiated wages up to 1990.

Table 28.4 Industry norm by bargaining round since 1998

Industry agreement by bargaining round	Duration	Industry norm or 'mark' (wage + other costs)	Average 'mark' by 12 months periods (not by calendar year)
March 1998–January 2001	35 months	6.9 %[4]	2.4 %
February 2001–March 2004	36–38 months	8.5 % (7.0 %), 7.3 % (5.8 %)[5]	ca 2.7 %, ca 2.3 %
April 2004–March 2007	Three years	7.3 % (6.9 %, 5.7 %)[6]	2.4 %
April 2007–March 2010	Three years	10.2 % (8.1 %)[7]	3.4 %
White-collar: April 2010–September 2011/January 2012	18 months	2.6 %	1.75 %
Blue-collar: April 2010–January 2012	22 months	3.2 %	1.75 %
February 2012–March 2013	14 months	3.0 %	2.6 %
April 2013–March 2016	Three years	6.8 %	2.3 %
April 2016–March 2017	One year	2.2 %	2.2 %
April 2017–March 2020	Three years	6.5 %	2.2 %
April 2020–October 2020	7 months*	0.0 %	–
November 2020–March 2023	29 months	5.4 %	2.2 %

Note: * Prolongation for seven months because of the Covid-19 pandemic *without wage compensation.*

Source: Yearbooks of the Swedish National Mediation Office, Danielsson Öberg and Öberg (2017: 154–155).

4 The agreement Metall – Association of Engineering Employers (wage increase of 5.7 per cent, shortened working-time 1.2 per cent).

5 Blue-collar 7.0 % wage increase (2.5 %+2.3 %+2.2 %) + 1.5 % shortened working-time (0.55 %+0.4 %+0.55 %) = 8.5 % cost increase (2.8 % per 12 months); white-collar 5.8 % wage increase (2.2 %+1.9 %+1.7 %) + 1,5 % shortened working-time (0.55 %+0.4 %+0.55 %) = 7.3 % cost increase (2,4 % per 12 months).

6 Blue-collar 6.9 % wage increase + 0.5 % shortened working-time = 7.4 % cost increase; white-collar 5.7 % + 0.5 % shortened working-time = 6.2 % cost increase.

7 Within the framework of wages in engineering rose by 8.1 per cent (2.8 per cent the first year, 2.5 per cent the second year and 2.8 per cent in the third year), on top of which came increased costs for pensions and other things.

Coordinated bargaining based on the industry norm is combined with different models of decentralized wage setting (Kjellberg 2019). While some industrial agreements are 'figureless' – most common in the public sector – others contain traditional wage scales or piece work. No blue-collar union has concluded a 'figureless' agreement, and to make the industry norm possible there is no such agreement in manufacturing, as the norm presupposes a specified wage increase. Some agreements guarantee individuals a fixed minimum wage increase, while the remaining pay increases agreed in industrial agreements are distributed at workplace level. Others have no such guarantees. In 2020, 28 per cent of all employees had some form of individual wage guarantee, to which can be added 8 per cent covered by general wage increases (Medlingsinstitutet 2021: 245).

When industrial agreements are implemented at workplace level, no or only small wage increases are added, with the result that wage drift has declined and is now almost non-existent (Kjellberg 2019). Local wage formation is above all an issue of distribution, but within fairly narrow limits. Groups with a strong market position may raise their wages relative to others. In 2019, for example, members of the TCO union, organizing nurses, midwifes and biomedical analysts, increased their wages by an average of 3.5 per cent and in 2020 by 4.1 per cent, well above the industry mark of 2.2 per cent (*Vårdförbundet* 2020, 2021). Although the more individually differentiated and performance-based wage setting entails, in a formal sense, increased employer discretion, the change in practice appears modest. The industry mark, translated into local budgets and wage frames, set rather narrow limits to workplace differentiation. Difficulties discerning substantial performance variations among most employees, normative expectations regarding continuously compressed wages and employee expectations also limit the space for wage differentiation (Ulfsdotter Eriksson et al. 2020).

The total coverage of collective agreements was 90 per cent in 2020 and in the private sector 85 per cent. In 2000 the corresponding shares were 88 and 81 per cent, respectively, and in 2010, 89 and 84 per cent (Kjellberg 2022a). Collective agreements cover both members and non-members at workplaces with agreements. Recruitment efforts and other union workplace activities are thus important for combating freeriding and establishing social norms that favour union membership. The latter are an additional explanation of high union density. At workplace level, particularly in the case of figureless industrial agreements, 'wage talks' are often held between the individual employee and the manager, or the workplace union negotiates for each individual. In both cases, it works best if the union and the employer together construct a local wage system in which the criteria for wage setting by members are perceived as transparent and fair. In *IF Metall* about eight out of ten workers are covered by local wage systems negotiated by the union at workplaces where the 'union clubs' have at least fifty members. The union's aspiration is to link individual wage development to development at work by rewarding workers who acquire more skills. At workplace level, besides wage negotiations, union clubs also participate in negotiations on codetermination and layoffs. At workplaces without clubs, union representatives may do this instead, but if there is no collective agreement only union officers from the regional branch have the right to negotiate. Negotiations on pensions, conversion and more take place at peak level, involving LO and the white-collar cartel PTK.

A challenge for all workplace negotiations is the declining coverage of union clubs and of workplace representatives at workplaces without clubs. In 2019 the total number of elected union representatives was 254,000, of whom 115,000 were blue-collar and 137,000 white-collar (Larsson 2020). They made up 11 per cent of the unionized blue-collar workers and more than 8 per cent of the white-collar members. Although the number of elected representatives as a proportion of union members has been relatively constant, the absolute number decreased from 360,000 in 1995 to 254,000 in 2019 because of declining union density. The share of union representatives was somewhat higher among female members (10 per cent) than among males (8 per cent), in particular among white-collar workers (10 and 6 per cent, respectively).

For the first time in many years the number of workplace clubs in *Unionen* increased in 2019, to 2,710. That is considerably fewer than the 3,325 clubs in 2008, however. During the same period the number of active *Unionen* members increased by 162,000. The combination of a decline in the number of clubs and the growth in the number of members, many of whom were attracted by the union income insurance, has meant a dramatic decrease in club coverage as a proportion of members. At workplaces without clubs in 2019 there were 3,471 workplace representatives. Between 2013 and 2019 the share of members covered by a club or workplace representative decreased from 51 to 46 per cent. In all, *Unionen* had 30,551 elected representatives at workplace, region and central level (35,069 in 2008), of whom 7,853 were safety representatives.

In 2020 *IF Metall* had 1,348 workplace clubs and 3,664 representatives at workplaces without clubs, 26,299 elected representatives in all. In 2006, 69 per cent of the members had a workplace club, 16 per cent a workplace representative, and 14 per cent had neither. In 2020 the corresponding shares were 64, 16 and 19 per cent. *IF Metall* clubs with at least 180 members usually have at least one elected representative paid full-time by the company to perform union tasks. The same applies to large clubs in other unions.

Industrial conflict

There are very few restrictions on conflict rights in Sweden. According to the laws on collective agreements and the labour court introduced in 1928, conflicts are not allowed before agreements expire, but sympathy action is allowed, provided that the primary conflict is legal. This means that the latter might not take place during the contract period. Sympathy action is important in forcing unorganized employers to conclude subsidiary collective agreements. During bargaining rounds, trade unions can trigger sympathy strikes to support the demands of other unions. In 2014 all LO unions except one gave notice of sympathy measures (strikes and blockades against specified companies) in the conflict between the LO union Seko and the SN-affiliated *Almega Tjänsteförbunden* (Almega Service Associations), but an agreement was concluded before the measures came into force. In 2016, *Akademikerförbundet SSR* (Union for Professionals, Saco) gave notice of strike action and a blockade at a number of companies and workplaces in the conflict on flexible pensions between the SN association *IT & Telekomföretagen* (Swedish IT and Telecom Industries) and *Unionen* (TCO) and *Sveriges Ingenjörer* (Association of Graduate Engineers, Saco), respectively.

Although there are few restrictions the Swedish labour market is very peaceful (see Appendix A1). There are several reasons for this. First, the 1997 Industry Agreement re-established the spirit of cooperation in manufacturing. Second, rising Swedish real wages since then have also limited the incentive to strike. Third, there is the new Swedish National Mediation Office (MI, *Medlingsinstitutet*), established in 2000, which primarily covers other parts of the labour market than manufacturing and other industries with negotiation agreements. It is explicitly ordered to foster the wage-leading role of the export sector by mediating in case of conflict and actively promoting norms backing up this role. The MI may resort to enforced mediation, but only in industries without negotiation agreements. The parties behind the Industry Agreement have their own mediation body, the group of 'impartial chairs' (OpO, *Opartiska ordföranden*). The MI, like the OpO, can postpone industrial action by up to fourteen days in an effort to prevent negotiations from descending into open conflict. Finally, strike notices are often sufficient to press employers' associations to make concessions in negotiations. A relative balance of power exists between unions and employers' associations equipped with large, centrally controlled strike and lockout funds. A tax-free benefit, equal to 80 per cent of the wage, is paid to striking or locked-out members, corresponding to their loss of income.

A power shift has occurred, however, at least since the 1990s or even earlier. The strong position of transnational companies in the Swedish economy means that trade unions in manufacturing risk production moving abroad (Kjellberg 2022c). Intensified international competition also discourages manufacturing unions from demanding too large wage increases. The exception is the 2010 paper workers' strike, whereby the Paper Workers' Union withdrew from the Industry Agreement and has remained outside since 2011. The predominantly home market 6F Alliance of LO unions do not feel such pressures and have criticized the industry norm. Consequently, all large strikes except the one mentioned previously have occurred in the home market sector since the 1997 Industry Agreement: the 1999 bus strike, the 2003 *Kommunal* public sector strike, the 2008 nurses' strike and the 2012 building workers' strike. Also, in recent years nurses and midwifes have resorted to spontaneous action in the form of collective job terminations, while student nurses have organized hiring blockades. Other forms of industrial action are overtime bans and physical blockades of workplaces. Blockades or notices of blockades against selected companies are common in case of sympathy conflicts (see above) and conflicts to force unorganized companies to accept collective agreements. They often occur during collective bargaining, such as when the Hotel and Restaurant Workers' Union in 2020 gave notice of a total blockade against the recruitment of new workers and hiring of staff from temporary agencies.

Political relations

High union density means that Swedish governments have to consider trade union views, whether they agree with it or not. Unions protested in vain against the considerably raised unemployment fund fees imposed by the centre-right government in 2007, but they did not organize mass demonstrations against the state. Since the 1930s, when the long period of social democratic government began, there has been no such tradition, and scarcely before that, in contrast to states with a more repressive attitude towards unions. Swedish unions prefer to influence governments by other means (Kjellberg 2021a: 24–26, 41–42). There two main channels for this purpose: the referral system (*remissförfarande*) and the close contacts between LO and the Social Democratic Party (*Sveriges Socialdemokratiska Arbetareparti*).

First, unions and employers' associations have access to the policy process via the referral system. Before laws are enacted, the government appoints a commission, which may ask both sides of industry for advice and information, for example on working environment issues. Sometimes the government invites the social partners to participate in reference groups assisting the commission. Lastly, the government sends the commission report to unions and other actors, who are invited to submit comments before the bill is presented to the parliament. But although unions were often directly represented in commissions dealing with labour market issues in the past century, this happens more seldom today. This diluted union representation in government commissions has weakened their political influence.[8] An exception is the present legal process to implement the 2020 basic agreement, which until 2022 requires a revised law on employment protection and legislation on economic support for competence development. The unions signing the agreement in 2020 (the bargaining cartel PTK, *Kommunal* and *IF Metall*) were represented in three government commissions, while others (e.g. LO) were offered the opportunity to submit their views via the referral system.

Second, the strong links between LO and the Social Democratic Party give the former easy access to the party and government. Collective affiliation of LO members to the Social Democratic Party was abolished in 1991, but LO is still represented on the party's board and executive committee and provides the party with financial resources and staff during election campaigns (Jansson 2017). Representatives of the party and LO

---

8 Up to the early 1990s, trade unions and employers' associations were represented in the boards of government agencies, such as the Labour Market Board. On the initiative of the employers, 'corporatist' representation was abolished. Their motive was to weaken trade unions.

also meet in a number of permanent and temporary committees. During certain periods there were severe tensions between LO and the party, labelled 'the War of the Roses', above all when, during the deep economic crisis in the 1990s, the party abandoned Keynesianism in favour of fighting inflation. Nevertheless, the decoupling of the party and the union movement evident in many other countries is still not very apparent in Sweden (Magnusson 2018). It is telling that in the government, installed in 2014, the former *IF Metall* president was the Prime Minister until he resigned in November 2021, but the former TCO president was still the Labour Market Minister and a former Saco president continued as the Minister of Education. The former LO president now became the Minister for Business, Industry and Innovation and the former president of the TCO union *Vision* became the Minister for Climate and the Environment.

Also, the fact that the white-collar confederations TCO and Saco are politically independent does not prevent them from expressing their views on all matters of interest to their members, or from attempting to influence the government in the desired direction. The existence of separate white-collar unions and confederations without political links has promoted the high union density of white-collar workers by preventing this category of workers from feeling union 'homeless'. That might have happened if they had had no alternative to social democratic blue-collar unions. During the Covid-19 crisis all political parties, employers and unions agreed to introduce a system of short-term layoffs.

Societal power

Trade unions have invested in the development of websites and other digital media, such as YouTube (Jansson and Uba 2019). In recent years Swedish unions have in general increased their public confidence. In 2020 this confidence reached its highest level since the SOM Institute started its surveys in 1986. This year, confidence in trade unions was the same as for newspapers and higher than for political parties, but smaller than for the parliament or radio/TV (SOM 2021). To influence public opinion, unions have three think tanks: *Arena* (a number of LO, TCO and Saco unions), *Katalys* (6F Alliance) and *Futurion* (TCO). They publish reports and arrange seminars, *Arena* in addition provides schools with information on labour relations. *Arena* has an online magazine. The unions themselves also publish reports and journals, write debate articles, organize campaigns and have communication departments with press officers to influence public opinion, the state and political parties. As already mentioned, LO has close links to the Social Democratic Party. They also act as lobby organizations in Sweden and towards the EU. The Covid-19 pandemic has also offered opportunities to influence public opinion. During its campaign against the use of precarious workers in elderly care and home care, *Kommunal* won the sympathy of the public. A growing proportion of health care assistants have the most insecure forms of temporary work, such as employment on a time or on-call basis. During the pandemic, it became obvious that their lack of training and insecure forms of employment facilitated the spread of the disease. Furthermore, if hourly paid workers have to stay at home because of sickness, they have no rights to sickness benefits and risk not being offered work again.

An example of NGOs fighting the exploitation of workers is Fair Play Bygg (founded by the Building Workers' Union and an association of building contractors), to which the public can report suspicions of fraud, 'black' labour and similar offences in construction. Others include the Union Centre for the Undocumented (founded by LO, TCO and a number of unions) and Fair Trade Sweden, all of which cooperate with Swedish unions.

Trade union policies towards the European Union

Sweden joined the EU in 1995 after a referendum (with a narrow majority of 52 per cent). The union rank and file opinion was so split that LO, TCO and Saco abstained from taking an official position. The unions in manufacturing and export trades, such as Metall, recommended that their members vote 'yes', however. The president of the LO Commercial Employees Union (Handels, *Handelsanställdas Förbund*) participated in the anti-EU campaign. In the 2003 referendum on whether Sweden should join EMU, 56 per cent voted 'no'. Again LO was split and had to take a neutral position. Metall campaigned for EMU, while Handels and Transport were against. Nevertheless, TCO, Saco and LO are all ETUC affiliates; they cooperate closely on several issues and take similar positions in relation to the government and the EU. They share an office in Brussels. They sometimes make great common efforts to influence the policy of the ETUC and the EU. While Swedish unions have traditionally been sceptical of EU labour market policies (Furåker and Bengtsson 2013), this sentiment has been strongly reinforced recently.

Two issues explain this: the *Laval* verdict of 2007 and, in 2020, the European Commission's proposal for a Directive on adequate minimum wages in the European Union. Both are considered to clash with the Swedish model of self-regulation, in which collective bargaining follows a voluntarist tradition without state intervention. Thus, in Sweden there is neither a statutory minimum wage nor an extension mechanism.

The *Laval* judgement seriously restricted the efforts of Swedish unions regarding posted workers. The judgement declared the actions of the Swedish Building Workers' Union in pursuit of a Swedish collective agreement for posted workers at a construction site of the Latvian building company Laval to be illegal (Thörnqvist and Woolfson 2012). Against the absence of national legislation on minimum wages and extension of collective agreements in Sweden can be set the right to start strikes and blockades against unorganized companies. Few workers posted to Sweden are union members. Because they are not nationally registered in Sweden, they are not included in the calculation of Swedish union density. Several hundred foreign construction companies employing posted workers have collective agreements, but no union members or union representatives. Consequently, it is hard for the Building Workers' Union to check whether the agreements are being applied. According to law, the regional safety representatives appointed by the unions have no access to workplaces without union members, even if there is a collective agreement. There is plenty of evidence suggesting a high prevalence of poor working conditions at many sites with posted workers. The Social Democratic Party-led government tried to change this in 2020, but the parliamentary majority of liberal and conservative parties rejected the proposal. After issuing a strike notice, however, the Building Workers' Union managed to obtain this right.

Consequently, the Swedish model of self-regulation via collective agreements paved the way for safety representatives' access to such workplaces (although only in construction) after the government failed to open the door for them by law. The leading employers' association, SN, however, would like to abolish regional safety representatives and replace them with local non-union safety representatives, assisted by officials from the Swedish Work Environment Authority (*Arbetsmiljöverket*). Obviously, the employers wish to exclude regional union safety representatives, who, with some authority, can demand improvements in the working environment in companies without local union safety representatives. Non-union safety representatives at such workplaces would hardly be able to represent the workers effectively in relation to the employer, in particular because they are often afraid of being dismissed if they contact a union. This is a problem for Swedish unions trying to organize posted workers in construction, where most are from Poland and often not formally employed. In construction the growing 'grey area' of bogus self-employed workers dependent upon a single employer is closely related to 'the frequent use of long subcontracting chains in which self-employed migrant workers are often to be found at the end-point of these supply-chains' (Thörnquist 2015: 419). Many of these problems are frequent also in road haulage companies with foreign drivers.

Another controversial issue is the EU Directive on adequate minimum wages in the European Union (European Parliament and Council of the European Union 2022), which was strongly opposed by Danish and Swedish unions. In Finland, where collective agreements are extended to whole industries, unions were less critical. The tensions caused by the Directive on adequate minimum wages were essentially based on different perceptions of the potential consequences for the Swedish model. In Sweden the Nordic model of collective agreements is widely considered to be superior to legislation as it allows greater flexibility, for example when implementing the EU working time directive. Above all, with an EU directive on minimum wages the labour market parties fear losing influence over wage formation to the state and the EU (Müller and Platzer 2020: 301). This perception has a long history. When Sweden joined the EU, the responsible commissioner at that time, Pádraig Flynn, promised that the Swedish labour market model would not be affected. This promise resulted in a letter, which in Sweden is known as the 'Flynn letter'. This letter was not legally binding, but in the introduction to the Directive on posted workers (point 22) it was asserted that 'this Directive is without prejudice to the law of the Member States concerning collective action to defend the interests of trades and professions'. The EU court, however, drew a different conclusion in the *Laval* case (Thörnqvist and Woolfson 2011: 16) and Swedish unions see a danger that it may do the same regarding minimum wages. Furthermore, the EU Directive on adequate minimum wages contains a provision that the adequacy of statutory minimum wages can be assessed in accordance with international standards, such as 60 per cent of the median and 50 per cent of the average wage. Even though Sweden has no statutory minimum wages, if applied, this could create downward pressure on minimum wages in Sweden for almost all employees because collectively negotiated minimum wages are, as a rule, higher than the standards foreseen in the Directive (Hällberg and Kjellström 2020). Furthermore, today collective agreements have a strong normative influence on wages for the 450,000 or so employees without such agreements, but if lower wages are legitimized by the EU, Swedish unions fear that this might change. The favourability principle prevents only organized employers and those with substitute agreements from deviating downwards. Although legislated minimum wages may not 'end up being a ceiling for low wages, rather than a floor' (Lovén Seldén 2020: 335) every EU intervention into wage formation by the labour market parties and the state is considered a break with the Swedish principle of self-regulation. The different views on the Directive on adequate minimum wages on the part of the Swedish unions and the ETUC and the majority of its affiliates have led to tensions within the European trade union movement and ultimately, in December 2021, prompted LO-Sweden to temporarily suspend payment of its membership fees to the ETUC because it no longer felt appropriately represented by the ETUC (Arbetet 20/12 2021). Furthermore, Swedish unions, such as the Transport Workers' Union, have also been very active on the cabotage issue, namely domestic transport of goods by foreign drivers on Swedish roads. A satisfactory solution seems to be in sight after many years of effort. Regarding posted workers and cabotage, union efforts to improve EU regulations in recent years have had considerable success: conflict rights have been extended and misuse of cabotage restricted.

Swedish unions participate actively in the European social dialogue, at both confederal (LO, TCO and Saco) and sectoral level. Regarding the European Semester, only a minor part of the social dialogue, they give higher priority to national social dialogue than to European social dialogue. Contributing to this situation are the fact that Sweden is not a member of EMU and its relatively strong national economy compared with many other EU countries, not to mention the fact that the national dialogue on the European Semester functions well (Jansson et al. 2019). At national level there are tripartite consultations regarding the European semester. Each year the unions and employers' organizations, in an appendix to the National Reform Programme, present how their activities have contributed to attaining the targets of the Europe 2020 Strategy. In 2012 when the EC pointed out the relatively high wages at the bottom of the wage scale as an obstacle to fighting the high unemployment among newly arrived immigrants, it was generally perceived as an 'attack' on the social partners' autonomy and heavily criticized (Jansson et al.

2019: 15, 21–23). The introduction of establishment jobs in 2020, mentioned above, emerged from a Swedish debate and concerns rather than in response to EU recommendations on how to employ newly arrived immigrants (Jansson et al. 2019: 23). The long-term goal of the unions, but to some degree also of the employer confederation SN, is to protect the Swedish model of industrial relations (Jansson et al. 2019: 17, 19–20). Swedish unions prefer working within ETUC to being in direct contact with the Commission (Jansson et al. 2019: 18). But when LO and the Social Democrats published a report in 2014 on the need for a Pillar of Social Rights, the unions considered influence via the new social democratic government as more important to ensure that it was included in the European Semester than influence through ETUC or contacts with the Commission (Jansson et al. 2019: 19–21). One of the aims of the Pillar was to prevent a race to the bottom on social issues. SN objected that the inclusion of the Pillar might threaten social partner autonomy. In contrast to, for example, Southern European unions, their Swedish counterparts have no domestic tradition of participating in protest demonstrations and for this reason hardly do so at European level either (Bengtsson 2017: 165–166; Bengtsson and Vulkan 2018: 118).

There is a close cooperation between the Nordic confederations and unions to strengthen their voice in the world. The Council of Nordic Trade Unions (*Nordens Fackliga Samorganisation*) represents sixteen national trade union confederations, representing almost 9 million members. Founded in 1972, the main task of NFS is to 'coordinate and foster regional trade union cooperation in the Nordic countries, particularly with regard to employment, economic and social policy and in relation to ETUC, ITUC, TUAC, ILO and PERC',[9] and in relation to the Nordic Council of Ministers. NFS has close ties with the Baltic Sea Trade Union Network (BASTUN). In relation to the ETUC, Nordic affiliates emphasize their autonomy, while for example Southern members are prepared to give ETUC a stronger mandate (Furåker and Larsson 2020: 35; Larsson 2015: 115). The well-prepared and coordinated Nordic unions often speak with one voice in ETUC (Kjellberg 2000: 543–544; Larsson 2015: 42, 99). The existence of strong Nordic 'meta-organizations' at the sectoral and cross-sectoral levels makes it possible to 'lobby directly at EU institutions without having to take a detour via the ETUC or the ETUFs' (Lovén Selden 2020: 332). Consequently, Swedish unions have several

9 NFS website: https://www.nfs.net/languages/english/about-nfs-9063699

options for influencing the EU, depending on the issue at stake and the current situation, including national dialogue, the ETUC and Nordic cooperation, among other things. Various combinations are also possible. In December 2021 LO-Sweden decided temporarily not to participate in ETUC meetings or pay contributions to 'an organisation that goes against us regarding European minimum wages' (Arbetet 20/12 2021).

Nordic cooperation is also strong at the industry level. *Nordiska Metall* (Nordic Metall), founded in the 1970s and focused on wage bargaining, merged in 2006 to form the cross-manufacturing *Industrianställda i Norden* (IN, Nordic Industrial Employees). IN has close contacts with German colleagues, which have a central position in cross-bargaining networks and transnational cooperation in general (Furåker and Larsson 2020: 45). Within the European Metalworkers' Federation, and later in its successor organization the European federation IndustriALL, the Nordic unions 'became a major actor through their joint strategies' (Larsson and Törnberg 2019: 4). In other European Trade Union Federations, the influence of Nordic unionists is strengthened by their strong joint preparations before meetings (Larsson and Törnberg 2019: 13). Metall played the role of forerunner because of its high exposure to competition, high transferability of production across borders and its resourceful unions (Larsson and Törnberg 2019: 5).

Because of the strong position of large transnational companies in Swedish economy (Kjellberg 2022c), unions work actively within European Works Councils (EWCs). The EWCs have proved to be useful bodies for the exchange of information with companies and offer opportunities to develop contacts between employees from different industrial relations systems. As transnational companies tend to play off the employees in different regions and countries against each other, the development of strong common norms and common positions among unionists from different parts of Europe is given high priority, for example by Unions in Manufacturing (FI, *Facken inom industrin*) (FI 2014). *IF Metall* (LO), *Unionen* (TCO) and the Association of Graduate Engineers are all affiliated to IndustriAll, which has developed binding guidelines for negotiating EWC agreements.

Conclusions

Sweden still belongs to a small group of countries with the highest union densities in the world. Almost seven out of ten employees are union members. In the absence of extension mechanisms, the right to industrial action, including sympathy measures, against unorganized employers is important to maintain the high coverage of collective agreements. Furthermore, Swedish employers' organizations, compared with, for instance, their German colleagues, have been more successful in recruiting and retaining members. Nine out of ten employees work in companies or public authorities affiliated to employers' organizations. The coverage of collective agreements is at about the same high level although lower in the private sector: 85 per cent in 2020. The high density of both unions and employers' organizations is a prerequisite for the Swedish model of self-regulation, in contrast to, for example, the French model of state regulation in which the high coverage of collective agreements is achieved by the implementation of extension mechanisms.

The industry norm, set by the bargaining parties in manufacturing, has a strong influence on all industrial agreements and at the workplace level, despite the tendency towards more individualized wage setting. The increased exposure to international competition, also affecting Swedish construction companies, is among the circumstances explaining the almost complete absence of local wage drift. Relatively small nominal wage increases, together with expectations from the employees not to obtain less than 'the mark', limit the space of local managers to increase wage dispersion. Despite the moderate nominal wage increases associated with the industry norm, Swedish real wages have increased steadily in contrast to Germany, where for several years they have declined or remained unchanged.

The Swedish model of industrial relations, however, is not without challenges. The declining coverage of union clubs and union representatives at workplace level may in the future circumscribe the unions' capacity to negotiate local wage systems. Another challenge is the growing gap between the density of employers' associations and union density: from being the same in 2000, namely about 75 per cent in the private sector, union density among private sector employees had declined to 64 per cent by 2020, while employer density increased somewhat.

There are widening gaps among employees, too. Before the remaking of the Swedish Ghent system, blue-collar and white-collar union density was the same, but in 2020 the union density of blue-collar workers was 12 percentage points lower than that of white-collar workers. Part of this divergence is explained by a third growing gap, that between foreign-born and domestic-born blue-collar workers. The large number of refugees from non-European countries entering the Swedish labour market in blue-collar jobs, often on fixed-term contracts in private sector services, makes recruitment more difficult. Compared with white-collar workers those with fixed-term jobs, employed part-time, young or born abroad are overrepresented among blue-collar workers. Other explanations of the growing white-collar/blue-collar divide are the considerably higher blue-collar fees to unemployment funds in the period 2007–2013 and the greater attractiveness and prevalence of union income insurance among white-collar workers than among blue-collar workers (Kjellberg and Nergaard 2022).

The declining union density of blue-collar workers, combined with their decreasing share of the labour force is changing the balance of power within the union movement. In December 2020 the white-collar private sector cartel PTK and the employer confederation SN concluded a new basic agreement (Kjellberg 2021b). The blue-collar confederation LO initiated negotiations in 2017, but because of internal tensions LO did not sign the agreement; the two largest LO unions, *Kommunal* and *IF Metall* signed it in the face of protests from the others. Almost a year later, in November 2021, after negotiations on conversion LO finally signed the agreement. Compared with the Danish LO, which in 2019 merged with the largest white-collar confederation, the Swedish LO has always included fewer white-collar workers. The strength of Swedish white-collar unions is shown by the fact that the 'industry norm' is set by *IF Metall* and two other LO manufacturing unions, but also by the white-collar *Unionen* (TCO) and the Association of Graduate Engineers (Saco). All five unions are members of Unions in Manufacturing. The two white-collar unions have together considerably more members than the three LO unions. In contrast, the Danish 'mark' is set only by former LO unions. The Danish equivalent of the Association of Graduate Engineers is not even recognized as a negotiating party by the Danish private sector employers' confederation.

In 2018 and 2019, average union density was unchanged (68 per cent). Blue-collar density did not decline any further. In the first two months of the Covid-19 pandemic (March and April 2020) the number of union members increased by almost 60,000, of whom about 20,000 were blue-collar. In 2020 union density was up to 69 per cent, while the number of active union members expanded by 75,000. It is hard to say whether this is a trend break reversing the longstanding decline. In 2021 union density reached 70 per cent.

Of the four scenarios presented by Visser (2019) regarding the future of the union movement – marginalization, dualization, substitution (with non-union arrangements), and revitalization – revitalization is the most likely outcome for Sweden. During the pandemic, Kommunal very actively fought to improve the poor conditions that many members experience in hospitals, elderly care and bus transport. That rewarded the union with substantial membership growth also during the second half of 2020, which most unions did not experience. Another example is the success of the unions at Volvo Cars engine plant in Skövde in persuading the company to invest €70 million in the production of electric engines. To address dualization tendencies revitalization efforts have to give high priority to foreign-born blue-collar workers. Both in 2019 and 2020 their union density increased, while that of the native-born was unchanged.

The Swedish model of self-regulation proved able to meet all challenges during the Covid-19 year of 2020. As in the 1930s, the labour market parties concluded a basic agreement, this time on employment protection, skills development and conversion. The aim was to keep the state out as much as possible. Nevertheless, the state assumed a larger role than in the 1930s as the law on employment protection had to be revised in accordance with the agreement. State financial support was necessary for implementing other parts of the agreement. That was also the case with the agreements on short-time working concluded by employers' associations and trade unions at industry level, rapidly followed by a very large number of local agreements. Companies without collective agreements, however, have to apply much more inflexible rules to obtain financial compensation from the state.

The future will show whether the EU directive on minimum wages will keep the Swedish labour market model intact. LO, TCO, Saco and all political parties fully agree on the desirability of this. Although the private sector TCO and Saco unions (the PTK unions), like the LO unions IF Metall and Kommunal, differed from the other LO unions regarding the 2020 basic agreement this will hardly affect the climate between the three confederations. The deep division instead occurred *within* LO, but it by no means paralysed the confederation. This was demonstrated in 2021, when almost all LO unions stood behind the decision resuming the negotiations with SN to obtain much more favourable conversion terms than those in the 2004 LO-SN agreement. It presupposed that LO would also sign the new basic agreement, which indeed happened in November 2021. In June 2022 it was finally signed by LO, PTK and SN together.

References

All links were checked on 8 December 2021.

Bengtsson E. (2017) Swedish trade unions and the ETUC, in Ciampini A. and Tilly P. (eds) National trade unions and the ETUC: a history of unity and diversity, Brussels, ETUI, 161–175. https://www.etui.org/publications/books/national-trade-unions-and-the-etuc-a-history-of-unity-and-diversity

Bengtsson M. and Vulkan P. (2018) After the Great Recession: unions' views on transnational interests and cooperation, Nordic Journal of Working Life Studies, 8 (3), 11–133.

Danielsson Öberg A. and Öberg T. (2017) Vem ska bestämma på lönemarknaden? Stockholm, Premiss.

European Parliament and Council of the European Union (2022) DIRECTIVE (EU) 2022/2041 OF THE EUROPEAN PARLIAMENT AND OF THE COUNCIL of 19 October 2022 on adequate minimum wages in the European Union, Official Journal of the European Union, L 275/33, 25.10.2022. https://eur-lex.europa.eu/legal-content/EN/TXT/PDF/?uri=CELEX:32022L2041&from=EN

FI (2014) Europeiska företagsråd, Stockholm, Facken inom industrin.

Frödin O. and Kjellberg A. (2018) Labor migration from third countries to Swedish low-wage jobs, Nordic Journal of Working Life Studies, 8 (1), 65–85.

Frödin O. and Kjellberg A. (2020) Anställningsbidrag: integration eller etnisk segmentering?, Arbetsmarknad & Arbetsliv, 26 (1), 30–52.

Furåker B. and Bengtsson M. (2013) Trade union cooperation in the EU: views among Swedish trade unions and their members, Nordic Journal of Working Life Studies, 3 (3), 117–132.

Furåker B. and Larsson B. (2020) Trade union cooperation in Europe. Patterns, conditions, issues, Basingstoke, Palgrave Macmillan.

Hällberg P. and Kjellström C. (2020) Collective agreements and minimum wages. A report from the Swedish National Mediation Office, Stockholm, Swedish National Mediation Office.

Jansson J. (2017) Two branches of the same tree? Party-union links in Sweden in the 21st century, in Haugsgjerd Allern E. and Bale T. (eds) Left-of-centre parties and trade unions in the twenty-first century, Oxford, Oxford University Press.

Jansson J. and Uba K. (2019) Trade unions on YouTube. Online revitalization in Sweden, Basingstoke, Palgrave Macmillan.

Jansson O., Jansson J. and Ottosson J. (2019) Neither sticks nor carrots: Swedish trade union involvement in the European Semester. Case study Sweden. National trade union involvement in the European Semester (INVOTUNES) project, OSE Working Paper Series 42, Brussels, European Social Observatory.

Kjellberg A. (2000) The multitude of challenges facing Swedish trade unions, in Waddington J. and Hoffmann R. (eds) Trade unions in Europe: facing challenges and searching for solutions, Brussels, ETUI, 529–573.

Kjellberg A. (2005) Sweden: mergers in a class-segmented trade union system, in Waddington J. (ed.) Restructuring representation. The merger process and trade union structural development in ten countries, Brussels, Peter Lang, 225–255.

Kjellberg A. (2011) The decline in Swedish union density since 2007, Nordic Journal of Working Life Studies, 1 (1), 67–93.

Kjellberg A. (2014) Union density and specialist/professional unions in Sweden, Studies in Social Policy, Industrial Relations, Working Life and Mobility. Research Reports 2013:2, Lund, Lund University.

Kjellberg A. (2017) Self-regulation versus state regulation in Swedish industrial relations, in Rönnmar M. and Julén Votinius J. (eds) Festskrift till Ann Numhauser-Henning, Lund, Juristförlaget i Lund, 357–383.

Kjellberg A. (2019) Sweden: collective bargaining under the industry norm, in Müller T., Vandaele K. and Waddington J. (eds) Collective bargaining in Europe: towards an endgame, Brussels, ETUI, 583–604 (+ an extra updated appendix).

Kjellberg A. (2020) Den svenska modellen i en oviss tid: Fack, arbetsgivare och kollektivavtal på en föränderlig arbetsmarknad, Stockholm, Arena Idé.

Kjellberg A. (2021a) Vad är facklig styrka? Arbetsplatsfacket centralt i den svenska partsmodellen, Stockholm, Futurion, 2021 (1).

Kjellberg A. (2021b) Den svenska modellen 2020: pandemi och nytt huvudavtal, Stockholm, Arena Idé.

Kjellberg A. (2021c) The successive merger of Swedish teachers' unions. Nio - Fem Tidskrift om arbetsliv & profession, 2021 (1). https://portal.research.lu.se/files/108974583/The_successive_merger_of_Swedish_teachers_unions.pdf

Kjellberg A. (2022a) Kollektivavtalens täckningsgrad samt organisationsgraden hos arbetsgivarförbund och fackförbund (The Coverage of Collective Agreements, Union Density and Density of Employers' Associations; Appendix 3 in English), Research Reports 2022:1, Lund, Department of Sociology, Lund University.

Kjellberg A. (2022b) The membership development of Swedish trade unions and union confederations since the end of the nineteenth century, Lund, Department of Sociology, Lund University.

Kjellberg A. (2022c) The shifting role of European unions in the social dialogue: Sweden in a comparative perspective, in Abrahamsson K. and Ennals R. (eds) Sustainable work in Europe. Concepts, conditions, challenges, Berlin, Peter Lang. For an earlier online version: https://portal.research.lu.se/portal/sv/publications/the-shifting-role-of-unions-in-the-social-dialogue(3762b0d8-0aca-4ddc-a9eb-9fdc76ebf42c).html

Kjellberg A. and Lyhne Ibsen C. (2016) Attacks on union organizing: reversible and irreversible changes to the Ghent-systems in Sweden and Denmark, in Larsen T.P. and Ilsøe A. (eds) Den danske model set udefra – komparative perspektiver på dansk arbejdsmarkedsregulering, København, Jurist- og Økonomforbundets Forlag, 279–302.

Kjellberg A. and Nergaard K. (2022) Union Density in Norway and Sweden: Stability versus Decline, Nordic Journal of Working Life Studies. Special issue S8, 51–72. https://portal.research.lu.se/sv/publications/union-density-in-norway-and-sweden-stability-versus-decline

Larsson B. (2015) Trade union channels for influencing European Union policies, Nordic Journal of Working Life Studies, 5 (3), 101–121.

Larsson M. (2020) Facklig anslutning år 2020, Stockholm, LO.

Larsson B. and Törnberg A. (2019) Sectoral networks of transnational trade union cooperation in Europe, Economic and Industrial Democracy, 42 (4), 1189–1209.

Lovén Seldén K. (2020) Challenges posed by the EU minimum wage initiative to the ETUC and European trade union cooperation, Transfer, 26 (3), 325–343.

Magnusson L. (2018) Trade unions in a changing political context: the case of Sweden, Transfer, 24 (2), 137–149.

Medlingsinstitutet (2021) Avtalsrörelsen och lönebildningen 2020, Medlingsinstitutets årsrapport, Stockholm, Medlingsinstitutet.

Müller T. and Platzer H.-W. (2020) The European Trade Union Federations within the European polity: ETUFs and international trade union activity, Transfer, 26 (3), 289–305.

SOM (2021) Svenska trender 1986–2020, Göteborg, Göteborgs Universitet, SOM Institute.

Thörnquist A. (2015) False self-employment and other precarious forms of employment in the 'Grey Area' of the labour market, International Journal of Comparative Labour Law and Industrial Relations, 31 (4), 411–429.

Thörnqvist C. and Woolfson C. (2011) Dog den svenska modellen i Vaxholm? Laval-målet och den svenska arbetsmarknaden, Arbetsmarknad & Arbetsliv, 17 (3), 9–22.

Thörnqvist C. and Woolfson C. (2012) When tender turns tough: posted workers and the tendering regime in the Swedish construction industry, Construction Management & Economics, 30 (7), 525–533.

Ulfsdotter Eriksson Y., Larsson B. and Adolfsson P. (2020) Under the surface of individual and differentiated pay in Sweden: a zero-sum game of performance-based pay?, British Journal of Industrial Relations, 59 (2), 398–417.

Vårdförbundet (2020) Annual report 2019, Stockholm, Vårdförbundet.

Vårdförbundet (2021) Annual report 2020, Stockholm, Vårdförbundet.

Visser J. (2019) Trade unions in the balance, ILO ACTRAW Working Paper, Geneva, ILO.

Abbreviations

6F *Fackförbund i samverkan* (Trade Unions in Cooperation; the LO unions of building workers, electricians, maintenance workers, painters and service & communication workers)

Akad *AkademikerAlliansen* (Alliance of Academics; negotiation council for Saco unions with members in local government)

EMU	Economic and Monetary Union
ETUC	European Trade Union Confederation
ETUF	European Trade Union Federation
EWC	European Works Councils
FI	*Facken inom industrin* (Unions in Manufacturing)
HRF	*Hotell- och Restauranganställdas Förbund* (Hotel and Restaurant Workers' Union)
IF Metall	*Industrifacket Metall* (Industrial Union Metall)
IN	*Industrianställda i Norden* (Nordic Industrial Employees)
ITUC	International Trade Union Confederation
Kommunal	*Svenska Kommunalarbetareförbundet* (Swedish Union of Municipal Workers)
LO	*Landsorganisationen i Sverige* (Swedish Trade Union Confederation)
LR	*Lärarnas Riksförbund* (National Union of Teachers in Sweden)
LS	*Lärarnas samverkansråd* (Teachers' Collaboration Council)
NFS	*Nordens Fackliga Samorganisation* (Council of Nordic Trade Unions)
OFR	*Offentliganställdas Förhandlingsråd* (Public Employees Negotiation Council)
PERC	Paneuropean regional council
PTK	*Förhandlings- och samverkansrådet PTK* (Bargaining and Cooperation Council), formerly *Privattjänstemannakartellen* (Bargaining Cartel of Private Sector White-collar Collar Workers)
SAC	Sveriges Arbetares Centralorganisation (Swedish Central Organization of Workers)
Saco	*Sveriges Akademikers Centralorganisation* (Swedish Confederation of Professional Associations)
Saco-S	Negotiation council for Saco unions with members in the state
SAF	*Svenska Arbetsgivareföreningen* (Swedish Employers' Confederation)

SKR	*Sveriges Kommuner och Regioner* (Swedish Association of Local Authorities and Regions)
SLF	*Skogs- och Lantbrukstjänstemannaförbundet* (Association of Forestal and Agricultural Employees)
SN	*Svenskt Näringsliv* (Confederation of Swedish Enterprise)
ST	*Fackförbundet ST* (Union of Civil Servants)
TCO	*Tjänstemännens Centralorganisation* (Swedish Confederation of Professional Employees)
Transport	*Svenska Transportarbetareförbundet* (Swedish Transport Workers' Union)
TUAC	Trade Union Advisory Committee to the OECD

Chapter 29

Conclusion: Trade Unions picking up the pieces from the neoliberal challenge

Jeremy Waddington, Torsten Müller and Kurt Vandaele

For about the past forty years trade unions in the European Union (EU) have had to cope with a neoliberal agenda that has challenged their organizational strength and restricted their capacity to act. This neoliberal agenda, pursued by employers and policymakers at national and European level, has been much more than merely a macroeconomic policy programme involving trade liberalization, fiscal discipline and inflation control at the expense of full employment. It has been a broader political programme, cutting across different policy areas, ostensibly to free markets from what the proponents of this programme saw as unduly bureaucratic political and corporatist control (Streeck 2013: 55). From this perspective trade unions, collective bargaining and other forms of joint regulation by collective actors are perceived as institutional 'rigidities' that obstruct the functioning of free markets and employers' discretion (Baccaro and Howell 2017; Gamble 2014). As a consequence, a range of structural reforms and policies were enacted that have negatively affected the unions' capacity to act.

Chapter 1 outlined the range of measures representing the 'neoliberal challenge' and their consequences for trade union organization and activities. In order to review trade union responses to these challenges it is important to recall three key elements of this challenge at this juncture. First, the reduction of the role and size of the state, as both a regulator and an employer. The liberalization and privatization of large parts of public services have led to a significant shrinking of public sector employment, which traditionally is a stronghold of unionization. Second, labour market reforms were designed to increase flexibility. This has involved measures to reduce employment protection and to boost low-wage and atypical employment, linked to fissured workplaces (Weil 2014), coupled with the decentralization and, in some instances, de-unionization of collective bargaining and wage-setting. Third, a general distancing of the state and political parties from union involvement in policymaking: for instance, by dismantling or downgrading the significance of tripartite arrangements for policy formulation, albeit to different degrees in different Member States (Ebbinghaus and Weishaupt 2021).

Trade unions have received little help from Europe. On the contrary, from the outset the asymmetry between market-creating and market-correcting measures has been a defining characteristic of the European integration process, which prompted Streeck to call the EU a 'liberalization machine' (2013: 148). The European-level push for neoliberal structural reforms reached its highpoint with the establishment of the new system of economic governance that began to emerge in 2010 in the wake of the management of the Great Recession of 2007–2009. The reforms pushed for in the context of the European Semester and by the Troika (comprising the European Commission, the European Central Bank and the International Monetary Fund) represented a 'new European interventionism' (Schulten and Müller 2013), which aimed at 'an overall reduction in the wage-setting power of trade unions' (European Commission 2012: 104). Only recently have there been signs of a more union-friendly shift in European-level discourse, acknowledging the importance of strong labour and social systems for economic development and political stability (Schulten and Müller 2021). This shift in discourse has found concrete expression in, for instance, the adoption of the European Pillar of Social Rights in 2017 and more recently, in autumn 2022, in the adoption of the Directive on adequate minimum wages in the EU. It remains to be seen whether the latter will help to provide a more supportive European-level framework for unions or whether, in light of the crisis caused by the Covid-19 pandemic and the war in Ukraine, there will be a return to neoliberal supply-side approaches.

While trade unions in all EU countries have had to cope with these neoliberal challenges, their impact on the unions' organizational strength and their capacity to act have differed markedly between Member States. This can be traced to three factors. First, in terms of the structural environment the extent of the neoliberal challenges varies markedly between countries (Baccaro and Howell 2017; Bohle and Grescovits 2012; Dølvik and Martin 2014). Exemplary of this variation is the impact of the management of the Great Recession on collective bargaining, which ranged from a 'frontal assault' (Marginson 2015) in the countries subjected to the measures prescribed by the Troika, to incremental adaptions in the Nordic countries, which aimed principally at stabilizing rather than undermining existing bargaining arrangements (Dølvik and Marginson 2018).

Second, the impact also depends on the state of trade unionism. The country chapters illustrate that unions in the various countries differ significantly in their capacity to resist the neoliberal challenge. Influencing their capacity to resist the neoliberal challenge were union differences in organizational strength – union density – (Vandaele 2019) and financial and material resources. Furthermore, trade unions' embeddedness in the existing institutional framework provided them with different opportunity structures to influence policymaking at national level. The handling of the Great Recession once again is instructive in this respect. Two different developmental paths can be distinguished (Bieling 2013): one path was followed by countries belonging to the model of Nordic corporatism or the continental European model of social partnership, for instance Austria and Germany, which enabled unions to cushion and moderate the crisis through 'crisis corporatism' (Urban 2015). This means that the trade unions had access to policymaking and were actively involved in crisis management. In the countries of southern Europe and throughout much of Central and Eastern Europe (CEE), however, such a crisis-corporatist path was blocked because institutional access to policymaking never existed or has been further weakened by the management of the crisis (Glassner 2013).

Third, and closely associated with the second point, is the absence of a viable counter-narrative to neoliberalism from within left-of-centre European political parties (Coates 2007; Glyn 2001; Haugsgjerd and Bale 2017). This is compounded by the absence, with the arguable exception of the Nordic countries, of a consensus, or even a shared view, regarding the relationship between left-of-centre parties and trade unions. In combination, points two and three reduce trade unions' capacity to secure support for preferred policy choices within Member States, suggesting that *most* trade unions are unable to rely on political allies to implement legislation that will externally support trade union renewal. As a consequence of the variation in both the extent of the neoliberal challenge and the unions' resilience, over time the existing divergence in European industrial relations, more generally, and the unions' capacity to act, more specifically, increased even further (Dølvik and Marginson 2018; Müller and Platzer 2016).

Against this background, this Conclusion reviews the range of trade union actions implemented to meet the challenges arising from neoliberalism. It comprises four sections. The first section focuses on trade union renewal within the Member States. It engages with unionization but also issues of union structure, democracy, resources and finance in order to map the measures taken within unions to improve their organizational strength. The second section examines and analyses the unions' interaction with external actors: potential members, employers and the state, and civil society organizations. The third section 3 addresses activities at European level, while the fourth section reviews the responses of our country experts to Visser's (2019) categories and speculates on future developments. It is acknowledged that trade union actions at and within Member State and European levels may be interconnected. Treating each level and action in a separate section, however, facilitates explanation and identification of the parameters that influence renewal. (Unless otherwise specified, all country references in the Conclusion refer to the country chapters.)

Trade union renewal

Although myriad challenges are facing trade unions within the EU, trade unionists retain some discretion in the countermeasures they implement to adapt to changed circumstances. The range of union countermeasures aimed at renewing or revitalizing their organization is vast and includes innovative experiments intended to equip unions with a membership, agenda and organization 'fit' to meet the neoliberal challenge (Bernaciak and Kahancová 2017a; Frege and Kelly 2004). To a degree, these experiments are contingent on national circumstances, particularly the degree of trade union institutional embeddedness. Hence the reliance in this publication on country chapters to elaborate them in detail. It is useful at this juncture, however, to review the range of union countermeasures to illustrate some of the principal features of trade union renewal. To this end recruiting and organizing new members, restructuring representation, servicing and organizing, and trade union finance are discussed. It is acknowledged from the outset that there are overlaps between these categories.

Recruiting and organizing new members

Many unions implement organizing campaigns with the intention of bringing new groups of workers into membership, known as 'greenfield organizing'; or attempt to deepen density where unionization is already present, known as 'brownfield organizing'. Organizing is understood among mainstream unions mainly in terms of recruitment and less so in terms of mobilization, let alone 'deep organizing' (Holgate et al. 2018; McAlevey, 2016; Vandaele 2020). Although it is now more than three decades since unions in the United States (US) launched the initial organizing campaigns, the meaning of organization in this sense remains ambiguous and contested. Some argue that organizing constitutes a radical break from union approaches based on the servicing of members and requires a reconceptualization of union operations and activities (Carter 2006). In contrast, others fail to see an absolute separation between organizing and servicing, and view organizing as a campaign tool that can be deployed selectively and directed towards specific short-term targets without a complete overhaul of union operations and objectives (de Turberville 2004; Simms 2012).

It appears that a number of conditions need to be met to engage with the organizing approach. First, it needs to be recognized within a trade union that its membership decline is a problem. In Ghent system countries, for example, the maintenance of relatively high membership levels may explain why trade unions adopted elements of the organizing approach later than other unions. Second, unionists need to recognize that the organizing approach is the preferred method. In southern Europe other approaches appear preferable: for example, in France union legitimacy is based on a 'unionism of activism' rather than mass membership (Sullivan 2009), whereas in Spain the elections of workplace representatives and works councils act as a focus for renewal (Martinez Lucio 2017). Third, the organizing approach requires the reallocation of resources or generation of new resources. Many trade unions in the EU16 are in a position to reallocate resources, whereas their counterparts in the EU11 tend to be more reliant on resources transferred for unions in the EU16, the ETUFs or EU project money for capacity building.

What is clear is that organizing requires a skill set that was not initially available among a sufficient number of full-time trade union officers to sustain long-term organizing campaigns. In consequence, several unions, primarily from Anglophone countries, set up organizing academies, introduced organizing skills sessions into training programmes and, in some instances, established networks of organizers to drive campaigns forward (Heery et al. 2000; Simms et al. 2013). It is also apparent that the appointment or election of senior unionists with a commitment to organizing underpins most organizing campaigns. The election of Detlev Wetzel as *Erster Vorsitzender* (President) of the Metalworkers' Union (IGM, *Industriegewerkschaft Metall*) in Germany, for example, resulted from his success in promoting organizing in North Rhine Westphalia, where he was the *Bezirksleiter* (Regional Secretary), and resulted in an intensification of organizing activities within the union as a whole (Schmalz and Thiel 2017). Accompanying a commitment on the part of senior unionists is intensive activity within the locality of the organizing campaign to promote union organization and to build cadres of activists (Arnholtz et al. 2016; Connolly et al. 2017). Similarly, organizing techniques need to vary from industry to industry within countries, as well as between countries if membership gains are to be made (Mrozowicki 2014; Mundlak 2020; Simms and Holgate 2010).

Superficially, there appears to be a convergence in union responses to membership decline through the organizing approach (Ibsen and Tapia 2017). The country chapters, however, illustrate huge variation in the form of organizing campaigns, and also its limited spread throughout the EU. Among these variations three features appear in many organizing campaigns, albeit in different forms: the head office or central identification of target groups of potential members; the allocation of resources to identify issues relevant to the target group at the place of work, coupled with the deployment of organizers; and the recruitment of new members, together with the identification of grassroots worker leaders who might increase the likelihood of the new group of members becoming self-sustaining within the union (McAlevey 2016). US-based research demonstrates that the success of organizing depends on the range and intensity of practices deployed during the campaign (Bronfenbrenner and Hickey 2004), confirming a requirement for specific organizing resources, strategic planning and member mobilization (Fletcher and Hurd 2001). Similarly organizing requires unions to identify the concerns of potential members and establish a connection between these concerns and the union (Connolly et al. 2017; Knotter 2017). It should be noted, however, that the split between the American Federation of Labor-Congress of Industrial Organizations (AFL-CIO) and the Change to Win trade unions in 2005 did not result in a statistically significant improvement in performance among the Change to Win trade unions, although they employed more organizing practices (Aleks 2015).[1]

In terms of aggregate national membership, organizing has at best merely slowed the rate of decline in union density. Specific unions, however, have recorded membership increases or membership stability as a result of deploying additional resources to organizing (Holgate et al. 2018; Pernicka and Aust 2007; Wetzel et al. 2013). The most likely targets of organizing campaigns are private sector services; women, young and migrant workers; and those employed in low quality precarious jobs, reflecting both current union organizational weaknesses and segments of growing employment (Martinez Lucio et al. 2017; Pulignano et al. 2016; Simms 2017). The central theme is to extend union organization to previously neglected segments of the labour force. The exceptions to this general observation are often the result of industrial union organization, which may limit the possible targets for organizing. In Germany, IGM, for example, has attempted to organize workers employed in the growing wind turbine segment of the metals industry: that is, workers in companies building new products. It has also tried to extend organization among white-collar workers within the metal industry from its largely blue-collar base, and is campaigning to organize workers subcontracted by engineering companies at which the union has members (Nicklich and Helfen 2019). In practice, IGM primarily campaigns to heighten density within the metal industry. The case of the Construction-Agriculture-Environment Union (IGBAU, *Industriegewerkschaft Bauen-Agrar-Umwelt*), however, demonstrates that industrial organization need not be an impermeable barrier to organizing in that, from a traditional membership in construction and agriculture, IGBAU has sustained a long-term campaign to organize cleaners in some large German cities, demonstrating that greenfield organizing is possible.

1 In 2005 seven trade unions split from the AFL-CIO to form a new union confederation called 'Change to Win'. The Change to Win unions argued that insufficient resources were allocated to organizing within AFL-CIO. The split was thus intended to ensure that organizing was prioritized to a greater extent within Change to Win. Analysis of ten years of data from the Labor Relations Board and the National Mediation Board shows that the effect of Change to Win policies on whether a union won a certification election and the number or percentage of workers successfully organized was not statistically significant (Aleks 2015). In short, the implementation of organizing practices by Change to Win trade unions did not improve organizing performance.

Irrespective of the chosen targets, organizing requires a shift of resources within trade unions to fund and sustain campaigns. This shift has created tensions within unions between those with a servicing background and brief, and the beneficiaries of additional resources engaged in organizing (Simms et al. 2013). The shift in resources has, in some instances, also created an imperative to secure additional members to compensate for the funds allocated to organizing. Financial difficulties have arisen where insufficient additional members are organized to compensate for the costs. In the Netherlands, for example, the Dutch Trade Union Federation (FNV, *Federatie Nederlandse Vakbewegung*) proposed to lay off 400 of 2,000 union employees because of such financial problems in 2018 (Winkel 2018).[2] Differences in commitment to organizing may also result in political disputes between unions. While in the EU there has been nothing comparable to the split within the AFL-CIO between the Change to Win trade unions, which advocated organizing, and other affiliates (Estreicher 2006), the reluctance of some unions to embrace organizing is concurrent with the emergence of 'radical unions' and grassroots movements in France and Poland, which make a space for participation and self-organization for groups of workers reluctant to participate in more traditional or mainstream trade unions (Denis 2012; Mathers 2017; Mrozowicki and Maciejewska 2017). Overall, however, 'radical unions' are in the minority and currently are limited to a few European countries (Connolly et al. 2014), although their tactics and strategies towards precarious and vulnerable workers may inspire mainstream unions (Però 2020: Vandaele 2021)

As the country chapters make clear, there are very different approaches to organizing within and between unions. The country chapters highlight the merits and limitations of this variation and explain why some unions have not engaged in organizing. Key to the variation in organizing strategies are the terms of the national social model and union strategies. Where periodic elections are required for works councillors, for example in Belgium (Vandaele 2020), Germany (Behrens 2009) and Spain (Martinez Lucio 2017), unions campaign in workplaces for votes, which raises their profile and may attract new members. Elsewhere, under different institutional circumstances, 'leverage' has been used to reveal a company's vulnerabilities, which may be exploited to promote union

2 As a result of strike action the number of proposed redundancies was reduced to 250.

organization (Ramesh 2021). Where trade unions are based on company or other restricted scopes of organization, resources and expertise are rarely available in sufficient quantities to implement wide-ranging organizing campaigns. In most of these instances organizing campaigns do not take place. In a limited number of such cases in CEE, support from European Trade Union Federations (ETUFs) and individual national unions based in western Europe in the form of resources and expertise have sustained organizing campaigns.

Restructuring representation

A second core area of union renewal concerns the restructuring of representation. As with organizing there is a huge variation within and between trade union movements. In this context union mergers, union democracy and shifts in the relationship between servicing and organizing within unions figure large.

Mergers

Throughout much of Europe, and linked to membership decline, is union structural change by means of mergers. 'Merger' is used as a collective term that includes amalgamations, in which two or more unions combine to form a new union; and acquisitions, usually involving a larger union's absorption of a smaller union (Waddington 2006; Waddington et al. 2005). Mergers take many forms, resulting in no small part from the confederal structure and constitutional power of the confederation(s) within each Member State. In Czechia, Germany and Slovakia, for example, confederations have very little constitutional authority over affiliated trade unions, with the consequence that mergers result from initiatives taken within affiliated trade unions. In contrast, in France, Italy and Spain confederations exert some constitutional authority over the constituent federations. As a result, mergers take place within confederal structures and usually along the lines agreed within the confederation. In Austria and the Netherlands intermediary positions have been established whereby confederations have some authority over affiliated unions, but some mergers and other structural changes have been completed without confederal agreement. Furthermore, in countries with multiple confederations there are instances of mergers between confederations, exemplified recently by mergers between the Danish Confederation of Trade Unions (*Landsorganisationen i Danmark*, LO) and the Confederation of

Professionals in Denmark (*Functionærernes og Tjenestemændenes Fællesråd*, FTF) in January 2019 to form the Confederation of Trade Unions (*Fagbevægelsens Hovedorganisation*, FH), and between the National Confederation of Hungarian Trade Unions (*Magyar Szakszervezetek Országos Szövetsége*, MSZOSZ) and the Autonomous Trade Union Confederation (*Autonóm Szakszervezetek Szövetsége*, ASZSZ) to form the Hungarian Trade Union Association (*Magyar Szakszervezeti Szövetség*, MASZSZ) in December 2013. The extent to which these confederal mergers promote mergers between affiliated unions remains to be seen.

Four further features are associated with the merger process. The first is that where industrial unionism is dominant the impact of membership decline is uneven. Mining, print, leather and textile unions, for example, have disappeared as independent trade unions in many countries as a result of the contraction of employment in these industries. In these circumstances the industrial union structure and attached constitutional arrangements prohibit recruitment beyond the agreed scope of the union, effectively preventing organization in new or expanding segments of the economy. More conglomerate unions with recruitment bases straddling several industries have thus emerged from the merger process (Visser 2012).

A second feature associated with the merger process is the concentration of membership in a few, relatively large trade unions. This raises questions of internal union democracy: how are members from different industries represented within post-merger trade unions? Similarly, the concentration of membership within fewer trade unions brings into question the relationship between confederations and affiliated trade unions. In many confederations, for example, decision-making is a function of votes taken by affiliates, which, in turn, is dependent on membership size. The concentration of membership into fewer unions has thus resulted in cases where very few affiliated unions can determine the policy of the confederation and calls into question the utility of confederal affiliation to the smaller trade unions, which can exert very little influence over policy direction. As noted in the country chapters, approaches to this dilemma vary. An exceptional example is the Dutch FNV, in which the two largest unions *FNV Bondgenoten* and *AbvaKabo FNV* came to represent about two-thirds of affiliated membership. Following a merger involving these two unions and several smaller FNV affiliates the resultant 'one big union' agreed to its division into twenty-three sectors, each with industrial, occupational, gender or age interests. In short, the pre-merger size of *FNV Bondgenoten* and *AbvaKabo FNV* necessitated radical restructuring to sustain confederal democracy.

A third feature associated with the merger process concerns the extent to which mergers are defensive or strategic. Continuing a long-standing pattern (Waddington 2006), the majority of recent mergers are defensive: unions may incur membership losses or financial pressures, or become subject to some other adverse event, as a consequence of which they seek a merger. In these circumstances the choice of merger partner may be influenced by the terms of the offers received rather than any 'industrial logic'. Where industrial bargaining is in place both or all pre-merger unions usually retain a degree of bargaining autonomy. It should be noted that in many defensive mergers post-merger restructuring results in reductions in the number of union employees and the rationalization of administrative units in attempts to cut post-merger costs. Much more infrequent are mergers with an unambiguous strategic intent, usually defined by reference to industrial or political circumstances. In Germany the merger to form the United Services Union (ver.di, *Vereinte Dienstleistungsgewerkschaft*) in 2001 combined almost all public and private services sector unionists,[3] while in Spain the General Union of Workers (UGT, *Unión General de Trabajadores*) reorganized its federal structure to comprise three main federations with responsibilities in public services, private sector services, and industry, construction and agriculture, respectively. The General Federation of Belgian Labour (ABVV/FGTB, *Algemeen Belgisch Vakverbond/ Fédération Générale du travail de Belgique*), with seven affiliates today, is also slowly moving in this direction.

A fourth feature arising from the merger process is not universal, but not uncommon either, and concerns relations between the post-merger union and members. The services to members provided by post-merger unions are comparable with those provided by the pre-merger unions (Baraldi et al. 2010; Behrens and Pekarek 2012). In some circumstances it is questionable, however, whether mergers promote renewal. In the Danish context, for example, shop stewards belonging to acquired unions are less likely to contact the headquarters of the post-merger union about

---

3 Two unions did not participate in the ver.di merger. They organize workers in the services sector: *Gewerkschaft Nahrung-Genuss-Gaststätten* (NGG, Food, Beverage and Catering Union) and *Gewerkschaft Erziehung und Wissenschaft* (GEW, Education and Science Union).

organizing activities than their counterparts in non-merged unions (Navrbjerg and Larsen 2018). This confirms that the re-establishment of working relationships in post-merger unions is a time-consuming process and may inhibit development within post-merger unions (Waddington 2006).

Union democracy

A further element of restructuring representation linked to changing union membership composition is exemplified by the increasing diversity of union membership, resulting from both mergers and labour market change. This process raises issues of representation within trade unions. Traditional approaches to union democracy were geographical and vertical in orientation, insofar as the region or industry was treated as the basic unit of democratic organization (Edelstein and Warner 1975; Webb and Webb 1897). The merger process resulted in a range of sections, trade groups and *Fachbereiche* within trade unions to accommodate the increasing range of industries in which members worked, but a basic unit of internal union democracy remained vertical. Such representative structures take little or no account of variation among the membership: sex and age, for example, were downplayed by comparison with industry. To adjust to the changing membership composition, a range of horizontal structures have been introduced, designed to bring together members with particular, often personal, characteristics. These horizontal structures supplement geographical and vertical forms of representation. Such horizontal structures allow, for example, the representation of women, young workers, unemployed workers, retired workers, workers with specific sexual orientations or gender identities, and workers with different ethnic origins, irrespective of their geographical or industrial location of employment (McBride 2001; Hodder and Kretsos 2015; Humphrey 2002). In some instances, these developments have been linked to systems of proportional representation whereby the composition of a committee is proportional to the composition of the membership represented by the committee: if 60 per cent of the membership is female, for example, women make up 60 per cent of the committee representing that membership (Terry 1996). In short, internal representative structures have become more complex and often more expensive in many unions to accommodate diversity within the membership.

Servicing and organizing

A third element of restructuring representation is directly related to organizing and concerns whether, or the extent to which, organizing displaces servicing as the principal union purpose. While organizing is unlikely to completely overwhelm the servicing function, it is commonplace for the relationship between the two functions within unions to change fundamentally. Within the Service Employees International Union (SEIU) in the United States, the stated intention of Andy Stern, the President elected in 2007, was to spend half the budget on organizing, although in 2020, 28.2 per cent of the budget of $255 million was spent on organizing Americans for Fair Treatment (Americans for Fair Treatment 2022).[4] The extent of the commitment to organizing within the SEIU is rarely replicated. Unions have introduced measures to mainstream or routinize organizing within their repertoire of activity (Simms et al. 2013) by adapting, reformulating and selectively using the organizing approach (Czarzasty et al. 2014; Geary and Gamwell 2019; Krzywdzinski 2010; Nicklich and Helfen 2019; Thomas 2016). Similarly, the establishment of organizing and leverage departments, often with direct access to senior union policymakers, coupled with teams of organizers that may be deployed anywhere within the union's remit are features of many unions as they commit to organizing. The point here is that unions' internal activities and the deployment of staff and resources have been restructured in unions that have committed to organizing: in part, the extent of this restructuring reflects the extent of the commitment to organizing.

Trade union finance

It is noteworthy that issues associated with the reform of systems of union financial management rarely appear in the renewal literature, yet union finances impinge on unions' capacity to campaign, deliver support to members and ensure member representation. In France, for example,

---

4 The same sources report that the SEIU spends 28.2 per cent of its budget on organizing compared with 19.4 per cent on political activities and lobbying; 13.9 per cent on investments and fixed assets; 11.5 per cent on member support; 11.0 per cent on general overheads; 6.3 per cent on benefits; 4.4 per cent on union administration; 1.8 per cent on per capita tax; 1.8 per cent on direct taxes; 0.9 per cent on contributions, gifts and grants; and 0.8 per cent on other expenses.

union management remains archaic, with damaging consequences for the collection of membership subscriptions and resource allocation within unions (Andolfatto and Labbé 2008). Elsewhere, some unions are subject to 'cost disease pressures'; in other words, costs rising at a faster rate than inflation, at least before 2021, in part as a result of issues associated with the management of collective action organizations (Willman et al. 2020). It is likely that increasing heterogeneity of membership and their representation will increase internal costs further. The country chapters indicate two key trends regarding union finance.

First, membership contributions remain a significant source of union income in all Member States. Membership decline or stagnation, however, is not necessarily associated with financial difficulties. Unions, particularly those in the EU16, have been able to raise membership fees, at least, to partially compensate for membership losses. Membership decline has been particularly financially damaging in two circumstances: where unions are small and where industrial union organization prevails. Where unions are small – such as company unions in the EU11 – membership decline may undermine them. As many of these unions are unable to support the employment of a full-time union official, resources to reverse membership decline are often absent. Where industrial union organization is still present, unions in declining industries sustain membership losses and financial difficulties because they are unable to extend organization into expanding segments of the economy where other unions have established recruitment bases. In these circumstances many of the declining industrial unions have sought a merger.

A second point emerging from the country chapters regarding union finance concerns the differences between the EU16 and EU11. In general terms, trade unions based in the EU16 tend to be more financially robust than their counterparts in the EU11. In part, this is because of the long-term accumulation of reserves and assets, and their relative size, which spreads the risk of membership decline over a wider area of the labour market. In contrast, many of the small company-based unions operating within the EU11 have neither accumulated reserves nor assets on which to draw to mitigate the impact of financial downturns. Such company unions also often do not have the capacity to recruit elsewhere and thus spread the risk of membership decline more widely. Although EU11 unions have access to funds from the sale and rent of property 'inherited' from the pre-1990 period, these funds tend to be at the disposal of confederations rather than workplace unions. Campaigning by unions in the EU11 is also supported by the transfer of funds from trade union organizations based in the EU16 and EU project funding intended to build capacity.

New services and servicing techniques

Within the financial constraints arising from membership decline, union renewal has seen the introduction of packages of financial services embracing, among other things, discounted insurance, health care and holidays intended to attract newly individualized potential members and to retain existing members. Some unions have claimed that members subscribing to these services can recoup the costs of their membership contributions. The costs to the unions of these financial services are marginal, as the service provider meets the costs of marketing (TUC 1988; Bassett and Cave 1993). Survey evidence from fourteen European countries, however, indicates that packages of financial services are of little attraction to members compared with 'traditional' trade union services of support at work and improved pay and conditions (Waddington 2014).

A further area of union innovation concerns the delivery of services. In several instances innovations are linked to organizing insofar as organizing required communications with members and potential members and surveys to ascertain the issues around which a campaign might be developed. The internet and social media were often used to conduct these communications and research. In addition to this relatively narrow usage the same tools are now envisaged as a means to communicate in real time during industrial disputes, to transform the practice of industrial democracy, to improve service delivery, and to introduce new forms of member engagement (Clark 2000: 106–124; Shostack 1991: 101–124). Subsequently gathered European evidence confirms that internet and social media tools have assisted organizing campaigns (Fitzgerald et al. 2012), membership involvement (Kerr and Waddington 2014), generating international solidarity (Martinez Lucio et al. 2017), union networking (Martinez Lucio and Stuart 2009), and the conduct of industrial disputes (Rego et al. 2016). The country chapters, however, show that there tend to be gaps between actual membership and members' engagement with the internet and social media. A particularly innovative illustration of the use of the internet and social media is ver.di's Mediafon initiative, designed to organize the self-employed (Haake 2017). This initiative of almost twenty years' standing uses electronic media to maintain contact with self-employed union members, many of whom have no stable workplace and may work at a number of locations during a given period. Where support and advice are requested by self-employed members it is dispensed via access to experts employed by ver.di in the relevant area of the member's concern. Other union organizations in Belgium, France, Italy and Spain have implemented the principles underpinning this approach to support solo self-employed workers and freelancers, including, on occasion, platform workers (Vandaele 2021).

A new policy agenda

Changes in the labour market and unions' political positions have promoted revisions of the union agenda and the means of its implementation. In particular, attention is now directed towards bringing workers previously outside unions into membership. Unions have thus introduced policies appropriate for these groups. Trade unions have also sought to establish new relationships with employers, the state and campaigning civil society organizations, and to set a union agenda on topical issues. These elements of a new policy agenda are outlined here to further illustrate the range of policy options being pursued by unions within the EU.

Policies towards potential members

Policies intended to protect: workers in precarious employment or in private sector services; young, migrant, and agency workers; black, Asian and minority ethnic workers; those on low pay; and workers in the 'gig' or platform economy are now found in various forms throughout Europe. In several cases the introduction of such policies represented a marked change in union approach. Precarious and migrant workers, for example, were initially viewed as outsiders, and unions acted to defend the interests of existing members. The policy shift to defend the 'new' groups of workers thus represents a shift from defending 'vested interests' to acting as a 'sword of justice' (Flanders 1970). Similarly, the introduction of statutory minimum wages in Germany (2015) was the result of long-running campaigns by unions with members concentrated in services, which eventually persuaded unions with memberships in manufacturing to support the introduction of a statutory minimum wage (Bruttel et al. 2018).

While organizing looms large in many of the policy initiatives directed towards workers previously regarded as outsiders, it is by no means the only policy approach employed. Trade unions have pressured employers with unionized workforces to set minimum standards for the employment of agency and outsourced work; have cooperated with regulatory bodies, such as labour inspectorates, in an attempt to enforce existing standards; have lobbied governments to regulate more robustly; and have campaigned for improved training and skill acquisition opportunities (Burgess et al. 2013; Doellgast et al. 2018; Heery and Abbott 2000). Many of these initiatives rely on existing industrial relations institutions and practices to facilitate campaigns.

Examples of union policies on migrant and young workers illustrate the breadth of the initiatives launched. Reference to the notion that unions are positioned differently in Member States with reference to markets, society and class (Hyman 2001) enables Connolly et al. (2017) to demonstrate that Spanish unions have tended to coalesce between class and social rights in using state resources and social services to further the interests of migrants, while in the Netherlands social rights and ethnicity guided union policy, integral to which was the promotion of a greater sensitivity to ethnic communities within social dialogue. Examination of the approaches to migrant workers among Italian unions also illustrates a strong commitment to organizational change and the representation of migrant workers' specific interests (Marino 2012). All of these initiatives remain national in orientation. Attempts by IGBAU to establish the European Migrant Workers' Union (EMWU) – an international union for migrant workers – with the intention of establishing branches in several European countries came to nothing as national unions defended their vested interests within the nation-state rather than cede authority to the EMWU (Greer et al. 2013).[5]

Although demand for union membership has been persistently high from young workers across the EU (Caraker et al. 2015; Turner and D'Art 2012; Vendramin 2007), young workers have very limited knowledge of unions (Fernández Rodríguez et al. 2015; Hodder 2019). Furthermore, young and older workers are less likely to be unionized than those in their forties and fifties (Blanchflower 2007; Blanchflower and Bryson 2020), while inter-generational unionization rates appeared to widen between

---

[5] This initiative is discussed below in the context of transnational developments.

2004 and 2014, with increases in the median age of union members in most Member States (Vandaele 2018, 2019).[6] In these circumstances it is thus not surprising that unions have launched a wide range of initiatives intended to bring more young workers into membership.

To this end unions have intensified the following: the use of outreach activities, including visits to schools, higher education institutions and job fairs; the availability of information on the social rights of young workers; links between unions and youth organizations; and campaigning on issues important to young people, such as the removal of the youth rate in national minimum wage schemes and reductions in the period of work before access to benefits is allowed (Hodder and Houghton 2015; Tapia and Turner 2018; Vandaele 2018). In addition, unions have 'tailored' their messaging thorough the use of internet and social media (Geelan 2015). Within unions, representative structures exclusively for young members have been established, and reduced membership contributions or free membership schemes are now commonplace (Vandaele 2012). The various measures directed specifically at young workers ensure that they continue to join unions, but the widening of inter-generational unionization rates (Vandaele 2018, 2019) and the overall decline in unionization rates demonstrate that young workers are not joining in sufficient numbers to replace older members that are leaving unions.

A further element of a new policy agenda concerns union agenda setting on topical issues, such as digitalization, low carbon economy, the platform economy and family-friendly policies. Again, the country chapters illustrate considerable variation in these initiatives as regards whether they are pursued and, if so, at what intensity and how. Among the factors that influence these policies are the industrial location and gender composition of the membership, coupled with the union's organizing intentions. Unions with significant membership employed in nuclear energy production, for example, are unlikely to campaign vigorously for the dismantling of nuclear power stations. It should also be acknowledged that different unions and trade unionists highlight different aspects of these topical issues. German unions emphasize issues of control and surveillance in the context of digitalization, whereas workplace representatives highlight the risks of job losses and downgraded wages and

---

6 Only in Austria, Hungary and Italy did the median age of trade unionists decline between 2004 and 2014.

working conditions (Ilsøe 2017). Elsewhere, gender inequalities, job security, skill degradation, and the distribution of productivity gains arising from digitalization have been brought to the fore (Drahokoupil and Vandaele 2021). The key point here is that unions are developing and implementing policies on topical issues. The country chapters demonstrate that these policy processes are uneven in their development and have been directed towards different objectives, contingent on national circumstances. Although several of these topical issues are international in coverage and effect, it is also apparent that national trade union initiatives, rather than a coordinated transnational response, loom large in the union response.

External relations: employers, the state and civil society

Revitalizing organizational strength is essential for unions' external relations in terms of their capacity to regulate the employment relationship in interactions with employers, policymakers and civil society. Union organizational strength in respect of union density and the capacity to mobilize members, however, is only one factor that determines the outcome of these interaction processes. Other important factors include broader institutional arrangements comprising the specific shape of labour law, the collective bargaining system, the system of company-level employee participation, the welfare state and trade union access to political decision-making processes more generally. These institutional arrangements are the result of previous interaction processes and struggles between unions, employers and the state and can therefore be seen as institutionalizing the existing balance of power between the actors involved in the regulation of industrial relations (Brinkmann et al. 2008). A further factor that influences unions' external interaction processes is the ability to influence the public discourse on relevant policy issues and to cooperate and forge alliances with other civil society actors to put pressure on employers and governments. The power resources approach conceptualizes these different dimensions as the interplay between unions' organizational, institutional and societal power resources (Lehndorff et al. 2017; Schmalz and Dörre 2013). In their interactions with external actors, the unions draw on all three sources of power but the specific mixture of the three depends on the national industrial relations framework and is therefore highly country- and sector-specific.

In order to achieve their objectives, unions use three principal channels or arenas, each characterized by a specific constellation of actors and a country-specific set of rules and practices that either promote or restrict unions' regulatory capacity (Hyman 2001). The first channel is the system of collective bargaining and company-level structures of employee interest representation. The second channel is the 'political system' from the standpoint of the unions' embeddedness in corporatist and tripartite decision-making arrangements and their links to political parties as allies in the legislative process. Civil society and the broader public constitute the third arena, in which the unions engage in a battle of ideas by successfully trying to set the agenda and to influence public opinion in support of their regulatory interests.

One common trend emerging from all twenty-seven country chapters, albeit to varying degrees, is the attempts by employers and governments to reduce the unions' regulatory capacity in the first two arenas. In the field of collective bargaining this involves three main processes: first, the employers' gradual withdrawal from industry-level bargaining or their refusal to enter into such bargaining arrangements in the first place; second, promoting the decentralization of collective bargaining by reducing the regulatory scope of industry-level agreements. This involves measures such as loosening up the favourability principle, allowing for company-level derogations from industry-level agreements, more restrictive criteria for the extension of collective agreements, and converting industry-level agreements into less substantive and specific framework agreements (Müller et al. 2019: 631–632). The third process for reducing unions' regulatory capacity in the area of collective bargaining is decreasing bargaining security, which includes factors that support the unions' bargaining role. This involves measures such as introducing more restrictive strike regulations or more restrictive rules on union recognition, for instance, through more restrictive representativeness criteria as a precondition of bargaining or by extending negotiating rights to non-union representation structures (Müller et al. 2019: 635–636).

In the second arena, the 'political system', measures to reduce unions' capacity to influence political decisions include the weakening of their corporatist involvement or changing the nature of existing tripartite arrangements, for instance by reducing their competences, downgrading them from real decision-making bodies to mere consultative structures. This essentially reduces them to what Bernaciak (2017) with reference to the situation in Poland called 'PR corporatism'. Another measure mentioned in the country chapters is the distancing of political parties that formerly served as political allies within the parliamentary system.

Unions' responses to these challenges vary and are fundamentally influenced by the scale of the attack and their capacity to resist them. This, in turn, depends on the unions' organizational strength and institutional embeddedness. In other words, unions' strategies for retaining or restoring their regulatory capacity to act vis-à-vis employers and the state depends on the (perceived) means available to them.

Concerning the unions' response to these challenges, a general trend that emerges from the country chapters is a shift in the relative importance of the three arenas. While the first two arenas of collective bargaining and political lobbying are still the dominant means of regulating the employment relationship, the unions have considerably increased their engagement in the third arena of the broader public through campaigns, mass mobilization and alliances with other civil society organizations to complement and support their activities in the first two arenas. Expressed in the terminology of the power resources approach: to some extent the unions tried to compensate for their loss of organizational and institutional power resources by increasing their societal power resources. By stepping up their activities in the public sphere the unions tried to restore their capacity to act in the field of collective bargaining and political decision-making. The description of this general trend masks important country- and sector-specific differences in the strategic mix the unions pursued to restore their capacity to act vis-à-vis employers, the state and the broader public. In full awareness of the trade-off between depth and breadth, the following examination summarizes some key elements that emerged from the country chapters.

To restore their capacity to act vis-à-vis employers in the field of collective bargaining the unions, to varying degrees, used all three arenas. The first set of measures refers to attempts to resist the push towards decentralization from within the collective bargaining system; for instance, by regaining some degree of control over the process of decentralization. To retain the regulatory capacity of industry-level agreements, the objective was to ensure a process of 'organized decentralization' (Traxler 1995), which guarantees industry-level actors some control over company-level bargaining. For this purpose, unions in several countries accepted arrangements, such as framework agreements or opening clauses, that allow for company-level derogations from industry-level agreements as long as they define the terms under which these derogations can take place (Ibsen and Keune 2018). These measures, however, presuppose union presence at company or workplace level to ensure sufficient articulation between the two bargaining levels. This strategy of retaining some degree of strength from within, therefore, was largely limited to those countries in which unions still enjoyed some degree of organizational strength and/or institutional support for bargaining security. Examples include Austria, Denmark, Finland, Germany and the Netherlands.

Another measure for retaining the regulatory capacity of industry-level agreements was to circumvent formal changes to the bargaining system in support of decentralization by ensuring the support of employers for industry-level bargaining. Italy and Spain are examples: the unions there managed to encourage some employers to maintain the previous hierarchy of bargaining levels and to refrain from the formal opportunity to opt-out of industry-level agreements (Lehndorff et al. 2017).

A third strategy to restore the capacity to act in the field of collective bargaining was to lobby in the political arena for a more supportive legal framework. In the countries hit hardest by the Great Recession and the corresponding crisis management measures, such as Greece, Portugal, Romania and Spain, this involved a call – albeit with limited success – to reverse the neoliberal reforms that had led to the diminution or even abolition of the previous system of industry-level collective bargaining. Calls for legislative changes to strengthen the collective bargaining system, however, were not limited to the 'crisis countries'. In Germany, for instance, unions also lobbied for a change in the extension mechanism and the inclusion of a requirement to be covered by a collective agreement among the criteria for public procurement.

The political arena seemed to be the most difficult area for the unions in their efforts to restore their capacity to act from within. With the notable exception of the Nordic states, in most countries unions lost their traditional allies in the political system with the decline of social democratic parties. As a consequence, unions tended to become more pragmatic in their choice of political allies. Furthermore, the unions used of what was left of their institutional embeddedness to engage in corporatist arrangements to deal with economic crises such as the Great Recession and more recently the Covid-19 crisis. The example of Germany illustrates that, irrespective of the substantive results of corporatist crisis management, the simple involvement and addressing of interests that went beyond their core constituency considerably improved unions' public reputation.

All these attempts to improve their capacity to act vis-à-vis the employers and the state in the area of collective bargaining and the political system were increasingly supplemented and supported by activities in the third arena, civil society. The use of campaigns and mass mobilization to support demands and initiatives in the first two arenas is nothing new in countries such as Belgium, France, Italy, Portugal and Spain, in which the mobilization of the broader public and political strikes are traditionally important elements in the unions' repertoire of action. But what emerges from the country chapters is a general shift in the relative importance of activities aimed at a stronger engagement in and with civil society in other countries, including Austria, Germany, the Netherlands and Sweden, where this was not a traditional feature of unions' repertoire.

It should be noted that all these activities to improve unions' capacity to act in the first two arenas require some degree of organizational strength and institutional support for collective bargaining and lobbying activities. There is a significant difference between the EU16 and the EU11 in this respect. Despite the neoliberal attack on unions' capacity to act, in most western European countries the unions could still rely on a basic level of organizational strength, institutional support for collective bargaining and involvement in corporatist political decision-making. In most CEE countries the unions operated under much more adverse conditions. In a nutshell, their situation is characterized by low density; a fragmented union movement; limited regulatory capacity of collective bargaining because of decentralized bargaining (with the notable exception of the public sector); low bargaining security and low collective bargaining coverage; and a low level of corporatist embeddedness in political decision-making – where tripartite structures exist, they often have only consultative competences and are unable to influence unilateral government decisions. Even in the third arena CEE unions faced more difficult conditions than their western European counterparts because of the weakly developed civil society in the post-communist region (Howard 2002), which means that labour advocacy coalitions were not a standard element of unions' repertoire of action.

The country chapters confirm the findings of Bernaciak and Kahancova (2017b) and Trif et al. (2021) that under these adverse conditions CEE unions had to be innovative in developing their regulatory capacity. In contrast to unions in western Europe, which focused more strongly on strengthening their capacity to act in the area of collective bargaining, the CEE unions focused more strongly on their capacity to influence government decisions. This, in turn, is not surprising given the more important role of the state and legislation in regulating the employment relationship. Given their limited direct access to government decision-making they relied more heavily on mass demonstrations, public protests and direct democracy, such as people's initiatives and referenda (Bernaciak and Kahancova 2017b). In so doing, unions in CEE, similar to western European unions, opened up their agendas to new and formerly neglected segments of the workforce, addressing wider societal goals and issues that go beyond the traditional concerns of their core membership. While these initiatives were not always successful in influencing government decisions it nonetheless helped to raise their public profile and legitimacy.

To summarize, the country chapters confirm that unions are attempting to seek new relationships with employers and the state, as well as alliances with campaigning social movements and community campaigns. In essence, these union initiatives are aimed at building bridges between unionists and non-unionists in the form of a shared narrative, leading some to suggest that the object of such initiatives is social movement unionism (Nissen and Rosen 1999). Underpinning these initiatives are attempts to reframe union narratives to generate shared identities and solidarity between unionists and social movement activists (Hyman and Gumbrell-McCormick 2017; Tarrow 2005). To this end unions have campaigned with and/or supported environmental, women's, living-wage and a wide range of local community campaigns, among others.

Alliances involving unions and civil society organizations, however, are far from straightforward. In particular, such alliances are likely to be irregular and project-based rather than entail wide-ranging organizational change (Heery et al. 2011). Furthermore, the service-oriented practices of unions differ from the relational culture of community organizations, thus jeopardizing long-term joint involvement on the part of members of both unions and community organizations (Tapia 2013). The shift from workplace to community or broader concerns also requires a reformulation of union practice to embrace demands beyond the workplace (Pocock 2011). This could be problematic, as workplace issues, support at the workplace and improved terms of employment are central to recruiting and retaining union members, while issues beyond the workplace are relatively marginal (Waddington 2014). To be successful, such a shift requires a more complex mobilization and organization of workers based on an intersectional analysis of demands and issues (Doellgast et al. 2021).

The strategic challenge at European level

The internationalization of trade union activity involves two parallel processes: the development of meaningful international trade union organization with sufficient capacity to act, and an international orientation within national trade unions that are willing to engage in transnationally coordinated activities. During the 'golden age' from about 1945 to about 1975 the almost exclusive focus of union activity was within the nation-state. The globalization of production and trade, coupled with the associated growth in the number and scale of multinational companies (MNCs); successive enlargements of the EU; and the increasing scope of EU regulation, however, have rendered such an exclusive focus on the nation-state obsolete, necessitating a more pronounced international focus of trade union activity. The absence of transnational regulation to accompany the global shifts in production and trade has resulted in an unregulated space within which unions wish to introduce regulation. Specifically, within the EU, the range of transnational regulations is burgeoning, particularly in relation to European integration, the establishment of the European single market and the introduction of the euro. Each of these developments within the EU has created a further imperative for transnational activity if unions are to influence the terms of the European regulatory framework.

Institution-building was at the core of much initial transnational union activity. Following the establishment of the ETUC in 1973, it increased its coverage through affiliation. While the ETUC was formed with seventeen affiliates from fifteen countries, today it comprises ninety-two affiliates from thirty-nine countries, including Christian and communist unions. By the end of the twentieth century ETUC coverage was representative of western European trade unionism and its position as political interlocutor with European institutions was secure (Dølvik 1999), albeit on the basis of structure before action: that is, institutional coverage was more advanced than the capacity to mobilize (Turner 1991). During the early years of the twenty-first century ETUC coverage was extended throughout CEE (Degryse and Tilly 2013).

The ETUC was reorganized in 1999 around a key division of labour: while the ETUFs would handle industrial matters within multinationals, the ETUC was to be the primary institution dealing with the European Commission in the political sphere. EU regulations directed towards minimum standards in worker participation at national and transnational levels and within the boards of European companies; the establishment of a wide range of sectoral social dialogue committees; and the introduction of arrangements for pan-European social dialogue involving the ETUC and employers' organizations comprise but a small part of the emergent EU regulatory framework. Each of these developments necessitated a trade union response in terms of a policy position and institution-building.

To assess how these and other developments have impacted on the development of trade unions in the EU this section advances in two stages. The first stage identifies the challenges facing union organization at European level as the rate of European social policy development has slowed. The second stage examines initiatives taken beyond the formal ETUC and ETUFs. In practice, of course, there are links between these two levels of activity, but examining them separately facilitates analysis. At the core of both levels of activity are tensions between institution-building and trade union action, and between national and European levels of trade unionism. Evidence presented in the country chapters and elsewhere demonstrates that institution-building has not been matched by transnational trade union action of similar scope.

European social policy development: 'Europe yes, but differently'[7]

From the late 1970s, and particularly during the Jacques Delors Presidency of the European Commission, 1985–1995, the EU fostered improvements in trade union security and internationalization within Europe as efforts were made to inject a 'social dimension' into the European integration agenda to accompany the single market (Anderson

---

7 The slogan 'Europe Yes, But Differently' is taken from a ver.di campaign (*Europa ja, aber anders*) that highlighted the trend towards neoliberal policy solutions at European level and the downplaying of social market solutions.

1995; Bercusson 1992).[8] This development was characterized by wide-ranging debates and procedural reforms intended to promote social policy measures; the proposal of hard law solutions to social policy matters; and the funding of institutions necessary for a European social market, including the ETUC (Falkner 1998: 55–77; Hantrais 2000: 1–20). The attractiveness of these policies promoted a more wide-ranging interest in 'Europe' among some trade unionists as a means of finding a European solution to the decline of national unions that went beyond a permissive consensus (Ross 1995). In short, the 'attractiveness' of Europe promoted a shift of material and political resources by trade unionists to influence the form and structure of the proposed European social dimension.

Following this 'high point', the EU, influenced by political shifts in Member States, subsequently 'distanced' itself, in practice if not rhetorically, from the promotion of a European social dimension, particularly during the Manuel Barroso Presidency, 2004–2014 (Natali and Vanhercke 2011; Roth et al. 2011). Elements of the neoliberal economic and social agenda informed EU policymaking; the social policy measures that were adopted comprised many soft law elements and weak minimum standards, and made no attempt to upwardly harmonize social policy. Furthermore, a series of European Court of Justice (ECJ) decisions prioritized the operation of the single market over the rights of labour, including the right to strike (Bücker and Warneck 2010; Sapir 2014; Fazi 2014). Compounding these developments was the impact of the policies of the Troika following the sub-prime and financial crisis of 2008–2009, which effectively dismantled long-standing industrial relations systems in which trade unions were embedded in several countries (Koukiadaki et al. 2016; Schulten and Müller 2015). The accentuation of the asymmetry between market-enforcing and market-correcting measures (Scharpf 2009), coupled with the rising social deficit apparent in economic and social union (Hinarejos 2016) raise four significant strategic challenges for trade unions at European level.

First, the ETUC has steadfastly supported European integration on the assumption that it comprises both economic and social dimensions (Lapeyre 2018). This support ensures that resources and recognition are afforded to the ETUC by European institutions in the form of financial

---

8 At the time there was wide-ranging criticism of the Delors-led Commission from both the political right and the left (Ross 1995). Only with the hindsight of experience of successive Commissions has criticism from the left tended to dissipate.

support and social partner status. The position of the ETUC has become increasingly contradictory with the diminution of the social dimension. The ETUC supports European integration in principle, but in the absence of a viable social dimension it is implicitly, but rarely explicitly, critical of the process of European integration (Fazi 2014; Martin and Ross 2004). The ETUC has thus to decide: if it is in favour of a particular form of integration that incorporates a meaningful social dimension, what action should be taken when integration follows a different path? Compounding this situation is the ETUC's call to defend 'social Europe': that is, its various national formulations (ETUC 2015). As outlined in every country chapter, however, many of these national variants of the European social model are undergoing rapid and fundamental change, raising the questions: what is the objective of the call to defend 'social Europe' and is such a call best mounted from Brussels or within Member States? The increase in the diversity of national social models implicit in enlargement emphasizes the challenge faced by the ETUC in this context.

A second strategic challenge faced by the ETUC concerns the generation of social policy objectives around which affiliates can cohere. This challenge is exacerbated by the subsidiarity of social to economic aspects of integration and the disparity in national variants of the social model. A range of measures that were relatively uncontroversial, in principle if not in practice, were promoted and/or accepted by the ETUC and affiliates in the period up to about 2000, for example, in the areas of information and consultation, sectoral social dialogue, working time, and part-time and agency work. In addition, the European Social Charter was fundamentally revised in 1996 and the Charter of Fundamental Rights of the European Union was incorporated into the Treaty of Lisbon in 2009. In short, a growing body of legislation and Charter commitments underpinned the development of a rudimentary social dimension. At a general or abstract level trade unions support the further strengthening of the social dimension. The formulation of more concrete proposals, however, exposes the diversity of union positions and the strategic challenge of the ETUC to formulate positions around which affiliates can cohere (Adamczyk 2018; Busemeyer et al. 2008).

The example of the ETUC's internal debate about the European Commission's initiative for a Directive on adequate minimum wages in the EU, which was adopted in autumn 2022 (European Parliament and Council of the European Union 2022), illustrates the scale of this challenge for the ETUC. The debate about a European minimum wage policy has a long and controversial history, which is dominated by two opposite positions. Whereas trade unions from CEE countries have campaigned for some kind of EU-level regulation on minimum wages, affiliates from the Nordic countries reject any European approach to the issue of minimum wages (Furaker and Lovén Seldén 2013; Schulten et al. 2015).

CEE unions strongly support a European minimum wage directive because it would provide a minimum wage floor to protect workers from in-work poverty and forced labour migration. In light of the highly fragmented and decentralized collective bargaining system in many CEE countries, marked by extremely low collective bargaining coverage and union density, a European minimum wage would, furthermore, strengthen the unions' bargaining position, especially if it could be linked with initiatives to support multi-employer bargaining to prevent social dumping (Müller and Platzer 2020; Stredula et al. 2020). In contrast, Nordic unions strongly resist a European minimum wage directive because they are concerned that it would interfere fundamentally with their voluntaristic tradition of industrial relations. From their perspective, a European minimum wage directive threatens to undermine collective bargaining autonomy, hamper the normative effect of collective agreements, exert negative pressure on wage levels, and weaken incentives for organization among both workers and employers (Dahl et al. 2020; Lovén Seldén 2020; Risgaard et al. 2020).

In the past, the ETUC managed to broker a compromise between these diametrically opposed positions by including in its resolutions various non-regression and guarantee clauses in order to protect systems with higher standards (ETUC 2017a). This allowed the Nordic unions to agree to resolutions, which in turn enabled the ETUC to speak with one voice vis-à-vis European policymakers.

The von der Leyen Commission initiative to introduce a legal instrument on minimum wages, however, was a game-changer because the debate was no longer about defining a position in favour of a European minimum wage policy more generally; now it was about how to shape a concrete legislative initiative which carries potentially far-ranging implications at the national level. This puts to the test the historic compromise reached between the ETUC affiliates because it dramatically increased the stakes for the affiliates. This makes the ETUC's task of developing a robust common position even more difficult because it sheds a harsh light on the fundamentally different positions of its affiliates (Müller and Platzer 2020). It should also be noted that the political opportunity structure of the von der Leyen Commission may prove to be more open than those of her predecessors. In addition to minimum wage initiative, for example, are the initiatives on the platform economy, the wage transparency directive and the revision of the European works councils directive. It remains to be seen whether these initiatives will constitute a change in overall direction, but the adoption of directive on adequate minimum wages can be viewed as a paradigm shift towards a more social Europe (Müller and Schulten 2022).

A third strategic challenge is long-standing and concerns attitudes towards European integration and involvement. Since the 'golden age' Europe has been a concern primarily among senior cadres of trade unionists (Busemeyer et al. 2008; Hyman 2005). The Irish Congress of Trade Unions (ICTU), the German Trade Union Confederation (DGB, *Deutscher Gewerkschaftsbund*) and the Swedish Trade Union Confederation (LO, *Landsorganisationen i Sverige*), for example, are affiliated with the ETUC, but they are organizations to which trade unions affiliate as member organizations. The political distance between trade union members and the ETUC is thus vast, articulated by multiple layers of trade union officialdom and raises challenges regarding international trade union democracy (Hyman and Gumbrell-McCormick 2020). Before the ascendency of neoliberal policies within the EU, EU scepticism among trade union members was widespread (Archer 2000; Teschner 2000; Wessels 1995). This was later exemplified by substantial numbers of Dutch and French trade unionists voting against the Treaty on European Union in 2005, many Irish trade unionists voting against the Lisbon Treaty in 2008, and many Danish (2000) and Swedish (2003) trade unionists voting to reject the euro, although a 'yes' vote was promoted by senior trade union leaders in each case (Hyman 2010). Furthermore, the core groups from which trade union membership is drawn, manual and white-collar workers with no university education, appear disproportionately to be eurosceptics (Hyman 2010).

The country chapters illustrate that this scepticism generates a wide range of responses. In Spain, for example, *Podemos*, a left-of-centre populist party, expresses a very critical view of neoliberalism within the EU and has attracted large numbers of trade unionists to vote for it. In contrast, in Italy substantial proportions of trade unionists vote for right-of-centre populist and nationalist parties (Leonardi and Carriere

2020: 279), whereas in Germany no fewer than 12.2 per cent of all trade unionists voted for *Alternative für Deutschland* (AfD) in the 2021 General Election, a right-of-centre populist party that opposes EU membership (DGB 2021).[9] Brexit, of course, represents an extreme example of this development as large swathes of trade unionists and workers targeted for membership by trade unions voted to leave, perhaps on the grounds that they viewed themselves as excluded from any benefits of EU membership. These developments place the ETUC and senior trade unionists in a strategic quandary. The ETUC supports European integration and generates policy prescriptions favouring integration and a more substantial social dimension. This position is compromised on two counts. First, the financial and political resources made available to the ETUC by European institutions, supplementing affiliation fees, may limit its capacity to oppose integration measures founded on neoliberal assumptions (Hyman 2005; Martin and Ross 1999). Second, the long-standing euroscepticism among many European trade unionists limits the ETUC's capacity to mobilize members and generate solidarity in support of a more social Europe (Mosimann et al. 2019). These points notwithstanding, however, various ETUC campaigns such as 'A New Path for Europe' in 2013–2014 and 'Europe Needs a Pay Rise' in 2017–2018 explicitly rejected austerity policies and argued for more demand-side approaches to promote sustainable growth and quality jobs (ETUC 2014, 2017b).

A fourth challenge faced by trade union organizations at the European level arises from the points elaborated above: namely, if the benefits of European-level trade union engagement decline, will the intensity of trade union engagement also diminish? For many trade unions based in CEE this issue is compounded by resource limitations, which restrict representatives' participation in international meetings. The country chapters highlight the participation of lay representatives in European works councils and, to a lesser extent, on European company boards: both instances in which the company meets the trade union representatives' expenses. Concerning participation elsewhere the country chapters are more sanguine. The wave of establishment of union offices in Brussels

---

9 Trade unionists voted in the following proportions for the other major parties in the 2021 election: *Sozialdemokratische Partei Deutschlands* (SPD) 32.1 per cent; *Christlich Demokratische Union Deutschlands* (CDU) 18.6 per cent; *Die Grünen* (Greens) 13.0 per cent; *Freie Demokratische Partei*; (FDP) 9.0 per cent; and *Die Linke* (Left) 6.6 per cent.

around the time of the Delors Presidency subsequently fell away. Trade union resources remain concentrated at national level, with the ETUC operating with markedly fewer staff than many western European national trade union confederations. Furthermore, since 2000 the number of ETUFs has been reduced from sixteen to ten by mergers, driven in no small part by the need to consolidate organization financially.[10] In short, it remains an open question whether national trade union movements will continue to support and finance European trade union organizations at the same level as previously, given the limited social advances achieved in recent years and the financial restrictions at national level arising from membership decline.

Beyond the ETUC and the ETUFs

In recognition of the point that many trade unions cannot now defend or promote their members' interests by acting within the nation-state alone, there are a host of formal and informal examples of cross-border trade union initiatives. Many of these are not independent of the activities of the ETUC and ETUFs and have developed from initiatives at European level. These initiatives can be bilateral, in the form of cooperation across the border separating two Member States; multilateral, involving trade unions from a range of Member States; or founded on transnational institutions, such as European works councils (EWCs), and serve a wide range of purposes. Apart from the information and consultation arrangements that figure large in EWCs and similar institutions, the principal purpose of many cross-border trade union initiatives is to promote convergence in living standards and union organization. As is the case with participation within the ETUC and ETUFs, more limited resources, the relatively infrequent presence of officials dedicated to international affairs, and language barriers are cited in several of the country chapters as restricting the range of cross-border initiatives involving trade unions from the EU11.

---

10 In particular, the formation of industriAll from the merger of the European Metalworkers Federation, the European Mine, Chemical and Energy Workers Federation and the European Trade Union Federation of Textiles, Clothing and Leather, and the formation of UNI-Europa from the merger of the European Federation of Commercial, Clerical, Professional and Technical Employees, the European Federation of Communications International and the European Federation of Media and Entertainment account for the reduction in the numbers of ETUFs.

European works councils

EWCs are a prime example of an institution created at European level that has promoted institution-building beyond formal requirements and has, in some instances, led to transnational union action. The EWC directive adopted in 1994 has led to the establishment of more than 1,100 institutions of transnational worker representation within MNCs (De Spiegelaere et al. 2022). The country chapters report that involvement in EWCs is a key example of transnational participation. Formally EWCs are institutions of European coverage, but in a few instances have promoted the formation of World Works Councils (WWCs) in recognition of the geographical scope of the MNCs within which they operate. Some EWCs have been involved in transnational campaigns to influence the terms of corporate restructuring. In a few cases these campaigns have included industrial action, albeit only when trade unions have been directly involved (Bartmann and Dehnen 2009; Hanké 2000). EWCs and ETUFs have established procedural arrangements whereby European Framework Agreements can be concluded, constituting a step towards the system of multi-level governance envisaged for Europe (Marginson and Sisson 2004; Rüb et al. 2013). Operationally, EWC representatives may include non-unionists, so the ETUFs have put institutions in place to prevent a decoupling of EWC activities from trade union strategies. To this end, most ETUFs have established standing committees to facilitate cooperation and strategic alignment between ETUFs and EWCs. To address company-specific challenges *ad hoc* trade union coordination groups may be convened. Taking a different tack that reflects low levels of union density in its area of operation, UNI Europa has in process a policy to establish trade union alliances (TUAs) to work in conjunction with each EWC. A trade union alliance comprises trade union officials from the unions with interests in the MNC in addition to some unionized representatives from the EWC (Rüb and Platzer 2015; Waddington 2016). The development of agreed policies, the implementation of campaigns to pursue these policies and institution-building at transnational level necessitate considerable resources, which may explain why some EU11 unions do not participate in such policymaking. The key point, however, is that the establishment of one institution, an EWC, has led to further institution-building and trade union action.

Interregional trade union councils

Interregional trade union councils (IRTUCs) may be both bilateral and multilateral and may involve trade unions from countries that are not EU Member States. Furthermore, there may be several IRTUCs within a single Member State: no fewer than nine are reported in Austria alone. The ETUC mentions the presence of more than forty IRTUCs formed to address the disparities that characterize terms and conditions of employment in border areas (ETUC 2009). While many IRTUCs are rudimentary organizations, others are relatively sophisticated. The IRTUC covering Western Hungary and Burgenland in Austria, for example, operates networks at industry level and within specific companies (Hammer 2010). More generally, IRTUCs tend to focus on measures to counter wage and social dumping, the exchange of information on collective bargaining and wage development, migration, vocational training and advice on workers' rights. Many IRTUCs are thus primarily transnational institutions of information exchange rather than a basis on which to initiate trade union actions. The issue of transforming structure into action that resonates throughout this section on transnational trade unionism thus also applies to IRTUCs. Polish workers employed at the Olkiluoto 3 construction site, for example, failed to enlist support from Finnish trade unions during their labour dispute (Lillie and Sippola 2011). Similarly, the transition from the exchange of information within an IRTUC to concerted trade union action involving the trade unions party to the IRTUC is reported as being relatively rare (Bähr and Albrecht 2014; ETUC 2009; Hammer 2010).

Union-driven initiatives

In addition to transnational ventures 'triggered' by EU institutions are a host of developments with different forms and objectives instigated by trade unions. The majority of these initiatives focus on lobbying, capacity building, recruitment and organizing, and migrant workers. The 'classic' and long-standing institution designed to facilitate the lobbying of European institutions is the Nordic Council of Trade Unions, which serves as a forum to generate agreed positions among participating unions. More recently the Nordic Council has been supplemented by the Baltic Sea Trade Union Network, which has conducted wide-ranging analyses of a series of issues pertinent to the area, including energy and climate policies, infringements of trade union rights, equal representation and labour migration (Ostrowski 2017). To date the Baltic Sea Trade Union Network has not acted as a lobbying organization of European institutions, although it has pressured more local institutions within its area of influence (Kall et al. 2019; Ostrowski 2017). It is noteworthy that similar formal arrangements have yet to be established in other geographical areas of the EU, although more informal exchanges involving Southern European- and Visegrad-based trade unions take place.[11]

At the core of transnational exchanges founded on capacity building, recruitment and organization is the transfer of resources from West to East. Several of the country chapters, for example, report trade unions based in CEE applying to the European Social Fund for project funding to build union capacity. UNI Europa has also set up three organizing centres: the Central European Organizing Centre in Poland (2016), Europe's Power and Organizing Centre to organize workers in commerce (2019), and the South-East European Organizing Centre in Romania (2021). These centres are intended to train local trade unionists in organizing skills, while also targeting specific multinationals in the organizing centre's industry or locality. Similarly, trade unions based in the EU16 have transferred resources to various – often neighbouring – countries with the object of deepening union density and enhancing capacity. To illustrate, IGM has established exchanges with and materially supported the Metalworkers' Trade Union Federation (Vasas, *Vasas Szakszervezeti Szövetség*) in Hungary; the Federation of Industry (FI, *Federación de Industria*) of the Workers' Commissions (CCOO, *Comisiones Obreras*) and the Federation of Industry, Construction and Agriculture (FICA, *Federación de Industria, Construcción y Agro*) of the General Union of Workers (UGT, *Unión General de Trabajadoras y Trabajadores*) in Spain; and the United Auto Workers at the Chattanooga, Tennessee plant of Volkswagen in the United States in order to consolidate union organization at German-owned automotive production sites. In addition, IGM operates a series of regional exchanges direct towards capacity building and the exchange of information pertinent to rounds of collective bargaining: IGM Bavaria with unions in Austria, Czechia, Hungary, Slovakia and Slovenia; IGM Nordrhine Westphalia with unions in Belgium and the Netherlands; and IGM Küste with unions in Denmark.

---

[11] The Visegrad nations include the EU Member States of Czechia, Hungary, Poland and Slovakia.

A third prominent form of transnational trade union initiative mentioned in the country chapters concerns the support of migrant workers. Such initiatives may take many forms. The most prominent is defence of migrant workers' interests by a trade union in the host country. Migrant Bulgarian workers, for example, may be supported by Austrian, Cypriot, German or Romanian unions as a result of collaborations between trade unions. Elsewhere unions have set up branches or similar local organizations to represent foreign workers where the number of workers of a particular nationality is large. The most ambitious project to represent migrant workers was the EMWU founded in 2004 by IGBAU, mentioned above. A combination of internal organizational flaws and resistance to the EMWU from other European construction workers unions led to its failure (Greer et al. 2013). In practice, national trade unions protected their interests within the Member State to the detriment of the EMWU.

The future

Visser (2019) argued that there are four possible scenarios for trade unions based on the dynamics of membership: *marginalization*, in which trade unions are effectively displaced and become ever weaker; *dualization*, where trade union representation covers the core and relatively stable segments of the workforce, but unions fail to establish organization in new and expanding segments of the workforce; *substitution*, where trade unions are replaced by alternative forms of social and non-governmental organizations; and *revitalization*, where trade unions reconnect with new worker constituencies and develop a myriad of innovative and alternative strategies. In aspirational terms all trade unions seek, at least rhetorically, some form of revitalization.

While there are many difficulties in allocating trade union organizations at an aggregated Member State level to one or other of Visser's (2019) categories, the authors of the country chapters indicate a range of national experiences. In some cases, for example, the authors identified the presence of more than one of these categories. In Ireland no tendency was identified as dominant. In contrast, in France two elements of polarization were viewed as likely: polarization between non-union small- and medium-sized companies and larger unionized companies, and between compromise-oriented and oppositional unions. The Irish and French cases are thus disregarded here. Similarly, several authors classified unions in their country as likely to be stable or exhibit continuity rather than by reference to a Visser category. With these provisos in mind, Table 29.1 outlines the authors' responses on twenty-five Member States. Table 29.1 shows that marginalization is the likely pattern of development in eleven countries, dualization in nine, substitution in one and revitalization in five. Authors identified eight countries as likely to be characterized by stability or continuity. Four points immediately emerge from these observations.

Table 29.1 Likely future developments using Visser's categories

Member state	Dualization	Substitution	Marginalization	Revitalization	Stability/ continuity
Austria					✓
Belgium					✓
Bulgaria			✓	✓	
Croatia			✓	✓	
Cyprus	✓				
Czechia	✓		✓		
Denmark					✓
Estonia					✓
Finland					✓
Germany				✓	✓
Greece	✓		✓		
Hungary			✓		
Italy	✓			✓	
Latvia					✓
Lithuania	✓				
Luxembourg			✓		
Malta					✓
Netherlands			✓		
Poland	✓		✓		
Portugal	✓		✓		
Romania			✓		
Slovakia			✓		
Slovenia	✓				
Spain	✓	✓			
Sweden				✓	

Source: authors' elaboration based on the country chapters.

First, despite the range of initiatives intended to adapt trade unions to changed circumstances, many of which are outlined in the country chapters, the majority of authors view marginalization or dualization as the most likely outcome. Implicit in these observations is the assumption that organizing initiatives to unionize private sector services are unlikely to have a marked impact in the foreseeable future. Second, seven of the EU11 Member States are allocated to the marginalization category and four to dualization, suggesting that the situation of trade unions based in the EU11 is particularly problematic and their priorities are likely to differ from those of many unions based elsewhere in the EU. Marginalization and dualization tendencies are considered to be almost absent in Germanic and Nordic Europe except for Luxembourg and the Netherlands, where marginalization is regarded as a possibility. Dualization is considered to be a possibility in southern Europe, particularly in Cyprus, Italy and Spain, whereas in Greece and Portugal both marginalization and dualization are regarded as possibilities. Third, three countries operating a variant of the Ghent system (Belgium, Denmark, Finland) are allotted to the stability or continuity category and the fourth (Sweden) to revitalization. State supported systems that promote unionization thus appear to underpin greater optimism for future developments. Similarly, Austria, with a consistently high rate of collective bargaining coverage because of the endurance of the *Arbeiterkammer* system (Table A1.H), is allocated to the stability or continuity category. Fourth, it is apparent that allocation of a country to the stability/continuity category arises from various circumstances. Stability/continuity in Estonia and Latvia, for example, suggests that unions are unlikely to exert a marked influence on the labour market or the political sphere in the foreseeable future, as outlined in these country chapters. In contrast, stability/continuity in Austria, Germany and the Ghent system countries implies a wider range of trade union policy options.

Against the backdrop of the country experts' sanguine assessment of the future development of trade unions in the EU, what can be identified as the key issues for the foreseeable future? To this end reference is made to the likely attitudes of employers, the state and trade unionists within this timeframe.

In general terms, private sector employers within the EU adopt different stances within the EU16 and the EU11. Within the EU16 employers have promoted the decentralization of collective bargaining, particularly in manufacturing, and have tended to resist unionization at small- and medium-sized enterprises in private sector services, even where legislation guarantees workplace representation. The introduction of minimum wage systems, for example, reflects the unions' failure to agree or enforce terms and conditions of employment through collective bargaining. Furthermore, it is apparent that where industrial bargaining remains in place many agreements are framework agreements rather than ones that set the actual terms and conditions of employment. The country chapters do not suggest that the views of private sector employers in the EU16 are likely to shift markedly from the stance adopted since before 2000. Within the EU11 employer resistance to collective bargaining, particularly industrial bargaining, is widespread, with the result that coverage is low; industrial bargaining is rare, with the exception of Slovenia; many collective agreements merely replicate terms laid out in legislation; and an unknown proportion of the industrial agreements that remain are framework agreements (Müller et al. 2019). Although some EU11 country chapters mention the tightening of labour markets as likely to pressure employers, there is no expectation that this will lead to more positive attitudes towards collective bargaining among private sector employers, particularly industrial bargaining, and unionization. Within both the EU16 and the EU11 managers continue to employ human resource management (HRM) techniques designed to encourage direct communication within the workforce rather than indirect communication via workplace representatives. Such techniques limit the impact trade unions can exert at the workplace and may limit the development of union organization at newly established or weakly organized sites.

The state is likely to impinge on the development of trade unions as an employer and as a legislator. As an employer, throughout the EU the state has tended to retain industrial collective bargaining to a greater extent than private sector employers, albeit with considerable devolution of bargaining competences to lower levels. This increases the pressure on local union organizations to negotiate on a wider range of issues and on higher levels to coordinate across the devolved settlements to ensure comparability. Given the relatively high coverage of collective bargaining in the public sector, however, there are opportunities for unions to reduce the extent of free riding.

The influence of the state as a legislator, of course, depends on the electorate. Where neoliberal oriented governments are elected the evidence presented here suggests that the trends outlined in many of the country chapters will continue unabated. In these circumstances trade unionism is likely to become more marginalized and the opportunities for revitalization more restricted. The election of social democratic or labour governments may promote unionization, although membership decline and the diminution in collective bargaining coverage have also occurred since 2000, when such governments have been in office. The impact of social democratic or labour governments depends on, among other things, the extent to which they reject neoliberal policy assumptions (see Portugal and Spain for example). What is clear is that the political distance between trade unions and political party 'allies' is now greater than in the past and reduces the chances of supportive legislation.

It should also be noted that European policy decisions have unknown effects. Trade unionists in CEE, for example, argue that the introduction of the Directive on an adequate European minimum wage (particularly Article 4) will assist extension of collective bargaining coverage where it is currently less than 70 per cent. It remains to be seen whether these expectations will be met in practice. Similarly, the outcome of initiatives taken by the ETUFs to build capacity and to extend workplace representation in the EU11 is uncertain.

What is clear is that union activity, either independently or in conjunction with allies will be at the centre of revitalization campaigns. It is also apparent that union activity at the workplace is key to both membership recruitment and retention (Waddington 2014). More problematic is the ignorance, indifference or resistance to renewal within a substantial number of trade unions, the challenges of internal reform required to ready unions for renewal campaigns, and the limited resources available to some unions, particularly many of those in the EU11. How the tension between these two sets of forces is resolved will determine whether trade unions in the EU can pick up the pieces left from the neoliberal challenge.

References

Adamczyk S. (2018) Inside the trade union family: the 'two worlds' within the European Trade Union Confederation, European Journal of Industrial Relations, 24 (2), 179–192.

Aleks R. (2015) Estimating the effect of 'change to win' on union organizing, ILR Review, 68 (3), 584–605.

Americans for Fair Treatment (2022) The big picture: national union spending of local chapter dues. https://americansforfairtreatment.org/resources-and-data/seiu-where-do-your-dues-go?

Andolfatto D. and Labbé D. (2008) Le financement clair-obscur du syndicalisme français, Histoire et Liberté, 33, 17–34.

Anderson J. (1995) The state of the (European) Union: from the single market to Maastricht, from singular events to general theories, World Politics, 47 (3), 441–465.

Archer C. (2000) Euroscepticism in the Nordic Region, European Integration, 22 (1), 87–114.

Arnholtz J., Ibsen C. and Ibsen F. (2016) Importing low density ideas to high density revitalisation: the 'organising model' in Denmark, Economic and Industrial Democracy, 37 (2), 297–317.

Baccaro L. and Howell C. (2017) Trajectories of neoliberal transformation: European industrial relations since the 1970s, Cambridge, Cambridge University Press.

Bähr H and Albrecht M. (2014) Interregional trade union councils: transnational orientation and interest intermediation of trade unions, Industrielle Beziehungen, 21 (3), 300–321.

Baraldi S., Sverke M. and Chaison G. (2010) Union absorptions in times of restructuring: the importance of attitude towards merger in predicting post-merger attachment levels, Industrial Relations Journal, 41 (1), 52–73.

Bartmann M. and Dehnen V. (2009) Cooperation versus competition: unions and works council strategies in the Delta site-selection process at General Motors Europe, in Hertwig M., Pries L. and Rampleltshammer L. (eds) European works councils in complementary perspectives, Brussels, ETUI, 301–328.

Bassett P. and Cave A. (1993) All for one: the future of trade unions, Fabian Pamphlet 559, London, Fabian Society.

Behrens M. (2009) Still married after all these years? Union organising and the role of works councils in German industrial relations, Industrial & Labor Relations Review, 62 (3), 275–293.

Behrens M. and Pekarek A. (2012) To merge or not to merge? The impact of union merger decisions on workers' representation in Germany, Industrial Relations Journal, 43 (6), 527–547.

Bercusson B. (1992) Maastricht: a fundamental change in European labour law, Industrial Relations Journal, 23 (2), 177–190.

Bernaciak M. (2017) Coming full circle? Contestation, social dialogue and trade union politics in Poland, in Lehndorff S., Dribbusch H. and Schulten T. (eds) Rough waters: European trade unions in a time of crisis, Brussels, ETUI, 151–172.

Bernaciak M. and Kahancová M. (2017a) Conclusions, in Bernaciak M. and Kahancová M. (eds) Innovative union practices in central-eastern Europe, Brussels, ETUI, 219–236.

Bernaciak M. and Kahancová M. (2017b) Introduction: innovation against all odds?, in Bernaciak M. and Kahancová M. (eds) Innovative union practices in Central-Eastern Europe, Brussels, ETUI, 7–20.

Bieling H.-J. (2013) Gewerkschaftspolitische Strategien in der Eurokrise – zwischen Krisenkorporatismus und sozialem Widerstand, in Rüb S. and Müller T. (eds) Arbeitsbeziehungen im Prozess der Globalisierung und Europäischen Integration. Ökonomische und soziale Herausforderungen im Zeichen der Euro-Krise, Baden-Baden, Nomos, 243–294.

Blanchflower D. (2007) International patterns of union membership, British Journal of Industrial Relations, 45 (1), 1–28.

Blanchflower D. and Bryson A. (2020) Now unions increase job satisfaction and well-being, NBER Working Paper 27720, Cambridge, National Bureau of Economic Research.

Bohle D. and Grescovits B. (2012) Capitalist diversity on Europe's periphery, Ithaca, Cornell University Press.

Brinkmann U., Choi H.-L., Detje R., Dörre K., Holst H., Karakayali S. and Schmalstieg C. (2008) Strategic unionism: aus der Krise zur Erneuerung?, Wiesbaden, VS-Verlag.

Bronfenbrenner K. and Hickey R. (2004) Changing to organize: a national assessment of union organizing strategies, in Milkman R. and Voss K. (eds) Rebuilding labor: organizing and organizers in the new union movement, Ithaca, Cornell University Press, 19–60.

Bruttel O., Baumann A. and Dütsch M. (2018) The new German statutory minimum wage in comparative perspective: employment effects and other adjustment channels, European Journal of Industrial Relations, 24 (2), 145–162.

Bücker A. and Warneck W. (2010) Viking-Laval-Rüffert: consequences and policy perspectives, Report 111, Brussels, ETUI.

Burgess J., Connell J. and Winterton J. (2013) Vulnerable workers, precarious work and the role of trade unions and HRM, International Journal of Human Resource Management, 24 (21–22), 4083–4093.

Busemeyer M., Kellerman C., Petring A. and Stuchlik A. (2008) Overstretching solidarity? Trade unions' national perspectives on the European economic and social model, Transfer, 14 (3), 435–452.

Caraker E., Høgedahl L., Jørgensen H. and Møberg R. (2015) Fællesskabet før forskellene. Hovedrapport fra APL III-projektet om nye lønmodtagerværdier og interesser, Copenhagen, FTF and LO.

Carter B. (2006) Trade union organizing and renewal: a response to de Turberville, Work, Employment and Society, 20 (2), 415–426.

Clark P. (2000) Building more effective unions, Ithaca, ILR Press.

Coates D. (2007) The category of labour: its continued relevance in social theory, in Gamble A., Ludlam S., Taylor A. and Wood S. (eds) Labour, the state, social movements and the challenge of neo-liberal globalisation, Manchester, Manchester University Press, 7–20.

Connolly H., Marino S. and Martinez Lucio M. (2017) Justice for Janitors goes Dutch: the limits and possibilities of unions' adoption of organizing in a context of regulated social partnership, Work, Employment and Society, 31 (2), 319–335.

Connolly H., Kretsos L. and Phelen C. (eds) (2014) Radical unionism in Europe and the future for collective interest representation, Oxford, Peter Lang.

Czarzasty J., Gajewska K. and Mrozowicki A. (2014) Institutions and Strategies: trends and obstacles to recruiting workers into trade unions in Poland, British Journal of Industrial Relations, 52 (1), 112–135.

Dahl M., Gideonsson S. and Linder M. (2020) An EU directive on minimum wages is unacceptable, 16/09/0020. https://www.svensktnaringsliv.se/english/an-eu-directive-on-minimum-wages-is-unacceptable_1146924.html

Degryse C. and Tilly P. (2013) 1973–2013: 40 years of history of the European Trade Union Confederation, Brussels, ETUI.

Denis J.-M. (2012) The case of SUD-rail: the limits of 'radical political unionism', European Journal of Industrial Relations, 18 (3), 267–272.

De Spiegelaere S., Jagodzinski R. and Waddington J. (2022) European works councils: contested and still in the making, Brussels, ETUI.

De Turberville S. (2004) Does the 'organizing model' represent a credible union renewal strategy?, Work, Employment and Society, 18 (4), 775–794 .

DGB (2021) Bundestagswahl 2021: So haben Gewerkschafter*innen gewählt, 26/09/2021. https://www.dgb.de/themen/++co++79fb7b60-1f79-11ec-88c8-001a4a160123

Doellgast V., Lillie N. and Pulignano V. (2018) Reconstructing solidarity: labour unions, precarious work and the politics of institutional change in Europe, Oxford, Oxford University Press.

Doellgast V., Bidwell M., Alexander J. and Colvin S. (2021) New directions in employment relations theory: understanding fragmentation, identity and legitimacy, ILR Review, 74 (3), 555–579.

Dølvik J.E. (1999) An emerging island?, Brussels, ETUI.

Dølvik J.E. and Martin A. (2014) European social models from crisis to crisis, Oxford, Oxford University Press.

Dølvik J.E. and Marginson P. (2018) Cross-sectoral coordination and regulation of wage determination in northern Europe: divergent responses to multiple external pressures, European Journal of Industrial Relations, 24 (4), 409–425.

Drahokoupil J. and Vandaele K. (eds) (2021) A modern guide to labour and the platform economy, Cheltenham, Edward Elgar.

Ebbinghaus B. and Weishaupt T. (eds) (2021) The role of social partners in managing Europe's great recession: crisis corporatism or corporatism in crisis? Abingdon, Routledge.

Edelstein J and Warner M. (1975) Comparative union democracy, London, Allen and Unwin.

Estreicher S. (2006) Disunity within the house of labour: change to win or stay the course?, Journal of Labor Research, 27 (4), 505–511.

ETUC (2009) Interregional trade union councils: collective bargaining, cross-border co-operation, Brussels, ETUC.

ETUC (2014) A new path for Europe: European Trade Union Confederation plan for investment, sustainable growth and quality jobs, Brussels, ETUC.

ETUC (2015) Paris Manifesto. 13th Congress, Paris, 29 September–2 October, Brussels, ETUC.

ETUC (2017a) For a common strategy on low and minimum wages, Adopted by the Executive Committee, Malta, 15–16 March 2017, Brussels, ETUC.

ETUC (2017b) Europe needs a pay rise – it's time for our recovery, 15/02/2017, Brussels, ETUC. https://www.etuc.org/en/pressrelease/europe-needs-pay-rise-its-time-our-recovery

European Commission (2012) Labour market developments in Europe 2012, European Economy 5, Luxembourg, Publications Office of the European Union. https://ec.europa.eu/economy_finance/publications/european_economy/2012/pdf/ee-2012-5_en.pdf

European Commission (2018) Report from the Commission to the European Parliament, the Council and the European Economic and Social Committee. Report on the implementation by member states of directive 2009/38/EC on the establishment of a European works council or a procedure in community-scale undertakings and community-scale groups of undertakings for the purposes of informing and consulting employees (Recast), COM (2018) 292 final, 15.05.2018.

European Parliament and Council of the European Union (2022) DIRECTIVE (EU) 2022/2041 OF THE EUROPEAN PARLIAMENT AND OF THE COUNCIL of 19 October 2022 on adequate minimum wages in the European Union, Official Journal of the European Union, L 275/33, 25.10.2022. https://eur-lex.europa.eu/legal-content/EN/TXT/PDF/?uri=CELEX:32022L2041&from=EN

Falkner G. (1998) EU social policy in the 1990s: towards a corporatist policy community, London, Routledge.

Fazi T. (2014) The battle for Europe: how an elite hijacked a continent and how we can take it back, London, Pluto Press.

Fitzgerald I., Hardy J. and Martinez Lucio M. (2012) The internet, employment and Polish migrant workers: communication, activism and competition in new organising spaces, New Technology, Work and Employment, 27 (2), 93–105.

Flanders A. (1970) Management and unions: the theory and reform of industrial relations, London, Faber and Faber.

Fletcher B. and Hurd R. (2001) Overcoming obstacles to transformation: challenges on the way to a new unionism, in Turner L., Katz H. and Hurd R. (eds) Rekindling the movement: labor's quest for relevance in the twenty-first century, Ithaca, ILR Press, 182–210.

Frege C. and Kelly J. (2004) Union strategies in comparative context, in Frege, C. and Kelly, J. (eds) Varieties of unionism, Oxford, Oxford University Press, 31–44.

Furaker B. and Lovén Seldén K. (2013) Trade union cooperation on statutory minimum wages? A study of European trade union positions', Transfer, 19 (4), 507–520.

Gamble A. (2014) Crisis without end? The unravelling of western prosperity, New York, Palgrave Macmillan.

Geary J. and Gamwell S. (2019) An American solution to an Irish problem: a consideration of the material conditions that shape the architecture of union organizing, Work, Employment and Society, 33 (2), 191–207.

Geelan T. (2015) Danish trade unions and young people, in Hodder A. and Kretsos L. (eds) Young workers and trade unions: a global view, Basingstoke, Palgrave Macmillan, 71–89.

Glassner V. (2013) Central and Eastern European industrial relations in the crisis: national divergence and path-dependent change, Transfer, 19 (2), 155–169.

Glyn A. (2001) Aspirations, constraints and outcomes, in Glyn A. (ed.) Social democracy in neo-liberal times: the left and economic policy since 1980, Oxford, Oxford University Press, 1–20.

Greer I., Ciupijus Z. and Lillie N. (2013) The European Migrant Workers Union and the barriers to transnational industrial citizenship, European Journal of Industrial Relations, 19(1), 5–20.

Haake G. (2017) Trade unions, digitalisation and the self-employed: inclusion or exclusion?, Transfer, 23 (1), 63–66.

Hammer N. (2010) Cross-border cooperation under symmetry: the case of an interregional trade union council, European Journal of Industrial Relations, 16 (4), 351–386.

Hanké B. (2000) European works councils and industrial restructuring in the European motor industry, European Journal of Industrial Relations, 6 (1), 35–59.

Hantrais L. (2000) Social policy in the European Union, 2nd edn, Houndmills, Macmillan.

Haugsgjerd Allern E. and Dale T. (2017) The relationship between left-of-centre parties and trade unions, in Haugsgjerd Allern E. and Dale T. (eds) Left-of-centre parties and trade unions in the twenty-first century, Oxford, Oxford University Press, 1–25.

Heery E. and Abbott B. (2000) Trade unions and the insecure workforce, in Heery E. and Salmon J. (eds) The insecure workforce, London, Routledge, 155–180.

Heery E., Simms M., Delbridge R., Salmon J. and Simpson D. (2000) Union organizing in Britain: a survey of policy and practice, The International Journal of Human Resource Management, 11 (5), 986–1007.

Heery E., Williams S. and Abbott B. (2011) Civil society organisations and trade unions: cooperation, conflict and indifference, Work, Employment and Society, 26 (1), 145–160.

Hinarejos A. (2016) Changes to economic and monetary union and their effects on social policy, The International Journal of Comparative Labour Law and Industrial Relations, 32 (2), 231–249.

Hodder A. (2019) Young people: attitudes to work, unions and activism, Birmingham, University of Birmingham Press.

Hodder A. and Houghton D. (2015) Union use of social media: a study of the University and College union on Twitter, New Technology, Work and Employment, 30 (3), 173–189.

Hodder A. and Kretsos L. (eds) (2015) Young workers and trade unions: a global view, Basingstoke, Palgrave Macmillan.

Holgate J., Simms M. and Tapia M. (2018) The limitations of the theory and practice of mobilization in trade union organizing, Economic and Industrial Democracy, 39 (4), 599–616.

Howard M. (2002) The weakness of civil society in post-communist Europe, Cambridge, Cambridge University Press.

Humphrey J. (2002) Towards a politics of the rainbow: self-organization in the trade union movement, Aldershot, Ashgate.

Huzzard T., Gregory D. and Scott R. (eds) (2004) Strategic unionism and partnership: boxing or dancing? New York, Palgrave.

Hyman R. (2001) Understanding European trade unionism, London, Sage.

Hyman R. (2005) Trade unions and the politics of European social model, Economic and Industrial Democracy, 26 (1), 9–40.

Hyman R. (2010) Trade unions and 'Europe': are the members out of step?, Relations Industrielles-Industrial Relations, 65 (1), 3–29.

Hyman R. and Gumbrell-McCormick R. (2017) Resisting labour market insecurity: old and new actors, rivals or allies?, Journal of Industrial Relations, 59 (4), 538–561.

Hyman R. and Gumbrell-McCormick R. (2020) (How) Can international trade union organisations be democratic?, Transfer, 26 (3), 253–272.

Ibsen C. and Keune M. (2018) Organised decentralisation of collective bargaining: case studies of Germany, the Netherlands and Denmark, OECD Social, Employment and Migration Working Papers 217, Paris, OECD Publishing.

Ibsen C. and Tapia M. (2017) Trade union revitalisation: where are we now? Where to next?, Journal of Industrial Relations, 59 (2), 170–191.

Ilsøe A. (2017) The digitalisation of service work: social partner responses in Denmark, Sweden and Germany, Transfer, 23 (3), 333–348.

Kall K., Lillie N., Sippola M. and Mankki L. (2019) Overcoming barriers to transnational organizing through identity work: Finnish–Estonian trade union cooperation, Work, Employment and Society, 33 (2), 208–225.

Kerr A. and Waddington J. (2014) E-communications: an aspect of union renewal or merely doing things electronically?, British Journal of Industrial Relations, 52 (4), 658–681.

Koukiadaki A., Távora I. and Martinez Lucio M. (2016) Joint regulation and labour market policy in Europe during the crisis, Brussels, ETUI.

Knotter A. (2017) Justice for Janitors goes Dutch: precarious labour and the trade union response in the cleaning industry (1988–2012): a transnational history, International Review of Social History, 62 (1), 1–35.

Krzywdzinski M. (2010) Organizing employees in Central Eastern Europe: the approach of Solidarność, European Journal of Industrial Relations, 16 (3), 277–292.

Lapeyre J. (2018) The European social dialogue: the history of a social innovation (1985–2003), Brussels, ETUI.

Lehndorff S., Dribbusch H. and Schulten T. (2017) European trade unions in a time of crisis – an overview, in Lehndorff S., Dribbusch H. and Schulten T. (eds) Rough waters – European trade unions in a time of crisis, Brussels, ETUI, 7–35.

Leonardi S. and Carriere M. (2020) Populism and trade union internationalism: the case of Italy, Transfer, 26 (3), 273–288.

Lillie N. and Sippola M. (2011) National unions and transnational workers: the case of Olkiluoto 3: Finland, Work, Employment and Society, 25 (2), 292–308.

Lovén Seldén K. (2020) Challenges posed by the EU minimum wage initiative to the ETUC and European trade union cooperation, Transfer, 26 (3), 325–343.

Marginson P. (2015) Coordinated bargaining in Europe: from incremental corrosion to frontal assault?, European Journal of Industrial Relations, 21 (2), 97–114.

Marginson P. and Sisson K. (2004) European integration and industrial relations: multi-level governance in the making, Basingstoke, Palgrave Macmillan.

Marino S. (2012) Trade union inclusion of migrant and ethnic minority workers: comparing Italy and the Netherlands, European Journal of Industrial Relations, 18 (5), 5–20.

Martin A. and Ross G. (1999) European unions face the millennium, in Martin A. and Ross G. (eds) The brave new world of European labor: European trade unions at the millennium, New York, Berghahn Books, 1–25.

Martin A. and Ross G. (2004) Euros and Europeans: monetary integration and the European model of society, Cambridge, Cambridge University Press.

Martinez Lucio M. (2017) Organising without knowing it? The curious case of para-organising style campaigns in southern Europe and the case of trade union elections in Spain, Transfer, 23 (1), 89–94.

Martinez Lucio M. and Stuart M. (2009) Organising and modernisation, in Gall G. (ed.) Union revitalisation in advanced economies, Basingstoke, Palgrave Macmillan, 17–37.

Martinez Lucio M., Marino S. and Connolly H. (2017) Organising as a strategy to reach precarious and marginalised workers, Transfer, 23 (1), 31–46.

Mather A. (2017) Solidaires, unitaires et démocratiques: social movement unionism and beyond, Transfer, 23 (1), 79–88.

McAlavey J.F. (2016) No shortcuts. Organizing for power in the new gilded age, Oxford, Oxford University Press.

McBride A. (2001) Gender democracy in trade unions, Aldershot, Ashgate.

Mosimann N., Rennwald L. and Zimmermann A. (2019) The radical right, the labour movement and the competition for the workers' vote, Economic and Industrial Democracy, 40 (1), 65–90.

Mrozowicki A. (2014) Varieties of union organising in Central and Eastern Europe: a comparison of the retail and automotive sectors, European Journal of Industrial Relations, 20 (4), 297–315.

Mrozowicki A. and Maciejewska M. (2017) The practice anticipates our reflections: radical unions in Poland, Transfer, 23 (1), 67–77.

Müller T. and Platzer H.-W. (2016) Gewerkschaften und Arbeitsbeziehungen im Europa der Krise – Strukturdaten und Entwicklungstrends im Vergleich, in Bsirske F. et al. (eds) Gewerkschaften in der Eurokrise – nationaler Anpassungsdruck und europäische Strategien, Hamburg, VSA-Verlag, 10–44.

Müller T. and Platzer H.-W. (2020) The European trade union federations within the European polity: ETUFs and international trade union activity, Transfer, 26 (3), 289–305.

Müller T. and Schulten T. (2022) Die europäische Mindestlohn-Richtlinie – Paradigmenwechsel hin zu einem Sozialen Europa, in: Wirtschaft und Gesellschaft, Vol. 48(3), 335-365.

Müller T., Vandaele K. and Waddington J. (2019) Conclusion: towards an endgame, in Müller T., Vandaele K. and Waddington J. (eds) Collective bargaining in Europe: towards an endgame, Brussels, ETUI, 625–668.

Mundlak G. (2020) Organizing matters: two logics of trade union representation, Cheltenham, Edward Elgar/ILO.

Natali D. and Vanhercke B. (2011) European paradox: is the EU running to stand still?, in Natali D. and Vanhercke B. (eds) Social developments in the European Union 2011, Brussels, ETUI, 11–24.

Navrbjerg S. and Larsen T. (2018) The effects of union mergers on internal restructuring: a bottom-up perspective by Danish shop Stewards, Industrial Relations Journal, 49 (4), 370–397.

Nicklich M and Helfen M. (2019) Trade union renewal and 'organizing from below' in Germany: institutional constraints, strategic dilemmas and organizational tensions, European Journal of Industrial Relations, 25 (1), 57–73.

Nissen B. and Rosen S. (1999) Community-based organizing: transforming union organizing programs from the bottom up, in Nissen B. (ed.) Which direction for organized labor?, Detroit, Wayne State University Press, 59–74.

Ostrowski P. (2017) Trade union cooperation in the Baltic region in the context of the 'Europe 2020' EU Strategy, Warsaw, European Commission.

Pernicka S. and Aust A. (eds) (2007) Die Unorganisierten gewinnen: Gewerkschaftliche Rekrutierung und Interessenvertretung atypisch Beschäftigter ein deutsch-österreichischer Vergleich, Berlin, Edition Sigma.

Però D. (2020) Indie unions, organizing and labour renewal. Learning from precarious migrant workers, Work, Employment and Society, 34 (5), 900–918.

Pocock B. (2011) Rethinking unionism in a changing world of work, family and community life, Relations Industrielles/Industrial Relations, 66 (4), 562–584.

Pulignano V., Ortíz Gervasi L. and de Franceschi F. (2016) Union responses to precarious workers: Italy and Spain compared, European Journal of Industrial Relations, 22(1), 39–55.

Ramesh R. (2021) Brains as well as brawn: UNITE's new General Secretary comes out fighting, The Guardian, 3 December, 17.

Rego R., Sprenger W., Kirov V., Thomson G. and Di Nunzio D. (2016) The use of new ICTs in trade union protests: five European cases, Transfer, 22 (3), 315–329.

Risgaard L., Gabrielson H.-C. and Svanströ T. (2020) EU legislation on minimum wages is not the solution, Social Europe Blog, 5.10.2020. https://socialeurope.eu/eu-legislation-on-minimum-wages-is-not-the-solution

Roth F., Novak-Leman D. and Otter T. (2011) Has the financial crisis shattered citizens' trust in national and European governmental institutions? Evidence from EU member states 1999–2010, CEPS Working Document 343, Brussels, Centre for European Policy Studies.

Ross G. (1995) Jacques Delors and European integration, Cambridge, Polity Press.

Rüb S. and Platzer H.-W. (2015) Europäisierung der Arbeitsbeziehungen im Dienstleistungssektor: Empirische Befunde, Probleme und Perspektiven eines Heterogenen Feldes, Berlin, Edition Sigma.

Rüb S., Platzer H.-W. and Müller T. (2013) Transnational company bargaining and Europeanization of industrial relations: prospects for a negotiated order, Frankfurt am Main, Peter Lang.

Sapir A. (2014) Still the right agenda for Europe? The Sapir report ten years on, Journal of Common Market Studies, 52 (1), 57–73.

Scharpf F. (2009) The double asymmetry of European integration. Or, why the EU cannot be a social market economy, MPIfG Working Paper 09/12, Cologne, Max Planck Institute for the Study of Societies.

Schmalz S. and Dörre K. (eds) (2013) Comeback der Gewerkschaften? Machtressourcen, innovative Praktiken, internationale Perspektiven, Frankfurt am Main, Campus.

Schmalz S. and Thiel M. (2017) IG Metall's comeback: trade union renewal in times of crisis, Journal of Industrial Relations, 59 (4), 465–486.

Schulten T. and Müller T. (2013) A new European interventionism? The impact of the new European economic governance on wages and collective bargaining, in Natali D. and Vanhercke B. (eds) Social developments in the European Union 2012, Brussels, ETUI/OSE, 181–213.

Schulten T. and Müller T. (2015) European economic governance and its intervention in national wage development and collective bargaining, in Lehndorff S. (ed.) Divisive integration: the triumph of failed ideas in Europe-revisited, Brussels, ETUI, 331–363.

Schulten T. and Müller T. (2021) A paradigm shift towards social Europe? The proposed directive on adequate minimum wages in the European Union, Italian Labour Law e-Journal, 14 (1), 1–19. https://illej.unibo.it/article/view/13368/12951

Schulten T., Müller T. and Eldring L. (2015) Prospects and obstacles of a European minimum wage policy, in Van Gyes G. and Schulten T. (eds) Wage bargaining under the European economic governance: alternative strategies for inclusive growth, Brussels, ETUI, 327–359.

Shostack A. (1991) Robust unionism: innovations in the labor movement, Ithaca, ILR Press.

Simms M. (2012) Imagined solidarities: where is class in union organising?, Capital and Class, 36 (1), 97–115.

Simms M. (2017) Unions and job quality in the UK: extending interest representation within regulation institutions, Work and Occupations, 44 (1), 47–67.

Simms M. and Holgate J. (2010) Organising for what? Where is the debate on the politics of organising?, Work, Employment and Society, 24 (1), 157–168.

Simms M., Holgate J. and Heery E. (2013) Union voices: tactics and tensions in UK organizing, Ithaca, ILR Press.

Stredula J., Radzikowski A., Duda P., Gardias D., Kordás L., Csóti C. and Kuti L. (2020) Statement of the trade unions from Czechia, Hungary and Poland endorsing the ETUC's reply to the second phase consultations of social partners under article 154 TFEU on a possible action addressing the challenges related to fair minimum wages. https://szef.hu/attachments/article/3741/Statement%20of%20Trade%20unions%20from%20PL%20Cz%20HU%20supporting%20ETUC%20response%20to%20EU%20initiative.pdf

Streeck W. (2013) Gekaufte Zeit – Die vertagte Krise des demokratischen Kapitalismus, Berlin, Suhrkamp.

Sullivan R. (2009) Density matters: the union density bias and its implications for labor movement revitalization, Mobilization, 14 (2), 239–260.

Tapia M. (2013) Marching to different tunes: commitment and culture as mobilizing mechanisms for trade unions and community organizations, British Journal of Industrial Relations, 51 (4), 666–688.

Tapia M. and Turner L. (2018) Renewed activism for the labor movement: the urgency of young worker involvement, Work and Occupations, 45 (4), 391–419.

Tarrow S. (2005) The new transnational activism, Cambridge, Cambridge University Press.

Terry M. (1996) Negotiating the government of UNISON: union democracy in theory and practice, British Journal of Industrial Relations, 34 (1), 87–110.

Teschner J. (2000) No longer Europe's Europhiles? Euroscepticism in Germany in the 1990s, Journal of European Integration, 22 (1), 59–86.

Thomas A. (2016) The transnational circulation of the 'organizing model' and its reception in Germany and France, European Journal of Industrial Relations, 22 (4), 317–333.

Traxler F. (1995) Farewell to labour market associations?, in Crouch C. and Traxler F. (eds) Organized industrial relations in Europe: what future?, Aldershot, Avebury, 3–19.

Trif A., Paolucci V., Kahancova M. and Koukiadaki A. (2021) Power resources and successful trade union actions that address precarity in adverse contexts: the case of Central and Eastern Europe, Human Relations. https://doi.org/10.1177/00187267211020189

TUC (1988) Meeting the challenge: first report of the special review body, London, TUC.

TUC (1999) Partners for progress: new unionism at the workplace, London, TUC.

Turner L. (1991) Democracy at work: changing world markets and the future of labor unions, Ithaca, NY, Cornell University Press.

Turner T. and D'Art D. (2012) Public perceptions of trade unions in countries of the European Union: a causal analysis, Labor Studies Journal, 37 (1), 33–55.

Urban H.-J. (2015) Between crisis corporatism and revitalisation: trade union policy in the era of European financial market capitalism, in Lehndorff S. (ed.) Divisive integration: the triumph of failed ideas in Europe – revisited, Brussels, ETUI, 269–294.

Vandaele K. (2012) Youth representatives' opinions on recruiting and representing young workers: a twofold unsatisfied demand?, European Journal of Industrial Relations, 18 (3), 203–218.

Vandaele K. (2018) How can trade unions in Europe connect with young workers, in O'Reilly J., Leschke J., Ortlieb R., Seeleib-Kaiser M. and Villa P. (eds) Youth labor in transition: inequalities, mobility, policies in Europe, New York, Oxford University Press, 660–688.

Vandaele K. (2019) Bleak prospects: mapping trade union membership in Europe since 2000, Brussels, ETUI.

Vandaele K. (2020) Newcomers as potential drivers of union revitalization: survey evidence from Belgium, Relations Industrielles/Industrial Relations, 75 (2), 351–375.

Vandaele K. (2021) Collective resistance and organization creativity amongst Europe's platform workers: a new power in the labour movement?, in Haider J. and Keune M. (eds) Work and labour relations in global platform capitalism, Cheltenham, Edward Elgar, 206–235.

Vendramin P. (2007) Les jeunes, le travail et l'emploi. Enquête auprès des jeunes salariés en Belgique francophone, Namur, Fondation Travail-Université.

Visser J. (2012) The rise and fall of industrial unionism, Transfer, 18 (2), 129–141.

Visser J. (2019) Trade unions in the balance, ILO ACTRAV Working Paper, Geneva, ILO.

Waddington J. (2006) The trade union merger process in Europe, Industrial Relations Journal, 37 (6), 630–651.

Waddington J. (2014) Trade union membership retention and workplace representation in Europe, Working Paper 2014:10, Brussels, ETUI.

Waddington J. (2016) Building trade union alliances: a UNI Europe strategy to strengthen transnational workers' representation in multinational companies, Brussels, Uni Europa.

Waddington J., Kahmann M. and Hoffmann J. (2005) A comparison of the trade union merger process in Britain and Germany, London, Routledge.

Webb S. and Webb B. (1897) Industrial democracy, London, Longmans.

Weil D. (2014) The Fissured Workplace, Cambridge, Mass: Harvard University Press.

Wessels B. (1995) Support for integration: elite or mass-driven?, in Niedermayer O. and Sinnot R. (eds) Public opinion and internationalized governance, Oxford, Oxford University Press, 137–162.

Wetzel D., Weigand J., Niemann-Findeisen S. and Lankau T. (2013) Organizing. Die mitgliederorientierte Offensivstrategie für die IG Metall, in Wetzel D. (ed.) Organizing. Die Veränderung der gewerkschaftlichen Praxis durch das Prinzip Beteiligung, Hamburg, VSA Verlag, 47–66.

Willman P., Bryson A. and Forth J. (2020) UK unions: collective action and the cost disease, British Journal of Industrial Relations, 58 (2), 447–470.

Winkel R. (2018) Verdienmodel vakbonden decennia onder druk, Financieel Dagblad, 9 July 2018.

Abbreviations

ABVV/FGTB	Algemeen Belgisch Vakverbond/Fédération générale du travail de Belgique (General Federation of Belgian Labour)
AFL-CIO	American Federation of Labor-Congress of Industrial Organizations
ASZSZ	Autonomous Trade Union Confederation (*Autonóm Szakszervezetek Szövetsége*)
CBI	Confederation of British Industry
CCOO	Workers' Commissions (*Comisiones Obreras*)
CEE	Central and Eastern Europe
ETUC	European Trade Union Confederation
ETUF	European Trade Union Federation
EMWU	European Migrant Workers Union
EU	European Union
EWC	European Works Council
FH	Confederation of Trade Unions (*Fagbevægelsens Hovedorganisation*)
FI	Federation of Industry (*Federación de Industria*)

FICA	Federation of Industry, Construction and Agriculture (*Federación de Industria, Construcción y Agro*)
FNV	Dutch Trade Union Confederation (*Federatie Nederlandse Vakbewegung*)
FTF	Confederation of Professionals in Denmark (*Functionærernes og Tjenestemændenes Fællesråd*)
HRM	Human resource management
IGBAU	Construction, Agriculture and Environment Union (*Industriegewerkschaft Bauen-Agrar-Umwelt*)
IGM	Metalworkers' Union (Industriegewerkschaft Metall)
ILO	International Labour Organization
IRTUC	Interregional Trade Union Council
LO	Danish Confederation of Trade Unions (*Landsorganisationen I Danmark*)
MASZSZ	Hungarian Trade Union Association (*Magyar Szakszervezeti Szövetség*)
MNC	Multinational company
MSZOSZ	National Confederation of Hungarian Trade Unions (*Magyar Szakszervezetek Országos Szövetsége*)
SEIU	Service Employees International Union
TUA	Trade Union Alliance
TUC	Trades Union Congress
UGT	General Union of Workers (Unión General de Trabajadoras y *Trabajadores*)
UK	United Kingdom
UNI Europa	Union Network International Europe
US	United States
Vasas	Metalworkers' Trade Union Federation (*Vasas Szakszervezeti Szövetség*)
ver.di	United Service Workers' Union (*Vereinte Dienstleistungsgewerkschaft*)
WWC	World Works Council

Appendix A1

Indicators relevant to trade unions in the European Union

The following tables comprise the raw data that are utilized in the graphs presented in Chapter 1 'Trade Unions in the European Union: identifying challenges'; they are referred to throughout the 27 country chapters. The 'standard' country acronyms set out in the table below are applied.

Country acronyms

Austria	AT	Italy	IT
Belgium	BE	Latvia	LV
Bulgaria	BG	Lithuania	LT
Croatia	HR	Luxembourg	LU
Cyprus	CY	Malta	MT
Czechia	CZ	Netherlands	NL
Denmark	DK	Poland	PL
Estonia	EE	Portugal	PT
Finland	FI	Romania	RO
France	FR	Slovakia	SK
Germany	DE	Slovenia	SI
Greece	GR	Spain	ES
Hungary	HU	Sweden	SE
Ireland	IE		

Sources

European Commission, AMECO Database.

Eurostat (ILC_ DI12). Last update: 4 November 2021.

OECD/AIAS (2021a) *ICTWSS database*, Paris, OECD.

OECD/AIAS (2021b) *ICTWSS database codebook*, Paris, OECD.

Visser J. (2019) ICTWSS Database. Version 6.1. November 2019, Amsterdam, Amsterdam Institute for Advanced Labour Studies (AIAS), University of Amsterdam.

Table A1.A Total trade union membership in the EU Member States in thousands, averages (1960s, 1970s, 1980s, 1990s) and annual data, 2000-2019

Year	AT	BE	BG*	HR*	CY*	CZ	DK	EE*	FI	FR	DE	GR*	HU*	IE	IT	LV*	LT*	LU*	MT*	NL	PL	PT*	RO*	SK*	SI	ES*	SE
1960s	*1,524*	*1,691*	-	-	-	-	*1,037*	-	*634*	*2,979*	*7,950*	-	-	*365*	*4,666*	-	-	-	-	*1,480*	-	-	-	-	-	-	*2,216*
1970s	*1,581*	*2,298*	-	-	*113*	-	*1,412*	-	*1,326*	*3,843*	*8,920*	*980*	-	*466*	*7,341*	-	-	-	*38*	*1,662*	-	*1,502*	-	-	-	*2,732*	*3,011*
1980s	*1,663*	*2,655*	-	-	*124*	-	*1,961*	-	*1,771*	*2,779*	*9,576*	*728*	-	*507*	*9,105*	-	-	*75*	*53*	*1,566*	-	*1,225*	-	-	-	*1,104*	*3,720*
1990s	*1,569*	*2,913*	*1,580*	-	*161*	*2,225*	*2,144*	*296*	*2,067*	*2,088*	*11,546*	*730*	*2,132*	*515*	*10,589*	*425*	*407*	*87*	*77*	*1,824*	*4,238*	*857*	*3,651*	*1,024*	*391*	*1,842*	*3,905*
2000	1,442	3,096	652	-	170	1,200	2,155	88	2,132	2,212	10,001	-	-	549	10,985	-	-	-	86	1,913	2,480	-	-	660	333	2,263	3,847
2001	1,421	3,113	-	-	175	1,048	2,151	85	2,173	2,262	9,677	696	966	556	11,062	-	253	253	87	1,919	2,278	-	-	630	329	2,344	3,835
2002	1,407	3,130	-	-	181	985	2,130	85	2,177	2,302	9,494	-	-	569	11,170	-	-	-	86	1,923	2,254	800	-	583	361	2,430	3,831
2003	1,385	3,110	568	-	195	962	2,110	75	2,168	2,274	9,195	-	911	578	11,293	187	182	182	86	1,921	2,262	816	2,035	538	350	2,511	3,824
2004	1,358	3,169	-	457	198	893	2,120	67	2,178	2,201	8,849	740	-	573	11,482	-	-	-	86	1,910	2,313	836	-	483	296	2,552	3,806
2005	1,335	3,217	-	-	203	849	2,114	65	2,185	2,191	8,620	-	801	583	11,551	-	-	-	86	1,899	2,495	-	-	453	302	2,626	3,772
2006	1,272	3,294	-	-	206	815	2,078	60	2,197	2,203	8,423	-	-	603	11,647	173	150	150	87	1,866	1,970	840	2,210	412	259	2,741	3,739
2007	1,248	3,335	-	-	206	796	2,059	55	2,236	2,216	8,293	784	-	610	11,814	166	115	115	88	1,878	1,952	-	-	382	253	2,998	3,550
2008	1,239	3,367	476	437	206	787	2,051	53	2,241	2,258	8,197	-	761	614	11,922	152	120	120	84	1,898	1,914	837	2,246	353	254	3,153	3,478
2009	1,222	3,408	-	424	193	760	2,046	46	2,254	2,293	8,101	-	-	581	12,003	129	115	115	83	1,887	1,889	-	-	320	332	3,166	3,470
2010	1,211	3,438	-	-	186	720	2,026	46	2,241	2,326	8,012	786	-	609	12,020	120	113	113	85	1,870	2,069	739	-	319	260	3,115	3,449
2011	1,206	3,460	-	-	182	684	2,049	43	2,237	2,355	7,977	-	-	591	11,930	110	109	109	87	1,876	2,069	692	-	282	286	3,067	3,450
2012	1,203	3,478	420	341	180	656	1,810	41	2,254	2,366	7,977	-	563	584	11,926	109	102	102	89	1,849	2,001	-	1,432	285	207	2,910	3,484
2013	1,199	3,472	-	369	175	550	1,794	39	2,214	2,350	7,973	682	-	578	11,805	108	95	95	92	1,792	-	-	-	278	197	2,724	3,515
2014	1,198	3,487	-	350	171	524	1,796	38	2,197	2,342	7,950	-	531	564	11,645	106	94	94	93	1,762	2,060	-	-	268	219	2,596	3,553
2015	1,197	3,445	-	321	166	496	1,807	33	2,176	2,340	7,962	-	-	551	11,482	105	92	92	94	1,734	-	596	-	259	182	2,482	3,595
2016	1,201	3,403	407	-	168	507	1,814	31	2,133	2,355	7,935	612	396	538	11,361	102	92	92	96	1,718	1,806	579	1,340	249	-	2,499	3,624
2017	1,206	3,362	-	313	-	504	1,821	31	2,085	2,154	7,900	-	-	534	11,061	102	92	92	99	1,703	1,747	-	-	247	-	2,508	3,641
2018	1,211	3,339	-	302	-	500	1,861	30	2,045	2,151	7,908	-	367	543	11,016	98	87	87	101	1,693	-	-	1,390	247	-	2,506	3,646
2019	1,217	3,295	-	-	-	-	1,868	30	2,024	-	7,885	696	-	552	11,020	-	90	90	104	1,602	-	-	-	-	-	2,471	3,649

Note: Total trade union membership is defined as the '(t)otal sum of trade (labour) union members (including self-employed workers and non-active union members, i.e. students, retirees or unemployed) at national level' (OECD/AIAS 2021b: 19). * One or more decade averages are calculated based on incomplete data.
Source: OECD/AIAS (2021a). Last update: 21 September 2021.

Table A1.B Gross union density in the EU Member States (%), averages (1960s, 1970s, 1980s, 1990s) and annual data, 2000-2019

Year	AT	BE	BG	HR	CY	CZ*	DK	EE*	FI	FR	DE	GR*	HU*	IE	IT	LV*	LT*	LU*	MT	NL	PL	PT	RO	SK*	SI*	ES*	SE
1960s	65.0	61.5	-	-	-	-	62.0	-	43.0	21.4	38.2	-	-	53.7	38.1	-	-	-	-	43.1	-	-	-	-	-	-	70.6
1970s	60.2	76.1	-	-	-	-	73.0	-	75.1	23.1	40.0	42.6	-	61.2	53.9	-	-	49.3	-	41.6	-	61.3	-	-	-	15.1	82.6
1980s	59.7	90.5	-	-	-	-	89.5	-	87.7	15.6	41.1	41.6	-	60.3	62.8	-	-	49.3	-	33.8	-	44.2	-	-	-	13.4	94.5
1990s	50.5	94.9	-	-	-	53.2	90.6	34.6	111.8	11.0	36.6	35.3	59.4	51.8	71.9	28.0	34.0	43.8	-	30.3	39.3	27.5	45.4	43.8	53.9	18.7	106.9
2000	44.8	89.9	27.3	-	76.2	30.2	87.0	16.5	105.8	10.8	31.0	-	-	39.9	72.7	-	-	-	68.3	27.4	23.5	-	-	34.2	44.2	18.3	103.1
2001	43.9	90.5	-	-	74.2	26.4	86.5	15.7	105.5	10.7	30.0	27.4	29.1	38.9	71.4	-	23.1	-	66.9	26.9	22.3	-	-	32.5	43.4	18.1	99.6
2002	43.7	90.9	-	-	74.5	24.8	86.2	15.6	105.3	10.8	29.7	-	-	39.0	70.5	-	-	-	67.7	26.7	22.8	21.4	-	30.1	47.1	17.8	99.2
2003	41.9	89.9	23.6	-	78.0	24.7	85.7	13.6	105.2	10.4	29.2	-	26.8	38.8	70.4	22.3	15.6	54.9	67.2	26.8	22.9	22.0	35.9	27.7	45.3	17.6	98.9
2004	42.2	90.1	-	38.1	77.0	22.9	85.1	12.3	105.6	10.1	28.3	26.5	-	37.3	71.3	-	-	54.5	68.8	26.8	22.9	22.5	-	25.4	37.1	17.2	99.3
2005	40.9	89.7	-	-	76.0	21.2	84.3	11.5	104.2	9.8	27.1	-	23.8	36.0	70.3	-	-	53.3	66.7	28.1	23.8	-	-	23.5	37.5	16.7	97.5
2006	38.2	91.0	-	-	73.3	20.2	81.5	10.0	103.2	9.9	25.8	-	-	35.2	69.6	19.0	12.6	51.8	66.9	27.3	17.9	22.0	36.0	20.6	32.2	16.7	94.5
2007	36.9	89.4	-	-	68.4	19.3	80.7	9.2	102.7	9.7	24.8	26.6	-	32.8	69.9	17.6	9.3	49.2	66.2	26.7	16.7	-	-	18.7	30.6	17.7	87.5
2008	35.9	88.4	16.2	31.2	67.1	18.8	80.5	8.8	101.5	9.7	24.1	-	22.5	33.6	69.3	16.1	9.5	47.0	61.3	26.5	15.7	21.6	35.6	16.9	29.7	18.7	84.5
2009	35.6	90.5	-	30.5	62.9	18.5	83.3	8.5	106.2	10.0	23.8	-	-	34.9	70.5	16.0	9.9	45.9	60.6	26.5	15.4	-	-	16.0	40.4	19.9	86.4
2010	35.0	89.6	-	-	57.8	17.9	83.8	8.8	105.7	10.2	23.9	27.8	-	38.2	71.4	15.9	10.2	45.1	61.2	26.6	17.4	19.6	-	16.4	32.5	20.0	85.6
2011	34.3	89.6	-	-	55.7	17.1	84.8	7.8	104.4	10.3	23.3	-	-	37.6	70.4	14.4	9.7	45.8	60.4	26.7	17.3	18.6	-	14.5	36.8	19.9	83.3
2012	33.9	89.8	16.2	27.1	56.1	16.5	75.4	7.3	105.0	10.4	23.1	-	16.7	37.3	70.4	14.0	9.0	44.1	59.3	26.2	16.6	-	25.0	14.5	26.7	20.0	83.5
2013	33.7	90.3	-	29.5	58.1	13.6	74.9	6.9	104.1	10.3	22.7	30.8	-	35.9	70.8	13.7	8.3	43.6	58.6	25.8	-	-	-	14.1	26.2	19.4	83.6
2014	33.6	89.9	-	26.5	57.4	12.9	74.1	6.7	104.4	10.3	22.4	-	14.6	34.1	69.4	13.6	8.1	42.9	56.4	25.7	16.5	-	-	13.4	29.4	18.2	83.0
2015	33.2	89.3	-	24.0	54.4	11.9	73.2	5.7	104.1	10.2	22.2	-	-	32.1	67.6	13.4	7.9	41.5	55.0	25.1	-	16.1	-	12.6	23.8	16.8	82.8
2016	32.6	87.2	15.3	-	54.0	11.9	72.0	5.3	101.3	10.3	21.5	25.3	10.2	30.1	65.7	13.1	7.7	40.2	53.6	24.5	14.1	15.3	21.6	11.8	-	16.4	82.0

Year	AT	BE	BG	HR	CY	CZ*	DK	EE*	FI	FR	DE	GR*	HU*	IE	IT	LV*	LT*	LU*	MT	NL	PL	PT	RO	SK*	SI*	ES*	SE
2017	32.3	84.6	-	22.0	-	11.7	71.2	5.2	97.1	9.3	21.2	-	-	28.8	62.6	13.0	7.7	40.1	52.7	23.8	13.4	-	-	11.5	-	16.0	80.4
2018	31.9	81.7	-	20.8	-	11.4	71.5	5.1	92.8	9.2	21.0	-	9.2	28.3	61.6	12.2	7.2	37.9	49.5	23.1	-	-	21.4	11.3	-	15.4	79.2
2019	31.8	79.6	-	-	-	-	70.8	5.0	91.2	-	20.6	-	-	27.8	61.1	-	7.4	35.2	48.4	21.4	-	-	-	-	-	14.8	78.9

Note: Gross union density is defined as the '(p)roportion of employees who are members of a trade union (…) among all employees (WSEE)', whereby WSEE is the '(t)otal number of employees mainly based on national labour force surveys and referring to all employees living in a particular country (national concept)' (OECD/AIAS 2021b: 19). Trade union membership thus includes non-active union members, such as students, the unemployed, the early retired or pensioners, if trade union rules, regulations or the law allow this. This generally implies that gross trade union density is somewhat higher than net density for most countries. The 'Ghent countries' are exceptional as the differences are more pronounced, and gross density may artificially surpass 100 per cent given the different definitions between nominator and denominator. * One or more decade averages are calculated based on incomplete data.

Source: OECD/AIAS (2021a). Last update: 21 September 2021.

Table A1.C Net trade union membership in the EU Member States in thousands, averages (1960s, 1970s, 1980s, 1990s) and annual data, 2000-2019

Year	AT	BE	BG*	HR	CY*	CZ	DK	EE*	FI	FR	DE	GR*	HU*	IE	IT	LV*	LT*	LU*	MT*	NL	PL	PT*	RO*	SK*	SI	ES*	SE
1960s	*1.377*	*1.114*	-	-	-	-	*997*	-	*561*	*2.824*	*6.889*	-	-	*328*	*3.671*	-	-	-	-	*1.377*	-	-	-	-	-	-	*2.054*
1970s	*1.394*	*1.489*	-	-	*113*	-	*1.304*	-	*1.106*	*3.622*	*7.543*	*749*	-	*420*	*6.159*	-	-	*59*	*38*	*1.496*	-	*1.602*	-	-	-	*2.732*	*2.643*
1980s	*1.417*	*1.494*	-	-	*124*	-	*1.682*	-	*1.411*	*2.605*	*7.973*	*661*	-	*456*	*6.349*	-	-	*72*	*53*	*1.334*	-	*1.225*	-	-	-	*1.053*	*3.205*
1990s	*1.302*	*1.659*	*1.580*	-	*137*	*1.820*	*1.793*	*294*	*1.443*	*1.851*	*9.421*	*665*	*1.965*	*463*	*5.536*	*225*	*311*	*87*	*73*	*1.491*	*4.238*	*842*	*3.651*	*1.024*	*391*	*1.774*	*3.080*
2000	1.190	1.951	652	-	145	1.080	1.845	75	1.496	1.942	7.928	-	775	494	5.262	-	-	-	79	1.554	2.480	-	-	660	333	2.168	3.022
2001	1.172	1.980	-	-	148	943	1.838	72	1.577	1.992	7.670	633	676	500	5.306	-	203	-	80	1.538	2.278	-	-	630	329	2.227	3.031
2002	1.160	1.958	-	-	154	887	1.818	72	1.565	2.032	7.520	-	-	512	5.339	-	-	-	79	1.544	2.254	768	-	583	361	2.296	3.013
2003	1.143	1.918	568	-	165	866	1.782	64	1.535	2.004	7.260	-	641	520	5.382	176	142	120	78	1.503	2.262	783	2.035	538	350	2.360	2.984
2004	1.120	1.946	-	457	168	804	1.786	57	1.517	1.951	6.936	673	600	516	5.470	-	-	121	78	1.518	2.313	802	-	483	296	2.386	2.930
2005	1.102	1.971	-	-	172	764	1.792	55	1.525	1.911	6.856	-	581	525	5.543	-	-	122	77	1.491	2.495	-	-	453	302	2.442	2.872
2006	1.049	1.946	-	-	175	734	1.778	51	1.531	1.923	6.720	-	-	543	5.624	164	116	124	78	1.465	1.970	806	2.210	412	259	2.550	2.858
2007	1.029	1.999	-	-	175	716	1.761	47	1.548	1.936	6.604	666	-	549	5.758	157	115	123	79	1.422	1.952	-	-	382	253	2.789	2.721
2008	1.022	2.035	476	437	175	708	1.753	45	1.542	1.978	6.476	-	516	553	5.841	144	112	123	75	1.436	1.914	803	2.246	353	254	2.933	2.659
2009	1.008	2.027	-	424	162	684	1.692	39	1.538	2.013	6.400	-	-	523	5.910	122	115	122	73	1.423	1.889	771	-	320	332	2.913	2.581
2010	999	2.035	-	-	155	648	1.647	39	1.513	2.046	6.330	628	-	548	5.945	114	113	122	75	1.370	2.069	739	-	319	260	2.834	2.558
2011	995	2.094	-	-	149	616	1.661	36	1.492	2.075	6.300	-	-	532	5.953	105	109	127	76	1.360	2.069	692	-	282	286	2.760	2.580
2012	993	2.095	420	341	146	590	1.656	35	1.485	2.086	6.310	-	423	526	6.009	103	102	126	78	1.330	2.001	-	1.432	285	207	2.590	2.601
2013	989	2.048	-	369	140	550	1.649	33	1.436	2.070	6.298	511	-	520	5.958	102	95	126	80	1.265	-	-	-	278	197	2.397	2.607
2014	988	2.050	-	350	137	524	1.660	32	1.426	2.062	6.281	-	401	508	5.939	100	94	127	81	1.244	2.060	-	-	268	219	2.258	2.643
2015	987	2.020	-	321	133	496	1.684	28	1.412	2.067	6.290	-	-	496	5.814	100	92	127	83	1.224	-	596	-	259	182	2.134	2.701
2016	991	2.014	407	-	135	507	1.696	27	1.382	2.075	6.268	459	356	484	5.811	97	92	127	85	1.213	1.806	579	1.340	249	-	2.124	2.727
2017	995	2.016	-	313	-	504	1.706	26	1.350	2.074	6.241	-	-	481	5.875	96	92	130	88	1.202	1.747	-	-	247	-	2.106	2.751

Year	AT	BE	BG*	HR	CY*	CZ	DK	EE*	FI	FR	DE	GR*	HU*	IE	IT	LV*	LT*	LU*	MT*	NL	PL	PT*	RO*	SK*	SI	ES*	SE
2018	999	2.043	-	302	-	500	1.757	26	1.322	2.071	6.247	-	332	489	5.840	93	87	128	90	1.209	-	-	1.390	247	-	2.105	2.764
2019	1.004	2.034	-	-	-	-	1.767	25	1.306	-	6.229	-	-	497	5.865	-	90	123	92	1.152	-	-	-	-	-	2.075	2.757

Note: Net trade union membership is 'derived for the total (labour) union membership (…) and adjusted, if necessary, for trade (labour) union members outside the active, dependent and employed labour force (i.e. retired workers, self-employed workers, students, unemployed)' (OECD/AIAS 2021b: 19). Net trade union membership is considered the nominator for calculating 'net union density'. * One or more decade averages are calculated based on incomplete data.

Source: OECD/AIAS (2021a). Last update: 21 September 2021.

Table A1.D Net union density in the EU Member States (%), averages (1960s, 1970s, 1980s, 1990s) and annual data, 2000-2019

Year	AT	BE	BG	HR	CY	CZ*	DK	EE*	FI	FR	DE	GR*	HU*	IE	IT	LV*	LT*	LU*	MT	NL	PL	PT	RO	SK*	SI*	ES*	SE
1960s	*58.7*	*40.5*	-	-	-	-	*59.6*	-	*38.0*	*20.3*	*33.1*	-	-	*48.3*	*30.0*	-	-	-	-	*40.1*	-	-	-	-	-	-	*65.5*
1970s	*53.1*	*49.3*	-	-	-	-	*67.5*	-	*62.8*	*21.7*	*33.8*	*48.2*	-	*55.1*	*45.2*	-	-	*46.4*	-	*37.5*	-	*64.7*	-	-	-	*31.3*	*72.5*
1980s	*50.9*	*50.9*	-	-	-	-	*76.7*	-	*69.9*	*14.6*	*34.2*	*37.8*	-	*54.2*	*43.8*	-	-	*50.5*	-	*28.8*	-	*44.2*	-	-	-	*12.8*	*81.4*
1990s	*41.9*	*54.0*	-	-	-	*43.6*	*75.8*	*45.9*	*77.8*	*9.8*	*29.9*	*32.1*	*53.9*	*46.6*	*37.5*	*28.0*	*26.0*	*43.8*	-	*24.7*	*39.3*	*27.0*	*45.4*	*43.8*	*53.9*	*18.1*	*84.1*
2000	36.9	56.6	27.3	-	65.1	27.2	74.5	14.0	74.2	9.5	24.6	-	23.8	35.9	34.8	-	-	-	63.1	22.3	23.5	-	-	34.2	44.2	17.5	81.0
2001	36.2	57.6	-	-	62.8	23.8	73.9	13.3	76.6	9.4	23.7	24.9	20.4	35.0	34.2	-	18.5	-	61.7	21.6	22.3	-	-	32.5	43.3	17.2	78.7
2002	36.0	56.9	-	-	63.3	22.4	73.6	13.3	75.7	9.5	23.5	-	-	35.1	33.7	-	-	-	61.9	21.4	22.8	20.5	-	30.1	47.1	16.8	78.0
2003	34.6	55.4	23.6	-	66.3	22.3	72.4	11.7	74.5	9.2	23.0	-	18.9	34.9	33.6	21.0	12.2	44.0	60.8	20.9	22.9	21.1	35.9	27.7	45.3	16.5	77.2
2004	34.8	55.3	-	38.0	65.5	20.6	71.7	10.5	73.5	8.9	22.2	24.1	17.9	33.6	34.0	-	-	43.4	61.9	21.3	22.9	21.6	-	25.4	37.1	16.0	76.4
2005	33.8	54.9	-	-	64.5	19.1	71.5	9.7	72.7	8.6	21.5	-	17.3	32.4	33.8	-	-	42.6	59.8	22.1	23.8	-	-	23.5	37.5	15.5	74.2
2006	31.6	53.8	-	-	62.4	18.1	69.7	8.5	71.9	8.6	20.6	-	-	31.7	33.6	18.0	9.8	41.4	60.3	21.4	17.9	21.1	36.0	20.6	32.2	15.6	72.3
2007	30.4	53.6	-	-	58.0	17.4	69.0	7.9	71.1	8.5	19.8	22.6	-	29.5	34.0	16.7	9.3	39.5	59.2	20.2	16.7	-	-	18.7	30.6	16.4	67.0
2008	29.6	53.4	16.2	31.2	57.2	16.9	68.8	7.4	69.9	8.5	19.0	-	15.3	30.2	33.9	15.2	8.9	37.6	54.6	20.0	15.7	20.7	35.6	16.8	29.7	17.4	64.6
2009	29.3	53.8	-	30.5	52.7	16.7	68.9	7.2	72.5	8.8	18.8	-	-	31.5	34.7	15.2	10.0	36.8	53.4	20.0	15.4	20.4	-	16.0	40.4	18.3	64.2
2010	28.9	53.0	-	-	48.0	16.1	68.1	7.5	71.4	9.0	18.9	22.2	-	34.4	35.3	15.1	10.1	36.1	53.8	19.5	17.4	19.6	-	16.4	32.6	18.2	63.5
2011	28.3	54.2	-	-	45.6	15.4	68.7	6.6	69.6	9.1	18.4	-	-	33.9	35.2	13.7	9.7	36.6	52.5	19.3	17.3	18.6	-	14.5	36.7	17.9	62.3
2012	28.0	54.1	16.2	27.1	45.3	14.8	69.0	6.2	69.2	9.1	18.3	-	12.5	33.6	35.5	13.2	9.0	35.3	52.1	18.8	16.6	-	25.0	14.5	26.8	17.8	62.4
2013	27.8	53.3	-	29.5	46.6	13.6	68.8	5.9	67.5	9.0	18.0	23.1	-	32.3	35.7	12.9	8.4	34.8	51.3	18.2	-	-	-	14.1	26.2	17.0	62.0
2014	27.7	52.9	-	26.5	45.8	12.9	68.5	5.6	67.8	9.0	17.7	-	11.0	30.7	35.4	12.8	8.1	34.1	49.3	18.1	16.5	-	-	13.4	29.4	15.8	61.8
2015	27.4	52.3	-	24.0	43.6	11.9	68.2	4.8	67.5	9.0	17.6	-	-	28.9	34.2	12.7	7.9	33.3	48.4	17.7	-	16.1	-	12.6	23.8	14.4	62.2
2016	26.9	51.6	15.3	-	43.3	11.9	67.4	4.5	65.7	9.0	17.0	19.0	9.2	27.1	33.6	12.4	7.7	32.3	47.5	17.3	14.1	15.3	21.6	11.8	-	13.9	61.7

Year	AT	BE	BG	HR	CY	CZ*	DK	EE*	FI	FR	DE	GR*	HU*	IE	IT	LV*	LT*	LU*	MT	NL	PL	PT	RO	SK*	SI*	ES*	SE
2017	26.7	50.7	-	22.0	-	11.7	66.7	4.4	62.9	8.9	16.7	-	-	25.9	33.2	12.3	7.7	32.1	46.7	16.8	13.4	-	-	11.5	-	13.4	60.8
2018	26.3	50.0	-	20.8	-	11.4	67.5	4.4	60.0	8.8	16.6	-	8.3	25.5	32.6	11.6	7.1	30.4	43.8	16.5	-	-	21.4	11.3	-	13.0	60.1
2019	26.3	49.1	-	-	-	-	67.0	4.2	58.8	-	16.3	-	-	25.0	32.5	-	7.4	28.2	42.9	15.4	-	-	-	-	-	12.5	59.6

Note: Net union density is defined as the '(p)roportion of employees who are members of a trade union (NUM) among all employees (WSEE)', whereby NUM is the 'union membership of employees derived for the total (labour) union membership (…) and adjusted, if necessary, for trade (labour) union members outside the active, dependent and employed labour force (i.e. retired workers, self-employed workers, students, unemployed)' and WSEE is the '(t)otal number of employees mainly based on national labour force surveys and referring to all employees living in a particular country (national concept)' (OECD/AIAS 2021b: 19). * One or more decade averages are calculated based on incomplete data.
Source: OECD/AIAS (2021a). Last update: 21 September 2021.

Table A1.E Share of women in union membership in the EU Member States (%), averages (1960s, 1970s, 1980s, 1990s) and annual data, 2000-2019

Year	AT	BE	BG*	HR*	CY*	CZ*	DK	EE*	FI*	FR*	DE	GR*	HU*	IE*	IT*	LV	LT*	LU*	MT*	NL	PL	PT*	RO*	SK*	SI*	ES*	SE*
1960s	*28.1*	-	-	-	-	-	*24.4*	-	-	-	*16.8*	-	-	*23.0*	-	-	-	-	-	*9.6*	-	-	-	-	-	-	*28.5*
1970s	*28.4*	-	-	-	-	-	*33.7*	-	*36.3*	*29.2*	*18.6*	-	-	*27.3*	-	-	-	-	-	*11.6*	-	-	-	-	-	-	*39.4*
1980s	*30.7*	-	-	-	-	-	*44.2*	-	*43.3*	-	*23.6*	-	-	*30.7*	*35.0*	-	-	-	-	*15.8*	-	-	-	-	-	-	*47.9*
1990s	*31.6*	-	-	-	35.4	-	*47.7*	-	*45.8*	-	*31.1*	-	-	*35.7*	-	*60.3*	-	*25.6*	-	*26.5*	-	-	*55.0*	-	-	*29.2*	*52.0*
2000	32.3	37.9	-	-	-	-	49.0	59.9	-	-	-	-	-	-	-	-	-	-	-	31.1	-	-	-	-	-	35.8	51.9*
2001	32.4	-	-	-	-	-	-	59.5	-	-	31.6	-	-	43.4	-	-	-	-	-	30.5	51.7	-	-	-	-	-	52.1*
2002	32.8	39.1	-	-	36.3	46.7	49.2	64.3	-	-	-	23.3	-	44.6	38.3	-	-	-	-	30.9	-	41.5	-	-	51.3	-	52.2*
2003	33.1	-	49.7	-	-	-	-	67.7	53.1	44.0	31.9	-	-	45.0	-	58.9	57.1	-	27.3	31.3	-	-	57.9	42.1	49.7	36.9	51.9*
2004	33.2	-	-	-	-	-	51.1	67.6	-	-	-	26.3	18.5	46.8	-	-	-	34.4	-	33.0	-	-	-	-	-	-	52.2*
2005	33.0	-	-	-	-	-	-	67.1	-	-	32.5	-	-	48.0	-	-	-	-	-	-	-	-	-	-	-	-	52.0*
2006	33.3	40.8	-	-	-	-	-	64.7	-	-	-	-	-	47.6	-	-	-	-	-	34.2	-	41.4	-	-	-	42.3	51.7*
2007	34.1	-	-	-	-	-	-	64.8	-	-	34.0	-	-	48.7	-	68.0	-	-	-	34.1	59.2	-	-	-	-	-	51.6*
2008	34.0	41.0	46.9	-	37.3	45.9	50.5	61.5	-	46.1	34.7	33.8	-	50.2	-	-	56.3	36.7	30.5	35.2	-	-	-	41.9	49.9	-	51.4*
2009	34.4	-	-	-	-	-	-	63.7	54.7	-	35.5	-	12.9	53.1	-	-	-	-	-	36.0	-	-	-	-	-	-	51.7*
2010	34.6	-	-	-	-	-	51.3	59.5	-	47.3	35.8	31.7	-	54.6	-	-	-	-	-	37.4	-	-	-	-	50.2	40.7	51.4*
2011	34.7	-	-	-	-	-	51.8	60.5	-	-	37.5	-	-	56.0	-	-	-	-	-	38.6	-	-	-	-	-	-	51.5*
2012	34.9	42.2	-	-	-	-	51.0	59.1	-	-	37.6	32.4	-	56.1	43.2	-	-	-	31.4	37.9	-	-	-	-	51.9	-	51.7*
2013	35.1	-	-	59.9	-	-	51.4	61.2	54.8	46.5	38.0	-	-	56.5	-	-	-	36.9	-	38.6	-	-	-	-	-	-	51.8*
2014	35.3	-	-	60.1	39.5	49.0	51.1	59.4	-	-	38.1	-	-	57.1	-	-	-	-	-	39.6	59.0	42.2	-	-	-	43.0	51.7*
2015	35.5	44.0	-	60.0	-	-	51.1	56.7	-	-	38.5	-	9.3	55.6	-	65.2	53.6	-	-	40.6	-	-	-	-	-	-	51.8*
2016	35.8	-	-	59.9	-	-	51.3	-	-	45.5	38.6	-	-	56.5	-	-	-	-	-	41.5	-	-	-	46.2	-	-	-
2017	35.9	-	-	-	-	-	51.3	-	-	-	38.7	-	-	-	-	-	-	-	-	41.5	-	-	-	-	-	-	-

Year	AT	BE	BG*	HR*	CY*	CZ*	DK	EE*	FI*	FR*	DE	GR*	HU*	IE*	IT*	LV	LT*	LU*	MT*	NL	PL	PT*	RO*	SK*	SI*	ES*	SE*
2018	36.1	45.6	-	-	-	-	51.1	-	-	-	38.8	-	-	-	-	-	-	-	-	40.0	-	-	-	-	-	-	-
2019	36.4	-	-	-	-	-	51.8	-	-	-	-	-	-	-	-	-	-	-	-	38.6	-	-	-	-	-	-	-

Note: Share of women in union membership is defined as the '(i)ncidence of women among total union membership of employees as derived from administrative data source' (OECD/AIAS 2021b: 19). * Decade average is calculated based on incomplete data for the 1970s for France, for the 1980s for Italy and Sweden, and for the 1990s for Cyprus, Denmark, Ireland, Latvia, Luxembourg, Romania and Spain.
Source: OECD/AIAS (2021a) except for * Visser (2019). Last update: 21 September 2021.

Table A1.F Union density of private sector workers in the EU Member States (%), averages (1960s, 1970s, 1980s, 1990s) and annual data, 2000-2019

Year	AT	BE	BG	HR	CY	CZ	DK	EE	FI	FR	DE	GR	HU	IE	IT	LV	LT	LU	MT	NL	PL	PT	RO	SK	SI	ES	SE
1960s	-	35.8	-	-	-	-	56.5	-	-	-	26.2	-	-	-	-	-	-	-	-	32.1	-	-	-	-	-	-	61.7
1970s	47.4	42.4	-	-	-	-	64.8	-	59.7	-	25.6	-	-	-	-	-	-	-	-	-	-	-	-	-	-	-	62.5
1980s	42.9	49.0	-	-	-	-	71.2	-	63.5	-	28.1	-	-	-	-	-	-	43.3	-	23.4	-	-	-	-	-	-	73.6
1990s	32.3	53.2	-	-	-	-	66.7	-	71.6	-	24.1	-	-	-	-	-	-	-	-	19.1	-	-	-	-	-	-	-
2000	-	-	-	-	-	-	64.4	-	64.5	-	-	-	-	-	-	-	-	-	-	17.1	-	-	-	-	-	-	-
2001	-	-	-	-	-	-	-	-	-	-	-	-	-	-	-	-	-	-	-	16.6	-	-	-	-	-	-	-
2002	-	53.8	-	-	-	-	-	-	-	-	-	-	-	-	-	-	-	-	-	16.1	-	-	-	-	-	-	-
2003	-	-	-	-	-	-	-	-	-	-	-	-	-	-	-	-	-	-	-	16.5	-	-	-	-	-	-	-
2004	-	-	-	-	-	-	59.2	-	-	-	-	-	-	-	-	-	-	-	-	16.6	-	-	-	-	-	-	-
2005	26.2	-	-	-	-	-	-	-	-	-	-	-	-	-	-	-	-	-	-	-	-	-	-	-	-	-	-
2006	24.1	-	-	-	-	-	-	-	-	-	17.5	-	-	-	-	-	-	-	-	16.0	-	-	-	-	-	-	-
2007	-	-	-	-	-	-	-	-	-	-	-	-	-	-	-	-	-	-	-	15.3	-	-	-	-	-	-	-
2008	-	-	-	-	-	-	-	-	-	-	-	-	-	-	-	8.3	-	-	-	15.7	-	-	-	-	-	-	-
2009	-	-	-	-	-	-	-	-	-	-	-	-	-	-	-	-	-	-	-	-	-	-	-	-	-	-	-
2010	23.2	-	-	-	-	-	-	-	-	-	16.3	-	-	-	-	-	-	-	-	-	-	-	-	-	-	-	-
2011	-	-	-	-	-	-	-	-	-	-	15.9	-	-	-	-	-	-	-	-	-	-	-	-	-	-	-	-
2012	-	-	-	-	-	-	-	-	-	-	-	-	-	-	-	7.5	-	-	-	-	-	-	-	-	-	-	-
2013	-	53.0	-	-	-	-	62.0	-	-	-	-	-	-	-	-	-	-	-	-	16.4	-	-	-	-	-	-	-
2014	-	-	-	-	-	-	-	-	-	-	-	-	-	-	-	-	-	-	-	-	44.0	-	-	-	-	-	-
2015	-	-	-	-	-	-	-	-	-	-	15.4	-	-	-	-	-	-	-	-	-	-	-	-	-	-	-	-

Year	AT	BE	BG	HR	CY	CZ	DK	EE	FI	FR	DE	GR	HU	IE	IT	LV	LT	LU	MT	NL	PL	PT	RO	SK	SI	ES	SE
2016	-	51.0	-	-	-	-	59.9	-	-	-	-	-	-	-	-	6.2	-	-	-	15.5	-	-	-	-	-	-	-
2017	21.2	-	-	-	-	-	-	-	-	-	-	-	-	-	-	-	-	-	-	-	-	-	-	-	-	-	-
2018	-	-	-	-	-	-	-	-	-	-	-	-	-	-	-	-	-	-	-	-	-	-	-	-	-	-	-
2019	-	-	-	-	-	-	-	-	-	-	-	-	-	-	-	-	-	-	-	-	-	-	-	-	-	-	-

Note: The union density of private sector workers is defined as the '[p]roportion of private-sector employees who are members of a trade union among private-sector employees as derived from administrative data source' (OECD/AIAS 2021b: 20).

Source: OECD/AIAS (2021a). Last update: 21 September 2021.

Table A1.G Union density of public sector workers in the EU Member States (%), averages (1960s, 1970s, 1980s, 1990s) and annual data, 2000-2019

Year	AT	BE	BG	HR	CY	CZ	DK	EE	FI	FR	DE	GR	HU	IE	IT	LV	LT	LU	MT	NL	PL	PT	RO	SK	SI	ES	SE
1960s	-	60.3	-	-	-	-	74.3	-	-	-	79.7	-	-	-	-	-	-	-	-	73.6	-	-	-	-	-	-	75.1
1970s	92.1	64.7	-	-	-	-	83.0	-	98.9	-	63.8	-	-	-	-	-	-	-	-	-	-	-	-	-	-	-	89.7
1980s	84.6	60.6	-	-	-	-	99.8	-	99.5	-	56.2	-	-	-	-	-	-	74.3	-	66.6	-	-	-	-	-	-	92.0
1990s	72.1	62.4	-	-	-	-	92.0	-	99.5	-	51.6	-	-	-	-	-	-	-	-	38.2	-	-	-	-	-	-	-
2000	-	-	-	-	-	-	96.4	-	98.4	-	-	-	-	-	-	-	-	-	-	35.9	-	-	-	-	-	-	-
2001	-	-	-	-	-	-	-	-	-	-	-	-	-	-	-	-	-	-	-	34.3	-	-	-	-	-	-	-
2002	-	63.0	-	-	-	-	-	-	-	-	-	-	-	-	-	-	-	-	-	35.0	-	-	-	-	-	-	-
2003	-	-	-	-	-	-	-	-	-	-	-	-	-	-	-	-	-	-	-	31.2	-	-	-	-	-	-	-
2004	-	-	-	-	-	-	97.1	-	-	-	-	-	-	-	-	-	-	-	-	31.9	-	-	-	-	-	-	-
2005	58.5	-	-	-	-	-	-	-	-	-	-	-	-	-	-	-	-	-	-		-	-	-	-	-	-	-
2006	55.9	-	-	-	-	-	-	-	-	-	29.3	-	-	-	-	-	-	-	-	28.7	-	-	-	-	-	-	-
2007	-	-	-	-	-	-	-	-	-	-	-	-	-	-	-	-	-	-	-	27.3	-	-	-	-	-	-	-
2008	-	-	-	-	-	-	-	-	-	-	-	-	-	-	-	39.0	-	-	-	26.2	-	-	-	-	-	-	-
2009	-	-	-	-	-	-	-	-	-	-	-	-	-	-	-	-	-	-	-	-	-	-	-	-	-	-	-
2010	45.6	-	-	-	-	-	-	-	-	-	25.6	-	-	-	-	-	-	-	-	-	-	-	-	-	-	-	-
2011	-	-	-	-	-	-	-	-	-	-	25.0	-	-	-	-	-	-	-	-	-	-	-	-	-	-	-	-
2012	-	-	-	-	-	-	-	-	-	-	-	-	-	-	-	30.2	-	-	-	-	-	-	-	-	-	-	-
2013	-	53.1	-	-	-	-	80.9	-	-	-	-	-	-	-	-	-	-	-	-	22.2	-	-	-	-	-	-	-
2014	-	-	-	-	-	-	-	-	-	-	-	-	-	-	-	-	-	-	-	-	12.3	-	-	-	-	-	-
2015	-	-	-	-	-	-	-	-	-	-	23.3	-	-	-	-	-	-	-	-	-	-	-	-	-	-	-	-
2016	-	52.6	-	-	-	-	81.5	-	-	-	-	-	-	-	-	31.5	-	-	-	21.5	-	-	-	-	-	-	-

Year	AT	BE	BG	HR	CY	CZ	DK	EE	FI	FR	DE	GR	HU	IE	IT	LV	LT	LU	MT	NL	PL	PT	RO	SK	SI	ES	SE
2017	42.0	-	-	-	-	-	-	-	-	-	-	-	-	-	-	-	-	-	-	-	-	-	-	-	-	-	-
2018	-	-	-	-	-	-	-	-	-	-	-	-	-	-	-	-	-	-	-	-	-	-	-	-	-	-	-
2019	-	-	-	-	-	-	-	-	-	-	-	-	-	-	-	-	-	-	-	-	-	-	-	-	-	-	-

Note: The union density of public sector workers is defined as the '[p]roportion of public-sector employees who are members of a trade union among public-sector employees as derived from administrative data sources' (OECD/AIAS 2021b: 20).
Source: OECD/AIAS (2021a). Last update: 21 September 2021.

Table A1.H Collective bargaining coverage in the EU Member States (%), averages (1960s, 1970s, 1980s, 1990s) and annual data, 2000-2019

Year	AT	BE	BG	HR	CY	CZ	DK	EE	FI	FR	DE*	GR	HU	IE	IT	LV*	LT	LU	MT	NL	PL	PT	RO	SK	SI	ES	SE
1960s	*95.0*	*80.0*	-	-	-	-	*79.5*	-	*67.3*	*50.0*	*85.0*	-	-	*70.0*	*100.0*	-	-	-	-	*82.6*	-		-	-	-	-	*75.0*
1970s	*95.0*	*87.5*	-	-	-	-	*80.5*	-	*74.3*	*70.0*	*85.0*	-	-	*70.0*	*100.0*	-	-	*60.0*	-	*81.4*	-	*68.5*	-	-	-	*54.0*	*81.5*
1980s	*95.0*	*96.0*	-	-	-	-	*82.5*	-	*77.3*	*87.1*	*85.0*	*85.0*	-	*70.0*	*100.0*	-	-	*60.0*	-	*82.7*	-	*72.7*	-	-	-	*89.1*	*89.5*
1990s	*98.0*	*96.0*	-	-	-	*44.6*	*84.0*	-	*83.0*	*94.0*	*76.8*	*100.0*	*41.8*	*60.3*	*100.0*	-	-	*60.0*	*59.7*	*81.5*	-	*78.4*	-	-	*100.0*	*92.9*	*90.7*
2000	98.0	96.0	-	-	65.1	42.4	85.1	-	85.0	-	67.8	100.0	38.4	44.2	100.0	-	12.5	60.0	-	81.7	25.0	78.3	100.0	52.0	100.0	84.8	87.7
2001	-	-	-	-	62.8	38.5	85.1	-	-	-	68.8	100.0	35.7	-	100.0	-	-	-	-	85.9	-		100.0	48.1	100.0	83.7	-
2002	-	-	36.4	-	63.3	38.5	84.9	-	91.0	-	67.8	100.0	33.8	-	100.0	-	-	-	56.6	92.7	-	77.7	100.0	-	100.0	80.6	-
2003	-	96.0	-	-	66.3	41.1	85.1	-	-	-	67.6	100.0	34.3	-	100.0	-	-	-	-	80.4	-	80.1	100.0	-	100.0	78.9	-
2004	-	96.0	-	-	65.5	40.4	85.1	-	91.4	97.7	65.8	100.0	34.5	-	100.0	-	-	-	-	84.9	-	80.3	100.0	40.0	100.0	77.7	-
2005	98.0	96.0	-	-	64.5	38.2	85.0	-	-	-	64.9	100.0	24.8	41.7	100.0	-	-	-	-	91.3	-	83.2	100.0	-	100.0	76.8	89.4
2006	98.0	96.0	29.3	-	62.4	37.0	85.0	14.5	87.7	-	63.4	100.0	22.7	-	100.0	34.2	10.4	-	-	70.3	-	80.4	100.0	-	100.0	76.5	88.7
2007	98.0	96.0	-	-	58.0	36.4	82.8	-	-	-	61.7	100.0	24.6	-	100.0	-	10.0	-	-	82.7	18.9	82.4	100.0	-	-	77.0	87.5
2008	98.0	96.0	-	-	57.2	38.2	82.6	-	87.5	-	61.3	100.0	22.8	-	100.0	-	9.5	59.0	52.4	81.8	18.7	82.6	100.0	40.0	-	80.3	88.9
2009	98.0	96.0	-	61.0	52.7	38.0	-	-	-	-	61.7	100.0	26.9	40.5	100.0	-	10.7	-	-	86.3	-	81.2	100.0	-	-	83.2	89.6
2010	98.0	96.0	26.8	-	48.0	36.0	-	15.7	-	98.0	59.8	100.0	27.3	-	100.0	32.9	10.9	-	-	90.6	18.6	77.8	100.0	-	70.0	79.4	88.7
2011	98.0	96.0	-	-	45.6	36.9	83.0	-	-	-	58.9	100.0	26.4	-	100.0	-	10.4	54.2	-	87.2	18.1	78.1	-	35.0	-	79.8	88.3
2012	98.0	96.0	-	55.1	45.3	36.7	83.7	-	-	-	58.3	51.5	26.9	-	100.0	-	9.6	-	-	85.1	17.7	75.5	-	-	-	80.1	88.8
2013	98.0	96.0	-	-	46.6	36.4	-	-	-	98.0	57.6	37.3	25.5	-	100.0	-	9.0	-	-	85.7	-	76.5	35.0	-	65.4	84.6	88.4
2014	98.0	96.0	25.7	52.7	45.8	34.3	-	14.1	91.9	-	57.8	29.2	25.4	-	100.0	32.4	8.7	-	-	85.9	-	74.0	-	-	69.2	83.4	88.6
2015	98.0	96.0	-	-	43.6	34.2	83.1	-	-	98.0	56.8	21.3	28.3	-	100.0	-	8.5	-	-	79.4	17.3	73.7	22.6	24.4	67.5	79.6	88.7
2016	98.0	96.0	-	-	43.3	32.9	-	-	-	-	56.0	14.3	28.1	-	100.0	-	8.3	-	50.1	79.3	-	74.1	-	-	70.9	80.8	88.6

Year	AT	BE	BG	HR	CY	CZ	DK	EE	FI	FR	DE*	GR	HU	IE	IT	LV*	LT	LU	MT	NL	PL	PT	RO	SK	SI	ES	SE
2017	98.0	96.0	-	-	-	33.6	-	-	88.8	-	55.0	14.2	23.3	34.0	100.0	-	8.3	-	-	77.1	-	73.1	15.0	-	78.6	78.9	87.7
2018	98.0	96.0	23.4	-	-	34.2	82.0	6.1	-	98.0	54.0	-	21.1	-	100.0	27.1	7.6	-	-	76.7	-	73.6	-	-	-	80.1	88.0
2019	98.0	96.0	-	-	-	34.7	-	-	-	-	-	-	21.8	-	100.0	-	7.9	-	-	75.6	13.4	-	-	-	-	-	-

Note: Adjusted coverage is defined as the '(n)umber of employees covered by collective (wage) agreements in force as a proportion of all employees with the right to bargain defined as the proportion of employees who are not excluded from collective bargaining' (OECD/AIAS 2021b: 23). Decade averages are calculated based on incomplete data, except for Italy. * The adjusted coverage is derived from survey data except for the period 1960–1994 in Germany.

Source: OECD/AIAS (2021a). Last update: 21 September 2021.

Table A1.I Days not worked due to industrial action in the EU Member States, average 1990s and annual data, 2000-2020

Year	AT	BE*	BG	HR	CY	CZ*	DK	EE*	FI	FR	DE	GR*	HU*	IE	IT	LV*	LT*	LU	MT	NL	PL	PT	RO	SK*	SI*	ES	SE
1990s	4	95	-	-	138	1	170	0	170	77	11	2,075	20	120	158	11	-	29	44	22	43	30	63	1	149	313	49
2000	1	77	-	-	5	-	51	2	124	120	0	-	198	72	59	0	9	12	38	1	7	11	96	0	9	295	0
2001	0	135	-	-	20	-	23	0	29	86	1	-	4	82	67	0	2	0	22	6	0	11	0	0	33	150	3
2002	3	18	-	-	29	-	78	0	36	47	10	-	0	15	310	4	3	3	6	34	0	29	6	0	29	365	0
2003	402	70	-	-	28	-	23	38	32	202	5	-	0	26	123	0	0	16	26	2	1	15	2	37	22	56	162
2004	0	47	-	-	36	-	31	3	20	33	4	-	2	14	43	0	0	35	13	9	0	12	4	0	5	304	4
2005	0	187	-	-	58	-	21	0	322	187	6	-	0	17	55	0	1	5	10	6	0	7	2	0	46	61	0
2006	0	25	-	-	97	-	34	0	40	145	50	-	5	4	33	0	0	36	23	2	3	12	4	10	5	57	1
2007	0	34	-	-	34	-	36	0	44	140	22	-	9	3	55	0	8	151	43	4	16	8	80	0	0	70	3
2008	0	69	-	-	3	-	743	0	7	141	16	-	7	2	42	4	26	-	13	16	23	-	22	0	-	90	26
2009	0	43	-	-	6	-	6	0	44	167	12	-	2	200	-	0	0	-	56	1	1	-	-	0	-	82	0
2010	0	42	-	-	1	-	8	0	149	356	5	-	5	4	-	0	0	-	0	8	1	19	-	0	-	43	7
2011	16	99	-	-	15	-	6	0	60	97	9	-	-	2	-	0	0	-	4	3	2	17	-	0	-	32	0
2012	0	90	-	-	151	-	4	55	8	62	18	-	0	5	-	1	3	-	8	31	1	32	-	0	-	89	9
2013	1	60	-	-	2,024	-	397	0	12	80	16	-	-	9	-	0	0	-	1	3	1	23	-	0	-	78	2
2014	1	221	-	-	100	-	7	0	19	81	11	-	-	27	-	0	2	-	5	6	0	7	-	0	-	44	1
2015	0	67	-	-	44	-	4	0	53	76	57	-	-	19	-	29	2	-	20	7	9	5	-	0	-	34	0
2016	0	124	-	-	116	-	6	0	3	133	13	-	9	41	-	0	31	-	0	3	1	3	-	0	-	26	2
2017	0	63	-	-	12	-	11	0	11	76	6	-	1	27	-	0	0	-	0	43	3	8	-	0	-	38	1
2018	2	104	-	-	72	-	8	2	99	113	28	-	9	2	-	0	28	-	-	33	0	13	-	0	-	56	0
2019	1	107	-	-	-	-	3	-	173	203	10	-	13	18	-	0	2	-	-	53	142	14	-	0	-	52	2
2020	-	77	-	-	-	-	3	-	82	-	9	-	-	11	-	0	-	-	-	29	0	-	-	0	-	34	0

Note: *The 1990 average is calculated based on incomplete data.

Source: ETUI based on national statistical offices and ILOSTAT. Last update: 22 November 2021.

Table A1.J Unemployment rate in the EU Member States (%), averages (1960s, 1970s, 1980s, 1990s) and annual data, 2000-2020

Year	AT	BE	BG	HR	CY	CZ	DK	EE	FI	FR	DE	GR	HU	IE	IT	LV	LT	LU	MT	NL	PL	PT	RO	SK	SI	ES	SE
1960s	*1.5*	*1.9*	-	-	-	-	*1.0*	-	*1.8*	*1.7*	-	-	-	*5.4*	*4.8*	-	-	*0.0*	-	*0.9*	-	*2.4*	-	-	-	*2.5*	*1.9*
1970s	*1.2*	*4.0*	-	-	-	-	*3.3*	-	*3.5*	*4.4*	-	-	-	*7.5*	*5.9*	-	-	*0.5*	-	*3.8*	-	*4.5*	-	-	-	*4.5*	*2.5*
1980s	*3.2*	*9.6*	-	-	-	-	*7.0*	-	*4.8*	*8.6*	-	-	-	*14.2*	*8.4*	-	-	*2.5*	-	*8.4*	-	*7.8*	-	-	-	*16.4*	*3.3*
1990s	*4.0*	*8.4*	*11.3*	-	*5.1*	*4.5*	*7.3*	*9.5*	*11.8*	*9.7*	-	*8.3*	*8.9*	*12.1*	*10.5*	*9.6*	*6.6*	*2.4*	*5.5*	*5.8*	*12.7*	*6.0*	*7.7*	*12.8*	*7.1*	*19.5*	*8.3*
2000	3.5	7.0	16.9	15.6	4.9	8.8	4.6	14.6	9.8	8.6	7.9	11.4	6.4	4.5	10.6	14.3	16.4	2.4	6.6	2.9	16.2	4.1	7.3	18.8	6.8	13.9	6.7
2001	3.6	6.6	20.3	16.0	3.9	8.2	4.6	13.0	9.1	7.8	8.0	10.8	5.7	4.2	9.6	13.7	17.3	2.3	6.9	2.3	18.3	4.1	6.8	19.3	6.2	10.6	4.9
2002	4.0	7.5	18.2	15.0	3.6	7.3	4.6	11.2	9.1	7.9	8.8	10.4	5.8	4.7	9.0	12.5	13.7	2.9	6.9	2.8	20.0	5.1	8.6	18.7	6.3	11.5	5.1
2003	4.3	8.2	13.7	14.2	4.3	7.8	5.4	10.3	9.0	8.5	9.9	9.8	5.9	4.8	8.7	11.6	12.5	3.7	7.6	3.7	19.7	6.4	7.0	17.6	6.7	11.5	5.7
2004	5.5	8.4	12.1	13.7	4.7	8.3	5.5	10.1	8.8	8.9	10.9	10.6	6.1	4.7	8.0	11.7	10.9	5.1	7.2	4.6	19.0	6.7	8.1	18.2	6.3	11.0	6.5
2005	5.6	8.5	10.1	12.8	5.3	7.9	4.8	8.0	8.4	8.9	11.2	10.0	7.2	4.6	7.7	10.0	8.3	4.5	6.9	5.9	17.8	7.7	7.2	16.3	6.5	9.2	7.5
2006	5.3	8.3	9.0	11.3	4.6	7.2	3.9	5.9	7.7	8.8	10.3	9.0	7.5	4.8	6.8	7.0	5.8	4.7	6.8	5.0	13.9	7.8	7.3	13.4	6.0	8.5	7.1
2007	4.9	7.5	6.9	9.9	3.9	5.3	3.8	4.6	6.9	8.0	8.7	8.4	7.4	5.0	6.1	6.1	4.3	4.1	6.5	4.2	9.6	8.1	6.4	11.1	4.9	8.2	6.2
2008	4.1	7.0	5.6	8.6	3.7	4.4	3.7	5.5	6.4	7.4	7.5	7.8	7.8	6.8	6.7	7.7	5.8	5.1	6.0	3.7	7.1	7.7	5.8	9.5	4.4	11.3	6.2
2009	5.3	7.9	6.8	9.2	5.4	6.7	6.4	13.5	8.2	9.1	7.8	9.6	10.0	12.6	7.8	17.5	13.8	5.1	6.9	4.4	8.2	9.6	6.9	12.0	5.9	17.9	8.4
2010	4.8	8.3	10.3	11.7	6.3	7.3	7.7	16.7	8.4	9.3	7.0	12.7	11.2	14.6	8.4	19.5	17.8	4.4	6.9	5.0	9.7	11.0	7.0	14.4	7.3	19.9	8.6
2011	4.6	7.2	11.3	13.7	7.9	6.7	7.8	12.3	7.8	9.2	5.8	17.9	11.0	15.4	8.4	16.2	15.4	4.9	6.4	5.0	9.7	12.9	7.2	13.6	8.2	21.4	7.8
2012	4.9	7.6	12.3	16.0	11.9	7.0	7.8	10.0	7.7	9.8	5.4	24.5	11.0	15.5	10.7	15.0	13.4	5.1	6.2	5.8	10.1	15.8	6.8	14.0	8.9	24.8	8.0
2013	5.4	8.4	13.0	17.3	15.9	7.0	7.4	8.6	8.2	10.3	5.2	27.5	10.2	13.8	12.2	11.9	11.8	5.9	6.1	7.3	10.3	16.4	7.1	14.2	10.1	26.1	8.1
2014	5.6	8.5	11.4	17.3	16.1	6.1	6.9	7.4	8.7	10.3	5.0	26.5	7.7	11.9	12.7	10.8	10.7	5.9	5.7	7.4	9.0	14.1	6.8	13.2	9.7	24.5	8.0
2015	5.7	8.5	9.2	16.2	15.0	5.1	6.3	6.2	9.4	10.4	4.6	24.9	6.8	10.0	11.9	9.9	9.1	6.7	5.4	6.9	7.5	12.6	6.8	11.5	9.0	22.1	7.4
2016	6.0	7.8	7.6	13.1	13.0	4.0	6.0	6.8	8.8	10.1	4.1	23.6	5.1	8.4	11.7	9.6	7.9	6.3	4.7	6.0	6.2	11.2	5.9	9.7	8.0	19.6	7.0
2017	5.5	7.1	6.2	11.2	11.1	2.9	5.8	5.8	8.6	9.4	3.8	21.5	4.2	6.7	11.2	8.7	7.1	5.5	4.0	4.9	4.9	9.0	4.9	8.1	6.6	17.2	6.7

(Continued)

Table A1.J Continued

Year	AT	BE	BG	HR	CY	CZ	DK	EE	FI	FR	DE	GR	HU	IE	IT	LV	LT	LU	MT	NL	PL	PT	RO	SK	SI	ES	SE
2018	4.9	6.0	5.2	8.5	8.4	2.2	5.1	5.4	7.4	9.0	3.4	19.3	3.7	5.8	10.6	7.4	6.2	5.6	3.7	3.8	3.9	7.1	4.2	6.5	5.1	15.3	6.4
2019	4.5	5.4	4.2	6.6	7.1	2.0	5.0	4.4	6.7	8.4	3.1	17.3	3.4	5.0	10.0	6.3	6.3	5.6	3.6	3.4	3.3	6.5	3.9	5.8	4.5	14.1	6.8
2020	5.4	5.6	5.1	7.5	7.6	2.6	5.6	6.8	7.8	8.0	3.8	16.3	4.3	5.7	9.2	8.1	8.5	6.8	4.3	3.8	3.2	6.9	5.0	6.7	5.0	15.5	8.3

Note: Unemployed persons from 15 to 74 years of age as a proportion of the labour force.

Source: Eurostat (UNE_RT_A_H). Last update: 3 November 2021.

Table A1.K Employment rate in the EU Member States (%), average (1992-1999) and annual data, 2000-2020

Year	AT	BE	BG	HR	CY	CZ	DK	EE	FI	FR	DE	GR	HU	IE	IT	LV	LT	LU	MT	NL	PL	PT	RO	SK	SI	ES	SE
1990s	*70.7*	*62.2*	-	-	*71.2*	*72.5*	*75.7*	*70.1*	*67.8*	*65.8*	*67.4*	*60.1*	*59.1*	*63.0*	*55.7*	*65.1*	*68.1*	*64.4*	*57.5*	*69.0*	*64.1*	*69.8*	*69.9*	*66.7*	*68.5*	*53.6*	*74.6*
2000	71.4	65.8	55.3	58.3	72.2	71.0	78.0	66.6	71.6	68.1	68.7	61.9	61.2	71.8	57.4	63.6	65.5	67.0	57.4	74.3	61.0	73.5	69.1	63.5	68.5	60.7	76.8
2001	71.3	65.0	54.8	56.9	73.9	71.2	78.3	67.4	72.6	68.8	68.9	61.5	61.3	72.4	58.5	64.5	64.2	67.5	57.4	75.4	59.4	74.0	68.3	63.5	69.4	62.1	78.7
2002	71.8	65.0	55.8	58.1	74.9	71.6	77.7	68.0	72.6	69.3	68.7	62.5	61.4	72.1	59.4	66.5	67.2	67.8	57.7	75.8	57.4	73.6	63.3	63.6	69.0	63.1	78.5
2003	72.0	64.7	58.0	58.4	75.2	70.7	77.3	69.6	72.2	69.8	68.3	63.6	62.4	72.0	60.0	67.8	68.9	67.2	57.8	75.2	57.1	72.9	63.7	64.8	68.1	64.3	77.9
2004	69.5	65.6	60.1	59.5	75.1	70.1	77.6	70.3	72.2	69.6	68.2	63.9	62.1	72.9	61.6	67.9	69.3	67.7	57.9	74.9	57.3	72.5	63.5	63.7	70.4	65.4	77.4
2005	70.4	66.5	61.9	59.9	74.4	70.7	78.0	72.0	73.0	69.4	69.4	64.4	62.2	74.0	61.5	69.1	70.7	69.0	57.4	72.7	58.3	72.2	63.6	64.5	71.1	67.5	77.9
2006	71.6	66.5	65.1	60.6	75.8	71.2	79.4	75.9	73.9	69.4	71.1	65.6	62.6	74.7	62.4	73.2	71.3	69.1	57.9	73.7	60.1	72.6	64.8	66.0	71.5	69.0	78.8
2007	72.8	67.7	68.4	63.9	76.8	72.0	79.0	76.9	74.8	69.9	72.9	65.8	62.3	75.1	62.7	75.2	72.7	69.6	58.6	75.5	62.7	72.5	64.4	67.2	72.4	69.7	80.1
2008	73.8	68.0	70.7	64.9	76.5	72.4	78.7	77.1	75.8	70.5	74.0	66.3	61.5	73.5	62.9	75.4	72.0	68.8	59.2	76.9	65.0	73.1	64.4	68.8	73.0	68.5	80.4
2009	73.4	67.1	68.8	64.2	75.3	70.9	76.1	70.0	73.5	69.5	74.2	65.6	60.1	68.0	61.6	66.6	67.0	70.4	59.0	76.8	64.9	71.1	63.5	66.4	71.9	64.0	78.3
2010	73.9	67.6	64.7	62.1	75.0	70.4	74.9	66.8	73.0	69.3	75.0	63.8	59.9	65.5	61.0	64.3	64.3	70.7	60.1	76.2	64.3	70.3	64.8	64.6	70.3	62.8	78.1
2011	74.2	67.3	62.9	59.8	73.4	70.9	74.8	70.6	73.8	69.2	76.5	59.6	60.4	64.6	61.0	66.3	66.9	70.1	61.6	76.4	64.5	68.8	63.8	65.0	68.4	62.0	79.4
2012	74.4	67.2	63.0	58.1	70.2	71.5	74.3	72.2	74.0	69.4	76.9	55.0	61.6	64.5	60.9	68.1	68.5	71.4	63.9	76.6	64.7	66.3	64.8	65.1	68.3	59.6	79.4
2013	74.6	67.2	63.5	57.2	67.2	72.5	74.3	73.3	73.3	69.5	77.3	52.9	63.0	66.5	59.7	69.7	69.9	71.1	66.2	75.9	64.9	65.4	64.7	65.0	67.2	58.6	79.8
2014	74.2	67.3	65.1	59.2	67.6	73.5	74.7	74.3	73.1	69.7	77.7	53.3	66.7	68.1	59.9	70.7	71.8	72.1	67.9	75.4	66.5	67.6	65.7	65.9	67.7	59.9	80.0
2015	74.3	67.2	67.1	60.6	67.9	74.8	75.4	76.0	72.9	70.0	78.0	54.9	68.9	69.9	60.5	72.5	73.3	70.9	69.0	76.4	67.8	69.1	66.0	67.7	69.1	62.0	80.5
2016	74.8	67.7	67.7	61.4	68.7	76.7	76.0	76.4	73.4	70.4	78.6	56.2	71.5	71.4	61.6	73.2	75.2	70.7	71.1	77.1	69.3	70.6	66.3	69.8	70.1	63.9	81.2
2017	75.4	68.5	71.3	63.6	70.8	78.5	76.6	78.3	74.2	71.1	79.2	57.8	73.3	73.0	62.3	74.8	76.0	71.5	73.0	78.0	70.9	73.4	68.8	71.1	73.4	65.5	81.8
2018	76.2	69.7	72.4	65.2	73.9	79.9	77.5	79.1	76.3	71.8	79.9	59.5	74.4	74.1	63.0	76.8	77.8	72.1	75.5	79.2	72.2	75.4	69.9	72.4	75.4	67.0	82.4
2019	76.8	70.5	75.0	66.7	75.7	80.3	78.3	79.7	77.2	72.1	80.6	61.2	75.3	75.1	63.5	77.4	78.2	72.8	76.8	80.1	73.0	76.1	70.9	73.4	76.4	68.0	82.1
2020	75.5	70.0	73.4	66.9	74.9	79.7	77.8	78.2	76.5	71.9	80.0	61.1	75.0	73.4	62.6	77.0	76.7	72.1	77.3	80.0	73.6	74.7	70.8	72.5	75.6	65.7	80.8

Note: The employment rate is defined as the number of persons in the labour force measured as a percentage of the total population from 20 to 64 years of age. The 1992–1999 average is calculated based on incomplete data, except for France.
Source: Eurostat (LFSI_EMP_A_H). Last update: 15 March 2022.

Table A1.L Employment rate of women in the EU Member States (%), average (1993-1999) and annual data, 2000-2020

Year	AT	BE	BG	HR	CY	CZ	DK	EE	FI	FR	DE	GR	HU	IE	IT	LV	LT	LU	MT	NL	PL	PT	RO	SK	SI	ES	SE
1990s	*61.2*	*50.9*	-	-	*56.6*	*63.1*	*69.7*	*65.2*	*64.7*	*57.5*	*58.0*	*42.3*	*51.5*	*49.1*	*39.2*	*60.0*	*64.4*	*48.2*	*33.4*	*57.4*	*56.9*	*60.4*	*63.5*	*58.7*	*63.7*	*36.8*	*72.5*
2000	62.3	56.0	50.7	51.7	59.1	61.9	72.9	62.8	68.2	60.5	60.8	45.5	53.9	59.2	42.2	59.3	63.9	53.1	33.2	64.1	54.2	65.1	63.0	57.2	63.6	44.5	74.6
2001	62.8	55.3	51.5	49.6	62.4	62.2	73.7	63.5	69.5	61.3	61.5	45.2	54.1	60.4	43.8	60.6	62.6	54.1	33.0	65.7	53.0	65.8	62.3	57.5	64.1	46.3	76.4
2002	64.1	55.8	52.3	50.7	64.6	62.3	73.1	64.3	70.4	62.6	61.8	46.8	54.3	61.0	44.9	62.3	63.9	55.0	34.4	66.8	51.4	65.7	56.8	57.2	63.8	48.3	76.6
2003	64.5	56.2	54.0	51.1	65.4	61.4	72.4	66.0	70.0	63.6	61.9	48.1	55.5	61.1	45.6	63.2	65.6	55.1	34.9	66.9	51.2	65.8	57.0	58.4	62.8	50.2	76.0
2004	62.7	57.2	56.0	52.0	64.6	61.1	73.0	67.3	69.7	63.6	62.0	49.0	55.3	62.2	48.5	63.5	65.3	56.2	34.3	66.9	51.2	65.9	57.4	56.7	65.4	52.1	75.3
2005	64.0	58.6	57.1	52.8	63.8	61.3	73.7	69.7	70.8	63.7	63.1	49.7	55.6	63.7	48.5	64.5	66.6	58.4	34.8	64.4	51.7	66.0	56.9	56.7	66.2	55.1	75.2
2006	65.2	58.8	60.4	53.6	65.9	61.8	74.8	72.5	71.5	63.9	65.0	51.3	55.6	64.6	49.6	68.4	68.0	59.4	35.7	65.7	53.1	66.3	58.5	57.5	66.5	57.1	75.8
2007	66.2	60.3	63.5	55.9	67.7	62.4	74.7	72.6	72.5	64.9	66.7	51.7	55.2	65.8	49.9	70.3	69.1	61.0	37.7	67.7	55.5	66.3	57.9	58.7	67.1	58.6	77.1
2008	67.6	61.3	65.4	57.0	68.2	62.5	74.3	72.9	73.1	65.5	67.8	52.6	54.8	65.4	50.6	71.9	68.7	60.1	39.4	69.4	57.3	67.1	57.3	60.3	68.5	58.9	77.2
2009	68.2	61.0	64.0	58.0	68.3	61.4	73.1	69.0	72.4	65.0	68.7	52.9	54.0	62.9	49.7	66.5	67.2	61.5	40.0	69.9	57.6	66.1	56.3	58.2	67.9	56.8	75.7
2010	68.8	61.6	60.8	56.4	68.8	60.9	72.0	65.9	71.5	64.9	69.7	51.8	54.6	61.1	49.5	64.5	65.0	62.0	41.6	69.8	57.3	65.6	56.5	57.4	66.5	56.3	75.0
2011	69.2	61.5	59.8	53.6	67.7	61.7	71.4	67.8	71.9	64.7	71.3	48.7	54.7	60.2	49.9	65.3	66.6	61.9	43.8	70.4	57.2	64.6	56.2	57.4	64.8	56.1	76.5
2012	69.6	61.7	60.2	52.6	64.8	62.5	71.1	69.4	72.5	65.1	71.6	45.2	56.2	60.2	50.5	66.4	67.9	64.1	48.0	71.0	57.5	63.0	56.7	57.3	64.6	54.6	76.8
2013	70.0	62.1	60.7	52.8	62.2	63.8	71.2	70.1	71.9	65.5	72.5	43.3	56.9	61.3	49.9	67.7	68.6	63.9	51.7	70.6	57.6	62.3	56.5	57.8	63.0	53.8	77.2
2014	70.1	62.9	62.0	54.2	63.9	64.7	71.0	70.6	72.1	66.1	73.1	44.3	60.2	62.3	50.3	68.5	70.6	65.5	54.3	69.7	59.4	64.2	57.3	58.6	63.6	54.8	77.6
2015	70.2	63.0	63.8	55.9	64.0	66.4	71.5	72.2	71.8	66.5	73.6	46.0	62.1	63.8	50.6	70.5	72.2	65.0	55.3	70.8	60.9	65.9	57.2	60.3	64.7	56.4	78.3
2016	70.9	63.0	64.0	56.6	64.1	68.6	72.5	72.4	71.7	66.8	74.5	46.8	64.6	65.4	51.6	71.8	74.3	65.1	58.0	71.6	62.2	67.4	57.4	62.7	66.7	58.1	79.2
2017	71.4	63.6	67.3	58.3	66.2	70.5	73.2	75.1	72.4	67.3	75.2	48.0	65.7	67.0	52.5	72.7	75.5	67.5	60.6	72.8	63.6	69.8	60.2	64.7	69.7	59.6	79.8
2018	71.7	65.5	68.3	60.1	68.9	72.2	73.9	75.5	74.5	68.1	75.8	49.1	66.8	68.1	53.1	74.8	76.7	68.0	64.1	74.2	65.0	72.1	60.6	65.5	71.7	61.0	80.2
2019	72.4	66.5	70.7	61.5	70.1	72.7	74.7	76.0	75.8	68.7	76.6	51.3	67.6	69.0	53.8	75.5	77.4	68.1	65.8	75.5	65.3	72.7	61.3	66.9	72.9	62.1	79.7
2020	71.5	65.9	68.9	61.3	69.1	71.9	74.3	75.2	75.0	68.5	76.9	51.8	67.0	67.4	52.7	75.2	75.8	68.5	67.8	75.5	65.7	71.9	61.0	66.1	72.4	60.0	78.3

Note: The employment rate of women is defined as the number of women in the labour force measured as a percentage of the total population of women from 20 to 64 years of age. The 1992–1999 average is calculated based on incomplete data, except for France.
Source: Eurostat (LFSI_EMP_A_H). Last update: 15 March 2022.

Table A1.M Proportion of the workforce in industry in the EU Member States (%), 1999-2020

Year	AT	BE	BG	HR	CY	CZ	DK	EE	FI	FR	DE	GR	HU	IE	IT	LV	LT	LU	MT	NL	PL	PT	RO	SK	SI	ES	SE
1999	32.5	27.8	-	-	25.2	41.7	27.1	33.1	29.1	27.1	35.5	28.1	36.0	30.4	35.2	29.7	32.4	22.8	-	22.2	-	39.6	46.8	38.8	42.6	33.2	25.7
2000	32.7	27.8	37.1	-	23.8	41.3	25.6	36.6	29.2	27.0	35.1	27.6	35.5	30.1	34.5	29.9	32.2	22.1	33.0	21.2	38.8	39.5	46.1	37.6	41.4	33.0	25.0
2001	31.9	26.9	36.5	-	24.2	41.8	25.6	34.8	28.2	26.7	34.3	27.6	36.1	30.4	34.0	28.9	32.3	22.2	31.7	21.3	38.8	38.5	45.8	37.1	42.4	33.6	24.2
2002	31.5	27.7	36.4	35.1	23.9	41.3	23.9	30.7	28.2	26.0	33.9	27.4	35.8	28.5	33.8	28.1	33.3	20.8	31.8	19.8	36.3	38.1	47.0	38.4	42.3	32.8	23.3
2003	31.4	26.3	36.3	36.4	23.7	41.0	23.8	31.8	27.6	24.5	32.8	26.6	34.8	28.3	33.9	29.7	32.8	20.0	30.5	19.9	35.7	37.3	45.7	38.1	40.2	32.2	22.9
2004	28.6	26.2	37.3	35.7	23.9	40.6	24.2	34.8	27.2	24.6	32.8	25.6	34.3	28.3	33.3	29.4	33.2	19.3	30.1	19.8	36.1	34.9	45.4	39.5	39.4	31.5	22.6
2005	29.8	26.0	38.0	34.5	23.7	40.3	24.1	34.6	26.6	24.1	31.3	25.5	33.8	28.2	33.0	28.3	33.2	18.0	30.3	20.7	35.9	34.3	44.4	39.0	40.2	30.5	22.1
2006	30.4	25.8	37.9	34.0	22.4	41.0	23.5	34.0	26.3	24.2	31.0	24.9	33.4	27.7	32.2	29.2	33.4	17.5	28.6	20.4	35.9	34.1	43.6	39.1	38.7	30.2	21.9
2007	29.6	25.4	38.7	34.8	22.1	41.2	23.8	35.6	26.4	23.7	31.3	25.3	33.7	25.9	32.1	30.1	33.2	17.5	26.2	19.6	36.5	33.9	44.1	39.3	38.1	29.9	21.7
2008	28.2	25.4	38.5	34.3	22.5	40.2	23.3	35.2	25.5	23.4	30.4	24.9	33.3	22.4	31.7	30.1	31.3	15.3	25.2	18.5	35.8	32.3	41.7	39.3	37.5	28.2	21.1
2009	26.9	23.9	37.0	32.6	21.2	38.1	20.5	31.0	24.2	22.7	29.9	23.6	32.2	19.2	30.9	24.9	28.2	12.8	24.8	17.3	34.6	30.8	39.5	36.8	35.5	24.5	19.9
2010	26.9	23.8	34.5	30.9	19.6	37.8	19.8	29.8	23.5	22.3	29.3	21.7	31.5	17.6	30.2	23.7	26.0	13.1	24.4	16.2	33.4	30.2	38.0	35.4	34.9	22.8	19.6
2011	27.9	23.5	33.0	31.6	20.3	38.6	20.0	32.2	23.1	22.3	29.3	19.5	31.8	17.5	29.9	23.4	25.8	13.3	23.9	15.6	33.8	29.1	37.6	36.0	33.7	21.7	19.5
2012	27.9	22.0	32.6	31.1	19.7	38.5	19.7	31.0	22.9	21.8	29.2	17.8	30.8	16.9	29.2	23.9	26.5	12.9	21.3	15.7	33.2	27.4	37.6	36.3	32.8	20.5	19.2
2013	27.8	21.9	31.5	30.1	16.9	37.7	19.5	30.1	22.9	21.3	28.7	16.7	30.9	17.0	28.7	24.5	26.8	12.2	21.2	15.2	32.9	25.9	37.3	34.6	33.3	19.7	18.7
2014	27.7	21.7	31.4	28.5	16.0	38.5	19.2	30.1	21.9	20.4	28.9	16.4	31.4	17.0	28.5	24.3	26.0	11.3	20.2	15.1	32.8	25.6	37.7	34.6	33.8	19.4	18.1
2015	27.5	21.5	30.8	28.6	16.0	38.8	19.3	30.7	21.7	20.2	28.6	16.4	31.2	17.7	28.3	24.0	26.2	11.8	19.3	15.4	33.1	25.8	35.5	35.1	33.8	19.8	17.9
2016	27.3	21.3	30.8	28.4	16.7	38.8	18.9	29.3	22.0	20.2	28.2	16.8	31.3	18.3	27.9	24.5	25.8	11.2	18.9	15.5	33.7	25.8	36.0	35.9	34.6	19.6	17.7
2017	26.6	20.9	30.7	27.4	17.1	38.9	18.6	29.8	22.1	20.4	28.2	17.2	32.3	18.4	27.7	23.6	25.8	9.2	18.7	15.2	33.8	25.9	36.1	36.2	35.2	20.1	17.7
2018	27.1	21.2	30.9	28.5	16.9	38.2	18.8	29.2	22.4	20.2	28.1	16.9	33.2	18.3	27.9	24.0	26.3	11.2	17.1	14.9	34.0	26.0	35.8	35.5	35.2	20.4	17.7
2019	26.9	20.9	30.4	28.8	18.7	38.0	18.4	28.4	21.7	20.3	27.9	17.0	33.0	18.3	27.9	23.9	25.9	10.3	17.9	14.6	34.1	25.8	35.5	35.2	35.5	20.6	17.9
2020	26.7	20.4	30.8	29.1	19.4	38.1	18.6	28.7	22.0	19.8	28.1	16.4	32.9	18.7	28.3	24.2	25.7	10.1	17.4	14.4	33.5	26.0	34.6	35.6	35.2	20.8	17.7

Note: 1999–2007 and 2008–2020: industries C–F. From 15 to 74 years of age.

Source: 1999–2007: Eurostat (LFSA_EEGANA); 2008–2020: Eurostat (LFSA_EEGAN2). NACE Rev. 2. Last update: 18 November 2021.

Table A1.N Proportion of the workforce in the private service sector in the EU Member States (%), 1999-2020

Year	AT	BE	BG	HR	CY	CZ	DK	EE	FI	FR	DE	GR	HU	IE	IT	LV	LT	LU	MT	NL	PL	PT	RO	SK	SI	ES	SE
1999	39.6	33.4	-	-	45.2	29.4	33.8	32.8	34.0	35.0	32.4	35.7	30.6	39.7	27.8	32.5	28.9	40.8	-	39.0	-	27.9	25.3	26.9	30.8	34.3	33.3
2000	39.3	33.3	29.8	-	44.5	28.7	35.1	33.3	34.3	35.1	33.0	36.4	31.5	40.5	28.9	34.1	28.9	40.4	36.0	40.0	29.6	28.5	25.8	27.7	32.1	35.6	34.1
2001	39.9	34.5	30.7	-	44.2	28.2	35.4	33.8	35.2	35.7	33.6	37.3	31.7	40.4	29.1	33.9	27.8	42.9	38.1	39.6	30.7	29.5	25.7	28.0	31.0	35.1	35.1
2002	39.7	34.7	31.6	34.4	43.5	28.7	34.9	37.6	35.4	36.0	33.6	37.0	31.9	40.2	29.9	31.9	29.0	41.5	36.7	38.1	31.5	29.9	24.6	28.0	31.2	35.5	35.4
2003	40.1	34.8	31.1	34.6	43.1	29.3	35.5	34.3	35.3	35.8	34.3	37.4	31.8	40.4	30.1	35.2	30.9	41.8	37.4	40.9	31.3	30.1	25.4	28.4	33.1	35.6	35.0
2004	42.0	33.5	31.0	35.0	42.6	29.7	35.1	32.5	35.4	35.9	34.0	36.6	31.9	40.0	32.3	35.1	31.2	40.2	37.1	39.9	31.5	31.6	27.2	27.8	32.2	36.4	35.3
2005	40.9	33.8	31.3	35.8	41.6	29.6	35.5	34.1	36.2	36.0	35.1	37.6	33.4	40.0	32.9	35.1	31.2	40.4	37.1	39.4	32.1	31.5	28.0	28.7	31.9	36.5	35.5
2006	40.1	34.2	32.1	37.1	41.4	29.7	36.1	34.7	36.4	36.4	35.4	37.1	34.1	40.2	33.4	37.3	33.0	41.4	38.1	39.6	32.2	32.0	29.5	29.7	32.3	37.3	35.9
2007	41.0	34.6	32.5	37.8	43.1	29.9	35.9	34.6	37.0	36.7	35.6	37.0	34.6	42.5	34.0	37.5	33.4	41.3	40.7	40.2	33.4	32.7	30.5	30.5	33.0	38.0	36.7
2008	47.0	40.0	36.7	42.4	54.1	34.4	41.9	39.7	43.1	43.3	42.2	44.0	39.1	49.9	40.8	42.8	39.7	52.4	45.2	43.6	36.3	40.4	34.7	33.9	38.4	47.6	42.5
2009	46.9	40.3	37.8	42.5	56.3	35.8	42.6	40.5	43.2	43.9	42.2	44.6	38.8	50.8	41.4	45.3	41.0	53.2	45.3	42.4	37.1	40.7	36.1	35.6	39.8	48.6	43.3
2010	46.5	40.6	40.1	43.2	57.3	35.4	42.3	40.9	43.5	43.9	42.3	45.1	38.6	50.7	42.1	45.6	42.7	51.7	44.8	41.1	37.6	40.9	37.2	35.6	39.5	48.9	43.6
2011	46.4	41.0	41.2	43.4	56.7	35.4	42.4	40.1	43.4	44.2	42.4	46.1	38.3	50.9	42.1	45.6	43.5	52.7	45.1	40.9	37.5	41.3	37.8	35.5	39.7	49.3	43.5
2012	46.3	41.7	41.6	43.5	58.6	35.0	42.5	40.5	43.5	44.1	42.3	46.4	39.2	51.7	42.9	45.4	43.4	53.2	46.7	41.8	38.0	41.7	38.3	35.5	40.0	50.1	43.6
2013	46.1	43.0	42.3	43.2	59.5	35.7	42.2	41.8	43.7	44.0	43.0	47.0	39.2	51.9	43.7	44.9	43.7	53.6	48.3	43.7	37.8	42.8	39.3	36.0	39.9	51.1	43.9
2014	45.7	42.4	42.0	42.7	58.4	35.0	42.6	41.8	44.3	43.7	42.6	48.2	38.3	52.1	43.8	46.1	44.2	54.6	49.4	44.2	38.1	43.4	39.9	35.5	38.9	51.3	44.1
2015	45.5	42.5	42.8	43.3	58.7	35.0	43.8	41.4	44.5	43.6	42.9	49.2	38.3	51.8	44.2	46.3	43.3	50.3	49.7	44.3	38.4	43.2	41.0	35.4	38.3	51.3	44.1
2016	45.9	42.1	43.5	45.2	58.2	34.7	44.2	43.9	44.3	43.7	43.2	48.7	38.0	51.9	44.6	45.7	43.8	50.1	51.8	44.3	38.2	43.6	41.1	35.4	38.0	51.6	44.3
2017	46.1	42.4	44.2	46.0	59.7	34.6	44.3	44.0	44.5	44.0	43.2	48.8	37.5	51.7	44.9	46.9	44.2	48.0	52.0	43.7	38.3	43.9	41.4	34.7	37.7	51.3	44.5
2018	46.0	42.9	43.7	44.9	60.1	35.4	45.0	44.4	44.5	44.3	43.1	49.1	36.9	51.8	45.1	47.2	44.3	51.8	53.2	44.0	38.2	42.9	42.1	35.3	38.2	50.9	44.5
2019	46.1	43.8	44.1	43.3	58.8	35.6	45.7	44.8	45.2	43.7	43.1	49.4	37.6	51.4	45.2	45.8	44.5	54.1	52.7	43.6	38.2	43.6	42.5	35.5	38.3	51.0	44.1
2020	45.8	42.6	43.0	42.6	57.2	34.7	44.8	43.7	44.5	43.7	41.7	49.2	37.6	50.1	44.2	45.4	45.0	53.5	52.8	42.4	38.3	42.9	43.1	35.0	37.8	49.7	44.0

Note: 1999–2007: Industries G–K; 2008–2020: industries G–N and R–U. From 15 to 74 years of age.
Source: 1999–2007: Eurostat (LFSA_EEGANA). NACE Rev. 1.1; 2008-2020: Eurostat (LFSA_EEGAN2). NACE Rev. 2. Last update: 18 November 2021.

Table A1.O Proportion of part-time employment in the EU Member States (%), average (1993-1999) and annual data, 2000-2020

Year	AT*	BE	BG	HR	CY*	CZ*	DK	EE*	FI*	FR*	DE	GR	HU*	IE*	IT	LV*	LT*	LU*	MT*	NL	PL*	PT	RO*	SK*	SI*	ES	SE*
1990s	14.9	14.6	-	-	5.9	5.1	21.5	7.5	11.4	16.9	16.6	4.7	3.2	15.8	6.6	11.6	9.0	9.4	6.2	37.3	8.6	7.4	13.4	2.1	6.2	7.3	23.0
2000	16.4	17.5	-	-	7.5	4.7	21.0	7.6	11.9	16.5	19.2	4.3	3.0	16.9	8.3	10.6	9.9	11.0	6.5	41.2	9.3	8.2	14.0	1.8	5.6	7.8	21.0
2001	17.3	18.4	2.8	-	7.3	4.3	19.6	7.8	11.8	16.1	19.9	3.8	3.1	16.9	8.3	9.8	9.7	11.4	7.0	41.9	9.2	8.0	14.1	2.2	5.4	7.9	19.7
2002	18.2	19.0	2.2	-	6.8	4.3	19.4	7.2	12.4	16.2	20.5	4.2	3.1	16.9	8.5	9.2	10.6	12.0	7.9	43.6	9.6	8.3	10.1	1.8	5.4	7.9	20.0
2003	18.4	20.3	1.9	6.9	7.6	4.5	20.7	7.4	12.6	16,7	21.3	4.1	3.7	17.2	8.4	9.6	9.2	13.4	8.8	44.6	9.4	8.8	10.2	2.2	5.5	8.1	22.0
2004	19.4	21.2	2.0	6.6	7.5	4.3	21.5	7.2	13.2	16.9	22.2	4.4	4.4	17.2	12.5	9.9	8.4	16.3	8.3	45.1	9.8	8.3	9.5	2.5	7.9	8.6	22.8
2005	21.0	21.7	1.8	7.6	7.6	4.4	21.5	6.8	13.2	17.1	23.4	4.8	3.9	17.6	12.7	7.6	6.9	17.4	9.0	45.1	9.8	8.2	9.2	2.4	7.8	12.0	23.5
2006	21.5	22.0	1.7	7.1	6.6	4.4	22.9	6.8	13.5	17.1	25.2	5.5	3.7	17.4	13.1	5.9	10.0	17.1	9.7	45.0	8.9	8.2	8.6	2.7	8.0	11.6	23.6
2007	22.0	21.9	1.4	6.1	6.4	4.4	23.0	7.1	13.4	17.2	25.4	5.4	3.9	17.9	13.4	5.6	8.6	17.8	10.6	45.7	8.5	8.9	8.6	2.5	8.1	11.4	23.5
2008	22.7	22.4	2.0	6.5	6.8	4.3	23.1	6.4	12.7	16.8	25.1	5.4	4.3	18.7	14.1	5.9	6.5	17.9	11.1	46.1	7.7	8.8	8.6	2.5	8.1	11.6	25.7
2009	23.9	23.2	2.1	6.5	7.5	4.8	24.6	9.4	13.3	17.2	25.3	5.9	5.2	21.3	14.1	8.2	7.9	17.6	11.0	47.0	7.7	8.5	8.5	3.4	9.5	12.4	26.0
2010	24.4	23.7	2.2	7.0	8.3	5.1	24.8	9.8	13.8	17.6	25.6	6.3	5.5	22.4	14.8	9.3	7.8	17.4	11.6	48.1	7.7	8.5	9.9	3.8	10.3	12.9	25.8
2011	24.5	24.7	2.2	7.2	9.0	4.7	24.3	9.3	14.1	17.6	25.9	6.7	6.4	23.3	15.2	8.8	8.3	18.0	12.6	48.3	7.3	10.3	9.5	4.0	9.5	13.5	25.2
2012	25.2	24.7	2.2	5.6	9.7	5.0	24.1	9.2	14.1	17.7	25.8	7.7	6.7	23.7	16.8	8.9	8.9	18.5	13.2	49.0	7.2	11.2	9.3	4.0	9.0	14.4	25.0
2013	26.0	24.3	2.5	5.4	11.9	5.8	24.0	8.9	14.0	18.1	26.6	8.4	6.4	23.7	17.6	7.5	8.4	18.7	14.0	49.8	7.1	11.1	9.0	4.5	9.3	15.7	24.7
2014	26.9	23.7	2.5	5.3	13.5	5.5	23.9	8.3	14.1	18.5	26.5	9.3	6.0	23.0	18.1	6.8	8.6	18.4	15.3	49.6	7.1	10.1	8.7	5.1	10.0	15.8	24.5
2015	27.3	24.3	2.2	6.0	13.0	5.3	23.8	9.5	14.1	18,3	26.8	9.4	5.7	22.2	18.3	7.2	7.6	18.4	14.3	50.0	6.8	9.8	8.8	5.8	10.1	15.6	24.3
2016	27.8	24.7	2.0	5.6	13.4	5.7	25.0	9.9	14.9	18.2	26.7	9.8	4.8	21.9	18.5	8.5	7.1	19.2	13.9	49.7	6.4	9.5	7.4	5.8	9.3	15.1	23.9
2017	27.9	24.5	2.2	4.8	12.2	6.2	24.7	9.5	15.0	18.2	26.9	9.7	4.3	20.1	18.5	7.7	7.6	19.5	13.7	49.8	6.6	8.9	6.8	5.8	10.3	14.9	23.3
2018	27.3	24.5	1.8	5.2	10.8	6.3	23.9	11.1	15.1	17.9	26.8	9.1	4.2	19.5	18.4	7.2	7.1	17.7	13.2	50.1	6.4	8.1	6.5	4.9	9.7	14.5	22.6

(*Continued*)

Table A1.O Continued

Year	AT*	BE	BG	HR	CY*	CZ*	DK	EE*	FI*	FR*	DE	GR	HU*	IE*	IT	LV*	LT*	LU*	MT*	NL	PL*	PT	RO*	SK*	SI*	ES	SE*
2019	27.2	24.9	1.9	4.8	10.2	6.3	24.2	11.3	15.5	17.4	27.2	9.1	4.4	19.7	18.7	8.3	6.4	16.9	12.2	50.2	6.1	8.1	6.1	4.5	8.4	14.5	22.5
2020	27.2	24.4	1.8	4.5	10.0	5.7	23.4	12.3	14.8	17.0	22.5	8.6	4.8	18.2	18.2	8.9	6.1	18.0	11.2	50.8	5.9	7.5	5.9	4.5	8.3	13.9	22.3

Note: Part-time employment is defined as 'employed persons not working full time. The distinction between full-time and part-time work is generally based on a spontaneous response by the respondent. The main exceptions are the Netherlands (…) where a 35 hours threshold is applied, Sweden where a threshold is applied to the self-employed (…)' (Eurostat, Metadata). Measured as a percentage of total employment from 15 to 64 years of age. * 1993–1999 average is calculated based on incomplete data.

Source: Eurostat (LFSI_PT_A_H). Last update 4 November 2021.

Table A1.P Proportion of employees on temporary contracts in the EU Member States (%), average (1993-1999) and annual data, 2000-2020

Year	AT	BE	BG	HR	CY	CZ	DK	EE	FI	FR	DE	GR	HU	IE	IT	LV	LT	LU	MT	NL	PL	PT	RO	SK	SI	ES	SE
1990s	6.7	5.6	-	-	7.9	5.3	9.7	2.0	14.5	12.6	10.4	6.2	5.2	8.4	5.6	6.6	4.8	2.7	3.5	10.0	3.6	9.5	1.9	3.7	9.5	25.5	10.8
2000	6.7	7.7	-	-	8.1	6.2	8.9	2.7	14.1	13.8	11.6	8.0	6.0	8.2	7.3	6.0	3.9	3.1	3.5	11.9	4.1	15.2	1.7	4.4	11.7	25.8	12.8
2001	6.9	7.5	4.8	-	8.0	6.1	8.3	2.5	14.3	13.3	11.3	8.1	6.4	7.5	7.1	6.6	4.8	3.5	3.7	12.6	8.5	15.6	1.8	4.4	10.9	25.9	13.4
2002	6.5	6.9	4.0	-	7.6	6.1	8.2	2.6	14.1	12.6	11.1	7.2	6.2	7.7	7.2	11.6	5.9	3.5	3.6	12.6	11.2	16.6	0.7	4.3	12.1	26.1	13.4
2003	6.1	7.2	5.0	8.9	9.6	7.0	8.4	2.4	14.3	11.9	11.2	6.9	6.5	7.9	7.3	9.7	5.8	2.9	3.1	12.7	14.3	15.8	1.3	4.3	11.9	26.2	13.4
2004	7.8	7.4	5.8	9.6	9.9	7.0	8.6	2.4	14.1	11.9	11.6	7.8	5.8	7.9	8.6	8.6	5.0	4.4	3.3	12.8	16.8	15.3	1.7	4.7	15.2	26.8	13.8
2005	7.9	7.5	5.1	9.6	11.0	6.7	9.0	2.5	14.4	12.4	12.6	7.8	6.1	8.1	9.1	7.7	4.5	4.9	3.7	13.3	19.3	15.3	1.6	4.2	14.9	27.5	14.1
2006	7.8	7.4	5.1	10.1	10.6	6.7	8.1	2.4	14.3	13.1	12.9	7.0	6.0	7.7	9.8	6.4	3.8	5.6	3.2	14.2	20.8	16.3	1.2	4.3	14.6	28.1	15.3
2007	7.7	7.4	4.4	10.7	10.8	6.6	8.2	2.0	14.0	13.4	13.0	7.2	6.4	7.8	9.9	3.7	3.2	6.3	4.4	15.3	21.8	17.8	1.1	4.3	15.8	26.2	15.5
2008	7.8	7.1	4.3	10.0	11.4	6.1	7.6	2.3	13.1	13.5	13.1	7.7	6.9	7.8	10.0	3.0	2.1	5.8	3.6	15.4	20.9	18.3	0.9	3.9	15.1	24.1	14.3
2009	7.9	7.0	4.0	9.7	11.3	6.3	7.8	2.2	12.6	12.9	13.0	8.1	7.4	7.9	9.5	3.8	2.0	6.6	4.2	15.5	20.6	17.7	0.7	3.6	13.9	21.1	13.5
2010	8.2	7.0	3.9	10.2	11.7	6.7	7.5	3.4	13.4	13.4	13.0	8.3	8.5	8.5	9.6	6.3	2.2	6.5	4.5	15.4	21.1	18.6	0.7	4.7	14.5	20.7	14.4
2011	8.4	7.7	3.6	10.8	11.9	6.5	7.8	4.1	13.6	13.6	13.0	7.6	8.0	9.1	10.1	5.9	2.4	6.5	5.7	15.4	20.9	18.2	1.0	5.5	15.2	21.1	14.9
2012	8.2	7.0	3.9	10.9	12.9	6.8	7.7	3.2	13.5	13.5	12.3	6.5	8.5	9.1	10.5	4.2	2.3	6.9	6.0	16.2	20.9	16.9	1.1	5.7	14.4	19.5	14.4
2013	8.1	6.9	4.9	12.1	14.7	7.5	7.8	3.2	13.4	13.7	12.0	6.5	9.7	9.0	10.1	3.8	2.4	6.4	6.6	17.0	21.1	17.6	1.0	5.8	13.8	19.1	14.7
2014	8.1	7.4	4.6	14.4	15.8	8.0	7.6	2.8	13.4	13.4	11.8	7.5	9.6	8.6	10.4	2.9	2.4	7.3	6.7	17.7	22.4	18.0	1.1	7.4	13.7	19.9	15.2
2015	8.0	7.7	3.9	17.2	15.9	8.3	7.7	3.1	13.1	14.1	11.8	7.9	10.1	8.1	10.8	3.3	1.8	9.1	6.5	16.7	22.2	18.7	1.0	8.9	15.1	20.9	15.1
2016	7.9	7.8	3.6	19.3	14.4	8.1	11.8	3.4	13.6	14.2	11.9	7.5	8.7	7.6	10.9	3.2	1.7	7.9	6.6	17.2	21.9	19.1	1.0	8.4	14.6	21.8	14.7
2017	8.1	9.0	3.9	18.2	13.5	8.0	11.3	2.8	13.9	14.8	11.7	7.6	7.9	7.8	12.1	2.6	1.5	8.1	5.1	18.1	20.9	19.0	0.9	8.0	15.2	22.4	14.7
2018	8.1	9.3	3.6	17.6	12.2	7.0	9.9	3.1	14.2	14.7	11.5	7.6	6.5	8.6	13.4	2.4	1.4	8.9	6.8	17.8	19.5	19.0	0.9	6.9	13.5	22.7	14.5
2019	7.7	9.4	3.9	16.0	12.0	6.5	9.9	2.8	13.6	14.3	11.0	8.7	5.9	8.4	13.4	2.8	1.3	8.3	7.8	16.9	17.4	17.9	1.1	6.6	11.5	22.3	14.3
2020	7.3	8.7	3.2	13.4	11.7	5.8	10.0	2.5	12.8	13.4	9.8	7.0	5.2	7.7	11.9	2.4	1.1	6.9	6.7	14.9	14.7	15.3	1.0	5.5	9.5	20.4	13.5

Note: Temporary contracts are defined as 'employees with a limited duration job/contract or employees whose main job will terminate either after a period fixed in advance, or after a period not known in advance, but nevertheless defined by objective criteria, such as the completion of an assignment or the period of absence of an employee temporarily replaced. The concept of fixed-term contract is only applicable to employees, not to self-employed' (Eurostat, Metadata). Measured as a percentage of total employment from 15 to 64 years of age.
Source: Eurostat (LFSI_PT_A_H). Last update: 4 November 2021.

Table A1.Q Real wage growth in the EU Member States (%), averages (1960s, 1970s, 1980s, 1990s) and annual data, 2000-2020

Year	AT	BE	BG*	HR*	CY*	CZ*	DK	EE*	FI	FR	DE	GR	HU*	IE	IT	LV*	LT*	LU	MT*	NL	PL*	PT	RO	SK*	SI*	ES	SE
1960s	*5.0*	*4.4*	-	-	-	-	*5.2*	-	*4.6*	*5.4*	*5.1*	*7.1*	-	*4.5*	*6.0*	-	-	*3.5*	-	*6.1*	-	*7.5*	-	-	-	*8.3*	*4.5*
1970s	*4.0*	*5.4*	-	-	-	-	*2.0*	-	*4.1*	*3.9*	*4.2*	*5.0*	-	*4.2*	*3.8*	-	-	*4.7*	-	*4.1*	-	*4.7*	-	-	-	*4.9*	*2.1*
1980s	*1.2*	*1.1*	-	-	-	-	*1.0*	-	*3.3*	*0.5*	*0.5*	*0.2*	-	*2.0*	*1.1*	-	-	*1.1*	-	*-0.2*	-	*2.0*	-	-	-	*0.9*	*0.3*
1990s	*1.6*	*2.2*	*-0.4*	*7.6*	*2.9*	*5.1*	*1.5*	*9.2*	*1.3*	*1.4*	*1.4*	*0.6*	*0.8*	*2.3*	*0.4*	*4.4*	*9.5*	*1.1*	*2.6*	*1.0*	*5.0*	*3.9*	*-1.2*	*5.2*	*2.4*	*1.2*	*1.3*
2000	0.2	-1.4	4.4	2.5	4.4	4.1	0.4	8.4	0.8	0.0	0.6	2.0	4.5	3.0	-0.8	6.2	1.4	2.5	4.9	2.8	0.4	2.2	23.6	4.6	2.5	-0.8	6.1
2001	-0.9	1.3	7.4	-2.6	2.0	4.7	1.5	3.3	0.9	0.4	-0.1	2.7	5.9	3.5	0.3	1.8	4.6	0.7	2.8	0.1	6.2	0.4	15.4	0.1	3.8	-0.6	2.3
2002	1.0	3.1	2.5	8.4	3.7	6.3	1.9	6.5	0.0	2.2	0.0	8.3	5.0	-0.1	0.4	-1.2	5.3	2.5	1.8	1.6	-0.5	0.0	-3.2	5.7	0.7	0.9	1.4
2003	0.2	0.4	3.4	5.4	5.6	7.7	2.4	9.5	1.1	1.1	0.2	5.0	5.8	2.5	1.1	6.6	10.7	-1.1	6.0	1.7	1.0	-0.4	9.8	1.2	2.4	-0.5	1.7
2004	0.3	-0.6	2.8	3.0	0.5	4.4	1.9	8.3	3.2	1.2	-0.7	1.0	6.1	3.4	1.1	7.9	12.3	1.3	-1.3	1.3	-2.2	1.0	4.1	0.7	4.6	0.3	3.7
2005	-0.4	-1.0	2.2	2.3	3.4	2.7	1.7	6.7	2.2	1.1	-0.7	5.4	4.5	3.7	0.9	15.1	11.5	0.9	-1.0	-0.1	-0.1	0.9	18.8	5.8	3.7	0.0	2.6
2006	1.0	0.7	4.0	-0.5	0.6	4.0	1.3	8.7	1.9	0.7	-0.2	-0.2	1.9	1.9	-0.2	11.1	15.3	1.6	2.4	-1.2	0.6	-1.7	7.3	3.0	3.0	0.6	2.3
2007	0.4	0.8	3.5	2.4	-1.8	3.2	1.9	16.5	1.2	0.2	-0.8	0.9	-0.3	2.6	0.2	20.7	7.8	1.9	2.0	1.1	3.5	0.1	0.4	6.0	1.9	0.8	4.1
2008	1.1	0.4	10.0	-0.9	-1.5	-0.2	0.9	2.1	0.8	0.0	0.2	-0.6	1.8	2.3	0.5	3.7	2.5	-0.4	0.1	1.8	4.1	-0.2	23.3	2.1	1.6	3.5	1.1
2009	1.3	2.0	7.4	-3.1	5.3	-1.5	1.6	-2.7	0.3	3.1	0.3	2.1	-7.3	5.8	2.7	-7.6	-13.1	2.5	0.9	4.4	0.7	4.4	-7.1	2.6	1.0	4.9	0.2
2010	-0.6	-0.4	7.9	0.7	-1.9	3.4	0.7	-1.1	0.6	1.8	1.0	-3.2	-2.1	-1.2	1.2	-4.2	-1.5	-0.1	0.4	-0.8	6.3	0.2	4.6	4.4	2.4	0.2	1.3
2011	-1.1	0.3	3.1	1.6	-0.6	1.1	-0.9	-3.0	0.1	0.7	1.2	-6.2	0.8	-0.7	-1.7	-3.4	1.7	0.8	1.0	0.3	0.2	-3.5	-6.6	-1.8	-0.3	-2.0	1.7
2012	0.3	1.0	4.7	-3.1	-0.8	-0.2	-0.5	1.8	-0.1	0.9	1.2	-4.8	-2.6	0.4	-2.3	4.1	0.9	-0.8	0.6	1.0	0.1	-4.8	-1.0	-1.0	-2.6	-2.4	2.5
2013	0.1	1.4	10.3	-2.8	-5.1	-0.7	0.7	2.6	-1.0	0.9	0.5	-6.7	-1.5	-2.5	0.1	5.2	4.6	1.6	0.7	-0.2	1.2	2.6	2.0	1.2	-1.6	0.3	1.4
2014	-0.2	0.2	4.2	-4.8	-2.9	1.9	0.9	5.7	-0.4	1.2	2.0	-2.1	-0.5	0.2	-0.2	6.8	4.6	1.3	0.3	0.8	2.4	-1.9	4.9	2.1	1.7	0.1	1.2
2015	0.5	-0.7	3.2	1.0	1.1	3.1	1.3	4.1	1.0	0.7	2.2	0.7	1.4	1.3	0.8	8.2	6.8	0.7	4.5	-0.4	3.2	-0.6	0.6	3.8	2.1	0.7	1.6
2016	0.9	-0.9	4.0	1.5	1.0	3.6	1.2	5.1	0.7	1.1	1.6	-2.8	1.4	2.1	0.0	6.0	5.4	-0.1	4.6	0.7	5.2	0.2	14.7	2.6	3.5	-0.8	1.7
2017	-0.2	0.0	5.7	-0.7	0.5	4.7	0.6	2.6	-2.1	1.1	1.1	1.1	3.6	2.0	-0.5	4.2	5.8	0.9	1.3	-0.4	3.7	0.7	11.8	3.6	1.4	-0.7	0.3

Year	AT	BE	BG*	HR*	CY*	CZ*	DK	EE*	FI	FR	DE	GR	HU*	IE	IT	LV*	LT*	LU	MT*	NL	PL*	PT	RO	SK*	SI*	ES	SE
2018	0.9	-0.2	7.1	2.5	0.3	5.4	1.0	4.7	0.0	0.1	1.5	-3.9	3.0	0.6	1.1	4.9	5.1	0.9	2.8	-0.3	6.3	2.3	8.8	3.6	1.9	-0.3	1.3
2019	1.1	0.6	4.8	-0.8	3.2	4.2	1.2	5.8	0.2	-1.1	2.0	0.6	2.3	1.2	1.2	4.7	8.3	0.3	1.6	0.3	4.8	4.0	5.2	4.0	3.6	1.7	0.9
2020	0.3	-2.0	7.8	1.9	-2.2	0.4	1.9	6.1	0.3	-3.7	-0.3	0.3	-1.1	2.0	3.1	4.7	6.4	-0.3	-1.4	3.1	0.5	1.2	4.5	1.4	4.0	1.3	1.4

Note: Real compensation per employee, total economy. Deflator private consumption. * 1990s average is calculated based on incomplete data.
Source: AMECO (RWCDC). Last update: 18 November 2021.

Table A1.R Productivity growth in the EU Member States (%), averages (1960s, 1970s, 1980s, 1990s) and annual data, 2000-2020

Year	AT	BE	BG*	HR*	CY	CZ	DK	EE	FI	FR	DE*	GR	HU*	IE	IT	LV	LT	LU	MT*	NL	PL	PT	RO	SK*	SI	ES	SE
1960s	*3.9*	*4.2*	-	-	-	-	*4.4*	-	*4.1*	*4.5*	-	*7.9*	-	*4.0*	*5.7*	-	-	*3.0*	-	*3.7*	-	*5.7*	-	-	-	*6.6*	*3.7*
1970s	*4.0*	*3.4*	-	-	-	-	*1.9*	-	*3.9*	*3.4*	-	*4.7*	-	*3.2*	*3.3*	-	-	*2.5*	-	*2.5*	-	*4.5*	-	-	-	*2.7*	*2.1*
1980s	*1.9*	*2.0*	-	-	-	-	*1.9*	-	*3.2*	*1.8*	-	*0.2*	-	*2.7*	*2.3*	-	-	*4.2*	-	*1.4*	-	*3.0*	-	-	-	*2.3*	*2.1*
1990s	*2.2*	*1.9*	*-1.6*	*4.0*	*2.7*	*0.3*	*2.1*	*5.7*	*1.5*	*1.6*	*1.2*	*1.4*	*1.7*	*6.2*	*1.4*	*-2.6*	*-2.8*	*3.3*	*3.9*	*2.7*	*3.6*	*3.2*	*-1.0*	*4.8*	*1.7*	*2.3*	*1.3*
2000	3.2	3.5	6.5	8.1	5.2	4.1	3.4	7.2	5.6	3.4	3.0	3.7	4.8	7.8	3.9	7.0	5.5	5.6	5.4	3.7	4.5	3.0	2.2	1.3	2.8	4.9	4.6
2001	0.9	0.6	6.1	2.9	2.5	3.5	0.5	6.7	2.6	1.3	1.6	3.6	4.3	3.7	1.7	6.6	6.9	1.9	-1.9	1.4	1.4	1.2	5.5	3.8	3.4	3.2	1.2
2002	1.1	1.2	7.1	5.7	2.9	1.8	0.1	8.4	1.4	0.3	-0.3	3.4	5.0	4.1	0.0	9.2	8.1	2.1	2.0	-0.3	2.1	0.6	9.4	4.8	3.3	1.3	1.9
2003	0.6	0.6	5.3	5.4	1.4	3.6	0.1	7.8	1.7	0.0	-0.6	5.6	4.4	1.2	-0.3	8.5	11.9	1.3	3.2	-0.3	3.5	-1.2	2.9	5.7	2.6	0.9	1.9
2004	2.2	3.0	7.6	4.2	3.7	4.8	2.4	7.2	3.6	2.3	1.3	4.7	5.2	5.1	0.7	10.4	6.7	2.8	-0.6	1.6	5.1	1.2	11.1	4.3	4.4	1.8	4.0
2005	1.4	1.8	7.1	4.3	3.1	6.3	2.0	10.1	2.4	0.6	0.9	0.5	4.5	3.2	0.3	11.8	10.0	0.9	2.5	1.6	3.5	0.6	5.0	7.3	3.6	1.7	2.4
2006	3.0	2.0	7.7	4.9	3.0	6.4	3.6	10.7	3.7	1.9	4.0	5.5	4.1	2.2	1.3	12.6	9.1	4.4	2.5	3.4	6.2	1.7	8.7	7.8	5.8	2.1	4.1
2007	3.4	2.8	7.1	4.9	2.9	5.0	0.5	8.3	5.0	1.9	3.0	2.8	0.4	2.2	1.0	11.2	12.5	6.4	4.2	3.6	7.3	2.3	8.8	10.8	6.0	1.7	2.7
2008	1.3	-0.3	6.7	2.0	0.8	1.6	-1.1	-4.5	0.2	-0.3	1.4	-0.5	1.2	-6.5	-2.0	-2.5	3.7	-2.1	3.4	1.7	4.1	0.0	11.4	5.7	3.6	-0.8	-1.2
2009	-4.0	-2.8	-2.7	-7.2	-4.5	-5.2	-5.4	-14.7	-8.6	-3.4	-5.4	-4.6	-6.5	-6.0	-5.7	-12.9	-14.3	-4.9	-2.2	-4.1	1.8	-3.3	-4.8	-5.4	-8.5	-4.5	-5.2
2010	1.6	2.0	1.8	-1.0	-0.4	2.2	1.4	2.3	2.9	1.3	4.5	-5.8	1.3	1.2	1.1	-2.0	4.2	1.8	5.1	0.8	3.6	1.7	-3.5	5.7	1.1	0.0	5.0
2011	2.6	0.3	5.4	0.1	-2.1	2.0	0.9	7.6	2.0	1.9	3.7	-9.8	2.2	0.7	0.3	4.0	9.0	-1.3	0.0	1.0	4.7	-1.1	2.6	3.1	0.5	-1.3	2.4
2012	0.2	0.0	0.9	-1.9	-5.2	-0.9	-0.1	3.5	-2.0	-0.3	0.3	-6.9	-0.7	-0.5	-3.1	8.7	4.6	-0.6	3.2	-1.2	1.4	-4.0	2.6	1.5	-2.7	-3.1	-1.3
2013	-0.7	0.0	0.0	-0.1	-6.4	-0.1	0.5	2.1	-1.3	0.0	0.3	-1.8	2.1	0.7	-2.2	2.7	5.3	0.5	4.2	-0.5	1.2	0.0	4.0	0.7	-1.1	-0.9	0.3
2014	0.0	1.1	1.7	0.1	-0.5	2.1	1.1	3.4	-0.8	0.6	1.7	1.3	4.5	7.9	0.0	3.5	4.2	0.2	5.5	1.0	3.5	1.2	3.9	2.2	2.2	1.4	1.6
2015	0.0	1.6	4.2	3.3	3.9	5.2	1.6	1.9	0.3	0.6	0.5	0.6	3.9	24.2	1.1	4.2	3.2	0.3	6.7	1.5	4.2	2.4	3.5	5.0	2.2	4.0	3.4
2016	0.8	0.5	4.0	4.4	6.2	2.3	2.4	3.2	2.3	0.9	1.6	0.0	2.5	0.9	1.5	3.2	3.1	2.3	1.8	1.7	3.2	2.3	5.3	2.0	3.2	3.0	0.8
2017	1.5	1.3	3.1	4.4	4.5	4.9	2.2	5.6	3.0	1.8	2.1	1.2	4.5	7.6	1.8	4.7	6.0	-0.8	7.9	2.4	5.0	3.4	7.9	2.7	4.6	2.9	1.2
2018	2.0	1.3	3.7	3.9	4.7	2.8	1.5	4.1	1.0	1.5	0.8	1.8	5.5	7.7	1.1	4.5	5.0	0.0	2.4	1.7	5.3	3.3	5.1	3.9	4.4	1.6	0.8
2019	1.2	1.6	4.3	4.0	3.7	2.6	1.7	3.4	1.2	1.5	1.0	1.8	4.6	3.5	0.7	3.6	4.7	1.1	1.6	1.4	4.9	2.6	4.7	2.5	2.4	1.2	1.0
2020	-7.1	-5.9	-3.4	-7.7	-6.3	-6.1	-2.3	-3.3	-2.9	-8.3	-4.9	-8.8	-4.5	4.7	-8.3	-3.4	0.0	-3.3	-10.2	-4.3	-2.5	-8.7	-3.3	-4.9	-5.1	-11.1	-3.5

Note: Gross domestic product at constant prices per head of population. * Decade average is calculated based on incomplete data.
Source: AMECO (RVGDP). Last update: 17 November 2021.

Table A1.S Wage share in the EU Member States (%), averages (1960s, 1970s, 1980s, 1990s) and annual data, 2000-2020

Year	AT	BE	BG*	HR*	CY*	CZ*	DK	EE	FI	FR	DE*	GR	HU*	IE	IT	LV*	LT*	LU	MT	NL	PL*	PT	RO	SK*	SI*	ES	SE
1960s	*63.7*	*55.8*	-	-	-	-	*59.5*	-	*66.6*	*63.1*	-	*65.3*	-	*64.9*	*64.5*	-	-	*51.2*	-	*62.5*	-	*67.2*	-	-	-	*63.5*	*66.6*
1970s	*63.1*	*61.7*	-	-	-	-	*61.1*	-	*64.4*	*64.1*	-	*53.2*	-	*64.3*	*64.3*	-	-	*55.5*	-	*68.0*	-	*76.9*	-	-	-	*65.8*	*64.4*
1980s	*61.2*	*63.4*	-	-	-	-	*58.8*	-	*62.4*	*62.9*	-	*55.3*	-	*61.6*	*61.4*	-	-	*56.4*	-	*64.9*	-	*60.8*	-	-	-	*62.2*	*62.4*
1990s	*58.7*	*61.9*	*44.0*	*62.7*	*53.4*	*45.2*	*55.9*	*52.4*	*58.3*	*57.3*	*59.0*	*49.6*	*49.6*	*54.5*	*55.2*	*49.6*	*47.6*	*52.2*	*51.3*	*61.5*	*58.9*	*59.2*	*66.2*	*44.6*	*63.5*	*60.5*	*58.3*
2000	56.0	60.5	49.4	67.2	51.7	45.9	53.9	49.4	52.9	55.9	59.0	49.5	49.7	47.4	50.9	48.7	48.7	49.8	49.1	59.3	56.7	60.2	72.2	44.7	61.8	58.8	52.9
2001	55.5	61.6	50.4	63.3	50.9	45.9	54.8	48.3	52.5	56.0	58.3	48.7	50.0	46.9	51.0	47.4	47.2	52.3	51.0	58.4	58.4	60.4	76.4	43.8	61.9	57.7	52.5
2002	55.0	62.2	48.7	64.4	52.3	47.7	55.3	47.5	52.6	56.5	58.0	51.4	49.2	44.9	51.3	44.6	47.9	53.4	50.3	58.9	55.9	59.8	61.6	43.9	61.1	57.2	52.6
2003	55.1	61.6	48.6	64.6	54.1	48.6	55.7	48.3	52.7	56.6	58.1	51.2	50.4	45.6	51.9	44.2	48.7	52.6	50.5	59.1	53.8	59.6	62.3	43.1	60.4	56.2	52.7
2004	54.1	60.0	47.0	63.4	53.3	48.1	54.5	48.3	52.4	56.1	57.1	50.6	50.6	46.2	51.8	43.9	49.3	51.9	50.4	58.3	50.5	58.7	55.1	41.6	60.5	55.9	52.4
2005	53.3	59.3	46.3	62.8	55.0	47.7	54.3	47.1	53.0	56.2	56.6	53.9	50.9	46.8	52.0	45.4	49.2	51.7	49.3	57.0	49.6	58.7	59.4	42.1	60.6	55.3	53.0
2006	53.0	59.2	44.6	61.2	54.1	47.7	54.2	47.4	53.2	56.0	55.3	51.7	50.1	47.1	52.1	46.7	51.7	49.5	50.2	55.7	48.4	57.3	57.1	41.6	60.0	55.1	53.2
2007	52.4	59.0	43.8	60.7	52.6	47.2	55.6	49.3	51.8	55.4	54.2	51.3	50.0	48.7	51.9	49.6	49.9	48.9	49.5	55.6	48.2	56.1	50.0	41.2	59.0	55.2	51.8
2008	53.4	60.8	45.6	60.2	51.8	48.1	56.4	53.6	53.2	55.7	55.2	51.8	50.0	52.9	52.7	53.5	49.8	49.4	49.2	56.3	50.0	56.6	53.1	41.8	60.0	57.2	53.2
2009	55.0	62.3	48.2	62.6	55.7	48.0	58.8	54.5	56.6	57.5	57.7	54.1	48.7	53.3	54.1	52.7	50.6	51.9	50.1	59.2	48.6	57.6	50.1	44.9	62.9	57.8	56.6
2010	54.6	60.7	49.8	61.7	54.3	48.8	56.4	50.9	55.4	57.5	56.7	53.8	47.2	50.4	53.8	48.3	45.9	49.6	48.1	57.9	48.9	56.6	54.1	43.7	63.8	57.2	55.4
2011	53.9	61.3	48.0	60.5	54.6	49.2	56.0	49.0	55.4	57.5	56.2	54.9	47.4	48.2	53.3	46.0	43.8	50.7	50.5	58.4	47.8	55.5	48.5	43.4	62.5	56.2	55.4
2012	54.5	61.8	49.5	58.9	54.6	50.1	55.2	49.1	56.5	58.1	57.3	54.7	48.5	47.6	53.2	45.2	43.6	50.1	50.4	59.2	47.8	54.0	47.9	43.4	62.7	54.9	56.5
2013	55.0	62.0	53.8	56.4	52.7	49.5	55.1	49.8	55.9	58.4	57.5	52.2	47.0	47.3	53.1	47.1	44.4	49.9	49.8	58.9	47.8	53.6	46.3	43.6	61.9	54.1	55.9
2014	55.0	61.3	55.8	55.0	51.4	48.8	54.9	50.4	55.5	58.5	57.3	52.4	45.8	45.1	52.7	48.5	45.4	49.4	48.3	58.8	47.9	52.6	47.0	44.0	61.0	54.2	55.5
2015	54.5	59.9	55.5	54.7	50.2	48.0	55.1	52.2	55.1	58.0	57.5	50.8	44.8	35.4	52.7	50.8	47.7	49.3	46.6	57.6	47.2	51.5	44.5	44.4	60.7	53.8	55.1
2016	54.5	59.1	55.5	53.2	49.1	48.8	54.8	52.8	54.3	58.1	57.5	51.2	46.0	36.6	52.3	52.6	49.8	49.2	48.8	57.9	48.1	51.0	47.3	45.8	61.3	53.2	54.3
2017	54.5	59.1	57.9	52.2	49.2	49.9	54.4	52.9	52.1	58.2	57.4	51.0	46.2	35.3	51.9	53.2	49.9	50.8	47.6	57.5	48.3	51.3	49.5	47.2	61.1	52.7	52.1
2018	54.6	59.1	59.3	53.0	49.2	51.6	54.6	53.6	52.4	58.1	58.1	50.5	45.5	34.0	52.4	54.0	50.7	52.1	48.1	57.4	49.3	52.1	50.5	48.2	61.5	52.8	52.4
2019	55.1	58.9	58.1	52.0	50.1	51.8	54.8	54.7	52.6	57.0	58.7	50.3	45.0	33.0	52.6	55.4	52.5	52.9	48.7	57.3	48.9	52.7	50.4	49.4	62.6	53.7	52.6
2020	57.7	60.7	61.0	57.2	51.6	53.5	55.4	57.9	52.7	58.1	60.3	54.6	45.0	31.9	53.1	59.2	54.7	52.9	53.7	60.7	49.9	56.5	53.1	51.3	66.5	56.4	52.7

Note: Total economy, percentage of GDP at current market prices. * 1990s average is calculated based on incomplete data.
Source: AMECO. Last update: 12 November 2021.

Table A1.T Gini coefficients in the EU Member States (%), average (1995-1999) and annual data, 2000-2020

Year	AT	BE	BG	HR	CY*	CZ	DK*	EE	FI*	FR	DE	GR	HU	IE	IT	LV	LT	LU	MT*	NL	PL	PT	RO	SK	SI	ES	SE*
1990s	25.6	28.0	-	-	29.0	-	20.3	-	22.5	28.8	26.2	34.6	-	33.0	31.4	-	-	27.0	-	27.0	-	36.4	-	-	-	34.0	21.5
2000	24.0	30.0	25.0	-	-	-	-	36.0	24.0	28.0	25.0	33.0	26.0	30.0	29.0	34.0	31.0	30.0	29.0	29.0	30.0	36.0	29.0	-	22.0	32.0	-
2001	24.0	28.0	26.0	-	-	25.0	22.0	35.0	27.0	27.0	25.0	33.0	25.0	29.0	29.0	-	31.0	29.0	29.0	27.0	30.0	37.0	30.0	-	22.0	33.0	24.0
2002	-	-	26.0	-	-	-	-	35.0	26.0	27.0	-	-	24.0	-	-	-	-	-	-	27.0	-	-	30.0	-	22.0	31.0	23.0
2003	27.4	28.3	-	-	-	-	24.8	-	-	-	-	34.7	-	30.6	-	-	-	30.6	-	-	-	-	-	-	-	-	-
2004	25.8	26.1	-	-	-	-	23.9	37.4	25.5	28.2	-	33.0	-	31.5	32.9	-	-	31.5	32.9	-	-	37.8	-	-	-	31.0	23.0
2005	26.3	28.0	-	-	28.7	26.0	23.9	34.1	26.0	27.7	26.1	33.2	27.6	31.9	32.7	36.2	36.3	31.9	32.7	26.9	35.6	38.1	-	26.2	23.8	32.2	23.4
2006	25.3	27.8	31.2	-	28.8	25.3	23.7	33.1	25.9	27.3	26.8	34.3	33.3	31.9	32.1	38.9	35.0	31.9	32.1	26.4	33.3	37.7	-	28.1	23.7	31.9	24.0
2007	26.2	26.3	35.3	-	29.8	25.3	25.2	33.4	26.2	26.6	30.4	34.3	25.6	31.3	32.0	35.4	33.8	31.3	32.0	27.6	32.2	36.8	38.3	24.5	23.2	31.9	23.4
2008	27.7	27.5	35.9	-	29.0	24.7	25.1	30.9	26.3	29.8	30.2	33.4	25.2	29.9	31.2	37.5	34.5	29.9	31.2	27.6	32.0	35.8	35.9	23.7	23.4	32.4	25.1
2009	27.5	26.4	33.4	-	29.5	25.1	26.9	31.4	25.9	29.9	29.1	33.1	24.7	28.8	31.8	37.5	35.9	28.8	31.8	27.2	31.4	35.4	34.5	24.8	22.7	32.9	26.3
2010	28.3	26.6	33.2	31.6	30.1	24.9	26.9	31.3	25.4	29.8	29.3	32.9	24.1	30.7	31.7	35.9	37.0	30.7	31.7	25.5	31.1	33.7	33.5	25.9	23.8	33.5	25.5
2011	27.4	26.3	35.0	31.2	29.2	25.2	26.6	31.9	25.8	30.8	29.0	33.5	26.9	29.8	32.5	35.1	33.0	29.8	32.5	25.8	31.1	34.2	33.5	25.7	23.8	34.0	26.0
2012	27.6	26.5	33.6	30.9	31.0	24.9	26.5	32.5	25.9	30.5	28.3	34.3	27.2	30.4	32.4	35.7	32.0	30.4	32.4	25.4	30.9	34.5	34.0	25.3	23.7	34.2	26.0
2013	27.0	25.9	35.4	30.9	32.4	24.6	26.8	32.9	25.4	30.1	29.7	34.4	28.3	30.7	32.8	35.2	34.6	30.7	32.8	25.1	30.7	34.2	34.6	24.2	24.4	33.7	26.0
2014	27.6	25.9	35.4	30.2	34.8	25.1	27.7	35.6	25.6	29.2	30.7	34.5	28.6	31.0	32.4	35.5	35.0	31.0	32.4	26.2	30.8	34.5	35.0	26.1	25.0	34.7	26.9
2015	27.2	26.2	37.0	30.4	33.6	25.0	27.4	34.8	25.2	29.2	30.1	34.2	28.2	29.7	32.4	35.4	37.9	29.7	32.4	26.7	30.6	34.0	37.4	23.7	24.5	34.6	26.7
2016	27.2	26.3	37.7	29.8	32.1	25.1	27.7	32.7	25.4	29.3	29.5	34.3	28.2	29.6	33.1	34.5	37.0	29.6	33.1	26.9	29.8	33.9	34.7	24.3	24.4	34.5	27.6
2017	27.9	26.1	40.2	29.9	30.8	24.5	27.6	31.6	25.3	28.8	29.1	33.4	28.1	30.6	32.7	34.5	37.6	30.6	32.7	27.1	29.2	33.5	33.1	23.2	23.7	34.1	28.0
2018	26.8	25.7	39.6	29.7	29.1	24.0	27.8	30.6	25.9	28.5	31.1	32.3	28.7	28.9	33.4	35.6	36.9	28.9	33.4	27.4	27.8	32.1	35.1	20.9	23.4	33.2	27.0
2019	27.5	25.1	40.8	29.2	31.1	24.0	27.5	30.5	26.2	29.2	29.7	31.0	28.0	28.3	32.8	35.2	35.4	28.3	32.8	26.8	28.5	31.9	34.8	22.8	23.9	33.0	27.6
2020	27.0	25.4	40.0	28.3	29.3	-	27.3	30.5	26.5	29.3	34.4	31.1	28.3	-	-	-	35.1	-	-	27.5	27.2	31.2	33.8	20.9	23.5	32.1	26.9

Note: Gini coefficient of equivalized disposable income – EU-SILC survey. * 1995–1999 average is calculated based on incomplete data.
Source: Eurostat (ILC_DI12). Last update: 4 November 2021.

“Work & Society”

The series “Work & Society” analyses the development of employment and social policies, as well as the strategies of the different social actors, both at national and European levels. It puts forward a multi-disciplinary approach – political, sociological, economic, legal and historical – in a bid for dialogue and complementarity.

The series is not confined to the social field *stricto sensu*, but also aims to illustrate the indirect social impacts of economic and monetary policies. It endeavours to clarify social developments, from a comparative and a historical perspective, thus portraying the process of convergence and divergence in the diverse national societal contexts. The manner in which European integration impacts on employment and social policies constitutes the backbone of the analyses.

Series Editor: Philippe Pochet, General Director ETUI-REHS (Brussels) and Digest Editor of the Journal of European Social Policy

Published books

No 86 – *Trade unions in the European Union. Picking up the pieces of the neoliberal challenge.* Jeremy Waddington, Torsten Müller and Kurt Vandaele (eds.), 2023, ISBN 978-2-87574-634-4

No 85 – *Les défis de la diversité culturelle dans le monde du travail au XXIe siècle. Politiques, pratiques et représentations en Europe et dans les Amériques,* Ariane Le Moing (Volume editor)Saïd Ouaked (Volume editor)Christèle Le Bihan (Volume editor), 2020, ISBN 978-2-8076-1082-8

No.84 – *Austerity and the Implementation of the Europe 2020 Strategy. Re-shaping the European Productive and Social Model: a Reflexion from the South,* Javier Ramos Díaz and Esther Del Campo (eds.), 2017, ISBN 978-2-8076-0436-0

No.83 – *The New Pension Mix in Europe Recent Reforms, their Distributional Effects and Political Dynamics,* David Natali (ed.), 2017, ISBN 978-2-8076-0265-6

N° 82 – *Accompagner vers l'emploi. Quand les dispositifs publics se mettent en action*, Christèle Meilland et François Sarfati (dir.), 2015, ISBN 978-2-87574-352-7

N° 81 – *Outiller les parcours professionnels. Quand les dispositifs publics se mettent en action*, Sophie Bernard, Dominique Méda, Michèle Tallard (dir.), 2016, ISBN 978-2-87574-351-0

N° 80 – *Politiques de la diversité. Sociologie des discriminations et des politiques antidiscriminatoires au travail*, Milena Doytcheva, 2015, ISBN 978-2-87574-290-2

No.79 – *Activation Policies for the Unemployed, the Right to Work and the Duty to Work*, Elise Dermine, Daniel Dumont (eds.), 2014, ISBN 978-2-87574-232-2

No.78 – *The Transnationalisation of Collective Bargaining. Approaches of European Trade Unions*, Vera Glassner, 2014, ISBN 978-2-87574-167-7

N° 77 – *L'Europe entre marché et égalité. La politique européenne d'égalité entre les femmes et les hommes, de l'émergence au démantèlement*, Sophie Jacquot, 2014, ISBN 978-2-87574-159-2

N° 76 – *Représenter le patronat européen. Formes d'organisation patronale et modes d'action européenne*, Hélène Michel (dir.), 2013, ISBN 978-2-87574-057-1

No.75 – *The Wage under Attack. Employment Policies in Europe*, Bernadette Clasquin & Bernard Friot (eds.), 2013, ISBN 978-2-87574-029-8

No.74 – *Quality of Employment in Europe. Legal and Normative Perspectives*, Silvia Borelli & Pascale Vielle (eds.), 2012, ISBN 978-90-5201-888-1

No.73 – *Renewing Democratic Deliberation in Europe. The Challenge of Social and Civil Dialogue*, Jean De Munck, Claude Didry, Isabelle Ferreras & Annette Jobert (eds.), 2012, ISBN 978-90-5201-875-1

No.72 – *Democracy and Capabilities for Voice. Welfare, Work and Public Deliberation in Europe*, Ota De Leonardis & Serafino Negrelli (eds.), 2012, ISBN 978-90-5201-867-6

N° 71 – *Trajectoires des modèles nationaux. État, démocratie et travail en France et en Allemagne*, Michèle Dupré, Olivier Giraud et Michel Lallement (dir.), 2012, ISBN 978-90-5201-863-8

No.70 – *Precarious Employment in Perspective. Old and New Challenges to Working Conditions in Sweden*, Annette Thörnquist & Åsa-Karin Engstrand (eds.), 2011, ISBN 978-90-5201-730-3

No.69 – *Europe 2020: Towards a More Social EU?*, Eric Marlier and David Natali (eds.), with Rudi Van Dam, 2010, ISBN 978-90-5201-688-7

No.68 – *Generations at Work and Social Cohesion in Europe*, Patricia Vendramin (ed.), 2009, ISBN 978-90-5201-647-4

No.67 – *Quality of Work in the European Union. Concept, Data and Debates from a Transnational Perspective*, Ana M. Guillén and Svenn-Åge Dahl (eds.), 2009, ISBN 978-90-5201-577-4

No.66 – *Emerging Systems of Work and Welfare*, Pertti Koistinen, Lilja Mósesdóttir & Amparo Serrano Pascual (eds.), 2009, ISBN 978-90-5201-549-1

No.65 – *Building Anticipation of Restructuring in Europe*, Marie-Ange Moreau (ed.), in collaboration with Serafino Negrelli & Philippe Pochet, 2009, ISBN 978-90-5201-486-9

No.64 – *Pensions in Europe, European Pensions. The Evolution of Pension Policy at National and Supranational Level*, David Natali, 2008, ISBN 978-90-5201-460-9

No.63 – *Building Anticipation of Restructuring in Europe*, Marie-Ange Moreau (ed.), 2008, ISBN 978-90-5201-456-2

No.62 – *Jobs on the Move. An Analytical Approach to 'Relocation' and its Impact on Employment*, Béla Galgóczi, Maarten Keune & Andrew Watt (eds.), 2008, ISBN 978-90-5201-448-7

N° 61 – *Les nouveaux cadres du dialogue social. Europe et territoires*, Annette Jobert (dir.), 2008, ISBN 978-90-5201-444-9

No.60 – *Transnational Labour Regulation. A Case Study of Temporary Agency Work*, Kerstin Ahlberg, Brian Bercusson, Niklas Bruun, Haris Kountouros, Christophe Vigneau & Loredana Zappalà, 2008, ISBN 978-90-5201-417-3

No.59 – *Changing Liaisons. The Dynamics of Social Partnership in 20th Century West-European Democracies*, Karel Davids, Greta Devos & Patrick Pasture (eds.), 2007, ISBN 978-90-5201-365-7.

No.58 – *Work and Social Inequalities in Health in Europe*, Ingvar Lundberg, Tomas Hemmingsson & Christer Hogstedt (eds.), SALTSA, 2007, ISBN 978-90-5201-372-5.

www.peterlang.com